Consumer Behaviour

ANDERSONIAN LIBRARY
WITHDRAWN
FROM
LIBRARY
STOCK
UNIVERSITY OF STRATHCLYDE

Consumer Behaviour

Applications in Marketing

Second Edition

obert East, Malcolm Wright and Marc Vanhuele

SAGE
Los Angeles | London | New Delhi
Singapore | Washington DC

Los Angeles | London | New Delhi
Singapore | Washington DC

SAGE Publications Ltd
1 Oliver's Yard
55 City Road
London EC1Y 1SP

SAGE Publications Inc.
2455 Teller Road
Thousand Oaks, California 91320

SAGE Publications India Pvt Ltd
B 1/I 1 Mohan Cooperative Industrial Area
Mathura Road
New Delhi 110 044

SAGE Publications Asia-Pacific Pte Ltd
3 Church Street
#10-04 Samsung Hub
Singapore 049483

Editor: Matthew Waters
Editorial assistant:
Production editor: Vanessa Harwood
Marketing manager: Alison Borg
Cover design: Jennifer Crisp
Typeset by: C&M Digitals (P) Ltd, Chennai, India
Printed by MPG Books Group, Bodmin, Cornwall

First published 2008
Reprinted 2008, 2009, 2011, 2012

This second edition published 2013

Library of Congress Control Number: 2012940757

British Library Cataloguing in Publication data

A catalogue record for this book is available from the British Library

ISBN 978-1-4462-1122-9
ISBN 978-1-4462-1123-6 (pbk)

Contents

ANDERSONIAN LIBRARY
WITHDRAWN
FROM
LIBRARY
STOCK
UNIVERSITY OF STRATHCLYDE

Praise for the previous edition

This book provides a wonderful (and very unusual) balance between areas of marketing that are often at odds with each other (or, worse yet, unaware of each other) […] I recommend it to any student, researcher, or manager in marketing.
Peter Fader, Frances and Pei-Yuan Chia Professor, and Professor of Marketing, Wharton School, University of Pennsylvania, USA

This textbook is exceptional for the amount of relevant research that is presented and explained. Students who have read and understood this text are likely to be much more of use to industry.
Fergus Hampton, Managing Director, Millward Brown Precis, London, UK

A serious, thoughtful consumer behaviour text, that focuses on substance rather than what's fashionable in academic circles.
Professor Byron Sharp, Ehrenberg-Bass Institute, University of South Australia

About the Authors

Robert East is professor of consumer behaviour in the marketing department of Kingston Business School, London and adjunct professor at the Ehrenberg-Bass Institute of the University of South Australia. He trained as a social psychologist and is a postgraduate of London Business School. His research has mainly focused on word-of-mouth patterns, where his new evidence has shown that some widely held beliefs are mistaken. As a teacher of consumer behaviour, he has been keen to deliver knowledge that is useful to students while not over-simplifying the subject. This book reflects both his iconoclastic research and his commitment to a curriculum that is both intellectual and useful.

Malcolm Wright is professor of marketing at Massey University, New Zealand, and adjunct professor at the Ehrenberg-Bass Institute of the University of South Australia. He applies empirical principles to marketing problems and has made interrelated discoveries about brand loyalty, the use of probability scales, new product forecasting and optimizing the advertising budget. He has also published many articles critically examining the foundations of popular marketing knowledge.

Marc Vanhuele holds a PhD from UCLA and is associate professor of marketing at HEC Paris. He has taught in MBA, Master of Science, executive and doctoral programmes on the topics of market orientation, consumer behaviour, pricing and communication. He also serves as consultant to consumer goods and market research companies. His research focuses on two different areas: how consumers deal with price information, and how a new use of marketing metrics can help managers to make better decisions.

Preface

Readership and Scope

We have designed this book to support courses in consumer behaviour at master's level. It is also suited to more advanced teaching at first-degree level. Our intended audience is those who see consumer behaviour as a research-based discipline that addresses problems raised by marketing and consumer policy. The problems we explore are found in all advanced and emerging economies and, for this reason, we believe that the book will be useful throughout the world.

This new edition continues the themes of the 2008 edition and, in addition, has one new chapter on Consumer Group Differences (Chapter 6). This covers cross-cultural comparisons and some segmentation issues. The remaining chapters have been updated with additional material, reflecting changes in the field in recent years, but their structure remains essentially as before. The book is selective in the research it covers, dealing in some detail with the areas chosen. As before, the chapters are quite short and are intended to support students who will also be reading original research papers. In updating and revising the book, we have found that we can often simplify and clarify the text and occasionally omit some elements that no longer seem so relevant. The result is a book that is easier to read and no longer than the previous edition.

Consumer Behaviour: Applications in Marketing stresses well-researched aspects of consumer behaviour that are of widespread importance. Following the Introduction, we describe the patterns of customer purchasing that are usually observed in market economies and the way these patterns can be explained and applied in marketing. We then look at research that has illuminated our understanding of consumer decision-making and show how this understanding can be used by marketers and public policy-makers. The last section of the book deals with the observed consumer response to market intervention and covers research findings on price, promotion, word of mouth and advertising.

Approach

Most textbooks in consumer behaviour are extensive and well illustrated, but may present the subject in a rather uncritical manner. Often, the treatment illustrates fashionable topics rather than providing evidence that helps us understand long-standing marketing problems. Such books do not make sufficient call on the expanding research in our field and, when they do cite research, may give limited attention to the uncertainties or opposing views that persist in our discipline. In practice, there are competing findings and explanations in all areas of consumer behaviour and marketing, and we have tried to recognize these and discuss their relative merits.

This touches on a problem familiar to those who teach business students. Some of these students find arguments from evidence to be quite unfamiliar and may instead provide accounts of current business practice as though these were conclusive. Our approach opposes such uncritical thinking. We believe that those who learn to use evidence as students acquire a technique that will serve them well as practitioners.

One hazard of research-based texts is the sheer weight of evidence. We have tried to emphasize the most recent work and key papers on topics while also acknowledging those early researchers who first identified problems in consumer behaviour – problems that are usually still current. We therefore make no apology for some of the more ancient citations in this book, as these help to describe the origin of current thinking.

As subjects become more fragmented, textbooks acquire importance as integrators of different perspectives. In scientific consumer behaviour, we can discern two rather different approaches to research and application. On the one hand, there is the tradition that dominates in the large conferences of the *Association for Consumer Research*. Put baldly, this endorses theorizing and hypothesis-testing, often within experimental designs, and tends to emphasize explanations in terms of the beliefs, preferences and the culture of consumers – a cognitive orientation. In contrast to this is the approach of those who belong to the *marketing science* grouping, who place emphasis on behaviour, measures rather than concepts, generalization from an accumulation of findings, and on the use of mathematical models rather than psychological theories for explanation. Textbooks have generally emphasized the cognitive tradition. We give more space than usual to the marketing science orientation; in particular, we emphasize behavioural explanations, the role of habit and the modelling of market patterns and market change. However, we also provide a full treatment of the techniques and theory that underlie the cognitive approach to consumer behaviour.

Consumer behaviour is a changing field. New research is giving answers to questions of major importance and, in due course, will give rise to a new breed of professional marketer. All three authors are active researchers and use their own research in this book; we hope that, in doing so, we manage to convey the excitement that new discoveries arouse.

Exercises

Good education gives students the confidence to use and criticize ideas. We try to enlarge this confidence through practical exercises that help the reader to apply and reflect on ideas about consumer behaviour. The exercises require self-appraisal, calculation, observation, measurement of attitudes and the use of computer programs. In many cases, they are quickly done and the reader will benefit by doing them as they occur.

Plan of the Book

The book is divided into four Parts. Part 1 (Chapter 1) introduces the reader to explanations for the different forms of consumer purchase. Part 2 (Chapters 2, 3, 4, 5 and 6) focuses on patterns of purchase; we cover customer loyalty and brand equity, the recurrent features of mature and changing markets, and relevant differences between cultures and consumer segments. Part 3 (Chapters 7, 8 and 9) focuses on decision-making; we deal with methods for predicting and explaining decisions, the way that decisions can be biased and the post-decision effects relating to satisfaction and quality. Part 4 (Chapters 10, 11, 12 and 13) focuses on the responses of consumers to conditions that affect consumption. These are price, the retail environment, social influence and advertising.

Acknowledgements

A number of people assisted us in the production of the previous edition: Dag Bennett, Brian Birkhead, Walter Carl, Cullen Habel, Kathy Hammond, Bruce Hardie, Paul Marsh, Jenni Romaniuk, Deborah Russell, John Scriven, Byron Sharp, Mark Uncles and Jim Wiley. For the present edition, we are particularly indebted to Kathy Hammond, Magda Nenycz-Thiel, Cathy Nguyen, Francesca Dall'Olmo Riley, Jenni Romaniuk, Deborah Russell, Jaywant Singh, Mark Uncles and Melissa Vignardi. Finally, we appreciate very much the influence of our students. With them in mind, we have tried to be relevant and clear.

Companion Website

Be sure to visit the companion website (www.sagepub.co.uk/east2e) to find additional teaching and learning material for both lecturers and students.

For lecturers:

- PowerPoint Slides
- Notes for Lecturers
- Example Questionnaire
- Sample Course Programme
- Software Notes
- SPSS Data Files

For students:

- References

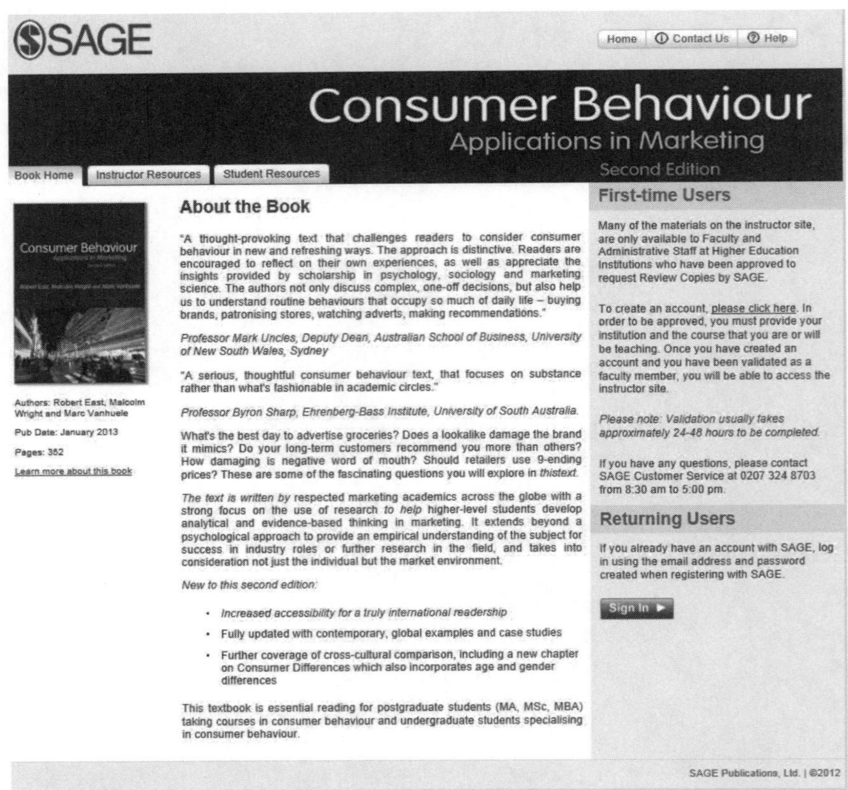

Part 1
Introduction

1 Ideas and Explanations in Consumer Research

LEARNING OBJECTIVES

When you have completed this chapter, you should be able to:

1. Explain why it is important to study consumer behaviour.
2. Discuss the limitations of a common-sense approach to consumer behaviour.
3. Compare and contrast different approaches to decision-making by consumers.
4. Discuss the effects of the consumer environment on choice.
5. Explain how markets are usually classified.

OVERVIEW

In this chapter, we show that findings about the way in which consumers behave when they buy and use products and services can be quite unexpected and that research is needed if we are to answer the questions posed by marketers and regulators. Then we describe three ways in which consumer choice can occur. Following this, we introduce some classifications that are commonly used to describe different types of marketing and consumer research.

SECTION 1: THE SCOPE OF CONSUMER BEHAVIOUR

How do people buy and use goods and services? How do they react to prices, advertising and store interiors? What underlying mechanisms operate to produce these responses? If marketers have answers to such questions, they can make better managerial decisions. If regulators have answers, they can design better policy. It is the role of consumer behaviour research to provide these answers.

In this book, we provide an up-to-date account of the main issues studied by consumer behaviour researchers, our current understanding based on these research findings, and show how our understanding can be applied to marketing problems. Knowledge has grown rapidly in some areas, and we have reflected these advances by describing some work in more depth. In such cases, we explain why an issue is important, how it is investigated and what the findings are. This approach culminates in *empirical generalizations*. These are general findings, based on evidence, that have stood the test of repeated investigation. Such general findings summarize the state of our knowledge and are useful to practitioners and researchers alike. All too often, popular pronouncements on marketing issues contain little evidence of this sort and it is our purpose to reverse this approach.

Where our knowledge is still sketchy, we have tried to indicate doubts about the evidence or its interpretation. Such uncertainty propels research and, as a result, creates new knowledge. Though not always welcome to students, doubt is part of good education. Students who see the uncertainties in consumer research should be more sceptical of unsupported opinions and may be better placed to interpret and adapt to new findings when these emerge. Each of the authors is an active researcher and has struggled to understand the complexities of consumer behaviour over many decades. We hope that this sharpens the account that we give. Inevitably, we have omitted some fields of knowledge; in particular, we have left out some topics that are well covered in more introductory consumer behaviour texts.

In this chapter we introduce some general ideas about consumer behaviour and marketing, which are explored further in following chapters. In Section 1, we look at the sort of *question* raised by marketing and the *answers* that are provided by consumer behaviour research. Section 2 of this chapter will discuss models that provide descriptions of *consumer decision processes* and Section 3 will focus on some of the *classifications* and *explanations* that we use to describe different types of consumer research.

Questions and Answers

There is a close affinity between marketing and consumer behaviour. In a sense, marketing is a customer of consumer research. Marketers want answers to a number of problems raised by their practices, and consumer researchers can provide these answers. Examples of marketing practices are:

- the use of price incentives
- the use of particular colours, music and aromas in the retail environment
- launching new products using existing brand names (brand extension).

Often, the direction of an effect fits common sense; for example, consumers buy more when the price is dropped. However, the benefit of a discount depends on the *amount* of extra sales generated by, say, a 10 per cent price cut and here common sense does not supply an answer. For informed action, we need to conduct systematic research, which allows us to measure the size of any effect. Evidence is gathered using the methods of market research, psychology and the social sciences. Using such methods, we seek answers to questions such as:

- How much do sales change when the price of a product is cut by 10 per cent? What happens to sales after a discount has ended? Why do these effects occur?
- How much do colours, music and aromas affect consumers' behaviour in a store? What underlying mechanisms explain any effects we see?
- When a new product is launched under an old brand name, how much does the old name affect purchase of the new product?

Another set of questions comes from legislators and regulators, who have to set rules that affect marketing. Examples of their questions are:

- How do consumers react to product benefits such as increased energy efficiency or high nutritional value? What explains their behaviour?
- Do childproof packs save lives? How are such packs used?

Sometimes, marketers give little attention to the explanation for an effect. An example is the identification of specific groups who are very heavy buyers of a product. If such people can be identified, they can be selectively targeted. This type of empirical approach can work well but explanation still helps. If we know *why* some groups buy a product much more than other groups, we may be able to design communications that capitalize on this and also predict other products that these groups will want.

In any applied subject, practitioners need to use their judgement when evidence is lacking. Those who have to take decisions cannot delay action until problems have been fully researched. However, it is important that practitioners do accept new evidence when this becomes available. Some apparently sensible practices may need to be adjusted because of new findings. For example, it has been assumed that the childproof packs for medicines decrease accidental poisoning, but this may be illusory. Viscusi (1984) found evidence that child-resistant bottle caps were associated with an *increase* in child poisoning, possibly because parents left medicines accessible when they thought that a cap was childproof, or because the child-proof closure was so much trouble for adults that they left the container open. Viscusi's work suggests that packs should carry more specific advice about use and possibly be redesigned so that they are less likely to be left open. More generally, this type of work reminds us that common sense does not replace empirical tests.

SECTION 2: CONSUMER DECISION MODELS

The traditional approach to problems in consumer behaviour employed a comprehensive model of the purchase decision process. Such models were often the centrepiece of

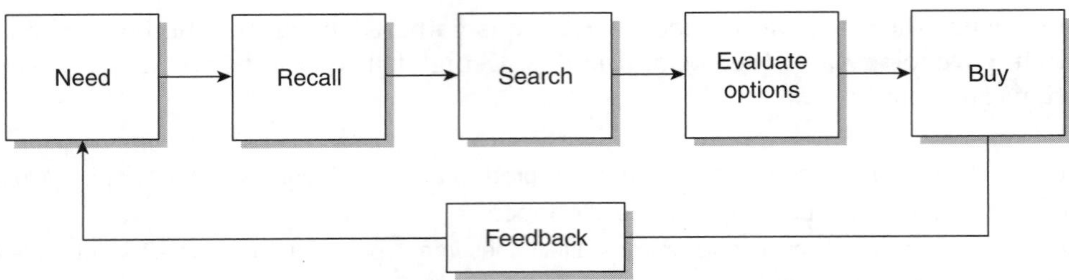

Figure 1.1 Is this how you choose?

undergraduate consumer behaviour texts and were expressed with boxes and arrows representing all the components and connections of an elaborate rational decision. In these models, the consumer is supposed to attend to product information and process it into their memory. The consumer retrieves the memory when a need emerges and, after further search and evaluation of all relevant alternatives, a purchase is made. After this, post-purchase evaluation may create satisfaction or dissatisfaction with the chosen product and this can result in a review of needs for later decisions. Figure 1.1 shows the basic form of such a model.

These days, there is less enthusiasm for such models. One problem has always been that they are hard to test because it is difficult to find satisfactory measures for all the components (Ehrenberg, 1988). Another problem with comprehensive models is that they overstate the rationality of how consumers choose. If there is plenty of time and the decision is important, then *sometimes* people will discover all the alternatives, evaluate them and select the one that seems to be the best, but we know from our own experience that we often simplify the process. Sometimes, we choose first and justify our behaviour afterwards, if we justify it at all. Thus, although rational decision models might suggest what people *ought to do* (normative), they are a poor guide to what people *actually do* (descriptive). In practice, managers want to know what people actually do since it is this behaviour that they seek to influence.

Textbooks now give more attention to 'partial decision models' where the rationality of the process is incomplete; also, it is accepted that much repeat purchase occurs automatically as a habit. Often, this range of decision making from rational to automatic is related to the degree of *involvement* with the product. People are likely to be more involved and give more thought to the choice when they are buying something for the first time and it has important outcomes. To explain decision-making in more detail, we focus on three models of consumer decision, which have different implications for managers (see Box 1.1). The models are:

1 **Cognitive**, treating purchase as the outcome of rational decision-making processes.
2 **Reinforcement**, treating purchase as behaviour which is learned and modified in response to the opportunities, rewards and costs present in the consumer's environment.
3 **Habit**, treating purchase as already learned behaviour, which is elicited by particular stimuli in the consumer's environment.

Box 1.1 Models of consumer choice

The cognitive model. This assumes rationality. The decision rests on beliefs about alternatives, which are investigated and compared. Marketers can influence cognitive decision-making by providing information that leads the consumer to prefer or reject alternatives.

The reinforcement model. Choice is controlled by factors in the environment that reward and facilitate some alternatives more than others. Marketing influence is achieved by changing the consumer's situation. However, what is rewarding to some persons may not be so to others and this limits influence.

The habit model. Choice is controlled by managing stimuli (brand name, logo, pack features, etc.) that have become associated with a product as a result of past purchases. Sometimes this is called stimulus control.

The Cognitive Model

When consumers make an important purchase for the first time, they may reflect on alternatives and discuss pros and cons with others with the intention of securing benefits and avoiding costs. This model, sometimes called *extended problem-solving*, has always had its critics. Olshavsky and Granbois (1979: 98–99) noted:

> for many purchases a decision never occurs, not even on the first purchase … even when purchase behaviour is preceded by a choice process, it is likely to be very limited. It typically involves the evaluation of few alternatives, little external search, few evaluative criteria, and simple evaluation process models.

It is quite hard to find behaviour that fits the elaborate sequence of extended problem-solving. Beatty and Smith (1987) found that people did not search much before the purchase of durables and Beales et al. (1981) found that few people in the USA consulted *Consumer Reports*. Carefully thought-out decision-making is only likely for first purchases but these are quite rare, even in consumer durable markets, since most purchasers are either buying a replacement for an existing product or making an additional purchase. In a study of white goods purchases in the USA, Wilkie and Dickson (1985) found that two-thirds of the purchasers had bought the category before and Bayus (1991), quoting US industry sources, found that 88 per cent of refrigerators and 78 per cent of washing machines were replacements. In these circumstances, a carefully thought-out comparison of brands is likely to be the exception rather than the rule.

But, when it does occur, is a carefully thought-out decision likely to result in the best choice? When people attempt to be rational about a first-time choice, they may make mistakes because they lack experience. However, they are likely to make a better choice than those who abandon any rational processing and plump for an alternative (see Box 1.2).

Box 1.2 When pension is converted to an annuity

People build up pension funds over their working lives and then convert the accumulated investment into an annuity when they retire. They may use their pension company for the annuity or search for better value from another company. According to Hargreaves Lansdown, a large financial services firm in the UK, the majority of people buy their annuity from their pension company. Since annuity rates across pension companies can vary by as much as 15 per cent, this careless choice can mean that many retirees lose income that they could have enjoyed for the rest of their lives. The most likely explanation for this behaviour is that the retirees had a very poor understanding of the issues and they plumped for the company with which they were familiar.

The tendency to simplify decision-making is also observed in industry. One study of investment decisions in British industry revealed that these were often made first and then justified later. Marsh et al. (1988) found that faulty financial analysis and lack of coherence with stated strategic objectives were common in major acquisitions and that the company rule books were often ignored. More generally, industrial decisions often fit a 'satisficing' model (Simon, 1957). Simon describes how executives tend to accept the first option that is good enough to solve a problem; this means that there is little comparison between alternatives. Klein (1989) found that many decisions in operational settings follow a pattern that is consistent with Simon's ideas. Typically, people assess the situation and generate a prospective action based on this assessment. Then, they evaluate this action to see whether it will provide a solution. If it fails, they generate another prospective action and evaluate this, but they do not usually compare prospective actions.

When the satisficing model applies, the order in which products are evaluated is important since the first satisfactory solution will be the one that is adopted. This means that more prominent alternatives have a better chance of selection (see Box 1.3). Managers and marketers may be able to use this fact to their advantage by keeping awareness of their brands high in consumers' minds.

Box 1.3 Diagnosis

Even in medicine, decisions may be simplified. Often, the symptoms are assessed and a preliminary diagnosis is made, taking account of common illnesses; then other symptoms are checked to see whether they confirm this diagnosis. Only if these other symptoms fail to support the first diagnosis is a second one considered. This procedure may lead to the over-diagnosis of common illnesses.

These examples of decision-making in industry and medicine suggest that the simplification of choice is the norm rather than the exception and we might expect consumers to follow much the same pattern. For example, if the freezer needs replacing and a preliminary inquiry establishes that there is an appropriate model in a convenient shop, consumers may complete the purchase there and then. If the shop does not offer a suitable freezer, they may then turn to other stores and look at other models.

Although satisficing may not result in the optimal solution, it may use time efficiently when this is scarce. However, when the outcome of the decision is important, consumers and managers would make better decisions if they considered a second alternative before deciding.

Influences on Decision-Making

It is easy to fall into the trap of assuming that decisions are made by people acting on their own. Many choices are made in groups and, even when people decide on their own, they are often influenced by word of mouth from other people. At other times, people may base their decisions on information received through the mass media (e.g. advertising, newspaper, television and Internet comment). People are particularly likely to seek advice on matters that are obscure or difficult to test in other ways; this is common when the recipient of the advice is choosing for the first time or acting under changed circumstances, such as when they move home and need to find service providers such as a dentist. In later chapters on word of mouth and advertising, we consider in more detail how these influences may affect choice.

Since advice affects consumer decisions, marketers need to take account of this process. For example, advertising can include information that is easily passed on in conversation, and the design of the ad can reflect the process of giving advice. However, word of mouth is under consumer control, not marketing control, so normally marketers can only affect it indirectly.

Exercise 1.1 Decision-making

Identify an important purchase that you have made, for example a holiday, electronic device, financial investment or education course.

- Were you clear about what you wanted?
- How much investigation did you do before purchase?
- Did you consider one option and move on to others if it was unsuitable, or did you keep several alternatives in mind before choosing?
- Did you use the Internet to search for others' opinions?
- Did you consult friends or relatives?

In retrospect, you may be able to see defects in your decision-making process. Often we lack enough prior experience, time or motivation to fully compare the options.

Purchase as Learned Behaviour

A person's environment controls behaviour in two ways. First, the environment makes some actions possible and other actions impossible to perform; for example, some physical items can only be bought if they are stocked by retailers and available to you either by post or to purchase at the store. Second, when actions lead to positive outcomes they are more likely to be repeated and, conversely, negative outcomes make it less likely that the action will be repeated. These reinforcement effects on behaviour have been examined in *learning theory*; this is a systematic description of the relationship between initial behaviour, its outcomes and subsequent behaviour. Learning theory is relevant to both the reinforcement and habit models.

Reinforcement

Early research in learning theory was done by Thorndike (1911), who confined a hungry cat to a cage and placed food outside. The erratic movements of the cat eventually released a simple catch and the cat escaped. The cat took less time on subsequent trials and eventually it released the catch immediately when it was placed in the cage. Thorndike called this *trial and error learning* and it has some relevance to consumption. People entering new markets are faced with a range of brands and may make near random trials of alternatives until they come upon a brand that they like.

In Thorndike's work, the cat's actions were driven by the outcomes: gaining food and freedom. Skinner (1938, 1953) called such outcomes *reinforcers*. Skinner defined a reinforcer as an experience that raises the frequency of responses associated with it, while a punisher reduces the frequency of such responses. Reinforcers may be rewards or reductions in cost while punishers may be costs or reductions in reward. Reinforcement has most effect when it occurs at the same time as, or just after, the response. Skinner placed emphasis on the way in which reinforcement changes the frequency of the response, but reinforcement also strengthens the association between stimulus and response and this is important for the habit model. Figure 1.2 illustrates the effect of reinforcement.

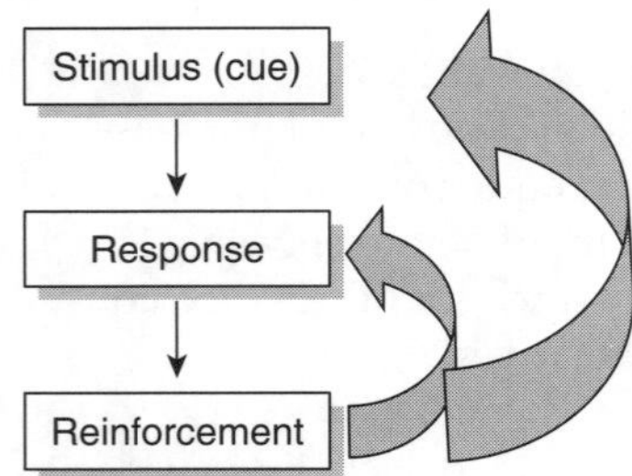

Figure 1.2 Reinforcement learning

The principles of reinforcement are applied in many sales promotions, such as discounts that offset the cost of a product. Skinner also introduced the idea of *shaping*, the process whereby behaviour is gradually shifted from one form to another by selectively reinforcing those performances that show change in the desired direction. Shaping is sometimes apparent in sales techniques where the salesperson moves the prospect towards the sales goal by reinforcing shifts in the preferred direction with nods, agreement and approval. Products also shape us. We become more expert at using computers and cars, partly because of the reinforcers that such products deliver; as a result of this, we may seek more sophisticated models.

Learning can be reinforced each time a response is produced, i.e. *continuously*, or it can be reinforced *intermittently*. Learning is faster if the reinforcement schedule is continuous but the final effect of a given amount of reinforcement is greater when it is used intermittently. This helps to explain why people are prepared to lose money by gambling on fruit machines. The cost of playing a slot machine is a fairly continuous punishment but the machine rewards intermittently. Over time, the gains are less than the losses, but the effect on behaviour of the irregular reward is greater than the effect of the regular cost.

Both stimuli and reinforcers can lose their effect if they are used too frequently. Stimulus satiation, called *desensitization*, helps people to put up with recurring unpleasant experiences. An important effect of desensitization in consumer behaviour is the way in which people get used to conditions that are inadequate or unpleasant and, as a result, may not complain or demand compensation. Examples of this are the way people tolerate litter in streets, overcrowding on public transport and being kept waiting 'on hold' on the phone. Similarly, consumers may put up with defective goods because they have grown used to the defects. Examples are the continuing use of lumpy mattresses, broken refrigerator shelves and inadequate carving knives. The job of the marketer is to overcome the inertia in these situations so that the consumer sees the problem afresh and seeks a solution.

Stimulus Control: Classical Conditioning

One type of learning, called classical conditioning, was studied by Pavlov (1927). Pavlov noticed that dogs started to salivate at the sight of the person who fed them. The older dogs showed this most and Pavlov thought that, over time, the salivation reflex that normally occurred at the presentation of food had become associated with a new stimulus, the dogs' handler. Pavlov set up a series of experiments to demonstrate this process of classical conditioning using the sound of a buzzer as the conditioned stimulus instead of the dogs' handler. Figure 1.3 illustrates this process.

Classical conditioning has considerable relevance to consumer behaviour. Packaging, brand names, colours, smells, music and the contexts of purchase and consumption may become associated with the buying of particular products. Some advertising is clearly intended to forge associations between brands and particular stimuli that can be used in further advertising and at the point of sale, e.g. McDonald's and the big 'M' sign, 'i' and phone, pod, pad, … and, more generally, all logos and their respective brands and companies. The idea here is that the conditioned stimulus may help in identification and add to

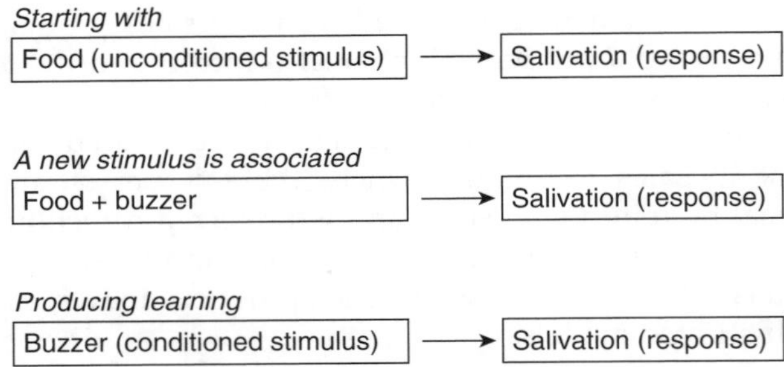

Figure 1.3 Classical conditioning: Pavlov's experiment

purchasing tendency. It is also noticeable that, to compete in some markets, manufacturers have to adopt the colours and pack shape that are conventional for that type of product. The power of such associations is revealed by a trip to an unfamiliar country. The absence of familiar features makes the high street confusing. A simple task, like posting a letter, requires investigation and effort in order to identify the colour, shape and location of the post box.

A stimulus that is associated with a rewarding product may induce a more generalized tendency to buy other products that appear similar. A direct application of such generalization in marketing is the use of an existing brand name for a new product. By this process of *brand extension*, some of the buying tendency (often termed *propensity* by marketers) that consumers have for the old brand may attach to the new brand. For example, Mars used the positive consumer propensity towards the brand when introducing Mars ice-cream and this was helped by the similarity in the appearance of the ice-cream and the confectionery bar.

Habits of Purchase

The cognitive and reinforcement models emphasize the *modification* of consumer behaviour and thus may explain the *changes* that occur in our purchasing. However, much consumption has a settled form; people buy the same brands and use the same stores over long periods. This habitual aspect of consumption is of great value to firms.

We say that people have a habit when they regularly produce much the same behaviour on encountering a particular stimulus. In the case of supermarket goods, important stimuli are the colour, size and shape of the pack. Williams (1966) found that colour positively affected buying behaviour most, followed by size then shape. Response to such stimuli is automatic, so that no conscious thought is required when we pick a laundry detergent brand in the supermarket. Habits sidestep cognitive decision-making and leave us free to concentrate on other problems where experience does not provide us with a ready response. However, even in novel situations people may trade on already acquired habits. Consider the person who is about to buy a car for the first time. Most first-time car purchasers are familiar with cars, have been to car showrooms before, may have bargained for goods before, may be knowledgeable about the ways of salespersons and may understand credit arrangements. Thus, even first-time car purchasing may draw on previous learning, some of which may have become habitual. Viewed in this way, even complex and novel behaviour may call upon behaviours in a habit repertoire.

The habit model of consumption excludes planning before action but does not imply that consumers never think about their habitual behaviour. People may reflect on their actions *after* purchase either because of discussion with others or because their purchase outcomes were exceptionally good or bad. But this is unusual; generally, habit restricts experimentation and, as a result, consumers may be unaware of improvements in products from which they could benefit. This suggests that, although habitual purchase is frequently satisfactory, it is not always the best solution. Exercise 1.2 draws your attention to habits that you may have which do not always lead to you choosing what best meets your needs.

Exercise 1.2 Habits

It is hard to detect habits that work against your own interests but consider two areas:

1 Taking sugar in tea and coffee are habits that add to body weight and contribute to tooth decay. When people give up sugar they get used to it fairly soon and after a few weeks may prefer unsweetened tea or coffee. Is this not a habit worth changing?
2 If you make a regular journey to work, is the route optimal? People can discover journey improvements after years of using a less suitable route that has become habitual.

How should marketers present new brands in markets where purchase is strongly habitual?

When purchase is habitual, a new brand must be marketed in a way that disrupts habit and provokes a review of past purchase. This is not easily achieved. Advertising may be ignored, while discounts and free samples may be used by consumers without much effect on later purchase. Most of the time, consumers carry on buying what they have bought before. But that's why marketers need to understand what types of marketing interventions work best for different customer groups in different environments.

How Free Are Consumers?

It is often claimed that the consumer is king but this may exaggerate the flexibility of action that consumers have. To be free you should be able to choose from more than one option without pressure, and be able to reject all options if they are unattractive. Many choices are controlled by the consumer's environment rather than by reflective thought by the consumer, and this casts doubt on how much freedom of action consumers can exercise.

The constraints on consumers are considerable and are not just environmental. Consumers may *lack knowledge* of alternatives when these are not displayed. Sometimes, people *have to use* products; they must put petrol in a car and laundry detergent in a washing machine and the fact that they have a choice between near identical brands is often, to them, a matter of indifference. Freedom of action is also affected by *limited access* to goods and services, by *physiological dependence* on products like cigarettes and alcohol and by *psychological dependence* when the consumer is a compulsive purchaser or gambler.

People do many things that they would prefer to avoid, e.g. going to work on congested public transport and waiting for flights in airports. In many areas, such as education, medicine and legal advice, the opportunity to influence a service by withdrawing custom or complaining is effectively limited by the continuing need to use the service. There are other areas where a lack of money prevents people from doing the things they might wish to do; large houses and luxurious cars are possible for only a few. For these reasons, we are sceptical of claims about the almost unlimited choice available to consumers and how much autonomy they have. However, the growth of the Internet has raised access to knowledge about goods and services and has assisted purchase; this may lead to a genuine increase in consumer choice.

Decision-Making on the Internet

The increased use of the Internet and the facilities that websites offer may change the rationality of choice. The ability to compare prices online generally drives down the average price of goods and services bought online. The proportion of UK shoppers who say they often consult the Internet before making a purchase is 78 per cent in 2011, unchanged from the previous year (Nielsen, 2011a). However, they seem to be making more purchases on the Internet. According to Nielsen, the proportion of shoppers claiming to use the Internet most days has increased from 50 per cent to nearly 80 per cent in the five years to January 2011, and those claiming never to use it has fallen from 25 per cent to just 7 per cent (see Figure 1.4). In the UK, the two leading sites for shopping are Amazon and eBay, each with a unique audience double that of the operator in third place. Grocery shopping via the Internet has doubled in the four years to 2011 and is now 5 per cent of total grocery shopping in the UK.

The Internet makes it easier to compare prices and specifications, and can take some of the effort out of shopping. Search engines such as Google.com assist in the identification of sources and products, while chat rooms and blogs often provide user comment on different brands. Comparison sites such as Shopping.com show the prices charged by different suppliers. Other sites, such as Uswitch.co.uk, can compute the best value among service providers and may facilitate transfer to a new provider. Websites for those buying houses, shares, books and many other items aid choice by providing easy comparison between alternatives. For example, an Australasian buyer can use a site such as realestate.com.au to specify properties by location, price and type, and can then inspect pictures of interiors. This helps to focus attention only on those properties that meet the needs of the buyer. A subscriber buying shares through a Web-based stockbroker such as Hargreaves Lansdown (hl.co.uk) can see the past return on specific shares over different periods, and can compare this performance with other shares and with standard indexes. On Amazon.com, customers can read reviews of a book before buying and be provided with

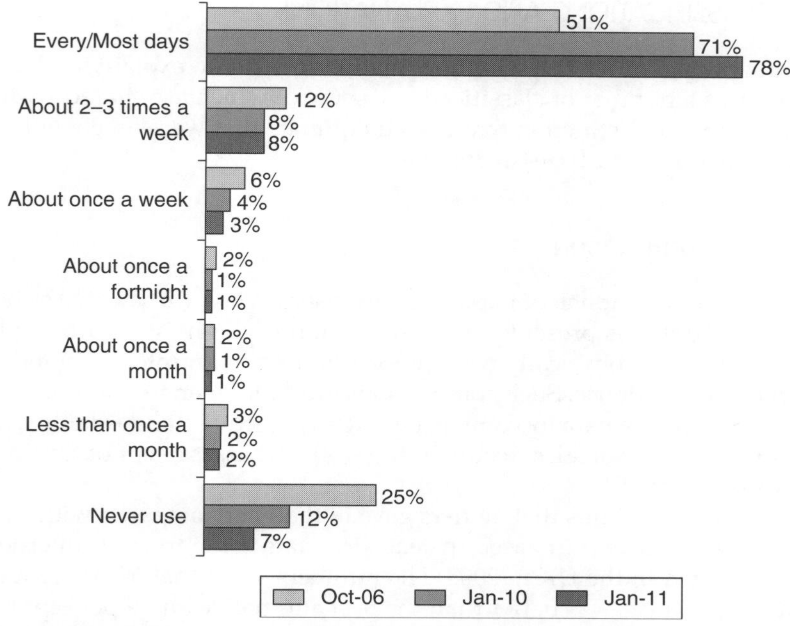

Figure 1.4 Five-year changes in the use of the Internet by UK shoppers (Nielsen, The State of the Nation, 2011)

information on new books that are related to their previous purchases. On airline sites such as ba.com, a traveller can pick travel times that are cheaper. Quite clearly, the Internet *can* be used by consumers to assess alternatives better, but how much do consumers do this to improve their choices and lower their costs?

A study by Zettelmeyer, Morton and Silva-Risso (2006) suggests that Internet customers may bring down the price that they pay for cars by an average of 1.5 per cent; this may seem modest but it accounts for 22 per cent of the dealer's gross margin. However, consumers who use the Internet may be more price-sensitive and these people might also drive a hard bargain in an offline context. Also, it appears that even Internet customers rarely secure the lowest price. According to Shopping.com, 80 per cent of Internet customers pay more than they have to. It seems that use of the Internet to obtain better value is restrained by loyalty to particular websites. Once they are familiar with a site, consumers may return to it later because it is easy to use and saves time. A consumer might agree that a book might be cheaper elsewhere but still use Amazon because of convenience – this convenience can be seen as considerable, as often customers allow trusted sites to store their credit card and delivery details, so purchasing really is a single click. Similarly, buyers normally use one online grocer because of the trouble of getting to know another site. In short, habits take over.

This evidence presents a somewhat confused picture. The Internet *can* assist people to make better decisions and buy more cheaply, but the technology may discourage experimentation when goods are regularly bought. In addition, there are some sectors, such as groceries, where choice limitations and delivery cost may raise the price that is paid online.

SECTION 3: CLASSIFICATIONS AND EXPLANATIONS

Disciplines must organize and classify information in order to explain it. Marketing is no exception and uses a number of classifications, some of which are shared with other subjects. We start with one distinction that is so ubiquitous that we scarcely notice it. This is the use of comparison in the assessment of evidence.

The Principle of Comparison

Any judgement rests on implicit or explicit comparison. When we say 'that's cheap', we are comparing the price that is presented with some standard. The standard might be given by another brand that is physically present, or it might be an internal standard that we have built up from experience. Such comparisons are fundamental to human judgements. We make sense of any raw data by comparing it with objective standards, or with personal or social norms. Comparison also occurs in the scientific assessment of findings. To illustrate this, consider Table 1.1.

This table shows the ratings that owners gave to their car compared with the best alternative that they could have purchased instead. The data come from an Internet survey of 495 owners conducted in the UK in 2003. The numbers show that 64 per cent of respondents thought that their car was better than the best alternative and 9 per cent thought that it was worse. This seems to show great confidence among respondents in their choice of car. Our finding reflects a general phenomenon called the endowment effect: objects are rated more highly once they are owned (Kahneman, Knetsch and Thaler, 1991a). However, the assessments shown in Table 1.1 are difficult to justify. When there are many alternatives, which are difficult to fully compare, it is quite likely that another brand would have been better than the one chosen. Thus, there seems to be an optimism bias in the assessment of possessions which is revealed by making the question comparative. In Chapter 8, we study these judgemental effects in more detail.

Sometimes, the standard of comparison that people use for judgements has an objective basis: for example, the average price of a basket of goods in the different supermarket chains or the fuel economy of different cars. But notice that consumers have to discover and accept such standards if these are to affect their judgements. Standards may be affected by marketing communications but, mostly, people appear to acquire price or

Table 1.1 How owners rated their current car

Rating in comparison to the best alternative make that could have been purchased instead	*Current car (%)*
Much worse	1
Worse	8
The same	27
Better	38
Much better	26

quality norms from experience. Such internal norms will be based on observations, discussions with other consumers and information from the media and are likely to be quite stable. In these circumstances, what changes when marketers are successful in modifying consumer behaviour? Usually, marketing activity alters the immediate perception rather than the internal norm. When the price is cut, and more people buy, it is because the new price is seen as cheap, compared with the norm.

Categories, Brands, Variants and SKUs

Classifications are also made on the basis of the context in which decisions are taken. We call anything a customer buys, whether good or service, a *product*. Then all products are divided into *categories* such as soup, wine, mobile phone airtime suppliers, cars and hotels. Within a category there will be a number of brands available for consumers to choose from. Brands are easily recognizable entities – such as Apple, Toyota and Disney – and customers can become attached to one brand rather than another when making repeated choices. Sometimes there are sub-brands, e.g. Volkswagen has Polo, Golf, Passat, etc. The branding is signalled primarily by name, but also by logo, and the shape, colour and design of the pack or product when this has a physical form. Advertising may attach other associations to the brand, such as cartoon animals and musical themes. In many cases, a company name is synonymous with the brand, e.g. BP, but in other cases, the company owns a variety of brand names, e.g. General Motors, Procter & Gamble and Unilever each manage many brand names (e.g. Unilever owns Ben & Jerry's, Bertolli, PG Tips, Dove, Lynx and Timotei among other brands). Variants are subdivisions of the product type so the Volkswagen Passat is available as a saloon or estate, and Heinz soups are available in different flavours.

In business, the term SKU (stock keeping unit) is used widely. This is a unique combination of brand, variety, pack size, etc. that is required for manufacturing or filling the shelves. The SKU is coded so that automated systems can specify it in production scheduling and stock control. Manufacturers and retailers often analyze consumer choice at the level of the SKU.

The consumer's preference to buy varying quantities of a specific brand from a specific outlet at a specific price point controls the profit that is made by the brand owner, retailer and other suppliers; marketing activities are therefore coordinated to promote brand or sub-brand preference. This means that the branding must be distinctive enough for consumers to distinguish one brand from another but, at the same time, the brands in a category often have features in common which help the consumer to recognize what they are buying when they search for the product on a shop shelf or on a website. As a result, brands often share characteristics such as pack size, colour and shape. In fact, one brand does not have to be physically different from other brands in a category. For example, at one time Volkswagen, Seat and Ford offered SUVs that were almost the same except for the name badge and the price. Similarly, there may be no detectable difference between the granulated sugar offered by two different manufacturers; consumers know this, but this does not stop them from regularly buying one brand rather than another. Often, each brand will cover much the same range of variants. Sugar brands will offer granulated, castor, icing and Demerara variants; soup brands will have much the same range of flavours; and car brands will be available in SUV, sports, saloon and estate forms. In fact, the differences between the variants of a single brand are often much greater than the differences between the corresponding variants of different brands.

The use of sub-brands can raise problems in the car industry when a new model comes out. Should the sub-brand be retained because of the value that consumers attach to it (brand equity) or is a new sub-brand needed to emphasize the novelty of the new model? Volkswagen retains sub-brand names, Citroën has tended to abandon them but has recently resurrected the DS name which was first used in 1955 on a model still revered by motoring enthusiasts (DS sounds like déesse, French for goddess).

In many categories, the brands compete only with each other for the customer's attention, e.g. Colgate versus Aquafresh toothpaste. However, in the food and entertainment fields this is less true. A frozen meal brand competes with home cooking and restaurant meals, as well as with other brands of frozen meals. Similarly, beer competes with wine and ten-pin bowling competes with the cinema.

Other differentiators beside brands are used to distinguish one market offering from another. An interesting example is provided by wine. French wine has traditionally been branded by the producer, sub-region and region, e.g. Château Cheval Blanc is a St Emilion production in the Bordeaux region. There are many other producers, and this produces a complex choice for the consumer. By contrast, Australasian wine is sold more on the basis of grape variety. Although there are many varieties of grape, a small number dominate the field (e.g. Cabernet, Chardonnay Malbec, Merlot, Shiraz, Pinot Noir, Reisling, Sauvignon and Tempranillo) and several of these varieties are grown in each region. This marks major differences between wines and provides an easy 'handle' for the consumer. When the grape variety has been chosen, regions like the Barossa, producers like Penfolds, and the year of the vintage may be used in the choice process of the more discriminating buyer.

Goods and Services

A familiar grouping of categories is into goods and services. A good has physical form, e.g. a can of soup or a bed, or in business-to-business (B2B) markets, aluminium sheets or bus wheels, whereas a service is intangible and is used by the recipient as it is created, e.g. a haircut, a visit to the dentist, professional advice or a phone call. Thus the essence of a service is that it exists in time and must be consumed at that time if a loss of sale is to be avoided. By contrast, goods, such as frozen peas, can be stockpiled by the consumer and supplied when there is demand. Most service products incorporate a goods component, e.g. the meal is consumed in a restaurant and your phone call is made from an electronic device such as a phone handset or a computer.

Goods can be subdivided into classes such as groceries, electronics and fashion, or in B2B markets, electronic components, food commodities, etc. Similarly, services divide into classes such as telephony, transport, surgery, entertainment and financial services. The fact that there are textbooks devoted to the marketing of services suggests that this is substantially different from the marketing of goods. One difference is that, because they are delivered over time, services can suffer problems of uneven demand, leading to inefficient use of resources and delay and frustration among customers. We cover research on the consumer response to delay in Chapter 9. There are also differences that arise from the interaction between the service supplier and the customer; Keaveney (1995) found that a large part of all service switching occurred because of failures in the face-to-face service encounter and this has no parallel with goods. Most goods can be examined before purchase and this helps consumers to assess how well they fit their needs. It may not be possible to examine services in this way and, as a result, those who are thinking of adopting a new service provider may seek advice from existing customers whose word of mouth provides a proxy for personal experience.

In other respects, goods and services are similar. Our three models of consumer decision-making apply to both, and so does the distinction between repertoire and subscription categories that we discuss below.

Vargo and Lusch (2004) have suggested that services rather than goods are the fundamental product form since goods are made by the service of workers. This new 'dominant logic' in marketing has echoes in the work of early economists, particularly in Marx's theory of value, first expounded in *Capital* (volume 1 was published in 1867), which relates value to the labour input. At the time, economists argued that the value of goods was defined by an exchange process; it is what others are prepared to give for the goods and no amount of labour input will raise the price of something that people do not want. The character of transactions may have changed and become more cooperative but, in our view, such exchanges remain the basis of value. Marketers must be concerned with profitable trading and, for this reason, we are sceptical about making service fundamental in marketing.

Repertoire and Subscription Categories

Categories can be divided into those that are repertoire, where consumers commonly purchase more than one brand over a fairly short time such as a year (e.g. most groceries, restaurants and airline flights) and subscription, where consumers mostly use only one brand at a time (e.g. current bank accounts, dentists and refrigerators). Research by Sharp, Wright and Goodhardt (2002) shows that most categories fall clearly into either the repertoire or the subscription division. In repertoire categories, we can measure a type of brand loyalty called *share-of-category requirement* (SCR). This is the percentage of category purchases that a customer gives to a specific brand over a period. For example, if a person buys instant coffee on ten occasions in a year and five purchases are Maxwell House, the customer's SCR for Maxwell House is 50 per cent. By contrast, loyalty in subscription categories is shown at the time of repurchase when the customer either retains the brand or switches to another.

Market Concentration

In many categories, there are relatively few brands. Laundry detergents, toothpaste and mobile phone airtime supply are examples. In other fields, such as wine, cheese and biscuits, there are a great many producers, none of which commands a large market share. In some other fields, such as supermarkets, fashion stores, chemists and investment advisers, a few large chains compete with many smaller suppliers in Western markets. When a few producers command a large part of the category, we describe the market as *high concentration*. Usually, large suppliers are more profitable because of economies of scale in manufacture, distribution and advertising. Retailers feel compelled to stock more familiar brands because of demand and this helps the manufacturer (the brand owner) to maintain the price paid by the retailer.

Consumers are not necessarily disadvantaged by high market concentration. The large scale and efficiencies of big producers mean that product development can occur and the wide distribution of big brands ensures that consumers can easily find the larger brand. One concern is that high concentration may reduce competition but it is not difficult to find high levels of competition in concentrated markets. For instance, the worldwide cola market is highly concentrated, yet both Pepsi and Coca-Cola remain fiercely competitive suppliers.

Market Share

Ehrenberg (1988) has explained that many aspects of aggregate consumer behaviour can be seen as an outcome of market share. For example, the average SCR loyalty for a big brand tends to be higher than that for a small brand (i.e. the evidence is that in general the bigger the brand the more likely that it is that customers will buy it again compared with the customers of smaller brands). In Table 1.2, we illustrate how another variable, the share of recommendation, relates to market share in the mobile phone category in data gathered before the advent of smartphones.

Table 1.2 shows that the share of brand recommendations closely follows the market share of the brand. There is no mystery about this. As we saw earlier with regard to cars, people are usually happy with the products that they own, and East, Romaniuk and Lomax (2011) found an average of 71 per cent of recommendations related to the informant's main brand. So, the bigger the brand, and therefore the greater the number of users, the larger will be the share of recommendations. For this reason, managers need to take account of market share before they assess the word of mouth about their brand. In Table 1.2, Motorola is doing well because the rate of recommendation is ahead of market

Table 1.2 Market share and share of recommendations of mobile phone brands (unpublished UK data gathered in 2005)

Brand	*Market share (%)*	*Share of recommendations (%)*
Nokia	40	40
Sony-Ericsson	25	21
Motorola	14	20
Samsung	10	11
Siemens	4	2
Others	7	4

Exercise 1.3 Do big brands get more, or less, negative word of mouth?

Recommendation is positive word of mouth. What about negative word of mouth? Develop ideas about how negative word of mouth is produced. What will be the resulting relationship between market share and the share of negative word of mouth?

When you get to Chapter 12, you will see our evidence on this topic.

share. If the rate of recommendation was assessed without taking account of market share, Nokia would come top, but we can see that its performance is just average for its size.

Consumer Segmentation and Causal Relationships

We often compare population segments: those who retain a brand versus those who switch, heavy TV viewers versus light viewers, high recommenders versus low recommenders, men versus women, etc. If we have evidence about the consumption habits of different segments, we can target those that appear to be most likely to purchase the category or most open to switch brands. Consumer segmentation is an approach that is very popular in marketing; it can work well even when we do not know why the behaviour of one segment differs from another. For example, a method used by those trying to harness word of mouth is to try to identify those consumers who give more advice than others (the *influentials*). Once they have been identified, the job of the marketer is to recruit them on behalf of a promoted brand.

However, in consumer behaviour, we want to explain behaviour, preferably by finding causes for it. Why is it that one segment is more active in giving advice to others than another segment? We can investigate how segments differ with respect to possible causes. As the picture of the different factors underlying recommendation builds up, a new strategy becomes available to marketers. Instead of identifying a segment that gives more word of mouth, marketers can try to influence the factors that cause word of mouth and this can be done *without* identifying the influentials.

Behaviourism and Cognitivism

Does a change in thinking cause a change in behaviour, or does a change in behaviour cause a change in thinking? The answer is that we can find support for both processes. In psychology, the primacy of behaviour is called *behaviourism*. This approach was developed by Skinner (1953). The traditional behaviourist rejects the idea that thought and feeling are the initiators of action. Instead, action is explained by reference to the environmental circumstances that act on a person. This fits the reinforcement and habit models of consumer decision-making.

In traditional behaviourist research, it used to be believed that thought and feeling are *effects but not causes*; like ripples on the surface of a pond they indicate the fish's movements but do not move the fish. If this account is correct, we can use people's thoughts and feelings as indicators of their potential behaviour but not as explanations for it. Such narrow behaviourism is usually rejected today. One reason is that it is difficult to describe action without taking account of the thoughts and feelings that lie behind it; words become insults or praise only through an understanding of the motives of the person uttering them. The traditional behaviourist position is not subtle enough to deal with this complexity in the nature of human behaviour.

Opposed to behaviourism is the view that thought and feeling can produce change in action directly. This is *cognitivism* and it lies behind rational accounts of consumer decision-making. In its strongest form, experience is interpreted and used to change attitudes and knowledge, which then control behaviour. From a cognitivist perspective, behaviour may be modified by communications that change attitudes and knowledge. Some support for the cognitivist position can be found in the way public information campaigns change behaviour (for example, anti-smoking advertising, featuring the hazards of smoking, has been shown to be effective; see Chapter 13).

There are also examples where behaviour precedes attitudes that support behaviourism. Clare and Kiser (1951) asked parents of completed families about the number and sex of the children that they thought were desirable. There was a strong tendency for parents to prefer both the size and the sex mix of the family that they already had; for example, if they had two girls they stated that they felt two girls was what they would like if they were to have their family again. At the time of the study, there were no ways of controlling the sex of offspring, so the preference for the same sex balance can only be explained as a product of experience.

In many other cases the causal direction between attitude and behaviour may be in doubt. The preferred number of children is a case in point. Parents might have had two children because they wanted two; or, having had two children, they might have come to prefer this number. Such alternative explanations can often be seen in the social sciences. For example, Marx argued that it was not ideology that determined social relations but that social relations determined ideology. This is the sociological equivalent of the primacy of behaviour over attitude and it is contrasted with Hegelian philosophy favouring the primacy of ideas. Sometimes Hegel's account fits; paradoxically, Marxism itself was a revolutionary ideology that created change.

Some studies in consumer research show the effect of prior behaviour. Bird and Ehrenberg (1966) found that two-thirds of those who have used a brand at some time express an intention to buy it. A declining brand has a long tail of past users and, as a result, a larger number of consumers state that they are going to buy it again, compared with a growing brand with the same share. There is also evidence that brand attitudes follow the purchase of groceries. Dall'Olmo Riley et al. (1997) found that brand attributions (e.g. that 'Persil washes whiter') may depend on recent purchase. Sandell (1981) examined the relationships between brand attitudes and purchase using consumer panel data and found that individual attitudes were aligned with purchase immediately after buying, but that, over time, people's attitudes reverted to the pre-purchase pattern.

SUMMARY

Key questions for consumer behaviour come from marketing strategy and consumer policy. In order to answer these questions we need an understanding of how consumers make decisions. When people face difficult and involving choices, the cognitive model of choice may describe the process of decision-making, but the process is often simplified, even when the decision is difficult. When action is steered by the environment, the reinforcement model provides an explanation of how purchasing or consumption patterns are learned: consumer action is constrained by the opportunities available and directed by the rewards and costs that are present. Once actions such as brand purchase are learned, they may be induced by specific stimuli, such as brand name, and the habit model can apply. To change the behaviour of consumers, the influencing agent (e.g. advertising, promotions, word of mouth, etc.) must either alter the beliefs and values involved in a complex decision or, where the context controls behaviour, modify the consumer's environment. Learning principles help us to explain some marketing practices, such as brand extension.

The growth of the Internet suggests that people are able to make better choices (more suitable brands, lower prices) but it is not clear yet how much this occurs.

In this chapter, we also introduced some of the ways in which data are organized to create meaning: the use of comparison, types of category, brands and variants, goods and services and market share.

Additional Resources

For an early challenge to comprehensive models of consumer behaviour, read Olshavsky and Granbois (1979).

Part 2
Consumption Patterns

2 Customer Loyalty

LEARNING OBJECTIVES

When you have completed this chapter, you should be able to:

1. Report the different terms and measures that have been used to describe customer loyalty.
2. Explain how different ideas about loyalty developed.
3. Explain how customer loyalty is divided between brands in repertoire categories.
4. Describe other habitual features of consumer purchase.
5. Discuss and criticize the main ideas in favour of encouraging retention in consumer markets.
6. Show how design features of loyalty programmes trigger differences in consumer behaviour.
7. Report research on the associations between different forms of loyalty.
8. Report on the reasons for defection in services.

(Loyalty schemes, which are really forms of retail promotion, are also covered in Chapter 11.)

OVERVIEW

There are three types of loyalty behaviour that consumers can show. First, when they buy several brands in a category, consumers can give a high share to one of them. Second, they can continue to buy a brand for a long time; this is retention. Third, they can give positive advice about a brand and, by this action, recruit new customers. These three forms of customer loyalty – share, retention and recommendation – ensure a continuing revenue stream to the brand owner and reduce the need for the parent company to promote the brand. Marketers therefore want to find and keep customers who exhibit these forms of loyalty and, where possible, they want to encourage this behaviour. Marketers are also keen to understand why customers switch away from a brand.

A second aspect to loyalty is the feeling that customers have about brands. We talk of being satisfied by or liking a brand, being committed to the brand and, in the case of business and service suppliers, trusting and being dependent upon them.

This subject is quite complicated. We have a common term, loyalty, but it has many different forms and one form of loyalty may have a strong or weak relationship with another. Also, the measure of loyalty that we use depends on the category. We use repeat purchase to show retention in consumer durables and duration as a customer to show retention for utilities and other services. In some fields where consumers have a portfolio of brands they regularly buy we can use both share and retention to show the loyalty of customers (e.g. to grocery brands, stores and airlines). To explore these issues, we approach the subject historically, show how different measures of loyalty originated, and examine some of the evidence associated with each form of loyalty.

SECTION 1: BRAND LOYALTY IN REPERTOIRE CATEGORIES

The Development of Panel Research

Research on brand loyalty, as a share of purchase, began with a paper by Copeland (1923) in the first issue of the *Harvard Business Review*. Copeland discussed a phenomenon, which he called brand insistence, which occurs when a consumer refuses to substitute one brand for another. Copeland was concerned with repertoire markets like groceries, where consumers often purchase more than one brand in a category. In these markets, brand insistence is an extreme form of share loyalty and is now called sole-brand loyalty.

Initially, research into this field was held back because there were no sound methods for measuring brand purchases. Retrospective surveys of purchase may be used but consumers can easily forget some of the purchases that they have made. To reduce this recall error, Churchill (1942) advocated the use of panels of consumers, who agreed to make regular reports about their household purchases. The methods for measuring purchases by panel members have evolved. Initially, members were asked to provide weekly reports of their household's purchases, usually by keeping a diary of daily purchases. An alternative form of measurement was the 'dustbin' method where the consumer retained all wrappers and agency staff counted purchases from the wrappers. But all wrappers may not be kept, so this method is also fallible. When bar codes became universal, panel members were given a bar-code reader and they used this to record their purchases when they brought their groceries home. Home scanning panels are still used worldwide by companies like Kantar (formerly TNS) and Nielsen. An alternative method is used by Information Resources Inc. (IRI) in the USA. They provide the checkout scanners in the stores of a number of communities where they conduct research. When panel members use a store they show an identification card and the store scanner sends data on their purchases directly to IRI for processing.

The first regular panel was run by a newspaper, the *Chigago Tribune*. Brown (1953) used data from this panel and found that brand loyalty in a household fitted one of four patterns:

- Sole-brand loyalty.
- Divided brand loyalty (polygamous).
- Unstable loyalty (switching, between brands).
- No brand loyalty (promiscuous).

Brown classified people on the basis of runs of purchase of brands in each category. Thus AAAAAA shows sole brand loyalty, a mix such as AABABA indicates loyalty divided between brand A and brand B, and AAABBB might indicate unstable loyalty with a switch from A to B, though it is not possible to distinguish true switching from divided loyalty without an extended period of measurement. It is now clear that divided (or multi-brand) loyalty is the usual pattern of grocery purchase (see Box 2.1).

Box 2.1 Reasons for divided loyalty

Why do people buy more than one brand in a category? There seem to be two sorts of explanation for having a portfolio of brands – which we call genuine and apparent.

Genuine portfolio

This may occur because:

1. There is little brand awareness and the consumer does not remember previously bought brands.
2. The category is one where consumers appreciate variety (biscuits, cereals, wine).
3. Customers buy discounted brands, which spreads their range of purchase.
4. The brand that the customer wanted was not available.

Apparent portfolio

1. The panel collects data on household expenditure. Members of a household may prefer different brands. Individually, they could be 100 per cent loyal but, as a household, they could show divided loyalty.
2. A household may buy different brands in sub-categories such as biological and non-biological detergent. The household could be 100 per cent loyal in each sub-category. We need to remember that the product groupings in the minds of consumers may differ from the categories used by market researchers.

Share of Category Requirement

Cunningham's (1956) share-of-purchase approach is now standard and is illustrated with invented data in Table 2.1. In the table, the last three numbers of row 1 show that, over one year, Household 1 devotes 50 per cent of purchases to Brand A, 30 per cent to Brand B and 20 per cent to Brand C. These percentages are the share-of-category requirement (SCR) measures that were introduced in Chapter 1. Another measure that is often used is

Table 2.1 Hypothetical brand purchase data for one category (assume only three brands in the category)

House-hold	*Purchases of Brands A, B and C in each month*												*Total purchases (all brands)*	*% over year*		
	Jan	*Feb*	*Mar*	*Apr*	*May*	*June*	*July*	*Aug*	*Sept*	*Oct*	*Nov*	*Dec*		*A*	*B*	*C*
1	A	B	B	A	C		A	C	B	A		A	10	50	30	20
2	B	C		C	A	AC		C	B		C	C	10	20	20	60
3	AA		AB	B	AA		AB	A	A	A	B	AB	15	67	33	0
4	C	A	A	B	C	CC	A	A	AC	B	A	A	14	50	14	36
5	AB		AB	A	B	C	A	A		A	A		11	64	27	9
6	A			A		A				A			4	100	0	0
7	A		C	C		A		AB		AC		A	9	56	11	33
8	C	C		A	A			A	C	A	C		8	50	0	50
9	A		A		A			B		A			5	80	20	0
10			A			A						A	3	100	0	0
Mean													**9**	**64**	**15**	**21**

first-brand loyalty. This is the share given to the most heavily bought brand (e.g. Household 1 has a first-brand loyalty of 50 per cent). We see in Table 2.1 how purchase patterns can vary and that some households buy very little.

The last three columns give the SCR loyalty to brands of each household and the means at the base of these columns give the average SCR per brand; Brand A, with a score of 64 per cent, is more popular than Brands B and C.[1]

Exercise 2.1 Market share and average SCR

How do average SCRs relate to market share? Are they the same or different? Think about this before looking below.

The average SCRs per brand are quite close to market share. Purchase frequencies differ across households and light buyers tend to focus on market leaders (like consumers 6 and 10 in Table 2.1). This means that the average SCR of brand leaders tends to be a little above their market share. Fifty-one of the 89 purchases in Table 2.1 are for Brand A, which gives it a market share of 57 per cent, slightly below the mean SCR of 64 per cent for Brand A.

Another measure is the average first-brand loyalty in a category. What is the average first-brand loyalty in Table 2.1? This is 50 + 60 + 67 + 50 + 64 + 100 + 56 + 50 + 80 + 100 divided by 10, which is nearly 68. Figures of 50–70 per cent for first-brand loyalty are common for grocery brands.

Customers who buy a brand only once in a period must have an SCR of 100 per cent; when the brand is bought twice, the SCR cannot be less than 50 per cent; and when it is bought three times, the minimum is 33 per cent. These small-number effects mean that customers who rarely purchase in a period tend to have higher SCRs than average and, conversely, those who are sole-brand loyal are often light buyers. When more cases are obtained by gathering data over a long period, the small-number effect disappears and then light buyers are found to be somewhat less loyal (Stern and Hammond, 2004).

Loyalty Proneness and its Correlates

Cunningham (1956) also wanted to know whether the loyalty that a consumer showed in one category was related to their loyalty in another; he called this *loyalty proneness*. In his research, Cunningham found little evidence of loyalty proneness. Among 21 correlations between share loyalties for individuals across different categories, the highest was 0.3. East et al. (1995) found correlations averaging 0.46 between share-loyalty measures across four grocery categories in a survey. This evidence indicates that it is realistic to average a consumer's loyalty scores across a range of categories to obtain a score for individual loyalty proneness. Using this method, East et al. found that a customer's share loyalty to grocery brands was correlated with their store loyalty (measured as share), total supermarket spending, lack of interest in discounts and household income.

The association between brand loyalty and store loyalty that East et al. found has been noted in other studies and a number of explanations have been offered. One possibility is that loyalty to retailer brands (own label, private label) explains the effect because the customer who buys more of a particular retailer brand has to do this by shopping with that retailer. However, Rao (1969) and East et al. (1995) both found that the correlation persisted after removing store-brand loyalty, and Flavián, Martínez and Polo (2001) support this view with their finding that brand-loyal customers bought fewer private label goods. Another explanation is that those who use a wider range of stores (low store loyalty) have a wider range of brands to choose from and this would tend to reduce their brand loyalty. A third possibility is that the correlation between brand loyalty and store loyalty may be explained if these forms of loyalty are habits, and that some people are more habit-prone. This explanation is supported by the finding that those with high brand and high store loyalty are more likely to show another habit by having a routine day for supermarket shopping (East et al., 2000). Habit proneness could relate to personality or lifestyle. Habits, by their nature, tend to exclude new experience but they may save time and effort (see Box 2.2).

Box 2.2 The habits of Gilbert & George (from the ***Observer Magazine***, 28 January 2007)

The artists Gilbert & George wear the same tailored suits day in, day out, and follow the same routines 365 days a year. They get up at 6.30am and go round the corner to a café for breakfast (they do not have a kitchen at home). They then work till 11, when it's back to the café for lunch, after which they put in a full afternoon until Paul O'Grady's show comes on ITV at 5pm. … Dinner is taken in the same Turkish restaurant in Hackney every night. …They are often asked about these routines and complain that no one ever seems to grasp that they stick to them, not for show, but to save time.

Other Habits

Purchase habits also apply to brands that we routinely *do not buy*. Most of us will admit to avoiding certain brands and service providers. Research by Hunt, Hunt and Hunt (1988) has thrown light on the way consumers hold grudges against such brands or providers. Hunt et al. find that grudges persist for a long time and usually begin with an emotionally upsetting experience as a customer. Grudge-holders often give negative word of mouth about the offending product when talking to others. Such brand avoidance could have dire consequences for a manufacturer but, despite this, it has received little systematic study.

Beside brands, there are other product differentiators, and consumers can be loyal to pack size, price level, country of origin, flavour and formulation characteristics. For example, Romaniuk and Dawes (2005) found that, although people bought a variety of different wines, they tended to have a consistent pattern of preference for price tiers. Singh, Ehrenberg and Goodhardt (2004) have illustrated regular patterns of purchase with regard to other category divisions. The point that we emphasize here is that no emotional commitment is needed for such effects. We argue that most patterns of purchase, including loyalty, reflect habit rather than deeply felt commitment.

SECTION 2: THE RISE OF RELATIONSHIP MARKETING: CUSTOMER LOYALTY AS RETENTION

Relationship marketing (RM) has been described as 'attracting, maintaining and enhancing customer relationships' (Berry, 1983: 25). In a business-to-business (B2B) context, RM is an industrial philosophy that replaces the competitive transaction between buyer and seller with a more cooperative relationship[2] (Grönroos, 1994). In a cooperative relationship, partners learn to trust each other and to reveal more detail about their needs to the other, which improves the quality of mutual support. Relationship marketing has also been applied in the business-to-consumer (B2C) field, particularly by those concerned with services. As in B2B, some service relationships (e.g. dentist and patient) can be characterized by trust and cooperation but this does not apply so well when the business is larger. There is still interdependence between a large firm and its customers but any initiatives are likely to come from the firm and to be automated with the help of the customer database. Firms call this customer relationship management (CRM). Much of the CRM conducted by large firms is designed to increase sales by exploiting customer purchase habits and this has little to do with cooperation. Most firms follow good-practice rules so that their customers can trust them to deliver consistent quality goods and services, but it does not go much further than that. For their part, customers can be quite calculating. For example, they may participate in loyalty schemes because they get a discount on purchases, or gain other benefits, rather than because they like the firm.

In relationship marketing there is more emphasis placed on retaining existing customers than attracting new ones. CRM can help here; for example, when a sudden lack of spending indicates that a customer has switched supermarkets, customized vouchers can be issued that may bring the customer back. Most firms are keen to see increases in satisfaction among customers because this is thought to retain customers. This emphasis on retaining customers is based on the idea that it is more expensive to acquire customers than to retain them. So, instead of losing a customer and gaining another, it is cheaper not to lose the customer in the first place. A review by Rosenberg and Czepiel (1984) suggested that the average company spends six times as much acquiring a customer as keeping a customer. The 'six times as much' rule has now become an item of marketing folklore; the reality is that the relative cost varies with the category. For example, supermarket customers are acquired at little cost whereas credit card customers are expensive to acquire because they must be checked with credit agencies and offered financial inducements to switch.

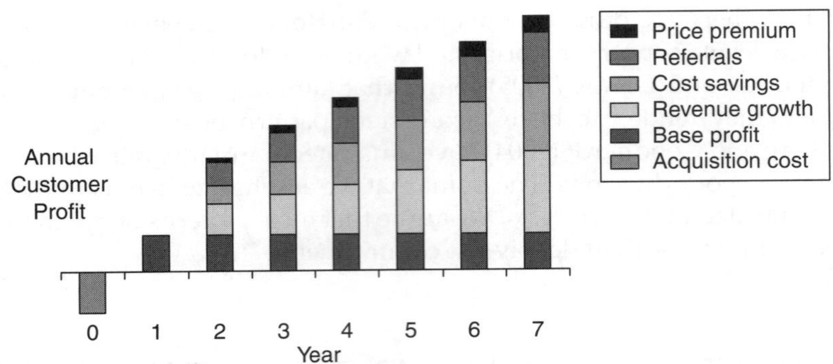

Figure 2.1 Factors in customer lifetime value (adapted from Reichheld, 1996b)

The idea that customer retention increases long-term profit was given added impetus by Reichheld and his associates in a series of papers (Reichheld and Kenny, 1990; Reichheld and Sasser, 1990; Reichheld, 1993; Jones and Sasser, 1995; Reichheld, 1996a). These ideas were brought together in a book by Reichheld (1996b). Reichheld suggests that the value of a customer grows with the length of time that they remain a customer (called customer tenure). The reasons for this are illustrated in Figure 2.1. Reichheld argues that, for each added year of tenure, the profit from a customer rises as the acquisition cost is amortized, and as the customer spends more (revenue growth), becomes easier to deal with (cost savings), introduces more new customers (referrals) and is more tolerant of higher prices (price premium). Also, and not shown in Figure 2.1, the longer customers stay, the more likely they are to remain in the following year. This means that those who are currently long-term customers are likely to give more profit in the future than current short-term customers. An admirable feature of Reichheld's work is that he is very precise about the potential effects of customer retention so that others can test these claims. Reichheld's own evidence tends to be based on case studies. Case studies serve well for teaching about management practice but, as evidence, they are not as valuable as systematic studies that are set up to test a hypothesis. Case study evidence is often already available when marketers begin to hypothesize and they may unintentionally focus on the evidence that fits their theory. Below, we review Reichheld's claims.

Customer Tenure and Profitability

We now review five assumptions for how customer loyalty might be turned into higher profits.

First, do long-term customers spend more? East, Hammond and Gendall (2006) reported on 17 services where customers were asked how much they spent and how long they had used the supplier. Examples of services were supermarkets, credit cards, dry cleaners, fashion stores, mobile phone airtime and car servicing. Of the 17 studies, only three showed a statistically significant positive association between tenure and spending:

credit cards (UK), outdoor clothing (USA) and mobile phone airtime (UK). The average correlation between tenure and spend for the 17 studies was 0.09. This shows that, usually, there is no substantial association between tenure and spending that would justify management attention. In a few categories, long-term customers may spend significantly more than new customers, but such cases need to be established by research and not assumed by managers.

Second, are long-term customers cheaper to serve? Long-term customers become familiar with company procedures and need less 'hand holding' but they may also exploit company services more. Dowling and Uncles (1997) first expressed doubt that long-term customers were cheaper to serve. Later, Reinartz and Kumar (2000, 2002) found that long-term customers in one firm made more use of the free services available, thus raising their cost to serve. They also found that loyalty programme costs increased with tenure. It seems that total costs do not routinely decline with tenure.

Third, do long-term customers refer more new customers than recently acquired customers? Long-term customers may value their providers more for two reasons. First they may *learn* more about the merits of the supplier's offering over time, and second, as those who dislike the supplier switch, the more appreciative customers remain. Despite these effects, Smith and Higgins (2000) and Fournier, Dobscha and Mick (1998) have illustrated how relationships can sometimes sour over time. Also, a brand may be salient when first acquired but may then become so familiar that consumers give it no thought and therefore do not talk about it. This loss of salience is more likely when the category does not change much (e.g. house insurance) and/or is frequently used (e.g. credit cards). When there is change, for example in the merchandise of a fashion store, the brand might be recommended again whereas a relatively unchanging product, for example motor insurance, does not merit a second recommendation.

In their review of previous evidence, East et al. (2005a) found either no association between recommendation rates and tenure (e.g. Kumar, Scheer and Steenkamp, 1995; Verhoef, Franses and Hoekstra, 2002) or a negative association (e.g. East, Lomax and Narain, 2001; Wangenheim and Bayón, 2004). In their own research, East et al. reported evidence from 23 studies on tenure and recommendation rates (shown in Table 2.2). They found that the overall association between tenure and recommendation was neutral (–0.01) but that individual associations ranged from significantly negative to significantly positive. The significant negative associations were for cheque accounts, credit cards and car insurance. The significant positive associations were for car servicing and main fashion stores (data for this latter category were gathered in Mexico). Car servicing is infrequent so it takes time for a new customer to be reassured about the quality of work. Car servicing was one of the service categories mentioned by Reichheld and, in this specific case, the evidence supports the assertion that long-tenure customers recommend more. Notice that East et al. studied credit cards and car servicing twice in the UK (with different samples); the pairs of studies gave similar results and this makes the work more convincing. Overall, East et al. (2005a) do not support Reichheld's claim that long-tenure customers normally recommend more than short-tenure customers. The association depends on the category and may be positive, negative or neutral.

Table 2.2 Correlations between customer tenure in 23 service studies (from East et al., 2005a)

Service (country)	*Customer tenure and recommendation*
Cheque book service (UK)	–.44*
Credit card (UK)	–.39*
Car insurance (UK)	–.36*
Credit card (UK)	–.28*
Main supermarket (UK)	–.09
Mobile airtime (UK)	–.04
Motor insurance (UK)	–.03
Dentist (UK)	–.03
Dry cleaning (UK)	–.02
Internet provider (UK)	0.02
Leisure centre (UK)	0.04
House contents insurance (UK)	0.04
Main supermarket (Mexico)	0.06
Main fashion store (UK)	0.07
Car insurance (Mauritius)	0.07
Favourite restaurant (UK)	0.08
Email (UK)	0.10
Hairdresser (Mexico)	0.12
Search engine (UK)	0.13
Main fashion store (Mexico)	0.18*
Car servicing (UK)	0.20*
Car servicing (Mauritius)	0.20*
Car servicing (UK)	0.25*
Mean	**–.01**

*Significant at $p < 0.05$

Fourth, are long-term customers more price-tolerant? Price tolerance is particularly exploited by providers of financial services. For example, firms may allow the interest paid on accounts to drop without telling the account holders. In addition, mortgage, insurance and credit card offers to new customers are often better than those to existing customers. These tactics rely on customer inertia and may produce short-term profit for the bank if a large proportion of existing customers do not notice the changes but, when customers do take note, they may be irritated and switch providers in order to get introductory discounts themselves. This behaviour can be very damaging to long-term profits. Reichheld makes it clear that this sort of exploitation of customers is likely to be detrimental in the longer run. However, in other fields there may be no long-term price premium. In three B2C companies that they studied, Reinartz and Kumar (2002) found that long-tenure customers did not pay more than short-term customers for the same goods. They also found that

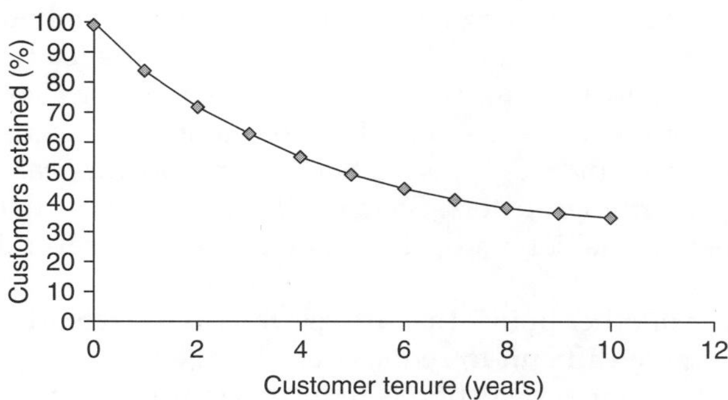

Figure 2.2 Normal customer survival pattern (adapted from Reichheld, 1996b)

long-tenure customers were *more* price-sensitive and that these customers expected better value when compared with recent customers.

Fifth, do defection rates decline with tenure? In general, this is true. Reichheld finds that a company typically loses about 15 per cent of its current customers in the first year and 50 per cent over five years. If we follow a cohort of customers and examine them over a period, we find that fewer and fewer customers defect each year and that the decay curve levels out, as shown in Figure 2.2. A study by East and Hammond (1996) estimated defection rates for a range of groceries and found an average of 15 per cent defection in the first year. In the second year, defection halved. This means that the customer's prospective lifetime value increases with tenure. However, there must come a time when changes in life stage (and even death) mean that customers no longer need the category and defection may then rise. In addition, there are some products and services which are only used for a limited period, for example disposable nappies and crèche facilities, and here we would see a different pattern from that shown in Figure 2.2.

In conclusion, Reichheld's claim that customer loyalty translates into long-term profit is more a plausible hypothesis than a fact. Each of the potential sources of the profit increase from loyal customers has been challenged by more recent research, and companies should examine to what extent loyal customers may be an advantage for their particular business.

The Strategy of Customer Retention

The evidence summarized above indicates that the benefit of customer retention in consumer markets has been exaggerated and that the benefits from retention differ substantially between categories. One implication of this evidence is that customer acquisition may bring more advantage, relative to retention, than is conventionally recognized. We need more evidence of the relative cost of sales gains through customer acquisition and retention and we also need more evidence on how increases in market share come about – are such increases due primarily to acquisition or retention of customers? Two relevant studies are by East and Hogg (1997) and Riebe, Sharp and Stern (2002). East and Hogg found that, when Tesco overtook Sainsbury in 1995 as the leading UK supermarket, the Tesco gains came equally from increased customer acquisitions and reduced defection. Sainsbury lost customers because of reduced recruitment, not increased defection. Riebe et al. found that increases in drug prescription among doctors came mainly from the acquisition of new prescribing doctors. Sharp (2010) also argues that brand gains come mainly from customer acquisition and presents evidence from several studies to support his view.

There are a number of other points that are relevant to the retention versus acquisition argument. First, it is quite difficult to reduce defection. Reichheld's calculations suggest large gains in profit if customer defection is reduced from 15 per cent to 10 per cent but a one-third drop in defection is a substantial amount. Reichheld did give some examples where defection averaged only a few per cent a year but, in services where there is a specific location for service delivery, a large part of the defection occurs because of the relative inaccessibility of the service. For example, East, Lomax and Narain (2001) found that 43 per cent of the defections from a main supermarket were because the customer had moved home or because a more convenient store had been built nearby. This sort of customer loss is very difficult to counter.

A second point is mentioned by Reichheld but is sometimes forgotten by those who espouse his arguments. This is that the customers who are retained by a successful marketing intervention or service improvement are not necessarily typical of the other customers of the service provider. Customers who defect are obviously more mobile; when these customers are retained through a marketing intervention, they may be more likely to defect later.

A third point is that it is in the nature of loyal customers that they stay put. They may not need incentives to stay; if this is so, investments in rewards and product improvements may give little return with this group. Similarly, it may be very difficult to prise away the loyal customers of competitors. This leads to a paradox of loyalty. The most loyal customers may have the highest value but they may not be the best segment for marketing intervention because of their inertia. So which customers should be targeted when we have evidence of their loyalty? Should you target your high-share customers, who cannot increase their share much and also may not be willing to change their habits?[3] Or medium-share customers, who can increase their share and may be more changeable? Or low-share customers, who can increase their share substantially or may change easily, but also may be prone to change again away from your brand later? This is a complicated problem which requires category-specific research.

Although customer retention is emphasized in relationship marketing, this evidence shows that customer acquisition may be more important. Reichheld (1996b) does not ignore customer acquisition. He gives the example of the MBNA credit card organization. This company managed to acquire high-spending and high-retention customers by the careful design of the service and by well-chosen targeting. It is also well accepted that not all customers are profitable. Company costs can exceed returns on small-spending customers and sometimes retail facilities are so overstretched that more profit is made when some customers defect.

Exercise 2.2 Brand switching

Consumers switch for many reasons which may vary across categories. Your own experience may be a guide. If you have switched banks, mobile phone companies, doctors, hairdressers, supermarkets or alcoholic beverages, why did you do this? Choose two categories in which you have switched your main brand:

1 List the key reasons for your switch.
2 Identify four things the supplier could have done to try to retain you.
3 Evaluate how effective each of these supplier initiatives would have been in your particular case.

Loyalty Programmes

Many B2C companies now have loyalty programmes. These programmes have been introduced for different reasons. Some companies saw a genuine interest in rewarding their most loyal customers, and business books like *The Loyalty Effect* (Reichheld 1996b) encouraged them in this direction. They often had to open up their programme to less loyal customers, which in some cases increased the costs up to a point where the expected gains from the overall programme were erased. Other companies felt forced to imitate their competitors for fear of losing customers. In some industries, loyalty programmes increased the overall costs for all players without real effect on loyalty (a zero-sum game). Overall, recent academic research suggests that loyalty programmes only generate small effects (Verhoef, 2003) or no effect (DeWulf, Odekerken-Schroder and Iacobucci, 2001; Mägi, 2003) on purchase behaviour. But these programmes nevertheless exist and should be optimized. Drèze and Nunes (2011) developed a programme of research to examine how insights from consumer behaviour can help marketers design and improve their loyalty programmes.

In most loyalty programmes rewards can be earned repeatedly (e.g. discount certificates at a retailer, free nights at a hotel chain, free tickets on an airline). Consumers work towards the goal of obtaining the reward and, once the reward is obtained, have to build up their reward credit again. Drèze and Nunes (2011) examine what happens to consumption behaviour after a reward has been obtained. One might expect a post-reward reset and deceleration in purchases after the consumer attains the reward. Using a large-scale dataset from a frequent-flier programme, the authors show that, instead, success is followed by an increase in effort to reach the same goal again. Interestingly, this effect is only obtained when success requires perseverance. Successes that come too easily, when small rewards are frequently obtained, do not have this effect. Creating larger rewards with greater purchase requirements leads to more overall effort. In a subsequent experimental study, Drèze and Nunes show that the consumer's self-perceptions of efficacy play an important role. Some form of self-learning takes place in the process of goal attainment which affects action designed to secure the second and subsequent rewards. Overall, this work shows that cleverly designed loyalty programmes really can stimulate purchases.

A loyalty programme can also be designed to give consumers additional incentives to purchase, without additional cost. In a field experiment at a professional car wash, Nunes and Drèze (2006) randomly distributed two types of loyalty cards. For the first type, eight car wash purchases were required for a free car wash. With the second type of card, ten purchases were necessary but, as part of a special promotion, two free stamps were given such that the number of required new purchases was also eight. The respective redemption rates were 19 per cent and 34 per cent. Framing the task as already begun apparently enhanced the effort to reach the reward goal, although the distance to the goal was no different between the two groups. Consumers in that framing condition also accelerated their purchases: they left 2.9 fewer days between washes.

Another design feature of loyalty programmes is that they can have a hierarchical structure with different tiers to give the 'best' customers (supposedly, the highest spenders) a special status. Companies have to decide on the number of tiers they want to introduce (a single tier is an option) and, in the case of multiple tiers, on the number of customers they want to admit to each. Drèze and Nunes (2009) show, in a series of experiments, that the desire for tier status can drive behaviour. Companies face the trade-off of making as many customers as possible feel special, without disenfranchising the very best customers by diluting their special status. The authors show that a three-tiered programme is more satisfying than a programme with two tiers, and this applies to all customers, not just those qualifying for elite status. The size of the top tier can be increased without decreasing the status perceptions of its existing members, as long as a second tier is added. Adding a third tier enhances self-perceptions of status of those in the second tier. (Note: other aspects of loyalty programmes are considered in Chapter 11).

SECTION 3: COMBINATION DEFINITIONS OF LOYALTY

So far we have described loyalty in terms of share, retention, recommendation and satisfaction. We have not combined these different forms of loyalty into a more complex definition. Most marketing scientists use a single behavioural definition, usually share or retention (see East et al., 2005a). By contrast, most of those who have theorized about loyalty suggest that loyalty is not behaviour alone, and many feel strongly that attitude should appear in the definition. For example, Jacoby and Olson (1970) defined loyalty as the biased (i.e. non-random) behavioural response (i.e. purchase), expressed over time, by some decision-making unit (e.g. household, person), with respect to one or more alternative brands, which is a function of psychological processes (decision-making, evaluation).

Customers who stay with suppliers because of unthinking habit or simple convenience are not regarded as loyal according to this definition because a feeling about the brand is required in addition to behaviour. Oliver (1999: 34) emphasized the role of feeling as well as behaviour when he described loyalty as 'a deeply held commitment to re-buy or re-patronize a preferred product/service consistently in the future, thereby causing

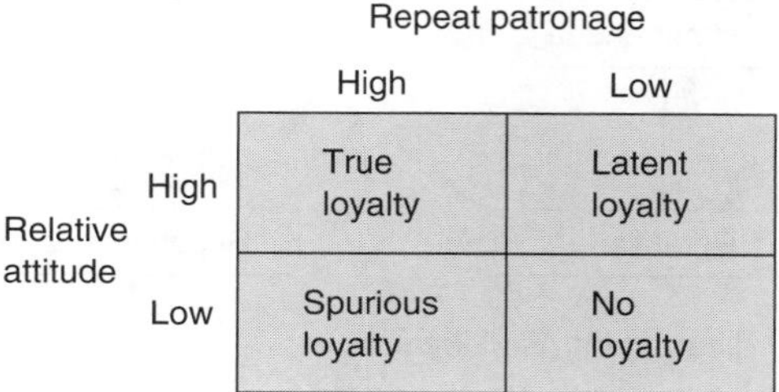

Figure 2.3 Forms of loyalty (adapted from Dick and Basu, 1994)

repetitive same-brand or same brand-set purchasing, despite situational influences and marketing efforts having the potential to cause switching behavior'. Also, Day (1969) suggested that 'true' or intentional loyalty occurred when there was a positive attitude to the brand and he distinguished this from 'spurious' loyalty where purchase of the brand was not supported by any commitment. Another widely quoted paper by Dick and Basu (1994) used Day's distinction and divided customers into four segments in the typology shown in Figure 2.3. True loyalty occurs in the top left-hand quadrant of Figure 2.3. Latent loyalty covers those who would like to buy the brand but who have not been able to do so in the past because it was not available, too expensive or because they had no need for it. Spurious loyalty occurs when consumers buy the brand but regard it as little better than others. In this typology, 'relative attitude' means that the attitude measure includes a term such as *compared with available alternatives*. Then, if a brand gets a high score, it is because it is rated much higher than the nearest alternative.

So should we see loyalty simply as behaviour or as behaviour with attitude? Ryanair and Wal-Mart can make profits from customers who use them regularly but may not like them. Indeed, for brands in some utilitarian categories like bleach and sugar it is difficult to generate much feeling. But when loyal behaviour is supported by a liking for the brand, retention may be greater and more profit may be made. There are brands like Harley-Davidson which are clearly liked a lot by their owners. Fournier and Yao (1997) studied how consumers experience their relationships with their favourite brand(s) of coffee from the perspective of interpersonal relationship theory. In-depth interviews with eight consumers show that the strength and character of loyalty relationships with brands can vary widely even if, on the surface, there may be not much difference in behaviour. For some consumers, their favourite brand is like a partner and provides sense and structure in their life. Even brands with a small share of use (SCR in our jargon) can play a very significant role in some people's consumption routines.

Definitions relate to the type of explanation that the researcher seeks to make. In Chapter 1, we introduced *segment comparisons* and *causal relationships*. Dick and Basu's typology allows researchers to make comparisons between the four segments with respect to retention, share, recommendation and overall profitability, though we have been unable to find research that does this. Pritchard, Havitz and Howard (1999) used the Dick and Basu typology to show a number of differences between travellers who were classified according to the four segments but the authors did not investigate behaviour

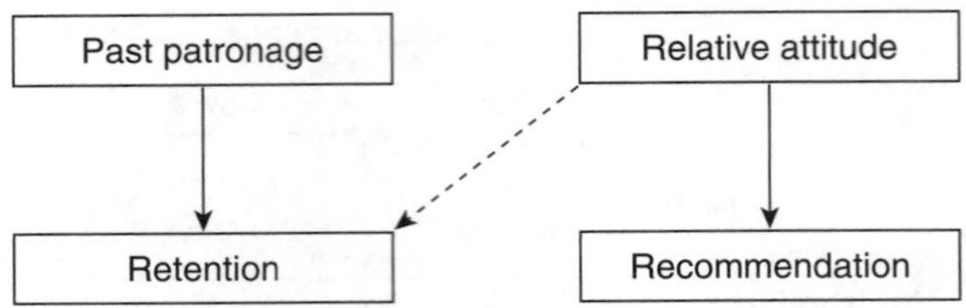

Figure 2.4 Consequences of different forms of loyalty

such as recommendation and retention. Macintosh and Lockshin (1997) also found significant differences between customers divided according to the Dick and Basu typology, but they investigated *intention* to repurchase rather than actual retention, and intention to repurchase may not relate closely to actual retention. Combination definitions of loyalty may be useful if retention and recommendation differ across segments, but we need to see evidence on this matter.

East et al. (2005a) investigated whether relative attitude and past patronage both predicted later retention and recommendation. For supermarkets and cars, they found that greater relative attitude was associated with more recommendation but had little relationship with retention. They also found that customers who bought mostly from one supermarket or who had bought the same make of car on the last two occasions (high past patronage) were somewhat more likely to retain the supermarket or buy the last make of car again at the next purchase, but that the level of past patronage had no effect on word of mouth. Figure 2.4 summarizes these relationships with the dotted line indicating a weak relationship. We conclude that retention and word of mouth have largely different causes. One simple way of explaining the relationships in Figure 2.4 is that 'like correlates with like'. Past patronage and later retention are alike because they are the same measure at different points in time. Relative attitude and recommendation are alike because the reasons that people have for liking a brand are likely to be much the same as the reasons they give when they recommend it.

Research studies have generally shown a weak positive association between satisfaction and retention. Crosby and Stephens (1987) found that life assurance renewal was slightly greater when customers were satisfied with the provider. Kordupleski, Rust and Zahoric (1993) found limited evidence that satisfaction increased retention in company research by AT&T. Reichheld (1993) reported that between 65 per cent and 85 per cent of customers who defected were satisfied with their former supplier. Ennew and Binks (1996) did not find clear evidence of a positive association between retention and service quality (the latter is usually closely related to satisfaction) and Hennig-Thurau and Klee (1997) generally found moderate associations between satisfaction and retention in a review of studies in this field. Against this weak evidence we can find a few stronger findings but these are where *dissatisfaction* has caused customers to switch. Andreasen (1985) studied ten patients who reported serious problems with their medical care and found that six of them switched physicians; Bolton (1998) found that dissatisfaction with a mobile phone airtime provider led to switching if the users had recently adopted the service and lacked knowledge of the supplier's longer-term performance. Winchester, Romaniuk and Bogomolova (2008) show that defection is indicated by prior negative beliefs about the product. Overall, the research evidence indicates that satisfaction with a brand or supplier provides a limited prospect of increased retention but dissatisfaction may be a spur to switching.

Some readers may find it puzzling that feelings like satisfaction have such a weak relationship with retention but there are some good reasons why this should be so. One reason is that, usually, the measure of satisfaction employed is not *relative*. People retain a supplier because of the *superiority* of that supplier over others and using a relative satisfaction measure is more sensitive to this relative difference between alternatives. A second reason for the weak association between satisfaction and retention can be found in the reasons for defection. In services, defection often occurs as a consequence of specific failures, price changes or the emergence of superior competition, as found by Keaveney (1995); such reasons are unlikely to be anticipated by an earlier measure of satisfaction. The same could be true of some goods. A third reason why satisfaction fails to predict defection well is that the defection may be involuntary, as was found by East, Lomax and Narain (2001). People who move house will change their main supermarket if their old one is now inaccessible; this does not mean that it was unsatisfactory.

What does all this mean? Those who propose combination measures of loyalty need to show that this approach is useful and that the segments in Dick and Basu's typology behave in different ways. In particular, they need to show that the top-left loyalty segment shows more retention, share loyalty and recommendation than other segments, at least in some categories. If they cannot do this, the case for such combination measures fails. Meanwhile, those who are interested in the prediction of retention and recommendation need to treat these behaviours separately because they do not appear to have much common causation.

SECTION 4: REASONS FOR DEFECTION

Retention is often based on inertia. Behaviourally, consumers remain loyal by continuing to do what they have done before. In some cases, the inertia can be quite thoughtless as people continue with savings accounts and utility suppliers, even when alternative suppliers offer much better value. In the case of consumer durables, where an act of repurchase is required for retention, there may be more thought but, even here, the process may be fairly automatic. A study by Lapersonne, Laurent and Le Goff (1995) on car purchase showed that 17 per cent of the respondents considered only the brand of their current car.

We have mentioned how existing customers can attract new ones through positive word of mouth. It turns out that defection is also contagious. Using data on one million customers of a cellular phone company, Nitzan and Libai (2011) show that exposure to a defecting neighbour in their close social network increases a person's chances of defection by 80 per cent. Consumers with more social connections are more affected. But heavy users and customers with a longer tenure are less affected by their neighbours' defections.

When people defect, they often have reasons. The reasons for defecting from service providers were studied by Keaveney (1995).

Table 2.3 Reasons for switching from a service (adapted from Keaveney, 1995)

	All reasons (%)	*When only one reason given (%)*	*Mean (%)*
Core service failures	25	25	25
Failed service encounters	19	20	20
Response to failed service	10	0	5
Pricing	17	20	18
Competition	6	7	6
Ethical problems	4	4	4
Inconvenience	12	10	11
Involuntary switching	4	7	5
Other	5	7	6

Keaveney used her postgraduate students as investigators. They gathered evidence from people outside the university, asking them to focus on their most recent service defection, report what the service was and describe what happened. The narratives of what happened were reviewed by judges, who produced a typology of eight reasons for defection plus an 'other' category. Then the frequency of the different reasons was assessed from the narratives. Some people had more than one reason for defection and, in Table 2.3, we show the percentages for all the reasons cited and the percentages when one reason was given. There is not much difference between these two sets of percentages and we treat the average as typical of what Keaveney found (column 4).

The method used by Keaveney, called Critical Incident Technique (CIT), is suitable for establishing the typology of reasons for defection but rather less appropriate for measuring the frequency of the different reasons since some memories are more easily recalled because of *retrieval bias*. This was described by Taylor (1982: 192), who states that 'colorful, dynamic, or other distinctive stimuli disproportionately engage attention and, accordingly, disproportionately affect judgments'. Events are more changing and distinctive than conditions and are thus more easily retrieved. In Keaveney's list of reasons, the first three (core service failures, failed service encounters and responses to failed service) are clearly events (50 per cent), whereas inconvenience and involuntary switching (16 per cent) are likely to relate to persisting conditions. Keaveney asserts that managers can make changes that prevent events, and can thus stop defection; and she argues that her data support action to retain customers. But if Keaveney's method raises the proportion of events reported at the expense of conditions, a strategy of customer acquisition may be more profitable.

East, Grandcolas, Dall'Olmo Riley and Lomax (2012) used a different method of measurement. They put Keaveney's reasons into one item of a questionnaire and asked survey respondents to state which of these reasons was the most important in their decision to defect. This method should have reduced retrieval bias because all the possible reasons were prompted. Keaveney aggregated the data on all services mentioned by respondents

Table 2.4 Condensed table of reasons for defection compared with Keaveney's results (percentages by row) (from East et al., 2012)

	N	*Service failure events*	*Pricing*	*Competition*	*Ethical problems*	*Conditions*	*Other*
Located services	523	12	12	23	1	47	6
Non-located services	369	27	35	20	0	8	9
All services	892	18	22	22	1	31	7
Keaveney	211	50	18	6	4	16	6

but East et al. report findings for specific services. They chose some services that were delivered in a particular location (e.g. a favourite restaurant) and some services where delivery was independent of location (e.g. mobile phone airtime). They reasoned that conditions would be much more important as a reason for defection when service delivery was located because the inaccessibility of some locations could cause inconvenience and involuntary switching. East et al. combined data on the three types of service failure event and the two types of condition and their aggregate results are shown in Table 2.4, together with Keaveney's frequencies for comparison.

Table 2.4 shows that East et al. found a much lower proportion of service failure events compared with Keaveney (18 per cent instead of 50 per cent) and a higher proportion of conditions (31 per cent versus 16 per cent). The conditions came mainly from the located services, as expected. This evidence suggests that it is difficult to retain customers in located services and, here, it may be better to go for a strategy of customer acquisition.

SUMMARY

Several behaviours indicate customer loyalty. These are share-of-category requirement (SCR) in repertoire markets, and retention and recommendation in all markets. Feelings also indicate loyalty. The main feelings are attitude, satisfaction, commitment and trust.

Early work investigated SCR in grocery purchase and showed that consumers frequently divided their purchasing across several brands in a category. Divided loyalty patterns persist over long periods and reflect consumer habits.

With the rise in relationship marketing, attention turned to the retention of customers, particularly with regard to services. Reichheld (1996b) argued that there was substantial profit to be gained if customers could be retained for longer periods; however, many of his assertions have been undermined by subsequent research. Loyalty programmes are nevertheless very common. They can be optimized by thinking carefully about the reward frequency and status perceptions when there are different tiers of loyalty.

Marketing scientists have generally used behaviour measures such as share and retention while others have argued that loyalty should be seen as a composite of attitude and behaviour and should be tested by segment comparisons. The best-known composite model is by Dick and Basu (1994); however, although differences in behaviour have been demonstrated between the population segments defined by this model, there is little evidence that these segments differ in respect of retention and recommendation.

Defection from services has been studied by Keaveney (1995), who developed a typology of eight reasons for defection. Keaveney found that many reasons for defection related to events that managers could control and thus thought that much defection could be prevented. However, recent work suggests that much defection may not be controllable, which turns attention to customer acquisition rather than customer retention.

Additional Resources

The papers by Reichheld and his colleagues are clearly written and are more concise than his book. Keaveney's (1995) paper is much cited and easy to follow. Reinartz and Kumar (2002) provide a critical review in this area.

Notes

1 We do not describe the average SCR per brand as *brand loyalty* because there is no consistent usage here.
2 User-generated content online has given more voice and initiative to the consumer. See Chapter 12.
3 Tesco estimate the share of each customer's grocery purchases that they get (they call it *share of stomach*).

3 Brand Knowledge, Brand Equity and Brand Extension

LEARNING OBJECTIVES

When you have completed this chapter, you should be able to:

1 Understand ideas about the mental representation of concepts.
2 Understand what is meant by brand image, brand awareness, brand strength and brand equity.
3 Explain the potential gains and losses from brand extensions.
4 Understand how brand shares alter when new brands enter a market.

OVERVIEW

Brands are represented in the minds of customers as ideas, associations, feelings and purchase dispositions. Managers search for ways of exploiting these mental representations of brands by introducing line extensions (new variants in a brand's category) and category extensions (products with the same brand name in different categories). These extensions are not without risk. If the extension fails to capture new sales or avoid losses, then marketing effort will have been wasted. In addition, if the new introduction reduces allegiance to the brand, all the sales associated with the brand could suffer. We start by considering how consumers store and process brand knowledge in a network of related concepts. Then, we consider the way in which this processing gives brands strength and value, and the way in which brand names are recalled and recognized. Building on this, we consider the idea of brand equity, that brands are capital that can be exploited by their owner. Finally, we examine research on brand extension and the way in which new entrants to a market take sales from existing players.

SECTION 1: THE MENTAL REPRESENTATION OF BRANDS

In this chapter, we are first concerned with the way in which concepts such as companies, brands, services and categories are represented in memory along with all the other concepts that we have. Psychologists have described this cognitive world using mental representations theory, which is reviewed by Smith and Queller (2001). The fundamental idea is that memory is an *associative network* of interlinked nodes in which each node is a concept. The meaning of a concept is therefore given by the interrelationships it has with other concepts. Applied to brands, the interrelationships define how the brand is perceived and what developments of the brand are most likely to be commercially successful. These interrelationships are established in people through direct experience, from information received from other persons and from the mass media. In mental representations theory:

- Perception activates nodes that correspond to the perceived object.
- Thinking occurs when these activated nodes spread activation to other linked nodes.
- Links between nodes are strengthened slowly over time by such activation.
- The concepts relating to more frequently activated nodes are more easily retrieved from memory.
- Nodes are valenced (positive or negative), thus forming the basis of attitude.
- Long-term memory is the single, large associative structure covering all concepts whereas short-term memory is a currently activated subset.
- Simultaneous activations may occur (parallel processing), but much of this processing is unconscious.

To illustrate this thinking we have set out one possible mental representation map for iPhone in Figure 3.1. The mental node for iPhone could be linked to a wide range of concepts and only some are shown. These include product features such as reliability, ease of use and cost as well as a wider range of ideas. iPhones may be associated with Apple stores, with their novel store layout and merchandising. Another connection is to the Apple Corporation and its founder, Steve Jobs, who is credited with a string of original product developments. Other links might be to the vast range of apps that can be downloaded, such as the one that allows the user to pop bubblewrap (virtually). Brands are often associated with their competitors; in this case we have shown Nokia and BlackBerry. iPhone and other smart phones are thought to have played a large part in the mobilization of dissent in the Arab world in 2011, as indicated in the figure.

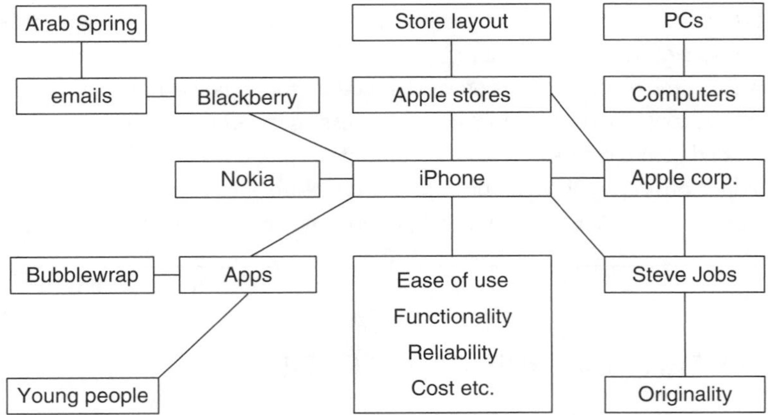

Figure 3.1 Concepts that might be associated with iPhone

We should be wary of drawing too close a parallel between mental representations and the evidence from brain research, but there is clearly some correspondence between the neurons in the brain which are connected to other neurons by synapses, and the nodes connected by links in mental representations theory. Brain research shows that consciousness is associated with the activation of hundreds of thousands of neurons and that each neuron has as many as two thousand synapses connecting it to other neurons (Greenfield, 1997). This suggests that mental-representations maps indicate only a very small part of the content and linkages involved when people think.

Brand Knowledge

The nodes and linkages in Figure 3.1 help us to describe two aspects of brand knowledge, *brand image* and *brand awareness*, which are discussed in the next two sections. Brand image is the set of ideas about the brand, as illustrated in Figure 3.1. Brand awareness is how these ideas are brought to mind, which depends on the nature of the linkages.

Brand Image

Gardner and Levy (1955) believed that brands have a social and psychological meaning as well as a physical nature and that these feelings and ideas about brands direct consumer choice; this thinking is also conveyed by terms such as 'the symbols by which we buy', 'brand personality' and 'brand meaning'. These ideas are created in consumers' minds by their experience with the brand, by word of mouth and through mass communications. To the extent that consumers have similar customer experiences and similar exposure to word of mouth and mass communication, we expect them to have similar brand images for products such as iPhone.

Applying the theory of mental representations, brand image is given by the concepts associated with the brand. These associations differ in respect of valence (positive or negative), number, uniqueness and linkage strength, as shown in Figure 3.2. Thus, we can break down brand image into a valence concept, brand attitude, and a cognitive concept, brand strength.

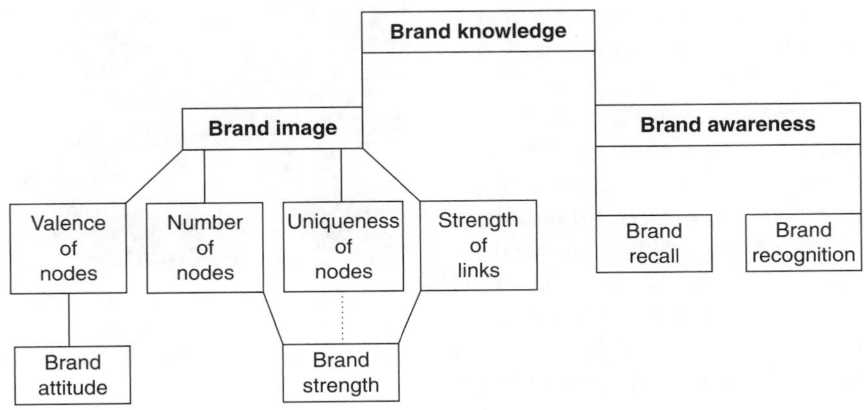

Figure 3.2 Main forms of brand knowledge

Brand attitude is given by the positive and negative feelings about brand features. Attributes like unreliability and cost are typically negative, while ideas such as ease of use and wide functionality are usually positive. In addition to this attribute basis for brand attitude, there is likely to be a 'mere exposure' effect whereby links become stronger on repeated exposure (usually usage but also exposure to advertising and word of mouth). This is explained further in Chapter 8.

Brand strength is important because it relates to the ease of retrieving the brand name from memory, together with the range of associations and the resistance to change in thought and feeling. If the number of links affects strength, we might expect brands in the choice set (the brands considered for purchase) to have an above average number of links. Supporting this, Romaniuk (2003) has shown that brands with more image attributes are more likely to be considered for choice, and Romaniuk and Gaillard (2007) have shown

Box 3.1 Consumer confusion and look-alike brands

The term 'consumer confusion' is used in a variety of ways. In courts of law, it relates to passing off, when one manufacturer makes a product that is very similar to that of another manufacturer. In these circumstances, consumers may make mistakes and buy the wrong brand. This has been a concern in marketing but there is often little confusion on the part of the consumer. For example, a person buying Perigan's gin will normally know that they are not buying Gordon's gin, despite some similarities of bottle shape, colour and label design. But Gordon's gin has built up a buying propensity that is associated with the uniqueness of its pack, and some element of this buying propensity may attach to look-alike competitors, even when consumers are well aware of the differences between brands. This means that Perigan's gin is using brand strength that it did not create. However, it is not clear that their product damages Gordon's gin – it could even strengthen this brand because it draws attention to the Gordon's design. Also, if a brand is sold at a distinctly different price from another in the same category, there will be limited direct competition.

Gordon's and Perigan's gin. Both spirits are in squared bottles, use yellow and orange on the labels and have similarities of label design.

that the biggest brands have more attributes. Romaniuk and Sharp (2003) also found that respondents stated that they were less likely to defect from brands with a greater number of positive attributes. Thus, more associations and more positive linkage help to anchor brand use so that it is difficult to change consumers' choice sets.

If brand strength is affected by the uniqueness of nodes, retrieval of the brand name from memory should be greater when nodes are uncommon and differentiated from others in the brand image. However, the evidence does not support this effect of uniqueness. Romaniuk and Gaillard (2007) did not find that consumers thought that the brand they bought had more unique attributes than brands they did not buy, and they also found that large and smaller brands had similar numbers of unique characteristics. Thus, although we have included uniqueness in Figure 3.2, it is likely that this feature is overemphasized in brand theory. Customers need to be able to differentiate brands but this can be accomplished through quite trivial differences (see Box 3.1).

The variation in brand strength will relate to the extent to which categories are promoted, their importance in everyday life and the awareness consumers' have of them (their salience) in the environment. Box 3.2 illustrates two brands with rather different strengths.

Box 3.2 Brand strength

A weak brand

Some years ago, one of the DIY store groups in the UK found that the extra sales raised by its advertising were much the same as the extra sales they received when their competitor advertised. It seemed that the public made little differentiation between DIY stores; advertising probably reminded them of work that they had intended to do and they got any necessary supplies from the most convenient store. Thus, the advertising of any one store group had the effect of promoting the DIY retail category as a whole, rather than the named store group. In situations like this, where brand awareness is weak, store groups may use sales promotions and advertise these. In this way, consumers only gain advantage when they patronize the store group offering the promotion.

A strong brand

In Britain, the case of Hellman's mayonnaise illustrates the way in which strong brand awareness can pay off (Channon, 1985). In 1981, Hellman's was priced well above other brands of mayonnaise and was open to fierce competition from these other brands, particularly retailer brands. The advertising used the term 'Hellman's' rather than 'mayonnaise' to reinforce the brand name. The campaign was successful in making Hellman's the effective name of the category and the brand still has a large share of the market. Becoming synonymous with the category has always been an attractive possibility for a leading brand. In the UK, 'Hoovering' (from the one-time market leader, Hoover) means vacuum cleaning and is one of the best known examples of this effect.

Brand strength is associated with the size of the brand and Ehrenberg (1993) suggested that, because of this, there is no need for the concept of brand strength – size or market share would serve instead. However, most people see market share as the outcome of the wide associations and ease of recall of a strong brand. Furthermore, there may be occasions when brands lose market share because of competitor innovation but retain their associations, at least for a while. Thus, we do not see brand strength and market share as equivalent.

A number of techniques are used for measuring the components of brand image. Driesener and Romaniuk (2006) review three commonly used methods: brands can be rated, ranked or all those with a characteristic can be named – the 'pick-any' method. These techniques can be used for evaluative criteria such as good value, or for more descriptive criteria such as French-made or organic.

Brand Awareness

Brand awareness concerns the way in which ideas are brought to mind. There are two mechanisms, *recall* and *recognition* (Bettman, 1979). When people recall something, they use the links between concepts in their mental representation to get to the idea that is recalled. For example, they might be told of an app and then think of iPhone. Recognition involves a direct match between an external stimulus and a mental representation; this occurs when a person sees an object or an image of it, for example, an iPhone, and knows what it is. When the stimulus is partial or the mental representation poorly defined, the recognition will be harder to achieve. Human beings have very great powers of recognition, e.g. the ability to recognize people from their face, voice and other cues. Recognition is a specific-to-general process; for example, the iPhone is recognized as a smart phone.

Recall is usually a general-to-specific process; for example, the thought of a smart phone might bring the idea of an iPhone to mind. Often, the cue is the category or a need for the category. Clearly, a number of alternative brands can be recalled and it is the business of marketers to make their brand come to mind more easily than other brands so that it is more often chosen or at least considered.

The strength of brand recall may be measured as a top-of-mind effect. Top of mind means the first brand retrieved in response to a category stimulus; for example, FedEx might be recalled when a courier service is needed. Ease of recognition may be measured as speed of response when a brand stimulus is presented. Accuracy of recognition might be estimated by asking people to report whether a particular brand is present when a picture of several brands is exposed briefly.

Brands are thought about and chosen in a variety of contexts and these contexts affect whether recall or recognition is used to retrieve a brand from memory. For example, a person might want to repair a broken jug and recall that Loctite will do the job. Alternatively, the person might be in a DIY store and see Loctite on the shelf, recognize it, and then recall that this product is needed to repair the jug. Brands with a physical form are generally suitable for recognition because the brand 'makes itself known' to the consumer in the store. Services are often harder to represent in the environment and here the need for the category often occurs first, and then the brand is recalled in response. Rossiter and Bellman (2005) use the distinction between recall and recognition as a cornerstone of their approach to designing effective advertising and choosing suitable media. Visual media such as television are good for the recognition of physical brands because they can display the product, but radio is good for strengthening the link from category to brand and this medium therefore aids recall.

The distinction between recall and recognition would have less relevance if advertising and brand experience facilitated recall and recognition equally. However, the linkages in the mental representation have direction and a person who has a *brand* → *category* recognition may not have the same degree of *category* → *brand* recall, even though the same nodes are linked. The measurement of brand awareness should test these links separately.

SECTION 2: BRAND EQUITY AND BRAND EXTENSION

Brand Equity

Biel (1991) describes brand equity as the value of a brand beyond the physical assets associated with its manufacture or provision and says that it can be thought of as the additional cash flow obtained by associating the brand with the underlying product. Because brand knowledge usually changes slowly, a brand that is currently profitable is likely to continue to be so (barring unforeseen disasters such as serious PR gaffs by company employees that devalue the brand).

We should therefore conserve and exploit brands in the same way that we do with other assets. Some marketers have taken a *financial* approach and have tried to value the additional profit potential offered by a brand. Indeed some companies now estimate the value of their brands on their balance sheets – and certainly brand equity is of crucial concern in company mergers and take-overs. A second *customer-based* research approach has focused on consumer responses to the brand as measured by image, awareness, quality, loyalty and specific market advantages (e.g. Aaker, 1991).[1] These are the precursors to financial benefit; without these consumer responses to the brand, there would be no extra revenue stream or scope for brand extension. In consumer behaviour, we are primarily interested in this second approach and Figure 3.3 shows brand equity as the outcome of brand attitude, brand strength and context. Context covers such matters as market size and category differences such as prominence of the category in everyday life.

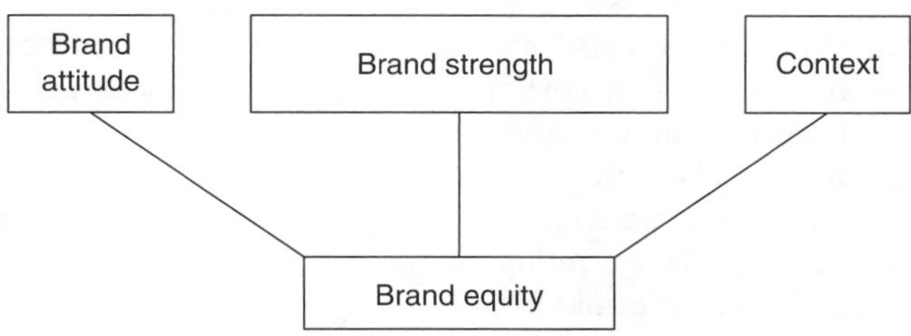

Figure 3.3 Determinants of brand equity

Because of the difficulty of measuring these different components of brand equity, and uncertainties about how they should be aggregated, customer judgements of quality are often used as a proxy for brand equity. For example, using brands of high and low quality, Krishnan (1996) compared the number of associations, valence, uniqueness and how the associations were formed (whether by experience or indirectly through communication). Krishnan's results were generally in the direction expected but there is a problem about using quality as a measure of brand equity; few people doubt the quality of Porsche but most people lack the means to buy such cars, which reduces Porsche's brand equity (hence the introduction of context in Figure 3.3). Kamakura and Russell (1991) and Keller (1993) have proposed an alternative measurement of brand equity. Instead of trying to measure aspects of brand knowledge, these researchers suggest that brand equity can be measured by comparing consumer responses to changes in the product specification, price, promotion and distribution of a named brand with the corresponding responses for an unnamed or unfamiliar product. The differences indicate the benefit conferred by the branding.

Exercise 3.1 The scope for brand extension

1. Put in order of brand quality the following brand names: Samsung, Toshiba, Sony, Bush.
2. What does this suggest about the profit potential of the four brands?
3. What, in particular, do you associate with Sony?

In western countries, Sony usually tops the list and Samsung does less well (but not in South Korea where it is a national premium brand). Sony's ascendancy probably reflects product quality, innovation and advertising over many years. However, Sony is particularly focused on electronic goods and the assurance offered by the brand name might be much weaker when applied to a field outside electronics such as kitchen utensils. This introduces the idea that the extension should fit the parent brand strengths.

New Brand or Brand Extension?

Brand equity will affect the success of line, category and geographical extensions. A line extension is a variant within the category of a parent brand (e.g. a new pack size). One form of line extension, known as a vertical extension, introduces new lines at different price points (e.g. a premium version and a basic version). A category extension occurs when a brand name used in one category is applied in another category (e.g. when Stella Artois, known for lager, introduced a cider). Some extensions are more of a leap (e.g. when Amazon moved from being solely a retailer to being a manufacturer, when it introduced the Kindle for reading electronic books).

A geographical extension occurs when a brand that is marketed in some countries is introduced to other countries (where it is often well known already – perhaps from films or other popular media) (e.g. the introduction of US car brands such as Chrysler to Europe).

Can Stella succeed in the cider category?

Stella cider

In addition to extensions, companies with a strong brand may gain by taking over other companies and extending their name to the acquired company's products. For example, a well-established hotel brand, like Marriott, may be able to make more profit out of another hotel company's physical assets because of the strength of the Marriott name. Similarly, co-branding combinations can work well, e.g. Intel and Dell. Alternatively, a firm with a strong brand will come to an arrangement with a manufacturer with much weaker brand presence; for example Caterpillar boots are made by Wolverine World Wide under licence.

How to use the brand and sub-brand are difficult decisions for car manufacturers (see Box 3.3).

Box 3.3 The model name dilemma

The launch of a new car raises branding problems. Should the old model (or sub-brand) name be abandoned or kept? Some equity attaches to a model name which is lost when the name is dropped. On the other hand, it is important to show the novelty of the new model, and a break with the past helps this. Some companies, such as Volkswagen, have a policy of retaining model names such as Golf and Passat, whereas other manufacturers, such as Peugeot, usually drop the model name (but when faced with the continuing popularity of the 205, they retained this name for a while).

Nesting a new model name with the old one is not normally used in the car industry but it had to be done in Australia when Daihatsu found that their rather bizarre model name, Charade, was better known than the parent brand, Daihatsu. When the time came to end the Daihatsu Charade, they introduced the new model as the Daihatsu Charade Centro in order to benefit from the positive brand image that the Charade had gained amongst consumers (*Sydney Morning Herald*, 7 July 1995).

Line extensions are very common. In the USA, Aaker (1991) estimated that about 90 per cent of new products in the packaged goods industry were line extensions, though there was some cutback in line extension when the Efficient Consumer Response movement got underway and reduced wasteful marketing activity (Buzzell, Quelch and Salmon, 1991; Kahn and McAlister, 1997). More recently, *Les Échos* (2004) reported that new launches divided into 18 per cent new brands, 17 per cent category extensions and 65 per cent line extensions. Generally, the description of a product as a line extension is appropriate when the variant can compete with its parent. For example, those who buy fun-size Mars bars will usually do so instead of buying the normal size Mars bar. Sometimes, a line extension will raise additional brand sales but often it is defensive and designed to counter competition and prevent sales erosion when new variants are introduced by competitors. Normally, category extensions do not compete with sales of the parent brand. For example, Porsche sunglasses do not compete with the sale of Porsche cars and Caterpillar boots will not compete with the sale of the company's earth-moving equipment. Exceptions to this rule occur in food and drink categories; for example, it is possible that instead of buying a Mars bar, a customer may buy a Mars ice-cream or Mars mini roll.

Although there may be substantial value attaching to a brand name, it is not easy to decide whether to introduce a product as a new brand or to extend an existing brand name. Sometimes, there will be an incompatibility between categories that makes it unrealistic to extend a name. Procter & Gamble might see problems in extending the Pampers brand (disposable diapers) to baby food though they might be able to use the name on baby clothing. The Toyota brand was deemed unsuitable for the launch of a new luxury car because of its mass-market positioning. As a result, Toyota developed Lexus. By contrast, high-quality brands such as BMW and Mercedes have chosen to offer smaller cars and utility vehicles under the parent brand name. This underscores a general observation that high-quality brands are more extendable than lower-quality brands.

If a new name is used, managers should check that it is (1) different from other brand names, (2) easy to remember, (3) translates well (the Vauxhall Nova was unsuitable in Spain because it implied that the car would not go), (4) available (many brand names are registered but unused by other manufacturers) and, most importantly, (5) extendable itself, since extensions of a new brand can make further profits and help to justify creating the new brand name. One reason for the loss of interest in descriptive names such as 'I Can't Believe It's Not Butter' is that such names offer limited scope for extension.

New brand names are expensive. McWilliam (1993) found that cost saving was the most frequent reason cited by marketing practitioners for using an extension. Smith and Park (1992) studied the effect of extensions on market share and advertising efficiency and concluded that extensions capture greater market share and can be advertised more efficiently than new brands. Doyle (1989) also found that extensions needed less advertising and noted that they are more readily accepted by distributors as well as by customers. Tauber (1988) found that an existing name helps a brand to gain shelf space in stores.

Smith and Park (1992) did not find that the efficiency of a new extension was reduced by the number of extensions already made. Similarly, Dacin and Smith (1993) found that consumer confidence in a new extension was unaffected by the number of existing extensions, provided that the new entrant was compatible with its predecessors. Dawar and Anderson (1993) found that new lines were more acceptable if they were introduced in an order that made them coherent with the products that had already been introduced.

However, failure with a brand extension may damage the parent brand. This may occur because the extension so enlarges the associations of the brand name that it loses impact and all products under that name suffer in consequence (Tauber, 1981). There may also be a negative effect on the brand in downward vertical extension. Heath, DelVecchio and McCarthy (2011) examined the effect on the parent brand of vertical line extension up and down the quality range. They found that lower-quality extensions tended to reduce the parent brand's rating a little and higher-quality brands tended to improve the rating quite substantially so that the effect was asymmetric. Dall'Olmo Riley, Pina and Bravo (forthcoming) found that the scale of the negative effect depended on the product and that prestige brands were more sensitive than luxury brands. However, they found that the effect was reduced when the downward extension had a much lower price.

Aaker and Keller (1990) found that potentially negative associations could be neutralized by focusing on the attributes of the new brand rather than the strengths of the parent brand. In a subsequent study, Keller and Aaker (1992) examined how consumers saw the extensions to a brand when there were, and were not, prior extensions. They found that, if the prior extensions were regarded as successes, they improved the evaluation of a new extension; if the prior extensions were unsuccessful, they diminished the evaluation of a new extension. This suggests that brand owners should be wary of extensions after a failure.

Consumer Acceptance of a Category Extension

Aaker and Keller (1990) took six well-known brand names and examined how consumers reacted to 20 hypothetical category extensions. For example, they suggested the idea of Crest toothpaste extending into chewing gum and also Vidal Sassoon offering perfume. They found that three factors were related to the attitude of consumers to the potential extension. One of these was the *fit* between the categories of the parent and offspring. A second was the quality of the parent brand. The third factor was whether the extension was seen as difficult to make by the owner of the parent brand. These relationships are shown in Figure 3.4.

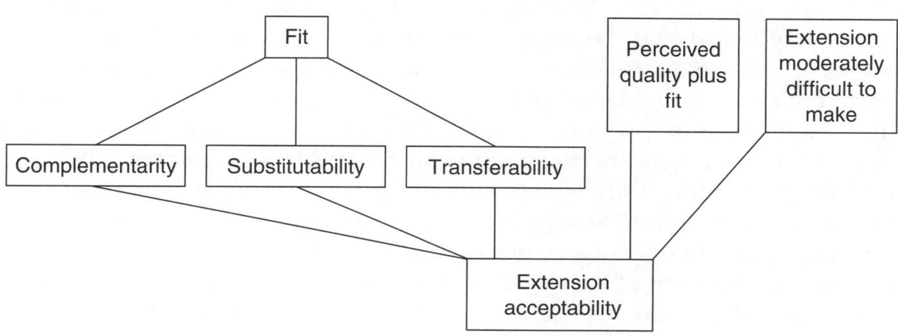

Figure 3.4 Factors contributing to extension success (adapted from Aaker and Keller, 1990)

Fit was positively associated with acceptability. It was measured as complementarity, substitutability and transferability. Complementarity concerns the matching of the new product with the parent expertise, thus skiing goggles would be a complementary product for a maker of skis. Substitutability applies when the new product could be used instead of the parent product; for example, snow boards would substitute for skis. Transferability relates to manufacture rather than usage; whether or not the producer of the parent product is believed to have the capacity to produce the offspring product. For example, a firm that made skis would not necessarily be seen as the best organization to manufacture snow-making equipment but would be acceptable for ice skates. This account of fit is neat but it may be inadequate when faced with brands like Chanel which embrace a wide variety of product types (e.g. fragrances, jewellery, clothing, skin care products). Although Chanel products share a quality image, they differ in other respects.

The second factor, the perceived quality of the parent brand, was positively associated with the acceptability of the extension according to Aaker and Keller, but only when there was a good fit. The third factor, the degree of difficulty perceived about making the extension, was positively associated when the difficulty was moderate: extensions that were very easy to make and very difficult to make were less acceptable. This may be explained in a number of ways. Aaker and Keller suggest that consumers might think that an easily made extension was overpriced. An alternative explanation relates to the cognitive effort involved. An easily made extension may take less effort to comprehend and may therefore not disturb a person's mental representation. When people have to do cognitive work on an idea, they may connect it with existing concepts, thus raising awareness of the extension. However, if the cognitive work required is too complicated, the extension may be rejected. Thus, an extension requiring moderate cognitive effort may be most acceptable. Related to this explanation, Hartman, Price and Duncan (1990) suggest that people will try to make sense of an extension but, if it differs too much from the parent product, they may dismiss the idea of the new product. Supporting Hartman et al., Meyers-Levy and Tybout (1989) showed that one unusual characteristic increased cognitive processing but too many unusual characteristics reduced it. In sum, the very obvious may be ignored and the inexplicable may be rejected.

Sunde and Brodie (1993) failed to replicate Aaker and Keller's (1990) findings. Following this, Bottomley and Holden (2001) reviewed the evidence on the acceptability of brand extension. They used data from the original Aaker and Keller (1990) study and from seven replications. They found that the original contentions of Aaker and Keller were broadly supported: fit makes an extension more acceptable and the quality of the parent brands increases acceptability provided that there is some fit. However, we should note that Aaker and Keller's method is quite weak; it rests on the judgement of respondents about how they will behave in hypothetical circumstances and this judgement can be mistaken.

Batra, Lenk and Wedel (2010) suggest that the success of an extension depends on the atypicality of the parent brand as well as the fit of the extension. By *atypicality* they mean having abstract (rather than concrete) associations since these can link to a wider range of categories. They suggest that a beer brand such as Corona, which has 'lifestyle' associations, is atypical compared to Heineken which is sold more on its performance as a beer. Batra et al. proposed a personality measuring procedure covering the brand and the category that permits assessment of atypicality. Their initial results are promising but this work still rests on the perceptions of consumers rather than their purchasing, which is the ultimate test. The circumstances governing the success of an extension are also covered by Keller and Lehmann (2006) in a wide-ranging review of the field.

Effective Marketing

Völckner and Sattler (2006) investigated ten factors that might predict extension success and found that fit was the most important; however, they found that marketing support and retailer acceptance were also needed. This suggests that marketing effectiveness may play a large part in brand extension success. Some poorly fitting extensions have worked because the appropriate marketing structures were available. Marks and Spencer, originally known for clothing, successfully diversified into food because they had an effective system of sourcing and distribution; Bic, known for disposable ballpoints and lighters, succeeded with a sailboard extension. Neither of these extensions were obvious fits. McWilliam (1993) points out that marketers are very reluctant to see a failure as the result of poor marketing, but this is often the reason. The potential of a category extension is affected by market size, product quality, market growth, economies of scale, distribution structures and profit margin, all of which should influence the marketing strategy. From this standpoint, some incongruous extensions may succeed because they are well marketed.

So, can we predict extension success?

It is clearly important that we understand how brands are accepted or rejected and therefore what scope there is for extracting more profit from a brand. However, the potential of a brand is difficult to measure. First, it seems likely that the unconscious cognitive activity involved in brand choice is large and, because it is unconscious, it is difficult to represent and measure this activity. Another problem is that brand choice is contextual. It occurs under a variety of circumstances and these different circumstances will relate to different parts of a consumer's mental representation map. This problem is aggravated when we take account of the way mental representations differ between people. The theory of mental representations may serve as a description of why certain effects are found, but it has limited value as a predictive model.

We are also rather sceptical about the methods used to determine the acceptability of potential extensions such as that by Aaker and Keller (1990). We do not dispute the findings of such work, now checked by Bottomley and Holden (2001). What we dispute is the generalizability of these findings to everyday life. Under research conditions, people will report on perceived quality and fit but, in the field, marketing activity and consumer adaptability may overcome lack of fit. In addition, until the work of Sattler et al. (2010), research in this area has focused on the acceptability of the extension without taking account of price and therefore profitability.

Despite these problems, there are some areas of promise. It is clear that brands do have value in the sense that people associate more benefits with some well-known brands and may pay more for a branded product than a functionally equivalent anonymous product. Tests based on such comparisons are likely to indicate brand strength and extension potential.

Exercise 3.2 Potential extensions

Nokia, Pampers, Shell and the BBC are brands that have few extensions. Suggest extensions which might be appropriate and successful for these brands. Give reasons for your suggestions. Why have these brands not been extended into these areas before?

SECTION 3: SALES LOSSES BY THE PARENT OF A LINE EXTENSION

Sometimes a new entrant enlarges a market so that all the brands gain. One example was when Pampers entered the disposable diapers market in South Africa (Broadbent, 2000). Their campaign helped the category to become established as an alternative to cloth diapers and this helped Pampers' competitors to sell more volume. But this is unusual. Normally, markets have fairly static aggregate sales over the medium term so that the sales gained by a new brand are another brand's loss. When this applies, it is important to know how a new entrant takes sales from the existing players since this helps to decide a manager's strategy. This sales effect is often large when a line extension is launched, because existing lines can easily be substituted by the new line: the new line *cannibalizes* the existing lines. Sometimes, cannibalization is enforced by retailers who refuse to give manufacturers additional shelf space for a new line and stipulate that some other line in their portfolio must be abandoned in order to provide space. 'Line in, line out' is the terse name for this retailer practice. When extra space is given and the new line can compete with the previously established brands, there are two sales patterns that can occur:

- Existing brands may lose sales to the new entrant in proportion to their market share. This is the basic effect that may be expected when there are no special affinities between brands.
- An extra loss of sales occurs among brands that are perceived to be similar to the new entrant. With a line extension, the main similarity is likely to be the common brand name, with the result that the parent loses more sales than would be expected from market share alone. Extra losses may also be incurred when there are similarities of formulation, packaging, pricing, positioning, targeting, distribution and physical proximity to other brands in the store.[2]

Some data on the British detergent market illustrate the way in which consumers shift support from existing brands to a new brand. Table 3.1 shows how, 20 weeks after launch, the first liquid detergent on the British market, Wisk, was taking customers from other brands (right-hand column). Wisk was a new brand and took share from other brands roughly in relation to their market share (the correlation is 0.85), though Surf, with its value-for-money positioning, seemed to resist loss better. Because the sales loss is proportional to existing share, big brands lose more volume than small brands.

This effect was further investigated in a study by Lomax et al. (1996). Using new data, this work confirmed that Wisk took share in relation to the market share of the other brands. A second study by Lomax et al. showed the cannibalization effect of the same

Table 3.1 Brand market shares and percentage of Wisk gain 20 weeks after Wisk launch (AGB Data, 1992)

Brand	*Midland market share before Wisk launch*	*Contribution to Wisk sales after launch*
Persil	28	27
Ariel	17	22
Surf	16	8
Bold	14	12
Daz	9	11
Other brands	16	15
No previous purchase	–	5

brand name when a concentrated version of a German detergent took disproportionately more sales from its parent than from other brands. In a third study, Lomax et al. examined the gains of the Ariel liquid detergent that followed Wisk onto the British market. Here there was a parent powder brand and it was anticipated that this would be cannibalized by the new liquid formulation, but this did not occur. Instead, Ariel liquid gained sales at the expense of the whole powder section. Though unexpected, this finding is consistent with a notion of *cannibalization barriers* introduced by Buday (1989). Consumers apparently saw the new product in relation to its formulation rather than its branding. In the language of mental representations, there may be limited linkage between versions of the brand across formulations. This seems to be an advantage but there is a danger that, when this occurs, the new entrant will gain less benefit from the common brand name. A fourth study examined the sales of Persil Liquid, which was launched after Ariel Liquid; again the impact on the parent powder was not disproportionate.

This work shows that cannibalization is not inevitable. More generally, it seems likely that it is reduced by pricing, targeting and positioning the brand so that it is more similar to competitor brands and less similar to the manufacturer's existing brands.

SUMMARY

Memory can be represented as a network of interlinked nodes. Thinking involves the activation of parts of this network. The whole network represents long-term memory. Short-term memory is the currently activated section of the network. Within this system, brand knowledge has two aspects: brand image – the range of brand associations – and brand awareness, which is the retrieval of the brand via the associations using recall or recognition.

Brand equity is the value added to the basic product by branding. It is thought that brand equity is greater when the attitude to the brand is more positive, when the range of associations is large and strongly linked, when awareness is high and where the brand is prominent, well marketed and has large market share. In practice, there is no coherent way of measuring and aggregating all these factors so either perceived quality is used as a proxy for brand equity or it is measured by showing the difference in the value created when branded and unbranded products are promoted.

Marketers want to know whether a category extension will succeed. This has been approached by examining consumer judgements about different extension propositions. Acceptance is greater when the proposed extension *fits* the parent because it complements or substitutes for the parent product and when the parent is seen as suited to producing the offspring product. Acceptance of a fitting product is increased when the parent is seen to be high quality. However, this approach has been criticized for ignoring marketing expertise in the launch of an extension. Some fitting extensions have failed and some non-fitting ones succeeded and it is likely that success or failure owes a great deal to effective marketing.

When line extensions are launched, they often take a large proportion of their sales from the parent. Sometimes, this is accepted as part of the evolution of the product, but it is attractive to get extra sales from a line extension. There has therefore been interest in how a new entrant to a market draws sales from existing players. Sometimes, the sales losses of the parent are modest because consumers use formulation, price or another factor to distinguish the new line from the parent.

Additional Resources

Read Keller and Lehmann (2006) to understand one approach to brand equity and the scope for predicting successful extensions. For a more comprehensive treatment read Dall'Olmo Riley's (2010) introduction to the four-volume book of papers titled *Brand Management*.

Notes

1 A well-known method of valuing brands in this way is by the Interbrand Group. Seven factors are considered: leadership, stability, market stability, internationalization, trend, support and protection. Simon and Sullivan (1993) describe a method that compares branded and unbranded cash flows. Others have used the stock market to indicate the value of brands by subtracting the value of fixed assets from the market valuation.

2 These affinity effects are also seen when consumers buy more than one brand in a category. When they do this, their selection of brands may be linked by a common characteristic such as brand name or product formulation. This is discussed in Chapter 4.

4 Stationary Markets

LEARNING OBJECTIVES

When you have completed this chapter, you should be able to:

1 Describe the typical patterns of purchase found in mature, stationary markets.
2 Explain the role of stationary market models in evaluating brand performance.
3 Discuss the importance to sales of both light and heavy buyers.
4 Explain how market regularities set limits to marketing objectives.

OVERVIEW

Research on market patterns is done by analysis of the data provided by market research companies. In particular, academic researchers use the findings of consumer panel studies, described in Chapter 2, which are conducted by companies such as IRI, Taylor Nelson Sofres (now in WPP's Kantar group), GfK and Nielsen. Consumer panels record the purchases of many hundreds or thousands of individual households for several years. From such records we can see that most mature consumer markets are approximately stationary (i.e. brand sales change little from year to year).

In order to judge how a consumer brand is performing in a stationary market, we need to know the patterns of purchase that are commonly found in such markets. Then we can see whether a brand is behaving in a normal manner, or whether there are exceptional aspects to its sales. Marketing scientists have established elegant mathematical models that are very effective at mimicking the patterns found in stationary markets that are revealed by panel data. These models have been so successful that they now provide us with sales norms that can be used to assess the performance of a brand. When brand performance differs from the stationary market prediction, we can investigate why this is so. This work applies primarily to consumer goods and services and to frequently purchased repertoire markets (where consumers often buy more than one brand in the category).

SECTION 1: MODELLING MATURE MARKETS

The Stability of Mature Markets

In this chapter, we are mainly concerned with established consumer markets rather than markets for new goods or services or business markets. Established, or mature, markets cover the majority of our purchases. An important feature of these markets is that they usually do not change much (in terms of the market shares of the major brands) and are therefore described as *near-stationary*. Changes do sometimes occur in mature markets: whole sub-markets may decline, e.g. the 1980s saw a decline in the consumption of bitter beer and a corresponding rise in lager drinking in the UK. Normally, such changes occur quite slowly over a period of years. Only exceptionally do we see rapid changes that become permanent for specific brands or for the whole category. Such changes may occur when adverse publicity about a product damages its reputation, or when an advertising campaign is particularly successful (e.g. Stella Artois gained substantial share in the British lager market in the mid-1980s following a very successful advertising campaign). Markets may also change over short periods because of sales promotions but, usually, these gains are not maintained when the promotion finishes (Ehrenberg and England, 1990; Ehrenberg, Hammond and Goodhardt, 1994a). Because promotions run for short periods, the gains they produce have little effect when averaged over several months and, often, promotional gains are counter-balanced by losses when competitors run promotions. As a result, the market looks quite stable over a period of several months or a year.

One reason for the relative stability of markets has been explained in Chapters 1 and 2. Individuals form habits of purchase that limit change. In Chapter 2, we noted that a typical brand loses about 15 per cent of its customers over a year, and that these customer losses are usually offset by customer gains.

The Value of Mathematical Models

If a market does not change, brand performance measures, such as repeat purchase, the relative number of heavy and light buyers and the pattern of cross-brand buying in a category, will be much the same each time they are measured for a period of the same length. An effective mathematical model will let us predict these brand performance measures from other simple brand statistics. If a model is routinely effective, it acquires diagnostic value. When the observed brand performance does not fit predictions from the model, we need to find out why this is so and we may have to adjust our marketing support for the brand. The model used to predict the purchase patterns for a single brand is the negative binomial distribution (known as the NBD), while a more complex model used for predicting purchasing and cross-buying for competing brands is the Dirichlet (pronounced: *Dir-eesh-lay*).

Early research on brand modelling was conducted by Ehrenberg (e.g. papers in 1959, 1969) and then brought together in *Repeat Buying: Theory and Applications* (Ehrenberg, 1988, first published 1972). This book attacked conventional beliefs in marketing and caused a reappraisal of some of the traditional ideas about brand loyalty, brand positioning, the effects of advertising and the way in which sales grow. It was followed by work in the USA investigating the mathematical properties of stationary market models. Morrison and Schmittlein (1981, 1988), for example, gave detailed attention to the precision of models and to the modifications that might improve this precision.

Mathematical models can also be applied to other forms of stable repetitive behaviour. Goodhardt, Ehrenberg and Collins (1975, updated 1987) used such a model to study television audiences. Another application has been to store choice, with store groups being treated as brands (Kau and Ehrenberg, 1984; Wright, Sharp and Sharp, 1998). It is also possible to model other category divisions such as a pack-size (Singh, 2008). Models can be used to predict the performance of brand aggregations (e.g. all private label brands in a category, or a combination of many small brands in an 'other brands' grouping).

Stationary market research does not explain *why* some people buy more than others and one brand rather than another. Some critics argue that the lack of attention to such motivational issues limits the application of these models, particularly when the marketer is trying to induce change. What do you put in advertisements if consumer motivations are unknown? Do those who buy more have different reasons from those who buy less? Why do people avoid some brands? When markets do expand or contract, these changes may reflect changes in motivation, income or other household circumstances. But theorists such as Ehrenberg do not claim to cover all the problems that arise in marketing and specifically exclude motivation. What they do describe is the quantitative form of stable markets; if a market is stationary, the numerical predictions from the model are usually very close to the observations derived from panel data. If the market is not stationary, the difference between the observed facts and the model prediction is often instructive and may help us to understand the relative performance of different brands.

Definitions

Before we examine the patterns of purchase found in mature markets, the reader should be clear about the meaning of a number of terms. First, we usually work with *purchase occasions* rather than sales. On a purchase occasion, a buyer buys one or more units of a brand. In most markets, consumers buy one unit at a time so that purchase occasions are approximately equal to sales. Other important definitions are:

- The *penetration, b,* which is the proportion of all potential buyers (in the population we are studying) who buy a brand at least once in a period. (Think: *b* for buyers.)
- The *purchase frequency, w,* which is the average number of purchases made by those who purchase *at least once* in a period. (Think: *w* for purchase weight.)
- The *mean population purchase rate, m,* the number of purchase occasions in the period made by an average member of the population. (Think: *m* for mean.) When *b* is expressed as a percentage, *m* will be the sales per hundred of the population.

These variables are linked by the *sales equation*:

$$m = bw$$

Thus when the penetration of Persil over three months is 0.25 and the purchase frequency is 4, $m = 0.25 \times 4$ or 1. (In words: when a quarter of the population buy Persil, on average four times, then the average purchase occasion rate in the whole population is one.)

When people buy more than one unit per purchase occasion, we multiply by a correcting factor to get the sales rate. For example, if people buy, on average, 1.2 units of Persil per purchase occasion then the mean population *sales rate* m_s, will be given by:

$$m_s = 0.25 \times 4 \times 1.2 = 1.2.$$

Exercise 4.1 Applying the sales equation

1 In a stationary market, the penetration of Senso toothpaste is 0.07 over 24 weeks. Over 24 weeks, there are 21 purchases of Senso per hundred people in the population. What is the purchase frequency?
2 How many purchase occasions per 100 consumers will there be in 48 weeks?
3 If the purchase frequency for the 48-week period is 4.6, what are the mean sales and penetration?

Answers:

1 0.21/0.07 = 3.
2 In a stationary market, you double the purchase occasions if you double the period: 42 per 100.
3 $m = bw$; therefore $0.42 = b \times 4.6$. So $b = 0.42/4.6 = 0.09$, or 9 per cent.

SECTION 2: SINGLE BRAND PURCHASE PATTERNS

The Impact of Recent Purchase

How does recent purchase experience affect the next purchase? In particular, is there a bias towards purchasing the same brand as last time? Consider two people who have both bought Persil and Ariel an equal number of times over the last six months, as below:

Philip: Ariel, Ariel, Persil, Persil
Elizabeth: Persil, Ariel, Persil, Ariel

Both Philip and Elizabeth have bought Persil twice. Who is most likely to buy Persil at their next purchase? If people learn more from their recent experience, Philip is more likely to buy Persil next time. This is a *first-order* explanation because it relates to the last purchase. A *zero-order* explanation takes no account of the order of prior purchases and here there would be no difference between Philip and Elizabeth in terms of their likelihood of purchasing Persil. When the explanation is zero-order we can predict the likelihood of a future brand purchase using only the ratio of past brand purchases.

Since people do occasionally switch brands, their most recent purchase should be a slightly better guide to their next purchase than earlier purchases. Kuehn (1962) found some evidence to support a first-order effect; however, a study by Bass et al. (1984) showed that the majority of purchases in most markets are zero-order. All studies have their weaknesses and Kahn, Morrison and Wright (1986) argued that, because *household* panel data were used by Bass et al., the first-order behaviour of *individuals* might have been obscured. However, on balance, it seems likely that a zero-order pattern of purchase is more common in stable markets and that habit, rather than learning, provides the best way of thinking about repetitive purchase.

Do Consumers Buy at Regular Intervals?

We have habits about *what* we buy, but are we also habitual about *when* we buy? Purchase time habits would show up in panel data as an individual tendency to buy a category once a week or once a month. Habits of this sort would mean that a purchaser's probability of buying rises sharply at intervals. This pattern is also found for some frequent purchases, such as newspapers or cigarettes. It also applies to shopping trips (Dunn, Reader and Wrigley, 1983). Kahn and Schmittlein (1989) report that households tend to be loyal to a particular day for grocery shopping, and East et al. (1994) found that the majority of supermarket users were also loyal to particular times of the day (Chapter 11).

Despite the routine timing of many shopping trips, brands are usually bought at irregular intervals. There are several reasons for this. First, we should note that most brands are bought quite infrequently. For example, a typical US household buys a specific coffee brand about three times a year and the category about nine times a year. This gives an average inter-purchase interval between purchases of any brand of instant coffee of five to six weeks. Actual intervals are quite varied because household consumption may fluctuate and shoppers may stockpile or run out. The prediction of when a specific brand will be rebought is even more irregular because other brands in a category may be bought instead. So, although there is a long-term average frequency of brand buying, brand purchase occurs at irregular times. Mathematicians describe this random pattern as a *Poisson* distribution.

However, people rarely buy a brand again immediately after purchasing it. Because of this 'dead time' after purchase, the Poisson distribution does not fit well for short periods (such as a week or less). Over the longer periods covered in panel research, the fit of the Poisson assumption is close and provides a basis for the mathematical models described later.

How Does Purchase Frequency Vary?

People differ widely in how much they buy of the category and of specific brands. The range of purchase frequencies in a sample of buyers has a form that is described by the *Gamma* distribution, like the one illustrated in Figure 4.1. This is a histogram of purchases of a frequently bought category in which the largest number of buyers usually occurs at the lowest purchase frequency.

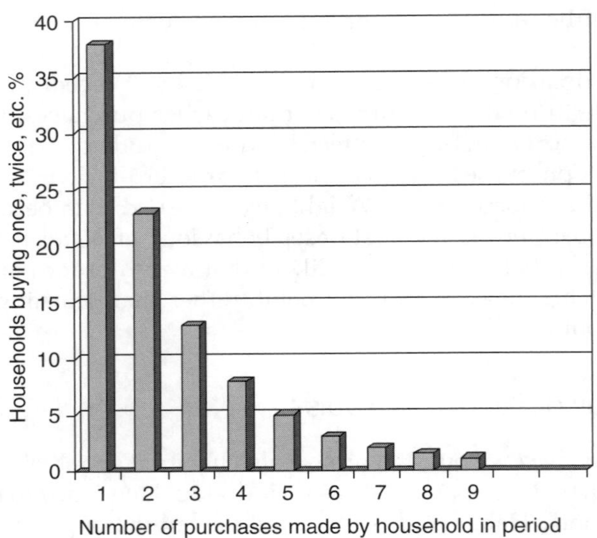

Figure 4.1 Gamma distribution of purchase for a brand showing that there are many light buyers and few heavy buyers

Few people buy heavily but those who do so are responsible for a large proportion of a brand's sales. Table 4.1 illustrates this with the purchases of Kellogg's Corn Flakes in the USA. In Table 4.1, you see that a sample of 100 households have bought 210 purchases of Kellogg's Corn Flakes, 2.1 per household, in three months. This average is based on the 55 per cent who bought once, 22 per cent who bought twice, 8 per cent who bought three times and so forth (a typical Gamma distribution). When we work out the sales from these sub-groups we get the NBD distribution, outlined in Section 1. This is the bottom row of Table 4.1 and it shows how important the few heavy buyers are for sales. Those who bought six or more times – 5 per cent of all purchasers – were responsible for 20 per cent of sales.

In general, a substantial proportion of purchases are made by relatively few heavy buyers; one rule of thumb, the *heavy-half* principle, is that the lighter-buying 50 per cent are responsible for about 20 per cent of all purchases while the heavier-buying 50 per cent

Table 4.1 Three-month sales of Kellogg's Corn Flakes in the USA (adapted from Ehrenberg and Goodhardt, 1979)

Penetration (%)	*Purchase frequency*	*Out of 100 purchasers, the number buying:*						
20	*2.1*	*Once*	*Twice*	*3 times*	*4 times*	*5 times*	*6+ times*	*Total*
		55	22	8	5	5	5	**100**
		Number of purchases:						
		55	44	24	20	25	42	**210**

are responsible for the other 80 per cent. When this rule applies, we find that the heaviest 20 per cent are responsible for about 50 per cent of sales. If you inspect Table 4.1 you will see that the 55 per cent buying once are responsible for 26 per cent of purchases and the heaviest 23 per cent (buying three or more times) are responsible for 53 per cent of purchases, so the data in Table 4.1 fit the heavy-half rule quite well. Other ratio rules are more extreme. The best known is the 80:20 rule, that 80 per cent of purchases are made by the heaviest buying 20 per cent of customers. The precise ratio depends partly on the category. For example, if we investigated those with savings accounts, we might find that very few heavy savers were responsible for a large part of the total savings in a savings institution. The ratio is less extreme when there is a natural ceiling on purchase within the time period being studied, e.g. people rarely buy more than one newspaper a day.

Ratios also depend on the period of time used to collect data. Because they buy frequently, most heavy buyers will be sampled in any short purchase period. Light buyers may not get round to buying in a short period but, as the period lengthens, more of them are captured. Therefore, if purchase data for instant coffee are collected over a period of years instead of months, a greater proportion of light buyers are recorded and the ratio moves from approximately heavy-half to approximately 80:20. Ratio rules were first highlighted by Pareto, an Italian economist, and they are reviewed by Schmittlein, Cooper and Morrison (1993).

The heavy-half principle shows that heavy buyers are an attractive segment in many markets and marketers may therefore try to focus their efforts on them. For example, promotions may give progressively more attractive benefits to those who buy more and the frequent-flyer schemes that airlines run are designed to benefit the heavier users. Sometimes, it is possible to target the heavy buyers by using a particular distribution system. For example, a wine warehouse, which sells wine by the case, may secure a larger proportion of heavy wine buyers than a supermarket. Also, it may be useful to focus research on heavy buyers since they are responsible for so much of the profit (e.g. Hammond and Ehrenberg, 1995). In B2B marketing, *key account management* has become a recognized speciality (the key accounts are the few big ones).

Ratio rules can apply to any phenomenon and Box 4.1 provides an interesting example. Another application has been to the imprisonment of offenders. If most crimes are committed by a relatively small group of offenders, crime will go down if these offenders are imprisoned for longer.

Box 4.1 Weight of consumption among feline consumers (Churcher and Lawton, 1987)

An interesting demonstration of how consumption varies was provided by a study of what the cat brought home to households in a Bedfordshire village. Over 70 domestic cats were studied over a year and their tendency to kill and bring home sparrows, frogs, rabbits, mice and so on was studied. One cat was responsible for 10 per cent of the total kill while, at the other end of the distribution, several cats brought back nothing in a whole year.

The ratio of light to heavy buyers depends on the break point chosen but we can compare the top 20 per cent of customers that is typically responsible for 50 per cent of sales with the bottom 80 per cent of customers that is responsible for the other 50 per cent. On this basis, light buyers are four times as numerous as heavy buyers. Because of their numbers, light buyers *in aggregate* may offer more scope for sales gain than the heavy buyers. However, when purchasers of a brand are considered *individually,* it is clear that more attention should be given to the few heavy buyers. This is partly because they could buy more and partly because their loss could be very damaging. Mass communications such as advertising are effective at reaching the large number of light buyers but, when marketing to customers needs substantial resources, it is better to concentrate on the heavy buyers.

It is easy to be confused by stationary market evidence. Although relatively few heavy buyers are responsible for a substantial proportion of sales, this does not mean that heavy buyers are responsible for most of the gain or loss when sales change. First, as noted, this depends on the proportion of buyers that are treated as 'heavy'. If this is only the heaviest 20 per cent, any change in buying patterns may be more obvious amongst the more numerous light buyers. Second, we find that light buyers tend to change their purchasing *proportionately* more than heavy buyers. As a result, light (and new) buyers are responsible for a large part of any gain in sales when a brand improves its market share. But when the new pattern of sales has stabilized, we are likely to still find that 20 per cent of buyers are again responsible for 50 per cent of sales as a number of light buyers will have been converted to heavy buyers. This analysis means that marketers must not ignore the light buyers since their purchasing is more changeable and, from their ranks, some new heavy buyers may emerge. Further, as discussed in Chapter 5, heavy buyers show some regression to the mean; that is, they do not necessarily stay as heavy buyers.[1] This evidence that sales gains come mostly from new and light buyers may surprise those who are wedded to relationship marketing with its emphasis on retaining customers. A popular book, *How Brands Grow* by Sharp (2010) has highlighted the fact that brands grow mostly by acquiring new buyers. This text draws on research by Riebe et al. (forthcoming) on pharmaceuticals and banking which shows that brands grow mainly because of customer acquisition and brands decline mainly because they fail to acquire new customers.

How Does the Type of Product Affect Purchase?

Brands in product categories that differ substantially (e.g. food products and household cleaners) may show similar patterns of customer purchase. For example, if two brands in quite different categories have the same purchase frequency and penetration, they will have much the same sole brand loyalty and repeat purchase rates. Effectively, the purchase characteristics of a brand are captured by purchase frequency and penetration, and a variety of other brand performance statistics can be predicted from these measures. This means that the specific brand or category need not be known in order to predict these brand performance measures, provided that we know the purchase frequency and penetration of the brand.

Repeat Purchase

If we compare any two adjacent sales periods, e.g. two quarters, we find that many of the buyers of a brand in quarter 1 (Q1) return in Q2, particularly the heavier buyers. But some do not return and these 'lapsed' buyers are replaced by an approximately equal number of 'new' buyers. These 'new' buyers are mostly light buyers of the brand, like those that they replace, and although they did not buy in Q1, they have usually bought the brand before and are not really new. At Q3 about the same proportion of Q2 buyers drop out and are replaced by others, including some of those who lapsed after Q1. This intermittent pattern of purchase does not show loss of loyalty but instead reflects the fact that many people buy a brand so infrequently that they often miss quarters. The change of buyers at each quarter is explained mainly as a probability effect, though a small part of the effect is due to more permanent acquisition of, and defection from, the brand.

This analysis helps us to understand that repeat purchase rates depend mainly on purchase frequency. A household that buys four times in one quarter is more likely to re-buy in the next quarter than one that bought only once, since the latter household may not need to buy again so soon. Because heavier buyers are more likely to repeat, we find that the purchase frequency of repeat purchasers is higher than the rate for the whole sample (by about 20 per cent). In addition, new purchasers tend to be light buyers and, whatever the category, their purchase rate usually does not rise much above 1.5 for any period.

Table 4.2 Repeat purchase for given purchase frequencies and penetrations

	Baseline case	*Tenfold increase in penetration*	*Tenfold increase in purchase frequency*
Penetration as %	2	2	20
Purchase frequency	2	20	2
Repeat purchase as %	57	85	60

Although repeat-purchase rates depend mainly on purchase frequency, penetration does have a small effect, illustrated in Table 4.2. Compare the baseline column with the next and you see that a tenfold increase in purchase frequency has a substantial effect on repeat purchase, raising it from 57 per cent to 85 per cent; compare the baseline column with the last and you see that repeat purchase moves only three points when the penetration increases tenfold. Note that it is the repeat purchase *rate* that is slightly affected by penetration. The *number* of repeat purchasers is directly affected by penetration; that is, as larger brands have more purchasers, they also have commensurately more repeat purchasers, even if the repeat purchase rate is little different.

Repeat purchase is an important diagnostic measure. If the purchase frequency for a reporting period indicates a repeat purchase rate of 50 per cent under stationary market conditions, then consistent deviations from this figure indicate that the market does not have the normal stationary characteristics. One application of this thinking was reported by Ehrenberg (1988: 97–98). A brand launched 18 months before was being heavily advertised but, despite this, sales were constant. Two explanations were possible:

- The advertising was ineffective and the brand was creating normal repeat purchase.
- The advertising was effective, consumers were trying the brand, but they were not repeat purchasing so the brand was not gaining sales.

To distinguish these two we derive the normal repeat-purchase rate for a stationary market and see whether this is what is found in the panel data. Evidence that repeat purchase is normal favours the first explanation and means that the advertising should be changed or stopped. Evidence that the repeat purchase is below the normal level supports the second explanation. In this case, the evidence suggested that the brand was weak, and that sales would collapse when the pool of potential trialists was exhausted, so the brand should be dropped before more advertising money was wasted. This case is presented in Exercise 4.4 below.

NBD (Negative Binomial Distribution) Theory

Negative binomial distribution (NBD) theory is a mathematical model that enables the prediction of repeat purchase and other brand performance measures from data on the penetration and purchase frequency of the brand for any given reporting period. NBD theory is based on the assumptions that the purchasing of a brand is stationary, that individual purchases follow a Poisson distribution, and that the long-run average purchase rates of individuals follow a Gamma distribution. These assumptions are set out by Ehrenberg (1988: ch4).[2]

Box 4.2 Does the NBD give the best prediction?

Marketing scientists have tried to improve on the predictions derived from the NBD by adjustment of the mathematics. One suggestion is that NBD theory might be modified to allow for the temporary loss of buying interest following a purchase. But any gain would be marginal since the theory is already very close to panel evidence. Usually, the random variation in consumer panel data is rather larger than any difference between the predictions of competing mathematical models. In a comparison of theories, Schmittlein, Bemmaor and Morrison (1985) concluded that the NBD model was hard to beat. A further paper by Morrison and Schmittlein (1988) identified three ways in which real behaviour tended to depart from NBD assumptions but noted that these effects tended to cancel each other out so that the NBD remained a good predictive model.

NBD Program

When purchase frequency and penetration are known, the NBD program (available from the Sage website) estimates a range of brand performance statistics. This computer program requires data on the penetration, purchase frequency and data collection period and computes repeat purchase and new purchase rates for different periods. The Gamma distribution of persons buying once, twice, etc. is worked out for each period and the proportion of sales attributable to different rates of purchase is calculated (the negative binomial distribution). These figures are tabled on the screen and the user then has options to change the rounding and to express data as proportions, percentages or actual numbers. A copy of the screened figures can be recorded as a file for printing.

Table 4.3 shows the output for Kellogg's Corn Flakes using the figures shown in Table 4.1 (a three-month penetration of 20 per cent and a purchase frequency of 2.1). Because the program does not have a three-month column, the figures were assigned to the 12-weeks period (highlighted). If you look down this column you see the input penetration and purchase frequency, then the predicted repeat purchase rate of about 62 per cent. Below this is the purchase frequency of repeat buyers, which is always found to be about 20 per cent higher than the purchase frequency of the whole group, and the purchase frequency of new buyers (usually not much greater than 1.5). The program estimates the number of buyers buying once, twice, etc. and then calculates the sale proportions contributed by these segments. In Table 4.4, the empirical data from Table 4.1 are compared with the theoretical predictions. If you inspect Table 4.4 you will see that the agreement is close.

Table 4.3 Output from NBD program (figures rounded to 2 decimal places)

	1 day	*1 wk*	*4 wks*	***12 wks***	*24 wks*	*48 wks*	*1 yr*
Penetration (*b*)	0.00	0.03	0.10	**0.20**	0.28	0.36	0.36
Purchase frequency (*w*)	1.02	1.11	1.40	**2.10**	3.04	4.73	5.01
Repeat purchase (%)	2.97	16.82	40.99	**61.65**	71.61	78.88	79.60
Purchase frequency of repeat buyers	1.03	1.18	1.63	**2.55**	3.67	5.60	5.91
Purchase frequency of new buyers	1.01	1.09	1.24	**1.38**	1.45	1.49	1.49
Proportion –							
not buying	1.00	0.97	0.90	**0.80**	0.72	0.64	0.64
buying once	0.00	0.03	0.07	**0.11**	0.11	0.11	0.11
twice	0.00	0.00	0.02	**0.04**	0.06	0.06	0.06
3 times	0.00	0.00	0.01	**0.02**	0.03	0.04	0.04
4 times	0.00	0.00	0.00	**0.01**	0.02	0.03	0.03
5 times	0.00	0.00	0.00	**0.01**	0.01	0.02	0.02
6 +	0.00	0.00	0.00	**0.01**	0.04	0.10	0.10
Proportion of sales due to those buying –							
once	0.97	0.82	0.52	**0.25**	0.14	0.07	0.06
twice	0.03	0.15	0.26	**0.21**	0.13	0.07	0.07
3 times	0.00	0.03	0.12	**0.15**	0.12	0.07	0.07
4 times	0.00	0.00	0.05	**0.11**	0.10	0.07	0.06
5 times	0.00	0.00	0.02	**0.08**	0.09	0.06	0.06
6 +	0.00	0.00	0.02	**0.19**	0.43	0.66	0.69

The output of the NBD program also allows us to see how penetration and purchase frequency change when periods of different duration are used. Table 4.5 shows how the penetration and purchase frequency rise as the period of time is successively doubled (Table 4.5 is obtained by assigning figures to incorrect time periods in program NBD, e.g. the 12-week figures are assigned to 48 weeks so that the tabled 12- and 24-week figures are then actually 3 and 6 weeks). Mean sales are given by the product of penetration and purchase frequency; in a stationary market, these must keep step with the time period, as recorded in the bottom row. Table 4.5 shows that each doubling in the period produces about the same absolute penetration increase. When the penetration is low, changes in sales are mainly related to changes in penetration. When penetration is high and approaching a ceiling, the sales changes appear as changes in purchase frequency.

Table 4.4 Quarterly sales of Corn Flakes in the USA (observed (O) and theoretical (T) values)

Out of 100 purchases, the number buying:

Once		*Twice*		*3 times*		*4 times*		*5 times*		*6+ times*	
O	T	O	T	O	T	O	T	O	T	O	T
55	53	22	22	8	11	5	6	5	4	5	6
Giving sales of:											
55	53	44	44	24	33	20	24	25	20	42	36

Table 4.5 Change in purchase data over time (theoretical)

	3 wks	*6 wks*	*12 wks*	*24 wks*	*48 wks*	*96 wks*	*192 wks*
Penetration (*b*)	0.08	0.13	0.20	0.28	0.36	0.44	0.51
Purchase frequency (*w*)	1.3	1.6	2.1	3.0	4.7	7.8	13.5
Mean sales (*bw*)	0.1	0.2	0.4	0.9	1.7	3.4	6.9

Program NBD is easy to use and is needed to answer questions in Exercises 4.2 to 4.4. It has one technical limitation: when the penetration is high and the purchase frequency is very low, the mathematical procedure for estimating the parameter *k* breaks down and the user must then extrapolate from results obtained with lower penetration figures.

Exercise 4.2 Using the NBD program: how the period affects the data

1 Assume that 0.05 of the population buys an average of 1.5 Snickers in each 4-week period. Use program NBD to establish the penetration, *b*, and the purchase frequency, *w*, and mean sales, *m* (= *bw*), for the given periods and fill in the table below. (If you enter the 4-week data as 1-week data all results will be for four times the tabled period.)

Weeks:	6	12	24	48	96	192
b:						
w:						
bw:						

2 Can you compute the proportion of the population who buy *no* Snickers in four years?
3 Notice that the purchase rate for new buyers is relatively constant for longer periods. See whether it remains so for different *b* and *w* input data.

Exercise 4.3 Collecting panel data for comparison with NBD predictions

NBD predictions can be tested against panel data gathered by the class. You – and others – could keep a diary and record when you engage in a consumer activity such as phoning your friends or drinking beer. Table 4.6 records data from 224 students for one day together with the distribution that is predicted from the NBD model. You can see that the fit is close.

Table 4.6 Number of students making 1, 2, 3, etc. telephone calls in a day

Number calling:	*Once*	*Twice*	*3 times*	*4 times*	*5 times*	*6+ times*
Observed:	75	30	8	0	0	1
Predicted:	75	28	8	2	0	0
b = 0.51; *w* = 1.46						

Exercise 4.4 Marketing analyses

1 Brand R was launched 18 months ago. With continuing advertising support it has maintained a penetration of 4 per cent and a purchase frequency of 1.4 per quarter, but is scarcely viable. Panel research shows a repeat purchase rate of 21 per cent. Should you stop the advertising? Withdraw the brand? Maintain both? To answer this you need to calculate, using the NBD program, the theoretical repeat purchase and see whether it agrees with the observed figure. If the actual repeat purchase is below the stationary market norm, the brand is failing. Also, see the earlier section on repeat purchase.
2 The consumption of soup rises in the winter and falls in the summer. Find out whether all those who buy soup reduce consumption in the summer or whether there are two groups: those who buy it all the year with much the same frequency, and those who buy it only in the winter. Panel data show that those who buy soup in the

summer show a penetration of 32 per cent and a purchase frequency of 5 over 12 weeks. When these people are followed into the higher consumption winter period, panel data show that their quarterly repeat purchase is 79 per cent. What do you conclude? You need to calculate, using program NBD, whether this repeat purchase is the norm for a stationary market for the given particular levels of penetration and purchase frequency. If it is, then you have two separate groups: the all-year stationary buyers and seasonal buyers who only enter the market in the winter. For more information, see Wellan and Ehrenberg (1990).

SECTION 3: PATTERNS OF PURCHASE IN THE WHOLE CATEGORY

We now address the following questions:

- How do penetrations and purchase frequencies vary in a product category?
- What changes do we see in penetration and purchase frequency when market share changes?
- Can we predict the buying frequency and penetration of a new brand if it achieves a given market share?
- When people buy more than one brand, how is their purchase distributed between the different brands?
- Does the evidence of cross-purchase support the idea of niche positioning?
- Is television watching like brand purchasing?
- How is multi-brand purchase modelled mathematically?

Purchase Frequencies and Penetrations in a Product Field

The double jeopardy 'rule'

Table 4.7 presents data on the UK shampoo market, ordered by average sales. You can see that bigger brands (shown by market share) have greater penetrations and slightly greater purchase frequencies. This is typical of what is found in most packaged goods markets. It means that changes in brand sales will be seen mainly as changes in penetration. The low variation in purchase frequency is not so surprising. Why should one brand of shampoo be used more often than another by the people who like it?

The relationship between penetration and purchase frequency in a product field fits the pattern known as *double jeopardy* (Ehrenberg, Goodhardt and Barwise, 1990). Double jeopardy (DJ) was described by the sociologist McPhee (1963: 133–140), who credits the original idea to the broadcaster Jack Landis. McPhee noted how less-popular radio presenters suffer in two ways – fewer people have heard of them and, among those who have heard of them, they are less appreciated. Applied to brands, DJ implies the pattern seen in

Table 4.7 Market share, penetration and purchase frequency in the UK shampoo market (Taylor, Nelson, Sofres, 2005)

Shampoo brand	*Market share %*	*Annual penetration*	*Purchase frequency*
Head & Shoulders	11	13	2.3
Pantene	9	11	2.3
Herbal Essences	5	8	1.8
L'Oréal Elvive	5	8	1.9
Dove	5	9	1.6
Sunsilk	5	8	1.7
Vosene	2	3	1.7
Average			**1.9**

Table 4.7, that less popular brands are not only bought by fewer people (lower penetration) but are also bought less often (lower frequency) by those who do buy them. Ehrenberg, Goodhardt and Barwise show that DJ is a ubiquitous phenomenon, occurring not only in the purchasing of groceries, but also in such fields as the viewing of TV programmes and the purchase of consumer durables, industrial goods and newspapers.

Although DJ is easily seen, the explanation for the effect is less clear. McPhee's explanation took account of differential awareness. People who are aware of less-popular presenters are usually also aware of more-popular presenters and thus are more likely to 'split their vote' compared with those who have only heard of the more-popular broadcasters. But the DJ effect is seen in categories, such as supermarkets, where consumers are likely to be fully aware of all the major brands in a market.

We see DJ as a statistical effect. Consider a board with 100 slots that can receive counters. If you throw counters on to the board, the early ones will each tend to get a slot on their own and each time that you do this, they raise the percentage of slots with a counter (the 'penetration'). As more counters are thrown on to the board, they will increasingly land on slots where there are already counters and this will raise the average number of counters in occupied slots (the 'frequency'). Figure 4.2 shows the theoretical relationship that applies; further analysis of the theoretical double jeopardy line can be found in Habel and Rungie (2005).

Notice that the relationship is approximately linear for much of the penetration range. The statistical relationship between penetration and frequency will be disrupted in a number of ways in real markets. In particular, there may be feedback effects so that, once consumers have bought a brand, they may be more, or less, willing to buy the brand again. A second empirical effect is that some consumers will never buy in some categories. For example, those who do not own a cat rarely (if ever) buy cat food. This 'out-of-the-market' effect will vary across categories and buying segments and it means that predicted penetrations will underestimate observed penetrations, which are based only on those who are in the market.

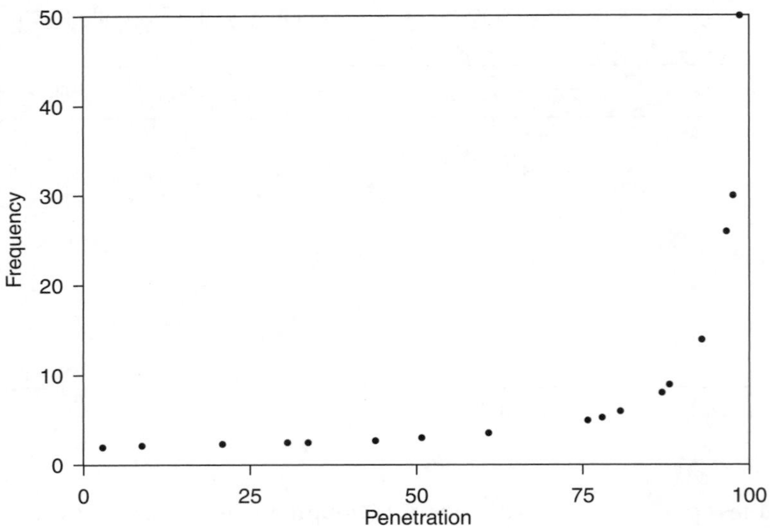

Figure 4.2 Theoretical relationship between penetration and frequency

What Else Changes When Sales Change?

Table 4.7 is useful in showing the way in which penetration and purchase frequency may be expected to change. Major changes over short periods of time are rare, but, looking at Table 4.7, if Vosene were to raise its share of sales to that of L'Oreal Elvive, it is very unlikely that it could do so by getting its existing buyers to buy two-and-a-half times as much of the brand as they currently do. The closeness of purchase frequencies across brands means that sales have to grow mainly by increasing their penetration. Sometimes a gain in frequency may be possible by persuading consumers to find new uses for a product, e.g. by eating cereals at tea-time, but this is a new use of the *category* which is likely to raise the purchase frequencies of all brands.

Some evidence on what changes when a brand gains sales comes from advertising cases. In 1982, advertising substantially increased the purchasing of Curly Wurly, a chocolate-coated toffee liked by children in the UK. Sales then remained approximately constant for the rest of the year (Channon, 1985: 168). From the published data, it appears that among children of 7–11, the two-monthly penetration increased by 60 per cent while the purchase frequency increased by a mere 6 per cent. Among adult purchasers the main gain was also in penetration. Thus, sales gains came mainly because the advertising attracted new buyers, in line with the DJ pattern. Other evidence comes from the sales of Hellman's mayonnaise (Box 4.3).

The relative constancy of purchase frequency is also important to those who are hoping to break into a market with a new brand. With enough advertising money and a sound product, marketers may occasionally achieve a high market share. If they succeed with the new brand, the DJ pattern will define how much of that success will come from penetration and how

Box 4.3 Attempts to raise purchase frequency

There are some situations where increased consumption of a brand might be expected to come from more frequent use by existing buyers rather than by increased penetration. One such situation arose in the case of Hellman's mayonnaise when it was new to the British market. The manufacturers found that the British used Hellman's mayonnaise on little else but salads, a habit they had probably learned from earlier experience with salad cream, which looks rather like mayonnaise. The advertising for Hellman's was therefore designed to expand the number of situations in which the product could be used.

The case report (Channon, 1985) shows that, following the advertising, 40 per cent of users were trying the product in the new ways suggested in the campaign. However, the sales increase that was noted was still largely due to a gain in penetration in line with the double jeopardy rule.

much from purchase frequency. Supporting this, Wellan and Ehrenberg (1988) found that, after rapidly establishing leadership in the UK market, a new soap called Shield registered a purchase frequency appropriate to its new position, i.e. slightly more than its competitors.

For the reporting periods used in market research, most sales changes affect penetration but Treasure (1975) pointed out that when sales are aggregated over longer periods, changes in purchase level appear to be based more on changes in purchase frequency and less on penetration. This difference arises because of the way in which light buyers are counted over short and long periods. Over short periods, an infrequent buyer tends to be a non-buyer in the reference period and is therefore registered as a penetration gain when he or she buys in a later period. Over longer periods, the infrequent buyer is more likely to purchase in the reference period and therefore any gain in purchase in later periods will be recorded as a purchase frequency gain. There is a danger of too rigid an interpretation of the double jeopardy pattern; the important matter here is that it is light buyers that produce most of the change in brand purchase.

Patterns of Multi-brand Purchase

As we saw in Chapter 2, most buyers buy more than one brand in the category. In many grocery markets, the average share-of-category requirement (SCR) is around 30 per cent; this means that for every three purchases of a given brand, the average buyer makes seven purchases of other brands. Ehrenberg (1988) remarks that 'your buyers are the buyers of other brands who occasionally buy you'.

Is there a pattern to this multi-brand buying? There are two possibilities. One is that certain brands are mutually substitutable. If most buyers see brands X and Y as almost the same, we would expect a higher than average purchase rate for Y among purchasers of X and vice versa. Such cross-purchasing of brands would create purchase sub-sets or *market partitioning*. Ehrenberg and Goodhardt (1979) demonstrate that this effect does occasionally occur, e.g. in children's cereals where those who buy one sweetened cereal are more likely to buy another sweetened cereal rather than an unsweetened brand. An alternative pattern is that the purchase of one brand is unrelated to the purchase of other brands, and purchase rates simply reflect the penetrations of the other brands. We find both effects in grocery markets. The basic pattern is that other-brand purchasing is directly proportional to the penetrations of the other brands. Ehrenberg (1988) calls this the *duplication of purchase law*. Superimposed on this pattern are some cases of market partitioning.

Some people expect more market partitioning because they see some brands as close alternatives. But, although many of us will have our own personally preferred groupings of brands, there may be little agreement between individuals. For example, in the toothpaste market, during the course of a year one person may buy Colgate and Aquafresh, another person Aquafresh and Macleans, a third Macleans and a retailer's private label. When these diverse combinations are put together, the different individual cross-preferences will average out so that, usually, there is not much evidence of market partitioning at an aggregate level. When partitioning does occur, it can usually be connected with distinct product features such as price, product form (e.g. flavour, pack type) or a common brand name, rather than with the less tangible claims of the brand that may be identified in advertising. Collins (1971) has reviewed this issue.

Table 4.8 shows how buyers of one brand of toothpaste also bought other brands. The brands are arranged in market share order by column and row. The bottom row shows the average cross-purchase (or purchase duplication, the mean percentage of people buying a 'column' brand in addition to their 'row' brand). Table 4.8 shows some partitioning. There is a higher level of cross-purchase between Colgate GRF and Colgate gel than is implied by average cross-purchase. Compare the 32 per cent for Colgate gel bought by Colgate GRF buyers with 24 per cent average duplication, and compare the 53 per cent for GRF bought by Colgate gel buyers with 35 per cent average cross-purchase. This effect is common where two products with the same brand name compete in the same field; it provides a basis for line extension since some of the tendency to buy a brand seems to pass to the new line (see Chapter 3).

Table 4.8 Cross-purchase in the British toothpaste market (AGB Data, 1992)

Buyers of:	*Who also bought:*						
	Market share %	*Colgate GRF %*	*Aquafresh %*	*Crest %*	*Macleans Fresh %*	*Mentadent %*	*Colgate gel %*
Colgate GRF	18	–	19	18	20	12	32
Aquafresh	9	30	–	26	28	14	23
Crest	8	32	28	–	23	17	24
Macleans Fresh	8	31	27	20	–	12	21
Mentadent	7	28	21	22	18	–	20
Colgate gel	7	53	24	23	23	15	–
Av. cross-purchase (all brands)		35	24	22	23	14	24

Cross-purchase and Positioning

Positioning is heavily emphasized in marketing. It is the set of beliefs about the brand that the manufacturer and advertising agency seek to establish in the minds of potential purchasers: in other words, it is an *intended brand image*. One implication of the cross-purchase evidence is that new brands do not need to have some unique formulation or brand image to succeed, a finding which has worried those who attach strong importance to brand positioning. If cross-purchase between brands depends largely upon penetrations with exceptions relating only to price, formulation or brand name, we must conclude that positioning, with its implication that each brand occupies a distinct niche in the minds of consumers, is poorly supported. When advertising does succeed, it may be because it has been effective at producing high brand awareness and not because the brand is seen as subtly different from other brands in its category. Indeed, many successful brands may do well because they are perceived as typical of other brands in the category, rather than as different from those brands. Thus, manufacturers often focus on the strategy which Ehrenberg (1988) called 'me-too', i.e. copying the formulation and appearance of existing successful brands and thereby trading on established purchase habits. This is a strategy much used by retailers when they offer private label brands.

Positioning assumptions are well established in marketing. It is hard to abandon the idea that a brand has a unique selling proposition (USP), which is appreciated by consumers. This approach leads to the common idea of a niche brand, one that is appreciated by some consumer segments but not by others, even though they could buy it. This sometimes happens in fashion (see Box 4.4). Of course, advertisers do need to show that their offering fits consumer expectations but these expectations may relate more to the whole category or to variants. (As we saw in Chapter 1, there are more differences between the variants of a brand than between brands.)

The Tesco pack has much the same shape and design as the more established Head & Shoulders brand of Procter & Gamble

Box 4.4 Niche brands

Niche brands are those that are bought by one section of the population but not by other sections that could afford to buy them (in this sense, expensive brands like Porsche are not niche brands). To identify niche brands it is necessary to compare the consumers who buy different brands to see whether they differ in terms of demography or beliefs (e.g. age or politics). One study compared the demographic profiles of brand buyers in different grocery categories (Hammond, Ehrenberg and Goodhardt, 1996). This work showed very little difference between the buyers of different brands except in the case of cereals where certain brands were bought only when there were children in the household. Given this evidence, the realistic assumption is that there is normally little difference between the buyers of any two brands in a packaged goods category. This is not so surprising when we remember that the buyers of one brand are often the buyers of another brand.

But niches can occur. One interesting case arose when the fashion designer Burberry launched a wide range of lower-price brand extensions which were taken up by 'chavs'. In the UK, chavs is a term for those perceived as 'uneducated and uncultured people' (Wikipedia). Their endorsement of Burberry was unwelcome for the fashion house because it could lead other potential buyers to avoid the brand. The chief executive, Rose Marie Bravo conceded that the adoption of Burberry by chavs may have been responsible for the half-year results (the *Daily Telegraph* (2005), 'Burberry boss is happy with the chav cheques' http://www.telegraph.co.uk/news/uknews/1480169/Burberry-boss-is-happy-with-the-chav-cheques.html).

The close association between other-brand purchase rates and penetration does not hold when brands lack a common distribution structure since the availability of brands obviously affects choice. Thus, local variation in distribution will produce local variation in other-brand purchases. This can occur with beer brands since many are regional and are not available in parts of the country. Uncles and Ehrenberg (1990) have shown this effect with stores; they found that, in the USA, the cross-purchase between two chains (Safeway and Lucky) was higher than predicted because these chains tended to have stores in the same areas.

Watching Television

Television viewing has been shown to have similarities to brand purchase (Goodhardt, Ehrenberg and Collins, 1987). When the programme is a serial, viewing the next episode is like repeat purchase and we can ask how much programme loyalty exists, as measured by repeat viewing. The evidence shows that there is loyalty, particularly for serials with very high ratings. In the UK, about 55 per cent of those watching a serial will repeat-view in the following week but this figure is derived from several different loyalties. Some people watch more than others (i.e. they are loyal to the medium) and this raises their chance of being a viewer of the next episode; some people are channel loyal so that serials on favourite channels have a better repeat-viewing chance; and some people watch more at particular times of the day so that time loyalty may enhance repeat viewing. These three loyalties ensure that people who have been watching a serial are quite likely to be tuned to the same channel at the same time of the week *after the serial has ended*. The difference between this end-of-serial viewing and the repeat viewing when the serial is running indicates the true loyalty to the programme. Such partitioning of loyalty can be applied to other categories, e.g. to the way in which loyalty to a car is divided between brand and model.

Goodhardt, Ehrenberg and Collins (1987) also found some programme partitioning, e.g. those who watch one sports programme are more likely to watch other sports programmes, but they also note that people watch a wide variety of programmes so that cross-viewing has limited partitioning. More recently, Lees and Wright (2012) found similar effects for radio audiences, with some limited partitioning between the 'talk' and 'music' formats.

Terrestrial TV is a *broadcast*, not a *narrowcast*, medium and this makes it difficult to target specific social groups accurately using the main television channels. However, television transmission by cable and satellite has increased the degree of partitioned viewing. Those interested in particular genres, such as sport or children's programmes, are able to access more of these channels, leading to increased duplication of viewing between these genre-specific channels. Collins, Beal and Barwise (2003) offer evidence on this point.

The Dirichlet Model

The Dirichlet is a mathematical model that predicts brand performance statistics for *all* the brands in a product field. It was described in work by Chatfield and Goodhardt (1975) and developed by Bass, Jeuland and Wright (1976). It was presented in a comprehensive form by Goodhardt, Ehrenberg and Chatfield (1984). The assumptions are similar to those for the single-brand NBD model but, in addition, it is assumed that the market has no partitioning. The model does not apply if there is appreciable evidence of brand clustering on any other basis than penetration.

Programs running Dirichlet analyses can give predictions of penetration, purchase frequency, sole buyers, sole-buyer purchase frequency, proportions of buyers at different frequencies and the repeat-purchase rates of those buying with different frequencies. Table 4.9 shows the real data for the US instant coffee market together with the Dirichlet norms. The fit is fairly close with the exception of Maxim and Brim which may be a sampling error effect since these are small brands.

The Value of Models in Marketing

Ehrenberg, Uncles and Goodhardt (2004) point out that mathematical models provide norms against which real markets can be assessed. One management application of such norms is to set out the realistic options that are open to those who want to improve the

Table 4.9 Observed and predicted annual penetrations and purchase frequencies in the US instant coffee market (Hallberg/MRCA, 1996)

		Penetration		*Purchase frequency (w)*	
	Market share	*Observed*	*Dirichlet*	*Observed*	*Dirichlet*
Folgers	24	11	12	3.2	3.1
Maxwell House	22	10	11	3.1	3.1
Taster's Choice	17	9	9	2.8	3.0
Nescafé	11	6	6	2.7	2.9
Sanka	9	5	5	3.0	2.8
High Point	1	1	1	2.6	2.6
Maxim	1	.3	.8	4.5	2.6
Brim	.3	.2	.2	2.1	2.6
Other brands	16	8	8	3.0	3.0

share of their brand or who want to launch a new brand on the market. Table 4.9 shows that the penetration and purchase frequency of a brand is anchored on its market share; brand share changes will relate mainly to changes in penetration rather than purchase frequency. Models also provide norms for cross-purchase in an unpartitioned market and show the long-run propensity to buy a repertoire of brands. When markets are partitioned, e.g. powdered and liquid detergent, we can see the extent to which this partitioning affects cross-purchase. In some cases the market analysis, coupled with Dirichlet norms, may help to show how much of a market is accessible to competition. For example, if a new environmentally friendly detergent is being contemplated, is the competition all detergents, or all detergents that make environmental claims, or some combination thereof?

A further value of this work lies in management education. An understanding of stationary markets helps managers to read their own brand statistics and to understand the ways in which change may, or may not, be brought about. When change does occur and the market stabilizes again, the new brand performance statistics will fit the Dirichlet norms.

One criticism of stationary market research is that it has generally been confirmatory in approach, showing the fit between data and models, rather than testing for exceptions. Exceptions need to be zealously pursued because it is information on such exceptions that may help us to see how to 'buck the market'.

SUMMARY

Over reporting periods of three months to a year the sales of most established consumer brands are approximately stationary: short-term fluctuations due to promotions are averaged out and longer-term trends are too slow-acting to have much effect. The steady state of such markets arises because most buyers in a category maintain their propensities to buy the same group of brands for long periods of time.

The penetration, purchase frequency and market share of a brand are key statistics. These measures encode most of the buying propensities of consumers so that there is no need to know anything more about the brand in order to predict other brand performance statistics. This makes mathematical modelling possible.

Brands have few heavy buyers but these are responsible for a large part of the sales; the heaviest 20 per cent of buyers typically account for about 50 per cent of the purchases. However, because there are many light buyers and some new buyers, a change in their purchasing can have a substantial effect on sales. Over shorter periods (3–12 months), sales changes are mostly seen as a change in penetration, as occasional buyers return to the category, with only a small change in purchase frequency in line with the rule of double jeopardy.

The NBD and Dirichlet models rest on assumptions that purchase incidence is Poisson, purchase rates in a population of buyers are Gamma, and that (in the case of the Dirichlet) there is no market partitioning. The predictions from such models usually fit the data derived from panel research. When the fit is poor, the model provides benchmark norms for interpreting the unusual brand performance.

Analysis of cross-purchase suggests that there is limited market partitioning. The absence of substitution patterns between specific brands indicates that the different brands in a category are seen by consumers in much the same way. In these circumstances, a positioning strategy based on brand differences may have little relevance.

Additional Resources

A clearly written but technical account of the NBD can be found in Morrison and Schmittlein (1988), while the phenomenon of double jeopardy is well explained by Ehrenberg, Goodhardt and Barwise (1990). For a useful review of the Dirichlet and its applications see Ehrenberg, Uncles and Goodhardt (2004). An exercise designed to bring home the features of stationary markets is available in Ehrenberg, Uncles and Carrie (1994b). A book designed for practitioners brings home the implications of research on stationary markets; this is *How Brands Grow* by Byron Sharp, Oxford: Oxford University Press (2010).

Notes

1 Firms sometimes conduct Pareto analyses and delete the worst-performing brands or discourage the customers who buy the least. It is important to consider whether such brands and customers could change. For example, a customer at a DIY store could buy little for several years but become a heavy buyer after moving house.

2 Within these assumptions it is possible to derive an expression for the probability of making r purchases in a period, p_r. For those interested in the technicalities: $p_r = [1-m/(m+k)]^{-k}$ where k is a parameter that is estimated from the purchase frequency and penetration. Expressions of the form $(1+x)^n$ are called binomial; the equation for p_r is a negative binomial because the exponent is negative. The calculation of the NBD requires the solution of the equation $1-b = (1+m/k)^{-k}$ to obtain the parameter k; this is done by the NBD program.

5 Market Dynamics

LEARNING OBJECTIVES

When you have completed this chapter, you should be able to:

1. Sketch a 52-week sales curve showing seasonality and sales promotions.
2. Explain what will happen if there is an imbalance between customer defection and customer acquisition.
3. Explain why the effects of marketing actions may take some time to become obvious.
4. Explain the social basis of diffusion theory.
5. Describe/sketch the technology substitution model, the Bass model and the typical trial growth curves for frequently bought products.

OVERVIEW

Chapter 4 described the regular patterns of purchase found in mature, stationary markets. But what if a market is not stable? Sales and market share do sometimes change and new products sometimes gather sales and become established. In this chapter, we explore aspects of this change.

In the first section, we discuss sales fluctuations in mature markets due to seasonality and sales promotions. These short-term changes can be large, making it harder to spot long-term trends. The second section describes the dynamic patterns in loyalty underlying stable markets. We document these, show how they lead to dynamic equilibrium and discuss the effects of disturbing this equilibrium. In doing so, we extend some of the material from Chapter 4. In the third section, we consider the launch of major innovations. These may create new markets or lead to the complete substitution of an old way of doing things. We draw on the theory of innovation diffusion, as described by Everett Rogers, introduce the technology substitution model and give an overview of Frank Bass's model of new product adoption. Finally, we consider frequently bought categories, such as grocery products. These categories exhibit recurrent minor product innovation, but arguably with a different social dynamic from that found in the work of Rogers and Bass. We document the growth of first purchases for these minor innovations, and discuss the development of loyalty to such new products.

SECTION 1: CHANGES IN AGGREGATE SALES

Variations in Demand – Seasonality and Sales Promotions

Most of the sales fluctuations seen in mature markets are transient, and do not affect underlying demand for a brand or category. Businesses typically experience large swings in demand that simply relate to the time of the year, holidays, sales promotions and other events. More butter and soup are sold in winter. There is little demand for Easter Eggs at Christmas. Americans buy barbecue sauce in summer, with demand skyrocketing for the 4th of July, assisted by heavy sales promotion. Similar patterns can occur in durables and business-to-business markets. The weather, holidays and tax refunds all nudge consumers towards buying certain products at particular times. Even sales targets and discounting policies can lead to seasonality in demand (see Box 5.1).

Box 5.1 Discounts create irregular sales

Early in his career, one of the authors worked for a large American computer company where the need to meet sales quotas led to a crescendo of effort at the end of the year. If sales were slow, management would authorize company-wide promotions in the final quarter, in the hope that they could still achieve their targets. Some IT customers responded to this by adjusting their capital purchase cycle. When pressed about low sales mid-way through the year, sales staff would tell management that their customers 'liked to buy at the end of the year, when the discounts are offered'.

It is important to be familiar with such temporary variations in demand. Figure 5.1 provides an example. The graph covers two and a half years of weekly data, and is representative of sales of widely used table condiments in a major western economy. The *x*-axis shows intervals of 13 weeks, or a quarter, which is a common management reporting period. The base of the *y*-axis is zero, so differences in the height of the graph are directly proportional to percentage differences in demand.

This figure shows spikes that increase sales by as much as 150 per cent above the baseline level. They tend to be about four quarters apart. In other words, the spikes occur at the same time (or season) every year. Why are these sales spikes so large? Because sales promotions are often timed to match holidays or seasonal upswings in demand, giving a large combined effect. As mentioned in Chapter 4, despite the magnitude of these changes there is usually little long-term increase in average yearly sales or in customer loyalty. This is because most of the extra sales come from a brand's existing users (Ehrenberg, Hammond and Goodhardt, 1994a; Gupta, Van Heerde and Wittink, 2003).

Many managers are surprised when they first see such period-to-period sales variations, so it is important to be aware of them. The size of these variations can cause

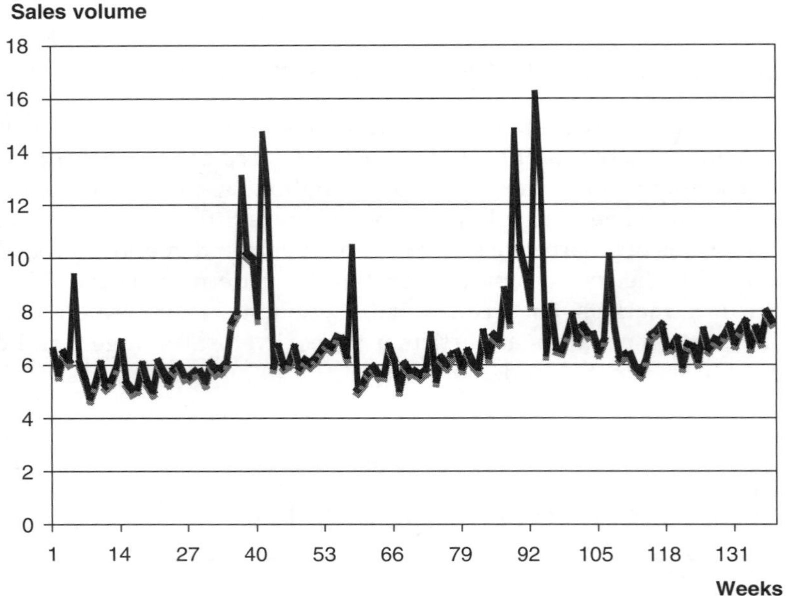

Figure 5.1 Category volume for a grocery product
Source: Simulated data based on known patterns

supply problems and managers should take steps to avoid stock-outs during periods of heavy demand, such as sales promotions.

Measuring Long-Term Sales Performance

These transient changes in demand make it difficult to identify underlying trends in sales. Figure 5.1, for example, shows an upward trend over time, although this is hard to pick out at first glance. One reason why market share is a popular measure of performance is that it controls for some of these fluctuations. Seasonality and holidays should affect all competitors equally, so market share is a more stable measure of performance than raw sales data. In addition, many companies measure market share using statistical techniques that reduce the period-to-period variation in the data and enable a clearer picture of trends in sales to emerge.

Some companies may apply seasonal decomposition to remove seasonality effects, or exponential smoothing to reduce the impact of random variations. Advanced econometric techniques, such as ARIMA (autoregressive integrated moving average), may combine both methods, include estimates of trend lines and use dummy variables for holiday effects. By using statistical models to identify the seasonal, promotional and holiday effects, the underlying trend is more clearly revealed.

SECTION 2: DYNAMIC EFFECTS AND BRAND LOYALTY

The Changes Underlying a Stable Market

Section 1 outlined the fluctuations in total sales that occur in stationary markets. In this section we examine fluctuations in individual consumer purchases. Even in a stationary market individual buying will fluctuate. Some of the commonly observed patterns include regression to the mean for heavy buyers, long-term erosion of loyalty, and churn (turnover in the customer base) as customers cease buying and are replaced.

We know from Chapter 4 that the NBD model describes the normal patterns of light buying, heavy buying and repeat purchase. We can expand on this, using a technique called conditional trend analysis (CTA). Conditional trend analysis was developed by Goodhardt and Ehrenberg (1967) to extend the NBD to different classes of buyers, so that repeat purchase can be predicted for light versus heavy buyers, or indeed for any group of buyers who made a specified number of purchases in the first period analyzed. Managers should be interested in this, because of the sales importance of heavy buyers, the desire to increase the purchase rate of light buyers, and the need to convert some proportion of zero buyers into regular customers. In particular, managers are often concerned that a loss of loyalty from heavy buyers presages a decline in brand sales and share. CTA reveals the level of repeat purchase that should usually be expected for each group of buyers – heavy buyers, light buyers, and even the purchase rate to be expected from people who were zero buyers in the previous period.

Consider a brand that is bought by 15 per cent of category purchasers, on average 1.6 times in a 13-week period, a fairly typical pattern. The NBD analysis in Chapter 4 tells us that the expected repeat purchase rate in the next 13-week period is about 50 per cent (i.e. half of the people who bought the brand in the first period will buy again in the second). But the NBD does not tell us how repeat purchase is distributed between light and heavy buyers. To compare actual repeat purchase with the norms for heavy buyers, we need to undertake CTA. Table 5.1 reports some results from both normal NBD analysis and CTA, broken down by the number of purchases made in the first period.

First, look at the set of buyers who made a single purchase in period 1. They are important, as they make up 65 per cent of all buyers. Given that they bought once in period 1, a manager may expect them to continue buying at the same rate. It may be a surprise to find that this set of buyers makes just 0.6 purchases (on average) in the second period. Likewise, the set of buyers who bought twice in the first period drops to 1.2 purchases in the second period and the heaviest buyers have gone from an average 4.8 purchases down to 2.7.

It would be easy to interpret this as an erosion of loyalty, and to conclude that you need to find the source of the problem and recruit replacement customers. That would be a mistake, though not an uncommon one. It is what Andrew Ehrenberg calls the 'Leaky Bucket Theory' (most recently, in Ehrenberg, Uncles and Goodhardt, 2004), the idea that customers are steadily leaking away, requiring replacement by freshly recruited buyers.

In fact, the values in Table 5.1 are theoretical norms, rather than observed values. They are exactly what we would expect in a normal, mature, stationary market. Period 1 shows familiar NBD patterns; most buyers make only one purchase, and 35 per cent of buyers

Table 5.1 Purchase and repeat purchase over consecutive 13-week periods

	Initial purchases – period 1		*Repeat purchases – period 2*	
Number of purchases	*% of buyers*	*% of sales*	*Average purchases per Period-1 buyer*	*% repeat buying*
1	65	41	0.6	40
2	21	26	1.2	61
3	8	15	1.7	74
4+ (av. 4.8)	6	18	2.7	87

account for 59 per cent of sales. In period 2, we simply see how the NBD plays out over time. We see how the 50 per cent repeat-purchase rate is distributed across heavier and lighter buyers, and that the average number of purchases for each group declines in period 2. Instead of thinking of this as undesirable, we should recognize it as the typical pattern of purchasing over time. Heavier buyers show higher repeat rates simply because they are heavier and more regular buyers to start with. Despite this, their purchases decline in the second period, exhibiting the familiar statistical phenomenon of regression to the mean.

Total sales remain stable because those who do not repeat purchase in period 2 are balanced by an influx of other regular buyers. These are households who did not purchase in period 1, but are nonetheless established buyers of the brand. Similarly, a reduction in purchase frequency by some buyers will be matched by an increase in purchase frequency by others. Rather than a 'leaky bucket' in need of constant replenishment, this is the normal pattern of buying in repertoire markets.

Some companies do monitor erosion of loyalty by examining repeat-purchase rates for heavy buyers. This is sometimes called buyer flow analysis and data for this is available from consumer panel companies. If you want to undertake buyer flow analysis, be sure to use the NBD and CTA for a benchmark. You will find that much apparent erosion is simply the normal pattern of occasional purchasing.

Erosion of Loyalty in Repertoire Markets

The previous section demonstrates that much apparent erosion in loyalty is simply due to customer purchase rates fluctuating from period to period. That is not to say that there is no true erosion of repeat-purchase loyalty. There is, but it is smaller than implied by a simple buyer flow analysis. True erosion is revealed by examining the decline in repeat-purchase rates for the whole customer base. For example, East and Hammond (1996) examined repeat-purchase rates for supermarket products and found that they declined from around 55 per cent to 47 per cent over a year. This is 8 percentage points, and 8/55 is 15 per cent of buyers. Similar observations can be found in Zufryden (1996). In a study of four brands in two segments, he observed year-to-year retention of first-brand loyalty ranging from 79 per cent to 86 per cent. Thus, erosion ranged from 14 per cent to 21 per cent. These values are a little higher than those of East and Hammond (1996), perhaps because a loss of first-brand loyalty does not necessarily represent a complete switch. It may simply be a downgrade to a lower position in a customer's repertoire, such as moving from favourite to second-favourite brand.

So, there is erosion but it occurs slowly. The leaky bucket theory is not wrong, but the holes are quite small.

Defection and Churn in Subscription Markets

Leakage is often more obvious in subscription markets, where consumers have only one supplier, such as insurance, banking, utilities and mobile phone airtime. These markets may be based on an annually renewable contract, as in the case of insurance, or they may be a 'tenure' contract in which the subscription continues until terminated, as with banking or utilities. Some markets, such as hairdressing or the family doctor, are thought to show the same kind of persistent subscription-like behaviour, even when choice is not constrained by a contract (Sharp, Wright and Goodhardt, 2002).

In subscription markets, a loss of loyalty often represents a complete loss of revenue from the customer concerned. Thus, the rate of defection (or retention) is a key performance metric and a leading indicator of a brand's fortunes. Sometimes, a loss of loyalty may represent a downgrade rather than a complete defection, but may nonetheless be treated as if it were a full defection. Banking is a prime example of this. Customers often have relationships with more than one financial institution, and these relationships tend to be long-lasting and valuable. Banks are interested in whether they are a customer's main bank, with the largest share of wallet, and therefore the best opportunities for cross-selling. So main bank defection rates are treated in a similar way to other types of defection.

Annual defection rates in subscription markets typically range from 4 per cent to 20 per cent of a brand's customer base. Lees, Garland and Wright (2007) report a figure of 3.6 per cent for a main bank. Gupta, Lehmann and Stuart (2004) found figures of 5 per cent for online stock trading and 15 per cent for a credit card company. Wright and Riebe (2010) calculated, but did not report, category switching rates in both consumer- and business-to-business markets. However, these were 4.1 per cent for the main bank and 20 per cent for annual industrial pipe contracts. Reichheld (1996b) claimed that defection varied quite widely but averaged about 15 per cent across a range of services.

Turnover in the customer base, often called churn, is not always due to defection to or from another supplier. First-time market entry and market exit both play a part. People may enter some markets as they reach independence or form new households, and leave them as they cease to support a family. There may also be churn due to upgrades or downgrades in the product used or because of competitive pricing.[1]

In some fields, change is linked strongly to life-stage. Consider banking. Over a lifetime an individual may move from a child's savings account, to an overdraft, to a mortgage, to an on-call cash management account. People may move house or be affected by a major life event such as their first job, marriage, birth of a child and so forth. This can affect the types of product and service they require and thus their loyalty to previously purchased brands. Some car models are suitable for young people, others for executives and others for families. Similarly, there are regional banks in many countries that cannot offer a full range of services in large cities. A young family that moves from a regional centre to a large city may be forced to change their bank.

Some evidence on the reasons for switching banks comes from Lees, Garland and Wright (2007). They found that, in New Zealand, a change of main bank was due to better offers 32 per cent of the time, product or service failures 31 per cent of the time, reasons beyond the bank's control (such as moving house) 22 per cent of the time and a combination of these reasons 15 per cent of the time. Bogomolova and Romaniuk (2009) examined brand defection for a business-to-business financial service, and found that 60 per cent of defection was for reasons that managers could not control. Chapter 2 carried evidence of defection in other categories.

Consequently, as with buyer flow in repertoire markets, there is a certain level of inevitable turnover in the customer base. When interpreting defection figures, theoretical norms should be used to determine how much defection is normal, and how much is unusual. Wright and Riebe (2010) provide a method of calculating such norms for subscription markets.

Change from Market Imbalance

If erosion, or switching, from a brand is exactly matched by customer acquisition, a dynamic equilibrium will exist in which market share for that brand remains constant. An imbalance between the two will lead to a change. For example, reducing a brand's defection rate while maintaining the rate of customer acquisition will lead to an increase in market share. Conversely, if the defection rate increases while acquisition remains stable, market share will decrease. Defection reduction has been recognized as a possible source of growth for some time (Reichheld and Sasser, 1990). More recently, Reichheld (2003) pursued the idea of growth coming from dynamic forces through his 'Net Promoter Score', which takes account of the propensity to give positive word of mouth (see Chapter 12). Recent work has also integrated defection rates into an understanding of customer lifetime value (Gupta, Lehmann and Stuart, 2004) and compared the relative returns of customer acquisition and defection reduction efforts (Reinartz, Thomas and Kumar, 2005) to support an optimal allocation of the marketing budget.

However, work in this area tends to overlook the fact that defection reduction is *bounded*. That is, if a brand has 6 per cent defection, it can only reduce it by this amount, or less. No matter how superior the product or service, some loss of customers will occur due to market exit, changes in customer requirements, or other matters beyond the control of managers.

Further, recent work has compared unusual defection and unusual acquisition as sources of dynamic changes in market share (Riebe et al., forthcoming). The evidence leads to the conclusion that acquisition rates are much more important than defection rates in explaining changes in market share for both growing and declining brands.

Exercise 5.1 Defection reduction and share growth

Question: Imagine you have a brand with a 3 per cent market share and an annual defection rate of 10 per cent. How long will it take to increase your market share from 3 per cent to 10 per cent, simply by halving your defection rate?

Answer: Assuming your market share has been in a dynamic balance and that all customers buy at the same rate, your 10 per cent annual defection rate will have been matched by a 10 per cent annual customer acquisition rate. If your defection rate halves to 5 per cent while your customer acquisition rate remains constant, you will grow by 5 per cent of your customer base per annum. That is, your market share after *T* years can be found by a simple compounding formula, as follows:

$3\% \times (1 + .05) \wedge T$

We suggest you conduct a simple spreadsheet analysis to find the answer. We did this and found that market share will rise above the 10 per cent threshold in the *24th year*. However, defection reduction can be an expensive exercise so there is a risk that market share growth will not be matched by profit growth.

Comment: This example is somewhat similar to that of MNBA, outlined in Reichheld and Sasser (1990). Reichheld and Sasser were more concerned with customer lifetime value than with growth. However, we hope our example makes it clear that brand growth requires a broader explanation than just defection reduction, especially when brands have a relatively low market share.

Ask yourself the question: what else could lead to brand growth?

Observing Market Change

One consequence of occasional buying and relatively low levels of erosion is that marketing actions can take a long time to bear fruit. Exposure to advertising, for example, cannot affect brand choice until the next purchase occasion. Similarly, defection-reduction programmes seek to plug a leak that may be fairly small to start with, while attempts to acquire customers will be limited by the number entering the market or looking to make a change. So it may take some time for marketing initiatives to play out in changes to sales. An exception is sales promotion, which tends to have a large effect during the period of the promotion, leading to the spikes in sales seen in Figure 5.1.

Similarly, market problems, such as a drop in perceived quality, may not be immediately noticeable. It may be some time before affected customers are ready to purchase the category again, or to renew a contract and have the opportunity to make a different choice. By that time, quite a weight of dissatisfaction may have accumulated so that many switch. This makes it important to use brand performance metrics such as satisfaction or perceived quality as well as average purchase frequency and, repeat purchase, as these more-qualitative data may indicate potential problems, allowing a manager to respond before the problems gather too much momentum.

SECTION 3: THE DYNAMICS OF NEW PRODUCT ADOPTION

So far we have examined change in mature markets. What about the more fundamental changes that result from the launch of new products? Whether they satisfy a previously unmet demand, or replace a previous technology, new products can result in more rapid and enduring change than is seen in mature markets.

How are such innovations adopted by a population of consumers? While there is a large literature on this topic, we will restrict ourselves to examining three approaches of particular importance to marketers. These are Rogers' innovation diffusion curve, Fisher and Pry's technology substitution model and the Bass model.

Rogers' Approach to Innovation Diffusion

Most marketers have some awareness of work on the diffusion of innovations. The most well-known author in this area is Everett Rogers (1962, 2003), whose book on the subject is a widely cited classic. Rogers brought together studies from many disciplines, but gave emphasis to sociology. He followed influential work by Gabriel Tarde (1903), who noted that cumulative adoption followed an S-shaped curve and saw adoption or rejection as a critical decision; George Simmel (1908), who introduced the idea of a social network; and Ryan and Gross (1943), who undertook a landmark study into adoption of hybrid corn. Later work incorporated Granovetter's finding (1973) that the spread of an innovation through a social system was helped if people were loosely bonded to many different groups.

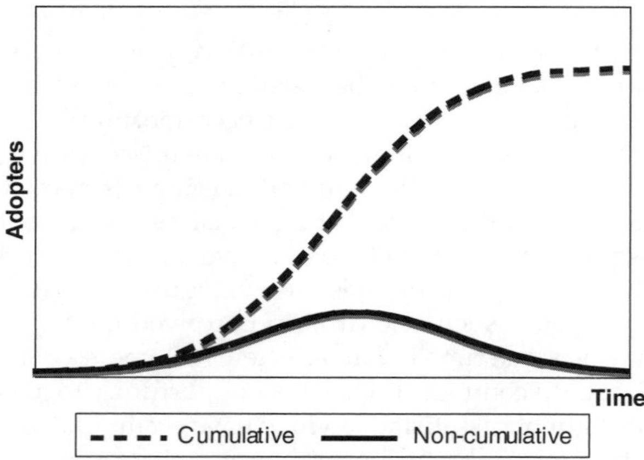

Figure 5.2 A normal adoption curve

In Rogers' work, these ideas are more fully developed and integrated, with diffusion defined as 'the process in which an innovation is communicated through certain channels over time among the members of a social system' (Rogers, 2003: 5). Rogers believed that adoption follows a normal distribution curve, with time as the x-axis and number of adopters as the y-axis. Figure 5.2 shows this normal curve. There are two versions: the standard normal curve of (non-cumulative) adoptions in each period and the S-shaped curve of total (cumulative) adoption. Historical examples of new products that become widely established include black and white televisions, computer chips, air conditioning units, facsimile machines and first-generation mobile telephones. Modern examples might include high-definition colour televisions, solar water heating, media recording devices and smart phones.

Characteristics of an Innovation

Innovations do not always follow this curve. They may fail. Or they may diffuse so slowly that the left tail, or lead-time, of the adoption curve extends for many years before rapid growth kicks in. Rogers cites as examples the Royal Navy's reluctance to use citrus juice as an anti-scurvy agent, resistance to the use of boiled water in Peru and the failure to displace the QWERTY keyboard on which this book has been rather inefficiently typed. He became interested in the characteristics affecting the innovation adoption rate and posited that it depended on:

- The *relative advantage* that an innovation has over previous methods of meeting the same need. Some innovations, such as text messaging and social networking tools, also have strong network effects, so that relative advantage increases with the number of adopters.
- *Compatibility*, or the consistency of an innovation with the existing experiences, needs and values of the adopting population. Cultural and religious incompatibilities may be particular risks for the adoption of innovations.
- *Complexity*, or how easy an innovation is to use and describe to others and whether it requires specialized expertise or substantial learning.
- *Trialability*, enabling experience to be gained with the innovation before purchase or full adoption.
- *Observability*, increasing both awareness and social influence, as we are influenced by seeing others use new products and tend to follow the consumption habits of the communities we live in.

There is also the perceived risk of an innovation. The higher the price, the less the confidence in after-sales service, or the harsher the returns policy the more reluctant people will be to adopt. Rogers' adoption characteristics also have an indirect impact on perceived risk, as this will be reduced by trialability or observability and increased by problems of compatibility or complexity.

Adopter Categories and Innovativeness

Perhaps the most famous part of Rogers' work is the division of the normal curve into adopter categories. People in the first 2.5 per cent of the normal curve in Figure 5.2 are labelled the innovators and the next 13.5 per cent the early adopters. Then we have the early majority (34 per cent), late majority (34 per cent) and laggards (16 per cent). These adopter categories are reproduced in most consumer behaviour textbooks, together with comments about their typical characteristics.

This approach has come in for some serious criticism. Bass (1969) famously described Rogers' approach as 'largely literary'. Wright and Charlett (1995) pointed out that Rogers' adopter categories were a *post hoc* tautological classification system, of no value for forecasting. This is because Rogers' categorization depends on the standard deviation from the mean time to adopt. Innovators are all those up to two standard deviations before the mean time to adopt; early adopters are between 2 and 1 standard deviations from the mean time to adopt and so on. Yet neither the mean nor the standard deviation can be calculated until the diffusion of the innovation is complete, at which point the adopter categories have little managerial value.

A counter-argument is that innovativeness is a normally distributed trait, associated with other consumer characteristics in a predictable manner, allowing innovators and early adopters to be identified and targeted. Rogers claimed that there were 26 characteristics that varied between adopter categories, including socio-economic variables, personality values and communication behaviour. However, empirical findings do not always support this claim. Taylor (1977) found that a striking characteristic of 'innovators' in grocery products was that they were simply heavy buyers of the category, a finding that was recently confirmed for pharmaceuticals (Stern and Wright, 2007). This hardly suggests an enduring personality trait. A more popular modern view is that innovativeness varies by product category (e.g. Crawford and Di Benedetto, 2006: 372).

The long lead-time that can occur before an innovation takes off is sometimes explained by the characteristics of the most innovative people. Rogers notes that innovators are often 'deviants', somewhat apart from the rest of the social system: they might be metaphorical hermits in the wood, dwelling apart from the community, or perhaps the archetypical computer geek. While such people may be innovative, they may have little social influence, so their behaviour has little effect on the broader community. Diffusion will only take off when more influential people, well connected within the social system, adopt the innovation. In a tribal village, this might be the chief or the chief's wife. In western social networks, it may be opinion leaders or celebrities, or people who offer marketplace advice to many others, such as Feick and Price's (1987) 'market mavens' (if they can be found; see Chapter 11). Rogers places such people in the early adopter category.

While these ideas offer insights into ways of speeding up adoption within particular social systems, they are not necessary to explain the S-shaped curve that we see in practice. A long lead-time can be explained through the cumulative effects of social forces, as we shall see later. Nonetheless, Rogers' work is very useful. The concept of an idea spreading through a social system via specific communication channels underlies much subsequent work on innovation diffusion. The insight that adoption follows a normal curve has been borne out in many product categories.

Fisher and Pry's Technology Substitution Model

Rogers' adopter categorization exploits the properties of the S-shaped normal distribution curve, but is not helpful for forecasting. Marketers need to make forecasts to assist launch decisions on new products, set targets against which performance can be assessed, and allocate marketing expenditure.

Fisher and Pry (1971) showed how to use an S-shaped curve to forecast the replacement of an inferior technology with a better one that meets the same need. This process is called technology substitution. They dealt with the problem of an indeterminate lead-time by assuming the substitute technology must achieve several per cent market share before complete substitution could be guaranteed to occur. They then treated substitution as a logistic function of time.[2] This has the practical effect of transforming the S-shaped cumulative adoption curve into a straight line. Extrapolation through regression then yields a forecast. They validated this model over 17 diverse data sets and found surprisingly accurate results.

Figure 5.3 is an example of the raw pattern of technology substitution, using some previously published data on diesel and steam locomotives in the USA. These data are expressed in relative percentages of the total number of locomotives. You will see that the growth curve for diesel locomotives is similar to the cumulative normal adoption curve shown in Figure 5.2.

Although quite old now, Fisher and Pry's (1971) model is likely to continue to be of great importance as we undergo accelerating technological substitution in areas such as telecommunications, computing and home electronics. This model has the useful feature of forecasting the dynamic decline of the old technology as well as the growth of the new one. This is potentially very helpful to companies in fields such as telecommunications, where there are substantial but declining revenue streams from products such as fixed-line telephone connections.

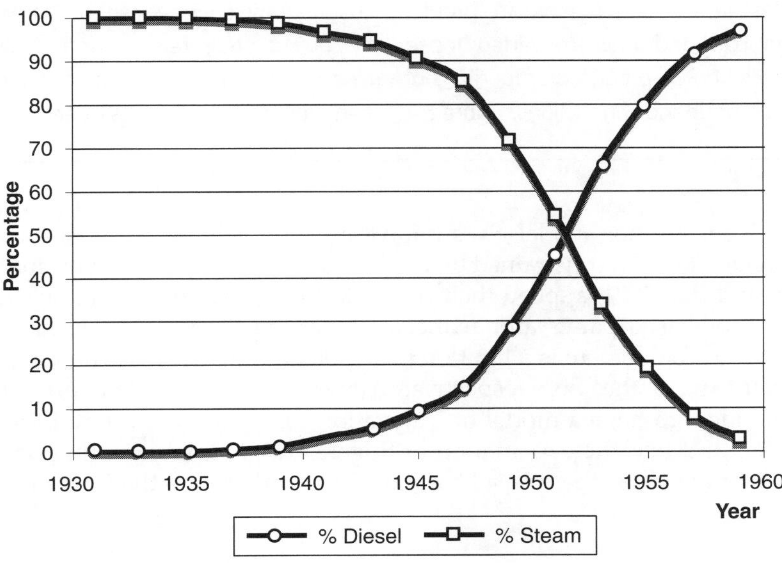

Figure 5.3 Cumulative substitution of locomotives

Source: Interstate Commerce Commission, Statistics of Railroads 1925–1960, as cited in Moore and Pessemier (1993: 79)

By way of example, consider the following forecast (Box 5.2). This applies the Fisher and Pry model to publicly available information on dial-up and broadband Internet connections in Australia. We describe the workings so you can see how easily the model is applied. Note that the date had to be adjusted to an equal interval scale to allow the statistical analysis to take place. Figure 5.4 graphs the example in Box 5.2, in this case in fractions rather than percentages.

Box 5.2 The growth of broadband

We applied the Fisher and Pry model to forecasting the decline of Australian dial-up Internet access and, conversely, the growth of broadband in that country. Using Nielsen net ratings figures published at http://www.dcita.gov.au, we converted the proportions of Internet users that had dial-up and broadband access to a log odds ratio (LOR) and ran an OLS regression. The OLS regression predicted that LOR = 3.214 −0.068 × adjusted date. (We had to use an adjusted date to ensure an equal interval scale, as the time between reports varied.) We put future dates into this equation to predict changes in LOR and then converted these changed LORs back to predicted proportions of dial-up and broadband connections. Figure 5.4 shows our forecasts. Forecasts like this give useful long-range expectations about the size of the customer base and the support infrastructure needed from capital equipment to call-centre staff. They are also useful to help forecast market potential for Internet services relying on a broadband connection, such as Internet TV.

Postscript: The forecasts were based on data up until June 2006, at which stage 71 per cent of Internet users had broadband. This was forecast to grow to 95 per cent by the end of 2008. In 2009 a press release from Nielsen online revealed that the actual figure for broadband penetration in 2008 was 97 per cent.

The technology substitution model gives impressive forecasting ability, but it does not offer much explanation. It is also constrained by the simplicity of the assumptions. In their original article, Fisher and Pry (1971) applied their model to the substitution of margarine for butter, water-based for oil-based paints and artificial for natural fibres. We now know that those substitutions are partial – there is a limit on their potential that is less than the total usage of yellow fats, paint and clothes fibre respectively. Sometimes, silk is still preferred to nylon.

It would be ideal to have a model of innovation diffusion that offered the forecasting ability of Fisher and Pry, the explanation of Rogers and a variable ceiling on the number of adopters. As it happens, there is such a model in marketing – the Bass model.

The Bass Model

Frank Bass's approach to diffusion of innovation (1969) is one of the most well-known models in marketing. Bass drew on epidemiological theory – the theory of the spread of

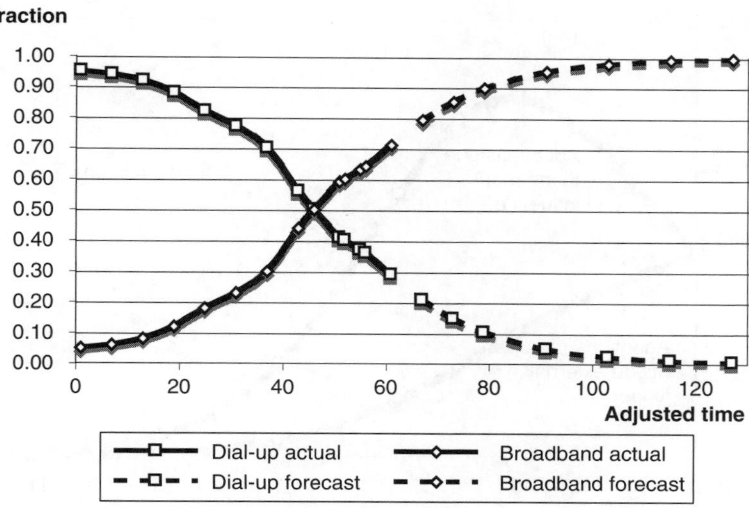

Figure 5.4 Cumulative substitution of Internet access

diseases – to examine the spread of an innovation throughout a connected social system. Bass modelled the effect of both innovative and imitative forces in promoting adoption up to a saturation point. He saw innovative forces as those external to the social system, such as advertising and personal selling. Innovation therefore acts throughout the diffusion process rather than being limited to the first 2.5 per cent of adopters. Conversely, imitative forces reflect social influence, which is internal to the social system. Therefore imitative forces are exerted by previous adopters as they model and recommend the innovation to others. For example, you might buy an iPad simply because you see an advertisement (innovation), but your purchase becomes more likely the more you see people using one, the more your friends and family own them, and the more they tell you about it or show you how it works (word of mouth). Unlike earlier researchers, Bass found a way to quantify these social influence variables within a mathematical model. An early success of the Bass model is illustrated in Box 5.3.

Box 5.3 A strong test of the bass model

The Bass model is lauded for having passed the key scientific test – prediction. Bass used his model to predict the peak of the colour television adoption curve in the USA. He was roundly criticized at the time by industry figures for his 'pessimistic' forecasts. However, when actual sales figures became available, he was proved right. Ignoring his forecasts led the consumer electronics industry to build too much production capacity, at considerable cost.

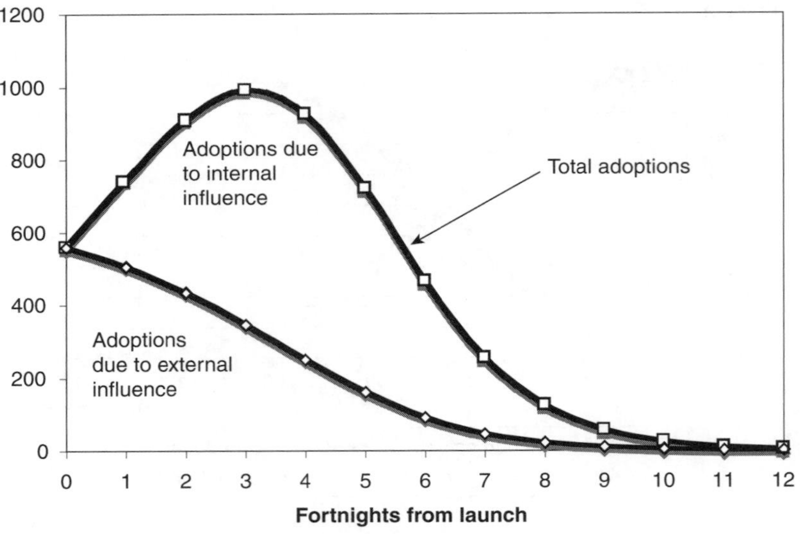

Figure 5.5 Adoption of an interactive telephone enrolment system (non-cumulative)

Source: Model parameters from Wright, Upritchard and Lewis (1997)

Parameters, Shape and Equations

Bass's model is elegant. It requires only three parameters: innovation (p), imitation (q) and the eventual number of adopters, known as market potential (m). The dependent variable is either cumulative or non-cumulative adoption by time period – $Y(T)$ or $y(t)$ respectively. Importantly, sales data can be equated with adoption data if the purchase is a high-value durable or service that is bought once and does not need replacement for some time.

In the first period (usually a year), the probability of adoption, given that no adoption has yet taken place, is simply p, and the predicted number of adopters is $p \times m$. However, as more of the population adopt, social influence (q) increases and the probability of adoption becomes $p + q \times [Y(T)/m]$. This basic equation can be expressed in a variety of forms, both algebraic and probabilistic and for either cumulative or non-cumulative adoption.

The mix between internal and external influence can be seen in the Bass curve in Figure 5.5, estimated on data for first-time use of a telephone enrolment system at Massey University in New Zealand. The parameters of this curve are $p = 0.10$, $q = 0.47$ and $m = 5{,}788$. This p value is quite high for Bass modelling, so the adoption curve starts at a point well above zero, peaks early and is over quickly. This shows the extra flexibility of the Bass model compared to a simple normal distribution curve.

Validation, Replication and the Extension of the Bass Model

Box 5.3 notes a famous case of forecasting success for the Bass model but Bass may have been lucky on this occasion. More cases are needed to assess the model. In a review of early replications, Wright, Upritchard and Lewis (1997) noted that a poor fit was sometimes found for the model outside North American and European settings. They also found that the predictive ability of the model was limited by variations in the early data. As early sales (or adoptions) are quite few, fluctuations are proportionately larger and so have a larger effect on long-term forecasting accuracy. Putsis and Srinivasan (2000) subsequently found that Bass model forecasts generally do not stabilize until the peak of the adoption process had passed. Also, the assumption of constant social influence may be an over-simplification. As we shall see in Chapter 12, word-of-mouth production may vary with the period a person has owned a product.

Notwithstanding this, there has been a wealth of successful research on the Bass model, including applications to other historical data sets, methodological improvements and many useful extensions, such as allowing population size to vary or modelling the successive generations of new technologies. Bass models have accurately described innovations in areas as diverse as consumer durables, consumer electronics, education, agriculture services, telecommunications and even United Nations membership. In these areas, only one purchase is normally made; thus sales (or membership) data give a direct measure of diffusion, up to the point where replacement purchases commence.

Using the Bass Model to Predict

To predict the sales of an innovation using the Bass model, we need to know the values of p, q and m. The usual way to estimate these is through non-linear regression against sales data for the first few periods. However, this requires several years of such data and some degree of statistical skill. Furthermore, as noted earlier, the results tend to be unstable until the data include the peak of the adoption process.

It would be much more helpful to apply the model before the launch of a new product. Then it could be used for initial sales forecasting, launch decisions, capacity planning and marketing budgeting. Two traditional approaches to doing this are to forecast by analogy or to use management judgement.

To forecast by analogy, known values of p and q from other innovations are used. Sultan, Farley and Lehmann (1990) report the results of a meta-analysis of these parameters, and tables of them have been published elsewhere (e.g. Lilien and Rangaswamy, 2002). However, Rogers' theory tells us that the characteristics of the innovation and the characteristics of the social system are the key drivers of adoption, so it is questionable whether p and q values are generalizable unless they are from a similar innovation in a very similar social system. For the m parameter, the value cannot be derived by analogy, but may be estimated through market research.

The techniques for applying managerial judgement are not made very clear in the literature and should generally be seen as a last resort. Managers may not understand the social basis or typical values of the Bass model parameters p and q. Managers will therefore have little basis to apply their judgement. Also, Armstrong (1985) has evaluated evidence on the performance of subjective estimates – managerial judgement – in forecasting. He found that they do not perform well compared to forecasts from objective methods and that integrating objective information with managerial judgement typically provided substantial improvements over managerial judgement alone (Armstrong, 1985: 387–420). So it is doubtful whether management judgement will show much accuracy unless the judge already has substantial experience with the Bass model and takes steps to combine this judgement with other, objective, information.

Lessons for Market Dynamics from the Bass Model

What lessons does the Bass model offer us in understanding market dynamics? First, consider the domain of the model. It concerns new products, not brands. It is typically applied to high-value products or services that have long inter-purchase times. These may be completely new or substantial technological improvements (although it can be applied to other behaviours if true adoption data is available, as in Figure 5.5). Bass modelling has shown that sales curves following the introduction of such products and services will be roughly normal or S-shaped.

Second, the exact shape of the curve will depend on social factors relating to the social system involved. Understanding the relative importance of these external and internal influences will give richer insights for marketing planning and more accurate forecasts of product sales growth.

Third, a long lead-in time can be explained simply by the values of the parameters. It will occur if the innovation parameter, p, is relatively low. Rapid acceleration of adoption will then occur if the innovation parameter, q, is relatively high.

Therefore, knowledge of the Bass model gives a good understanding of market dynamics following the introduction of a new product, at least for durables or high-involvement services. However, the Bass model has little to say about frequently bought products or new brands in established markets. We address this in the final section of this chapter.

Exercise 5.2 The flexibility of the Bass curve

The following graphs show how changes to the parameters affect the shape of the Bass curve. Examine each one of the four examples and then consider the questions that follow.

1 For each curve, identify a social system and innovation it could be describing. (Hint: think about the level of innovation and the extent of word-of-mouth recommendation.)
2 Consider Rogers' innovation characteristics. How might they affect the shape of the cumulative adoption curve?
3 Which do you think are the most and least common shapes? Justify your answer.

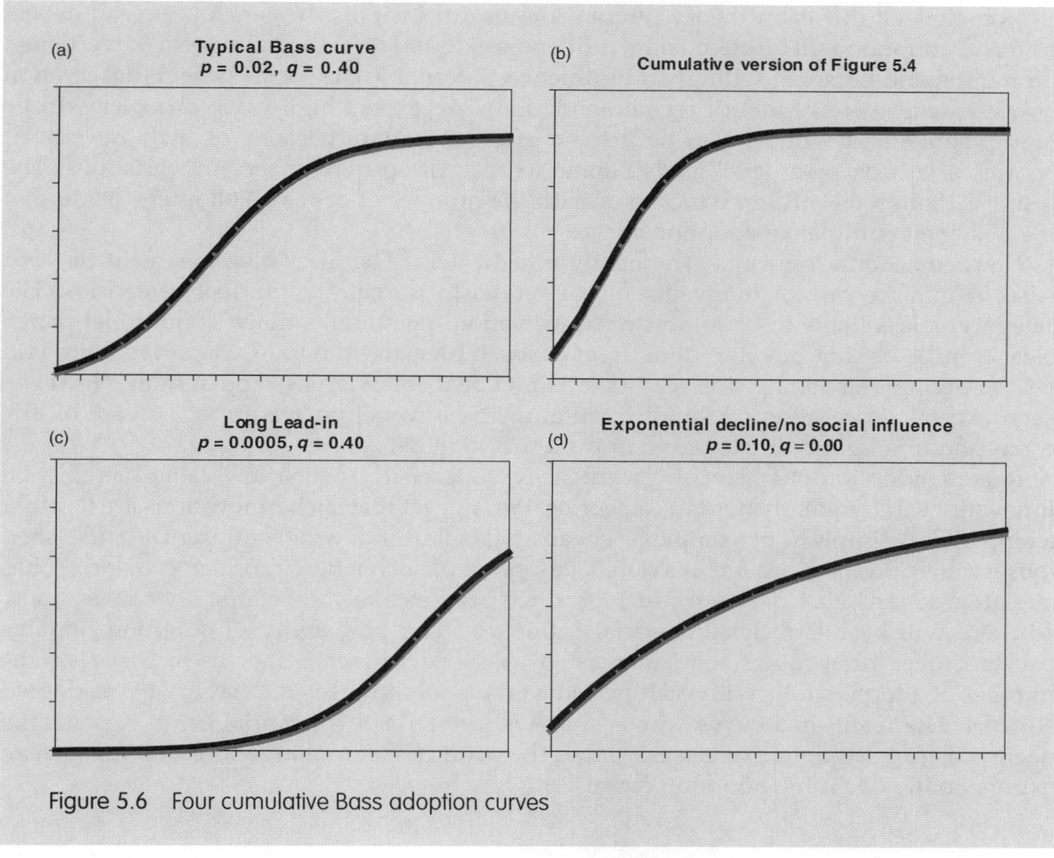

Figure 5.6 Four cumulative Bass adoption curves

SECTION 4: THE SALES DYNAMICS OF FREQUENTLY BOUGHT CATEGORIES

Low-Innovation Products

Section 3 described what we know about sales changes that occur when new categories are introduced, or when technological substitution causes a wave of change in an existing durable category. Yet most new products are much more mundane, and involve incremental 'me-too' products in familiar, frequently bought, low-value and low-involvement categories. We cannot expect that the same dynamic processes will necessarily apply in such different circumstances. Rather, new products in these frequently bought, low-involvement categories rely on familiarity and existing memory structures, as discussed in Chapter 3, and most sales come from repeat purchases rather than from the initial adoption decision. Occasionally, there may be a major innovation, such as the first olive oil spread or low-fat calcium-enriched milk. However, even these are typically presented as new brands launched into a familiar category (yellow fats and milk, respectively).

Nonetheless, diffusion theory offers some useful insights. In general, we can expect trial and adoption will be affected by influences external to the social system (advertising, promotion and personal selling) and influences internal to the social system (observation of others and word-of-mouth recommendation). We expect high-value durables will be more visible, and will tend to be a topic of conversation, because of their novelty or because the high price level leads people to seek pre-purchase recommendations. The result is that social influence increases with the number of previous adopters, leading to the S-shaped cumulative adoption curve.

Now, consider a low-value, frequently bought item. The low value means lower risk. Also, it may be one of many dozens of regularly purchased product categories. The category is less likely to be a topic of conversation – who talks much about toilet paper, bleach, milk, baking powder, flour, light bulbs, butter and the like? Of course there will be exceptions – a cooking club may talk a great deal about a new type of flour. However, such exceptions represent a small fraction of the buyers and we are not aware of any corresponding light bulb-changing or milk-drinking clubs.

Rogers' adoption characteristics can easily be applied to such low-value incremental innovations in frequently bought categories. We suggest that such innovations are familiar (compatible), simple (not complex), cheap (trialable) and widely present on the shelf (observable). So there are few barriers to adoption of such a new product, provided it has a relative advantage. Conversely, such products are less likely to be topics of conversation, so there will be relatively little social influence.[3] The probability of adoption remains constant over time rather than increasing as social influence increases; however, the number of adopters falls with each period as the pool of those who have not yet adopted shrinks. The result is a curve whose shape is known as exponential or an exponential decline. Figure 5.6(d) in Exercise 5.2 shows the pattern of cumulative adoption for such an exponentially declining adoption curve.

Exercise 5.3 Sketch an exponential decline curve

It's easy to see for yourself how an exponential decline curve works. Imagine that a population of 100 people has an adoption rate of 10 per cent. In the first period, 10 will adopt; in the second period, 9 (10 per cent of the remaining 90 who had not yet adopted); in the third period 8.1 are expected to adopt (10 per cent of the remaining 81) and so on.

1 In Excel, calculate the number of adopters for each of the first 20 periods. Assume a population of 100 and an adoption rate of 10 per cent. (Hint: you might find it helpful to have columns for those yet to adopt, adopters in the period, and total adopters to date.)
2 Graph both the cumulative and non-cumulative adoption curves.
3 Repeat the exercises for adoption rates of 30 per cent and 5 per cent.

Empirical Patterns in First Purchases

The shape of adoption curves for frequently purchased products has been studied empirically. Wright and Stern (2006) examined 12 national product launches and 19 controlled test market product launches for a variety of frequently bought categories. Figure 5.7 sketches some of their findings. It is noteworthy that the individual product launches showed similar patterns, despite varying degrees of innovativeness in the product or brand being launched. Similar curves are presented in Du and Kamakura (2011).

These curves are not obviously S-shaped and so show little evidence of an increasing word-of-mouth effect (although see note 3). They show an exponentially declining pattern of growth in first purchases. There is a slight bend in the curve for national launches, although this may be due to distribution growth. Yet, even with this, the curve still generally follows the declining exponential pattern. Nonetheless, it is worth remembering that while changes to distribution are beyond the scope of this chapter, they are nonetheless a primary cause of permanent sales change. Availability is a necessary precursor to purchase.

After the First Purchase

For durable products, adoption and sales are measured by the simple act of a purchase. However, the picture is not so clear for frequently bought items such as groceries. Exponential models of cumulative first purchase do not assume that the first purchase is an adoption, or tell us what the long-term purchase frequency will be. We might instead expect buyers of these new products to make one or two trial purchases before choosing either to drop the new product or to include it in their repertoire. This is the traditional view in most consumer behaviour texts and is consistent with Rogers' theories on innovation diffusion, with exposure being followed by evaluation and then an adoption or rejection decision.

This traditional view turns out to be surprisingly controversial. Light buyers may only buy the category two or three times a year, so trial will continue for some time and it is hard to say when a light buyer will have completed their evaluation, or even whether such a question is meaningful. If somebody makes a low-involvement purchase of a brand once or twice a year, it is not clear that this involves much cognition or post-purchase evaluation, as is expected by traditional theory.

Evidence on this point is provided by Ehrenberg and Goodhardt (2001), who found that the long-term average purchase rates for a new brand are achieved very quickly. In a study of 22 grocery product launches, they compared average purchase frequencies for new brands with those of the existing brands. In the first quarter, the new brands had an average purchase frequency of 1.4 – a little lower than established brands, which averaged 1.9. In subsequent quarters, the new brands showed purchase frequency of 1.8, 1.9 and 2.0, virtually identical with the established brands. Wright and Sharp (2001) found similar results for an Australian grocery product launch. These findings are inconsistent with the traditional idea of a trial purchase followed by an adoption or rejection decision.

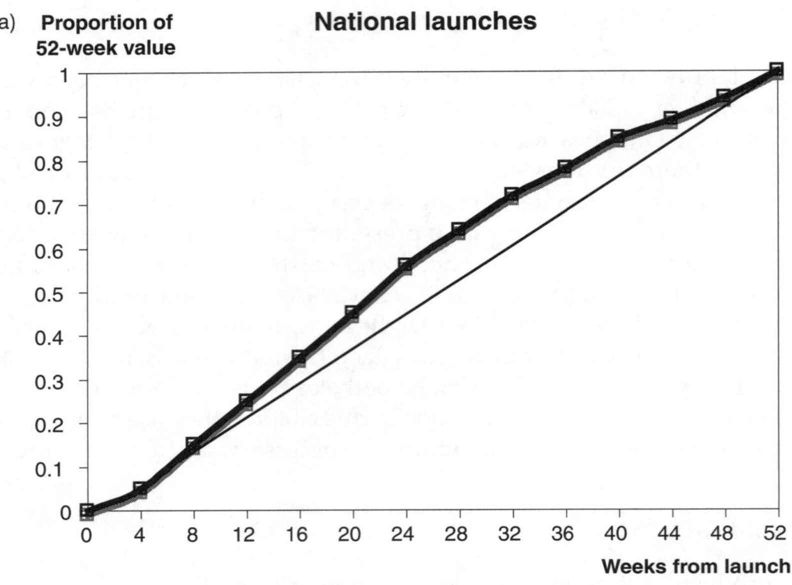

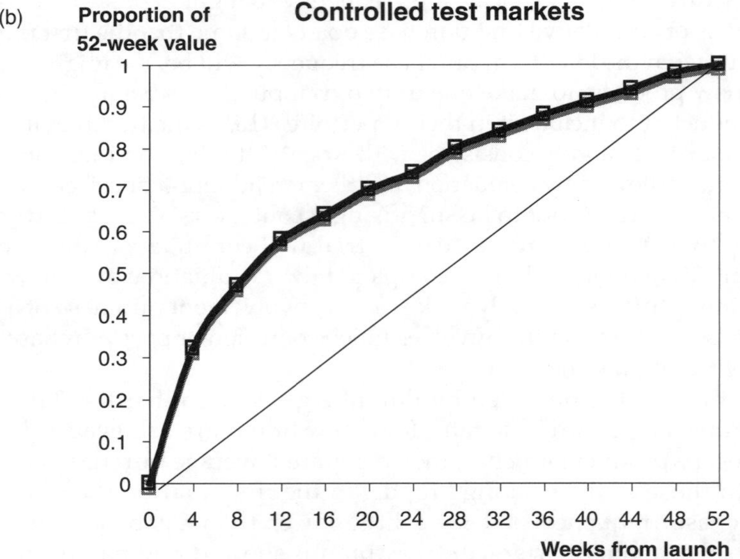

Figure 5.7 Cumulative first purchases for 52 weeks from launch

Source: Values reported in Wright and Stern (2006), partly derived from data downloaded from www.brucehardie.com

How could such near-instant loyalty come about? One explanation is that new brands in low-involvement categories are immediately included in the consumer's repertoire. The trial curve may then just reflect distribution growth, the occasional nature of category purchases and the shuffling of purchases around the consumer's repertoire.

This explanation remains somewhat unsatisfying. Intuition tells us that consumers sometimes simply do not like a new product. They may buy it once, and then decide it tastes awful, or does not work for their household. The reliance of the near-instant loyalty hypothesis on *average* purchase rates, rather than *repeat* purchase rates, excludes this effect altogether.

Repeat-purchase rate is therefore a more direct measure of loyalty, and has greater face validity. Yet there is surprisingly little evidence on patterns in repeat-purchase rates for new products. One difficulty is that early buyers are more likely to be heavy buyers; Taylor (1977) demonstrated this, Fourt and Woodlock (1960) made a similar assertion and Stern and Wright (2007) have confirmed it. These heavy buyers may complete trial purchases and evaluations quickly. Therefore, initial repeat-purchase figures may be misleading, as they combine heavy buyers, whose repeat-purchase rate has settled down, with lighter buyers who may still be making evaluative purchases. So the overall repeat-purchase figure will keep changing until light buyers have finished making evaluative purchases.

Eskin (1973) sought an early indication of final repeat-purchase rates by separating out heavy buyers and examining their repeat-purchase rates. Yet we know from Chapter 4 that the top 20 per cent of buyers only account for 50 to 60 per cent of sales, and CTA leads us to expect that heavy buyers will have different repeat-purchase rates from light buyers, and that these purchase rates will regress to the mean in subsequent periods. So Eskin's approach, which has been highly influential, seems incomplete.

Fader, Hardie and Huang (2004) took a different approach. They adapted a standard trial-repeat model to allow consumers' purchase rates to be revised after experiencing the new product. The result was an extremely accurate forecasting performance for the single brand that they examined. This suggests that their assumption, that purchase rates are revised *slightly* following experience, is a reasonable one, although replication across other data sets would give more confidence in their conclusions.

Some indirect support is provided by Singh et al. (2012), in a study of sales growth for 47 brand extensions in the United Kingdom. They found that, in the third quarter after launch, those with a positive sales trend had an average repeat purchase rate of 32 per cent while those with a negative sales trend had an average repeat purchase rate of 22 per cent. This difference is consistent with a post-experience revision of purchase probabilities suggested by Fader et al. (2004). Such work is needed on the evolution of repeat-purchase rates, for both successful and unsuccessful new packaged goods. As a practical matter, it would be helpful to have empirical studies that identify the typical evolution of repeat-purchase rates across a wide range of conditions. This would enable managers to benchmark the repeat-purchase performance of their new brands against an existing knowledge base.

SUMMARY

Markets undergo sales change for many reasons. First, time of year, holidays, sales promotions and other events have a temporary effect. Second, a dynamic equilibrium underlies stable markets, with buyers churning between brands or migrating between heavy and light buying. Disturbances to this equilibrium may result in changes to market share. However, changes often occur slowly due to the low rate of erosion or switching and the long inter-purchase times of occasional buyers.

Third, the launch of new products is a major source of more rapid and enduring change. Sociology helps us to understand the underlying forces, while models such as the technology substitution model and the Bass model provide tools for analysing and forecasting new product adoption. Fourth, social forces may be different for low-value, frequently bought items. We can capture the first purchase process in these markets with exponential models (which assume little social influence). For repeat purchase, the analysis is a little more complicated, due to early trial by heavy buyers, the large number of light buyers and the unclear role of evaluative purchases. One approach is to assume near-instant loyalty. Another is to use statistical models that allow purchase rates to be revised after experience with the new product. Recent evidence shows that differences in repeat purchase rates for succeeding and failing brand extensions can be detected in the third quarter after launch.

In studying or managing markets, you need to know what fluctuations can be expected, even in stable markets, and also how genuine change will play out over time. From this chapter, we hope you have developed a good understanding of the mechanisms that underlie changes in sales figures.

Additional Resources

The classic text on the diffusion of innovations, Rogers (2003), gives a good review of the diffusion literature and offers many interesting examples, although it has little on alternative models. For an appreciation of the technological substitution model, go straight to Fisher and Pry (1971), which remains readable and interesting and has a number of case studies. An overview of the Bass modelling literature can be obtained by reading Bass (1995), Mahajan, Muller and Bass (1990) and Sultan, Farley and Lehmann (1990). Finally, if you wish to know more about new product development, there are many excellent textbooks in the area, such as Crawford and Di Benedetto (2006).

Notes

1 The term *churn* is widely used in industry but, if the defection and recruitment rates are different for a brand, what is the churn? We prefer to use 'churn' to describe the average replacement rate in a category. Average defection and acquisition will be the same across the category if it is stationary.

2 A logistic function is a function of logits, or log-odds ratios. Odds ratios are simply the ratio of possible outcomes. If a football team is expected to win 80 per cent of the time, the odds of victory are 8:2 (or 4:1), and the natural logarithm of this is ln(4), which is 1.39. The logit is widely used in some other types of market modelling, such as the multinomial logit choice model.

3 An alternative view has recently been put forward by Du and Kamakura (2011), who argue that weak contagion effects can be observed in new consumer packaged goods, provided the modelling of such effects properly controls for potential sources of bias.

6 Consumer Group Differences

LEARNING OBJECTIVES

When you complete this chapter you should be able to:

1. Identify consumer differences that are relevant and those that are less useful to marketers.
2. Categorize cultures along the dimensions proposed by Hofstede.
3. Give examples of how these dimensions have been used in consumer research.
4. Understand the criticisms of Hofstede's approach.
5. Describe how values can be used to understand fundamental consumer motivations.
6. Explain how gender and age are related to consumption.

OVERVIEW

Marketers need to take account of group differences when they design and promote products, since what may appeal to one group may be of no interest to another. Group differences may reflect local conditions or history and may be related to ways of viewing the self and others in society. Some differences, such as individualism versus collectivism, can be seen as orientations shaping consumer consciousness; these have interested social scientists who seek to characterize pervasive features of whole societies. Other differences relate to divisions within society and we focus on age and gender since there are new developments here.

We start by asking what differences are relevant in consumer research and note that many personality differences are hard to use because it is difficult to target people with a particular disposition unless this is associated with physical segregation or differential consumption of media. Deep-seated cultural differences are approached via Hofstede's (1980, 2001) five dimensions and Rokeach's (1973) value system. We look at the use of these ideas in consumer research and show that it may be quite difficult to derive predictions from them. We also note that there may be simple social differences in consumption that are best revealed by market research rather than academic study.

Contrasted with consumer group differences is the idea of convergence – that a process of globalization is ongoing and that societies, at least in market practice, are becoming similar. We explore this idea and look in particular at China, comparing it with the west. On age, we focus particularly on the older members of society. The proportion of over-65s is growing rapidly and represents a considerable burden on more productive, younger groups. Though many are poor, much wealth is held by the older generation and recent work has focused on the relatively conservative decision-making of older consumers. On gender differences, there is evidence that women make more interpersonal bonds than men, which affects their loyalty patterns.

In this book, we do not cover segmentation by brand. This is because there is a body of robust evidence showing that there is generally little difference between the customers of any two brands in a category. Brands do not usually differ enough to appeal to different sub-groups in the population. Uncles et al. (2011) summarized the empirical evidence on comparisons of user profiles of directly competing brands. Through a series of replication studies and extensions, these authors reconfirmed that user profiles of directly competing brands seldom differ. The study used data spanning 25 years, across 50+ categories and 60 data sets, and confirmed lack of user segments for brands in emerging markets, private labels, variants and composite segments. Similar findings are reported in other studies. For example, in a study on Japanese buyers' purchase intentions, Singh et al. (2012) showed demographic similarity across the users of top Japanese grocery brands. Similar findings were also reported by Uncles and Lee (2006) amongst Australian customers and in the UK by Singh, Ehrenberg and Goodhardt (2008).

SECTION 1: RELEVANT DIFFERENCES FOR CONSUMER RESEARCH

Segmentation, a fundamental notion in marketing, means grouping consumers into discrete segments according to their similarities or differences. The segments may differ in needs, consumption habits, responsiveness to marketing actions, etc. Although it is useful to diagnose differences between consumers concerning a specific product or issue with dedicated market research, understanding the fundamental drivers that account for differences across a broad range of behaviour has more potential.

Socio-demographic characteristics were the first fundamental drivers examined in marketing. Some characteristics like social class and profession have lost appeal to marketers over time because the significance of the social norms attached to them has faded. Other characteristics have remained important but have taken on a different meaning. Gender and age for instance still account for important consumption differences, but in new ways, partly because of the changed economic conditions. We address research linking these two factors to loyalty in Chapter 2.

Personality traits are obviously an important determinant of consumption behaviour. For instance, Venkatraman and Price (1990) show that a consumer's openness to innovation correlates with his or her impulsivity and inclination towards social risk taking. This type of finding is not easy for marketers to apply because, if managers want to target consumers with certain personality traits, they not only have to identify them, but also they need to find ways to communicate with a specific segment without too much spillover to other segments.

Identification ideally requires a personality survey, difficult to apply in practice, unless indirect indicators are available (like the types of activities a consumer engages in). However, a person's dispositions and behaviours are not only affected by his or her personality make-up, but also by the norms and beliefs of the cultural environment (Triandis, 1989). Culture shapes people's personal perceptions, dispositions and behaviours. More concretely, the cultural environment stimulates individual dispositions that fit that environment and restrains those dispositions that are not a good fit (Triandis, 1989). Hofstede (2001) talks about 'mental programs' developed in early childhood in the family and reinforced later on in schools and other organizations. Most research in this area studies the influence of national culture and reviewing this work is the main topic of this chapter. This nationally defined cultural environment is much easier to identify for marketers and there is substantial research that examines its influence on consumption behaviour.

SECTION 2: NATIONAL CULTURAL DIFFERENCES

Hofstede's Five Dimensions

Analyses of cultural differences among people have often been influenced by the seminal work *Culture's Consequences* by Hofstede (1980, 2001). Hofstede reports an analysis of more than 116,000 questionnaires filled out by IBM employees from 50 subsidiaries around the world. This research on the influence of national culture has become a classic for both academics and practitioners. In an era of increasing globalization, Hofstede's work drew attention to the importance of cultural differences on attitudes to work in an international organization.

In his analyses, Hofstede aimed to capture cultural differences between nations in four dimensions: power distance, uncertainty avoidance, individualism–collectivism, and masculinity-femininity. For instance, the first dimension – power distance – was based on three items, of which the central one was 'How frequently, in your experience, does the following problem occur: Employees expressing disagreement with their managers'. An additional dimension, long- versus short-term orientation, was added in a new book, a decade later. Some of these dimensions had been around in the social science literature for some time but Hofstede provided quantitative data on the differences in responses across nations (see Table 6.1).

Table 6.1 Hofstede's five dimensions categorizing national cultures

Name of dimension	*Description of dimension*
Power distance	The degree of acceptability, by the less powerful members of an organization, of the inequality of the distribution of power
Uncertainty avoidance	Intolerance of the unpredictable, ambiguous or uncertain
Individualism versus collectivism	The degree to which individuals are supposed to look after themselves or remain integrated into groups (usually around the family)
Masculinity–femininity	Economic and other achievements. Taking care of other people
Long- versus short-term orientation	The degree to which people accept delayed gratification or their material, social and emotional needs

Exercise 6.1 Where would you place these countries?

Hofstede presents the aggregate scores for individuals from each country in two-dimensional maps. For this exercise, focus on individualism versus collectivism, and weak and strong uncertainty avoidance, and assign two countries to each of the quadrants of Hofstede's map below (eight countries in total). In alphabetical order these countries are: Canada, France, Great Britain, Hong Kong, Italy, Mexico, Singapore and South Korea. (Answers in endnote 1.)

	Weak uncertainty avoidance	Strong uncertainty avoidance
Collectivistic		
Individualistic		

A CRITICAL ANALYSIS

Hofstede produced a monumental study that was, and is, referenced by virtually all those dealing with cultural differences. His work clearly has implications for individuals working in another culture than their own and for companies operating across different cultures. His findings have also often formed the basis for consumer research on cultural differences, as we will see later on in this chapter.

Although Hofstede's work was very influential, it also met with criticism. A fundamental concern was that he carried out an eclectic analysis of data, based on theoretical reasoning and correlation analysis. In other words, although his framework is based on hard data, he uses some creativity in the analysis. McSweeney (2002) summarized this verdict in the title of his article 'A Triumph of Faith – A Failure of Analysis'. He also attacks the assumption that one can extrapolate the results of IBM employees to an entire nation. IBM employees may not be representative for their nation. McSweeney thinks they may even be atypical. Moreover, the number of relevant questions in the IBM questionnaire was limited, and they may not be adequate to test Hofstede's propositions fully. The questionnaire was not designed to identify national cultures, and purposely designed questionnaires by other researchers have produced different results (see below). A third critique is that what Hofstede uncovered in the workplace may be situationally specific and not transferable to other situations (e.g. home, retail behaviour, recreational consumption). Fourth, again on the method side, McSweeney objects to the way in which Hofstede sought to validate his results by an analysis of historical and contemporary events, and he claims that these illustrative stories ignore counter-evidence. The 2001 edition of the book also presents cross-validation with other studies and claims that the findings are consistent with those from 140 other studies. A further criticism comes from Ailon (2008), who argues that, rather than capturing and mapping differences in societal values, Hofstede's work actually constructs reality and is therefore a product of a specific cultural milieu and knowledge-producing tradition. It therefore reaffirms a scheme in which western values are always the idealized reference point. Hofstede anticipated this criticism; he realized that his personal value system might influence the results and therefore outlined in the book his personal position on various questionnaire items. Revealing this potential bias does of course not eliminate it.

There is a danger of stereotyping. *On average,* one population may differ from another but plenty of people in the two populations could still share the same values and react in the same way to innovations. Work continues in this area; one recent paper by deMooij and Hofstede (2010) reviews the work and applies it to work on global branding and advertising strategy.

THE UNIVERSAL CONTENT AND STRUCTURE OF VALUES

It was Hofstede's intention to analyze the values held by his respondents. Rokeach (1973: 159–160), the key reference on this topic, defines values as enduring beliefs 'that a specific mode of conduct or end-state of existence is personally and socially preferable to alternative modes of conduct or end-states of existence'. These values are fairly general and Rokeach suggests they are activated in a large variety of situations. As already implied in this definition, Rokeach distinguishes between terminal values, referring to desirable end-states that a person would like to achieve during his or her lifetime, and instrumental values that are modes of behaviour to achieve the terminal values. When taking the Rokeach Value Survey (see Table 6.2), respondents have to order lists of values according to the importance each has as a guiding principle in their lives. Using this instrument, those in different cultures and sub-cultures can be compared.

Exercise 6.2 The Rokeach Value Survey

Take the Rokeach Value Survey (Table 6.2). Arrange the 18 terminal values, followed by the 18 instrumental values, into an order of importance to YOU, as guiding principles in YOUR life (Rokeach, 1973: 27). To what extent does your ranking relate to your consumption behaviour? How do you explain divergences?

It is interesting that the work on cultural values discussed here was done by psychologists. Until the 1980s, culture was still thought of as 'out there' rather than an individual disposition (Triandis, 2004). Most psychologists therefore held the view that cultural differences were a topic for anthropologists to work on. A major turning point came with

Table 6.2 The Rokeach Value Survey

Terminal values	*Instrumental values*
1. True friendship	1. Cheerfulness
2. Mature love	2. Ambition
3. Self-respect	3. Love
4. Happiness	4. Cleanliness
5. Inner harmony	5. Self-control
6. Equality	6. Capability
7. Freedom	7. Courage
8. Pleasure	8. Politeness
9. Social recognition	9. Honesty
10. Wisdom	10. Imagination
11. Salvation	11. Independence
12. Family security	12. Intellect
13. National security	13. Broad-mindedness
14. A sense of accomplishment	14. Logic
15. A world of beauty	15. Obedience
16. A world at peace	16. Helpfulness
17. A comfortable life	17. Responsibility
18. An exciting life	18. Forgiveness

the publication of a review by Markus and Kitayama (1991) that showed major cultural differences in cognition, emotion and motivation.

The programmatic work of Schwartz and Bilsky (1987, 1990) provides a comprehensive academic reference on cross-cultural research into values. They developed a theory of a universal psychological structure of human values and tested it with an analysis of data from the Rokeach Value Survey. Their theory received empirical support from 97 studies in 44 countries with 25,000 respondents. The analysis is an interpretation into groupings and mapping of all the values as shown in Figure 6.1. It turns out that the groupings are stable across samples and they correspond to ten value types. The value types also always have the same neighbours. In fact, the five value types that primarily serve individual interests (power, achievement, hedonism, stimulation, self-direction) form a contiguous region opposite to another contiguous region formed by the three value types that serve primarily collective interests (benevolence, tradition, conformity). Universalism and security serve both types of interests and are located on the boundaries between these regions. The relationship among value types can also be summarized in terms of four higher-order value types that form the bipolar dimensions of Figure 6.1:

- Openness to change (following your own intellectual and emotional interests) versus conservation (preserving the status quo and the certainty it provides).
- Self-enhancement (advancing personal interests, even at the expense of others) versus self-transcendence (promotion of the welfare of others and nature).

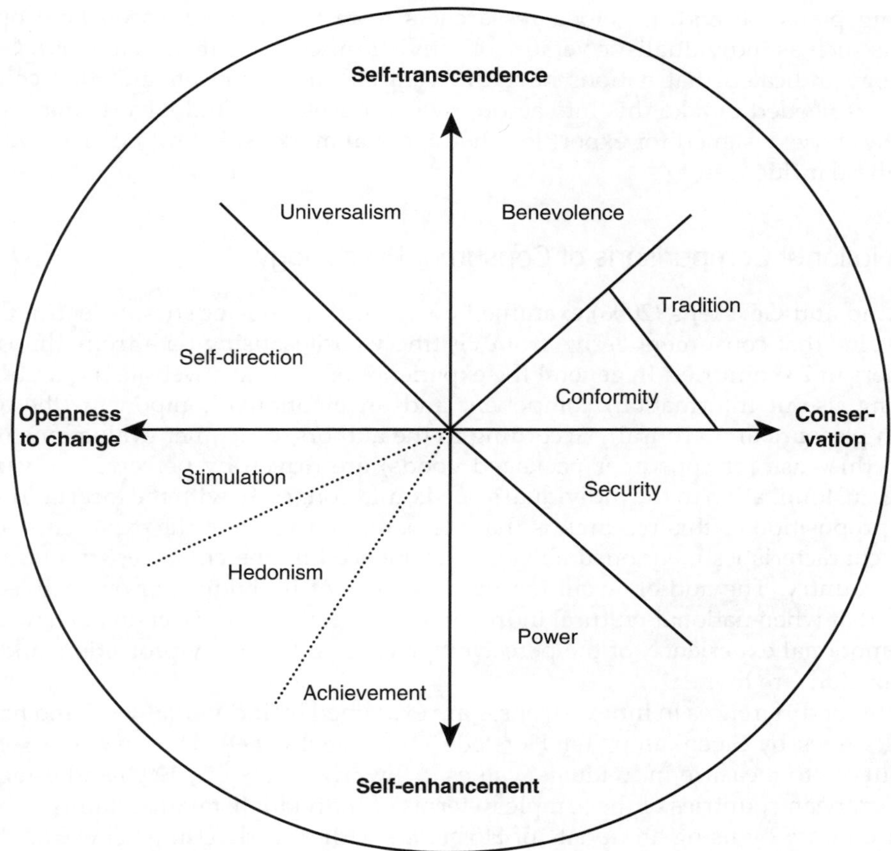

Figure 6.1 Relations among motivational types of values (Schwartz, 1992)

Note: the dotted lines around the hedonism wedge signal that this value is linked both to openness to change and to self-enhancement

Different societies share different values and value types, but not all combinations are possible. The simultaneous pursuit of some value types is possible while other combinations are incompatible.

SECTION 3: CULTURAL DIFFERENCES IN CONSUMER RESEARCH

The research in cultural psychology discussed in the previous section influenced consumer research and marketing in two ways. First, it helped us to segment markets and to understand their differences so that they could be targeted with different strategies and marketing plans. Second, it helped researchers to test their theories on how opposite mindsets such as individualistic versus collectivistic affect consumer behaviour. Cultural psychology indicated that nations have different cultural mindsets and that consumer researchers needed to take this into account when developing and advertising products, especially those designed for export to other national markets. Below we give two examples of these influences.

Cross-National Comparisons of Consumer Psychology

Steenkamp and Geyskens (2006) examine how country characteristics influence the perceived value that consumers derive from visiting websites, using data from almost 9,000 consumers in 23 countries. In general the experience of visiting a website has a utilitarian (acquiring useful information) component and an emotional component (the authors focus on pleasure and arousal). According to the authors, consumer evaluations of websites (in this case for consumer packaged goods) are driven by perceived privacy and security, customization to the individual's needs, and congruity with the local culture. The central proposition of this research is that the perceived value of the experience and the website characteristics mentioned above are influenced by the characteristics of the consumer's country. The authors examine the influence of individualism/collectivism and propose that when national-cultural individualism is higher, the effect on perceived value of the emotional experience, of the perceived privacy and security protection, and of the customization, are higher.

Consumer differences in innovativeness are explained by individual-level and national-cultural values by Steenkamp, Ter Hofstede and Wedel (1999). They use the Schwartz Value Survey to measure individuals' values (Schwartz and Sagiv, 1995) and categorized the 11 European countries of the sample in terms of individualism, uncertainty avoidance and masculinity by using an update of Hofstede's earlier work. Using Schwartz's bipolar value dimensions they hypothesize that a consumer's tendency to seek out new products and brands is impacted negatively by conservation and positively by self-enhancement (see Figure 6.1). In terms of Hofstede's cultural dimensions, individualism would be expected to have a positive effect and uncertainty avoidance a negative effect. Masculinity stands for assertiveness (versus nurturance) and should have a positive effect on innovativeness. In this large-scale consumer survey all hypothesized effects were supported but the finding for self-enhancement was not statistically significant.

Cultural Differences as Contrasts in Consumer Research

Aaker and Williams (1998) examine the effectiveness of emotional appeals in advertising. More specifically, they compare ego-focused (e.g. pride) and other-focused (e.g. empathy) advertising appeals. The contrast between individualist and collectivistic cultures in this work represents the effect of self-perception (referred to as self-construal) that is either independent (a focus on qualities of uniqueness) or interdependent (the self as inseparable from others and from the social context). According to the authors, these cultural differences lead to differences in the accessibility of certain types of emotions: ego-focused emotions should be more accessible in individualistic cultures and other-focused emotions in collectivistic cultures. This in turn should have a positive influence on the ability to process the respective emotions when they are presented in persuasive messages. As a test of their hypotheses, they presented a print ad for a fictitious new beer with one of the two following appeals (Aaker and Williams, 1998: 245):

- 'Acing the last exam. Winning the big race. Receiving deserved recognition. Ohio Flag Beer. Celebrating life's accomplishments.'
- 'Reminiscing with old friends. Enjoying time together with family during the holidays. Relaxing near the fire with best friends. Ohio Flag Beer. Celebrating the relationships that matter most.'

They compared the effect of each appeal on two samples: Chinese students (born and raised in China), as members of a collectivistic culture, and North American students, as members of an individualistic culture. The results showed a pattern opposite to the expectations: Chinese students showed more positive attitudes towards the advertisement and brand when exposed to the ego-focused emotions, as compared to the other-focused emotions, while for American students the scores were reversed. As explanation, the authors propose the novelty of the appeal as the driving factor. For members of a collectivistic culture, ego-focused appeals are more unusual and therefore trigger more attention. Similarly, the North American students may have found the collectivist messages unusual and were therefore more responsive to them. This idea was tested in a new study with ads for colour film that showed either (individual) happiness or peacefulness. The results confirmed that the novel thoughts provoked by an unusual appeal drove the subsequent attitudes to the advertisement and to the brand.

Members of collectivist cultures are generally considered to be caring and understanding. Does this also mean that they are easier to satisfy as consumers and that they are more tolerant of service failures? A recent review of the literature on cross-cultural services seems to indicate so (Zhang, Beatty and Walsh, 2008). But Chan, Wan and Sin (2009) addressed a different facet of collectivism: the need for attention and care. They proposed that, in some situations, consumers from more collectivistic cultures may be less tolerant of failure than those from individualistic cultures. The criterion is whether the service failure is social (e.g., status and esteem) or non-social (e.g. money and time). They developed a scenario for each and exposed it to American or Chinese students (a between-subjects design where each student sees one scenario). The students had to imagine going to a restaurant where either the waiter does not smile, messes up the order and does not apologize or the restaurant ran out of the food they selected and does not have the second choice available. The Asians were indeed more dissatisfied with a social failure than the westerners and less dissatisfied with a non-social failure. This research also examines the factors that drive this effect. The Asians' belief in fate explains their higher tolerance of non-social failure. Their concern for face (i.e. a positive image of self that is affirmed by interaction with others) makes them more sensitive to failures in a social context.

Box 6.1 Back-translation and other problems

A particular challenge for cross-cultural research, be it academic or commercial, is the translation of the measurement instrument. When questionnaire items are translated into another language, there may be no exact way of rendering the same meaning. This problem has been addressed by back-translating the translation into the original language to see whether the original and the back-translation have the same meaning. Brislin (1970) claimed that a functionally equivalent translation can be demonstrated when responses to the original and target versions are compared and found to be near-identical. However, it is pointed out that some bad translations that merely substitute terms (as in a machine translation) are easy to back translate, but may be poor in conveying the same meaning.

It seems reasonable to argue that meaning differences that are introduced in translation may be a basis for apparent cross-cultural differences. Such concerns are alleviated when studies using different methods and measures converge on the same outcome – if they do. Note that this problem is not necessarily removed by conducting all studies in English since this restricts sampling to those familiar with English, and even in such sub-groups, there may be differences of usage.

Other problems in comparing across cultures include differential response rates, differing responses to incentives and variation in the tendency to please interviewers.

MARKET-RELEVANT FACTS

Broad cultural differences between nations are of great interest but sometimes quite specific facts about difference in practice and thinking are important. For example, when Levi 501s were relaunched in Europe by BBH and McCann, they argued that jeans were perceived differently in the USA and Europe and, because of this, the existing US advertising was inappropriate for Europe (see Box 6.2).

There are other cases where cultural differences have particular forms that marketers should know about. For example, it is common practice on the Indian Subcontinent to stay with relatives. Indians and Bangladeshis have been heard to complain about the discomfort that occurs when relatives squeeze up to make room for a visitor. Sometimes the visitor would prefer to stay in a hotel but this would cause offence. Hotel firms in the west that seek to expand in other countries need to know about such practices.

Globalization

Up until now we have stressed the cultural differences among consumers living in different regions of the world. However, with the globalization of markets, these differences may be diminishing and the debate of globalization versus localization has concerned

Box 6.2 A small difference in perception

When Bartle Bogle Hegarty and the McCann agencies handled the relaunch of *Levi* 501 jeans in Europe in 1985 they refused to use the US advertising (Feldwick, 1990). Their analysis was that, in the USA, jeans were workaday clothes and increasingly old-fashioned but, in Europe, wearing jeans could still be a fashion statement. Moreover, 501s had genuine provenance and were worn by a small number of opinion leaders. Thus the agencies sought to re-establish the slightly baggy 501s as 'the right look' for young people, the definitive classic jean. To do this, they needed different advertising.

A set of commercials was developed of which the most famous was 'launderette' featuring Nick Kamen sitting in the *launderette* in his boxer shorts as he waited for his 501s to wash; the music backing was Marvin Gaye's 'I Heard It Through the Grapevine'. It is still to be found on YouTube if you search using 'Levi' and 'launderette'. These ads multiplied Levi's sales twenty-fold in the next three years at a higher price and it was claimed that even the sale of boxer shorts increased.

The point of this example is that the successful strategy related to a difference in perception about jeans – hardly a matter of cultural difference but immensely important to the success of the advertising. Such differences of perception are more a matter of market research than cross-cultural investigation but they cannot be ignored by marketers.

international marketing practitioners in the past few decades. Advocates of globalization stress convergence of consumer attitudes and behaviours across geographical boundaries and try to identify and reach consumer segments across boundaries with common products and marketing programmes. In this context, three Dutch researchers segmented European consumers from 11 different countries using a means-ends chain survey (Ter Hofstede, Steenkamp and Wedel, 1999). A means–ends chain examines how consumers connect to a product by asking questions about the link between attributes (e.g. organically produced, low fat) and benefits (e.g. spending less money, good taste) and that between benefits and values (e.g. self-respect, warm relationships). They identified four cross-national segments that then were linked to descriptive data on socio-demographics, product consumption and media usage, and information on personality and attitudes.

Marketing in China

China, as well as being the home of a large part of the world's population, shows a spectacular rate of GDP growth. In 2010 it was 10.4 per cent (World Bank) and eased to an annual rate of 8.1 per cent by the first quarter of 2012. Meanwhile, western markets recorded low or negative growth.[2] Because of its importance, we have compared China with western markets. How different is China? Although Chinese consumers buy different foodstuffs from the west, many other aspects of purchase are very similar and the Chinese are purchasing a large number of luxury brands from the west, from perfume to whisky. Uncles (2010) believes that the main theme is convergence – 'Significant aspects of the Chinese retail landscape now conform to what might be described as an international norm and, superficially at least, consumer attitudes and behaviours appear to be more alike.' Uncles (2010) notes that 'retail formats, institutions, infrastructures, and management practices are becoming similar to those seen in international markets'. In grocery retailing, hypermarkets and supermarkets are rapidly growing and took 62 per cent of grocery sales in 2008, a figure not far behind that of many Western countries. By comparison, traditional retailing such as wet markets are stationary. Uncles notes that much of the modern retail expansion is driven by international companies such as Carrefour and Tesco who often work in partnership with Chinese companies. This speeds the transfer of western business practice.

Chinese consumers accept the new pattern of retailing. One reason for this is environmental determinism. In Chapter 1 we noted that behaviour is moulded by the conditions under which people live; the environment defines what actions are possible and rewards and punishes behaviour according to how it fits the environmental conditions. It is hardly surprising that attitudes and values develop that broadly endorse a retail system that meets consumer needs and it would be naïve to assume that values always come first and systems are developed to be consistent with them. This control by the environment is enhanced when urban renewal projects replace the traditional market with a western format. Uncles notes that more traditional retailing practices persist in China but points out that there are corresponding traditional forms in the west.

Uncles, Wang and Kwok (2010b) studied brand performance metrics to see whether patterns familiar in the west are also found in China. They found the double jeopardy effect with toothpaste and soy sauce in two different cities, Shanghai and Xi'an, which was consistent over five years. They also showed that multi-brand loyalty was the norm, just as it is in Europe, Australasia or the USA. In two other studies, Uncles and Kwok (2008, 2009) examined patterns of category purchase by store. Again, the Dirichlet patterns were found, so what people buy may differ but how they buy fits patterns of behaviour found in the west.

In another study, Thøgersen and Zhou (2012) investigated the take-up of organic food. They found that Schwartz's universalism value lay behind the adoption of organic food in China, as in the west. Furthermore, buying organic food was strongly linked to beliefs about health, taste and care for the environment in both the west and China. Thus, this research suggests that globalization has proceeded fast in China and that, in many respects, there is convergence in the consumption patterns of China and the west.

SECTION 4: AGE AND GENDER DIFFERENCES IN CONSUMPTION

Age

The present scale of population ageing is 'unprecedented, pervasive, enduring and has profound implications for many facets of human life' (United Nations, 2002). The post-retirement proportion of the population is rising and many members of this group are becoming richer. Euromonitor (2011) reports that the percentage of the world's inhabitants over 65 has moved from 5.9 in 1980 to 8.0 in 2011 and that, in western Europe, the percentage is 16.5. In Japan, it is 23 per cent. Moreover, the current over-65s are closely followed by an even larger group of those born between 1946 and 1964 (the 'baby-boomers') who are now beginning to retire; these people also vary widely in their spending, social commitments and lifestyle and are, collectively, the wealthiest group of older people in history (Euromonitor, 2006). Marketers and policy-makers must take account of these changes and understand them because they will change economic priorities. Central to this understanding is how older consumers buy (Uncles and Lee, 2006).

Market research has focused on the goods and services that are typically bought by consumer segments. However, to explain preferences among older consumers, it is necessary to study how the *process* of decision-making varies with age. So far, this aspect of decision-making has focused mainly on variation in cognitive and affective processes as people age (Cole et al., 2008; Drolet, Schwarz and Yoon, 2010; Lambert-Pandraud and Laurent, 2010; Lambert-Pandraud, Laurent and Lapersonne, 2005).

Lambert-Pandraud et al. (2005) examined the impact of age on loyalty. They analyzed the answers of 30,000 respondents to a survey of recent new-car buyers who had replaced a previous car. The survey covered the purchase process of both the recently acquired and the previous car. Because a car purchase is one of the most involving consumer purchases, one would expect consumers to engage in at least some information search and comparison. In fact, 21 per cent of consumers between the ages of 60 and 74 considered only one brand, and among consumers 75 or over, 27 per cent were in this group. Many respondents purchased the same make of car and, as age rose, so did the repeat-purchase rate, shown in Figure 6.2. The effect of age remained strong in a multivariate model that includes contextual variables and other socio-demographics. Older car-purchasers showed other characteristics. They considered fewer car models when they considered more than one, they dealt with fewer dealers and, when they did change the make of their car, they were likely to buy a familiar national brand. They were also more prone to defer purchase, a matter that should interest marketers (and governments when economies are stagnating).

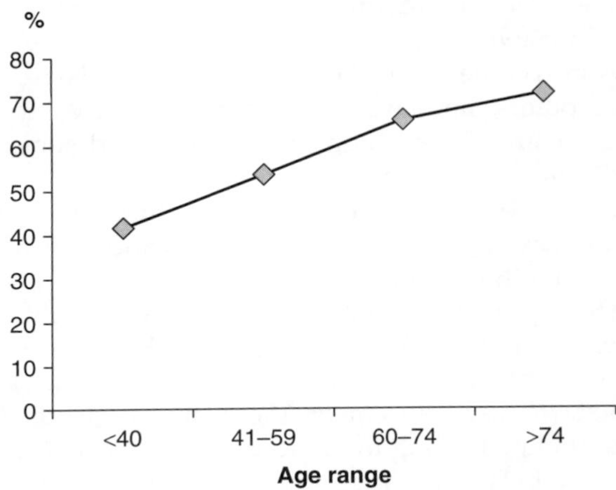

Figure 6.2 The repeat purchase of cars by age group (from Lambert-Pandraud, Laurent and Lapersonne, 2005)

Taking all these facts together, we can see that the decision-making of the older consumer can be described as *conservative*.

The conservatism of older buyers could relate to *cognitive decline*, which increases the cognitive effort in decision-making and pushes the older person towards decision heuristics such as choice repetition or purchase deferral (Lambert-Pandraud et al., 2005; Phillips and Sternthal, 1977). However, there is evidence that it is the speed rather than the ability to process information that is measured in tests of cognitive process (Cole and Houston, 1987; Roedder-John and Cole, 1986). This suggests that older people may have the capacity to decide effectively but make less use of this capacity because of their slower processing speed.

A second explanation is *socio-emotional selectivity*: that older persons tend to have more activation of emotional centres leading to a focus on affective information as age advances. This leads to more attention to established emotional contacts and less to gaining new information, which results in older consumers having fewer social interactions and concentrating on the people they know well (Castensen, Isaakowitz and Charles, 1999). This could explain the smaller choice set of car brands/dealers among older people found by Lambert-Pandraud et al. (2005).

A third mechanism producing conservative behaviour is *change aversion* (Wallach and Kogan, 1961). Change aversion leads to purchase deferral and draws decision-makers toward more familiar options where risks may be lower. However, such change aversion may relate to a justifiable cynicism about brand differences that grows with experience and therefore age. *Risk aversion* was studied by Simcock, Sudbury and Wright (2006). They found that older buyers of cars were more likely to express risk-related concerns.

These three explanations for age-related conservatism suggest a fairly inexorable process of change as people age that is difficult to influence. However, it is possible that this work has focused too much on individual processes and not enough on the social element in consumer decision-making. We know that many decisions occur because advice from others draws attention to new alternatives and pushes the individual to think through the possibilities. To explore this, 16 accumulated studies on word of mouth (WOM) conducted at Kingston University were reviewed to see whether there were any age-related differences in volume of word of mouth received. These studies covered bank accounts, cameras, computers, holidays, credit cards, and two studies each of mobile phones, mobile phone airtime, coffee shops, restaurants and supermarkets. The results were startling and are shown in Figure 6.3.

From Figure 6.3 we can see that word of mouth about brands received by respondents falls sharply with age. On average, respondents aged 65 and over receive 1.5 instances of WOM compared with 3.9 by those aged 25. Men tend to report receiving more WOM than women except in the 65+ segment. A number of explanations could fit these findings. The older respondents might recall fewer instances of advice because of cognitive decline but, against this, the effect is fairly continuous and seems to start before the age when cognitive decline is believed to start. Also, retirement, the death of friends and the departure of children from the household – leading to reduced social contact – are consistent with the decline in advice observed. The same research also examined the period of time that respondents had owned their current brand in seven categories and this period jumped to

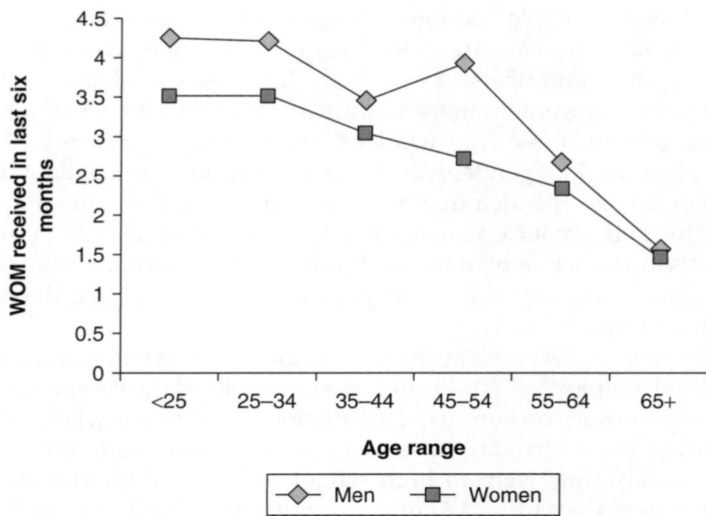

Figure 6.3 Average sum of received positive and negative word of mouth about brands by age and sex (2600 respondents from 16 studies)

nearly twice the level for the post-65-year-olds. Using regression analysis the researchers examined whether word of mouth received was related to the length of time that the current brand had been owned (which was seen as evidence of purchase deferral). It was found that the volume of positive advice did have a significant effect, reducing purchase deferral, so we can say that those respondents who received a greater volume of positive advice were more likely to state that they had changed their brand of bank account, mobile phone, credit card, etc.

This evidence therefore suggests another explanation for conservative behaviour by the older consumer: that, compared to younger consumers, they have lower levels of social influence. If this is so, the older consumer may be induced to consume more if marketers can influence those who give advice, such as children, or if the deficit in advice can be covered by increased advertising designed for this age group. There is clearly more to find out about age differences. We have not discussed how the importance of different categories changes as people get older; older people may process decisions like younger people when the decision is more important to them, for example when it concerns finance or medical decisions.

Gender

It is a common stereotype that men show lower levels of sexual loyalty than women. How about consumer loyalty? Melnyk, van Osselaer and Bijmolt (2009) make the distinction between loyalty towards people and towards companies. They present a series of studies indicating that female customers are more loyal to individuals, whereas male customers are more loyal to groups and firms. They cite work (Cross and Madson, 1997) that shows that in western cultures, women, more than men, want to connect to other people and maintain existing relationships. Thus women focus on interdependence. One view is that men see themselves as independent and focus on uniqueness and individuality but Melnyk et al. also discuss the idea that both women and men are interdependent, but in different ways. In their account, women attach more importance to close relationships with specific individuals while men focus on relationships with larger and more abstract groupings of people. Thus, men are interdependent too but their interdependence is with groups rather than individuals.

Applying this thinking, Melnyk and her co-authors propose that women may be more loyal to individual employees while men are more loyal to companies/brands. In a scenario study, the authors present participants with a situation where instead of going to the closest bakery for a birthday cake, there is the option of going to a bakery owned and run by somebody they went to high school with. In an alternative condition, the word *somebody* is replaced by a group of people. In subsequent studies they asked participants directly whether they were more loyal to individual service providers or to companies in different categories for their actual consumption behaviour. Across these studies they show that women do not always exhibit more consumer loyalty than men. But their loyalty does indeed extend to individual employees, while men show more loyalty towards companies. They also found evidence that these types of loyalty are driven by the quest for relational versus collective interdependence, for women and men respectively.

The difference in loyalty between men and women found by Melnyk et al. could be underpinned by genetic difference or adjustment to social norms. The generalizability of the findings will depend on which explanation applies; if the difference relates to role differences that are widely found in western economies, we might find different patterns of loyalty in other societies where the role relationships are different. This would mean that the loyalty difference is more cross-cultural than inherent in genetics. From the findings of Melnyk et al., we might expect women to talk more about categories where interpersonal relationships were common. Some unpublished work at Kingston University indicates the product fields that women talk about to others more than men. Men talk more about mobile phones, airtime suppliers for mobile phones, computers, credit cards and bank accounts while women talk more about holiday destinations, luxury brands, supermarkets, restaurants and coffee shops. These differences fit gender roles. Women may give more advice about supermarkets because they do so much more food shopping than men (Chang-Hyeon, Arentze and Timmermans, 2006), but women use phones more than men according to Nielsen (2011b) in evidence from the USA and, despite this, men appear to talk more about mobiles. Perhaps devices like phones, being impersonal, attract more interest from men. Whatever the bases for these differences, they are of importance to marketers and ad agencies making decisions about the targeting and content of communications.

SUMMARY

The cultural environment in which an individual is raised and lives obviously shapes his or her perceptions, dispositions and behaviour. National cultural differences have been studied extensively, largely under the influence of the seminal work of Hofstede. Hofstede categorizes countries on the level of power distance that is accepted by their members, their tolerance for uncertainty, the degree to which economic achievement versus caring for other people is valued, the degree to which the delay of gratification is accepted, and the degree to which individuals are supposed to look after themselves or remain integrated in groups. This last dimension, referred to as individualism versus collectivism, has been much used in consumer research. An excellent mapping of all relevant cultural differences is provided by Schwartz and Bilsky (1990); based on the Rokeach Value Survey, they identify ten value types.

As examples of how consumer researchers have used these classifications of cultures, we described how the perceived value of visiting websites and consumer innovativeness are influenced by differences in individualism-collectivism. We also examined differences between American and Chinese consumers in their sensitivity to ego-focused and other-focused appeals in advertising and in their tolerance to service failures.

National differences between consumers continue to influence marketing communications and service format but at the same time we observe convergence. We illustrated this with an international segmentation study and a study of consumption behaviour in China.

Understanding consumer group differences is useful for market segmentation. Behavioural differences between individuals and groups are often easy to observe but understanding the fundamental drivers of this behaviour has broader application potential. We examined the reasons for increased brand loyalty of older consumers. We also compared loyalty of men and women and found that men are more loyal towards companies while women more so towards individual employees.

Further reading on cross-cultural studies

This chapter examined the most relevant consumer differences that also received research attention. For the reader specifically interested in cross-cultural issues from a marketing practitioner's point of view, we recommend the following handbooks:

de Mooij, M. (2011) *Consumer Behavior and Culture: Consequences for Global Marketing and Advertising*, 2nd edition, London: Sage Publications Ltd.

de Mooij, M. (2010) *Global Marketing and Advertising: Understanding Cultural Paradoxes*, 3rd edition, London: Sage Publications.

Usunier, J.C. and Lee J. (2011) *Marketing Across Cultures*, 5th edition, Prentice Hall.

Notes

1 Answer to Exercise 6.1:

	Weak uncertainty avoidance	Strong uncertainty avoidance
Collectivistic	Hong Kong Singapore	Mexico South Korea
Individualistic	Canada Great Britain	France Italy

2 Some of the spectacular growth in consumption in China is attributable to the one-child policy in the country. Demographers have drawn attention to the resources that have to be spent on servicing an increasing population. If the population increases by 2 per cent each year, so must the schools, firms and other social institutions if the new generation is to have the same opportunities as before. This is called the demographic investment and it holds back development. The problem is made worse by the fact that a growing population contains a larger proportion of children who do not assist the economy and who need the attention of adults, thus further restricting economic activity. China has avoided the demographic investment. The one-child policy has the eventual consequence that the ratio of old to young shifts and a large older population has to be supported by a smaller workforce. However, by then, China may have established the economy at a higher level so that everyone can benefit. In India, population growth has continued at a rate of 1.6 per cent per year (Rosenberg, 2011) and this helps to explain why India's economy is not expanding as rapidly as that of China.

Part 3
Explaining Decision-Making

7 Predicting and Explaining Behaviour

LEARNING OBJECTIVES

When you have completed this chapter, you should be able to:

1 Define attitude, belief and intention, and explain how these concepts are measured.
2 Understand the expected-value theory of attitude applied to products.
3 Report on the research linking attitude and intention to behaviour.
4 Describe the theory of planned behaviour, its applications, strengths and weaknesses.
5 Understand the problems of predicting behaviour.

OVERVIEW

The cognitive approach to consumer behaviour relates consumers' attitudes, beliefs and intentions to their behaviour. Among the theories used, the theory of planned behaviour has been most successful, although a number of problems with this theory remain. We first examine the nature and measurement of attitudes, beliefs and intentions and their relationship with behaviour, and then we explain how the theory of planned behaviour can be used to predict and explain behaviour. This has a clear relevance to marketing: we need to predict purchase and to understand why people prefer one brand to another if we are to create products in the right quantity and of the right quality.

SECTION 1: DEFINITIONS AND MEASUREMENTS

Attitudes are what we feel about a concept, which may be a brand, category, person, theory or anything else we think about and attach feelings to. An important class of concepts are *actions*, particularly commercially relevant behaviour such as buying, renting, using and betting. We focus on attitudes to such actions because these attitudes help us to predict the consumer behaviour that concerns marketers. Thus, it is the attitude to *playing* the National Lottery or *buying* a smart phone that most interests us. The attitude to the object (the National Lottery or the smart phone itself) is less directly related to the action.

A person's attitude may be inferred from his or her actions or measured using a systematic questioning procedure. According to the mental representations model, introduced in Chapter 3, a concept is a node linked to other nodes. The linkages to other nodes can be seen as beliefs about the central concept. When the concept is an action, the beliefs often concern the outcomes of the action. If I play the National Lottery, there are outcomes such as dreaming of untold wealth, being excited by the draw and, usually, being disappointed by the result. Such beliefs have an outcome likelihood (or belief strength) and an evaluation which can be measured by the scales below:

If I play the National Lottery I will be excited by the draw

unlikely	1	2	3	4	5	6	7	likely
	extremely	*quite*	*slightly*	*neither*	*slightly*	*quite*	*extremely*	

Being excited by the draw is:

bad	–3	–2	–1	0	1	2	3	good
	extremely	*quite*	*slightly*	*neither*	*slightly*	*quite*	*extremely*	

The first scale measures the likelihood of the outcome, the second measures the value of the outcome if it occurs. These seven-point measures, called semantic differential scales, were first used in research by Osgood, Suci and Tannenbaum (1957). We usually denote the likelihood measure as b (for belief) and the evaluation measure as e. The full outcome measure is the product of b and e, which we call the *expected value* of the outcome. An expected value can be negative as well as positive because the evaluation can be negative.

The Expected-Value Theory of Attitude

Most of the alternatives from which we choose are *multi-attribute*. To assess the value of going to Wales for a holiday, I have to take account of weather, cost, travelling effort, food, opportunities for recreation, etc. Using the method above, we can measure an expected value for each outcome, and my overall (or global) attitude to going to Wales for a holiday is given by the sum of the expected values. So, if A is the global attitude:

$$A = b_1e_1 + b_2e_2 + b_3e_3 + \ldots$$

or $A = \sum b_ie_i$

Rosenberg (1956) pioneered this approach in attitude theory and Fishbein (1963) tested the relationship by separately measuring the global attitude, *A*, and the sum value, $\sum b_i e_i$. If the theory is correct and *A* is related to $\sum b_i e_i$, then subjects with high scores on one measure will have high scores on the other. Thus, by correlating respondents' scores on the two measures, we can find out how much *A* is related to $\sum b_i e_i$. Fishbein found a correlation between the sum score and the global measure of 0.80, which gave strong support to the idea that global attitudes are based on the sum of the expected values of the attributes. Fishbein's expected-value treatment of attitude has been confirmed in a large number of subsequent studies though the correlations are generally lower than 0.8 (typically, in the range 0.4 to 0.6).

Fishbein's treatment of attitude assumes a process of compensation: for example, that the unspoilt beaches can offset wet weather in Wales. At best, compensation is likely to be partial. Just taking account of the main outcome of one alternative requires some thought and when several outcomes are involved the assessment is obviously more complicated. As noted in Chapter 1, extended thought before choice is a rarity but we probably consider more attributes when important decisions are taken. People choosing between several options usually take the one with the largest expected value. Edwards (1954) described this as the subjective expected utility (SEU) model of decision. This way of thinking about decisions treats any product as a bundle of expected gains and losses.

Modal Salient Beliefs

Fishbein's theory of attitude is about what *individuals* think and feel, but it has to be tested on *groups* of people and each member of the group may have a somewhat different basis for their attitude. To take account of this, some studies have asked each person separately about the attributes that he or she thought were important, e.g. Budd (1986) on cigarette use and Elliott and Jobber (1990) on company use of market research. This technique increases the observed association between global and sum measures but is laborious. Fortunately, on many issues there is substantial agreement between people on the factors that are important, and the same questionnaire can be used on all respondents with only a modest loss of precision.

To establish the commonly held beliefs about a concept it is necessary to perform an *elicitation*, which is described in Exercise 7.1. This is a series of questions about the positive and negative associations of the concept which are put to members of the target group. The beliefs that come easily to mind are recorded and those that occur frequently in a group, called *modal salient beliefs*, are used for the questionnaire. In an elicitation, the questioning should be low pressure. Fishbein and Ajzen (1975) ('Ajzen' is pronounced 'Eye-zen') argue that beliefs which have to be dredged up from the recesses of the mind are unlikely to have much effect on behaviour. Exercise 7.1 covers not only the gains and losses of a prospective action, but also factors discussed later in the chapter – the influence of other people and the personal and environmental factors that make the action easier or more difficult to perform.

Exercise 7.1 Eliciting salient beliefs

1 **Define the action clearly**. For example, 'buying Snickers', 'getting a new computer', 'giving blood when the blood transfusion service comes to the campus'.
2 **Define clearly the target group**. For example, you might be particularly interested in children buying Snickers, or women computer buyers.
3 **Elicit salient beliefs**. In a sample of people from the target group, ask each person questions about the advantages and disadvantages of the defined action. After each response prompt with: 'anything else?' but do not press hard for ideas. Record the responses for each person. A typical encounter might be:

   Q. Can you tell me what you think are the advantages of getting a new computer?
   A. You get a lot for your money now.
   Q. Anything else?
   A. Probably more reliable.
   Q. Anything else?
   A. Not really.
   Q. Can you tell me what are the disadvantages of getting a new computer?
   A. It will have to be set up with the right programs.
   Q. Anything else?
   A. I'll have to get used to new versions of Word and PowerPoint.
   Q. Is there anything else that you can think of about getting a new computer?
   A. No.

4 **The negative action**. Certain actions may have different salient beliefs associated with *not* doing the action. For example, 'not having children' and 'not taking drugs' may be seen as actions with their own rationale and are not just the opposites to having children and taking drugs. For such negative actions, it is wise to also elicit salient beliefs about the negative action.
5 **Salient referents**. Ask each respondent in the sample whether there are people or groups who think that the respondent should do the defined action. Repeat with 'should not'. Ask if there are other people or organizations that come to mind when they think of the action. Use the prompt 'anyone else?' but do not press for responses. (Recent work has often included measures of what salient referents think the respondent *will* do as well as *should* do.)
6 **Control factors**. Ask each respondent about conditions that make the action easier or harder to perform. Again, prompt with 'anything else?'
7 **Refine the list of beliefs**. Combine similar beliefs. Compile a list of modal salient beliefs using the ones most frequently mentioned. The decision to include a belief depends on the frequency with which it is mentioned and the time and money available to support the research. When the questionnaire is intended to be used *both before and after* exposure to advertising or the product, it is important to include beliefs that may *become* salient as a result of this exposure.
8 You can use the computer program NEWACT (available from Sage) to create a questionnaire according to the methods of planned behaviour theory.

After similar responses have been grouped together, the list of modal salient beliefs is usually quite short. Complex issues, such as getting married or using oral contraceptives, may have about ten salient beliefs relating to attitude; simpler issues, such as buying specific chocolate bars, will have fewer.

Do Attitudes Predict Action?

Our interest in attitudes is partly based on the belief that they predict behaviour. Following Allport (1935), an attitude is usually seen as 'a preparation or readiness for response' and thus should be a predictor of behaviour, except when freedom of action is restricted. However, when Wicker (1969: 65) reviewed 47 studies on attitudes and behaviours, he concluded that: 'It is considerably more likely that attitudes will be unrelated or only slightly related to overt behaviors than that attitudes will be closely related to actions.'

Schuman and Johnson (1976) suggested that other unreported variables affected behaviour in addition to attitude. This was supported in work by Fishbein and Ajzen (1975), Ajzen and Fishbein (1980) and Ajzen (1985, 1991). These researchers showed that, in addition to attitude, behaviour is controlled by beliefs about the wishes of people and groups important to the respondent and by beliefs about the way personal ability and the environment can promote or restrict behaviour.

In addition to the 'other variables' explanation for the poor prediction of behaviour, Ajzen and Fishbein (1977) pointed out that researchers frequently measured the wrong attitude. The correct attitude for predicting behaviour is the attitude to that specific behaviour. Fishbein and Ajzen (1975: 360) concluded that 'many of the studies that have been viewed as testing the relation between attitude and behaviour are actually of little relevance to that question'. Thus, if you want to predict quitting smoking, it is the attitude to quitting smoking not the attitude to cigarettes, or even smoking in general, that should be measured. This lack of compatibility between the attitude and behaviour measures is neatly demonstrated by an unpublished study conducted on 270 women by Jaccard, King and Pomazal (reported by Ajzen and Fishbein, 1977). In this work, three attitudes relating to birth control were measured and correlated with the use of birth control. As the attitude comes closer to the specification of the behaviour, the correlation rises (see Table 7.1). This effect is readily explicable if we think of the motivations of different women. For example, a woman who wanted to become pregnant would neither use the pill nor be positive in her attitude to using it (giving a high correlation between her behaviour and her attitude), but she might still be positive about the pill and birth control in general (giving a low correlation with her non-usage of the pill). Similar results were obtained in another study of the correlations between attitudes to 'religion', 'church', 'attending church this Sunday' and actual church attendance this Sunday.

Another example of using the wrong attitude takes the form of trying to predict what people *will* do from measures of *past* satisfaction. As we saw in Chapter 2, satisfaction can be a poor predictor of future behaviour because people can be positive about their past experience with a product without necessarily wanting to use it in the future. Needs change and sometimes products change so that what was satisfactory in the past may not be expected to be satisfactory in the future. A somewhat better prediction of retention would be obtained by using the attitude to 'buying the product again'.

Table 7.1 Correlations are greater when measures of attitude and behaviour are more compatible (Ajzen and Fishbein, 1977)

Attitude to:	*Correlation with use of the birth control pill*
Birth control	0.16
The birth control pill	0.34
Using the birth control pill	0.65

Specifying Measures

From this work it is clear that the more compatible the measures of attitude and behaviour, the more they will correlate. Compatibility is specified by target, action, context and time (think TACT). In the case of oral contraceptive use, the target is the oral contraceptive, the action is using it and the context/time is implicit in its use. In other cases, the context and time could be more important. For example, shopping in my local supermarket on a Saturday morning might be avoided because the local store is so busy at that time. In addition to the TACT variables, it is important to ensure that respondents are talking about their own attitudes and behaviour rather than some general idea. Ajzen and Fishbein (1977) applied these compatibility criteria in a meta-analysis of 142 attitude–behaviour associations. They sorted the studies into those with low, partial and high compatibility between the measures and sub-divided the last group because some measures were not clearly specified. Table 7.2 shows their findings. It is clear that low compatibility between attitude and behaviour explains why many previous studies showed a weak connection between attitude and behaviour.

Another measurement challenge occurs when attitudes embrace a *set* of behaviours rather than one specific behaviour (Ajzen and Fishbein, 1977). For example, a measure of a person's attitude to the environment might give a rather low prediction of their bottle recycling behaviour because specific factors may affect the decision to recycle bottles. If a multiple-act measure of environmental behaviour is constructed that also includes use of recycled paper, use of low-energy bulbs, installing insulation, recycling of metals and newsprint, donations to environmental groups, refusal to buy tropical hardwoods,

Table 7.2 Analysis of attitude–behaviour studies (adapted from Ajzen and Fishbein, 1977)

Compatibility	*Significance of attitude–behaviour relationship*		
	Nil	Low	High
Low	26	1	0
Partial	20	47	4
High–questionable measures	0	9	9
High–appropriate measures	0	0	26

boycotting the products of environmentally suspect firms, criticizing women in fur coats, etc., we would expect this measure to have a stronger correlation with the attitude to the environment. This is because the specific factors affecting single actions tend to cancel each other out in the combined measure leaving the common theme of helping the environment. Consistent with this, Weigel and Newman (1976) found that the attitude to environmental preservation correlated better with a multiple-act measure of environmentally concerned behaviour than with single measures.

In consumer research, the compatibility principle means that attitudes to the *purchase*, *hiring* and so on of the product must be measured if it is these actions that we want to predict. This simple lesson about using compatible measures has not been well learned. Usually attitudes to the brand are studied rather than attitudes to purchasing the brand. Often there is substantial overlap between these measures but, as Ajzen and Fishbein show (1980: ch. 13), this is not always so. Many of the early studies reviewed by Wicker (1969) in this field used incompatible measures, thus explaining the low association that he found between attitude and behaviour. The notion of compatibility has much improved attitude research.

Exercise 7.2 Compatibility test

Circle the numbers that are closest to your feelings:

Swimming is:

bad	−3	−2	−1	0	1	2	3	good
	extremely	*quite*	*slightly*	*neither*	*slightly*	*quite*	*extremely*	

Swimming in my local swimming pool is:

bad	−3	−2	−1	0	1	2	3	good
	extremely	*quite*	*slightly*	*neither*	*slightly*	*quite*	*extremely*	

For me, going swimming in my local swimming pool over the next month is:

bad	−3	−2	−1	0	1	2	3	good
	extremely	*quite*	*slightly*	*neither*	*slightly*	*quite*	*extremely*	

I will go swimming in my local swimming pool over the next month:

unlikely	−3	−2	−1	0	1	2	3	likely
	extremely	*quite*	*slightly*	*neither*	*slightly*	*quite*	*extremely*	

In Exercise 7.2, we are not able to measure behaviour so a measure of intention, the last scale, is used as a proxy. The scores of students in a class can be entered on a data file and the correlations between the last intention measure and each of the other measures calculated. You should find that the more compatible a concept is with the intention measure, the higher the correlation between the measures.

Purchase Intentions

Intentions may predict behaviour but do not tell us why the behaviour is undertaken; for this, reasons are required. However, sometimes in marketing, prediction of behaviour may be all that is needed.

Purchase behaviour may be predicted either from stated intention or from a person's estimate of their purchase probability. Measures of intention have been well tested in the field of consumer durable purchase. In early research in this area, Pickering and Isherwood (1974) found that 61 per cent of those who said they were '100 per cent likely to purchase' actually did so; this compares with the 5 per cent of respondents who made a purchase even though they had expressed no intention to purchase the durable in the next 12 months. These findings were close to those obtained by Gabor and Granger (1972) in a similar early study.

Since intention-to-buy measurements can discriminate quite well between prospective buyers and non-buyers it is possible to compare prospective purchasers and non-purchasers in the same way that users and non-users are compared. In this way, it should be possible to find out what makes products attractive before they are bought and to improve them or their marketing at an early stage.

There are two reasons for discrepancies between predicted and actual purchase: first, the true probability of purchase may be inaccurately measured by the scale point checked by the respondent and, second, people may change their intention or be unable to fulfil it (Bemmaor, 1995). The second inaccuracy is difficult to avoid but the first type of discrepancy is reduced by improved scaling. Juster (1966) used an 11-point, verbally referenced scale to measure the likelihood of purchase (see Box 7.1). In a review of intention measurement, Day et al. (1991) argue that the best results are obtained using a Juster scale, and Wright and MacRae (2007) show that predicted purchase proportions obtained using the Juster scale were unbiased estimates of the actual purchase proportions found from panel data or purchase recall.

Box 7.1 The Juster scale

This is an 11-point scale with verbal descriptions and probabilities associated with each number:

10	Certain, practically certain	(99 in 100)
9	Almost sure	(9 in 10)
8	Very probable	(8 in 10)
7	Probable	(7 in 10)
6	Good possibility	(6 in 10)
5	Fairly good possibility	(5 in 10)
4	Fair possibility	(4 in 10)
3	Some possibility	(3 in 10)
2	Slight possibility	(2 in 10)
1	Very slight possibility	(1 in 10)
0	No chance, almost no chance	(1 in 100)

Intention measures are used in the planned behaviour research reported next. In planned behaviour research, the seven-point semantic differential scale has usually been used (rather than the eleven-point scale described above), either as a direct measure of intention or as a self-prediction by the respondent that he or she will perform some behaviour. Often, there is little difference between the two measures but self-prediction seems likely to be more accurate because it may take more account of conditions that may prevent action. For example, people may intend to give up cigarettes but be more realistic, if asked to estimate the likelihood that they actually will give up. However, Sheppard, Hartwick and Warshaw (1988) reviewed a large number of attitude–behaviour studies and found only marginal superiority for self-prediction over true intention measures.

Normally, with durable goods like cars, a large majority of people express no intention of buying in the next year so that even a small percentage of this group who do buy provides a large fraction of the total number of buyers. Pickering and Isherwood (1974) found that 55 per cent of all buyers came from the group expressing no intention to buy. Theil and Kosobud (1968) in the USA, and Gabor and Granger (1972) in Britain, found that 70 and 65 per cent of purchasers respectively were in the group stating a zero purchase probability.

The extent to which people fulfil their intentions was reviewed by McQuarrie (1988), who assembled data from 13 studies. McQuarrie found that those who intended to purchase did so, on average, 42 per cent of the time whereas those not intending to purchase did not purchase 88 per cent of the time; this asymmetry is probably related to the fact that it is easier not to do something than to do it (see Box 7.2).

Box 7.2 Reasons for inaction

Why don't people do what they intend? East (1993) found that only two-thirds of those intending to apply for shares in British government privatizations actually did so. When the other third were asked why they hadn't followed through on their intention, they were equally divided between changing their mind (e.g. because the investment looked less advantageous) and inertia (e.g. forgetting, too much trouble). Pickering (1975) investigated failure to follow through an intention to buy consumer durables. In this case, respondents had usually changed their mind due to unforeseen circumstances, such as lack of money, or because their current durable was lasting better than expected.

Discrepancies between attitude and behaviour may also increase with the period that elapses between attitude measurement and behaviour measurement. The longer the period, the more opportunity people have to change their minds in response to new information or changed circumstances. For example, the attitude to voting for a political party may be affected by unfolding political events, and a measure of voting attitude taken close to an election should naturally be expected to have more predictive value than one taken a year before. However, although this effect of time lapse seems common sense,

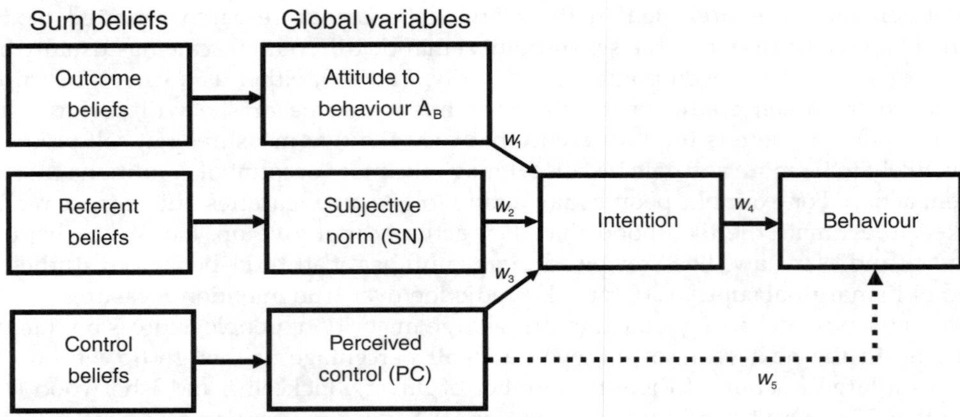

Figure 7.1 The theory of planned behaviour (TPB)

a study by Randall and Wolff (1994) found no evidence that the length of the interval was related to the correlation between intention and behaviour.

One study has raised some concern about the prediction of behaviour from intention. Chandon, Morwitz and Reinartz (2005) found that correlations in surveys between intention and subsequent behaviour are artificially increased by the process of asking about the respondent's intentions. It appears that the research process affects the respondents so that, after questioning, they are more likely to do what they said they were going to do.

SECTION 2: THE THEORY OF PLANNED BEHAVIOUR

Attitudes, intentions and behaviour have been combined in a comprehensive model of consumer choice called the theory of planned behaviour. Figure 7.1 illustrates this theory and Figure 7.2 shows it applied to playing the UK National Lottery.

The theory of planned behaviour (TPB) was developed over a long period, starting with Fishbein's (1963) expected-value theory of attitude. This theory was extended in a number of studies to predict intention and behaviour (e.g. Ajzen and Fishbein, 1969; Ajzen, 1971; Ajzen and Fishbein, 1972). In addition to attitude (A_B), the authors included subjective norm (SN) as a determinant of intention. SN measures the person's beliefs about what other people think they should do. This extended model was renamed the theory of reasoned action by Ajzen and Fishbein (1980) in a book in which they applied the theory to practical concerns such as health, consumer behaviour and voting. In 1985, Ajzen introduced the theory of planned behaviour by adding perceived control (PC) as a determinant of intention. PC measures a person's beliefs about the opportunities for an action which are based on the environment and their own abilities. The relative strengths of A_B, SN and PC in determining an action are given by the weights w_1, w_2 and w_3. Since

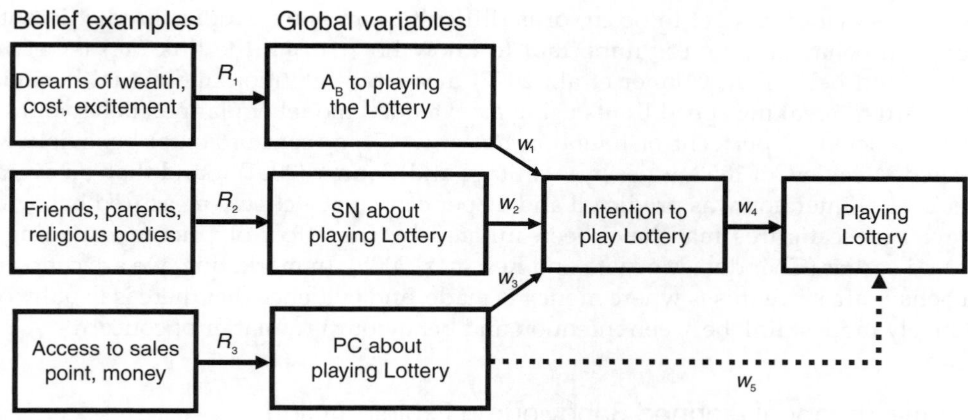

Figure 7.2 The theory of planned behaviour applied to playing the National Lottery

these weights vary from category to category, they are established empirically, using regression analysis or structural equation modelling.

As can be seen from Figure 7.1, the three global variables determine intention, which then determines behaviour. The weight w_4 reflects the fact that circumstances may stop people from realizing their intentions, or that their intentions could change. Finally, the model includes a second direct effect of perceived control on behaviour, with weight w_5. This covers behaviours such as giving up smoking and eating less where lack of personal control can undermine intention. This might apply to compulsive gamblers who find the National Lottery difficult to resist.

This theory also covers altruistic behaviour, which can be driven by the subjective norm, and it takes account of a person's self-assessed abilities and opportunities. As such, it is an advance on simple subjective expected utility (SEU) models that do not allow for such influences. The subjective norm is an internalized influence, exerting its effect through the agent's memories and values. The social agents that are recalled need not be present, or even exist, for them to have an effect. In recent work, a measure called the descriptive norm has been added. This is what others expect that the respondent *will* do (as opposed to *should* do). For example, Forward (2009) found that adding a descriptive norm variable to the model improved prediction of driving violations. Similarly, White et al. (2009) found that the addition of descriptive norm improved the prediction of recycling behaviour. Among the many behaviours to which the TPB has been applied are: taking exercise, attaining college grades, condom use, health self-examinations, escaping addiction, blood donation, mothers' diet management of their babies, food choice, recycling, buying environmentally friendly products, Internet use, reducing risky driving, accident avoidance, seeking funding, buying gifts, applying for shares in initial public offerings, and complaining. It is suitable for any behaviour where there are reasons for action but it is more appropriate for explaining category use than brand use if there are few differences in beliefs and attitudes between brands.

When behaviour has yet to occur, or is difficult to measure, studies predict intention rather than behaviour, so it is important to know how strong the link (w_4) is between intention and behaviour. Conner et al. (2007) measured intention and actual behaviour with regard to breaking speed limits using an extended model of planned behaviour. The model predicted 82 per cent of intention but only 17 per cent of actual behaviour was predicted. A review of 185 studies by Armitage and Conner (2001) found that, on average, 39 per cent of intention was predicted and 21 per cent of objectively measured behaviour. However, these figures may have been inflated by the effect of prior questioning, as indicated earlier (Chandon, Morwitz and Reinartz, 2005). In marketing, we are concerned with behaviour, since this is where money is made, and evidence that there is usually only a relatively modest link between intention and behaviour is a matter of concern.

Using the Theory of Planned Behaviour to Explain Action

The TPB can be used in three ways to explain actions.

Level 1: Behaviour

The immediate precursors of behaviour in the TPB are intention and perceived control, so one form of explanation concerns the relative impact of these two factors. This has been examined by Madden, Ellen and Ajzen (1992) who found that usually perceived behavioural control is the weaker factor and may have no direct impact on behaviour.

Level 2: Intention

Next, we need to know the relative importance of A_B, SN and PC in predicting intention. This varies from application to application. For example, Jaccard and Davidson (1972) found that, among college women, the use of the contraceptive pill was associated more with A_B than with SN; this probably reflected the importance of avoiding pregnancy for this group at that time. Davidson and Jaccard (1975) found that among married women with children, the intention to use the contraceptive pill was more determined by SN.

Level 3: Specific Factor Explanations

The third type of explanation relates specific outcome, referent and control beliefs to intention or behaviour. In the theory, specific beliefs relate to intention through the appropriate global variable but it is not always clear which global variable a factor belongs to when a research study is being conducted. For example, embarrassment about complaining might be seen as an outcome or as a control factor. East (2000) found that embarrassment acted primarily as a control factor, obstructing complaining, rather than as an emotional cost if a complaint was made. At a practical level, this issue can be resolved by correlating beliefs directly with intention.

Sometimes, the obvious reason for an activity is not its prime motivation. Membership of sports clubs may be driven by the need to meet people, for example. East (1993) found that application for shares in state privatizations was driven more by access to finance,

Box 7.3 An application to giving up cigarettes

In 1978, the UK Joint Committee on Research into Smoking recommended that a new study should be undertaken on attitudes towards smoking. One stimulus for this work was a 1977 report on attitudes and smoking behaviour prepared by Fishbein for the US Federal Trade Commission. This recommended a shift of focus from 'attitudes to smoking' to 'attitudes to giving up cigarettes'. The new study was conducted by the Office of Population Censuses and Surveys by Marsh and Matheson. The findings were published by the government in 1983 but the main features appear in a paper by Sutton, Marsh and Matheson (1990). The research measured A_B and confidence in being able to stop smoking, which was a form of PC measurement, but did not measure SN. This work provided one of the most substantial tests ever given to a theory in social psychology.

The researchers predicted behaviour on the basis of the difference between the expected values of stopping and continuing to smoke. It is this difference that shows the personal gain or loss of taking one option rather than the other. The research showed that the majority of smokers accepted that smoking caused lung cancer (73 per cent) and heart disease (59 per cent), but the study showed that most of these people believed either that they did not smoke enough to do any damage or that any damage was already done and was irreversible. For such people, cessation held little promise of reduced risk. The only smokers who saw a benefit from stopping were the minority who believed both that they had an enhanced risk and that cessation would diminish this risk. The researchers predicted that these people would make more attempts to stop and this was confirmed when smokers were followed up six months later. This evidence therefore supports a causal process from attitude to action.

This research showed where to place emphasis in health education in order to get people to try to quit smoking; for example, by explaining that the risk from cigarettes is related to the number smoked, that there is no threshold at which health hazards begin and that there are health benefits for nearly all people who stop smoking. The study also showed that eventual success in quitting was strongly dependent on confidence and that health education should therefore emphasize 'how to stop' methods which would build this confidence.

a PC factor, than by the expected financial outcomes, an A_B factor. This suggests that business people should not become too focused on the good value of their product or service since many of the people who might buy it may be constrained by finance or other control factors.

Level 3 explanations help us to choose intervention strategies. For example, if a firm wants to encourage customers to let it know about service failures, the key factors affecting complaining must be addressed. If many people lack confidence about complaining, it is best to provide a clear procedure, explain that it is supported by the company, and draw attention to this procedure on receipts and on the company website.

Exercise 7.3 Research using planned behaviour theory

1 Choose an action that is individually performed and voluntary, e.g. watching a popular TV programme, carrying an organ donor card, installing solar water heating, going to the dentist regularly or playing the National Lottery. Make sure that the action is appropriately specified in terms of target, action, context and time.
2 Choose the target group.
3 From a sample of the target group elicit the salient outcome, referent and control beliefs about the action, using Exercise 7.1. Ideally, about 20 people should be used. Reduce the salient beliefs by merging similar ones and dropping those that are rare.
4 Use the NEWACT program to create a planned behaviour questionnaire. The program asks for:

- the title of the questionnaire
- the intention
- the outcome beliefs
- the referent beliefs
- the control beliefs.

The program sets up the different scales for each item and the form of the items from input. Mistakes and poor grammar in the questionnaire need to be eliminated by word processing. Often the phraseology for control items is clumsy and needs adjustment. Some items are added automatically but these may be deleted if not required. The questionnaire will usually cover two sides of paper when printed in two-column landscape format. The questionnaire looks better if scale referents such as 'extremely', 'quite' and 'slightly' are italicized. The scaling is designed for a proportional font such as Times Roman.

5 Gather data from 50+ respondents.
6 Analyze the data.

Use the COMPUTE function in SPSS to:

a) Create products between outcome probability and outcome evaluation (and the corresponding products for the referent and control beliefs, but see later comment, Multiplying Ordinal Measures).
b) Produce three sum measures by aggregating products for the outcome, referent and control items.
c) Aggregate measures for each of the global variables and intention when more than one scale is used. (A reliability test may be appropriate here to check that each scale is measuring the same variable.)

Next:

d) Test the correlations between sum and global measures.
e) Perform a structural equation analysis or regression analysis to test the theory and establish the relative weights of A_B, SN and PC in the prediction of intention. (If you use regression, ordinal regression is appropriate.)

7 Examine your analysis and answer the following questions:

- Is intention most related to A_B, SN or PC?
- Do the sum measures correlate with the corresponding global measure better than with the other two global measures?
- Which belief factors correlate most with intention?
- Which belief factors might be used to improve the product's design or positioning, if any?
- What are the shortcomings of this study and analysis?

Applying Evidence from Planned Behaviour Research

When the findings from planned behaviour research are used to influence others, the influence attempt may not succeed for a number of reasons. First, correlations do not mean that there is a causal relationship. Second, beliefs may be strongly anchored and resist change, or may not change because of a ceiling effect (no room for change). Third, the attempt at influence may be interpreted in an unexpected way that does not bring about the intended change. Fishbein and Ajzen (1981) stated that studies of the existing basis for action give only an indication of where to place emphasis in an influence attempt; tests are needed to clarify this. Even so, planned behaviour research can suggest what may be important in decisions on product development, positioning and advertising themes.

SECTION 3: PROBLEMS WITH THE THEORY OF PLANNED BEHAVIOUR

Multiplying Ordinal Measures

In planned behaviour research, scales may be unipolar (1 to 7) or bipolar (–3 to +3). Bagozzi (1984) and others have explained that the scale measurement used in planned behaviour research is ordinal, but it is treated as ratio-scale when a two numbers from scales, such as outcome likelihood and evaluation, are multiplied to form a product. This introduces error and alters correlations with other variables. This alteration can be substantial when a switch is made between bipolar to unipolar scales. In this situation, Ajzen (1991) recommends *optimal scaling*, i.e. adding a constant to each scale to produce the highest correlation between the sum and global variables. This procedure gives some benefit to random effects and there is no specific justification for taking the scaling that gives the best correlation. An alternative method is to use the four combinations of 1 to 7 and –3 to +3 to see whether the results vary much. If similar results are obtained, whatever the scaling, there is more assurance about the results. The NEWACT program numbers all the scales 1 to 7 but the scales can be recoded in the analysis.

The Principle of Sufficiency

The TPB is based on beliefs. Therefore, any change in global variables, intention or behaviour must come about through the acquisition of new beliefs or the modification of existing beliefs. In other words, belief changes are a *sufficient* explanation for subsequent changes in global variables and intention. Ajzen and Fishbein (1980) accept that variables *external* to the theory, such as past experience, personality, age, sex and other social classifications, will be associated with behaviour but they argue that this occurs only because these variables are related to relevant beliefs and hence to A_B, SN or PC. They state:

> Although we do not deny that 'external' variables of this kind may sometimes be related to behaviour, from our point of view they can affect behaviour only indirectly. That is, external variables will be related to behaviour only if they are related to one or more of the variables specified by our theory. (Ajzen and Fishbein, 1980: 82)

Thus, beliefs and the other components of the TPB should mediate the effect of external variables as shown in Figure 7.3. This argument has been tested in a number of studies by including external variables in the regression analysis to see whether these significantly improve the prediction of intention compared with the global variables alone. Often, demographic variables have little effect; for example, Marsh and Matheson (1983) found no direct effects of age or sex on intention in their study on smoking cessation and Loken (1983) found no direct effect of external variables on television watching.

However, it is usually found that past experience has a direct effect on intention and behaviour (Bagozzi and Kimmel, 1995). In the Marsh and Matheson (1983) study, the previous experience of attempting to stop smoking had a direct effect on intention and a small direct effect on attempts to stop smoking. Similar direct effects of past behaviour on both intention and subsequent behaviour have been found by Bentler and Speckart (1979, 1981), Fredricks and Dossett (1983) and Bagozzi (1981). One possible explanation is that people are partly controlled by their environment as a result of habits set up by experience but that this control is not fully captured by the global measures (Bentler and Speckart, 1979; Fredricks and Dossett, 1983; Triandis, 1977). This may be because habits are sometimes controlled by stimuli that are not consciously recalled.

The Development of A_B, SN and PC

As experience increases, people become more informed and the belief basis for future action is changed. This is a situation that is particularly relevant to consumer behaviour. Consumers are naïve when they enter markets that are new to them and, as they repeat purchase, they become more experienced. When the experience is positive, intention will be enhanced in a positive feedback loop; if the experience is negative, intentions will be reduced and further trial curtailed. Thus, under the voluntary conditions that attach to most consumer behaviour, we would expect to find that those who are highly experienced have stronger intentions. Applying the TPB, there should be changes in A_B, SN and PC as intention develops, as illustrated in Figure 7.3. This can occur because the beliefs underlying the global variables become more numerous and more strongly linked to the behaviour. If experience makes the belief basis of planned behaviour more complicated, we may ask whether it has the same effect on A_B, SN and PC. East (1992) suggested that the progression from novice to expert consumer involves a movement from actions based mainly on SN to

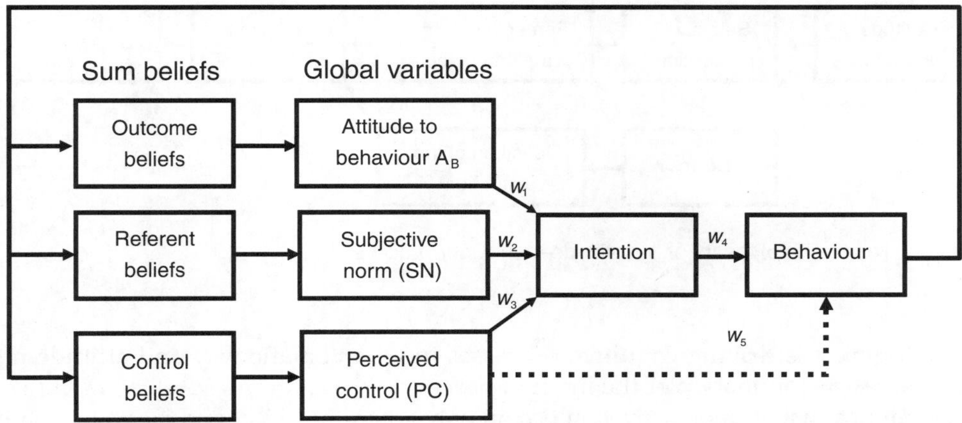

Figure 7.3 Feedback from experience should affect beliefs

actions based more on A_B and PC. This proposal is founded on the idea that, in the absence of detailed knowledge, people have to make decisions on the basis of naïve ideas, and that 'what others think I should do' is better known, or more easily guessed, than the benefits and opportunities related to an unfamiliar prospect. East identified three minor studies that supported the idea that SN gave way to A_B and PC as people became more experienced. However, as further studies accumulated, no clear-cut pattern emerged and the work was not published. This issue has yet to be resolved. The studies that did not support the theory were mainly financial decisions, such as the purchase of endowments and pensions, and these may not have permitted much development of knowledge from experience.

Despite the lack of support for the theory, the issue of how experience affects the different beliefs underlying global variables is important and deserves further study. In many TPB studies, SN is a relatively weak determinant of behaviour and there has been some tendency to downgrade it (e.g. Sheppard, Hartwick and Warshaw, 1988). Armitage and Connor (2001) found that part of the weakness could be attributed to poor measurement. It seems quite likely that the contribution of SN in the determination of intention depends on the experience of respondents.

Deliberate and Spontaneous Action

Fazio (1990) divides the explanation of behaviour into two fields. Where decision-making is deliberate, Fazio supports the TPB, but when the decision is spontaneous, he proposes a different model in which attitude comes first. This second model is shown in Figure 7.4.

In Fazio's (1986) account, attitudes are automatically activated by observation of the attitude object. The attitude then guides perception and the individual becomes aware of aspects of his or her environment related to the attitude. The definition of the event then occurs as these perceptions are associated with a normative understanding of the situation and, out of this definition of the event, behaviour may follow. The main point here is that

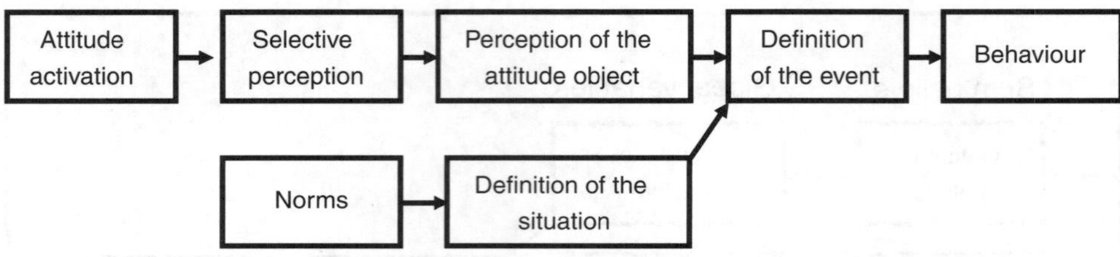

Figure 7.4 Fazio's (1986) theory of the attitude–behaviour process

the environment is driving cognitive processes in an automatic way and attitude rather than belief is the foundation of the internal process.

Fazio argues that attitude activation occurs only when the object and its evaluation have been well established in memory, usually through direct behavioural experience. Thus spontaneous production of behaviour is restricted to familiar contexts, leaving planned behaviour to explain the more unusual situations. However, this rather cosy division of the field has been disrupted by evidence from Bargh et al. (1992) that a wide range of objects can elicit attitude-driven effects. This casts doubt on the separation between the automatic and deliberate control of behaviour. It seems possible that these two types of explanation may often work together. Fazio (1990) showed that responses in measurements of deliberate behaviour are affected if people are asked to focus on emotion-evoking objects before measurement. Baldwin and Holmes (1987) found that systematically different measurements were obtained when different social referents were visualized before response. These findings reflect the effect of automatic processes even when people are making considered responses.

Adjustments and Alternatives to the Theory of Planned Behaviour

A number of researchers have suggested modifications of the theory. Bagozzi and Kimmel (1995) and Bagozzi (1992) suggest distinctions between intention, desire and self-prediction, and Armitage and Conner (2001) find some support for these distinctions. There have also been proposals to include a moral norm to cover the respondent's personal normative control, but this has been found to have an additional predictive function only for some actions.

Ajzen and Driver (1992) distinguish between the short-term and expressive consequences of action and the longer-term and more cognitive consequences of action. Often, a short-term pain has to be balanced against a long-term gain. On this basis, A_B should be seen as having two components.

In its present form, the theory includes only one type of subjective norm – what respondents think that others think that they *should* do. As noted earlier, what others actually do (descriptive norm) exerts an additional influence on behaviour (Deutsch and Gerard, 1955). When descriptive norms are included, predictions are usually better supported (Rivis and Sheeran, 2003). Other developments are possible; Armitage and Conner (2001) separate measures for the control element in the theory into the control that a person has by virtue of his or her abilities and the control that is made possible by the environment. However, all these adjustments raise the complexity of the theory and make it harder to use.

In the consumer behaviour context, the technology acceptance model (TAM) has been offered as an alternative method of predicting the intention to use new systems (Davis, 1989). This theory bases behavioural intention on two factors: perceived usefulness and perceived ease of use. This model has the advantage of simplicity and avoids elicitation but it applies to some situations only and may not give as much explanation as a belief-based model. In TAM, usefulness has some correspondence with A_B, and ease of use with PC, and while the theory originally did not include SN, Venkatesh and Davis (2000) have modified the TAM model to incorporate SN.

Reviewing Planned Behaviour Theory

The development of the theory of planned behaviour has been a success story. Social psychologists have emerged from the dark days of 1969 when Wicker claimed that there was little or no connection between attitude and behaviour. We now have a predictive and explanative model which works effectively though there remains a nagging doubt about the scale of behaviour prediction.

However, there is a concern about the methods that have been used to test the theory. If the theory is causal, it should be possible to instigate change by supplying information and then to follow how the effects of that change 'cascade' through the components of the theory. This requires research designs in which comparisons are made between experimental conditions that induce changes of belief. The fact that there is little published evidence of this sort may indicate that little has been done in this area or that the results of such research have not been conclusive.

Finally, there is a need to apply the theory more effectively in marketing. It may be used to study the activities of marketers – why they opt for or against particular practices (e.g. Elliott, Jobber and Sharp, 1995) – and it applies to a host of consumer practices. The theory is of limited use in explaining the preference for one brand over another, unless the brands are markedly different (e.g. one restaurant versus another, or one holiday destination rather than another). The main strength of planned behaviour research is at the category level. It can explain why categories are liked and, therefore, it can assist managers to position brands, target more responsive population segments and select themes for advertising.

SUMMARY

Attitudes are an evaluative response to a concept. The concept is a cluster of attribute beliefs about a particular topic, and each belief has values attaching to it. Thus the attitude to the concept should relate to the aggregate value of the attribute beliefs. Generally, this view of attitude has been upheld by research and it fits the idea that the purchase of a product can be seen as the acquisition of a bundle of expected costs and rewards.

In many studies the correlation between attitude and behaviour measures is found to be weak. There are two reasons for such weak relationships. The first is that 'other variables' may swamp the association between attitude and behaviour. The second reason is that the measures of attitude and behaviour may not be compatible, i.e. these measures may not refer to the same action, target, context and time. A mismatch here means that the wrong attitude is being used to predict behaviour.

The closest prediction of behaviour is provided by measures of intention – those who state that they will buy a product are, unsurprisingly, found to be much more likely to buy it than those who state that they will not buy it.

The theory of planned behaviour (Ajzen, 1985, 1991) formalizes this link between beliefs, attitudes, intentions and behaviour. In this theory, there are three global variables – attitude to a behaviour, subjective norm and perceived control. These three variables have a combined effect on intention. Behaviour is predicted by intention and perceived control. The global variables rest on beliefs about the outcomes of behaviour, the referents who think that a person should or should not engage in the behaviour, and the ability and opportunity to engage in the behaviour. The theory of planned behaviour provides different levels of explanation which can be used in product positioning, development and advertising themes.

Additional Resources

Issues on the nature of attitudes and their relationship with behaviour are well discussed in chapter 4 of Eagly and Chaiken (1993) and by Eagly and Chaiken (2005). A review of the theory of planned behaviour is provided by Ajzen (2002) and by Armitage and Conner (2001). Ajzen's website is www.people.umass.edu/aizen/faq.html (note: 'aizen' is an alternative spelling).

8 Information Processing and Decision-Making

LEARNING OBJECTIVES

When you have completed this chapter, you should be able to:

1. Understand the way schemas and response competition are involved in thinking.
2. Explain what is meant by a heuristic mechanism and describe how these mechanisms may bias decision-making.
3. Describe how human beings respond to objective probability and value.
4. Understand the ideas of framing, mental accounting and editing.
5. Describe how this work can be used to influence others and improve consumer choice.

OVERVIEW

In the previous chapter, the theory of planned behaviour was described. Though it assists prediction, this theory does not really describe how people think. People do not assign likelihoods and evaluations, multiply them and sum the products to form their attitudes. Planned behaviour theory works *as if* people figure out their interests in this way, but no claim is made that they actually do so.

An alternative approach, described here, focuses on automatic mechanisms that guide information-seeking and choice. This approach seems to get closer to the thought processes (often unconscious) that govern behaviour. We deal first with the way structures called schemas can guide thought and recognition. Then we consider the situation where there is no clear schema available to interpret a stimulus, which leads to response competition and sustained attention as alternative schemas are tried. When such ambiguous stimuli are repeatedly exposed, they may be liked more as response competition is reduced. After this discussion of how people think, the majority of the chapter is devoted to findings relating to prospect theory. This work by Kahneman, Tversky and many of their colleagues has transformed thinking about the way human beings process information and make choices. Kahneman and Tversky show that human decision-making is modified by local conditions. Their methods have mainly involved simple choices, presented to participants, with a count of the preferences expressed. Using such methods, they have documented many instances where judgement is biased away from a rational model, and decision-making departs from economic assumptions.

SECTION 1: SCHEMAS AND ATTENTION

Schemas

According to Crocker, Fiske and Taylor (1984: 197), a schema is:

> an abstract or generic knowledge structure, stored in memory, that specifies the defining features and relevant attributes of some stimulus domain, and the interrelationships among those attributes. ... Schemas help us to structure, organize and interpret new information; they facilitate encoding, storage and retrieval of relevant information; they can affect the time it takes to process information. ... Schemas also serve interpretive or inferential functions. For example, they may fill in data that are missing or unavailable in a stimulus configuration.

The notion of the schema was implicit in the early work by Bartlett (1932) on remembering. Bartlett wrote of the 'effort after meaning' and showed how unusual structures that fell short of representing any object were interpreted by reference to more familiar ideas. One of Bartlett's stimuli was a diagram of an ambiguous object that was variously recognized as a battleaxe, turf cutter, anchor or key, although it was not quite like any of them. People used a schema for a more familiar object to make sense of the ambiguous object.

More frequently encountered stimuli are more easily retrieved. In addition, stimuli with particular characteristics are recognized or recalled more easily. 'Colorful, dynamic, or other distinctive stimuli disproportionately engage attention and, accordingly, disproportionately affect judgements' (Taylor, 1982: 192). This leads to the idea that thinking is based on cognitive accessibility. The more rapidly an idea can be brought to mind, the more likely it is to figure in cognition and subsequent processing. This *retrieval bias effect* has parallels with accessibility in the physical environment. For example, people buy more from those supermarkets that are nearby. Internet search engines use a related process when they take account of the frequency of past interest in the search outcomes. Retrieval bias is quite efficient because it ensures that the more likely candidates are considered first. However, concepts that occur infrequently or are hard to visualize for other reasons will tend to be left out of cognitive processing. In general, experience-based concepts are more easily retrieved than communication-based concepts, events are favoured over states, recent occurrences over long-past occurrences and the clearly defined concept over those that are obscure. Bartlett's example involves the simplest of schemas, those used to classify objects. More elaborate schemas include classifications of persons or groups, grammatical forms and social roles. In their most abstract form, schemas may cover relationships like logical validity, causality and symmetry.

When more than one schema fits a situation, people experience *response competition* as they struggle to give meaning to the stimulus (see Box 8.1). This leads to extended attention as people grapple with the problem.

Box 8.1 Response competition

Response competition is demonstrated by the Stroop test. In this test you are asked to call out the colour that is written the moment that it is displayed. In one condition, the word is RED written using a red colour; in the other condition, RED is written using a blue colour and, in this second case, respondents take longer to respond than in the first condition. In the second case, two competing responses are aroused – to say 'red' (reading the word) and to say 'blue' (noting the colour of the text) – and the competition delays the production of the correct response.

Managing Schemas

Since thought is guided by schemas, it follows that negotiation and other forms of influence may succeed by manipulating the selection of schemas that people use to interpret their experience. One standard ploy in negotiation is to try to anchor the discussion around a particular range of outcomes. Early in the discussion, a negotiator might say, 'The normal rate for this type of work is £1,000 a day'. This can constrain offers to those fairly close to the rate mentioned. Turning to advertising, schemas may be used to develop the product concept. For example, 'No FT, no comment' implies that those who read the *Financial Times* are likely to be better informed – it conjures up the notion of the business expert dispensing wisdom. Often public relations exercises can be seen as attempts to manipulate the schemas used in judgement. For example, firms may play up their green credentials by drawing attention to their energy-saving actions. Some interesting examples of schema management are shown in Box 8.2.

Do People Like Response Competition?

Jokes are often based on response competition. People may anticipate one outcome and have their expectations confounded at the punch line. But other forms of response competition may be disliked. Even jokes may be disliked when a person is under stress. The explanation for this variable reaction is that it depends upon the degree of arousal of the person involved. Boredom (low stimulation) and high stress (high stimulation) are both conditions of high

Box 8.2 New schemas for old

An activist group took on the tobacco companies in Australia in the 1980s. The group was called the Billboard Utilising Graffitists Against Unhealthy Promotions (BUGA UP) and they specialized in 'refacing' tobacco posters. When a cigarette company offered a car as a prize, their poster was given the caption 'From the people who put the 'car' in carcinogen'. The adjustments to the posters, and the speeches in court when members of the group were prosecuted, gave entertainment to many Australians, who much appreciated the sight of multinational tobacco companies being humbled in this way.

When a tobacco company sponsored work at the Sydney Opera House, well-dressed members of BUGA UP distributed leaflets expressing regret at this unsavoury association between tobacco and the arts. Another BUGA UP enterprise sabotaged a Marlboro 'Man of the Year' competition in Australia. BUGA UP proposed their own candidate – a man disabled by smoking, confined to a wheelchair, and smoking through the hole in his throat provided by a tracheotomy operation. The man himself was a willing accomplice and starred in a poster which was printed and sold in large numbers. The schema of the strong heroic figure that Marlboro had tried to cultivate was ridiculed. In its place were put the schemas of disease and disability which are more accurately related to smoking cigarettes. A further 'anti-promotion' counteracted the distribution of free cigarettes in shopping malls. To most people a gift is a kindness and the giver is regarded as well-meaning. To oppose such promotions, BUGA UP arranged for children to parade around the mall with banners saying 'DANGER – DRUG PUSHERS AT WORK'. This changed the perception of the tobacco companies' motives from kindness to self-interest. Tobacco companies have a squalid history of refusing to admit to the hazards of their products; they are licensed drug sellers and an important part of their public relations has been to counter such facts by sponsoring orchestras, sport and research. BUGA UP's achievement was to reassert the drug seller schema as the one by which the tobacco companies' actions could be judged.

arousal. People prefer an intermediate level of stimulation because, in this region, arousal is lower. Conceptual conflicts may be welcome when people are inactive or bored (e.g. when watching television) because the extra stimulation will reduce arousal; at other times, unusual stimuli may raise arousal (Berlyne, 1965; Berlyne and McDonnell, 1965) and, when this occurs, the stimuli may be disliked. This explains why Harrison (1968) and Saegert and Jellison (1970) found that the stimulating objects were often disliked.

Mere Exposure

Response competition has been used to explain an interesting phenomenon first reported by Zajonc (pronounced Zi-onse, 1968). Zajonc observed that repeated exposure to a new stimulus often made people like it more. This effect of *mere exposure* was so called because the change in the observer's evaluation occurs without the use of reinforcement (discussed in Chapter 1). Zajonc observed this effect in both laboratory and field experiments, using nonsense words, obscure characters and photographs of unknown faces as the unfamiliar stimuli. For example, in Zajonc and Rajecki's (1969) field experiment, nonsense words such as NANSOMA were printed like advertisements in campus newspapers. Later, the researchers got large numbers of students to rate the words on evaluative scales and there was clear evidence that the frequency of exposure correlated positively with the evaluative rating. Zajonc's explanation for this was that the nonsense words created response competition in the minds of readers and that this was reduced as people developed a familiarity with the nonsense word after repeated exposure. If the response competition created by nonsense words is generally disagreeable, a reduction in competition (e.g. through familiarity with the nonsense word) should produce a more positive evaluation. Harrison (1968) measured response competition as the time delay before any response to the stimulus and found that the delay was reduced as the number of exposures increased. Lee (1994) offered another ingenious explanation which is based on the availability heuristic discussed later in this chapter: repeated exposure speeds up recognition; the stimuli that we recognize more easily tend to be those that we like; this association guides judgement and leads us to give the stimuli higher evaluations.

However, not all stimuli become more liked on repeated exposure. This suggests that prospective brand names (which are often like nonsense words) should be pre-tested to see whether they are well liked after they have become familiar.

The Response to Thought and Feeling Stimuli

We tend to think that recognition is a necessary precursor to any evaluation of a stimulus. If you do not know what the concept is, how can you have any affective response to it? Strangely, it seems that we can have an evaluative response without recognition. Zajonc (1980) showed that thought and feeling are initially processed independently and Kunst-Wilson and Zajonc (1980) found that evaluative responses occurred slightly ahead of recognition. Zajonc points to the survival value attaching to a fast response to dangerous stimuli: it is better to jump without thought than to recognize that it is a car that is hitting you!

In a further experiment, Marcel (1976) used an instrument called a tachistoscope to present stimuli at speeds and levels of illumination at which they were hard to recognize. The stimuli were either words or blank spaces, with equal likelihood. Words were either short or long and either 'good' or 'bad'. A good word might be 'food' while a bad word might be 'evil'. If the participants in the experiment thought they saw a word, they were asked to judge its length against comparison words and also to give an evaluative judgement, to say whether the word was good or bad. The duration of exposure was reduced until the subjects were guessing the presence of words at chance level and could not therefore have been recognizing anything. At this duration, Marcel found that word-length judgements (also cognitive) were at chance level too. However, at this point the subjects were still scoring at above chance on their evaluative judgements of words when these were present, indicating that the evaluative response was generated faster than the recognition response. Vanhuele (1994) reviews this work.

Fast recognition judgements of the sort studied by Zajonc are quite different from the choices typically faced by consumers, but these studies show how unconscious mechanisms can underlie consciously experienced thought and feeling.

Attention and Value

In decision-making, the observable action is often restricted to the overt choice. However, when the alternatives are physically present, it is possible to observe the direction of gaze and to infer from this which alternative a person is thinking about. Gerard (1967) used this method of investigation; he employed two projectors to show two alternatives (Impressionist paintings), while light reflecting off a mirror attached to the back of the participant's head showed which alternative was receiving attention. A multi-channel recorder logged the data. Gerard reported that the participants looked most at the alternative that they did *not* choose and suggested that they were trying to come to terms with not having this alternative.

To test Gerard's result, East (1973) conducted two experiments using a battery of slide viewers connected to a hidden time recorder (illustrated). As in the earlier study by Gerard (1967), the choice was made between French Impressionist paintings. The participants were led to believe that they would get a poster of the picture that they chose.

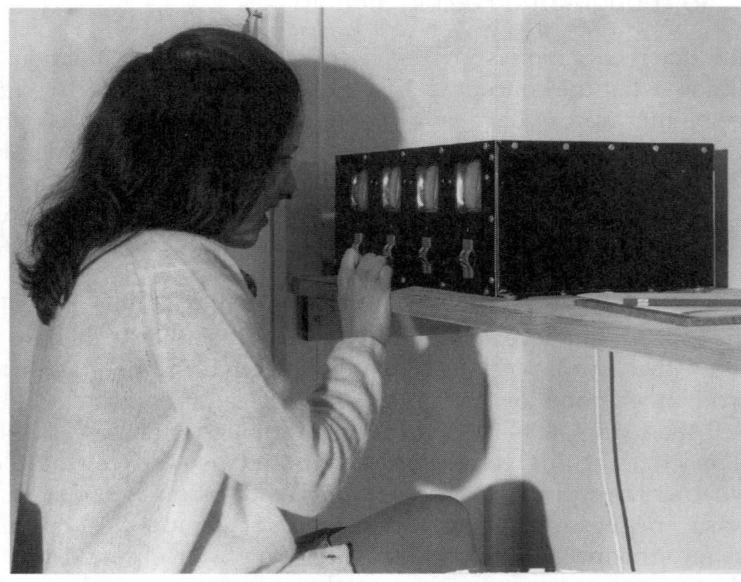

Using the slide viewer equipment (East, 1973)

Control of the viewing equipment was left entirely in the hands of the participant so that the time spent on the different alternatives was unconstrained.

East's first experiment presented subjects with two alternatives, while a second experiment presented three alternatives. Both experiments had two levels of choice difficulty: high, between alternatives that had previously been rated equally by the subject, and low, between alternatives that had been rated unequally.

The results showed that the subjects spent more time looking at the alternatives that they liked, so that the ratio of attention times was an approximate function of the ratio of the evaluations (see Table 8.1). East's result was the opposite of Gerard's reported findings and it is possible that, with Gerard's rather complicated method for recording attention, the records were inadvertently linked to the wrong alternative. A later study by Russo and Leclerc (1994) supports East's finding. Russo and Leclerc used video equipment in a simulation supermarket situation and measured the number of eye fixations on alternatives (rather than duration of time spent) at different phases in the decision sequence. They found that in the main phase of the decision the number of fixations clearly favoured the alternative later chosen. In another study, Pieters and Warlop (1999) also found more attention to the alternative that was eventually chosen.

Thus there is a simple mechanism that directs attention to the more valued alternative. This mechanism is unconscious; when asked about their potential behaviour, people do not know which alternative they would look at most. This evidence suggests that the more valued features of a person's environment generally get more attention compared with those of lesser value. We can see that this mechanism helps people to benefit from their environment. To avoid harm, it is possible that people attend more to unpleasant stimuli than neutral ones but we do not have data on this.

If evaluation guides attention, it means that second and third preferences will get proportionately less attention and their worthwhile attributes are less likely to be discovered. Only when investigation of the first preference leads to it being down-rated will more time will be allocated to lesser alternatives. This mechanism therefore carries a bias in favour of existing preferences but it is an efficient way of using time since it ensures that little time is wasted on low-rated prospects. Given this evidence, people may be encouraged

Table 8.1 Mean durations of attention to alternatives in choice experiments (East, 1973)

	Order of evaluation	*Two alternatives: Time spent (seconds)*	*Three alternatives: Time spent (seconds)*
High choice difficulty	1	46	25
	2	37	23
	3	–	*21*
Total time		**83**	**69**
Low choice difficulty	1	24	24
	2	18	16
	3	–	*9*
Total time		**42**	**49**

to buy an initially lower-rated brand if information about this brand is attached to a message on the initially preferred alternative since, in this arrangement, it is more likely to receive attention. This may be done by using comparative advertising, and there is evidence that small brands benefit from this procedure (Grewal et al., 1997).

SECTION 2: HEURISTICS

Exercise 8.1 Availability effects

In the UK, approximately 600,000 people die each year from all causes. How many people die prematurely each year from the following two causes? Enter the figures that you think apply:

Smoking:
Road accidents:

We now consider biases that may affect everyday decision-making. *If you want to find the river, go downhill!* This is a heuristic rule which often helps but may mislead when there is no river in the valley. The term 'heuristic' was used by Kahneman, Slovic and Tversky (1982) to cover inexact or rule-of-thumb processes which may be used consciously or unconsciously to assess the likelihood of an uncertain event. Kahneman et al. argue that people do not appear to follow the statistical theory of prediction when making such judgements. Instead, they rely on a limited number of heuristic processes which often yield reasonable judgements but sometimes lead to error. In particular, people seem to attach higher probability to ideas that are easily retrieved; this is called the *availability heuristic*. This arises because frequently experienced concepts become easier to retrieve; as a result higher probability and ease of retrieval become associated in heuristic thinking.

Markus and Zajonc (1985) provide an example of the way in which availability may quite unjustifiably support the prestige of the medical profession. People often get better without treatment but, when treatment has been given, there is a tendency to assume that this treatment was the cause of the recovery. The treatment is more cognitively available as a cause of recovery than ideas about the natural processes counteracting disease that occur unseen within the body. As a result, people may judge therapy to be more effective than it is.

The judgement of risk is notoriously erratic. Some of the reason for this may lie in the poor information about actual risks in the media but judgement may also be distorted by the action of heuristics. Lichtenstein et al. (1978) suggested that the risk of occurrences that are referred to often in the media becomes exaggerated because of the availability heuristic. Those who completed Exercise 8.1 are likely to have overestimated the risk of death from road accidents because these events are more salient in media reports. Smoking deaths are less well reported and are likely to be underestimated. The approximate annual numbers of deaths in the UK by cause are:

All causes	600,000
Smoking	100,000
Road accidents	2,000

Misjudgement of risk has also affected the use of oral contraceptives. Exaggerated fears of potentially harmful side-effects have caused women to abandon the pill, even when the identified risk was very small in absolute terms. In 1996, a 10 per cent increase in legal abortion in Britain was attributed to earlier announcements that a number of contraceptive pills should be phased out because of small associated risks.

People seem to have difficulty in taking account of background risk and may focus instead on large percentage increases. For example, women may be shocked to hear that those who are over 35 and who smoke and take the contraceptive pill have 18 times the risk of pulmonary embolism compared with those who do neither of these actions. The '18 times' fact seems to be more available and to dominate in judgement, but embolisms are very rare in the 35–45-year-old range so this is 18 times a very small number and other hazards present far more risk. A more responsible way of handling the data would be to report the personal increment in the risk for smokers of using the pill. For example, that a smoker who takes the pill has an extra risk of dying of one in a million. The effect of the information on embolism was to encourage women to abandon the pill. They would have done better to quit smoking since this causes smokers to lose, on average, about six years of life.

Exercise 8.2 Who was to blame? (Abridged from Tversky and Kahneman, 1980: 62)

Solve the following problem:

A cab was involved in a hit-and-run accident at night. Two cab companies, the Green and the Blue, operate in the city. You are given the following data:

- 85 per cent of the cabs in the city are Green and 15 per cent are Blue.
- A witness identified the cab as a Blue cab. The court tested his ability to identify cabs under appropriate visibility conditions. When presented with a sample of cabs (half of which were Blue and half of which were Green) the witness made correct identifications in 80 per cent of the cases.

Question: What is the probability that the cab involved in the accident was Blue rather than Green?

Decide on your answer before reading on.

The tendency to ignore base rates such as market share is the basis of the *representativeness heuristic*. Likelihood is judged by reference to visible similarities rather than background probabilities. For example, a person may be seen as a barrister because of features of dress and delivery of speech. In this case, the judgement draws on the stereotype of a barrister, but such a judgement takes no account of the low number of barristers in society which makes it unlikely that a person belongs to this group.

Exercise 8.2 (continued)

Tversky and Kahneman (1980) put this problem to several hundred participants; the median response was an 80 per cent likelihood that the cab was Blue. Thus participants tended to take note of the witness's skill in recognizing cabs and ignored the market shares of the two cab companies. Clearly, if there had been no Blue cabs, the witness could not have been right so the proportion of Blue cabs is relevant. The probability that the witness was right is the ratio of correct identification of cab colour as blue to total identification as blue (both correct and incorrect). The chance that the cab was Blue (0.15) and was recognized correctly (0.8) is 0.15×0.8 and the chance that the cab was Green (0.85) and was recognized wrongly as Blue (0.2) is 0.85×0.2. The required ratio of correct identification to total identifications is therefore:

$$\frac{(0.15 \times 0.8)}{(0.15 \times 0.8) + (0.85 \times 0.2)}$$
$$= 0.41$$

So there is 41 per cent chance the cab was Blue.

In Exercise 8.2, the bias towards the witness test and away from the market shares of the two cab companies probably relates to the fact that the witness test is an event. As previously reported, events are more available than continuing states such as market share. We seem to be tuned to change and direct our thinking to the more active aspects of a problem. In contrast, data dealing with an unchanging background do not attract as much attention. This mechanism serves a useful purpose by drawing attention to aspects of the environment that require response but it can cause mistakes in some cases. In particular, it means that consumer financial decisions may be related to more active features of the environment rather than their impact on wealth. Wealth is a state rather than an event and does not usually figure in individual judgements even though, normatively, it should.

People are also prone to give more weight to causal data, which is related to change. For example, respondents are more likely to agree with the proposition that *a girl has blue eyes if her mother has blue eyes* than *a mother has blue eyes if her daughter has blue eyes* though the two events are equally probable (Tversky and Kahneman, 1980). The mother-to-daughter inheritance is causal, unlike the daughter-to-mother relationship and it is this that influences respondents.

The focus on events rather than states and the different heuristic rules were described by Kahneman (2002) as intuitive thinking in his presentation following his award of the Nobel Prize for economics. Kahneman likens such thinking to the way perception seems to be governed by mechanisms over which we have little conscious control. What we perceive is a function of the context from which reference points are drawn. Small changes in problems can affect the reference points and change the judgement. There are criticisms of this work; see, for example, Gigerenzer (1991), who has raised questions about the interpretation of effects (response by Kahneman and Tversky, 1996).

Relevance to Marketing and Management

The greater cognitive availability of events and causal data has a relevance to marketing. For example, we may exaggerate the impact of market interventions, such as a brand extension. As we saw in Chapter 4, conditions such as market share control the likely outcome of such interventions, but these conditions may get less attention than they deserve because of their constancy.

In addition, retrieval bias will move decisions towards the option that is easiest to bring to mind. This may lead us away from the prevention of undesirable occurrences before they happen (proaction) so that we have to respond to undesirable occurrences after they have happened (reaction). The choice between proaction and reaction depends on costs. Sometimes, it is best to let things happen and then to focus resources on the problem – management by exception – but in other cases, for example avoiding accidents, prevention is usually best. Our point is that there is a bias against proactive intervention because successful prevention produces no visible outcome and this choice is therefore less cognitively available. In addition to supporting reactive solutions, retrieval bias will operate in favour of the visible, well-defined events and against those that are hard to bring to mind. This suggests that people may:

- give too much support to the status quo: what is happening is available, but what could happen is harder to bring to mind;
- make poor assessment of the opportunity cost, which is the alternative use of resources when a course of action is selected;
- find it easier to sell products that have a physical form that is easily seen.

SECTION 3: PROCESSING VALUE AND PROBABILITY

Objective value, expressed in money or other units, and objective probability, the likelihood of something occurring, are processed by human beings to produce subjective evaluations

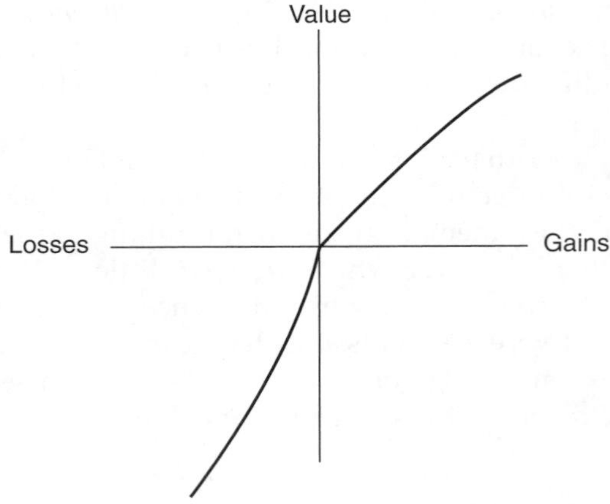

Figure 8.1 The value function (from Kahneman and Tversky, 2000)

(or utility) and subjective estimates of probability. These subjective representations do not exactly correspond with the objective forms and this affects decision-making.

Value

The relationship between objective value and utility has a long history going back to Bernoulli (1738), who described how the curve of utility against wealth flattens as wealth increases, and marginal utility therefore diminishes with each increment in wealth. Benoulli gave the example of a pauper who, finding a lottery ticket offering an equal chance of winning 20,000 ducats or getting nothing, might quite reasonably ensure a gain by exchanging his ticket for a guaranteed 9,000 ducats. The value function is curved, so that half the *utility* of 20,000 ducats is less than the utility of 9,000 ducats.

This curvature assists exchanges. To a person who has enough of a good, the marginal utility of additional supplies is low and this will encourage exchanges with others who possess different goods that the person needs. Both parties in such an exchange can gain in utility. However, Benoulli was mistaken to think that such exchanges were reckoned against total wealth. Normally, people assess gains or losses against a more salient criterion – and this is often the zero point. This relationship between gains and losses relative to zero, and utility, is shown by the curve in Figure 8.1. You can see that the curve is concave to the *x*-axis for both gains and losses and that the response to losses is larger than the response to gains. This relationship has been established by observing the preferences expressed by individuals about different choices. Comparisons between positive and negative choices have been particularly interesting (see Exercise 8.3).

Exercise 8.3 Positive and negative choices

1 Which do you prefer?

A: £9,000 for certain, or
B: £10,000 with a probability of 0.9; otherwise nothing.

2 Which do you prefer?

C: Losing £9,000 for certain, or
D: Losing £10,000 with a probability of 0.9; otherwise nothing.

In Exercise 8.3 people generally prefer A to B. The shape of the value–utility relationship for gains explains why people prefer £9,000 for certain rather than have 0.9 × £10,000. They also prefer D to C. The shape of the value function in the negative region means that losing £10,000 with a probability of 0.9 is less painful than losing £9,000 for certain and people prefer the smaller disutility. These outcomes mean that people are generally *risk averse on gains but risk prone on losses*. This pattern of preference reversal is regularly found and is called the *reflection effect*. However, in 1992, Tversky and Kahneman suggested that the data were more consistent with the idea that people are risk averse on gains and risk prone on losses when outcomes had medium or high probability; for low probability outcomes they suggest the reverse risk profile occurs. This modification arises because of the way people weight low probabilities, as we explain later.

Figure 8.1 shows another interesting effect. This is the steepness of the negative part of the value function in comparison to the positive part. This effect is captured by the aphorism *losses loom larger than gains* and, more formally, as *loss aversion*. Loss aversion is behind the *endowment effect* which is that people often demand much more to give up an object than they would be willing to pay to acquire it. The endowment effect has been demonstrated in a number of studies reviewed by Kahneman, Knetsch and Thaler (1991a). One simple example of the effect is the reluctance of people to engage in a 50:50 win/lose bet. On average, people will only wager a dollar on a coin toss if they can win more than two dollars. Generally, people will be reluctant to trade what they own, except at a high price. Not surprisingly, the endowment effect has been tested by critics; see for example Shogren et al. (1994).

As we stated, gains and losses relate to some reference point. In some cases it will be a prior cost. For example, a person may see the $20,000 cost of building work on a newly acquired house as an addition to the $1million price paid for the house. Viewed like this, the $20,000 seems a modest increment to the purchase price but, ten years later, when the purchase of the house had faded into the past, further building work costing $20,000 will be evaluated on its own and will be psychologically more painful. Thaler (1999) points out that the extent to which a cost is psychologically linked to a benefit can vary. When people pay a fixed cost for a service, irrespective of their amount of use, usage is decoupled from the payment since any extra use is free. Another decoupling occurs when a credit card is used. This postpones payment and also aggregates costs into one bill which reduces the total psychological cost compared with the sum of several smaller separate costs.

Probability

What are your answers to Exercise 8.4?

Exercise 8.4 The Allais paradox (Allais, 1953)

Allais asked one group of subjects to choose between the two options:

- A: $4,000 with a probability of 0.8; otherwise nothing.
- B: $3,000 for certain.

Which do you prefer?

Another group were asked to choose between:

- C: $4,000 with a probability of 0.2; otherwise nothing.
- D: $3,000 with a probability of 0.25; otherwise nothing.

Which do you prefer?

Faced with the choices in Exercise 8.4, Allais found that 80 per cent of respondents preferred option B to A but 65 per cent preferred option C to D. This seems paradoxical because the ratio of the probabilities is the same in each choice pair. One explanation for this pattern is that probability is weighted as it is converted to subjective probability. Figure 8.2 shows how the weighting of objective probability reduces the subjective impact of high probabilities and increases the impact of low probabilities. The *x*-axis is objective probability and the *y*-axis is the weighted outcome. Applied to the data in Exercise 8.4, the weighting reduces the appeal of A and increases the appeal of C.

No mathematical expression has been given for the probability weighting function; it is determined empirically. One partial explanation for the effect is that a rule of diminishing sensitivity with distance from a reference point applies. The probability function has two natural reference points, 0 and 1; the weights, or relative differences between subjective and objective probability, initially increase with distance from these anchors. However, as these relative differences are in opposite directions, they must come together again somewhere in the central area.

The weighting of small objective probabilities fits the evidence that people are positive about insurance and like to place long-odds bets. Above an objective probability of 0.40, the weighting depresses subjective probability so that risks are subjectively discounted; for example, a 50 per cent probability is nearer to 40 per cent, subjectively. At the extremes,

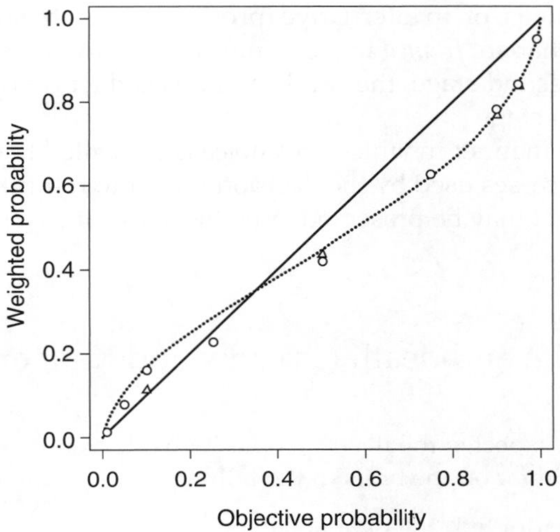

Figure 8.2 The probability function (from Kahneman and Tversky, 2000)

the weighting is unstable; a one in a thousand chance may be dismissed as no chance or taken seriously (bettors on national lotteries accept very long odds).

The sensitivity near the reference point (0, 1) is illustrated by Exercise 8.5.

Exercise 8.5 Risk preferences

Suppose that you have a 99 per cent chance of getting $1,000. How much would you pay to move that probability to certainty?

Suppose that you have a 50 per cent chance of getting $1,000. How much would you pay to move that probability to 51 per cent?

Suppose that you have 0 per cent chance of getting $1,000. How much would you pay to move that probability to 1 per cent?

Most people will pay more in the 0 per cent and 99 per cent conditions for a one per cent increment in probability but the long-run benefit of a one-per-cent gain in probability is the same at any point on the probability range.

Prospect Theory

Kahneman and Tversky (1979) and Tversky and Kahneman (1992) incorporate the subjective conversion of value and probability into a theory of choice called prospect theory, and they propose that the choice of an alternative (prospect) is established in two stages. In the first stage, the choices that are *framed* in a communication are restructured or *edited* by the receiver. Then, in the second stage, the receiver chooses the best option based on the values assessed in the first stage.

Framing refers to the manner in which the choice is presented to the decision-maker, and editing refers to the processes used by the decision-maker to rethink the choice. In framing, an alternative or prospect may be presented either as a loss or as a gain, as in Exercise 8.6.

Exercise 8.6 Life and death (Tversky and Kahneman, 1981: 453)

An unusual disease is expected to kill 600 people. Two interventions are proposed. Which intervention do you prefer on the basis of the following information?

- If programme A is adopted, 200 people will be saved.
- If programme B is adopted, there is ⅓ probability that 600 people will be saved and ⅔ probability that no people will be saved.

When you have decided, consider how you would react to these alternatives:

- If programme C is adopted, 400 people will die.
- If programme D is adopted, there is ⅓ probability that no one will die and ⅔ probability that 600 people will die.

The second pair of alternatives in Exercise 8.6 is the same as the first (A = C, B = D). Yet Tversky and Kahneman found that 72 per cent preferred programme A to B and 78 per cent preferred programme D to C. By framing the problem in terms of the gains (lives saved), it is possible to steer preference to the risk-averse option, A, rather than B. In the second-choice pair, the framing in terms of lives lost makes people risk prone, and steers them to option D. Using the appropriate frame is clearly a 'must' for anyone in the field of persuasive communication.

Thaler (1985) suggests some interesting implications of framing for those presenting gains and losses to others. Losses are best presented in aggregate, to minimize their impact, and gains are best presented singly to maximize their effect. It may also be better to offset some losses against gains because, separately, losses have more impact than gains. Framing effects seem to apply to the presentation of discounts. A saving of $10 on a $50 item may be presented as such or as a 20 per cent discount. When the percentage discount is small it may be best to present it as an absolute cost reduction.

In the editing phase of decision-making, complex choices may be simplified. Thus a person may see the price of a car not as $20,000, but as $2,000 less than he or she expected to pay; another edit by the prospective buyer may be to aggregate the cost of extra features with the basic price so that there is a single purchase price.

Box 8.3 Overpaid?

The way bond traders are paid may help them to get very high remuneration. Bond dealers typically work on commissions that are very low percentages. A commission of 0.1 per cent does not seem much. However, if it is based on a principal of $100 million, it is $100,000. In general, people assess costs in proportional terms and will take more trouble to save $5 off a $20 item than $5 off a $100 item.

In negotiation, our editing processes may lead us into a poor deal and we should beware of the way the other side frames choices. It is wise to focus on the total cost of a deal. Give way on small items but resist concessions on the larger ones. It could even be worthwhile to include small items in a proposal so that you can concede them later.

Thaler (1999) introduced the term *mental accounting*, which covers some of these editing functions. This uses the metaphor of accounting to explain the way in which people organize, evaluate and keep track of financial activities. As in accounting proper, people maintain separate accounts for different activities; for example they may accept the idea of flying business class to Australia at an extra cost of $6,000 but find it difficult to justify spending $6,000 to save two days' discomfort in another area of their life. Also people may close an account after a defined period; gamblers on the race track tend to think of gains or losses over a day and investors in the stock market may operate with a one-year horizon.

Box 8.4 The Nudge Unit

Thaler and Sunstein (2008) have written a popular book called *Nudge* in which they argue that national administration can be much more effective if it incorporates the known findings from mental accounting and other psychological research. They focus on activities such as paying taxes, investing in pensions and securing organ donation. These ideas have caught the interest of governments. In the UK, the Cabinet Office is advised by a 'Nudge Unit' which claims to have saved substantial sums of money by simple changes such as the redrafting of letters to tax payers.

SECTION 4: FINANCIAL APPLICATIONS OF PROSPECT THEORY

Prospect theory provides explanations for some puzzling behaviour. We now provide several examples of its explanatory power, drawing on a review by Camerer (2000).

Investment

One of the effects of loss aversion is that people tend to hang on to losers and sell winners in share markets. Investors may have some equilibrium concept in mind, believing that the swing of the pendulum will take a losing stock back towards its purchase price and that a rising stock could similarly fall. They may also be reluctant to sell a losing stock because this turns a potential loss into an actual loss, so that it is more painful. From a rational standpoint, the buying price is sunk cost and should not figure in the decision to sell shares, except for calculating capital gains tax. The selection of an alternative to sell should be based on prospective return, based on the current valuation of the share.

A bias in favour of selling winners and keeping losers has been demonstrated experimentally by Weber and Camerer (1998) and in real data by Odean (1998). Such behaviour appears to be a mistake since Odean estimated that investors lost an average of 3.4 per cent in the subsequent year compared with selling losers and keeping winners. However, this behaviour by investors may contribute to the effective operation of share markets. These markets are potentially unstable since a loss of confidence can precipitate selling, which may further aggravate the loss of confidence and lead to a collapse of the market. In practice, panic selling on a large scale is rare and markets show corrections but do not usually collapse. If the market has fallen, many investors will bide their time and refuse to sell. There seems to be evidence that market professionals are much more willing to realize a loss (see Box 8.4). They may operate with a momentum rather than an equilibrium concept of the market. Computerized share trading may lead to more market instability if it circumvents the effects of loss aversion.

Box 8.5 'Mutual-fund pros panicked in peso crisis while small investors stood their ground' (Headline in the *Wall Street Journal*, 13 January 1995)

Among share-trading professionals the folklore is to stay in a rising market and sell when it turns. Loss aversion suggests that small investors might find this difficult. In particular, once they see that the market has fallen, and that they have made a loss by reference to recent prices, they may resist selling because now they are risk prone. Also, by selling, they close the account so that the potential loss becomes a real loss. The headline above suggests that ordinary investors follow loss aversion but that the professionals have learned to reverse it.

The Equity Premium

Equities have traditionally provided a greater return on investments than fixed interest investments (bonds). Sometimes bonds give a return that is little better than inflation, while equities have given an average return in the USA of about 10 per cent over the period

1926–2003 and 9.6 per cent in the UK over the period 1900–2003 (Dimson, Marsh and Staunton, 2004). Traditionally, the equity premium has been explained as a compensation for the greater risk associated with equities but an alternative explanation has been offered by Benartzi and Thaler (1995). A feature of equity markets is that they rise and fall in market value much more than bond markets. Investors who look at their equity investment a month after purchase are about equally likely to see a gain or a loss compared with the purchase price but, after ten years, there is nearly always a gain. Since losses loom larger than gains (the ratio of the dis-attraction of losses to the attraction of gains is about 2.25), an investor with a short-term horizon will suffer more pain from the losses and may be put off from investing in equities. Benartzi and Thaler therefore explain the equity premium as the additional return required to compensate for the loss aversion effect. This explanation would be still more convincing if there were evidence that those investors with longer-term horizons held a greater proportion of their portfolios in equities rather than bonds.

Long-Shot Bias and the Value Premium

As noted, when the probabilities are low, the psychological weighting of probability makes long odds more attractive. This seems to operate in betting. In racetrack betting there is a tendency to back outsiders or long shots – horses with high odds that are unlikely to win. This may reflect the overweighting of small probabilities. Bookmakers tend to offset risk so that disproportionate betting on outsiders will tend to reduce the odds on these horses and raise the odds on favourites. The result is that, in the long run, long shots do worse than favourites. This effect becomes more pronounced over the course of the day as bettors lose money. Their mental accounting period is a day and, in order to end up 'in the money', they increasingly need to win on a long shot, so still more money goes on such horses. Under these circumstances, an each way bet on the favourite for the last race will make money, on average, even allowing for a 15 per cent tax on winnings (Ali, 1977). If you want to test this out yourselves, when visiting the racetrack it is best to place the bet on the Tote which compensates for weight of betting more effectively.

Long-shot bias, or something rather similar, may lie behind the persistent value premium effect in share investment. Value or income stocks typically give fairly high dividends and sell at prices that are rather lower than is justified by their fundamentals. Value stocks are contrasted with growth stocks that pay low dividends. With growth stocks, investors forgo current income and hope for more rapid growth. By analogy, the growth stock is rather like a long shot and some companies like Google and Apple emerge to give spectacular results. However, the fundamentals are just that and Dimson, Marsh and Staunton (2004) find that, in the long run, value stocks give a distinctly better performance and show a premium of about 3 per cent over growth stocks. This effect is transnational. In a comparison of 14 countries, only one country (Italy) showed a superior return from growth stocks.

Impact on Economics

Economics is founded on rational assumptions. These include an assumption that the accumulation of wealth drives individual behaviour and that alternatives should be assessed against this wealth criterion. However, it is apparent that individuals do not think about their wealth but instead about gains and losses relative to norms defined by the context. Furthermore, they operate with a number of accounts so that a gain in one is not necessarily offset (in their minds) by a loss in another. This pattern of behaviour violates the principle of fungibility, that money in one account is as good as money in another account. Also, it is possible to construct choices where preferences violate the principle of dominance. People may prefer A to B and B to C, but C to A.

Thus, people do not think according to the canons of economic logic, and traditional economics has been severely challenged by prospect theory. Previously, economists have argued that wealth will increase most rapidly if people act rationally and money is fungible. This is a normative theory. They claim that those who do not apply normative economic principles will lose out, so that self-interest or reinforcement will direct behaviour towards a rational pattern. Thus, actual economic behaviour will be driven towards the rational pattern. But if people do not act rationally, normative economics needs to take this into account. The most rational policy is to anticipate the irrationality of others and adapt to it. Therefore, a study of everyday decision-making is needed so that the rational person (or policy-maker) can exploit the systematic biases in the choices of others.

Problems with Prospect Theory

The possibility of using prospect theory to explain behaviour, choose profitably and negotiate successfully has seized the imagination of researchers but the potential may be reduced when the theory is more widely evaluated. Van der Plight and van Schie (1990) gathered evidence on risk aversion and risk proneness among European populations. Their work confirmed Kahneman and Tversky's findings, but the effects were less strong. In addition, Leclerc, Schmitt and Dubé (1995) find that people making decisions under risk were often risk averse about time loss when, according to prospect theory, they should be risk prone.

Many of the studies on prospect theory have used hypothetical and rather artificial examples. In these studies, the judgement of the majority has been used to decide response and it would be interesting to know more about those people who do not fit the model. However, there is plenty of field evidence which supports the theory though, often, only after *ad hoc* assumptions have been made about the mental accounting period and the separation of accounts.

The more fundamental problem with prospect theory is the lack of an underlying rationale that could relate the different phenomena that are reported. Why do losses loom larger than gains? Why do costs affect consumers less than other losses? Why is time different from money in terms of loss aversion? What we have in prospect theory is an accumulation of important findings but no fundamental explanation. One possibility is that the effects we see are related to the relative frequency of different types of occurrence. We have seen that frequency affects availability but it may have a wider relevance. If there are generally more positive than negative events, reference points will tend to be based on the positives. As a result, negative outcomes are more at variance with assumptions and are therefore more disturbing. This is the explanation offered by Fiske (1980) for the greater impact of negative information (considered in Chapter 11). However, more research is required before this provides a coherent explanation.

SUMMARY

This chapter is about the automatic mechanisms involved in recognizing, evaluating, judging, investigating and deciding. One process that seems to underlie a person's thought processes is the use of schemas – cognitive structures that are fitted to information to make sense of it. When the fit is poor, people may give more attention to the stimulus until a fit is achieved. Repeated exposure of a stimulus that is initially obscure often leads to increases in the evaluation of that stimulus.

The evaluative response to stimuli is often faster than the cognitive response and these evaluative responses, in the initial stages at least, seem to involve relatively independent processing. When we make choices, attention is related to the evaluation of alternatives.

When making judgements, people use simplifying processes called heuristics. They make more use of information that is more available – that is discrete, eventful, recent or established through personal experience – and they tend to neglect information dealing with persisting conditions. More available information is also given higher probability.

We convert objective value and probability into subjective forms. The effect of this is that people are risk averse on gains and risk prone on losses at medium and high probabilities. The value function is steeper in the negative region. This gives rise to loss aversion and makes people more reluctant to part with things that they own.

The way choices are presented (framed) and the information processing of receivers (editing) affect the way in which decisions are made. If the framing is manipulated, people can be pushed towards particular alternatives. People tend to think in terms of different accounts which may be closed after different periods. Thus, mental accounting, loss aversion and risk tolerance will affect the evaluation of prospects.

These processes produce effects that are contrary to axioms in economics but they help to explain a number of puzzles. These include the preference for selling winning rather than losing shares, reluctance to fully invest in shares as opposed to bonds, and a tendency to buy growth shares rather than income shares.

Additional Resources

In 2002, Kahneman was awarded the Nobel Prize for economics – no mean achievement for a psychologist. The lecture that he gave at the time is available at: http://nobelprize.org/nobel_prizes/economics/laureates/2002/kahneman-lecture.html.

Much of the work referenced here has come from two volumes edited by Kahneman, Slovic and Tversky (1982) and Kahneman and Tversky (2000). In particular, read Thaler (1999) 'Mental accounting matters' (reprinted in Kahneman and Tversky, 2000: 241–260). Kahneman (2012) has incorporated many of the findings from this research stream in his book *Thinking Fast and Thinking Slow.* This book brings out the practical implications for decision-making and national policy in a thoughtful and accessible way.

9 Consumer Satisfaction and Quality

LEARNING OBJECTIVES

When you have completed this chapter, you should be able to:

1. Describe theories of consumer satisfaction/dissatisfaction (CSD).
2. Measure customer satisfaction and service quality.
3. Know the evidence on the relationship between satisfaction and company profit.
4. Understand research on consumer complaining behaviour (CCB).
5. Report on research on how consumers respond to service delay.

OVERVIEW

In the USA, Hunt and Day set up the first conference on consumer satisfaction in 1976 and work in this field grew rapidly. In 1993, Perkins noted over 3,000 academic references relating to this area. In Europe, consumer satisfaction and dissatisfaction (CSD) has received rather less emphasis than in the USA and, starting with the work of Grönroos (1978), the focus has been more on the perception of quality, particularly with regard to services. Customer satisfaction often depends on the quality of goods and services and, therefore, CSD research is closely associated with quality research. The measurement of quality has been developed in the USA by Parasuraman and his colleagues but this work has been widely criticized. This chapter reviews the field, describes measurement of satisfaction and quality, examines theories of CSD, reports research linking satisfaction and company profit, and sets out evidence on complaining behaviour. This chapter relates to work on the effects of CSD on customer retention/defection described in Chapter 2.

SECTION 1: INTRODUCTION

It is not a surprise that customers are sometimes dissatisfied with products or services that they have purchased. However, quantifying this dissatisfaction and comparing levels of satisfaction reliably across different product categories or in different countries has not always been straightforward. Andreasen (1988) quoted a general figure of 15–25 per cent dissatisfaction across a range of goods and services in the USA; Stø and Glefjell (1990) found similar figures for a range of goods and services in Norway. Peterson and Wilson (1992), who reviewed this topic, found lower levels of dissatisfaction; for example, 83 per cent were satisfied, with the remainder divided between neutrality and dissatisfaction. This suggests that, roughly, there is one dissatisfied customer for every ten that are satisfied.

Much of the work on consumer satisfaction and dissatisfaction has focused on services. Maintaining the quality of a service is difficult because of the nature of services. A service is consumed as it is produced and any mistake by the provider becomes part of the service delivered. In contrast, mistakes in the production of goods can often be corrected before sale. Quality is usually raised by uniformity in goods but attempts to make services uniform can be counter-productive. Service providers need to adapt to the needs of the customer and what suits one person may not suit another; for this reason, service standardization can produce a rather formulaic interchange with customers, which may not meet their requirements. Getting services right is important because they constitute an increasingly large fraction of modern economies. In most OECD countries, services accounted for more than 70 per cent of GDP (OECD, 2000); the European Service Forum reported 71 per cent in 2007, indicating little change. Given the greater difficulty in delivering services, it is likely that these will cause more problems than goods and, in a study conducted by Technical Assistance Research Programs (TARP, 1979), unsatisfactory service quality was responsible for most of the complaints reported (see Table 9.1).

There are several reasons for an interest in satisfaction and quality. People like to deliver something that is appreciated but it also pays to deliver quality. Buzzell and Gale (1987) showed that when a firm's quality was high, profit margins were larger and firms could grow more easily. Reichheld (1996b) and others have argued that it costs less to retain existing customers than to gain new ones, and that quality helps to retain customers (Chapter 2). Brand extensions are likely to be more successful when the brand has higher perceived quality (Chapter 3). Thus, those who deliver a lower quality than their competitors may lose market share (see Box 9.1). Hirschman (1970) suggested that unsatisfactory delivery of goods and services led to two types of consumer response, which he described succinctly as *exit* and *voice*. Exit is switching to other products or suppliers. Voice has a number of forms: complaining to suppliers and seeking redress, negative word of mouth to other consumers and, occasionally, formal complaints through legal or trade authorities. In Chapter 2, we noted that dissatisfaction is related to defection. However,

Table 9.1 Reasons for complaint (TARP, 1979)

Problem	*Households reporting a problem (%)*
Unsatisfactory repair or service	36
Store did not have advertised product for sale	25
Unsatisfactory product quality	22
Long wait for delivery	10
Failure to receive delivery	10

although repurchase intentions are much reduced by dissatisfaction, Oliver (1980), Oliver and Swan (1989), Feinberg et al. (1990) and Fornell (1992) find that many consumers are reluctant to change. For example, Feinberg et al. (1990) found that, after an unsatisfactory warranty repair, repurchase intentions for different goods were still 47–84 per cent compared with more than 90 per cent repurchase intention when the repair was satisfactory. Often, it is not feasible to change a supplier; sometimes the product is satisfactory in other respects and there may be substantial switching costs.

Box 9.1 Quality in all things (abridged from *The Guardian*, 11 August 1993)

Heidi Fleiss, accused of running an expensive call-girl circuit for the elite of Hollywood, rebutted criticism from Madam Alex, the previous leader of the circuit, who claimed that she had stolen her clients. 'In this business', Heidi Fleiss is reputed to have said, 'no one steals clients. There is just better service.'

SECTION 2: THEORIES OF CONSUMER SATISFACTION

The Confirmation Model

Early thinking about satisfaction treated it as meeting consumer expectations. This is the *confirmation model* of consumer satisfaction which is illustrated in Figure 9.1. Oliver (1989) described the outcome as *contentment*; for example, we are contented when a refrigerator continues to keep food cold. This low arousal state is matched by low-arousal *discontent* when negative expectations are met. Such discontent applies to the routine use of inadequate services, such as congested roads, late buses and long queues at airport security, and to unsatisfactory products such as dripping taps, lumpy mattresses and toasters that eject the toast prematurely. In these situations, the discontent is subdued because of habituation. People get used to a problem and no longer notice it. As a result, it does not occur to them to do anything about it and any effect on behaviour is weak (shown as a dotted line in Figure 9.1). Consumer contentment and discontent may not be expressed but are revealed when people are questioned, or when other factors raise the salience of a product's performance; for example, others may comment on the dripping tap or an ad for beds may make people think of their own bedtime discomfort.

The toleration of product deficiencies is explained by adaptation theory (Helson, 1964). In this theory, perceptions are relative to some standard which itself is a function of all previously experienced outcomes. As long as positive and negative deviations from expectation are small, they will be accommodated and will have little effect on thinking and behaviour.

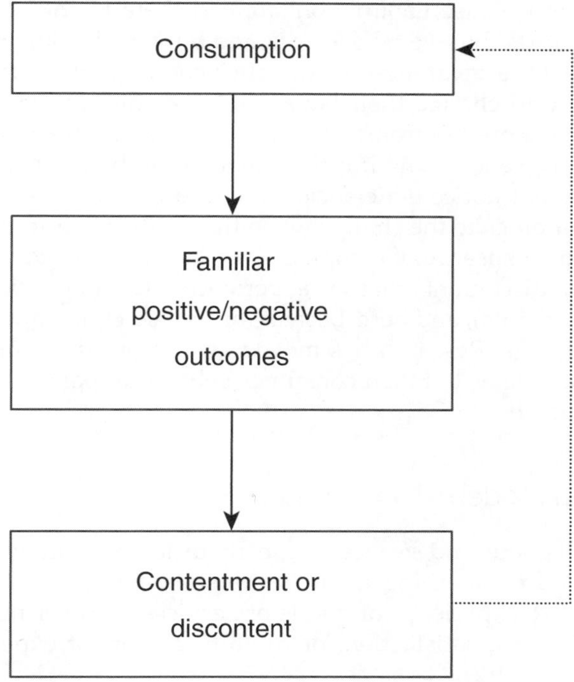

Figure 9.1 The confirmation model of consumer satisfaction: meeting expectations

Exercise 9.1 Recognizing dissatisfactions

Think of everyday products that you use, for example, refrigerators, shoes and clothing. Are these satisfactory? If you look at these products with a more critical eye, are there weaknesses that could be corrected? Does your refrigerator ice up or fail to drain condensation? Are your shoes too worn? Are you using clothes sizes (bras, collars, etc.) that are no longer appropriate? Such generally unrecognized problems often occur because what was once satisfactory has slowly become less so – too slowly to be noticed. What should advertisers do to draw your attention to the needs that you have not recognized yourself?

Some problems persist for a long time before a solution is found. Many of these solutions could have been invented earlier; what is often missing is the idea, rather than new technology. Consider the wheels on luggage which are now so common. These could have been produced years before they became common. Often, people may not have had the idea for the innovation because habituation stopped them from recognizing a problem. Can you think of products that we take for granted but which could be made better?

If consumers have little awareness of the shortcomings of everyday products, they will feel little pressure to change their behaviour and this can be a matter of concern. Our tendency to adjust to our environment may be to our disadvantage. When poor products are frequently experienced, any improvement would be frequently experienced too. Although people may not notice deficiencies in currently used goods and services, they may well notice and appreciate the change when the product is improved; thus, it is a pity if habituation leads to an absence of complaint or a lack of effort to find a better product. However, many of the discontents that we experience relate to public services (e.g. transport and parking constraints), and here, because of limited choice and influence, it may be difficult to achieve change. Research has moved away from the confirmation model but we can see this model relates to much consumer behaviour, particularly the toleration of delay, which is considered later.

The Disconfirmation Model

If our experience with goods and services is greatly different from what we expect, we are usually motivated to do something about it. Most research has focused on this high arousal condition where experience of goods or services disconfirms expectation, either by exceeding it and giving satisfaction, or by falling short of expectation and causing dissatisfaction (see Figure 9.2).

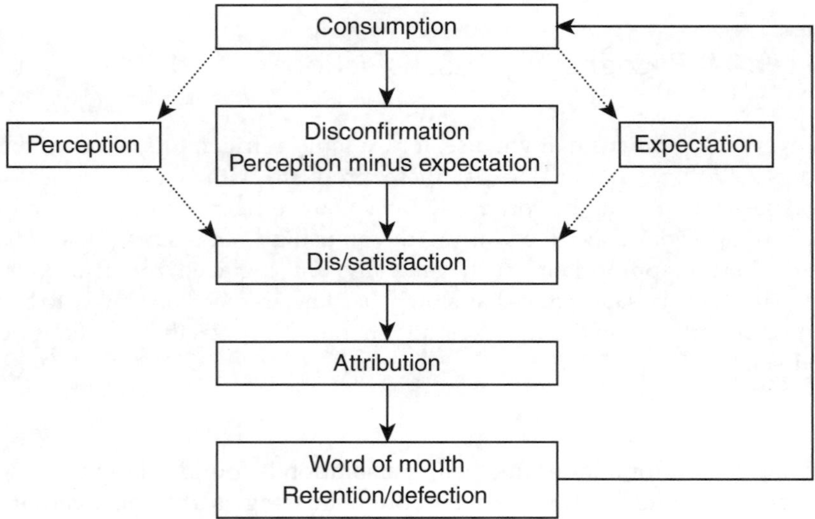

Figure 9.2 The disconfirmation model: exceeding or falling short of expectations

In the disconfirmation model the consumer is surprised by product features that are better or worse than expected.[1] The magnitude of surprise is related to the size of the discrepancy between expectation and experience. Two additional determinants are shown in Figure 9.2 – we show these with dotted lines because they are not part of the core disconfirmation model. The perception of the performance of the goods or services affects satisfaction directly; the better it is, the more we like it. Expectation also has a direct effect. There is variation in the emphasis placed on the different factors affecting satisfaction. Some researchers (e.g. Oliver, 1980, 1981; Swan and Trawick, 1981) have emphasized expectations, while others (e.g. Churchill and Surprenant, 1982; LaTour and Peat, 1979; Tse and Wilton, 1988) have given attention to perceptions. Several studies (e.g. Oliver, 1980; Swan and Trawick, 1980) found that satisfaction is influenced mainly by disconfirmation. At odds with these results, Churchill and Surprenant (1982) found that satisfaction with a video disc player was determined by perceived product performance, and any disconfirmation had no additional impact on satisfaction. It is quite likely that the relative importance of the different components of the model depends on the category.

The disconfirmation explanation of satisfaction has gradually evolved. Cardozo's (1965) laboratory work is often cited as the first empirical treatment of disconfirmed expectation and Howard and Sheth (1969: 145) were among the first to suggest that people use standards of assessment in judging products when they wrote that satisfaction was 'the buyer's cognitive state of being adequately or inadequately rewarded for the sacrifice he has undergone'. Oliver suggests that the emotion felt from disconfirmation of expectations decays into the attitude to the product:

> ... the summary psychological state resulting when the emotion surrounding disconfirmed expectations is coupled with the consumer's prior feelings about the consumption experience. Moreover, the surprise or excitement of this evaluation is thought to be of finite duration, so that satisfaction soon decays into (but nevertheless greatly affects) one's overall attitude toward purchasing products. (Oliver, 1981: 34)

Attribution

Disconfirmations may be interpreted in different ways by consumers. The model in Figure 9.2 therefore has an *attribution* stage where a causal explanation is developed in reaction to the product experience that generated the dis/satisfaction. This attribution will affect later behaviour by the consumer. When consumers explain a positive experience as a chance effect, they are unlikely to recommend the product but if a negative experience is attributed to neglect by the service provider, negative word of mouth and complaint to the provider may ensue. Burns and Perkins (1996) cover a wide range of possible responses in such situations. The attribution that consumers make may be affected by other conditions and, in particular, the *availability of explanations* and types of *causal inferences* have been studied. Exercise 9.2 relates to attribution.

Sometimes subtle cues can change the attribution that is made and therefore influence the satisfaction with a consumption experience. Pham, Goukens, Lehmann and Stuart

(2010) show that the presence of mirrors increases the likelihood that consumers attribute service outcomes to themselves, rather than to the service provider. As a result, unfavourable outcomes create less expressed dissatisfaction. The downside of the phenomenon is that favourable outcomes also lead to less expressed satisfaction. Self-awareness is the key driving factor here: cues that increase self-awareness (e.g. the small talk of a sales person centred on the customer) make self-attributions more likely. The effect is shown both in experimental scenarios in a lab setting and in real-life shopping situations. Interestingly, it also operates for the evaluation of past experiences. A limiting condition is that consumers have to bear some responsibility for the negative outcome (e.g. returning or exchanging previously purchased items).

Exercise 9.2 Your experience

The apparently fresh Brie is acrid, the new vacuum cleaner blocks or the waiter in an expensive restaurant is unhelpful; here the dissatisfactions arise because we expected a better experience. Conversely, we may be pleasantly surprised and satisfied when expectations are surpassed, e.g. when the roads are unusually clear, the fruit in supermarkets is ripe or the plane arrives early.

Think back to the last time you were surprised by your experience as a consumer. Did the surprise make you satisfied, dissatisfied or neither? How would you explain what happened? Who was responsible?

Availability

According to the availability heuristic, vivid events are more easily brought to mind than routine occurrences and, in addition, these vivid events are judged more probable than they are in reality (see Chapter 8). Folkes (1988) gives an interesting example of how this can work. She asked people who were approaching the escalators to their apartment in a six-storey building how often the escalators broke down. The escalators only went to the fourth floor so that those who lived on the fifth and sixth floors always had to climb the stairs for the last part of their ascent. Those who always had to use the stairs for part of their journey estimated that the escalators broke down *less* often than the people who used the first four floors, for whom an escalator failure (leading to the unusual event of climbing the stairs) was more vivid. The distinctiveness of a product failure raises its vividness, and the availability heuristic raises the *perceived* likelihood that it will occur again (chapter 8). This, in turn, raises dissatisfaction. The supplier should, therefore, try to make failures less distinctive. For example, if customers are occupied in some way when service quality is reduced, they may form a less distinct memory of the poor performance.

Worse-than-expected outcomes have more impact than better-than-expected outcomes (DeSarbo et al., 1994). This difference could be explained as an example of losses looming larger than gains (Chapter 8).

Causal Inferences

Weiner (1980, 1990) has examined the explanations given for success and failure and has suggested three causal dimensions that are relevant to consumer response: *stability, locus of causality* and *controllability*. Stability occurs when the cause can be consistently attributed to a particular person or feature of the environment; locus of causality relates to whether the purchaser, the supplier or some other party is seen to be at fault; and controllability reflects the ability of an agent to intervene and change outcomes. An unstable negative event may not trigger negative attributions by consumers; for example, an out-of-stock item may be seen as exceptional (unstable) and unlikely to be repeated. It is, therefore, better for a seller if the cause of their failure is seen as unstable by the customer. By contrast, it is better to have stability in product success since this encourages continued usage. Folkes (1984) suggests that, when failure is perceived to be stable, a consumer will prefer to have a refund for a product failure since a replacement carries the same risk as the original; if the failure is seen as unstable, consumers will be more willing to accept a replacement. Stability may vary across customer segments. Bolton (1998) examined defection from the service supplier as a consequence of the failure of a mobile phone network. If the customer was long-term, the failure was offset against past good performance and seen as unstable, so the customer was disinclined to defect. Recent customers who lacked this experience were more likely to see the failure as stable, blame the supplier, and defect.

Weiner's other dimensions also affect consumer response after product failure. For example, with respect to locus of causality, customers may blame themselves when they purchase a poor product, and therefore expect no redress; but if they see the failure as the responsibility of the manufacturer or retailer, they may then expect a replacement or refund. If people feel that they have no control over their outcomes, they may feel anger towards those whom they think do have control, for example when public transport services are inadequate.

Exercise 9.3 Managing satisfaction

Understanding the implications of research findings on CSD can help us create better goods and services and to manage the process better when things go wrong. Create a scenario in which a major service failure is occurring and you are managing the service.

What are you going to say to customers? Consider the attributions they will make and the response they will want. What are the customer expectations and how can you manage these so that the failure is more acceptable? What compensation should you give, if any?

SECTION 3: MEASURING SATISFACTION AND SERVICE QUALITY

Satisfaction

Satisfaction with a product is experienced by a customer or ex-customer. In this respect, it is more restricted than the attitude to the product and assessments of quality, which may be given by anyone, customer or not. However, satisfaction with the product is an attitude; people are satisfied for reasons that can be measured, as reported in Chapter 7, and they will give an overall satisfaction like the global attitude described in the theory of planned behaviour. This overall satisfaction can be measured by a question such as:

Considering your main supermarket, would you say you are:

Very satisfied [7]
Quite satisfied [6]
Slightly satisfied [5]
Neither satisfied nor dissatisfied [4]
Slightly dissatisfied [3]
Quite dissatisfied [2]
Very dissatisfied [1].

However, as we saw in Chapter 2, if we are trying to predict what people will do, a relative measure is better because it indicates the advantage of one product over another. Once relativity is admitted, we have a choice of comparators. In the American Customer Satisfaction Index (ACSI, www.theacsi.org), Fornell, Johnson and Anderson (1996) use three questions about recently purchased brands that relate to overall satisfaction, expectancy disconfirmation and perceived performance compared with ideal performance (see Box 9.2).

Box 9.2 The American Consumer Satisfaction Items

1 Please consider all your experiences to date with your main supermarket. Using a ten-point scale on which '1' means "very dissatisfied" and "10" means "very satisfied", how satisfied or dissatisfied are you with your supermarket overall?

Write in number (1 to 10) ....

2 To what extent has your main supermarket fallen short of your expectations or exceeded your expectations? Using a ten-point scale on which "1" now means "falls short of your expectations" and "10" means "exceeds your expectations", to what extent has your supermarket fallen short of or exceeded your expectations?

Write in number (1 to 10) ....

3 Forget your main supermarket for the moment. Now imagine an ideal supermarket. How well do you think your supermarket compares with that ideal supermarket? Please use a ten point scale on which "1" means "not very close to the ideal" and "10" means "very close to the ideal".

Write in number (1 to 10) ....

Here, the latter two items are relative to two different comparators. For practical purposes, the ACSI is the average of responses to the three items, though Fornell and his associates use different weights for specific predictions. When a firm markets several brands, a composite ACSI score for the firm can be derived from the scores for each brand. The ACSI items are part of a larger set of questions that cover complaints, loyalty, expectations, value and quality.

There has been less research emphasis on the components of satisfaction – the specific reasons why a product is liked or disliked. We can measure this using the methods of the theory of planned behaviour discussed in Chapter 7, treating satisfaction as a reaction to a bundle of costs and benefits. Westbrook (1980) tested this approach. He examined the way in which customers combined the dis/satisfactions relating to a store and found that a global measure of retail satisfaction correlated well with a simple addition of the satisfactions and dissatisfactions customers felt about different aspects of store service.

Quality

Whereas satisfaction measures focus on the global attitude, quality measures tend to give more attention to the reasons why a product is high quality. The field of service quality measurement has been dominated by an instrument called SERVQUAL, designed to assess any service using one standard set of questions. It was developed by Parasuraman, Zeithaml and Berry (1985, 1988). SERVQUAL measures customers' expectations of what firms should provide in the industry being studied and their perceptions of how a given service provider performs against these criteria. The 1988 version of the instrument contained 22 expectation questions covering such specific service facilities as up-to-date equipment, visually appealing premises and polite employees. In 1991, Parasuraman, Berry and Zeithaml modified the instrument slightly. They changed two items and altered the wordings of some others; the negative scoring on some items was removed and the wording of the expectation measures was changed so that respondents were asked what an 'excellent service would provide', rather than what 'firms in the industry should provide'. Box 9.3 shows the expectation items in the 1991 scale, applied to telephone companies. A second set of questions (not shown) would deal with the perceptions about a specific telephone company.

Parasuraman, Zeithaml and Berry (1988) showed that these 22 items could be allocated to five dimensions – tangibles, reliability, responsiveness, assurance (knowledge and courtesy of employees and their ability to inspire trust and confidence) and empathy (caring and individual attention to customers). However, the five-factor structure has not been well supported; Cronin and Taylor (1992) found only one general factor.

The idea that SERVQUAL will apply to a variety of services without much modification has also been contested. Carman (1990) found that some functions require additional measures for adequate explanation. Koelemeijer (1992) and Finn and Lamb (1991) found that the SERVQUAL instrument performed poorly in retail contexts. Dabholkar, Thorpe and Rentz (1996) developed a scale for retail quality measurement which customized the measure to the retail context. It is easy to argue that some of the items are inappropriate for certain services, e.g. religious services having modern-looking equipment or neat appearance in academic settings. Thus, customization of SERVQUAL seems to be required

Box 9.3 SERVQUAL expectation components and classification (from Parasuraman, Berry and Zeithaml, 1991: 446–447)

Tangibles

1 Excellent telephone companies will have modern-looking equipment.
2 The physical facilities at excellent telephone companies will be visually appealing.
3 Employees of excellent telephone companies will be neat-appearing. [Did they really say this? Or is it neat in appearance?]
4 Materials associated with the service (such as pamphlets or statements) will be visually appealing in an excellent telephone company.

Reliability

5 When excellent telephone companies promise to do something by a certain time, they will do so.
6 When customers have a problem, excellent telephone companies will show a sincere interest in solving it.
7 Excellent telephone companies will perform the service right first time.
8 Excellent telephone companies will provide their services at the time they promise to do so.
9 Excellent telephone companies will keep error-free records.

Responsiveness

10 Employees of excellent telephone companies will tell customers exactly when services will be performed.
11 Employees of excellent telephone companies give prompt service to customers.
12 Employees of excellent telephone companies will always be willing to help customers.
13 Employees of excellent telephone companies will never be too busy to respond to customer requests.

Assurance

14 The behaviour of employees of excellent telephone companies will instil confidence in customers.
15 Customers of excellent telephone companies will feel safe in their transactions.
16 Employees of excellent telephone companies will be consistently courteous with customers.
17 Employees of excellent telephone companies will have the knowledge to answer customer questions.

Empathy

18 Excellent telephone companies will give customers individual attention.
19 Excellent telephone companies will have operating hours convenient to all their customers.
20 Excellent telephone companies will have employees who give customers personal attention.
21 Excellent telephone companies will have the customers' best interests at heart.
22 The employees of excellent telephone companies will understand the specific needs of their customers.

for application to different services and, although Parasuraman, Zeithaml and Berry (1994) accepted this, the changes in questions may need to be substantial.

The computation of quality judgement from the questionnaire responses has also raised problems. SERVQUAL uses the difference scores between expectation and perception but expectations tend to be uniformly high and show little variance. Although the difference measures correlate reasonably well with an overall measure of quality (Babacus and Boller, 1992; Cronin and Taylor, 1992; Parasuraman, Berry and Zeithaml, 1991), the low variance in the expectation measures makes these irrelevant to the score so that perception-only scores are equally predictive. For this reason, Cronin and Taylor (1992) recommended that the measure be restricted to performance perceptions (which they call SERVPERF), giving a questionnaire of half the length. An alternative to this is to measure the gap between expectation and perceived performance with a single question that combines the two elements. Babacus and Boller (1992) suggested a way of phrasing this and Box 9.4 shows the binary form and the combined measure. In a review of SERVQUAL's history, Smith (1995) concludes that few of the original claims remain undisputed. The aim of generic measurement of service quality is attractive, but this goal may be unobtainable because of variation in the nature of services and because of a lack of agreement about concepts and measures.

Box 9.4 Alternative scales

1 SERVQUAL expectation and perception scales:

Firms in XYZ's field should have modern-looking equipment:

strongly disagree	1	2	3	4	5	6	7	strongly agree

Firm XYZ has modern-looking equipment:

strongly disagree	1	2	3	4	5	6	7	strongly agree

2 Combined item:

XYZ's modern-looking equipment:

greatly falls short of my expectations	1	2	3	4	5	6	7	greatly exceeds my expectations

SECTION 4: OUTCOMES OF SATISFACTION AND DISSATISFACTION

Does Increased Satisfaction Lead to Increased Profit?

If managers can increase product and service quality and hence customer satisfaction, a number of beneficial effects may follow for the supplier, as detailed in Figure 9.3. These

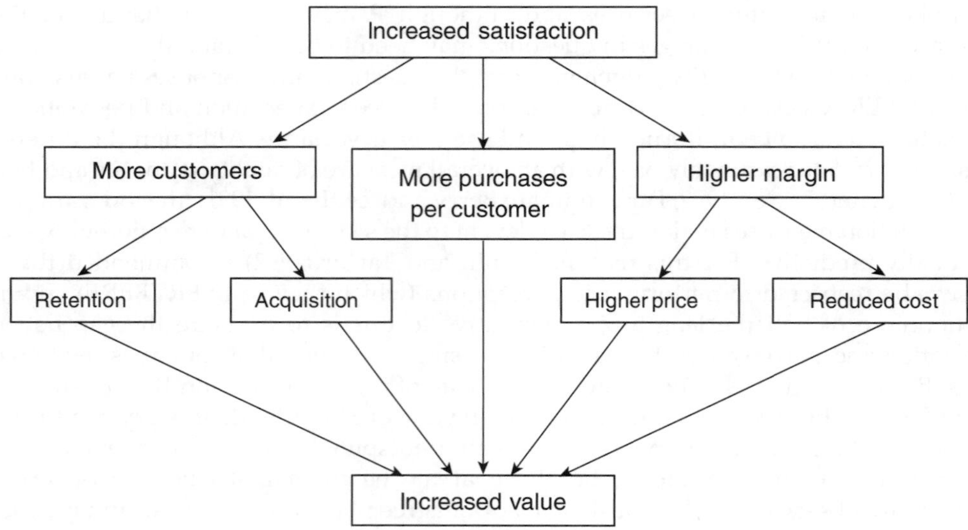

Figure 9.3 Routes to increased value

are more customers (either by retention or acquisition), additional purchases per customer and a higher profit margin, either through an increase in price or a reduction in costs per sale. There are, however, also additional costs associated with innovation and quality management. Thus, evidence is needed on whether an increase in satisfaction is normally associated with increased profit and, if so, how this comes about.

To investigate the consequences of increased satisfaction, the measure of satisfaction developed for the American Customer Satisfaction Index (ACSI) is often used. This is because the ACSI, and similar indexes in other countries, provide comprehensive measures across a range of industries, in the case of ACSI for more than 200 specific companies. In a review of studies using such measures, Zeithaml (2000) found a generally positive association between quality and profit and suggested that this was mediated by improved customer retention. Using the Swedish Customer Satisfaction Barometer, Anderson, Fornell and Lehmann (1994) were able to demonstrate small increments in return on investment over five years as a result of increases in satisfaction. These authors suggest that the connection between satisfaction and profit could be mediated by a range of effects. They cite greater retention, reduced price elasticity, lack of interest in competitor offerings, reduced costs for future transactions, reduced costs from failure, lower costs of customer acquisition, advertising and new product advantage through increased reputation of the firm, more customer recommendation, greater willingness to try products and stronger relationships with suppliers. These more specific explanations are largely covered by the aggregate effects shown in Figure 9.3.

Anderson, Fornell and Mazvancheryl (2004) have shown that increases in customer satisfaction are associated with increases in shareholder value, as measured by Tobin's *q* (see note 2). Anderson et al. argue that higher customer satisfaction may raise the bargaining power of a firm with its suppliers and other partners because these partners value relationships with companies who 'own' a valuable customer base. Increased bargaining power may assist margin and sales and may thus contribute to shareholder value. Gruca and Rego (2005) found satisfaction influenced shareholder value by both increasing cash flows and reducing their variability; this provides a financial account of the relationship, but tells us little about the underlying changes in consumer behaviour. Fornell et al. (2006) examined the growth obtained from investing in stock portfolios of high satisfaction companies. They found impressively high returns compared with standard investment indices and they argue that this extra gain was achieved without incurring greater risk. This study was conducted over 1997–2004 but, subsequently, Fornell, Mithas and Morgeson (2006) report that, up to October 2008, the investment portfolio had generated an average return of 15.1 per cent compound in the previous eight years while the S&P 500 index changed little. Aksoy et al. (2008) also find that changes in the satisfaction score predict stock value changes, but only when the economy is expanding. Anderson and Mansi (2009) make the connection between satisfaction and the corporate bond market. They show that firms with higher customer satisfaction ratings (as measured by ACSI) benefit from better credit ratings and lower debt costs and therefore obtain a financing advantage. Luo, Homburg and Wieseke (2010) also check the impact of satisfaction on financial markets and analyze the relationship between ACSI satisfaction scores, recommendations of financial analysts and company value, for about 100 firms over a 12-year period. Customer satisfaction is informative for the analysts because it predicts the growth and volatility of future cash flows. Luo et al. (2010) find that firms with higher levels of customer satisfaction receive more positive stock recommendations from analysts. The effect is higher in more competitive markets and also in situations of higher uncertainty in financial markets. They also show that satisfaction impacts financial returns, both directly and indirectly through the analysts' recommendations.

Although there is little *evidence* favouring any specific pathway from quality/satisfaction to increased value, there has been some tendency to emphasize the retention route (Anderson and Mittal, 2000; Zeithaml, 2000). This emphasis on retention may be misplaced, since a review of the connection between satisfaction and retention generally found weak associations (Chapter 2). In addition, Wangenheim and Bayón (2007) show that increased customer satisfaction does lead to new customer acquisition via increased word of mouth. We suspect that this is the main route to increased profit but definitive research is needed here. Word of mouth is considered further in Chapter 12.

Complaining

Factors Affecting Complaining Behaviour

People are often reluctant to complain when they are dissatisfied with goods or services. There is evidence that the degree of dissatisfaction has a modest relationship with the likelihood of complaint (Day, 1984; Malafi et al., 1993; Oliver, 1981, 1987; Singh and Howell, 1985). Oliver (1981) reports a correlation of about 0.4 between dissatisfaction and complaining. However, there is considerable inertia: Andreasen (1988) and Stø and Glefjell (1990) both found that 60 per cent of dissatisfied consumers did nothing, while Benterud and Stø (1993) found that 95 per cent of those dissatisfied with their TV shopping did not complain.

Day (1984) and Singh and Howell (1985) have noted that complaining is affected by how people explain product failure, their expectation of redress and the likely time-cost and effort involved. Research on complaining needs to take account of all the possible reasons that people might have for this behaviour. We can cover these reasons by using Ajzen's (1985, 1991) theory of planned behaviour, as discussed in Chapter 7. This deals with three types of influence.

1. **Expected outcomes**. Hirschman (1970) suggested that complaining by customers was related to the expected returns and costs. Positive outcomes may include replacement, apology and better goods or service in the future, while negative outcomes may include lost opportunities, wasted time and embarrassment. The perceived likelihood of success in obtaining redress has been found to be associated with complaining in a number of studies (Day and Landon, 1976; Granbois, Summers and Frazier, 1977; Richins, 1983, 1987; Singh, 1990). Richins (1985) also found evidence that the importance of the product affects the likelihood of complaining.
2. **Normative influences**. Consumers may also be influenced by what they believe others think they should do, even when these other people are not present. Normative influences on complaining have not been studied systematically, although Richins (1981) has noted instances where consumers felt that they *ought* to complain.
3. **Control factors**. These are knowledge, skills, time and other factors that can make complaining easier or harder. Examples are the ease of access to key personnel, an understanding of the workings of the organization causing dissatisfaction, and confidence about complaining. Control factors help us to distinguish between those who complain and those who do not. Two studies (Caplovitz, 1967; Warland, Herrmann and Willits, 1975) found that non-complainers seemed powerless and had less knowledge of the means of redress. Grønhaug (1977) found that there were more complaints to a Norwegian consumer protection agency from citizens who lived closer to it. Grønhaug and Zaltman (1981) also recognized the importance of resources such as time, money and confidence and this study is cited by Yi (1990) as important in showing differences between complainers and non-complainers. A matter of concern is that vulnerable consumers (the old, ill and disadvantaged) complain less than others (Andreasen and Manning, 1990) and this is likely to be related to the reduced control that such consumers have.

East (2000) used the theory of planned behaviour to investigate complaining in the UK. He found that complaining was focused mainly on getting a refund or replacement, standing up for one's rights, doing what friends expected and confidence about being able to complain. Such evidence helps us to see what factors may encourage complaining. For example, in order to increase confidence, suppliers should make it clear that they welcome complaints and should explain a clear procedure for handling them.

The Benefits of Receiving Complaints

Fornell and Wernerfelt (1987) argue that, within cost limits, it is profitable to gather and evaluate complaints from dissatisfied customers. Companies increasingly put toll-free telephone numbers and e-mail addresses on goods packaging for this purpose. One reason for the profitability of receiving complaints is that these supply information about product deficiencies, which can then be corrected. A second reason is to gather further sales when the complainer gets in touch. For example, the complainer may be advised that there is a newer version of software or an improved design of outdoor clothing and this information may lead to a further purchase. A third reason is that an effective response to the aggrieved customer by the company may reduce negative word of mouth to other potential customers, which could damage sales. Finally, if the complaint is well handled, the company may be able to stop defection or recover customers who have already left.

There is evidence that customers who are retained after a service failure may be more satisfied than they are without the failure. This is called the service recovery paradox (SRP). One explanation is that, if customers appreciate the efforts of the company to satisfy their concerns, they may recommend it more and be more inclined to repurchase. Examples of SRP were found by TARP (1979) and Gilly and Gelb (1982) but Solnick and Hemenway (1992) found that those who complained about health provision were over four times more likely to defect than those who did not. More patronage after complaint may occur because the complaint handling resolved the customer's dissatisfaction and exceeded expectation, but it is also possible that those who intend to remain with the supplier complain because they want to benefit from any changes resulting from their complaining.

Magnini et al. (2007) used role-play studies to investigate the SRP. They found that the effect occurred when the failure was not severe, the firm had not failed the customer before, the cause of the failure was seen as unstable and the customer believed that the company had little control over the failure. In a meta-analysis, De Matos et al. (2007) found a significant SRP effect for satisfaction but not for repurchase intention or word of mouth.

Response to Delay

Delay in the delivery of service is a perennial feature of retailing and other services. Indeed, it is an inherent liability of something that is produced and consumed during an interval of time. Consumers wait for counter service in post offices, for train tickets in booking offices and at the checkout in supermarkets; they also wait for public transport and get held up in traffic jams; they may have to wait to talk to someone on the telephone. For the individual, delay is frustrating and for the economy it is wasteful because people waiting in line are neither producing nor consuming. Bitner, Booms and Tetreault (1990) noted that delay was a major feature of incidents causing dissatisfaction. Pruyn and Smidts (1993) found that Dutch consumers waited, on average, over half an hour per day for various services and that supermarket checkout delay was the most irritating hold-up. In Britain, 70 per cent of respondents in a Consumers' Association report on supermarkets (*Which?*, February 1990) mentioned 'a lot of staffed checkouts' as desirable, placing it fourth in importance compared with other store features, and another report on post offices (*Which?*, September 1989) put cutting queuing time at the top of service improvements suggested by respondents, even though the research recorded an average wait of only 3.5 minutes.

Queuing for crêpes in Hampstead

It appears that dissatisfaction with waiting can affect the total service experience: the longer the wait, the lower the evaluation of the whole service (Feinberg, Widdows and Steidle, 1996; Katz, Larson and Larson, 1991; Taylor, 1994; Tom and Lucey, 1995). Organizations may not see delay in the same way as their customers. Feinberg and Smith (1989) found that the customer at the checkout thought the average delay was 5.6 minutes when the staff though it was 3.2; the actual time was 4.7 minutes.

It is likely that people are less bothered by delay when it is expected (Maister, 1985). Supporting this, an experiment on bank queues by Clemmer and Schneider (1989) showed that the more unexpected the delay, the more it was disliked. This suggests that we can identify two types of dissatisfaction with delay: a low involvement discontent when the delay is predicted and a high involvement disconfirmation effect when it is unanticipated. As delays get more common they also become more predictable and, paradoxically, consumers may put up with them more easily. This may be why Taylor (1994) did not find that common delays were associated with significantly more irritation.

People also tolerate a wait better if they know how long it is. The provision of delay information is standard for airlines, and London Transport provides display boards reporting the wait before the next train or bus arrives. This information seems to be much appreciated despite the fact that it does nothing to reduce the waiting time. A similar facility is queue position information for those waiting on the telephone for their turn to speak to a customer service representative.

Maister also notes that people are less irritated by delay if they are occupied in some way. One example here is the way in which Disneyland entertains its queues with costumed characters; another is the provision of mirrors in places where people have to wait, for example at lifts. Taylor (1995) used two groups in an experiment to test the effect of occupying people when they had to wait. Both groups were delayed by ten minutes but only one was allowed activities to offset the delay. In this study, the evaluation of the service was reduced by delay but the reduction in evaluation was less when people were occupied. In fact, some of those who were delayed did not even realize that they had been held up and most of these people were in the 'occupied' group. One explanation for this effect of keeping people occupied is that, with this distraction, they do not retrieve expectations about acceptable delay and therefore do not form an assessment of their experience. Taylor's work also suggested that, if the service provider was thought to have control, customers assessed the service more negatively. This is consistent with Weiner's (1980, 1990) suggestion that people become more irritated when they believe that the service provider has control of the situation.

Studies by Dubé-Rioux, Schmitt and Leclerc (1989) show that when delay occurs at the beginning or end of a process, in their example a restaurant meal, it was evaluated more negatively than mid-process delays. For example, it was better for waiters to take the order, and then impose the delay, than to wait before taking the order. However, it is not always clear when a service starts and finishes. For example, delays to air travel occur when going to the airport, at check-in, baggage check, passport control, the departure lounge, in the plane before take-off, before landing, at baggage reclaim and again at passport control and customs. People may think of this sequence as a number of services or just one, and the way they regard it may affect how they tolerate delay at different points.

A study of the service experiences of UK customers by East, Lomax and Willson (1991) showed that 31 per cent did not mind waiting at the checkout in supermarkets. In banks and post offices, this figure rose to 50 per cent and in building societies to 57 per cent. A cynic might see this as evidence of British stoicism, and Maister (1985) has noted dryly that, if the British see a queue, they join it. However, further evidence showed that most people (52 per cent in the UK and 63 per cent in the USA), either did not mind, or minded a little, when delayed at the checkout (East et al., 1992). The data could indicate that delay is tolerated better in the USA than in the UK. However, the dislike of delay was related to how long people expected to be delayed; the US respondents expected delays to be briefer and this probably explains their greater tolerance.

Dislike of queuing is also likely to be related to the reason for waiting and the amount of spare time that people have. Table 9.2 shows the evidence on post offices subdivided by age and whether the customer was paying or receiving money. Older people, who might be expected to have more spare time, were more tolerant of delay. People were also more tolerant when they were receiving a benefit rather than paying for something.

Table 9.2 Percentage who dislike waiting at the post office (East, Lomax and Willson, 1991)

Age	*Those buying stamps, licences or paying bills (%)*	*Those receiving pensions, allowances or other benefits (%)*
Under 65	61	49
65+	50	18

Perceived Responsibility for Delay

Of particular interest is the way people explain who is responsible when they have to wait for service. If customers see the service provider as responsible, they are likely to be more irritated by the delay and complain more (Weiner, 1980; Taylor, 1995). Folkes, Koletsky and Graham (1987) found that customers became angrier and expressed more resistance to repurchase when they felt that a delay was avoidable by management. Taylor (1994) also found that those who blamed management were angrier about the wait.

In the study by East, Lomax and Willson (1991), respondents were asked whom they held responsible when they were delayed at the checkout of a supermarket. Table 9.3 shows that more of the people who blamed management disliked waiting. The investigations of delay in post offices, building societies and banks gave very similar results. We see from the bracketed numbers in Table 9.3 that few people are self-blaming; they are much more likely to blame other customers than themselves. This is consistent with the actor–observer bias (Jones and Nisbett, 1972), that an actor tends to see others as choosing and therefore responsible for their behaviour while the actor sees the same behaviour in himself as caused by the situation (e.g. circumstances or other people).

Table 9.3 Those held responsible for delay in the supermarket (East, Lomax and Willson, 1991)

Response to delay	*No one (99) (%)*	*Self (9) (%)*	*Other customers (96) (%)*	*Checkout staff (19) (%)*	*Management (208) (%)*	*Total (431) (%)*
Don't mind	48	33	46	37	16	31
Dislike it	52	67	54	63	84	69

When serious delays occur, managers may receive much of the blame. Often the cause is accidental or brought about by other service providers on whom a firm had relied. This suggests that management needs to distinguish between the cause of the delay and responsibility for its consequences. Staff should clearly accept responsibility for remedying a problem, but it will help if, when appropriate, they can explain that they did not create the problem, since Taylor (1994) has shown that the service is liked less when blame is attributed to the service provider. For example, the cause of an aircraft take-off delay may be that a service company has failed to deliver airline food on time, a mechanical fault has been revealed by standard checks before take-off, bad weather has delayed the plane's arrival, or that airport congestion is worse than normal. In all these cases, timely announcements may help to deflect blame.

Queues can be organized as either multiple-line or as single-line. Sometimes it is possible to use a queuing ticket system, which allows people to conduct other business while they wait. The relative attraction of these three systems was tested by East, Lomax, Willson and Harris (1992) in their investigation of bank and building society use (see Table 9.4). The single-line queuing system is much preferred to queuing at each counter despite the fact that this introduces a slight delay as customers make their way to a vacant counter.

Box 9.5 Delay management

Research on the response to delay helps us to understand how to manage this service problem better. There are three approaches:

1. **Operations management**. Where feasible, managers should try to avoid delays by increasing service supply in line with demand. For example, supermarket managers can count shoppers entering the store and open checkouts in advance of the calculated demand; also they can try and use their fastest checkout operators at peak times.
2. **Influencing demand**. The second approach uses regulation and incentives to draw demand away from busy periods and towards quiet periods. A reservation system is used for many services and differential pricing may also shift demand, e.g. Monday is often a cheap day at the cinema in Britain. However, East, Lomax, Willson and Harris (1994) judged that the scope for promoting the off-peak periods in supermarkets was limited (see more on this in Chapter 11).
3. **Perception management**. The third approach is to try to ensure that the customer sees the delay in a way that does least damage. Tom and Lucey (1995) suggest putting literature at the checkout and advise that this is a good location for free samples. Maister (1985) also recommends diverting the queue but the form of the diversion should be chosen carefully; it is easy to irritate customers with mindless music on the telephone and irrelevant advertising on screens set up for the queue. Such arrangements imply that the delay is normal (stable) and management is interested in alleviating, rather than eliminating, the discomfort of waiting.

Table 9.4 If there were queues, would you rather have …? (East, Lomax, Willson and Harris, 1992)

System	*Banks (%)*	*Building societies (%)*	*Mean (%)*
… separate queues at each counter	15	12	14
… a single queuing system	78	81	79
… queuing tickets	7	7	7

The advantages of single-line systems are twofold: delays are approximately equal and therefore fair and they are more predictable since excessive delays at one counter will not affect waiting time much when there are several counters in use. A single-line system seems particularly useful when the start of a service is imminent, for example, in train stations where there is a danger of missing the train. Work by Pruyn and Smidts (1993) indicates that, although people may prefer the single line, the queuing system is of less consequence than the duration of delay and the quality of the waiting environment.

Waiting as a Cue for Quality

Although our coverage of waiting has so far considered it as a negative experience, we should not forget that consumers can also be attracted to service providers with long waiting times. A long line outside a restaurant or nightclub can be perceived as the promise of a great experience. Consumers often rely on the behaviour of others for guidance, and other people waiting in line is an easily observable cue. In a series of four experiments, with either scenarios or actual waiting experiences, Giebelhausen, Robinson and Cronin (2011) show that a required wait can increase purchase intentions and experienced satisfaction. They also examine different moderators of this effect. It appears more pronounced when the product or service is difficult to evaluate because of a lack of familiarity or objective criteria and when quality, as opposed to convenience, is a decision criterion.

SUMMARY

Consumer satisfaction, dissatisfaction, quality perception and complaining behaviour are important because they relate to profit via word of mouth and repeat purchase. A particular emphasis in this field has been on the quality of services because these are more prone to failure than goods and constitute a large and growing proportion of modern economies.

Consumers are contented when products meet positive expectations and are discontented with goods and services that show expected weaknesses, but this fulfilment of expectations normally produces little arousal and, therefore, little 'exit' or 'voice' by the customer. Much research has focused on those occasions where product performance surprises the consumer (the disconfirmation model). Surprise is arousing and causes more behavioural response and, therefore, more potential impact on profit. There is some variation in the way researchers describe the detail of the disconfirmation model but there is agreement that the discrepancy between expectation and perception is the main focus; expectations and perceptions may have additional direct effects on dis/satisfaction. In addition, researchers now recognize an interpretative phase in which consumers' explanations of their experience may modify their responses to it.

There are a number of consequences of satisfaction, some of which were covered in Chapter 2. An important concern is the association between satisfaction and profit. Companies that increase satisfaction have been found to show subsequent increases in profit. This gain in profit does not appear to be fully anticipated in the share price so that buying shares in companies that show satisfaction gains appears to be a sensible investment strategy.

When customers are dissatisfied, they rarely complain. Companies can benefit from complaints being expressed and research has been conducted to explain the motivation to complain. Delay is a general liability of service provision that causes dissatisfaction. Unexpected delay (causing disconfirmation) is particularly disliked. When it occurs, delay is tolerated better if people understand why they are delayed and how long it will last. Also, if consumers can occupy their time they are less dissatisfied. It is better to start a service and then impose a delay than to begin or end with the delay. In some cases, delays can be a signal of success of the product and therefore a cue for quality.

Additional Resources

For reviews of SERVQUAL, see Smith (1995) and Buttle (1996). For evidence of the impact of satisfaction on shareholder value, see Anderson et al. (2004) and Gruca and Rego (2005).

Notes

1 Expectations are often reported as though they are held in mind prior to the experience and then compared with the delivered product, but the experience, pleasant or unpleasant, usually causes us to bring to mind what would be appropriate in the circumstances, which we then call our expectation.

2 A firm's q value is the ratio of its market value to the current replacement cost of its assets (Tobin, 1969). Thus it is higher for those firms that are perceived to be using their assets more effectively.

Part 4
Market Response

10 Consumer Response to Price and Sales Promotions

LEARNING OBJECTIVES

When you have completed this chapter, you should be able to:

1 Describe how consumers process price information.
2 Explain how marketers assess consumers' price sensitivity.
3 Evaluate the different tactics you observe in the marketplace to present prices and price changes.
4 Assess the effectiveness of promotions by distinguishing between possible sources of extra sales.
5 Compare the advantages and disadvantages of price discounting versus couponing.
6 Discuss the long-term effectiveness of promotions.
7 Assess the effectiveness of the customization of promotions for both Internet and 'bricks-and-mortar' stores.

OVERVIEW

Consumers verify the prices of products in order to make sure they buy at the right price and, for expensive items, stay within budget. Buying at the right price means getting good value for money, compared with alternative products and this may involve buying at the right moment and place. Benchmark prices may be externally available but often consumers have to rely on their memory of previously encountered prices to make comparisons. Price memory, unfortunately, appears to be rather unreliable.

Marketers have developed different methodologies to estimate how consumers react to price changes. Price increases, though often necessary and justified, are unpopular and are often considered unfair. Consumer researchers have examined the conditions under which perceptions of fairness or unfairness occur. Prices also influence the perceived quality and even the emotional experience of using the product.

Price decreases are usually sales promotions. Two decades of access to scanner data has given researchers the opportunity to develop sophisticated quantitative models to evaluate promotion effectiveness. Combining a price cut with additional promotional activities, such as in-store displays and advertising features, may have a synergistic effect. Promotions usually have large short-term effects on sales, but there is doubt about their long-term effectiveness and contribution to profit. Customization of promotions, to adapt them to the characteristics and purchase habits of individual consumers or consumer segments, seems to hold promise. However, initial results show that customization is not necessarily more profitable compared to mass promotions, especially in 'bricks-and-mortar' retailing.

SECTION 1: CONSUMER RESPONSE TO PRICE

Reference Prices

A price is rarely treated in isolation: prices become informative by relating them to other prices, a phenomenon studied under the heading of reference price. A price in combination with a reference price, whether accurate or not, allows a consumer to determine if it is better to buy here and now or to wait and buy elsewhere. When a product is cheaper than expected it is more likely to be purchased and vice versa.

The concept of reference price was introduced to marketing by Monroe (1973). It was inspired by Helson's (1964) adaptation-level theory that states that stimuli are judged with respect to internal norms. These internal norms represent the aggregate effect of past and present stimulation. There are two views on the origin of reference prices. According to the first view, consumers call on their memory of past prices they paid or encountered. They hold what is referred to as internal reference prices (IRP). The second view posits that reference prices are formed during the shopping occasion itself, based on prices observed, known in the literature as external reference prices (ERP).

Interestingly, most research on reference price does not ask consumers for their reference prices but instead infers them from choice models estimated on panel data (Winer, 1986). These models include as explanatory variables the elements of the marketing mix, including price, but also a reference price term. This term captures the difference between the current price of the product and some mathematical function of past prices (in the case of IRP) or currently observable other prices (in the case of ERP). The fact that this difference variable helps explain choice is taken as evidence that consumers make comparisons with reference prices. The wide availability of individual-level scanner data has permitted an extremely productive stream of research in this area (see the review in Mazumdar, Raj and Sinha, 2005).

Researchers have provided a broad range of reference price models. Hardie, Johnson and Fader (1993) compared a model with ERP and one with IRP and found that, at least for orange juice, the category they examined, ERP, was a better representation of reference price. Briesch et al. (1997), however, showed that IRP gave a better model fit in other categories. It is of course possible that the use of IRP or ERP varies across consumers and situations. Mazumdar and Papatla (2000) pursue this idea and show that there are indeed segments of consumers that differ in the extent to which they use IRP or ERP. They also show that IRP is more frequently used for more expensive product categories while ERP is more often used in categories with a longer interpurchase time and greater frequency of promotions.

Although most research examines ERP and IRP as defined above, a number of alternative definitions of reference price have been proposed. People may compare with the price they *usually* pay but they may also compare with the price they would *like* to pay, the price they *expect* to pay, given the expected evolution of prices, or the price they regard as *fair*. Winer (1988) even proposed eight different possible definitions of price reference.

Although most research treats reference prices as precise points, it may be that consumers actually have price zones in mind. Kalyanaram and Little (1994) estimate a 'latitude of acceptance' around the reference price. This is a zone in which the consumer is indifferent to deviations between the observed price and the reference price. As with most reference price models, they also find the asymmetric price effect predicted by prospect theory (see Chapter 8), with stronger negative responses to price increases than positive responses to price decreases.

Exercise 10.1 Your price knowledge

Keep the till receipt of one of your next trips to the supermarket. When you get home, unpack your products and, without looking at your receipt, write down the prices you paid. Indicate each time whether you think you remember the price accurately or whether you are just making an estimate. Also indicate how accurate you think you are (very accurate, rather accurate, not accurate). Score your responses according to whether they are exactly right, within 10 per cent or outside this range. Compare your results with others.

1 How easy or difficult was it to determine whether your knowledge is directly drawn from memory? In other words, how good is your introspective access to the cognitive processes you use to answer the questions?
2 Is there any evidence that frequently bought items are better remembered?
3 Do you have other hypotheses about why you remembered some prices better than other ones?
4 How can these hypotheses be tested in a study?
5 Are students likely to remember prices better than other consumers? If so, why?

Price Memory

If consumers use IRP to assess the attractiveness of an offer, it is interesting to verify how accurate their knowledge of prices is. Dickson and Sawyer (1990) found that less than half of US shoppers could give the correct price for the item that they had just put into their shopping trolley. They mention in their article that marketing executives and academics who attended presentations of this study were surprised by how imperfect shoppers' attention to, and retention of, price information was at the point of purchase. Nevertheless, the finding was corroborated by Le Boutillier, Le Boutillier and Neslin (1994) for coffee, but not for soda, where 71 per cent could recall the exact price they paid. In addition, using the same interviewing procedure, Wakefield and Inman (1993) report percentages of correct responses ranging from 52 to 78 per cent for four product categories.

These in-the-aisle price knowledge surveys have received two types of response. Some researchers consider that these survey results bring reference price findings into question, because price knowledge is much lower than most researchers intuitively expected (Kalyanaram and Winer, 1995). A second type of response concerns the interpretation of the results. The Dickson and Sawyer results are often interpreted as indications that price memory is poor. Vanhuele and Drèze (2002) point out that what may be measured in these in-the-aisle surveys is short-term memory, not long-term price memory.

Vanhuele and Drèze (2002) examined how price information is stored in long-term memory and, based on theories from numerical cognition, hypothesized that three types of coding are used: verbal (similar to recording your voice), visual (photographic) and magnitude coding (you remember that the price was somewhere between 35 and 40). They show that recall questions measure only part of price memory. Recognition memory is clearly better and some knowledge is also only present in an approximate form in memory. The Dickson and Sawyer results are therefore not necessarily in conflict with reference price research.

Overall, price knowledge surveys may suggest that the current price is of no consequence to many purchasers but this simplifies the issue too much. Although consumers may take prices on trust on many occasions, they may, at other times, check on how much they are paying and react against suppliers who are seen to overcharge. In addition, the price of a limited number of goods may be used as a key to the overall value for money offered by a store. Even if there is only a small segment of consumers who examine prices carefully most of the time, this segment of so-called price vigilantes (Wakefield and Inman, 1993) may be sufficiently important for retailers to keep prices low.

Although some price learning may be incidental and unconscious – and therefore less available to recall (Monroe and Lee, 1999; Vanhuele and Drèze, 2002) – other price learning may be intentional and conscious, especially for motivated price-sensitive consumers. What if we are motivated to learn prices? How good can we become at price recall? How well is our cognitive system adapted to memorizing prices? With a series of experiments Vanhuele, Laurent and Drèze (2006) examined how immediate memory for prices functions. Participants had to keep prices for two or three products in a given category (DVDs, cameras and candy) in memory for five seconds before feeding them back. Analyses of the responses confirmed that the three types of numerical coding discussed by Vanhuele and Drèze (2002) are used: verbal, visual and magnitude coding. Most intriguing is the effect of verbal coding. If people want to hold a price (or whatever other information) in short-term memory, they cycle it through a sub-system of working memory. Because the capacity of this sub-system is restricted to 1.5 to 2 seconds of length of speech, prices that take longer to pronounce are less well remembered. Also, consumers who speak slower have poorer immediate memory, because of this capacity restriction. And consumers who do not respect the official pronunciation of prices and use shortcuts instead (e.g. twelve ninety instead of one thousand two hundred and ninety) have a memory advantage. An implication of this finding, not examined in the article, is that, across regions, language differences handicap some consumers in their price memory. For the French, for instance, a price of 90 euros is 'quatre-vingt-dix euros', but French-speaking Belgians and Swiss know it in a shorter form as 'nonante euros'.

The Price–Quality Relationship

When comparing different goods, consumers may use price as an indicator of quality. In a review of over 40 studies, Rao and Monroe (1989) found robust but moderate evidence that consumers indeed use price as a proxy for product quality. When such inferences occur, they may actually be mistaken. An analysis of US studies by Tellis and Wernerfelt (1987) found a mean correlation between price and *objective* product quality of only 0.27. Zeithaml (1988) reviewed nearly 90 studies and only found mixed support for a relationship between price and *subjectively* assessed quality. It seems that the inference of quality from price is therefore rather weaker than has been supposed. One important reason is probably that quality perceptions obviously depend on a number of factors in addition to price, such as the appearance of the product, the reports of others, the brand and the store that sells the product. Consumers who believe that price and quality are related may persist in this belief because they selectively focus on cases that confirm their belief, i.e. they attend most to high-price/high-quality and low-price/low-quality products. Kardes et al. (2004) show, however, that belief-inconsistent information can be processed for price–quality inferences when consumers are motivated and have the opportunity to do so.

Combining this review with that on reference price, we see that price can influence acceptability either because of quality inferences or because of the comparison with reference prices that highlight the economic sacrifice. This gives us the model shown in Figure 10.1. Notice that, as price rises, the acceptability of the product is raised by the price–quality relationship but reduced by the comparison against reference prices. Normally we expect the reference price effect to be stronger since otherwise sales would rise with increase in price, which is not usually observed. In a series of experiments, Bornemann and Homburg (2011) showed that when consumers evaluate a product for consumption in the distant future, the price–quality relationship receives more weight, while for near future consumption, price is instead interpreted as a sacrifice. (For example, participants in the experiments had to imagine the launch of an electronic book reader that would be available in the university book store in two days or six months.)

In a variation on the price–quality inference theme, Shiv, Carmon and Ariely (2005) show that consumers who pay a discounted price for an existing energy drink that is thought to enhance mental acuity are, after consumption of the drink, able to solve fewer word-jumble puzzles than consumers who paid the regular price. An additional surprising finding is that the effect, which in the medical world would be called a placebo effect, is apparently unconscious. Plassmann et al. (2008) demonstrate that when we believe that a wine is more expensive, we experience more pleasure while drinking it. They presented

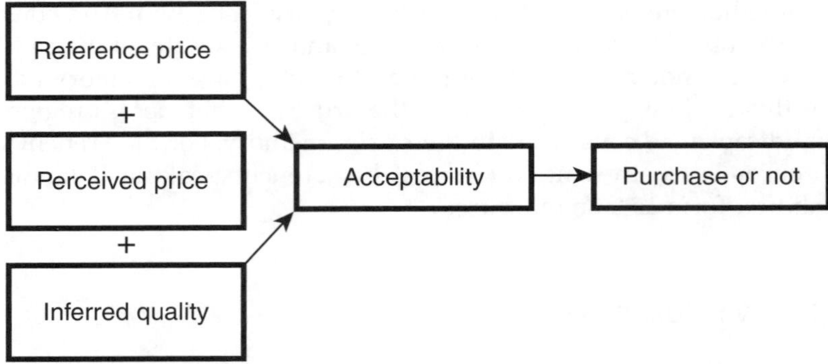

Figure 10.1 Price, acceptability and purchase

the same wines at different prices. A 90-dollar wine was in fact presented twice, once at its real price and once marked at 10 dollars. Similarly a 5-dollar wine was also presented at 45 dollars. Subjects in this study rated the pleasantness of each wine but the researchers also used fMRI scans to measure activity in the part of the brain that is involved in the experience of pleasantness and showed increased activity in that area for higher-priced wines. The fMRI scans indicate that the ratings cannot be dismissed as rationalizations and are the result of genuinely experienced pleasantness.

SECTION 2: ESTIMATING PRICE SENSITIVITY

The sensitivity of sales to changes in prices is usually quantified as price elasticity. Price elasticity is the ratio of sales change to price change, expressed in relative terms. Thus, if sales go up 20 per cent when the price is cut by 10 per cent (a negative change), the price elasticity would be –2. For some products, for instance prescription drugs, price changes produce very little change in demand. Price elasticity is close to zero and demand is called 'inelastic'. Conversely, the price elasticity for any supplier in a commodity market is highly 'elastic' and the absolute value of price elasticity is very high, indicating that sales will drop steeply if price is increased and will increase considerably when price is dropped. It is important to keep in mind that price elasticities are not the same at all price levels. A price elasticity estimation is therefore only valid for the region of prices used for its estimation. Price elasticities can, of course, also change with general economic conditions or changes in specific market factors (for instance, the development of new distribution channels such as the Internet).

In consumer markets three methods are used to estimate price sensitivity. For new products, customer surveys are often used. For new and established products, price experiments can be run. When historical information on the market is available, econometric modelling can be applied. Quantitative research in marketing has made enormous progress over the past 15 years in developing models to evaluate the impact of marketing actions in general and price in particular. In particular, the wide use of checkout scanners and other forms of information technology has permitted detailed recording of transaction data. The result has been an enormous increase in the ability of researchers to evaluate price effects.

Customer Surveys

There are two approaches to surveying consumers to assess their price sensitivity. In the direct-survey approach, consumers receive a product description, or are exposed to the product itself and then have to react to potential prices. This method, developed in the 1960s, is simple to apply and easily understood by respondents (Gabor and Granger, 1961, 1966; Wedel and Leeflang, 1998). There are a number of biases that typically lead consumers to overstate their willingness to pay, but corrections are possible. An important drawback is, however, that price is treated in isolation in these surveys while, in real-life choices, product characteristics have to be weighed against price.

Conjoint analysis (Green and Krieger, 2002) is a widely used customer survey method that presents consumers with simplified product descriptions and asks them for their preference among these products while considering all information conjointly. Price sensitivity and the sensitivity to changes in other attributes are then inferred using estimation methodology. Conjoint analysis is widely applied for new product designs in general, not just for price analysis. Running conjoint surveys by computer and on the Internet has now become standard practice. The method is rarely used in consumer research but has become a standard tool for commercial market researchers and a large number of applications have been published (see reviews in Green, Krieger and Wind, 2001; Wittink, Vriens, and Burhenne, 1994).

Price Experiments

The objective of an experiment is to control factors that influence the outcome of interest (usually sales) but which are not the object of the study. Sales are not only influenced by price changes but also by all the other marketing actions of the firm, those of its competitors and changes in the context. Running a price experiment in one store and comparing sales at the end of the experiment with sales before is therefore rarely conclusive; an observed change in sales can usually be attributed to other factors that have changed.

The art of running a good price experiment is in selecting a good comparison basis, usually called the control group, which cancels out the influence of other factors. Price experiments can be carried out in a simulated shopping environment, but large market research companies, such as Kantar, Nielsen and GfK in Europe, have test cities in different countries in which they run experiments with consumer goods on a regular basis. All the variables of the marketing mix can be controlled during these experiments (for an example see Fader, Hardie and Zeithammer, 2003). Price experiments can also be conducted on the Internet (see Box 10.1).

Ehrenberg and England (1990) investigated price elasticity using a field experimental method. Staff made fortnightly home visits to housewives and offered a limited selection of cereal, confectionery, soup, tea and biscuit brands for sale at prices that were a little below those in local supermarkets. After two visits, the prices of some brands were raised or lowered. The order of price changes was altered for different sub-groups so that any effects based on price sequence could be detected. The authors found that the response to price changes was immediate and was unaffected by the order of earlier changes, i.e. it was zero order. Price increases had slightly less percentage impact on sales than decreases. The mean elasticity obtained by Ehrenberg and England (weighted by brand size) was –2.6.

Box 10.1 Price experiments on the Internet

Technically, the Internet allows price experimenting on a constant basis. In practice, consumer reactions may complicate things (but see Exercise 10.2). In early September 2000, *Computerworld* reported that consumers logging on to Amazon at about the same time could be charged very different prices for the same DVD. For example, at 2.40 pm a search for the *Planet of the Apes* DVD on the Amazon site using a Netscape Web browser turned up a quoted price of $64.99 – 35 per cent off the original price of $99.98 but, several seconds later, a similar search performed with Microsoft Corp.'s Internet Explorer browser resulted in a price of $74.99 for the same product. A company spokesperson acknowledged that Amazon was running price experiments. 'Some customers will pay the same for a certain item as customers paid last week, some will pay more and some will pay less', she said. In a statement several weeks later, Amazon formally denied published rumours that the price differences in the test were based on customer demographic information and said that the price reductions, which were in the 20–40 per cent range, aimed at determining how much sales are affected by lower prices. Amazon also promised that, if they ever were to run such a test again, they would automatically refund customers who purchased at a price higher than the lowest test price for the same item.

Econometric Estimation

Econometric estimation of price elasticities has a long history and research has sought to combine the knowledge accumulated over decades of pricing research. A meta-analysis by Tellis (1988b) brought together 367 elasticities, drawn from 42 prior studies using a variety of estimation methods. Tellis showed that a number of market factors were related to elasticity and that the mean elasticity across all the studies was –1.8.

Bijmolt, van Heerde and Pieters (2005) presented a more recent meta-analysis, and across 1,851 price elasticities drawn from 81 studies, they found a substantially larger average of –2.6. They examined the evolution over time between 1961 and 2004 and found that the (absolute) sales elasticity became larger each year, at a rate of one percentage point per 25 years. They also compared different market and category characteristics and found that price elasticities have greater magnitude in the introduction and growth stages of the product life cycle compared with the maturity and decline stages. Consumers are more price sensitive for durables than for other products. Inflation also increases the magnitude of price elasticity. They found no effects of country, income, data source (firms, retail panels, household panels) and brand ownership (private labels versus manufacturer brands).

SECTION 3: PSYCHOLOGICAL REACTIONS TO PRICES AND PRICE CHANGES

Perceived (Un)fairness of Prices and Price Changes

Consumers can react to prices and price changes by purchasing now – and even stockpiling – if the current price is attractive, or by cancelling or postponing a planned purchase if the current price is unattractive. They may also develop perceptions of fairness or, more commonly, unfairness about the seller. These perceptions can lead to negative attitudes about a company or an entire industry (e.g. 'pharmaceutical prices should be controlled more strongly because of the excess profits of the industry'), boycotts and negative word of mouth.

What is considered as fair or unfair? Fairness is a judgement about the justness, reasonableness or acceptability of an outcome (the price) or the process to reach the outcome (often communicated by the seller as a reason for a change, or inferred by the consumer). It is a judgement that is induced by a comparison to another outcome, such as 'I paid more than another customer did' or 'I paid more than I usually do' (Xia, Monroe and Cox, 2004).

Kahneman, Knetsch and Thaler (1991a, 1991b) identified, in a series of surveys and experiments, the price conditions that consumers consider as fair or unfair. They developed the principle of dual entitlement as an explanation, arguing that fairness perceptions are determined by a belief that firms are entitled to a certain profit and customers are entitled to a certain price. Increasing prices to increase profits when there is heavy demand is considered unfair, but it is fair to protect profit from rising costs. The classic example is that a retailer is entitled to raise the price of snow shovels in reaction to an increased wholesale price, but not in response to extra demand brought about by a snowstorm.

Campbell (1999) expands on the dual entitlement principle and identifies two important factors that affect the perceived fairness of a price change: consumers' inferences about the firm's motive for a price change, and inferred profit, relative to the past. The core idea is that consumers make inferences about a marketer's motive or intention for a particular price increase. This idea is based on evidence from attribution research that people search for causal explanations for negative and unexpected events. When consumers infer that the firm has a negative motive (e.g. exploiting a sudden increase in demand), the increase is considered unfair. When the firm has a good reputation, consumers give it the benefit of the doubt. Even when the scenario suggests a negative motive, if the firm does not appear to make extra profit, consumers infer a more positive motive.

Exercise 10.2 Price discrimination

Yield management is a pricing practice in which prices are adapted over time to optimize profits and capacity usage. It is used in industries where capacity is fixed, such as the hotel and airline business. Marginal revenue at a low price may be worthwhile if the room or seat would otherwise be empty, but not if it forces a reduction of the overall price level. So, while tourists might get a concessionary rate on the weekend, because they book well in advance and have flexible travel times, this should not undermine the full price charged to business travellers. It is now commonly accepted that, on any given flight, passengers pay widely varied prices for their tickets as a result of the use of yield management pricing software.

Pick with a friend a couple of flying destinations that are served by a low-cost carrier (like Ryanair, EasyJet or Virgin Blue). Agree on a departure date and hour and check the prices of your flights a couple of times over the next week. Do prices change? By how much and in which direction? Why do they change? Under what conditions would you find it acceptable if your friend found a lower price than you for a given flight? What if you both logged on at the same time, and got a different price quote?

Bolton, Warlop and Alba (2003) examine, in ten different studies, how information about prices, profits and costs influences consumer perceptions of price fairness. They show that consumers underestimate inflationary trends, even when provided with explicit quantitative information, and therefore overestimate the profits that sellers are drawing from price increases. When comparing the price of the same product in different types of store (such as a department store versus a discount store), they tend to attribute price differences to different profit motives instead of to different cost levels. Some marketing strategies are considered unfair, even when they are not under the store's control. When they are given information about the cost structure of a firm, consumers tend to focus on the cost of goods sold and ignore other cost categories. In conclusion, unfavourable comparisons seem to dominate: consumers apparently have a tendency to believe that the selling price of a good (or service) is substantially higher than its fair price.

Framing of Price and Price Reductions

Sometimes prices can be presented in different ways in order to make them look more attractive, a practice that is referred to as 'framing'. Likewise, temporary price reductions can be presented in different formats, such as 'up to 50% off', '30–50% off' or 'buy two get one free'. Rationally speaking, consumers should be indifferent to different frames that result in the same cost. However, Chapter 8 showed how framing can affect people's judgements. The frequency of use of price framing suggests that it is an effective pricing tool.

To encourage subscriptions, magazines present their per-issue subscription price. Membership fees of clubs can be framed in terms of the amount per day (only $2.50 per day) instead of the actual total amount to pay ($912). Internet-based suppliers may separate packaging and delivery ($4.95) from the cost of the product ($24.95). Charitable donations explain the benefits you can bring to children in poverty 'for less than a dollar per day'. Gourville (1998) posits that consumers evaluate unfamiliar single-alternative transactions by comparing them to known transactions that involve similar expenses. Different frames therefore foster the retrieval of different comparison bases and influence the evaluation of the offer and compliance. The 'pennies-a-day' frame, as Gourville describes it, triggers comparisons to small ongoing expenses like buying a cup of coffee or a train ticket, which makes the transaction more acceptable.

The effect of the face value of foreign currencies can be considered as an extreme example of framing. Consumers confronted with prices in foreign currencies that have an exchange rate that is a multiple of their own currency tend to underspend because the price looks higher. The reverse happens when the exchange rate is a fraction of the consumers' currency (Raghubir and Srivastava, 2002). This effect occurs even though the exchange rate is provided.

The Effect of Price Endings

Prices often fall just below a round number, a practice referred to as odd pricing. A price of, for instance, $10 is converted to $9.99. According to some counts, between 30 and 65 per cent of all prices end in the digit 9 (Schindler and Kirby, 1997; Stiving and Winer, 1997). The clearest demonstration of the effect of 9-endings on sales comes from Anderson and Simester (2003), who varied prices on identical items in different clothing catalogues that were sent to tens of thousands of randomly selected customer samples. In the different experiments demand for the items with 9-ending prices increased by 7 to 35 per cent. The effect was stronger for new items.

There are two dominant explanations of the phenomenon. A first theory posits that consumers ignore the right-most digits or at least do not give them sufficient weight because of left-to-right processing. A price starting with a 2 therefore looks a lot smaller than a price starting with a 3, even if the complete price is 2.99. Thomas and Morwitz (2005) indeed show that the phenomenon only occurs when the leftmost digit drops by a unit (3 to 2.99) and not when it remains unchanged (3.60 to 3.59). According to a second theory, the 9-ending signals a good deal or a promotion. Schindler (2006) analyzed retail price advertisements and found that 99-ending prices are much more often used in advertisements that carry other low-price cues. He hypothesizes that consumers' repeated exposure to this form of advertising leads to an association between 99-ending prices and low prices. Manning and Sprott (2009) compared choice situations between two alternatives with round or 9-ending prices. A round price difference between (a) 2 and 3 dollar can be presented as (b) 2.00 and 2.99, (c) 1.99 and 2.99 and (d) 1.99 and 3.00. The lower-priced option attracted the highest choice share with frame (d), and the lowest share with frame (b). There was no difference between the two other options.

SECTION 4: CONSUMER RESPONSE TO SALES PROMOTIONS

The effectiveness of sales promotion started receiving attention in the 1980s when the use of promotions increased considerably with the arrival of scanner data. Before the introduction of checkout scanning, companies had to rely on store audit data, collected by auditors on a sample of stores, which were released on only a bimonthly basis. These data did not have the detail necessary to see the real effect of promotions that are usually run on a week-to-week basis. When weekly data became available and marketers realized the full size of the boost to sales, they started investing much more in promotions. Promotions usually have a clearly identifiable impact on sales. Graphs of sales over time show a sales spike after a promotion launch, a phenomenon that is much less apparent for advertising (unless, of course, the advertisement communicates a promotion). Despite enthusiasm for promotions, the consulting company Accenture found, in 2001, that 80–90 per cent of trade promotions do not generate a positive return on investment.

In reaction to the increased use of promotions, academics oriented their research attention to the analysis of promotional effectiveness, usually by using sophisticated quantitative modelling. In his 1995 review of the promotion literature, Chandon counted 200 academic studies published over the previous ten years, while for the period between 1965 and 1983 he only found 40.

Promotions can take many forms but promotional campaigns are usually short-lived (see Box 10.2). The distinction has to be made between promotions offered by retailers and manufacturers to consumers, and trade promotions offered by manufacturers to retailers. Examples of trade promotions are co-op advertising funds and display allowances. The retailer may or may not pass on cost savings to the consumer (called the 'pass-through').

Most research focuses on price promotions, feature advertising, display and couponing. In recent years the interest of promotions has been questioned. Advertising agencies tend to dislike them since they may take part of the ad budget, although this attitude has somewhat changed now that many advertising agencies have converted themselves into full-service agencies that handle all forms of communication, including promotions.

Box 10.2 Types of promotion

- **Direct price reduction** – also known as 'discounts' or, in the USA, as 'deals'.
- **Couponing** – refers to the distribution of certificates that can be redeemed for a discount when purchasing.
- **Rebates or cash back** – price refunds that can only be obtained after the purchase by mailing an application, for instance.
- **Display** – refers to in-store display.
- **Feature advertising** – refers to stand-alone circulars, also known as flyers, that consumers receive in their postbox. This is a form of cooperative advertising in which manufacturers pay retailers to feature their products.
- **Games and contests**.
- **Multibuy** – for example, three for the price of two.
- **Extra quantity** – for example, 10 per cent extra length on a chocolate bar.
- **Bonus offers** – buy product X and get product Y free.

Supplying companies also have mixed feelings about promotions because they have to carry the costs of administration, pack changes and the production and inventory costs associated with peaks and dips in demand. On top of this, a successful promotion may bring retaliation from competitors, which damages later profits. In aggregate, the effects of competing sales promotions may cancel out, leaving a cost that has to be added to the price of goods. Maybe all players (except the sales promotion agencies) would be better off if discounting in mature markets was limited (see Exercise 10.3).

Much of our evidence on sales promotions comes from the USA, where marketing practices are rather different from those applying in Europe. In the USA, we find:

- more lines are normally offered on deal
- discounts are usually larger
- promotion periods are usually a week – shorter than in Europe – and they are often driven by short-life coupons. In other countries coupons are less popular.

Exercise 10.3 Coupon war

In autumn 2002, Tesco and Sainsbury became involved in a coupon war in the UK. Sainsbury had issued coupons on its home delivery service, offering, for instance, discounts of £2 for every £20 of shopping. Tesco reacted by announcing that it would itself honour these coupons on its own service. In retaliation, Sainsbury printed thousands of coupons to send to customers in areas where it was not present, hoping that customers would redeem them with Tesco. Its objective was to decrease Tesco's margins. A Tesco spokesperson replied: 'It is usually our job to promote shopping with Tesco, but if our competition want to do that as well, that is fine with us … The risk is that by encouraging consumers to get discounts with us, it actually makes them more loyal to the Tesco brand.'

Analyze the moves of the two players. Were there alternatives? Under what conditions is there an interest in this type of escalation and for whom? What would you do next if you were Sainsbury?

Sources of Extra Sales

Observing a promotional sales spike or bump does not necessarily mean the promotion was effective. Whether a sales promotion is beneficial, from a managerial perspective, depends on whether the additional sales can be attributed to brand switching (usually good news for the manufacturer, but the retailer's evaluation depends on the relative margins of the competing brands), category expansion effects (even better news, both for manufacturer and retailer) or purchase acceleration and stockpiling (usually mixed news because this can be considered as 'borrowing' sales from the future). Researchers therefore have built sophisticated econometric models to decompose the promotional bump into these three sources of sales.

Initial results were conflicting, with some researchers finding that most promotional sales volume comes from brand switchers (e.g. Gupta, 1988; Totten and Block, 1987) and others observing that category expansion is a more important source of additional sales (e.g. Chintagunta, 1993). One possible explanation of the contrasting findings is product category differences. When comparing category expansion, brand switching and purchase acceleration, Pauwels, Hanssens and Siddarth (2002) found a breakdown of 66/11/23 for a storable product (canned soup) and 58/39/3 for a perishable product (yoghurt). In the most recent analysis to date, van Heerde, Leeflang and Wittink (2004) found that each source contributes to about one-third of the sales bump on average; they used four products, two from an American and two from a Dutch data set.

As already mentioned, stockpiling is considered the least interesting contributor to promotional sales, because it is assumed that consumers would otherwise buy the brand later, at the regular price. However, Ailawadi et al. (2007) demonstrate that stockpiling can also have benefits in two forms – category consumption can increase because consumers have (more of) the product at home, and the extra inventory of the promoted brand may pre-empt the purchase of a competing brand. They observe that the first benefit is the most important and that, together, the two benefits offset the downside of stockpiling.

Price promotions are an important competitive tool for retailers. In a large-scale experiment over 16 weeks in 86 stores across 26 product categories, Hoch, Drèze and Purk (1994) compared an everyday low price (EDLP) strategy (more or less constant low prices) with a Hi-Lo strategy (higher prices but with frequent promotions). For the EDLP condition, they lowered prices by 10 per cent while they increased those for the Hi-Lo condition by 10 per cent. As a result, sales increased by 3 per cent in the EDLP condition while they decreased by 3 per cent in the Hi-Lo condition. There were, however, also large differences in profitability, but now in the opposite direction. EDLP reduced profits by 18 per cent and Hi-Lo increased them by 15 per cent. The authors explain that in general the results depend on how the customer base is divided among price-sensitive store switchers and store-loyal customers. The main interest of the EDLP strategy is that it attracts switchers from other stores. If many consumers are loyal, this will not work well and the profit level will fall because everyone will pay a lower price. In the Hi-Lo strategy, loyal customers purchase their product basket both when the products are on deal and when the price is at the normal level. On average they therefore generate more profit than in the EDLP strategy. Store switchers, on the other hand, will buy more when prices are lower. Overall, the Hi-Lo strategy is therefore a good price discriminator, while the drawback of EDLP is that it offers low prices to everyone, irrespective of price sensitivity.

The Combined Effect of Discount, Display and Ad Features

Research reports by practitioners and consulting agencies claim that the best promotion campaigns are built on synergies between price deals, feature advertising and display. For instance, IRI (1989) have circulated an analysis of these effects based on their 1988 data on sales in 2,400 grocery stores in 66 markets in the USA. The data are normalized on a price

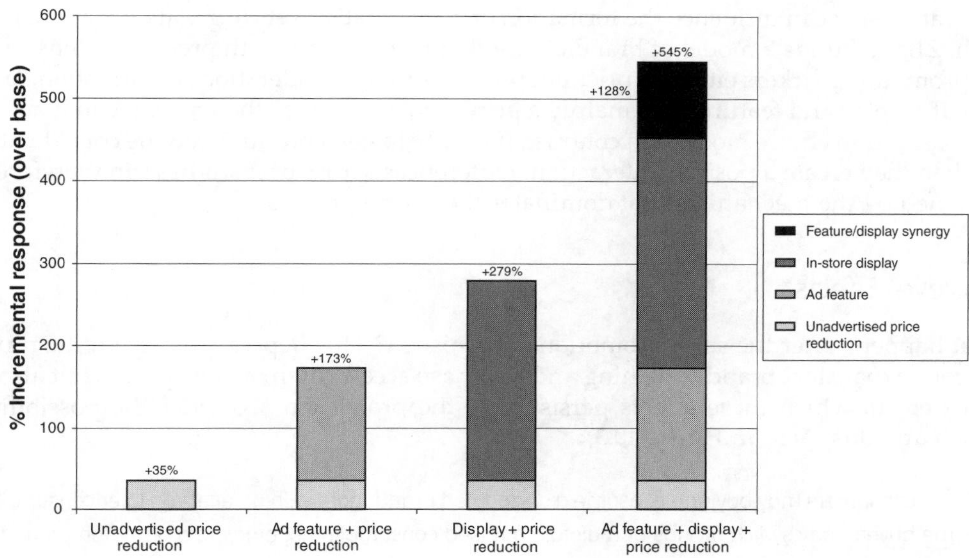

Figure 10.2 The combined effects of discount, display and ad feature

cut of 15 per cent. The main findings are shown in Figure 10.2. The price cut on its own increases sales by 35 per cent (an elasticity of –2.3). When the discount is coupled with an ad feature the effect is 173 per cent, i.e. 138 per cent more than the price cut on its own. When the price cut is paired with an in-store display the sales gain is 279 per cent, 244 per cent more than the sales gain alone. Of particular interest is what happens when price cut, ad feature and display are combined. The sales effects could simply add together, thus:

35% + 138% + 244% = 417%

Figure 10.2 shows instead that there is a gain of 128 per cent above the 417 per cent, which suggests that the three components of promotion act synergistically.

Later academic research, however, reported mixed findings. Gupta (1988) observed negative interactions of display and feature with price cuts, which he attributes to a possible overlap or substitutability among these promotional instruments. Lemon and Nowlis (2002) found, across different brands, a mix of small positive and negative interactions of display and price cut and a negative interaction of feature and price cut. In an experimental setting, East, Eftichiadou and Williamson (2003) found no synergistic effect for a double, as opposed to a single, display. Zhang (2006) provided an explanation of these mixed patterns. She observes first that promotion markers can serve as a proxy for a price cut, as shown by Inman, McAlister and Hoyer (1990); a promotion signal is in this case taken as a cue for a price cut that influences choice even in the absence of a real reduction in price. Second, another stream of research has shown that in-store displays and feature ads can influence the formation of consideration sets (e.g. Allenby and Ginter, 1995). Zhang builds a model of brand choice that incorporates both processes: consumers use promotion markers either as price cut proxies, or for consideration set formation, or for both. If display and feature have mainly a price cut proxy effect, then negative interactions are observed in choice models. In contrast, if they help get a product into the consideration set, then they create a positive interaction. Differences across past studies can therefore be explained by the mechanism that dominates the choice process.

Carryover Effects

What happens after the sales promotion has finished? This depends partly on the mix of category expansion, brand switching and purchase acceleration or stockpiling, but also on the extent to which these effects persist after the promotion. Consider the possibilities (which are illustrated in Figure 10.3):

- Some consumers may buy and consume a discounted brand more with no effect on later consumption.
- Some buyers may switch brands or maintain a raised consumption after trying a brand on promotion.
- Some regular consumers may accelerate purchase and stockpile a brand on a deal; as a result they may buy less later. This requires more planning than is usually found among consumers of frequently purchased goods.

The availability of scanner data has made research on the carryover effect more feasible and the *overall* picture shows little carryover effect. The most comprehensive study in this area is by Ehrenberg, Hammond and Goodhardt (1994a) using panel data from Britain, Germany, America and Japan on 25 established grocery products. The researchers identified 175 sales peaks of 25 per cent or more for different brands in these product fields

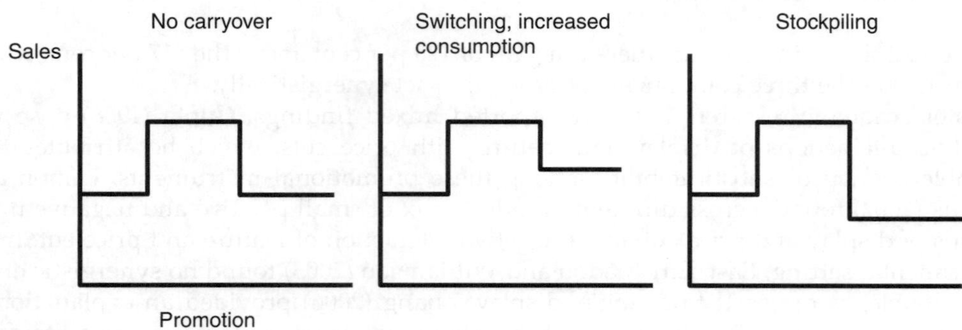

Figure 10.3 Post-promotion sales

and compared sales levels before and after these promotional episodes. The procedure excluded cases where the sales pattern was irregular either before or after the peak.

The overall outcome of this study was a sales increase of 1 per cent which is effectively no effect. A check was made by measuring the repeat buying rates for the 8-week period after the peak; the average was 43 per cent, almost the same as the 44 per cent inferred from NBD theory (see Chapter 4) which showed that buying was stationary in the post-promotion period. Differences between countries were small and there was no evidence that categories showed a consistent movement when data were available on the same category from more than one country.

In sum, these studies show little evidence of carryover effect. A lack of carryover effect is quite difficult to explain. How is it that a spike of extra sales, often several times the normal level, does not disturb the base-level sales? One explanation offered by Ehrenberg et al. is that deals touch only a minority of the brand's customer base; many regular buyers would not see a promotion and their behaviour could not be affected. A second explanation offered by Ehrenberg et al. is that the extra purchasers attracted by the deal were nearly always people who had bought the brand in the past (see Table 10.1); thus a promotion does not introduce *new* buyers to the brand. Those who respond to promotions are past and current buyers who are already familiar with the brand characteristics.

A thoughtful paper by Neslin and Stone (1996) compared seven different explanations for the lack of post-promotion effect. They suggest that many people are insensitive to the stock of purchases already made so that household inventory has little effect on purchase decisions. But the enlarged inventory will eventually slow purchasing and produces a generally lower sales level rather than a post-promotion dip. So, the effect of discount sales is to reduce base-level sales; without promotions the base rate would rise.

Table 10.1 Percentage of those buying on promotion who had bought the brand before (adapted from Ehrenberg, Hammond and Goodhardt, 1994a)

	Bought promoted brand in previous:			
Product	*6 months (%)*	*1 year (%)*	*2 years (%)*	*$2\frac{1}{2}$ years (%)*
Ground coffee (Germany)	78	83	91	95
Detergent (USA)	76	76	88	93
Yogurt (USA)	71	78	90	91
Ketchup (USA)	52	68	88	91
Detergent (Germany)	61	90	98	na
Soup (USA)	75	90	91	na
Carbonated drinks (Germany)	70	79	90	na
Instant coffee (USA)	70	80	90	na
Crackers (USA)	55	65	78	na
Average	**68**	**79**	**89**	**93**

Long-Term Effects of Promotions

There has been concern that there may be a long-term negative effect of promotions that is not revealed in the shorter-term studies that test for carryover effect. Broadbent (1989) and Ogilvy (1987) are among those who have suggested that the heavy use of sales promotions will degrade brand equity.

There are four bases for concern about promotional activity. The first comes from reference price research. Promotional prices may become integrated in the reference price and consumers therefore start perceiving the normal, non-promoted price as high (Kalwani and Yim, 1990). A second basis for concern comes from attribution theory, suggesting that consumers make causal attributions of promotional events; they wonder why the brand is promoted. Lichtenstein and Bearden (1989), for instance, concluded that consumers' reactions are more positive when they think that a promotion aims to attract customers, as opposed to when they think the promotion's objective is to get rid of unwanted goods. Third, customers may see the lower price as evidence of poorer quality. Finally, frequent promotions may condition consumers to only buy on deal. Bolton (1989) and Raju (1992), for instance, observed that the sales spikes are smaller when promotions are more frequent.

In a review of research up to 1995 on the possible negative effect of promotions, Blattberg, Briesch and Fox (1995) conclude that, given the mixed evidence, the 'jury is still out'. However, more recent studies, based on time-series analysis, converge on an absence of positive and a possibility of negative long-term effects. Dekimpe, Hanssens and Silva-Risso (1999) find positive effects for only one brand out of 13 in an analysis of four categories. Nijs et al. (2001) examine the possibility of category expansion but find this type of effect in only 36 of 560 product categories. Pauwels, Hanssens and Siddarth (2002) find no permanent effects of promotions for purchase incidence or purchase quantity. In only one of the 29 cases do they find permanent effects on brand choice.

Couponing

Couponing is vastly popular in the USA. For packaged goods a total volume of almost 300 billion coupons were printed in 2005. For groceries specifically, the total face value of coupons issued that year added up to $190 billion, of which $3 billion were effectively redeemed (Hartnett, 2006). Research has mainly focused on whether and, if so, how coupons create incremental sales. Coupons can increase category consumption (Ailawadi and Neslin, 1998), encourage brand switching (Neslin, 1990), trigger trial (Neslin and Clarke, 1987), and also reward brand loyalty. Neslin (2002: 49) reports several studies that show that brand-loyal consumers are more likely than others to redeem coupons.

Coupons can be considered as an instrument for price discrimination. Instead of giving a discount to all buyers, coupons reserve the discount for consumers who make the effort to obtain the saving. Coupons have to be found, stored, organized and redeemed before expiry for the correct product. The 'cost' associated with this effort, including the opportunity cost of time, is higher for some individuals than for others. Narasimhan (1984) develops this argument in more detail and his analyses conclude that users of coupons are more price-sensitive than non-users of coupons.

American consumers are attached to coupons (see Box 10.3). An explanation for consumers' attachment to coupons is that highly coupon-prone consumers are not only drawn to reduced prices but also are seeking psychological benefits. For instance, they get a sense of achievement by purchasing products on deal and view themselves as smart shoppers, an idea Garretson and Burton (2003) confirmed in a store exit survey.

Box 10.3 Life without coupons?

Procter & Gamble launched in January 1996 an 18-month 'no-coupon' test in upstate New York, a region where 90 per cent of shoppers used coupons. Procter & Gamble believed that across-the-board lower prices offered more efficient savings than coupons. In a survey by the trade journal *Supermarket Business*, 80 per cent of manufacturers and 69 per cent of retailers and wholesalers considered that Procter & Gamble was on the right track and some manufacturers followed its lead (Partch, 1996). However, consumers reacted fiercely with public hearings, petition drives and boycotts. Some put up 'Save Our Coupons' signs on their front lawns. A county official claimed that the elimination of coupons by the 'big guys' was intended to hurt the 'average Joe'. The *Wall Street Journal* observed that 'coupons, to many people, are practically an inalienable right' (Narisetti, 1997: 1). Procter & Gamble stopped the test after 14 months.

Heilman, Nakamoto and Rao (2002) examine responses to in-store instant coupons such as electronic shelf coupons and peel-off coupons on product packages. They show that these 'surprise' coupons increase market basket sales for two reasons – unplanned purchases are made as the result of the psychological income effect in reaction to the unexpected financial gain, and the coupons raise the consumers' mood.

In conclusion, coupons – and promotions in general – are not just forms of price reduction. As Chandon, Wansink and Laurent (2000) show, promotions give consumers hedonic benefits (opportunities for value expression, entertainment and exploration) in addition to utilitarian benefits (savings, the possibility to upgrade to higher product quality and improved shopping convenience).

Customized Promotions

To increase the effectiveness of promotions, marketers have recently explored the use of customization, both in online and offline ('bricks-and-mortar') stores. In an offline environment, coupons are usually printed at the checkout register or sent by mail. They can be redeemed on the next purchase trip. In an online setting, the store interface can be customized for each visit and promotions therefore can be offered for the current shopping occasion. Zhang and Wedel (2009) compare the effect of the degree of customization in these two settings, using a model of purchase incidence, product choice and quantity. The depth and frequency of discounts can be customized at a segment level or at the level of the individual customer. The authors also compare two types of promotions: 'loyalty promotions', aimed at customers who bought the now promoted product at the previous purchase occasion, and 'competitive promotions' for customers who bought a different brand previously. The data come from a large supermarket chain that also sells its products through an internet store. After the estimation of the model parameters they determine the profit maximizing promotional strategy in 300 different scenarios. The authors find that loyalty promotions are more profitable in online stores than in offline stores, while the reverse holds for competitive promotions. This result is driven by the fact that customers of online stores are in general more loyal than those of regular stores. Inducing switching is therefore easier in an offline environment. Surprisingly, individual-level customization is only slightly more profitable than segment-based customization or no customization at all. The effects of customization are particularly small for offline stores. The main problem here is the very low redemption rates of targeted coupons. In an online environment, customization has more potential, but only for promotion-sensitive product categories.

Exercise 10.4 Optimal discounts

Plus is a canned soft drink selling at $1 for a four-pack. The margin is 50 cents and the elasticity is –4.

1 Assuming no additional fixed costs or competitor retaliation, would a discount of 12.5 per cent make money?
2 What is the optimal discount? The profit is given by the number sold multiplied by the margin, i.e. profit = $(100 + 4d)(50 - d)$ where d is the discount as a percentage. If you multiply this out, differentiate, equate the differential to zero (the slope is zero at highest point), you can calculate the optimum discount.
3 Is the promotion still profitable if sales over the period of the promotion are 1 million and fixed costs for the promotion are $40,000, ignoring competitor response?
4 If competitor retaliation reduces subsequent profits by $20,000, is the promotion still worthwhile?

Answers:

1 For every 100 sales at normal price there will be $100 + 4 \times 12.5$ sales at the 12.5 per cent discount, i.e. 150 sales, and the profit will be $0.375 \times 150 = \$56.25$ instead of $0.5 \times 100 = \$50$. Therefore the discount is more profitable than the usual price, assuming no other costs.
2 Multiplying out, profit $= 5000 + 100d - 4d^2$. Differentiating, slope $= 100 - 8d$. Therefore, equating slope to zero, $d = 12.5$ per cent. In words, the optimal discount is 12.5 per cent.
3 On a million sales the profit is $0.375 \times 1{,}000{,}000 = \$375{,}000$ and without the discount the profit on the reduced sales would be $333,333. The profit advantage is $41,667, reduced to $1,667 after taking account of fixed costs.
4 If competitor retaliation costs a further $20,000 the exercise would be loss making.

SUMMARY

Consumers compare observed prices to reference prices in order to determine their interest in buying a particular product at a particular time and place. Reference prices can be externally available or recalled from memory. Price memory is, unfortunately, not reliable for many people. One reason is that prices are not encoded correctly because of their verbal length.

When comparing different products, consumers do not necessarily prefer the product with the lowest price because many associate low price with low quality. In reality, however, price is not a good predictor of quality, but that is not how consumers perceive it.

Market researchers apply different methodologies to assess consumers' price sensitivity. For hypothetical new products they often use conjoint analysis and direct questioning. To examine reactions to large changes in existing prices or to alternative prices for new products, price experiments are used. When historical data are available, econometric estimation of price elasticity is possible.

Consumers react to price changes by adapting their purchase behaviour, but they may also express their agreement or disagreement in ways that affect a company's image and, possibly, its brand equity. There is a clear tendency to interpret price increases as unfair. If companies do not give explanations for price increases that show that increasing profit is not the motive, consumers often infer that profit is the motive. Interestingly, the way a price (or discount) is presented can influence the perception of expensiveness.

Promotions can clearly boost sales temporarily, but long-term positive effects seem to be absent. Even the obvious short-term effects have to be interpreted with caution, because promotions ultimately risk becoming a costly zero-sum game among competitors. Everything depends on the source of the additional sales. If promotions increase switching and bring new customers to the market, they can be profitable. If they just offer the product at a lower price to brand-loyal customers, they may be counter-productive. Customizing promotions could target them more efficiently but recent research indicates that customization is only profitable in certain conditions.

Additional Resources

An excellent overview of pricing research is given in Gijsbrechts (1993). This overview not only shows what the main findings are but also explains how they were obtained. It is not restricted to pricing and also covers some promotion issues. Schindler has published a lot of research on odd pricing and 9-endings. Schindler (2006) is a nice example of how simple observations of the marketplace can be very insightful. This chapter referred several times to meta-analyses. A good recent example of this type of analysis can be found in DelVecchio, Henard and Freling (2006).

11 The Retail Context

LEARNING OBJECTIVES

When you have completed this chapter, you should be able to:

1 Understand the main ideas about gravity models.
2 Discuss the reasons why people use different types of retail store and how they use them at different times.
3 Report on the factors related to loyal, heavy and compulsive shoppers.
4 Discuss the evidence on store atmospheric effects and explain these effects.

OVERVIEW

First, we consider how store location affects shopper choice according to aggregate models. Then, at the individual level, we examine the reasons that individual shoppers give for their choice of supermarket and consider the way in which store use varies over time. We focus on three types of customer: loyal, heavy and compulsive shoppers. We also briefly review loyalty schemes. In conclusion, we assess the ways in which the store environment can influence spending, particularly research on atmospherics, and the impact on shoppers of music, smell, colour and crowding in the store.

SECTION 1: SHOPPER CHOICE

Gravity Models

The number of people who buy from a particular store depends upon nearby population densities, transport access, the store type and the presence of competing retail locations. Gravity models are used to analyze retail data and show how shops, stores, shopping centres and cities draw customers from the surrounding environment.

The early research in this area focused on the attraction exerted on a shopper by two cities at varying distances. Reilly (1929) argued that trade was attracted in direct proportion to the population of each city and inverse proportion to the square of the distance from the city. The similarity with Newton's explanation for the movement of planets under gravity led to theories of this sort being called *gravity models*. Reilly's model implies that there will be a *breaking point* between two cities where customers are equally attracted to each city. The model was tested on 30 pairs of cities and found to be quite accurate. However, it does not allow for the strong appeal of particular stores. However, distance is only an approximate indicator of the travel effort and cost which really control customer demand; Reilly's model is less applicable when good transport facilities make distant locations easily accessible. In addition, neighbourhoods vary in their preferences and spending power so that population size is only a crude indicator of expenditure per head.

As store location models became more sophisticated, Huff (1962, 1981) modelled the pulling power of a retail centre within a city. In this model the attraction of a centre, A_1, is a function of its selling area (S), divided by a power λ (lambda) of the travel time (T):

$$A_1 = S/T^{\lambda}$$

The probability of a consumer using a shopping area is a function of A_1 divided by the sum of the attractions of all the available shopping centres, i.e.

$$p = A_1/\Sigma(A_1 \ldots A_n)$$

Wee and Pearce (1985) found that Huff's model was well supported and that the exponent, λ, was approximately two, as Reilly hypothesized. Huff's approach includes all the possible shopping centres, although in practice a consumer might rule many of these out. Wee and Pearce modified Huff's model and used only the shopping centres that the shopper considered. With this adjustment, predictions were better but even the improved model gave an R^2 of only 0.25, showing that much of location preference remained unexplained. This is hardly surprising since a gravity model cannot take account of the detail of a particular shopping environment or of the exact way in which information is processed. For example, Foxall and Hackett (1992) found that stores that were located at path junctions were better remembered. One use of gravity models is to calculate the impact on sales in existing stores when a new store is opened in a particular location. Using Wee and Pearce's (1985) approach, it is possible to estimate the loss of trade.

Because shoppers are attracted to retail centres, store growth also happens at these centres. *Central place theory* (Christaller, 1933; Losch, 1939) uses the importance of a centre and the economic distance as basic concepts to explain how centres develop and how retail units tend to cluster together, with each taking advantage of the custom generated by the others. Businesses in the same field can benefit from proximity since together they increase the total custom. We can find examples of this effect in most cities; one example is the concentration of restaurants in particular locations (see Box 11.1).

Box 11.1 Retail clusters

Some quite small locations can become specialists in a particular field. In and around the ancient Shropshire town of Ludlow there are seven restaurants with entries in the *Michelin Guide*. People can take a long weekend in Ludlow and eat excellent cuisine. As a result, Ludlow may draw gourmets from great distances. A similar effect is found in Ireland, at Kinsale, which again is a hub for award-winning restaurants.

Store Preferences

Gravity models and central place theory provide explanations of retail attractiveness at an aggregate level. At an individual level, we can ask about the shoppers' preferences for store types and assemble the reasons given for using stores. We can also investigate when the stores are used, and how frequently. Complete Exercise 11.1 below on your personal use of supermarkets.

Exercise 11.1 Supermarket use

Which supermarket do you use most? What is the reason for this? Do you have a regular day and time of day for doing your shopping? Many people do have regular times – why do you think this is so? Would you say that you were loyal to your main supermarket? What does this mean?

Try to answer these questions now. In the sections below, we provide answers from data gathered over twenty years.

Reasons for Using Supermarkets

In the 1990s, surveys of supermarket use were conducted in the UK at Kingston University in concert with colleagues in the USA and New Zealand. These surveys sought the reasons why respondents used their main supermarket (the one where they spent most). Table 11.1 shows the principal reasons across different years and continents. One message from Table 11.1 is that the reasons for shopping at supermarkets do not vary that much between different advanced economies. The two most important criteria were location and good value; these account for an average of 55 per cent of the main reasons given for patronizing a specific supermarket. There was more interest in good value in the USA and New Zealand, compared with the UK. When the figures are compared for 1992 and 1994, we find that, in the USA, good value dominates in 1992, probably because of a recession at that time. Recession hit the UK rather later and we see an increase in the importance of good value there in 1994. Then, as the economy became more settled from 1994 to 1998, the

Table 11.1 Reasons for patronizing main supermarkets

Reason	1992 UK (%)	1992 USA (%)	1994 UK (%)	1994 USA (%)	1998 UK (%)	1998 New Zealand (%)	Mean (%)
Location (easy to get to)	32	25	29	33	31	24	29
Good value/lowest price/sales promos	14	34	24	29	20	35	26
Good quality	15	15	14	11	14	5	12
Wide choice	18	13	13	12	10	7	12
Other (familiarity with store, parking, etc.)	21	13	20	15	25	29	21

Sources: Consumer Research Unit, Kingston University, UK; Debra Perkins, Florida Memorial University, USA; Phil Gendall, Massey University, New Zealand

importance of good value eased slightly. This evidence shows that supermarket choice criteria can change in response to economic conditions; retailers are alert to such changes and adjust their offerings and communications accordingly. Thus, with the onset of the global economic crisis in 2008, there has been an increased emphasis on price. This can be seen in Figure 11.1 in data provided by Nielsen for the UK. Focus is on the main store shopping which is mostly done in supermarkets.

We see that in the severe economic conditions of 2011, getting good value is important for the main shopping trip since 'value for money' together with 'low prices' and 'in-store promotion' account for 82 choices out of 200. Convenient location gets only 27 out of 200 for the main store while range and quality criteria combined get 63 out of 200. We should be wary about direct comparison between Table 11.1 and Figure 11.1 because of the

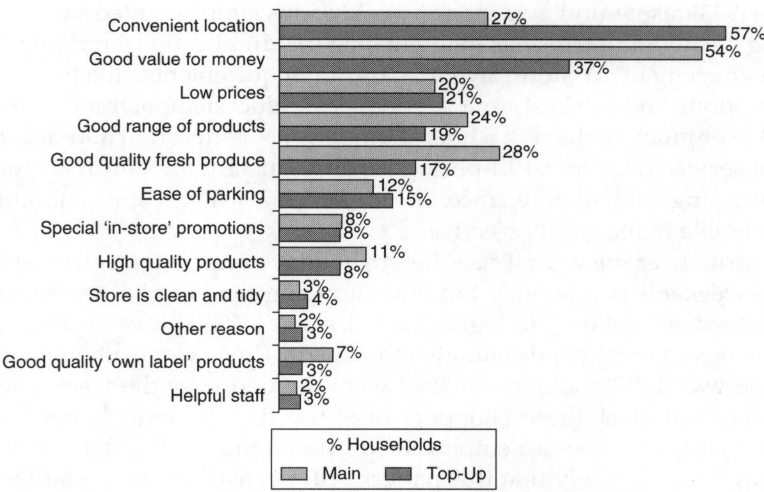

Figure 11.1 Which of the following factors are most important when choosing where to do your shopping? (Check two reasons) (UK data supplied by Nielsen for 2011)

different methods used for gathering data but if we compare top-line findings, it appears that, compared with the 1990s, in 2011 low prices are considerably more important, location less so and quality/range much the same.

In the past location has been the main advantage for convenience stores but, since supermarket groups have invaded the convenience field with their small store formats, the independent convenience stores have little protection from the competition of the big supermarket groups. What then is the future for the small independent grocer? In the UK, the big four, Tesco, Asda, Sainsbury and Morrison accounted for 75 per cent of all grocery sales in 2010, according to the Kantar Worldpanel reported in *The Guardian* (2011). However, there do seem to be some hazards for the big groups. As often happens when firms get larger, there has been a groundswell of resistance to some aspects of modern store management. There has been worry about the power exerted by retailers over suppliers and about their ability to outspend local authorities that oppose new store developments. There have been complaints about the air freighting of vegetables from Africa to Europe because of carbon emissions and demands for more local sourcing. Despite this last criticism, small stores have failed to capitalize on the demand for local sourcing which has been met by farmers' markets in many countries.

Shopping Trip Patterns

The previous section outlined the reasons shoppers give for their choice of store. However, it is important to understand not just why and where people shop but also how often and when. While consumers go shopping for a great variety of goods, researchers have mostly studied grocery shopping (partly because of the wealth of detailed data available from consumer panels). Households tend to have a routine of supermarket shopping that often includes one weekly main trip and one or more top-up trips. In the USA, McKay (1973), Frisbie (1980) and Kahn and Schmittlein (1989) found this pattern. In Britain, Dunn, Reader and Wrigley (1983) also found evidence of weekly trips supplemented by secondary trips.

The timing of shopping trips has many managerial implications, ranging from staffing and stock management to store layout, parking requirements, likely effectiveness of in-store promotions and the best time to conduct product demonstrations. The store may be little used over much of the day while, at other times, congestion and delay may reduce the quality of service delivered. Off-peak periods are useful for staff relaxation, cleaning, restocking, training and maintenance, as Sasser (1976) notes, but smoothing demand remains a desirable managerial objective.

Store use varies over the year; it rises before holiday periods and can be affected by bad weather. The weekend is a holiday too and shopping tends to be heavier on Thursday, Friday and Saturday, as shown in Figure 11.2. East et al. (1994) investigated whether fully employed customers used supermarkets at different times from other shoppers; Figure 11.2 shows the way 1,012 shoppers in 1992 were divided over the week and Figure 11.3 shows the distribution of these shoppers over the day, by employment status. These figures show that those who are employed full-time tend to shop later in the week and later in the day and it is likely that this pattern still persists. We can infer from these two distributions that those shopping late on a Friday or on Saturday are very likely to be employed full-time. This separation of the employment segments could be useful to store

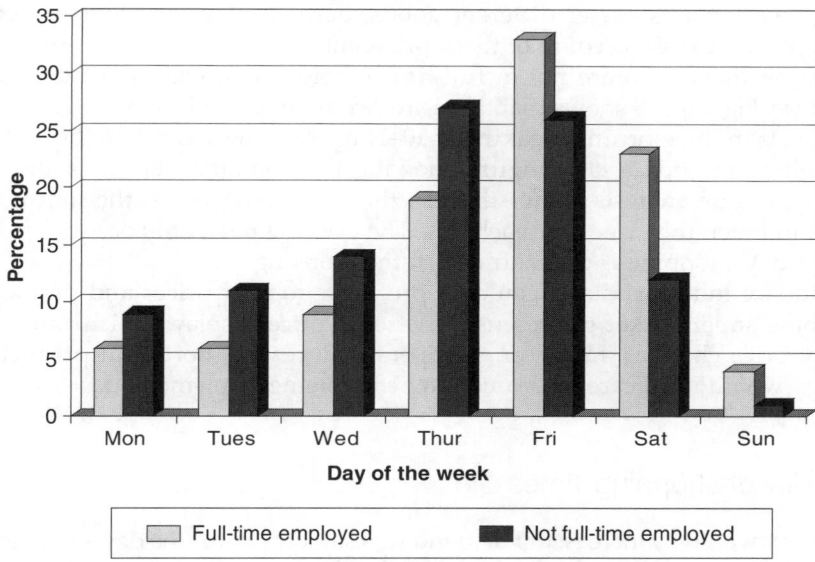

Figure 11.2 Percentage of shoppers on each day by employment status (East et al., 1994)

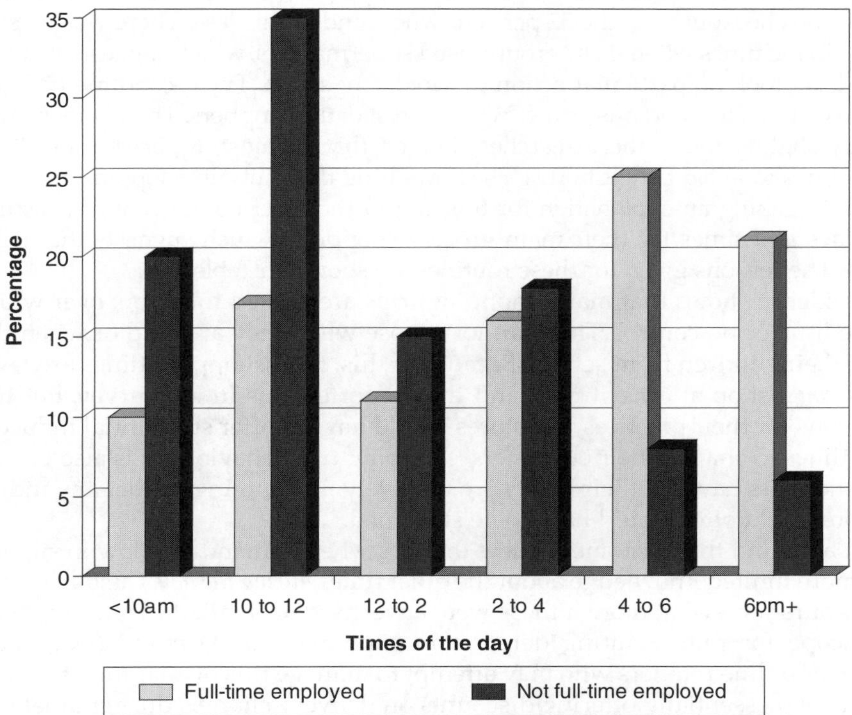

Figure 11.3 Percentage of shoppers at different times of the day by employment status (East et al., 1994)

owners; if these groups prefer different goods, both displays and in-store promotions could be switched to take account of these preferences.

Focusing on those who are not in full-time employment, who make up much of the customer base, Figure 11.3 shows that there are two main periods of high demand over the day. The first is in the morning, peaking at 10–11am, and the second, in the early evening. It is difficult to provide a clear figure showing the combined effect of day and hour preferences but our analysis shows that, as the week progresses, the morning peak is distributed in much the same way each day. The evening peak only occurs Wednesday to Friday. Saturday shopping is concentrated in the morning.

This evidence indicates that it could be profitable to alter prices and promotions over the day. Some supermarket groups use electronic price display, which can be used for time-of-day price changes. However, shoppers may resent short-term price changes, so this strategy would need careful evaluation before being implemented.

The Flexibility of Shopping Times

Store efficiency would be increased if demand was smoother over the day and over the week. East et al. (1994) investigated the flexibility of the times of use of stores and, in particular, whether shoppers deliberately avoided busy times. This was tested in supermarkets in two ways. The first method compared the times of shopping of the 48 per cent who disliked being held up at the checkout with the 52 per cent who minded this less. There was no significant difference in the times when these groups used supermarkets, which suggests that those who disliked delay took no particular action to avoid congestion. The second method compared those who claimed to avoid busy times with the rest of the shoppers. The 'avoiders' used quiet times only slightly more; the researchers judged that, at most, 6 per cent of all shoppers changed times to avoid congestion. This shows little flexibility in shopping times and East et al. (1994), seeking an explanation for this, found that over 60 per cent of consumers had routine days and times for their main grocery shopping, which suggests that habits limit flexibility. The reasons given for these routines are shown in Table 11.2.

This evidence shows that many shopping trips are related to factors over which shoppers have little or no control. They cannot choose when they are paid or when they have to collect their children from school. Because of this, their shopping times are fairly rigid; shoppers *could* shop at other times, and they reported this in the survey, but they have good reasons for their practices and stores would have to offer substantial inducements at off-peak times to change their customers' shopping trip behaviour. It is also clear that the reasons shoppers have for their habits are relatively unchanging so that any inducements that a store might offer would have to be sustained.

East et al. found that customers knew the *days* when demand was low in supermarkets but had more limited knowledge about the quiet times *during the day*. Customers might use off-peak hours somewhat more if these were advertised. Overall, these findings suggested limited scope for redistributing demand in supermarkets. Demand peaks are also a headache for online retailers who may attempt to manage this by manipulating the fee for home-delivery, essentially offering discounts on delivery charges during quiet times and premiums for deliveries at weekends.

Table 11.2 What was your main reason for shopping on …? (East et al., 1994)

On a specific day	*%*	*At a specific time of day*	*%*
Near weekend	28	Fitted in with other shopping	25
Day not working	16	Store less busy	25
Store less busy	13	Left work then	15
Ran out of food, needed item	13	Car/lift/help available	13
Wages/pension day	12	Ran out of food, needed item	6
Car/lift/help available	12	On route to/from work	5
Food fresher/better stocked	5	On route to/from school	4
Open late	2	Easier parking	4
		Happened to pass store	3
		To meet people	1

Exercise 11.2 Analysis of store data

On the website associated with this book (www.sagepub.co.uk/east) you will find UK98, which is the data in SPSS format from a survey conducted in the UK. Findings from this survey were used for this chapter. The questionnaire for the survey is supplied as SU6. Use SPSS to compare stores (question 3) in respect of comparative checkout delay, how much the store is recommended and the relative share of requirements (questions 13, 16 and 21). Use **Compare means, means**, to get the means per store.

For all stores, what factors are associated with the rating of the store? To do this, select potential predictors and run an ordinal regression to predict the answers to question 17. Is rating related to recommendation and share of requirement? Use a Spearman correlation to test for this.

How strong are these findings? What alternative explanations are there for the associations you find?

SECTION 2: CUSTOMER TYPOLOGIES

Textbooks sometimes contain classifications of customer types. These may be hypothetical or derived empirically from data. For example, one might hypothesize that shoppers divide into 'prospecting' and 'reluctant' shoppers. The 'prospectors' are generally positive about shopping and see the retail environment as a hunting ground for new ideas, fashions and bargains; these people play a game with retailers in which they feel they have won when they get good value for money. The 'reluctants' have little interest in shopping and see it as a necessary means for achieving other goals. Using this classification, we might be able to predict other behaviour. For example, we might expect more window shopping by prospectors.

Perhaps the most sophisticated classification of shoppers is made by the Dunnhumby agency in their analysis of Tesco's loyalty data. Dunnhumby uses a selection of frequently bought products to classify customers on 30 criteria. For example, a large size of oven-ready chips will indicate positively for budget consciousness and negatively for health consciousness or gourmet propensity. Those who purchase organic produce indicate another type of concern and those who buy Tesco's own label disproportionately may be classified as Tesco loyalists. These behaviour-based classifications are used to ensure that coupons go to those who will appreciate them, and new products are promoted to customers who are likely to buy them.

In this section, we consider three types of store customer: store-loyal, heavy, and those whose shopping behaviour seems out of control – compulsive customers. The first two are important for profit; the last indicates a social problem that may concern us.

Store-Loyal Customers

Like brand loyalty (Chapter 2), store loyalty can be defined in a number of ways. The attitude to, or satisfaction with, the store provides one measure of loyalty. As behaviour, loyalty can be measured by *share-of-category requirement* (SCR), which is the proportion of spending in a specific store or group. Interest tends to focus on the SCR to the primary store, called *first-store loyalty*. Another behavioural measure is *retention* of the store in the shopper's store portfolio; high retention loyalty occurs when customers patronize the store for a long time. Despite the assumption that different loyalty measures have some common basis (discussed in Chapter 2), these measures may show little association. East et al. (2005a) found that the SCR for the primary store and attitude to the store showed only weak correlations of 0.13 and 0.15 in UK and New Zealand studies.

Store loyalty can be investigated using the market regularities described in Chapter 4. We may use models like the Dirichlet to show the relationship at an aggregate level between SCR requirement and factors such as penetration, purchase frequency and market share (Kau and Ehrenberg, 1984; Uncles and Ehrenberg, 1990; Uncles and Hammond, 1995; Wright, Sharp and Sharp, 1998). We may also search for economic, demographic, behavioural or attitudinal factors that predict SCR or retention at an individual level. Such variables include age, the frequency of store use, the accessibility of the store, brand loyalty, shopping on a particular day, the amount spent in the retail category, income, attitude to the store and free time. Retailers will also be interested in whether the customers of different store groups show differences in average loyalty (Box 11.2).

Box 11.2 Average supermarket loyalty

Average levels of loyalty to different stores depend on the retail category, market concentration, average store size and the period of time taken for measurement. For supermarkets in the UK, AGB (1992) reported that over an 8-week period approximately 75 per cent of expenditure took place in the primary supermarket. Also in the UK, Mason (1991) reported that the SCR for the primary store was 72 per cent over one month, 65 per cent over 12 weeks and 60 per cent over 24 weeks. Loyalties to the store group are slightly higher than the loyalty to the individual store. In keeping with the double jeopardy rule (Chapter 4) bigger stores and larger store groups tend to have higher SCRs.

Box 11.3 Purchase and loyalty on the Internet

In Chapter 1, we drew attention to the rapid growth of Internet purchase. In the early days of Internet use, it was argued that this channel was particularly suited to 'bit-based' products such as music, booking travel, share purchase, banking, gambling and pornography. These fields have certainly prospered but the Internet is now frequently used to purchase a range of physical products. Some of these are familiar, such as groceries, books, CDs and clothing, while others benefit from the ability to search the Web for unusual products. For example, if you want to find a specialized product that might not be sold in your neighbourhood such as an orthopaedic back support or home fire-escape ladder these are easily located online and delivered to your door. Thus, some use of the Internet is driven by the convenience of this method of purchase. The ability to deliver relevant information is a powerful incentive in other cases, e.g. for the purchase of stocks and shares, and this could raise loyalty.

From the standpoint of the supplier, the Internet may save costs, particularly for bit-based products that can be distributed 'down the wire'. The customer can also save because price comparison is easy on the Internet. Nielsen (*Online Shopping*, 2011a) found that 30 per cent agreed strongly and 37 per cent slightly that you could save money on groceries by buying on the Internet. However, there are drawbacks and the Nielsen study showed that the inability to select for oneself when buying groceries on the Internet was the most common problem reported about Internet grocery purchase. Internet grocery shopping is well established in the UK and has been growing at 20 per cent a year but still only accounts for five per cent of all grocery shopping and ranks twentieth in every-day usage of the Internet (Nielsen, *Online Shopping*, 2011a).

Grocery buying has been studied to see whether brand loyalty is stronger when purchase is made on the Internet. Degeratu, Rangaswamy and Wu (2001) found that brand names played a stronger role in choice and that fewer brand switches were made in the online environment. But Degeratu et al. studied relatively early adopters of online shopping and also compared those who shopped online with those who shopped offline and any differences may be due to the different abilities and interests of the two groups rather than to the channel used. Arce and Cebollada (2006) improved the analysis by comparing the online and offline grocery purchasing of the same people. They confirmed that there was less brand switching online. One explanation for this is that, on the Web, buyers may work from a list of past purchases and take less advantage of the discount opportunities available. As a result, they stick to the same brands and have high loyalty.

Heavy Shoppers

Some shoppers are obviously more important than others; in particular, heavy buyers and loyal buyers should be a focus of management attention. According to the 'heavy half' principle (Chapter 4), the heaviest 50 per cent of buyers will make about 80 per cent of all purchases. Retailers want to identify these heavy buyers and aim to target promotions to these shoppers in order to recruit and retain them.

It might be thought that those who spend more would use more shops and therefore have lower first-store loyalty but Dunn and Wrigley (1984) and Mason (1991) found that first-store loyalty did not change with increasing total expenditure in supermarkets. Knox and Denison (2000) found a small positive association ($r = 0.24$) between store loyalty and total spending for supermarkets but a negative relationship for other types of retail outlet. If bigger spenders in supermarkets are more loyal, it follows that they are doubly attractive to the retailer who gets their main custom. Not only do they spend more but a larger proportion of this spending goes to their favourite store. Stores with loyalty data may be able to identify heavy buyers directly from their spending and direct promotions to them. (Note that loyalty data only show purchases at the single store chain but spending in other stores may be inferred from the goods bought in the single chain.)

Unpublished data gathered at Kingston University on heavy supermarket shoppers suggests that, more than other segments, heavy shoppers tend to have larger incomes and households, be under age 45, prefer large out-of-town stores, shop later in the day, less often, and have a regular day for shopping.

Compulsive Shoppers

In the USA, 15 million people are estimated to exhibit the deviant pattern of compulsive purchase; they buy clothes, shoes and other goods which they do not need and sometimes never use (Arthur, 1992). Scherhorn, Reisch and Raab (1990) have reported on compulsive shopping in Germany and Elliott (1993, 1994) has researched this phenomenon in the UK. Faber and O'Guinn (1988) saw this type of shopping as part of a wider range of compulsive behaviour, which they describe as: 'A response to an uncontrollable drive or desire to obtain, use, or experience a feeling, substance, or activity that leads an individual to repetitively engage in behaviour that will ultimately cause harm to the individual and/or others.' Compulsive purchase has been reviewed more recently by Black (2007) who reports that nearly six per cent of the US population fit this classification and that this compulsive pattern is associated with other compulsive behaviour.

Compulsive shopping is clearly a serious problem, which often causes financial and psychological distress to the shoppers themselves and to their families. One reason for compulsive shopping could be the more attractive shopping environment of the present day but, to explain why some people suffer from this compulsion more than others, we need to focus on the behaviour and background of the compulsive shopper. D'Astous (1990) argues that this type of behaviour is the extreme end of a continuum and that many people have strong urges to buy that they can barely hold in check.

Compulsive shoppers tend to be owners of credit cards (D'Astous, 1990); 92 per cent are women, and they tend to be younger and to have lower self-esteem (Faber and O'Guinn, 1992). Research in this area is by survey and it is difficult to assign cause and effect; compulsive shoppers may have low self-esteem because of their behaviour but it seems more likely that it is a cause, rather than an effect.

Compulsive shoppers appear to get some emotional release, or temporary 'mood repair', out of the process of buying. Elliott, Eccles and Gournay (1996) interviewed 50 compulsive shoppers and probed their thinking and motivation. The respondents accepted that their behaviour was abnormal and potentially very damaging but they could not easily control it. In this respect it functioned rather like a drug and Elliott et al. emphasize this by describing the behaviour as addictive. Elliott et al. also found that this type of shopping was often related to unsatisfactory relationships with partners. Women whose partners worked excessively, ignored them, or were controlling, were more likely to be compulsive shoppers. In many cases, their behaviour was a form of revenge or was deliberately designed to rile their partner. In other cases, their treatment by their partner may have lowered their self-esteem and made compulsive shopping more likely.

Dittmar, Beattie and Friese (1995) suggested that the way in which products are bought reflects the way in which people see themselves. These researchers suggested that the sexes might differ in this respect. They found that men tend to buy instrumental and leisure items impulsively, reflecting their independence and activity, while women tend to buy symbolic and self-expressive goods concerned with appearance and the emotional aspects of self. The researchers suggested that similar patterns might be found in compulsive shoppers. Dittmar (2005) stresses that materialistic values are one key to compulsive shopping. Those with low self-esteem can only get mood repair from shopping if possessions have importance to them (see Figure 11.4).

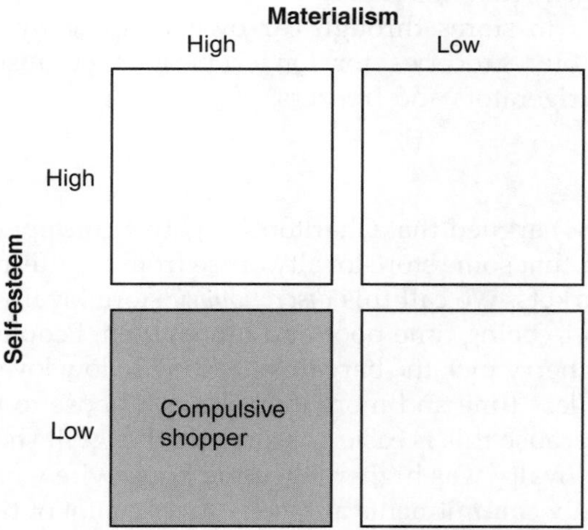

Figure 11.4 Compulsive shopping as a product of high materialism and low self-esteem

Theories of Store Loyalty

There may be no overarching explanations for giving most of one's shopping spend (high SCR) to one store, or for remaining loyal to a specific store for many years (high retention). These effects may be the result of a large number of weak influences that have little in common. However, it is reasonable to look for one or two mobilizing influences that are responsible for much of the effect and here there have been two competing theories about the nature of store loyalty. We report these theories and suggest a third possibility.

Resource Constraint

The first theory of store loyalty was suggested by Charlton (1973), who drew on earlier work by Enis and Paul (1970). In this theory, store loyalty is the outcome of limited resources: those who lack money, time and transport, or whose environment lacks choice (Tate, 1961), are forced to use one store much of the time and are therefore obliged to be loyal. Carman (1970) offered a variation of this model, suggesting that some people had little interest in shopping and therefore did not use the choice that they had. Such people had commitments outside the home, full-time work, little home entertaining and a lack of interest in deals, advertising and shopping. As a result, they were loyal to both brands and stores because they did not seek alternatives. However, East, Harris, Willson and Lomax (1995b) found that shoppers with different loyalty levels gave similar ratings for the pleasantness of supermarket shopping, which does not support Carman's lifestyle theory.

Carman (1970), and Enis and Paul (1970), found that those with low incomes were more loyal, so resource constraint probably did affect loyalty at the time when the research was conducted but it is unlikely that this still applies. Shoppers now have more choice because they have wider access to stores through car ownership or by shopping online, and, specifically, they can buy groceries for longer periods because of almost universal availability of home refrigerators and freezers.

Discretionary Loyalty

Dunn and Wrigley (1984) argued that Charlton's negative concept of store loyalty needed review. They suggested that some store loyalty arose from a pattern of one-stop shopping, often in large supermarkets. We call this *discretionary* store loyalty. Discretionary loyalty could be an adaptation to being time poor and money rich. People can spend less if they use several stores and cherry pick the bargains (leading to low loyalty) but this takes time and effort. Those with less time and more money may choose to buy most of what they need from one outlet because this is easier; as a result, they will show high loyalty. Mason (1991) found that store loyalty was higher when the housewife worked and was under 45 years of age (when family commitments are likely to take a lot of time). Flavián, Martínez and Polo (2001) found general support for discretionary loyalty in Spain. However, East et al. (2000) found that neither free time nor income was significantly related to SCR in a regression analysis covering many factors and this leaves some doubt about the basis of discretionary loyalty.

Loyalty as Habit

An alternative way of thinking about loyalty is that it is a habit. The habit may be set by the conditions under which a person lives; for example, those with routine work patterns are free at specific times and may fit shopping at a particular store into one of these times;

after a while, this arrangement will become routine. Another basis for habit is personal disposition; some people may find routines more attractive than other people. Either way, we would expect to find that those with high store loyalty tend to have other similar habits, such as brand loyalty and a regular day for shopping. Evidence from East et al. (2000) gave support to this explanation.

The Effects of Loyalty Schemes

Loyalty schemes take a variety of forms. All schemes have some form of customer incentive. Many schemes, such as supermarket loyalty programmes, give cash or product incentives. Some schemes raise service levels for a more valuable part of the customer base, for example the provision of executive lounges for frequent air travellers. A loyalty scheme has two potential effects. First, the incentives may raise customer acquisition, share of wallet and retention by directly influencing customers. Second, when data on the purchases of different card holders are collected, the store owner may use those data to target shopper segments more accurately and produce further gains in customer acquisition, spending and retention.

Incentives are very expensive. They take about one per cent of turnover; thus, if the store group makes 5 per cent on turnover, the incentives reduce margin by 20 per cent and sales must be increased to compensate for this. Furthermore, competitors can run loyalty schemes which may cancel out any gains. In an effort to reduce the effect of competitor response, some schemes, such as Air Miles and Fly Buys, only allow one retailer in each sector. If Shell gives Air Miles, BP, Esso and others are excluded. However, competitors can still run alternative schemes.

A loyalty scheme provides a database covering most customers together with information about their purchases. Retailers can use this information to ensure that promotions (often by vouchers) are well targeted. Tesco, with its analysis agency Dunnhumby, is recognized as a world leader in this field. Tesco is interested in the types of purchase made – and not made – by a card holder. If the customer buys no meat, vouchers for meat are never sent, to avoid offending vegetarians, but if the customer does not buy toothpaste at Tesco, vouchers might be used in an effort to switch their purchasing of toiletries to Tesco. A similar inducement might be given to those who appear to buy most of their wine elsewhere; alternatively, the wine buff may be invited to wine tasting events. In other cases, vouchers may be for what the customer already buys, and act as a reward. The database also reveals customers who have switched to competitors (they can differentiate this from going on holiday by the nature of the purchases before the customer leaves). Defecting customers can be sent vouchers in order to recover them. Customer purchase information also helps to sell items that never go through the stores, such as gardening equipment and baby buggies (certain other items purchased, together with a customer's age, can indicate when she may be pregnant). The customer database allows Tesco to launch financial products, such as credit cards and insurance, with less risk than its competitors. The pattern of demand in stores allows the management to tailor the inventories for different stores. Tesco can also sell data to manufacturers because the system shows the relative performance of brands.

This sophisticated operation has helped to expand Tesco's total business and, in the view of the company, it is the information rather than the direct incentive effect that justifies the scheme. However, researchers remain interested in the incentive effect of loyalty cards; this is difficult to measure because other factors may be involved. For example, Tesco took share from Sainsbury when the loyalty scheme was introduced in 1995 but much of this change might have happened in any case because Tesco built more stores, many of which were in Sainsbury territory (East and Hogg, 1997). Although Tesco gained market share, the firm's customers did not show a disproportionate increase in the share-of-category requirement (SCR). This is despite the fact that Tesco was targeting those with intermediate loyalty to the store in an effort to expand their SCR. The data in Table 11.3 from Taylor Nelson Sofres show that in 1996, a year after the introduction of the loyalty scheme, Tesco had a slightly greater market share than Sainsbury in 1994, but the same SCR. Thus, Tesco's loyalty scheme seems to have built the customer base by gaining new customers rather than by getting their existing customers to buy more. This seems to be the normal pattern for share gains that was noted in Chapter 4.

Table 11.3 Market share and share-of-category requirement for five UK store groups, 1994–7

	1994		*1996*		*1997*	
Store group	*MS*	*SCR*	*MS*	*SCR*	*MS*	*SCR*
Tesco	18	44	21	46	22	48
Sainsbury	20	46	19	45	20	48
Asda	11	42	12	42	13	44
Safeway	9	34	10	35	10	36
Somerfield	7	31	6	29	5	28

Source: Data from Taylor Nelson Sofres

Meyer-Waarden (2007) has reviewed studies of incentive effect. In general, there is little or no effect of SCR from loyalty schemes; for example, Sharp and Sharp (1997) found that the firms in the Fly Buys scheme in Australia did not show a significant increase in SCR compared with Dirichlet norms. Meyer-Waarden used panel data in his own research and found that customers who were holders of one card showed single-figure percentage increases in lifetime duration (retention) and more share of wallet but customers with several cards did not show these effects.

In these studies, loyalty membership may involve self-selection; if those who join a loyalty scheme are already highly loyal customers, it is difficult to attribute effects to the loyalty scheme. Leenheer et al. (2007) took account of self-selection effects in a study of loyalty schemes in Dutch supermarkets. They found that, if self-selection was ignored, loyalty schemes increased share of wallet by 30 percentage points but, when self-selection effects were taken into account, the increase in share of wallet attributable to loyalty programme membership averaged 4 per cent. The size of the effect varied slightly between schemes and reduced as the customers joined additional loyalty programmes. A four per cent gain in customer loyalty is probably not going to cover the cost of the scheme but it is a mistake to focus only on share of wallet since customer acquisition and retention may also give a return. Another study on the long-term effect of loyalty programmes by Liu (2007) found that these did not affect heavy buyers but low- and moderate-weight buyers increased spending. An influential early paper on loyalty schemes was quite sceptical about their benefits (Uncles, Dowling and Hammond, 2003). This review tends to support this verdict with regard to their incentive effect but it appears that loyalty schemes may be justified when the wider advantages derived from loyalty data are included.

SECTION 3: THE STORE ENVIRONMENT

Store Layout, Location and Space

Actions occur when the environment presents opportunities, stimuli and rewards. The store layout should therefore be designed to increase spending opportunities, present purchase cues and make the store an easy and pleasant place to be. These different considerations do not always coincide; for example, IKEA uses a layout that requires the customer to move through the whole store in order to reach the exit; this may raise spending opportunities but it can be a near-claustrophobic experience for some customers who find it difficult to get out.

In supermarkets, specific locations in the store are associated with different rates of purchase, probably because they provide a more powerful stimulus to shoppers. For example, the end-aisle position induces more purchase and eye-level shelves sell nearly twice as much as the lowest shelf. One of the applications of scanner technology, called direct product profitability (DPP), is to measure the profit from a given stock keeping unit (SKU) in a specific location. This technology identifies 'hot-spots' in the store and SKUs can be moved to optimize profit. However, sales gains for items given more space or better locations are offset by the lower sales of items that lose space or go to a worse location. Drèze, Hoch and Purk (1994) showed a potential profit difference of about 15 per cent when comparing the worst and best configurations of location and space but, in practice, the authors estimated that the feasible changes would produce a much smaller gain.

Early experimental studies on varying shelf space in grocery categories show that a doubling of space leads to sales increases in the region of 20 per cent (Cox, 1970; Curhan, 1972; Kotzan and Evanson, 1969; Krueckeberg, 1969). However, Drèze et al. found that more effect came from location than from the amount of space given to an SKU. The display of goods has been found to be important in supermarkets as a large proportion of grocery purchase decisions are made at the point of purchase (Dagnoli, 1987).

Atmospherics

Store Features

The store environment includes the amount of space employed, and the layout, fittings, colours, aromas, sound and density of customers present. There are some standard display features used by stores that affect the impression given by the store. For example, discount stores sell out of cases to emphasize low prices, shopping centres create central areas with entertaining features, and fashion shops use music that suits the age and taste of their clientele. These features help to define the store offering and to differentiate it from that of other stores (and from the sellers on the Internet). In this sense, store design and the display of goods have parallels with advertising and packaging.

Exercise 11.3 Assessing atmospheric features

Describe a shop which you find attractive *and* stimulating. What is the basis for this? How is space, colour, sound and odour used? Do these environmental features affect your spending in the store?

Kotler (1973) suggested that store features create an *atmosphere*, modifying the buyer's knowledge and mood and thus effect behaviour. Kotler also noted that atmospherics could be used to de-market; for example, State liquor stores in some countries are deliberately off-putting environments. There is no doubt that environmental features can have a strong effect on in-store behaviour. On colour, Bellizzi, Crowley and Hasty (1983) found that people were more aroused by red than blue or green and suggested that red will speed up behaviour and might be appropriate where quicker action is more profitable, e.g. in fast-food restaurants. Babin, Hardesty and Suter (2003) report that blue was associated with greater purchase intention, compared to orange, but this effect was much weaker under subdued lighting. Milliman (1982) found that fast-tempo music speeded up supermarket customers and this reduced their purchasing. When customers moved more slowly with slow-tempo music, they spent 38 per cent more. Areni and Kim (1993) conducted an experiment and showed that, compared with popular music, classical background music in a wine store led to the choice of more expensive wines. North, Hargreaves and McKendrick (1999) followed up Areni and Kim's study by using either French accordion music or German beer cellar music in a supermarket. More French wine was sold when the French music played and more German wine was sold when the German music played and customers were unaware of this influence on their behaviour.

Another study by Yalch and Spangenberg (2000) showed that music could raise sales in a departmental store. The music had to be appropriate for each department; for example, music in departments with younger customers had to be played at high volume. Other work has looked at the way different stimuli work together. For example, Mattila and Wirtz (2001) showed that, when music and scent were similar in terms of arousing properties, they worked together to increase the evaluation of the environment. Similarly, a 'Christmas' scent raised the evaluation of the store environment only when accompanied by Christmas music (Spangenberg, Grohmann and Sprott, 2005). Bosmans (2007) also found that scents that were congruent with the product had a powerful influence on

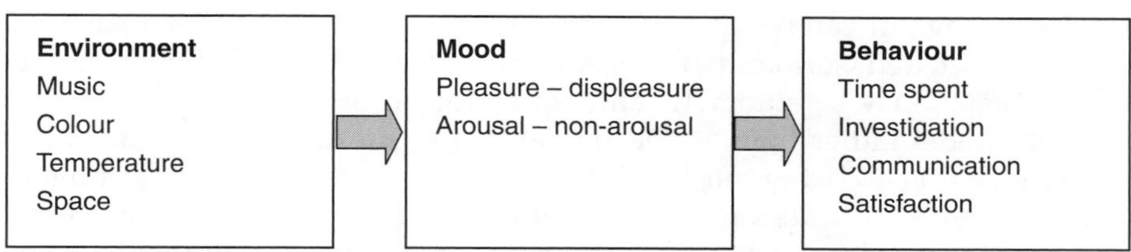

Figure 11.5 The role of moods in mediating atmospheric effects on shopping behaviour

evaluations. Intuitively, it seems reasonable that congruent stimuli will be more effective at raising evaluations.

Another explanation for atmospheric effects is that they affect mood which in turn affect purchasing. Donovan and Rossiter (1982) used a classification of mood states described by Mehrabian and Russell (1974). They found that a store's atmosphere produced mood effects in consumers which could affect the time and money spent in the store. Figure 11.5 shows this stimulus → organism → response (SOR) model with the intervening moods of pleasure and arousal. Donovan and Rossiter expected high arousal to act with pleasure to raise spending/time in store and with displeasure to reduce spending/time in store. The first was supported but there were too few unpleasant environments to test the second effect.

Smith and Sherman (1992) showed that store image was associated with mood, which then predicted the amount of time and money spent in the store. Mehrabian and Russell (1974) suggested that more novel and complex environments would raise interest and Gröppel (1993) observed that supermarkets with high novelty and complexity levels did give more pleasure, that customers spent more time and bought more in such stores. Swinyard (1993) argued that only the more elaborate processing of the highly involved consumer would be affected by mood and that this mood change would affect shopping intentions. This was supported in a scenario-based experiment, i.e. only the highly involved shoppers claimed that they would modify their shopping intentions. Sharma and Stafford (2000) showed that store design affected the persuasiveness of sales personnel, an effect that may be mediated by mood. Eroglu, Machleit and Davis (2003) even found support for mood effects in an online environment.

Donovan et al. (1994) reviewed research in this area. They noted weaknesses in their earlier paper and those of others. In particular, they suggested that it was necessary to distinguish moods induced by the environment from emotions associated with purchase. Donovan et al. conducted a further study which avoided these problems. They found that pleasure did contribute to time in the store and extra spending and that arousal did reduce spending in environments rated as unpleasant, but arousal did not increase spending when the environment was pleasant. The increase in time without increase in spending indicates more window shopping. In some retail sectors, window shoppers are as common as active shoppers (Nielsen, 2005) and we need to know how valuable window shoppers are: do they buy later or encourage others to buy through word of mouth?

While mood may act as an intervening variable to modify levels of spending, there are cases where this explanation is inadequate. In particular, the North et al. (1999) study indicates that behaviour can be modified directly by the French and German music cues (there are no French and German moods). Also, the effect of the tempo of music, observed by Milliman (1982), may be automatic and not mediated by mood. This fits a stimulus–response (SR) model rather than a SOR model. Many stimuli affect behaviour without much awareness; this is part of our low involvement response to the environment which helps us to cope with the wide variety of stimuli that impinge on our senses. By acting in this way, we leave ourselves free to concentrate on other features of the environment. One SR explanation comes from North et al. (2004) who looked at congruent elements in advertising; they suggest that one stimulus will activate or prime related processes so that a response occurs more easily when a second congruent stimulus is encountered. This priming process can be seen as readying an individual for certain types of stimulus but not others so that thought, feeling and action are channelled in particular directions. Such an account would explain the wine store results of Areni and Kim, and North et al., as well as the joint effect of congruent stimuli.

The work on atmospherics indicates powerful effects but limited explanation. Morin, Dubé and Chebat (2007) suggest a dual model whereby stimuli can affect shoppers' perceptions by two paths. Ambient environmental cues, such as smells, operate at an unconscious level – as pre-attentional signals – and induce limited processing, but focal cues with more value may be selected for conscious attention. The authors suggest that some stimuli, such as pleasant music, may influence behaviour through both channels. One route to influence, which involves conscious thought, is social. Some retail interiors may cause so much interest that these places are easily mentioned in conversations and lead more people to visit the store, for example, the vastness of the Mall of America and the aquarium and ski slope in the Dubai Mall. One other explanation for customer response to atmospheric effects comes from attribution theory. In this theory, an individual seeks to interpret and control his environment, and particularly to understand why and how things happen. The theory suggests some biases in reasoning of which the most important is fundamental attribution error. This is the tendency to find reasons for behaviour in the motivational dispositions of people rather than their environment. Attribution effects could guide inferences about the purpose of retail environments, and the behaviour of store staff and customers. Brown and Dant (2009) note a number of accounts of retail behaviour that fit this theory.

Crowding

A common problem in stores, banks, post offices, restaurants and other retail services is the level of congestion or crowding. People have a complex response to crowding and, in different contexts, may find it attractive or aversive. Hui and Bateson (1991) found that an important factor in determining whether crowding was liked or disliked is the control that customers feel that they have in the situation. In Hui and Bateson's study, high densities of people were associated with *increased* control in a bar and *reduced* control in a bank. People go to banks for instrumental reasons and bars for recreation and it seems likely that this different usage is associated with the way crowding affects perceived control since crowding is more likely to obstruct activity in banks than in bars. In shops, therefore, people are likely to dislike densities that impede action, and store designs should aim to reduce such congestion. However, there may be some recreational shoppers with little to buy who enjoy store congestion. It is also likely that people are put off when a store appears empty. Wicker (1984) has suggested that every setting has an optimal number of occupants. For example, some people feel reluctant to go into a near-empty restaurant. Here, people may attribute the emptiness of the restaurant to lack of quality. This may be true but other reasons could apply, for instance that the restaurant gets its custom mainly at a different time of day.

Milgram (1970) saw crowding as stressful, making people quicker, less exploratory and more inclined to omit purchases. The impact of stress is to narrow concentration so that central tasks may be performed better but more complex operations, which require more peripheral perceptions and memories for their completion, may be performed less efficiently. This means that the key functions of shopping may be done more efficiently under crowded conditions but shoppers may forget items that are peripheral to their needs. Anglin, Stuenkel and Lepisto (1994) found that shoppers who scored high on measures of stress engaged in more comparison shopping and were more price-sensitive; these behaviours might be seen as central to shopping. This is another reason why stress-reducing atmospheric factors may raise spending. Michon, Chebat and Turley (2005) found that scents made people more positive about their environment when the shopping density was at a medium level. This may be because scents tend to reduce stress. In psychology, it has been found that there is a preferred level of stimulation: people seek minimum arousal; they are more aroused when there are no stimuli (and they are bored) and also when there are many stimuli (and they cannot process them all). This model is shown in Figure 11.6. This suggests that store interiors, including the effects of crowding, can be too stimulating or not stimulating enough and that the optimum will vary across consumers and types of outlet.

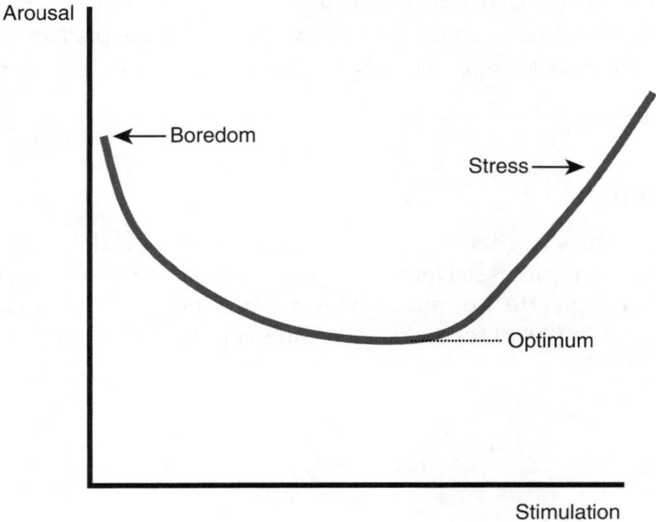

Figure 11.6 There is an optimum level of stimulation

SUMMARY

Retail use is explained at the aggregate level by gravity models and at the individual level by identifying the preferences of customers. Shoppers are mainly affected by convenience, price, range of choice and quality. In times of recession, price assumes more importance. Retail use varies by day, and time of day, and stores are under-used much of the time. Many of the reasons for use of stores at different times relate to the shopper's personal situation and this limits the scope for changing time of use. Fully employed people shop later in the day and later in the week compared with those who are not in full-time employment.

A number of typologies have been suggested for shoppers. One important group for retailers is high spenders. Among grocery shoppers these heavy buyers are found to be wealthier, have larger households and to use a car. A second group is high-loyalty customers. Store loyalty, like brand loyalty, has two basic behavioural forms: share-of-category-requirement loyalty is the proportion of patronage given to a store in the retail category, and retention is the duration of patronage. Early studies suggested that people were more loyal (measured as a proportion) when they lacked the time, money, transport resources or interest to spread their custom. A second theory, called discretionary loyalty, was that certain people, who had resources, used them to concentrate shopping. The latter are time poor and money rich and can afford to save time by spending a little more by shopping at one store. Evidence in the UK fitted a third theory, that store loyalty was a habit that was associated with other habits such as brand loyalty and regularity in time of shopping. Compulsive shoppers buy things that they do not need and may not use. This pattern of behaviour has raised concern because of the financial devastation that uncontrolled spending can produce. These people tend to have low self-esteem, which is temporarily alleviated by shopping.

In all types of store, spending may be affected by *atmospherics*, which is the impact of variations in space use, colour, sound, odour and crowding. Atmospheric changes produce quite strong effects on spending but the explanations for these effects need more development.

Additional Resources

There is a large literature in this area, as well as a major specialist journal, the *Journal of Retailing*. For particular topics, see Donovan et al. (1994) for store atmosphere, Morin, Dubé and Chebat (2007) for the effect of music, Meyer-Waarden (2007) on loyalty programmes, and Arce and Cebollada (2006) for work on online versus offline shopping behaviour.

12 Word-of-Mouth Influence

LEARNING OBJECTIVES

When you have completed this chapter, you should be able to:

1. Discuss the difficulty of conducting research on word of mouth (WOM).
2. Describe how product decisions in different categories are affected by WOM.
3. Report on the relative occurrence and impact of positive and negative WOM in familiar categories.
4. Describe variations in WOM that affect its impact.
5. Report how WOM relates to the current and past usage of brands and to market share.
6. Describe ways in which WOM may build up support for a product in social networks.
7. Suggest how marketers might apply knowledge about WOM.

OVERVIEW

Much of the evidence on WOM is quite recent and this new research focus has probably been stimulated by the growth of the Internet. Comment on the Internet is regarded as a form of WOM, which marketers are keen to use to promote products and predict sales.

In this chapter, we show how consumers use WOM to choose brands in different categories. We describe problems in researching this field and report findings on the relative frequency of positive and negative WOM (PWOM, NWOM) and the circumstances that stimulate people to give WOM. We provide evidence on the relative impact of PWOM and NWOM and we explain how different factors contribute to that impact. We describe how WOM production is related to market share, and review applications of WOM research.

SECTION 1: THE NATURE OF WORD OF MOUTH

In Chapter 5, we described the way in which innovations are adopted by consumers. At the centre of the adoption process is the communication of information. A person who adopts a new idea or product must find out about it, either through mass media (advertising, promotions, editorial content), through personal discovery (e.g. seeing it in a shop) or from other people (salespersons, other consumers). This chapter is concerned with the last way of finding out, through the influence of others. Sometimes, consumers just see what others do and copy them but often they receive advice as word of mouth (WOM). In addition to guiding the adoption of new products, WOM is involved in the switching from one brand to another in established markets. There are some specialized exchanges which differ from normal WOM. Sometimes compliments and complaints to a supplier are treated as WOM but we do not do this and have covered complaints separately in Chapter 9. WOM also sometimes occurs as rumour (see Box 12.1).

Box 12.1 Rumour

Rumours are unverified topical beliefs that circulate between people. Early thinking about rumour was presented by Knapp (1944) and by Allport and Postman (1947). Rumours may be based on hope, fear or hatred and may involve claims about conspiracies or dangers. The Internet now provides a means for the rapid circulation of rumours and many companies have suffered from this hazard. The financial marketplace is particularly susceptible to rumour (Kimmel, 2004). Rosnow (2001) argues that uncertainty, credibility and personal relevance are the primary drivers of rumours, which will spread faster in contexts of high anxiety (for example when investments are at risk). Kimmel and Audrain-Pontevia (2007) found that roughly three-fifths of rumours were negative, one-fifth positive and one-fifth neutral. They confirmed that uncertainty, credibility and importance of the topic were the key factors in rumour transmission. For a recent review of research on rumours and their influence see Kimmel (2010).

WOM advice now covers direct face-to-face exchanges, telephone, text messages, mail, email, blogs, message boards and social networking websites. Much of this WOM is interactive so that a receiver can follow up and ask a sender further questions. When this applies, the advice can be tailored to and focused on the needs of the receiver, and this adds to its power.

WOM may be positive (PWOM – recommendation, advocacy) or negative (NWOM – advising against). Some exchanges contain both positive and negative comment and some are neutral. When it is about a brand, PWOM usually increases, and NWOM reduces, the receiver's probability of purchasing that brand. Some advice occurs in a commercial context, for example, from sales personnel and on sponsored websites. Commercial advice is different from consumer-to-consumer advice because it is potentially biased. However, Carl (2008) studied the responses of consumers to advice from BzzAgents (people who are given products by BzzAgent and asked to talk about these products to others); he found that three-quarters of respondents trusted the BzzAgent to give them good advice when they knew that he/she was a BzzAgent. In fact, the effect of the BzzAgent's advice was often greater when their affiliation was known. If such trust extends generally to sales personnel, their advice may be quite influential despite the potential for bias.

Many of the classic studies on WOM were concerned with innovations and new categories rather than established brands; for example, Whyte (1954) on air conditioners, Coleman, Katz and Menzel (1957) on the prescribing of new drugs by physicians, and Katz's (1961) work on new farming practices. These really new products may produce exceptional comment when compared with well-established products but there is clearly a gradation from the very novel to the familiar. Sometimes brands will have new features not offered by others and here, choice may be more like the adoption of a new product. For example, the widespread acceptance of smart phones was clearly driven by the new features that they offered. But, as the category matures and brands become more familiar, the reason for choice may not be an innovation but some simple advantage that can be drawn to a consumer's attention. For example, one person might advise another about the relative cost of mobile phone brands, or their performance in weak-signal areas. This is useful information to a prospective buyer but it is not an innovative feature of the product.

In this chapter, we focus less on the adoption of new categories and more on brands in mature categories. Research on WOM is limited because it is difficult to measure. Ideally, we would observe WOM as it occurs and then monitor its consequences. In practice, WOM occurs too rarely for it to be observed systematically, and usually any effect is delayed, so that direct observation of the outcomes of WOM may be impossible. As a result, other methods have to be used, which are reviewed below.

Text Mining on the Internet

Although we cannot observe WOM as it happens, we may be able to measure it as comments posted on the Internet. WOM is not hard to find in consumer-generated media, but there are two challenges. First, those who set up websites may encourage more PWOM or NWOM than is typical in everyday life and, second, those who post comments on the Internet, and those who read these comments, may be different from those who give and receive offline advice. Godes and Mayzlin (2004b) did not find that the volume of online comment about TV programmes was predictive of viewing but Liu (2006) was successful in predicting box office returns from the volume of online comment about movies, and Qin (2012) also found that the volume of the WOM predicted movie sales. Interestingly, Liu did not find that the valence of the WOM (i.e. whether it was positive or negative) was predictive of sales. However, a later paper by Liu (2012) on Twitter comments suggests that the valence is more predictive than the volume of comments. More work is required here.

Internet research usually deals with aggregate effects. We can count the posts and obtain data on box office receipts. We may be able to predict returns from such data but we do not know quite how individuals have used the online information. We want to understand as well as predict and, for this, we need individual-level data so that we can connect individual responses to individual experience. Individual-level data are obtained in experiments and surveys.

Box 12.2 Online advice

The predictive value of online comment depends, in part, on how much this medium is used, compared to other media. If it is only a small part of total advice on brands, it may not be a reliable guide to sales. Surveys show that online comment remains a modest part of the total. In 2006, Keller and Fay found that WOM was:

Face-to-face	70%
Phone	19%
Email	4%
Text message	3%
Online chat or blog	1%
Other	3%

Subsequently, the share of online WOM (eWOM) has not changed much. In 2010, the Keller Fay Group reported that 7 per cent of WOM was offline in the US, UK and Australia, though this rose to 15 per cent for the teen group in US measurements. In 2011, Keller Fay reported that, in the UK, 81 per cent of WOM was face-to-face, 10 per cent via phone and 9 per cent online (including email, texting and social networking sites). Thus, the Internet is not the dominant channel for advice by any means. Even so, some categories like restaurants, holidays and hotels attract much more online comment and it is likely that, in these fields, the Internet is a more reliable guide to demand.

There are, however, some differences between Web and face-to-face advice. First, some online advice is one-way and not interactive. Second, in many contexts, such as online reviews or on Twitter, online advice from one source may be received by many others, which is uncommon for offline advice. Third, the Web may allow a degree of deception – those reviews on Amazon may include some that are 'arranged'; because of this, people may be more suspicious of positive comment on the Web than they are when it occurs face-to-face. Fourth, offline WOM is more often between close ties but, on the Web, a larger amount of weak-tie contact is likely to occur (e.g. in discussion groups or anonymous product reviews).

Experiments

A number of experiments have examined the impact of positive and negative information (e.g. Ahluwalia, 2002; Herr, Kardes and Kim, 1991). The main problem here is that the artificiality of the laboratory situation restricts generalization to naturally occurring WOM. This artificiality has several aspects:

1 The stimulus is not like real WOM. In experiments, the 'WOM' is often prepared written information rather than spontaneous exchanges between people (e.g. Herr, Kardes and Kim, 1991). Such prepared advice cannot be asked for, which is often a feature of real WOM, and the advice is unlikely to be well tailored to the needs of the receiver.
2 The response measures may be inappropriate. Experimental studies of WOM have used attitude towards a product or brand and belief items to measure impact (e.g. Ahluwalia, 2002); marketers are generally more interested in the impact on purchase or purchase probability.

lack of information on a product and little opportunity to find out about it through direct experience.

In early work, WOM was credited with very large effects. Dichter (1966) claimed that advice figured in as many as 80 per cent of brand decisions. Katz and Lazarsfeld (1955) claimed to show that WOM was seven times as effective as newspapers and magazines, four times as effective as personal selling and twice as effective as radio advertising in influencing consumers to buy products. These early studies applied more to the adoption of new categories than to brand switching, so these claims may not tell us much about brand choice in familiar categories. However, WOM clearly has impact on brand choice; Keaveney (1995) found that about 50 per cent of service provider replacements occurred primarily through WOM.

East et al. (2005b) asked people about the *main* source of information influencing their choice when they changed brand or started using a service for the first time. Table 12.1 shows the results. The main source of information was divided into recommendation, personal search, advertising and 'other'. The 'other' category included non-commercial editorial advice in the mass media and situations where people had no choice because of contracts, gifts or other circumstances that were compelling. At the base of the table, we see that recommendation was the main influence in about one-third of the brand choices.

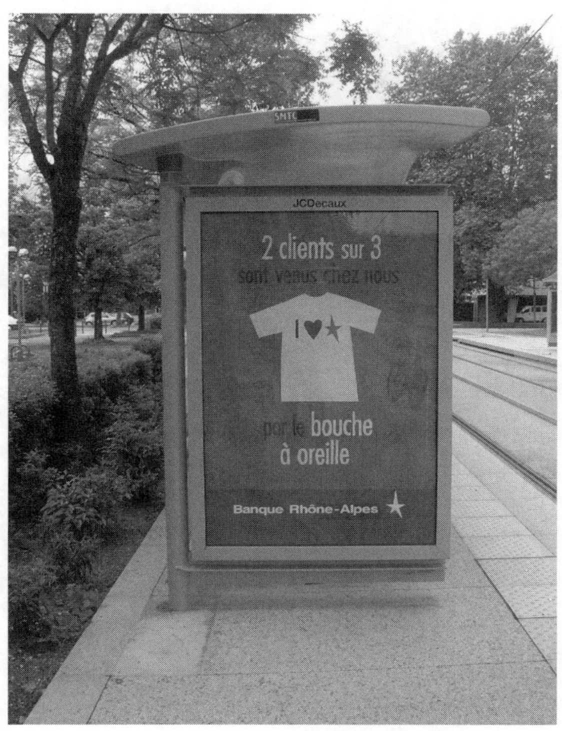

Two out of three customers come to us by word of mouth

In this research, each study involved asking respondents about two or three categories, and the data are grouped accordingly in Table 12.1. Within each survey grouping, you can see that categories differ in the way they get their customers. In the first grouping, coffee shops and mobile airtime providers are more often chosen on recommendation than credit cards. The evidence from Table 12.1 shows that WOM is less often a source of information for cars (13 per cent) and for retail services such as supermarkets (10 per cent and 9 per cent). This is not surprising since durables and supermarkets can be tried out and are the objects of substantial advertising.

By contrast, we might expect social networking sites to recruit largely via WOM and here Trusov, Bucklin and Pauwels (2009) showed a very substantial effect from referrals compared

Table 12.1 Choice of brand provider when switching buying a category for the first time (East et al., 2005b)

	Main source when choosing new brand/provider (%)			
Category (country)	*Recommendation*	*Personal search*	*Advertising/ Promotion*	*Other*
Coffee shop (UK)	65	20	1	14
Mobile phone airtime provider (UK)	50	24	6	20
Credit card (UK)	20	16	20	44
Car insurance (Mauritius)	60	16	6	18
Car servicing (Mauritius)	56	17	3	14
Dentist (UK)	59	3	9	30
Current car (UK)	13	42	13	33
Education institution (UK)	48	19	2	31
Mobile phone airtime provider (UK)	25	22	9	44
Optician (UK)	21	16	8	56
Bank (UK)	43	20	13	24
Mobile phone brand (UK)	21	26	16	37
House contents insurance (UK)	33	12	34	21
Car insurance (UK)	27	19	34	20
Car servicing (UK)	32	9	1	58
Dry cleaning (UK)	14	26	4	56
Hairdresser (Mexico)	32	29	5	34
Fashion store (Mexico)	13	27	43	17
Supermarket (Mexico)	10	36	33	21
Mobile phone airtime provider (UK)	29	13	21	37
Internet service provider (UK)	24	26	26	24
Fashion store (France)	15	47	9	29
Supermarket (France)	9	29	8	54
Means	**31**	**22**	**14**	**32**

with traditional marketing activity. Furthermore, both Trusov et al. and Villanueva, Yoo and Hanssens (2008) found that the customers derived from WOM were more valuable than those found by conventional marketing activity. Customers may be more valuable because they show greater retention and because they recommend the brand more to others.

How Does WOM Occur?

There is a widespread belief in marketing that PWOM comes from satisfied and NWOM from dissatisfied customers (see Box 12.4). But think back to the last advice that you gave. Was it driven by satisfaction or dissatisfaction, or were you trying to provide information that would help someone else with their decision? Our satisfaction or dissatisfaction with a product may be the main basis for giving advice but, often, we are influenced by other factors, such as the need for advice of the receiver.

Box 12.4 Comparing satisfied and dissatisfied consumers

Marketing textbooks such as Heskett, Sasser and Schlesinger (1997) and Hanna and Wosniak (2001) report NWOM to PWOM ratios of two or three to one *when comparing satisfied and dissatisfied customers*. The origin of these reports is work by a US agency, the Technical Assistance Research Program (TARP), which finds that NWOM from dissatisfied customers occurs about twice as frequently as PWOM from satisfied customers, though the ratio varies with the category (Goodman and Newman, 2003). Anderson's (1998) comprehensive study also showed greater WOM among those who were very dissatisfied compared with those who were very satisfied, but he commented: 'The widespread belief in a high degree of word of mouth by dissatisfied customers may be unwarranted. In fact, in a sizable proportion of cases, the difference between the two is probably not significant' (Anderson, 1998: 15).

People may confuse the WOM from dis/satisfied customers with WOM in general. This may be why Silverman (2001: 134) claims that studies have shown that most WOM is negative. In Figure 12.1, we see from Anderson (1998) that WOM is also produced by those who are neither satisfied nor dissatisfied and Mangold, Miller and Brockway (1999) found that only a small part of WOM is driven primarily by satisfaction and dissatisfaction (Table 12.2). To establish the ratio of all PWOM to NWOM, we need studies on the general occurrence of PWOM and NWOM, not just studies where the WOM is based on dis/satisfaction.

The fact that advice may be unrelated to satisfaction is indicated by a study conducted by Anderson (1998), who used the Swedish Customer Satisfaction Barometer and the American Customer Satisfaction Index, which cover many industries in each country. The results were very similar for the two countries and Figure 12.1 illustrates the data for Sweden. We see that there is a little more WOM when people are very satisfied or very dissatisfied, but that, when

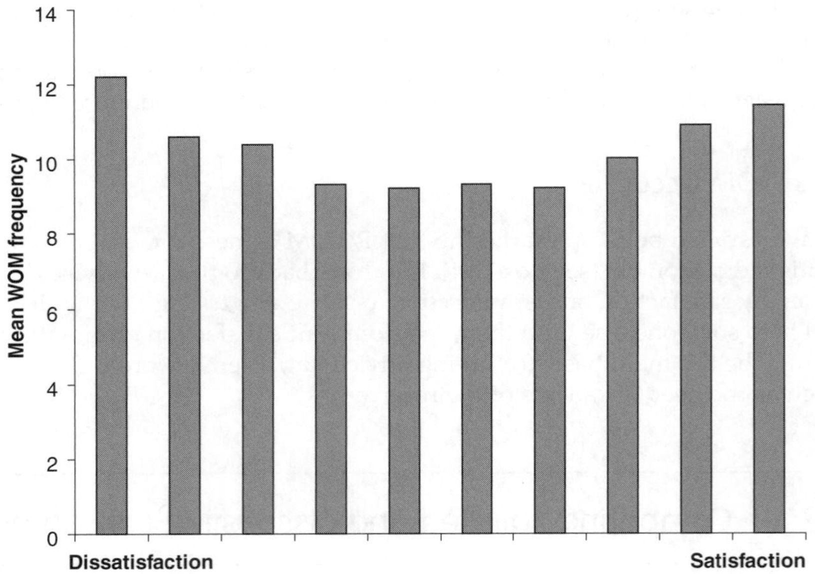

Figure 12.1 Frequency of word of mouth in relation to satisfaction and dissatisfaction in Sweden (adapted from Anderson, 1998)

they are neutral about an issue, WOM is still produced at about 80 per cent of the maximum level. This indicates that satisfaction and dissatisfaction need not be involved in the production of WOM and implies that other circumstances are relevant.

These other circumstances are illustrated by Mangold, Miller and Brockway (1999), who asked respondents to describe the last time they received positive or negative advice about a service. Mangold et al. identified ten catalysts that set off WOM, which are shown in Table 12.2. The most common catalyst was the receiver's felt need, which was either implicit in the situation or made explicit by a request for advice. Coincidental conversation occurred when a conversation led to advice, for example, when a discussion of weekend plans led to a destination recommendation. The communicator's dis/satisfaction with the service (as judged by the receiver) was the third catalyst and this made up 12 per cent of the total. The fourth catalyst occurred when the recipient made a comment that related to the service, for example, about the communicator's hair, which led the communicator to recommend her hairdresser. The fifth catalyst was the effort to make a joint decision, such as which restaurant to go to together. This work does *not* show that consumer satisfaction and dissatisfaction have little to do with WOM. What Mangold et al. found is that it is unusual to find that satisfaction and dissatisfaction are the main factors that cause WOM.

Mangold et al. only considered the catalysts from the standpoint of the receiver but Mazzarol, Sweeney and Soutar (2007) gathered data on both the giver and receiver of WOM, using focus groups, and found that 'felt need' was again the trigger for much of the WOM. This evidence means that researchers who have gathered evidence on WOM in

Table 12.2 Catalysts that stimulate word of mouth (adapted from Mangold, Miller and Brockway, 1999)

Stimulus	*Positive communication (%)*	*Negative communication (%)*	*Total (%)*
Receiver's felt need	54	47	50
Coincidental communication	16	21	18
Communicator's dis/satisfaction	5	13	9
Receiver's comment about effect of service	9	4	7
Joint decision on service	6	6	6
Marketing organization's promotion	2	5	3
Receiver's dis/satisfaction	3	3	3
Another's comment about the effect of service	4	1	2
Media exposure (not marketing organization)	1	1	1
Unsolicited comment	1	0	1

relation to dis/satisfaction have focused on only a part of the WOM that is produced. Richins (1983) treated NWOM in this way when she described NWOM as communication that *denigrated* the product. Halstead (2002) saw both NWOM and complaints as products of dissatisfaction. Similarly, Wetzer, Zeelenberg and Pieters (2007) concentrate on NWOM that arises from dissatisfaction and Goldenberg et al. (2007) also define NWOM in this way. In contrast to this, Asugman (1998) observed that NWOM was an everyday occurrence and need not be associated with dissatisfaction. It seems likely that dis/satisfaction is a condition for much WOM but the evidence from Mangold et al. suggests that it is not normally the main cause of it. However, there is a need for more research here; Mangold et al. used a method called critical incident technique and Mazzarol et al. used focus groups, but neither method is well designed for gathering frequencies.[1]

A feature of Mangold et al.'s study is the similarity of the catalyst frequencies for PWOM and NWOM; these have a correlation of 0.96. This shows that there is not much difference in the circumstances governing positive and negative advice. Clearly, PWOM makes the choice of a brand more likely and NWOM makes it less likely, but often they are both helpful advice.

Some products generate more WOM than others. Berger and Schwartz (2011) point out that some categories are more interesting than others – one would expect iPhones to get more comment than soap. However, they also observed that some products are more accessible than others; these may be cued by usage or be visible because they are frequently present in the environment. Such products (e.g. mobile phones) may stimulate more WOM than those that drop from sight after use, such as films. Berger and Schwartz found that the cued and visible products received more WOM than the interesting but short-term products. The latter were talked about a lot immediately after consumption but WOM then fell away. In a field experiment, they found that WOM could be increased by linking a product to a recurrent feature of the environment. The authors also suggest that advertising could be more effective when this sort of linkage is made.

Motives for Giving WOM

Mangold et al. researched catalysts to WOM; these relate to the situational circumstances as well as motives. Others have looked more narrowly at the motivation for WOM. There are circumstances in which people deliberately go out of their way to give advice, most notably when they write product assessments and give advice online, and it is worth understanding why they choose to do this. In an early study before online advice existed, Dichter (1966) reported on the motivation to talk about products. He analyzed interviews and found that people gave advice because this gave them standing with the receiver. The recommendations which people gave were based on experience with the product, involvement with the product, the needs of the receiver and public information (such as ads) on the product. Also using interviews, Sundaram, Mitra and Webster (1998) found that PWOM was motivated by altruism, product involvement, self-enhancement and assisting the company producing the product. The motives for giving NWOM were altruism, anxiety reduction, vengeance and as a response to others seeking advice. Hennig-Thurau et al. (2004) turned attention to online advice. Using an online questionnaire, they found that advice was motivated, as in offline, by wanting to vent negative feelings, concern for other consumers, social benefits, economic incentives, helping the company and advice seeking but there were two other factors related to the online environment; one was a form of self-enhancement coming from expressing positive feelings and a second was the assistance provided by the platform to express advice. Related to the second point, Berger and Iyengar (2012) found that more interesting topics are covered online because the medium gives more time to consider topics and to write reviews. One problem with online studies is that the research method may evoke particular forms of PWOM and NWOM that are atypical; a second problem is that the motives are likely to vary with the product category so that aggregate findings are of limited value; and a third problem is that, by asking about motives, researchers may miss important situational determinants of WOM such as the need of the receiver, revealed by Mangold et al.

Is there More PWOM than NWOM?

Naylor and Kleiser (2000) studied users of a health and fitness resort and found more positive comment than negative. Chevalier and Mayzlin (2003) found that the majority of book reviews on two websites were positive. Godes and Mayzlin (2004b) studied TV comment on websites and found that positive appraisals occurred nearly twice as often as negative appraisals. Romaniuk (2007) found four times as much PWOM as NWOM when assessing advice about television programmes. The Keller Fay Group conducts surveys of 'branded' conversations that have taken place over the last 24 hours in the USA and the Group has provided us with data for 2009. Sixty-five per cent of these conversations were mainly positive, 8 per cent mainly negative, 15 per cent mixed and 12 per cent neutral. If we assume that people hearing mixed comment on a brand state that they have received both PWOM and NWOM, these data indicate a ratio of 3.5 to 1. East, Hammond and Wright (2007b) examined the ratio of PWOM to NWOM in 15 different studies, covering all the brands in a range of widely used categories (mostly services). In every case, the PWOM incidence exceeded the NWOM incidence and the average ratio was 3.1 to 1. This work was conducted by asking respondents about the PWOM and NWOM that they had *given* in the last six months. In follow-up studies, respondents were asked about the WOM they had *received* in the last six months and the WOM they *would give, if asked*. These latter follow-up studies gave PWOM:NWOM ratios of of 2.4 to 1 and 3.4 to 1 respectively. From this evidence, it is clear that there is more PWOM than NWOM, though the ratio varies by category.

Why is there more PWOM? One explanation may be that there are not many negative things to say about goods and services. Mostly, people are satisfied with what they get according to Peterson and Wilson (1992), whose work suggested an average 10:1 ratio of satisfied to dissatisfied (Chapter 9). A second possibility is that PWOM is seen as more useful. Most consumer choices are about selecting one from many brands. NWOM may eliminate an option but this does not settle the choice if more than one option remains. By contrast, PWOM may be used by a receiver to make a final decision. Thus, if people are trying to help others with their advice, saying what is good may be more constructive than saying what is bad.

How much Do People Talk about Their Current Brand?

East, Romaniuk and Lomax (2011) investigated whether the brand that was referred to in PWOM and NWOM was currently used, previously used or never used (Table 12.3). Across 15 studies, they found that, on average, 71 per cent of PWOM was about the currently used brand, 22 per cent about a previously used brand and only 7 per cent about a never-used brand. For NWOM, 22 per cent was about the currently used brand, 55 per cent about a previously used brand and 22 per cent about a never-used brand. Wangenheim (2005) also found that NWOM was often about previously owned brands and Winchester and Romaniuk (2008) found that, when people expressed negative beliefs about brands, these were often about previously owned brands. Table 12.3 also shows that people are more willing to give NWOM than PWOM on brands they have not used and this suggests that, sometimes, brands become widely discussed because of their deficiencies. This is a serious worry for managers. Note that the previous work showing more PWOM than NWOM was about *all* the brands in a category. Individual brands could be the object of more NWOM than PWOM.

How Does the Occurrence of WOM Relate to the Market Share of the Brand?

Bigger brands, with more users, will get more recommendations because, as we see above, most recommendations are about the current main brand. As a result, the volume of recommendation will tend to relate to market share. WOM for previously owned brands will reflect the market share that applied at an earlier time and, if the market has not changed much, this will approximate to the current market share. This means that NWOM volume will also relate to market share, but less so than PWOM because it relates to an earlier market structure. This was tested by Uncles, East and Lomax (2010a). They analyzed data from 13 surveys and found an average correlation between market share and PWOM volume of 0.92. This was significantly greater than the corresponding correlation for NWOM which was 0.73.

This evidence shows that if one brand gets more PWOM than another, it is not necessarily performing better. To do well, a brand must get more PWOM and less NWOM than would

Table 12.3 The ownership of brands cited in given PWOM and NWOM (adapted from East, Romaniuk and Lomaz, 2011)

	PWOM			*NWOM*		
Category (year data were collected)	*Current main brand %*	*A previous brand %*	*Never owned %*	*Current main brand %*	*A previous brand %*	*Never owned %*
Camera (2007)	88	12	0	33	34	33
Mobile phone handset (2005)	81	15	5	20	71	9
Mobile phone airtime supplier (2005)	79	9	12	19	56	26
Mobile phone handset (2007)	78	10	9	55	29	16
Main coffee shop (2008)	75	25	0	15	82	4
Mobile phone airtime supplier (2007)	73	20	7	33	44	23
Main coffee shop (2006)	72	27	1	18	71	12
Bank account (current) (2007)	72	22	6	30	39	30
Computers (2006)	70	19	12	24	19	58
Skin care products (2008)	70	25	6	4	96	0
Main credit card (2007)	67	29	4	18	54	24
Current bank account (2009)	64	26	10	11	45	44
Luxury leather goods (2006)	63	29	8	7	69	24
Main supermarket (2008)	63	36	1	28	69	4
Luxury brands (2006)	51	32	17	17	53	30
Means	**71**	**22**	**7**	**22**	**55**	**22**

be expected on the basis of the market-share norm. Sometimes, new brands may get much more PWOM than their market share warrants; for example, some unpublished evidence at Kingston showed that, when smart phones first arrived, iPhone was well above the norm for PWOM and its subsequent success has vindicated this early interest.

Factors Associated with Word-of-Mouth Production

In studies by researchers and students at Kingston University, we have found that the volume of recommendation is often related to:

- The relative attitude to the brand. Relative attitude is the rating of the brand compared with other available brands and, for practical purposes, this is the same as relative satisfaction.
- Whether a person was recruited to the brand by recommendation or not. In the main, those who are recruited by recommendation tend to give more recommendations themselves. This was also found by Wangenheim and Bayón (2004) when they investigated German utility customers. This effect is likely to depend on the size of a person's circle of friends. Those who interact more with others have more opportunity both to receive and to give advice. Related to this, Godes and Mayzlin (2004a) incentivized PWOM and found that the extra sales that resulted were related to the size of a person's social circle.

- Whether the communicator recommends other categories. This reflects a disposition, called *mavenism*, to give advice across a wide range of products (Feick and Price, 1987).
- Age. The pattern here is that people tend to give and receive less WOM as they age, particularly when they are over 65. This may depend on opportunity, since there is likely to be a loss of social contact as people age, stop work and their children leave home. This topic is covered in more detail in Chapter 6.
- Whether a brand owner has heard others recommend their brand. We discuss this in Section 4.

Other factors relating to WOM production depend on the categories:

- Customer tenure (duration of time as a customer of the brand). The relationship between tenure and PWOM was described in Chapter 2. In brief, East et al. (2005a) found that recommendations fell as tenure increased in the case of credit cards, bank accounts, motor insurance and supermarkets, but recommendation rose in the case of car servicing and fashion shops. In other categories there was no significant effect.
- Weight of purchase. Heavy buyers quite often give more WOM but not always. Perhaps, in some categories, they habituate to the brand and then become less interested in talking about it.

Interestingly, share-of-category requirement is not usually related to PWOM. High-share customers, by their nature, have more limited experience of brands other than their main one and this may limit their ability to give advice when this involves comparing brands.

SECTION 3: THE IMPACT OF WORD OF MOUTH

What Is the Impact of Positive and Negative Word of Mouth on Brand Choice?

NWOM may be less common than PWOM, but perhaps it has more impact when it does occur? There seems to be a belief among marketers that an instance of NWOM has more effect than an instance of PWOM, and there is some evidence suggesting that this might be true. Arndt (1967) showed twice as much impact on purchase from NWOM than from PWOM, but he studied only one brand. Also, a series of studies has shown a 'negativity effect' – that negative information has more impact on attitudes than positive information (Anderson, 1965; Chevalier and Mayzlin, 2003; Fiske, 1980; Herr, Kardes and Kim, 1991; Mittal, Ross and Baldasare, 1998; Mizerski, 1982). In these attitude studies, negative information is less common than positive information and Fiske (1980) has explained that the rarity of negative information makes it more useful than positive information because the latter is what most people already think. Thus, it is the gap between the position supported by the message and the position currently held by the receiver that is the basis for the negativity effect. For example, evidence that a brand is unreliable might be more useful than evidence that the brand is reliable because most people assume that modern products are reliable. Exceptionally, when the receiver's expectation is negative and the information received is positive, there could be a 'positivity effect'. Research on the negativity effect is reviewed in detail by Skowronski and Carlston (1989). However, some work has not supported the negativity effect. For example, Ahluwalia (2002) compared responses to written positive and negative information when participants were familiar or unfamiliar with the brand. When the brand was familiar, there were no significant differences in the impact of positive and negative information.

Much of this work has used measures of impact based on change in attitude or thinking. However, in marketing, impact may instead be measured in terms of change in purchase or purchase propensity. People might receive NWOM and change their attitude but not change their intention to purchase. This would happen if, prior to the NWOM, they had zero probability of purchase. East, Hammond and Lomax (2008) used the shift in purchase probability to measure the impact of WOM; they showed that positive advice will have more effect if the receiver has a low likelihood of purchase before the PWOM is received because this leaves more 'room for change'. Conversely, NWOM will have more effect when the initial probability of purchase is high. This applies the gap notion of the negativity effect to the intention measure of impact. In Table 12.4, we show East et al.'s average results from 19 studies. Respondents were asked what their probability of purchase was before and after hearing the WOM using the Juster (1966) scale, described in Chapter 7, to measure purchase probability.

The mean probability of purchase before WOM was 0.43 for those who received PWOM and 0.40 for those receiving NWOM so that there was slightly more 'room for change' in the purchasing probability for the receivers of PWOM (1 – 0.43 = 0.57) than NWOM (0.40). In addition, the impact of PWOM was correspondingly greater in magnitude than that of NWOM (0.20 versus –0.11). These findings suggest that PWOM usually has more impact on brand choice than NWOM when impact is measured as a change in intention. However, as we stated at the beginning of this chapter, it is difficult to study WOM effects, and estimates of past probabilities of purchase could easily be biased by selective recall. For this reason, we should be cautious about these research findings.[2]

What Variables Affect the Impact of WOM?

East et al. (2008) measured how six variables affected WOM impact, where impact was measured as change in the intention to buy. These were: the prior probability of purchase; how strongly expressed the WOM was; whether the WOM was about the main brand; the closeness of the communicator and receiver (that is, whether a close friend/relative, or not); whether the WOM was sought, or not; and how much advice the respondent reported *giving* on the category that was studied. These factors were used in a regression analysis to predict impact. Table 12.5 shows the output from the analysis. We see that the prior probability of choice is the most significant factor, supporting the argument in the previous section. For PWOM, the greater the prior probability, the less the change (and the reverse for NWOM). The strength of WOM expression, a variable noted by Mazzarol et al. (2007) as important, is a strong determinant of impact. Also, PWOM about the currently used main brand has more effect than PWOM on other brands, while NWOM on the main brand has less impact than NWOM on other brands. The closeness of the communicator and whether the advice was sought are only significant for PWOM, and the amount of WOM given by the respondent is only significant for NWOM. An interesting feature of Table 12.5 is the similarity in the magnitude of the different determinants, as shown by the beta coefficients. Remember that we have argued that PWOM and NWOM are similar in kind since they are often both intended to help the recipient. Table 12.5 supports this claim.

Table 12.4 The mean impact of PWOM and NWOM on brand choice probability (adapted from East, Hammond and Lomax, 2008)

	Probability of purchase before WOM %		*Impact (shift in probability of purchase)*	
Category	*Prior to PWOM*	*Prior to NWOM*	*PWOM*	*NWOM*
Supermarket	0.43	0.39	0.16	–0.16
Mobile phone airtime	0.40	0.41	0.16	–0.09
Mobile phone handset	0.50	0.42	0.08	–0.19
Current bank account	0.40	0.47	0.28	–0.11
Camera	0.45	0.38	0.01	–0.17
Computer	0.53	0.49	0.20	–0.20
Mobile phone airtime	0.32	0.41	0.19	–0.10
Main credit card	0.37	0.48	0.28	–0.17
Luxury brands	0.38	0.20	0.12	–0.06
Leather goods	0.48	0.46	0.23	–0.14
Camera	0.53	0.34	0.17	–0.12
Holiday destination	0.48	0.42	0.18	–0.19
Coffee shop	0.54	0.42	0.19	–0.11
Holiday destination	0.41	0.38	0.06	–0.06
Mobile phone handset	0.39	0.36	0.20	–0.07
Restaurant, favourite	0.35	0.59	0.39	–0.47
Restaurant, ethnic	0.36	0.41	0.34	–0.23
Hair colorant	0.51	0.28	0.19	–0.08
Restaurant, Iranian	0.44	0.22	0.31	–0.03
Means	**0.43**	**0.40**	**0.20**	**–0.11**

Table 12.5 Variables related to impact (multiple regression analysis) (adapted from East, Hammond and Lomax, 2008)

	PWOM		*NWOM*	
Variable	*Beta*	*Sig.*	*Beta*	*Sig.*
Prior probability of purchase	0.43	<.001	0.37	<.001
Strength of expression of WOM	0.22	<.001	0.22	<.001
WOM about main brand	0.16	<.001	–0.21	<.001
Closeness of communicator	0.10	<.001	0.06	0.06
Whether advice was sought	0.06	0.03	0.04	0.17
Amount of WOM given	0.04	0.13	0.08	0.01
Adjusted R^2	0.23		0.21	

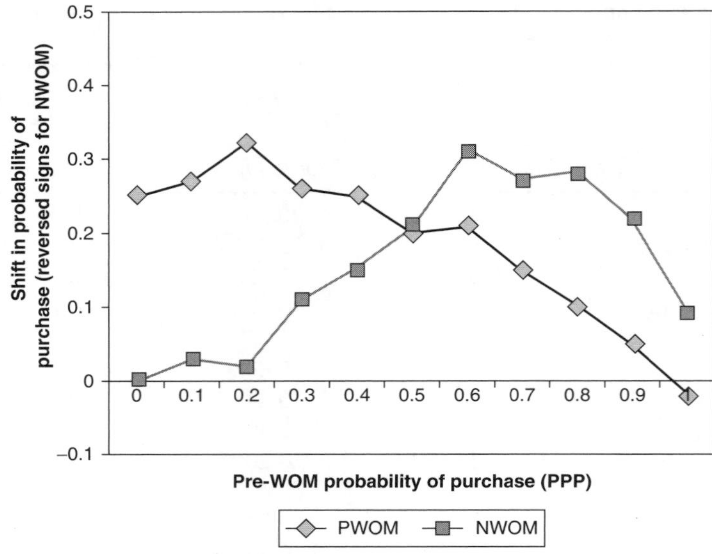

Figure 12.2 Shift in probability of purchase (impact) as a function of the probability of purchase before receiving WOM

Previous work has shown that close ties have more direct effect than distant ties (Brown and Reingen, 1987) and that sought advice is more influential than advice that is unsought (East et al., 2005a; Bansal and Voyer, 2000). The weak associations shown in Table 12.5 may relate to the method of analysis. When multiple regression is used, other variables that are associated with both the predictor and outcome variables can assume part of the explanation.

The Effect of Brand Commitment

East et al. (2008) analyzed the shift in purchase probability against the probability of purchase prior to receiving WOM. The result is shown in Figure 12.2. For most of the range, there is a close relationship between impact, measured as shift in purchase probability, and prior probability of purchase. However, people who are very likely to buy a brand give less weight to NWOM on that brand and people who are very unlikely to buy a brand give less weight to PWOM on the brand, perhaps because they intend to buy another brand. Thus, Figure 12.2 shows how commitment to brands can make people resistant to advice about alternatives. Figure 12.2 is useful because it helps us to see how consumers differ in their response to information, depending on their prior probability to purchase.

SECTION 4: WOM IN THE SOCIAL NETWORK

One stimulating development has been work by Watts and Dodds (2007), who cast a critical eye over the two-step flow model of mass media influence which was proposed by Lazarsfeld, Berelson, and Gaudet (1944) and refined by Katz and Lazarsfeld (1955). In this

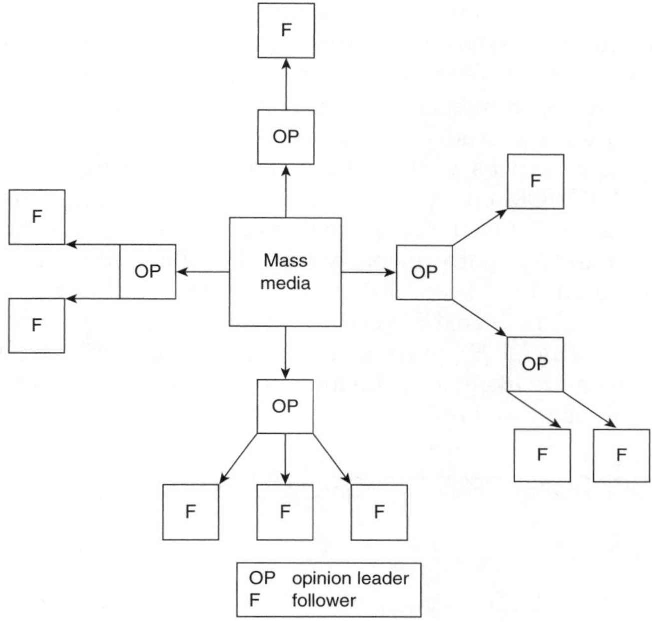

Figure 12.3 Flow of influence via opinion leaders

model, mass-media communications are processed by a small group of opinion leaders, who are well meshed into the mass media and, by interpreting, filtering and selectively passing on ideas, may promote or oppose change. Sometimes an opinion leader may recruit a further opinion leader to spread the word, as shown in Figure 12.3. Watts and Dodds suggest that the opinion leader is usually only modestly more influential than average. They argue that influence may flow in both directions in networks of individuals (unlike the two-step flow model). In the more fluid social network that they propose, their computer simulations suggest that innovations take off when a critical mass of easily influenced individuals has been reached. When this occurs, there is a large-scale cascade of adoption.

If WOM is a lubricant to the adoption of innovations, how does it act in the social network? We have shown that most WOM is expressed by those who have already used a brand. How can this WOM be amplified? In some unpublished work at Kingston University, we asked respondents whether they had heard others recommending a service that they had recently used and we asked them how many times they had recommended the service themselves in the preceding four weeks. We found that, on average, those who had heard others recommend a service gave nearly twice as many recommendations compared with those who had not heard their brand recommended. Even after removing the effect of some co-variates, the effect remained. One explanation for this is that people can easily repeat recommendations that they hear. This provides a mechanism whereby influence can travel over the network of existing users in any direction. What is interesting about this mechanism is that it creates positive feedback. Suppose that, by some means, we induce extra recommendations in a social network; users who hear such recommendations will then produce more recommendations themselves and this will induce still more recommendations by other users, and so on. The amount of feedback will depend on the proportion of the population that are users and the extent to which hearing a recommendation raises the level of giving recommendations. It is possible that a process similar to this could underpin Watts and Dodds' cascade of influence.

Such ideas may also help us to understand how advertising can affect WOM. It is known that the level of WOM on a product rises in response to advertising (Bayus, 1985; Graham and Havlena, 2007). One mechanism that could cause this is that the ad increases the salience of the brand so that previously used PWOM scripts are more likely to be expressed after the ad has been seen. Brand salience may also be increased by conversations *about the ad*, since 20 per cent of WOM discussions refer to paid advertising content according to Keller and Fay (2009). In some cases the ad may supply a script that a receiver can repeat; this seems more likely for print and radio ads where information is already in a verbal form that can be passed on.

SECTION 5: APPLICATIONS OF WORD-OF-MOUTH RESEARCH

Net Promoter Score

The Net Promoter Score (NPS) is intended to measure the number of people who are positive about a brand/company (promoters) and the number who are negative (detractors) (Reichheld, 2003). The score is computed as shown in Figure 12.4. The NPS asks about future recommendation, but Romaniuk, Nguyen and East (2011) found that responses are usually influenced by the WOM that responders have given in the recent past; apparently, when asked what they will do, people check on what they have done. In these circumstances, it might be better to measure past WOM in the first place.

In the NPS, detractors are meant to give much of the NWOM on a brand. This seems doubtful; those who give little PWOM may just be disinclined to give WOM in any form. This

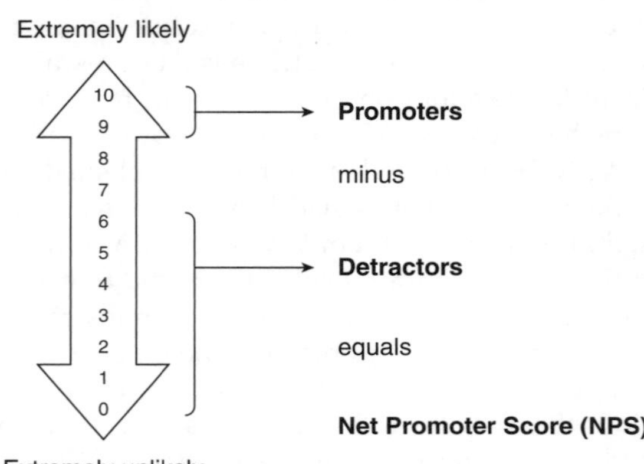

Figure 12.4 Measuring the Net Promoter Score

was tested by East, Romaniuk and Lomax (2011a). They identified promoters and detractors in three categories and found out how much of the total PWOM and NWOM these groups had produced in the last six months. The detractors produced very little NWOM and, in two of the categories, they gave more PWOM than NWOM. Bear in mind that the NPS is based on *customers* and much of the NWOM on a brand is produced by *ex-customers* who were included in the East et al. study but are not included in the NPS measure. It appears that the NPS provides a good indication of PWOM but not NWOM because of the focus on current customers. Also, if we wish to evaluate the way that WOM supports a brand, it would be better to measure the amount of WOM received (the NPS is based on the amount of WOM *given*).

One of Reichheld's contentions is that the NPS is a better measure of company performance than satisfaction. The best-known measure of satisfaction is the American Customer Satisfaction Index (ACSI), first developed in Sweden by Fornell (1992) and discussed in Chapter 9. The predictions of the ACSI and the NPS have been compared (e.g. Morgan and Rego, 2006; Keiningham et al., 2007) and generally the ACSI has been superior. However, because both the NPS and the ACSI are restricted to recent customers, there is potential for a better WOM-based measure that covers all consumers.

Reichheld's thesis has recently been restated (Reichheld and Markey, 2011) but this book gives no answers to NPS critics. Instead, it emphasizes a corporate philosophy of designing management systems that deliver to customers the product that they like and will talk about. It is difficult to argue with this but what people like and dislike needs measurement and the NPS clearly could be improved as a measure.

Influentials or Current Users?

In the two-step flow model, advertising is relayed by a limited group of 'influentials' or opinion leaders who recommend widely. Thus, a popular strategy is to identify these influentials and direct communications to them. As we have seen, Watts and Dodds (2007) criticized the two-step flow model and suggested that influence was more widely spread in the network. Related to this, Balter and Butman (2005) argue that WOM is more effective when it is delivered by ordinary people. Furthermore, research by Goodey and East (2008) showed that those who scored high on the mavenism index (Feick and Price, 1987) did not give much more WOM than those who scored low, so it may be difficult to identify truly influential people.

To some extent, the best strategy depends on cost. If costs are low (as when the Internet is used), it makes sense to target all those on a customer database. However, the messages need to differ between current users (responsible for most of the PWOM) and ex-users (responsible for most of the NWOM). If costs are high, it may pay to focus on the influentials; this is what happens when BzzAgents are given products to talk about. However, whether all users or just influentials are targeted, there is a need for research to find out what sort of information people pass on and what impact different forms of information have on receivers.

A popular method of using WOM from current customers is the referral programme. This is a managed intervention designed to add to naturally occurring PWOM. Often there is a reward for the person making a successful referral and sometimes an incentive for the person referred. There is evidence that the customers acquired through such campaigns are more valuable (Schmitt, Skiera and Van den Bulte, 2011).

Stopping Negative and Promoting Positive Comments

Suppliers may be able to use their customer databases to direct information to groups who could be criticizing the product. In Table 12.3, we showed that about one-fifth of negative advice relates to the communicator's main brand. Some of this negative advice is not because the brand is disliked but because the communicator thinks that it is unsuitable for another person and it is probably unrealistic to try to reduce this sort of NWOM. However, some of the NWOM about a currently used brand may reflect dissatisfaction with the brand and, where possible, this sort of WOM should be counteracted. Even if it is impossible to detect the minority who criticize their main brand, it may still be possible to deal with common complaints by communicating with all customers. By doing so, both NWOM and defection may be targeted.

Most cases of NWOM come from past customers, who are usually still on databases. Normally, past customers are contacted with a view to recovering them but there may also be value in contact designed to counteract NWOM. When products have improved, those who no longer buy them are unlikely to know about the improvement and may continue to criticize their previous brand offering on the assumption that it is unchanged. By sending past customers information about brand improvements, suppliers may be able to lessen NWOM. East et al. (2007) found that those who gave NWOM were much more likely to give PWOM (probably on another brand); this suggests that a person who stops giving NWOM could become a strong recommender.

Information, Not Hearsay

When there are widespread misunderstandings in research evidence, there is a danger that strategies will be misjudged. Many beliefs about WOM appear to have been mistaken. It is not true that NWOM is more common than PWOM according to the evidence that has now accumulated and it does not appear that there is much evidence that NWOM has more impact. The role of satisfaction or dissatisfaction in the genesis of WOM has probably been over-emphasized. Nor is it generally true that long-term customers usually recommend more than short-term customers. More research findings are needed to displace such hearsay and to inform well-based marketing strategies.

SUMMARY

PWOM and NWOM are powerful influences on consumer choice but they are difficult to study. Internet research deals with only a small fraction of those giving advice, experimental research lacks relevance to natural settings, and survey research is prone to bias. In the absence of good evidence, some misunderstanding has occurred. It now appears that much of WOM is given to help others, and dis/satisfaction, though relevant, may not be needed for WOM. Therefore, comparisons between satisfied and dissatisfied customers are inappropriate for determining the occurrence and impact of PWOM and NWOM.

PWOM tends to be about the communicator's current main brand and NWOM about previously owned brands. These patterns produce a strong association between the volume of PWOM and market share and a somewhat weaker association between NWOM volume and market share. Market share thus provides a norm for the amount of PWOM and NWOM that brands should receive on average and this allows measurement of better or worse performance for individual brands.

Research evidence shows that PWOM is more common than NWOM and that, in general, PWOM has somewhat more impact on the probability of purchase than NWOM. Impact is related to the probability of purchase before the WOM is received, the strength of expression of WOM, and whether the WOM is about the current main brand or not. Those people who are very likely to buy a brand give less weight to NWOM on this brand and those who are very unlikely to purchase the brand give less weight to PWOM on it.

There is uncertainty about the process whereby influence passes through the social structure. The two-step flow model (in which the mass media affect opinion leaders who then pass the message on to followers) has been criticized by Watts and Dodds (2007) who argue that influence is more dispersed and is bi-directional. One suggestion is that WOM production is increased by product users when they hear others recommend their brand, and this would make influence omni-directional and more dependent on ownership than opinion leadership. Managers, seeking to influence WOM, may target opinion leaders, if they can be identified, or they can seek to influence their whole customer base. The best strategy depends on costs; when these are low it is better to target the whole customer base.

The Net Promoter Score (Reichheld, 2003) is a measure of WOM, but this measure, along with the American Consumer Satisfaction Index, is based on customers and it is ex-customers who express most of the negative sentiment about brands. The Net Promoter Score measures PWOM but is a poor measure of NWOM.

Additional Resources

To see how word-of-mouth impact varies between categories and for a further review of the literature, see East, Hammond and Lomax (2008) and Mangold, Miller and Brockway (1999) who are concerned with the circumstances under which WOM is produced. It is worth checking the websites for the WOM agencies mentioned earlier, www.bzzagent.com, www.business.tremor.com and also www.womma.org. One marketing text has tried to apply the new thinking covered in this chapter, namely Allan Kimmel's (2010) *Connecting with Consumers*, Oxford: Oxford University Press. Some very interesting new work is coming from Wharton; check the Internet.

Note

1 However, some recent work, so far unpublished, suggests that Mangold et al.'s method (critical incident technique) may have affected his data. Using a survey method, satisfaction and dissatisfaction appear to be more common factors inducing WOM.

2 A critic might argue that a better measure of impact would relate the shift in probability to the movement necessary to reach certainty. On this basis, the effect of PWOM would average 0.20/0.57 = 0.35 compared with 0.11/0.40 = 0.28 so, even on this basis, PWOM has more effect. Note that this is an average effect; in some categories NWOM is clearly more influential as Table 12.4 indicates.

13 The Response to Advertising

LEARNING OBJECTIVES

When you have completed this chapter, you should be able to:

1 Describe what is meant by effective advertising, giving examples.
2 Discuss the issues relating to the effective frequency and concentration of ads.
3 Explain how advertising could have primary and secondary effects on sales.
4 Report evidence on the rate at which advertising effects decay.
5 Discuss which product fields and which customer segments are more responsive to advertising.
6 Consider how new media and changes to television viewing have changed advertising.

Exercise 13.1 What do you expect?

Go through the objectives above and decide what you think will be reported in the following pages. This helps you to take in the evidence presented in this chapter.

OVERVIEW

Advertising sometimes has a powerful impact on consumption, but its effect is variable and quite often there is no discernable outcome. We review research on the frequency and concentration of ad exposures, and how these affect the impact of advertising. There is evidence that high concentrations of ads may break through the resistance established by competitor brands.

Sales effects resulting from advertising appear to have two components: a short-term effect that is largely dissipated within a month and a long-term effect, which can last for more than a year, but which only occurs if there is a short-term effect. We discuss the bases for these effects.

Ads have more effect in certain product fields and more impact on certain consumer segments. We illustrate these effects, and consider which segments provide most extra sales volume. The Internet, mobile telephony and other developments are offering new ways of communicating with consumers.

SECTION 1: EFFECTIVE ADVERTISING

Ads may affect our beliefs and attitudes, but ultimately they must change or reinforce behaviour if they are to be useful. In social applications, ads can reduce accidents, increase voting rates, promote healthy eating, or get people to report suspicious behaviour that might indicate terrorist activity. In commercial applications, advertising can increase purchase and subscription, or maintain purchase rates when the price goes up. Sometimes the profit-making behaviour occurs at the end of a chain of prior actions, and the links in this chain may be strengthened by advertising, e.g. by getting consumers to go to a showroom or to check a product on the Internet.

Ambler and Broadbent (2000) discuss how advertising campaigns vary in effectiveness (how much change they achieve) and in efficiency (how much change they achieve for a given cost). Effectiveness depends in part on decisions about copy such as whether to write informative or emotional ads, the prominence given to the brand, whether to include a unique selling proposition, the use of a celebrity endorsement, the length of the ad, the creative idea and so forth. Efficiency depends on the quality of the ad and on media planning and buying, which should ensure that ads reach the target audience in a cost-effective manner. Decisions about content and media schedules depend on theories about how viewers consume media and how they process advertisements, so different theories will lead to different recommendations. The optimal approach may vary with the product category, whether the brand is already familiar to the consumer, and whether the purpose is to communicate an offer, remind people to keep buying the brand or to stimulate a substantial change in behaviour.

In the commercial arena, three particular outcomes may be derived from advertising, which we discuss in more detail in the following sections. These are:

- Price support: buyers pay more per unit and so the profit on a sale is increased.
- Sales support: buyers buy more than they would have done without the advertising. This is the most widely used criterion of ad effectiveness.
- Cost saving: costs are reduced as advertising stabilizes sales and makes intermediaries more compliant.

These outcomes can occur via a number of mechanisms. Advertising may:

- be based on a new analysis of the product range and consumer segments (a relaunch). For example, Virgin focused more on its younger customers when it relaunched the Australian service in 2004 (*Effective Advertising 8*, 2006).[1]

- induce word of mouth and media comment that eventually results in purchase. Murray-Burton, Dyke and Harrison (2007) report on a live Monopoly game, which could be played over the Internet and which generated measurable WOM.
- increase retailer stocking, raising the opportunity to purchase. The Felix cat food campaign (Broadbent, 2000) boosted distribution so that a third of the extra sales effect came from this source. In many cases, expanded distribution produces a sales gain without the help of advertising.
- raise demand for scarce items such as property and shares. In the case of the One2One (now T-Mobile) telephone company, ads lifted share values so that capital could be raised at lower cost (Kendall, 1998).

Price Support

Some ads make consumers aware of discounts and the possibility of saving money. This price-related advertising tends to be associated with increased price sensitivity on the part of the consumer (Bolton, 1989; Kaul and Wittink, 1995). When this occurs margins may be squeezed, so any benefits must come via increased sales. By contrast, most brand advertising is designed to raise perceptions of quality and thus increase appreciation of the brand. This tends to reduce price sensitivity, allowing the brand owner to raise margins. For example, Broadbent (2000) showed that price sensitivity about Lurpak butter dropped in regions that received more advertising for this brand. Hamilton, East and Kalafatis (1997) found that well-advertised brands usually had either slightly lower price elasticity or were more highly priced than others; brand leaders advertised twice as heavily as follower brands, and the main difference in price sensitivity occurred between these leader and follower brands. This combination of high adspend and high price is a common pattern for leading brands (Farris and Reibstein, 1991). Sometimes, it is suggested that the high level of advertising could be a consequence of the brand's success but several case histories provide quite good evidence that the reduction in price sensitivity *follows* the advertising. For example, in the Stella Artois case, the ads seemed to lead the sales (see Box 13.1). Binet and Field (2009) found that ad campaigns that tried to reduce price sensitivity were more effective than those that tried to increase sales.

Box 13.1 Stella Artois

Price support has been demonstrated by the success of Stella Artois advertising in Britain (Baker, 1993). Stella was advertised as 'reassuringly expensive', to imply high quality. It attracted a large proportion of lager drinkers despite a trade price premium of 7.5 per cent. Publicans more than recovered this premium when they sold Stella at its higher retail price. In 1999, Stella was priced 14 per cent above the premium lager average and the profit increment was estimated at six times the ad cost (Broadbent, 2000).

Mela, Gupta and Lehmann (1997) studied the impact of brand advertising and sales promotion on price sensitivity over an 8-year period. They focused on a mature product where life-cycle effects were minimal and found that *reductions* in brand advertising were associated with increased price sensitivity. Most of this effect occurred among the less brand-loyal customers, showing that price support from advertising occurs mainly because it affects low-loyalty buyers.

Squeezing the Retailer

Steiner (1973, 1993) found that advertising in the toy industry could both reduce the price to the customer and raise manufacturer margin. He showed that advertising created a consumer demand for products that compelled retailers to stock them, so they had to pay the manufacturer's asking price. At the same time, competition between retailers forced them to reduce the selling price. As a result, consumers and manufacturers did well at the expense of retailers. This effect is likely to be particularly strong when the product is a 'must have', such as the last Harry Potter book (see Box 13.2). Farris and Albion (1980) reviewed this subject and concluded that advertising exerted pressure on retailers' margins and that the net effect of such advertising often lowered the price to the consumer. When retailers have great power, as in the case of the leading UK supermarket groups, this effect may be less apparent but even in groceries there is evidence that manufacturers have adjusted production to emphasize the stronger brands where they have more leverage on price. In the 1990s, Procter & Gamble and Unilever dropped a large number of small brands and focused on the *power brands* which supermarkets had to stock.

Evidence from Hanssens (2009) and Ataman et al. (2010) shows that distribution has six to ten times the sales impact of advertising. Thus, to the extent that advertising promotes additional distribution of this sort, its effect is greatly multiplied. *Advertising Works 20* (Snow, 2011) gives the example of Marie Curie Cancer Cure changing their traditional annual advertising campaign to focus on distribution, and soliciting people to act as collectors rather than as donors. For an outlay of £184,000 they recruited an additional 5,219 collectors, who generated an extra £634,583 in donations.

Box 13.2 The trouble with Harry (from *The Guardian*, 4 May 2007)

Waterstone's owner HMV yesterday defended its decision to sacrifice profits and offer the forthcoming Harry Potter book at half price, suggesting a price war had left it with little choice.

HMV chief executive Simon Fox said the whole market for the final instalment of the boy wizard's tale would be at half price and cited Ottakar's, now owned by HMV, as an example of the price to be paid for not joining in a Harry Potter price battle. 'Not being price competitive on the book seemed to set a perception that the store was high price. There are very few books that have that level of publicity,' said Mr Fox. 'If we try to be anything other than half price we are setting the Waterstone's brand off as high price and that's something we are trying to change.

When Supply is Limited

When supply is relatively fixed – as in auctions, the services of top professionals and houses for sale – increased demand will result in an increase in price. In equity markets, where the available stock is fixed in the short term, corporate advertising may have a direct effect on the share price. Evidence for this effect is sketchy but Moraleda and Ferrer-Vidal (1991) showed that advertising raised the intention to apply for shares in the Spanish oil company, Repsol, in the run-up to privatization.

In monopoly situations, customers may feel their forced choice of a single product may be poor value. Here, advertising can be used to raise perceived value. Kendall (1998) showed how ads were used to raise the evaluation of North West Water in the United Kingdom (where water companies have monopolies). Before the advertising, customers were hostile to the company and objected to increases in their water costs. The advertising drew attention to the benefits offered by the company and raised the perceived value of the service.

Sales Support

The cases in the *Advertising Works* (UK) and *Effective Advertising* (Australia) series demonstrate that advertising can increase sales. On rare occasions the effect is large, as in the case of Levi 501 jeans in the UK. Here, campaigns from 1984 to 1987 raised sales 20 times (Feldwick, 1990). But the Levi 501 case was quite exceptional. Even when the best campaigns are reviewed, sales gains of 100 per cent or more are uncommon and tend to go to small brands, which can sometimes increase share substantially. In *Advertising Works 15* (Green, 2007), a small-volume brand, Actimel, secured a year-on-year sales gain of 426 per cent while the much bigger company O_2 gained about 35 per cent on contract customers and 100 per cent on pre-pay customers as a result of a very successful campaign in a rising market. The payback of a campaign can be very substantial when the brand is big. The O_2 payback was as much as 80 times the ad cost when all possible benefits were included. The Actimel payback was much lower at about 1.7 times because of the small size of the brand. Other examples from *Effective Advertising 8* (2006): the Sunbeam electric blanket brand gained 83 per cent but the return payback was only 1.8 because the market was relatively small. Compare this with a campaign for Australian lamb that raised sales by about 25 per cent over five years; the payback in this big market was 53 times the ad cost. So, ad campaigns can give very good returns for big brands but it is hard to show a large payback for small brands, even when market share is substantially increased.

Australian lamb was a generic campaign. Small brands may sometimes be able to band together and fund generic advertising for the whole industry. This works when suppliers are trying to overcome consumer inertia rather than displace each other. An example might be beds, where weak brand awareness makes individual brand advertising risky. Collectively, bed manufacturers might show a good return on advertising designed to get consumers to replace sagging beds and lumpy mattresses.

The Australian lamb advertising corrected a long-term decline in lamb sales, so the 25 per cent gain on sales at the start of the campaign was probably an underestimate of the advertising achievement. Sometimes, even static sales are an achievement if, without the advertising, there would have been a decline. In Australia, Hahn Premium light beer expected to lose its leading position because of a build-up of intense competition but its campaign successfully countered the attack and the brand even gained a little share (*Effective Advertising 8*, 2006).

One very successful campaign in the UK was conducted by the ad agency TBWA for Wonderbra. This ad probably drew attention because it was puzzling. The model was unconventionally provocative and the quote was mysterious to those unfamiliar with the work of the filmstar, Mae West. These ads featured a self-assured model (Eva Herzigova) and enigmatic captions. The cost of the initial four-month campaign was only £330,000 as billboards were the predominant medium used (Baker, 1995). Over a two-year period, a gain in sales of 120 per cent was achieved even though Wonderbra was selling above the price of many other brands. The key to this success was almost certainly the substantial editorial comment and word of mouth (WOM) that the advertising provoked, including discussion of how advertising could distract drivers and cause accidents (see Box 13.3). Although this is

Box 13.3 Successful ads

The wide variation in the effectiveness of ads has led to speculation among practitioners about which elements of an ad make it effective. It might be thought that copy tests would isolate the key factors but, although these tests differentiate between alternative ads once they have been prepared, they are not useful in helping create good ads. The supposed key elements of a good ad refer to rather obvious features of the ad. For example, Moldovan (1984) focused on ad credibility and Brown (1986) on the power of the ad to arrest attention. These claims are sensible but they are of limited value to those trying to create good copy.

By its nature, creativity cannot be anticipated. But, after its creation, we can see features of an ad that help to make it successful. For example, the Wonderbra campaign was noticed because it created curiosity at a number of levels. Among these were the enigmatic and challenging character of the model, the oddity of putting such ads on billboards and, in the ad shown, uncertainty about the origin of captions such as 'or are you just pleased to see me?'. This comes from a line Mae West says to Cary Grant in the film *She Done Him Wrong*. The full line is 'Is that a pistol in your pocket, or are you just glad to see me?'

an extreme example, WOM is an important secondary effect of advertising. Keller and Fay (2009) found that 32 per cent of online WOM and 21 per cent of offline WOM referred to paid advertising, and that this involved more recommendation than other WOM.

The *Advertising Works* and *Effective Advertising* cases are selected because they are successful. Most advertising for established brands produces far less sales response. This is illustrated by a report by Riskey (1997) on 23 Frito-Lay ad campaigns. This study compared brand sales when ads were running with a no-ad control condition. The study was conducted using the BehaviorScan method of Information Resources Inc. (IRI), which is described in more detail in Box 13.4. Twelve campaigns showed measurable effects, and these cases produced an average sales increase of 15 per cent.

Box 13.4 BehaviorScan

Information Resources Inc. (now SymphonyIRI Group) uses cable TV in specific towns to test ads. Households are recruited to a panel and agree to receive television that may be modified by IRI. The BehaviorScan technology swaps commercials so that some households receive trial ads or extra exposures of normal ads when compared with other households. The former allows *copy* tests to be conducted, the latter *weight* tests. Members of the panel show an identification number when they buy groceries in town. IRI finances the scanners in the town's stores and downloads sales information each night from these scanners. This system allows sales to be tied to households receiving different frequencies of advertising. Malec (1982) describes the system in more detail. GfK has used the same technology in Germany (Litzenroth, 1991).

This system permits experimental tests but suffers from some weaknesses:

- Members of the household may not be watching a TV set when it is on.
- Out-of-town purchases (out-shopping) are missed.
- The tests exclude trade response. National advertising may generate more retailer stocking and competitor advertising than in the test communities.
- The brands that are tested are chosen for commercial reasons and this may bias the sampling.
- There may be a 'hothouse' effect if panellists guess that commercials are on test and, as a consequence, take more interest in them.

As a method of testing copy, the BehaviorScan procedure takes a long time and is expensive. The ARS Persuasion Measure is a cheaper, quicker but less reliable method; this uses the shift in intention to purchase after exposure to ads (Blair and Rabuck, 1998).

Armstrong (2010) offers guidelines for developing effective copy. He summarizes findings from 3,000 studies into around 200 normative principles on how to write effective ads. For example, Principle 3.1.1 notes 'Do not mix rational and emotional appeals', and Principle 6.9.2 notes 'Attack ads should employ objective information, not emotion'. Copy that follows his principles should be more effective. However, while all the principles are evidence based, their effectiveness when used to generate better ad copy has not yet been tested. Also, while these principles might help copywriters to avoid mistakes, creativity is still required to produce ads that gain attention and engagement from the audience.

Cost Saving

In some cases, advertising produces efficiencies that reduce cost. For example, Volkswagen saved on storage costs when extra demand meant that they had fewer cars unsold (Kendall, 1998). Costs may also be saved when advertising is accurately targeted so that irrelevant inquiries are avoided. Internet job advertising can get replies from anywhere in the world and such ads should be designed to cut out applicants who cannot be appointed by virtue of their location or nationality. Kendall (1998) showed the value of well-targeted advertising in the campaign to recruit personnel to the British Army. In 1994, one person from every 6.7 inquirers was enlisted. Following the advertising campaign, the conversion ratio improved to 1 in 3.4. In the analysis, it was estimated that this change in ratio saved the Army £16 million after deducting the cost of the advertising. In addition, it appeared that better recruits were enlisted since they were less likely to drop out during the period of initial training.

The Effects of Social Advertising

Large paybacks are quite often found in social applications of advertising. For example, a £31 million campaign to raise rear seat belt usage in the UK gave a directly quantifiable return of £18 million, and, when further assumptions were made about the costs of injury and death, the return was £73 million (Broadbent, 2000). Another campaign in Australia achieved a drop in smoking of over 7 per cent, equivalent to 190,000 fewer smokers. The healthcare saving was estimated at $24 million (*Effective Advertising 6*, 2001). Often, social advertising has no opposing advertising but has to work against consumer inertia (e.g. energy saving) or self-indulgence (e.g. eating less).

SECTION 2: ADVERTISING FREQUENCY AND CONCENTRATION

Schedules

Advertising is presented in media according to a schedule. Traditionally, for TV, radio or print media, ad exposures may be *continuous* (delivered at a steady frequency per month) or in *bursts* (e.g. one month on and two months off). When the bursts are short-interval (e.g. a week) this pattern may be called *pulsing*. Sometimes, a low level of advertising or *drip* is maintained in the gaps between bursts. The choice of schedule should be determined primarily by its sales impact on consumers. Continuous schedules spread the advertising across a larger number of people so that each person tends to see fewer

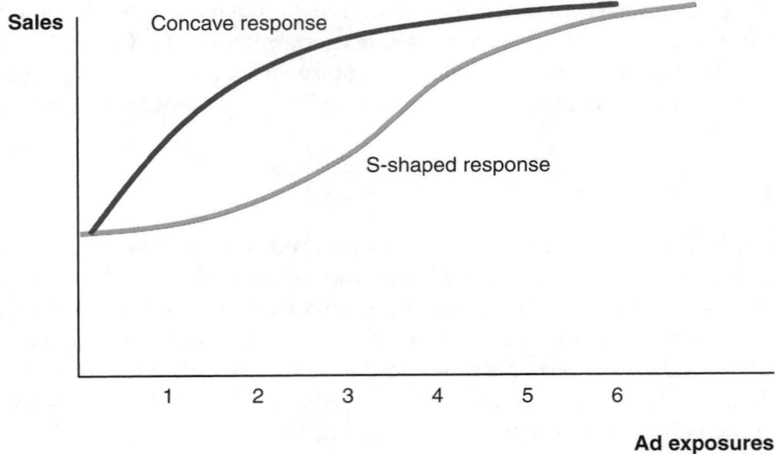

Figure 13.1 Concave and S-shaped responses to exposures

exposures compared with bursting. As the time for the burst is reduced, there is more *concentration* (the exposures occur over a shorter period).

In order to choose the most effective schedule, we need to know how individuals respond to each additional ad exposure and how they react to the same number of exposures when these are concentrated into different time intervals. Work in this field has been hampered in the past by the poor quality of the data available. Now, with actual sales data on individual respondents, the effect of each extra exposure can be measured. If each additional exposure produces a smaller sales effect than the last, the response is *concave to the x-axis* and is an example of *diminishing marginal returns* (see Figure 13.1). When this occurs, the most cost-effective number of exposures (known as the *effective frequency*) is *one per person* and it is best to use a continuous schedule that spreads the advertising across the target population as widely as possible. In this way, more people are reached at lower frequencies. But if additional exposures produce increasing and then decreasing increments in sales, which is an *S-shaped* response curve, then the best strategy is to use a schedule that takes the audience quickly to the point where their sales response is steepest. This strategy sacrifices ad penetration for ad frequency. It is achieved best by bursting and pulsing schedules.

S-Shaped or Concave Response?

Simon (1979) analyzed data from a study by Zielske (1959) and found that the second and later exposures gave a concave response (diminishing returns). In further evidence, Simon and Arndt (1980) reviewed 37 advertising studies and established that the great majority showed a concave response function. Roberts (1996) found that the response curve was concave in 15 out of 17 cases of mature brands. McDonald (1995) also argued that the true pattern of sales response to advertising exposures is concave for mature brands; his earlier work (McDonald, 1970) supported this when it was re-analyzed.[2] McDonald was influenced in part by work done by Jones on single-source data (Jones, 1995a, 1995b, 1995c), which showed little gain after the first exposure. In studies by Adams (1916) and by Burnkrant and Unnava (1987), three showings of different ads for a brand were compared with three showings of the same ad. There was more effect on purchase propensity when the ads were different. This indicates that the second and third exposures of the same ad had less effect than a new ad; the curve was concave.

Despite this evidence, there is practitioner support for the S-shaped response function. This is partly because the difficulties of research in this field make results uncertain. In particular, there is a problem posed by the decay of any ad effect as the period of time between exposure and measurement increases. Also, the time between exposures can vary, thus varying the concentration. Broadbent (1998) pointed out that there is very little agreement among researchers and practitioners on the period over which exposures should occur when frequency effects are studied; three exposures could occur in a day, a week or a month.

In addition, there are good reasons why the response to exposures *should be* S-shaped. An important argument is based on the idea of *breakthrough*, getting over a threshold of attention so that the audience cannot miss the message (Broadbent, 1998). This is discussed in more detail in the section below ('Explaining Breakthrough'). An S-shaped response is also implicit in Krugman's (1972) three-hit theory. Krugman argued that on first exposure, viewers are curious, on the second the meaning of the ad may become clear and they endorse or reject the message, and on the third and subsequent exposures they are reminded of the message again and may take action. In this account, the second and third exposures are more effective than the first. An influential book by Naples (1979) endorsed the three-hit theory.

Aggregate evidence supports an S-shaped response function. Lodish and Lubetkin (1992) analyzed IRI data and found that both new and established products did better when the advertising was initially concentrated, rather than spread over time. This suggests that exposures need to exceed some threshold level if they are to have optimum effect. This evidence has left considerable uncertainty, but this may be resolved by work on concentration, below.

Concentration

Roberts (1999) provided evidence on the way concentration affects the outcome of repeated exposures to ads. He used a UK data set on 750 households from Taylor Nelson Sofres' Superpanel, which was gathered by TVSpan. Each household was equipped with a TV 'setmeter' so that viewing could be recorded. Ad exposures were related to household purchases recorded through Superpanel. One hundred and thirteen brands from ten categories were studied. These were advertised over a two-year period from March 1996 to March 1998. This method does not produce data that controls for co-variates, and care must be taken to reduce the effects of such biases. Roberts controlled for two major co-variates: concurrent sales promotions and weight of television viewing. He compared respondents who had received exposures on a brand with *these same respondents* when, over another period, they had not received any ad exposures on the brand for 28 days.

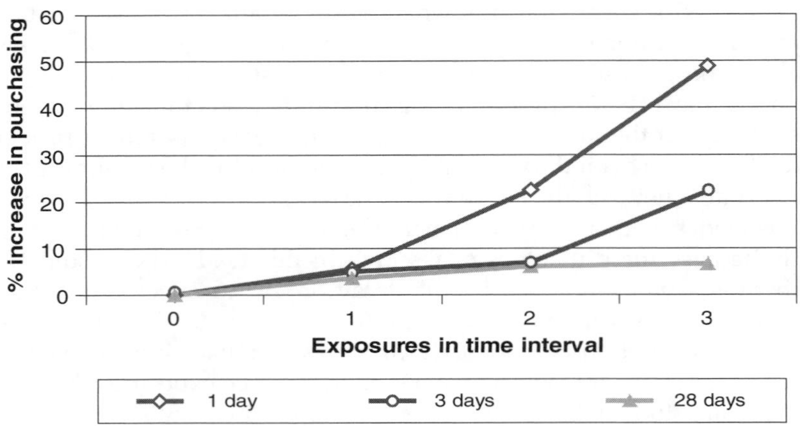

Figure 13.2 Percentage increase in sales for different frequencies and concentrations (from Roberts, 1999)

Roberts (1999) conducted a number of analyses. Here, we focus on the effects of three exposures in three different intervals: one day, three days and 28 days. Figure 13.2 shows the sales recorded after the end of the exposure interval. When the exposures occur over 28 days the additional effect of the second and third exposures is small and follows the familiar concave pattern. When all three exposures occur in the same day (and in practice this is often over a few hours) the effect of the second and third exposures is large and produces a convex sales response, which could be the lower part of an S-curve. Over three days, the pattern is more linear. There appears to be an interaction between exposures when these occur over a short period but not over a long period. Thus, multiple exposures, when close together, assist each other to achieve breakthrough. In further work, Roberts confirmed that the extra sales achieved by a high concentration decayed at the same rate as sales achieved by low concentration.

In a further unpublished analysis, Roberts calculated how concentration might affect sales under continuous, monthly burst and weekly pulse schedules. One-week pulsing had the most effect and continuous the least. The degree of superiority of pulsing over the continuous schedule was estimated to be from 4 to 13 per cent depending on the total weight of advertising employed.

Roberts' evidence, though persuasive, is still the main published evidence there is on ad concentration and it should be closely scrutinized. First, we note that the data are gathered in Britain where ad clutter is relatively low. This raises the possibility that stronger effects from ad concentration might be observed in high-clutter environments. Second, the study is restricted to groceries. Third, doubts may be felt about the effectiveness of the control comparison used in this work (the purchases made by the same respondents when they have not been exposed to the advertising for 28 days). However, in this study, control subjects had shown themselves to be in the market by making purchases in other categories and this limits the possible differences between control and test groups.

Explaining Breakthrough

Breakthrough relates to the psychological concept of interference, which occurs when a change in the strength of one concept affects the strength of another concept. In the competition between brands in a category, more recent ads for brand A tend to displace the propensity to buy brand B by retroactive interference, i.e. the new learning about brand A displaces the previously learned responses to buy brand B. Prior ads for brand B prevent this by proactive interference, i.e. previous learning makes it harder to acquire new learning that is similar to the previous learning. Breakthrough occurs when more concentrated exposure to ads for brand A overcomes the proactive interference set up by other brands.

A study by Burke and Srull (1988) showed proactive and retroactive interference effects in the recall of advertising. In their study, the target brand ad frequency was manipulated from 1 to 3 exposures while competitive advertising was manipulated from 0 to 3 exposures. The findings showed that, as competitive brand advertising was increased, the recall of target brand details decreased. This evidence of interference adds support to the argument that Roberts' results were obtained because the greater concentration overcame any interference from competitive brand ads. A weakness of this study is that it was based on recall and lacked any observation of sales effect but now the effect has been found in market data by Danaher, Bonfrer and Dhar (2008), who examined the impact on sales of a focal brand when competitors advertised within a week and found a substantial reduction compared with the sales that would have occurred without the competitor advertising. Practitioners have always been concerned to measure share of voice, the proportion of advertising exposure that a brand gets compared to its competitors. The research by Danaher et al. suggests that this simplifies the issue too much. Consider a situation in which two brands, A and B, which put out the same amount of advertising and have equal strength so that the ad for one always displaces the other brand from the minds of consumers. If the ads for brand A immediately follow those for brand B and then there is a delay before brand B advertises again, brand A's ad schedule will have more impact although the two brands have equal strength, advertise equally and their share of voice is the same.

Share of voice relates to the associative network discussed in Chapter 3. Interference should vary with the closeness and the linkage strength of competitive brands – some competitors are more of a threat than others. There is also a background level of interference set up by all the advertising received. This inhibits response to any ad and concentrated exposures may also help to overcome this clutter, thus increasing attention to the focal brand. These interference effects are more apparent when the content of the ad that is remembered is trivial, which fits most advertising.

SECTION 3: A MODEL OF ADVERTISING EFFECT

Some ads are aired a great number of times. This suggests some incremental effect after many exposures – probably, the brand name repetition helps to keep the brand salient relative to competitors. One mechanism for this is the effect of mere exposure, which was discussed in Chapter 8 (Zajonc, 1968; Zajonc and Rajecki, 1969). Therefore, we need a model

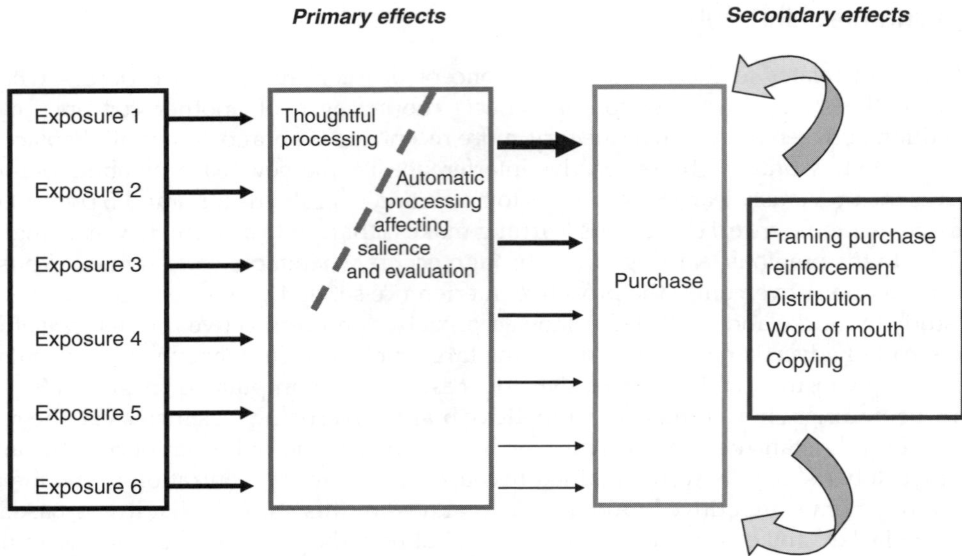

Figure 13.3 Primary and secondary responses to advertising

of advertising effect that describes the consequence of early exposures, as well as the continuing effect from what is often a large number of subsequent exposures. Figure 13.3 illustrates such a model in which advertising has two types of *primary* effect on an audience.

We suggest that the first few presentations of the ads may secure attention and may sometimes modify thinking about a brand. It is likely that this thoughtful initial response has a substantial sales effect when it occurs but that this response is not usually repeated on later exposures when only the second primary effect occurs. This second primary effect is produced by low-involvement automatic mechanisms that help to maintain brand awareness. Mechanisms of this sort produce weak effects but may continue to work over many repetitions. This dual-process account has some parallel in work on persuasion by Fazio (1990) and Petty and Cacioppo (1985). Even if existing consumers of a brand do not pay much attention to a new ad, they may still be affected by these passive low-involvement processes.

Figure 13.3 also shows secondary processes that may occur later. These secondary effects generally produce weak effects on sales but, because they are sustained over long periods, may contribute substantially to the total sales benefit from advertising. Studies of the connection between primary and secondary effects consistently show that a secondary effect occurs only when there has been a primary effect on sales. Abraham and Lodish (1990) reported that, if advertising tests do not show an effect after six months, they are unlikely to show any effect later. Jones (1995a) found that no one-year ad effect was observed if a short-term effect was not detected in the first seven days after exposure. Riskey (1997) observed that longer-term effects in 12 ad campaigns occurred only when there were shorter-term effects. Lodish et al. (1995b) found no delayed effects from ads that were ineffective in their test year. This evidence shows that any secondary effect is an outcome of the primary effect; however, a primary effect does not guarantee a secondary effect because it could be countered by competitor communications.

The secondary effect could arise in a number of ways. There may be framing when ads modify thinking and produce a persistent change in the way that a product or brand is perceived. For example, ads may persuade customers to think of their phone as a replacement for their camera. Usually, the changes produced by advertising involve a more modest change in thinking that adjusts the positioning of the brand, rather than its categorization. For example, ads may establish that a car model is more economical than previously thought. These shifts in thinking, whether dealing with the category or the attribute, are likely to be first produced by the thoughtful primary processes rather than by automatic mechanisms.

Another process that could produce a secondary effect is *purchase reinforcement*. When the short-term effect of an ad is to induce extra purchase, this additional purchase experience may strengthen the propensity to buy the brand in the future. Purchase reinforcement could occur because, after buying a brand, it comes to mind more easily, as experience-based information is more easily recalled (Fazio, 1986; Fazio, Powell and Herr, 1983; Fazio and Zanna, 1981). Purchase reinforcement could also be based on knowledge of where to buy the brand – which store and the location in the store. One objection to the purchase reinforcement explanation for the secondary effect of advertising is that there can be no such effect in the case of consumer durables; people who have just bought a new cooker are not in the market for another one. Because of this, Givon and Horsky (1990) suggest that advertising induces a different effect for durables. They suggest that those who receive the advertising may become *potential* adopters and then may find out more about the product from others, particularly those who have already acquired it.

A third secondary effect occurs when advertising raises *distribution* and reduces *stock-outs* so that the product is more easily purchased. More efficient stocking may occur either because retailers anticipate demand and order more when they are advised about forthcoming ad campaigns, or because the extra demand from an ad campaign forces retailers to increase stock. Retailers may maintain the higher stock level after the advertising has finished, thus further boosting sales.

A fourth process is social influence, either as positive word of mouth when consumers recommend the product to others or as copying when publicly used products catch the attention of others, as with fashion goods. The idea that new usage and brand switching is often started by recommendation is undeniable. The role of social influence is implicit in the diffusion of new ideas and products (Chapter 5) and is often explicitly cited when people replace one brand with another. In Chapter 12, we reported evidence that word of mouth was increased by advertising (Bayus, 1985; Graham and Havlena, 2007) and discussed mechanisms that might bring this about.

How Long Do Advertising Effects Last?

Decay of advertising effect occurs when the extra propensity to buy declines over time. This decay process will affect both the primary and the secondary effects of advertising. Decay usually shows an exponential pattern, like that of radioactivity; the rate of decay is constant but, since it applies to a diminishing quantity, the change in the whole becomes less and less as it approaches some base level. Such patterns are usually described by their half-life, the period of time required for activity to decay to half its original level. Some of the decay may be due to forgetting and some to interference effects from competitive brands.

Short-Term Decay

To a large degree, the short-term decay relates to primary effects of advertising and the long-term decay to the secondary effects. Early studies estimated advertising half-lives on the assumption that there was a single process of ad decay. On this basis, Broadbent (1984) claimed that, for most brands, half-lives were in the region of 4–6 weeks and a meta-study of 70 brands by Clarke (1976) indicated half-lives in the range of 4–12 weeks. Subsequently, Broadbent and Fry (1995) suggested that ad decay had both short-term and long-term components and Roberts (1999) measured average short-term ad decay for frequently purchased brands. He found that this fitted an exponential curve with a half-life of 16 days. This means that, on average, an exposure loses 4.4 per cent of its sales effect each day and 72 per cent after 28 days. This rapid loss of effect has practical implications (see Exercise 13.2).

Exercise 13.2 Which day should you advertise?

Groceries have an uneven pattern of purchase over the week. Spending is heavier on Thursday, Friday and Saturday when compared with Sunday, Monday, Tuesday and Wednesday. The Nielsen figures are shown below.

Weekly supermarket sales by day of the week (percentage of total, Nielsen 2005):

Monday	Tuesday	Wednesday	Thursday	Friday	Saturday	Sunday
11.7	12.1	12.8	15.8	19.5	20.2	7.9

Which day should you advertise if the impact of your ads decays each day?
What factors beside decay might affect your decision?

Long-Term Decay

Lodish and Lubetkin (1992) used IRI data on upweight tests to measure the persistence of ad-induced sales gains. In their study, 44 brands received 50–100 per cent extra advertising during a test year and sales of these brands were then followed for the ensuing two years when ad spending had returned to normal. These were compared with a control condition where there was no uplift in the test year. Approximately half of the brands showed a sales increase in the test year. Lodish and Lubetkin analyzed the extra sales for these brands and compared results with consumers who had not received extra advertising. Table 13.1 shows the extra sales in the upweight group over three years and shows that the extra sales that occurred in years 2 and 3, after the upweight had finished, were roughly equal

Table 13.1 Percentage gain in upweight group (adapted from Lodish and Lubetkin, 1992)

	Test year %	*Year 2* %	*Year 3* %
Sales gain	22	14	7

to the extra sales during the test year. This work was criticized for excluding cases where there was no sales impact from increased weight since these cases might have shown a response in later years but Lodish et al. (1995b) checked and found that there was no such later response.

Roberts (2000) divided customers into those who had – and those who had not – been exposed to advertising for grocery brands in the previous 28 days. His analysis took account of weight of viewing, concurrent promotions and brand size. He found that repeat purchase of the brand in the subsequent 12 months was higher if the ad had been seen. Roberts assessed the extra sales in the year as 5.6 times the short-term increase in sales over a month. When these extra sales are taken into account, advertising will often pay off over a year. Hanssens, Parsons and Schultz (2001) also find evidence of a substantial long-term ad effect.

Figure 13.4 shows both short- and long-term effects of advertising. In Figure 13.4, a burst of advertising produces a short-term primary effect. The long-term secondary effect is based on the extra sales generated by the short-term effect; it has a much smaller

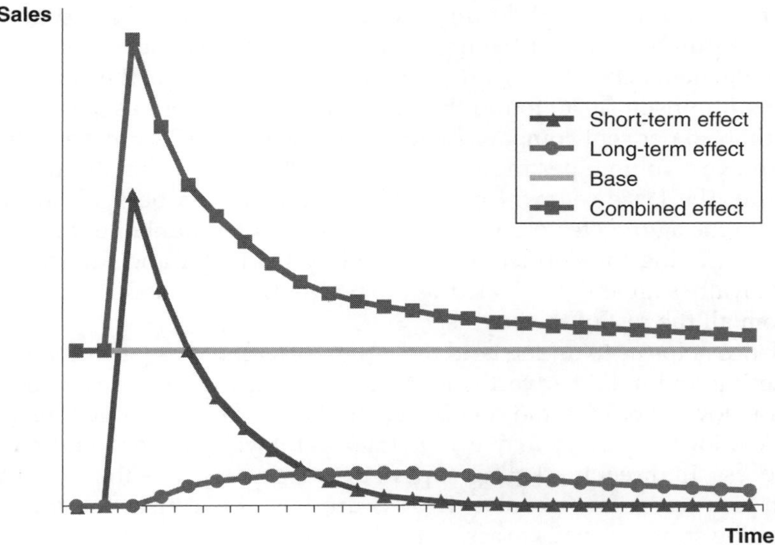

Figure 13.4 How primary and secondary effects of advertising may combine with base sales

amplitude but lasts much longer. The combined effect aggregates the base sales, long-term and short-term effects. Hanssens (2011) has reviewed evidence on the long-term effect of advertising.

SECTION 4: SPECIFIC EFFECTS

Segments

Advertising will have greater effect on some customer segments than others. Identifying such segments helps us to understand how advertising works and, more practically, how it may be profitably used.

Loyalty

Raj (1982) found the maximum sales response to advertising occurred among those with a share-of-category requirement (SCR) loyalty of 50–70 per cent. Raj found that the purchases of other brands were not much affected when the focal brand gained – the extra sales in the 50–70 per cent loyalty group came mainly from an increase in category volume. Tellis (1988a) studied one mature product category and also found that ads had more sales effect on loyal buyers with an SCR greater than 50 per cent. Those who had not bought the brand before showed only a small volume sales response to the advertising compared with loyal buyers.

Roberts (1999) looked at percentage increase rather than volume increase. He found that, on average, the low-loyalty segment (SCR less than 10 per cent) showed the greatest percentage increase and the high-loyalty group (SCR more than 50 per cent) the least. But the higher base purchase rate of the high-loyalty buyers means that the absolute volume increase among members of this group is large compared to the low-loyalty buyers. Baldinger and Rubinson (1996) found that there were three times as many buyers with an SCR of less than 10 per cent compared with buyers with an SCR greater than 10 per cent. Although the extra volume per individual low-loyalty buyer is small, the aggregate volume gain from the large segment of low-loyalty buyers can be very substantial when compared with the aggregate volume gain from the smaller number of buyers in the high-loyalty segment. Using the segment sizes found by Baldinger and Rubison, we calculate that the low-loyalty segment (SCR less than 10 per cent) gave a larger increment in volume than that from all the rest of the buyers.

This evidence helps us to understand the rather different roles performed by one-to-one direct marketing and media advertising. Media advertising provides access to the large number of low-loyalty buyers and non-buyers that can provide a large total of extra sales. Also, some low-loyalty buyers may evolve into high-loyalty buyers, and advertising can start this process. In direct marketing, it pays to focus on those with high initial loyalty if an approach to a buyer is expensive. If costs are low, this constraint does not apply. A sound marketing strategy needs to assess the likely outcomes and costs of both advertising and direct marketing before deciding on the appropriate mix.

Heavy and Light Buyers

Some of the previous discussion about low and high loyalty segments also applies to light and heavy buyers. In Chapter 4, we saw that the distribution of buyers' purchase frequencies follows a Gamma distribution. This means that there are many more light than heavy buyers so that the small volume changes made by many light buyers (and non-buyers) can aggregate to a much bigger increase in sales than the large volume changes made by few heavy buyers. This is what we see: sales growth comes principally from the light buyer/non-buyer segment. Advertising can reach light buyers and non-buyers and is usually involved when a brand gains share. The parallel with high and low loyalty is not exact, as some light buyers are 100 per cent loyal – all those who buy only once, for example, must be 100 per cent loyal by definition. Nonetheless, a similar argument applies to both situations; sales growth principally comes from those who are not yet heavy buyers of the brand.

Heavy and Light Television Viewers

Heavy TV viewers have been found to be relatively less responsive to television ads. Roberts (1999) divided households into the 40 per cent with the lightest viewing pattern and the rest. When he compared these light and heavy viewers, the light viewers had over twice the sales response of the heavy viewers. Roberts suggests that the greater responsiveness of light viewers is a 'share-of-mind' effect, i.e. the light viewer experiences less clutter so that each ad has more effect. Light viewers tend to watch during the peak evening period – it is their extra viewing that makes it a peak period. Roberts compared off-peak-only and peak-only viewers and showed that peak-only viewers had three times the sales response of the off-peak-only viewers.

Do Some Brands Get More from Their Advertising?

Big Brands

Brands are big mainly because they have more buyers rather than because each buyer buys them more frequently (Ehrenberg, 1988). If the sales response from advertising depends mainly on the number of buyers, big brands will get more total volume uplift from an ad campaign, other things being equal. But the evidence often shows stronger gains for smaller brands. Riskey (1997) found that ads for small brands delivered greater volume increases than ads for big brands and suggested that this may be because the small-brand ads tend to report some advance in the brand and these 'newsy' ads were more effective. Sometimes, the buyer base of the small brand is actually quite large, even though purchases in a given period are relatively low; long-established small brands can have a large number of past buyers who may be activated by advertising. Another factor against big brands is that they may have reached a ceiling where there are few potential recruits; when this applies, advertising serves to retain buyers rather than to increase sales. In addition, the advertising of small brands is often infrequent and this may make it more effective when it does occur. An example of a small brand that benefited from advertising is the Co-operative Society (Broadbent, 2000). Here, an old and relatively small store brand, which was very well known and had not advertised for some time, did very well when it returned to advertising.

In summary, although big brands usually have more buyers, a small brand may get a good response from advertising if it has not advertised for a while, has something new to say and has a long history.

New Brands

New brands are often introduced by advertising. Unless the new brand can be directly marketed, it must use media advertising to let potential customers know that it exists. The responsiveness to ads, measured as advertising elasticity, is high for new brands. Advertising elasticity is the ratio of the proportional increase in sales to proportional increase in advertising. Lodish et al. (1995a) found an elasticity of 0.05 for established brands and 0.26 for new brands. The novelty of a product may help it to gain attention but, even though a new brand shows a high elasticity, the gain in volume can still be very modest because there are few base sales. Furthermore, buyers of new brands may not stay. If they are willing to try new brands, they may later move to try yet newer brands.

Elastic Categories

In some fields the boundaries between categories have little meaning to buyers. Consumers may replace Coca-Cola with beer and the cinema may replace the theatre. Thus, an increase in consumption of one brand may occur at the expense of other brands in the category *or* brands in another category. As a result, the whole category can grow and the sales of individual brands may be more responsive to advertising. Because of gains from other categories, food and drink brands are particularly responsive to advertising in comparison to toiletries and cleaners, where brands can usually only gain at the expense of other brands in the category. Supporting this effect, unpublished Unilever research shows a greater ad response among food and drink categories than among cleaning and toiletry products. However, the greater ad response of food and drink brands has its reverse side since, in these fields, gains in sales can be whittled away by same-category competitors *and* by brands in other categories.

SECTION 5: ADVERTISING, NEW MEDIA AND CHANGES TO TELEVISION VIEWING

The growth of the Internet is changing the face of advertising. Blogs, message boards, emails and personal websites allow large numbers of people to put ideas into the public domain with great ease. As a result, an increasing proportion of consumer choice is directed by consumer-generated media, over which suppliers have limited control. Because the Internet is used so widely, more and more of the ad budget goes to this medium. Much of this spending is related to search engines because of the exceptional precision of search-related advertising, and because the act of search pre-qualifies a customer as more likely to buy. Other major types of Internet activity include expenditure via display or banner ads and the use of websites, social media and other portals to promote customer engagement and interaction with the brand.

Digital marketing involves other new media as well. Smartphones offer search and web browsing, with associated opportunities for advertising. In addition, the geo-location of smartphones allows ads to be delivered in locations where consumption can occur. Smartphone apps enable companies to interact with customers through micro-website, games and other applications. *Advertising Works 20* (Snow, 2011) provides the example of a homeless charity, Depaul UK, developing the iHobo game app, allowing users to look after a virtual hobo and providing the opportunity to donate in-game. Their modest £6,000 budget was extended by seeding the app to two technology bloggers for a viral campaign, leading to 600,000 downloads, 95 times as many donors as in previous campaigns, and 1,021 young people added to their donor database.

The character of ads on new media may have altered audience expectations. The Internet can present material that would not be aired on commercial television. For example, the Trojan Games website shows risqué videos of sham sexual athleticism with voice-overs that are reminiscent of a darts match commentary. Visitors to the website who are amused can easily pass on the website link to others. As a result, people have become aware of the Trojan brand of condoms at a very low cost. A further case is a video of a suicide bomber detonating a bomb in a Volkswagen Polo. The bomb explodes but the Polo, 'small but tough', contains the explosion without breaking up. This ad, which may still be found on YouTube, was not made for Volkswagen but it probably enhanced the Polo's reputation for toughness.

Blogs and discussion sites have much of the character of personal communication, even though the communicators and receivers are usually not personally acquainted. Generally, comment on the Internet is treated as an electronic form of word of mouth (eWOM), which may be passed on from consumer to consumer, either as face-to-face WOM or by giving the link in emails. This emphasis on WOM seems to have refocused ad agencies on producing copy that people talk about. In the USA, some Burger King ads have been deliberately bizarre so that people discuss them. Public relations has always been concerned with creating comment, either between consumers or in editorial content. One example of this was the launch of the telephone directory inquiry number 118 118 in the UK. To emphasize the number, twins were used in the advertising. The twins were portrayed as runners and one technique was for them to run through public areas so that people saw them and talked about them to their friends. This case is reported by Hoad (2005).

Companies such as Facebook and Twitter now actively promote WOM through sharing functions within their online social networks. By seeking to make recommendation easy and relevant, they may increase the amount of WOM over time. More importantly, these companies create a forum for social engagement which they control, enabling them to inject advertising messages into personal interactions.

Exercise 13.3 Where are new media going to take us?

How is advertising on the Web and mobile phones going to develop? How is this going to affect other forms of advertising?

Television, as an advertising medium, faces competition from other media; with the growth of online/mobile media; there is fragmentation due to satellite and terrestrial digital television offering much more channel choice; and ad effectiveness may decline as viewers with digital video recorders zip through ads. Surprisingly, TV advertising has remained relatively unaffected. Average channel shares have dropped, due to the larger number of channels, but total viewing has not declined and viewer behaviour follows the same patterns it has for decades (Sharp, Beal and Collins, 2009). Nor has TV ad effectiveness declined – if anything it has increased (Rubinson, 2009). In addition, it has been found that fast-forwarding of ads does not seem to affect ad recall (du Plessis, 2009), perhaps because fast-forwarding requires that the viewer attend to the ad break, instead of engaging in ad avoidance behaviour.

Fulgoni and Morn (2009) examined how Internet advertising changed behaviour. Despite low click-through rates, they found that mere exposure to display ads and search marketing (such as Google Adwords) increased site visits, search behaviour and both online and offline purchasing. For now, Internet advertising seems to have simply added an additional medium that operates in a familiar manner.

SUMMARY

Commercial advertising targets behaviours that affect profit, such as purchase and rental. Social advertising may target behaviours such as smoking and dangerous driving. The benefit from commercial advertising may be via more sales, greater margins or lower costs. Ad campaigns usually have quite small effects on sales but, in large markets, the payback on advertising can be many times the expenditure.

We now understand better how individuals react to different frequencies and concentrations of advertising. Extra exposures tend to give increasing sales effects when these exposures are concentrated into a short interval; otherwise, extra ads have a diminishing effect. This is probably because concentrated exposures give better breakthrough. This evidence suggests that a schedule of short concentrated periods of advertising (pulsing) is the most effective.

We present a model in which ads may have two sorts of primary effect: one is thoughtful, and the effect is quite strong, if it occurs; the other is automatic and weak. Thoughtful processes occur early in the sequence of ad exposures if they occur at all; automatic mechanisms can occur at each exposure so ads can continue to have some effect for a long period.

When primary effects occur, there may be consequential secondary effects that include framing (persisting change in thinking about the brand), purchase reinforcement (later purchase is facilitated by the occurrence of the earlier purchase), better distribution, word of mouth and copying.

Corresponding to these primary and secondary effects, sales appear to have short-term and long-term decay rates. In one study, the short-term component had an average half-life of 16 days. The long-term component can persist for a year or more after the advertising has finished.

While low-loyalty and light buyers show less individual volume response to advertising, the large number of these buyers ensures that these segments provide more sales gain. Advertising is effective at reaching light and non-buyers and contrasts with direct marketing, which is better when there is a need to focus on the smaller number of high-loyalty or heavy buyers. In their reaction to television advertising, light viewers are more responsive than heavy viewers.

While the rise of new media and changes to television viewing present superficial challenges to traditional advertising methods, research shows that TV advertising continues to be effective and Internet advertising generates the kinds of offline sales lifts that have been traditionally expected from other media. However, the growth of recommendation on the Internet may create greater changes over time.

Additional Resources

You should read at least one of the cases in the *Advertising Works* series (or the equivalent in another country). These cases indicate the concerns of ad agencies and the difficulties of measuring advertising effects. If you are more interested in the decisions that have to be made in ad agencies, one textbook that is based on advertising research is Rossiter and Bellman (2005). If you are interested in Armstrong's rules, you can read his book or visit his site www.advertisingprinciples.com, where the rules can be downloaded free of charge.

Notes

1 The Advertising Federation of Australia (AFA) supports the publication *Effective Advertising* and, in the UK, the Institute of Practitioners in Advertising (IPA) supports *Advertising Works*. These publications are dedicated to showing how competent and creative advertising can bring returns to the advertiser.

2 There is more agreement between researchers and practitioners on ad frequency when the advertising or product is new or complex. It is widely held that a linear or S-shaped response may be expected under these conditions. Roberts (1996) found that the response was effectively linear in five out of seven cases where the brand was new or relaunched.

References

Aaker, D.A. (1991) *Managing Brand Equity: Capitalizing on the Value of a Brand Name*, New York: The Free Press.

Aaker, D.A. and Keller, K.L. (1990) Consumer evaluations of brand extensions, *Journal of Marketing*, 54(1), 27–41.

Aaker, J.L. and Williams, P. (1998) Empathy versus pride: the influence of emotional appeals across cultures, *Journal of Consumer Research*, 25(3), 241–261.

Abraham, M.M. and Lodish, L.M. (1990) Getting the most out of advertising and promotion, *Harvard Business Review*, 68(3), 50–60.

Adams, H.F. (1916) *Advertising and its Mental Laws*, New York: Macmillan.

AGB (1992) Revealed: the nation's shopping habits, *SuperMarketing*, 14 August.

Ahluwalia, R. (2002) How prevalent is the negativity effect in consumer environments?, *Journal of Consumer Research*, 29 (September), 270–279.

Ailawadi, K.L. and Neslin, S.A. (1998) The effect of promotion on consumption: buying more and consuming it faster, *Journal of Marketing Research*, 35(3), 390–398.

Ailawadi, K.L., Gedenk, K., Lutzky, C. and Neslin, S.A. (2007) Decomposition of the sales impact of promotion-induced stockpiling, *Journal of Marketing Research*, 44(3), 450–467.

Ailon, G. (2008) Mirror, mirror on the wall: culture's consequences in a value test of its own design, *Academy of Management Review*, 33(4), 885–904.

Ajzen, I. (1971) Attitude vs. normative messages: an investigation of the differential effects of persuasive communications on behavior, *Sociometry*, 34(2), 263–280.

Ajzen, I. (1985) From intentions to actions: a theory of planned behavior. In J. Kuhl and J. Beckmann (eds), *Action-Control: From Cognition to Behavior*, Heidelberg: Springer, 22–39.

Ajzen, I. (1991) The theory of planned behavior. In E.A. Locke (ed.), *Organizational Behavior and Human Decision Processes*, 50, 179–211.

Ajzen, I. (2002) Perceived behavioral control, self-efficacy, locus of control and the theory of planned behavior, *Journal of Applied Social Psychology*, 32(4), 665–683.

Ajzen, I. and Driver, B.L. (1992) Application of the theory of planned behavior to leisure choice, *Journal of Leisure Research*, 24(3), 207–224.

Ajzen, I. and Fishbein, M. (1969) The prediction of behavioral intentions in a choice situation, *Journal of Experimental Social Psychology*, 5(4), 400–416.

Ajzen, I. and Fishbein, M. (1972) Attitudinal and normative beliefs as factors influencing behavioral intentions, *Journal of Personality and Social Psychology*, 21(1), 1–9.

Ajzen, I. and Fishbein, M. (1977) Attitude–behavior relations: a theoretical analysis and review of empirical research, *Psychological Bulletin*, 84, 888–918.

Ajzen, I. and Fishbein, M. (1980) *Understanding Attitudes and Predicting Social Behavior*, Englewood Cliffs, NJ: Prentice-Hall.

Aksoy, L., Cooil, B., Groening, C., Keiningham, T. and Yalçın, A. (2008) The long-term stock market valuation of customer satisfaction, *Journal of Marketing*, 72(4), 105–122.

Ali, M. (1977) Probability and utility estimates for racetrack bettors, *Journal of Political Economy*, 85, 803–815.

Allais, M. (1953) Le comportement de l'homme rationel devant le risque: critique des postulats et axiomes de l'ecole americaine, *Econometrica*, 21(4), 503–546.

Allenby, G.M. and Ginter, J.L. (1995) The effects of in-store displays and feature advertising on consideration sets, *International Journal of Research in Marketing*, 12(1), 67–80.

Allport, G.W. (1935) Attitudes. In C. Murchison, (ed.), *A Handbook of Social Psychology*, Worcester, MA: Clark University Press, 798–844.

Allport, G.W. and Postman, L. (1947) *The Psychology of Rumor*, New York: Holt, Rinehart and Winston.

Ambler, T. and Broadbent, S. (2000) A dialogue on advertising effectiveness and efficiency, *Admap*, July/August, 29–31.

Anderson, E.I. and Simester, D. (2003) Effects of $9 price endings on retail sales: evidence from field experiments, *Qualitative Marketing and Economics*, 1(1), 93–110.

Anderson, E.W. and Mansi, S.A. (2009) Does customer satisfaction matter to investors? Findings from the bond market, *Journal of Marketing Research*, 46(5), 703–714.

Anderson, E.W. and Mittal, V. (2000) Strengthening the satisfaction–profit chain, *Journal of Service Research*, 3(2), 107–120.

Anderson, E.W., Fornell, C. and Lehmann, D.R. (1994) Customer satisfaction, market share and profitability, *Journal of Marketing*, 58(3), 53–66.

Anderson, E.W., Fornell, C. and Mazvancheryl, S.K. (2004) Customer satisfaction and shareholder value, *Journal of Marketing*, 68(4), 172–185.

Anderson, N.H. (1965) Averaging versus adding as a stimulus-combination rule in impression formation, *Journal of Experimental Psychology*, 70, 394–400.

Andreasen, A.R. (1985) Consumer responses to dissatisfaction in loose monopolies, *Journal of Consumer Research*, 12(2), 135–141.

Andreasen, A.R. (1988) Consumer complaints and redress: what we know and what we don't know. In E.S. Maynes (ed.), *The Frontier of Research in Consumer Interest*, Columbia: University of Columbia and American Council of Consumer Interest, 675–721.

Andreasen, A.R. and Manning, J. (1990) The dissatisfaction and complaining behavior of vulnerable consumers, *Journal of Consumer Satisfaction, Dissatisfaction and Complaining Behavior*, 3, 12–20.

Anglin, L.K., Stuenkel, J.K. and Lepisto, L.R. (1994) The effect of stress on price sensitivity and comparison shopping. In C.T. Allen and D.R. John (eds), *Advances in Consumer Research*, 21, 126–131.

Arce, M. and Cebollada, J. (2006) The role of loyalty in online and offline shopping behaviour: an empirical application to the grocery industry, *Conference Proceedings of the European Marketing Academy*, Athens.

Areni, C.S. and Kim, D. (1993) The influence of background music on shopping behavior: classical versus top-forty music in a wine store. In L. McAlister and M.L. Rothschild (eds), *Advances in Consumer Research*, 20, 336–340.

Armitage, C.J. and Conner, M. (2001) Efficacy of the theory of planned behaviour: a meta-analytic review, *British Journal of Social Psychology*, 40(4), 471–499.

Armstrong, J.S. (1985) *Long-range Forecasting: From Crystal Ball to Computer*, 2nd edition, London: Wiley.

Armstrong, J.S. (2010) *Persuasive Advertising: Evidence-Based Principles*, Basingstoke: Palgrave Macmillan.

Arndt, J. (1967) The role of product-related conversations in the diffusion of a new product, *Journal of Marketing Research*, 4 (August), 291–295.

Arthur, C. (1992) Fifteen million Americans are shopping addicts, *American Demographics*, March, 14–15.

Asugman, G. (1998) An evaluation of negative word-of-mouth research for extensions, *European Advances in Consumer Research*, 3, 70–75.

Ataman, M.B., Van Heerde, H.J. and Mela, C.F. (2010) The long-term effect of marketing strategy on brand sales, *Journal of Marketing Research*, 47(5), 866–882.

Babacus, E. and Boller, G.W. (1992) An empirical assessment of the SERVQUAL scale, *Journal of Business Research*, 24(3), 253–268.

Babin, B.J., Hardesty, D.M. and Suter, T.A. (2003) Color and shopping intentions: the intervening effect of price fairness and perceived affect, *Journal of Business Research*, 56(7), 541–551.

Bagozzi, R.P. (1981) Attitudes, intentions and behavior: a test of some key hypotheses, *Journal of Personality and Social Psychology*, 41(4), 607–627.

Bagozzi, R.P. (1984) Expectancy-value attitude models: an analysis of critical measurement issues, *International Journal of Research in Marketing*, 1(4), 295–310.

Bagozzi, R.P. (1992) The self-regulation of attitudes, intentions and behaviors, *Social Psychology Quarterly*, 55, 178–204.

Bagozzi, R.P. and Kimmel, S.K. (1995) A comparison of leading theories for the prediction of goal-directed behaviours, *British Journal of Social Psychology*, 34(4), 437–461.

Baker, C. (1993) *Advertising Works 7*, Henley-on-Thames: Institute of Practitioners in Advertising, NTC Publications.

Baker, C. (1995) *Advertising Works 8*, Henley-on-Thames: Institute of Practitioners in Advertising, NTC Publications.

Baldinger, A.L. and Rubinson, J. (1996) Brand loyalty: the link between attitude and behavior, *Journal of Advertising Research*, 36(6), 22–34.

Baldwin, M.W. and Holmes, J.G. (1987) Salient private audiences and awareness of the self, *Journal of Personality and Social Psychology*, 52(6), 1087–1098.

Balter, D. and Butman, J. (2005) *Grapevine: The New Art of Word-of-Mouth Marketing*, New York: Penguin Portfolio.

Bansal, H.S. and Voyer, P.A. (2000) Word-of-mouth processes within a services purchase decision context, *Journal of Service Research*, 2(3), 166–177.

Bargh, J.A., Chaiken, S., Govender, R. and Pratto, F. (1992) The generality of the automatic activation effect, *Journal of Personality and Social Psychology*, 62(6), 893–912.

Bartlett, F.C. (1932) *Remembering*, Cambridge: Cambridge University Press.

Bass, F.M. (1969) A new product growth model for consumer durables, *Management Science*, 15(5), 215–227.

Bass, F.M. (1995) Empirical generalizations and marketing science: a personal view, *Marketing Science*, 14(3), Part 2 of 2, G6–G18.

Bass, F.M., Jeuland, A.P. and Wright, G.P. (1976) Equilibrium stochastic choice and market penetration theories: derivation and comparisons, *Management Science*, 22(10), 1051–1063.

Bass, F.M., Givon, M.M., Kalwani, M.U., Reibstein, D. and Wright, G.P. (1984) An investigation into the order of the brand choice process, *Marketing Science*, 3(4), 267–287.

Batra, R., Lenk, P. and Wedel, M. (2010) Brand extensions strategy planning: empirical estimation of brand-category personality, *Journal of Marketing Research*, 47(2), 335–347.

Bayus, B.L. (1985) Word of mouth: the indirect effects of marketing efforts, *Journal of Advertising Research*, 25(3), 31–39.

Bayus, B.L. (1991) The consumer durable replacement buyer, *Journal of Marketing*, 55 (January), 42–51.

Beales, H.J., Mazis, M.B., Salop, S.C. and Staelin, R. (1981) Consumer search and public policy, *Journal of Consumer Research*, 8(1), 11–22.

Beatty, S.E. and Smith, S.M. (1987) External search effort: an investigation across several product categories, *Journal of Consumer Research*, 14(1), 83–95.

Bellizzi, J.A., Crowley, A.E. and Hasty, R.E. (1983) The effects of color in store design, *Journal of Retailing*, 59(1), 21–44.

Bemmaor, A.L. (1995) Predicting behavior from intention-to-buy measures: the parametric case, *Journal of Marketing Research*, 32(2), 176–191.

Benartzi, S. and Thaler, R.H. (1995) Myopic loss aversion and the equity premium puzzle, *Quarterly Journal of Economics*, 110(1), 73–92. Reprinted in Kahneman, D. and Tversky, A. (2000) *Choices, Values, and Frames*, New York: Russell Sage Foundation, Cambridge University Press, 301–316.

Bernoulli, D. (1738) Specimen Theoriae Novae de Mensura Sortis. *Comentarii Academiae Scientiarum Imperiales Petropolitanae*, 5, 175–92. Translated by L. Sommer in *Econometrica*, 1954, 22(1), 23–36.

Benterud, T. and Stø, E. (1993) TV shopping in Scandinavia: consumer satisfaction, dissatisfaction and complaining behavior, *Journal of Consumer Satisfaction, Dissatisfaction and Complaining Behavior*, 6, 196–203.

Bentler, P.M. and Speckart, G. (1979) Models of attitude–behavior relations, *Psychological Review*, 86(5), 452–464.

Bentler, P.M. and Speckart, G. (1981) Attitudes 'cause' behaviors: a structural equation analysis, *Journal of Personality and Social Psychology*, 40, 226–38.

Berger, J. and Iyengar, R. (2012) How interest shapes word of mouth over different channels, http://rady.ucsd.edu/faculty/seminars/papers/berger.pdf.

Berger, J. and Schwartz, E.M. (2011) What drives immediate and ongoing word of mouth?, *Journal of Marketing Research*, 48(October), 869–880.

Berlyne, D.E. (1965) *Structure and Direction in Thinking*, London: Wiley.

Berlyne, D.E. and McDonnell, P. (1965) Effects of stimulus complexity and incongruity on duration of EEG desynchronisation, *Electroencephalography and Clinical Neurophysiology*, 18(2), 156–161.

Berry, L.L. (1983) Relationship marketing. In L.L. Berry, G.L. Shostack, and G.D. Upah (eds), *Emerging Perspectives on Service Marketing*, Chicago: American Marketing Association, 25–28.

Bettman, J.R. (1979) *An Information Processing Theory of Consumer Choice*, Reading, MA: Addison-Wesley.

Biel, A.L. (1991) The brandscape: converting brand image into equity, *Admap*, Oct, 41–46.

Bijmolt, T.H.A., van Heerde, H.J. and Pieters, R.G.M. (2005) New empirical generalizations on the determinants of price elasticity, *Journal of Marketing Research*, 42(2), 141–156.

Binet, L. and Field, P. (2009) Empirical generalizations about advertising campaign success, *Journal of Advertising Research*, 49(2), 130–133.

Bird, M. and Ehrenburg, A.S.C. (1966) Intentions-to-buy and claimed brand usage, *Operational Research Quarterly*, 17, 27–46.

Bitner, M.J., Booms, B.H. and Tetreault, M.S. (1990) The service encounter: diagnosing favourable and unfavourable incidents, *Journal of Marketing*, 54(1), 71–84.

Black, D.W. (2007) A review of compulsive buying disorder, *World Psychiatry*, 6(1), 14–18.

Blair, M.H. and Rabuck, M.J. (1998) Advertising wearin and wearout: ten years later – more empirical evidence and successful practice, *Journal of Advertising Research*, 38(5), 7–18.

Blattberg, R.C., Briesch, R. and Fox, E.J. (1995) How promotions work, *Marketing Science*, 14(3), G122–G132.

Bogomolova, S. and Romaniuk, J. (2009) Brand defection in a business-to-business financial service, *Journal of Business Research*, 62(3), 291–296.

Bolton, L.E., Warlop, L. and Alba, J.W. (2003) Consumer perceptions of price (un)fairness, *Journal of Consumer Research*, 29(4), 474–491.

Bolton, R.N. (1989) The relationship between market characteristics and promotional price elasticities, *Marketing Science*, 8(2), 153–169.

Bolton, R.N. (1998) A dynamic model of the duration of the customer's relationship with a continuous service provider: the role of satisfaction, *Marketing Science*, 17(1), 45–65.

Bornemann, T. and Homburg, C. (2011) Psychological distance and the dual role of price, *Journal of Consumer Research*, 38(3), 490–504.

Bosmans, A. (2007) Scents and sensibility: when do (in)congruent ambient scents influence product evaluations?, *Journal of Marketing*, 71(3), 32–43.

Bottomley, P.A. and Holden, S.J.S. (2001) Do we really know how consumers evaluate brand extensions? Empirical generalizations based on secondary analysis of eight studies, *Journal of Marketing Research*, 38(4), 494–500.

Briesch, R.A., Krishnamurthy, L., Mazumdar, T. and Raj, S.P. (1997) A comparative analysis of reference price models, *Journal of Consumer Research*, 24 (September), 202–214.

Brislin, R.W. (1970) Back-translation for cross-cultural research, *Journal of Cross-Cultural Psychology*, 1(3), 185–216.

Broadbent, S. (1984) Modelling with Adstock, *Journal of the Market Research Society*, 26(4), 295–312.

Broadbent, S. (1989) *The Advertising Budget: The Advertiser's Guide to Budget Determination*, Henley-on-Thames: NTC Publications.

Broadbent, S. (1998) Effective frequency: there and back, *Admap*, May, 34–38.

Broadbent, S. and Fry, T. (1995) Adstock modelling for the long term, *Journal of the Market Research Society*, 37(4), 385–403.

Broadbent, T. (2000) *Advertising Works 11*, Henley-on-Thames: Institute of Practitioners in Advertising, World Advertising Research Centre (WARC).

Brown, G. (1986) Monitoring advertising performance, *Admap*, 22(3), 151–153.

Brown, G.H. (1953) Brand loyalty, *Advertising Age*, 24, 28–35. Reproduced in A.S.C. Ehrenberg and F.G. Pyatt (eds), *Consumer Behaviour*, Harmondsworth: Penguin Books, 28–35.

Brown, J.J. and Reingen, P.H. (1987) Social ties and word-of-mouth referral behavior, *Journal of Consumer Research*, 14(3), 350–362.

Brown, J.R. and Dant, R.P. (2009) The theoretical domains of retailing research: a retrospective, *Journal of Retailing*, 85(2), 113–128.

Buday, T. (1989) Capitalizing on brand extensions: lessons of success and failure, *Journal of Consumer Marketing*, 6(4), 27–30.

Budd, R. (1986) Predicting cigarette use: the need to incorporate measures of salience in the theory of reasoned action, *Journal of Applied Social Psychology*, 16, 663–685.

Burke, R.R. and Srull, T.K. (1988) Competitive interference and consumer memory for advertising, *Journal of Consumer Research*, 15(1), 55–68.

Burnkrant, R.E. and Unnava, H.R. (1987) Effects of variation in message execution on the learning of repeated brand information. In M. Wallendorf and P. Anderson (eds), *Advances in Consumer Research*, 14, 173–176.

Burns, D.J. and Perkins, D. (1996) Accounts in post-purchase behavior: excuses, justifications and meta-accounts, *Journal of Satisfaction, Dissatisfaction and Complaining Behavior*, 9, 144–157.

Buttle, F. (1996) SERVQUAL: review, critique, research agenda, *European Journal of Marketing*, 30(1), 8–32.

Buzzell, R.D. and Gale, B.T. (1987) *The PIMS Principles: Linking Strategy to Performance*, New York: The Free Press.

Buzzell, R.D., Quelch, J.A. and Salmon, W.J. (1991) The costly bargain of trade promotion, *Harvard Business Review*, 68(2), 141–149.

Camerer, C.F. (2000) Prospect theory in the wild. In D. Kahneman and A. Tversky (eds), *Choices, Values and Frames*, New York: Russell Sage Foundation, 288–300.

Campbell, M.C. (1999) Perceptions of price unfairness: antecedents and consequences, *Journal of Marketing Research*, 36(2), 187–199.

Caplovitz, D. (1967) *The Poor Pay More*, 2nd edition, New York: The Free Press.

Cardozo, R.N. (1965) An experimental study of consumer effort, expectation and satisfaction, *Journal of Marketing Research*, 2(3), 244–249.

Carl, W.J. (2008) The role of disclosure in organized word-of-mouth marketing programs, *Journal of Marketing Communications*, 14(3), 225–241.

Carman, J.M. (1970) Correlates of brand loyalty: some positive results, *Journal of Marketing Research*, 7(1), 67–76.

Carman, J.M. (1990) Consumer perceptions of service quality: an assessment of the SERVQUAL dimensions, *Journal of Retailing*, 66(1), 33–55.

Castensen, L.L., Isaakowitz, D.M. and Charles, S.T. (1999) Taking time seriously: a theory of socioemotional selectivity, *American Psychologist*, 54(March), 165–181.

Chan, H., Wan, L.C. and Sin, L.M. (2009) The contrasting effects of culture on consumer tolerance: interpersonal face and impersonal fate, *Journal of Consumer Research*, 36(2), 292–304.

Chandon, P., Wansink, B. and Laurent, G. (2000) A benefit congruency framework of sales promotion effectiveness, *Journal of Marketing*, 64(4), 65–81.

Chandon, P., Morwitz, V.G. and Reinartz, W.J. (2005) Do intentions really predict behavior? Self-generated validity effects in survey research, *Journal of Marketing*, 69(2), 1–14.

Chang-Hyeon, J., Arentze, T. and Timmermans, H. (2006) Characterisation and comparison of gender-specific utility functions of shopping duration episodes, *Journal of Retailing and Consumer Services*, 13(4), 249–259.

Channon, C. (1985) *Advertising Works 3*, London: Holt, Rinehart and Winston.

Charlton, P. (1973) A review of shop loyalty, *Journal of the Market Research Society*, 15(1), 35–51.

Chatfield, C. and Goodhardt, G. (1975) Results concerning brand choice, *Journal of Marketing Research*, 12(1), 110–113.

Chevalier, J.A. and Mayzlin, D. (2003) The effect of word of mouth on sales: online book reviews, *Journal of Marketing Research*, 44(3), 345–354.

Chintagunta, P.K. (1993) Investigating purchase incidence, brand choice and purchase quantity decisions of households, *Marketing Science*, 12(2), 184–208.

Christaller, W. (1933) *Central Places in Southern Germany*, translated by C.W. Baskin (1966), Englewood Cliffs, NJ: Prentice-Hall.

Christiansen, T. and Tax, S.S. (2000) Measuring word of mouth: the questions of who and when?, *Journal of Marketing Communications*, 6, 185–199.

Churcher, P.B. and Lawton, J.H. (1987) Predation by domestic cats in an English village, *Journal of Zoology*, 212, 439–455.

Churchill, G.A. Jr and Surprenant, C. (1982) An investigation into the determinants of customer satisfaction, *Journal of Marketing Research*, 19(4), 491–504.

Churchill, H. (1942) How to measure brand loyalty, *Advertising and Selling*, 35(24), 34–50.

Clare, J.E. and Kiser, C.V. (1951) Preference for children of a given sex in relation to fertility. In P.K. Whelpton and C.V. Kiser (eds), *Social and Psychological Factors Affecting Fertility*, New York: Milbank Memorial Fund, 621–673.

Clarke, D.G. (1976) Econometric measurement of the duration of advertising effect on sales, *Journal of Marketing Research*, 13(4), 345–357.

Clemmer, E.C. and Schneider, B. (1989) Towards understanding and controlling dissatisfaction with waiting during peak demand times. In M.J. Bitner and L.A. Crosby (eds), *Designing a Winning Service Strategy*, Chicago: American Marketing Association, 87–91.

Cole, C., Laurent, G., Drolet A., Ebert, J., Gutchess, A., Lambert-Pandraud, R., Mullet, E., Norton, M.I. and Peters, E. (2008) Decision making and brand choice by older consumers, *Marketing Letters*, 19(3/4), 355–365.

Cole, C.A. and Houston, M.J. (1987) Encoding and media effects on consumer learning deficiencies in the elderly, *Journal of Marketing Research*, 24(1), 55–63.

Coleman, J., Katz, E. and Menzel, H. (1957) The diffusion of an innovation among physicians, *Sociometry*, 20(4), 253–270.

Collins, M. (1971) Market segmentation – the realities of buyer behaviour, *Journal of the Market Research Society*, 13(3), 146–157.

Collins, M., Beal, V. and Barwise, P. (2003) Channel use among multi-channel viewers: patterns in TV viewing, *Report 15 for Corporate Sponsors*, Ehrenberg-Bass Institute for Marketing Science Adelaide Australia.

Conner, M., Lawton, R., Parker, D., Chorlton, K., Manstead, A.S.R. and Stradling, S. (2007) Application of the theory of planned behaviour to the prediction of objectively assessed breaking of posted speed limits, *British Journal of Psychology*, 98(3), 429–453.

Copeland, M.T. (1923) Relation of consumer's buying habits to marketing methods, *Harvard Business Review*, 1, 282–289.

Cox, K.K. (1970) The effect of shelf space upon sales of branded products, *Journal of Marketing Research*, 7(1), 55–58.

Crawford, C. and Di Benedetto, A. (2006) *New Products Management*, 8th edition, New York: McGraw-Hill/Irwin.

Crocker, J., Fiske, S.T. and Taylor, S.E. (1984) Schematic bases of belief change. In J.R. Eiser (ed.), *Attitudinal Judgement*, New York: Springer-Verlag.

Cronin, J.J., Jr and Taylor, S.A. (1992) Measuring service quality: a re-examination and extension, *Journal of Marketing*, 56(3), 55–68.

Crosby, L.A. and Stephens, N. (1987) Effects of relationship marketing on satisfaction, retention, and prices in the life insurance industry, *Journal of Marketing Research*, 24(4), 404–411.

Cross, S.E. and Madson, L. (1997) Models of the self: self-construals and gender, *Psychological Bulletin*, 122(1), 5–37.

Cunningham, R.M. (1956) Brand loyalty – what, where, how much?, *Harvard Business Review*, 34 (Jan./Feb.), 116–128.

Curhan, R.C. (1972) The relationship between shelf space and unit sales in supermarkets, *Journal of Marketing Research*, 9(4), 406–412.

D'Astous, A. (1990) An inquiry into the compulsive side of normal consumers, *Journal of Consumer Policy*, 13(1), 15–32.

Dabholkar, P.A., Thorpe, D.I. and Rentz, J.O. (1996) A measure of service quality for retail stores, *Journal of the Academy of Marketing Science*, 24(1), 3–16.

Dacin, P.A. and Smith, D.C. (1993) The effect of adding products to a brand on consumers' evaluations of new brand extensions. In L. McAlister and M.L. Rothschild (eds), *Advances in Consumer Research*, 20, 594–598.

Dagnoli, J. (1987) Impulse governs shoppers, *Advertising Age*, 5 October, 1993.

Dall'Olmo Riley, F.D. (2010) *Brand Management*, London: Sage.

Dall'Olmo Riley, F.D., Ehrenberg, A.S.C., Castleberry, S.B., Barwise, T.P. and Barnard, N.R. (1997) The variability of attitudinal repeat-rates, *International Journal of Research in Marketing*, 14(5), 437–450.

Dall'Olmo Riley, F., Pina, J.M., Bravo, R. (forthcoming) Step-down extensions: consumer evaluations and feedback effects, *Journal of Business Research*. http://dx.doi.org/10.1016/j.jbusres.2012.07.013

Danaher, P.J., Bonfrer, A. and Dhar, S. (2008) The effect of competitive advertising interference on sales for packaged goods, *Journal of Marketing Research*, 45(2), 211–225.

Davidson, A.R. and Jaccard, J.J. (1975) Population psychology: a new look at an old problem, *Journal of Personality and Social Psychology*, 31, 1073–1082.

Davis, F.D. (1989) Perceived usefulness, perceived ease of use, and user acceptance of information technology, *MIS Quarterly*, 13(3), 319–339.

Dawar, N. and Anderson, P.F. (1993) *Determining the Order and Direction of Multiple Brand Extensions*, INSEAD Working Paper 93/17/MKT.

Day, D., Gan, B., Gendall, P. and Esslemont, D. (1991) Predicting purchase behaviour, *Marketing Bulletin*, 2(May), 18–30.

Day, G.S. (1969) A two-dimensional concept of brand loyalty, *Journal of Advertising Research*, 9, 29–35.

Day, R.L. (1984) Modeling choices among alternative responses to dissatisfaction. In Kinnear, T.C. (ed.), *Advances in Consumer Research*, 11, 496–499.

Day, R.L. and Landon, E.L. (1976) Collecting comprehensive complaint data by survey research. In B.B. Anderson (ed.), *Advances in Consumer Research*, 3, 263–268.

De Matos, C.A., Henrique, J.L., Vargas, R. and Carlos, A. (2007) Service recovery paradox: a meta-analysis, *Journal of Service Research*, 10(1), 60–77.

de Mooij, M. (2010) *Global Marketing and Advertising, Understanding Cultural Paradoxes*, 3rd edition, London: Sage Publications Ltd.

de Mooij, M. (2011) *Consumer Behavior and Culture: Consequences for Global Marketing and Advertising*, 2nd edition, London: Sage Publications Ltd.

Degeratu, A.M., Rangaswamy, A. and Wu, J. (2001) Consumer choice behavior in online and traditional supermarkets: the effects of brand name, price, and other search attributes, *International Journal of Research in Marketing*, 17(1), 55–78.

Dekimpe, M.G., Hanssens, D.M. and Silva-Risso, J.M. (1999) Long-run effects of price promotions in scanner markets, *Journal of Econometrics*, 89(1/2), 269–291.

DelVecchio, D., Henard, D.H. and Freling, T.H. (2006) The effect of sales promotion on post-promotion brand preference: a meta-analysis, *Journal of Retailing*, 82(3), 203–214.

DeSarbo, W.S., Huff, L., Rolandelli, M.M. and Choi, J. (1994) On the measurement of perceived service quality. In R.T. Rust and R.L. Oliver (eds), *Service Quality: New Directions in Theory and Practice*, London: Sage, 201–222.

Deutsch, M. and Gerard, H.B. (1955) A study of the normative and informational influences upon individual judgment, *Journal of Abnormal and Social Psychology*, 51(3), 629–636.

DeWulf, K., Odekerken-Schroder, G. and Iacobucci, D. (2001) Investments in consumer relationships: a cross-country and cross-industry exploration, *Journal of Marketing*, 65 (October), 33–50.

Dichter, E. (1966) How word-of-mouth advertising works, *Harvard Business Review*, 44(6), 147–166.

Dick, A.S. and Basu, K. (1994) Customer loyalty: towards an integrated framework, *Journal of the Academy of Marketing Science*, 22(2), 99–113.

Dickson, P.R. and Sawyer, A.G. (1990) The price knowledge and search of supermarket shoppers, *Journal of Marketing*, 54(3), 42–54.

Dimson, E., Marsh, P. and Staunton, M. (2004) Low-cap and low-rated companies, *The Journal of Portfolio Management*, Summer, 1–12.

Dittmar, H. (2005) Compulsive buying – a growing concern? An examination of gender, age, and endorsement of materialistic values as predictors, *British Journal of Psychology*, 96(4), 467–491.

Dittmar, H., Beattie, J. and Friese, S. (1995) Gender identity and material symbols: objects and decision considerations in impulse purchases, *Journal of Economic Psychology*, 16(3), 491–512.

Donovan, R.J. and Rossiter, J.R. (1982) Store atmosphere: an environmental psychology approach, *Journal of Retailing*, 58(1), 34–56.

Donovan, R.J., Rossiter, J.R., Marcoolyn, G. and Nesdale, A. (1994) Store atmosphere and purchasing behaviour, *Journal of Retailing*, 70(3), 283–294.

Dowling, G.R. and Uncles, M.D. (1997) Do customer loyalty programs really work? *Sloan Management Review*, 38(Summer), 71–82.

Doyle, P. (1989) Building successful brands: the strategic options, *Journal of Marketing Management*, 5(1), 77–95.

Drèze, X. and Nunes J. C. (2009) Feeling superior: The impact of loyalty program structure on consumers' perception of status, *Journal of Consumer Research*, 35 (6), 890–905.

Drèze, X. and Nunes, J. (2011) Recurring goals and learning: the impact of successful reward attainment on purchase behavior, *Journal of Marketing Research*, 48(2), 268–281.

Drèze, X., Hoch, S.J. and Purk, M.E. (1994) Shelf management and space elasticity, *Journal of Retailing*, 70(4), 301–326.

Driesener, C. and Romaniuk, J. (2006) Comparing methods of brand image measurement, *International Journal of Market Research*, 48(6), 681–698.

Drolet, A., Schwarz, N. and Yoon, C. (2010) (eds). *The Aging Consumer: Perspectives from Psychology and Economics*, New York: Routledge, Taylor and Francis Group, ch. 4.

Du, R.Y. and Kamakura, W.A. (2011) Measuring contagion in the diffusion of consumer packaged goods, *Journal of Marketing Research*, 68(February), 28–47.

du Plessis, E. (2009) Digital video recorders and inadvertent advertising exposure, *Journal of Advertising Research*, 49(2), 236–239.

Dubé-Rioux, L., Schmitt, B.H. and Leclerc, F. (1989) Consumers' reactions to waiting: when delays affect the perception of service quality. In T.K. Srull (ed.), *Advances in Consumer Research*, 16, 59–63.

Dunn, R.S. and Wrigley, N. (1984) Store loyalty for grocery products: an empirical study, *Area*, 16(4), 307–314,

Dunn, R.S., Reader, S. and Wrigley, N. (1983) An investigation of the assumptions of the NBD model as applied to purchasing at individual stores, *Applied Statistics*, 32(3), 249–259.

Eagly, A.H. and Chaiken, S. (1993) *The Psychology of Attitudes*, Orlando, FL: Harcourt, Brace, Jovanovitch.

Eagly, A.H. and Chaiken, S. (2005) Attitude research in the 21st century: the current state of knowledge. In D. Albarracín, B.T. Johnson and M.P. Zanna (eds), *The Handbook of Attitudes*, Mahwah, NJ: Erlbaum, 743–767.

East, R. (1973) The duration of attention to alternatives and re-evaluation in choices with two and three alternatives, *European Journal of Social Psychology*, 3(2), 125–144.

East, R. (1992) The effects of experience on the decision making of expert and novice buyers, *Journal of Marketing Management*, 8(2), 167–176.

East, R. (1993) Investment decisions and the theory of planned behaviour, *Journal of Economic Psychology*, 14(2), 337–375.

East, R. (2000) Complaining as planned behavior, *Psychology and Marketing*, 17(12), 1077–1095.

East, R. and Hammond, K. (1996) The erosion of repeat-purchase loyalty, *Marketing Letters*, 7(2), 163–172.

East, R. and Hogg, A. (1997) The anatomy of conquest: Tesco versus Sainsbury, *Journal of Brand Management*, 5(1), 53–61.

East, R., Lomax, W. and Willson, G. (1991) Factors associated with service delay in supermarkets and post offices, *Journal of Consumer Satisfaction, Dissatisfaction and Complaining Behaviour*, 4, 123–128.

East, R., Lomax, W., Willson, G. and Harris, P. (1992) *Demand Over Time: Attitudes, Knowledge and Habits that Affect When Customers Use Banks and Building Societies*, Working Paper, Kingston Business School.

East, R., Lomax, W., Willson, G. and Harris, P. (1994) Decision making and habit in shopping times, *European Journal of Marketing*, 28(4), 56–71.

East, R., Harris, P., Willson, G. and Hammond, K. (1995) Correlates of first-brand loyalty, *Journal of Marketing Management*, 11(5), 487–497.

East, R., Uncles, M., Romaniuk, J. and Hand, C. (forthcoming) Distortions in retrospective word-of-mouth measurement, *International Journal of Market Research.*

East, R., Hammond, K., Harris, P. and Lomax, W. (2000) First-store loyalty and retention, *Journal of Marketing Management*, 16(4), 307–325.

East, R., Lomax, W. and Narain, R. (2001) Customer tenure, recommendation and switching, *Journal of Consumer Satisfaction, Dissatisfaction and Complaining Behavior*, 14, 46–54.

East, R., Eftichiadou, V. and Williamson, M. (2003) Point-of-purchase display and brand sales, *International Review of Retail, Distribution and Consumer Research*, 13(1), 127–134.

East, R., Gendall, P., Hammond, K. and Lomax, W. (2005a) Consumer loyalty: singular, additive or interactive?, *Australasian Marketing Journal*, 13(2), 10–26.

East, R., Hammond, K., Lomax, W. and Robinson, H. (2005b) What is the effect of a recommendation?, *Marketing Review*, 5(2), 145–157.

East, R., Hammond, K. and Gendall, P. (2006) Fact and fallacy in retention marketing, *Journal of Marketing Management*, 22(1–2), 5–23.

East, R., Hammond, K.A. and Wright, M. (2007) The relative incidence of positive and negative word of mouth: a multi-category study, *International Journal of Research in Marketing*, 24(2), 175–184.

East, R., Hammond, K. and Lomax, W. (2008) Measuring the impact of positive and negative word of mouth on brand purchase probability, *International Journal of Research in Marketing*, 25(3), 215–224.

East, R., Romaniuk, J. and Lomax, W. (2011) The NPS and the ACSI: a critique and an alternative metric, *International Journal of Market Research*, 53(3), 327–346.

East, R., Grandcolas, U., Dall'Olmo Riley, F.D. and Lomax, W. (2012) Reasons for switching service providers, *Australasian Marketing Journal*, 20(2), 164–170.

Edwards, W. (1954) The theory of decision making, *Psychological Bulletin*, 51(4), 380–417.

Effective Advertising 8 (2006) Sydney: Advertising Federation of Australia Advertising Effectiveness Awards.

Ehrenberg, A.S.C. (1959) The pattern of consumer purchases, *Applied Statistics*, 8, 26–41.

Ehrenberg, A.S.C. (1969) The discovery and use of laws of marketing, *Journal of Advertising Research*, 9(2), 11–17.

Ehrenberg, A.S.C. (1986) Pricing and brand differentiation, *Singapore Marketing Review*, 1, 5–15.

Ehrenberg, A.S.C. (1988) *Repeat Buying: Theory and Applications*, 2nd edition, London: Charles Griffin & Co. (first published in 1972 by North Holland).

Ehrenberg, A.S.C. (1993) If you're so strong, why aren't you bigger?, *Admap*, 28(1), 13–14.

Ehrenberg, A.S.C. and England, L.R. (1990) Generalising a pricing effect, *The Journal of Industrial Economics*, 39(1), 47–68.

Ehrenberg, A.S.C and Goodhardt, G.J. (1979) *Essays on Understanding Buyer Behavior*, New York: J. Walter Thompson Co. and Market Research Corporation of America.

Ehrenburg, A.S.C. and Goodhardt, G.J. (2001) New brands: near-instant loyalty, *Journal of Targeting, Measurement and Analysis in Marketing*, 10(1), 9–16.

Ehrenberg, A.S.C., Goodhardt, G.J. and Barwise, T.P. (1990) Double jeopardy revisited, *Journal of Marketing*, 54(3), 82–90.

Ehrenberg, A.S.C., Hammond, K.A. and Goodhardt, G.J. (1994a) The after-effects of price-related consumer promotions, *Journal of Advertising Research*, 34(4), 11–21.

Ehrenberg, A.S.C., Uncles, M.D. and Carrie, D. (1994b) *Armed to the Teeth: An Exercise in Brand Management*, Cranfield, UK: European Case Clearing House (reference M94-005:594-039-1/594-039-4/594-040-1/594-040-4).

Ehrenberg, A.S.C., Uncles, M.D. and Goodhardt, G.J. (2004) Understanding brand performance measures: using Dirichlet benchmarks, *Journal of Business Research*, 57(12), 1307–1325.

Elliott, R. (1993) Shopping addiction and mood repair. In M. Davies et al. (eds), *Emerging Issues in Marketing: Proceedings of the Marketing Education Group*, Loughborough: Loughborough University Press, 287–296.

Elliott, R. (1994) Addictive consumption: function and fragmentation in postmodernity, *Journal of Consumer Policy*, 17, 159–179.

Elliott, R. and Jobber, D. (1990) Understanding organizational buying behaviour: the role of cognitions, norms and attitudes, *Proceedings of the 23rd Marketing Education Group Conference*, Oxford Polytechnic, 402–423.

Elliott, R., Jobber, D. and Sharp, J. (1995) Using the theory of reasoned action to understand organizational behaviour: the role of belief salience, *British Journal of Social Psychology*, 34(2), 161–172.

Elliott, R., Eccles, S. and Gournay, K. (1996) Man management? Women and the use of debt to control personal relationships, *Proceedings of the XXnd Marketing Education Group Conference*, Strathclyde, available on compact disc, 'Buyer Behavior' track.

Enis, B.M. and Paul, G.W. (1970) Store loyalty as a basis for marketing segmentation, *Journal of Retailing*, 46(3), 42–56.

Ennew, C.T. and Binks, M.R. (1996) The impact of service quality and service characteristics on customer retention: small businesses and their banks in the UK, *British Journal of Management*, 7, 219–230.

Eroglu, S.A., Machleit, K.A. and Davis, L.M. (2003) Empirically testing a model of online store atmospherics and shopper responses, *Psychology and Marketing*, 20(2), 139–150.

Eskin, G. (1973) Dynamic forecasts of new product demands using a depth of repeat model, *Journal of Marketing Research*, 10(2), 115–129.

Euromonitor (2006) *Boomers: Now they are Sixty: Changing Consumption Habits of 40–60 Year-Olds to 2010*. Euromonitor, Global Report – Strategy Briefing.

Euromonitor (2011) *The World's Oldest Populations*. Euromonitor, Special Report.

Faber, R.J. and O'Guinn, T.C. (1988) Compulsive consumption and credit abuse, *Journal of Consumer Policy*, 11, 97–109.

Faber, R.J. and O'Guinn, T.C. (1992) A clinical screener for compulsive buying, *Journal of Consumer Research*, 19(3), 459–469.

Fader, P.S., Hardie, B.G.S. and Zeithammer, R. (2003) Forecasting new product trial in a controlled test market environment, *Journal of Forecasting*, 22(5), 391–410.

Fader, P.S., Hardie, B.G.S. and Huang, C.Y. (2004) A dynamic changepoint model for new product sales forecasting, *Marketing Science*, 23(1), 50–65.

Farris, P.W. and Albion, M.S. (1980) The impact of advertising on the price of consumer goods, *Journal of Marketing*, 44(3), 17–35.

Farris, P.W. and Reibstein, D.J. (1991) How prices, ad expenditures, and profits are linked, *Harvard Business Review*, 57(6), 173–184.

Fazio, R.H. (1986) How do attitudes guide behavior? In R.M. Sorrentino and E.T. Higgins (eds), *The Handbook of Motivation and Cognition: Foundations of Social Behavior*, New York: Guilford Press, 204–243.

Fazio, R.H. (1990) Multiple processes by which attitudes guide behavior: the mode model as an integrative framework. In M.P. Zanna (ed.), *Advances in Experimental Social Psychology*, 23, 75–109.

Fazio, R.H. and Zanna, M. (1981) Direct experience and attitude–behavior consistency. In L. Berkowitz (ed.), *Advances in Experimental Social Psychology*, 14, New York: Academic Press, 161–202.

Fazio, R.H., Powell, M.C. and Herr, P.M. (1983) Toward a process model of the attitude–behavior relation: accessing one's attitude upon mere observation of the attitude object, *Journal of Personality and Social Psychology*, 44, 723–735.

Feick, L.F. and Price, L.L. (1987) The market maven: a diffuser of marketplace information, *Journal of Marketing*, 51(1), 83–97.

Feinberg, R.A. and Smith, P. (1989) Misperceptions of time in the sales transaction. In T. Srull (ed.), *Advances in Consumer Research*, 16, 56–58.

Feinberg, R.A., Widdows, R., Hirsch-Wyncott, M. and Trappey, C. (1990) Myth and reality in customer service: good and bad service sometimes lead to repurchase, *Journal of Consumer Satisfaction, Dissatisfaction and Complaining Behavior*, 3, 112–113.

Feinberg, R.A., Widdows, R. and Steidle, R. (1996) Customer (dis)satisfaction and delays, *Journal of Consumer Satisfaction, Dissatisfaction and Complaining Behavior*, 9, 81–85.

Feldwick, P. (1990) *Advertising Works 5*, Institute of Practitioners in Advertising, London: Cassell Educational Ltd. 181–195.

Finn, D.W. and Lamb, C.W., Jr (1991) An evaluation of the SERVQUAL scale in a retail setting. In R.H. Holman and M.R. Solomon (eds), *Advances in Consumer Research*, 18, 483–490.

Fishbein, M. (1963) An investigation of the relationships between beliefs about an object and attitudes to that object, *Human Relations*, 16, 233–240.

Fishbein, M. and Ajzen, I. (1975) *Belief, Attitude, Intention and Behavior*, Reading, MA: Addison-Wesley.

Fishbein, M.F. and Ajzen, I. (1981) On construct validity: a critique of Miniard and Cohen's paper, *Journal of Experimental Social Psychology*, 17, 340–350.

Fisher, J.C. and Pry, R.H. (1971) A simple substitution model of technological change, *Technological Forecasting and Social Change*, 3, 75–88.

Fiske, S.T. (1980) Attention and weight in person perception: the impact of negative and extreme behavior, *Journal of Personality and Social Psychology*, 38(6), 889–906.

Flavián, C., Martínez, E. and Polo, Y. (2001) Loyalty to grocery stores in the Spanish market of the 1900s, *Journal of Retailing and Consumer Services*, 8(2), 85–93.

Folkes, V.S. (1984) Consumer reactions to product failure: an attributional approach, *Journal of Consumer Research*, 10(4), 398–409.

Folkes, V.S. (1988) The availability heuristic and perceived risk, *Journal of Consumer Research*, 15(1), 13–23.

Folkes, V.S., Koletsky, S. and Graham, J.L. (1987) A field study of causal inferences and consumer reaction: the view from the airport, *Journal of Consumer Research*, 13(4), 534–539.

Fornell, C. (1992) A national customer satisfaction barometer: the Swedish experience, *Journal of Marketing*, 56(1), 6–21.

Fornell, C. and Wernerfelt, B. (1987) Defensive marketing strategy by customer complaint management: a theoretical analysis, *Journal of Marketing Research*, 24(4), 337–346.

Fornell, C. and Wernerfelt, B. (1988) A model for customer complaining management, *Marketing Science*, 7(3), Summer, 187–198.

Fornell, C., Johnson, M.D., Anderson, E.W., Cha, J. and Bryant, B.E. (1996) The American Customer Satisfaction Index: nature, purpose, and findings, *Journal of Marketing*, 60(4), 7–18.

Fornell, C., Mithas, S., Morgeson, F.V., III and Krishnan, M.S. (2006) Customer satisfaction and stock prices: high returns, low risks, *Journal of Marketing*, 70(1), 3–14.

Forward, S.E. (2009) The theory of planned behaviour: the role of descriptive norms and past behaviour in the prediction of drivers' intentions to violate, *Transportation Research Part F: Traffic Psychology and Behaviour*, 12(3), 198–207.

Fournier, S. and Yao, J.L. (1997) Reviving brand loyalty: a reconceptualization within the framework of consumer-brand relationships, *International Journal of Research in Marketing*, 14(5), 451–472

Fournier, S., Dobscha, S. and Mick, D.G. (1998) Preventing the premature death of relationship marketing, *Harvard Business Review*, January/February, 42–51.

Fourt, L.A. and Woodlock, J.W. (1960) Early prediction of market success for new grocery products, *Journal of Marketing*, 25(2), 31–38.

Foxall, G. and Hackett, P.M.W. (1992) Consumers' perception of micro-retail location: wayfinding and cognitive mapping in planned and organic shopping environments, *International Review of Retail, Distribution and Consumer Research*, 2(3), 309–327.

Fredricks, A.J. and Dossett, K.L. (1983) Attitude–behavior relations: a comparison of the Fishbein–Ajzen and the Bentler–Speckart models, *Journal of Personality and Social Psychology*, 45, 501–512.

Frisbie, G.A., Jr (1980) Ehrenberg's negative binomial model applied to grocery store trips, *Journal of Marketing Research*, 17, 385–390.

Fulgoni, G.M. (1987) The role of advertising – is there one?, *Admap*, 262, 54–57.

Fulgoni, G. and Morn, M. (2009) Whither the click? How online advertising works, *Journal of Advertising Research*, 49(2), 134 –142.

Gabor, A. and Granger, C.W.J. (1961) On the price consciousness of consumers, *Applied Statistics*, 10, 170–188.

Gabor, A. and Granger, C.W.J. (1966) Price as an indicator of quality: report on an inquiry, *Economica*, 32, 43–70.

Gabor, A. and Granger, C.W.J. (1972) Ownership and acquisition of consumer durables: report on the Nottingham consumer durables project, *European Journal of Marketing*, 6(4), 234–248.

Gardner, A.G. and Levy, S.J. (1955) The product and the brand, *Harvard Business Review*, 33(March–April), 33–39.

Garretson, J.A. and Burton, S. (2003) Highly coupon and sale prone consumers: benefits beyond price savings, *Journal of Advertising Research*, 43(2), 162–172.

Gerard, H.B. (1967) Choice difficulty, dissonance and the decision sequence, *Journal of Personality and Social Psychology*, 35(1), 91–108.

Giebelhausen, M., Robinson, S. and Cronin, J. J. (2011) Worth waiting for: increasing satisfaction by making consumers wait, *Journal of the Academy Of Marketing Science*, 39(6), 889–905.

Gigerenzer, G. (1991) How to make cognitive illusions disappear: beyond 'heuristics and biases'. In W. Stroebe and M. Hewstone (eds), *European Review of Social Psychology*, 2, 83–115.

Gijsbrechts, E. (1993) Prices and pricing research in consumer marketing: some recent developments, *International Journal of Research in Marketing*, 10(2), 115–151.

Gilly, M. and Gelb, B. (1982) Post-purchase consumer processes and the complaining consumer, *Journal of Consumer Research*, 9(3), 323–328.

Givon, M. and Horsky, D. (1990) Untangling the effects of purchase reinforcement and advertising carryover, *Marketing Science*, 9(2), 171–187.

Godes, D. and Mayzlin, D. (2004a) *Firm-created Word-of-mouth Communication: a Field-based Quasi-Experiment*, Harvard Business School Marketing Research Papers No. 04–03.

Godes, D. and Mayzlin, D. (2004b) Using online conversations to study word-of-mouth communication, *Marketing Science*, 23(4), 545–560.

Goldenberg, J., Libai, B., Moldovan, S. and Muller E. (2007) The NPV of bad news, *International Journal of Research in Marketing*, 24(3), 186–200.

Goodey, C. and East, R. (2008) Testing the market maven concept, *Journal of Marketing Management*, 24(3/4), 265–282.

Goodhardt, G.J. and Ehrenberg, A.S.C. (1967) Conditional trend analysis: a breakdown by initial purchasing level, *Journal of Marketing Research*, 4(2), 155–161.

Goodhardt, G.J., Ehrenberg, A.S.C. and Collins, M.A. (1975) *The Television Audience: Patterns of Viewing*: Lexington, MA: Lexington Books.

Goodhardt, G.J., Ehrenberg, A.S.C. and Chatfield, C. (1984) The Dirichlet: a comprehensive model of buying behaviour, *Journal of the Royal Statistical Society*, A, 147, 621–655.

Goodhardt, G.J., Ehrenberg, A.S.C. and Collins, M.A. (1987) *The Television Audience: Patterns of Viewing: An Update*, Aldershot: Gower.

Goodman, J. and Newman, S. (2003) *Understanding customer behavior and complaints*. TARP (Technical Assistance Research Programs), available via www.asq.org.

Gourville, J.T. (1998) Pennies-a-day: the effect of temporal reframing on transaction evaluation, *Journal of Consumer Research*, 24(4), 395–409.

Graham, J. and Havlena, W.J. (2007) Finding the 'missing link': advertising's impact on word of mouth, Web searches, and site visits, *Journal of Advertising Research*, 47(4), 427–435.

Granbois, D., Summers, J.O. and Frazier, G.L. (1977) Correlates of consumer expectation and complaining behavior. In R.L. Day (ed.), *Consumer Satisfaction, Dissatisfaction and Complaining Behavior*, Bloomington, Indiana University, 18–25.

Granovetter, M.S. (1973) The strength of weak ties, *American Journal of Sociology*, 78(6), 1360–1380.

Green, L. (2007) *Advertising Works 15*, IPA Effectiveness Awards 2006, Henley-on-Thames: World Advertising Research Center (Warc).

Green, P.E. and Krieger, A.M. (2002) What's right with conjoint analysis?, *Marketing Research*, 14(1), 24–27.

Green, P.E., Krieger, A.M. and Wind, Y. (2001) Thirty years of conjoint analysis: reflections and prospects, *Interfaces*, 31(3), S56–S73.

Greenfield, S. (1997) *The Human Brain: A Guided Tour*, London: Phoenix.

Grewal, D., Kavanoor, S., Fern, E.F., Costley, C. and Barnes, J. (1997) Comparative versus noncomparative advertising: a meta-analysis, *Journal of Marketing*, 61(4), 1–15.

Grönroos, C. (1978) A service-oriented approach to marketing service, *European Journal of Marketing*, 12(8), 588–601.

Grönroos, C. (1994) From marketing mix to relationship marketing: towards a paradigm shift in marketing, *Management Decision*, 32(2), 4–20.

Gröppel, A. (1993) Store design and experience-orientated consumers in retailing: comparison between United States and Germany. In W.F. van Raaij and G.J. Bamossy (eds), *European Advances in Consumer Research*, 1, 99–109.

Grønhaug, K. (1977) Exploring complaining behavior: a model and some empirical results. In W.D., Perreault, Jr (ed.), *Advances in Consumer Research*, 4, 159–163.

Grønhaug, K. and Zaltman, G. (1981) Complainers and noncomplainers revisited: another look at the data. In K.B. Monroe (ed.), *Advances in Consumer Research*, 8, 83–87.

Gruca, T.S. and Rego, L.L. (2005) Customer satisfaction, cash flow and shareholder value, *Journal of Marketing*, 69(3), 115–130.

Guardian (2011, 16 August) Supermarkets changing market share, http://www.guardian.co.uk/business/2011/aug/16/supermarkets-market-share-kantar.

Gupta, S. (1988) Impact of sales promotions on when, what, and how much to buy, *Journal of Marketing Research*, 25(4), 342–355.

Gupta, S., Van Heerde, H.J. and Wittink, D.R. (2003) Is 75% of the sales promotion bump due to brand switching? No, only 33% is, *Journal of Marketing Research*, 40(4), 481–491.

Gupta, S., Lehmann, D.R. and Stuart, J.A. (2004) Valuing customers, *Journal of Marketing Research*, 41(1), 7–18.

Habel, C. and Rungie, C. (2005) Drawing a double jeopardy line, *Marketing Bulletin*, 16, Technical Note 1, 1–10.

Hallberg, G. (1996) *All Consumers Are Not Created Equal*, Hoboken, NJ: John Wiley & Sons.

Halstead, D. (2002) Negative word of mouth: substitute for or supplement to consumer complaints?, *Journal of Consumer Satisfaction, Dissatisfaction and Complaining Behavior*, 15, 1–12.

Hamilton, W., East, R. and Kalafatis, S. (1997) The measurement and utility of brand price elasticities, *Journal of Marketing Management*, 13(4), 285–298.

Hammond, K.A. and Ehrenberg, A.S.C. (1995) Heavy buyers: how many do you have? How important are they? In M. Bergardaà (ed.), *Marketing Today and for the 21st Century*. 24th EMAC Conference Proceedings, ESSEC, Paris, 1651–1656.

Hammond, K.A., Ehrenberg, A.S.C. and Goodhardt, G.J. (1996) Market segmentation for competitive brands, *European Journal of Marketing*, 30(12), 39–49.

Hanna, N. and Wosniak, R. (2001) *Consumer Behavior: An Applied Approach*, Englewood Cliffs, NJ: Prentice-Hall.

Hanssens, D.M. (2009) Advertising impact generalizations in a marketing mix context, *Journal of Advertising Research*, 49(2), 127–129.

Hanssens, D.M. (2011) What is known about the long-term impact of advertising. http://www.anderson.ucla.edu/faculty/dominique.hanssens/Website/content/Long-Term%20PUP%202011%20-Hanssens.pdf.

Hanssens, D.M., Parsons, L.J. and Schultz, R.L. (2001) *Market Response Models: Econometric and Time Series Analysis*, 2nd edition, Dordrecht, The Netherlands: Kluwer Academic Publishers.

Hardie, B.G.S., Johnson, E.J. and Fader, P.S. (1993) Modeling loss aversion and reference dependence effects on brand choice, *Marketing Science*, 12(4), 378–395.

Harrison, A.A. (1968) Response competition, frequency, exploratory behavior and liking, *Journal of Personality and Social Psychology*, 9(4), 363–368.

Hartman, C.L., Price, L.L. and Duncan, C.P. (1990) Consumer evaluation of franchise extension products. In M.E. Goldberg, G. Gorn and R. Pollay (eds), *Advances in Consumer Research*, 17, 110–127.

Hartnett, M. (2006) Coupons still king, *Frozen Food Age*, 55(3) October.

Heath, T.B., DelVecchio, D. and McCarthy, M.S. (2011) The asymmetric effects of extending brands to lower and higher quality, *Journal of Marketing*, 75(4), 3–20.

Heilman, C.M., Nakamoto, K. and Rao, A.G. (2002) Pleasant surprises: consumer response to unexpected in-store coupons, *Journal of Marketing Research*, 39(2), 242–252.

Helson, H. (1964) *Adaptation Level Theory*, New York: Harper & Row.

Hennig-Thurau, T. and Klee, A. (1997) The impact of customer satisfaction and relationship quality on customer retention: a critical reassessment and model development, *Psychology and Marketing*, 14(8), 737–764.

Hennig-Thurau, T., Gwinner, K.P., Walsh, G. and Gremler, D.D. (2004) Electronic word-of-mouth via consumer-opinion platforms: what motivates consumers to articulate themselves on the Internet?, *Journal of Interactive Marketing*, 18(1), 38–52.

Herr, P.M., Kardes, F.R. and Kim, J. (1991) Effects of word-of-mouth and product-attribute information on persuasion: an accessibility-diagnosticity perspective, *Journal of Consumer Research*, 17(March), 454–462.

Heskett, J.L., Sasser, W.E., Jr and Schlesinger, L.A. (1997) *The Service Profit Chain*, New York: The Free Press.

Hirschman, A.O. (1970) *Exit, Voice and Loyalty: Responses to Decline in Firms, Organizations and States*, Cambridge, MA: Harvard University Press.

Hoad, A. (2005) *Advertising Works 13*, Henley-on-Thames: Institute of Practitioners in Advertising, World Advertising Research Center, 123–144.

Hoch, S.J., Drèze, X. and Purk, M.E. (1994) EDLP, Hi-Lo, and margin arithmetic, *Journal of Marketing*, 58(4), 16–28.

Hofstede, G. (1980) *Culture's Consequences: International Differences in Work-Related Values*, Beverly Hills, CA: Sage.

Hofstede, G. (2001) *Culture's Consequences: Comparing Values, Behaviors, Institutions, and Organizations across Nations*, 2nd edition, Thousand Oaks, CA: Sage.

Howard, J.A. and Sheth, J.N. (1969) *The Theory of Buyer Behavior*, New York: Wiley.

Huff, D.L. (1962) *Determination of Intra-Urban Retail Trade Areas*, Los Angeles: University of California, Real Estate Research Program.

Huff, D.L. (1981) Retail location theory. In R.W. Stampfl and E.C. Hirschman (eds), *Theory in Retailing: Traditional and Non-Traditional Sources*, Chigago: American Marketing Association, 108–121.

Hui, M.K. and Bateson, J.E.G. (1991) Perceived control and the effects of crowding and consumer choice on the service experience, *Journal of Consumer Research*, 18(2), 174–184.

Hunt, H.K., Hunt, D. and Hunt, T. (1988) Consumer grudge holding, *Journal of Consumer Satisfaction, Dissatisfaction and Complaining Behavior*, 1, 116–118.

Inman, J.J., McAlister, L. and Hoyer, W.D. (1990) Promotion signal: proxy for a price cut?, *Journal of Consumer Research*, 17(1), 74–82.

IRI (1989) Larger sample, stronger proof of P-O-P effectiveness. Reprinted from IRI which enlarges on a report that first appeared in *P-O-P Times*, March/April, 28–32, 1989.

Jaccard, J.J. and Davidson, A.R. (1972) Toward an understanding of family planning behaviors: an initial investigation, *Journal of Applied Social Psychology*, 2(3), 228–235.

Jacoby, J. and Olson, J.C. (1970) *An Attitudinal Model of Brand Loyalty: Conceptual Underpinnings and Instrumentation Research*. Purdue Papers in Consumer Psychology, No. 159, Purdue University, West Lafayette, IN.

Jones, E.E. and Nisbett, R.E. (1972) The actor and observer: divergent perceptions of the causes of behavior. In E.E. Jones, D.E. Kanouse, H.H. Kelley, R.E. Nisbett, S. Valins and B. Weiner (eds), *Attribution: Perceiving the Causes of Behavior*, Morristown, NJ: General Learning Press, 79–94.

Jones, J.P. (1995a) *When Ads Work: New Proof that Advertising Triggers Sales*, New York: Lexington Books.

Jones, J.P. (1995b) Single source research begins to fulfill its promise, *Journal of Advertising Research*, 35(3), 9–16.

Jones, J.P. (1995c) Advertising exposure effects under a microscope, *Admap*, February, 28–31.

Jones, T.O. and Sasser, W.E. (1995) Why satisfied customers defect, *Harvard Business Review*, Nov.–Dec., 88–99.

Juster, F.T. (1966) Consumer buying intentions and purchase probability: an experiment in survey design, *Journal of the American Statistical Association*, 61(September), 658–696.

Kahn, B.E. and McAlister, L. (1997) *Grocery Revolution: The New Focus on the Consumer*, Reading, MA: Addison-Wesley.

Kahn, B.E. and Schmittlein, D.C. (1989) Shopping trip behavior: an empirical investigation, *Marketing Letters*, 1(1), 55–69.

Kahn, B.E., Morrison, D.G. and Wright, G.P. (1986) Aggregating individual purchases to the household level, *Marketing Science*, 5(3), 260–268.

Kahneman, D. (2002) Presentation following the award of the Nobel Prize for Economics. http://nobelprize.org/nobel_prizes/economics/laureates/2002/kahneman-lecture.html.

Kahneman, D. (2012) *Thinking Fast and Thinking Slow*, London: Penguin Books.

Kahneman, D. and Tversky, A. (1979) Prospect theory: an analysis of decision under risk, *Econometrica*, 47, 263–291. Reprinted in D. Kahneman and A. Tversky (2000), *Choices, Values, and Frames*, New York: Russell Sage Foundation, Cambridge University Press, 17–43.

Kahneman, D. and Tversky, A. (1996) On the reality of cognitive illusions, *Psychological Review*, 103(3), 582–591. Also available at: http://psy.ucsd.edu/~mckenzie/KahnemanTversky1996 PsychRev.pdf.

Kahneman, D. and Tversky, A. (2000) *Choices, Values, and Frames*, New York: Russell Sage Foundation, Cambridge University Press.

Kahneman, D., Slovic, P. and Tversky, A. (1982) *Judgment under Uncertainty: Heuristics and Biases*, Cambridge: Cambridge University Press, 117–28.

Kahneman, D., Knetsch, J. and Thaler, R. (1991a) Anomalies: the endowment effect, loss aversion, and status quo bias, *Journal of Economic Perspectives*, 5(1), 193–206. Reprinted in D. Kahneman and A. Tversky (2000), *Choices, Values, and Frames*, New York: Russell Sage Foundation, Cambridge University Press, 159–170.

Kahneman, D., Knetsch, J.L. and Thaler, R.H. (1991b) Fairness as a constraint on profit seeking: entitlements in the market. In R.H. Thaler (ed.), *Quasi Rational Economics*, New York: Russell Sage Foundation, 199–219.

Kalwani, M.U. and Yim, C.K. (1990) A price expectations model of customer brand choice, *Journal of Marketing Research*, 27(3), 251–262.

Kalyanaram, G. and Little, J.D.C. (1994) An empirical analysis of latitude of price acceptance in consumer package goods, *Journal of Consumer Research*, 21(3), 408–419.

Kalyanaram, G. and Winer, R.S. (1995) Empirical generalizations from reference price research, *Marketing Science*, 14(3), G161–G170.

Kamakura, W.A. and Russell, G.J. (1991) *Measuring Consumer Perceptions of Brand Quality with Scanner Data: Implications for Brand Equity*, Report 91–122, Cambridge, MA: Marketing Science Institute.

Kardes, F.R., Cronley, M.L., Kellaris, J.J. and Posanac, S.S. (2004) The role of selective information processing in price-quality inference, *Journal of Consumer Research*, 31(2), 368–374.

Katz, E. and Lazarsfeld, P.F. (1955) *Personal Influence*, Glencoe, IL: The Free Press.

Katz, E. (1961) The social itinerary of technical change: two studies on the diffusion of innovation, *Human Organization*, 20(Summer), 70–82.

Katz, K., Larson, B. and Larson, R. (1991) Prescription for waiting-in-line blues: entertain, enlighten, and engage, *Sloan Management Review*, 32, 44–53.

Kau, A.K. and Ehrenberg, A.S.C. (1984) Patterns of store choice, *Journal of Marketing Research*, 21(4), 399–409.

Kaul, A. and Wittink, D.R. (1995) Empirical generalizations about the impact of advertising on price sensitivity and price, *Marketing Science*, 14(3, Part 2 of 2), G151–G160.

Keaveney, S.M. (1995) Customer switching behavior in service industries: an exploratory study, *Journal of Marketing*, 59(2), 71–82.

Keiningham, T.L., Cooil, B., Andreasson, T.W. and Aksoy, L. (2007) A longitudinal examination of 'net promoter' and firm revenue growth, *Journal of Marketing*, 71(3), 39–51.

Keller, E. and Fay, B. (2006) Single-source WOM measurement: bringing together senders' and receivers' inputs and outputs. In W.J. Carl (ed.), *Measuring Word of Mouth* (Vol. 2), Chicago: Word of Mouth Marketing Association, 31–41.

Keller, E. and Fay, B. (2009) The roles of advertising in word of mouth, *Journal of Advertising Research*, 49(2), 154–158.

Keller, K.L. (1993) Conceptualizing, measuring, and managing customer-based brand equity, *Journal of Marketing*, 57(1), 1–22.

Keller, K.L. (2002) Branding and brand equity. In B. Weitz and R. Wensley (eds), *Handbook of Marketing*, London: Sage Publications Ltd, 155–178.

Keller, K.L. and Aaker, D.A. (1992) The effects of sequential introduction of brand extensions, *Journal of Marketing Research*, 29(1), 35–52.

Keller, K.L. and Lehmann, D.R. (2006) Brands and branding: research findings and future priorities, *Marketing Science*, 25(6), 740–759.

Kendall, N. (1998) *Advertising Works 10*, Henley-on-Thames: NTC Publications.

Kimmel, A.J. (2004) Rumors and the financial marketplace, *Journal of Behavioral Finance*, 5, 232–239.

Kimmel, A. and Audrain-Pontevia, A.-F. (2007) Consumer Response to Marketplace Rumors: An Exploratory Cross-Cultural Analysis. *Proceedings of the 36th EMAC Conference*, Reykjavik University, Iceland.

Kimmel, A.J. (2010) *Connecting with Consumers*, Oxford: Oxford University Press.

Klein, G.A. (1989) Recognition-primed decisions. In W.B. Rouse (ed.), *Advances in Man–Machine System Research*, 5, Greenwich, CT: JAI Press, 47–92.

Knapp, A. (1944) A psychology of rumor, *Public Opinion Quarterly*, 8, 22–27.

Knox, S.D. and Denison, T.J. (2000) Store loyalty: its impact on retail revenue. An empirical study of purchasing behaviour in the UK, *Journal of Retailing and Consumer Services*, 7(1), 33–45.

Koelemeijer, K. (1992) Measuring perceived service quality in retailing: a comparison of methods. In K. Grunert (ed.), *Marketing for Europe – Marketing for the Future: Proceedings of the 21st Annual Conference of the European Marketing Academy*, Aarhus, Denmark, 729–744.

Kordupleski, R.E., Rust, R.T. and Zahoric, A.J. (1993) Why improving quality does not improve retention (or whatever happened to marketing?), *California Management Review*, Spring, 82–95.

Kotler, P. (1973) Atmosphere as a marketing tool, *Journal of Retailing*, 49(4), 48–63.

Kotzan, J.A. and Evanson, R.V. (1969) Responsiveness of drug stores sales to shelf space allocations, *Journal of Marketing Research*, 6(4), 465–469.

Krishnan, H.S. (1996) Characteristics of memory associations: a consumer-based brand equity perspective, *International Journal of Research in Marketing*, 13(4), 389–405.

Krueckeberg, H.F. (1969) The significance of consumer response to display space reallocation, *Proceedings of the American Marketing Association Fall Conference*, 30, 336–339.

Krugman, H.E. (1972) Why three exposures may be enough, *Journal of Advertising Research*, 12(6), 11–14.

Kuehn, A.A. (1962) Consumer brand choice as a learning process, *Journal of Advertising Research*, 2(December), 10–17.

Kumar, N., Scheer, L.K. and Steenkamp, J.-B.E.M. (1995) The effects of supplier fairness on vulnerable resellers, *Journal of Marketing Research*, 32(1), 54–65.

Kunst-Wilson, W.R. and Zajonc, R.B. (1980) Affective discrimination of stimuli that cannot be recognised, *Science*, 207, 557–558.

Lambert-Pandraud, R. and Laurent, G. (2010) Why do older consumers buy older brands? The role of attachment and declining innovativeness, *Journal of Marketing*, 74 (5), 104–121.

Lambert-Pandraud, R., Laurent, G. and Lapersonne, E. (2005) Repeat purchasing of new automobiles by older consumers: empirical evidence and interpretations, *Journal of Marketing*, 69(August), 97–113.

Lapersonne, E., Laurent, G. and Le Goff, J.-J. (1995) Consideration sets of size one: an empirical investigation of automobile purchases, *International Journal of Research in Marketing*, 12(1), 55–66.

LaTour, S.A. and Peat, N.C. (1979) Conceptual and methodological issues in consumer satisfaction research. In W.L. Wilkie (ed.), *Advances in Consumer Research*, 6, 431–437.

Le Boutillier, J., Le Boutillier, S.S. and Neslin, S.A. (1994) A replication and extension of the Dickson and Sawyer price-awareness study, *Marketing Letters*, 5(1), 31–42.

Leclerc, F., Schmitt, B.H. and Dubé, L. (1995) Waiting time and decision making: is time like money?, *Journal of Consumer Research*, 22(1), 110–119.

Lee, A.Y. (1994) The mere exposure effect: is it a mere case of misattribution? In C.T. Allen and D.R. John (eds), *Advances in Consumer Research*, 21, 270–275.

Leenheer, J., van Heerde, H.J., Bijmolt, T.H.A. and Smidts, A. (2007) Do loyalty programs really enhance behavioral loyalty? An empirical analysis accounting for self-selecting members, *International Journal of Research in Marketing*, 24(1), 31–47.

Lees, G. and Wright, M. (2012) Does the duplication of viewing law apply to radio listening?, *European Journal of Marketing*, in press.

Lees, G.J., Garland, B.R. and Wright, M.J. (2007) Switching banks: old bank gone but not forgotten, *Journal of Financial Services Marketing*, 12(2), 146–156.

Lemon, K.N. and Nowlis, S.M. (2002) Developing synergies between promotions and brands in different price-quality tiers, *Journal of Marketing Research*, 39(2), 171–185.

Les Échos (2004) Étendre sa marque, un pari souvent gagnat. No. 19301, 7 December, 15. http://archives.lesechos.fr/archives/2004/LesEchos/19301-50-ECH.htm (accessed 2012).

Lichtenstein, D.R. and Bearden, W.O. (1989) Contextual influences on perceptions of merchant-supplied reference prices, *Journal of Consumer Research*, 16(1), 55–67.

Lichtenstein, S., Slovic, P., Fischoff, B., Lyman, M. and Combs, B. (1978) Judged frequency of lethal events, *Journal of Experimental Psychology: Human Learning and Memory*, 4, 551–578.

Lilien, G.L. and Rangaswamy, A. (2002) *Marketing Engineering: Computer-assisted Marketing Analysis and Planning*, 2nd edition, Upper Saddle River, NJ: Prentice-Hall.

Litzenroth, H. (1991) A small town in Germany: single source data from a controlled micromarket, *Admap*, 26(5), 23–27.

Liu, H.-S. (2012) How does online word-of-mouth influence revenue? Evidence from Twitter. http://www.citi.uconn.edu/cist07/1a.pdf (draft).

Liu, Y. (2006) Word of mouth for movies: its dynamics and influence on box office revenue, *Journal of Marketing*, 70(3), 74–89.

Liu, Y. (2007) The long-term impact of loyalty programs on consumer purchase behavior and loyalty, *Journal of Marketing*, 71(4), 19–35.

Lodish, L.M. and Lubetkin, B. (1992) How advertising works. General truths? Nine key findings from IRI test data, *Admap*, February, 9–15.

Lodish, L.M., Abraham, M., Kalmansen, S., Livelsberger, J., Lubetkin, B., Richardson, B. and Stevens, M.E. (1995a) How TV advertising works: a meta-analysis of 389 real-world split cable TV advertising experiments, *Journal of Marketing Research*, 32(2), 125–139.

Lodish, L.M., Abraham, M., Livelsberger, J., Lubetkin, B., Richardson, B. and Stevens, M.E. (1995b) A summary of fifty-five in-market experiments on the long-term effect of TV advertising, *Marketing Science*, 14(Part 2 of 2), G133–G140.

Loken, B. (1983) The theory of reasoned action: examination of the sufficiency assumption for a television viewing behavior. In R.P. Bagozzi and A.M. Tybout (eds), *Advances in Consumer Research*, 10, Ann Arbor, MI: Association for Consumer Research, 100–105.

Lomax, W., Hammond, K., Clemente, M. and East, R. (1996) New entrants in a mature market: an empirical study of the detergent market, *Journal of Marketing Management*, 12(4), 281–295.

Losch, A. (1939) *The Economics of Location*, translated by W.H. Woglom and F. Stolper (1954), New Haven, CT: Yale University Press.

Luo, X., Homburg, C. and Wieseke, J. (2010) Customer satisfaction, analyst stock recommendations, and firm value, *Journal of Marketing Research*, 47(6), 1041–1058.

Macintosh, G. and Lockshin, L.S. (1997) Retail relationships and store loyalty: a multi-level perspective, *International Journal of Research in Marketing*, 14(5), 487–497.

Madden, T.J., Ellen, P.S. and Ajzen, I. (1992) A comparison of the theory of planned behavior and the theory of reasoned action, *Personality and Social Psychology Bulletin*, 18(1), 3–9.

Mägi, A.W. (2003) Share of wallet in retailing: the effects of customer satisfaction loyalty cards and shopper characteristics, *Journal of Retailing*, 79(2), 97–106.

Magnini, V.P., Ford, J.B., Markowski, E.P. and Honeycut, E.D., Jr (2007) The service recovery paradox: justifiable theory or smouldering myth, *Journal of Services Marketing*, 21(3), 213–224.

Mahajan, V., Muller, E. and Bass, F.M. (1990) New product diffusion models in marketing: a review and directions for research, *Journal of Marketing*, 54(1), 1–26.

Maister, D.H. (1985) The psychology of waiting lines. In J.A. Czepiel, M.R. Solomon and C.F. Surprenant (eds), *The Service Encounter*, Lexington, MA: D.C. Heath, 113–124.

Malafi, T.N., Cini, M.A., Taub, S.L. and Bertolami, J. (1993) Social influence and the decision to complain: investigations on the role of advice, *Journal of Consumer Satisfaction, Dissatisfaction and Complaining Behavior*, 6, 81–89.

Malec, J. (1982) Ad testing through the marriage of UPC scanning and targetable TV, *Admap*, May, 273–279.

Mangold, W.G., Miller, F. and Brockway, G.R. (1999) Word-of-mouth communication in the service marketplace, *Journal of Services Marketing*, 13(1), 73–89.

Manning, K.C. and Sprott, D.E. (2009) Price endings, left-digit effects, and choice, *Journal of Consumer Research*, 36(2), 328–335.

Marcel, J. (1976) Unconscious reading: experiments on people who do not know they are reading. Paper presented at the British Association for the Advancement of Science, Lancaster, UK.

Markus, H. and Kitayama, S. (1991) Culture and self: implications for cognition, emotion and motivation, *Psychological Review*, 98(2), 224–253

Markus, H. and Zajonc, R.B. (1985) The cognitive perspective in social psychology. In G. Lindzey and E. Aronson (eds), *Handbook of Social Psychology*, 3rd edition (Vol. 1), New York: Random House, 137–230.

Marsh, A. and Matheson, J. (1983) *Smoking Attitudes and Behaviour: An Enquiry Carried Out on Behalf of the Department of Health and Social Security*, London: HMSO.

Marsh, P., Barwise, P., Thomas, K. and Wensley, R. (1988) *Managing Strategic Investment Decisions in Large Diversified Companies*, Working Paper, London Business School, reviewed in *The Economist*, 9 July, 1988.

Marx, K. (1930) *Capital*, Vols 1, 2 and 3. London: J.M. Dent & Sons Ltd.

Mason, N. (1991) *An Investigation into Grocery Shopping Behaviour in Britain*, Headington, Oxford: Nielsen Consumer Research.

Mattila, A.S. and Wirtz, J. (2001) Congruency of scent and music as a driver of in-store evaluations and behavior, *Journal of Retailing*, 77(2), 273–289.

Mazumdar, T. and Papatla, P. (2000) An investigation of reference price segments, *Journal of Marketing Research*, 37(2), 246–258.

Mazumdar, T., Raj, S.P. and Sinha, I. (2005) Reference price research: review and propositions, *Journal of Marketing*, 69(4), 84–102.

Mazzarol, T., Sweeney, J. and Soutar, G.N. (2007) Conceptualizing word-of-mouth activity, triggers and conditions: an exploratory study, *European Journal of Marketing*, 41(11/12), 1475–1494.

McDonald, C. (1970) What is the short-term effect of advertising? *Proceedings of the ESOMAR Congress*, Barcelona, 463–485.

McDonald, C. (1995) *Advertising Reach and Frequency*, Chicago: NTC Business Books.

McKay, D.B. (1973) A spectral analysis of the frequency of supermarket visits, *Journal of Marketing Research*, 10(February), 84–90.

McPhee, W.N. (1963) *Formal Theories of Mass Behavior*, Glencoe, IL: The Free Press.

McQuarrie, E.F. (1988) An alternative to purchase intentions: the role of prior behaviour in consumer expenditure on computers, *Journal of the Market Research Society*, 30(4), 407–437.

McSweeney, B. (2002) Hofstede's model of national cultural differences and their consequences: a triumph of faith – a failure of analysis, *Human Relations*, 55, 89–118.

McWilliam, G. (1993) The effect of brand typology on the evaluation of brand extension fit: commercial and academic research findings. In W.F. Van Raaij and G.J. Bamossy (eds), *European Advances in Consumer Research*, 1, 485–91.

Mehrabian, A. and Russell, J.A. (1974) *An Approach to Environmental Psychology*, Cambridge, MA: Massachusetts Institute of Technology Press.

Mela, C.F., Gupta, S. and Lehmann, D.R. (1997) The long-term impact of promotion and advertising on consumer choice, *Journal of Marketing Research*, 34(2), 248–261.

Melnyk, V., van Osselaer, S.M.J. and Bijmolt, T.H.A. (2009) Are women more loyal customers than men? Gender differences in loyalty to firms and individual service providers, *Journal of Marketing*, 73(4), 82–96.

Meyer-Waarden, L. (2007) The effects of loyalty programs on customer lifetime duration and share of wallet, *Journal of Retailing*, 83(2), 223–236.

Meyers-Levy, J. and Tybout, A.M. (1989) Schema congruity as a basis for product evaluation, *Journal of Consumer Research*, 16 (1), 39–54.

Michon, R., Chebat, J.-C. and Turley, L.W. (2005) Mall atmospherics: the interaction effects of the mall environment on shopping behaviour, *Journal of Business Research*, 58(5), 576–583.

Milgram, S. (1970) The experience of living in cities, *Science*, 167, 1464–1468.

Milliman, R.E. (1982) Using background music to affect the behavior of supermarket shoppers, *Journal of Marketing*, 46(3), 86–91.

Mittal, V., Ross, W.T. and Baldasare, P.M. (1998) The asymmetric impact of negative and positive attribute-level performance on overall satisfaction and repurchase intentions, *Journal of Marketing*, 62(1), 33–47.

Mizerski, R.W. (1982) An attributional explanation of the disproportionate influence of unfavorable information, *Journal of Consumer Research*, 9(1), 301–310.

Moldovan, S.E. (1984) Copy factors related to persuasion scores, *Journal of Advertising Research*, 24(6), 16–22.

Monroe, K.B. (1973) Buyers' subjective perceptions of price, *Journal of Marketing Research*, 10(1), 70–80.

Monroe, K.B. and Lee, A.V. (1999) Remembering versus knowing: issues in buyers' processing of price information, *Journal of the Academy of Marketing Science*, 27(2), 207–225.

Moore, W.L. and Pessemier, E.A. (1993) *Product Planning and Management: Designing and Delivering Value*, Singapore: McGraw-Hill.

Moraleda, P. and Ferrer-Vidal, J. (eds) (1991) *Proceedings of the 1990 ESOMAR Conference*, Monte Carlo.

Morgan, N.A. and Rego, L.L. (2006) The value of different customer satisfaction and loyalty metrics in predicting business performance, *Marketing Science*, 25(5), 426–439.

Morin, S., Dubé, L. and Chebat, J.-C. (2007) The role of pleasant music in servicescapes: a test of the dual model of environmental perception, *Journal of Retailing*, 83(1), 115–130.

Morrison, D. and Schmittlein, D.C. (1981) Predicting future random events based on past performances, *Management Science*, 27(9), 1006–1023.

Morrison, D. and Schmittlein, D.C. (1988) Generalizing the NBD model for customer purchases: what are the implications and is it worth the effort?, *Journal of Business and Economic Statistics*, 6(2), 145–166.

Murray-Burton, G., Dyke, M. and Harrison, T. (2007) Monopoly here and now. In L. Green (ed.), *Advertising Works 15*, IPA Effectiveness Awards 2006, Henley-on-Thames: World Advertising Research Center (Warc).

Naples, M.J. (1979) *Effective Frequency: The Relationship Between Frequency and Advertising Effectiveness*, New York: Association of National Advertisers.

Narasimhan, C. (1984) A price discrimination theory of coupons, *Marketing Science*, 3(2), 128–148.

Narisetti, R. (1997) Move to drop coupons puts Procter & Gamble in sticky PR situation, *Wall Street Journal*, 17 April, 1, A10.

Naylor, G. and Kleiser, S.B. (2000) Negative versus positive word-of-mouth: an exception to the rule, *Journal of Satisfaction, Dissatisfaction and Complaining Behavior*, 13, 26–36.

Neslin, S.A. (1990) A market response model for coupon promotions, *Marketing Science*, 9(2), 125–146.

Neslin, S.A. (2002) *Sales Promotion*, Cambridge, MA: Marketing Science Institute.

Neslin, S.A. and Clarke, D.G. (1987) Relating the brand use profile of coupon redeemers to brand and coupon characteristics, *Journal of Advertising Research*, 27(1), 23–32.

Neslin, S.A. and Stone, L.G.S. (1996) Consumer inventory sensitivity and the postpromotion dip, *Marketing Letters*, 7(1), 77–94.

Nielsen (2005) *Retail Pocket Book, 2006*. Oxford: WARC and AC Nielsen.

Nielsen (2011a) Online Shopping, http://www.ukom.uk.net/media/Online%20Grocery%20Shopping_A4Final.pdf.

Nielsen (2011b) Phone usage, women v. men, http://www.marketingcharts.com/direct/teens-sendreceive-3700-monthly-texts-15579/nielsen-phone-usage-women-v-men-jan11gif/.

Nijs, V.R., Dekimpe, M.G., Steenkamp, J.-B.E.M. and Hanssens, D.M. (2001) The category–demand effects of price promotions, *Marketing Science*, 20(1), 1–22.

Nitzan, I. and Libai, B. (2011) Social effects on customer retention, *Journal of Marketing*, 75(6), 24–38.

North, A.C., Hargreaves, D.J. and McKendrick, J. (1999) The influence of in-store music on wine selections, *Journal of Applied Social Psychology*, 84(2), 271–276.

North, A.C., Hargreaves, D.J. and Hargreaves, J.J. (2004) The uses of music in everyday life, *Music Perception*, 22(1), 41–77.

Nunes, J.C. and Drèze, X. (2006) The endowed progress effect: how artificial advancement increases effort, *Journal of Consumer Research*, 32(4), 504–512.

Odean, T. (1998) Are investors reluctant to realize their losses?, *Journal of Finance*, 53(5), 1775–1798. Reprinted in D. Kahneman and A. Tversky (2000) *Choices, Values, and Frames*, Cambridge: Russell Sage Foundation, Cambridge University Press, 371–392.

OECD (2000) *The Service Economy*. Business and Industry Policy Forum Series. Paris: Organization for Economic Cooperation and Development. http://www.oecd.org/dataoecd/10/33/2090561.pdf.

Ogilvy, D. (1987) Sound an alarm!, *International Journal of Advertising*, 6, 81–4.

Oliver, R.L. (1980) Cognitive model of the antecedents and consequences of satisfaction decisions, *Journal of Marketing Research*, 17(4), 460–469.

Oliver, R.L. (1981) Measurement and evaluation of satisfaction processes in retail settings, *Journal of Retailing*, 57(3), 25–48.

Oliver, R.L. (1987) An investigation of the interrelationship between consumer (dis) satisfaction and complaint reports. In Wallendorf, M. and Anderson, P. (eds), *Advances in Consumer Research*, 14, 218–222.

Oliver, R.L. (1989) Processing of the satisfaction response in consumption: a suggested framework and research propositions, *Journal of Consumer Satisfaction, Dissatisfaction and Complaining Behavior*, 2, 1–16.

Oliver, R.L. (1999) Whence customer loyalty?, *Journal of Marketing*, 63(Special Issue), 33–44.

Oliver, R.L. and Swan, J.E. (1989) Consumer perceptions of interpersonal equity and satisfaction in transactions: a field survey approach, *Journal of Marketing*, 53(2), 21–35.

Olshavsky, R.W. and Granbois, D.H. (1979) Consumer decision making – fact or fiction?, *Journal of Consumer Research*, 6(2), 93–100.

Osgood, J.F., Suci, G.J. and Tannenbaum, P.H. (1957) *The Measurement of Meaning*, Urbana: University of Illinois Press.

Parasuraman, A., Zeithaml, V.A. and Berry, L.L. (1985) A conceptual model of service quality and its implications for future research, *Journal of Marketing*, 49(4), 41–50.

Parasuraman, A., Zeithaml, V.A. and Berry, L.L. (1988) SERVQUAL: a multiple-item scale for measuring consumer perceptions of service quality, *Journal of Retailing*, 64(1), 12–40.

Parasuraman, A., Berry, L.L. and Zeithaml, V.A. (1991) Refinement and reassessment of the SERVQUAL scale, *Journal of Retailing*, 67(4), 420–450.

Parasuraman, A., Zeithaml, V.A. and Berry, L.L. (1994) Reassessment of expectations as a comparison standard in measuring service quality, *Journal of Marketing*, 58(1), 111–124.

Partch, K. (1996) Still inching toward efficient promotion, *Supermarket Business*, 51, 16.

Pauwels, K., Hanssens, D.M. and Siddarth, S. (2002) The long-term effects of price promotions on category incidence, brand choice, and purchase quantity, *Journal of Marketing Research*, 39(4), 421–439.

Pavlov, I.P. (1927) *Conditioned Reflexes*, translated by G.V. Anrep, London: Oxford University Press.

Peterson, R.A. and Wilson, W.R. (1992) Measuring customer satisfaction: fact or artifact, *Journal of the Academy of Marketing Science*, 20(1), 61–71.

Petty, R.E. and Cacioppo, J.T. (1985) The elaboration likelihood model of persuasion. In L. Berkowitz (ed.), *Advances in Experimental Social Psychology*, 19, New York: Academic Press.

Pham, M., Goukens, C., Lehmann, D. and Stuart, J. (2010) Shaping customer satisfaction through self-awareness cues, *Journal of Marketing Research*, 47(5), 920–932.

Phillips, L.W. and Sternthal, B. (1977) Age differences in information processing: a perspective on the aged consumer, *Journal of Marketing Research*, 14(November), 744–757.

Pickering, J.F. (1975) Verbal explanations of consumer durable purchase decisions, *Journal of the Market Research Society*, 17(2), 107–113.

Pickering, J.F. and Isherwood, B.C. (1974) Purchase probabilities and consumer durable buying behaviour, *Journal of the Market Research Society*, 16(3), 203–226.

Pieters, R. and Warlop, L. (1999) Visual attention during brand choice: the impact of time pressure and task motivation, *International Journal of Research in Marketing*, 16(1), 1–16.

Plassmann, H., O'Doherty, J., Shiv, B. and Rangel, A. (2008) Marketing actions can modulate neural representations of experienced pleasantness, *Proceedings of the National Academy of Sciences of the United States of America* (published online).

Pritchard, M.P., Havitz, M.E. and Howard, D.R. (1999) Analyzing the commitment–loyalty link in service contexts, *Journal of the Academy of Marketing Science*, 27(3), 333–348.

Pruyn, A.Th.H. and Smidts, A. (1993) Customers' evaluations of queues: three exploratory studies. In W.F. Van Raaij and G.J. Bamossy (eds), *European Advances in Consumer Research*, 1, 371–382.

Putsis, W.M. and Srinivasan, V. (2000) Estimation techniques for macro diffusion models. In V. Mahajan, E. Muller and Y. Wind (eds), *New Product Diffusion Models*, Norwell, MA: Kluwer Academic Publishers, 263–291.

Qin, L. (2012) *An empirical investigation of online word-of-mouth dynamic in different online communities*, http://www.swdsi.org/swdsi2012/proceedings_2012/papers/Papers/PA104.pdf.

Raghubir, P. and Srivastava, J. (2002) Effect of face value on product valuation in foreign currencies, *Journal of Consumer Research*, 29(3), 335–347.

Raj, S.P. (1982) The effects of advertising on high and low loyalty segments, *Journal of Advertising Research*, 9(1), 77–89.

Raju, J.S. (1992) The effect of price promotions on variability in product category sales, *Marketing Science*, 11(3), 207–220.

Randall, D.M. and Wolff, J.A. (1994) The time interval in the intention–behaviour relationship, *British Journal of Social Psychology*, 33(4), 405–418.

Rao, A.R. and Monroe, K.R. (1989) The effect of price, brand name, and store name on buyers' perceptions of product quality: an integrative review, *Journal of Marketing Research*, 26(3), 351–358.

Rao, T.R. (1969) Consumer's purchase decision process: stochastic models, *Journal of Marketing Research*, 6(3), 321–329.

Reichheld, F.F. (1993) Loyalty-based management, *Harvard Business Review*, 71(2), 64–73.

Reichheld, F.F. (1996a) Learning from customer defections, *Harvard Business Review*, 74(2), 56–69.

Reichheld, F.F. (with Teal, T.) (1996b) *The Loyalty Effect*, Boston: Harvard Business School Publications.

Reichheld, F.F. (2003) The one number you need to grow, *Harvard Business Review*, 81(12), 46–54.

Reichheld, F.F. and Kenny, D.W. (1990) The hidden advantages of customer retention, *Journal of Retail Banking*, 12(4), 19–23.

Reichheld, F. and Markey, R. (2011) *The Ultimate Question 2.0*, Boston: Harvard Business Review Press.

Reichheld, F.F. and Sasser, W.E. (1990) Zero defections: quality comes to services, *Harvard Business Review*, 68(5), Sept.–Oct., 105–111.

Reilly, W.J. (1929) *Methods for the Study of Retail Relationships*, Austin, TX: Bureau of Business Research Studies in Marketing, No. 4.

Reinartz, W. and Kumar, V. (2000) On the profitability of long-life customers in a non-contractual setting: an empirical investigation and implications for marketing, *Journal of Marketing*, 64(4), 17–36.

Reinartz, W. and Kumar, V. (2002) The mismanagement of customer loyalty, *Harvard Business Review*, 80(7), July, 86–94.

Reinartz, W., Thomas, J.S. and Kumar, V. (2005) Balancing acquisition and retention resources to maximize customer profitability, *Journal of Marketing*, 69(1), 63–79.

Richins, M.L. (1981) An investigation of the consumer's attitudes towards complaining. In Mitchell, A. (ed.), *Advances in Consumer Research*, 9, 502–506.

Richins, M.L. (1983) Negative word of mouth by dissatisfied consumers, *Journal of Marketing*, 47(1), 68–78.

Richins, M.L. (1985) The role of product importance in complaint initiation, *Proceedings of the Eighth and Ninth Conferences on Consumer Satisfaction and Complaining Behavior*, Baton Rouge, Louisiana and Phoenix, Arizona, 50–53.

Richins, M.L. (1987) A multivariate analysis of responses to dissatisfaction, *Journal of the Academy of Marketing Science*, 15(3), 24–31.

Riebe, E., Sharp, B. and Stern, P. (2002) An empirical investigation of customer defection and acquisition rates for declining and growing pharmaceutical brands. *Australian and*

New Zealand Marketing Academy (ANZMAC) 2002 Conference Proceedings, available at: http://members.byronsharp.com/7716.pdf.

Riebe, E., Wright, M., Stern, P. and Sharp, B. Growing the base of loyal customers, acquisition versus retention, *Journal of Business Research*, forthcoming.

Riskey, D.R. (1997) How TV advertising works: an industry response, *Journal of Market Research*, 34(2), 292–293.

Rivis, A. and Sheeran, P. (2003) Descriptor norms as an additional predictor in the theory of planned behaviour: a meta-analysis, *Current Psychology: Developmental, Learning, Personality, Social*, 22(3), 218–233.

Roberts, A. (1996) What do we know about advertising's short-term effects?, *Admap*, February, 42–45.

Roberts, A. (1999) Recency, frequency and the sales effects of TV advertising, *Admap*, February, 40–44.

Roberts, A. (2000) tvSpan: the medium-term effects of TV advertising, *Admap*, November, 12–14.

Roedder-John, D. & Cole, C.A. (1986) Age differences in information processing: Understanding deficits in young and elderly consumers. Journal of Consumer Research, 13(3), 297–315.

Rogers, E.M. (1962) *Diffusion of Innovations*, 1st edition, New York: The Free Press.

Rogers, E.M. (2003) *Diffusion of Innovations*, 5th edition, New York: The Free Press.

Rokeach. M.J. (1973) *The Nature of Human Values*, New York: The Free Press.

Romaniuk, J. (2003) Brand attributes – 'distribution outlets' in the mind, *Journal of Marketing Communications*, 9(2), 73–92.

Romaniuk, J. (2007) Word of mouth and the viewing of television programs, *Journal of Advertising Research*, 47(4), 462–471.

Romaniuk, J. and Dawes, J. (2005) Loyalty to price tiers in purchases of bottled wine, *Journal of Product and Brand Management*, 14(1), 57–64.

Romaniuk, J. and Gaillard, E. (2007) The relationship between unique brand associations, brand usage and brand performance: analysis across eight categories, *Journal of Marketing Management*, 23(3–4), 267–284.

Romaniuk, J. and Sharp, B. (2003) Brand salience and customer defection in subscription markets, *Journal of Marketing Management*, 19(1–2), 25–44.

Romaniuk, J., Nguyen, C. and East, R. (2011) The accuracy of self-reported probabilities of giving recommendations, *International Journal of Market Research*, 53(4), 507–531.

Rosenberg, L.J. and Czepiel, J.A. (1984) A marketing approach to customer retention, *Journal of Consumer Marketing*, 1(2), 45–51.

Rosenberg, M. (2011) http://geography.about.com/od/obtainpopulationdata/a/india population.htm

Rosenberg, M.J. (1956) Cognitive structure and attitudinal affect, *Journal of Abnormal and Social Psychology*, 53, 367–372.

Rosnow, R.L. (2001) Rumor and gossip in interpersonal interaction and beyond: a social exchange perspective. In R.M. Kowalski (ed.), *Behaving Badly: Aversive Behaviors in Interpersonal Relationships*, Washington, DC: American Psychological Association, 203–232.

Rossiter, J. and Bellman, S. (2005) *Marketing Communications*, Sydney: Pearson Education.

Rubinson, J. (2009) Empirical evidence of TV advertising effectiveness, *Journal of Advertising Research*, 49(2), 220–226.

Russo, J.E. and Leclerc, F. (1994) An eye-fixation analysis of choice processes for consumer non-durables, *Journal of Consumer Research*, 21(2), 274–290.

Ryan, B. and Gross, N.C. (1943) The diffusion of hybrid seed corn in two Iowa communities, *Rural Sociology*, 8, 15–24, as cited in E.M. Rogers (2003) *Diffusion of Innovations*, 5th edition, New York: The Free Press.

Saegert, S.C. and Jellison, J.M. (1970) Effects of initial level of response competition and frequency of exposure on liking and exploratory behavior, *Journal of Personality and Social Psychology*, 16(3), 553–558.

Sandell, R. (1981) *The dynamic relationship between attitudes and choice behaviour in the light of cross-lagged panel correlations*, Dept. of Psychology, University of Stockholm, Report no. 581.

Sasser, W.E. (1976) Match supply and demand in the service industry, *Harvard Business Review*, 54(6), 133–138.

Sattler, H., Völckner, F., Riediger, C. and Ringle, C.M. (2010) The impact of brand extension success drivers on brand extension price premiums, *International Journal of Research in Marketing*, 27(4), 319–328.

Scherhorn, G., Reisch, L.A. and Raab, G. (1990) Addictive buying in West Germany: an empirical study, *Journal of Consumer Policy*, 13, 355–387.

Schindler, R.M. (2006) The 99 price ending as a signal of a low-price appeal, *Journal of Retailing*, 82(1), 71–77.

Schindler, R.M. and Kirby, P.N. (1997) Patterns of rightmost digits used in advertised prices: implications for nine-ending effects, *Journal of Consumer Research*, 24(2), 192–201.

Schmitt, P., Skiera, B. and Van den Bulte, C. (2011) Referral programs and customer value, *Journal of Marketing*, 75(1), 46–59.

Schmittlein, D.C., Bemmaor, A.C. and Morrison, D.G. (1985) Why does the NBD model work? Robustness in representing product purchases, brand purchases and imperfectly recorded purchases, *Marketing Science*, 4(3), 255–266.

Schmittlein, D.C., Cooper, L.G. and Morrison, D.G. (1993) Truth in concentration in the land of (80/20) laws, *Marketing Science*, 12(2), 167–183.

Schuman, H. and Johnson, M.P. (1976) Attitudes and behavior, *Annual Review of Sociology*, 2, 161–207.

Schwartz, S.H. (1992) Universals in value content and structure, *Advances in Experimental Social Psychology*, 25.

Schwartz, S.H. and Bilsky, W. (1987) Toward a universal psychological structure of human values, *Journal of Personality and Social Psychology*, 53(3), 550–562.

Schwartz, S.H. and Bilsky, W. (1990) Toward a theory of the universal content and structure of values: extensions and cross-cultural replications, *Journal of Personality and Social Psychology*, 58(5), 878–891.

Schwartz, S.H. and Sagiv, L. (1995) Identifying culture-specifics in the content and structure of values, *Journal of Cross-Cultural Psychology*, 26(1), 92–116.

Sharma, A. and Stafford, T.F. (2000) The effect of retail atmospherics on customers' perceptions of salespeople and customer persuasion: an empirical investigation, *Journal of Business Research*, 49(2), 183–191.

Sharp, B. (2010) *How Brands Grow*, Oxford: Oxford University Press.

Sharp, B. and Sharp, A. (1997) Loyalty programmes and their impact on repeat purchase loyalty patterns, *International Journal of Research in Marketing*, 14(5), 473–486.

Sharp, B., Wright, M.J. and Goodhardt, G.J. (2002) Purchase loyalty is polarised into either repertoire or subscription patterns, *Australasian Marketing Journal*, 10(3), 7–20.

Sharp, B., Beal, V. and Collins, M. (2009) Television: back to the future, *Journal of Advertising Research*, 49(2), 211–219.

Sheppard, B.H., Hartwick, J. and Warshaw, P.R. (1988) The theory of reasoned action: a meta-analysis of past research with recommendations for modifications and future research, *Journal of Consumer Research*, 15(3), 325–343.

Shiv, B., Carmon, Z. and Ariely, D. (2005) Placebo effects of marketing actions: consumers may get what they pay for, *Journal of Marketing Research*, 42(4), 383–393.

Shogren, J.F., Shin, S.Y., Hayes, D.J. and Kliebenstein, J.B. (1994) Resolving differences in willingness to pay and willingness to accept, *American Economic Review*, 84(1), 255–270.

Silverman, G. (2001) *The Secrets of Word-of-Mouth Marketing*, New York: AMACOM.

Simcock, P., Sudbury, L. Wright, G. (2006) Age, perceived risk and satisfaction in consumer decision making: A review and extension. *Journal of Marketing Management*, 22(3), 355–377.

Simmel, G. (1908) *The Sociology of Georg Simmel*, translated by Kurt H. Wolf, New York: The Free Press, 1964, as cited in E.M. Rogers (2003) *Diffusion of Innovations*, 5th edition, New York: The Free Press.

Simon, C.J. and Sullivan, M.W. (1993) The measurement and determinants of brand equity: a financial approach, *Marketing Science*, 12(1), 28–52.

Simon, H.A. (1957) *Administrative Behavior*, New York: Macmillan.

Simon, J.L. (1979) What do Zielske's real data show about pulsing?, *Journal of Marketing Research*, 16(3), 415–420.

Simon, J.L. and Arndt, J. (1980) The shape of the advertising response function, *Journal of Advertising Research*, 20(4), 11–28.

Singh, J. (1990) Voice, exit, and negative word-of-mouth behaviors: an investigation across three categories, *Journal of the Academy of Marketing Science*, 18, 1–15.

Singh, J. and Howell, R. (1985) Consumer complaining behaviour: a review and prospectus. In H.K. Hunt and R.L. Day (eds), *Consumer Satisfaction, Dissatisfaction and Complaining Behavior*, Bloomington: Indiana University Press, 41–9.

Singh, J., Ehrenberg, A. and Goodhardt, G. (2004) Loyalty to product variants – a pilot, *Journal of Customer Behaviour*, 3(2), 123–132.

Singh, J., Ehrenberg, A. and Goodhardt, G. (2008) Measuring loyalty to product variants, *International Journal of Market Research*, 50(4), 513–523.

Singh, J., Dall'Olmo Riley, F., Hand, C. and Maeda, M. (2012) Measuring brand choice in older customers in Japan, *International Journal of Market Research*, 54(3).

Skinner, B.F. (1938) *The Behaviour of Organisms*, New York: Appleton Century Crofts.

Skinner, B.F. (1953) *Scientific and Human Behavior*, New York: Macmillan.

Skowronski, J.J. and Carlston, D.E. (1989) Negativity and extremity biases in impression formation: a review of explanations, *Psychological Bulletin*, 105(1), 131–142.

Smith, A.M. (1995) Measuring service quality: is SERVQUAL now redundant?, *Journal of Marketing Management*, 11, 257–276.

Smith, D.C. and Park, C.W. (1992) The effects of brand extensions on market share and advertising efficiency, *Journal of Marketing Research*, 29(3), 296–313.

Smith, E.R. and Queller, S. (2001) Mental representations. In A. Tesser and N. Schwarz (eds), *Intra-individual Processes*, Oxford: Blackwell Publishing.

Smith, R.B. and Sherman, E. (1992) Effects of store image and mood on consumer behavior: a theoretical and empirical analysis. In L. McAlister and M.L. Rothschild (eds), *Advances in Consumer Research*, 20, 631.

Smith, W. and Higgins, M. (2000) Reconsidering the relationship analogy, *Journal of Marketing Management*, 16(1–3), 81–94.

Snow, C. (2011) *Advertising Works 20: Proving the Payback on Marketing Investment, Case Studies from the IPA Effectiveness Awards 2011*, London: Institute of Advertising Practitioners.

Solnick, S.J. and Hemenway, D. (1992) Complaints and disenrollment at a health maintenance organization, *Journal of Consumer Affairs*, 26(1), 90–103.

Spangenberg, E.R., Grohmann, B. and Sprott, D.E. (2005) It's beginning to smell (and sound) a lot like Christmas: the interactive effects of ambient scent and music in a retail setting, *Journal of Business Research*, 58(11), 1583–1589.

Steenkamp, J.M. and Geyskens, I. (2006) How country characteristics affect the perceived value of web sites, *Journal of Marketing*, 70(3), 136–150.

Steenkamp, J.M., Ter Hofstede, F. and Wedel, M. (1999) A cross-national investigation into the individual and national cultural antecedents of consumer innovativeness, *Journal of Marketing*, 63(2), 55–69.

Steiner, R.L. (1973) Does advertising lower consumer prices?, *Journal of Marketing*, 37(4), 19–27.

Steiner, R.L. (1993) The inverse association between the margins of manufacturers and retailers, *Review of Industrial Organisation*, 8, 717–740.

Stern, P. and Hammond, K. (2004) The relationship between customer loyalty and purchase incidence, *Marketing Letters*, 15(1), 5–19.

Stern, P. and Wright, M. (2007) *Predicting the Innovator*, European Marketing Academy Conference (EMAC).

Stø, E. and Glefjell, S. (1990) The complaining process in Norway: five steps to justice, *Journal of Consumer Satisfaction, Dissatisfaction and Complaining Behavior*, 3, 92–99.

Stiving, M. and Winer, R.S. (1997) An empirical analysis of price endings with scanner data, *Journal of Consumer Research*, 24(1), 57–67.

Sultan, F., Farley, J.U. and Lehmann, D.R. (1990) A meta-analysis of applications of diffusion models, *Journal of Marketing Research*, 27(1), 70–77.

Sundaram, D.S., Mitra, K. and Webster, C. (1998) Word-of-mouth communications: a motivational analysis. In Alba, J.W. and Hutchinson, J.W., *Advances in Consumer Research*, Vol. 25, 527–531.

Sunde, L. and Brodie, R.J. (1993) Consumer evaluation of brand extensions: further empirical results, *International Journal of Research in Marketing*, 10(1), 47–53.

Sutton, S., Marsh, A. and Matheson, J. (1990) Microanalysis of smokers' beliefs about the consequences of quitting: results from a large population sample, *Journal of Applied Social Psychology*, 20(22), 1847–1862.

Swan, J.E. and Trawick, I.F. (1980) Satisfaction related to predicted versus desired expectations. In H.K. Hunt and R.L. Day (eds), *Refining Concepts and Measures of Consumer Satisfaction and Complaining Behavior*, Bloomington: School of Business, Indiana University, 7–12.

Swan, J.E. and Trawick, I.F. (1981) Disconfirmation of expectations and satisfaction with a retail service, *Journal of Retailing*, 57(3), 49–67.

Swinyard, W.R. (1993) The effects of mood, involvement and quality of store experience on shopping intention, *Journal of Consumer Research*, 20(2), 271–280.

Tarde, G. (1903) *The Laws of Imitation*, translated by Elsie Clews Parson, New York: Holt (reprinted University of Chicago Press, 1969), first published in 1890 as *Les Lois de l'Imitation* and available on http://archive.org/details/lesloisdelimita00tarduoft.

TARP (Technical Assistance Research Programs) (1979) *Consumer Complaint Handling in America: A Summary of Findings and Recommendation*, Washington, DC: US Office of Consumer Affairs.

Tate, R.S. (1961) The supermarket battle for store loyalty, *Journal of Marketing*, 25(6), 8–13.

Tauber, E.M. (1981) Brand franchise extension: new product benefits from existing brand names, *Business Horizons*, 24, 36–41.

Tauber, E.M. (1988) Brand leverage: strategy for growth in a cost-conscious world, *Journal of Advertising Research*, 28(4), 26–30.

Taylor, J.W. (1977) A striking characteristic of innovators, *Journal of Marketing Research*, 14(1), 104–107.

Taylor, S. (1994) Waiting for service: the relationship between delays and evaluations of service, *Journal of Marketing*, 58(2), 56–69.

Taylor, S. (1995) The effects of filled waiting time and service provider control over the delay on evaluations of service, *Journal of the Academy of Marketing Science*, 23(1), 38–48.

Taylor, S.E. (1982) The availability bias in social perception and interaction. In D. Kahneman, P. Slovic and A. Tversky (eds), *Judgment under Uncertainty: Heuristics and Biases*, Cambridge: Cambridge University Press, 190–200.

Tellis, G.J. (1988a) Advertising exposure, loyalty and brand purchase: a two-stage model of choice, *Journal of Marketing Research*, 25(2), 134–144.

Tellis, G.J. (1988b) The price elasticity of selective demand: a meta-analysis of economic models of sales, *Journal of Marketing Research*, 25(4), 331–341.

Tellis, G.J. and Wernerfelt, B. (1987) Competitive price and quality under asymmetric information, *Marketing Science*, 6(3), 240–254.

Ter Hofstede, F., Steenkamp, J.-B. and Wedel, M. (1999) International market segmentation based on consumer-product relations, *Journal of Marketing Research*, 36(2), 1–17.

Thaler, R. (1980) Toward a positive theory of consumer choice, *Journal of Economic Behavior*, 1, 39–60. Reprinted in D. Kahneman and A. Tversky (2000), *Choices, Values, and Frames*, New York: Russell Sage Foundation, Cambridge University Press, 269–287.

Thaler, R. (1985) Mental accounting and consumer choice, *Marketing Science*, 4(3), 199–214.

Thaler, R. (1999) Mental accounting matters, *Journal of Behavioral Decision Making*, 12, 183–206. Reprinted in D. Kahneman and A. Tversky (2000), *Choices, Values, and Frames*, New York: Russell Sage Foundation, Cambridge University Press, 241–268.

Thaler, R. and Sunstein, C. (2008) *Nudge*, Yale: Yale University Press.

Theil, H. and Kosobud, R.F. (1968) How informative are consumer buying intentions surveys?, *Review of Economics and Statistics*, 50, 50–59.

Thøgersen, J. and Zhou, Y. (2012) Chinese consumers' adoption of a 'green' innovation – the case of organic food, *Journal of Marketing Management*, 8(3–4), 313–333.

Thomas, M. and Morwitz, V. (2005) Penny wise and pound foolish: the left-digit effect in price cognition, *Journal of Consumer Research*, 32(1), 54–64.

Thorndike, E.L. (1911) *Animal Intelligence*, New York: Macmillan.

Tobin, J. (1969) A general equilibrium approach to monetary theory, *Journal of Money, Credit, and Banking*, 1(1), 15–29.

Tom, G. and Lucey, S. (1995) Waiting time delays and customer satisfaction in supermarkets, *Journal of Services Marketing*, 9(5), 20–29.

Totten, J.C. and Block, M.P. (1987) *Analyzing Sales Promotion: Text and Cases*, Chicago: Commerce Communications Inc.

Treasure, J. (1975) How advertising works. In M. Barnes (ed.), *The Three Faces of Advertising*, London: The Advertising Association, 48, 52.

Triandis, H.C. (1977) *Interpersonal Behavior*, Monterey, CA: Brooks Cole.

Triandis, H.C. (1989) Self and social behavior in differing cultural contexts, *Psychological Review*, 96, 506–520.

Triandis, H.C. (2004) The many dimensions of culture, *Academy of Management Executive*, 18(1), 88–93.

Trusov, M., Bucklin R.E. and Pauwels, K. (2009) Effects of word-of-mouth versus traditional marketing: findings from an Internet social networking site, *Journal of Marketing*, 73(5), 90–102.

Tse, D.K. and Wilton, P.C. (1988) Models of consumer satisfaction formation: an extension, *Journal of Marketing Research*, 25(2), 204–212.

Tversky, A. and Kahneman, D. (1981) Causal schemas in judgements under uncertainty. In Tversky, A. and Kahneman, D. (1981) The framing of decisions and the psychology of choice, *Science*, 211, 453–458.

Tversky, A. and Kahneman, D. (1992) Advances in prospect theory: cumulative representation of uncertainty, *Journal of Risk and Uncertainty*, 5, 297–323. Reprinted in D. Kahneman and A. Tversky (2000), *Choices, Values, and Frames*, New York: Russell Sage Foundation, Cambridge University Press, 44–65.

Uncles, M.D. (2010) Retail change in China: retrospect and prospects, *International Review of Retail, Distribution and Consumer Research*, 20(1), 69–84.

Uncles, M.D. and Ehrenberg, A.S.C. (1990) The buying of packaged goods at US retail chains, *Journal of Retailing*, 66(3), 278–296.

Uncles, M.D. and Hammond, K.A. (1995) Grocery store patronage, *International Journal of Retail, Distribution and Consumer Research*, 5(3), 287–302.

Uncles, M.D. and Kwok, S. (2008) Generalizing patterns of store-type patronage, *International Review of Retail, Distribution and Consumer Research*, 18(5), 473–493.

Uncles, M.D. and Kwok, S. (2009) Patterns of store patronage in urban China, *Journal of Business Research*, 62(1), 68–81.

Uncles, M.D. and Lee, D. (2006) Brand purchasing by older consumers: an investigation using the Juster scale and the Dirichlet model, *Marketing Letters*, 17(1), 17–29.

Uncles, M.D., Dowling, G.R. and Hammond, K. (2003) Customer loyalty and customer loyalty programs, *Journal of Consumer Marketing*, 20(4), 294–316.

Uncles, M., East, R. and Lomax, W. (2010a) Market share is correlated with word-of-mouth volume, *Australasian Marketing Journal*, 18(3), 145–150.

Uncles, M.D., Wang, C., and Kwok, S. (2010b) A temporal analysis of behavioural brand loyalty among urban Chinese consumers, *Journal of Marketing Management*, 26(9–10), 921–942.

Uncles, M.D. et al. (2011) *Perspectives on Brand Management*, Tilde University Press.

United Nations (2002) *World Population Ageing: 1950–2050*, New York: United Nations, Department of Economic and Social Affairs, Population Division.

Usunier, J.C. and Lee J. (2011) *Marketing Across Cultures*, 5th edition, Harlow: Pearson.

Van der Plight, J. and van Schie, E.C.M. (1990) Frames of reference, judgement and preference. In W. Stroebe and M. Hewstone (eds), *European Review of Social Psychology*, 1, Chichester: Wiley and Sons, 61–80.

van Heerde, H.J., Leeflang, P.S.H. and Wittink, D.R. (2004) Decomposing the sales promotion bump with store data, *Marketing Science*, 23(3), 317–334.

Vanhuele, M. (1994) Mere exposure and the cognitive-affective debate revisited. In C.T. Allen and D.R. John (eds), *Advances in Consumer Research*, 21, 264–269.

Vanhuele, M. and Drèze, X. (2002) Measuring the price knowledge shoppers bring to the store, *Journal of Marketing*, 66(4), 72–85.

Vanhuele, M., Laurent, G. and Drèze, X. (2006) Consumers' immediate memory for prices, *Journal of Consumer Research*, 33(2), 163–172.

Vargo, S.L. and Lusch, R.F. (2004) Evolving to a new dominant logic for marketing, *Journal of Marketing*, 68(1), 1–17.

Venkatesh, V. and Davis, F.D. (2000) A theoretical extension of the technology acceptance model: four longitudinal field studies, *Management Science*, 46(2), 186–204.

Venkatraman, M.P. and Price, L.L. (1990) Differentiating between cognitive and sensory innovativeness: concepts, measurement, and implications, *Journal of Business Research*, 20(4), 293–315.

Verhoef, P.C. (2003) Understanding the effect of customer relationship management efforts on customer retention and customer share development, *Journal of Marketing*, 67(October), 30–45.

Verhoef, P.C., Franses, P.H. and Hoekstra, J.C. (2002) The effect of relational constructs on customer referrals and number of services purchased from a multiservice provider: does age of relationship matter?, *Journal of the Academy of Marketing Science*, 30(3), 202–216.

Villanueva, J., Yoo, S. and Hanssens, D.M. (2008) The impact of marketing-induced versus word-of-mouth customer acquisition on customer equity growth, *Journal of Marketing Research*, 45(1), 48–59.

Viscusi, W.K. (1984) The lulling effect: the impact of child resistant packaging on aspirin and analgesic ingestions, *American Economic Review*, 74(2), 324–327.

Völckner, F. and Sattler, H. (2006) Drivers of brand extension success, *Journal of Marketing*, 70(2), 18–34.

Wakefield, K.L. and Inman, J.J. (1993) Who are the price vigilantes? An investigation of differentiating characteristics influencing price information processing, *Journal of Retailing*, 69(2), 216–234.

Wallach, M.A. and Kogan, N. (1961) Aspects of judgment and decision making: interrelationships and changes with age, *Behavioral Science*, 6(1), 23–36.

Wangenheim, F. v. and Bayón, T. (2004) Satisfaction, loyalty and word of mouth within the customer base of a utility provider: differences between stayers, switchers and referral switchers, *Journal of Consumer Behaviour*, 3(1), 211–220.

Wangenheim, F. v. (2005) Postswitching negative word of mouth, *Journal of Service Research*, 8(1), 67–78.

Wangenheim, F. and Bayón, T. (2007) Behavioral consequences of overbooking service capacity, *Journal of Marketing*, 71(4), 36–47.

Warland, R.H., Herrmann, R.O. and Willits, J. (1975) Dissatisfied customers: who gets upset and what they do about it, *Journal of Consumer Affairs*, 9(Winter), 152–162.

Watts, D.J. and Dodds, P.S. (2007) Influentials, networks, and public opinion formation, *Journal of Consumer Research*, 34(December), 441–458.

Weber, M. and Camerer, C.F. (1998) The disposition effect in securities trading: an experimental analysis, *Journal of Economic Behavior and Organization*, 33, 167–184.

Wedel, M. and Leeflang, P.S.H. (1998) A model for the effects of psychological pricing in Gabor–Granger price studies, *Journal of Economic Psychology*, 19(2), 237–261.

Wee, C.H. and Pearce, M.R. (1985) Patronage behavior toward shopping areas: a proposed model based on Huff's model of retail gravitation. In E.C. Hirschman and M.B. Holbrook (eds), *Advances in Consumer Research*, 12, 592–597.

Weigel, R.H. and Newman, L.S. (1976) Increasing attitude–behavior correspondence by broadening the scope of the behavioral measure, *Journal of Personality and Social Psychology*, 33, 793–802.

Weiner, B. (1980) *Human Motivation*, New York: Holt, Rinehart and Winston.

Weiner, B. (1990) Searching for the roots of applied attribution theory. In S. Graham and V.S. Folkes (eds), *Attribution Theory: Application to Achievement, Mental Health and Interpersonal Conflict*, Hillsdale, NJ: Lawrence Erlbaum Associates, 1–16.

Wellan, D.M. and Ehrenberg, A.S.C. (1988) A successful new brand: shield, *Journal of the Market Research Society*, 30(1), 35–44.

Wellan, D.M. and Ehrenberg, A.S.C. (1990) A case of seasonal segmentation, *Marketing Research*, 1, 11–13.

Westbrook, R.A. (1980) Intrapersonal affective influences upon consumer satisfaction, *Journal of Consumer Research*, 7(1), 49–54.

Wetzer, I., Zeelenberg, M. and Pieters, R. (2007) 'Never eat in that restaurant, I did': exploring why people engage in negative word-of-mouth communication, *Psychology and Marketing*, 24(8), 661–680.

White, K.M., Smith, J.K., Terry, D.J., Greenslade, J.H. and McKimmie, B.M. (2009) Social influence in the theory of planned behaviour: the role of descriptive, injunctive, and ingroup norms, *British Journal of Social Psychology*, 48(1), 135–158.

Whyte, W.H. (1954) The web of word of mouth, *Fortune*, 50(November), 140.

Wicker, A.W. (1969) Attitude vs actions: the relationship of verbal and overt behavioral responses to attitude objects, *Journal of Social Issues*, 25, 41–78.

Wicker, A.W. (1984) *An Introduction to Ecological Psychology*, Monterey, CA: Brooks/Cole.

Wilkie, W.L. and Dickson, P.R. (1985) *Shopping for Appliances: Consumers' Strategies and Patterns of Information Search*, Cambridge, MA: Marketing Science Institute Research Report No. 85–108.

Williams, L.G. (1966) The effect of target specification on objects fixed during visual search, *Perception and Psychophysics*, 1, 315–318.

Winchester, M. and Romaniuk, J. (2008) Negative brand beliefs and brand usage, *International Journal of Market Research*, 50(3), 1–20.

Winchester, M., Romaniuk, J. and Bogomolova, S. (2008) Positive and negative brand beliefs and brand defection/uptake, *European Journal of Marketing*, 42(5/6), 553–570.

Winer, R.S. (1986) A reference price model of brand choice for frequently purchased products, *Journal of Consumer Research*, 13(2), 250–256.

Winer, R.S. (1988) Behavioral perspectives on pricing: buyers' subjective perceptions of price revisited. In T.M. Divinney (ed.), *Issues in Pricing*, Lexington, MA: Lexington Books, 35–57.

Wittink, D.R., Vriens, M. and Burhenne, W. (1994) Commercial use of conjoint analysis in Europe: results and critical reflections, *International Journal of Research in Marketing*, 11(1), 41–52.

Wright, M.J. and Charlett, D. (1995) New product diffusion models in marketing: an assessment of two approaches, *Marketing Bulletin*, 6, 32–41.

Wright, M.J. and MacRae, M. (2007) Bias and variability in purchase intention scales, *Journal of the Academy of Marketing Science*, 35(4), 617–624.

Wright, M. and Riebe, E. (2010) Double jeopardy in brand defection, *European Journal of Marketing*, 44(6), 860–873.

Wright, M. and Sharp, A. (2001) The effects of a new brand entrant on a market, *Journal of Empirical Generalisations in Marketing Science*, 6, 15–29.

Wright, M.J. and Stern, P. (2006) *Extending consumer trial models to national panel data*, Working Paper, Victoria University of Wellington, New Zealand.

Wright, M.J., Upritchard, C. and Lewis, A. (1997) A validation of the Bass new product diffusion model in New Zealand, *Marketing Bulletin*, 8, 15–29.

Wright, M., Sharp, A. and Sharp, B. (1998) Are Australasian brands different?, *Journal of Product and Brand Management*, 7 (6), 465–480.

Xia, L., Monroe, K.B. and Cox, J.L. (2004) The price is unfair! A conceptual framework of price fairness perceptions, *Journal of Marketing*, 68(4), 1–15.

Yalch, R. and Spangenberg, E. (2000) Using store music for retail zoning: a field experiment. In L. McAlister and M.L. Rothschild (eds), *Advances in Consumer Research*, 20, 632–636.

Yi, Y. (1990) A critical review of consumer satisfaction. In V.A. Zeithaml (ed.), *Review of Marketing*, Chicago: American Marketing Association, 68–113.

Zajonc, R.B. (1968) Attitudinal effects of mere exposure, *Journal of Personality and Social Psychology Monograph Supplement*, 9(2, Part 2), 1–27.

Zajonc, R.B. (1980) Feeling and thinking: preferences need no inferences, *American Psychologist*, 35, 151–175.

Zajonc, R.B. and Rajecki, D.W. (1969) Exposure and affect: a field experiment, *Psychonomic Science*, 17, 216–217.

Zeithaml, V.A. (1988) Consumer perceptions of price, quality, and value: a means–end model and synthesis of evidence, *Journal of Marketing*, 52(3), 2–21.

Zeithaml, V.A. (2000) Service quality, profitability, and the economic worth of customers: what we know and what we need to learn, *Journal of the Academy of Marketing Science*, 28(1), 67–85.

Zettelmeyer, F., Morton, F.S. and Silva-Risso, J. (2006) How the Internet lowers prices: evidence from matched survey and auto transaction data, *Journal of Marketing Research*, 43(2), 168–181.

Zhang, J. (2006) An integrated choice model incorporating alternative mechanisms for consumers' reactions to in-store display and feature advertising, *Marketing Science*, 25(3), 278–290.

Zhang, J. and Wedel, M. (2009) The effectiveness of customized promotions in online and offline stores, *Journal of Marketing Research*, 46(2), 190–206.

Zhang, J., Beatty, S.E. and Walsh, G. (2008) Review and future directions of cross-cultural consumer services research, *Journal of Business Research*, 61(3), 211–224.

Zielske, H. (1959) The remembering and forgetting of advertising, *Journal of Marketing*, 23(3), 239–243.

Zufryden, F.S. (1996) Multibrand transition probabilities as a function of explanatory variables: estimation by a least squares approach, *Journal of Marketing Research*, 23(2), 177–183.

Author Index

Subject Index

FLAME RETARDANTS '90

Proceedings of the Flame Retardants '90 Conference held at Queen Elizabeth II Conference Centre, Westminster, London, UK, 17–18 January 1990.

Organised by
The British Plastics Federation
The Plastics and Rubber Institute

in collaboration with
The Association of Plastics Manufacturers in Europe
The Fire Retardant Chemicals Association (USA)

ORGANISING COMMITTEE

S. J. Grayson *(Chairman)*	Queen Mary College
P. Claus	Association of Plastics Manufacturers in Europe
I. Brown	Croxton & Garry
D. L. Buszard	Ciba-Geigy Industrial Chemicals
S. D. Christian	The Home Office
R. C. Kidder	Fire Retardant Chemicals Association (USA)
K. T. Paul	RAPRA Technology Ltd
M. Peacock	Plastics and Rubber Institute
P. J. Youle	Albright & Wilson Ltd
S. Wolf	British Plastics Federation
P. Lynchy	British Plastics Federation
A. Eagar	British Plastics Federation

FLAME RETARDANTS '90

Edited by

The British Plastics Federation

ELSEVIER APPLIED SCIENCE
LONDON and NEW YORK

ELSEVIER SCIENCE PUBLISHERS LTD
Crown House, Linton Road, Barking, Essex IG11 8JU, England

Sole Distributor in the USA and Canada
ELSEVIER SCIENCE PUBLISHING CO., INC.
655 Avenue of the Americas, New York, NY 10010, USA

WITH 96 TABLES AND 116 ILLUSTRATIONS

British Library Cataloguing in Publication Data

Flame Retardants '90 Conference: London, England
Flame Retardants '90.
1. Materials. Flame-retardant polymers
I. Title II. British Plastics Federation III. Plastics and Rubber Institute
620.1'9204217

ISBN 1-85166-461-0

Library of Congress CIP data applied for

Printed in Great Britain by Galliard (Printers) Ltd, Great Yarmouth

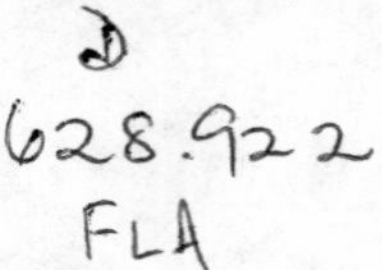

Preface

This proceedings is of the fourth conference in the series. It contains papers on flame retardants and their effect on the performance of polymers under extreme heat and fire conditions, as well as focuses on standards, legislation and testing. The book includes many of the latest developments in flame retardants and the views of flame retardant product manufacturers, specifiers, end-users, Government departments and those who deal directly with the consequences of fire.

The meeting is organised jointly by the British Plastics Federation and the Plastics and Rubber Institute in association with the Association of Plastics Manufacturers in Europe and the Fire Retardant Chemicals Association of the USA.

The British Plastics Federation is the principal trade association representing the interests of plastics raw material and machinery suppliers, together with plastics processors, in the United Kingdom. Its major role is to liaise with UK and EC Government agencies, trade bodies and customer industries and to actively promote both plastics materials and products and the industry at large. It handles commercial, technical and regulatory issues on behalf of the plastics industry and embraces a research and development function through its strong support for the Polymer Engineering Group. It also provides a computerised information service for industry through its Plastics and Rubber Advisory Service.

The Plastics and Rubber Institute was founded in 1921 and is a professional and qualifying body with an international membership of more than 10,500 individuals. It exists to serve the interests of its members and for the public good by advancing standards and methods of education in plastics and rubber and by providing opportunities for an exchange of knowledge between persons connected with these materials. The PRI is both a materials and an engineering society, and is active in organising conferences, meetings and symposia and in journal and book publishing. All members receive, completely free of charge, the PRI's leading journal *Plastics and Rubber International*, which is issued six times each year.

The Association of Plastics Manufacturers in Europe is the Brussels-based organisation of the plastics manufacturing industry in Western Europe. With some fifty member companies, APME represents more than 90% of the plastics production capability in the European member countries of the OECD. The main activities of the Association are concerned with health, safety and environmental protection and with international trade policy and statistics collection. The areas of particular interest are food contact and medical applications, fire safety, post-consumer solid waste management, and worker and consumer health protection aspects of chemicals used in plastics production. The overriding objective is to generate useful information to counteract undue discrimination of plastics, to safeguard free trade conditions, and to promote effective solutions to problem situations involving plastics.

The Fire Retardant Chemicals Association is the industry organisation of companies in the USA which market and use fire retardant chemicals, or related products and services. FRCA member companies, through application of appropriate chemical technology, contribute to achievement of an increasing array of consumer and industrial products that are more fire-resistant, leading to improved fire safety. FRCA maintains a co-operative and informative working liaison with government agencies, standards-writing organisations, model building codes organisations, insurance underwriters, research and testing organisations, and the fire service community. FRCA also conducts two technical meetings each year for the presentation of new and timely advancements in the field of fire safety and issues a quarterly newsletter to update members on fire safety trends and activities.

The British Plastics Federation

Contents

List of Contributors

V. Babrauskas, Head, Flammability and Toxicity Measurement, Center for Fire Research, National Institute of Standards and Technology, Gaithersburg, Maryland 20899, USA.

R. L. Bentley, Ciba-Geigy Industrial Chemicals, Tenax Road, Trafford Park, Manchester M17 1WT, UK.

A. Bevilacqua, Montefluos SpA, Via Principe Eugenio 1/5, 20155 Milano, Italy.

G. A. Bonner, Ethyl Corporation, PO Box 14799, Baton Rouge, Louisiana 70808, USA.

S. C. Brown, Alcan Chemicals Ltd, Chalfont Park, Gerrards Cross, Bucks. SL9 0QB, UK.

D. L. Buszard, Ciba-Geigy Industrial Chemicals, Tenax Road, Trafford Park, Manchester M17 1WT, UK.

S. E. Calewarts, Ethyl Corporation, PO Box 14799, Baton Rouge, Louisiana 70808, USA.

R. A. Carter, ICI Soda Ash Products, PO Box 4, Mond House, Winnington, Northwich, Cheshire CW8 4DT, UK.

D. Chaplin, Alcan Chemicals Ltd, Chalfont Park, Gerrards Cross, Bucks SL9 0QB, UK.

O. Cicchetti, Montefluos SpA, Via Principe Eugenio 1/5, 20155 Milano, Italy.

P. A. Cusack, International Tin Research Institute, Kingston Lane, Uxbridge, Middlesex UB8 3PJ, UK.

G. H. Damant, Chief, California Bureau of Home Furnishings, Department of Consumer Affairs, 3485 Orange Grove Avenue, North Highlands, California 95660-5595, USA.

D. D. Drysdale, Unit of Fire Safety Engineering, University of Edinburgh, The King's Buildings, Edinburgh EH9 3JL, UK.

L. Ekman, Volvo Car Corporation, Dept 93240 PV 1B, S-405 08 Gothenburg, Sweden.

E. Gal, Research Institute for Cables and Insulating Materials, Tovarenska 14, 815 71 Bratislava, Czechoslovakia.

U. Göransson, Swedish National Testing Institute, PO Box 857, S-501 15 Borås, Sweden.

J. Green, Senior Research Associate, FMC Corporation, PO Box 8, Princeton, New Jersey 08543, USA.

J. Hume, Director, Warrington Fire & Materials Centre, 101 Marshgate Lane, Stratford, London E15 2NQ, UK.

C. S. Ilardo, Occidental Chemical Corporation, 2801 Long Road, Grand Island, New York 14072, USA.

J. Jenc, Polyol International BV, The Netherlands.

W. J. Kennelly, Director, Technology and Operations, Climax Performance Materials Corporation, 447 Marlpool Drive, Saline, Michigan 48176, USA.

R. C. Kidder, Executive Vice-President, The Fire Retardant Chemicals Association, 851 New Holland Avenue, Lancaster, Pennsylvania 17604, USA.

D. A. King, Beaverfoam Manufacturing Ltd, Bluebell Close, Clover Nook Industrial Park, Alfreton, Derby DE55 4RD, UK.

G. Kirschbaum, Technical Service Manager, Martinswerk GmbH, Postfach 1209, D-5010 Bergheim, Federal Republic of Germany.

R. L. Markezich, Occidental Chemical Corporation, 2801 Long Road, Grand Island, New York 14072, USA.

R. F. Mundhenke, Occidental Chemical Corporation, 2801 Long Road, Grand Island, New York 14072, USA.

T. O'Neill, Du Pont (UK) Ltd, Maylands Avenue, Hemel Hempstead, Herts HP2 7DP, UK.

A. Pagliari, Montefluos SpA, Via Principe Eugenio 1/5, 20155 Milano, Italy.

A. Pal, Research Institute for Cables and Insulating Materials, Tovarenska 14, 815 71 Bratislava, Czechoslovakia.

D. J. Parry, ICI Soda Ash Products, PO Box 4, Mond House, Winnington, Northwich, Cheshire CW8 4DT, UK.

K. T. Paul, Rapra Technology Ltd, Shawbury, Shrewsbury, Shropshire SY4 4NR, UK.

K. Pettett, Warrington Fire & Materials Centre, 101 Marshgate Lane, Stratford, London E15 2NQ, UK.

F. A. Pettigrew, Ethyl Corporation, PO Box 14799, Baton Rouge, Louisiana 70808, USA.

D. A. Purser, Huntingdon Research Centre Ltd, Huntingdon, Cambridge PE18 6ES, UK.

R. Rothon, Technical Department, ICI Chemicals and Polymers Group, PO Box 8, The Heath, Runcorn, Cheshire WA7 4QD, UK.

J. Rychly, Polymer Institute, Centre of Chemical Research, Slovak Academy of Sciences, 842 36 Bratislava, Czechoslovakia.

R. A. Schleifstein, Ethyl Corporation, PO Box 14799, Baton Rouge, Louisiana 70808, USA.

K. Tarapcikova, Research Institute for Cables and Insulating Materials, Tovarenska 14, 815 71 Bratislava, Czechoslovakia.

H. E. Thomson, Unit of Fire Safety Engineering, University of Edinburgh, The King's Buildings, Edinburgh EH9 3JL, UK.

B. M. Valange, Manager, Polymers, Ethyl SA, Avenue Louise 523, BTE19, B-1050 Brussels, Belgium.

U. Wickström, Head of Fire Technology, Swedish National Testing Institute, PO Box 857, S-501 15 Borås, Sweden.

THE FUTURE OF EUROPEAN TESTING

ULF WICKSTRÖM
Statens Provningsanstalt, Fire Technology
P O Box 857, S-501 15 BORÅS

It is time to introduce modern technology in fire testing for classification. Europe shall harmonize testing and classification before the end of 1992. Modern testmethods are available based on new technology; a better understanding of the physics has allowed development of an entirely new generation of tests.

The Internal Market in Europe shall be completed before the end of 1992. Before then testing and classification must be harmonized. According to the new approach formulated by the European Commission (CEC), a common European classification shall be available for various essential safety aspects. Local authorities may then require various classes or levels of safety depending on their needs and preferences.

The European Council of Ministers accepted the Construction Products Directive in December 1988. Common classification rules shall thereafter be agreed within 30 months, that is already June 1991. The essential requirements in the Directive require to be translated into terms of performance specifications consisting of test procedures together with translation documents to be eventually transformed into a common European classification system. Translation documents shall give for each test procedure performance levels corresponding to the current requirements in the national codes. The national authorities may then operate their current systems and at the same time specify levels for products coming from other countries.

For testing of wall and ceiling linings three test methods (the 'three sisters') are proposed in a draft mandate to CEN (CEN/TC127 N79), i.e. the French 'Epiradiateur', the German 'Brandschacht', and the British 'Surface Spread of Flame'. To get a certificate, which allows a products to be marketed in every EC countries, it will be neccessary to test according to all these three methods. It will, however, be difficult to establish a common integrated European classification system based on all the three methods. They often rank products in different orders. That is one of several reasons why another solution is needed, at least for the long term.

The problem of fire testing of wall and ceiling linings was intensively discussed at the first meeting of CEN/TC 127 'Fire Safety in Buildings'. The proposal of the 'three sisters' was accepted although several countries voted against it. It was, however , also unanimously agreed to form a Working Group (WG2 'European reaction-to-fire classification')to make a proposal using new methods proposed by ISO. This group has started and has agreed to focus its work on investigating the Swedish proposal of using just the Cone Calorimeter (Figure 1) and the Room/Corner Test (Figure 2) for evaluation of wall and ceiling linings, see below or for further information e.g. [1].

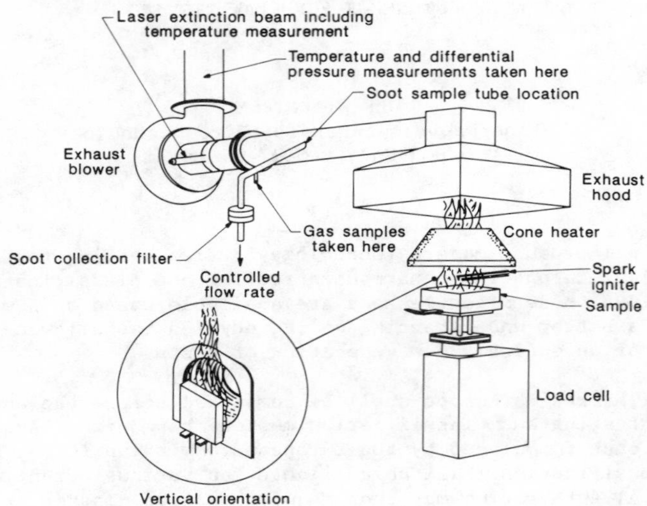

Figure 1 The Cone Calorimeter can be used for classification of building products.

Before a new system can finally be accepted experience of testing of various products are needed. The Nordic countries are coordinating their efforts in a comprehensive R&D program called EUREFIC. Important work are at the same time being carried out in several other countries. Fire research station in the UK studies the Room/Corridore scenario and an Italian laboratory investigates measurements of smoke. The fire laboratory in Dortmund (FMPA) exchange test results and coordinate choices of products to be tested with the EUREFIC program.

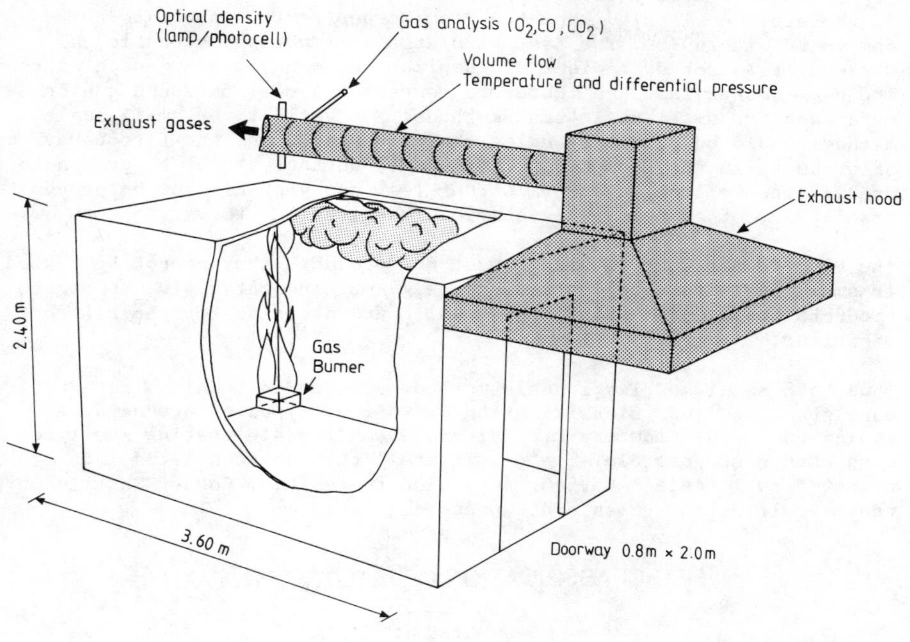

Figure 2 The Room/Corner Test is a reference for classification of surface linings.

WHY NOT USE THE BEST TEST METHODS?

There seems to be no objection among fire experts that the Cone Calorimeter is generally the best method available for evaluating reaction-to-fire properties of materials and products. Ignition and burning properties as well as the propensities to produce smoke and toxic gases can be evaluated at the same time. So, why not use the best method when it is available? Approximately 20 Cone Calorimeters are already installed or ordered by fire laboratories in seven or eight European countries. The world population now exceeds 40 and is growing at a rate of about 20 per year with the most significant growth being ing Western Europe. ISO has worked with the method and it will soon be put on ballot as a draft international standard.

By definition, however, the best possible estimate of the flammability of products is a full scale experiment. A standardized full scale test is therefore desirable. Thus the Room/Corner Test is about to be completed within ISO. The test simulates an importand scenario, a wastepaper basket or a piece of furniture burning in a corner of a room. The Room/Corner Test can therefore represent a real fire and can be a reference for small scale test methods. The validity of small scale methods could be proven by using them for predicting the fire behaviour of products in the Room/Corner Test. Methods that cannot be proven to predict the well defined Room/Corner Test can probably not be proven to predict any other relevant scenario either, or can they?.

The Room/Corner Test is also needed for products that cannot be tested in small scale for various reasons, e.g. melting materials, composite products or products with joints, which are decisive for their fire behaviour.

Thus both small and large scale methods are needed to allow for consistent and just classification of various types of products. As indicated in the flow chart of Figure 3 small scale testing shall be used when ever possible. The result shall then be translated into expected full scale behaviour according to the Room/Corner Test in which the classification rules are expressed.

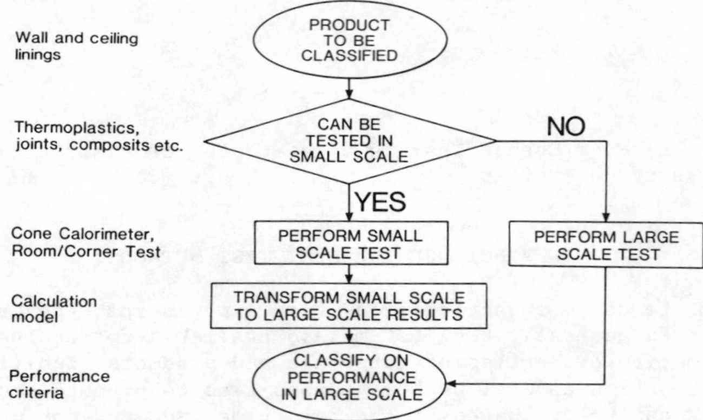

Figure 3 Principles of a testing and classification scheme emplying the Cone Calorimeter and the Room/Corner test. Large scale testing is only performed when small scale testing is not possible.

not believe there are any hazards connected with these products based on results that are found today. They concur with the efforts and conclusions that the BFRIP research efforts have conducted. The Environmental Protection Agency in the United States has been kept appraised of all these research projects and to date have felt there was no need for any regulatory activities or any cautions on the use of these products. Research work will be continued by the BFRIP to better understand the use of their products and any possible toxicity that might come from them.

In conclusion, toxicity of products of combustion remain the overriding issue of concern in the United States for fire safety of plastic materials. The industry is working diligently to develop improved tests that can give a more realistic determination of the hazard or potential risk for fire safety and/or develop information on the use of existing products which some have believed could have toxic consequences. This work will continue and it is hoped that it can have worldwide understanding and benefits.

NEW TEST METHODS FOR ASSESSING SMOKE, TOXIC PRODUCTS, CORROSIVE PRODUCTS, AND HEAT RELEASE IN FIRES[1]

VYTENIS BABRAUSKAS
Center for Fire Research
National Institute of Standards and Technology
Gaithersburg, MD 20899, USA

ABSTRACT

The existing inventory of various national tests for determining properties is gradually being supplanted by a new generation of test methods. These methods, unlike the earlier empirically designed ones, have been based on theoretically sound principles. The data from these new test methods are not arbitrary, but are suitable for quantitative fire engineering, and specifically as needed input data to fire models. Several such new methods are discussed in the areas of smoke, toxic products, corrosive products, and heat release.

INTRODUCTION

There is currently a huge number of available national test methods for fire testing. For example, one such compilation of only the ASTM methods on fire [1] tabulates some 77 tests! Based on this, the person new to the fire testing area might conclude that fire test methods are highly-refined, well-tuned to specific areas, and that he only has to find the right-fitting one. Of course, the reality is very different. The methods on the books have, in many cases, been developed 40 years ago, did not rely on any understanding of the physics of the situation being represented, and present their results as totally arbitrary numbers. Meanwhile, during the last decade or so, sound, physics-based design methods have come to be available to the fire engineer. These methods include both simpler, closed-form calculational formulas and complete fire computer fire models. An example is the HAZARD I model [2], which may be the most ambitious such software package yet made available for general design purposes. Such computer fire models require as input data variables which have not been available from traditional test methods. In some other cases, the requisite data may have been available from existing tests, but had unacceptable errors associated with them. During the last few years, methods to address these needs

---

1 This paper is a contribution of the U.S. National Institute of Standards and Technology and is not subject to copyright.

have either been developed or, in some cases, are at least under active development. In this paper we will examine some of these new methods, consider their salient features, and illustrate how they can be used in quantitative studies. Emphasis will be laid on the interrelation between bench-scale and full-scale methods.

FULL-SCALE AND BENCH-SCALE METHODS

Until the early 1970's, almost all of the testing for 'reaction-to-fire' (or 'flammability'), as opposed to fire endurance, was done in bench scale. The tests used were generally purely arbitrary bench-scale tests, with no proven relation to real fire scenarios. By 1973, however, the U.S. Federal Trade Commission thought that misrepresentation of the burning properties of plastics in bench-scale tests had become of such concern as to require an action against some two dozen manufacturers [3]. ASTM itself also became concerned and adopted a policy attempting to discourage such unwarranted faith in bench-scale techniques which may be misleading [4]. It was appropriate to deprecate such misleading use of bench-scale test methods; however, the question then came up – What is the user to do? Not only were better bench-scale test methods not on the books, but neither were there any suitable full-scale test methods.

The role of the full-scale room fire test method is rather special. The full-scale method is the only kind that can have intrinsic validity, without reference to another method. It still is required that the fire scenario used in the test be a good representation of the actual hazard, that the instrumentation and test arrangements be competently done, and so forth. Once these points are assured, a full-scale room fire test that is conducted **is** the true representation of reality. Any other tests can only be considered valid if they are validated against such full-scale room fire tests.

ROOM FIRE TESTS

Room fire tests of various types have been conducted for quite some while. The measurements made from them, however, did not have much general useability. The main reason was that neither mass loss rates nor heat release rates could be successfully measured in the typical room fire test of the early 1970's. The heat release rate is, of course, the single most important measure of a room fire, since it quantifies the question How big is the fire? The subsequent development of the oxygen consumption principle, which is described below, did allow for the development of useful, standardized room fire tests.

ASTM published in 1982 [5] a draft proposal for such a standard room fire test, where the heat release rate would be measured by oxygen consumption. The room was 2.4 m wide, by 3.7 m long, and 2.4 m high, with a single doorway opening in one wall, 0.76 m wide by 2.03 m high. The test method prescribes a standard ignition source, which is a gas burner, placed in a rear corner of the room, giving an output of 176 kW. The method is primarily intended for testing combustible wall and ceiling linings, although floor-standing combustibles could also be tested.

ASTM has not, as of this date, adopted this method as a formal standard. NORDTEST, however, has adopted a room fire test method quite similar to the one which was proposed by ASTM. The NORDTEST method [6] uses a room of essentially the ASTM dimensions, 2.4 by 3.6 m by 2.4 m high, with an 0.8 by 2.0 m doorway opening. The NORDTEST method uses a gas burner set to the 100 kW level. If no ignition is achieved in 10 minutes, the heat output is then raised to 300 kW. The NORDTEST room fire tests forms the basis of the method being currently considered by the ISO (the International Organization for Standardization) [7].

OXYGEN CONSUMPTION PRINCIPLE

It has long been known that there is an empirical relationship between the amount of heat produced in combustion systems and the oxygen consumed from the air stream. While this knowledge, in fact, dates to the turn of the century, the foundation for using the principle in fire test methods is based on the works of Huggett and Parker. Huggett [8] made a detailed study of a wide variety of materials. He found that for most combustible materials, which included polymers, organic liquids, and natural materials, 13.1 MJ of heat is released for each kg of oxygen consumed from the air. Deviations from this average value are typically on the order of only ±5%. (It must be emphasized that this constant must not be confused with the heat of combustion, which is defined as the heat released, per kg of fuel consumed. Heats of combustion for common materials vary readily by a factor of 2 and more and would not be considered at all constant.)

Huggett also noted that the material does not need to burn fully to CO_2 for the above relationship to hold. Typical reactions yielding part of the combustion products as CO or as soot do not significantly affect the accuracy of the results. The constant 13.1 MJ/kg O_2 holds very closely for all hydrocarbons (C, H materials) with only a very few exceptions. These exceptions are known, *e.g.*, the value for acetylene is 15.7. For combustibles which have significant fractions of O, N, Cl, Br, F, or S, the relationship may be less exact. Detailed values of this constant are tabulated for many combustibles [9].

The basic understanding of the oxygen consumption principle is simple: For each Joule of combustion heat generated, there is a fixed number of oxygen molecules that are removed from the exhaust stream. This understanding immediately makes it clear that the results of the method are unchanged when one changes the exhaust rate of the combustion products, or if one introduces an additional dilution stream. Neither an additional stream nor a changed flow rate will change the number of oxygen 'holes' travelling through the system. In practice, one does not count oxygen molecules; rather, measurements of flow rate and oxygen concentration are made. Thus, there are some practical limits to the extent of possible dilution if the resultant data are not to be noisy.

The actual implementation of the oxygen consumption equations has to be concerned with matters such as the mole change between the inflow and the outflow streams, trapping of certain species from gas analyzer lines, and so forth. The resultant equations are not necessarily simple, but they have been worked out in detail by Parker [10] for most conditions of concern. These equations are the starting point for the implementation of apparatuses based on oxygen consumption calorimetry.

HEAT RELEASE – LARGE SCALE

The ultimate in large-scale testing is full room fires, as discussed above. In such a test, all of the combustion products are collected through a large hood, where oxygen concentration and flow rate measurements are used to compute the instantaneous heat release rate. For a combustible wall lining, this is the only way that a proper full-scale test can be conducted. For floor-standing combustibles, that is, furniture, furnishings, stored goods, etc., a simpler test can be conducted. It was empirically demonstrated [11] that the heat release rate of a furniture item is generally the same, whether the item is in a fully-furnished room, or if it is burned out in the open. There are limitations to this relationship, and the reader interested in those details should consult the original reference.

The realization, that it is possible to obtain heat release data in an open-burn test, allowed a family of apparatus, generally termed 'furniture calorimeters,' to be designed. At NIST, the first such device was described in 1982 [12]. More recently, NORDTEST have adopted a similar scheme and have issued a standard, the NORDTEST NT FIRE 032 [13]. Figure 1 shows a view of the NORDTEST furniture calorimeter. The apparatus consists primarily of an instrumented exhaust duct system. In the exhaust duct, flow rate and oxygen concentration are measured, allowing the heat release rate to be computed. Additional gas analyzers can also be used to measure CO, CO_2, and other gases of interest. The exhaust stream also contains a smoke photometer for measuring the smoke being evolved from the specimen. Finally, a load cell is used to determine the specimen's mass loss rate. When combined with the heat release rate, an effective heat of combustion can then also be computed.

The basic variable measured in the furniture calorimeter is the heat release rate. For full-scale testing, this has the units of kW. Also, the total heat released during the entire test can be computed, using the units of MJ (megajoules).

HEAT RELEASE – BENCH-SCALE

Measurement of heat release in bench-scale is not new. For instance, ASTM has a method on the books (ASTM E 906, the OSU Calorimeter [14]) which was originally developed around 1970. Its results, however, when compared against other measurement methods, have been found to substantially underestimate the heat release rate [15]. A number of other instruments were also designed during the 1970's, but were limited because of either poor validity or practical operational difficulties. With oxygen consumption calorimetry coming into use, however, it became obvious that an entirely new instrument should be built which is specifically designed to make use of this principle.

The development work led to a practical instrument, known as the Cone Calorimeter. The apparatus (Figure 2) makes use of an electric heater in the form of a truncated cone, hence its name. The apparatus is a general-purpose one, which may be used to test products for various applications. Thus, the heater had to be capable of being set to a wide variety of heating fluxes; the actual capability spans 0 to 100 kW/m^2. The design of the heater was influenced by an earlier ISO test on radiant ignition, ISO 5657 [16]. The requirements for the Cone Calorimeter went beyond the design parameters of the ISO 5657 cone, thus the actual heating cone in the Cone Calorimeter is a new design. The Cone Calorimeter represented such a significant step forward in fire testing instrumentation that it was awarded the prestigious R&D•100 award in 1988 [17]. The technical features are documented in several references [18], [19], [20], and [21]. Here, we will merely point out some of the most salient features:

- horizontal or vertical specimen orientation
- composite and laminated specimens can be tested
- continuous mass loss load cell readings
- feedback-loop controlled heater operation
- heat flux calibration by heat flux meter with in-built alignment fixture
- heat release rate calibration using methane metered with mass flow controller

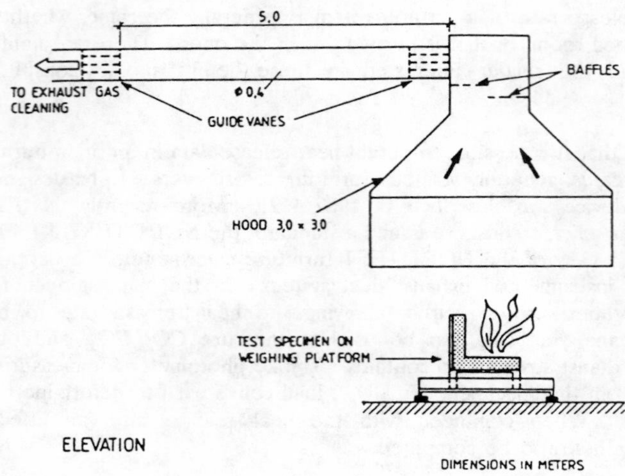

Figure 1. NORDTEST furniture calorimeter

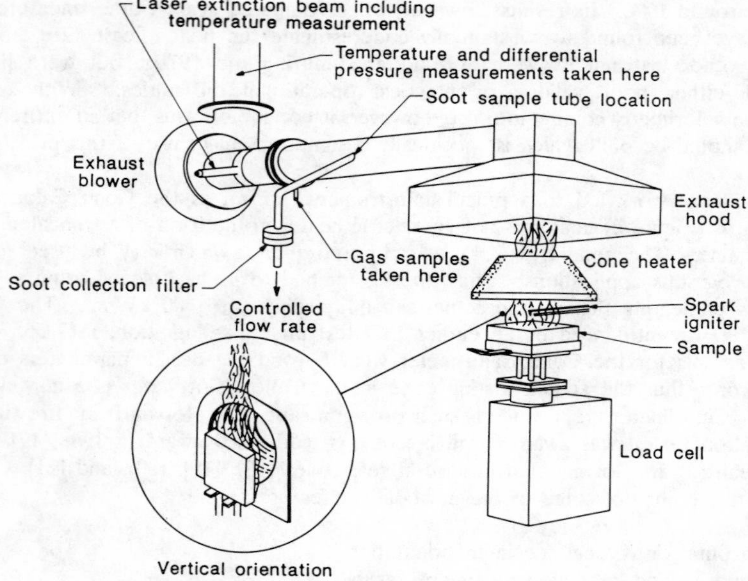

Figure 2. A schematic view of the cone calorimeter

- smoke measured with laser-beam photometer and also gravimetrically
- provision for analyzing CO, CO_2, H_2O, HCl, and other combustion gases

The method was originally issued by ASTM as a draft document [22], and is now nearing final adoption. A parallel standard is also being developed in ISO [23]. The equipment is made by 5 different manufacturers and is now used by close to 40 laboratories.

Data from bench-scale heat release rate measurements are reported in kW/m^2. The extra m^2, compared to the full-scale results, comes from the fact that in the full scale, one is interested in the total heat being produced by the burning object. In bench scale, by contrast, the area of the specimen has no intrinsic significance, and results have to be reported on a per-unit-area basis. To go from bench-scale data to full-scale predictions, then, requires that an 'm^2 factor' be supplied. This factor – in the simplest case of uniformly burning materials – is the area of flame involvement, at any given time of the fire. Today's methods for estimating the full-scale heat release rates do not, typically, treat this area-of-flame-involvement factor explicitly, but rather subsume it into the general predictive correlation.

For validating against the full scale, the state of the art is such that validations must be done on a product class basis – one cannot simply validate a bench-scale method for all applications. For the Cone Calorimeter, two such validation efforts have already been completed, one for combustible wall linings [24] and another for upholstered furniture [25]. The general means by which a proper validation is accomplished are detailed in [26] and [27]. For combustible wall linings, the method developed at the Statens Provningsanstalt, in Sweden, uses the time to ignition as an indicator of the flame spread rate, and, therefore, of the area of flame coverage. The predictive relationship, then, uses two data items obtained from the Cone Calorimeter – the peak heat release rate, and the time to ignition. Figure 3 shows the predictive results obtained. The method for upholstered furniture requires, in addition to heat release rate information (in this case, not the peak, but the average over the 180 s after ignition), some data about the full-scale article. Such data include the combustible mass and the frame type. The latter must be specified separately since Cone Calorimeter tests are done only on fabric/padding composites, whereas the full-scale behavior is influenced also by the thermostructural response of the frame. The reader should consult the above references for details of the actual implementation of these predictive methods.

SMOKE

Typically, the methods for measuring smoke in bench-scale have been closed box methods. Two of those are in common use – the NBS single-chamber test (ASTM E 662) [28] and the dual-chamber test developed in Germany. Both of these methods have been under consideration by ISO [29], [30]. The dual-chamber test has been used in Germany, Holland, and Italy, while the NBS test has been used in numerous countries worldwide. Nonetheless, a study showed that any closed-box type test has some very pronounced intrinsic limitations [20]. Thus, it became appropriate to consider a test with a flow-through geometry. Since the Cone Calorimeter already had other needed prerequisites (well-controlled uniform irradiance, accurate load cell, good control of airflow rates, etc.) it was decided to base a new smoke measuring apparatus on the combustion system already available with the Cone Calorimeter. Figure 4 shows a view of the laser-beam photometer which is used. The photometer uses monochromatic, rather than white, light, since it was shown that substantial errors can occur when using the Beer-Lambert law with white light sources [31]. The system is also notable in that windows (which are a

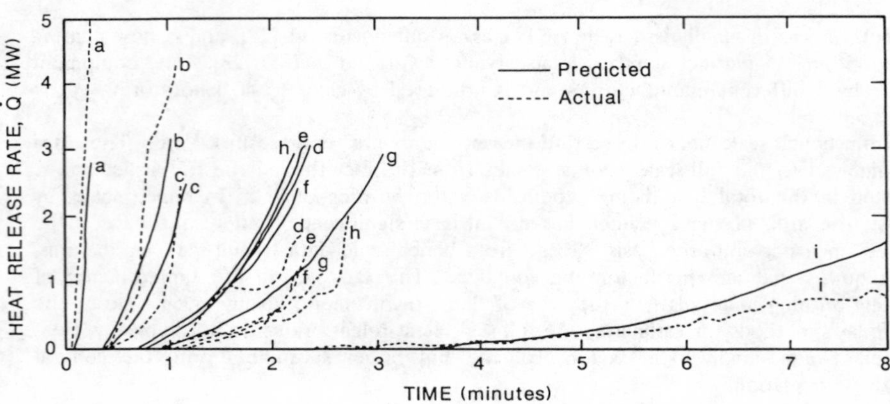

Figure 3. Prediction of combustible wall linings (notations *a* through *i* refer to 9 different materials tested)

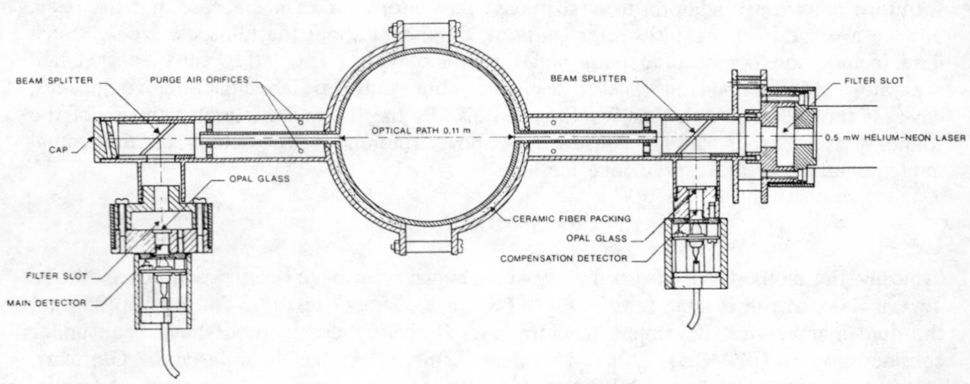

Figure 4. View of the smoke measuring system used with the cone calorimeter

substantial source of drift in those apparatuses where they are used) are not needed because of a pressure-difference purging arrangement. A discussion of the other design details is given in [20].

The Fire Research Station recently evaluated a number of bench-scale instruments for measuring smoke, and found that the Cone Calorimeter arrangement was subject to the least measurement bias [32].

The bench-scale smoke data are reported in the form of *specific extinction area*. This is defined as the area (m^2) of smoke generated per mass (kg) of specimen decomposed; thus the units are m^2/kg. It must be emphasized that load cell measurements are needed so that the specimen mass loss rate can be included. This variable is based on a theoretically sound analysis of the optical properties of fire smokes, and is not simply an arbitrary index, as has been used with some other smoke tests.

In large-scale tests, the measurement issues are generally similar. Early versions of the Furniture Calorimeter [12] used a simple white-light beam. In more recent years, a laser beam photometer very similar to the one used with the Cone Calorimeter is being fitted to furniture calorimeters and exhaust ducts associated with room fires.

Data analysis from large-scale tests can proceed in two different ways. For furniture calorimeter tests, where load cell data are usually available, the analysis can be done in exactly the same way as for the bench-scale data. This is sometimes referred to as the *yield* of smoke, since it is the extinction area generated per unit specimen mass. In the case of room fires, load cell data are usually not available. Even if load cell data are available, in many cases it is desired to evaluate fire hazard according to the total amount of smoke produced. This is termed the *production* of smoke, and is meaningful only as an integral over the entire test period. In other words, the extinction area flowing by per second (m^2/s) is integrated over time to give the total production (m^2). The instantaneous values of m^2/s are generally not used directly by themselves.

In addition to being described by its optical properties, smoke can also be measured as the amount of **soot** generated on a gravimetric basis. Soot measurements can be done equally well in large scale or in bench scale. The soot amount is measured by sampling a small fraction of the exhaust gas stream and collecting its soot on an inert filter. The filter is weighed to determine the soot deposited. The analysis, then, involves determining the yield of soot as (mass soot generated/mass specimen lost). Since the units for soot yield are kg/kg, they are dimensionless. Under certain circumstances there is linear relationship between the soot yield and the specific extinction area (smoke yield); Ref. [20] gives details of this relationship.

The validation of bench-scale smoke data against the full scale is still in its infancy. For optical measurements, the normal procedure would be to compare the test-average smoke yield (total m^2 smoke produced/total kg of specimen mass lost). Note that this is **not** equivalent to simply averaging the instantaneous yield readings over time, since a mass-weighted average is effectively required. For gravimetric soot measurements, the yields would be directly compared for bench scale against full scale. Some initial efforts have recently been reported [33], [20], but comprehensive validation efforts still remain to be attempted.

CORROSIVE PRODUCTS

The widespread realization of the importance of fire damage through corrosion dates, perhaps, to a conference [34] organized in Sweden in 1969. During the intervening years, a number of tests for the corrosivity of combustion products have been proposed. These typically were simple pH tests. On an even more extreme basis, some regulatory bodies have taken steps to restrict usage of materials based solely on the content of halogen atoms (Cl, Br, etc.), without any consideration of actual corrosion performance. The first actual performance test to achieve recognition was a test developed by the French telecommunications agency CNET. The method [35], like most recent efforts in this area, focuses exclusively on damage to electronic equipment, since this has been the area of the greatest public concern. It involves a single, closed box, which contains a test sample, a heater, and a target. The target is a printed circuit board; the performance measured is the increase in the resistance of the circuit trace. This increase is taken to be an indication of metal loss due to corrosion.

Recently ASTM appointed a Task Group, ASTM E5.21 T.G. 70, to study available fire corrosivity tests and to make recommendations. The task group, while finding the CNET test to be the best of the currently available methods, did not feel that it was a fully satisfactory performance test. The reasons had to do with practical difficulties in testing, with heating conditions which were considered unrealistic, and with inadequacies of both the target and its measurement technique. The Task Group made a number of recommendations, including the fact that it saw the need for a '3-part' target. It was felt that in addition to measuring simple loss of metal, a practical test method should also measure two other aspects of non-thermal fire damage: ohmic bridging (which can short out electric circuits), and contact fouling (which can make relay and switch contacts non-functional). While the Task Group has not yet finished its work, it has commissioned a number of exploratory experiments and has proposed a candidate method [36].

Figure 5 shows the method as currently envisioned. The Task Group considered various apparatus configurations and is currently working with a system where the combustion chamber is of a flow-through type, with the target exposure chamber being a large sampling syringe. The syringe is filled using a servo-controlled stepper motor, so that the filling time coincides with the actual specimen burning time. The syringe is then closed, disconnected, and allowed to remain for 24 h in a temperature-controlled room. The actual target has three pieces: a serpentine trace for metal loss, a set of discontinuous traces for ohmic bridging, and sets of relay contacts for contact fouling determinations. Electrical measurements are made on the target after the 24 h period has elapsed. The method has not been fully realized yet, and substantive changes may still be made by the Task Group.

As far as validation goes, there is currently no reliable full-scale data base against which bench-scale methods might be validated. Full-scale tests have been few and *ad hoc*.

TOXIC PRODUCTS

Over the last two decades, the design of a suitable apparatus for measuring the toxic potency of combustion products has interested quite a few researchers. Several dozen of these methods have been described in the literature; the better-known ones have been reviewed in depth in [37]. In the last several years the number of suggested new designs has rather decreased. Most recently there is a substantial amount of effort being put into

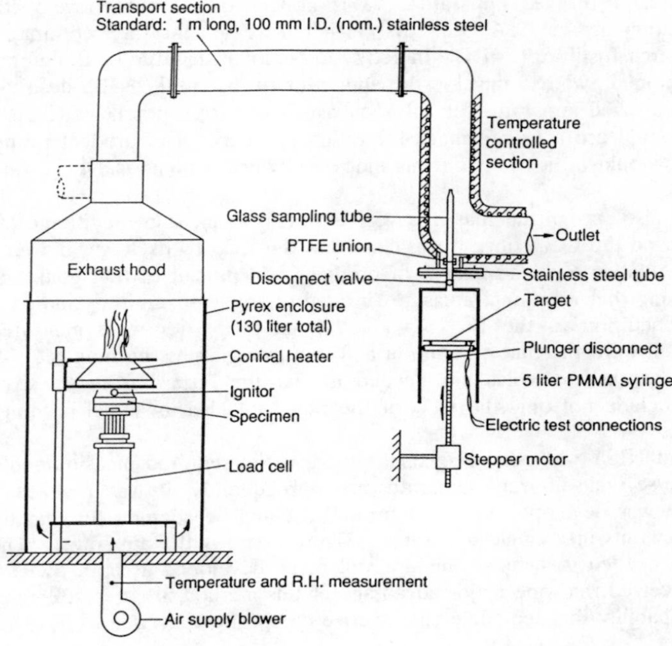

Figure 5. View of smoke corrosion test being developed by ASTM E 5.21 T.G. 70

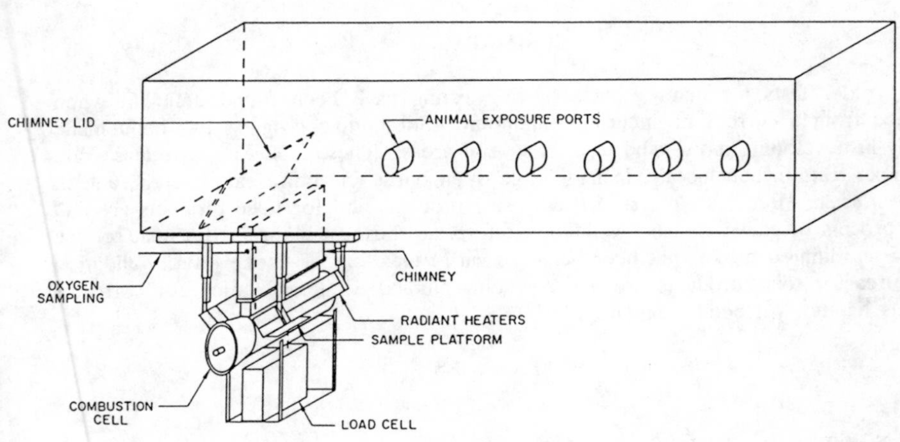

Figure 6. The radiant furnace toxicity apparatus

work with a radiant furnace apparatus. This apparatus was first developed at the Weyerhaeuser Company in 1984 [38]. Its further development then continued at the Southwest Research Institute (SwRI). In 1987 the National Institute of Building Sciences (NIBS) commissioned SwRI to develop the apparatus further [39]. NIBS desired, in fact, not simply an improved apparatus for actual measuring of toxic potencies (LC_{50}'s), but a method which would use a hazard index for rating products. The product rating, in the NIBS approach, would be a result on this index scale, not a numerical LC_{50} value.

At NIST it was also recognized that it is very desirable to measure additional properties of products, beyond the LC_{50}, since it was clear that the LC_{50} by itself was not an accurate measure of the relative *toxic fire hazard* of products. In pursuit of that goal, an analysis was made, showing that a rational measure (instead of solely an arbitrary index) could be obtained if, in addition to the LC_{50}, two additional properties were measured. The properties needed were the time to ignition and the average mass burning rate [40]. The reason that such other variables are needed is that the hazard from the combustion products must include not only the LC_{50} of the item, but also its actual burning rate.

At the time that NIST was proposing this approach, the required measurements had to be made using several different apparatuses. Subsequently, it was realized that the apparatus which was developed by SwRI for NIBS could be adapted for making all the needed measurements in a single apparatus. Figure 6 shows the apparatus. The details of the protocol needed to achieve this are still being developed at both SwRI [41] and NIST. It is perceived that one major advantage of this method, if successfully developed, would be its capability to adequately characterize composite specimens.

Validation of bench-scale fire toxicity data against the full scale has been a vigorously debated issue in recent years. Since the issues have not been resolved in any definite way, during the course of 1989 NIST has been conducting a pilot project to establish the proper bases for such a validation effort and to illustrate the approach with some experimental data. The intended result of this work is not, in itself, to produce a list of validated and non-validated methods, but rather to recommend a suitable strategy by which such validations could be carried out.

SUMMARY

Existing older tests for many aspects of fire testing have been found deficient when examined from a current engineering standpoint. Substantive progress has been made recently in developing more valid tests in several areas. These include heat release rate and smoke tests in bench-scale, in large-scale open burns (furniture calorimeter), and in full room scale. Bench-scale tests for corrosive products and for toxic products are still in the process of active design. Validation efforts are farthest along in the heat release area. Some limited success has been achieved with validations of smoke tests. Validation procedures for toxic products are actively being studied, while validation for corrosive products has not yet been tackled.

REFERENCES

1. **Fire Test Standards**, Second Edition, American Society for Testing and Materials, Philadelphia (1988).

2. Bukowski, R.W., Peacock, R.D., Jones, W.J., and Forney, C.L., Technical Reference Guide for the HAZARD I Fire Hazard Assessment Method (NIST Handbook 146, 3 Volumes). [U.S.] Natl. Inst. Standards and Technology (1989).

3. Federal Trade Commission Complaint on the Flammability of Plastic Products, File No. 732-3040, May 31, 1973.

4. ASTM Policy Defining Fire Hazard Standards, Limiting the Scope of Properties Description Standards and Establishing a Committee on Fire Hazard Standards, American Society for Testing and Materials, Philadelphia (18 September 1973).

5. Proposed Standard Method for Room Fire Test of Wall and Ceiling Materials and Assemblies, **1982 Annual Book of ASTM Standards**, Part 18. American Society for Testing and Materials, Philadelphia (1982).

6. Surface Products: Room Fire Tests in Full Scale (Nordtest Method NT FIRE 025). NORDTEST, Helsingfors, Finland (1986).

7. Room Fire Test in Full Scale for Surface Products, ISO DP 9705, International Organization for Standardization (1989).

8. Huggett, C., Estimation of Rate of Heat Release by Means of Oxygen Consumption Measurements, **Fire and Materials. 4**, 61-5 (1980).

9. National Fire Protection Association, **Fire Protection Handbook**, 16th edition, Section on Tables and Charts, NFPA, Quincy, MA (1986).

10. Parker, W.J., Calculation of the Heat Release Rate by Oxygen Consumption for Various Applications, **J. Fire Sciences. 2**, 380-395 (1984).

11. Babrauskas, V., Upholstered Furniture Room Fires – Measurements, Comparison with Furniture Calorimeter Data, and Flashover Predictions, **J. of Fire Sciences. 2** 5-19 (1984).

12. Babrauskas, V., Lawson, J.R., Walton, W.D., and Twilley, W.H., Upholstered Furniture Heat Release Rates Measured with a Furniture Calorimeter (NBSIR 82-2604). [U.S.] Natl. Bur. Stand. (1982).

13. Upholstered Furniture: Burning Behaviour – Full Scale Test. (NT FIRE 032). NORDTEST, Helsinki, Finland (1987).

14. Standard Test Method for Heat and Visible Smoke Release Rates for Materials and Products (ASTM E 906), American Society for Testing and Materials, Philadelphia.

15. Babrauskas, V., Comparative Rates of Heat Release from Five Different Types of Test Apparatuses, **J. of Fire Sciences. 4**, 148-159 (1986).

16. Fire tests – Reaction to fire – Ignitability of building products, International Standard ISO 5657, International Organization for Standardization (1986).

17. 1988 R&D 100 Award Winners, **Research & Development. 30**, 62-104 (October 1988).

18. Babrauskas, V., Development of the Cone Calorimeter – A Bench Scale Heat Release Rate Apparatus Based on Oxygen Consumption, **Fire and Materials. 8**, 81-95 (1984).

19. Babrauskas, V., and Parker, W.J., Ignitability Measurements with the Cone Calorimeter, **Fire and Materials, 11,** 31-43 (1987).

20. Babrauskas, V., and Mulholland, G., Smoke and Soot Data Determinations in the Cone Calorimeter, pp. 83-104 in **Mathematical Modeling of Fires** (ASTM STP 983). American Society for Testing and Materials, Philadelphia (1987).

21. Babrauskas, V., The Cone Calorimeter – A Versatile Bench-Scale Tool for the Evaluation of Fire Properties, pp. 78-87 in **New Technology to Reduce Fire Losses & Costs**, S.J. Grayson and D.A. Smith, eds., Elsevier Applied Science Publishers, London (1986).

22. Proposed Test Method for Heat and Visible Smoke Release Rates for Materials and Products using an Oxygen Consumption Calorimeter (E-5 Proposal P 190), **Annual Book of ASTM Standards**, Vol. 04.07, pp. 1221-1237, American Society for Testing and Materials, Philadelphia (1986).

23. Fire Tests – Reaction to Fire – Rate of Heat Release from Building Products. ISO Draft Proposal DP 5660..

24. Wickström, U., and Göransson, U., Prediction of Heat Release Rates of Surface Materials in Large-Scale Fire Tests Based on Cone Calorimeter Results, **J. Testing and Evaluation. 15,** 364-370 (1987).

25. Babrauskas, V., and Krasny, J.F., **Fire Behavior of Upholstered Furniture** (NBS Monograph 173). [U.S.] Natl. Bur. Stand. (1985).

26. Babrauskas, V., and Wickström, U.G., The Rational Development of Bench-Scale Fire Tests for Full-Scale Fire Prediction, pp. 813-822 in **Fire Safety Science – Proc. of the Second International Symposium** (1988). Hemisphere Publishing, New York (1989).

27. Babrauskas, V., Fire-Related Standards and Testing, pp. 31-41 and 119-130 in **Spacecraft Fire Safety** (NASA Conference Publication 2476), NASA Lewis Research Center, Cleveland, OH (1987).

28. Standard Test Method for Heat and Visible Smoke Release Rates for Materials and Products (ASTM E 906), American Society for Testing and Materials, Philadelphia.

29. Plastics – Smoke generation – Single chamber test. Part 1: Determination of specific optical density (DP 5659). ISO/TC 61/SC 4/WG 2/N 19 (1989).

30. Fire Tests – Reaction to Fire – Smoke Generated by Building Products (Dual Chamber Test). Draft International Standard DIS 5924 (ISO/TC 92/SC 1/WG 4/N 64), 1986.

31. Mulholland, G., How Well Are We Measuring Smoke?, **Fire and Materials. 6**, 65-67 (1982).

32. Morgan, H., and Geake, P.J., Smoke Particle Sizes: A Preliminary Comparison between Dynamic and Cumulative Smoke Production Tests, Fire Research Station, Borehamwood, England (1988).

33. Mulholland, G.M., Henzel, V., and Babrauskas, V., The Effect of Scale on Smoke Emission, pp. 347-357 in **Fire Safety Science – Proc. of the Second International Symposium** (1988). Hemisphere Publishing, New York (1989).

34. **SKYDD 69 (Protection 69): Plastics – Fire – Corrosion**, Proc. Intl. Symp. and 15th Nordic Fire Protection Day, Stockholm, April 23, 1969, Swedish Fire Protection Association, Stockholm (October 1969).

35. Fire Performance: Determination of the Corrosiveness of Effluents (158 CNET/LAB/SER/ENV). National Centre for Telecommunications Studies (CNET), France (1983).

36. Ryan, J.D., Babrauskas, V., O'Neill, T.J., and Hirschler, M.M., Performance Testing for the Corrosivity of Smoke, to appear in ASTM STP (1989).

37. Kaplan, H.L., Grand, A.F., and Hartzell, G.E., **Combustion Toxicology.** Technomic Publishing, Lancaster, PA (1983).

38. Alexeeff, G.V., and Packham, S.C., Use of a Radiant Furnace Fire Model to Evaluate Acute Toxicity of Smoke, **J. Fire Sciences. 2**, 306-320 (1984).

39. Grand, A.F., Development of a Product Performance Combustion Toxicity Test (SwRI Project 01-1744-001), final report to be issued. Southwest Research Institute, San Antonio, TX.

40. Babrauskas, V., Toxic Hazard from Fires: A Simple Assessment Method, pp. 16.1 to 16.10 in **Fire: Control the Heat...Reduce the Hazard**, QMC Fire & Materials Centre, London (1988); to appear in **Fire Safety J.**

41. Grand, A.F., Development of a Strategy for Evaluating the Potential Toxic Hazard of Items in Fires using the SwRI Radiant Combustion/Exposure System (SwRI Project 01-2926-001), final report to be issued. Southwest Research Institute, San Antonio, TX (1989).

NORDTEST FULL-SCALE FIRE TESTS

ULF GÖRANSSON
Swedish National Testing Institute
Department of Fire Technology
Borås, Sweden

ABSTRACT

All fire test results are a combination of material parameters of the product that is tested. Most test methods also give results that can give a basis for ranking materials or for classification.

Problems occur however if you want to make a better, a more adequate evaluation. Then there are two ways to choose between. Either you can put in a big effort in analysing small scale test methods so that you find the parameters that are important in your specific scenario. Or you can test the product in a test method that gives more adequate results. This is where a full-scale test can be valuable.

The fire hazards that we try to protect us from are full-scale fires. Full-scale tests therefore give results that are easy to interpret, even for a non-expert. If the test is well designed, it will also give more adequate information than a small-scale test can give.

Nordtest, which is a joint Nordic organisation, has financially supported the development of a series of full-scale tests. These tests are intended as reference tests or tests for special products.

In the Nordic countries there are Nordtest full-scale test methods for:

a) Surface materials in the room/corner test,
NT FIRE 025/ISO DP 9705.

b) Pipe insulation in the room test. A test method used in Sweden and Norway for classification of pipe insulation,
NT FIRE 036.

c) Upholstered furniture, a chair or a sofa is completely burnt in free excess to air,
NT FIRE 032.

d) Free-hanging curtains and draperies. A test that is just developed and has not yet been numbered.

These four test methods all use the same hood that collects all fire gases which means that the rate of heat release can be measured with the oxygen depletion technique. Other parameters are measured and observed during the tests as well.

In this paper the four full-scale test methods will be described. The test scenarios are motivated and there is a discussion of what products that can be tested in the different methods.

INTRODUCTION

Several full-scale tests have lately been developed on behalf of NORDTEST, a joint Nordic organisation for testing. The tests all use the oxygen consumption method to calculate the heat release rate as the main indication of the fire hazard.

The tests are developed with the two aims to provide a test method used in a classification system and to help fire modellers and researchers to evaluate the fire risk of a product.

To introduce full-scale tests in regulations does not necessarily have to create problems. It is more a question of being used to the idea that large-scale tests generally give more adequate results than small-scale tests. For most scenarios this is probably true and therefore it is preferable to classify after a large-scale test performance.

Full-scale tests are today used in the Nordic countries. Surface linings have been tested in an older version of a full-scale test for many years that have worked as reference test to the Nordic classification test (NT FIRE 004) for products that are hard to test in small scale. All pipe insulations are tested according to NT FIRE 036 for classification in Sweden and Norway since 1987.

WHERE FULL-SCALE TESTS SHOULD BE USED

When interpreting results from fire tests it is very important that there is a connection between the fire test and the fire scenario or threat that you want to be protected from. Often there are more than one fire threat and then it must be investigated if the fire test is good enough to protect you from all threats.

A full-scale test is designed to be a good picture of one scenario and can hopefully also evaluate other large fires well.

Another advantage with a full-scale test is that it yields a lot of information. It can give you information of all parts of fire safety ignitability, flame spread, smoke production and even products extinguishing properties.

Full-scale tests are especially interesting for people not normally involved in fire testing. As the test is more looking like a real fire, authorities and users can by themselves see what the consequencies are if you choose between products of different fire performance levels or when you decide what performance level that is required.

If the main fire threat is large fires that can kill many people and cost lots of money it is obvious that a large-scale test can describe this scenario better than a small-scale.

As the full-scale test normally is much easier to interpret than a small-scale test, one obvious field of application for a full-scale test is as basis for classification. Tests can still be carried out in small scale as long the results are possible to interpret to a large-scale test performance [1].

The biggest disadvantage of full-scale tests is that they are expensive. The need of material, testing staff and equipment are higher than for most small-scale test. Therefore a full-scale test shall only be a regular classification test for very special purposes. As reference test, a full-scale test is not too expensive, considering that the test costs are only one part of the costs for classification. Compared to the information that is gained a full-scale test is probably quite cheap.

One area where full-scale tests often are used are as ad hoc tests. Here they can show how a fire can develop in a specified scenario. Ad hoc tests can be used to asses the fire risk of one special application but the information is harder to interpret than from a standardized full-scale test as the result analysis cannot be based on experience. Heat release measurement equipment as in the Nordtest methods can, however, be used to make results more valuable.

FIRE TEST RESULTS

In almost all testing of materials reaction-to-fire you look to evaluate the burning behaviour and the smoke production from the material tested.

The burning behaviour of a product can be expressed in terms of ignitability and heat release rate. The flame spread properties can probably be considered as a function of the other two.

The properties of the smoke production are accordingly light obscuration, toxicity and volume of produced smoke. Obscuration and production of toxic gases are rather easy to determine in a specified scenario. Two scenarios can, however give very different results. The amount of produced smoke is more a function of burning behaviour than of smoke production properties.

When designing, or choosing, a test method you usually want to get as adequate information as possible of these four properties.

CHOOSING TEST PRINCIPLE

To be able to evaluate what information that is adequate you need to choose a test principle. A test can describe one scenario that is important, or one or many tests can give information that can be used to evaluate different fire scenarios. Either of these two alternatives can be used for classification purposes or when evaluating a product for a specified application.

A full-scale fire test is designed to be a good representation of one scenario, a specified ignition source and configuration. For this particular scenario, and for similar scenarios, the full-scale test gives much more adequate results than any other test method.

For a scenario that is very unlike the full-scale test, small-scale test methods can give results that give as much information as the full-scale test. The hardest thing to generalise, both in small and large scale, is the ignition source. Products are sensitive to different ignition sources and how is very hard to anticipate without having performed tests with different ignition sources.

NT FIRE 025 - FOR SURFACE LININGS

The full-scale test method that now is most discussed in the Nordic countries is NT FIRE 025, a test method for surface linings, walls and ceiling [2]. It is a room test with a gas burner placed in one corner. Three walls and the ceiling are covered by the tested material. The propane gas burner is a rather big ignition source (100 kW) simulating the fire of a filled waste paper basket.

The main principle of the method is to collect all combustion products that leave the room by a large hood so that gas samples can be taken to analyse contents of O_2, CO etc. The smoke production is measured by a lamp/photocell system. The rate of heat release, calculated from oxygen consumption, production rate of CO and other toxic gases and production rate of smoke can then be given as functions of time.

In the test you can make also many other types of measurements and observations. Radiant heat, gas temperature, flame spread rate etc. It is also possible to calculate an energy balance of the room.

The test method can be used as reference test and thus be used for classification of products not easily tested in small scale [3]. The test method is good as classification basis since the range of materials with different fire properties that can be tested is very wide.

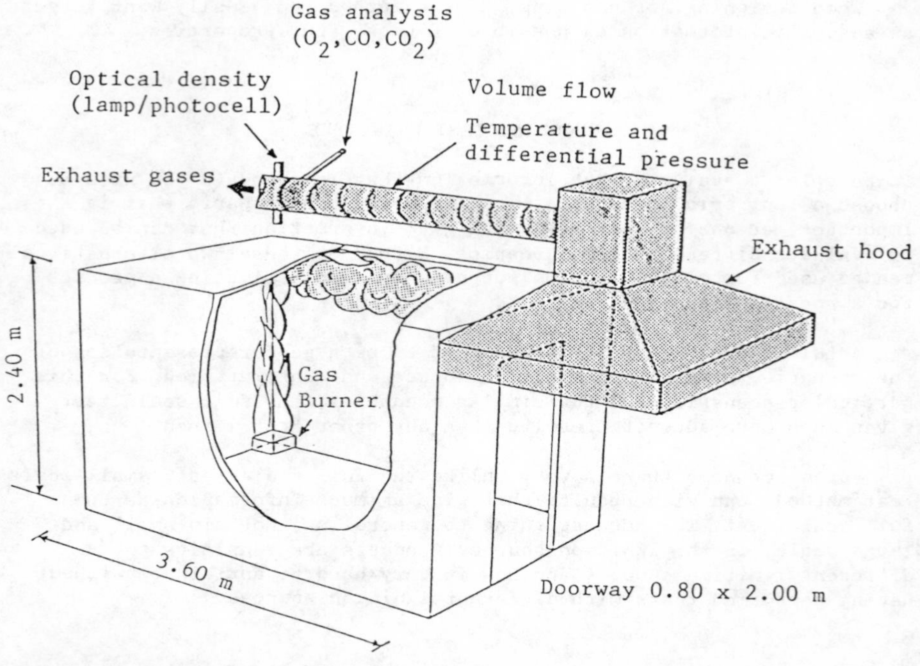

Figure 1. NT FIRE 025 - A full-scale test method for surface linings. The test material is mounted on the walls and ceiling.

The test method can also be used to obtain better information about properties not easily gained in small scale such as smoke and toxic gas production. A third application is when a fire modeller needs input to advanced fire designing and a fourth is for showing people how different materials react in a fire.

NT FIRE 036 - FOR PIPE INSULATION

For pipe insulation, a variaty of the NT FIRE 025 has been developed [4]. The method is similar to the surface products test except for the ignition source and the amount of tested material. When testing pipe insulation only the ceiling is covered by test material. The gas burner is placed 1 m above the floor level and has a heat output of 150 kW. The flames impinge on about 1 m^2 of the ceiling. The burner is moved from the corner to avoid edge effects of the pipe insulation so the heat output have to be raised to get flames large enough to break through a thin protective surface. For this position of the burner no material is needed on the walls to obtain adequate results. This method is since 1987 used in Sweden and Norway as classification test method for all pipe insulations.

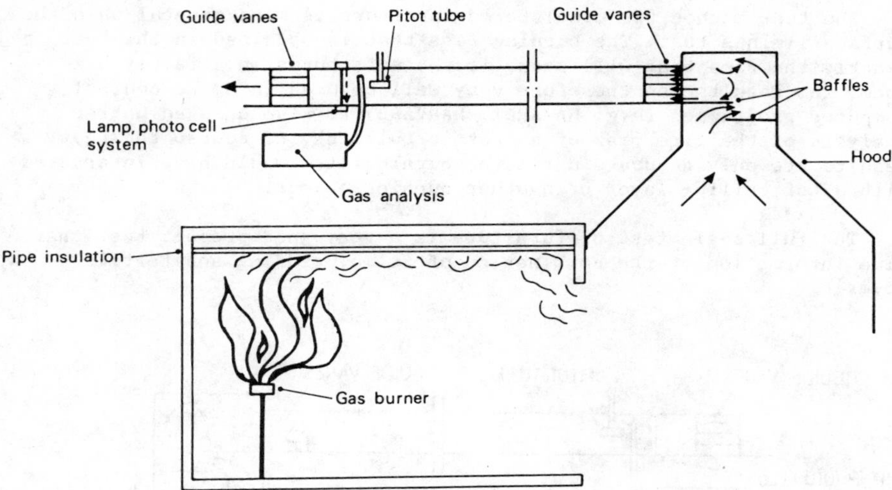

Figure 2. Pipe insulation tested in full scale according to NT FIRE 036. The insulation is mounted on bars 20 cm from the ceiling

NT FIRE 032 - FOR UPHOLSTERED FURNITURE

Furnishings represent one of the bigger fire threats in homes and public buildings. If the fire properties are not considered a chair or a sofa can develop a large fire in only a few minutes. Upholstered furniture is as important as surface lings for the fire hazard of a building but the fire safety requirements are usually much lower for furniture.

This full-scale test - NT FIRE 032 - is a test for assessing the fire properties of a piece of furniture in case of a fire [5]. It describes how the burning rate develops and thus how big fire risk the furniture represents. It is not an ignitability test and it could very well be complemented with ignitability test for small ignition sources such as BS 5852.

All types of upholstered furniture can be tested, chairs, sofas and also beds. The only restriction is that you test one item at the time so that you can compare your results.

The basic test principle is the same as in the surface linings test. A rather big ignition source, e.g. BS5852 crib 7, ignites the product and it is from measurements in the exhaust duct possible to determine burning rate, smoke production rate etc. In this test method the specimen is also placed on a weighing platform which gives information of mass loss rate and net heat of combustion when compared to the rate of heat release measurements.

The test method for upholstered furniture is more general than the surface linings test. The burning rate that is obtained in the test is exactly the same that will occur if the sofa burns in a fairly big room. The results can therefore very well be used in smoke control computer programmes (e.g. HAZARD1, HARVARD) to give an even better analysis of the fire risk of a certain building. Of course the test results are only accurate until the burning item would have interacted with a hot ceiling layer or another burning object.

The full-scale test of furniture is a very good product test that give information of the combination of frame, padding and textile covering.

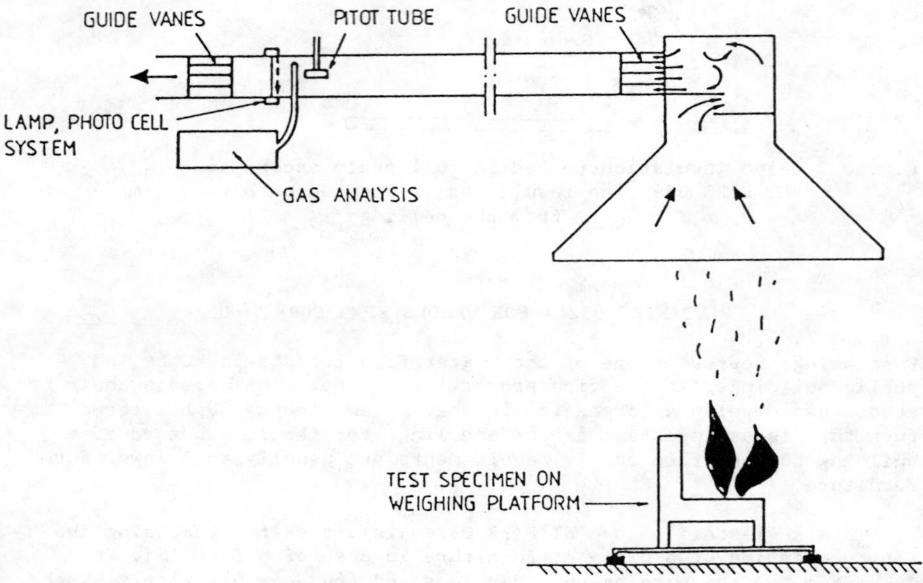

Figure 3. NT FIRE 032 - Full scale fire testing of furniture. The test specimen is placed on a weighing platform so that the mass loss rate can be recorded.

A NEW FULL-SCALE TEST METHOD FOR CURTAINS AND DRAPERIES

The test method for curtains and draperies, developed in 1988 [6], is intended for public buildings such as hotels, restaurants and theatres and not primarily for dwellings. The reason for a large-scale test method for textiles is that the present small-scale test methods mostly are ignitability tests for textiles exposed to small flames only. Textiles can, however, have a different behaviour when exposed to larger flames. It is also hard to distinguish between the better products when using a small flame only.

The test method is designed to test a material, not a ready-made product. The test specimen shall be without hems but sewn together to achieve the 3m by 3m specimen size.

A reason for a textile test method with a powerful ignition source is also that free-hanging textiles should be able to be compared with surface linings usually tested in tougher test methods given in the building regulations. Especially for textiles used as decorations to cover a whole wall or for theatre and cinema curtains there is need for a large-scale test.

There are two main risks with a burning textile. The flame spread can be very rapid which will involve a large burning area and quite a big heat release rate. The other main risk is that burning drops or parts of the curtain may fall down and ignite other items such as upholstered chairs etc. This could lead to a very serious fire in a very short period of time.

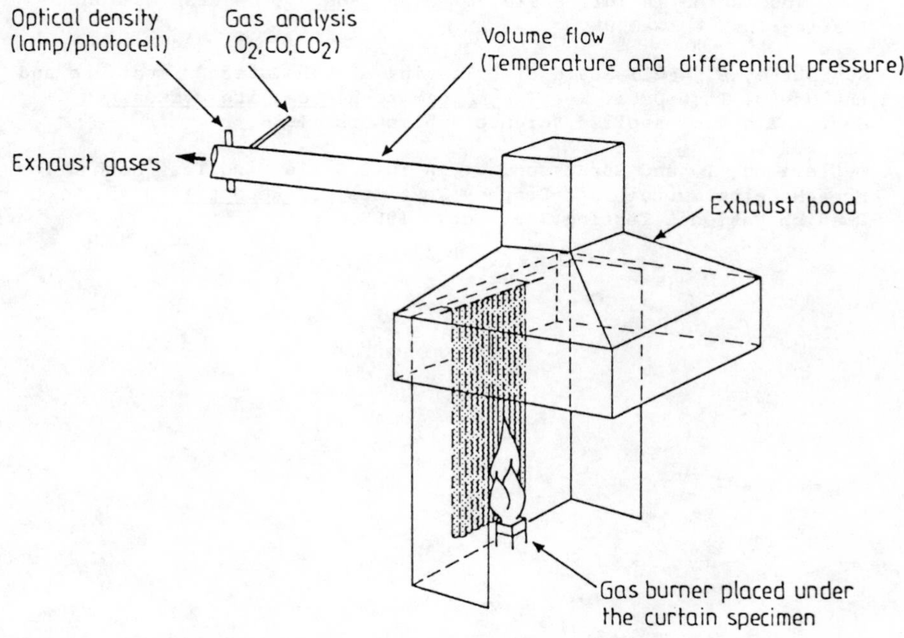

Figure 4. Full-scale fire test method for curtains. The flames reach about half the height of the curtain.

REFERENCES

1. Wickström, U. and Göransson, U., Prediction of Heat Release Rates of Surface Materials in Large-Scale Fire Test Based on Cone Calorimeter Results, ASTM Journal of Testing and Evaluation, nov 1987.

2. Sundström, B., The New ISO Full Scale Fire Test Procedure for Surface Linings, The First Yugoslav Scientific Meeting with International Participation - On Behaviour of Materials and Constructions in Fire, 1987.

3. Sundstöm, B., Göransson, U., Possible Fire Classification Criteria and their implications for Surface Materials Tested in Full Scale According to ISO DP 9705 or NT FIRE 025, SP-Report 1988:19, Swedish National Testing Institute, 1988.

4. Wetterlund, I. and Göransson, U., New Method for Fire Testing of Pipe Insulation in Full Scale, SP-Rapp 1986:33, Swedish National Testing Institute 1986.

5. Sundström, B., Full-Scale Fire Testing of Upholstered Furniture and the Use of Test Data, New Technology to Reduce Fire Losses and Costs, Elsevier Applied Science Publishers, 1986.

6. Wetterlund, I. and Göransson, U., A Full Scale Fire Test Method for Free-Hanging Curtain and Drapery Textiles, SP-Report 1988:45, Swedish National Testing Institute, 1988.

THE HEAT & FLAME RESPONSE OF FLAME RETARDANT HALOGENATED AND NON-HALOGENATED POLYMERS & COMPOUNDS

THOMAS O'NEILL
Du Pont (UK) Ltd
Hemel Hempstead, Herts HP2 7DP

ABSTRACT

The Author reviews the contribution that can be made to reducing fire risk by material selection based on performance assessment in small-scale "fire property" tests and underlines the restriction that limitations of scale impose in such tests. The predominating importance of the susceptibility of materials to ignition, flame spread and heat release in the overall fire risk assessment is discussed using experimental data derived from a programme of standard tests conducted on a series of halogenated and non-halogenated polymers and compounds. The relative advantages and disadvantages of each material class are compared and contrasted. As a label, "non-halogenated" is used rather than the deprecated term, "halogen-free" which is considered, in the same way as the term "halogen-deficient", to be insufficiently precise for the purposes of material specification.

INTRODUCTION

Fire is a complex phenomenon, the growth and severity of which depend on a multitude of interrelated factors. As it is impossible to standardise a fire, there is no possibility that a single test could be divised to predict the performance of materials in a real fire. It is conceivable, however, as in the case of the cone calorimeter, that from a knowledge of certain material properties, the likely behaviour pattern in some typified fire scenarios may be predicted. Generally, however, the way in which a combustible material behaves in fire depends on a large number of factors, relating both to the material and to its environment. In fact this behaviour can depend even more on the environment and mode of use than on the nature of the material itself, [1]. This makes the question of fire performance particularly difficult to deal with in specifications. Unlike, for example, electrical and mechanical performance, which can be related to measurable properties of the materials, the fire performance cannot be so determined as it is not a material property per se.

The identification of the main components of the fire growth process has led, however, to the adoption of a number of terms which have come to be regarded as "fire properties" of the materials themselves, such as ease of ignition, rate of flame spread, rate of heat release, smoke density and the like. This is unfortunate, for these aspects of fire behaviour cannot be assessed in isolation from the conditions of the fire itself.

The present paper is devoted to a report of experimental results obtained within a "fire property" test programme covering a range of diverse polymer materials, both halogenated and non-halogenated, commonly used in electrical wire and cables. The materials reported on here are listed below:-

Flame retardant PVC compound (FR-PVC)
Standard PVC cable insulation compound
Chlorosulphonated polyethylene (CSP)
Polytetrafluoroethylene (PTFE)
ATH-filled EVA (thermoplastic)
ATH-filled EVA (silane cross-linked)

With the exception of PTFE, which is a pure polymer, the materials are filled compounds with filler contents around 50 phr for the two PVC compounds, 100 phr for CSP and 140 phr in the case of the EVA compounds.

Heat and flame response has been appraised using recognised standard tests from ISO, IEC, ASTM, UL, and BSI. In the case of effluent corrosiveness the method of the French National Telecommunications Laboratory (CNET) has been used, and pH/conductivity measurements on aqueous solutions of the combustion products have been conducted according to the procedure of the UK Central Electricity Generating Board (CEGB). Table 1 provides the list of the tests included in our programme. The reader is referred to the designated documents for a complete description of apparatus and method.

IGNITABILITY

The experimental results given in Table 2 are particularly interesting in that they point to significant differences in response between the halogenated and the non-halogenated materials depending on whether the ignition source is impingeing or non-impingeing.

Thus with the exception of PTFE (which in this whole series of tests demonstrates its remarkable unwillingness to get involved in fire!) the halogenated materials appear to be more

TABLE 1
"Fire Property" test programme

"FIRE PROPERTY"	TEST	DESIGNATION
IGNITABILITY	CRITICAL FLUX TO IGNITION	ASTM E5 P-190 (1986)
	RADIANT CONE	ISO 5657
	GLOW WIRE	IEC 695-2-1
	NEEDLE FLAME	IEC 695-2-2
FLAMMABILITY	VERTICAL FLAMMABILITY	UL 94
	FLAMMABILITY TEMPERATURE*	ISO DP 9306
	VERTICAL FLAME SPREAD	IEC 332-1
RATE OF HEAT RELEASE	CONE CALORIMETER	ASTM E5 P-190 (1986)
SMOKE CORROSIVENESS	CNET (F)	DEC-0611/C 3rd edition
ACIDITY/ CONDUCTIVITY	CEGB (UK)	E/TSS/EX5/8056 part 3 (1984)
SMOKE DENSITY	NBS CHAMBER	ASTM E662-79
	CONE CALORIMETER	ASTM E5 P190 (1986)

* Temperature corresponding to an Oxygen Index of 21% (formerly called the Temperature Index)

readily ignited than the filled EVA compounds when subjected to a radiant, non-impingeing source. This is found to be the case in both the ISO radiant cone procedure and the ASTM cone calorimeter.

This effect can be attributed to the higher density, thermal conductivity and heat capacity of the highly filled EVA compounds, the thermal inertia of which retards the rate of temperature increase at the surface of the specimen. This is also apparent in the CSP data. The lower thermal inertia of the less highly filled PVC compounds results in more rapid temperature rises and consequently in the more rapid development of a combustible mixture of evaporation and degradation products at the surface of the specimen.

When the source impinges directly on the material, however, the situation is reversed and the non-halogenated compounds tend to be inferior to all of the halogenated materials with the possible exception of the conventional wire and cable grade of PVC. Under these test conditions the intensity of the localised heat source is such that the thermal inertia differences among the materials is of less importance than the differences in thermal stability. These results thus demonstrate that ethylene-vinyl acetate copolymers generate combustible mixtures of decomposition products at lower temperatures than is observed in the case of the halogenated materials under the conditions of these tests.

TABLE 2
Ignitability test results

MATERIAL	RADIANT CONE (s)	CRIT. IGN.FLUX (kW/m²)	NEEDLE FLAME	GLOW WIRE (°C)
Flame retardant PVC compound	23	9.4	NI	960
Standard PVC compound	23	5.9	I	850
Chlorosulphonated polyethylene (CSP)	28	12.9	NI	960
Polytetrafluoro-ethylene (PTFE)	193	25.4	NI	960
ATH filled EVA (thermoplastic)	63	16.4	I	850
ATH filled EVA (cross-linked)	74	13.6	I	750

(a) Radiant Cone data indicate time in seconds to ignition under a heat flux of 50kw/m^2.

(b) Needle Flame edge-application for 120s to 1mm thick sample (NI = no ignition, I= ignition with flaming debris).

(c) Glow Wire data give minimum wire temperature for ignition (30s application time, 1mm sample thickness).

FLAMMABILITY

The data given in Table 3 provide further confirmation of the superiority of the halogenated materials when they are subjected to an impingeing source of heat. In the UL94 tests, neither of the filled EVA compounds were classifiable (meaning that the sample underwent complete combustion and caused ignition of the lint). Most of the halogenated materials, on the other hand, were either V-0 or V-1.

In the case of the flammability temperature measurements, i.e. the ambient temperature at which the oxygen index of the sample equals 21%, the results show that no non-halogenated compound gives a result higher than 250 degrees C where as three out of the four halogenated materials have values higher than 300 degrees C.

TABLE 3
Flammability test results

MATERIAL	UL 94 1mm	UL 94 2mm	FLAMMABILITY TEMPERATURE (°C)	IEC 332-1
Flame retardant PVC compound	V-O	V-O	350	Pass
Standard PVC compound	V-1	V-2	180	Pass
Chlorosulphonated polyethylene (CSP)	V-1	V-0	330	Pass
Polytetrafluoro-ethylene (PTFE)	V-O	V-O	>>400	Pass
ATH filled EVA (thermoplastic)	U	U	250	Fail
ATH filled EVA (cross-linked)	U	U	240	Fail

U = Unclassifiable (complete combustion + lint ignition)

When the materials are tested for flame spread as insulation on single wires, the results are in alignment with those reported above. Thus when subjected to direct impingement by the 175mm premixed propane flame specified by the International Electrotechnical Commission standard for vertical flame propagation on single wires or cables (IEC 332-1), all of the halogenated materials pass and neither of the non-halogenated compounds meets the standard.

CONE CALORIMETRY

The cone calorimetry data given in Table 4 serve to corroborate some of the results discussed above. Thus, again with the exception of PTFE, the thermal inertia effect is seen from the times to ignition to play in favour of the EVA compounds. When it comes to their heat release characteristics, however, the inherently greater combustibility of these non-halogenated materials is clearly seen.

TABLE 4
Cone calorimetry test results

MATERIAL	CRITICAL IGNITION FLUX (kW/m^2)	MAX RATE OF HEAT RELEASE (kW/m^2)
Flame retardant PVC compound	11	220
Standard PVC compound	8	280
Chlorosulphonated polyethylene (CSP)	16	152
Polytetrafluoro-ethylene (PTFE)	33	65
ATH filled EVA (thermoplastic)	16	300
ATH filled EVA (cross-linked)	13	542

The excellence of PTFE in its response to high heat exposures is once again demonstrated. In addition the results confirm the low resistance to ignition of the standard PVC grade, and highlight the difference between this material and the improved FR-PVC and ATH-filled EVA compound. CSP exhibits higher resistance to ignition than all of the others with the exception of PTFE.

CORROSIVENESS

Two test methods were used in this work, viz:-

(a) The pH/conductivity approach (measurement of pH and ionic conductivity of a standard aqueous solution of combustion products)

(b) The CNET method, i.e. assessment of the corrosion of a copper printed circuit board by condensed combustion products. This method is currently under study by ISO for elaboration as an international standard.

The results presented in Table 5 confirm that, by suitable compounding, chlorinated polymers can be significantly improved from the point of view of acid emission and corrosive attack under standard test conditions. This can be demonstrated most dramatically in the CNET test where unplasticised PVC would give a corrosion reading of around 80% (corresponding to an increase of about 80% in the PCB resistance after 1 hour's exposure) whereas the flame-retardant compound lies below 10%. The importance of compounding as a means of decreasing corrosive attack is even more strikingly demonstrated in the case of CSP.

TABLE 5
Acidity, conductivity and corrosiveness test results

MATERIAL	CEGB		CNET
	pH	μScm^{-1}	% *
Flame retardant PVC compound	2,51	1500	8,8
Standard PVC compound	2,08	3350	14,2
Chlorosulphonated polyethylene (CSP)	3,58	50	5,6
Polytetrafluoro-ethylene (PTFE)	3,49	172	10,4
ATH filled EVA (thermoplastic)	3,84	32	0.6
ATH filled EVA (cross-linked)	4,44	20	0.9

* % increase in circuit resistance after 1h exposure to condensed combustion products.

The data on PTFE, which is an uncompounded pure polymer, confirm work reported by other authors showing the lower corrosiveness of combustion products from fluoropolymers on most substrates except glass [2].

The highly filled EVA compounds give relatively low acidity/conductivity/ CNET corrosiveness values as one might expect under such small scale test conditions. The experimental results given in Table 5 also highlight the fact that, in the CNET test, where a real corrosion effect is at play, it is relatively simple to assess performance within the limitations of the small scale test scenario. The pH and conductivity data do not lend themselves so readily to such interpretation.

SMOKE DENSITY

The results shown in Table 6 show that relatively low levels of smoke are generated by the ATH-filled EVA compounds under the conditions of these tests. Chorosulphonated polyethylene shows up relatively well also, producing as it does smoke of only moderate opacity. The absence of plasticiser and the higher filler content that can be compounded into this elastomer (compared with PVC) account for this more favourable behaviour.

In common with all completely fluorinated polymers, PTFE produces minimal quantities of opaque smoke when it burns, and the present test data confirm that fact.

TABLE 6
Smoke density test results

MATERIAL	NBS BOX DsMax (corr)		CONE CALORIMETER Spec. Ext. Area (m^2/kg)
	Flame	No Flame	
Flame retardant PVC compound	611	318	1240
Standard PVC compound	322	354	1660
Chlorosuphonated polyethylene (CSP)	201	162	405
Polytetrafluoro-ethylene (PTFE)	5	4	65
ATH Filled EVA (thermoplastic)	46	177	334
ATH filled EVA (cross-linked)	70	196	326

It is, of course, an over-simplification to consider smoke density test data in isolation from the materials' rates of burning. Indeed, a material which produces a high yield of smoke in one of the standard tests could well prove to be a more satisfactory choice than a low smoke-producer, if the low smoke producer can be easily ignited, or exhibits a much higher rate of surface spread of flame. In addition, it should be remembered that smoke density is highly dependent on the conditions to which the material is subjected, such as ventilation and incident flux levels.

TOXICITY

More than 20 years of intensive research world-wide have established that the toxic hazard of the smoke and gases from burning materials, be they natural or synthetic, is determined far more by the factors which control the rate of fire growth than by differences in the chemistry of the materials, as discussed in references [3] and [4]. On burning, every combustible material converts itself more or less rapidly into complex and highly toxic mixtures of many decomposition products whose effective toxic hazard is more often determined by the conditions prevailing at the scene of the fire (heat flux, ventilation levels and fuel loads) than by the compositions of the effluent mixtures which themselves vary as a function of time ambient temperature, available oxygen concentrations and contributing co-combusting materials. As summarised in reference [4]:-

"In general, laboratory fire effluent toxicity tests are unable to demonstrate practical quantitative differences between most materials - differences which can be used with confidence for choosing one material over another in the interest of improving fire safety. Experience has shown that most common materials, both natural and synthetic, do not differ widely in the toxicity of fire effluents produced from combustion. Some of the differences observed, even though of statistical significance, are of questionable practical significance from the viewpoint of impact on hazard to life safety in a fire".

In view of this state of affairs and of the dominating influence of combustibility characteristics in determining toxic hazard in fire, no attempt was made in this experimental programme to categorise materials on the basis of any small scale toxicity test.

CONCLUSIONS

This paper has been intended as a tool to help to clarify some of the complexities involved in writing specifications for materials with a view to improving the fire performance of wire and cable systems, particularly as to their potential contribution to post-fire corrosion damage.

No material is perfect. Specifications and standards, therefore, necessarily involve compromises where improved performance in one set of properties generally has to be paid for by some sacrifice within some other property set. Specifications for improved fire performance, however, are beset by the fact that "fire properties" in no way correspond to other sets of intrinsic material properties. This is because "fire properties" can depend as much on the test conditions as on the nature of the material being tested.

The temptation to oversimplify the problem by portraying certain classes of materials as being inherently worse than others on the basis of their chemical make-up rather than on their real performance is to be resisted in the interests of durable progress. Fire is admittedly a complex affair and some simplifying working hypotheses are often needed, but as Albert Einstein's word has it: "Things should be made as simple as possible...and no simplier!"

REFERENCES

1. Drysdale, D., An Introduction to Fire Dynamics, Wiley Interscience Publications, Chichester and New York (1985).

2. Sandmann, H. and Widmer, G., Fire and Materials, 140, 11-19 (1986).

3. Fardell, P.J. and Woolley, W.D., The State of the Art of Combustion Toxicity", Proc. Int. Conf. "Control the Heat - Reduce the Hazard", London, October 1988, No. 12.

4. International Organisation for Standardisation, ISO/TR 9122, "Toxicity Testing of Fire Effluents."

PROGRESS IN INTUMESCENT TECHNOLOGY BASED ON SPINFLAM$^{(R)}$ FLAME RETARDANTS

O. CICCHETTI, A. PAGLIARI and A. BEVILACQUA
Montefluos S.p.A. (Montedison Group)
Via Principe Eugenio, 1/5 20155, MILANO, ITALY

ABSTRACT

The halogen-free intumescent Spinflam$^{(R)}$ flame retardants, which have been commercially available for some years, are obtaining an ever increasing industrial success because of their high FR performance, (especially in polyolefins and polyurethanes), low smoke and toxic or corrosive gas emission, the absence of halogens and Sb_2O_3. In fact, these characteristics are in agreement with the issue of ever more restrictive regulations and market requirements on fire behaviour of polymer compounds.

Moreover, being low-loaded, polymeric compounds containing Spinflam$^{(R)}$ are characterised by low density, good processability, and physical, mechanical and electrical properties closer to the properties of the un-loaded polymer than those of similar compounds containing halogenated flame retardants or inorganic hydrates.

This paper reports results concerning the above aspects for polymer systems based on polyolefins and thermoplastic polyurethanes.

INTRODUCTION

It is well known that in modern life, the noticeable growth in the use of synthetic polymers materials has caused the number of serious fires to increase dramatically because of their easy ignitability and combustion propension.

Consequently the number of deaths and injuries to people and damage to properties has been rising (1).

Statistical data on fires in buildings (1) (2) show that the majority of deaths (80%) are due to the inhalation of smoke and not to the fire itself.

So, parallel to the growth of the plastics industry the use of flame retardants in polymers in order to reduce fire hazards has increased greatly in the recent years and growth will continue in the future.

Traditionally, a major industrial class of flame ritardants is that of the halogenated products (at least for certain types of polymers), generally used in synergic combination with Sb_2O_3, and/or other metallic compounds.

No doubt that they have given a great contribution to the increase in fire safety by increasing ignition resistance and reducing burn rates of the polymers (3) (4).

This class of commercial additives, however, have problems associated with their use. In particular, they are known to cause an increase in the amount of obscuring smoke and toxic or corrosive gases generated by plastics during combustion in event of fire.

In addition, many traditional flame retardants pocess undesirable toxicological properties themselves (5). Therefore, there is great interest in finding and introducing innovative safer additives as well as in substituting intrinsically halogenated and/or smoke-producing polymers.

As a result, several inorganic compounds, specially hydrates, have been introduced more recently in this field, and alumina trihydrate is the highest volume flame retardant (6).

While inorganic compounds are not toxic themselves and make a great contribution to reduction of combustion toxicity, they, however, must be used at exceptionally high loadings to be effective thus causing other types of drawbacks to substrates e.g. difficult processability and poor physical-mechanical (and wet-electrical) properties, even if improvements have been obtained by technologies of surface treatments and modifications of the powders (7).

Now, because of their action mechanism (char formation) and consequent high effectiveness, the halogen-free intumescent Spinflam$^{(R)}$ flame ritardants, illustrate high potential for the resolution of problems shown by both the traditional classes of flame retardants (8).

Unfortunately, selection processes of flame retarded polymers for specific applications and characteristics of products reaching market place are influenced and tempered by many factors mainly those resulting from requirements set by various regulatory and specifying agencies. Now, existing fire testing standards and regulations are tailor-made for the traditional technologies and thus the standards to be complied with not always are of real value for fire safety progress increasing in demand by the public and the end users.

In this situation, potential high value innovations can often be stalled or blocked only because of their apparent deficiency in a regulated or specified property of lesser value (9).

Accordingly, also Spinflam$^{(R)}$ technology may present some deficient properties in relation to existing specifications.

This paper reports results on five basic flame retarded polymer systems with particular reference to formulations, processing/ compounding and developmental applications of polyolefins and thermoplastic polyurethanes.

These systems are aimed to show an interesting balance of advantages and potential of Spinflam$^{(R)}$ technology and to suggest ideas to compounders, processors, designers and end users for developing commercial innovative applications, which could contribute significant improvements to fire safety of synthetic polymer materials if hopefully this type of technology is kept in mind by specifiers when reviewing existing testing standards and regulations.

RESULTS AND DISCUSSION

Extrusion polypropylene copolymer (Electrical Conduits)

The growing interest in finding alternatives to halogenated polymers (mainly PVC) as materials for extruded electrical conduits and cable trunkings is pressing for the development of halogen-free FR polyolefins. In this case, existing fire specifications and technical requirements based on PVC-made items must be met by a totally different base material.

Matrices based on polypropylene copolymers and polyethylene and/or their blends can be used.

Our results refer to a PP copolymer characterized by medium flow (MFI 3.5) and high impact strength.

The influence of Spinflam MF82/PP content on technical properties of the compound is shown in TABLE 1.

TABLE 1

Influence of Spinflam MF 82/PP on technical properties of PP copolymer

Spinflam content %	MFI dg/min (D 1238)	Charpy, 23°C KJ/m^2 (D 256)	Flex. Modulus MPa (D 790)	LOI % (D 2860)
-	3.5	17.0	1480	17.4
25	3.2	4.7	2250	35.7
30	2.8	3.8	2580	39.7
34	2.6	3.4	2640	43.7

It can be seen that Spinflam acts as a filler, increasing stiffness and lowering impact strength at values which are still acceptable. On the basis of these results and bearing in mind the desired properties of the final items, a compound was made containing 28% of Spinflam MF 82/PP in a large quantity to study its compounding and extrusion behaviour and properties with respect to required specifications.

As first articles from this polymer system an electrical conduit (ID = 16.0 mm; thickness = 1.4 mm) and a U-shaped cable trunking (square section) were made in cooperation with specialized fabricators.

Technical and fire reaction properties of the material are exposed in TABLE 2 and TABLE 3, respectively.

This compound appears useful to produce electrical conduits and cable trunkings safer than those required by the existing standards set forth by European Electrical Committee (EEC 614) and by Comitato Elettrotecnico Italiano (CEI 23-19) for fire safety.

TABLE 2

Technical properties of PP copolymer containing 28% of Spinflam MF 82/PP

Property	Unit	ASTM Method	Value
Specific gravity	g/cm^3	D 792	1.05
Melt Flow Rate	dg/min	D 1238	3.0
Tensile strength at yield	MPa	D 638	21.2
Elongation at break	%	D 638	>200
Flexural elastic modulus	MPa	D 790	2180
Charpy impact strength, 23°C	KJ/m^2	D 256	4.2
" " " -5°C	"		2.3
" " " -25°C	"		2.2
Izod impact strength, 23°C	"		3.2
HDT, 1.8 MPa	°C	D 648	73
" 0.46 MPa	°C		92

TABLE 3

Fire behaviour of PP copolymer containing 28% of Spinflam MF 82/PP

Property	Unit	Method	Value
. Gas corrosivity		UITP E8	
acidity	pH		9.26
conductivity	$S.cm^{-1}$		100
. Smooke Density	%	Arapahoe	3.5
. LOI	%	ASTM D 2863	39.7
. Vertical flame test at 1/16"	Rating	UL 94	V-0
. Flame propagation resistance	Rating	Modified CEI 23-19 (flame application time 45 sec)	Pass
. Glowing wire resistance	°C	CEI 23-19	960
. Arc resistance	sec	ASTM D 495	60

Injection molding polypropylene copolymer (Electronic applications)

An interesting potential application for halogen-free FR polyolefins is forecast in the electronic industry.

In this case, besides absence of corrosive gases emissions from burning halogens, frequently a UL 94 V-0 rating at low thickness (about 1 mm) and resistance to repeated ignitions (UL 94 5V test) are requested (10). We have found that of primary importance to obtain these results with the Spinflam(R) technology is the chemical constitution of the base polymer as well as Spinflam loading. Good results have been obtained in our labs using block PP copolymers also with addition of an impact modifier.

In TABLE 4 some examples of useful compositions are shown; while UL 94 V-0 ratings at low thicknesses up to 1.6 mm are obtainable with all the tested polyolefines matrices also at relatively low FR loadings, to achieve the same ratings at very low thicknesses (1 mm or lower) it is not sufficient to increase FR loading; but it is essential also the presence, in the compounds, of a certain amount of polyethylene sequences. The effectiveness improves ranging from PP block to PP bloc/Impact modifier blend.

It is interesting to note that these results are obtained in spite of the opposite behaviour of LOI values, which are, as expected, in agreement with the well known major difficulty to flame retard polyethylene-based polymers in comparison to polypropylene.

Thus, polyethylene contribution can be attributed to its propension to crosslink during fire testing, which retards, in combination with effective intumescent flame retardants such as Spinflam products, melting and dripping also of thinner specimens (11).

Further improved performances seem to be obtainable using more recent formulative modifications; preliminary results show that it is possible to obtain PP compounds with 0.8 mm UL 94 V-0 and 2.0-2.4 mm UL 94 5V ratings. The results discussed seem very interesting and enable Spinflam-retarded PP compounds as improved competitors of more costly polymers in sophisticated electronic applications where very thin sections and absence of corrosive combustion-gases are required as well as excellent electrical properties.

TABLE 4

Low thickness UL 94 rating polypropylene compounds.

	Spinflam %	LOI % (D 2863)	UL 94 rating at 3.2 mm	UL 94 rating at 1.6 mm	UL 94 rating at 1.0 mm	UL 94 5VA rating 3.2 mm
Homo PP(MFI=12)	25	37.0	V-0	V-0	V-2	Fail
	30	42.7	V-0	V-0	V-2	Pass
	34	46.0	V-0	V-0	V-2	Pass
Homo PP(MFI= 2)	25	35.8	V-0	V-0	V-2	Fail
Homo PP(MFI=1.5)	25	35.4	V-0	V-2	V-2	Fail
Copo PP Block (MFI=15)						
	25	34.5	V-0	V-2		
	30	40.0	V-0	V-0		
Copo PP Block (MFI=3.5)						
	25	35.7	V-0	V-2	B	Fail
	30	39.0	V-0	V-0	V-2	Fail
	34	43.7	V-0	V-0	V-0	Pass
Copo PP Block (MFI=3.5) + Impact Modifier						
	25	31.3	V-0	V-2	V-2	
	30	34.3	V-0	V-0	V-0	
	34	37.7	V-0	V-0	V-0	Pass

Glass fiber reinforced polypropylene

Spinflam technology also performes very well in GFR polypropylene systems as previously reported (8), so that development projects are in progress in cooperation with different compounders/fabricators.

To successfully compound this type of materials an improved technology has been adopted. It is based on the use of a Montedison's proprietary coupling agent (chemically bond) for glass fibers, special twin-screw design to assure good Spinflam dispersion (and incresed FR effectiveness) without damaging glass fibers and a suitable temperature profile (max temperature: 250 °C) to increase extruder productivity and homogenization avoiding any thermal decomposition.

Composites so obtained can be injection molded or extruded to produce articles having good dimensional stability and thermal behaviour, useful as load-bearing structural parts in automotive, electrical, electronic, aerospace and domestic appliances applications, where metals are increasingly substituted by reinforced thermoplastics (12).

In TABLE 5 main properties are reported of a PP homopolymer composite containing 16% of glass fibers and 20% of Spinflam MF 82/PP which pocess good processing performance during compounding and molding.

TABLE 5

Properties of FR glass fiber reinforced PP

Property	Unit	Method	16% GFR-PP	16% GFR-PP with Spinflam
Specific gravity	g/cm^3	ASTM D 792	1.00	1.17
Vertical Burning Test at 1.7mm	-	UL 94	Burns	V-O
Vertical Burning Test at 3.2 mm	-	UL 94-5V	Fail	Pass
Tensile strength	MPa	ASTM D 638	65	65
Flex Elastic Modulus	MPa	ASTM D 790	3700	3900
Izod impact, notched	J/m	ASTM D 256	80	80
HDT, 1.8 MPa	°C	ASTM D 648	146	134
Vicat, 49 N	°C	ASTM D 1525	125	124

The interesting balance of properties is evident, including mechanical and thermo-mechanical characteristics as well as flammability performances which make this type of compounds very promising.

Crosslinkable PE

Halogen-free cables are increasingly requested in sectors such as military equipment, nuclear or electrical power plants and undergrounds, where there is necessity to limit, in case of fire, emission of acidic smokes, corrosive for costly and vital apparatus involved (13) and/or toxic for humans (14).

The solution to this problem is now found with inorganic fillers incorporated in different polymer matrices (LDPE, EVA, EPR, etc.).

However, as previously mentioned, the large loadings (about 60%) requested, while hardly be sufficient to pass fire standards imposed, reduce greatly workability and physical-mechanical properties of final items (15).

Now, Spinflam[(R)] flame retardants, which has been early reported as suitable halogen-free additives for thermoplastic LDPE and EVA (8), can represent an innovative alternative to obtaining halogen-free cable jacketings showing excellent processability as well as improved mechanical properties.

In TABLE 6 data are shown concerning an industrial development project of a crosslinkable LDPE compound for wire and cable jacketings in comparison with PVC and ATH-filled PE-based polymers.

The formulation used contains 40% of Spinflam MF-82/PE-1, which is a special grade studied to eliminate interferences of peroxides and carbon black normally used in this type of technology.

It is useful to note the interesting balance of the various properties which is very promising to develop fire safer and more easily processable cables. In fact, high conductivity value can not be considered, in our case, as a measure of corrosivity of the combustion-gases because they do not contain any corrosive acids.

Thermoplastic polyurethane

Spinflam technology, industrially applied to PU foams since some years, is useful also to flame retard TPU, which is increasingly used for sophisticated applications such as metal conduits and wire and cable coatings.

Lab results on flammability properties of a commercial TPU compounded with two different commercial Spinflam[(R)] flame retardants are shown in TABLE 7.

TABLE 6

Typical properties of compounds for cable jacketing

Property	XLPE Spinflam	XLPE ATH (16)	EVA ATH (17)	PVC (14)(16)
LOI, % (ASTM D 2863)	33	32	35	35
Temperature index, °C (NES 715)	270	255	270	260
Smoke index (NES 711)	23	14	<20	151
Smoke density (ASTM E 662)				
. flaming (D max)	150	158	50	750
. smoldering (D max)	70	80	n.a.	885
Toxicity index (NES 713)	5	2.2	<1	25
Acid gas evolution (VDE 0472/813)				
. pH	> 5.6	> 4	4.2	2.4
. conductivity, μS/cm	385	< 40	31	4500
Tensile strength, MPa (ASTM D 638)	10.2	10.5	13	12.5
Elongation, % (ASTM D 638)	600	160	180	125
Specific gravity, g/cm^3 ((ASTM D 792)	1.1	1.46	1.58	1.4

To the moment, Spinflam MF 80/TPU has found application in TPU for use as extrusion coating of flexible metal conduit by Anamet Inc. (Connecticut, USA), which has also filed data of the combustion toxicity to the Office of Fire Prevention and Control of New York State as requested by the local law (18).

TABLE 7

Flammabiity of TPU Estane 58315 with Spinflam flame retardants.

Type of Spinflam	Loading %	LOI, % (ASTM D 2863)	UL 94 rating at 1.6 mm
MF 80/TPU	30	26.0	V-0
MF 82/TPU	30	27.3	V-0

The relevant compound, designed J-Plast Halogen-free TPU, is produced by J. Von Inc., Mass. USA; reportedly it produces reduced levels of smoke and toxic emissions when burned, and produces excellent mechanical properties (TABLE 8).

TABLE 8

Properties of TPU compound containing Spinflam MF 80

Property	Unit	Method	Value
Specific gravity	g/cm^3	ASTM D792	1.09
Hardness, Shore A	-	ASTM D2240	90.0
Tensile strength	MPa	ASTM D638	7.0
Elongation	%	ASTM D638	>300
Flexural modulus	MPa	ASTM D790	175.0
Dielectric Constant at lKHz	-	ASTM D150	3.24
Dissipation factor at lKHz	-	ASTM D150	0.0656
Smoke density, flaming	-	ASTM E662	212
Smoke density, non-flaming	-	ASTM E662	177
LOI	%	ASTM D2863	30
Vertical flame test at 1.6 mm	Rating	UL 94	V-0

This material is also said to provide excellent oil, chemical and abrasion resistance, and can be easily processed by extrusion, injection and blow molding, to be used in applications in subways, shipping and in high-rise buildings.

CONCLUSIONS

1) Effective intumescent technology is now available as improved alternative to both halogenated and inorganic flame retardants.

2) Spinflam$^{(R)}$ technology shows interesting balance of properties and performances, particularly:
   . high FR-efficiency with non-dripping characteristics
   . low smoke
   . non-corrosive combustion-gas
   . environmentally safe

3) Spinflam$^{(R)}$ technology is easy to be industrially applied (processability) and shows great potential for a wide range of polymer matrices and commercial applications.

4) Specifying and regulatory bodies, which have greatest influence on determining performance criteria and, hence, market success of FR compounds, should review and re-evaluate existing fire testing standards and regulations, based on older FR additives, in light of the advances of fire safety technology.

   New and/or modified standards, balanced for physical/mechanical requirements and fire safety should be developed.

   Accordingly, industrial availability of intumescent technology should be carefully considered as capable of significant contribution to progress in fire safety of polymer materials.

REFERENCES

1. Cusack, P.A., Paper presented at "Dynamics of Current Developments in Fire Safety of Polymers", Grenelefe, Florida, 20-23 March, 1988.

2. Harmathy, T.Z., Fire Technology, 1983, 19, 31

3. Babrauskas, V. and other, Paper presented at "Dynamics of Current Developments in Fire Safety of Polymers", Grenelefe Florida, 20-23 March, 1988.

4. Kidder, R.C., Paper presented at "Fire Retardant Coatings and Technical Research Developments for Improved Fire Safety, Annapolis, Maryland, 2-5 October, 1988.

5. Mischutin, V., Specialty Chemicals, 1982, 2, 27.

6. Anon., Mod. Plast. Int., 1984, 15, 63.

7. Brown, S.G., Evans, K.A. and Godfrey, E.A., Paper presented at "Flame Retardants '87", London, 26-27 Novembre 1987.

8. Cicchetti O., Fontanelli, R. and Pagliari, A., Paper presented at "Flame Retardants '85", London, 28-29 November, 1985.

9. Keogh, M.J., Paper presented at "Dynamics of Current Developments in Fire Safety of Polymers", Grenelefe, Florida, 20-23 March, 1988.

10. Sutker, B.J., Flame Retardants in Ullman's Encyclopedia of Industrial Chemistry, Vol. All, p. 123.

11. MacLaury, M.R. and Schrol, A.L., J. Appl. Polym. Sci., 1985, 30, 461.

12. Theberge, J.E., Crosby, J.M. and Thalley, K.L., Plastics Engineering, 1988, August, 47.

13. Anon., Plastics and Rubber Weekly, 1987, October 24, 3.

14. Artingstall, S., Pyle, A.J. and Taylor, J.A., Wire Industry, 1988, April, 315.

15. Murfitt, P.S., Paper presented at "Flame Retardants '87", London 26-27 November, 1987.

16. Brown, M. and Vaidya, U.J., Rubber World, 1986, November, 21

17. Warding, G., AFICEP Regional Meeting, Lyon, November 1981.

18. New York State Uniform Fire Prevention and Building Code, Art. 15, Part 1120, Combustion Toxicity Testing, 1987.

NEW HORIZONS FOR SAYTEX® HBCD FLAME RETARDANT

B.M. VALANGE, S.E. CALEWARTS, G.A. BONNER
F.A. PETTIGREW and R.A. SCHLEIFSTEIN
Ethyl S.A. and Ethyl Corporation
P.O. Box 14799
Baton Rouge, LA 70808, USA

ABSTRACT

For a number of years, the primary application for hexabromocyclododecane (HBCD) was in expanded polystyrene. A small loading of this rather high bromine containing (74%) species and the absence of Sb_2O_3 characterized it usage. However, at this time market forces have dictated that HBCD applications expand into conventional injection molded grades of plastic as well. These applications have necessitated the use of HBCD with Sb_2O_3. Moreover, the use of HBCD in these applications involves subjecting the compound or concentrate to be subsequently diluted to additional thermal stresses, necessitating caution in its formulation.

This paper will deal with the following points:

- The isomeric nature of HBCD and the properties imparted by the isomeric make-up.
- The formulation of HBCD into UL-94 V-2 grade of impact polystyrene (HIPS).
- The inherent thermal instabilities of the above polymer containing HBCD. Problems that can occur with HBCD formulations.
- The development of stabilizer packages to address the various aspects of thermal and color degradation.

INTRODUCTION

For a number of years, the primary flame retardant application for hexabromocyclododecane (HBCD) was in expanded polystyrene. In this application, no synergist is used because none is needed. Likewise, stabilizers are not used since the use levels are typically low and any effect on polymer properties caused by the instability of HBCD is negligible. In contrast, more recent applications for this highly brominated compound necessitated the development of thermal stabilizers to protect polymer viscosity and color. In some applications, the use of antimony trioxide as a synergist has been deemed desirable, thus leading to further demands on stabilizer systems.

The nature of HBCD

HBCD is a white, crystalline solid that contains about 74 wt% bromine. It has a melting range that varies from 172-184°C for the low melting versions to 201-205°C for the highest melting version. The range of melting points is due to the fact that commercially available HBCD consists of a mixture of isomers. Although the structure of HBCD is commonly depicted as the cross-shaped planar structure shown in Figure 1, this is not representative of the actual structure.

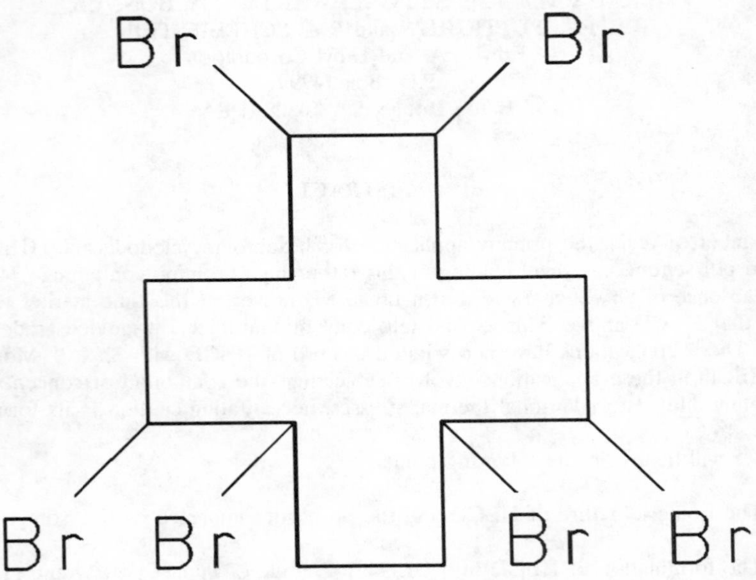

Figure 1. Simplified Cross Structure of HBCD

More correct structures of the three principal isomers are shown in Figure 2.

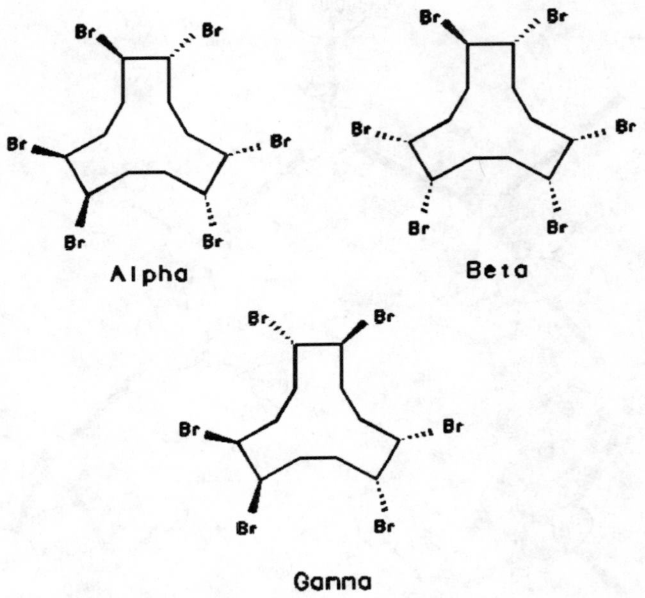

Br Br Br Br Br Br
Alpha

Br Br Br Br Br Br
Beta

Br Br Br Br Br Br
Gamma

Figure 2. HBCD Isomers

We had the structures of the alpha and gamma isomers determined by X-ray crystallography. They are far more complex than the structure shown in Figure 2.

The actual structure of the alpha isomer is shown in Figure 3.

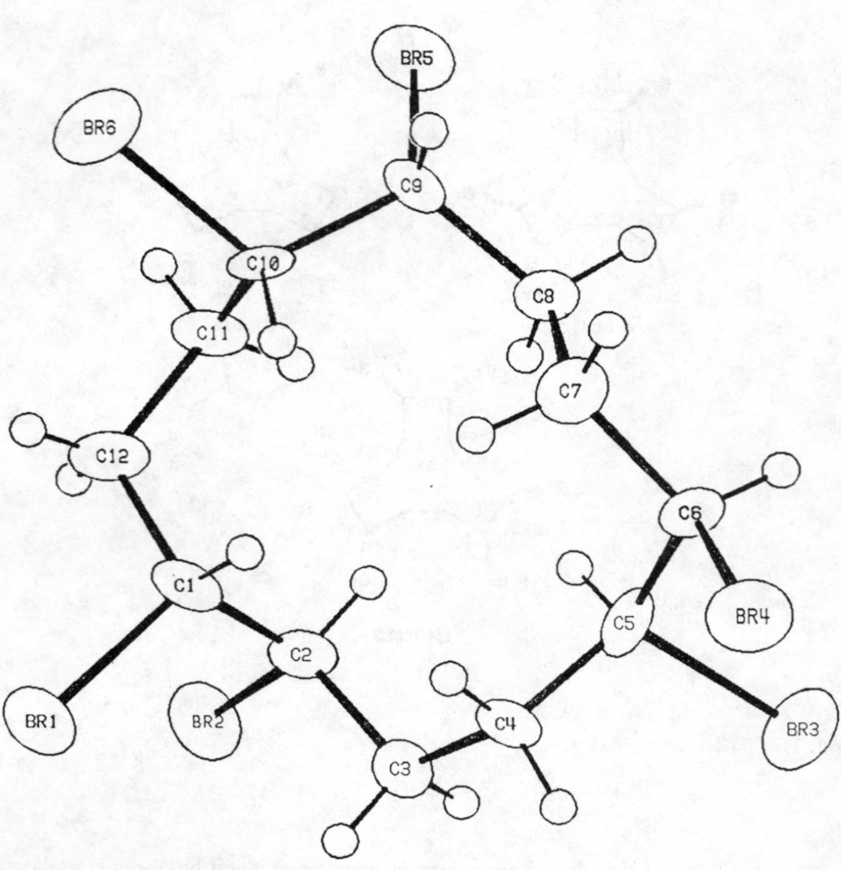

Figure 3. X-Ray Crystal Structure of Alpha HBCD

and that of the gamma isomer is shown in Figure 4.

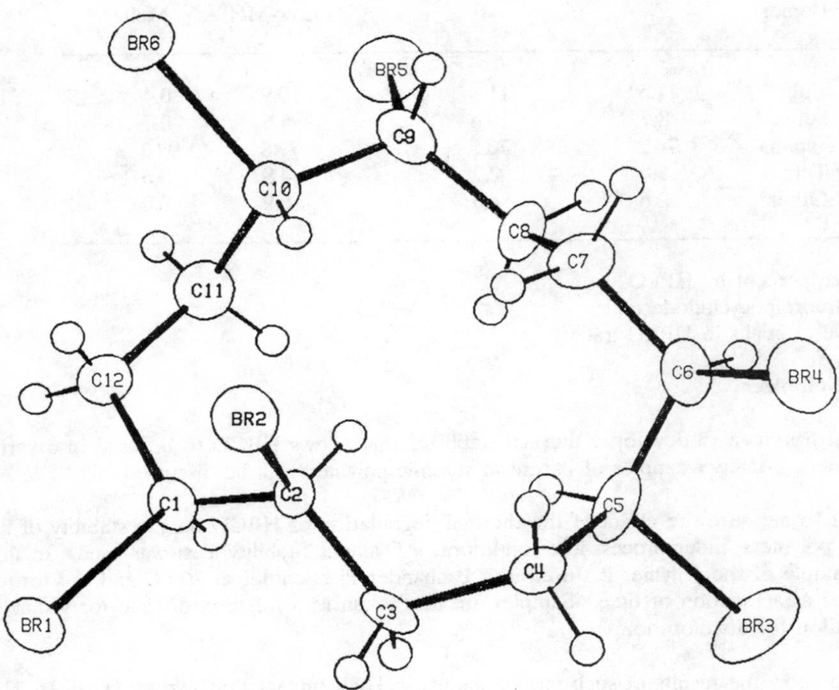

Figure 4. X-Ray Crystal Structure of Gamma HBCD

As mentioned above, the melting range observed for a particular sample of HBCD is determined by its isomeric composition. The readily available low-melt grades typically consist of 20-25% alpha and beta isomers and 70-75% gamma isomer. The highest melting HBCD products are essentially 98+% gamma isomer. Essentially all commercial HBCD products have some amount of tetrabromocyclododecene as an impurity. Low-melt versions often contain a few percent of unknown impurities. The isomeric distributions of some commercially available HBCD products are compared to that of a sample of high-melt HBCD in Table 1.

TABLE 1
Isomeric Composition of HBCD Samples

Isomer[1]	A	B	Ethyl Low-Melt	High-Melt
alpha	11.5	11.8	10.9	0.4
beta	8.7	10.4	5.6	0.7
gamma	74.2	70.5	77.8	98.3
Tetra[2]	3.0	2.7	4.8	0.6
Other[3]	2.6	4.6	0.9	0.0

1 = Area percent by HPLC
2 = Tetrabromocyclododecene
3 = Several peaks in HPLC trace

HBCD Stabilizer

Our goal has been to develop a thermal stabilizer that allows HBCD to be used in a variety of polymers. A few examples of its use in styrenic polymers will be discussed.

In order to measure the effect of the thermal degradation of HBCD on the stability of styrenic polymers under process-like conditions, a Dynamic Stability Test was used. In this test a sample of the polymer is fluxed in a Brabander Plasticorder at 200°C and the torque is measured as a function of time. Samples are also taken as a function of time for visual examination for discoloration.

Figure 5 show the results of such measurements in High Impact PolyStyrene (HIPS). The data is for a formulation containing 7% low-melt HBCD, which gives a UL-94 V-2 rating. The neat resin is included for reference. In the absence of any stabilizer, loss of viscosity due to degradation of the HBCD is quite severe. Our former stabilizer gives a dramatic improvement. However, our new stabilizer gives even further improvement. Note especially the leveling effect seen with the new package. The torque is virtually constant after the five minute reading.

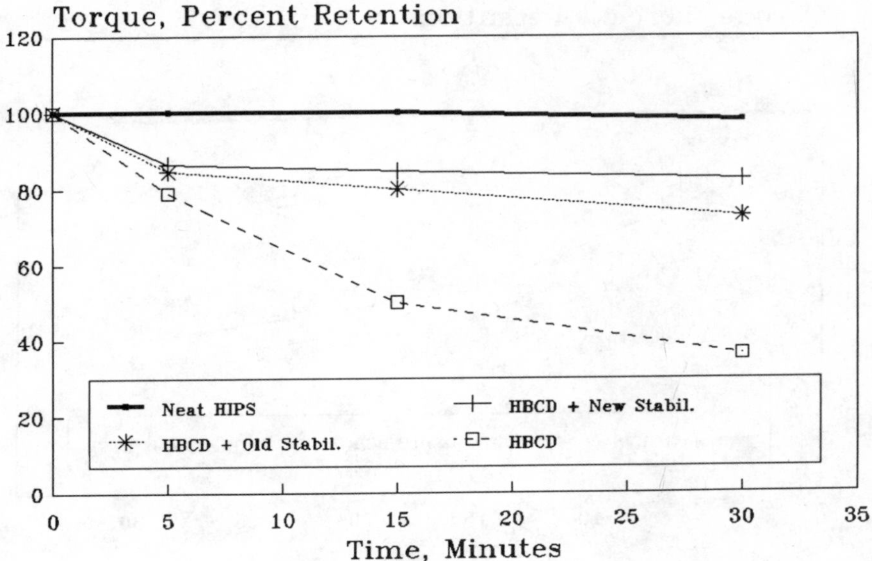

Figure 5. 7% Low-Melt HBCD in V-2 HIPS

Conventional wisdom taught that high-melt HBCD is more thermally stable than low-melt HBCD in various formulations. Figure 6 shows the results of a comparison of the two HIPS under the Dynamic Stability Test conditions. Here we see the torque curve for the neat resin compared to the resin with 7 wt% low-melt and high-melt HBCD added. Again, this formulation gives a UL-94 V-2 rating. Note that the stability of the low-melt HBCD to thermal degradation under these conditions is at least equivalent to that of the high-melt material. From this it can be concluded that for applications in HIPS there is no advantage to the high-melt version, contrary to conventional wisdom. The slight difference in viscosity between the two HBCD samples may be due to differences in the inherent plasticizing ability of the HBCD compositions and not to a difference in thermal stability. The fact that the distance between the two curves is constant from 5 to 30 minutes supports this conclusion.

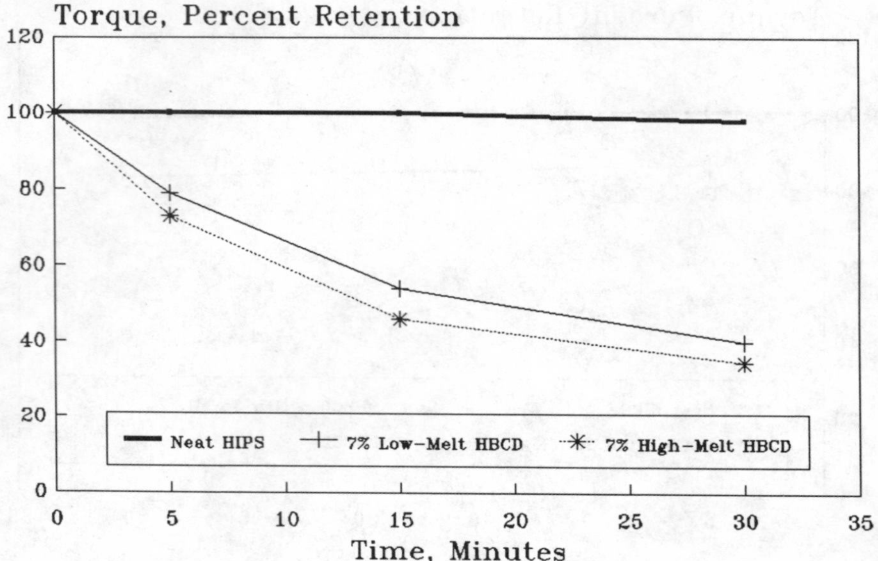

Figure 6. Unstabilized HBCD in V-2 HIPS

Figure 7 shows the effect of the stabilizer on these same low-melt and high-melt HBCD products in V-2 HIPS formulations. As before, in V-2 HIPS we see no obvious advantage to the high-melt HBCD under our laboratory test conditions.

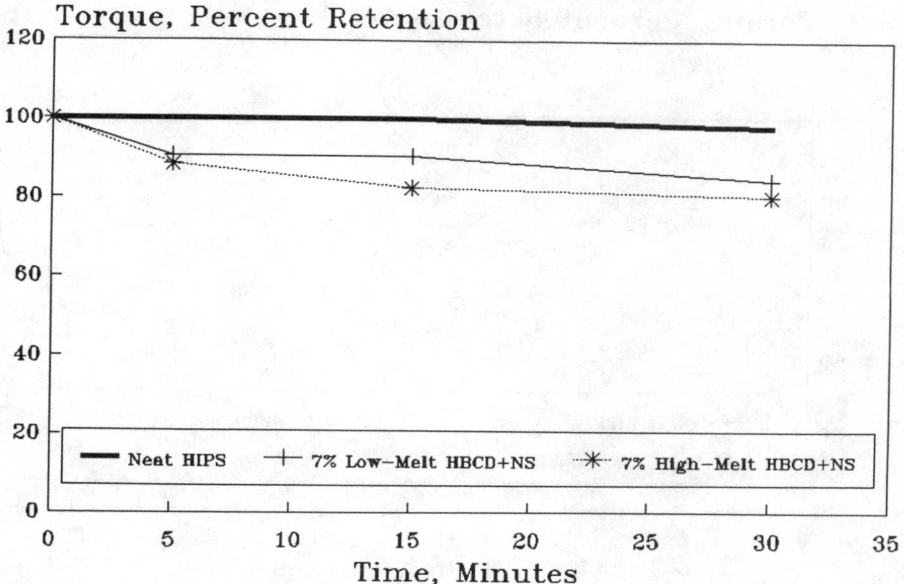

NS = New Stabilizer

Figure 7. Stabilized HBCD in V-2 HIPS

Stabilizer with Antimony Oxide

Conventional wisdom also taught that antimony oxide promotes the degradation of HBCD or other aliphatic bromine flame retardants, and we have found this to be true. Interestingly, this is not always evidenced by loss of viscosity.

In Figure 8 a 7% low-melt HBCD formulation was used as the control and a 4/1 HBCD/Sb_2O_3 formulation was evaluated with and without our new stabilizer.

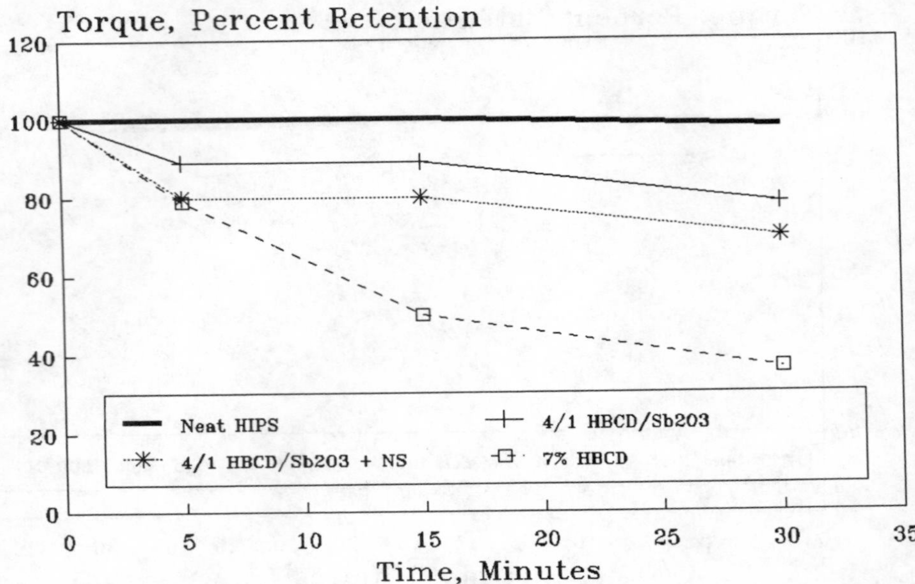

NS = **New Stabilizer**

Figure 8. Low-Melt HBCD in V-2 HIPS

All three of these formulations give UL-94 V-2 ratings. In this case, the deleterious effect of the antimony oxide is seen in the color of the HIPS. The HBCD/Sb_2O_3 combination, in the absence of the stabilizer, causes the HIPS to turn dark brown, whereas little or no change in color is observed in the presence of the new stabilizer. Note that the 4/1 HBCD/Sb_2O_3 formulation appears to be more stable that the 7% HBCD formulation by viscosity measurement alone. Comparing the two HBCD/Sb_2O_3 runs in Figure 8, one can see that the viscosity decrease is slightly greater with the new stabilizer than without. This may indicate that this particular stabilizer is not optimum for this particular grade of HIPS. Nevertheless, it is very apparent that the new stabilizer does prevent visual degradation, that is, a darkening of the resin.

A different effect was seen in the use of HBCD in General Purpose PolyStyrene (GPPS), where a 3/1HBCD/Sb_2O_3 or 5% HBCD formulation is sufficient to give a V-2 rating. Figure 9 shows the dramatic effect that the antimony oxide has on the melt viscosity compared to the 5% HBCD loading used as the control.

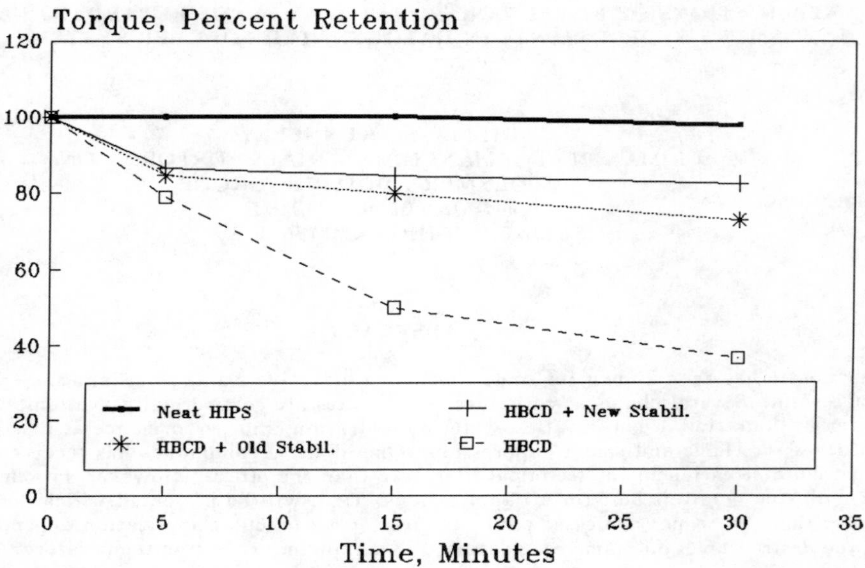

Figure 9. Low-Melt HBCD in V-2 GPPS

The addition of the new stabilizer virtually eliminates the loss in viscosity and again a leveling effect is observed. As before, less color degradation is observed in the presence of the new stabilizer. The improvement is less dramatic than in the case of antimony oxide in HIPS since the antimony oxide does not badly discolor the GPPS.

Conclusions

Our new stabilizer definitely helps maintain resin viscosity and color in our Dynamic Stability Test that simulates processing conditions. The method at present does not allow quantification of color degradation, only subjective observation. Ultimately, the new stabilizer will be evaluated under more realistic process conditions.

APPLICATIONS OF NOVEL ZINC BORATES AS FLAME RETARDANTS AND SMOKE SUPPRESSANTS IN HALOGENATED POLYMER SYSTEMS

WILLIAM J. KENNELLY
CLIMAX PERFORMANCE MATERIALS CORPORATION
POLYMER ADDITIVES GROUP
447 MARLPOOL DRIVE
SALINE, MICHIGAN 48176, U.S.A.

ABSTRACT

Zinc borate has been known for some time as an effective flame retardant and smoke suppressant. Several chemically distinct zinc borates are commercially available which differ in their zinc to boron ratios, water of hydration, and performance as plastics additives for flame and smoke suppression. One of these compounds has received much more attention in the technical literature than the others. However, no one form of zinc borate is best for all applications. Data will be presented which demonstrates that the proper choice of a zinc borate for a particular application depends on the desired level on flame retardation, the maximum processing temperature, and the particular resin selected. Results of rate of heat release calorimeter studies and other standard fire tests will be presented for poly(vinylchloride) and halogenated polyester resins.

INTRODUCTION

Zinc borates have been recognised as effective flame retardants for many years. These materials have been shown to be additives in both halogenated and non-halogenated polymer systems and are currently used in many applications in the plastics industry.

There are twenty-five different zinc borates listed in the Chemical Abstracts Registry, differing in their zinc to boron ratios, the amount of water of hydration, their crystal structure, particle size and range, and their chemical and physical properties. Many of these materials are available commercially and are sold for use as flame retardants in a variety of polymeric and coatings applications.

One major difference between various forms of zinc borate is the amount of water of hydration and the temperature at which it is lost. Zinc borates with the same zinc to boron ratio can have different numbers of waters of hydration and chemically bound more or less tightly depending on the crystal structure of the compound.

For applications in plastics compounding it is generally desireable to select a zinc borate which does not lose its water of hydration under normal thermal processing conditions. The relative advantages and disadvantages of two such thermally stable zinc borate hydrates are detailed here. These materials are ZB-223 ($2ZnO{\cdot}2B_2O_3{\cdot}3H_20$) and ZB-467 ($4ZnO{\cdot}6B_2O_3{\cdot}7H_20$). Applications are discussed in a number of plasticised PVC systems and in thermoset polyester resins.

EXPERIMENTAL

The zinc borates used were Climax Zinc Borate ZB-223 and Climax Zinc Borate ZB-467. Other materials were standard grades of commercially available products used without further treatment.

The PVC samples were prepared on a heated 2 roll mill and then pressed to the desired thickness in a heated press. The standard test methods used for flammability were the Limiting Oxygen Index (L.O.I.) method (ASTM D-2863) and Underwriters Laboratory vertical burn test (UL-94). Smoke formation was measured using the Arapahoe smoke chamber (ASTM D-4100) and the NBS smoke chamber (ASTM E-662) in both flaming and smoldering modes. Arapahoe test results are reported without decharring the burned test sample. This will result in higher levels of smoke reported for char forming additives (like zinc borate) than if the sample had been decharred. The Ohio State University Rate of Heat Release Calorimeter (ASTM E-906) was also used to measure rate of heat release and smoke.

Thermal gravimetric analysis used an ASI TGA. The TGA's were run at heating rates of 5°C/min. Thermal stabilities of PVC formulations were measured by placing 1 inch square plaques in an isothermal oven and removing them at 15-minute intervals. The time to the first formation of black marks was recorded.

NBS smoke chamber and OSU RHR tests were performed by contract laboratories. All other tests were performed at the AMAX R&D Center, Golden, Colorado.

Representative formulations were used to evaluate the performance of zinc borate. The flexible PVC wire insulation formulation consisted of: 100 parts Geon 103EP F76 PVC resin, 30 phr DIDP, 7 phr tribase, 0.4 phr DS-207, 0.4 phr Acrowax C, plus varying amounts of Sb_2O_3 and zinc borate. The ATH filled PVC cable jacket formulation consisted of: 100 parts Geon 103EP F76 PVC resin, 40 phr Santicizer 711 alkyl phthalate plasticiser, 15 phr Hydral 710 alumina trihydrate, 5 phr tribase lead stabiliser, 0.5 phr Bareco 500 wax, plus varying amounts of Sb_2O_3 and zinc borate. The PVC plastisol formulation tested consisted of: 100 parts Geon 121 PVC resin, 50 phr DOP, 5 phr Paraplex G-62 epoxidized soya oil, 3 phr Mark 2077 Ba-Cd-Zn stabiliser, plus varying amounts of Sb_2O_3 and zinc borate.

Thermoset polyester samples were prepared with 25% chopped strand fiberglass mat (1.5 oz/ft^2). Samples were catalyzed with 1% Lupersol DDM, MEK peroxide, based on resin weight. Resins studied included Hetron 92 AT (a chlorinated resin from Ashland Chemical), Dion 6692T (a brominated resin from Reichhold Chemical), Atlac 711-05A (a brominated resin from ICI Americas), and 2160-2 (a general purpose resin from Reichhold Chemical).

RESULTS AND DISCUSSION

Zinc Borate ZB-223 and ZB-467 both retain their water of hydration at normal PVC process temperatures. A comparison of the TGA showing water loss for ZB-223 and ZB-467 is presented in Table 1.

TABLE 1
TGA of Zinc Borates.

	ZB-223	ZB-467
1% wt loss	200°C	280°C
5% wt loss	245°C	380°C
10% wt loss	285°C	420°C
Total water	15.2%	14.5%

As can be seen from this data either compound would be suitable, in terms of water loss, for incorporation into flexible PVC.

Rigid PVC generally does not need the addition of a flame retardant because of its inherent non-flammability. If a rigid formulation were to require the incorporation of zinc borate the higher water retention temperatures of ZB-467 may be a factor in flame retardant selection, but as will be shown, other characteristics of the two products can influence the choice.

The results of flammability tests on two different flexible PVC formulations are given in Tables 2 and 3. As can be seen by this data, both ZB-223 and ZB-467 give comparable results in increasing the degree of flame retardancy as measured by the oxygen index. The use of antimony trioxide with the zinc borate does give higher oxygen indices than the use of zinc borate alone, but zinc borate can be used by itself to raise the L.O.I. in those cases where the use of antimony is undesirable.

Tables 2 and 3 also give the thermal stability times for the formulations which were tested. Although there is a trend to higher stability for ZB-467 over ZB-223 the thermal stability of both of these products is sufficiently high to avoid any processing problems in most applications.

TABLE 2
Flammability Properties of Flexible PVC Wire Insulation with Zinc Borates[1]

Additive	Oxygen Index	UL-94 Vertical Test Rating	UL-94 Vertical Afterflame Time, Seconds[2]	ASTM E-906[3]	Heat Stability Time in Minutes at: 185°C	Heat Stability Time in Minutes at: 200°C
0.5 phr Sb_2O_3	31.0	V-0	6		>180	180
1 phr Sb_2O_3	31.5	V-0	0		>180	>180
2 phr Sb_2O_3	32.5	V-0	0		>180	>180
2 phr ZB-223	31.5	V-0	13	90.9	>150	20
2 phr ZB-467	31.0	V-0	11	95.5	>180	45
1 phr Sb_2O_3 Plus						
1 phr ZB-223	35.0	V-0	5	73.3	150	45
1 phr ZB-467	33.0	V-0	2	78.4	>180	75
2 phr ZB-223	34.5	V-0	0	74.2	135	40
2 phr ZB-467	34.5	V-0	0	79.0	>180	75
0.5 phr Sb_2O_3 Plus						
2 phr ZB-223	32.5	V-0	4		150	40
2 phr ZB-467	33.0	V-0	8		>180	60

[1]Samples were tested at a thickness of 75 mils.
[2]Total afterflame time for 10 ignitions.
[3]Maximum heat release at 20 kW/m^2.

TABLE 3
Flammability Properties of Alumina Trihydrate
Filled PVC Cable Jacket Containing Zinc Borate[4]

Additive	Oxygen Index	UL-94 Vertical: Test Rating	UL-94 Vertical: Afterflame Time, Seconds[5]	ASTM E-906[6]	Heat Stability Time in Minutes at: 185°C	Heat Stability Time in Minutes at: 200°C
No Additives	24.5	Fail	>250	114.4	>180	>180
1.5 phr Sb_2O_3	28.5	V-0	1	79.9	>180	>180
3 phr Sb_2O_3	31.0	V-0	0		>180	>180
3 phr ZB-223	30.0	V-0	10	97.9	45	< 15
3 phr ZB-467	29.0	V-0	24	110.9	120	< 30
1.5 phr Sb_2O_3 Plus 1.5 phr ZB-223	32.0	V-0	0	79.1	75	< 15
1.5 phr Sb_2O_3 Plus 1.5 phr ZB-467	31.0	V-0	3	85.5	180	45
1 phr Sb_2O_3 Plus 2 phr ZB-223	32.5	V-0	3		60	< 15
1 phr Sb_2O_3 Plus 2 phr ZB-467	32.0	V-0	3		120	20

Tables 4 and 5 show the smoke properties for these same formulations which were presented in tables 2 and 3. This data shows that although both ZB-467 and ZB-223 act as smoke suppressants, ZB-223 is clearly the more effective additive. ZB-223 consistently gives lower smoke values than the corresponding ZB-467 formulation by both the Arapahoe and NBS test methods. In the ATH filled cable jacket the use of as little as 3 phr of ZB-223 reduced the NBS SMOKE level from 935 to 201 in the flaming mode.

[4]Tested at a thickness of 75 mils (1.9 mm).
[5]Total afterflame time for 10 ignitions.
[6]Maximum heat release at 20 kW/m^2.

TABLE 4
Smoke Properties of Flexible PVC Insulation with Zinc Borates[7]

Additive	Arapahoe Smoke Data, % Smoke[8]	NBS Smoke Chamber Data Flaming Dmc[9]	NBS Smoke Chamber Data Smoldering Dmc	ASTM E-906 Total SMOKE at 20 kW/m^2
1 phr Sb_2O_3	13.9	522	427	
2 phr Sb_2O_3	16.2	696	426	
2 phr ZB-223	8.0 (51)	244 (65)	270 (37)	479.4
2 phr ZB-467	9.3 (43)	322 (54)	317 (26)	516.5
1 phr Sb_2O_3 Plus				
1 phr ZB-223	9.5 (41)	411 (41)	322 (22)	397.5
1 phr ZB-467	11.2 (31)	495 (29)	339 (20)	423.0
2 phr ZB-223	9.6 (41)	324 (53)	281 (34)	280.0
2 phr ZB-467	10.8 (33)	432 (38)	298 (30)	323.2

TABLE 5
Smoke Properties of Alumina Trihydrate Filled PVC Cable Jacket Containing Zinc Borate[10]

Additive	Arapahoe Smoke Data, % Smoke[11]	NBS Smoke Chamber Data Flaming Dmc	NBS Smoke Chamber Data Smoldering Dmc	ASTM E-906 Total SMOKE at 20 kW/m^2
No Additives	12.4	935	309	540.8
1.5 phr Sb_2O_3	11.1	407	284	417.2
3 phr Sb_2O_3	11.3	536	284	
3 phr ZB-223	5.6 (50)	201 (63)	197 (31)	398.9
3 phr ZB-467	7.5 (33)	253 (53)	215 (24)	412.8
1.5 phr Sb_2O_3 Plus				
1.5 phr ZB-223	7.5 (34)	277 (48)	223 (21)	323.1
1.5 phr ZB-467	9.7 (14)	316 (41)	223 (21)	387.0

---

[7]Samples were tested at a thickness of 75 mils (1.9 mm), except for the NBS smoke samples which were tested at a thickness of 40 mils (1.0 mm).
[8]Numbers in parentheses are percent change in smoke compared to the value for 2 phr Sb_2O_3 control formulation.
[9]Dmc is the corrected maximum smoke density.
[10]Samples were tested at a thickness of 75 mils (1.9 mm), except for the NBS smoke samples which were tested at a thickness of 40 mils (1.0 mm).
[11]Numbers in parentheses are percent change in smoke compared to the value for 3 phr Sb_2O_3 control formulation.

Tables 6 and 7 present data on the use of ZB-223 to reduce flammability and smoke in a PVC plastisol. These tables show that the same trends which held in the flexible formulations also apply to the plastisol. That is zinc borate will help reduce the flammability of the plastisol relative to the non-flame retarded formulation and replacement of some antimony with zinc borate reduces smoke relative to the formulation with antimony as the sole flame-retardant synergist. The formulation with 5 phr antimony trioxide and 5 phr ZB-223 has the same L.O.I. as the antimony only formulation (at 10 phr), but the smoke is reduced by 24% in the flaming mode and 55% in the smoldering mode of the NBS test.

TABLE 6

Flammability Properties of 50 phr DOP Plastisol Containing Zinc Borate ZB-223[12]

Additive	Oxygen Index	UL-94 Vertical Test Rating	UL-94 Vertical Afterflame Time, Seconds[13]	ASTM E-906[14]
No Additives	24.5	Fail	>250	159.7
5 phr Sb_2O_3	31.0	V-0	0	115.7
10 phr Sb_2O_3	31.5	V-0	0	109.9
2.5 phr Sb_2O_3 + 2.5 phr ZB-223	28.5	V-0	8	105.8
5 phr Sb_2O_3 + 5 phr ZB-223	31.5	V-0	0	99.0

TABLE 7

Smoke Properties of 50 phr DOP Plastisol Containing Zinc Borate ZB-223[15]

Additive	Arapahoe Smoke Data, % Smoke[16]	NBS Smoke Chamber Data Flaming Dmc[9]	NBS Smoke Chamber Data Smoldering Dmc	ASTM E-906 Total SMOKE at 20 kW/m^2
No Additives	12.4	308	324	1147.8
5 phr Sb_2O_3	15.1	326	294	983.1
10 phr Sb_2O_3	14.2	307	333	924.4
2.5 phr Sb_2O_3 + 2.5 phr ZB-223	10.1 (33)	234 (28)	249 (15)	835.9
5 phr Sb_2O_3 + 5 phr ZB-223	9.6 (32)	234 (24)	149 (55)	767.7

[12]Samples were tested at a thickness of 125 mils (3.2 mm).

[13]Total afterflame time for 10 ignitions.

[14]Maximum heat release at 20 kW/m^2.

[15]Samples were tested at 125 mils (3.2 mm) in the Arapahoe test and 25 mil (0.6 mm) in the NBS Smoke Chamber.

[16]Numbers in parentheses are percent change in smoke relative to the Sb_2O_3 control with the same total FR/SS loading.

Table 8 gives data on the amount of char formation as measured by decharring samples which were tested in the Arapahoe smoke chamber. This data clearly shows that both ZB-223 and ZB-467 promote char formation relative to a formulation containing antimony trioxide alone. The data also shows that ZB-223 is a slightly better char former than ZB-467. Char formation may be a contributing factor in the mechanism by which zinc borate helps reduce flammability and smoke formation.

TABLE 8
Char Formation of Flexible PVC Insulation Samples With Zinc Borates[17]

Additive	Oxygen Index	Arapahoe Chamber Data[18] Percent Smoke Original	De-charred	% Char Formed
2 phr Sb_2O_3	32.5	16.2	13.3	14.3
4 phr ZB-223	31.5	8.0 (51)	5.1 (62)	30.3
4 phr ZB-467	32.5	9.8 (40)	9.1 (32)	25.8
0.5 phr Sb_2O_3 plus:				
2 phr ZB-223	32.5	9.0 (44)	6.2 (53)	26.1
2 phr ZB-467	33.0	11.0 (32)	8.2 (38)	21.1

The effectiveness of zinc borate in a thermoset polyester is very much dependent on the properties of the particular resin with which it is used. Tables 9, 10, and 11 show the flame and smoke test results with zinc borate ZB-223 and ZB-467 in chlorinated, brominated, and non-halogenated resins respectively. In all of the resins evaluated both of these zinc borates behaved similarly. Halogenated formulations containing zinc borate in place of antimony oxide showed a reduction in smoke at the expense of a slight decrease in oxygen index. In the general purpose resin a multi-component FR system containing zinc borate, ATH, and Phoschek P30 had to be used to achieve a good level of flame retardance, but this combination did achieve low flammability, low smoke test results in a non-halogenated formulation.

[17]Samples tested at a thickness of 75 mils.

[18]Numbers in parentheses are percent change in smoke compared to the value for the relevant control formulation. After weighing the burned sample, char was removed from the sample by rubbing with a paper towel. The sample was reweighed to obtain the percent de-charred smoke and percent char values.

TABLE 9
Effect of Zinc Borate in a Chlorinated Resin

Additive[19]	Oxygen Index	UL-94 Rating	Arapahoe Test %Smoke
Hetron 92 AT Resin			
No additives	32.0	V-0	13.0
1.2% Sb_2O_3	42.0	V-0	15.0
2.4% Sb_2O_3	45.0	V-0	13.4
4.8% Sb_2O_3	45.0	V-0	13.7
4.8% ZB-223	36.0	V-0	12.1
4.8% ZB-467	36.0	V-0	12.0
1.2% Sb_2O_3 + 1.2% ZB-223	43.0	V-0	12.4
1.2% Sb_2O_3 + 1.2% ZB-467	42.0	V-0	12.9

[19]Percent additive by weight excluding the glass fibers.

TABLE 10
Effect of Zinc Borate in a Brominated Resin

Additive[20]	Oxygen Index	UL-94 Rating	Arapahoe Test %Smoke
Dion 6692T Resin			
No additives	28.5	V-0	11.5
1.5% Sb_2O_3	37.0	V-0	15.8
2.9% Sb_2O_3	41.0	V-0	16.7
2.9% ZB-223	35.5	V-0	11.2
2.9% ZB-467	35.5	V-0	11.8
1% Sb_2O_3 + 1.9% ZB-223	38.5	V-0	14.6
1% Sb_2O_3 + 1.9% ZB-467	39.0	V-0	15.0
Atlac 711-05A Resin			
No additives	27.0	Fail	20.1
2.4% Sb_2O_3	31.0	V-0	24.7
4.8% Sb_2O_3	33.5	V-0	24.5
2.4% Sb_2O_3 + 2.4% ZB-223	31.0	V-1	23.0
2.4% Sb_2O_3 + 2.4% ZB-467	34.0	V-0	22.7

[20]Percent additive by weight excluding the glass fibers.

TABLE 11
Effect of Zinc Borate in a General Purpose Resin

Additive[21]	Oxygen Index	UL-94 Rating	Arapahoe Test %Smoke
Dion 6692T Resin			
40% ATH	25.0	Fail	1.8
50% ATH	29.0	V-1	0.9
30% ATH + 10% ZB-223	25.5	Fail	2.6
30% ATH + 10% ZB-467	24.5	Fail	3.9
40% ATH + 10% ZB-223	27.5	Fail	1.2
40% ATH + 10% ZB-467	28.0	Fail	1.3
30% ATH + 10% Phos-chek P-30	27.5	V-0	6.5
30% ATH + 10% Phos-chek P-30 + 10% ZB-467	31.0	V-0	4.7

CONCLUSIONS

Zinc borates are effective additives for reducing flammability and smoke formation in flexible PVC formulations. Various zinc borates behave slightly differently in their contributions to the properties of the polymer formulation. Although ZB-223 and ZB-467 both contribute to flame and smoke suppression, they do not behave identically. The proper selection of a zinc borate for a given application will depend on the relative importance of smoke reduction in the end product and the processing conditions used in thermoforming the plastic. Applications in which reducing the smoke formation is critical should consider the use of ZB-223. Applications with unusually high processing temperatures or unusually long processing time may require ZB-467.

In thermoset polyester formulations zinc borate is a modest flame retardant. The use of zinc borate will generally improve the oxygen index of a formulation, but not as much as the equivalent amount of antimony oxide. Unlike the PVC case, zinc borate does not have a strong influence on the amount of smoke generated by a polyester, but it does not have the negative influence on smoke that antimony oxide has.

The actual performance of zinc borates will vary from one formulation to another. Best results will be obtained by evaluating both zinc borates separately in the specific formulation of interest.

---

[21] Percent additive by weight excluding the glass fibers.

RECENT ADVANCES IN FLAME RETARDING ABS, HIPS, NYLON AND EPOXIES

R. L. Markezich, C. S. Ilardo and R. F. Mundhenke
Occidental Chemical Corporation
Technology Center
Grand Island, New York 14072

ABSTRACT

Dechlorane Plus®, the Diels-Alder diadduct of hexachlorocyclopentadiene and 1,5-cyclooctadiene has been used for years as a flame retardant in various polymers.

This paper discusses the recent results of Dechlorane Plus in the following areas:

1. The use of non-antimony oxide synergists in FR-nylon. With Dechlorane Plus in nylon 66 and 6, other synergists such as zinc oxide, zinc borate and iron oxides can be used to give flame retardancy. With the brominated flame retardants, only antimony oxide works as a synergist to give flame retardancy.

2. Mixed synergist systems that lower the level of flame retardants needed in flame retarded nylons.

3. New flame retarded epoxy resin formulations. The use of alternate synergists can also be used in epoxies to give flame retardancy.

4. New FR-ABS and FR-HIPS formulations that have improved UV stability, an increase in heat distortion temperature, excellent thermal stability, and are non-blooming.

INTRODUCTION

The synergistic action between antimony oxide and halogenated organic compounds to impart flame retardancy to plastics is well known.[1,2] Today, many highly efficient antimony oxide/halogenated additive systems are used to give flame retardant properties to a wide variety of polymers. Other complete or partial substitutes for antimony oxide in certain polymers have been reported. They are ferric oxide, zinc oxide and zinc borate.

Ferric Oxide or Zinc Oxide. In 30% glass-reinforced nylon 66, Dechlorane Plus flame retardant additive, with ferric oxide or zinc oxide as a synergist, gives a flame retarded material.[3] The flammability requirement met is V-O as measured by the UL-94 test procedure.

Zinc Borate. Zinc borate, in combination with antimony oxide and Dechlorane Plus, has been reported to impart flame retardancy to plastics.[4] An ICI patent discusses the use of zinc borate in combination with antimony oxide and Dechlorane Plus to give a non-burning 30% glass-reinforced nylon 66.[5] The level of zinc borate used was 15% with only 1 to 4% antimony oxide. Rhone-Poulenc has a patent in several European countries on the use of zinc borate/antimony oxide with Dechlorane Plus to produce a flame retarded nylon 66.[6]

The effectiveness of various synergists and synergist combinations with Dechlorane Plus has been discussed at three recent ANTEC Meetings[7,8,9] and at an FRCA Meeting.[10]

MATERIALS AND PROCEDURES

The additives used and their sources:

Diels-Alder adduct of hexachlorocyclopentadiene and 1,5-cyclooctadiene	Dechlorane Plus®	Occidental Chemical
Antimony Trioxide	Thermoguard® S	M&T Chemical
Zinc Oxide	Kadox 15	New Jersey Zinc
Zinc Borate	Firebrake® ZB	U. S. Borax
Ferric Oxide (Fe_2O_3)		J. T. Baker
Iron Oxide-Black (Fe_3O_4)	Akrochem® E-8846	Akron Chemical
Iron Oxide-Yellow ($Fe_2O_3.H_2O$)	YLO-2288D	Pfizer

DATA AND RESULTS

In nylon 66, ferric oxide is the most effective synergist (Table I). It gives a UL-94 material down to 1.6 mm thickness with only a 12% loading of Dechlorane Plus and 3% ferric oxide. This compares to 18% flame retardant and 9% of the other synergists: antimony trioxide, zinc oxide or zinc borate. Zinc borate seems slightly better than either antimony trioxide or zinc borate as the synergist. The zinc oxide formulation gives a CTI of 600 volt, while the zinc borate only gives a 325 CTI (Comparative Tracking Index).

Table 2 gives FR-nylon 66 formulations that are V-O down to 0.4 mm thickness. By using a mixture of zinc borate and antimony trioxide with Dechlorane Plus, a UL-94 V-O is achieved with just a 22% FR system loading. Ferric oxide in combination with zinc borate is the most effective synergist. It gives a V-O material with an FR system loading of only 15%.

The zinc borate/antimony trioxide combination also gives a material with a CTI of 450 volts.

Table 3 compares the efficiency of the two zinc compounds, zinc borate and zinc oxide, in nylon 66 with Dechlorane Plus. The zinc borate gives a UL-94 material down to 0.4 mm while the zinc oxide only gives a V-O down to 1.6 mm. The FR system loading level in each case consists of 10% zinc compound and 20% Dechlorane Plus. The zinc oxide synergist gives a material with a CTI of 600 volts.

Different iron oxides are available as the synergist with Dechlorane Plus in nylon 66. In Table 4 we give the results of the evaluation of various iron oxides to give UL-94 V-O materials. By using one of the various iron oxides, one can achieve both color and flame retardancy in a very cost-effective system.

The UV stability of Dechlorane Plus is greater than the brominated flame retardants (Table 5). After one week exposure in an Atlas Weather-O-Meter, the FR nylons using the chlorinated flame retardant only showed a change of 0.7 to 1.2 in the yellowness index. The nylon using the brominated material as the flame retardant showed a change of 30 in the yellowness index.

Table 6 gives the FR system loading levels necessary to achieve a UL-94 V-O at 0.4 mm in glass-reinforced nylon 66.

The most effective single synergist is iron oxide; only 3% with 12% Dechlorane Plus gives a V-O material.

Zinc synergists may also be used with Dechlorane Plus in glass-reinforced nylon 66 (Table 7). The best results obtained was a V-1 at 0.8 mm, but the CTI values was only 375 V.

In nylon 6, zinc borate is not an effective enough synergist with Dechlorane Plus to achieve any level of flame retardance (Table 8). But the combination of antimony trioxide with zinc borate gives UL-94 materials to 1.6 mm. In the case of nylon 66, a V-O material is achieved with an 18% FR system loading, but with nylon 6, an FR system loading of 24% is needed.

Also in nylon, ferric oxide is the most effective single

synergist, giving a UL-94 V-O down to 1.6 mm with 20% Dechlorane Plus and 5% ferric oxide (Table 9). A V-O at 0.4 mm can be achieved in nylon 6 by using 5% antimony trioxide with 5% of any of the iron compounds and 20% Dechlorane Plus. As in the case of nylon 66, all Dechlorane Plus/nylon 6 formulations are non-dripping.

Table 10 gives the results of 25% glass-reinforced nylon 6 using Dechlorane Plus and various synergists. A UL-94 at 1.6 mm can be obtained, depending on formulation.

Besides antimony trioxide, zinc borate or ferric oxide can also be used as a synergist with Dechlorane Plus to flame retard epoxy resins as shown in Table 11.

ABS

Brominated flame retardants have been used for years to impart flame retardancy to ABS. Decabromodiphenyl oxide (DBDPO) and octabromodiphenyl oxide (OBDPO), in combination with antimony oxide, are two of the flame retardants used in FR-ABS. They perform satisfactorily but their use may result in poor UV stability, surface blooming, and a drop in heat distortion temperature.

We have now developed flame retardant formulations for ABS using Dechlorane Plus 35 and low levels of proprietary additives. Dechlorane Plus 35 is Dechlorane Plus that has been ground to a mean particle size of 2 microns or less. These additives can be used with Dechlorane Plus 35 to produce FR-ABS's with a notched Izod of up to 200 J/m as shown in Table 12. These FR-ABS's have improved UV stability, an increase in heat distortion temperature, excellent thermal stability and are non-blooming.

In Table 13 we compared the Dechlorane Plus 35 FR-ABS formulation to FR-formulations using brominated flame retardants. The UV stability of the ABS using the chlorinated flame retardant is much better than the ABS's using the brominated flame retardants. The heat distortion temperature of the Dechlorane Plus 35 materials is higher than the brominated materials.

Dechlorane Plus can also be used to flame retard HIPS, as shown in Table 14. In HIPS, 1% of ATH (alumina trihydrate) is added to control afterglow.

A comparison of different flame retardants used in HIPS is shown in Table 15. The UV stability of the FR-HIPS using Dechlorane Plus as the flame retardant is improved over the brominated flame retardants.

TABLE 1
FR-Nylon 66 Using Different Synergists

Formulation (weight %)		1	2	3	4	5
Nylon 66		73	70	73	73	85
Dechlorane Plus		18	20	18	18	12
Antimony Trioxide		9	10	-	-	-
Zinc Oxide		-	-	9	-	-
Zinc Borate		-	-	-	9	-
Ferric Oxide		-	-	-	-	3
Performance						
UL-94	3.2 mm	V-O	V-O	V-O	V-O	V-O
	1.6 mm	V-O	V-O	V-O	V-O	V-O
	0.8 mm	NA**	V-O	NC*	V-O	V-O/V-2
	0.4 mm	NA	V-O	NC	NC	V-O/V-2
Tensile Strength (MPa)		NA	58.2	60.1	61.3	62.1
CTI Kc (volts)		NA	275	600	325	NA
Kb (volts)		NA	NA	600	225	NA

*No class.
**Not available.

TABLE 2
FR-Nylon 66 Using Mixed Synergists

Formulation (weight %)		1	2	3	4
Nylon 66		70	78	82	85
Dechlorane Plus		20	16	14	12
Antimony Trioxide		10	2	-	-
Zinc Borate		-	4	-	1.5
Ferric Oxide		-	-	4	1.5
Performance					
UL-94	3.2 mm	V-O	V-O	V-O	V-O
	1.6 mm	V-O	V-O	V-O	V-O
	0.8 mm	V-O	V-O	V-O	V-O
	0.4 mm	V-O	V-O	V-O	V-O
Tensile Strength (MPa)		58.6	67.1	71.6	70.2
CTI (volts)		275	450	275	350

TABLE 3
FR-Nylon 66 Using Zinc Synergists

Formulation (weight %)			1	2	3	4	5
Nylon 66			73	73	70	70	70
Dechlorane Plus			18	18	20	20	20
Zinc Borate			9	-	10	-	5
Zinc Oxide			-	9	-	10	5
Performance							
UL-94	3.2 mm		V-O	V-O	V-O	V-O	V-O
	1.6 mm		V-O	V-O	V-O	V-O	V-O
	0.8 mm		V-O	NC**	V-O	NC	V-O
	0.4 mm		NC	NC	V-O	NC	V-O
Tensile Strength		(psi)	8884	NA*	8603	8262	9484
		(MPa)	61.3		59.3	56.9	65.3
CTI Kc (volts)			325	600	300	600	375

*Not available.
**No class.

TABLE 4
Iron Oxides Used as a Synergist in Nylon 66

Formulation (weight %)	1	2
Nylon 6	82	85
Dechlorane Plus	14	12
Zinc Borate	-	1.5
Iron Oxide*	4	1.5
UL-94 V-O down to 0.4 mm thickness		

*Color	Iron Oxides	Source
Brick Red	Fe_2O_3	J. T. Baker Akron Chemical E-4129
Dark-Red Brown	$(FeO)_x(Fe_2O_3)_y$	Akron Chemical E-4102
Brown	$(FeO)_x(Fe_2O_3)_y$	Mineral Pigments E-4172
Black	Fe_3O_4	Akron Chemical E-8846
Yellow	$Fe_2O_3.H_2O$	Pfizer YLO-2288D
Mustard		Akron Chemical E-6982

TABLE 5
Comparison of Different Halogen-FR and UV-Stability

Formulation (weight %)		1	2	3
Nylon 66		70	78	70
Dechlorane Plus		20	16	-
Poly(tribromostyrene)		-	-	21
Antimony Trioxide		10	2	9
Zinc Borate		-	4	-
UL-94	3.2 mm	V-O	V-O	V-O
	1.6 mm	V-O	V-O	V-O
	0.8 mm	V-O	V-O	V-2*
	0.4 mm	V-O	V-O	V-1*
Yellowness Index (Y)				
Initial		15.4	24.5	28.1
One Week Exposure**		16.1	25.7	57.9
▲YI		0.7	1.2	29.8

*Samples drip.
**One week exposure in an Atlas Weather-O-Meter.

Table 6
FR-Nylon 66 (25% Glass-Reinforced) UL-94 V-O at 0.4 mm

Formulation (weight %)		1	2	3	4
Nylon 66		49	55	60	60
Fiberglass		25	25	25	25
Dechlorane Plus		18	16	12	12
Antimony Oxide		8	2	-	-
Zinc Borate		-	2	-	1.5
Iron Oxide		-	-	3	1.5
Ul-94	3.2 mm	V-O	V-O	V-O	V-O
	1.6 mm	V-O	V-O	V-O	V-O
	0.8 mm	V-O	V-O	V-O	V-O
	0.4 mm	V-O	V-O	V-O	V-O
Tensile Strength (MPa)		122.6	126.6	103.3	104.0
CTI (Kc) (volts)		225	350	200	200

TABLE 7
FR-Nylon 66 (25% Glass-Reinforced) Using Zinc Synergists

Formulation (weight)		1	2	3	4	5
Nylon 66		51	51	48	49	48
Fiberglass		25	25	25	25	25
Dechlorane Plus		16	16	18	18	18
Zinc Borate		8	-	-	4	9
Zinc Oxide		-	8	9	4	-
UL-94	3.2 mm	V-O	V-O	V-O	V-O	V-O
	1.6 mm	V-1	V-O	V-O	V-O	V-O
	0.8 mm	V-1	NC**	V-1	V-2	V-1
Tensile Strength (MPa)		NA*	NA	96.9	100.4	120.8
CTI (Kc)(Volts)		NA	NA	350	375	375

*Not available.
**No class.

TABLE 8
FR-Nylon 6 Using Different Synergists

Formulation (weight)		1	2	3	4	5
Nylon 6		73	70	74	76	70
Dechlorane Plus		18	20	21	16	20
Antimony Trioxide		9	10	2.5	6	-
Zinc Borate		-	-	2.5	2	10
Performance						
UL-94	3.2 mm	V-O	V-O	V-O	V-O	NC*
	1.6 mm	V-O	V-O	V-O	V-O	NC
Tensile Strength (MPa)		NA**	47.4	50.7	52.5	NA
CTI (Kc) (volts)		NA	325	425	375	NA

*No class.
**Not available.

TABLE 9
FR-Nylon 6 Using Iron Synergists

Formulation (weight %)	1	2	3	4
Nylon 6	75	70	70	70
Dechlorane Plus	20	20	20	20
Antimony Trioxide	-	5	5	-
Zinc Borate	-	-	-	5
Ferric Oxide	5	5	-	-
Iron Oxide (Black)	-	-	5	5
UL-94 3.2 mm	V-O	V-O	V-O	V-O
1.6 mm	V-O	V-O	V-O	V-O
0.8 mm	NC*	V-O	V-O	NC
0.4 mm	NC	V-O	V-O	NC
Tensile Strength (MPa)	48.4	49.5	50.2	51.1
CTI (Kc) (volts)	275	275	275	325

*No class.

TABLE 10
FR-Nylon 6 (25% Glass-Reinforced) Using Different Synergists

Formulation (weight)	1	2	3
Nylon 6	47	50	45
Fiberglass	25	25	25
Dechlorane Plus	22	20	20
Zinc Borate	-	-	7
Antimony Trioxide	6	-	3
Ferric Oxide (Red)	-	5	-
Performance			
UL-94			
3.2 mm	V-O	V-O	V-O
1.6 mm	V-O	V-O	V-O
Tensile Strength (MPa)	99.9	84.7	113
CTI (Kc) (volts)	250	125	350

TABLE 11
FR-Epoxies Using Dechlorane Plus*

Formulation (phr)	1	2	3	4	5
Dechlorane Plus	25.5	25.5	25.5	25.5	25.5
Antimony Trioxide	5	-	-	2.5	-
Zinc Borate	-	5	-	2.5	2.5
Ferric Oxide	-	-	5	-	2.5
<u>Performance</u>					
Oxygen Index (%)	27	28	26	28	28
UL-94 3.2 mm	V-1	V-1	V-O	V-O	V-O

*The epoxy used was Epon 828 from Shell Chemical. The curing agent was triethylene-tetramine (TETA) at a 13 phr level.

TABLE 12
FR-ABS Using Dechlorane Plus

Formulation (weight %)	1	2	3	4	5	6
ABS	77.0	76.0	72.6	74.0	70.6	73.6
Dechlorane Plus 35	16.9	16.9	16.9	16.9	16.9	16.9
Sb_2O_3	6.1	6.1	6.1	6.1	6.1	6.1
Additive A[1]	-	1.0	1.0	-	-	-
Additive B[2]	-	-	-	3.0	3.0	-
Additive C[3]	-	-	3.4	-	3.4	3.4
<u>Performance</u>						
Ul-94 3.2 mm	V-O	V-O	V-O	V-O	V-O	V-O
Notched Izod J/m	70	118	198	105	202	191

[1]"A" Air Products XFB41-57 (Polysiloxane Surfactant).
[2]"B" Struktol TR 060 (Process aid/mixture of aliphatic resins with a molecular weight <2000).
[3]"C" Acrylontrile (Butadiene) Copolymer (27% Acrylonitrile) (Impact Modifier)

TABLE 13
Comparison of FR-ABS

	Dechlorane* Plus 35	OBDPO	Bis(tribromo-phenoxy-ethane)
% FR plus 6.1% Sb_2O_3	16.9	13.8	15.7
% Halogen	11	11	11
Performance			
UL-94 3.2 mm	V-O	V-2	NC
Notched Izod J/m	208	283	309
Tensile Strength			
Yield (MPa)	32.3	39.8	36.8
Break (MPa)	24.1	29.6	26.5
Elongation at Break (%)	17	10	14
HDT 1/8" x 1/2" Bar (°C)	77	71	71
UV Aging Yellowness Index**			
Initial	31.5	32.9	28.6
1 Week	31.7	91.5	44.4
Change	0.2	58.6	15.8

*Contains "B" and "C".
**Atlas Weather-O-Meter, Temperature 60°C.

TABLE 14
FR-HIPS Using Dechlorane Plus

Formulation (weight %)	1	2	3	4	5
HIPS[(1)]	100	63	63	75	77
Dechlorane Plus	-	22	22	20	18
Sb_2O_3	-	4	4	4	4
SBS[(2)]	-	10	-	-	-
BR[(3)]	-	-	10	-	-
ATH[(4)]	-	1	1	1	1
UL-94 1/8" 3.2 mm	NC	V-O	V-O	V-O	V-O
Notched Izod J/m	267	85	107	53	64
Tensile					
Yield (MPa)	35.6	19.5	19.6	29.2	29.9
Break (MPa)	30.6	17.5	14.5	23.7	24.3
Elongation (%)	9.7	17	4.4	5.6	12

[(1)]Amoco Chemical H3E - 7.5% polybutadiene.
[(2)]Kraton D1102 (Shell Chemical) (Styrene-butadiene-styrene block copolymer).
[(3)]Solprene 25p (Housmex) (polybutadiene rubber).
[(4)]Solem 6325A/added to control afterglow.

TABLE 15
Comparison of FR-HIPS

Formulation (weight %)		1	2	3	4	5	6
HIPS (Amoco H3E)	%	100	75	63	63	78.1	78.1
Kraton D1102	%	–	–	10	–	–	–
Solprene	%	–	–	–	10	–	–
Dechlorane Plus	%	–	20	22	22	–	–
OBDPO	%	–	–	–		17.9	–
DBDPO	%	–	–	–	–	–	17.2
Sb_2O_3	%	–	4	4	4	4	4
ATH	%	–	1	1	1	–	–
UL-94 1/8" 3.2 mm		NC*	V-O	V-O	V-O	V-O	V-O
Notched Izod	J/m	238	48	85	90	112	96
UV Aging Yellowness Index							
Initial		0	10	10	8	8	8
1 Week		15	23	23	21	77	69
Change		15	13	13	13	69	61

*No class.

REFERENCES

(1) K. Otherm; Encyclopedia of Chemical Technology, Vol. 10, Third Edition (1980).

(2) I. Touval; "Antimony Oxide: Synergism in Flame Retardants," Plastics Compounding, September/October 1982.

(3) C. S. Ilardo; "Chlorine-Containing Flame Retardants, Part I," Plastics Compounding, January/February 1985.

(4) K. K. Shen; "Zinc Borate," Plastics Compounding, September/October 1985.

(5) J. Maslen and W. H. Taylor, U. S. Patent 4,105,621 (1978).

(6) R. Troncy and J. Cerny; Belg. BE 858,884 (1977), Ger. Offen. DE 2,656,883, Nepth. Appl. NL 76/13460, Brit. BG 1,512,300, all (1978).

(7) R. L. Markezich; "Synergists: Effectiveness with Halogen Flame Retardants," SPE 44th ANTEC, Page 1158 (1986).

(8) R. L. Markezich; "Use of Non-Antimony Oxide Synergists with Halogen Flame Retardants," SPE 45th ANTEC, Page 1298 (1987).

(9) R. L. Markezich and C. S. Ilardo; "Evaluation of Synergists with Halogen Flame Retardants," SPE 46th ANTEC, Page 1412 (1988).

(10) R. L. Markezich; "Use of Alternate Synergists with Dechlorane Plus Flame Retardant in Nylon," FRCA Spring Meeting, 1987.

BROMINATED AROMATIC PHOSPHATE ESTER FLAME RETARDANT

JOSEPH GREEN
FMC Corporation
P.O. Box 8
Princeton, N.J. 08543

ABSTRACT

Engineering thermoplastics are generally flame retarded with decabromodiphenyl oxide or polymeric bromine compounds with antimony oxide or sodium antimonate as the synergist. A brominated triaryl phosphate ester was shown to be a highly efficient flame retardant for polycarbonates, PBT, PET, and alloys including PC/ABS alloy. Antimony is generally not needed as a synergist. The brominated phosphate disperses readily into engineering plastics and also aids molding. The brominated phosphate has excellent thermal and high temperature color stability. Flammability and property data are reported for various thermoplastics containing the brominated phosphate and compared with commercial flame retardants.

INTRODUCTION

Commercially available flame retardants include chlorine- and bromine-containing compounds generally used with antimony oxide as synergist, phosphate esters used in modified polyphenylene oxide polymers, cellulose acetate and PVC, and chloroalkyl phosphates used in polyurethanes. This paper describes the use of a brominated aromatic phosphate ester in high temperature thermoplastic application. The use of this brominated phosphate does not require antimony synergist, not is it desirable, in many polymer systems.

Adapted with permission from Green J. In Fire and Polymers; Nelson, G.L., Ed.; ACS Symposium Series; American Chemical Society: Washington, DC, in press, March 1990.

0097-6156/90/0425-0000$06.00/0

The brominated aromatic phosphate ester described here contains 60% aromatic bromine and 4% phosphorus and is known as PB-460. Figures 1 and 2 compare its thermal stability with some commercial flame retardants by thermogravimetric analysis (TGA) and by differential scanning calorimetry (DSC). The phosphate ester melts at 110°C and shows a 1% weight loss at 280°C. When heated in a glass tube at 300°C for 30 minutes it remains a water-white liquid. This was compared with commercial bromine-containing flame retardants which melt below this temperature; they all turn color. The excellent thermal and color stability of this brominated phosphate ester makes it suitable for the high temperature processing of engineering plastics.

This aromatic phosphate is very soluble in methylene chloride (43%), toluene (25%), and methyl ethyl ketone (11%) and is insoluble in methanol (0.3%) and water (<0.1%). It is believed that the high solubility of this flame retardant in aromatic solvent accounts in part for the ease of compounding into aromatic engineering polymers.

The commercial flame retardants studied for comparison include a brominated polycarbonate oligomer chain capped with tribromophenol (58% bromine), a brominated polystyrene (68-70% bromine) and bis-(tribromophenoxy)ethane (70% bromine). In the tables, the brominated polycarbonate oligomer will be described simply as a brominated polycarbonate and the brominated aromatic phosphate ester simply as a brominated phosphate.

Flame Retardant Polycarbonates

The brominated aromatic phosphate ester is an efficient flame retardant for polycarbonate resin. UL-94 ratings of V-0 with oxygen index values of greater than 40 are obtained. Polycarbonate resin containing the brominated phosphate processes with greater ease than resin containing the commercial brominated polycarbonate oligomer as measured by injection molding spiral flow measurements. The heat distortion temperature is reduced and the high Gardner impacts are retained. The resultant products are transparent and water-white (Table 1).

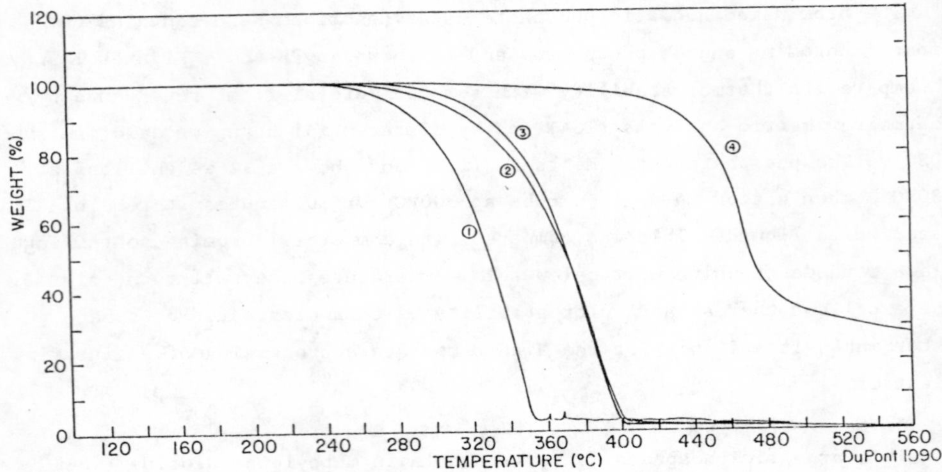

Figure 1. Thermogravimetric analysis (TGA) of brominated flame retardants - 10C/min. under nitrogen.
1. bis-(tribromophenoxy)ethane; 2. octabromodiphenyl oxide; 3. brominated phosphate ester; 4. brominated polycarbonate oligomer

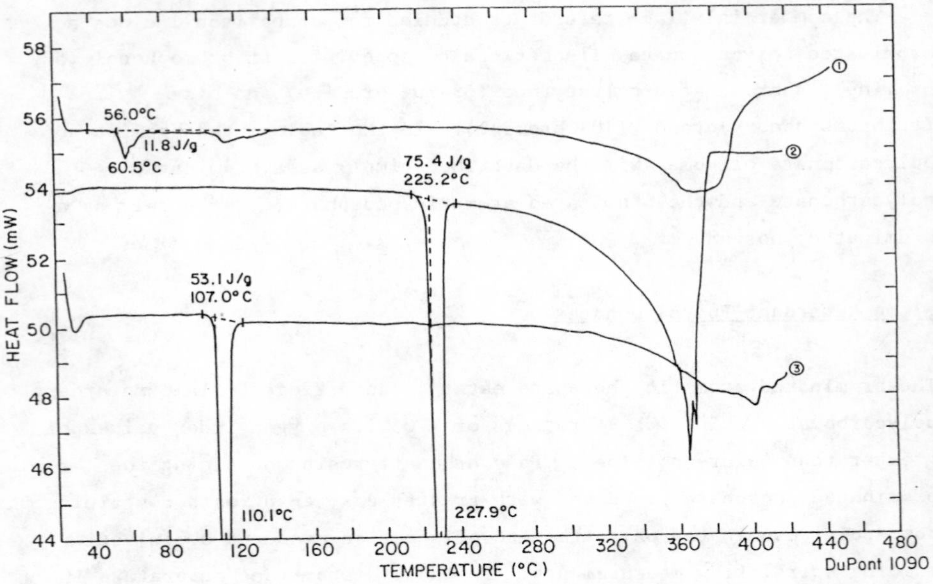

Figure 2. Differential scanning calorimetry (DSC) of brominated flame retardants - 10C/min. under nitrogen
1. octabromodiphenyl oxide; 2. bis-(tribromophenoxy)ethane
3. brominated phosphate ester

Flame retardant sulfonate salt polycarbonate resin gives a UL-94 rating of V-0 at 1/16 inch thickness. At 1/32 inch thickness, however, the product drips to give a V-2 rating. The addition of 3% brominated phosphate renders the product V-0 at 1/32 inch thick (Table 2). The addition of the flame retardant gives a resin with an increased melt index.

TABLE 1.
Flame Retarding Polycarbonate Resin

Polycarbonate Resin	93	93
Brominated polycarbonate	7	-
Brominated phosphate	-	7
Oxygen Index	32.1	>39.6
UL-94, rating (1/16")	V-O	V-O
time, sec.	3.8	2.4
Heat Distortion Temp. @ 264 psi, ^{o}F	261	239
Gardner Impact, in. lbs.	>320	>320
Spiral Flow, Inj. Molding, in.	23.5	29.5
	transparent, water-white	

TABLE 2.
Flame Retardant Polycarbonate Resin

FR Polycarbonate (sulfonate salt)	100	99	97
Brominated phosphate	-	1	3
Oxygen Index	33.6	34.8	37.5
UL-94			
@ 1/16" rating	V-O	V-O	V-O
sec.	1.2	1.9	0.9
@ 1/32" rating	V-2	V-2	V-O
sec.	4.7	2.4	1.4
Melt Index, g/10 min. (250°C)	7.0	-	9.1

Flame Retardant Polybutylene Terephthalate (PBT)

Mineral filled PBT polyester resin containing 12% brominated phosphate and 4% antimony oxide yields a V-0 product with a 29.7 oxygen index. A product containing 16% flame retardant and no antimony oxide is also V-O with a 31.2 oxygen index. The use of the brominated polycarbonate requires the use of antimony oxide as a synergist. This shows phosphorus to be highly effective as a flame retardant in PBT (Table 3).

TABLE 3.
Flame Retarding Mineral-Filled PBT

PBT Mineral Filled	84	84	84	84
Brominated polycarbonate	12	-	16	-
Brominated phosphate	-	12	-	16
Antimony Oxide	4	4	-	-
Oxygen Index	31.8	29.7	29.1	31.2
UL-94, Rating (1/16")	V-O	V-O	B	V-O
Time, sec.	0	3.7	-	3.1

Lower oxygen index values are obtained for the brominated phosphate/antimony system without effecting the UL-94 rating or burning time. Antimony and phosphorus appear to be somewhat antagonistic in a high oxygen environment. The UL test is therefore considered a better comparative test in these flame retardant resin systems.

With 30% glass filled PBT, the brominated phosphate requires the use of antimony oxide. A drip inhibitor was used in these studies and as little as 0.3% Teflon 6C fibrous powder is adequate to inhibit dripping. As little as 10% brominated phosphate will give a V-O product (Table 4).

TABLE 4.
Flame Retarding Glass Filled PBT

PBT/30% Glass	86.5	82.5	86.5	82.5
Brominated Polystyrene	10	14	-	-
Brominated Phosphate	-	-	10	14
Antimony Oxide	3.5	3.5	3.5	3.5
Teflon 6C	0.5	0.5	0.5	0.5
Oxygen Index	28.2	30.6	27.9	30.0
UL-94, Rating (1/16")	V-O	V-O	V-O	V-O
Sec.	1.4	0.2	2.4	1.6

Brominated phosphate, brominated polycarbonate and brominated polystyrene flame retardants are compared in Table 5. The brominated phosphate disperses readily into the resin presumably due to its high solubility in aromatics. Resin containing the brominated polycarbonate is relatively difficult to process as measured by injection molding spiral flow measurements.

TABLE 5.
Flame Retardant PBT/30% Glass

PBT/30% Glass	82.5	82.5	82.5
Antimony Oxide	3.5	3.5	3.5
Teflon 6C	0.3	0.3	0.3
Brominated Phosphate	14	-	-
Brominated Polystyrene	-	14	-
Brominated Polycarbonate	-	-	14
UL-94, rating (1/16")	V-0	V-0	V-0
sec.	0.9	0	0.1
Oxygen Index	29.7	32.7	33.0
HDT, 264 psi, ^{o}C	197	204	200
Izod Impact (1/8")	1.3	1.0	1.1
Spiral Flow, in.*	47	46	37
Melt Index, g/10 min. (250°C)	13.6	13.0	12.5
Flex Strength, psi	24,600	22,800	26,500
Flex Modulus x 10^6 psi	0.83	1.13	1.15

*Control (no FR) gives 48 inches flow

Properties of the resins are similar with the brominated phosphate containing resin showing a slightly lower heat distortion temperature and a slightly higher Izod impact.

Flame Retardant Polyethylene Terephthalate (PET)

Table 6 shows that sodium antimonate is antagonistic with the phosphorus/bromine flame retardant in 30% glass filled PET polyester resin. V-0 products with high oxygen index values are obtainable using only the brominated phosphate. The brominated phosphate is more effective than the brominated polystyrene/sodium antimonate combination (Figure 3).

TABLE 6.
Flame Retardant PET/30% Glass Resin

PET/30% Glass	82	80	80
Brominated Phosphate	18	20	15
Sodium Antimonate	-	-	5
Teflon 6C	0.5	0.5	0.5
Oxygen Index	30.6	36.0	29.4
UL-94, rating (1/16")	V-2	V-0	V-2
sec.	1.2	0.1	5.1

Flame Retardant Polycarbonate/PBT Polyester Blend

A 50/50 blend of polycarbonate resin and PBT polyester containing 13.5% brominated phosphate and no antimony oxide results in a product with a V-0 rating and an oxygen index of 33. An equivalent product containing the brominated polycarbonate has a low oxygen index and burns in the UL-94 test (Table 7).

TABLE 7.
Flame Retarding Polycarbonate/PBT Blends
(No Antimony)

Polycarbonate	43	43
PBT Polyester	43	43
Teflon Powder	0.5	0.5
Brominated Polystyrene	13.5	-
Brominated Phosphate	-	13.5
Oxygen Index	24.8	33.0
UL-94, rating (1/16")	Burn	V-0
time, sec.		0.9

Various blend ratios of polycarbonate and PBT polyester were flame retarded with brominated phosphate, brominated polystyrene, and brominated polycarbonate. These data are shown graphically in Figure 4. Brominated phosphate is the most efficient and brominated polycarbonate the least efficient flame retardant. At 50% and greater polycarbonate concentration, the brominated phosphate is significantly more effective than brominated polystyrene.

Flame Retardant Polycarbonate/PET Polyester Alloy

The flame retardant performance of the various flame retardants was compared in a commercial polycarbonate/PET polyester alloy. The brominated

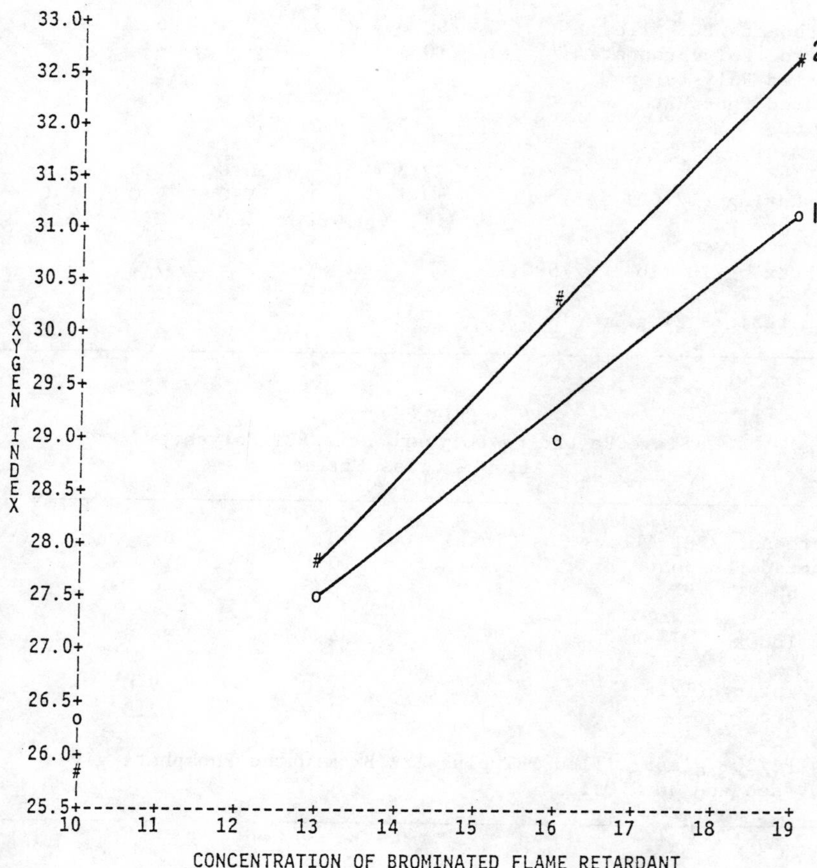

Figure 3. Flame retarding 30% glass filled PET
1. brominated polystyrene with sodium antimonate (3/1)
2. brominated phosphate ester

phosphate is a very efficient flame retardant as measured by oxygen index and UL-94 (Table 8 and Figure 5).

Brominated phosphate flame retardant was also evaluated in a commercial glass filled polycarbonate/PET polyester alloy. A concentration of 10% gives a V-0 rating with an oxygen index value of about 35 (Table 9).

TABLE 8.
Flame Retarding Polycarbonate/PET Polyester Alloy

Polycarbonate/PET Alloy	90	86	90	86	90	86
Brominated Polycarbonate	10	12	-	-	-	-
Brominated Polystyrene	-	-	10	12	-	-
Brominated Phosphate	-	-	-	-	10	12
Teflon 6C	0.5	0.5	0.5	0.5	0.5	0.5
Oxygen Index	27.3	27.9	30.6	30.9	31.2	35.4
UL-94, Rating (1/16")	V-1	V-1	V-0	V-0	V-0	V-0
sec.	11.3	6.1	1.0	2.7	4.9	2.3
Melt Index, g/10 min.* (275°C)	-	20	-	37	-	71

*Virgin resin - 24 g/10 min.

TABLE 9.
Flame Retarding Polycarbonate/PET Polyester
Alloy - Glass Filled

Polycarbonate/PET Alloy (20% Glass)	90	86	82
Brominated Phosphate	10	14	18
Teflon 6C	0.5	0.5	0.5
Oxygen Index	34.8	36.6	>39.6
UL-94, rating (1/16")	V-0	V-0	V-0
sec.	1.9	2.5	0

*44/44 PC/30% glass filled PET plus 12% Brominated Phosphate gives V-0/0.9 sec.and 36.9 O.I.

Flame Retardant Polycarbonate/ABS Alloy

The flame retardant performance of various flame retardant additives in a commercial polycarbonate/ABS alloy were compared. No antimony oxide was

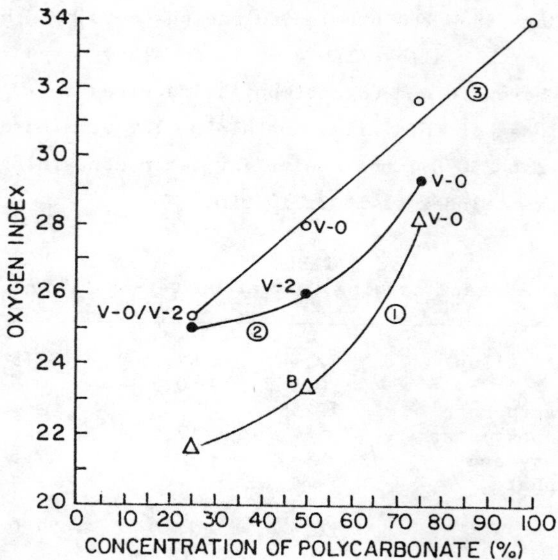

Figure 4. Flame retarding polycarbonate/PBT blends (12% flame retardant). 1. brominated polycarbonate oligomer; 2. brominated polystyrene; 3. brominated phosphate ester

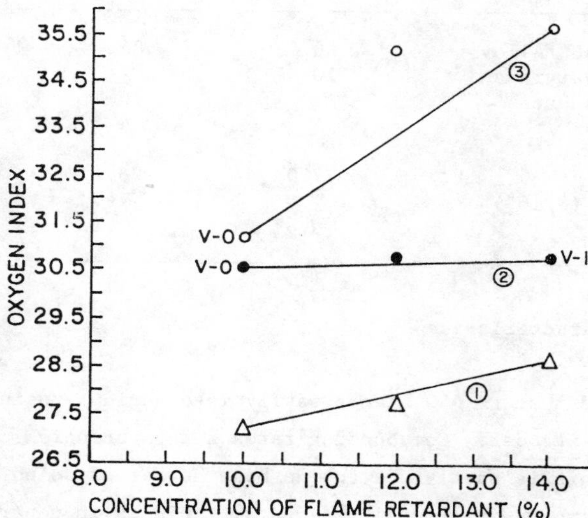

Figure 5. Flame retarding polycarbonate/PET alloy 1. brominated polycarbonate oligomer; 2. brominated polystyrene; 3. brominated phosphate ester

required. The data show the brominated phosphate to be a highly efficient flame retardant in this alloy (Table 10). An alloy composition containing 14% brominated phosphate and no antimony oxide gives a V-0 rating (Table 11). The melt index of this alloy containing 12% brominated polystyrene was 7.6g/10 min (at 250°C); the equivalent resin containing brominated phosphate had a melt index of 13.3g/10 min.

TABLE 10.
Flame Retarding Polycarbonate/ABS Alloy

Polycarbonate/ABS Alloy	82.5	82.5	82.5	82.5
Teflon 6C	0.5	0.5	0.5	0.5
Brominated Polycarbonate	17.5	-	-	-
bis-(tribromophenoxy)ethane	-	17.5	-	-
Brominated Polystyrene	-	-	17.5	-
Brominated Phosphate	-	-	-	17.5
Oxygen Index	26.4	27.0	27.0	28.2
UL-94, Rating (1/16")	V-1	V-0	V-0	V-0
sec.	22	2.0	2.6	1.4

TABLE 11.
Flame Retarding Polycarbonate/ABS Alloy

Polycarbonate/ABS Alloy	86	86	86
Brominated Polystyrene	10	-	-
Brominated Phosphate	-	10	14
Antimony Oxide	4	4	-
Oxygen Index	27.0	26.1	25.8
UL-94, Rating (1/16")	V-0	V-0	V-0
sec.	0.8	0.1	1.3

Compounding Characteristics

It was observed that PB-460 blends easily into various resins in a single or twin screw extruder. Compounding rates also are increased. It has been assumed that this is partly due to the high degree of solubility of the brominated phosphate in aromatic solvents. This is in contrast with the polymeric flame retardants which are more difficult to incorporate or compound into various resins.

A study was conducted in a Brabender Plasti-Corder. The brominated phosphate was compared with the commercial brominated polystyrene flame retardant. Various resins with and without glass were used and the temperature adjusted for the resin. When the polymeric flame retardant is added (in increments), the viscosity increases to a point and then decreases and plateaus at the original viscosity or frequently at a higher viscosity. When brominated phosphate is added in increments the viscosity decreases immediately and then plateaus, at a lower viscosity than the starting viscosity.

CONCLUSIONS

A brominated aromatic phosphate ester, PB-460, was shown to have excellent thermal stability and excellent retention of color at high temperature. The brominated phosphate is a highly efficient flame retardant in engineering thermoplastics and alloys such as polycarbonates, PBT polyester, PET polyester, and polycarbonate alloys with PBT, PET and ABS. With many polymers antimony oxide or sodium antimonate is not needed presumably due to the presence of the highly effective phosphorus. Brabender Plasti-Corder studies show the brominated phosphate to blend easily into resins, presumably due to its high aromatic solubility, unlike polymeric flame retardants which can be difficult to blend into engineering thermoplastics. This confirms the ease of compounding observed in a single or twin screw extruder. Increased melt index and greater spiral flow when brominated phosphate is used confirms the observed ease of injection molding.

ACKNOWLEDGMENTS

I wish to acknowledge the excellent contributions of Charles A. Tennesen for compounding and testing, Ray Skok for the flammability testing and John Jessup for the mechanical property testing.

FLAMTARD - A NEW RANGE OF FLAME AND SMOKE RETARDANTS

D CHAPLIN AND S C BROWN
Alcan Chemicals Limited
Chalfont Park, Gerrards Cross, Bucks., SL9 0QB, UK.

ABSTRACT

The fire performance of new materials, Flamtard H and Flamtard S, was studied in flexible PVC. The performance was compared to that of antimony trioxide. Emphasis was placed on measurements of smoke evolution and carbon monoxide emission.

The general trends observed were that in PVC formulations containing Flamtard, significantly lower smoke levels and less carbon monoxide emission were found compared to those containing equivalent levels of antimony trioxide.

PVC formulations containing low loadings of Flamtard addition plus chalk filler gave the most dramatic reductions in both smoke evolution and carbon monoxide generation versus antimony trioxide. Enhanced performance was obtained with tri-basic lead sulphate versus a Barium/Cadmium Stabiliser.

INTRODUCTION

PVC is one of the most widely used plastic materials. The large variability in formulation possibilities means that it can be modified to produce materials with a wider range of properties than any other polymer. In particular flexible PVC is used in a wide range of applications including floor coverings, clothing, films, cables and foams.

Rigid PVC is of course inherently flame retardant due to its high chlorine content. However, the production of flexible PVC by the addition of some of the more commonly used plasticisers such as phthalates acts to greatly diminish this flame retardancy. For many of its applications flame retardant flexible PVC is essential. This is usually done by two possible methods. Firstly the flammable plasticiser and can be replaced by other materials which act as plasticisers or plasticiser extenders and which offer some degree of flame retardancy. These include chlorinated waxes and phosphate esters. Alternatively, solid particulate materials can be added. Commonly used solid flame retardants include antimony trioxide, aluminium trihydroxide and zinc borate. Using some of these materials, or combinations of them, excellent degrees of flame retardancy can be obtained.

There is currently a move to replace PVC in some applications with various low smoke zero halogen (LSOH) materials. This is particularly applicable for underground mass transit systems and computer / telecommunications installations. These often comprise EVA or EPDM highly filled with aluminium hydroxide or magnesium hydroxide. PVC has a price advantage and an advantage in physical properties over these materials.(1)

It's serious disadvantage lies in secondary fire characteristics, namely smoke and corrosive fume emissions, whilst burning. Unmodified PVC is notoriously bad in terms of smoke and acid gas characteristics. It has also been found to produce higher levels of carbon monoxide than many other polymers whilst burning.

Although carbon monoxide poisoning is a major cause of death in fires, carbon monoxide emission is one of the least studied effects in the flame retardant industry. Almost no standards exist to include it. Some data is available from the National Bureau of Standards. This has been produced from the cone calorimeter(2). Much of this data suggests that flame retardant polymers actually produce more carbon monoxide than the base polymer, producing materials with perhaps more dangerous secondary fire effects. This is certainly true of many materials and the findings in PVC presented later in this paper confirm that the antimony trioxide traditionally used does generate more carbon monoxide. However, it has also been found that the use of new Flamtard materials can produce equivalent or even lower levels than the base polymer in some formulations.

Antimony Trioxide

The most commonly used flame retardant for PVC is antimony trioxide. This compound is a highly effective flame retardant at low levels, and has shown benefit by producing fire retardant products which have contributed to overall safety. It does however possess some disadvantages and the Flamtard products have been developed to address these problems. It is generally understood that antimony trioxide acts in the vapour phase to produce antimony halides.

Reaction via these halides provides a lower energy route for decomposition, thus decreasing the energy feedback to the decomposition process (3). The presence of these vapours just above the surface of the polymer may also act as a cushion which impairs the ability of oxygen to reach the surface.

As less oxygen reaches the polymer it would be expected that a greater proportion of the carbon in the polymer chains is oxidised to carbon monoxide rather than carbon dioxide. Results presented later in this paper suggest that this may take place in the presence of antimony trioxide. Rapid production of carbon monoxide was found from burning PVC containing antimony trioxide.

PVC produces more smoke during combustion than many other materials. The use of antimony trioxide usually increases still further generation of smoke. This is possibly again due to the vapour phase form of action. Less oxygen can reach the burning polymer. Thus a greater proportion of the decomposition products being evolved cannot be fully oxidised to carbon dioxide and water. They remain in the solid phase as smoke or soot. The mode of decomposition of PVC via conjugated polyenes is very conducive to the subsequent generation of fused aromatics that are the common constituents of smoke.

Antimony trioxide has one other important undesirable feature. This is its potential toxicity [4,5], and there is growing concern over the possible carcinogenicity of this material. This situation is particularly applicable to users who do not possess advanced and expensive enclosed handling facilities. Workers exposed to the material are also shown to experience other health problems such as antimony 'fleas' or 'measles'.

Flamtard H and Flamtard S

There is obviously a desire within the industry to retain the use of PVC wherever possible. There is also interest within the PVC industry to remove toxic materials from compounding plants wherever possible. One way to improve the acceptability of PVC is to bring it some way towards the low smoke properties of the LSOH compounds. This is a difficult undertaking.

It would appear that one way to improve some of the secondary fire characteristics would be to reduce the levels of material operating in the vapour phase. The antimony trioxide could be replaced by established materials such as aluminium trihydroxide or magnesium hydroxide which predominantly operate in the condensed phase. These products have to be used at high loadings which can be to the detriment of mechanical properties.

In addition new products are now commercially available as direct replacements for antimony trioxide. These are Flamtard H and Flamtard S. They are, proprietary performance additives available from B A Chemicals.

Flamtard H and Flamtard S - General Properties

Flamtard H and S are fine white powders of around one to two microns median particle size. They are recommended for addition to halogen containing polymers at low levels (1-15 phr) or with the addition of supplementary halogen to other polymers. Currently, two grades are available, but eventually a range of materials of different purities, particle sizes, morphologies and surface coatings will be available.

As measured by TGA, Flamtard H starts to decompose at above 180°C but Flamtard S is thermally stable in all polymer systems during processing. It has also been found that Flamtard H can actually be processed at temperatures far higher than its apparent decomposition point and has been extruded at temperatures of 210°C without problem.

The lower specific gravity of Flamtard H and S of 3.3 and 3.9 respectively compared to 5.7 of antimony trioxide enables fabrication of lighter articles.
Toxicity and ecotoxicity studies, carried out to comply with EEC Directives relating to new chemical substances, indicate that Flamtard H and Flamtard S pose negligible threat when handled in accordance with normal standards of good industrial hygiene.

TABLE 1
Physical Properties

	FLAMTARD H	FLAMTARD S
Median Particle Size (μm)	2.5	1.7
Surface Area (m^2/g)	4.5	3.3
Decomposition Temp. (°C)	>180	>600
Oil Absorption	18	25
Specific Gravity	3.3	3.9
Free Moisture (%)	<1	<1
Whiteness [(6)]	87	87
Oral LD_{50} (rats) (mg/kg)	>5000	>5000

Flamtard H and S have been tested in a variety of polymer systems. Conclusions are that the products are good flame retardants and smoke suppressants. Because of the chemistry involved during combustion temperatures it was expected and demonstrated that reductions in carbon monoxide evolution would also be possible. Like antimony trioxide it does work best in the presence of halogen be, it present as part of the polymer base or when added separately as a synergistic fire retardant.

Experimental

PVC Formulations

The following basic flexible PVC formulation was used in the work and various modifications to the formulation were also studied as indicated.

100 phr	PVC VY110/51	(supplied by Hydro Polymers)
50 phr	DOP Reomol	(supplied by Ciba Geigy)
3 phr	Stabiliser Irgastab BC26	(supplied by Ciba Geigy)
0.7 phr	Wax Irgawax 371	(supplied by Ciba Geigy)
1-10 phr	Flame Retardant	

The basic formulation was modified in several ways to determine the influence of stabiliser, use of filler and addition of supplementary chlorine.

1. Replacing Barium Cadmium stabiliser with Tri Basic Lead Sulphate (TBLS) (supplied by Chemson Ltd).

2. Adding 100 phr chalk, Sturcal, 6 μm.

3. Adding chlorinated paraffin wax, Cereclor S52, (supplied by ICI) added at twice phr loading of the flame retardant.

Compounding was carried out on a two roll mill at 130°C. All components were added at the same time. The polymer was compression moulded at 20 tons per square inch pressure and 170°C. 2mm thick strips were used for COI determination to BS2782 part 1 and 0.8mm thick plaques for testing in the NBS smoke chamber. Smoke was measured to BS6401 but with half inch wire mesh placed in front of the sample. This is necessary to prevent the sample from expanding out and fouling the furnace interior, which renders the test null and void.

A continuous carbon monoxide monitor was fitted to the NBS chamber via a port in the roof. In the following figures, only values of carbon monoxide taken two minutes after commencement of the test are quoted.

Results

Critical Oxygen Index

Fig. 1 shows comparative oxygen index values for Flamtard H, S and antimony trioxide in the basic formulation. This shows that the flame retardancy of the Flamtard materials as measured by COI is not as high as that of antimony at low levels. It has been found that the performance of antimony levels off at around 8-10 phr but the flame retardant efficiency of the Flamtard grades continues to increase with higher loading. This change in performance with loading of the additives is demonstrated more clearly in Fig. 2. The COI values for formulations containing antimony trioxide or Flamtard S are the same at 9-10 phr, but thereafter the Flamtard S curve continues to rise.

FIG.1. EFFECT ON COI OF THE BASIC UNFILLED PVC FORMULATION

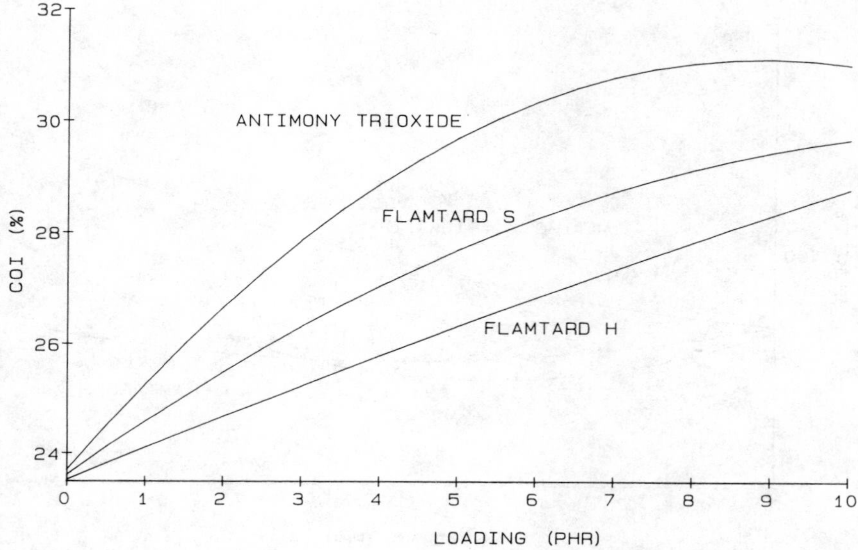

FIG.2. EFFECT ON COI OF THE PVC FORMULATION CONTAINING CERECLOR AND 100 PHR CHALK

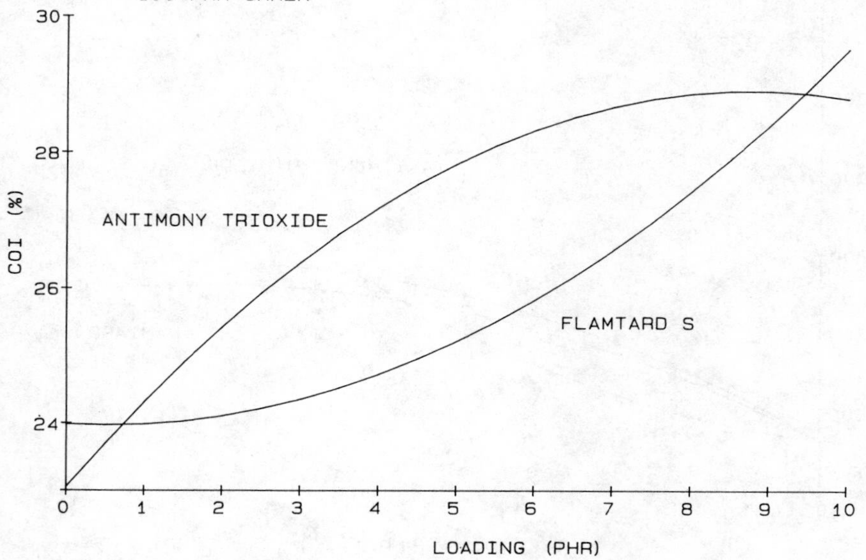

FIG.3. EFFECT ON SMOKE OF THE BASIC UNFILLED PVC FORMULA

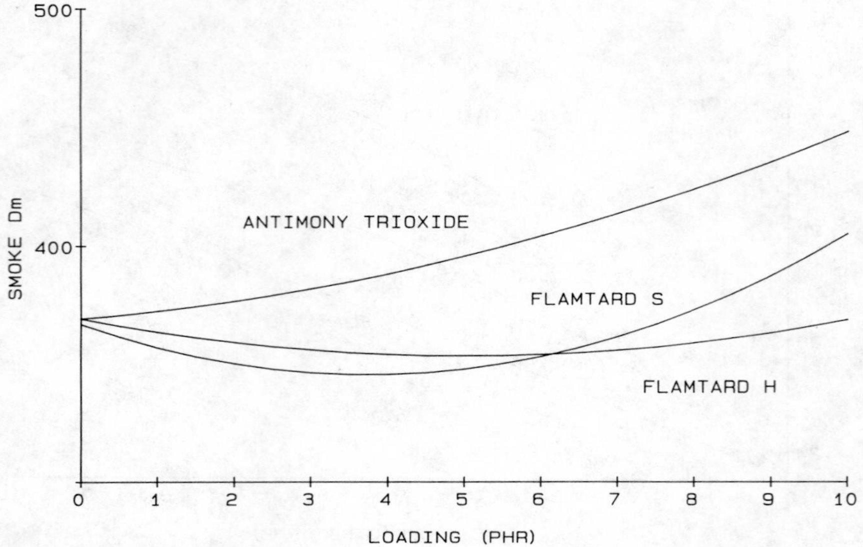

FIG.4. EFFECT ON CARBON MONOXIDE OF THE BASIC UNFILLED PVC FORMULATION

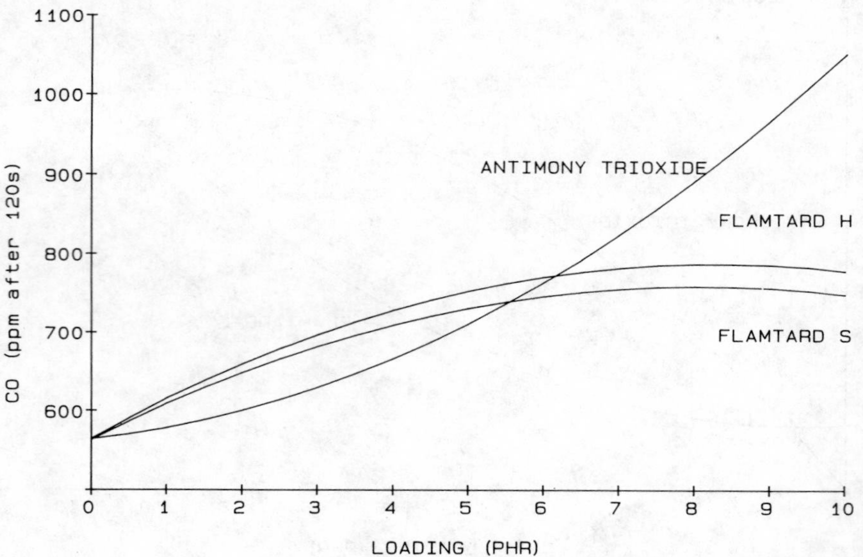

FIG.5. EFFECT ON SMOKE OF THE PVC FORMULATION CONTAINING TBLS STABILISER

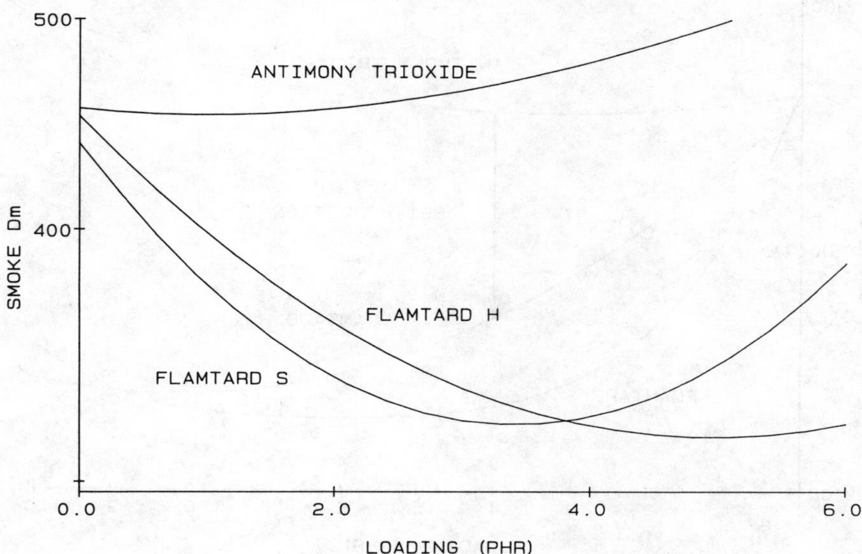

FIG.6. EFFECT ON CARBON MONOXIDE OF THE PVC FORMULATION CONTAINING TBLS STABILISER

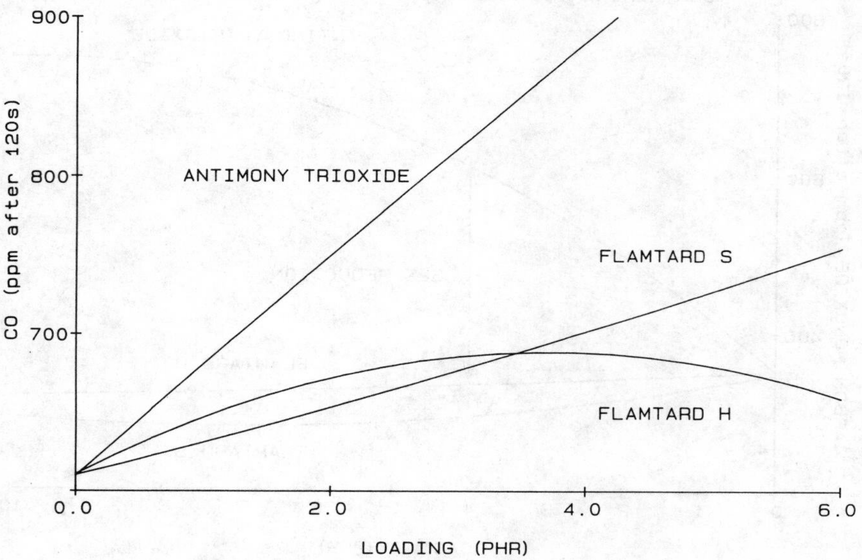

FIG.7. EFFECT ON SMOKE OF THE PVC FORMULATION CONTAINING 100 PHR CHALK

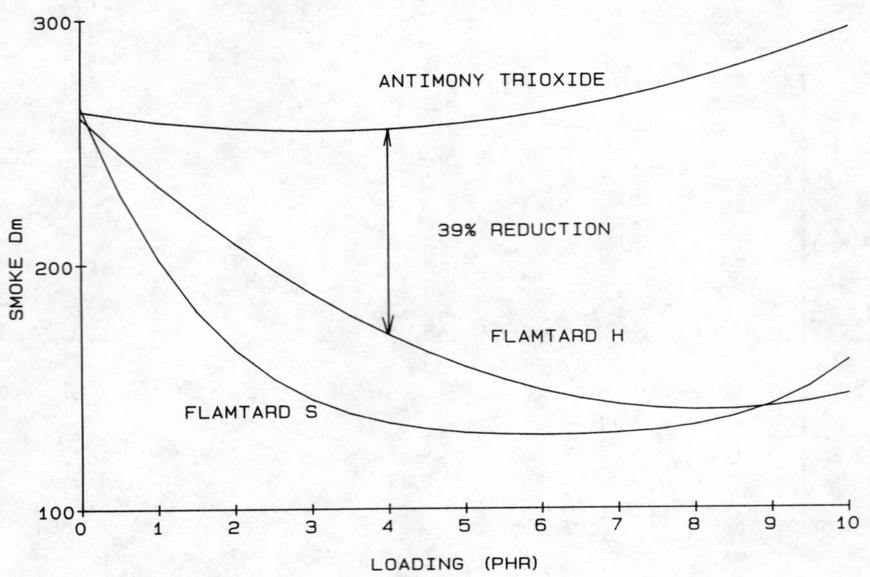

FIG.8. EFFECT ON CARBON MONOXIDE OF THE PVC FORMULATION CONTAINING 100 PHR CHALK

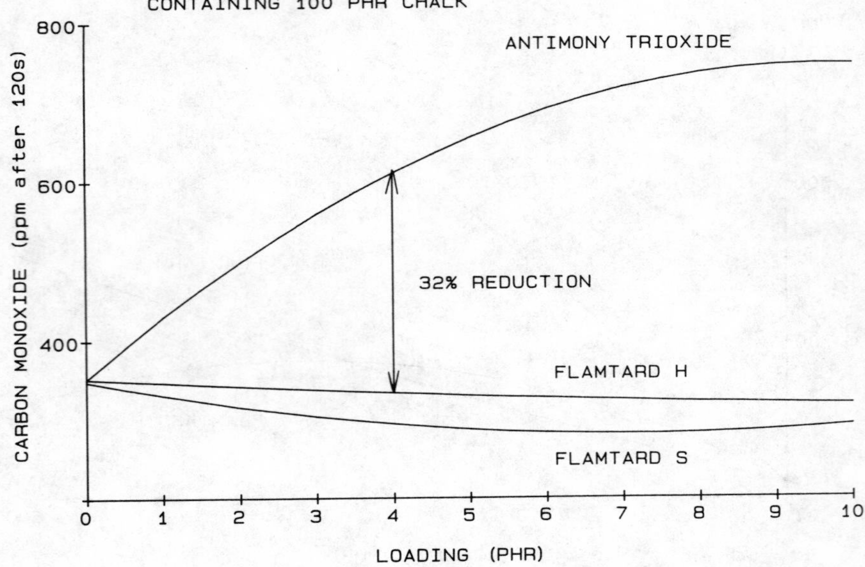

FIG.9. EFFECT ON SMOKE OF THE PVC FORMULATION CONTAINING CERECLOR AND 100 PHR CHALK

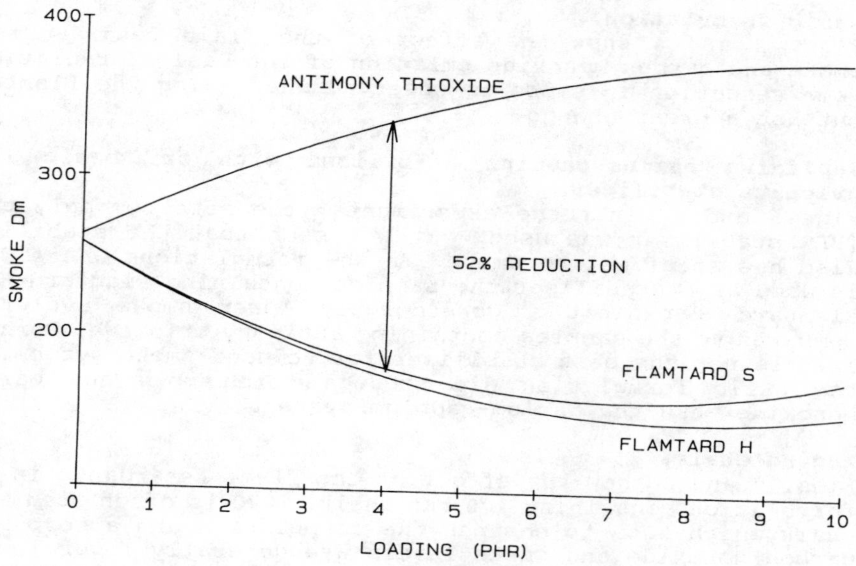

FIG.10. EFFECT ON CARBON MONOXIDE OF THE PVC FORMULATION CONTAINING CERECLOR AND 100 PHR CHALK

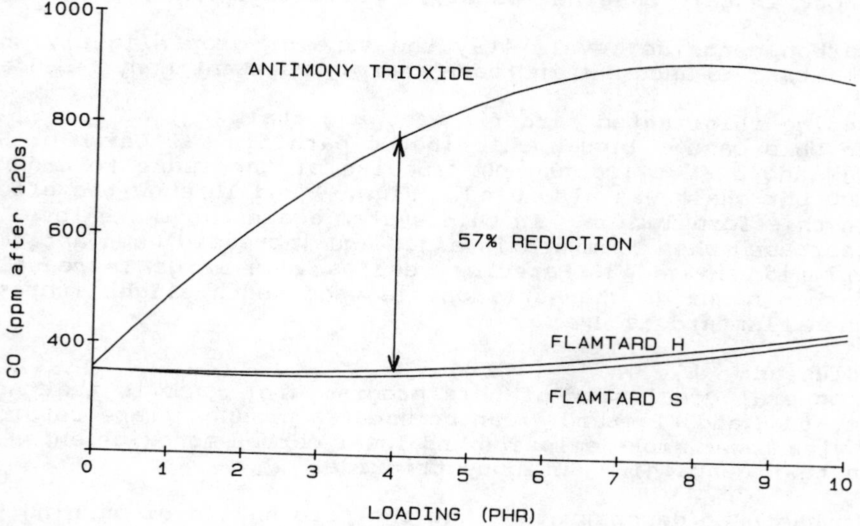

Smoke and Carbon Monoxide

1. **Basic formulation.**
   Figs. 3 and 4 show the effect of the flame retardants on smoke and carbon monoxide emission of the basic formulation. Some reduction in smoke is observed when using the Flamtard but not a great change.

2. **Replacing barium-cadmium stabiliser with tri basic lead sulphate stabiliser.**
   Figs 5 and 6, in these experiments, the more commonly used TBLS stabiliser was used. It was seen that the stabiliser also has an effect on smoke. In the formulations where TBLS is used as a stabiliser the samples containing Flamtard H or Flamtard S exhibit a considerably lower smoke evolution compared to the samples containing antimony trioxide. Perhaps TBLS is not the best stabiliser for reduced smoke systems as the basic formulation did produce more smoke and carbon monoxide than the barium-cadmium system.

3. **Adding Chalk.**
   Figs. 7 and 8 show the effect of the flame retardants in the formulation containing 100 phr chalk. PVC is often used with chalk which acts to cheapen the formulation and absorb HCl. Carbon monoxide and smoke levels are generally lower in the chalk containing formulations due to dilution effects. In this formulation addition of Flamtard significantly reduces the smoke compared to the non flame retarded formulation.

   The antimony trioxide interestingly does not greatly affect smoke in this case but is still worse than the Flamtard.

   Carbon monoxide levels stay the same or drop slightly when Flamtard is used but increase sharply when antimony is added.

4. **Adding chlorinated paraffin wax, and chalk.**
   In this case a liquid chlorinated paraffin wax Cereclor S52 was added at twice the phr loading of the flame retardant. 100 phr chalk was also used. Figs. 9 and 10 show the effect in this formulation. In this system again the smoke level is decreased when Flamtard is added and increased when antimony trioxide is added. Cereclor results in a large increase in carbon monoxide when antimony is used and a slight increase when Flamtard is used.

Conclusions

The general conclusion of this programme of work is that both Flamtard H and Flamtard S can be used to produce flame retarded PVC with lower smoke emission and lower carbon monoxide emission than that containing antimony trioxide.

It has been demonstrated that the fire hazard of burning PVC can be greatly reduced by use of the new Flamtard H and Flamtard S materials. Flame retardant PVC can be formulated to give lower smoke production and lower carbon monoxide emission than was perhaps previously possible.

It is expected that these materials will act as useful safer replacements for antimony trioxide in the future and will become an important constituent in reduced smoke, reduced toxicity, flame retardant PVC formulations.

Note
It should be noted that these tests were carried out in laboratories on small scale samples. There is now widespread concern that such testing may not represent the actual large scale fire situation. However, these laboratory tests are currently accepted as the only realistic way to develop products. We are now engaged in testing representative products in large scale fire tests.

Acknowledgement
The authors of this paper wish to acknowledge the considerable assistance and help of Mrs. L. R. Tingley.

REFERENCES

1. Matheson, A.F. and Corneliussen, T. Flexible PVC compounds with improved fire performance for cable insulation and sheathing. Flame Retardants 87, PRI/BPF Publication, London, 1987, 8/1.

2. Babrauskas, V. Smoke and gas evolution rate measurements on plastics with the cone calorimeter. Flame Retardants 87, PRI/BPF Publication, London, 1987, 20/1.

3. Flame Retardancy of Polymeric Materials. Vol 1. Marcel Dekker, New York, 1973, P163.

4. Groth, D.H., Settler, L E., Burg, J.R., Busey, W.M., Grant, G.C. and Wang, L. J.Toxicol.Environmental Health, 18:607. (1986).

5. Kanematsu, N.N. Hora and Kada, T. Mutation Research 77:109. (1980).

6. Elrepho whiteness meter (filter R457 no 10 and 11).

FULL-SCALE FIRE TESTING OF AUTOMOBILES

LENNART EKMAN
Volvo Car Corporation
Product Engineering / Dept. 93240 PV 1B
S-405 08 Gothenburg, Sweden

ABSTRACTS

As a part of the work to get high safety in cars, Volvo Car corporation performes full scale fire tests of cars. This report is intended to describe one of the full scale tests, carried out in recent years. This full-scale test shows that it is not a big problem to prevent rapid fire spread from the engine to the passenger compartment. It is more difficult to prevent the smoke generation. The test also shows that the design of a component or a system may be just as important for fire safety as chosing flame retardant material. The test does also show the velocity of forming toxic gases in the passenger compartment during a fire.

INTRODUCTION

Compared with other accidents fire in cars is not a big problem. There are, however, a number of causes which could lead to a fire. In the engine compartment there are combustable materials, fuel for instance, and during and shortly after run, several hot parts. The temperature on the exhaust system may be as high as 500 °C. A turbo system may reach temperatures up to 700 °C. In cars with catalytic emission control the catalytic converter works at temperatures between 400 and 600 °C. In spite of this, modern cars are very safe to fire. The designers are aware of these facts and the full scale tests are a part of the work to get high fire safety.

All interior trim materials in Volvo cars meet the requirements of the FMVSS 302. However the FMVSS 302 is a material standard and doesn't regulate fire safety in complete cars. The fire safety in cars depends on the material combination and the position in the car as well as the material. The flame spread in the car can differ in a very wide range, from selfestinguishing to a passenger compartment being in flames within two to three minutes, depending on the choice of material combination.

Therefore Volvo Car Corporation has performed full scale fire tests of cars since the beginning of the seventies. With full scale tests mean tests where complete cars are used, and the fire spread is measured in some way. Examples of full scale tests are testing of the fire wall, testing of the fuel tank, testing of the floor, testing of wall between trunk and passenger compartment and so on. In these tests, contrary to laboratory tests of materials, we try to simulate a real fire as far as possible.

TEST PERFORMANCE

This report will describe the testing of the fire wall and some results and conclusions of this test. Trials were done to carry out theese tests outdoors, but the wind and the climate had such influence on the results that it was impossible to get any reproducibility at all from test to test. Now these tests are performed indoors at the Swedish National Testing Institute.

For these tests standard cars are used. A vessel of petrol is placed on each side of the engine, close to the fire wall. Figure 1 shows the placing of the vessels, and the position of the thermocouple for temperature measuering. The quantity of petrol in the vessels shall be enough for five minutes burning. Before the ignition of the petrol, the engine shall run for at least 15 minutes in order to reach the same temperature in the engine compartment as at normal driving. After ignition the engine shall be shut off but the ignition key shall be in position on. The bonnet shall be closed during the test. In order to get the smoke out of the passenger compartment there shall be a hole in the roof of the car.

For documentation two video cameras are used. Figure 2 shows a typical camera arrangement.

The temperature is measured on the compartment side of the fire wall on 10 - 15 positions.

In some of the tests the concentration of certain toxic gases has been measured. The gases measured have been carbon monoxide, hydrogen chloride, hydrogen cyanide and some organic substanses. The carbon monoxide was measured continuously. The hydrogen chloride and the hydrogen cyanide were measured in intervals. The intervals for these gases were 0-2 minutes, 2-3 minutes, 3-4 minutes and 4-5 minutes after the ignition of the fire. Also some organic substanses have been measured. Theese have been determined as an average during a five minutes period. In theese cases the passenger compartment has to be closed and it was very difficult to take a film of the interior of the car depending on the high density of the smoke.

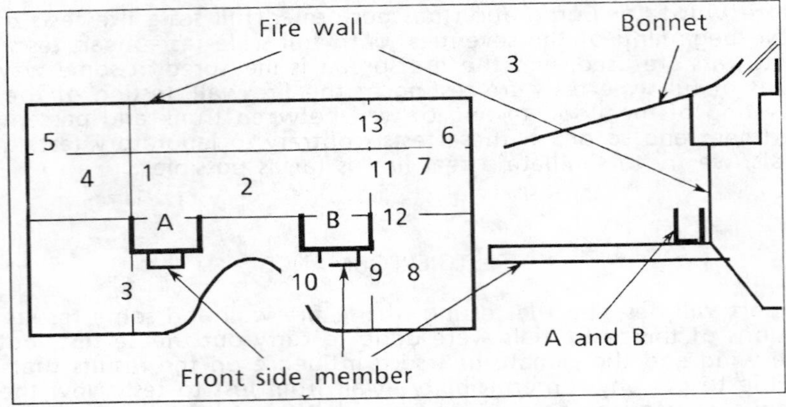

Figure 1. Shematic sketch of the fire wall. The vessels of petrol are placed at A and B. The figures 1-13 shows the position of the thermocuople.

Figure 2. Camera arrengment

RESULTS

Diagram in figure 3 shows the temperature on five positions on the fire wall. It will illustrate that the temperature differ in a very wide range at different positions on the wall.

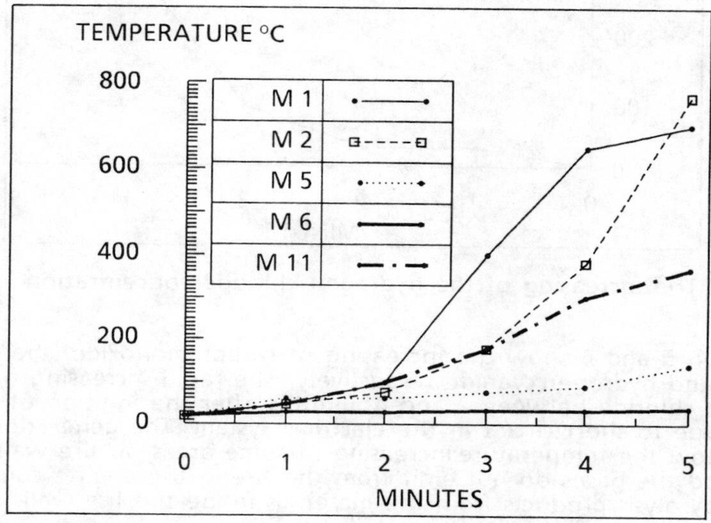

Figure 3. The temperature of the fire wall as a function of the burning time according to this test

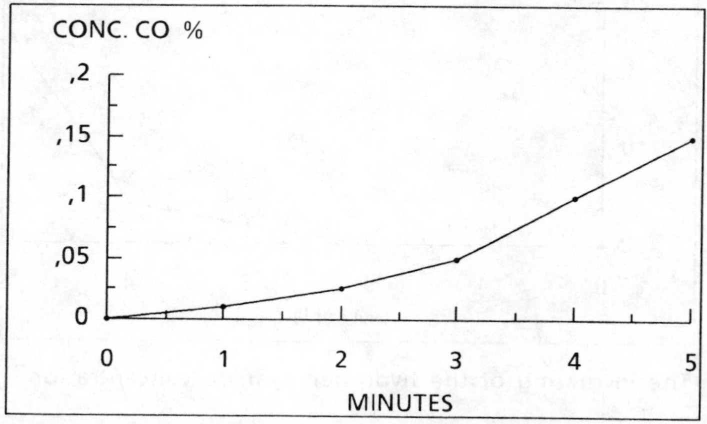

Figure 4. The concentration of carbon monoxide as a function of the burning time

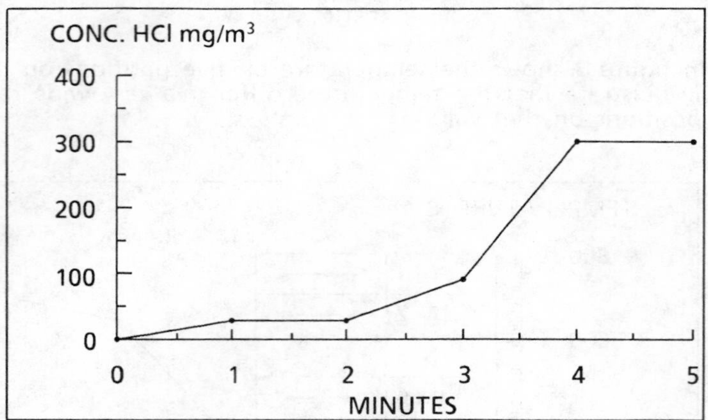

Figure 5. The increasing of the hydrogen chloride concentration.

Diagram 4, 5 and 6 show the increasing of carbon monoxide, the hydrogen chloride and hydrogen cyanide respectively. The rapid increasing of the hydrogen chloride between 2 and 4 minutes after the ignition of the fire may be due to short circuit in the electrical system. The generation of the gases follow the temperature increasing at some areas on fire wall. The smoke and the gases do not emit from the fire in the engine compartment but are pyrolysis products from the materials inside the fire wall.

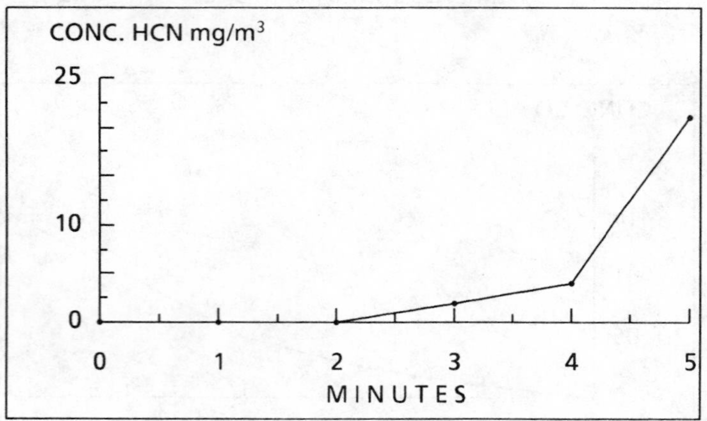

Figure 6. The increasing of the hydrogen cyanide concentration.

Two main groups of organic substanses have been identified in the smoke. Theese are chlorinated and aromatic hydrocarbons. Theese substanses are also pyrolysis products from the materials inside the fire wall. Table 1 and 2 show the average concentration of theese substanses.

TABLE 1 Concentration of some chlorinated hydrocarbons

Chlorinated hydrocarbons	Concentration mg/m^3
Dichlor- metane	100
1,2 dichlor- etane	50
1,1,1 trichlor- etane	35

TABLE 2 Concentration of aromatic hydrocarbons

Aromatic hydrocarbons	Concentration mg/m^3
Bensen	30
Toluen	100
Styrén	35
Ethylbensen	15

This is the same type of organic substanses which can be detected when rubber and plastics pyrolysis at a temperature of 600 -700 °C. Also the organic gases are pyrolysis products from the interior material.

CONCLUSIONS

The temperature measuring on the fire wall shows that it is possible to divide the wall into areas more or less appropriate for grommets and plugs Figure 7 shows such a division of the wall. The crossed-out areas are inappropriate for grommets. The other areas are ranked from 1 to 10 where 1 is the best and 10 is the worst area for fire safety.

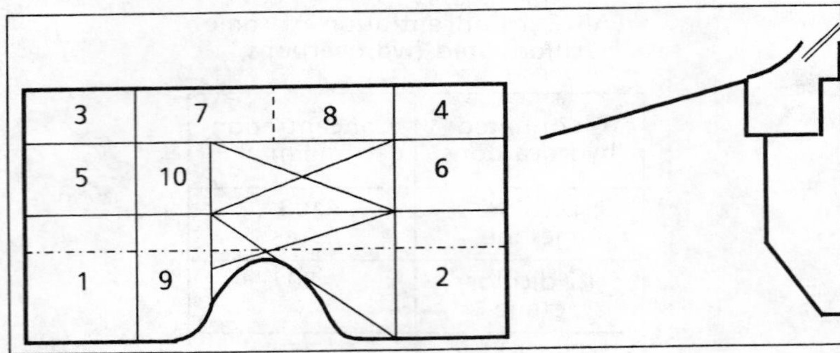

Figure 7. The most and less appropriate areas for plugs and grommets on the fire wall

The design of components such as grommets and plugs may be just as important as chosing flame-resistant materials. Figure 8 shows a grommet (A) wich is better fore fire safety than those shown in figure 9 (B and C). Even if the grommet A is made of standard EPDM material and (B) and (C) are made of a more flame-resistant material, for instance chloroprene. This depends on the fact the grommet (A) melts and tighten against smoke and fire. The thick one (C) swells by the heat and pops out from its hole. The thin one (B) will be destroyed by heat much faster than (A).

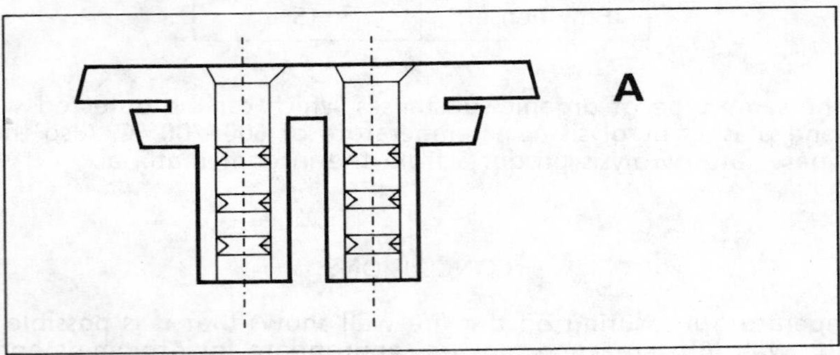

Figure 8. Grommet designed for high fire safety.

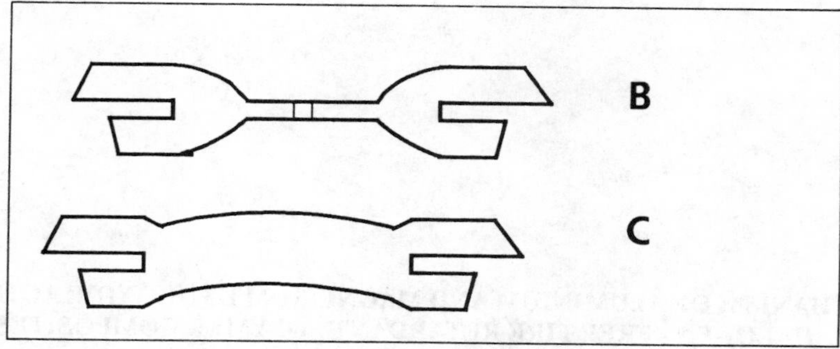

Figure 9 Grommet ,B, and plug ,C.

It is comparatively easy to prevent the fire spread from the engine compartment to the passenger compartment. However the temperature on the fire wall increases very fast. After 3 minutes the temperature on the inside of the fire wall is more than 400 °C. This means that the fire does not go through the wall, but the interior material may ignite by itself. The self-ignition temperature of untreated organic materials is about 400°C. To prevent self-ignition it is necessary to use flame resistant materials.

However the main problem is the smoke. The difficulty is that the smoke is generated inside the passenger compartment at least during the first five to ten minutes of the fire. The smoke generates by pyrolysis of the interior materials such as insulating materials and carpets. The passenger compartmet in a car is very small compared with other vehicles, buses for instance. That means that the concentration of smoke will increase rather fast. The smoke density has not been measured, but the intensity of the smoke increases very fast and follows the temperature on the fire wall.

Even if the interior materials are highly flame resistant, i e are self-extinguishing and won't ignite by heat or ignite at a very high temperature, that won't influence the smoke generation. Some materials with flame retardant generate more smoke than the same material without flame retardant.

Hence, it seems that it is necessary to combine the flame retardants with additives, which will depress the smoke generation. Such materials are not available on the market at the moment, but may be in the future.

Of course, without fire, no smoke. If it is possible to prevent the fire to start, there will be no smoke. Therefore, the main work has to be done at the design of the car. The design of parts and systems is just as important for fire safety as the use of flame-resistant materials. However a combination of good design and the right choice of materials will prepare the ground to get a high fire safety in cars. As long as we use organic materials we have to use flame-retardants, but they have to be combined with smoke depressing additives.

MECHANISM OF ALUMINIUM AND MAGNESIUM HYDROXIDE ACTION IN HALOGEN - FREE FIRE RETARDANT POLYMER COMPOSITES

E. GAL, A. PAL ,J. RYCHLY*, K. TARAPCIKOVA
Research Institute for Cables and Insulating Materials,
Tovarenska 14, 815 71 Bratislava, Czechoslovakia
*Polymer Institute, Centre of Chemical Research, Slovak Academy of Sciences,
842 36 Bratislava, Czechoslovakia

ABSTRACT

The flame retardant effect of aluminium and magnesium hydroxide in in polyethylene and ethylene - vinyl acetate is investigated. The flame retardancy action of hydroxides is attributed mainly to the water released during heating.However, these fillers influence also the rate of polymer volatilisation.An attempt is made to investigate the connection between hydroxides decomposition, volatisation of polymers and flammability characteristics of composites.

INTRODUCTION

The need of noncorrosive, smoke suppressing fire retardants in cable industry has attracted the research interest to inorganic halogenfree fillers. In particular aluminium and magnesium hydroxides are studied as an alternative for the halogen based fire retardants.

The retardant effect of these fillers is attributed mainly to the endothermic decomposition reaction and the acompanied release of water, resulting in cooling of the polymer matrix, dilution of flammable gases and protecting of polymer surface from air oxygen.Relatively little attention has been paid to the study of the way in which these apparently inert fillers affect the decomposition of polymers during heating. Although, some autors have called attention to the catalytic effect of hydroxides on thermal oxidation of polymers, which can influence their combustion characteristics (1-3).

In this work the effect of metallic hydroxides on both the combustion behaviour and decomposition processes is investigated. A correlation between decomposition processes, as received by nonisothermal TG measurments flammability characteristics, is searched for.

EXPERIMENTAL

Samples containing 60 and 67 weight % of aluminium hydroxide and magnesium hydroxide were prepared.As a polymer base very low density polyethylene was used (PE - VLD) with melt index 0,9 g/10 min and density 0,9 g/cm^3, and ethylene - vinyl acetate copolymer (E/VAC) with vinyl acetate content of 50%.

Composites with PE were prepared on calender and samples moulded at 130°C.

Composites with E/VAC were mixed in Brabender Plastograph where also Dicumylperoxide was added and samples were crosslinked by molding at 170°C for 12 min.

Decomposition profiles of samples were measured at 1090 b Du Pont Thermoanalytic System, consisting from TGA and DSC modules.The ammount of samples used was up to 10 mg, the heating rate was 10°C/min and the air flow 10 liters/h.

Self-ignition characteristics were determined using Setchkin-like apparatus (4).A sample (3g) was placed in a reactor maintained at a given temperature and scavenged by an air flow of 6 liters/min.Time to self-ignition at various temperatures was recorded.As a self-ignition temperature the value was taken at which the sample ignits 15 min after its insertion into the apparatus.

Oxygen indices, as well as temperature indices, were measured according to ASTM D - 2836 on a Stanton - Redcroft apparatus, moduli FTA and HFTA.

Time to ignition was measured according to IEC - 707, Method FV, but with flame applications for 10 s until flame combustion in duration of least 10 s has occured.

RESULTS

The effect of inorganic hydroxides on flammability characteristics of PE and E/VAC is summarized in table 1.

As seen from the results in the table, higher values of flammability characteristics have been obtained with the samples where as a polymer base E/VAC was used.If the effect of the fillers is compared, the results are not as univocal. Higher values of temperature indices were observed in both polymers when aluminium hydroxide was used as a filler.On the other hand self-ignition temperature increased more significantly in composites with magnesium hydroxide. In PE, higher values of LOI have been obtained with aluminium hydroxide than with magnesium hydroxide, in E/VAC again $Mg(OH)_2$ has been more effective.

The effect of hydroxides used on self-ignition characteristics is illustrated in Figure 1, in which the time to self-ignition versus temperature of oven is plotted for the composites containing 67 weight % of fillers.

TABLE 1

Flammability characteristics of PE and E/VAC filled with aluminium and magnesium hydroxide

Filler	% w	Polymer	LOI (%)	TI (°C)	T_{sig} (°C)	tig (s)
$Al(OH)_3$	60	PE	29	248	430	55
"	"	E/VAC	37	301	443	88
"	67	PE	40	300	433	101
"	"	E/VAC	43	341	435	118
$Mg(OH)_2$	60	PE	29	240	453	47
"	"	E/VAC	46	288	450	102
"	67	PE	33	269	465	120
"	"	E/VAC	57	311	449	-

TI = temperature index
T_{sig} = temperature of self-ignition
t_{ig} = time to ignition

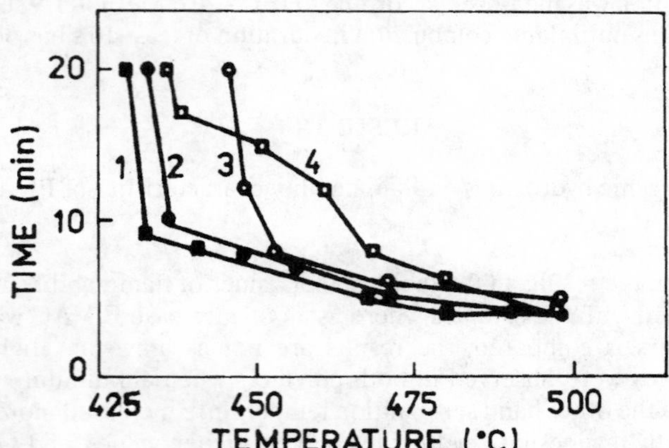

Figure 1. Time to self-ignition versus temperature of oven.
1 - PE + $Al(OH)_3$; 2 - E/VAC + $Al(OH)_3$; 3 - E/VAC + $Mg(OH)_2$;
4 - PE + $Mg(OH)_2$

The way in which these fillers interfere with the polymer decomposition has been evaluated by TGA.Decomposition profiles as revealed by TGA measurements are shown in Figure 2.

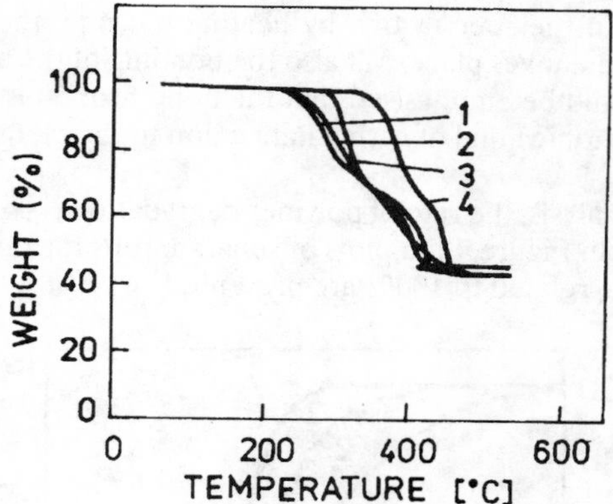

Figure 2. TG plots of the composites containing 67 weight % of the filler. 1 -PE + $Al(OH)_3$; 2 - E/VAC + $Al(OH)_3$; 3 - E/VAC + $Mg(OH)_2$; 4 - PE + $Mg(OH)_2$

In all TG curves only two decomposition waves were observed. It is surprising in the case of E/VAC, since it itself decomposes in two waves, first corresponding to acetic acid and the second to the decomposition of the rest of the polymer. As found in (3) the release of water from $Al(OH)_3$ always precedes the wave of acetic acid from E/VAC, while that from $Mg(OH)_2$ follows it. So the TG curve of the composite should, theoretically, yield three waves.

The fate of the acetic acid in the course of the composite heating may be revealed by IR analysis.The IR spectra of E/VAC composite with $Mg(OH)_2$ before (A) and after heating in TG furnace up to 400°C (B) are presented in Figure 3.

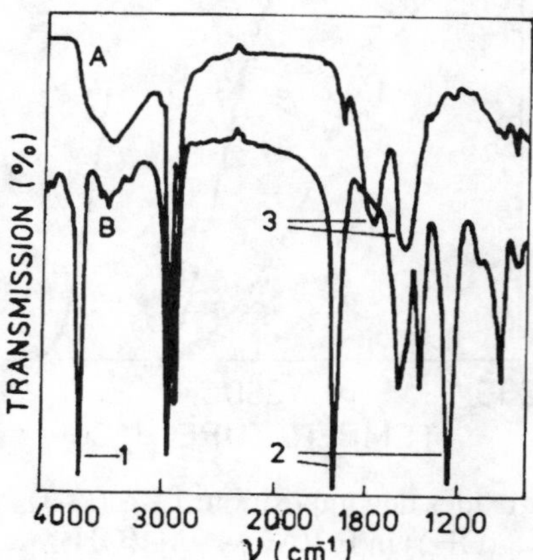

Figure 3. IR spectra of E/VAC + 60 weight % of $Mg(OH)_2$, A - unheated; B - heated up to 400°C. 1 - $Mg(OH)_2$; 2 - vinyl acetate; 3 - carboxylate anion bonded on metal cation.

It can be seen from the spectra that by heating not only the decomposition of hydroxide and vinyl acetate takes place, but also the bonding of the acetate to the metal hydroxide residue.It should be emphasised that the bond formed is not a covalent one of metal acetate, but the ionic bond of carboxilate anion to the metal cation.

As shown by TG analysis, the rate of polymer degradation is considerably changed by inorganic hydroxides.In Figure 4 the plots of separate runs for the second wave, that of polymer volatilization, related to 100% are presented.

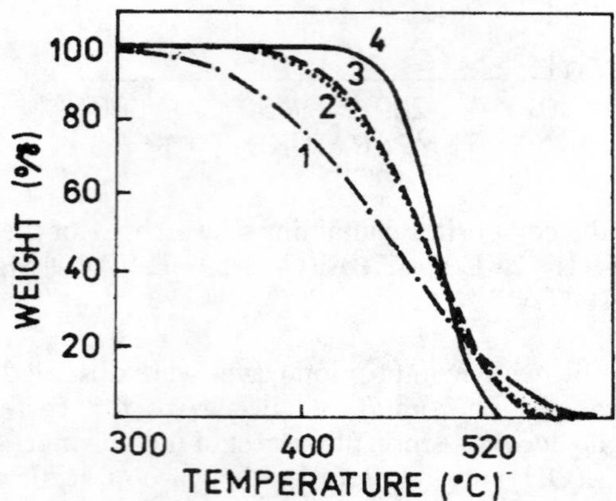

Figure 4. TG plots of polymer decomposition. 1 - PE + $Al(OH)_3$; 2 - E/VAC + $Al(OH)_3$; 3 - E/VAC + $Mg(OH)_2$; 4 - PE + $Mg(OH)_2$

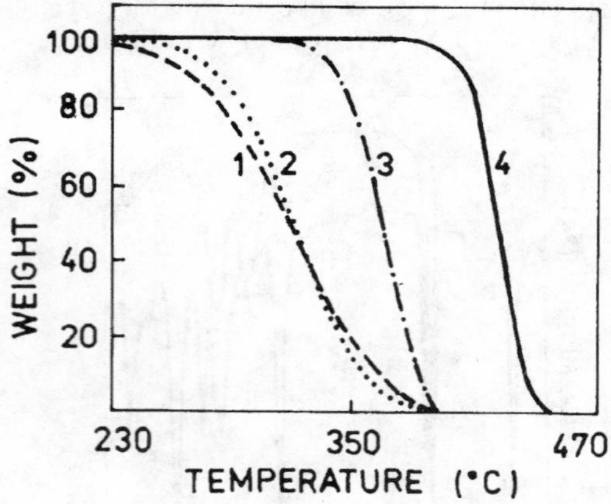

Figure 5. TG plots of hydroxides decomposition. 1 - $Al(OH)_3$ in PE 2 - $Al(OH)_3$ in E/VAC; 3 - $Mg(OH)_2$ in E/VAC; 4 - $Mg(OH)_2$ in PE

Not only hydroxides affect the polymer degradation, but also polymers affect the rate of hydroxides decomposition, as shown in Figure 5, where the separate runs for the first wave of hydroxides decomposition, related to 100%, are shown.

The mutual influence of polymers and hydroxides on the rate of their decomposition can be seen from Table 2.In the table the activation energies of both processes, i.e. the hydroxide decomposition and polymer degradation are summarized.The activation energies have been calculated according to the procedure developed by Rychly (5) for the quantitave analysis of nonisothermal thermoanalytical curves.

TABLE 2
Activation energies of the decomposition of samples

Filler	% w.	Polymer	E_1 (kJ/mol)	E_2 (kJ/mol)
$Al(OH)_3$	60	PE	92	51
"	"	E/VAC	69	55
"	67	PE	102	33
"	"	E/VAC	90	29
$Mg(OH)_2$	60	PE	210	239
"	"	E/VAC	160	100
"	67	PE	-	-
"	"	E/VAC	167	143

E_1 = activation energy of hydroxide decomposition
E_2 = activation energy of polymer

DISCUSSION

During the combustion of PE and E/VAC the inorganic fillers show combined retardant and stabilizing effect.They increase the LOI values as well as self-ignition characteristics and influence also the oxidation characteristics of polymers.

As illustrated by figure 4 and summarized in table 2, hydroxides significantly affect rate of polymer degradation.The weight loss of polymers in the presence of $Al(OH)_3$ occurs in much larger temperature interval than it is in the presence of $Mg(OH)_2$.This is reflected by the differences of activation energies, which are 29 to 51 kJ/mol for composites with aluminium hydroxide and 100 to 239 kJ/mol for those with magnesium hydroxide.The effect of $Al(OH)_3$ on the lowering of activation energy of polymer degradation can probably be explained by the increase of the production of char residue during the thermooxidation of polymers (5).On the other hand, the increase of the activation energy in the presence of magnesium hydroxide is due probably to the blanketing of the polymer surface from air oxygen by the water which released from $Mg(OH)_2$ at much higher temperatures than it is in the case of $Al(OH)_3$.The blanketing effect is reflected also by the activation energy, which is nearly the same as it is in nitrogen (210 kJ/mol) (5).

Lower temperature of water release in the case of $Mg(OH)_2$ in E/VAC as compared to PE (Figure 5) could be ascribed to the interaction with acetic acid formed by the degradation of copolymer.In the case of $Al(OH)_3$, which decomposes at lower temperatures than the acetic acid is released, no significant effect of polymer has been observed.

An interesting fact is the relation between ignitability of samples and nonisothermal TG characteristics of hydroxides decomposition. In Figure 6 self-ignition temperatures are plotted against activation energies of hydroxides decomposition.

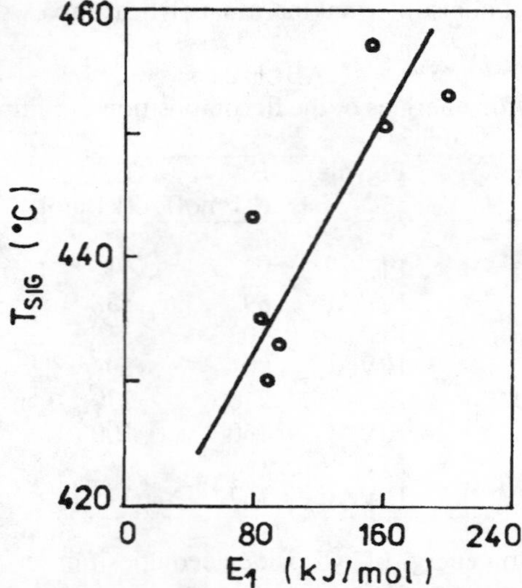

Figure 6. Plot of temperature of self-ignition (T_{sig}) versus activation energy of hydroxide decomposition (E_1)

The most significiant increase of T_{sig} related to pure polymer was observed for $Mg(OH)_2$ in PE (T_{sig} of pure PE is 400°C),where the value raised within 65°C.E/VAC displays lower increase,since T_{sig} of pure copolymer is 430°C and the maximal increase received by filler was 20°C,obtained with 67% $Mg(OH)_2$.

According to the work of Johnson (6) the LOI has to increase linearly with the decrease of the combustion heat of samples.Assuming that inorganic fillers reduce the combustion heat proportionelly to their content,it can be calculated from the known values of pure polymers, which are 48 kJ/g for PE and 36 kJ/g for E/VAC.In Figure 7 a plot of combustion heat calculated versus limit oxygen indices measured is shown.

As seen from correlation in Figure 7 ,higher limit oxygen indices obtained with composites where E/VAC was used as a polymer base can be ascribed to the lower combustion heat values.Interesting are values of LOI obtained for E/VAC filled with $Mg(OH)_2$,which are higher as one would suppose from the correlation between combustion heat and LOI.Most probably the catalytic effect of $Mg(OH)_2$ or of the products of its interaction with acetic acid has to be taken into account.However further work is required to explain this fact.

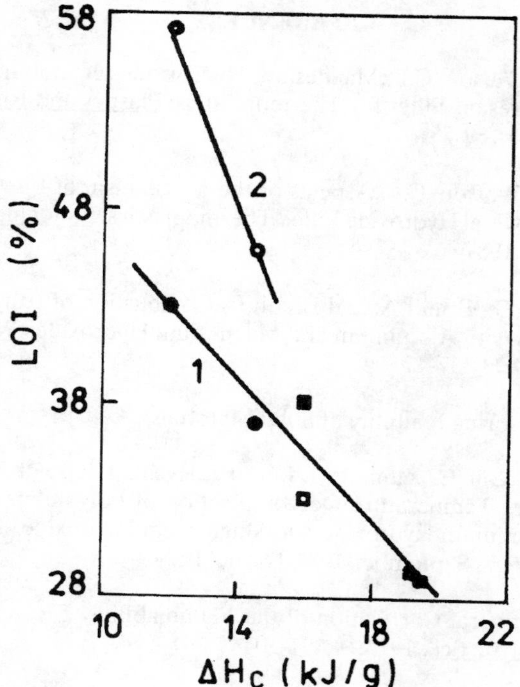

Figure 7. Plot of limit oxygen index (LOI) versus combustion heat (Hc).■ - PE + Al(OH)3;□ - PE + Mg(OH)2; ● E/VAC + Al(OH)3; o - E/VAC + Mg(OH)2

CONCLUSION

Nonisothermal TG records were used to explain the differences in ignitability characteristics of PE and E/VAC composites with aluminium hydroxide and magnesium hydroxide.

Synchronisation of hydroxides decomposition and polymer volatilisation has been reported as one of the major factors influencing fire resistency (2).Perhaps this is a reason of the increased limit oxygen indices found in the case of $Mg(OH)_2$ in E/VAC.In this composite the rate of water release from hydroxide seems to be affected by the acetic acid released from E/VAC.

The influence of hydroxides on thermal oxidative stability of polymers was observed by TG analysis.Although, the significance of this is unclear.Some correlation between the rate of polymer decomposition, temperature indices and time to flame has been observed, but more investigations are neede here.

REFERENCES

1. Hornsby, P.R. and Watson, C.L.,Magnesium Hydroxide - a Combined Flame Retardant and Smoke Suppresant Filler for Thermoplastics. Plastics and Rubber Processing and Application,1986,**6**,169-75

2. Hornsby, P.R. and Watson, C.L.,Aspects of the Mechanism of Fire Retardancy and Smoke Suppresion in Metal Hydroxide Filled Thermoplastics. Fundamentals of Polymer Flammability,London,1987

3. Delfosse,L., Baillet,G., Brault,A. and Brault,D.,Combustion of Ethylene-Vinyl Acetate Copolymer Filled with Aluminium and Magnesium Hydroxides.Polymer Degradation and Stability,1989,**23**,337-47

4. CSN 64 0149 - Measuring Ignibility of Solid Materials

5. Rychly,J., Vesely,K. Gal, E., Zummer,J. Jancar,J.,Rychla,L. Use of Thermal Methods in Characterizations of Temperature Deccomposition of Polyolefins Filled With Calcium Carbonate, Aluminium Hydroxide and Magnesium Hydroxide. Thrid Meeting on Fire Retardant Polymers, September 1989 Torino, Italy.

6. Johnson,P.R., A General Correlation of the Flammability of Natural and Synthetic Polymers. J. Appl. Polym. Sci., 1974,**18**,491-504

ALUMINIUM HYDROXIDE AND MAGNESIUM HYDROXIDE – NEW DEVELOPMENTS AND THEIR APPLICATION TO POLYMER COMPOUNDING

DR. GEORG KIRSCHBAUM
Technical Service Manager
Martinswerk GmbH
Kölner Straße 110, D-5010 Bergheim

ABSTRACT

Aluminium hydroxide is the best known halogen free flame retardant available with a low electrolyte content and specified particle size offering good mechanical and electrical properties in polymer compounds. A range of new, specially developed surface treatments, has provided for improved properties in rubber and polyester applications.

For applications using polypropylene and polyamide a new range of special magnesium hydroxide products are offered which tolerate processing temperatures up to 340°C before decomposing.
Using these grades polypropylene compounds will meet UL94 VO at about 60% loadings. Recently developed surface treatments retain tensile and impact strength even in heavily loaded compounds.

Non treated and specially surface treated grades of magnesium hydroxides offer excellent flame retardant properties and low smoke densities combined with good electrical and mechanical properties in rubber compound, and are recommended for use in cable manufacture.

INTRODUCTION

Economical manufacturing methods for mass production and improvements of properties of finished products have in many applications greatly contributed to replace traditional materials like metals or wood with plastics and rubbers.

The use of these organic polymer systems, which for the most part are flammable, leads to greater fire risks and thus to growing importance of flame retardants.

Traditional flame retardants based on halogen compounds, often combined with synergistic antimony oxides, act in the gas phase by splitting under formation of radicals, thereby capturing the radical molecule 0_2 and suppressing the burning reaction.

Flame retardant reaction in the gas phase usually leads to increased soot formation and smoke density and thereby affecting the escape of personnel and fire fighting. Special smoke suppressing systems in these formulations have not yet lead to the desired success.

Recent evaluations in the United Kingdom and the USA have shown that most fire fatalities in these countries were not caused by direct burns but by the effect of smoke and toxic combustion gases (1). The use of halogenated diphenyl ethers bears significant risks by forming polyhalgenated dibenzodioxines and dibenzofuranes at elevated temperatures, as found in investigations by the German Federal Bureau of Environment (2).

The conclusions described above are the main reasons for the great increase in demand for halogen free flame retardants.

MATERIALS AND METHODS

Aluminium Hydroxide grades used:

MARTINAL (TRIHYDE) OL-104, OL-107, OL-111 LE - Standard grades of aluminium hydroxide with 1.8, 1.1 and 0.7 microns median particle size respectively.

MARTINAL (TRIHYDE) OL-104/s, OL-107/s - Silane treated ATH-grades with a.m. particle size.

MARTINAL (TRIHYDE) OL-104/k, OL-107/k, OL-111/k - special surface treated grades for rubber applications.

MARTINAL (TRIHYDE) ON-310 - ground ATH, median particle size 8-10 microns.

MARTINAL (TRIHYDE) ON-920/v - standard product with special granulometry and surface treatment for UP-applications, med. particle size approximately 25 microns.

MARTINAL (TRIHYDE) VPF 8826 - development product, special granulometry and surface treatments for UP-applications, med. particle size approx. 6 microns.

All the ATH-grades used were produced by Martinswerk GmbH

Magnesium Hydroxide grades used:

VPF 8812 - Standard grade, non treated, med. particle size 0.9-1.1 microns

VPF 8813 - silane treated VPF 8812 for rubber applications

VPF 8814 - VPF 8812 with special surface treatment for PP-applications

VPF 8824 - VPF 8812 with special surface treatment for PA-applications

VPF 8927 - silane treated VPF 8812 for PP-applications

The new Magnesium hydroxide grades were developed in cooperation of Martinswerk GmbH and Veitscher Magnesitwerke AG.

Formulations

EPDM-compounds:	EPDM-rubber	100	pts
	ATH or Mg.-hyd.	220	pts
	Plasticizer	20	pts
	ZnO	5	pts
	Polyethyleneglycol	5	pts
	Silane	2	pts
	TAC	1	pts
	Curing agents	5.5	pts

PP-compounds: PP-Homopolymer
MG-hydroxide

PA-compounds: PA-6 Homopolymer
Mg-hydroxide

Methods:

All methods used for analysis and testing are indicated in the text.

RESULTS

New surface treated Aluminium Hydroxides for Rubber Applications

Finely precipitated ATH-grades have been standard products in halogen free flame retardant formulations for demanding rubber applications such as cable insulation and sheathing for more than 20 years.
Large amounts are processed to achieve effective flame retardancy in combination with good physical properties in the final products. In standard processes organic additives, such as fatty acid derivatives and silanes, are used for surface treatment of the flame retardant filler to give a better dispersion in the compound and an increased adhesion between A1-hydroxide and polymer matrix:
Silane treated ATH-grades are known to improve tensile strength and electrical properties of rubber compounds compared to the corresponding non-treated grades with their disadvantage of having a high price.
A new generation of surface treated ATH (the MARTINAL K-grades) has made possible an even better set of properties under more favourable economic conditions.
Additives usually used to improve workability of rubber compounds during processing, e.g. organic alcohol and ester derivatives, have the tendency of plasticising the compound thus decreasing tensile strength (see figure 1).

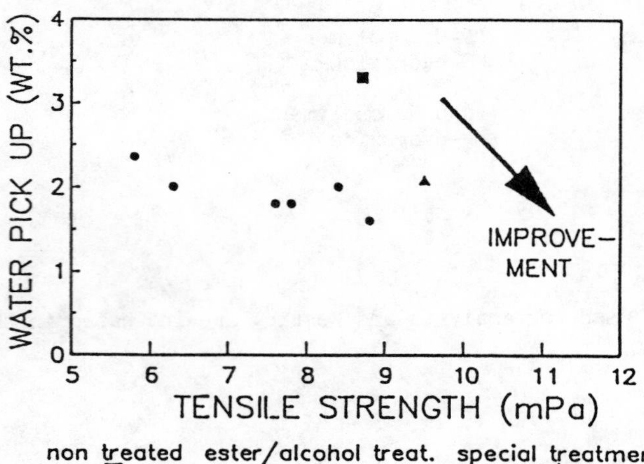

Figure 1. Al-hydroxides in EPDM compounds. Properties of different surface treatments on EPDM compound.

The new agent for surface treatment (indicated as "special treatment" in figure 1) shows advantages for nearly all determined compound properties. Tensile strength and volume resistivity are improved, water pick up and working viscosities of the corresponding compounds are decreased (see figures 2 to 5).

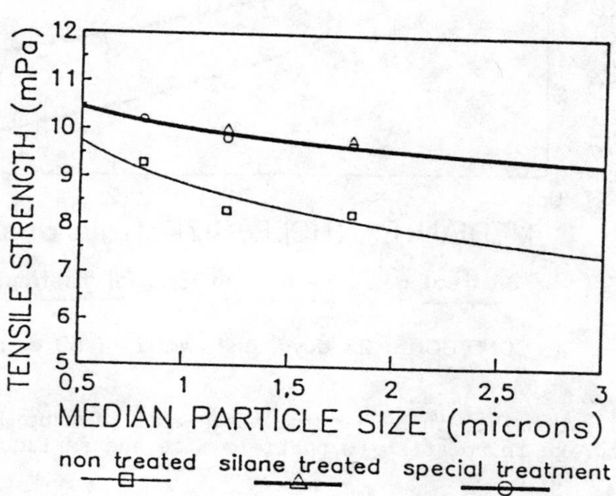

Figure 2. Al-hydroxides in EPDM compounds. Tensile strength in relation to particle size and surface treatment.

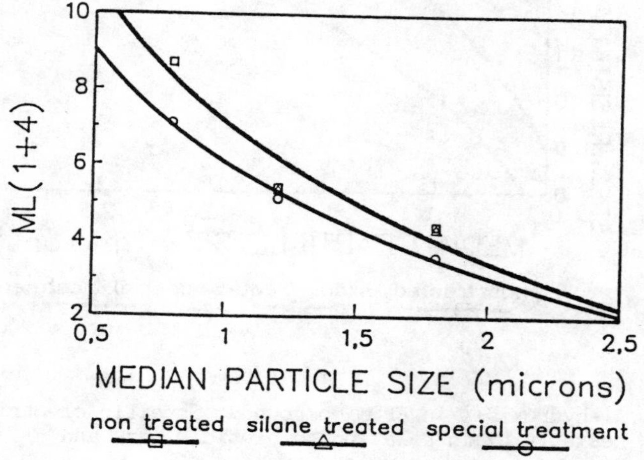

Figure 3. Al-hydroxides in EPDM compounds. Compound viscosity (before curing) in relation to particle size and surface treatment.

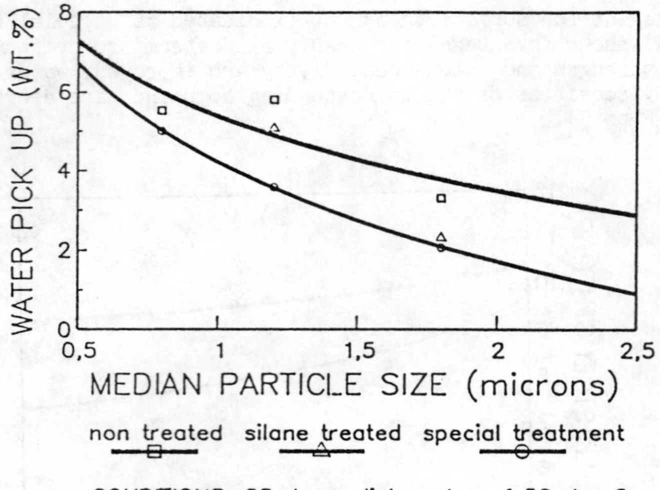

Figure 4. Al-hydroxides in EPDM compounds. Water pick up during water storage in relation to particle size and surface treatment.

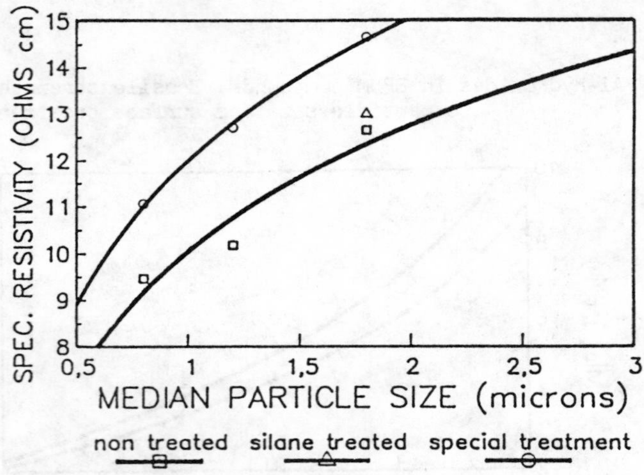

Figure 5. Al-hydroxides in EPDM compounds. Specific electrical resistivity in relation to particle size and surface treatment

As shown above the new surface treated MARTINAL K-grades open new possibilities for halogen free flame retardancy with Al-hydroxides for extremely demanding rubber applications, e.g. special cables.

Aluminium hydroxides in UP-resins

Besides the above mentioned application halogen free flame retarded UP (e.g. SMC, BMC) consumed large amounts of ATH worldwide. For processing highly filled UP-compounds it is important to reach the lowest possible compound viscosities. Adjusting the particle size distribution of precipitated or ground ATH and special surface treatments are two possible ways to achieve significant reductions in viscosity.
Recently developed ATH-grades permit high filling levels combined with, in comparison to standard grades, very low compound viscosities (see figure 6).

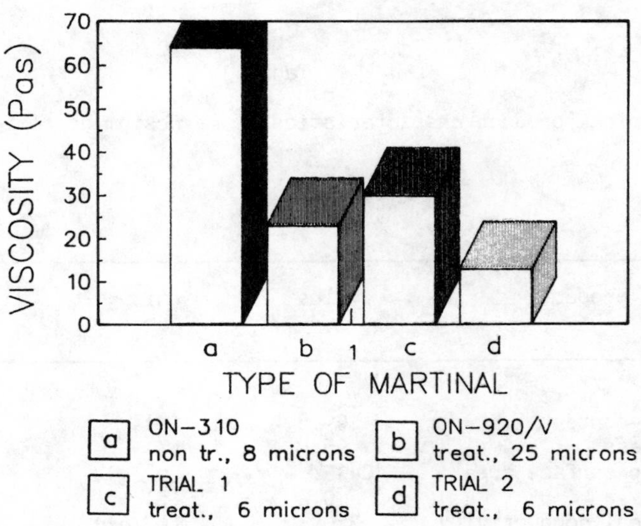

Figure 6. Al-hydroxides in UP-resins. Compound viscosities at a 175 phr loading level.

New Aspects for Thermoplastic Applications with Special Magnesium Hydroxides

Consumption and processing of plastics and especially polypropylene is increasing worldwide. As processing temperatures of these thermoplastics such as PP, PA and PE are above 200°C, Aluminium hydroxide cannot be used as a flame retardant in these systems because of its decomposition temperature. For all these applications Magnesium hydroxide with a decomposition temperature of 340°C opens up new areas for halogen free flame retardants. Most of the $Mg(OH)_2$ based flame retardants available up to now have been unable to comply with the combined requirements of flame retardancy and physical properties.

Traditional Magnesium hydroxides, derived from sea water by precipitation, possess high specific surface areas and sizeable quantities of ionic impurities, thus leaving workability and physical properties unsatisfactory.

a special process, patented by Veitscher Magnesitwerke AG, makes it possible to produce an ultrapure magnesium hdyroxide with regular crystals and low specific surface from a mineral raw material source.

Table 1 gives an overview of the characteristic product parameters.

Table 1

Typical product characteristics of magnesium hydroxide VPF 8812

product property	value	unit	method
$Mg(OH)_2$-content	99.8	(%)	XRD/XRF
Brightness	95	(%)	DIN 53163
Specific surface area	10-12	(m^2/g)	DIN 66131
Humidity	0.2	(%)	3h, 105°C
Electrical conductivity	350	(µS/cm)	DIN 53208
Median particle size	1	(microns)	(Laser-scattering)

With increasing amounts of magnesium hydroxide, elongation and impact strength are decreasing, as expected. Oxygen index is increasing, and UL 94 classification VO is passed with 60% $Mg(OH)_2$ loading and more.

Classification VO according to UL 94 is dependant on the sample thickness:

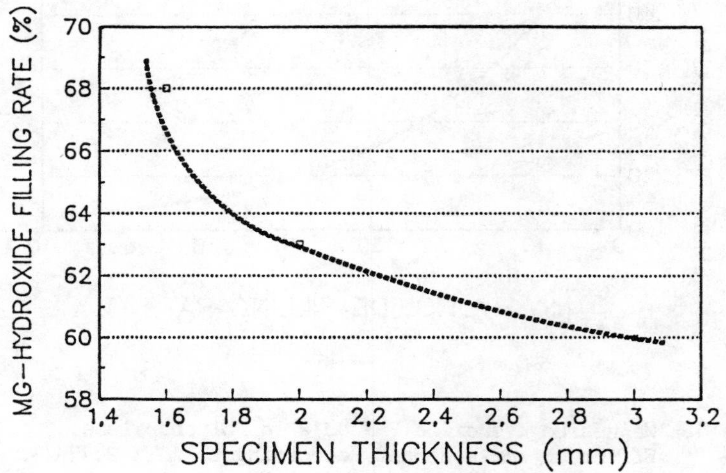

Figure 7. Magnesium hydroxide VPF 8812 in Polypropylene. Necessary filler levels to meet UL 94 VO.

The fine $Mg(OH)_2$ reduces smoke density of PP compounds very effectively:

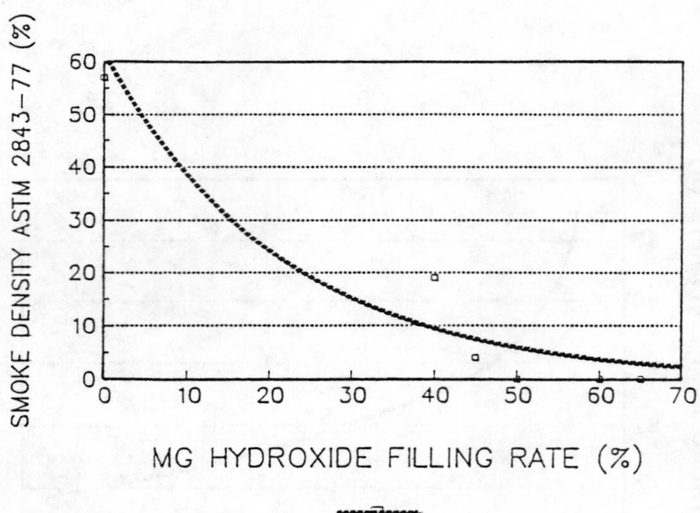

Figure 8. Magnesium hydroxide VPF 8812 in Polypropylene. Effect on smoke density according to ASTM 2843-77

High proportions of mineral fillers in plastic compounds often lead to evident and sometimes undesired changes of compound properties (see Table 2). By modifying the surface of $Mg(OH)_2$ VPF 8812, extensive adaptations to the specific requirements of the various PP applications are possible. Special grades lead to acceptable physical properties even at higher filler loadings.

Table 2
Magnesium hydroxides in Polypropylene. Influence of special surface treatments on compound properties.

product property	values				unit	method
PP	40	40	40	40		
VPF 8812	60	-	-	-		
VPF 8814	-	60	-	-		
VPF 8927	-	-	60	-		
$Mg(OH)_2$[1]	-	-	-	60		
Tensile strength	25	20.8	30.5	18.2	N/mm^2	DIN 53455
Elongation	0.04	0.34	0.05	0.03	m/m	DIN 53455
Impact strength	10	o.B.	34	3	KJ/m^2	DIN 53453
Oxygen Index	27	-[2]	26.5	-[2]	%	ASTM D - 2863-77
UL 94	VO	V1	V1	V1		

1) seawater derived material, med. particle size approx. 5 microns
2) not determined

Table 3
Magnesium hydroxide in Polyamide 6. Influence of filler's surface treatment on compound properties.

product property	values			method
PA 6	100	50	50	
VPF 8812	-	50	-	
VPF 8824	-	-	50	
Impact strength	o.B.	20	40	DIN 53453
UL 94[1)]	HB	V-1	V-2	

1) 3mm specimen

CONCLUSIONS

The above shown results demonstrate that development of special surface treating agents and methods for their applications can open new dimensions of effective halogen free flame retardants based on Al- and Mg- hydroxide.

Even well known products such as fine precipitated ATH can be modified resulting in highly filled compounds with astonishing properties.

New raw material sources, production processes and exact adjustment during crystallisation of magnesium hydroxides, as well as specific modification of their surface, open doors to halogen free flame retardancy in thermoplastic applications that were hardly possible before.

Technical polymer systems, such as thermoplastic elastomers based on polyester or polyurethane, present future applications for special $Mg(OH)_2$ grades.

References

1. Steorts, N.H., CPSC'S Comicitment to Fire Safety, FRCA-Conference "Flame Retardancy Advances in Fire Safety", March 28-30, 1984 New Orleans

2. a) Sachstand "Polybromierte Dibenzodioxine, polybromierte Dibenzofurane", Umweltbundesamt, 1989

   b) Pohle, H., The Future of Brominated Diphenyloxide based Flame Retardants - a Discussion of the Dioxine issue", Flame Retardants '87, Nov. 26-27 1987, London

THE EMERGENCE OF MAGNESIUM HYDROXIDE AS A FIRE RETARDANT ADDITIVE

ROGER ROTHON
Technical Department, ICI Chemicals and Polymers Group,
P.O. Box 8, The Heath, Runcorn, Cheshire WA7 4QD.

ABSTRACT

Hydrated inorganic compounds, such as metal hydroxides, are of growing interest as fire retardant additives for polymers.

Aluminium hydroxide has dominated this market for many years. Recently there has been growing interest in magnesium hydroxide.

This paper examines the types of magnesium hydroxide available, its fire retardant performance, the history of its development in this application and the reasons for it's growing acceptance.

The main advantage over aluminium hydroxide is greater thermal stability. Calcium hydroxide is even more stable and much less expensive. It's fire retardant performance is poor however. The reason for this is also briefly discussed.

INTRODUCTION

The principle of reducing polymer flammability by utilising high loadings of a filler which decomposes endothermically releasing water at pyrolysis temperatures has been known and exploited since the 1960's [1].

A variety of inorganic materials are suitable for this use, but until recently the commercial scene has been dominated by one material, aluminium hydroxide (alumina trihydrate, ATH).

Among the other possibilities is magnesium hydroxide. This was described in the patent literature at least as early as 1963 [2]. However, until recently this material has not been widely used. As the number of papers at this conference shows, this situation is now changing and magnesium hydroxide is set to play a more important role in the future.

Virtually all the literature concerning the performance of magnesium hydroxide as a flame retardant filler is either in patents or in product promotional form. This makes an objective appraisal of it's advantages and limitations and of the relative performance of its various physical forms very difficult.

As a company we have a wide interest in magnesium hydroxide. This includes its use in our own polymer composites, as a substrate for our specialised filler coating technology and also as a potential addition to our range of effect fillers.

This broad spread of interests has enabled us to carry out an extensive study of the material, its manufacture and properties.

Drawing on this experience and published literature this paper examines;

(i) the reasons why magnesium hydroxide is now beginning to find more widespread application.

(ii) the various types of product available.

(iii) the main factors influencing performance.

(iv) the use of surface modification to improve performance.

WHY MAGNESIUM HYDROXIDE?

The principles behind the effectiveness of fire retardant fillers are well known, with the most important features being the size of the decomposition endotherm and the volume of water released.

These values are listed in Table 1 for aluminium, magnesium and calcium hydroxides, together with the approximate decomposition temperatures (from DTA Measurements). As volume fraction is the most important factor in filled systems, these parameters are expressed in volume, rather than weight or molar terms.

TABLE 1

Thermal Decomposition of Metal Hydroxides

Mineral	Approximate Temperature of Decomposition °C	Enthalpy of Decomposition Cal/cc (Complete Decomposition)	Water Release g/cc (Complete Decomposition)
$Al(OH)_3$	180	-675	0.84
$Mg(OH)_2$	300	-820	0.73
$Ca(OH)_2$	450	-865	0.58

It can be seen that all three hydroxides possess similar properties with increasing heat absorption on going from aluminium to calcium hydroxide being offset by reduced water release.

On this basis the fire retardant performance of all three might be thought to be very similar.

However, while both aluminium and magnesium hydroxides are of proven effectiveness, calcium hydroxide gives disappointing results [3,4]. This has been shown to be due to the formation of the carbonate (an exothermic process) rather than oxide during polymer combustion [4].

The main difference between the hydroxides is their stabilities which increase markedly from aluminium to calcium hydroxide.

It is the relatively low thermal stability of ATH that limits its usefulness and drives the interest in alternatives. Higher stability allows higher processing temperatures and enables the filler to be used in a wider range of polymers. This is especially true of thermoplastics such as polypropylene and nylon which are difficult, if not impossible, to fill with ATH. Even with other polymers the use of higher processing temperatures can increase throughput and markedly improve economics.

As calcium hydroxide is ruled out by its poor performance, magnesium hydroxide is the material of choice in these applications. It is this factor which is leading to its more widespread use.

FIRE RETARDANT EFFECT OF MAGNESIUM HYDROXIDE

As stated earlier the primary fire retardant effect of magnesium hydroxide is due to its endothermic decomposition, accompanied by water release.

It is therefore worth examining this decomposition in more detail as it is somewhat more complex than would appear from idealised commercial literature.

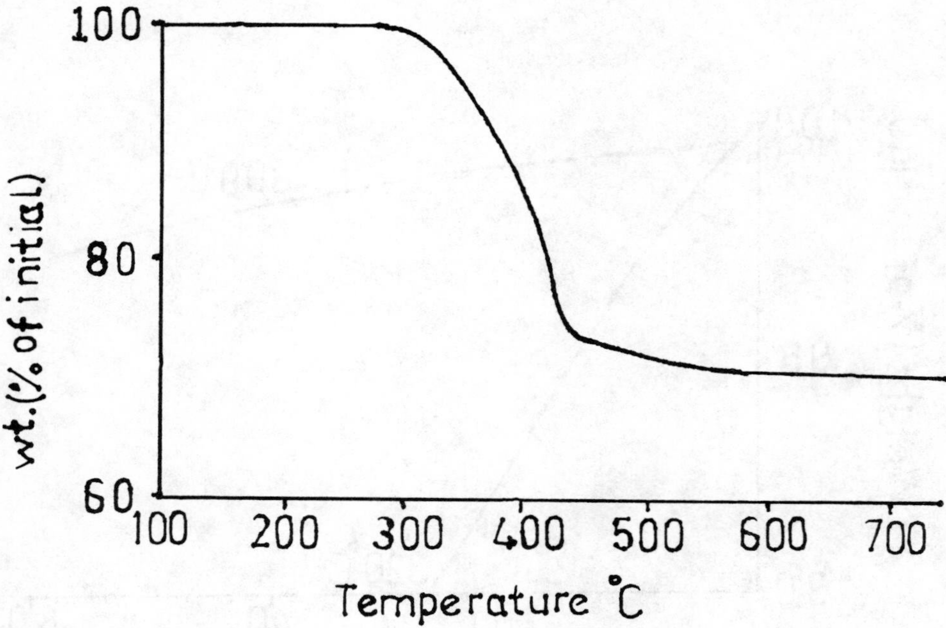

Figure 1. Typical thermogravimetric trace for magnesium hydroxide.

From the TGA trace in Figure 1 it can be seen that the decomposition is not the simple sharp, one step process that is generally depicted. Instead it occurs in two stages [5]. The first stage comprises conversion to a high surface area, disordered magnesium oxide lattice. The surface of this material is still heavily hydrated. Only at temperatures well above 500°C does this lattice rearrange to a more stable phase and lose surface area and water by sintering. This second step comprises about 15 per cent of the overall endotherm and water loss but may not contribute to the fire retardancy effect.

Our work has also caused us to question the decomposition temperature, generally quoted as being at least 330°C.

This value is derived from temperature programmed decomposition studies which can be misleading. Isothermal studies are more meaningful and typical decomposition curves obtained under these conditions are presented in Figure 2. Slow decomposition is seen to occur about 300°C and this must be regarded as the safe processing temperature limit.

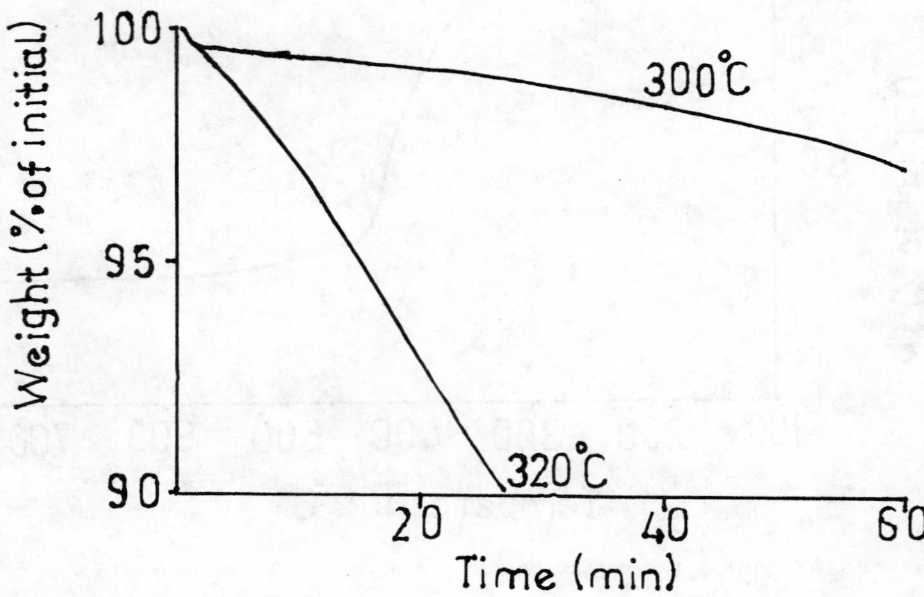

Figure 2. Isothermal weight loss of magnesium hydroxide.

Despite these modifications to the claims normally made for magnesium hydroxide it remains a very useful fire retardant.

The decomposition temperature is still well above ATH and sufficient for many polymers. Fire retardancy has been demonstrated by a number of studies in a wide range of polymers including ethylene vinylacetate, polypropylene and nylons.

Like ATH, magnesium hydroxide gives much lower smoke than halogen based formulations. There is also a claim that, by promoting char formation, it gives even lower smoke levels than ATH [6]. This has not been corroborated however.

TYPES OF MAGNESIUM HYDROXIDE AVAILABLE AND THEIR DEVELOPMENT

Three forms of magnesium hydroxide can be distinguished; small synthetic crystals, large synthetic crystals and naturally occurring materials.

The small synthetic crystal form is the easiest to produce. The crystals are less than 0.1 micron in size and are produced by adding alkali to a magnesium salt solution under a wide range of conditions [7,8]. The small crystals are usually tightly aggregated and it is these aggregates which are normally in the size range 1 - 10 micron that constitute the effective particles in most applications. This form will be referred to as polycrystalline in the remainder of this paper.

The large synthetic crystal form is generally more difficult and expensive to produce. Crystal size ranges from 0.5 to 5 micron. Aggregation is much less and the crystal size approaches the effective particle size. These will be called large crystal forms in this paper.

Finally there are the natural forms. Magnesium hydroxide occurs in a variety of forms in various parts of the world. Most of these deposits are too impure or too small for exploitation as a fire retardant but this may change as new deposits are discovered. Such forms should be inherently cheaper unless extensive processing is needed.

It is generally held that the large crystal material performs better than the polycrystalline types [9].

This is an oversimplification largely due to the fact that when intertest in fire retardant fillers first developed the only forms available in commercial quantities and at a reasonable price were the polycrystalline intermediates used in refractory magnesia production.

In crude form these usually give very poor results. This probably delayed industrial acceptance of the value of magnesium hydroxide as well as giving the polycrystalline form a poor reputation.

Although large crystal forms were known at the time [10,11,12] they only became commercially available in the mid 1970's. At this time Japanese producers developed an industrial route to such products [13] and began commercial manufacture and exploitation.

Since then others have developed routes to such product forms [14]. Credit for establishing magnesium hydroxide as an effective fire retardant additive must however largely be given to the Japanese.

Producers of the polycrystalline form have however been steadily improving their materials [15]. More recently filler producers have been adding their expertise, particularly in terms of coating technology. As a result products with performance equal to the larger crystal form are now appearing.

With the high level of activity in the area, further improved forms of both types can be expected to emerge.

SURFACE CHEMISTRY AND SURFACE TREATMENTS

The surface chemistry of a filler is a key factor of its performance in polymer composites.

Unfortunately there is virtually no information concerning the surface chemistry of magnesium hydroxide although one might expect it to be heavily carbonated.

Various surface modifications are claimed to improve performance.

Fatty acids are claimed to be effective in some thermoplastics with unsaturated acids being claimed as being particularly useful in polypropylene [9]. Silanes and carboxylated polybutadienes both produce beneficial effects in elastomers, although both these modifications can under certain circumstances adversely affect oxygen index [Table 2].

TABLE 2

Effect of surface modification on oxygen index of magnesium hydroxide filled, cross-linked, ethylene vinylacetate.

FILLER SURFACE TREATMENT	OXYGEN INDEX %
None	43
3% Carboxylated Polybutadiene	28
2% Vinyl Silane	32

This effect has been shown to probably result from increased cross-link density promoting spalling of the ash under the test conditions [4]. It is not thought to imply any deterioration in real fire resistance.

Further advances in surface modifications are likely and should lead to more widespread use of magnesium hydroxide in thermoplastics.

REFERENCES

1. Belgian 645,879, 1964.

2. British 1,080,468, 1967 (U.S. Appl. 1963).

3. Nishimoto, K. National Technical Report (Japan). 21 Part 3, 1975, 367-380.

4. Ashley, R.J., and Rothon, R.N., Use of Inorganic Fillers to Reduce the Flammability of Polymers, Paper 13, Filplas Conference (PR1/BPF), Manchester, April 1989.

5. Green, J., Calcination of Precipitated Magnesium Hydroxide, Journal of Materials Science, 18, 637-651 (1983).

6. Keating, L., Petric. S., and Beekman, G., Plast Compd. 9 (4) 40 (July/August 1986).

7. Copperthwaite. M., and Brett, N.H., Sci. Ceram., 8, 85-99, (1975).

8. Phillips, V.A., Kolbe, J.L., and Opperhauser, H., Journal of Crystal Growth 41, 228-234 (1977).

9. Miyata, S., Imahaski, T., and Anabuki, H., Fire Retarding Polypropylene with Mangnesium Hydroxide, Journal of Applied Polymer Science, 25, 415-425 (1980).

10. Cheremukhin, E.P., Karasik, E.M., and Priima, T.V., Study of particle Structure and Morphology of Magnesium Hydroxide Crystallites, Zh. Prikl. Khim. (Leningrad), 43 (Part 3), 533-8, (1970).

11 Nelson, S.M., Newman, A.C.D., Tomlinson, T.E., and Sutton L.E., Trans. Far Soc., 55 2186, (1959).

12 Livey, D.T., Wanklyn, B.M., Hewitt, M., and Murray, P., Trans. Brit. Ceram. Soc., 56, 677, (1957).

13. British Patent 1,514,081.

14. European Patent 0,214,494.

15. European Patent 0,243,201.

ICI "CEEPREE" - UNIQUE FIRE BARRIER FROM A VERSATILE FILLER

DR DAVID J PARRY, RUSSELL A CARTER
Commercial Department, ICI Soda Ash Products
Mond House, Winnington, Northwich, Cheshire, CW8 4DT, UK

ABSTRACT

ICI have launched a new versatile additive for plastics, coatings, adhesives and sealants. Ceepree* fire barrier filler, unlike conventional flame retardants, increases the fire resistance of materials by virtue of its unique composition of powdered specially-designed glasses. Ceepree melts over a wide temperature range (350-900°C) to encapsulate and fuse with combustible material, char, reinforcing fibres and other fillers. In this way Ceepree confers in situ integrity, crystallinity and high temperature strength up to 1100°C which protects against the thermal degradation of plastics and other materials and prevents the passage of flames, smoke and toxic fumes. Ceepree is uprating the fire resistance and high temperature strength of adhesives, sealants and protective surface coatings and making it possible to use plastics for greater design flexibility in new applications in building and construction, mass transit, aerospace, military and offshore industries where compartmentation of fire is essential.

*Ceepree is a trademark, the property of ICI Chemicals & Polymers Ltd.

INTRODUCTION

It has been suggested that for a structure to be truly "Resistant to Fire" then ideally it should:

- contain the fire
- not sustain or contribute to the fire
- not propagate a fire due to transmission of heat
- retain structural integrity
- not emit smoke or toxic fumes
- not melt to produce hot droplets that can propagate fire.

Relevant fire tests are therefore extensive and include:

- BS 476 : Parts 20-24 : 1987 Resistance to Fire Test

- BS 476 : Part 4 : 1970 Non-Combustibility Test for Materials
- BS 476 : Part 5 : 1979 Ignitability Test
- UL-94 : Ignitability of Plastics
- Brandschacht Test
- Epiradiateur Test
- BS 476 : Part 7 : 1968 Surface Spread of Flame Test
- BS 2782: Part 1 : 1978 and ASTM D-2863 Oxygen Index Tests
- FAR : Parts 25.853 : 1986: Ohio State University Heat Release Test
- NBS Smoke Chamber
- Airbus ATS.1000
- NBS Cone Calorimeter

Clearly these are stringent requirements for any material to meet, especially when functional and design considerations are imposed, such as:

- aesthetic appeal
- workability
- weight
- colour
- strength
- design flexibility

Glass reinforced plastics (grp) certainly are the materials of choice as far as the physical properties are concerned, but traditionally they have been regarded as having extreme shortcomings regarding their resistance to fire, shortcomings which have limited their use as major components in building and construction, mass transit, aerospace, military and offshore industries. The grp industry has certainly gone a long way in addressing these problems with flame retardant additives such as antimony oxide, alumina trihydrate and halogen and phosphorus compounds which tackle the problems of flammability and smoke emission but improvements in fire containment, structural integrity and toxic fume emission have been harder to achieve.

The launch of ICI's Ceepree Fire Barrier Filler represents the opportunity to improve in a simple yet versatile way what we perceive as weaknesses of grp, that is the ability to retain structural integrity and contain fire.

CEEPREE COMPOSITION AND MODE OF ACTION

In BS 476 : Parts 20-24 : 1987 Resistance to Fire Test, as in a real fire situation, the temperature climbs rapidly from ambient at time zero, to 556°C at t=5 mins reaching 718°C at t=15 mins (Figure 1). In practice, therefore, conventional flame retardants in grp subjected to this thermal gradient will be exposed to temperatures above their decomposition range within the first few minutes of the test. Their effectiveness during prolonged exposure to high temperatures in a fire is therefore limited. In contrast, Ceepree has been designed to uprate the high temperature performance of many host materials and can be used independently or formulated with a range of flame retardants to give the required fire resistance.

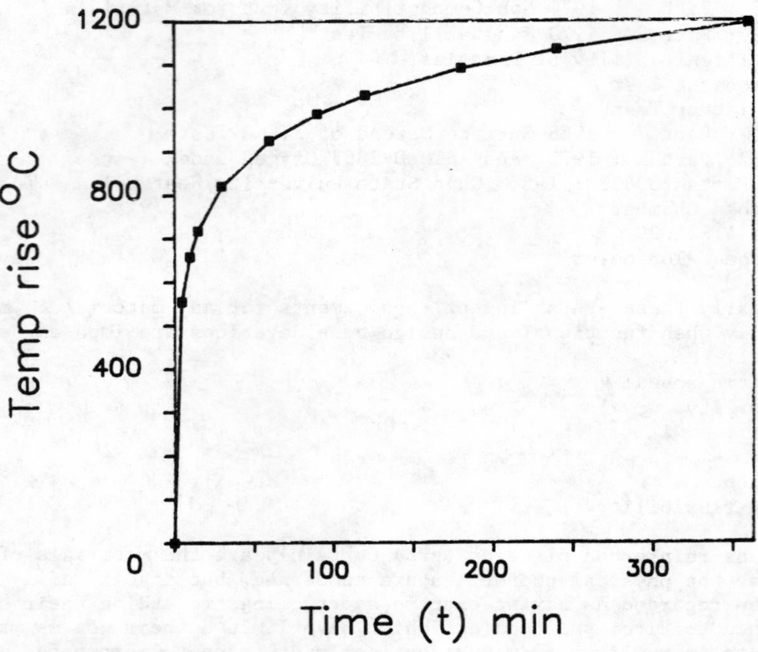

Figure 1. Standard time/temperature curve of BS 476 : Parts 20-24 : 1987 Resistance to Fire Tests.

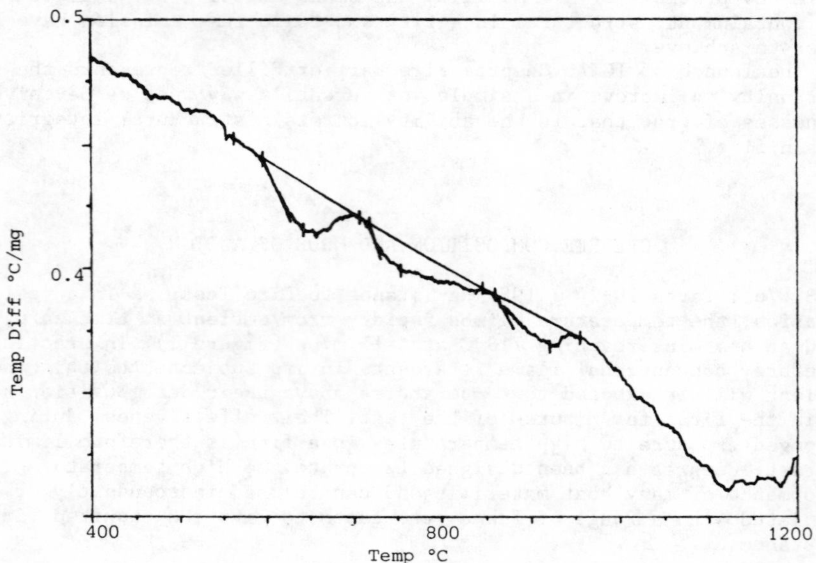

Figure 2. Differential Thermal Analysis (DTA) of Ceepree C200 grade.

Early work on Ceepree using experts in ceramics, was therefore directed at developing formulations of glasses with widely different melting ranges to continuously remove heat endothermically and to ensure that encapsulation of the host material and protection from degradation was maintained over the temperature/time profile covered by the Fire Resistance test (Figure 2). It was important that the inclusion of potentially highly toxic elements in the formulations was avoided. Furthermore, in order to ensure that the molten Ceepree glasses did not simply flow out of the grp during test, a component was included which devitrified at 900°C to effectively crystallise the grp as a hard, strong integral component which resisted fire penetration (Figure 3).

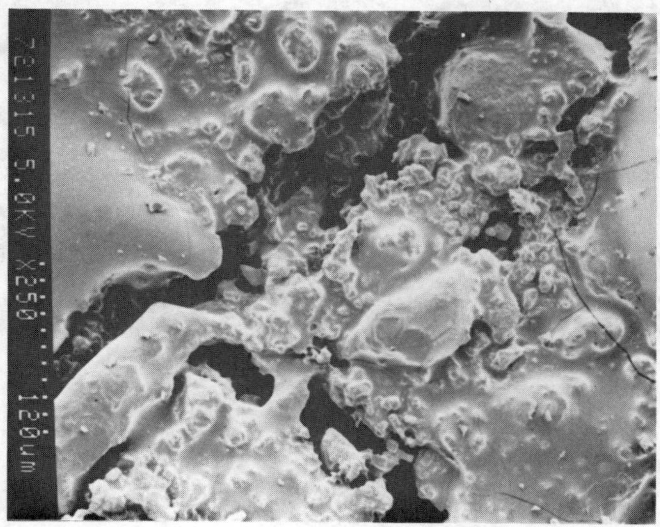

Figure 3. Ceepree Fire Barrier Filler in phenolic GRP heated to 1000°C in BS 476 : Parts 20-24 : 1987 (250 X magnification).

CEEPREE PHYSICAL CHARACTERISTICS, TECHNICAL AND SAFETY INFORMATION

The physical appearance of Ceepree is that of a near-white powdered glass produced by milling, the particles showing a characteristic "shattered" appearance under magnification (Figure 4).

Ceepree has been launched with at present one commercially available grade - C200. This grade has been chosen to have a wide particle size distribution range (Figure 5) and a mean of about 50 microns. It has been shown to be suitable for compounding in polyester, phenolic, epoxy and ICI Modar grp, prepregs and other end-uses (technical data is given in Table 1). Development samples of other grades such as microfine are available to meet the specific processing or materials demands of particular customers.

Ceepree can be easily compounded with most thermosets and thermoplastics or suspended in resin for pre-pregging or encapsulation using conventional methods and equipment. Generally, the filler loadings necessary to achieve the desired effects are lower than for other diluent or flame retardant fillers such as calcium carbonate or alumina trihydrate; its effect on the mechanical properties of most plastics is neutral. Ceepree is considered to represent a low hazard and should be treated as a low toxicity dust. Due to its chemical composition Ceepree makes no contribution to smoke or toxic products of combustion from grp.

Figure 4. Ceepree C200 (250 X magnification).

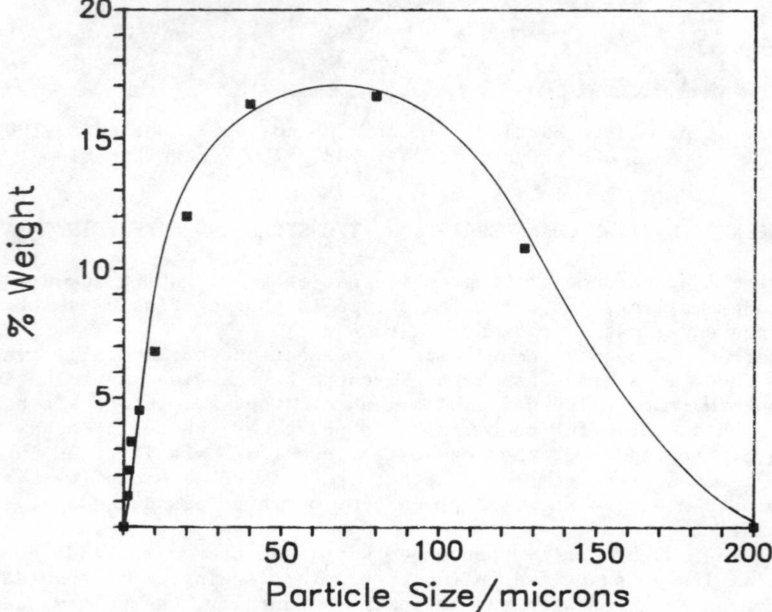

Figure 5. Particle size distribution of Ceepree C200.

TABLE 1
Technical data (typical values) Ceepree C200 grade

True Density[1] (g/cm^3)	2.68
Oil Absorption[2] (g/100g)	20
Specific Surface Area[3] (m^2/g)	0.7
Pouring Density (g/cm^3)	1.06
Mohs Hardness	4
Colour[4]	64.6
	68.7
	74.0
pH[5]	9.8
Refractive Indices[6] (+/- 0.002)	1.518
	1.576

NOTES
1 Quantachrome stereo pyknometer using Helium displacement
2 ASTM D - 281
3 Flowsorb II 2300 (nitrogen adsorption)
4 Minolta CR200 Chroma Meter (tristimulus value CIE 1931)
5 10% w/w aqueous suspension
6 Binary composite material

APPLICATIONS AND FIRE TESTING

Ceepree is now being successfully used in a number of significant applications which demonstrate its versatility to meet the requirements of fire resistance and high temperature strength. The following examples and fire tests illustrate this point.

We have worked in conjunction with Freeman Chemicals Ltd and Pyrofite Ltd to develop a range of fire resistant polyester dough moulding compounds based on Ceepree. These compounds exhibit fire resistances in certificated tests (e.g. Figure 6) of up to four hours as measured by BS 476 : Part 22, extremely low smoke and toxic fume release and oxygen indices as high as 72%. Applications include fire door glazing rings (Figure 7) where the design and manufacture of unlimited original design profiles is now possible together with exceptional fire resistance and low weight. Military aircraft components (Figure 8) which combine low ignitability with high temperature integrity may also be manufactured from Ceepree - containing dough moulding compounds.

The building and construction industry views resistance to fire as a major requirement, particularly in environments where means of escape are somewhat limited. In conjunction with Ceeward Technology Ltd a flooring tile has been developed based on a sandwich construction including cement-bonded particle board encapsulated with a resin/Ceepree envelope. The floor tile has four hour fire resistance together with high mechanical strength. On a similar theme, Primco Ltd have developed a phenolic/glass/Ceepree pre-preg material which has been passed for use in platform structures by London Underground. Honeycomb grade Ceepree pre-preg on a "Nomex" core sandwich is currently under test in the aerospace industry. These pre-pregs exhibit low heat release in OSU tests, V-0 in UL-94 flammability test, low smoke and toxic gas in addition to their fire resistance.

Figure 6. Fire test on DMC glazing ring to BS 476 : Part 22 : 1987 (Photo courtesy of Pyrofite Ltd).

Figure 7. Fire resistant glazing rings.

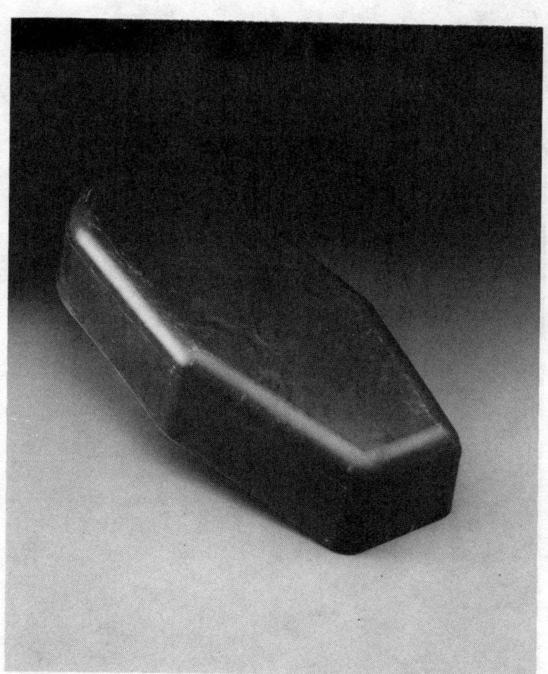

Figure 8. Tornado aircraft fuel tank jettison switch cover (photo courtesy of EPS Logistics Technology Ltd).

Ceepree is finding applications in adhesive formulations for improved fire performance in industries such as aerospace and offshore. In a joint testing program with AaBe Fabrieken bv, fabric/adhesive combinations have been developed which when applied to typical "Nomex"-cored substrate panels used extensively in aerospace, give heat release ratings lower than any system currently available (Figure 9). Similarly, in a project between Wimpey Offshore and British Alcan Aluminium to develop a lightweight offshore accomodation "Modulite" (Figure 10) Ceepree-containing adhesives are used extensively for bonding primary structural members of aluminium and mineral fibre to achieve A60 fire ratings.

Paint systems incorporating Ceepree have been developed by H Marcel Guest Ltd to increase the high temperature integrity and fire resistance of coatings. Figure 11 shows a two pack polyepoxide coating system achieving Class 1 surface spread of flame at Warrington Fire Research Centre.

Figure 9. Ohio State University (OSU) heat release test on aircraft panelling incorporating Ceepree in the adhesive (photo courtesy of British Aerospace).

CONCLUSIONS

Ceepree is a versatile additive which can easily be incorporated into a diverse range of materials, particularly plastics, to give new composites which are extremely resistant to fire penetration. Ceepree composite materials are ideal for applications where fire compartmentation and high temperature strength are required and consequently Ceepree is increasingly being used in building and construction, aerospace, mass transit and offshore industries.

Patents

Ceepree compositions and applications are described extensively in UK, European and ROW patents e.g. Nos. 8815593, 8708733, 8707656, 8703084 and 8523190.

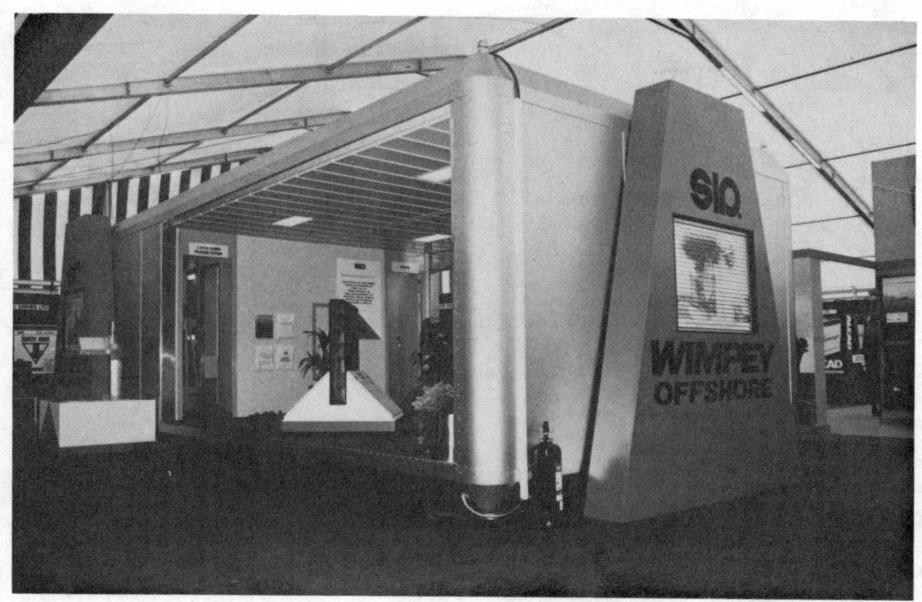

Figure 10. Lightweight offshore "Modulite" using Ceepree-containing adhesive (photo courtesy of Wimpey Offshore).

Figure 11. Class 1 low FST paint in BS 476 : Part 7 : 1971 surface spread

FLAME-RETARDANT INORGANIC TIN ADDITIVES WHICH SUPPRESS SMOKE AND CARBON MONOXIDE EMISSION FROM BURNING POLYMERS

PAUL A. CUSACK
International Tin Research Institute,
Kingston Lane, Uxbridge,
Middlesex, UB8 3PJ, U.K.

ABSTRACT

In view of the current demand for novel, non-toxic flame- and smoke-suppressant systems for synthetic polymers, certain inorganic tin compounds have been evaluated as fire retardants in a number of halogen-containing and halogen-free plastic and elastomeric substrates. Compounds which have been tested include anhydrous tin(IV) oxide, hydrous tin(IV) oxide, and various metal hydroxystannates and stannates. Whilst good performances have been obtained with each of these additives, the best results were demonstrated with zinc hydroxystannate, $ZnSn(OH)_6$, and zinc stannate, $ZnSnO_3$.

The tin compounds appear to act primarily in the condensed phase by a char-promoting mechanism, and this leads to a significant decrease in the amounts of smoke and toxic gases evolved during polymer combustion. The observed carbon monoxide-suppression in certain systems is particularly interesting, since CO inhalation is now known to be the cause of death in the vast majority of fire fatalities.

INTRODUCTION

The fire hazards associated with the widespread use of organic polymers in construction, transport and household applications have generated much public concern. As a result, the plastics industry is undertaking extensive research in order to develop novel, safer fire-retardant compositions.

Although it is possible to exercise a reasonable degree of control over the flammability characteristics of plastics, many of the additives used impart detrimental properties to the substrate. In particular, antimony trioxide - halogen systems tend to increase smoke production during combustion of the associated polymer (1), and also result in undesirable rigidity and/or brittleness (2), in addition to a strong pigmentation (3). Furthermore, recent health and environmental issues have focussed attention on the possible toxicity/carcinogenicity of Sb_2O_3 (4,5), and consequently, its use as a flame retardant has been subject to intense scrutiny.

Two novel tin-based additives, zinc hydroxystannate and zinc stannate, have recently been introduced as potential replacements for antimony trioxide in halogenated polymer formulations (6, 7). This paper reports the results of recent studies into the flame-retardant and smoke-suppressant properties of these inorganic tin compounds in a number of halogen-containing and halogen-free plastic and elastomeric compositions.

EXPERIMENTAL PROCEDURE

Tin additives

Zinc hydroxystannate and zinc stannate were synthesised according to previously reported procedures (8,9):

$$Na_2Sn(OH)_6 + ZnCl_2 \xrightarrow{H_2O} ZnSn(OH)_6\downarrow + 2NaCl$$

$$ZnSn(OH)_6 \xrightarrow{\Delta} ZnSnO_3 + 3H_2O$$

The identities of the products were confirmed by infrared spectroscopy and x-ray powder diffraction patterns. Properties of these inorganic tin compounds are presented in Table 1.

Test methods

Flammability: Limiting oxygen indices (LOI's) of polymer samples, in the form of thin strips of approximate dimensions of 120mm x 7mm x 3mm, were determined according to the procedure described in ASTM D2863 (10), using a Stanton Redcroft FTA module. High temperature LOI's were determined using a Stanton Redcroft HFTA instrument. Underwriters Laboratories UL-94 vertical burning tests were carried out on strips measuring 127mm x 12.7mm, with a thickness of 3.2mm, according to the UL-94 Standard for Safety Bulletin (11).

TABLE 1
Properties of zinc hydroxystannate and zinc stannate

Property	$ZnSn(OH)_6$	$ZnSnO_3$
Appearance	white powder	white powder
Analysis (approx.)	41%Sn 23%Zn	51%Sn 28%Zn
Specific gravity	3.3	3.9
Decomposition temperature	>180°C	>570°C
Oral toxicity, LD_{50} (rats)	>5000mg/kg	>5000mg/kg

Smoke density: Optical density measurements on the smoke evolved from burning polymer samples were carried out using a Stanton Redcroft NBS-type Smoke Box. The samples, which measured 76mm x 38mm, with a thickness of 2mm, were burned in the flaming mode for 10 mins, in accordance with BS 6401 (12). Specific smoke density (Ds) values reported are the averages of three independent determinations. Maximum specific optical density values (Dmc) were corrected for soot deposition on the optical windows, and the data are expressed as Ds/g and Dmc/g in order to normalize for sample weight.

Carbon monoxide evolution: The concentration of CO present in the Smoke Box at the end of combustion experiments (i.e. 10 mins after sample ignition), was determined using colorimetric 'Gastec' detector tubes (Detectawl Ltd., Milton Keynes). Quoted values, [CO]m, are the numerical averages of three independent determinations. The data are expressed as [CO]m/g to normalize for sample weight.

Carbon dioxide evolution: The concentration of CO_2 present in the Smoke Box at the end of combustion experiments was determined using colorimetric 'Gastec' detector tubes, and $[CO_2]m$ and $[CO_2]m/g$ were determined in a similar manner to the corresponding CO evolution parameters.

RESULTS AND DISCUSSION

Halogenated polymers

The flame-retardant action of chlorine and bromine compounds, either as physically incorporated additives to an organic polymer or as part of the polymer structure itself, is well established (13). Indeed, halogenated compounds find extensive commercial use as flame retardants (14), and these are often used in conjunction with synergists, such as antimony trioxide or phosphorus derivatives (1, 3, 13). However, halogen-containing polymers often evolve large amounts of smoke and corrosive gases during combustion (15), and there is a great demand for novel smoke-suppressant formulations.

Polyester resins: One of the most important growth areas for fire retardants in recent years has been their use in unsaturated polyester resins (16). These thermosetting polymers, which are often used in conjunction with fillers or glass-fibre reinforcement, are widely used in a number of building and transport applications which generally demand a high degree of flame-resistance (17).

Earlier studies at ITRI have demonstrated the effectiveness of tin(IV) oxide, both in its anhydrous and hydrous forms, as a flame- and smoke-retardant additive for halogenated polyester resin formulations (18). Recent work, carried out in collaboration with a major UK plastics manufacturing company, has involved the incorporation of inorganic tin compounds into a range of commercial chlorine- and bromine- containing polyesters, and evaluation of the fire performance of the resulting compositions. The halogenated reactive intermediates used are shown in Figure 1.

Extensive studies have been undertaken on polyesters based on dibromoneopentylglycol (DBNPG). Antimony trioxide, β-stannic acid (hydrous stannic oxide), zinc hydroxystannate and zinc stannate were incorporated at levels of 1-10 phr (parts per hundred of resin) into a resin containing 28% Br as DBNPG. No processing problems were encountered and the samples cured satisfactorily to give rigid, opaque strips.

The relationship between additive level and the LOI of the resin is

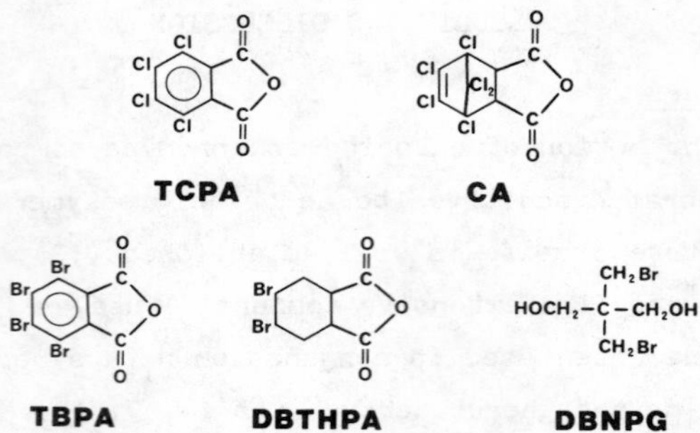

Figure 1. Reactive halogenated flame retardants used in polyester resins.

shown in Figure 2. The incorporation of Sb_2O_3 into the polyester leads to an interesting flammability effect: optimum flame retardancy is observed when the Sb_2O_3 level is in the range 1-3 phr, and further addition of the compound results in a dramatic decrease in LOI. Of the tin additives studied, the anhydrous and hydrated zinc stannates, $ZnSnO_3$ and $ZnSn(OH)_6$ respectively, are considerably more effective flame-retardant synergists with the bromine present in the plastic than β-stannic acid. In addition, $ZnSnO_3$ and $ZnSn(OH)_6$ both outperform Sb_2O_3 at levels $\geqslant$ 2 phr, and, in fact, 1 phr $ZnSnO_3$ is at least equivalent, in terms of LOI elevation, to 2 phr Sb_2O_3.

Evaluation of the smoke generated during flaming combustion of brominated polyester resins has been carried out using an NBS-type Smoke Box. The data obtained, illustrated graphically in Figure 3, clearly indicate that $ZnSn(OH)_6$ significantly reduces both the total amount and the rate of production, of smoke evolved from the burning resin. Similar effects have been recorded on $ZnSnO_3$-containing polyesters (19), but Sb_2O_3 is found to be slightly detrimental to the smoke emission characteristics of the plastic.

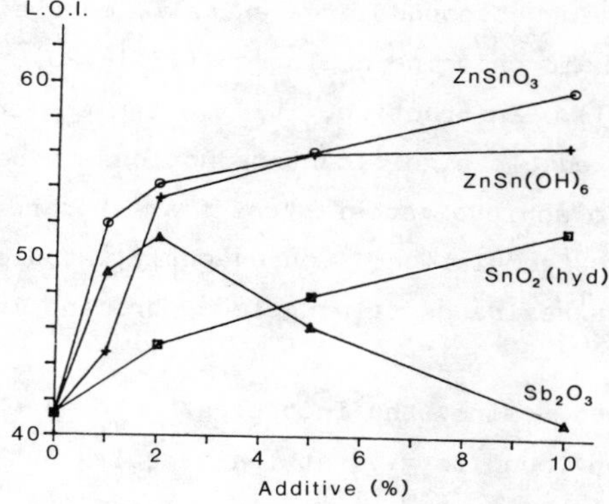

Figure 2. Effect of inorganic additives on the flammability of 28%Br DBNPG-based polyester resin.

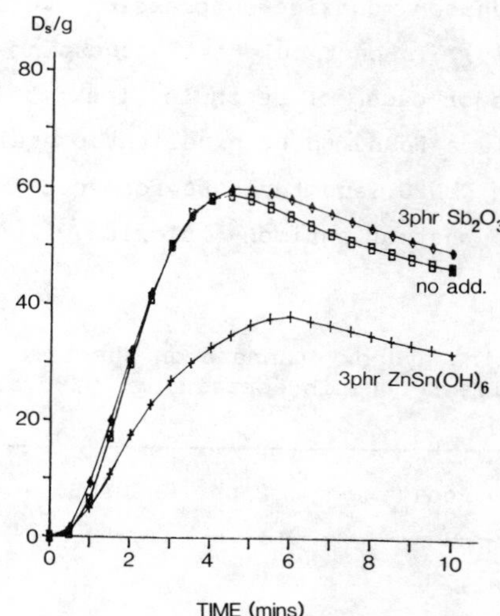

Figure 3. Effect of inorganic additives on the smoke evolved from 28%Br DBNPG-based polyester resin.

Although bromine compounds are generally more efficient as flame retardants than their chlorine analogues (13,16,20), they are considerably more expensive (21). In practice, it is often commercially attractive to use synergists to enable significant reductions to be made in the levels of Br necessary to achieve satisfactory flame-retardant performance in a particular polymer formulation. Consequently, studies have been undertaken on polyester resins containing lower bromine levels.

In DBNPG-based resins, the incorporation of 1 phr $ZnSnO_3$ or 2 phr $ZnSn(OH)_6$ has been found to give at least equivalent flame retardancy to that of 2 phr Sb_2O_3, in polyesters containing 5-28% Br (19). In addition, a $ZnSn(OH)_6$ level of 2 phr is sufficient to raise the UL-94 performance of a 10% brominated DBNPG resin from a fail to a VO pass classification (Table 2). The phenomenal improvement in flame resistance is accompanied by marked reductions in the smoke-, carbon monoxide- and carbon dioxide-emission characteristics of the polymer during flaming combustion (Table 2). The observed carbon monoxide-suppression, which is also evident in the 28% Br resin (19), is particularly interesting since CO inhalation is known to be a major cause of death in fire fatalities (22). Hence, the zinc stannates are found to be excellent overall fire retardants for polyesters based on DBNPG, and their performance in these systems is clearly superior to that of antimony trioxide.

TABLE 2
Effect of zinc hydroxystannate on the fire properties of a polyester resin containing 10%Br as DBNPG

Property	No additive	2 phr $ZnSn(OH)_6$	Effect
UL-94(3.2mm)	Fail	VO	
LOI	25.6	32.8	+7.2 units
Dmc/g	69.2	56.0	19% redn.
CO/g	141.7	106.8	25% redn.
CO_2/g	1800.8	997.1	45% redn.

Preliminary studies indicate that zinc hydroxystannate is less effective as a flame retardant and smoke suppressant in halogenated polyesters based on reactive intermediates other than DBNPG (23). However, a degree of flame-retardant synergism is evident and low levels (< 5phr) of $ZnSn(OH)_6$ are sufficient to enable resins containing 10%Br as either TBPA or DBTHPA, or 21% Cl as TCPA, to meet VO standard in the UL-94 test (Table 3). Although the incorporation of $ZnSn(OH)_6$ into these plastics results in a decrease in smoke emission during combustion, the level of smoke inhibition is variable. Work is currently being undertaken at ITRI in order to develop tin-based flame-retardant systems with significantly improved smoke- and toxic gas- suppressant properties.

TABLE 3
Effect of zinc hydroxystannate on the flammability and smoke evolution characteristics of halogenated polyester resins

Halogen content	$ZnSn(OH)_6$ content, phr*	ΔLOI	Smoke reduction
10%Br : DBNPG	2	25.6→32.8	19%
10%Br : TBPA	3	24.9→27.8	9%
10%Br : DBTHPA	4	24.2→30.5	3%
21%Cl : TCPA	1	28.5→31.0	13%

* UL-94 : VO (3.2mm thickness)

Other halogen-containing systems: In addition to the aforementioned ITRI studies on polyester resins, zinc hydroxystannate and zinc stannate are currently being evaluated as fire-retardant synergists in a wide range of halogen-containing polymers. Encouraging results have been obtained in rigid and flexible PVC, chlorinated elastomers and in paint formulations and thermoplastics, where the halogen is introduced as a supplementary additive (23).

Halogen-free polymers

In recent years there has been increasing concern about the toxicity and corrosive nature of the smoke and gases generated during the combustion of halogen-containing polymers (24). Consequently, there is a considerable demand for plastics which comply to the specification 'low smoke zero halogen' (LSOH) flame retardancy, particularly for use in underground transport, shipping and power stations. As a result, there has been much interest in the use of non-toxic inorganic additives and fillers, and the market for these compounds is likely to continue its rapid growth in the years ahead (14).

Ethylene-acrylic rubber: The use of PVC as a wire and cable insulation material has declined in recent years, and it has been replaced to a significant extent by halogen-free elastomeric compositions. At the present time, such formulations are made flame-retardant by the incorporation of alumina trihydrate (ATH). Although it is essentially non-toxic and relatively inexpensive, high addition levels are necessary for effectiveness, and this often results in a marked deterioration in the mechanical properties of the polymer (25). While recent advances in production technology and surface coating have mitigated some of the problems associated with high filler loading (26), improved systems comprising combinations of ATH with other additives are under investigation.

A collaboration has been undertaken with the Admiralty Research Establishment, Poole, UK, in which the fire-retardant properties of a number of inorganic tin compounds in a non-halogenated, ATH-filled ethylene-acrylic rubber formulation, are being assessed. Preliminary results have indicated that a marked flame-retardant synergism exists between certain tin compounds (at a 2.5% level) and ATH (50% loading), and an increase in LOI from 27.5 (for no tin additive) to 33.0 was observed for the $ZnSn(OH)_6$ containing formulations. It has been reported (27) that an ATH loading of 60% is necessary to raise the LOI of ethylene-acrylic rubber to a value of 33, and that such a formulation meets the MOD Naval Specification NES 518. Hence, it appears that lower total additive levels are required for adequate performance when ATH-$ZnSn(OH)_6$ combinations are used than when ATH is incorporated alone. This significant reduction in the filler content may prove advantageous in terms of the mechanical properties of the polymeric substrate.

Elevated temperature LOI data (Figure 4) indicate that the tin-containing elastomers retain their flame-retardant superiority up to a temperature of 250°C, above which the samples undergo extensive thermal degradation and determination of LOIs becomes impractical. It is of interest to note that the polymer containing $ZnSn(OH)_6$ does not burn in air even at 250°C and, accordingly, this composition has a temperature index of at least 50°C above that of the rubber containing ATH alone. The LOI and high temperature LOI data therefore provide substantial evidence as to the benefit of using $ZnSn(OH)_6$ as a flame-retardant synergist with alumina trihydrate filler.

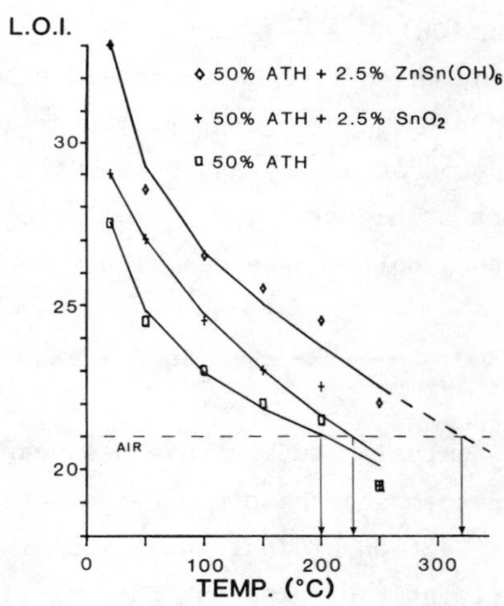

Figure 4. Effect of temperature on the LOI's of ethylene-acrylic rubber samples.

Other non-halogenated systems: The effectiveness of inorganic tin compounds, including $ZnSn(OH)_6$ and $ZnSnO_3$, as flame- and smoke-retardants, both alone and in combination with commercial inorganic fillers, is currently under investigation at ITRI. Preliminary data indicate that tin-containing systems can exhibit significant beneficial properties in certain halogen-free plastic and elastomeric formulations (23) and it is thought that their use in such materials should merit serious consideration.

Mechanistic studies

Although there have been many studies on the mode of action of fire retardants generally (13), the mechanistic behaviour of tin additives is less clear and may depend on several factors including the ratio of halogen: tin in the system.

Simultaneous thermogravimetry/differential thermal analysis studies of zinc hydroxystannate have indicated that dehydration of this compound occurs at temperatures > *ca*. 180°C, with a loss of 19.1% of its initial weight, corresponding to 3 moles of water (19):

$$ZnSn(OH)_6 \longrightarrow ZnSnO_3 + 3H_2O$$

This thermal dehydration, which obviously imposes a temperature limitation on the processing of $ZnSn(OH)_6$ in organic polymers, is accompanied by a large endotherm (absorption of heat), as previously reported (9). A secondary process occurs at higher temperatures (> 580°C), accompanied by a broad exotherm, due to a solid state reaction in which no weight loss is observed (9):

$$ZnSnO_3 \longrightarrow \tfrac{1}{2}Zn_2SnO_4 + \tfrac{1}{2}SnO_2$$

Extensive thermal analysis studies have been carried out on the DBNPG-based polyester system and these are reported elsewhere (19). An insight into the mode of action of individual additives is provided by simple combustion experiments, carried out in air. Table 4 shows that the yield of involatile carbonaceous char, formed when the brominated resin is burned to completion, is more than doubled when 5 phr additions of either β-stannic acid or zinc stannate are made to the plastic, this observation being consistent with condensed phase behaviour. Elemental analysis of the residues suggests that, although in the case of β-stannic acid only a small fraction of the tin is volatilised during combustion, very significant proportions of both the tin and the zinc are volatilised from the zinc stannate-containing polymer, which may be indicative of vapour phase action. Interestingly, the extent of bromine loss is significantly reduced for tin-containing samples, particularly those containing zinc stannate. Antimony trioxide, which undergoes almost complete volatilisation during polymer combustion, shows little char-enhancing behaviour and operates primarily in the gas phase. The apparent ability of $ZnSnO_3$ to act in both the condensed and vapour phases may account for its overall flame-retardant superiority to SnO_2 and Sb_2O_3 in the DBNPG-based resin system.

TABLE 4
Residual char yields and extents of volatilisation from 28%Br DBNPG-based polyester resin, during combustion in air

Sample	Char yield(%)	Elemental volatilisation Br(%)	Metal(%)	Primary phase of action*
No additive	24.1	95.9	-	-
5phr β-SnO_2(hyd.)	53.0	85.1	18.4(Sn)	condensed
5phr $ZnSnO_3$	52.8	74.0	42.9(Sn) 34.3(Zn)	condensed + vapour
5phr Sb_2O_3	33.5	94.4	93.0(Sb)	vapour

* With regard to metallic element; bromine itself acts almost exclusively in the vapour phase (13)

In general, it appears that $ZnSn(OH)_6$ and $ZnSnO_3$ operate as fire retardants in halogen-containing polymer systems by a combined condensed/ vapour phase action (23). The tin additives alter the initial decomposition stages of the plastic and promote halogen volatilisation, probably in the form of metallic halides or oxyhalides. These species may subsequently act as vapour phase flame inhibitors. In addition, tin compounds act in the condensed phase by promoting the formation of a thermally-stable, cross-linked char, at the expense of volatile, flammable products. This reduction in the amount of fuel supplied to the flame leads to the observed smoke- and CO-suppressant effects. The mode of action of tin additives in halogen-free polymers has not been studied in detail, but is thought to involve a predominantly solid phase mechanism (23).

SUMMARY

Two novel tin-based additives, zinc hydroxystannate and zinc stannate, are effective fire retardants in a number of polymer systems. They appear to have advantages over certain existing commercial flame retardants:

* Non-toxicity
* No discolouration of substrate
* Effectiveness at low levels
* Synergism with halogens and/or fillers
* Reduced smoke emission
* Carbon monoxide suppression
* Wide range of application

ACKNOWLEDGEMENTS

The International Tin Research Institute, Uxbridge, U.K., is gratefully acknowledged for permission to present this paper. The author would also like to express his appreciation to Messrs. R.S. Bains, A.W. Monk and J.A. Pearce, and Ms. S.J. Reynolds, I.T.R.I., for experimental assistance, Ms. J. Ratcliffe, I.T.R.I., for the design of slides for this presentation, and Drs. B.O. Brown and B. Kerr, Freeman Chemicals Ltd., Ellesmere Port, U.K., for generous gifts of polyester resins.

REFERENCES

1. Pitts, J.J., Inorganic flame retardants and their mode of action. In Flame Retardancy of Polymeric Materials, vol. 1, ed. W.C. Kuryla and A.J. Papa, Marcel Dekker, New York, 1973, pp. 133-194.

2. Rhys, J.A., Flame retarding of plastics materials. Chem. Ind. (London), 1969, 187-191.

3. Cullis, C.F., Metal compounds as flame retardants for organic polymers. Dev. Polym. Degrad., 1981, 3, 282-314.

4. Groth, D.H., Stettler, L.E., Burg, J.R., Busey, W.M., Grant, G.C. and Wong, L., Carcinogenic effects of antimony trioxide and antimony ore concentrate in rats. J. Toxicol. Environmental Health, 1986, 18, 607-626.

5. Kanematsu, N., Hara, M. and Kada, T., Rec assay and mutagenicity studies on metal compounds. Mutation Research, 1980, 77, 109-116.

6. Cusack, P.A. and Fontaine, P.E., Investigations into tin-based flame retardants and smoke suppressants. Speciality Chemicals, 1989, 9, 194-202.

7. Cusack, P.A., Killmeyer, A.J., Brown, S.C. and Tingley, L.R., Flame-retardant inorganic tin additives which suppress smoke and carbon monoxide emission from burning polyester resins. Presented at the 44th Annual Conference of the Composites Institute, Dallas, Texas, U.S.A., 6-10th February, 1989.

8. Dupuis, T., Duval, C. and Lecomte, J., Molecular spectroscopy - the structure of various hexahydroxystannates by infrared absorption spectroscopy. Compt. Rend., 1963, 257, 3080-3085.

9. Ramamurthy, P. and Secco, E.A., Studies on metal hydroxy compounds. Part XIII. Thermal analyses and decomposition kinetics of hydroxystannates of bivalent metals. Can. J. Chem., 1971, 49, 2813-2816.

10. ASTM D2863: 1970, Flammability of plastics using the Oxygen Index method.

11. UL-94: 1980, Tests for flammability of plastic materials for parts in devices and appliances.

12. BS 6401: 1983, Measurement, in the laboratory, of the specific optical density of smoke generated by materials.

13. Hirschler, M.M., Flame retardant mechanisms: recent developments. Dev. Polym. Stab., 1982, 5, 107-152.

14. Baker-Counsell, J. and Whitehead, J., Flame retardants. Plastics & Rubber Weekly, 1988 (11th June), 12-23.

15. Maahs, G. and Schuler, R., The determination of smoke density and of smoke evolution rate in the NBS chamber and the influence of flame-proofing agents and smoke retarders. J. Fire & Flammability, 1981, 12, 281-300.

16. Stepniczka, H.E., Flame retardant thermoset polyester resins. J. Fire Retard. Chem., 1976, 3, 5-21.

17. Nicholson, J.W. and Nolan, P.F., The behaviour of thermoset polymers under fire conditions. Fire & Materials, 1983, 7, 89-95.

18. Cusack, P.A., An investigation of the flame-retardant and smoke-suppressant properties of tin(IV) oxide in unsaturated polyester thermosets, Fire & Materials, 1986, 10, 41-46.

19. Cusack, P.A., Monk, A.W., Pearce, J.A. and Reynolds, S.J., An investigation of inorganic tin flame retardants which suppress smoke and carbon monoxide emission from burning brominated polyester resins. Fire & Materials, in press.

20. Ram, A. and Calahorra, A., Flame retardant polyesters based on bromine derivatives. J. Appl. Polym. Sci., 1979, 23, 797-814.

21. Cullis, C.F., Bromine compounds as flame retardants. Proc. 12th Intern. Conf. on Fire Safety, San Francisco, California, U.S.A., 12-16th January, 1987, pp. 307-323.

22. Levin, B.C., Paabo, M., Gurman, J.L., Harris, S.E. and Braun, E., Toxicological interactions between carbon monoxide and carbon dioxide. Toxicology, 1987, 47, 135-164.

23. Cusack, P.A., unpublished work.

24. Woolley, W.D. and Fardell, P.J., Basic aspects of combustion toxicology. Fire Safety J., 1982, 5, 29-48.

25. McAdam, B.W., Flame retardant additives for polymers. Speciality Chemicals, 1982, 2, 4-10.

26. Brown, S.C., Evans, K.A. and Godfrey, E.A., New developments in alumina trihydrate. Presented at "Flame Retardants '87", London, U.K., 26-27th November, 1987.

27. Anon., Martinal as a flame-retardant filler for cables. Martinswerk GmbH Data Sheet No. 2/2, Bergheim, West Germany, 1986.

IGNITION OF PUFs: A COMPARISON OF MODIFIED AND UNMODIFIED FOAMS

D.D. DRYSDALE & H.E. THOMSON
Unit of Fire Safety Engineering,
University of Edinburgh,
The King's Buildings,
Edinburgh, EH9 3JL, UK.

ABSTRACT

Ignition behaviour of several commercially available PUFs has been studied. Where possible, unmodified and modified foams from the same manufacturer have been compared. Techniques have been developed to allow measurement of surface temperature (firepoint temperature - T_{ig}) and rate of emission of volatiles (critical mass flux - $\dot{m}''_{cr}$) of foamed polymers at piloted ignition. The aim of this work is to develop a method of characterising the firepoint condition of organic solids in terms of their physical and chemical properties. The relevance of these data to the characterisation of fire behaviour is discussed with reference to a simple computer model which is able to account for some of the results.

INTRODUCTION

The development of synthetic cellular polymers began in earnest in the late 1940s with the development of a continuous process for the commercial manufacture of flexible polyurethane foam. Since then, the share of cellular polymers in the World plastics market has climbed steadily.

It has long been appreciated that in a fire situation cellular polymers will behave very differently to conventional materials. Over the last decade, concern has been growing about the fire hazards of such materials to life (rather than to property) with particular emphasis on polyurethane foams. The range of end uses of polyurethanes is extensive (Figure 1) and polyurethane foams have been implicated in numerous fires where very rapid fire development has occurred and death or injury has resulted from the spread of combustion products within very short time periods. Control of the hazard can only be achieved by gaining a sound understanding of ignitability, flame spread, heat release and smoke/-toxic gas production of cellular materials and by development of economically viable alternative formulations with acceptable physical properties and improved fire behaviour characteristics.

Recent advances in this field have produced a new generation of polyurethane foams with increased resistance to ignition and/or reduced potential for smoke and toxic gas production under fire conditions. This paper examines the pilot ignition behaviour and subsequent burning of four such materials and compares them with two standard polyurethane foams and a solid cast polyurethane.

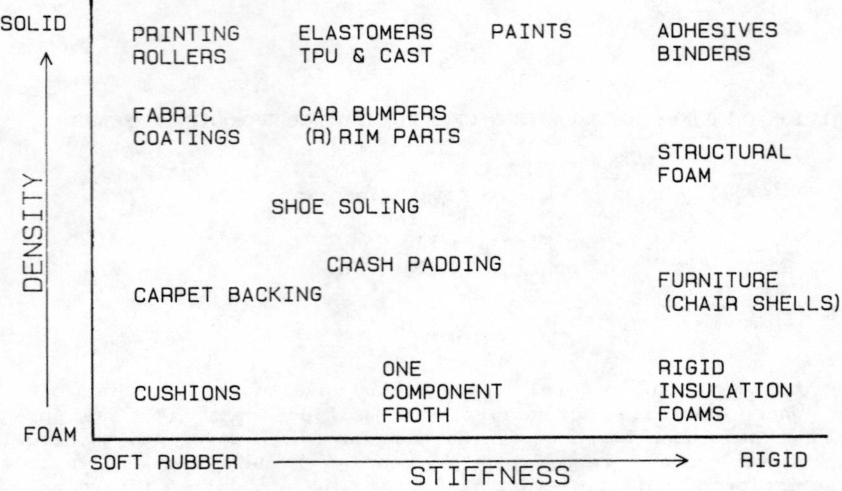

Figure 1. Property Matrix of Polyurethanes (1)

Materials

Six foams with a range of nominal densities between 21 and 75 kg/m^3 were studied. The four combustion modified foams were selected to represent different means of imparting modified fire behaviour. In addition, a batch of unfoamed polyurethane was cast in the laboratory. Details are given in Table 1.

TABLE 1
Details of Materials Used

Foam	Appearance	Formulation	Density (kg/m^3)
S1	White	Standard PU foam	21
S2	Green	Standard PU foam	30
G1	Black	Contains graphite	75
G2	Grey	Contains graphite	37
C1	White	Contains melamine	25
C2	Blue	Contains hydrated alumina	35
PU(Cast)	Brown	Diphenylmethane 4,4' diisocyanate + Polyol	1040

Experimental Procedure

Firepoint Temperature: The surface temperature at the moment of sustained ignition by a pilot source was determined for each of the six polyurethane foams using the apparatus shown in Figure 2 which has been described in detail previously (2). Firepoint temperature measurements were made at each of three different radiant heat fluxes between 15 and 37 kW/m^2 . The conical heater was maintained at a constant temperature of 1023°K using a temperature feedback control mechanism and the radiant heat flux was varied by adjusting the separation between the sample surface and the heater. The radiant intensity in the plane of the sample surface was measured using a Gardon type heat flux meter (3).

A needle was used to thread fine chromel and alumel wires (0.06mm diameter) through the foam samples (65 x 65 x 28mm) from opposite sides as shown in Figure 3. The two wires emerging from the centre of the sample surface were twisted together and silver soldered to form a junction. The wires were then gently retracted until the junction lay flush with the sample surface. Glass fibre sleeving was used to insulate the exposed wires. The sample was then wrapped in aluminium foil and placed in a metal holder which allowed exposure of a disc 60mm in diameter. The foil was carefully peeled away from this area to uncover the upper surface of the foam.

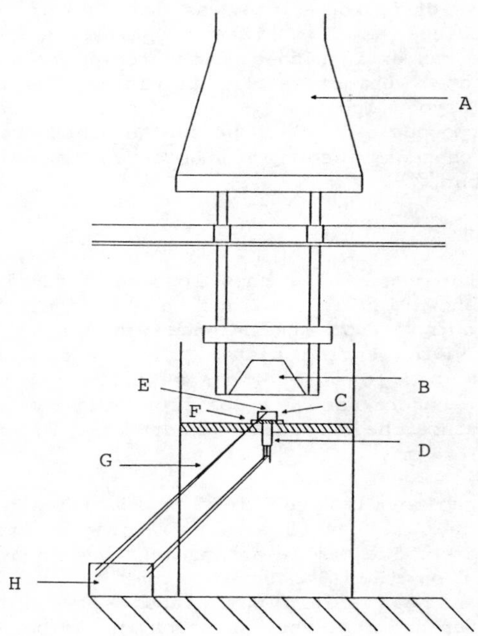

Figure 2. Apparatus for Measurement of Firepoint Temperature
A extract hood; B conical heater; C sample in holder; D radiant heat flux meter; E location of pilot flame; F guide rails; G surface mounted thermocouple; H junction box for data logging system.

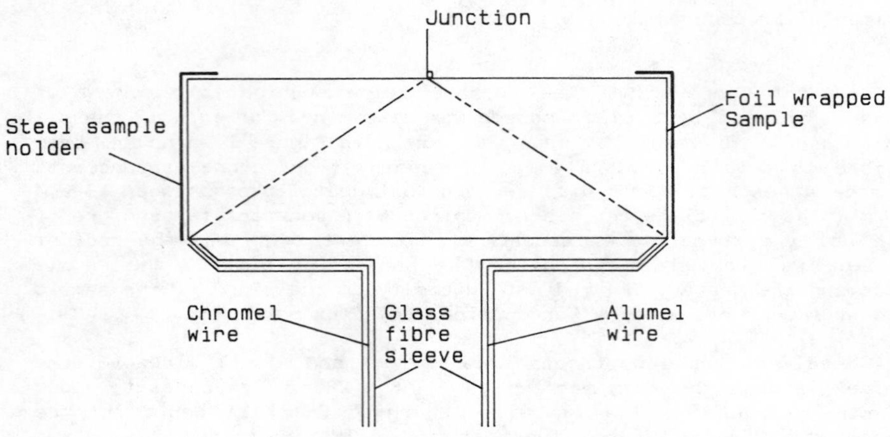

Figure 3. Thermocouple Attachment to Foam Sample

The sample assembly was positioned below the equilibrated conical heater using the fixed guide rails. The thermocouple output was monitored at 1s or 0.5s intervals using a data logging system. A small, non-luminous hydrogen diffusion flame was located at a position 1cm above the sample surface until sustained ignition occurred at which point the pilot flame was extinguished. Times to ignition and extinction (if observed) were noted. Unfortunately, it was not possible to monitor surface temperature beyond ignition as surface regression occurred so rapidly that the thermocouple junction became detached from the surface. This occurrence was characterised by a substantial increase in noise on the thermocouple output.

Mass Loss

The apparatus used to measure the mass loss of a sample subjected to radiant heating is shown in Figure 4 and has been described in detail elsewhere (4). The output from the balance was logged at 1s or 0.5s intervals using the data logging system. Mass loss measurements were made for each of the six foams at the same three radiant heat fluxes (constant heater temperature/variable position mode) as were considered in experiments to measure the firepoint temperature. In addition, S2 and G2 were examined at $10kW/m^2$.

Foil wrapped foam samples (65 x 65 x 28mm) were placed in the sample holder and the foil peeled away to expose a circular area of surface 60mm in diameter. The sample arrangement backed by Supalux board was placed centrally on the platform so that it did not touch the surrounding collar. A heat shield was placed between the heater and sample until the heater had achieved its operating temperature.

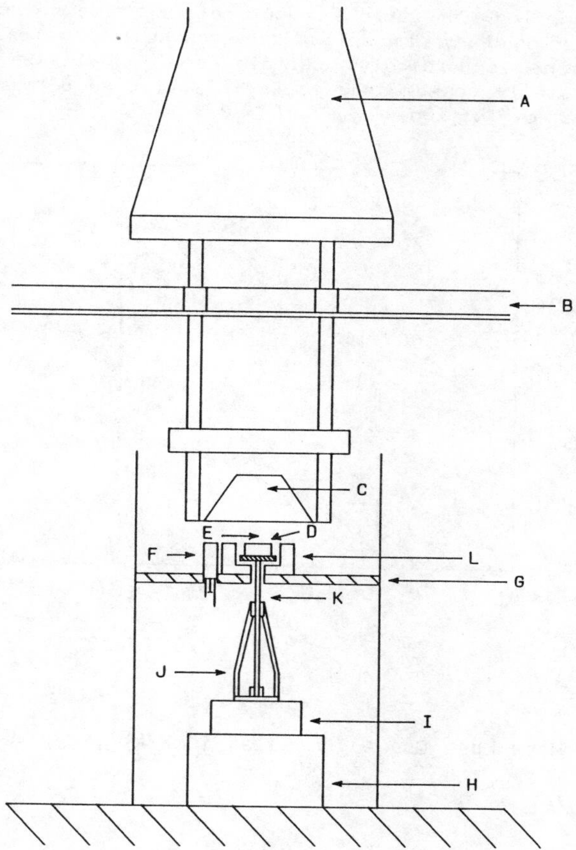

Figure 4: Apparatus for Measurement of Mass Loss
A extract hood; B support bar; C conical heater; D sample in holder; E location of pilot flame; F radiant heat flux meter; G base board; H concrete plinth; I Sartorius balance; J tripod; K glass rod; L collar.

A small H_2 diffusion flame was used to ignite the fuel volatiles as before, and extinguished after sustained ignition had occurred. The critical flowrate of volatiles at the firepoint was derived from the limiting slope of the mass loss curve at the instant that sustained flame became established at the surface which corresponded to a sudden rapid increase in mass loss (Figure 5). The critical mass flux at the firepoint was calculated from

$$\dot{m}''_{cr} = \frac{1}{a} \cdot \frac{dy}{dx} \tag{1}$$

where dy/dx is the slope of the tangent to the mass loss curve at the firepoint and 'a' is area of sample exposed.

Peak burning was taken to occur at the time corresponding to the maximum gradient of the mass loss curve. Mass loss rates at peak burning were determined accordingly. Certain samples self-extinguished before they were totally consumed by fire. This allowed determination of mass loss rates at extinction.

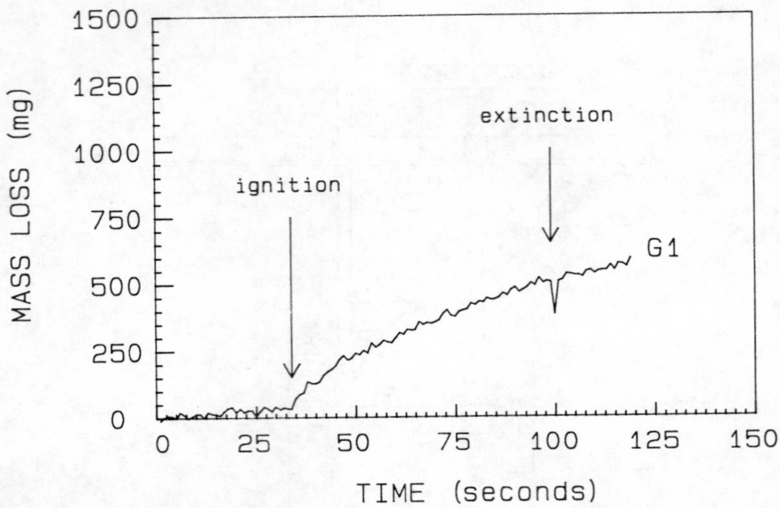

Figure 5. Mass Loss Curve for G1 at $15kW/m^2$

RESULTS

All results quoted are based on a minimum of six replicates. Sustained ignition was assumed for flame durations in excess of 5s. Flame which endured for less than 3s was considered to be flashing ignition.

TABLE 2
Ignition Delay Times

FOAM	Ignition Delay Time (s) 10kW/m²	15 kW/m²	26 KW/m²	37 kW/m²
S1		29	9	4
S2	49	25	8	2
G1		31	8	4
G2	59	28	8	3
C1		NI*	112 (t_f=11s)	61 (t_f=8s)
C2		NI*	152 (t_f=15s)	88 (t_f=12s)
PU		205 (t_f=170s)	57 (t_f=25s)	21

*NI signifies non-ignition.
t_f indicates time to onset of flashing ignition. (Flashing observed only where t_f values are indicated.)

TABLE 3
Firepoint Temperatures

FOAM	FIREPOINT TEMPERATURE (°C) 15 kW/m²	26 kW/m²	37 kW/m²
S1	-	324	333
S2	-	326	331
G1	306	312	318
G2	310	318	320
C1	NI*	-	T_f=306
C2	NI*	-	T_f=319
PU	271	280	276

*NI signifies non-ignition.
\- indicates measurements not possible.
T_f indicates surface temperature at flashpoint.

TABLE 4
Mass Loss Measurements

	10 kW/m^2	15 kW/m^2	26 kW/m^2	37 kW/m^2
S1				
$\dot{m}''_{cr}$ (g/m^2.s)		0.61	–	–
$\dot{m}''_{peak}$ (g/m^2.s)		11.05	11.50	12.63
S2				
$\dot{m}''_{cr}$ (g/m^2.s)	0.47	0.39	–	–
$\dot{m}''_{peak}$ (g/m^2.s)	7.93	7.69	8.31	10.09
G1				
$\dot{m}''_{cr}$ (g/m^2.s)		0.32	–	–
$\dot{m}''_{peak}$ (g/m^2.s)		4.18	5.20	6.32
$\dot{m}''_{ext}$ (g/m^2.s)		1.10	1.90	2.10
G2				
$\dot{m}''_{cr}$ (g/m^2.s)	0.51	0.39	–	–
$\dot{m}''_{peak}$ (g/m^2.s)	6.04	6.32	7.61	8.96
$\dot{m}''_{ext}$ (g/m^2.s)	1.38	1.05	1.61	1.64
C1				
$\dot{m}''_{cr}$ (g/m^2.s)		–	2.51	2.94
$\dot{m}''_{peak}$ (g/m^2.s)		–	14.06	14.40
C2				
$\dot{m}''_{cr}$ (g/m^2.s)		–	3.01	3.81
$\dot{m}''_{peak}$ (g/m^2.s)		–	13.96	13.68
PU				
$\dot{m}''_{f}$ (g/m^2.s)		0.51	0.60	0.54
$\dot{m}''_{cr}$ (g/m^2.s)		1.21	1.36	1.61
$\dot{m}''_{peak}$ (g/m^2.s)		14.10	15.64	15.88

DISCUSSION

Previous work (2,4) suggests that it is reasonable to assume that ignition of a combustible solid will occur when the surface temperature reaches a critical value (T_{ig}) which is associated with a critical mass flux of volatiles. For piloted ignition, this is the lowest temperature at which ignition of the products of decomposition (by means of a 'pilot' source) results in sustained burning. The concept is similar to that of the firepoint of a combustible liquid, but differs in that it refers to a surface temperature rather than a bulk temperature as measured in the Cleveland Open Cup Apparatus (5).

This concept allows the limiting condition for ignition of a solid to be discussed in terms of simple heat transfer models where attainment of the firepoint temperature is assumed equivalent to ignition. Such models are based on the assumption that the solid is chemically inert and does not melt or flow during exposure to the source of heat. Analytical solutions to the heat transfer equations in one dimension exist. That for a semi-infinite solid exposed to convective heating is as follows

$$\frac{T_s - T_o}{T_\infty - T_o} = 1 - \exp \frac{h^2 t}{k\rho c} \text{ erfc. } \frac{h\sqrt{t}}{\sqrt{(k\rho c)}} \qquad (2)$$

where h is the coefficient of convective heat transfer, t is time, k is thermal conductivity, ρ is density and c is thermal capacity. From equation (2), $k\rho c$ (thermal inertia) is seen to have a strong influence on the rate of surface temperature rise in response to an imposed heat flux.

Table 5 gives the thermal properties of a range of common materials. A simple numerical analysis model of one dimensional heat transfer analogous to the Schmidt graphical method and based on an inert, semi-infinite solid exposed to a uniform radiant heat flux perpendicular to one face has been developed. Figure 6 shows the temperature-time curves which this model predicts for the three materials given in Table 5 and illustrates the effect of thermal inertia on the rate of surface temperature rise. Thus, polyurethane foam which has a low thermal inertia responds very rapidly to an imposed heat flux. This is reflected by comparison of the short ignition delay times for standard polyurethane foams with the considerably longer ignition delay times for solid cast polyurethane indicated in Table 2.

TABLE 5
Thermal Properties

Material	k (W/m.K)	C_p (J/kg.K)	ρ (kg/m^3)	$k\rho C_p$ ($W^2/m^4.K^2$)
PMMA	0.19	1420	1180	3.18×10^5
Fibreboard	0.041	2090	229	1.96×10^4
PU Foam	0.034	1400	30	1.43×10^3

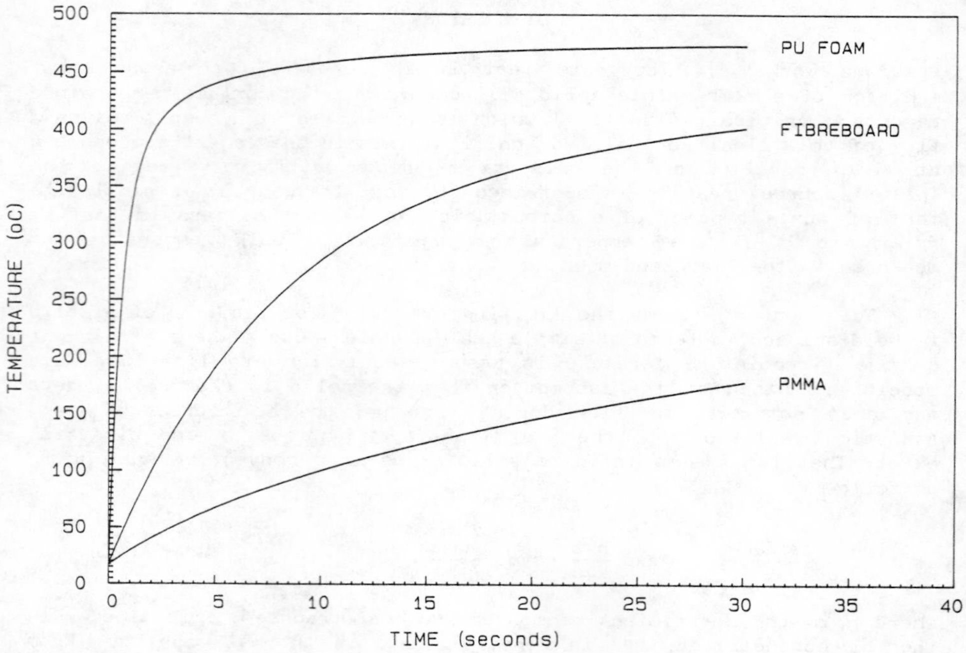

Figure 6. Theoretical Temperature - Time Curves at 25 kW/m2

Low thermal inertia is characteristic of the cellular structure of foamed polymers and it is not possible to substantially increase this value without losing some of the more desirable properties of the foam. Hence, fire retardant additives are used. These are effective by one or more of the following mechanisms:

1. Filling with substances which decompose to yield incombustible gases, e.g. water, carbon dioxide.

2. Addition of compounds which are either (a) gas phase active, such as halogenated fire retardants, where the retardant species (Cl, Br) inhibits the flame reactions, or (b) condensed phase active and modify the decomposition of the polymer, e.g. by inducing char formation which insulates lower layers from imposed heat flux.

3. Filling with materials which decompose endothermically at, or below the firepoint temperature.

The effect of various additives on the ignition of polyurethane was examined by measuring ignition delay times, firepoint temperatures and critical mass fluxes for several polyurethane foams under pilot ignition conditions.

Firepoint Temperature

Figure 7 illustrates the decomposition pathway for flexible polyurethane foams. Earlier work (6) has established that thermal degradation of PU foams proceeds via the relatively low temperature (~250°C) scission of urethane bonds to yield a nitrogen rich material ('yellow smoke') and a polyol component which undergoes further degradation at higher temperatures to yield small organic molecules (alkenes, alkynes, aldehydes, ketones, etc.) and ultimately particulate carbonaceous material - 'black smoke'. The yellow smoke decomposes at temperatures in excess of 800°C to yield 'black smoke' and organic nitriles including HCN.

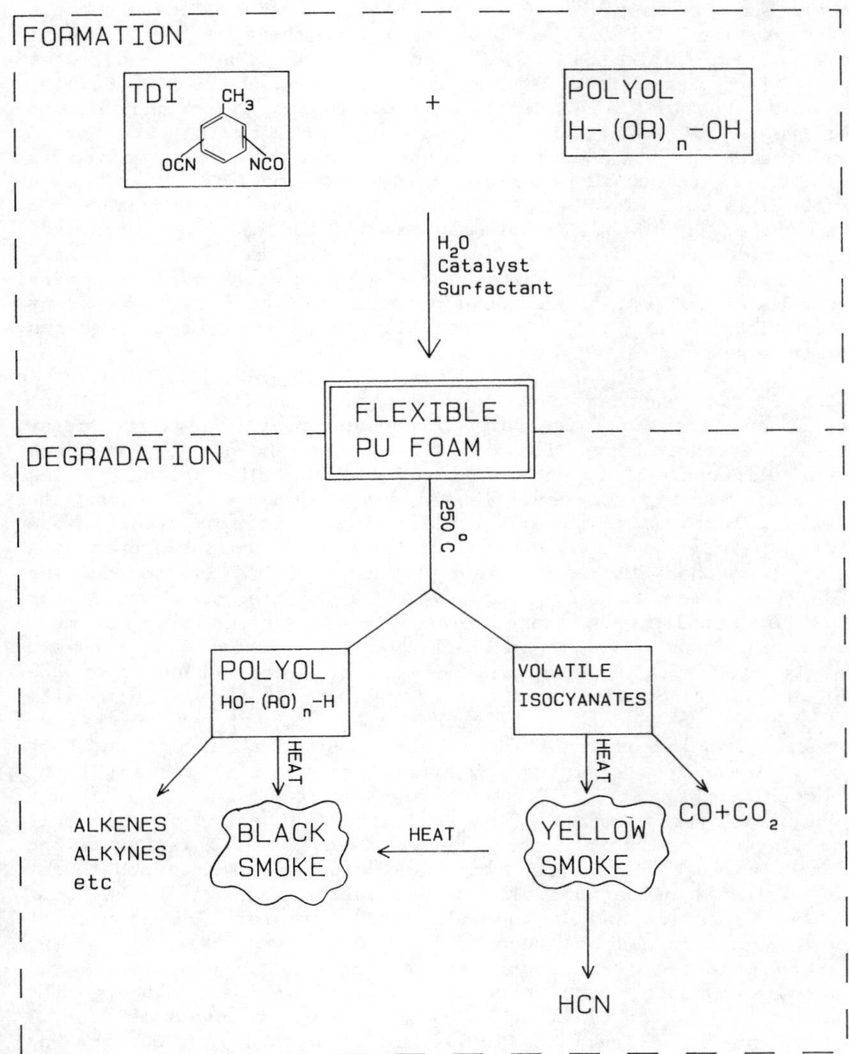

Figure 7. Formation and Degradation of Polyurethane Foam

Rapid structural breakdown of PU foams at temperatures well below the firepoint temperature resulted in problems with the measurement of surface temperatures. Melting and rapid surface regression lead to detachment of the thermocouple junction from the sample surface. This proved to be a particular problem at the lowest radiant heat flux considered and it was possible only to obtain firepoint temperature measurements at $15kW/m^2$ for the G1 and G2 foams which did not melt and regress. The two standard foams (S1 and S2) were found to have similar firepoint temperatures around 330°C while those of the two foams containing exfoliated graphite (G1 and G2) were also similar but approximately 10-20°C lower. The remaining two foams (C1 and C2) were considerably more resistant to ignition and determination of firepoint temperatures was not possible at any of the radiant heat fluxes because sustained ignition did not occur until the samples were almost completely molten. Unlike S1, S2, G1 and G2, both C1 and C2 underwent flashing ignition at surface temperatures of 319°C and 306°C, respectively. Solid, cast PU also displayed flashing ignition and had an average firepoint of 266°C which is 30-50°C lower than that for any of the foamed materials. A possible explanation for this observation is that solid PU, at temperatures slightly in excess of 250°C, produces a sufficiently high concentration of 'yellow smoke' rich in isocyanates to support sustained ignition. Foamed polyurethane, on the other hand, may not be capable of generating a sufficiently high 'yellow smoke' concentration to support sustained ignition. Therefore, attainment of firepoint would be delayed until the breakdown products of the polyol component made a significant contribution to the volatiles. This process requires temperatures in excess of 300°C.

Tables 2 and 3 indicate that the combustion modified foams, G1 and G2, have lower firepoint temperatures and comparable ignition delay times to the two standard foams (S1 and S2). However, there are substantial differences in post-ignition behaviour. The standard foams achieve steady burning very rapidly following ignition and burn with large, yellow, luminous flames until all the fuel is exhausted. In the absence of a pilot source, both standard foams will achieve spontaneous ignition in less than 30s at the highest radiant heat flux tested. The G1 and G2 foams take longer to achieve steady burning and burn with smaller, blue, non-luminous flames. The exposed surface does not melt and regress but forms a vermiform black char which appears to insulate lower levels of foam. After varying periods of time, dependent on the intensity of the imposed radiant heat flux, the G1 and G2 foams will self-extinguish. Subsequent re-ignition with sustained burning is not then possible. Spontaneous ignition is not observed at any of the heat fluxes considered. The remaining two combustion modified foams (C1 and C2) are considerably more resistant to sustained ignition although flashing ignition is observed at an early stage. These two foams melt and regress even more rapidly than the standard foams. This causes the surface to 'shrink' away from the heat source. Thus, subsequent behaviour in 'real' situations will depend on the original thickness of the foam, its location and on the method of restraint. In the present experiments, ignition did not occur at the lowest heat flux. At the two higher heat fluxes, sustained ignition occurred after the sample had formed a molten puddle in the base of the sample holder. Although the ignition delay times for C1 and C2 were much greater than those for G1 and G2, when sustained ignition finally did occur, vigorous burning was observed with large, yellow, luminous flames similar to those produced by burning standard PU foams. Burning continued until only a small quantity of char remained.

Critical Mass Flux

The concept of critical mass flux ($\dot{m}''_{cr}$) for solids, below which sustained ignition is not possible, was first proposed by Bamford et al. in 1946 (7) and has been supported by subsequent studies (4, 9-11). The critical condition for sustained ignition may be expressed in terms of the critical mass flux as follows:

$$(\dot{Q}''_{flame})_{cr} = \emptyset . \Delta Hc . \dot{m}''_{cr} \qquad (3)$$

where ΔHc is heat of combustion and $\emptyset$ is the maximum fraction of heat released in the flame that may be lost to the surface by convection without causing extinction.

The steady rate of burning expressed in terms of a mass flux ($\dot{m}''$) is:

$$\dot{m}'' = \frac{\dot{Q}''_{flame} + \dot{Q}''_{ext} - \dot{Q}''_{loss}}{L_v} \qquad (4)$$

Substituting from equation (3) into equation (4) for the firepoint condition leads to

$$S = (\emptyset \Delta Hc - L_v)\dot{m}''_{cr} + \dot{Q}''_{ext} - \dot{Q}''_{loss} \qquad (5)$$

where 'S' is the net 'sensible heat' entering the fuel and equals zero for 'steady burning' at the firepoint. Thus if 'S' is negative, then surface will cool, $\dot{m}''$ will decrease and the flame will extinguish and if 'S' is positive, the surface temperature will rise, $\dot{m}''$ will increase the flame will grow.

The main contribution to the term $\dot{Q}''_{loss}$ in equation (5) at the firepoint is conduction into the bulk of the solid. Thus for PU foams, this term will be much less than that for solid cast PU simply because conductive losses into the foams are low due to their low thermal conductivity (k).

$$\dot{Q}''_{loss} = \varepsilon \sigma T_s^4 + k\left(\frac{dT}{dx}\right)_s \qquad (6)$$

where ε is surface emissivity, σ is the Stefan-Boltzmann constant, T_s is the surface temperature (K) and $(dT/dx)_s$ is the temperature gradient immediately below the surface.

The accurate experimental determination of critical mass flux has proved difficult. Piloted ignition of the standard (S1 and S2) and graphite filled (G1 and G2) foams was rapid and the resolution of the mass loss/time curves was not sufficient to permit determination of critical mass fluxes at any but the lowest radiant heat flux (15kW/m^2). However, previous work (4) suggests that for standard materials, $\dot{m}''_{cr}$ is independent of the intensity of imposed radiant flux in the range considered.

Earlier studies on the measurement of critical mass flux at firepoint for solid plastics (4) indicated that hydrocarbon polymers (e.g. PE, PP, PS) have $\dot{m}''_{cr}$ values around $1g/m^2.s$ while those of oxygenated polymers (e.g. PMMA, POM) are approximately $2g/m^2.s$. Hence, the present values of $\dot{m}''_{cr}$ for S1, S2, G1 and G2 which range from .32-.61 $g/m^2.s$ are surprisingly low by comparison. However, the critical mass flux of solid cast PU with an average value of $1.5g.m^2.s$ lies midway between the values obtained previously for the two groups of solid polymers. This would seem to suggest that the physical structure of the foams is facilitating the ignition process and allowing sustained ignition to occur at a lower volatile concentration than expected. In fact, the critical mass flux at firepoint for the standard and graphite loaded foams is similar to the mass flow rate of volatiles at the flashpoint for solid cast PU. It may be possible to explain this in terms of the differences in the response of solid and foamed PU to heat transfer.

It was observed at all heat fluxes considered that solid PU underwent flashing ignition prior to sustained ignition. However, with the exception of C1 and C2, PU foams did not 'flash'. Thermal conductivity for solid PU is more than five times greater than for foamed PU. Hence, heat transfer by convection from flashes of flame between flashpoint and firepoint for solid PU is rapidly conducted away from the surface. Foams, on the other hand, have characteristically low thermal conductivities and tend not to exhibit flashing ignition. One possible explanation is that the heat transferred to the surface by the first flash of premixed flame propagating through the volatile mixture above the surface of the foam is sufficient to raise the surface temperature above the firepoint value and generate a steady burning diffusion flame.

The similarity of t_{ig}, T_{ig} and $\dot{m}''_{cr}$ results for standard foams (S1, S2) and G1 and G2 suggests that the addition of exfoliated graphite has little influence on volatile composition but is effective by promoting the formation of an inert insulating layer of ash which protects deeper levels of undegraded foam, that is, it is the post ignition behaviour that determines the improved fire properties.

C1 and C2 were considerably more resistant to ignition than the standard and graphite loaded foams. Piloted ignition was only possible at the higher two heat fluxes and flashing ignition was observed prior to sustained ignition. Sustained ignition did not occur until the samples were almost totally molten causing the exposed surface to have regressed by approximately 2.5cm. This corresponded to an effective reduction in incident radiant heat flux of 27% at the highest heat flux considered. When sustained burning was finally achieved, the flames were large and luminous and self extinction was not observed. The critical mass fluxes at firepoint were approximately 5 times greater than those of the standard (S1, S2) and graphite loaded (G1, G2) foams and showed some dependency on the intensity of imposed radiant heat flux. Previous work on fire retarded and unmodified polymethylmethacrylate and polypropylene (11) suggests that these observations are due to the presence of gas phase active fire retardants whose effect is progressively diminshed with extended heating.

CONCLUSIONS

The above work relates specifically to the pilot ignition of exposed horizontal samples of commercially available polyurethane foams. The fire behaviour of these materials is dominated by their characteristically low thermal inertia. This causes a very rapid surface response to an imposed heat flux resulting in fast achievement of ignition and development of peak burning rate and should be regarded as the major hazard of polyurethane foams. Additives can modify the fire behaviour of polyurethane foams in various ways but given sufficiently severe conditions, most will still ignite and burn. Further data on a wider range of combustion modified foams is required for better understanding of the influence of additives on the piloted ignition of cellular materials.

REFERENCES

1. Allport, D.C., Plastics and Rubber Processing and Applications, 1984 **4(2)**, 173.

2. Thomson, H.E. and Drysdale, D.D., Fire and Materials, 1987, **11**, 163.

3. Wraight, H.G.H., J. Physics E., 1971, **4**, 786.

4. Drysdale, D.D. and Thomson, H.E., Fire Safety Journal, 1989, **14**, 179.

5. Standard Test Method for Flashpoint and Firepoint by the Cleveland Open Cup Test Method D92-78. American Society for Testing and Materials, Philadelphia (1978).

6. Woolley, W.D., British Polym. J., 1972, **4**, 27.

7. Bamford, C.H., Crank, J. and Malan, D.H., Proc. Cambridge Phil. Soc.,1946, **42**, 166.

8. Deepak, D. and Drysdale, D.D., Fire Safety Journal, 1983, **5**, 167.

9. Rasbash, D.J., Proc. Int. Symposium on Fire Safety of Combustible Materials, Edinburgh University, 1975, p.169.

10. Tewarson, A. "Flame Retardant Polymeric Materials", vol. 3, Plenum Press, New York, 1982, p.97.

11. Thomson, H.E. and Drysdale, D.D. "Ignition of Fire Retarded Plastics" Paper Presented at Flame Retardants '87, London, November 1987, The Plastics and Rubber Institute.

THE DEVELOPMENT OF TOXIC HAZARD IN FIRES FROM POLYURETHANE FOAMS AND THE EFFECTS OF FIRE RETARDANTS

DAVID A. PURSER
Department of Inhalation Toxicology
Huntingdon Research Centre Ltd., Huntingdon, Cambs PE18 6ES, U.K.

ABSTRACT

Toxic hazard in a fire depends upon growth rate, toxic product yield and the toxic potency of the products. The yield of toxic products from flexible polyurethane foams depends upon the decomposition conditions. Smouldering/non-flaming yields mainly isocyanates and CO. Well ventilated flaming of objects up to chair size yields some CO, HCN and NOx. Fully developed large fires give high yields of CO and HCN. Small scale tests were found to give good predictions of full-scale yields if appropriate decomposition conditions were used. Flame retarded and other combustion modified foams were found to give higher yields of toxic products than standard foams during smouldering/non-flaming decomposition and in chair-sized well ventilated flaming fires, which increased the rate of hazard development. Fire growth and product yield were greater for all foams when flaming followed a period of smouldering.

INTRODUCTION

Concerns about the increasing incidence of injury and death in the UK resulting from exposure to smoke from fires in furniture and bedding [1] have led to the introduction of new types of flexible polyurethane foams (FPUs) with fire-retardant (FR) or other combustion modifying (CM) additives in an attempt to improve the ignitability and flame spread characteristics of building contents, with the assumption that this will lead to a reduction in fire casualties. The development of toxic hazard in a fire depends upon two major factors:

1. The dose of toxic products delivered to a victim, which depends upon:

   i. The fire growth curve in terms of the mass-loss rate of the fuel (kg/s) and the volume into which it is dispersed (kg/m^3)
   ii. The yield of toxic products (kg/kg fuel).

2. The toxic potency of the products (dose $kg.m^{-3}.min$ required for toxic effects)

Due to their improved ignitability and flame-spread characteristics, FR materials normally have improved performance in some situations with regard to fire growth rate, but this may be achieved at the expense of a greater yield of common toxic products [2,3,4,5]. In some cases extra toxic products not evolved from untreated materials may be released from the decomposing fire retardant or may be formed in the combined thermal decomposition products from the combination of the retardant with the base materials, and this may lead to an overall increase in toxic potency [6]. There are also concerns that some FR substances give rise to exotic products when heated (halogenated dibenzodioxins and dibenzofurans) that may produce serious long term toxic effects in people exposed to very low concentrations [7,8]. If we are to be sure that the introduction of these materials will lead to a net safety gain it is important to assess their performance by comparing the development of toxic hazard in fires involving both standard and FR or CM foams. In this paper a method for carrying out such a hazard analysis is applied to small-scale, large-scale and full-scale fire test data on standard and FR foams of various types used in armchair construction. In particular, use is made of data from a series of experiments ranging from small-scale to full-scale tests, performed at the U.S. National Institute of Standards and Technology (NIST - formerly the National Bureau of Standards - NBS) on a standard and FR foam covered with Haitian cotton covers.

Fire types and hazard situations

It is possible to identify three main types or stages of fires and hazard situations:

Non-flaming/smouldering fires
Early or small flaming fires
Fully developed large scale (post-flashover) fires.

Non-flaming/smouldering fires

Many accidental fires begin with materials being overheated and/or involve self sustaining smouldering. This may continue for several hours, after which flaming may occur followed by rapid fire growth. A common hazard situation exists where people are in the room of fire origin, possibly sleeping, and are exposed for a long period to gradually increasing concentrations of toxic gases from non-flaming decomposition. This may lead to incapacitation, so that the victim cannot escape when rapid flaming growth occurs. Victims are commonly found dead near a burned -out chair or bed, where there is evidence that long-term smouldering occurred prior to flaming. It is therefore important to determine how high reslience (HR), FR and CM foams behave under these conditions, in terms of toxic gas production during non-flaming, and flaming following prolonged smouldering.

Early or small flaming fires

Another fire hazard relates to rapidly growing, early flaming, fires where the victim is in the room of origin, or in a nearby location (e.g. adjoining room) and is overcome before being able to escape. The improved ignitability and flame spread characteristics of FR materials should confer great benefits in this situation, firstly by rendering flaming ignition much less likely to occur from the application of small sources, and secondly by slowing the rate of fire growth and hence the rate of development of toxic hazard, giving victims more time to escape. However, it is important in this situation to determine whether the improved fire growth rate is offset by an increased yield of toxic products.

Fully developed large scale (post-flashover fires)

The hazard in this situation is to persons in remote locations, and many non-fatal and fatal casualties are overcome by toxic gases in this situation. In general FR materials are most effective in inhibiting the early stages of fire growth, and have less effect in fully developed fires. There is little information on their contribution to the toxic potency of smoke produced in such fires.

THE TOXIC POTENCY OF THERMAL DECOMPOSITION PRODUCTS FROM FPU FOAMS

Small-scale tests

In order to assess the toxic potency of the thermal decomposition and combustion products from flexible polyurethane foams it is first necessary to determine the yields of common toxic gases and other toxic products when the materials are subjected to the reactive chemical environment, in terms of temperature, oxygen supply and flame, encountered during the main types and stages of the fires described above. Small-scale toxicity tests are used in attempts to create these conditions so that toxic potency can be assessed by animal experiments and the chemical composition of the products can be measured. The basic chemisty and toxicity of the thermal decomposition of FPUs is well known [9,10,11,12]. At temperatures of approximately 300°C FPU decomposes into the polyol, which forms a liquid pool, and toluene diisocyanate, which polymerizes to form a yellow isocyanate smoke. Some decomposition of the polyol gives rise to low yields of CO and CO_2, but the most important toxic product under non-flaming conditions is the isocyanate smoke, which is a potent lung irritant [12]. As the temperature of decomposition increases to mid-range temperatures around 600°C the isocyanate fraction starts to decompose, releasing CO and HCN, and at high temperatures of around 800°C the yield of HCN approaches the theoretical maximum of approximately 80 mg/g foam, and high yields of carbon oxides are also formed [10]. Under non-flaming, or oxygen vititated, conditions the main toxic products are therefore isocyanates at low temperatures and CO and HCN at high temperatures. However if the temperature and air supply are sufficient to support flaming, then the actual product mix will vary with the conditions. If flaming is well ventilated, as during the early stages of flaming fires, then most of the carbonaceous fuel will be oxidized to CO_2 and water, and fuel containing nitrogen is oxidized to a mixture of NOx and N_2, normally with a high yield of NO_2 [13,4,14]. If flaming is oxygen vitiated, particularly when large masses of FPUs are burned and compartment temperatures are high, then very high yields of CO and HCN are formed [15]. The most likely effect of FR and CM treatments will be to delay flaming and and reduce combustion during early flaming, thereby decreasing combustion efficiency and increasing the yields of CO, HCN and other pyrolysis products.

This basic chemical decomposition picture is supported by the results of small scale toxicity tests. Using a variant of the DIN 53436 method on FPU decomposed under nitrogen, Purser and Grimshaw [11] obtained principally yellow smoke at 300 and 600°C, which caused death by post-exposure lung irritation, and a smoke-free atmosphere consisting principally of CO and HCN at 900°C, which caused toxicity by narcosis. The effect of flaming decomposition at 600°C is illustrated by other work using the DIN method, when a thermoplastic polyurethane in an untreated form, and a form treated with decabromophenyl oxide and antimony trioxide were decomposed (Table 1). The non-FR sample burned with a steady flame and the atmosphere produced was low in CO, HCN and smoke (and therefore isocyanates). It was therefore found to be low in narcotic and irritant toxicity. For the FR material flaming was intermittent and inefficient, so that CO and HCN yields were high (HCN yield approximately 10 mg/g foam). The smoke density and irritancy were also high, indicating a high yield of irritant pyrolysis products.

TABLE 1

Composition of test atmospheres from flaming samples of thermoplastic polyurethane (600°C, 8.0 mg/l mass charge)

	CO ppm	CO_2 ppm	HCN ppm	Smoke OD/m	Irritancy RD_{50} mg/l
Normal	350	13000	11	0.07	4 approx
FR version	4200	6000	77	1.23	0.2 approx

In these tests the FR material was approximately 10x more potent in terms of the known toxic gases CO and HCN, and approximately 20x more irritant to mice than the normal material.

In the U.K., furniture is now required to contain foams with an acceptable flammability performance according to British Standard tests. Two commonly used types of these CM foams are graphite-containing and melamine-containing, and are of a higher density than existing (standard and high resilience [HR] foams). There is a danger that by modifiying the burning behaviour and by increasing the carbon and nitrogen content of the foams, the yields of CO and HCN from CM foams will be greater in fires than those obtained from standard or HR foams.

Workers at NIST have carried out a number of studies on the toxicity of thermal decompostion products from both standard and FR-treated FPUs using the NBS toxicity test method. This method, in which samples of material are decomposed in a cup furnace, has proved to be a reasonably good model for the conditions during early, well-ventilated, flaming fires. In a series of experiments on a standard FPU the rat mass loss LC_{50} under non-flaming conditions (375°C) was 32 mg/l (LCt_{50} 950 $mg.l^{-1}.min$), with low CO concentrations, only traces of HCN, and all the deaths occurring after exposure. These deaths were therefore most likely caused by irritant pyrolysis products, probably mainly isocyanates. Under flaming conditions (425°C) the yields of CO and HCN were higher, but still insufficient to cause death, and no deaths occured either during or following exposure at 40 mg/l, demonstrating that the irritant pyrolysis products were largely destroyed in the flame, and that insufficient NOx had been formed to cause a problem.

In another study two similar FPUs were tested, one containing a chlorinated phosphate so that it was cigarette and flame ignition resistant [2]. Under non-flaming conditions at 375-400°C the LC_{50} of the standard foamd was 38±2 mg/l (mass charge) and 34 mg/l (mass loss), giving an LCt_{50} of 1020 $mg.l^{-1}.min$. The yield of CO was somewhat higher than with the previous sample (approximately 1000 ppm, 46 mg/g foam - Table 2), but there was only a trace of HCN. As previously deaths occurred after exposure, indicating that toxic concentrations of irritants were present. Under flaming conditions (450°C) the main gaseous product was CO_2, and no deaths occurred at concentrations of up to 40 mg/l mass loss. For the FR foam under non-flaming conditions the LC_{50} was lower than that from the standard foam at 28 mg/l mass charge and 23 mg/l mass loss, equivalent to a lethal dose of 690 $mg.l^{-1}.min$. As with the standard foam, deaths occurred mainly post-exposure, but one animal died during exposure. It is therefore likely that the increased toxicity was due mainly to an increased yield of irritant pyrolysis products from the FR foam, but it is possible that some other toxic species was also present. The greatest difference between the

TABLE 2
Yields of gases from NBS(NIST) cup furnace:

Experiment	CO mg/g	HCN mg/g	CO_2 mg/g	CO_2/CO mg/g	CO/HCN v/v	LC_{50} mg/l
Standard foam:						
Non-flaming 400°C	46	0.35	73	1/1	71/1	39
Flaming 450°C	23	1.7	1579	43/1	15/1	40
NF-ramp 375-800°C		11				
CM foam:						
Non-flaming 375°C	35	0.2	35	1/1	123/1	28
Flaming	45	5.24	1533	20/1	10/1	27
NF-ramp 375-800°C		14				

two foams was under flaming conditions, when the LC_{50} of the FR foam was 27 mg/l mass charge (25 mg/l mass loss, lethal dose 750 $mg.l^{-1}.min$). The increased toxicity was partly due to a threefold increase in HCN yield, which together with doubled CO yield caused deaths during exposure, but since the majority of deaths occurred after exposure, it is likely that the main cause of death was lung irritancy from isocyanates and other pyrolysis products escaping the flame zone, or from some other factor related to the fire retardant, as under non-flaming conditions. These results are in agreement with those obtained from the TPU samples in the DIN furnace, showing that under non-flaming and early flaming conditions, the toxic potency of FR materials can be greater than non-FR materials.

Another aspect of the evolution of cyanide from small samples of foams decomposed in the NBS toxicity apparatus were studied by Levin et al [2]. In particular they attempted to mimic the common full-scale condition of a sample smouldering for some time and then flaming. This was achieved by heating samples of the two foams in the cup furnace at 370-375°C for 30 minutes and then ramping the cup temperature up to 800°C. The results showed that under non-flaming decomposition conditions at 370-375°C very little cyanide was evolved, but a greater amount of nitrogen-containing char was formed from the FR foam. When the samples were ramp heated, cyanide was evolved from the char, at 11 mg/g foam for the non-FR foam and 14 mg/g for the FR foam. In similar experimemts on other non-FR and FR foams, the HCN yields were 7 mg/g and 12 mg/g [3].

The basic findings from all these small-scale experiments therefore confirm the predictions from the fire chemistry of FPUs, that under low temperature, non-flaming, conditions irritant isocyanates are an important problem, with some contribution from CO. Under early flaming conditions toxicity is relatively low when combustion is efficient (although irritant effects from NOx may be a problem), but with FR foam in particular, toxic yields of CO, HCN and irritants are evolved, and flaming following smouldering is likely to result in considerably increased HCN yields. For large, post-flashover, fires high yields of CO and HCN can be expected from standard, FR and CM foams, and therefore a high toxic potency, depending upon the temperature, the nitrogen and carbon content of the foams and the degree of oxygen vitiation.

Full-Scale Tests

These small-scale tests do provide some infomation on the likely behaviour of FPUs in different fire conditions, and this toxic potency information can be used in conjunction with other small scale data (such as heat-release data) as inputs to toxic hazard analysis calculations for full-scale fires. However, all these test results are of dubious value unless it can be shown that the yields of toxic gases produced under small-scale conditions provide a true reflection of gas yields in full-scale fires. Unfortunately we often cannot be sure that this is the case, as very few attempts have been made to validate these tests against full-scale fire conditions with materials in their end-use configuration, and in many full-scale fires, particularly fully developed fires, the decomposition conditions, and therefore the yields of toxic gases, may be determined more by the general conditions in the full scale scenario than by material-related properties [5]. However, In theory, the chemical decomposition environment produced by these small-scale tests under non-flaming and flaming conditions should provide a reasonable simulation of the conditions in smouldering and in early or small (moderate temperature, well ventilated) fires, and under these conditions it is to be expected that material-related properties will influence both the rate of burning and the yields of toxic gases. A series of experiments which illustrate this point and confirms the findings from the small-scale data on standard and FR foams is summarized in Table 3.

In these tests samples of the two foams shown in Table 2, and Haitian cotton covering material, were tested in both the NBS toxicity test method and the cone calorimeter (from which CO, CO_2 yields, and heat release data were obtained. The materials were then made up into upholstered chairs (combustible mass 5.7 kg), which were tested with flaming ignition of the seat back, and smouldering ignition caused by one or two cigarettes placed in the seat angle for approximately one hour, followed by flaming ignition using a small butane torch. This was designed to simulate spontaneous ignition following prolonged smouldereing. The chairs were tested in a furniture calorimeter, for heat and toxic gas release, and in a full-scale scenario where rodent toxicity was measured in addition. The full-scale scenario was a closed system (volume 100.96 m^3) consisting of a burn room (2.34 x 2.35 x 2.16 m high), connected via a corridor 12.19 m long with a target room (2.24 x 2.22 x 2.43 m high).

For flaming ignition, steady-state burning mass loss rates were 25 g/s for standard foam chairs and 16 g/s for CM foam chairs. The CO and CO_2 concentrations in the burn room reached a peak briefly, and then decreased to a level close to that in the target room. By the end of the test the air in the closed system was well mixed, with little evidence of layering, and the final oxygen concentration was approximately 12%. From the gas concentrations in the system and the mass loss from the chairs it is possible to calculate the mass yields of different gases. The results in terms of toxic gas yields from the two types of materials and chairs are shown in Table 3. With tests involving flaming following smouldering, the smoke layer had reached floor level before the flaming was initiated, but there was a concentration gradient between the burn room and the target room. During smouldering the mass loss from the chairs was approximately 1 kg for both foam types, and the average mass loss concentration was approximately 13 g/m^3 for the burn room and 7 g/m^3 in the target room. For flaming the yields of both CO and HCN from the CM foam were higher than those from the standard foam, while the CO_2 was somewhat lower. The rate of decomposition was slightly lower for the CM foam. For flaming following

TABLE 3
Comparison of toxic gas yields from small and large-scale tests

Experiment	Temp °C	CO kg/kg	HCN kg/kg x 10^{-3}	CO_2 kg/kg	CO_2/CO v/v	CO/HCN v/v
STANDARD FOAM:						
Flaming decomposition:						
NBS Cup	450	0.023	1.7	1.58	43/1	15/1
Cone cal		0.013		2.34	115/1	
Furn cal		0.05	0.62	2.00	25/1	86/1
Room/corridor	680	0.037	0.59	3.10	54/1	67/1
Non-flaming (NS) or smouldering (S) decomposition:						
NBS Cup (NS)	400	0.046	0.35	0.073	1/1	71/1
Cone Cal (NS)		0.040		1.71	27/1	
Furn cal (S)		0.24	1.43	13.00	34/1	179/1
Rm/corridor(S)	61	0.15	0	1.0	4.2/1	
Flamimg decomposition following smouldering:						
NBS Cup (Ramp to 800°C) HCN only			11			
Cone cal No data						
Furniture Cal		0.12	1.09	3.60	19/1	117/1
Rm/corridor	673	0.062	2.74	3.18	32/1	25/1
FR FOAM:						
Flaming decomposition:						
NBS Cup	425	0.045	5.24	1.53	20/1	10/1
Cone cal		0.045		1.13	15/1	
Furn cal		0.09	1.75	1.90	13/1	55/1
Room/corridor	500	0.054	1.57	2.16	27/1	34/1
Non flaming (NF) or smouldering (S) decomposition						
NBS Cup(NF)	375	0.035	0.2	0.035	1/1	123/1
Cone cal(NF)		0.039		0.74	12/1	
Furn cal(S)		0.35	0.46	8.00	15/1	
Rm/corridor(S)	40	0.17	0	0.7	2/1	
Flaming decomposition following smouldering						
NBS Cup (HCN only)			14			
Cone cal No data						
Furn cal		0.13	7.00	1.90	9/1	20/1
Rm/corridor	640	0.088	3.64	2.53	18/1	27/1

smouldering the yields of both CO and HCN were higher than following direct flaming. All the flaming atmospheres were lethal to the animals, which is consistent with the combination of toxic gases measured in the exposure chambers.

Comparison of yields of toxic gases obtained from large and small-scale tests

During the small-scale tests on standard and FR foams, the yields of CO and HCN were greater from FR foams, and it is possible that this might counteract their desirable ignition resistance and lower fire growth characteristics. Table 3 shows that in the NIST study the yields of these gases and the differences between the foam types were similar in the small-scale tests (NBS toxicity test and cone calorimeter), the large scale test (furniture calorimeter), and the full-scale fire. The full-scale fire tests consisted of a small fire load (5.7 kg) in a well ventilated fire compartment which was part of a closed system (analogous to a small, single floor, appartment). The volume of air in the system was approximately twice that that needed to decompose the materials completely, so that when the fire finished, the oxygen concentration in the system was approximately 12% and the minimum concentration in the burn room was 10%.

Flaming ignition fires

Following flaming ignition the standard foam took approximately 3 minutes to burn, and the CM foam approximately 5 minutes. The basic fire condition was therefore of a small, reasonably well ventilated fire reaching a moderate compartment temperature (maximum 680°C for the standard foam and 500°C for the CM foam). This is therefore similar to the general conditions theoretically simulated by the NBS cup furnace and the cone calorimeter, and in the furniture calorimeter, where open burning is used. The yields of HCN are generally low as expected. Total conversion of available nitrogen to HCN would yield 80 g/kg, and total conversion of carbon to CO_2 would yield 2242 g/kg. The actual yields of cyanide were much lower than 80 g/kg at 0.6 g/kg for standard foam chairs and 1.6 g/kg for FR chairs, and were 2-3 times less than those obtained in the NBS cup. This may be due to recirculation of nitrogen-containing products through the hot cup furnace in the NBS test, leading to increased decomposition. Carbon dioxide yields were high, showing almost complete combustion of available carbon to CO_2. For standard foam the CO_2/CO ratio was 54/1, and 27/1 for the FR foam, indicating less efficient combustion. No measurements of NOx concentrations were made.

Flaming following smouldering

When the chairs were ignited by a burner following smouldering, the rate of fire growth was much more rapid than under direct flaming and the period of flaming was shorter at 1-1.5 minutes. For the standard foam the mass loss rates during steady burning after smouldering were similar to those following direct flaming ignition (approximately 20 g/s compared to 25 g/s), but for the FR foam the mass loss rate was much more rapid than following direct ignition (30 g/s compared to 16 g/s). This rapid burning resulted in a severe, temporary, oxygen vitiation in the fire compartment (0.5-2.5% for standard foam and 2.5-5.6% for CM foam). This short period of oxygen vitiation may be part of the reason that CO yields were doubled compared to flaming ignition, but in general CO_2/CO ratios were not very different from those obtained under direct flaming conditions, so that the period of oxygen vitiation was too short to alter the efficiency of combustion greatly. HCN yields were approximately 2-5 x that following direct flaming, just as was found in the NBS cup simulation.

Smouldering
During smouldering very little HCN was evolved and the yields of CO were higher than under flaming conditions, with CO_2 ratios of approximately 2/1 or 4/1. CO yields were higher for the FR foam.

TOXIC HAZARD TO POTENTIAL VICTIMS IN ROOM/CORRIDOR/ROOM FACILITY FIRES

The full-scale NBS tests provide a good model for the real life situation of a fire involving a single armchair, with burning restricted to the item first ignited, in a small appartment consisting of a living room joined by a corridor to a bedroom on the same floor, with the connecting doors being left open. The problem is to assess the effect of substituting the FR-foam for the standard foam on the time to incapacitation and death of a potential human fire victim in the burn room and the target room, following direct flaming ignition and flaming after smouldering. For this purpose the Purser [16] model for calculation of time to incapacitation and death for human fire victims has been applied to the full-scale fire data. The results of the calculations are shown in the Appendix (Tables 8 and 9), and are summarized in Table 4. The calculation is perfomed by calculating the fraction of an incapacitating dose of the major toxic gases each minute during the fire, and integrating the dose received with time until the fraction reaches unity, at which point it is calculated that an incapacitating dose has been received. Death is assumed to occur when the dose received exceeds twice the incapacitating dose.

Flaming decomposition

When chairs were ignited by a gas burner there appears to be an improved performance from the FR foam chairs, in terms of time to incapacitation due to narcois, in that time from burner application to incapacitation is increased from 8.5 to 11.5 minutes (burn room) and from 13 to 15 minutes (target room). However, stable ignition of the FR foam chair required 6 minutes of flame application compared to 4 minutes for the standard foam chair. If time from ignition is taken there is little difference between the two foams. Also, during the NBS cup tests, the FR foam caused late deaths, probably due to lung irritation, with an LCt_{50} of approximately 760 $mg.l^{-1}.min$ (mass loss). The mass loss dose up to the time of incapacitation due to narcotic gases was approximately 300-400 $mg.l^{-1}.min$. It is therefore likely that a person rescued at this point would suffer some degree of post-exposure lung damage from the FR foam, but considerably less from the standard foam.

Smouldering decomposition

Under smouldering conditions the concentrations of carbon monoxide in both the burn room and target room were higher for the FR-foam chair. Incapacitation from narcotic gases is therefore predicted earlier for the FR foam, at 54 minutes in the burn room (64 minutes for standard foam) and 72 minutes in the target room (insufficient for incapacitation in the target room for the standard foam). For the FR foam it is likely that death would occur before the smouldering phase was completed at approximately 84 minutes. It is also likely that a subject rescued at the point of incapacitation would have inhaled a mass loss dose of irritants capable of causing death from lung damage some hours after exposure (one rat exposed to smoke from the target room died following exposure). For a subject escaping at the end of the smouldering phase of the standard foam it is also likely that some lung damage might occur, and this might possibly prove fatal to some subjects, but the hazard is less than that from the FR-foam chair. For both types of foam, subjects present in either

TABLE 4
Predicted times to incapacitation and death from the effects of toxic gases for chairs made from standard and FR foams.

Test		Burn room		Target room	
		Time to I	Time to D	Time to I	Time to D
Flaming:	Standard foam chair	8.5	9	13	16
	FR foam foam chair	11.5	13	15	18
Smouldering to flaming:					
	Standard foam chair:				
	Smouldering phase	63	no D	no I	no D
	Flaming phase	already I	seconds	I seconds	D in 1 min
	FR foam chair:				
	Smouldering phase	54	84	72	no D
	Flaming phase	already I	already D	already I	D 1 min

I = Incapacitation
D = Death

the burn room or target room when flaming occurred following smouldering would become incapacitated within seconds and dead within a minute. Thus for example if persons entered the room/corridor system after 70 minutes of smouldering, and if (as commonly occurs) the act of entering were to cause the initiation of flaming, then they would be incapacitated very rapidly by the ensuing fire.

OTHER SMALL ROOM FIRE TESTS INVOLING POLYURETHANE FOAMS

Another series of tests confirming that cyanide yields are relatively low with small room fires involving single chairs, was performed by Alarie et al [17]. In these tests, chairs containing FPU cushions smouldered following cigarette ignition for approximately 60 minutes before flaming. Peak gas concentrations are shown in Table 5.

TABLE 5
Peak gas concentrations from single chair room fire [17]

CO	10,000 ppm for 5-10 minutes
CO_2	9%
O_2	8%
HCN	100 ppm

The smoke was found to be very irritant to mice during both smouldering and flaming phases. Time to the development of incapacitation and death for potential victims in another fire following flaming ignition of an FPU upholstered chair has been modelled in Purser [16].

Prager et al. [14] reported a series of fully furnished room fire, and single chair tests. Many of these tests resulted in small flaming fires, with room temperatures of only a few hundred degrees centigrade. These resulted in relatively low concentrations of CO (1000-2000 ppm, peaking at 6000 ppm in one test), and low concentrations of HCN with CO/HCN ratios of approximately 19/1 (80 ppm for 40 minutes in one room fire test of FPU with a polyamide/polyimide interliner). However oxides of nitrogen were measured, and these reached high concentrations (NOx 200-300 ppm), suggesting that in small, well ventilated fires, the nitrogen-containing materials are indeed oxidized to NOx as predicted by Woolley and Fardell [13].

TOXIC GAS YIELDS FROM LARGER AND POSTFLASHOVER FIRES INVOLVING POLYURETHANE FOAMS

With larger flaming fires in fully furnished rooms where flashover occurs, oxygen vitiation tends to be greater and yields of CO and HCN are increased. A series of tests were performed by Grand et al. [18] on a fully furnished hotel room mock-up (room - open corridor rig with a side room containing animals adjoining the corridor). The door to this room was closed 5 minutes after a flashover temperature (650°C) was obtained in the burn room. In addition to other fuels the major nitrogen containing materials in the burn room were 52 kg FPU, 16 kg of acrylic and a nylon carpet. The peak concentrations of gases are shown in Table 6.

TABLE 6
Peak gas concentrations in burn room and side room during hotel-room fire test

	BURN ROOM	SIDE ROOM
Temp °C	850°C	59°C
O_2	0.2%	14.2%
CO_2	13.8%	3.55%
CO	67,000 ppm	11,500 ppm
HCN	1340 ppm	145 ppm
HCl	2000-3000 ppm	475 ppm
NOx	120 ppm	50 ppm
CO/HCN	50/1	79/1
CO/NOx	558/1	230/1
CO_2/CO	2/1	3/1

Despite the door-sized opening to the fire room, these data show the typical conditions of a ventilation controlled, post-flashover, fire involving a relatively large fuel load. The temperature in the fire compartment was relatively high (850°C), and the compartment atmosphere was very oxygen vitiated (0.2%). If the small-scale predictions of toxic gas concentrations derived from the small scale experiments [9,10,11] are correct it is to be expected that CO and HCN concentrations would be much higher than those obtained from small (single chair) fires, with a CO_2/CO ratio of less than 10 and CO/HCN ratios in the 20/1 to 100/1 range. This was indeed the case as Table 6 shows. Another important point with regard to post-flashover fires, where the main consideration is conditions outside the fire compartment, is the extent to which secondary combustion of fire products occurs outside the compartment, where more air mixes with the hot plume. It is interesting in this case to compare the ratios of gases in the side room with those in the fire compartment. Table 6 shows that the CO_2/CO ratio in the side room is 3/1, compared to 2/1 in the fire compartment. This means that relatively little secondary combustion occurred in the plume, since ratios of greater than 10/1 would have been expected if this had occurred. However, the degree of oxidation of HCN also been (relatively) slightly greater, since the CO/HCN ratio has increased from 50/1 to 79/1, and this is consistent with the increase in the CO/NOx ratio by approximately a factor of two.

Yields of CO and HCN from large compartment fires involving FPU as the only fuel were obtained by Kirk and Stark [15], who burned large loads of foams in a room (volume 32 m^3) and corridor facility. Three types of foam were used for these tests:

Foam A: Standard polyether + toluene diisocyanate (TDI) 26.6 kg/m^3
Foam B: as A + brominated alkyl phosphate
Foam C: HR grade (non-FR) 33.3 kg/m^3

Each foam was tested twice, on one occasion with a foam load of approximately 130-290 kg in the compartment only, and on one occasion with an additional load of approximately 20 kg in the corridor, in order to examine effects on combustion in the system. One test was also performed with a smaller load (66 kg) of foam C, and another with 136 kg of wood for comparison. The results are summarized in Table 7.

TABLE 7
Yields of toxic gases evolved from fires involving large loads of polyurethane foams

Foam and mass kg	Compartment Temp Max°C	Compartment Minimum O_2%	Compartment CO g/kg	Compartment HCN g/kg	Compartment CO/HCN	Corridor Minimum O_2	Corridor CO g/kg	Corridor HCN g/kg	Corridor CO/HCN
A 127	1090	2.7	1937	31.5	62/1	9.2	346	5.5	63/1
127+14	1070	2.6	610	46.1	13/1	9.2	67	22.0	3/1
B 159	1110	3.2	302	27.6	11/1	5.8	201	11.3	18/1
159+18	1140	2.3	232	25.4	9/1	7.6	164	29.4	5/1
C 285	1120	7.2	989	23.5	42/1	6.6	95	9.8	10/1
134+36	1100	2.2	365	10.0	36/1	9.7	88	19.0	5/1
66	925	16.1	30	3.0	10/1	17.5	36	6.0	6/1
Wood 136	920	4.0	66			4.0	6		

As with the previous example, the large fire loads used in these tests produce a large, high temperature, ventilation-controlled fire with severe oxygen vitiation in the fire compartment. This produced very high yields of CO and HCN in the fire compartment at high concentrations (CO 5,700-14,000 ppm, HCN 1090-3690 ppm). The yields of CO were approximately 25-100% of the theoretical maximum yield from FPU of 1400 mg CO/g foam, and the yields of HCN were approximately 13-57% of the theoretical maximum of approximately 80 mg HCN/g foam, and were comparable to those obtained from small-scale experiments [9,10,11](53 mg/g in [11]) performed under similar decomposition conditions. Unfortunately CO_2 concentrations were not reported, but from the CO yield data they must have been less than 4/1. CO/HCN ratios are also low ranging from 9/1 to 62/1. Once the effluents pass down the corridor, the yields of CO are reduced, suggesting that oxidation has continued to occur in the plume from the entrained air. This means that the plume temperature in the corridor must be hotter than that in the corridor outside the previous (hotel room) fire, and indeed temperatures of 600-900°C were measured in the corridor. These reactions do not seem to have reduced the HCN yields, which are in fact increased when some of the fuel was placed in the corridor. The smaller foam fire load, and the wood fire, produced considerably lower yields of fire gases. Also, in these tests the FR-treated foam produced somewhat lower yields of CO than did the non-FR foam.

CONCLUSIONS

The results of these studies demonstrate that small-scale tests, when conducted under appropriate decompostion conditions, can be used to predict the yields and potencies of toxic products in full-scale fires involving flexible polyurethane foams, and together with other small-scale and large scale fire performance data, can be used to predict the development of toxic hazard in full-scale fires. However, an area that particulaly requires more research is the prediction of toxic gas yields in full-scale fires.

With regard to the substitution of standard foams by fire-retarded and other types of combustion modified foams, the results show that the development of toxic hazard depends upon a combination of ignitability, fire growth rate, gas yield and toxic potency. Although there may be a safety gain from their use by reducing the incidence of smouldering and flaming fires, once smouldering or flaming begins, the rate of hazard development is scenario-dependent and in some situations the use of FR or CM foams may be a disadvantage unless other measures are taken to improve fire performance.

REFERENCES

1. Central Fire Brigades' Advisory Councils Joint Fire Prevention Committee. Report of the technical Sub-committee on the fire risks of new materials. Home Office Fire Department, 1978, pp. 1-29.

2. Braun, E., Levin, B.C., Paabo, M., Gurman, J., Holt, T. and Steel, J.S., Fire toxicity scaling. U.S. Department of Commerce. National Bureau of Standards Report No. NBSIR 87-3510, 1987.

3. Levin, B.C., Paabo, M., Fultz, M.L. and Bailey, C.S., Generation of hydrogen cyanide from flexible polyurethane foam decomposed under different combustion conditions. Fire Mater., 1985, 9, 125-134.

4. Levin, B.C., Paabo, Bailey, C.S. and Harris, S.E., Toxicity of the combustion products from a flexible polyurethane foam and polyester fabric evaluated separately and together by the NBS toxicity test method. In Fire Safety Science. Proceedings of the First International Symposium. eds. C.E. Grant and P.J. Pagni, Hemisphere, Washington, 1986, pp. 1111-1122.

5. Purser, D.A., Toxicity in fire, are we studying the right problems? In International Conference on Fires in Buildings. Technomic, Lancaster PA., 1989, pp.95-100.

6. Petajan, J.H., Voorhees, K.L., Packham, S.C., Baldwin, R.C., Einhorn,

I.N., Grunnet, M.L., Dinger, B.G., and Birky, M.M., Extreme toxicity from combustion products of a fire-retarded polyurethane foam. Science, 187, 742-744.

7. Troitzsch, J.H., New trends in the use of halogenated flame retardants in Germany. International Progress in Fire Safety, Proceeding of the Fire Retardant Chemicals Association meeting New Orleans. March 22-25. 1987. pp. 141-150.

8. Eduljee, G.H., Dioxins in the environment. Chemistry in Britain, December 1988, 1223-1226.

9. Woolley, W.D., Nitrogen-containing products from the thermal decomposition of flexible polyurethane foam. Br. Polym. J.,1972, 4, 27-43.

10. Woolley, W.E. and Fardell, P.J., The prediction of combustion products. Fire Research, 1977, 1, 11-21.

11. Purser, D.A. and Grimshaw, P., The incapacitative effects of exposure to the thermal decomposition products of polyurethane foams. Fire Mater., 1984, 8, 10-16.

12. Purser, D.A. and Buckley, P. Lung irritance and inflammation during and after exposure to thermal decompostion products of polymeric materials. Med. Sci. Law. 23, 142-150.

13. Woolley, W.D., Fardell, P.J., Atkinson, A.P. and Verall, A.P. Conversion of fuels containing nitrogen to oxides of nitrogen in hydrogen and methane flames. Fire Mater., 1978, 2, 122-131.

14. Prager, F.H., Darr, W.C. and Wood, J.F., The contribution of upholstered furniture to residential fire risks. Cellular Polymers, 1984, 3 161-194.

15. Kirk, P.G. and Stark, G.W.V., Flexible polyurethane foam - large scale fires of industrial loads of seating cushions. Her Majesty's Stationery Office, London 1975, pp. 1-18.

16. Purser, D.A., Toxicity assessment of combustion products in: SFPE Handbook of Fire Protection Engineering, ed. C.L. Beyler. National Fire Protection Association, Quincy, MA. 1988. Chapter 1-14 pp. 1-200 to 1-245.

17. Alarie, Y., Stock, M.F., Matijak-Schaper, M. and Birky, M.M. Toxicity of smoke during chair smouldering tests and small scale tests using the same materials. Fund. Appl. Toxicol., 1983. 3, 619-626.

18. Grand, A.F., Kaplan, H.L., Beitel, J.J.III, Switzer, W.G. and Hartzell, G.E., An evaluation of toxic hazards from full-scale furnished room fire studies. Special Technical Publication 882. American Society for Testing and Materials, 1986, pp. 330-353.

APPENDIX

TABLE 8

Concentrations of toxic gas and FIDs* in burn room and target room following flaming ignition of armchairs made from standard and fire-retarded flexible polyurethane foam with Haitian cotton covers.

Time min	CO ppm	HCN ppm	CO2 %	O2 %	CO FID	HCN FID	xCO2 FID	O2 FID	FID SUM	TFID£
Burn room					STANDARD FOAM					
1-4	275	2	0.3	21	0.009	0.005	1.102	0	0.015	0.060
5	800	6	0.8	18	0.028	0.005	1.212	0.001	0.041	0.101
6	1400	12	1.5	17	0.050	0.006	1.385	0.002	0.080	0.181
7	1400	32	4.0	15	0.050	0.009	2.229	0.007	0.139	0.320
8	3000	60	7.5	11.5	0.111	0.018	4.339	0.047	0.607	0.927
9	3000	80	10.0	9	0.111	0.029	6.982	0.182	1.159	2.086
10	1100	68	8.5	10.5	0.039	0.022	5.248	0.081	0.401	2.487
Target room										
1-5	0	0	0.1	21						0
6	100	0	0.3	20	0.003	0.005	1.102	0	0.009	0.009
7	200	3	1.0	19	0.007	0.005	1.259	0.001	0.016	0.025
8	400	11	3.5	17	0.014	0.006	2.027	0.002	0.043	0.068
9	1000	20	6.5	13	0.035	0.007	3.587	0.021	0.172	0.240
10	700	26	8.5	11.5	0.024	0.008	5.248	0.047	0.215	0.455
11	800	25	8.2	12	0.028	0.008	4.957	0.036	0.214	0.669
12	1500	23	7.5	12.5	0.054	0.008	4.339	0.027	0.296	0.965
13	1500	21	7.0	13	0.054	0.007	3.945	0.021	0.262	1.227
14	1500	21	7.0	13	0.054	0.007	3.945	0.021	0.262	1.489
15	1500	21	7.0	13	0.054	0.007	3.945	0.021	0.262	1.751
16	1500	21	7.0	13	0.054	0.007	3.945	0.021	0.262	2.013
Burn room					FIRE-RETARDED FOAM					
1-4	225	0	0.1	21	0.008	0.005	1.061	0	0.014	0.056
5	500	0	0.2	21	0.017	0.005	1.082	0	0.024	0.080
6	600	6	0.4	21	0.021	0.005	1.123	0	0.029	0.109
7	1000	16	1.1	20	0.035	0.007	1.284	0	0.054	0.163
8	1500	30	2.0	18	0.054	0.009	1.523	0.001	0.097	0.260
9	1800	43	3.0	17	0.065	0.012	1.843	0.002	0.144	0.404
10	2100	57	4.0	15	0.076	0.017	2.229	0.007	0.214	0.618
11	3000	64	4.5	14.5	0.111	0.020	2.451	0.009	0.330	0.948
12	3000	78	5.5	13.0	0.111	0.027	2.965	0.021	0.430	1.378
13	3700	100	7.0	11.5	0.137	0.045	3.945	0.047	0.765	2.143
Target room										
1-4	0	0	0.04	21						0
5-6	100	0	0.1	21	0.003	0.005	1.061	0	0.008	0.016
7	100	2	0.2	20	0.003	0.005	1.082	0	0.009	0.025
8	300	3	0.3	20	0.010	0.005	1.102	0	0.017	0.042
9	200	9	0.8	20	0.007	0.006	1.212	0	0.016	0.058
10	500	21	2.0	18	0.017	0.007	1.523	0.001	0.038	0.096
11	1100	32	3.0	16	0.039	0.009	1.843	0.004	0.092	0.188
12	1400	43	4.0	15	0.050	0.012	2.229	0.007	0.145	0.333
13	1300	64	6.0	13	0.047	0.020	3.261	0.021	0.239	0.572
14	1500	65	6.1	12.9	0.054	0.020	3.324	0.022	0.268	0.840
15	2000	62	5.8	13.2	0.073	0.019	3.139	0.019	0.308	1.148
16	2200	68	5.8	13.2	0.080	0.022	3.139	0.019	0.339	1.487
17	2200	61	5.7	13.3	0.080	0.018	3.080	0.018	0.320	1.807
18	2200	61	5.7	13.3	0.080	0.018	3.080	0.018	0.320	2.127

* FID=Fractional Incapacitating Dose

£ TFID intergated FID

Times of incapacitation and death underlined

TABLE 9

Concentrations of toxic gas and FIDs* in burn room and target room for smouldering followed by flaming ignition of armchairs made from standard and fire retarded flexible polyurethane foam with Haitian cotton covers.

Time min	CO ppm	HCN ppm	CO2 %	O2 %	CO	HCN	xCO2	O2	FID /min	TFID£
Burn room					STANDARD FOAM					
0-13	180	0	0.11	21	0.006	0	1.019	0	0.006	0.078
13-27	300	0	0.16	21	0.010	0	1.032	0	0.010	0.218
27-40	360	0	0.18	21	0.012	0	1.037	0	0.013	0.387
40-53	700	0	0.30	21	0.024	0	1.069	0	0.026	0.725
53-67	700	0	0.30	21	0.024	0	1.069	0	0.026	1.089
67-75	1000	0	0.40	21	0.035	0	1.096	0	0.039	1.401
75-76	10000	1320	15.0	3	0.386	Death within seconds				

Mass loss concentration of irritants = 8.5 mg/l x 70.6= 600 mg/l.min

Rat mass loss LCt_{50} = 1014 mg/l.min, one death from smouldering products.

Therefore lung damage likely and possibly fatal after 70.6 minutes.

Time min	CO ppm	HCN ppm	CO2 %	O2 %	CO	HCN	xCO2	O2	FID /min	TFID£
Target room										
0-13	0	0	0.04	21						0
13-27	0	0	0.04	21						0
27-40	100	0	0.08	21	0.003	0	1.012	0	0.003	0.039
40-53	270	0	0.15	21	0.009	0	1.030	0	0.009	0.156
53-67	550	0	0.20	21	0.019	0	1.042	0	0.020	0.436
67-75	800	0	0.30	21	0.028	0	1.069	0	0.030	0.676
75-76	2700	125	9.00	13	0.099	0.080	5.772	0.021	1.054	1.730
76-77	2000	120	8.50	14	0.073	0.072	5.248	0.012	0.773	2.503

Mass loss dose of irritants approx. 300 mg/l.min, therefore lung damage unlikely to be serious.

Time min	CO ppm	HCN ppm	CO2 %	O2 %	CO	HCN	xCO2	O2	FID /min	TFID£
Burn room					FIRE RETARDED FOAM					
0-13	180	0	0.10	21	0.006	0	1.017	0	0.006	0.079
13-27	360	0	0.18	21	0.012	0	1.037	0	0.013	0.260
27-40	640	0	0.30	21	0.022	0	1.069	0	0.024	0.572
40-53	800	0	0.36	21	0.028	0	1.085	0	0.030	0.962
53-67	800	0	0.36	21	0.028	0	1.085	0	0.030	1.382
67-80	800	0	0.36	21	0.028	0	1.085	0	0.030	1.772
80-90	1000	0	0.40	21	0.035	0	1.096	0	0.039	2.162
90-91.5	8000	1360	15	5	Death within seconds					

Mass loss concentration of irritants = 8.5 mg/l

Rat mass loss LCt50 = 750 ppm.min lethal dose received in 88 min

Time min	CO ppm	HCN ppm	CO2 %	O2 %	CO	HCN	xCO2	O2	FID /min	TFID£
Target room										
0-13	100	0	0.08	21	0.003	0	1.012	0	0.003	0.039
13-27	136	0	0.08	21	0.004	0	1.012	0	0.004	0.056
27-40	227	0	0.13	21	0.008	0	1.024	0	0.008	0.199
40-53	545	0	0.26	21	0.019	0	1.058	0	0.020	0.459
53-67	727	0	0.29	21	0.025	0	1.066	0	0.027	0.837
67-80	900	0	0.40	21	0.032	0	1.096	0	0.035	1.292
80-90	1100	0	0.50	21	0.039	0	1.124	0	0.044	1.732
90-92.5	4000	158	7.00	13	0.149	0.159	3.945	0.021	3.088	4.820

Mass loss concentration of irritants = 4.25 mg/l

Dose of 383 mg/l.min received in 90.3 minutes, therefore possible lung damage.

* FID=Fractional Incapacitating Dose

£ TFID intergated FID

Times of incapacitation and death underlined

REDUCING SMOKE AND TOXIC GASES FROM BURNING POLYURETHANE FOAM

D. L. BUSZARD and R. L. BENTLEY
Ciba-Geigy Industrial Chemicals,
Tenax Road, Trafford Park,
Manchester M17 1WT
United Kingdom

ABSTRACT

Polyurethane (PU) foam burns with the evolution of large quantities of thick, black smoke and toxic gases, principally carbon monoxide and hydrogen cyanide. Statistics indicate that these combustion products are the major causes of death in domestic fires involving upholstered furniture. Although researchers have reported smoke-suppression systems for polyurethane foam, these have not proved to be commercially viable. Ciba-Geigy has now developed a novel additive which can be incorporated into flexible polyurethane foam at the production stage and which significantly reduces the amount and rate of formation of smoke and toxic gases. This effect has been demonstrated in bench-scale tests and in a simulated fire situation using full-scale upholstered chairs.

INTRODUCTION

In the last decade considerable attention has been focused on the fire hazards of flexible polyurethane foams, particularly in upholstered furniture. Fires involving polyurethane foam furniture often have the following characteristics:

- prolonged ignition times from smouldering sources e.g. cigarettes
- rapid growth of fire from larger flaming ignition sources or in the later stages of smouldering ignition
- rapid generation of large volumes of hot, dense yellow/black smoke
- rapid generation of carbon monoxide, carbon dioxide and hydrogen cyanide

Statistics [1,2] indicate that deaths from such polyurethane foam upholstered furniture fires are disproportionately higher than from other domestic fire situations. In the majority of cases the causes of death are the products of combustion, that is the smoke and toxic gases evolved, rather than the actual fire itself. The large volumes of thick, black smoke impede escape from the fire situation, even in rooms removed from the fire source, and seriously hinder fire brigades in rescuing people and putting out the fire. The accompanying toxic gases, principally carbon monoxide and to a lesser extent hydrogen cyanide, are the actual causes of death.

Much effort has been expended in developing foams with improved resistance to ignition, and recently 'combustion modified' or 'CM foams' have been successfully developed. However, it has proved to be impracticable so far to produce foams which do not ignite and burn and generate large volumes of smoke and toxic gases when a sufficiently large ignition source is encountered.

Polyurethane foams are prepared by the reaction of a polyhydroxy compound (polyol) with a di- or polyisocyanate. Conventional slabstock flexible polyurethane foam, traditionally used for furniture and bedding applications, is manufactured in a continuous process by reacting a long-chain polyether polyol with toluene diisocyanate (TDI) as shown in figure 1. The cellular foam structure is obtained by including water in the formulation. This reacts with additional TDI to generate carbon dioxide, which functions as a blowing agent. Other adjuvants include catalysts to increase reaction rates, and surfactants to control the cell structure.

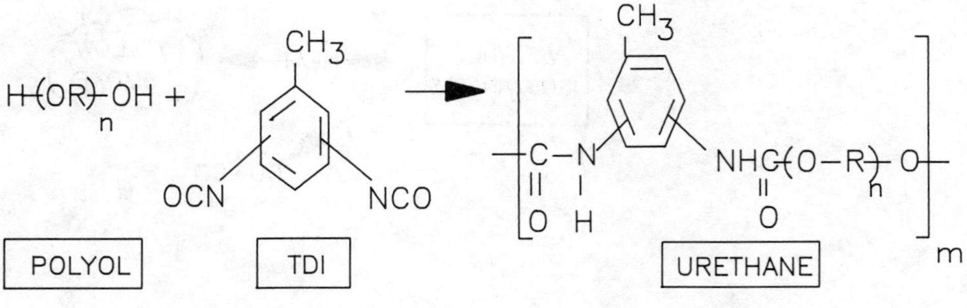

$H\text{-}(OR)_n\text{-}OH$ + TDI (toluene ring with CH_3, OCN, NCO) $\longrightarrow$ $[-C(=O)-N(H)-C_6H_3(CH_3)-NHC(=O)-(O-R)_n-O-]_m$

POLYOL TDI URETHANE

Figure 1. Preparation of polyurethanes.

Conventional polyether flexible polyurethane foam is readily ignited by a small flame source, and because of its low density and open-cell structure, it burns rapidly with a high rate of heat release and evolution of smoke and toxic gases, particularly carbon monoxide.

The mechanism of the formation of smoke and toxic gases from burning flexible PU foam is illustrated in figure 2. Degradation of the polymer begins with scission of the urethane bonds at 250 C to yield a relatively non-volatile polyol component and a volatile isocyanate component. As the fire develops, further degradation of the polyol residue at higher temperatures gives small organic molecules (alkenes, alkynes, aldehydes, ketones etc.) and ultimately particulate carbonaceous material - 'black smoke'. The volatile aromatic isocyanate fraction, containing the nitrogen of the polymer, degrades further giving carbon monoxide and a nitrogen-containing 'yellow smoke' which at higher temperatures degrades to 'black smoke' and hydrogen cyanide. An additive that can effectively trap the volatile isocyanate fraction will therefore have a substantial influence in reducing the smoke output.

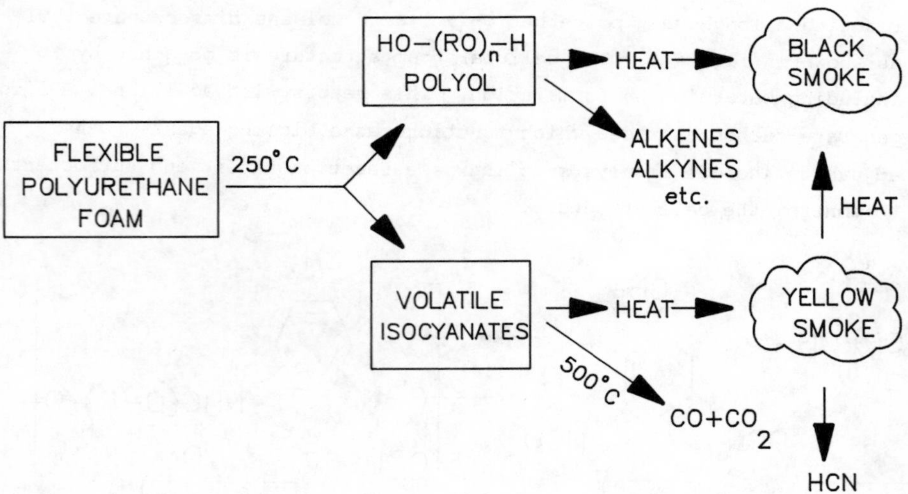

Figure 2. Thermal degradation of flexible polyurethane foam.

Researchers have used this mechanistic approach [3,4,5] to develop an additive system which reduces the formation of smoke and toxic gases from burning polyether foam.

This additive system, however, has a high reactivity towards the isocyanates and catalysts which prevents its addition at the foam production stage in the 'one-shot' continuous process used in the industry. The post-impregnation method used to develop this system is not a viable commercial process.

The criteria for a commercially acceptable additive are:

- it should preferably be a liquid
- it should be possible to add it direct to the foam formulation
- it must not interfere with the foam chemistry
- it must have minimal effect on the physical properties of the foam
- it must have good durability and ageing properties

We have developed a novel additive which essentially meets these criteria and which will significantly reduce both the overall levels of smoke and toxic gases as well as the rate at which they are evolved under realistic fire conditions.

MATERIALS AND METHODS

A conventional polyether polyol foam formulation was used to develop the additive. Bench-scale tests were carried out on hand-mixed box foams. For the full-scale chair tests, large foam blocks were produced on a pilot-scale foam dispensing machine. The following test protocols have been used to assess the effectiveness of the additive in reducing smoke and toxic gas formation.

NBS smoke density chamber

This apparatus is widely used for the measurement of smoke from burning plastics [6]. A modified procedure is used whereby cubes of foam are ignited by a small flame rather than by use of the furnace. The maximum smoke output is measured in terms of optical density per gram of foam, and the results are expressed as the percentage smoke output relative to a standard control foam. (i.e. without additive). Additionally, the optical density is recorded at ten-second intervals to give a measure of the rate of smoke production. The percentage of unburnt char and liquid melt produced relative to the initial foam weight is also measured.

Cone calorimeter

This instrument [7] has been developed as a bench-scale apparatus for the measurement of critical fire parameters, such as rate of heat release and smoke and toxic gas evolution. Samples of polyurethane foam with and without the additive have been tested in an horizontal orientation using an irradiance of 30 kw/m^2.

Full-scale chair tests

In order to validate the results of the bench-scale tests and to examine the effectiveness of the additive under real fire conditions, foam samples, with and without additive were tested as covered and uncovered chairs using the room and corridor test rig (figure 3) at Warrington Fire and Materials Centre [5].

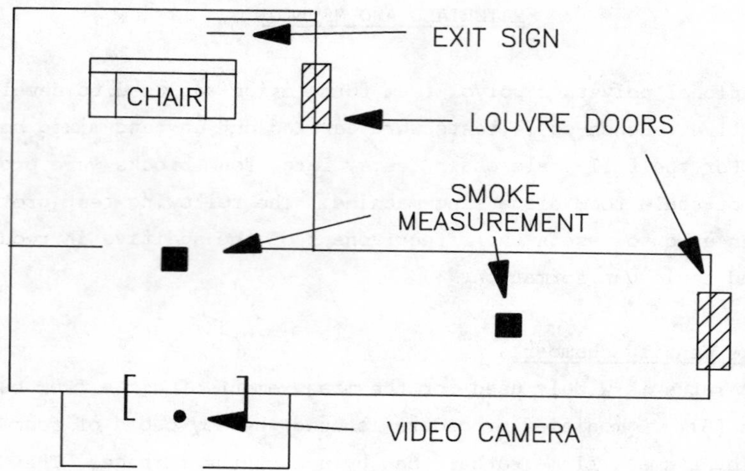

Figure 3. Room and corridor test rig.

Mock-up chairs were tested with four cushions (back, seat and two arms) on a metal frame rig using a No. 5 wooden crib [8] as ignition source. The parameters which were measured were smoke output, the time to obscuration of a standard 'EXIT' sign and gas levels (oxygen, carbon monoxide and carbon dioxide). The values given are mean results obtained from triplicate tests. A visual record of the tests was also made on video.

RESULTS AND DISCUSSION

The results obtained in the NBS smoke chamber test are given in figures 4 and 5.

In this test, the additive reduces the total smoke output by over 50% and gives a significant increase in the amount of unburnt char and reduction in the amount of liquid melt formed (figure 4).

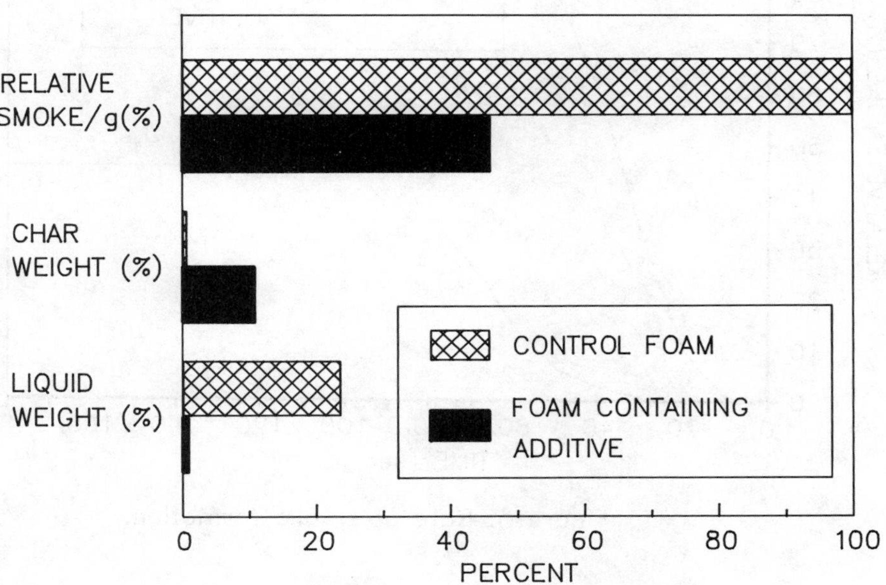

Figure 4. NBS smoke chamber test data.

The formation of the residual char is a key element in the mechanism of smoke reduction by this additive. Furnace pyrolysis studies at 240 C show that the residual char obtained from the additive-containing foam contains 68% of the original nitrogen content of the foam compared with only 35% retained in the char from the control foam without additive.

The additive therefore functions, at least in part, by preventing the smoke-forming aromatic isocyanate moieties from volatilising into the vapour phase by the formation of a stable char structure.

Figure 5 illustrates the effectiveness of the additive in reducing the rate of smoke formation. The control foam burns rapidly, producing all its smoke within one minute. By comparison, the foam containing the additive produces less than 20% of this smoke level during the first minute of combustion.

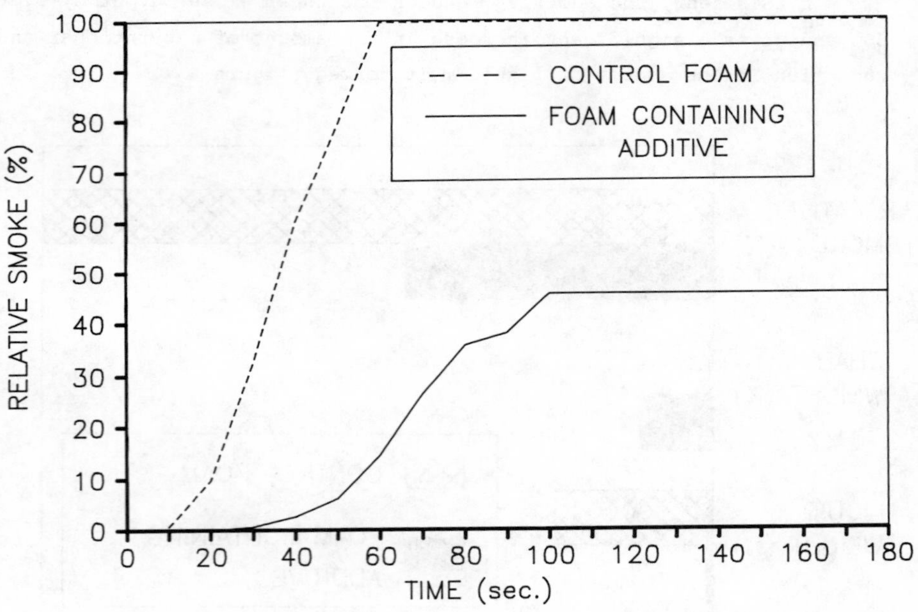

Figure 5. Rate of smoke formation.

Typical results obtained on the cone calorimeter are summarised in Figure 6.

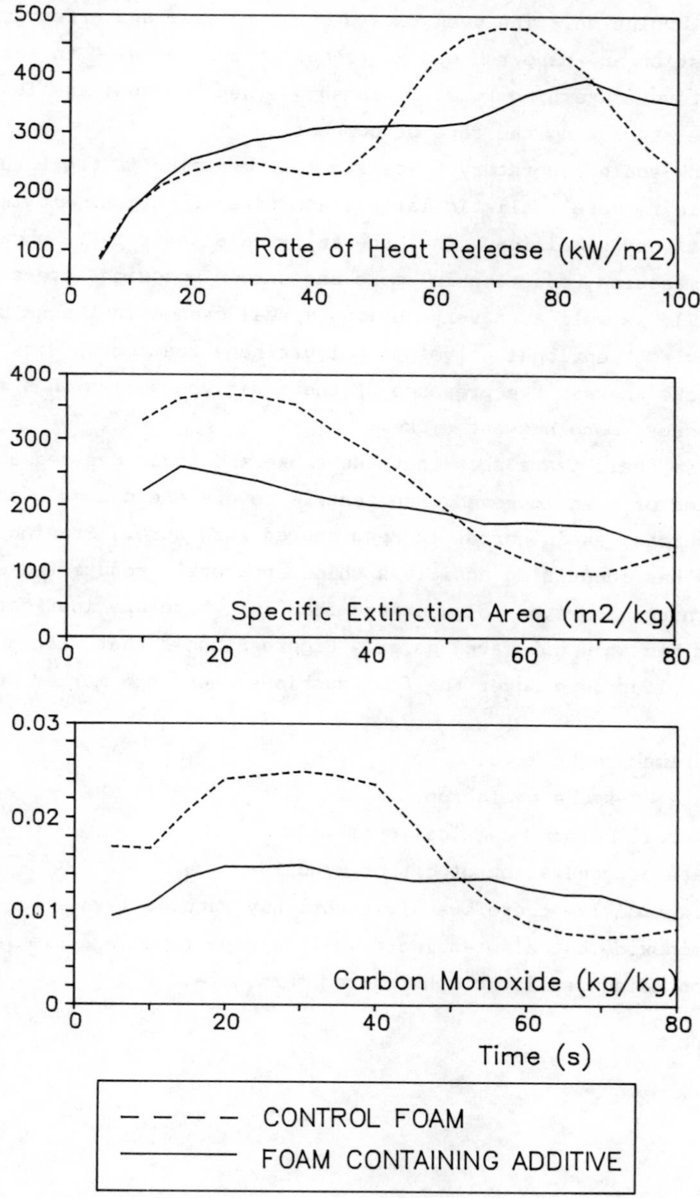

Figure 6. Cone calorimeter test data.

In this test the additive reduces the peak smoke output (specific extinction area) by 30% and gives a 30% reduction in peak carbon monoxide evolution. The peak rate of heat release and effective heat of combustion are also reduced and occur at a later time in the case of the additive-containing foam. This shows that the additive is effective at slowing the rate of combustion.

Bench-scale laboratory tests are only of value if the results are applicable to more realistic large-scale fire scenarios. It is therefore very significant that the full-scale chair tests show an even greater measured reduction in smoke and carbon monoxide levels (figure 7), as well as a very obvious visual change in the nature of the smoke. Conventional polyether polyurethane foam burns with a heavy black smoke whereas the presence of the additive results in a much lighter grey, more buoyant smoke.

These chair tests show that the smoke and toxic gas reduction is maintained or even improved when textile covers are placed over the foam cushions, as is normal in upholstered furniture. Previous work [3] has identified additives which apparently reduce the smoke from burning uncovered polyurethane foam but which are ineffective when the foam has an upholstered cover. Figure 8 shows that with a viscose velour cover over the foam cushions there are marked reductions in:

- the maximum smoke level
- the rate of smoke evolution
- the overall carbon monoxide level
- the rate of generation of carbon monoxide

This additive therefore gives not only reduced levels of smoke and carbon monoxide but also an increase in escape time in a simulated fire situation using realistic upholstered furniture.

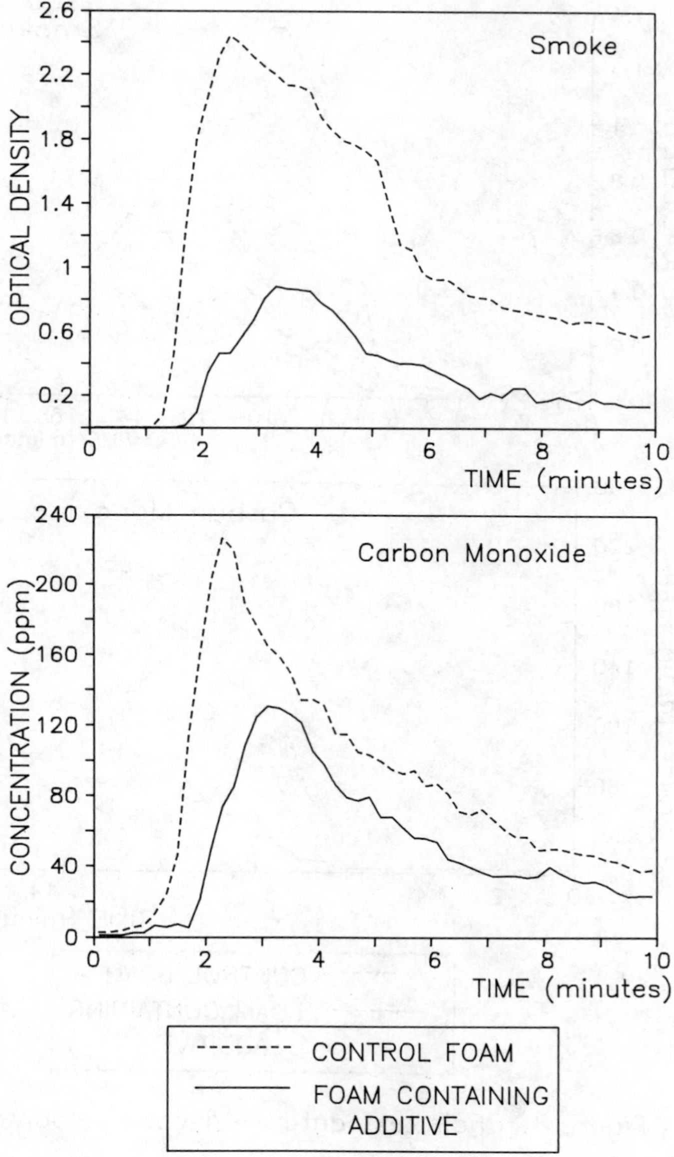

Figure 7. Chair test data — Uncovered foam.

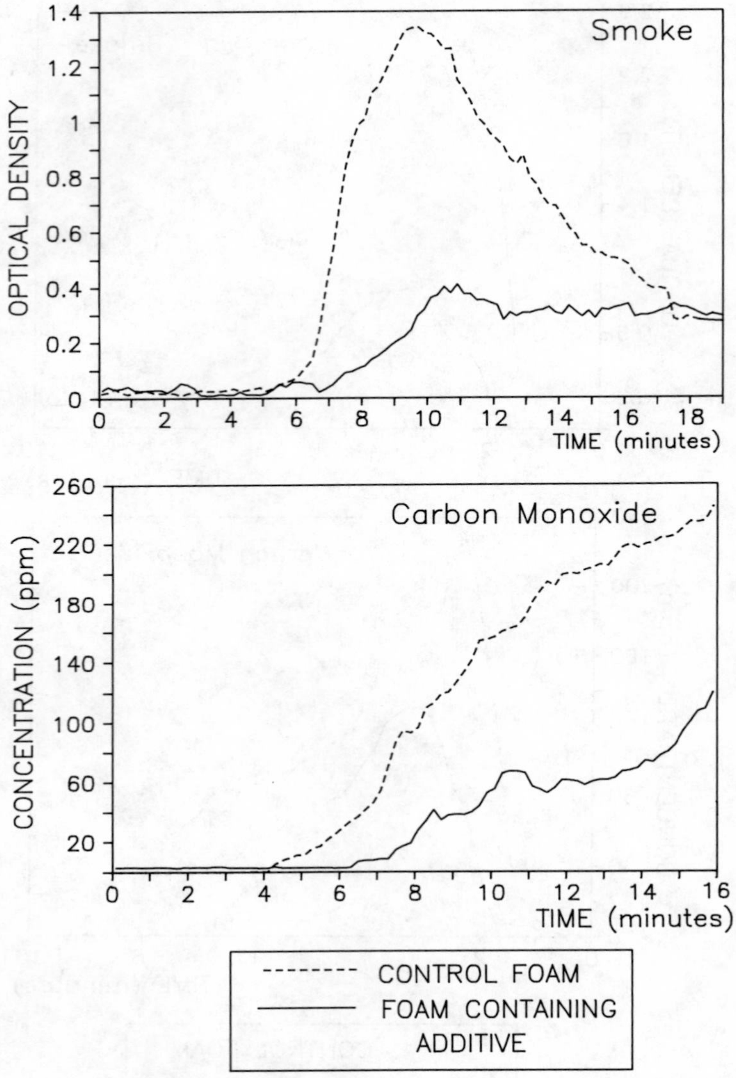

Figure 8. Chair test data — Viscose velour cover.

CONCLUSIONS

A novel chemical additive has been identified which can be added to a flexible polyurethane foam system during the manufacturing process and which will significantly reduce the smoke and toxic gases evolved from the foam when it burns. The effect is clearly apparent in large-scale chair burn tests with upholstered cushions, as well as in smaller scale laboratory tests. Further development work is in hand, including full-scale foam plant trials, and some tailoring of the additive system to optimise processing conditions and to minimise any effects on the physical and ageing properties of the foams.

REFERENCES

1. Fire Statistics, United Kingdom 1986, The Home Office, London (1988).

2. Report of the Technical Sub-Committee on the Fire Risks of New Materials. The Home Office, London. November (1978)

3. Grayson, S.J., Hume, J., and Smith, D.A., Smoke and Toxic Gas from Burning Plastics, Conference Proceeding, QMC Industrial Research, London. 6/19. (1982).

4. Grayson, S.J., Hume, J., Kumar, S., and Smith, D.A., Cellular Polymers, 2, 87-98 (1983).

5. Grayson, S.J., Hume, J., Smith, D.A., U.K. Patent. 2,107,369.

6. ASTM, E662-79.

7. Babrauskas, V., Fire and Materials. 8, 81-95 (1984).

8. BS 5852:Part 2:1982.

Cone Calorimetry of CMHR Polyurethane Foam: An Evaluation of the Effects of Melamine Additive

J Hume and K Pettett. Warrington Fire & Materials Centre
J Jenc. Polyol International BV (Wholly owned subsidiary of Dow Chemical Company)

Introduction

The advent of legislation in the United Kingdom to enforce the use of combustion modified foam in all upholstery applications has resulted in considerable activity in the research and development on foams of this type. The foam has to pass the BS5852 part 2 test which requires a weight loss of not more than 60g following combustion of a No 5 crib. The major type of foam with this performance is designated CMHR foam and contains melamine additive (usually 20-30 pphp) together with a chlorinated phosphate Fire Retardant (5 pphp).

The BS5852 test is simply a tool for testing compliance and does not give any insight into the role of the additives in modifying the burning characteristics of the foam. In particular the effect of varying levels of additive do not correlate well with measurements made in this test.

Cone calorimetry is much more useful in this regard since several fire characteristics are measured. Also the properties examined, rate of heat release (rhr), effective heat of combustion (ehc), smoke (as specific extinction area, sea) and gas yields relate more directly to the burning behaviour of the material. These advantages have been demonstrated to result in good correlation with results obtained in full scale fire tests on upholstered furniture (1).

Samples

Model foams were prepared by hand in paper boxes (200x200x200mm). Melamine was predispersed in the polyol using a high speed mixer (2000 rpm). The polyol used, Polyurax U-14.08, is a graft styrene-acrylonitrile polymer polyol which provides improved stabilisation of the melamine dispersion over conventional polyols, aids foam processing and enhances foam physical properties. After conditioning the polyol-melamine blend to room-temperature it was added to the other foam components in a conventional CMHR formulation.

The foam density was adjusted by varying the water added (2.5 to 3.1 pphp), diethanolamine (1.0 to 1.4 pphp) and blowing agent (F-11, 2 to 9 pphp). The aim was to obtain the same foam density for all melamine loadings. This is an necessary feature for an accurate assessment of melamine effects since flammability behaviour will vary with foam density.

Low melamine loadings are desirable during processing to reduce the viscosity of the melamine-polyol mix (Fig 1). Foam physical properties such as hardness, compression sets etc. will also vary with melamine content. For this reason a fire test which relates fire behaviour to melamine content is most useful to manufacturers desiring to optimise their formulations.

Instrumentation

The cone calorimeter used was built by Fire & Materials staff to the original NBS specification (2). Some non-essential modifications were employed where local supplies saved time and cost. The instrument utilises the oxygen consumption principle (3) to determine heat release during a test and our model also has provision for the optical measurement of smoke and continuous infra-red measurement of oxides of carbon.

All the samples were tested in the horizontal orientation and were wrapped in aluminium foil such that drips were contained and burnt in the original sample volume. This arrangement has the advantage of providing good repeatability but neglects a safety feature of CMHR foams which is the reduced flammability due to liquid retreat and extinguishment at cold surfaces.

The samples were all irradiated by the cone using a heat flux of 35 kW/m^2. Ignition was by the standard spark igniter. The samples were all tested in triplicate and it should be noted that the variation observed in the measurements are due to inhomogeneities within box-foamed samples as well as factors inherent in the apparatus.

Results

The significance of the differences observed will obviously depend upon the repeatability of the experimental results. In general for identical specimens the cone calorimeter gives very good repeatability with most scalar values varying by less than five percent in repeat runs. In this work the specimens have been cut from box foams and will vary to some extent and so the results should be considered with this in mind. The reliability can be seen from Table 1 which lists scalar data for three samples tested in triplicate and Figure 2 which shows rate of heat release against time for one material in triplicate.

The effect of melamine additive on heat and smoke release is shown in Table 2 and the effect of varying the FR level is presented in Table 3. For clarity these tables are also presented as trend lines in Figures 3 and 4.

Graphs of vector data for rate of heat release, effective heat of combustion, specific extinction area and carbon monoxide release are given in Figures 5 to 8.

Discussion

The reliability of the results from fire experiments has in general not been high in statistical terms. Table 1 suggests however that in this work variations between replicate experiments are such that the significance of observed differences is real.

The effect of the melamine additive can be seen most clearly on the peak rate of heat release. This parameter is considered to relate most strongly to the fire hazard and an average reduction of 37 kW/sq. m for every 10 pphp is observed. A similar, but smaller, reduction can be seen for average rates of heat release. Average heats of combustion are, as expected, only affected slightly by the inclusion of melamine. This points to an important feature in the mechanism of the action of melamine in that the overall fuel load is only slightly decreased but the rate of burning is greatly decreased. Smoke yields also decrease with melamine content and this is explained mainly by the reduced heat per unit time available to soot formation reactions.

The effect of fire retardant content is similar to melamine in heat release rate reduction but opposite in smoke yield.

Melamine is a colourless crystalline compound melting at 354 deg. C. It sublimes unchanged at temperatures below its melting point but can also when conditions allow polymerise under the action of heat losing ammonia. Differential scanning calorimetry shows an endotherm at 370 deg. C and this appears to be critical in limiting the fuel supply rate to an ignition source. As an organic compound melamine will be combustible but its high oxygen requirement will limit the rate of combustion. The overall effect is thus the reduction of peak values and an increase in the time to peak heat release rate coupled with an increased burn time. Burning polyurethane has a tendency to form a char by polymerisation of isocyanates and this is enhanced by reducing the combustion rate. These effects can be seen in Figures 5 to 8 which show increasing times to peak release for heat, smoke and carbon monoxide as the melamine content increases. Figure 8 shows that heat of combustion is increasing as the residue has a higher carbon content.

Conclusion

Cone calorimeter results correlate well with Melamine content. They can be used to elucidate its mechanistic action and may help to optimise foam formulation.

References

1. Babrauskas V and Walton W D (1986), Fire Safety Journal, 11 (1986) 181-192

2. Babrauskas V, Fire and Materials, Vol 8, (1984), 81-95

3. Huggett C, Fire and Materials, Vol 4, (1980), 61-65.

	PEAK HRR kW/m²	AVG HRR kW/m²	PEAK EHC MJ/kg	AVG EHC MJ/kg	PEAK SEA m²/kg	AVG SEA m²/kg
Example 1 - Sample 500, Melamine (30 pphp), FR (5 pphp)						
	484	291	28.5	23.1	447	213
	451	276	29.5	22.7	430	215
	485	287	35.3	22.6	566	213
Average	473	285	31.1	22.8	481	214
Std. Dev.	16	6	3.0	0.2	60	1
Example 2 - Sample 501, Melamine (40 pphp), FR (5 pphp)						
	440	282	29.5	22.7	448	196
	399	257	29.3	23.1	465	186
	428	251	36.0	22.4	451	208
Average	422	263	31.6	22.7	455	197
Std. Dev.	17	13	0.4	0.3	8	9
Example 3 - Sample 502, Melamine (30 pphp), FR (2.5 pphp)						
	512	289	29.7	23.7	527	190
	491	284	30.0	23.0	415	185
	528	295	30.0	22.9	504	196
Average	510	289	29.9	23.2	482	190
Std. Dev.	15	4	0.1	0.4	48	4

TABLE 1. TRIPLICATE CONE CALORIMETER MEASUREMENTS

Melamine pphp	PEAK HRR	AVG. HRR	PEAK EHC	AVG. EHC	PEAK SEA	AVG. SEA
20	501	301	31.2	22.9	507	273
30	473	285	31.1	22.8	481	214
40	422	263	31.6	22.7	455	197
50	388	244	29.1	22.2	376	167
60	357	231	29.2	22.1	380	146
70	313	205	29.8	22.3	303	139

TABLE 2. THE EFFECTS OF MELAMINE CONTENT

MELAMINE = 30 pphp

T101	PEAK HRR	AVG. HRR	PEAK EHC	AVG. EHC	PEAK SEA	AVG. SEA
0.0 pphp	506	295	30.8	24.2	250	107
2.5 pphp	510	289	29.9	23.2	482	190
5.0 pphp	473	285	31.1	22.8	481	214

TABLE 3. THE EFFECTS OF FR CONTENT

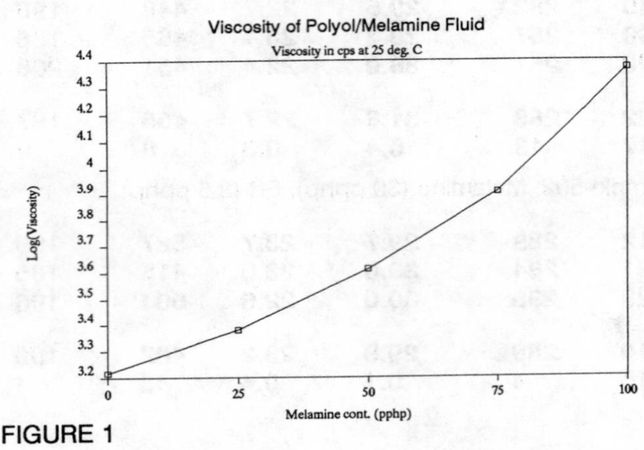

FIGURE 1

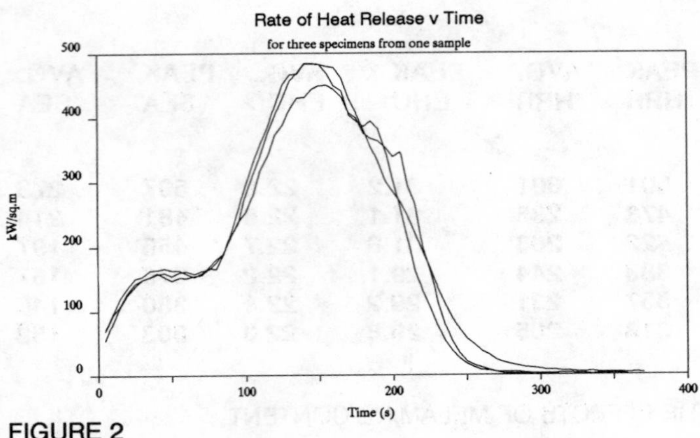

FIGURE 2

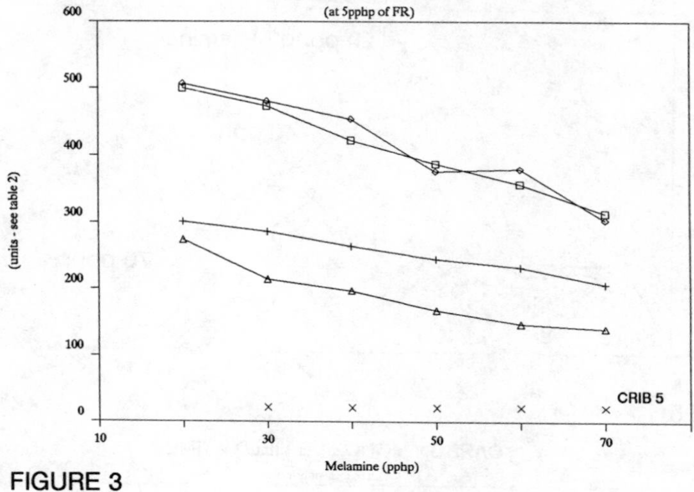

FIGURE 3

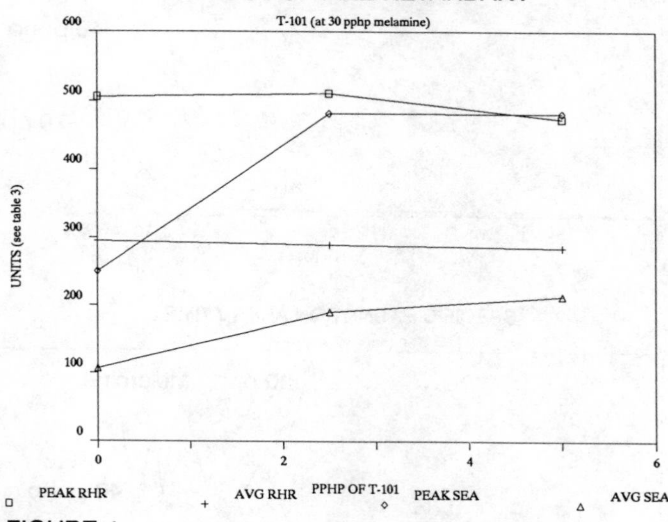

FIGURE 4

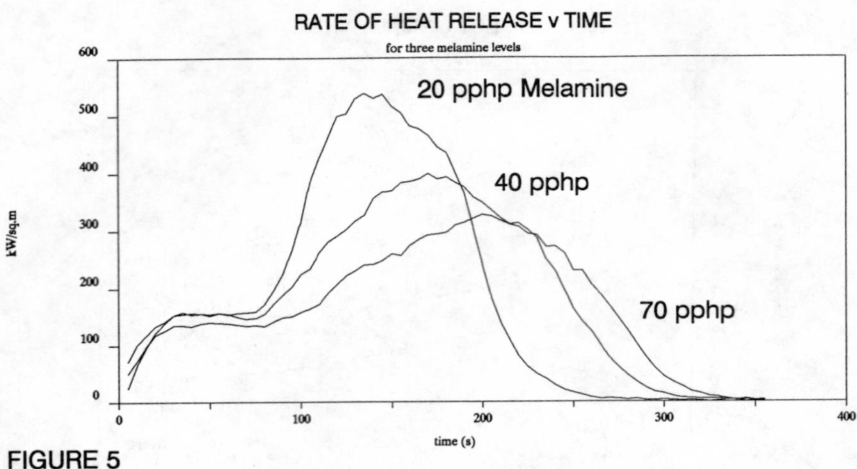

FIGURE 5

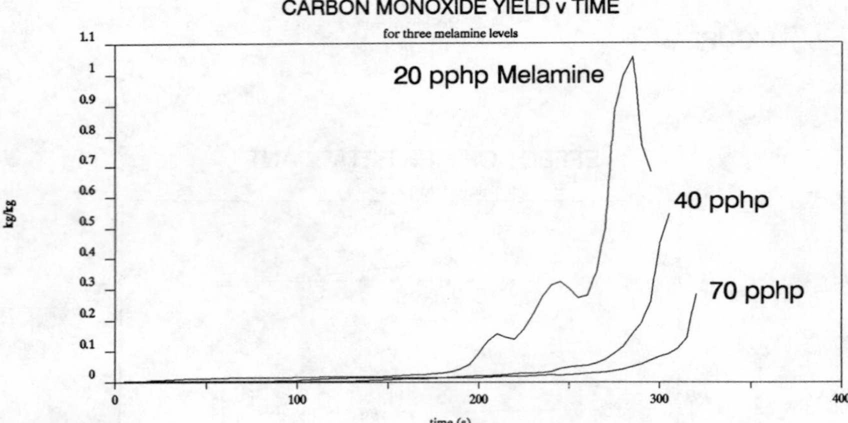

FIGURE 6

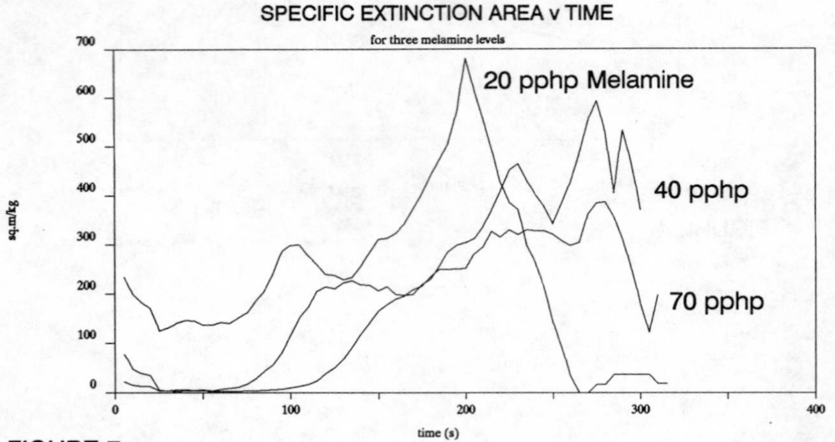

FIGURE 7

EFFECTIVE HEAT OF COMBUSTION v TIME

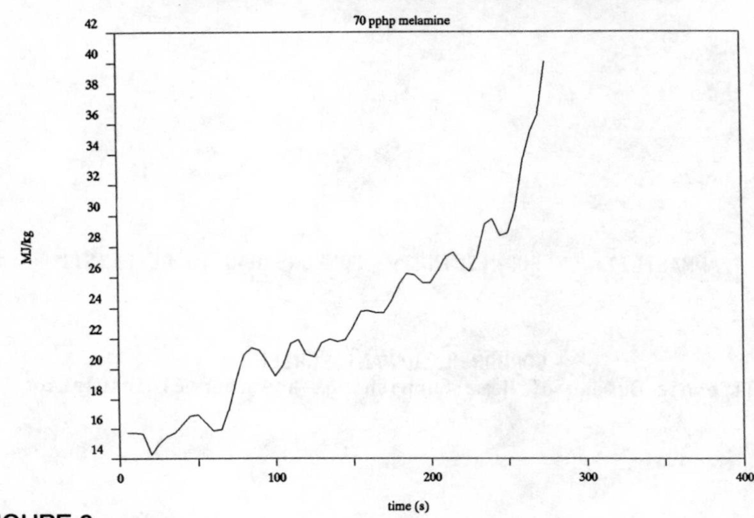

FIGURE 8

FLAMMABILITY OF FURNISHINGS: SOMEONE HAD TO BE FIRST!

GORDON H. DAMANT, CHIEF
California Bureau of Home Furnishings and Thermal Insulation

INTRODUCTION

In recent years considerable world-wide effort has been expended in investigating the flammability characteristics of upholstered furniture (1-14). Analysis of U.S. fire data collected from a number of sources indicates that the primary hazards associated with fires where upholstered furniture is the first item to ignite, are smoking materials. Specifically cigarettes, and to a much lesser degree cigars and pipes. In addition the data indicate that the typical scenario for fire fatality incidents involving upholstered furniture include an elderly smoker, whose reflexes may have been dulled and mobility restricted by fatigue, old age, infirmity or the influence of alcohol and/or prescribed drugs, who falls asleep while smoking in the living room. The cigarette-probable a filter tip-drops onto an item of furniture. The resulting smoldering combustion generates considerable quantities of smoke, toxic gases and heat, with the most likely cause of death, anoxia, resulting from inhalation of toxic combustion products.

In a survey of data to identify and rank what appears to be the most frequent scenarios for fire death in the United States, Clark and Ottoson (15) established that, "The most common fire scenario, by far, is the residential furnishings fire caused by smoking materials, which alone accounts for 27 percent of the U.S. fire deaths." When all ignition sources are considered, residential furnishings, which include mattresses, bedding and upholstered furniture, account for 36 percent of U.S. fire deaths. A further analysis of this data shows that about 15 percent of all U.S. fire deaths can be attributed to the scenario involving smoking materials and upholstered furniture.

Most articles of upholstered furniture consist of three essential parts:

1. The support structure or frame,
2. Stuffing or filling materials, and
3. Fabrics or coverings.

In terms of cigarette induced ignition of upholstered furniture the structure or frame is of very little concern, since it is highly unlikely that structural components would be directly ignited by cigarettes. Therefore, disregarding the frame, the furniture/cigarette hazard totally involves the interaction of the ignited cigarette with the fabric initially and then perhaps the interior stuffing materials. The nature and constituent components of fabrics and furniture stuffings may critically influence the combustion characteristics of the furniture piece. However, the total fuel load of the furniture structure and, therefore, the nature of the structural components, may be an important consideration in an ongoing fire, or when the furniture piece becomes a secondary rather than a primary ignition source.

LEGISLATIVE HISTORY

Legislation passed in California in 1972 (16) required all upholstered furniture offered for sale in California to be "fire retardant," and also specified that all such furniture should meet the requirements, regulations and standards developed by the California Bureau of Home Furnishings.

It is important to notice that the legislative mandate required:

A. All California furniture to be flame retardant,
B. The Bureau to develop fire performance standards for all such furniture, and
C. The effective date of such regulations to be October 1, 1975.

The legislative mandate did not require the Bureau to:

A. Establish a finding of need for a furniture flammability standard,
B. Perform any hazard/risk/benefit assessment,
C. Produce an economic impact statement or analysis,
D. Address any environmental impact of the regulation, or
E. Validate the standard by a subsequent assessment of effectiveness.

In essence the California Legislature said to the Bureau, "We have determined that there is a need for an upholstered furniture flammability standard in California, the Bureau will produce a standard by October 1, 1975."

Under California law the essential definition of upholstered furniture is: "Any product containing a concealed filling material which can be used to support any part of the body of limbs of a person while in a sitting or reclining position."

The legislative mandate was therefore very broad, covering almost every conceivable furniture article under the flammability umbrella, and contained no provision that would allow the exemption of any product from the Bureau's flammability requirements.

Subsequent California legislation introduced at the request of the furniture industry and enacted in 1975 indicated that: The Chief of the Bureau of Home Furnishings was authorized to exempt from the flammability requirements any furniture product which in his judgment did not constitute a serious fire hazard.

As a result of this clear-up legislation, the Bureau has exempted from the flammability requirements the following furniture products by product class:

A. Any furniture manufactured and sold solely for outdoor use,
B. Cushions manufactured and sold solely for decorative purposes, and
C. Any furniture containing one-half inch or less of a stuffing material in which the horizontal and vertical surfaces do not meet.

In addition the Bureau has exempted furniture designed purely for recreational purposes, such as weight-lifting benches, gymnasium equipment, etc.

TECHNICAL BULLETINS 116 AND 117

The essential features of California's upholstered furniture flammability standard are contained in two documents known as Technical Bulletin 116, "Requirements, Test Procedure and Apparatus for Testing the Flame Retardance of Upholstered Furniture" and Technical Bulletin 117, "Requirements, Test Procedure and Apparatus for Testing the Flame Retardance of Resilient Filling Materials Used in Upholstered Furniture." (17-18) As originally proposed in 1972 these Technical Bulletins required that by October 1, 1975, all furniture component materials used in furniture offered for sale in California must meet the flaming and smoldering requirements shown in Table I.

In addition to the requirements in Table I, Technical Bulletin 117, Section F, required that all upholstery fabrics be flame retardant by October 1, 1977; and Technical Bulletin 116, a test for the finished furniture piece, required that all furniture offered for sale in California after October 1, 1977, be totally cigarette resistant. It was under this format and test scheme that California's furniture flammability standard become fully effective on October 1, 1975.

TABLE I

Table I. California Furniture Test Requirements

	FLAMING	SMOLDERING
Cellular Foams (Polyurethane Foams, Latex Foam Rubber, Neoprene, etc.)	T.B. 117, Sec. A, Pt. I	T.B. 117, Sec. D
Shredded Foams	T.B. 117, Sec. A, Pt. II	T.B. 117, Sec. D
Polyestyrene Beads	T.B. 117, Sec. A, Pt. III	T.B. 117, Sec. D
Non-Manmade Fiber Battings, (Cotton, Wool, Kapok, etc.)	T.B. 117, Sec. B, Pt. I	T.B. 117, Sec. D
Feathers and Down	T.B. 117, Sec. B, Pt. II	T.B. 117, Sec. D
Man-Made Fiber Battings (Polyester, Nylon, Acetate, Acrylic, etc.)	T.B. 117, Sec. C	T.B. 117, Sec. D
Upholstery Fabrics	T.B. 117, Sec. E	

DEVELOPMENT

In March, 1977, the Bureau made several technical modifications to the flammability standard. Section F of Technical Bulletin 117, requiring that all upholstery fabrics be flame retardant was deleted from the standard, on the basis that technology did not exist to allow industry to uniformly comply with this requirement. In addition Technical Bulletin 116 requiring all finished furniture articles offered for sale in California to be totally cigarette resistant by October, 1977, was modified to initially be a voluntary standard with the provision and intent that at some future time it would become a mandatory requirement. The modification to the enforcement of Technical Bulletin 116 was again necessitated by considerations of the available technology, or lack of, which would enable furniture manufacturers to make all California furniture cigarette resistant. In particular, smoldering problems caused by the extensive use of fabrics consisting predominantly of cellulosic fibers such as cotton, rayon and linen, did not appear to be solvable in a reasonable and economic manner at that time.

By January 1, 1978, a flammability labeling requirement was added to the Bureau's standard. Under the provisions of this requirement all furniture in compliance with the mandatory requirements of Technical Bulletin 116 are labeled as follows:

NOTICE

> THIS ARTICLE MEETS ALL FLAMMABILITY REQUIREMENTS OF CALIFORNIA BUREAU OF HOME FURNISHINGS' FLAMMABILITY REQUIREMENTS. CARE SHOULD BE EXERCISED NEAR OPEN FLAME OR WITH BURNING CIGARETTES.

Furniture articles in compliance with Technical Bulletin 117, but not the requirements of Technical Bulletin 116, are labeled:

NOTICE

ONLY THE RESILIENT FILLING MATERIALS CONTAINED IN THIS ARTICLE MEET CALIFORNIA BUREAU OF HOME FURNISHINGS' FLAMMABILITY REQUIREMENTS. CARE SHOULD BE EXERCISED NEAR OPEN FLAME OR WITH BURNING CIGARETTES.

And products which have been exempted by the Bureau from the provisions of both Technical Bulletins 116 and 117 must be labeled:

NOTICE

THIS ARTICLE DOES NOT MEET THE CALIFORNIA BUREAU OF HOME FURNISHINGS' FLAMMABILITY REQUIREMENTS - TECHNICAL BULLETIN 117. CARE SHOULD BE EXERCISED NEAR OPEN FLAME OR WITH BURNING CIGARETTES.

Thus all furniture offered for sale in California must show one of the above three types of flammability labeling.

The Bureau's approach to flammability regulation of upholstered furniture has always recognized that such regulations are not, and must not be, set in concrete. The Bureau does not consider its furniture standard to be the ideal solution to a very complex problems, nor does the Bureau claim that furniture manufactured to the Bureau's specifications will not burn under any reasonable circumstances. On the contrary, the Bureau recognizes the imperfections in the regulation and is also cognizant of areas of the standard where improvements must be made, as technology becomes available, if the regulation is to achieve the ultimate goal of offering the California consumer the safest furniture in the United States, at a reasonable increase in cost.

Because of this recognition, the Bureau has attempted to maintain a degree of flexibility in the furniture standard which allows it to modify the standard, to take advantage of the latest technological developments in materials and supplies. This approach has also enabled the Bureau to suggest to industry the direction it should be moving to improve the flammability characteristics of its products. The Bureau believes that this dynamic approach to regulation is in the best interest of both the consumer and the industry, provided that such an approach is reasonable, is conducted in a cooperative spirit with the effected industries, and attempts to keep pace with technology rather than outstrip it.

The first major modification in the Bureau's furniture flammability standard occurred in January, 1980, when the Bureau published revisions of the Flammability Information Package including some substantial revisions in Technical Bulletins 116 and 117. The major change proposed by this revision addressed for the first time a realistic test procedure for evaluating the smoldering resistance of cellular foam. This procedure, known as Technical Bulletin 117, Section D, Part II, ideally complemented the Bureau's open flame test procedure for foams in Section A, Part I. As a result of this new procedure, all cellular foam used in any furniture offered for sale in California, irrespective of the point of manufacture, must be both flame retardant (FR) and smolder resistant (SR). Other modifications in the January, 1980, document consisted of a general "Tidying-up" of a number of technical points of Technical Bulletins 116 and 117, and additional clarification of some test requirements.

A STATUS REPORT

By October 1, 1985 the California Furniture Flammability Standard had been enforced for 10 years. Although the furniture industry estimates that the typical life of residential furniture is 20-30 years, and therefore, the full impact of furniture regulations might not be felt for about two decades, it was of interest to the Bureau to determine the impact of the regulation during the initial passes of its implementation.

The California Fire Incidents Reporting System (CFIRS) administered by the California State Fire Marshal's office was examined covering the years 1974-1985, for California fires where upholstered furniture was reported as the first item ignited. Figure I shows an approximate 50 percent decline in furniture fires, where furniture was ignited, during the ten year reporting period.

In reviewing this decline there are several factors which should be considered:

A. The increased use of smoke detectors in California residences clearly contributed to the decline in furniture fires, and a direct cause and effect relationship between the Flammability Standard and the decline in the number of furniture fires cannot be demonstrated.

B. In addition a general reduction in the number of smokers could be demonstrated, potentially resulting in fewer fires. However,

C. The decline in California furniture fires from 1974-1985 also coincided with a significant California population growth during that period, and thus at lease the potential for an increase in the number of reported furniture fires.

Therefore it is the opinion of the Bureau and the State Fire Marshal's office that the California Furniture Flammability regulations have had a significant impact in reducing furniture initiated fires in California, and have clearly resulted in safer furniture being offered for sale to California consumers.

FIGURE 1

UPHOLSTERED FURNITURE FIRES

Item First Ignited

California Fire Incidents Reporting System - California State Fire Marshal

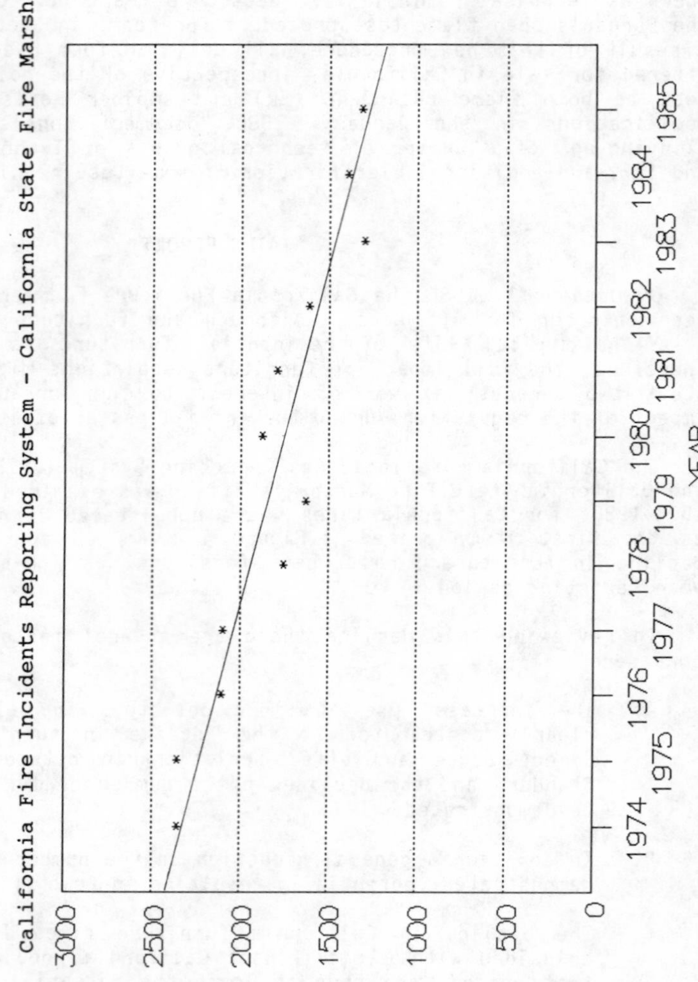

FURNITURE FIRES

FURNISHINGS - PUBLIC BUILDINGS

The clear intent of California's initial approach to the flammability of upholstered furniture, as proposed in Technical Bulletin 116 and 117, was to address the significant fire risk in residential occupancies. These standards therefore become mandatory for all furniture sold in California for residential use, as well as becoming the minimum standard expected in public buildings although Technical Bulletins 116 and 117 were never intended as an appropriate or suitable approach to furniture flammability in public buildings.

It is well known to fire safety investigators that furnishings are major contributors to the rate of fire growth and are often responsible for much of the energy released during an unwanted fire. This fact is particularly important to public occupancies, such as hospitals, nursing care facilities, etc. According to National Fire Protection Association statistics, 33 percent of United States hotel fires begin in interior furnishings. Furniture and other soft articles contribute significantly to the fuel load of a building. Materials in upholstered furnishings are often the first to ignite, and according to NFPA, 53 percent of civilian hotel fire injuries and 42 percent of civilian hotel fire deaths can be traced to the ignition of flammable furnishings. In California alone, from 1980 through 1984, soft goods and furnishings were the materials first ignited in 36 percent of the state's hotel/motel fires and 34 percent of the state's nursing home fires, according to the California Fire Incidence Reporting System.

Full scale room burns conducted by various organizations have shown that furniture constructed to be fire resistance, on the basis of small-scale product testing, may not effectively impede ignition and spread of fire. Most small-scale tests are conducted on the individual component parts of furnishings. For example, the cover fabric might be subjected to one test procedure and the fillings will be tested using a different test procedure. Full-scale tests are conducted on finished articles of furniture. A full-scale test looks at the composite of the furniture; therefore, the cover fabric and fillings are tested together as a unit. In full-scale testing, design features of the furniture may have an impact on the test results. Moreover, correlations between full-scale and small-scale testing of materials and finished products often do not exist and are difficult to obtain. Consequently, testing furniture using full-scale test procedures gives a more accurate picture of how that piece of furniture will perform in a real fire situation.

DEVELOPMENT OF TECHNICAL BULLETIN 133 TEST

In response to the need for full-scale fire testing of furnishing products; Technical Bulletin 133 (TB 133) was developed by the California Bureau of Home Furnishings and Thermal Insulation and first published in May 1984 (19-21). TB 133 is designed to evaluate seating furniture intended for use in public occupancies. The test evaluates the furniture based on its propensity to produce a potentially hazardous environment: elevated temperature, increased smoke obstruction, excessive concentration of carbon monoxide and excessive mass loss. It was developed in response to numerous requests from fire departments, architects, specifiers, and procurement personnel. These individuals and agencies were looking for a test procedure which provided greater fire protection than test procedures already developed for residential occupancies. They were interested in specifying, approving and providing furniture for buildings that were identified or considered to be higher risk than residential occupancies, and where there was greater potential for catastrophic loss of life and extensive property damage if a fire should occur. These occupancies could include correctional facilities, jails, prisons, penal institutions, health care facilities, hospitals, nursing care homes, convalescent homes, child day care centers, public auditoriums, hotels, and motels. These types of occupancies may present special fire hazards: such as intentionally set fires; evacuation problems due to security measures, limited mobility or lack of mobility of patients; unfamiliarity of occupants with exits; large numbers of people trying to rapidly exit public assembly facilities; and inadequate fire detection, notification and suppression systems. The hazards of fires in such occupancies occur in the form of elevated temperatures and toxic gases which may cause injury or death; smoke obstruction which may hinder escape by reduced visibility and increased disorientation; and ignition and rapid flame spread of combustible materials.

Since the first publication of TB 133, it has gained considerable popularity. The Bureau has recently proposed regulations which would adopt TB 133 as a legal standard for seating furniture sold in California for use in public occupancies. In 1987, a survey of 300 of the largest California fire departments showed a universal need for a flammability standard for seating furniture in public occupancies and support for the use of TB 133. Some individual cities and counties in California already require seating furniture to meet TB 133. The City of San Francisco requires that any seating furniture purchased for installation or use in any public assembly shall meet TB 133. In addition, legislation sponsored by the International Association of Fire Fighters in several other states would require seating furniture used in certain specified public occupancies to comply with TB 133.

TB 133 TEST

TB 133 was first published in May 1984 and was issued in its most recently revised form in April 1988 (22). The development of TB 133 was accomplished by evaluating three different test protocols. The test protocols differed in the size of the ignition source and/or the size of the metal ignition box. The Bureau conducted full-scale tests on 139 cushions composed of various combinations of nine different foams and six different fabrics. The data was evaluated to select the TB 133 test procedure and test criteria.

TEST FACILITY

TB 133 tests are conducted in a test room, 12 by 10 feet with an 8-foot ceiling height. The room has a door opening approximately 38 by 81 inches, located at the corner of a longer side wall.

The test room is instrumented for smoke opacity, gas concentrations, temperature, and weight measurements. Thermocouples are positioned in five locations: ceiling above the sample, four feet above the sample, floor, test room entrance, and exhaust hood entrance. The ceiling thermocouple is positioned over the geometric center of the ignition box one inch below the ceiling. The 4-foot thermocouple is positioned three feet in front of the ignition box, four feet below the ceiling. These two temperature measurements constitute two of the test criteria of TB 133. A gas sampling port is positioned at the corner of the room above the sample location. It is positioned 6 1/2 inches below the ceiling and 6 1/2 inches from the corner. The sample gas line is electrically heated to the gas analyzers entrance point. Three smoke opacity monitors are positioned at three different levels - floor, 4-foot, and ceiling - to record the opacity percentage of the smoke produced during burning of the test sample. Time varying concentrations of permanent combustion gases, i.e. CO (ppm), CO_2 (%), CO (%), and total hydrocarbons [THC] are recorded using infrared non-dispersive gas analyzers. Oxygen concentration is recorded by a Paramagnetic Beckman O_2 analyzer. Test sample weight is continuously monitored using a tensile stress load cell hanging from the ceiling of the test room.

The ignition source consists of five double sheets of loosely wadded newsprint contained in an ignition box. Three different ignition boxes are used: (1) Ignition box A for furniture with a seat/back crevice; (2) Ignition box B for furniture that does not have a crevice; and (3) Ignition box C for furniture that has a gap in the crevice area.

TEST PROCEDURE

After gas analyzers, smoke opacity monitors, and weighing scale are calibrated, the test sample is positioned on the weighing platform according to the TB 133 test specifications (22). The weighing platform supports the base of the furniture 5 ± 2 inches above the floor. The ignition box is placed in the designated location and the newsprint is ignited with a match. Simultaneously the data acquisition system is activated and data are recorded in the computer. Combustion is allowed to continue until: (1) all combustion has ceased, or (2) 1 1/2 hours of testing has elapsed, or (3) flame over or flashover appears to be inevitable, or (4) one or more of the test criteria have been exceeded.

TEST CRITERIA

Seating furniture fails to meet the requirements of TB 133 if any of the following criteria are exceeded:

A: A temperature increase of 200°F or greater at the ceiling thermocouple.

B: A temperature increase of 50°F or greater at the 4-foot thermocouple.

C: Greater than 75% opacity at the 4-foot smoke opacity monitor.

D: Greater than 50% opacity at the floor smoke monitor.

E: Carbon monoxide concentration shall not continuously exceed 1000 ppm for one minute.

F: Greater than 10% weight loss in the first 10 minutes of the test.

G: Greater than 90% weight loss of the readily combustible materials at the end of the test.

The April 1988 revision of TB 133 predominately made changes in the test criteria. Temperature criteria were changed to temperature increases from specific temperature levels. This was done to prevent bias caused by different initial temperatures. A weight loss criteria at the end of the test was added to deal with samples which satisfied the 10 minutes weight loss criteria, but lost most of their readily combustible materials by the end of the test. In addition, it was discovered that potentially safe seating furniture was failing TB 133 due to high concentrations of carbon monoxide gas produced for short periods of time; therefore, the carbon monoxide criteria was changed to include a one minute time frame.

TB 133 TESTS: RESULTS AND DISCUSSION

The Bureau has tested 229 articles of seating furniture submitted for TB 133 testing during the past 6 years. In addition, a number of mock-up tests have been performed on different types of cushions. The results of these tests, however, will not be discussed in this report. Technical Bulletin 133 was developed based on these results and was modified as mentioned earlier. The TB 133 tests are generally performed directly on finished products submitted by manufacturers. The Bureau, therefore, has no control over the sample obtained for testing. The contents of interior fillings and batting materials of the submitted articles are often unknown prior to the test, unless provided by the manufacturer. In addition, samples have been submitted by manufacturers doing considerable research and development work; consequently, some submitted samples were expected to fail the criteria and these were used as a basis for comparison by manufacturers. In addition, the Bureau's records do not always indicate the specific type of filling material, but may only indicate the generic type. For example often the Bureau simply knew that polyurethane foam was used and other times the Bureau was able to ascertain from the furniture manufacturer that the foam was a melamine polyurethane foam or a combustion modified high resiliency (CMHR) polyurethane foam. Consequently, many of the foams designated as polyurethane in the Bureau's data base may have been melamine or CMHR polyurethane foams. Recently the Bureau has drafted a special form in which suppliers of articles are asked to provide necessary information about the type of fabrics and/or filling materials that have been used in the construction of the furniture. Furthermore, for those articles for which a portion is unburned a piece of the cover and interliner materials are chemically analyzed. However, the Bureau has generated enough test data to draw some conclusions about seating furniture tested for compliance with TB 133.

Of the 229 TB 133 tests, 136 were reported in an earlier publication (23). However, those results were analyzed based on the original TB 133 test criteria. The additional 93 tests conducted since October 1988, were judged based on the newly modified version of the TB 133 test criteria. As indicated by the results, the modified test criteria had a definite effect on the test results, i.e., whether an article passed or failed. For instance, requiring that the concentration of carbon monoxide shall not continuously exceed 1000 ppm for one minute, as opposed to simply having 1000 ppm concentration as the criterion, caused many articles to pass the test which would have failed otherwise. In this report, the results of the previous 136 tests are summarized, and the results of 93 additional tests are discussed in detail.

The samples that were tested, consisted of a variety of types of seating furniture, mostly upholstered items. The 229 seating articles, included 83 stacking chair (36%), 36 office chairs (16%), 35 arm chairs (15%), 10 auditorium chairs (4%), 21 recliners and similar upholstered items (9%), 5 folding chairs (2%), 36 chairs (miscellaneous types) (16%), and the rest were miscellaneous types of furniture, such as sofas, corner chairs, modular seating, etc.

TEST CRITERIA STATISTICS

Over the past 6 years of TB 133 testing, the overall percentage of submitted furniture meeting the TB 133 test criteria was 64% for the first 136 tests (based on the May 1984 version of TB 133), and 57% for the additional 93 articles tested based on the April 1988 revision of TB 133. The latter shows the results of the tests mostly conducted during the first half of 1989.

The results of the initial 136 tests showed that 87 furniture articles or 64% met all six test criteria, 16.2% failed TB 133 based on the failure of one test criteria, 8.1% failed TB 133 based on the failure of two criteria, and 11.7% failed TB 133 based on the failure of three or more test criteria as shown in Figure 2. The results of the recent 93 tests indicate that 53 articles or 57% met all six test criteria, 7.5% failed TB 133 based on the failure of one test criteria, 8.6% failed TB 133 based on two test criteria, and 26.9% failed TB 133 based on three or more test criteria as shown in Figure 3. Generally, the majority of the submitted samples were in full compliance with TB 133. In addition, if 7.5% which failed only one criteria were slightly modified then the compliance rate would be about 65%. It must be mentioned that although the rate of compliance with TB 133 shows a decline in 1989, the recent data shows a significant increase in the number of tests being performed and more variety of furnishing products being tested. In the first 4 1/2 years TB 133, 136 pieces of furniture were tested, whereas, since October 1988, 93 articles were tested, an average increase of more than 200%. More data on samples tested based on the new version of TB 133 will more clearly show the actual trend of the compliance.

Results of recent tests, based on each criteria are shown in Figure 4. Similar results for the previous 136 tests are also shown in Figure 5. As shown in Figure 4, ceiling temperature, 4-foot temperature, and 4-foot smoke were most frequently associated with a TB 133 failure. This is

Fig 2: NUMBER OF FAILED CRITERIA

(For 136 tests based on 1984 version)

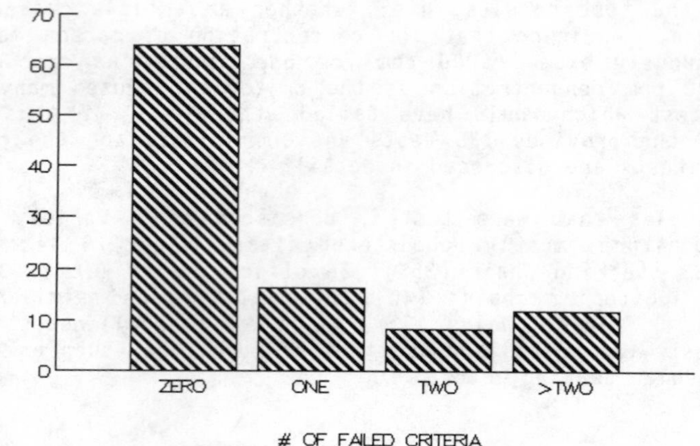

Fig 3: NUMBER OF FAILED CRITERIA

(For 93 tests based on 1988 version)

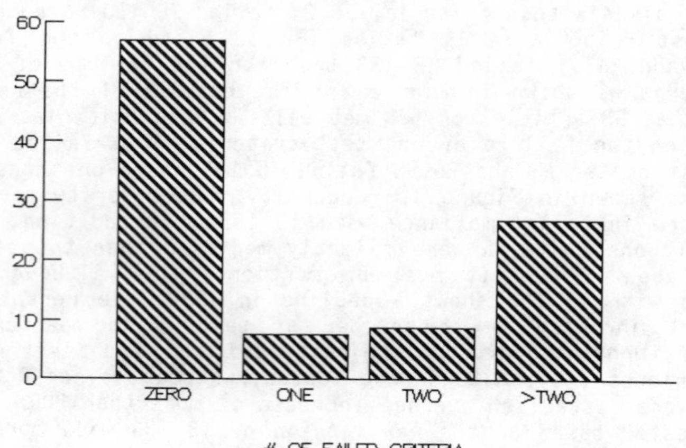

Fig 4: MOST FREQUENTLY FAILED CRITERIA

(For 93 tests based on 1988 version)

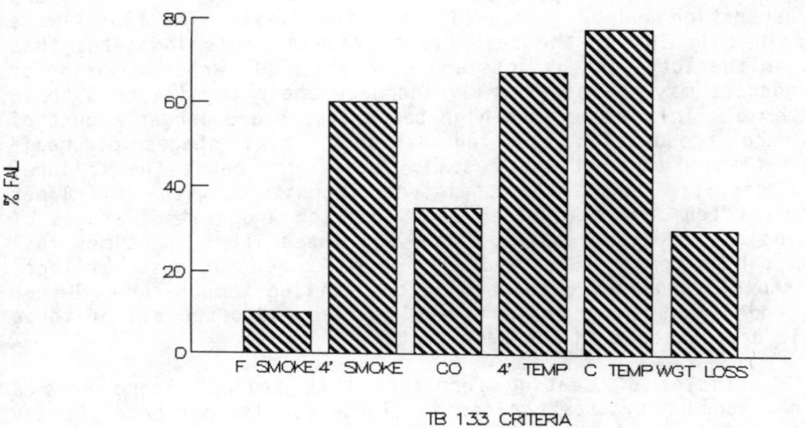

Fig 5: MOST FREQUENTLY FAILED CRITERIA

(For 136 tests based on 1984 version)

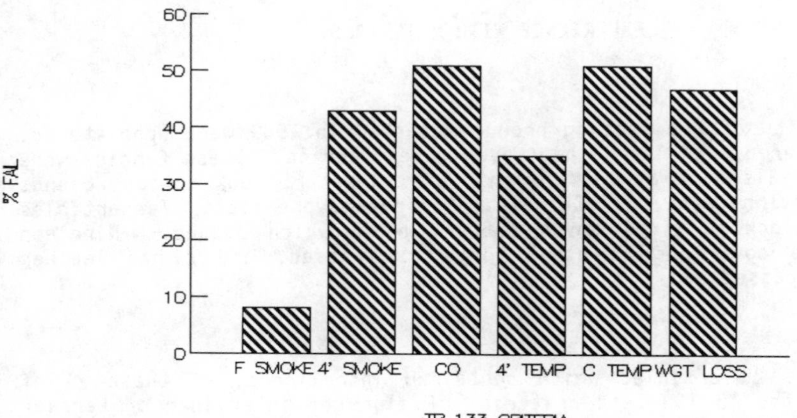

followed by carbon monoxide concentration and 10% weight loss as the next frequently occurring failure criteria. In the 40 tests where the seating furniture failed to meet one or more of the criteria, 77.5% exceeded the ceiling temperature criterion, 67.5% exceeded the 4-foot temperature criterion 60.0% exceeded 4-foot smoke criterion, 35% exceeded and carbon monoxide concentration and 30% exceeded 10% weight loss. The floor-smoke was exceeded in only 10% of the tests that failed. This indicates that improvements in the total weight loss and generation of carbon monoxide of furnishing products may not necessarily increase their compliance with TB 133 test criteria. This is because high temperatures and larger amount of smoke which are frequently generated during initial stages of rapid pyrolysis and flaming combustion of solid fuels, can cause the failure. For example, results show that upholstered furniture with interliner materials would often self extinguish upon ignition and initial stages of burning showing small weight losses. However, these items sometimes fail the test due to high temperatures and/or high smoke generations. In fact, as Figure 4 shows, frequency of exceeding the ceiling temperature, 4-foot temperature, and 4-foot smoke criteria are similar and often all of these three criteria are exceeded in the same test.

Of the 40 articles of seating furniture that failed, there were 8 products which exceeded two test criteria. These furnishings products may be slightly modified to achieve a pass on TB 133. There were 11 articles which exceeded 3 test criteria, 9 articles which exceeded 4 criteria, and 5 samples that failed 5 of the test criteria. It is likely that any improvements that can cause the article to pass either of the ceiling temperature, 4-foot temperature, and 4-foot smoke criteria can lead the third group of furnishings to achieve a pass on TB 133 . However, results for other groups indicate that a manufacturer must specifically design a product to meet higher flammability standards in order for that product to pass TB 133.

EXPERIENCE WITH MATERIALS

FABRICS

The majority of the seating products tested in 1989 were upholstered. Of 69 upholstered articles 53 had woven cover fabrics. These fabrics were various materials such as 100% nylon, 98% polyester, 100% cotton, blends of wool and nylon, etc., 23 of these (58%) passed the test. Ten articles had "flame blocker" vinyl cover fabric, 5 of which passed. Nineteen articles were covered with other vinyl, 11 passed, and 2 had leather fabric which passed.

INTERLINERS

There were 28 articles which contained interliners, of these 21 of those passed the TB 133 test criteria. Failure of interliner or barrier systems frequently resulted from the use of a non fire retardant sewing thread, which caused the barrier to be compromised during combustion.

FILLING MATERIALS

Data corresponding to the filling materials are as follows: 85 articles had foam filling. The type of filling material and the test results can be summarized as follow:

TABLE II

Type of Filling	Total No. of Articles	Total Passed	% Passed
Neoprene	2	2	100
CAL 117	7	4	57
Melamine & Code Red II	7	5	71
PU Foam (unknown type)	46	24	52
CMHR	9	5	55
IMPAK	6	4	67
Boston Fire Code	2	1	50

Of 46 articles that were identified to have generic PU foam filling, 14 had barrier materials 13 of which passed the test. Therefore, of 24 articles with generic PU foam filling that met the test criteria, 13 (54%) had a barrier. Of a total of 23 products that had barriers, 19 of them (83%) met the test criteria, demonstrating the effect of barriers on the fire performance of upholstered furniture.

As a general principle, seating furniture is most likely to meet the criteria of this test if the materials exhibit little or no weight loss, particularly small weight loss rate peaks at the early stages of pyrolysis and burning. These materials, therefore, produce little or no temperature increase, visible smoke, or carbon monoxide. Cover fabrics and filling materials which exhibit little weight loss or burning rate under the conditions of this test result in seating furniture are most likely to meet the criteria of the test.

When filling materials suffer significant weight loss and combustion, the use of strongly fire resistant cover fabrics may prevent or limit the involvement of the filling material, and the use of the fire barriers or interliners may reduce the weight loss attributable to the filling material. Barriers and interliners also reduce the production of carbon monoxide and smoke. However, barriers and interliners used with incompatible combinations of filling materials and cover fabrics may fail to prevent increase in temperatures, smoke and carbon monoxide, resulting in exceeding the criteria of TB 133. This was the case when interliners were used with California 117 foam. This combination sometimes showed the interliner to be ineffective. However, more data is needed to draw definite conclusions about any particular combinations of cover fabrics, foams, and barriers.

Interliners, especially fiberglass interliners, are most effective when the ignition source does not penetrate the interliner material. Post test examination of those samples that included fiberglass interliners which met TB 133 revealed that the interliners were severely charred, but remained intact. However, heat from the ignition source often caused minor degradation of the filling material beneath the interliner.

It is important to note that penetration of the interliner material can occur due to several reasons. The first and foremost is the type of sewing thread used in constructing the interliner. When using any interliners, fiberglass or noncombustible thread is needed. If thread is used that burns, seams will most likely open and allow the filling material to come in direct contact with the ignition source, and thus cause the seating furniture to fail TB 133. If, however, fiberglass or noncombustible thread is used, the likelihood of seam breakage is greatly reduced.

The design of seating furniture along with the structural configuration of furniture may also determine the effectiveness of the interliner. In an office chair with a gap between the seat and back where the back is attached by a post to the seat, penetration of the interliner material may occur where the post is inserted into the back. Flames may then come into direct contact with the filling material.

Filling materials which are not fire retarded are likely to undergo high weight loss, resulting in an increased buildup of carbon monoxide and elevated temperatures. Such filling materials include non-fire retarded polyurethane foam and polyester fiber batting, which may melt and burn as liquids. Of the 6 pieces of seating furniture containing polyester fiber batting without interliners, none met TB 133 . The addition of a polyester fiber batting did not achieve a barrier or interliner effect; instead, the additional fiber batting added to the fuel load once the sample started to burn. It was also noted that the addition of polyester fiber batting to some furniture systems has caused failure of systems which had met all the test requirements without the polyester fiber batting.

Materials which are resistant to cigarettes and small flame ignition, and thus meet California Technical Bulletins 116 and 117, are not necessarily resistant to ignition by the substantial flame source represented by TB 133. Materials which melt away from a cigarette may melt and burn as a liquid when exposed to substantial flame. The results of the previous 136 tests indicate that of the 7 pieces of seating furniture with foams identified as California 117 foam and no interliner, none met the requirements of TB 133. Similar results are observed in the recent data.

The analysis of the original 136 test articles showed that high performance foams exhibited significantly better performance than California 117 foams. Fourteen articles of seating furniture were identified as containing melamine foam. Five of the melamine foam articles were constructed with an interliner and all five met the criteria of TB 133. Of the nine remaining melamine foam articles, 5 failed to meet the criteria. Four of these failures were due to excessive levels of carbon monoxide. All of these failing articles had vinyl cover fabrics. The fifth melamine foam failure was due to exceeding the ceiling temperature criteria. Three articles of seating furniture were identified as containing CMHR foam without an interliner. Two of these articles passed and the third failed to meet the criteria of TB 133. The article that failed used rigid structural plastic in the design which rapidly became involved in the flaming combustion and quickly failed all six criteria. In the original 136 tests, the Bureau identified 4 pieces of seating furniture that contained neoprene foam all of which met the criteria of TB 133. The results of the recent 63 tests also confirm these trends. As the results indicate, most of the high performance foams exhibited much better performance than California 117 foams.

Thermoplastic parts, fabrics or filling materials which are not fire retarded are likely to be substantially consumed resulting in high weight loss, and increases in temperature and carbon monoxide. The melting of thermoplastic parts and their subsequent rapid burning as liquids contributed to the failure of some samples to meet the test criteria.

EXPERIENCE WITH DESIGNS

Seating furniture can be designed to meet the test criteria of TB 133 in a variety of ways. TB 133 currently lists 7 test criteria which are intended to measure the fire performance of seating furniture and discourage furniture production methods which do not necessarily improve the fire safety of the furniture.

The 10% weight loss in the first 10 minutes criteria appears to be the easiest criteria to design around. It is possible to reduce the percent weight loss of the sample by increasing the weight of the frame and/or reducing the weight of the filling material. Seating furniture with heavy metal frames are less likely to exhibit 10% weight loss in the first 10 minutes than seating furniture with the lightest frames allowed by strength requirements.

An additional weight loss criteria requires the furniture's post-test weight loss not to exceed 90% of the readily combustible materials. This was added to deal with samples which exhibited less than 10% weight loss in the first 10 minutes of the test, but subsequently lost most of their readily combustible material. In these tests, the cover fabric and filling materials burned completely which may pose a potentially hazardous situation; however, the resulting fire did not cause any other test criteria to be exceeded. This was particularly evident in stacking chairs which individually contained a small fuel load. These chairs typically lost all their readily combustible material during the test but met all other criteria of TB 133. Stack chairs may, however, produce a significant flammability hazard when large numbers of these chairs are stacked in a single location.

The existence and size of a gap between the seat and the back appears to be a significant design factor affecting flammability. In Bureau tests this gap design showed an interesting pattern on TB 133 results. When a gap was present, flames from the ignition source could extend through the gap and ignite the rear side of the chair back. This exposed the rear side of the chair back to direct flames. Flame from the ignition source also extended down through the gap and ignited the back of the seat itself which provided the opportunity for the flame to spread under the seat. This direct flame impingement on the rear side of the chair back and the underside of the seat may not have been anticipated by manufacturers and therefore precautions may not have been taken to make these locations fire resistant. Consequently, materials in these areas would often ignite and contribute significantly to the failure of the seating furniture.

Fig 6: % PASS BASED ON GAP SIZE

(For 93 tests based on 1988 version)

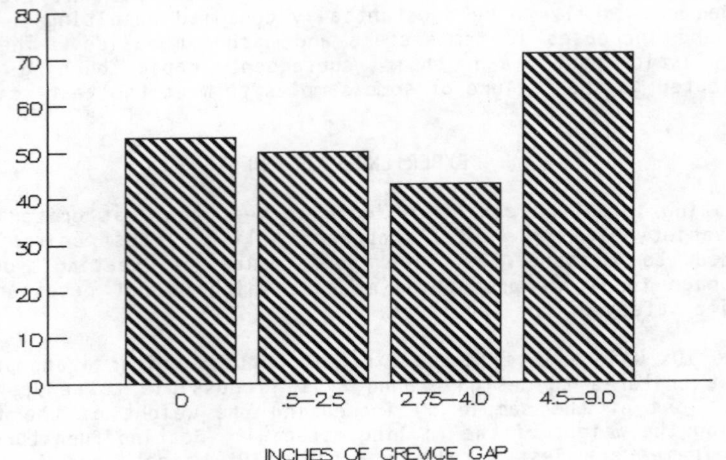

Fig 7: % PASS BASED ON GAP SIZE

(For 136 tests based on 1984 version)

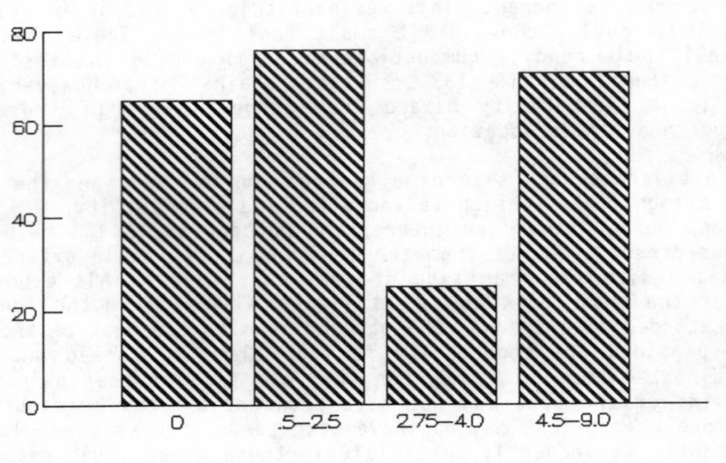

In the 136 furnishing articles tested, it was observed that seat/back gaps in a certain size range seemed to be associated with greater vulnerability to ignition than smaller and larger gaps. When the seating furniture had no gap between the seat and back, the Bureau's tests showed 65% of the samples passed TB 133 as shown in figure 6. The Bureau tested 29 samples which had a gap of .5 to 2.5 inches and these samples had a compliance rate of 76%. The Bureau evaluated 16 samples with a gap of 2.7 to 4.0 inches, with a compliance rate of 25%. Finally, the Bureau tested an additional 34 samples with a gap of 4.5 to 9.0 inches and a compliance rate of 71%. Gaps of 2.7 to 4.0 inches seem to be associated with the greatest vulnerability. The results of the recent 93 tests also basically show similar trend (Figures 6 and 7). The size of the gap between the seat and the back may be a design weakness of some seating furniture with regard to flammability. However, it was not possible in this test series to evaluate identical furniture construction with differing gap size.

The Bureau tested 54 articles of seating furniture with no gap in the seat-back crevice and no seat-arm crevice. These articles had a 65% compliance rate with TB 133. The Bureau also tested 15 pieces of seating furniture with no gap in the seat-back crevice but with seat-arm crevices. It was found that 53 percent met the criteria. Styles without arms appeared to be more likely to meet the criteria than styles with arms. Seating furniture with arms showed a greater propensity to fail TB 133. The addition of arms increased the fuel load, and if the filling materials were not properly fire retarded or if an interliner material was not included, these showed a greater tendency to ignite and burn. The presence of arms introduced two new areas which must be resistant to either direct flame impingement or direct radiant heat from the ignition source depending on the closeness of the arms to the ignition source. Furniture designed with a wide seat area and arms some distance from the ignition source are more likely to meet the criteria of TB 133 than narrower construction. When arms did ignite, due to re-radiation from these burning surfaces, a more intense fire resulted with an increased probability of failing the criteria of TB 133.

The integrity of the construction of the seating furniture also appeared to be a significant design factor. If the rear cover of the furniture back separated at the bottom, flame spread upward into the interior of the back. If the rear cover of the furniture back separated at the top, the rear cover peeled off downwards and sometimes spread flame to the underside of the seat, exposing flames to the interior of the back. In addition, it was important that the seat maintain enough integrity and strength to support the ignition box. In the case of solid plastic seating furniture, without cushioning, if the ignition box burned through the seat and was carried by its own weight through the seat to the floor, flames impinging on the bottom of the seat accelerated the burning of the remainder of the sample.

CONCLUSIONS

The Bureau has tested 93 articles of seating furniture which were analyzed based on the revised version of TB 133 test criteria. The results of these tests, indicate that ceiling temperature, 4-foot temperature, and 4-foot smoke opacity were the most frequently failed criteria. Carbon monoxide concentration and weight loss ranked next as most frequently occurring failure causes. In most cases, carbon monoxide was associated with failure when only one criteria was exceeded. Temperatures were also sometimes associated with a single failure criteria. From comparison of these tests and the 136 tests previously performed based on the May 1984 version of TB 133, it was concluded that although an article might not exhibit excessive weight loss and/or carbon monoxide production, however, high temperatures and smoke generated during rapid initial pyrolysis and flaming of the furniture could cause failure of TB 133. It was also confirmed that materials which meet the criteria of the California Technical Bulletin 117 will not generally meet the criteria of TB 133. As a general rule, materials which exhibit low rate of production combustible gases, are likely to pass TB 133 test unless some dramatic events such as rupture of interliners and exposure of the filling materials to intense heat cause the furnishing article to fail the test.

Seating furniture is most likely to meet the criteria of TB 133 if it is constructed of cover fabrics and filling materials exhibiting low weight loss or burning peaks under the conditions of this test. Seating furniture designed with a minimum of combustible material improves the chances of acceptable performance. The use of effective barriers or interliners can achieve increased fire performance. The integrity of construction may affect the seating furniture's ability to prevent involvement of the filling material. Furniture design features, such as the presence and size of a gap between the seat and back cushions, tend to have an impact on the furniture's fire test performance. The addition of arms adds a greater fuel load and additional surfaces which are subjected to the ignition source. Large areas of decorative plastics often contributed to failing results if the plastic components became involved in the flaming combustion.

California Technical Bulletin 133 is providing guidance and incentive in the development of seating furniture intended for public occupancies, and has continued to grow in popularity since it's inception in 1984. The Bureau has tested 117 articles of seating furniture which are in full compliance with TB 133.

SUMMARY

Fires in the United States involving articles of furnishings result in more deaths and injuries than any other product class. Fires involving cigarette smoldering and small, open-flame ignition of furnishings have been shown to be a serious cause of death, injury, and property loss. This paper has summarized the efforts of California since 1970 to address this issue. Standards for residential furnishings have been reviewed and their efficacy assessed.

In addition, many occupancies may be considered to be higher risk than residential occupancies, where great potential for catastrophic loss of life and extensive property damage exists in the event of fire. These occupancies might include: correctional facilities, jails, prisons, penal institutions, health care facilities, hospitals, nursing care homes, convalescent homes, child day care centers, public auditoriums, hotels, and motels. These types of occupancies may present special fire hazards: such as intentionally set fires; evacuation problems due to security measures; limited mobility or lack of mobility of patients; unfamiliarity of occupants with exists; or large numbers of people trying to rapidly exit public assembly facilities; and inadequate fire detection and suppression systems.

This paper has also summarized attempts by California to develop flammability standards, such as California Technical Bulletin 133, for public building occupancies.

REFERENCES

1. Hafer, C. A. and Yuill, C. H. "Characterization of Bedding and Upholstery Fire," NBS Contract No. CST-792-5-69, Southwest Research Institute (1970)

2. Yuill, C. H., "The Life Hazard of Bedding and Upholstery Fires," J. of Fire and Flammability, Vol. 1, 312-323 (October 1970).

3. Hilado, C. J., Atkins, K. E. and Fisher, J. A., "Fire Studies of Furniture Materials," J. of Consumer Product Flammability, Vol. 2, pp. 154-169 (June 1975).

4. Palmer, K. N. and Taylor, W., "Fire Hazards of Plastics in Furniture and Furnishings: Ignition Studies," U. K. Building Research Establishment Current Paper 18/74. Borehamwood (1974).

5. Palmer, K. N., Taylor, W. and Paul, K. T., "Fire Hazards of Plastics in Furniture and Furnishings: Characteristics of the Burning," U. K. Building Research Establishment Current Paper 3/75. Borehamwood (1975).

6. Palmer, K. N., Taylor, W. and Paul, K. T., "Fire Hazards of Plastics in Furniture and Furnishings: Fires in Furnished Rooms," U. K. Building Research Establishment Current Paper 21/76. Borehamwood (1976).

7. Damant, G. H., "Flammability Aspects of Upholstered Furniture," J. of Consumer Product Flammability, Vol. 3, 21-61 (May 1976).

8. Damant, G. H., "A Survey of Upholstery Fabrics and their Flammability Characteristics," J. of Consumer Product Flammability, Vol. 2, p. 5-57 (March 1975).

9. Vickers, A. K. and Tovey, H., "Hazard Analysis of Upholstered Furniture in Fire Incidents," Office of Information and Hazard Analysis, National Bureau of Standards (October 1, 1974).

10. Damant, G. H., "Flammability Aspects of Flexible Polyurethane Foams Commonly used in Upholstered Furniture," J. of Consumer Product Flammability, Vol. 3, pp. 73-127 (June 1976).

11. Damant, G. H., and Young, M. A., "Smoldering Characteristics of fabrics used as Upholstered Furniture Coverings," J. of Consumer Product Flammability, Vol. 4, pp. 60-113 (March 1977).

12. Damant, G. H., "The Effects of Aging on Fire Retardant Flexible Polyurethane Foams Commonly used in Upholstered Furniture," J. of Consumer Product Flammability, Vol. 3, pp. 277-287 (December 1976).

13. Hilado, C. J., Kolb, E. L. and Furst, A., "Fire Safety in the Home: Relative Toxicity of the Pyrolysis Products from some Upholstery Fabrics," California Bureau of Home Furnishings Laboratory Report No. SP-77-3 (June 1977).

14. Damant, G. H. and Young, M. A., "Flammability Classification of Fabrics used as Upholstered Furniture Coverings," J. of Consumer Product Flammability, Vol. 4, pp. 329-345 (December 1977).

15. Clark, F. B., III and Ottoson, J., "Fire Death Scenarios and Fire Safety Planning," Fire Journal, Vol. 70, No. 3, pp. 20-23 (May 1976).

16. California Assembly Bill No. 1522, Chapter 749, 1972.

17. California Bureau of Home Furnishings Technical Bulletin 116, "Requirements, Test Procedure and Apparatus for Testing the Flame Retardance of Upholstered Furniture," (January 1980).

18. California Bureau of Home Furnishings Technical Bulletin 117, "Requirements, Test Procedure and Apparatus for Testing the Flame Retardance of Filling Materials Used in Upholstered Furniture, (January 1980).

19. Wortman, P. S., Williams, S. S. and Damant, G. H., "Development of a Fire Test for Furniture for High Risk and Public Occupancies", <u>Proceedings of the International Conference on Fire Safety</u>, Vol. 9, 55-67 (January 1984).

20. Damant, G. H., Williams, S. S. and Wortman, P. S., "Development of a Fire Test for Furniture for Use in High-Risk Occupancies and Public Buildings", <u>Proceedings of the 28th SPI Annual Conference</u>, 169-173 (November 1984).

21. Wortman, P. S., Williams, S. S. and Damant, G. H., "Development of a Fire Test for Furniture Used in High Risk and Public Occupancies", <u>Proceedings of the International Conference on Fire Safety</u>, Vol. 10, 9-22 (January 1985).

22. California Technical Bulletin 133, "Flammability Test Procedure for Seating Furniture for Use in Public Occupancies" (April 1988).

23. Damant, G. H., McCormack, J. A., Mikami, J. F., Wortman, P. S., "The California Technical Bulletin 133 Test: Some Background and Experience", Proceedings of The International Conference on Fire Safety, Vol. 14, 1-12, (January 1989).

THE BURNING BEHAVIOUR OF DOMESTIC UPHOLSTERED CHAIRS CONTAINING DIFFERENT TYPES OF POLYURETHANE FOAMS

K.T.Paul (Rapra Technology Limited) and
D.A.King (Beaverfoam Manufacturing Limited).

ABSTRACT

This paper describes a series of domestic armchair burning tests carried out by Rapra Technology Limited and sponsored by the Beaverco group of companies. The tests compared a series of actual chairs containing flexible standard and high resilience polyurethane foam with chairs containing combustion modified high resilience polyurethane foam developed by Beaverco PLC (Tradename Safeguard) based on melamine/PIPA technology.

Upholstered armchairs containing different types of polyurethane foams and covered by various popular fabrics were burned in a room/corridor test rig. A limited number of chair designs was used and an important feature of these tests was the three series of armchairs of constant design in which only the fabric and polyurethane foam upholstery was varied. The chairs typified the various stages of UK domestic furniture requirements up to and including the post-1990 requirements for cigarette resistant composites, match resistant covers and combustion modified high resilience PU upholstery foams.

Each chair was ignited by the source required to cause sustained burning and measurements were continuously made of ceiling temperature, smoke density and volume; carbon monoxide, carbon dioxide, oxygen, and nitrogen oxide concentrations. Hydrogen cyanide measurements were made using chemical reagent tubes.

The results of these tests relate specifically to single chairs burning freely in a brick room (3 x 4½ x 2½m high) ventilated by a single, open, domestic sized door.

INTRODUCTION

This paper describes a series of domestic armchair burning tests carried out by Rapra Technology Limited and sponsored by the Beaverco group of companies. The tests compared a series of actual chairs containing flexible standard and high resilience polyurethane foam with chairs containing combustion modified high resilience polyurethane foam developed by Beaverco PLC (Tradename Safeguard) based on melamine/PIPA technology

BACKGROUND

It is nearly 20 years ago that the unacceptable fire behaviour of "modern" upholstered furniture became highlighted in the UK by Fire Brigade reports of domestic fires. The poor performance was blamed on the use of flexible polyurethane foam upholstery and demands were made to ban polyurethane foam or at least to insist on the use of flame retarded polyurethane foam.

The early 1970s saw three major research programmes to investigate the fire performance of furniture and furnishings. These programmes, (1), (2), (3), not surprisingly, produced similar conclusions that the adverse fire behaviour of upholstered furniture and made-up beds arose because of easy ignition by small everyday sources (cigarettes and matches) and rapid burning producing high rates of heat, smoke and toxic fire gas generation. Major contributory factors were the use of smoulderable and easily ignitable fabrics, melting fabrics and flexible polyurethane foams. Recommendations were to use materials which did not smoulder, to use fabrics which were not easily ignited by small flames, and to restrict the amount of flammable materials used. The use of interliners and barrier fabrics and foams was demonstrated and also the adverse effects of using certain types of flame retarded polyurethane foam (previously demanded) with flammable fabrics.

Various government authorities and especially The Crown Suppliers were already "fire conscious" and further extended the use of fabrics of reduced flammability, barrier fabrics and foams, and high resilience polyurethane foams in their purchase specifications for upholstered furniture and bed assemblies for use in the Crown Estate, public buildings, hospitals etc. Typically, products were required to meet cigarette and No.5 crib sources when tested to Crown Suppliers Tests (4). Full scale tests with domestic furniture in the late 1970s showed, regrettably, that not only had domestic upholstered furniture design and construction not followed the recommendations of early research, but that the fire performance of such furniture had arguably deteriorated.

In 1978, the Home Office report (5) specifically criticised the fire performance of upholstered domestic furniture and recommended manufacturers to improve ignition resistance, to reduce flammability, and to reduce the rates of smoke and toxic gas generation.

In 1980 the Consumer Protection Act (6) required manufacturers to take reasonable steps to ensure that fabric - soft infill composites (only) of domestic furniture resisted the cigarette test of BS5852: Part 1. Home Office Codes of Practice (7) were gradually extended to additional public areas and now advised similar ignition performance to that originally used for public areas, i.e. a minimum ignition resistance of cigarette and crib No.5 of BS5852,

Parts 1 and 2 (8) (9). The ignition test for bedding was published as BS6807 (10). The Consumer Protection Amendment of 1983 (11) required specified children's furniture to resist Source 5 of BS5852: Part 2. In the USA, cigarette testing of upholstered composites was introduced (UFAC) while California required that all components of upholstered furniture were small flame resistant. Other areas, e.g. prisons, also introduced various ignition controls while California developed single room based temperature, smoke and carbon monoxide generation tests for critical applications (12).

The next stage in the evolution of fire tests for upholstered furniture in the UK occurred in 1988 (13) and was largely triggered by the development of combustion modified polyurethane foams.

DEVELOPMENT OF COMBUSTION MODIFIED POLYURETHANE FOAM

The polyurethane foam industry has developed a series of grades of flame retarded and ignition resistant flexible PU foams. Early flame retarded polyurethane foams used additives e.g. chloro and bromophosphates or formulations which tended to melt e.g. high resilience polyurethane foam while polyurethane foam impregnated with resin bonded hydrated alumina was first developed as a fire barrier. The latter was subsequently developed and is now used for institution mattresses which are required to resist large ignition sources even when fully vandalised. Neither the barrier foam-high resilience polyurethane foam composites nor the full depth impregnated polyurethane foams were particularly suitable for use in domestic upholstery because difficulties with the inherent furniture production methods of the former and the unsatisfactory physical characteristics and especially resilience of the latter. The next major improvement was the development of combustion modified polyurethane foams (14).

The original combustion modified high resilience polyurethane foam was developed in the USA and was used in institutions, public buildings, hotels etc. It was made in a single operation and contained hydrated alumina and flame retardants (15). This was followed by a melamine containing high resilience polyurethane foam and a polyurethane foam containing exfoliated graphite. These latter two foams have been intensively developed in the UK. It was the production of these materials which encouraged the next legislative step towards improving the fire behaviour of domestic furniture since they permitted significant fire behaviour improvements to be made without the use of barrier fabrics and/or foams.

This is a very important factor because the primary function of upholstered furniture, mattresses and bed assemblies is to provide comfortable seating which is durable as well as aesthetically pleasing. The development of suitable fabrics, foams and other materials is therefore of great importance and is a factor that can be overlooked in the pursuit of improved fire performance.

A comparison of the properties of different types of polyurethane upholstery foams is given in Table 1.

TABLE 1

Comparison of Polyurethane Upholstery Foams

Test Method		Standard PU foam	High Resilience PU foam	Flame Retarded PU foam	Combustion Modified PU Melamine	Combustion Modified PU Hydrated Alumina + Flame Retardant	Post-treated PU foam
Standard Tests on uncovered PU foams							
BS4735							
Mean dist.mm		150	24-41	93-125	10-30	31-38	33-38
Mean rate mm/s		1.6-4.2	1.4-2.2	0.5-1.8	0.5-2.0	0.5-0.6	0.5-0.6
BS5111							
Smoke Density %		44	28	43-94			
Rate of Heat Release (12)							
NBS Cone KW/m^2		>400	-	>400	<280	<160	-
Ignition tests to BS5852: Part 1 on fabric covered PU foams							
Acrylic pile	C	N	N	N	N	N	N
	M	I	I	I	I^b	I^a	I^a
Cotton pile	C	I	I	N	N	N	N
	M	I	I	I	I^b	I^a	I^a
Polypropylene	C	N	N	N	N	N	N
	M	I	I	I	I	I	I^a
Modacrylic pile	C	N	N	-	N	N	N
	M	N	N	-	N	N	N
Polyester	C	N	N	N	N	-	N
	M	I	N	N	N	-	N
Wool pile	C	N	N	N	N	N	N
	M	N	N	N	N	N	N

Key
C = cigarette
M = No.1 gas flame
I = Sustained burning of specimen
I^a = Burning largely limited to fabric
I^b = Limited burning of foam (approx.30-60%) and fabric
N = No ignition.

Selection of Chairs

All of the chairs selected comprised a single fabric covered, polyurethane foam upholstered chair with a wooden frame. (Table 2). Typical domestic covering fabrics were selected.

The chairs selected included those expected to fail and to pass the cigarette test of BS5852: Part 1: 1980, Consumer Safety Regulations, cigarette resistant chairs, with flammable fabrics and combustion modified high resilience polyurethane foam conforming to the first phase of the 1988 Consumer Safety Regulations and chairs with ignition resistant fabrics and combustion modified high resilience polyurethane foams conforming to the final phase of the 1988 Consumer Safety Regulations.

A suggested method of regulation at one stage was to change from standard to high resilience polyurethane foam and 3 chairs containing this foam are included.

In addition three used chairs were also tested. These had been taken from scrap and were dusty, slightly torn and had compressed polyurethane foam cushions which resulted in rather slack fabric coverings.

In order to minimise the effect of chair design on the burning behaviour, three series chairs were built to a constant design but with different fabric/polyurethane foam combinations. Other chairs varied in both design and fabric/foam combinations (Table 3).

TABLE 2

Chairs used in Burning Tests

Covering Fabric	Soft Upholstery Foam	Upholstered Chair Conforming to:- Pre-1980 Not Cig. Resist	Pre-1988 Cig.Resist	Pre-1990 Cig.Resist CMPU Foam	Post-1990 Cig.Resist CMPU Foam Ignt.Resist. Fabric
Acrylic pile	SPE		A,C,S		
Acrylic pile	HRPE		A,C		
Acrylic pile	CM35			A	
Acrylic pile	CM50			A	
Woven cotton	SPE	B			
Woven cotton	CM35			B	
Woven cotton	CM50			B	
Woven FR Cotton	CM35				B
Woven Wool/Cotton	CM35				N
Viscose pile	SPE	C			
Viscose pile	HRPE		C		
Cellulose pile	SPE	S			
Woven Polypropylene	SPE		N,S		
Woven Polypropylene	HRPE		N		

<u>Key</u>

A,B,C	Standard designs
S	Soiled chairs, non-standard design
N	Non-standard design

TABLE 3

Ignitability of Upholstered Chairs

Design Code	Upholstery Fabric	Upholstery Foam	Cigarette	No.1	Source Used to Initiate Burn Test
A	Acrylic Pile	SPE	P	F	1
A	"	HRPE	P	F	1
A	"	CM35	P	F	1
A	"	CM50	P	F	1
C	"	SPE	P	F	1
C	"	HRPE	P	F	1
S	"	SPE	F*	F	1
B	Woven Cotton	SPE	F	F	1
B	"	CM35	P	P/F	1
B	"	CM50	P	FT	7
B	FR Woven Cotton	CM35	P	P	7
N	Woven Wool/Cotton	CM35	P	P	4
C	Viscose Pile	SPE	F	F	5
C	"	HRPE	F/P	P/F	5
S	"	SPE	F	F	1
N	Woven Polypropylene	SPE	P	F	1
N	"	HRPE	P	F	1
S	"	SPE	P	F	1

* Composite resisted but viscose rouching of chair would have caused failure if added to test specimen.

P/F Borderline result.
FT Technical fail, with flaming of limited duration.

Test Techniques and Equipment

Ignition Source for Chair Burns: The ignition resistance of the upholstered composites is given in Table 3. When selecting an ignition source for burning tests, it is important that the source should be large enough to cause sustained burning of the chair but should not be excessively large so as to dominate the burn. The chairs typically weighed 25-35 Kg and burned to a residue of 5-10 Kg.

Many of the composites were readily ignited with a No.1 gas flame of BS5852: Part 1, and this was used for most tests. Chairs which were known to resist Source 1 or which gave variable results in small scale ignition tests were ignited with Sources 4 or 5 while the more resistant chairs were ignited by ignition Source 7 (Table 4).

TABLE 4

Burning Behaviour of Ignition Sources (16)

Ignition Source	1	4	5	7
Duration of Burning Secs.	20	215*	203*	392*
Theoretical Heat of Combustion KJ	21.7	143	285	2100
Max. heat flux (below)	30-45	18	18	49

* Average of recorded values.

Test Environment: All tests were carried out in the Rapra Technology test room which effectively simulated a domestic sized room (3m x 4½m x 2½m high) ventilated by an open, domestic sized doorway. The room/corridor facility comprised a brick structure with a concrete floor and roof. The inner single brick wall is separated from the outer double brick wall by a standard cavity, 11-12 cm wide. The burning room measuring 4.6m x 3m x 2.4m high and corridor measuring 1.8m x 2.4m x 15m are connected by an internal domestic sized door. The fire test room had a volume of $34m^3$. At the end of the corridor is an extractor fan and an after burner.

The air flowed through a duct entering the actual burning room via the door from the corridor. The top of the duct was in the neutral plane between the incoming and the outgoing smoke which passed down the corridor and was destroyed in the after burner. The air flow into the chamber was recorded using a rotating vane anemometer positioned in the air entry duct. The linear air velocity was multiplied by a factor of 0.6 to allow for the velocity distribution in the air entry duct. This factor has been determined experimentally during previous tests. Smoke was measured using a horizontal lamp/ photo cell system positioned in the corridor (Figure 1). The system comprised a tungsten filament bulb and a selenium barrier photo cell. The amount of smoke was calculated from its density, temperature and the flow rate of air entering the fire chamber.

Continuous gas samples were passed through filters to remove soot etc. and then through two non-dispersive infra-red meters to measure carbon monoxide and carbon dioxide and a paramagnetic oxygen meter. Hydrogen cyanide gas was measured using chemical reagent tubes. Nitrogen oxides were measured using a chemiluminescence meter. Temperatures were measured using chrome-alumel thermocouples positioned at the ceiling above the chair, at the room exit lintel, and in the corridor near the horizontal smoke measuring point. The test chair was placed in a sand tray supported by two strain gauge load cells and the mass of the chair recorded throughout the test.

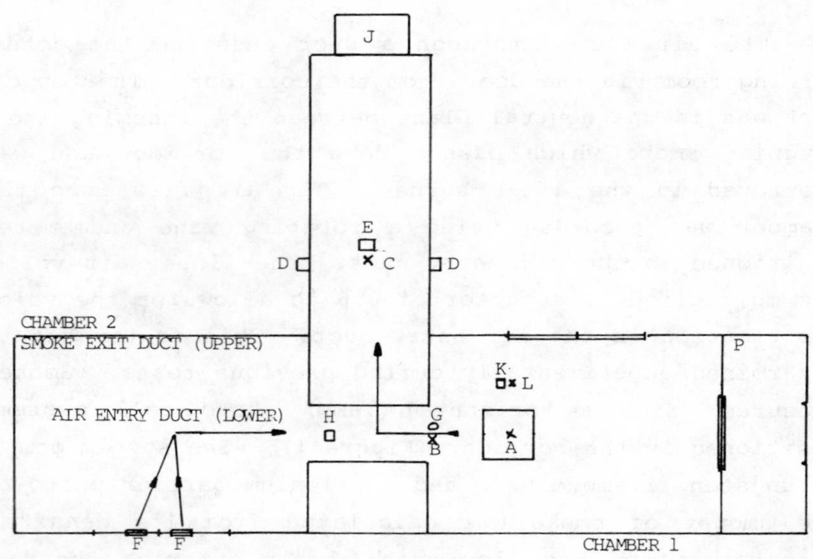

KEY

X - A - Thermocouple on ceiling
X - B - Thermocouple on lintel
X - C - Thermocouple at eye level in corridor
D - Smoke Measuring Apparatus (eye level) Horizontal Beam
E - Smoke Measuring Apparatus Vertical Beam
F - Air Entry ports
o - G - Toxic Gas Probe (for CO; CO_2; O_2)
- H - Air Flow Movement
J - After Burner and Extractor fan
K - Heat Flux Meter
X - L - Thermocouple Positioned 61 cm from edge of chair
P - Observation Room

Fig. 1. Layout of fire chamber and instruments for burning chair tests.

THE BURNING BEHAVIOUR OF UPHOLSTERED CHAIRS CONTAINING DIFFERENT TYPES OF POLYURETHANE FOAMS

A brief description of the burning behaviour of upholstered chairs is given in this section. Test data are summarised in Tables 5 to 7.

CHAIRS CONTAINING STANDARD POLYURETHANE FOAM (SPU)

Viscose pile fabric covered SPU chair

Viscose pile fabrics have a tendency to smoulder when used over standard polyurethane foam and may be ignited with a No.1 gas flame to BS5852/Pt.1 although the results depend considerably on the individual fabric used.

The full scale chair burns, ignited with a No.5 crib, showed that the onset of rapid burning was delayed compared to the acrylic covering fabrics and the standard polyurethane foam containing chairs took about 10 minutes to achieve the maximum temperature. The design of the used, cellulosic fabric covered chair differed from that of the chair described above, the main difference being a slightly higher back. The chair was ignited by a No.5 crib and it burned steadily reaching its peak temperature after about 9 minutes. The maximum smoke density was rather higher than the viscose pile covered chair, but the temperature and carbon monoxide concentrations were similar and the chair burned in a generally similar manner.

Acrylic pile fabric covered SPU chairs

Two acrylic pile fabric chairs of different design were burned. Each was easily ignited with a No.1 gas flame and then burned rapidly reaching their maximum temperatures after 2½ and 5½ minutes respectively. The chairs produced considerable amounts of smoke which restricted visibility in the fire room. The soft upholstery had largely been burned within about 5 minutes of ignition and only the damaged frames remained after about 12-15 minutes.

The acrylic pile fabric covered used chair burned in a generally similar manner to the new chairs except that the chair took 8 minutes to reach its peak temperature and produced rather less smoke. It is considered that the age of the chair had caused the polyurethane foam to compress and that the covering fabric was not tensioned. This, combined with the cotton backing of this acrylic fabric, delayed the time at which the fabric char ruptured to expose the polyurethane foam upholstery. Another factor which would have altered the ignition behaviour of the chair was the use of viscose rouching around the cushions. Acrylic fabric/standard polyurethane foam upholstery composites will resist a cigarette when tested to BS5852: Part 1, but the insertion of viscose rouching along the vertical/horizontal junction of the test rig is sufficient to cause a cigarette to initiate progressive smouldering in the composite.

Woven Cotton Fabric Covered SPU Chair

This chair was ignited with a No.1 gas flame and took 5 minutes to reach its peak temperature. Temperatures, smoke densities, carbon monoxide and other gas concentrations and rates of smoke production, were significantly less than for the acrylic covered standard polyurethane foam chair.

Woven Polypropylene Fabric Covered SPU Chair

The polypropylene fabric covered chair was easily ignited and burned rapidly. The armchair reached its peak after 4 minutes. It gave generally similar results to the fast burning acrylic fabric covered chairs. A feature of this burn was that the fabric tended to melt to expose the foam ahead of the flame front.

CHAIRS CONTAINING HIGH RESILIENCE POLYURETHANE FOAM (HRPU)

Viscose pile fabric covered HRPU chair.

This chair behaved in a generally similar manner to the viscose pile fabric chair containing standard polyurethane reaching the peak temperature after about 10 minutes. The high resilience polyurethane foam chair produced higher ceiling temperatures and smoke densities with slightly higher peak carbon monoxide concentrations.

Acrylic Pile Fabric Covered HRPU Chair

The acrylic pile fabric covered chairs containing high resilience polyurethane foam also burned rapidly reaching their peaks after 4 and 8½ minutes. Peak temperatures were lower than those of the standard polyurethane foam chairs. The rates of generation of smoke were also lower for the high resilience foam chair although the maximum smoke densities were significantly higher for the high resilience foam chairs. The foam upholstery of the high resilience foam chair was largely consumed by 6 and 10 minutes. The peak carbon monoxide concentrations for the high resilience foam containing chairs was similar to or greater than that of the standard foam containing chairs. The apparent difference between the 2 types of chair was probably due to the 2 types of acrylic fabric used and to differences in chair design.

Woven Polypropylene Covered HRPU Chair

Flames initially spread slowly across the width of the chair back and then up to the top of the back. This initial slow period developed quickly into a fire which was similar to that of the polypropylene covered standard polyurethane foam chair although the smoke and carbon monoxide were higher.

COMBUSTION MODIFIED PU FOAMS. HIGH RESILIENCE (CMHRPU) LOW-MEDIUM DENSITY

The CMHRPU foams used in these chairs were typical of those used for domestic seating.

Acrylic pile fabric covered (CMHRPU) chair

The acrylic covered chair containing the lower density, combustion modified high resilience polyurethane foam upholstery peaked after 6-7 minutes giving lower peak temperatures, carbon dioxide and hydrogen cyanide concentrations, considerably lower smoke density and carbon monoxide concentrations than the chair containing standard polyurethane foam. The rate of smoke generation was slightly less than that of the high resilience foam and the upholstery was largely consumed by 7 minutes.

Woven cotton fabric covered (CMHRPU) chair

The woven cotton covered chair was also ignited by the No.1 gas flame but burned very slowly during the initial period of the test. The chair reached its maximum temperature after 19 minutes with similar smoke densities and carbon monoxide concentrations to the equivalent acrylic covered CM35 PU foam chair. A major difference was observed in the burning pattern during the early stages because the fabric and polyurethane foam surface tended to burn slowly leaving a charred surface on the remaining foam. The chair eventually burned to completion.

COMBUSTION MODIFIED HIGH RESILIENCE POLYURETHANE FOAMS MEDIUM-HIGH DENSITY

The density of the combustion modified high resilience polyurethane foams used in these chairs were typical of those used for contract and public area seating.

Acrylic pile fabric covered CMHRPU chair

The acrylic fabric covered chair containing the higher density combustion, modified high resilience polyurethane foam upholstery, burned in a completely different manner to the other acrylic covered chairs. Combustion was largely limited to the fabric cover and the outer layer of the upholstery foam. The rate of smoke generation was less than that of the other chairs. This chair peaked at 16-18 minutes with relatively low temperatures, heat flux values, and carbon monoxide concentrations. The hydrogen cyanide peak was about half of the peak of the standard and high resilience polyurethane foam chairs. After 30 minutes, a significant proportion of the foam upholstery remained.

Woven cotton fabric covered CMHRPU chair

The woven cotton fabric covered chair was initially ignited by a No.1 flame but this extinguished after about 11 minutes. A No.7 crib in the seat/back/arm junction was used to initiate the burn test. This chair burned slowly but then increased more rapidly to reach its peak after about 37-40 minutes.

COMBUSTION MODIFIED HIGH RESILIENCE POLYURETHANE FOAMS (CMHRPU). MEDIUM DENSITY WITH IGNITION RESISTANT FABRICS

Wool/cotton fabric covered CMHRPU chair

This chair was of the Chesterfield type design and was ignited by a No.4 crib in the seat/back/arm junction. The chair burned fairly slowly and the fire penetrated through the seat/back/arm junction and developed slowly in the lower seat and back after about 11-12 minutes. The chair produced relatively low smoke densities and temperatures, carbon monoxide concentrations at its peak which occurred after about 17 minutes.

Flame retarded cotton fabric covered CMHRPU chair

The flame retarded cotton covered chair containing the medium density combustion modified high resilience polyurethane foam resisted ignition Sources 1 and 5 when applied to the seat/back junction. A No.7 crib, in the seat/back/arm junction was used to ignite the chair.

The fire burned slowly in the seat area and appeared to descend into the base of the chair. The chair burned slowly with relatively low flames above the seat level and only minor flames were visible after about 10 minutes. The fire in the base of the chair increased slowly and then more rapidly after 23 minutes. The chair reached its peak after 26-27 minutes. The fire gave similar peak temperatures, smoke densities, to the chair with non-flame retarded cotton fabric and standard polyurethane foam ignitable by source No.1 although the rate of smoke generation and peak, toxic gas concentrations (except for carbon monoxide) were lower. The chair burned essentially to completion.

TABLE 5

Fire Test Data for Acrylic Fabric Covered Chairs, Test Series A

Upholstery Foam		Std.PU	HRPU	CMHR35	CMHR50
Fabric		Acrylic	Acrylic	Acrylic	Acrylic
Design		A	A	A	A
Ignition Source (BS5852)		1	1	1	1
Fire Intensity					
Max. Ceiling Temp.	°C	706	661	490	94
Time to max. temp.	mins.	2½	4	6	15
Smoke					
Max. Optical Density	OD/m	1.7	2.1	0.8	1.0
Time to max.	mins.	3	5	6	18
Max. Smoke temp.	°C	491	463	375	89
Max. Smoke rate	m^3/min	37	32	18	10
Fire Gases					
Max. carbon monoxide conc.	%	0.14	0.22	0.06	0.02
Max. carbon dioxide conc.	%	8.5	7.9	6.4	0.9
Min. oxygen conc.	%	12.4	12.5	14.9	19.7
Time to max.gas conc.	mins	2-4	4-5	6-7	15-17

TABLE 6

Fire Test Data for Cotton Fabric Covered Chairs, Test Series B

Upholstery Foam Fabric Design		Std.PU Cotton B	CMHR35 Cotton B	CMHR50 Cotton B	CMHR35 FR Cotton B	CMHR35 Wool/Cotton N
Ignition Source (BS5852)		1	1	7	7	4
Fire Intensity						
Max. Ceiling Temp.	°C	630	145	674	702	300
Time to max. temp.	mins.	3	19	37	26	17
Smoke						
Max. Optical Density	OD/m	0.9	0.7	0.9	1.7	0.8
Time to max.	mins.	4-5	19-21	37-40	26-27	17-20
Max. Smoke temp.	°C	313	88	430	366	237
Max. Smoke rate	m^3/min	3.4	5.4	7	12	20
Fire Gases						
Max. carbon monoxide conc.	%	0.1	0.05	0.17	0.28	0.08
Max. carbon dioxide conc.	%	6.3	1.1	9.5	8.9	2.9
Min. oxygen conc.	%	13.8	19.5	11.3	16.9	17.3
Time to max.gas conc.	mins	3-7	16-20	37-40	25-27	17-19

TABLE 7

Fire Test Data for Viscose Fabric Covered Chairs, Test Series AC

Upholstery Foam		Std.PU	HRPU	Std.PU	HRPU
Fabric		Viscose	Viscose	Acrylic	Acrylic
Design		C	C	C	C
Ignition Source (BS5852)		5	5	5	5
Fire Intensity					
Max. Ceiling Temp.	°C	350	435	415	395
Time to max. temp.	mins.	10	10½	5½	8½
Smoke					
Max. Optical Density	OD/m	3.3	3.8	3.1	3.8
Time to max.	mins.	10-11	10½-12	5-6	9-10
Max. Smoke temp.	°C	380	540	505	440
Max. Smoke rate	m^3/min	-	-	-	-
Fire Gases					
Max. carbon monoxide conc.	%	0.07	0.09	0.05	0.06
Max. carbon dioxide conc.	%	5.7	9.5	4.4	5.5
Min. oxygen conc.	%	16.3	13.9	14.1	15.0
Time to max.gas conc.	mins	11-14	11-15	5-7	9-11

TABLE 8

Fire Test Data for Polypropylene Fabric Covered Chairs(N) and for Used Chairs(S)
Test Series N and S

Upholstery Foam Fabric Design		Std.PU Polyprop. N	HRPU Polyprop. N	Std.PU Acrylic S	Std.PU Cotton S	Std.PU Polyprop. S
Ignition Source (BS5852)		1	1	1	5	1
Fire Intensity						
Max. Ceiling Temp.	°C	430	520	482	343	402
Time to max. temp.	mins.	4	4	3	9	4
Smoke						
Max. Optical Density	OD/m	1.7	2.6	1.6	>4.5	1.0
Time to max.	mins.	4½-5	4½-5	7-9	7-12	4
Max. Smoke temp.	°C	300	270	340	381	359
Max. Smoke rate	m^3/min	31	41	46	-	25
Fire Gases						
Max. carbon monoxide conc.	%	0.03	0.15	0.09	0.09	0.06
Max. carbon dioxide conc.	%	4.5	3.7	6.0	5.7	8.0
Min. oxygen conc.	%	16.4	16.4	14.7	15.0	12.5
Time to max.gas conc.	mins	4½-5	3½-4½	9-12	8-10	4

Comparison of burning characteristics of upholstered chairs

A comparison of the burning behaviour of the chairs is given in Figure 2 and data/time curves for a limited number of chairs in Figures 3 to 6.

All chairs were ignited in the seat/back or seat/back/arm junction. Chairs with acrylic, cellulosic and polypropylene fabrics with standard polyurethane or high resilience polyurethane foam burned in a generally similar manner. Flames spread up and across the chair back and more slowly across the chair seat. The flames on the chair back radiated heated onto the seat which began to burn more rapidly. The arms started to scorch and pyrolyse and then ignited. Flames penetrated through to the rear of the chair and eventually through the front of the chair below the seat. At this stage the fire reached its peak and the smoke typically formed a layer down to or below the top of the chair back. The fires continued to burn leaving a fire damaged frame after about 15-20 minutes.

There was no significant difference between the burning pattern of the chairs which had been in use for many years and the new chairs. The major differences were due to the type of fabric. Polypropylene fabrics and some acrylic pile fabrics burned rapidly and split open to allow the foam to burn directly. Viscose pile and cellulosic fabrics burned more slowly until the charred fabric split open.

In general the use of high resilience polyurethane foam gave a slightly slower burn rate than similar chairs containing standard polyurethane foam but the difference was typically only about 1-2 minutes which, in real fire terms, is probably not significant. The smoke density produced from the chairs containing the high resilience polyurethane

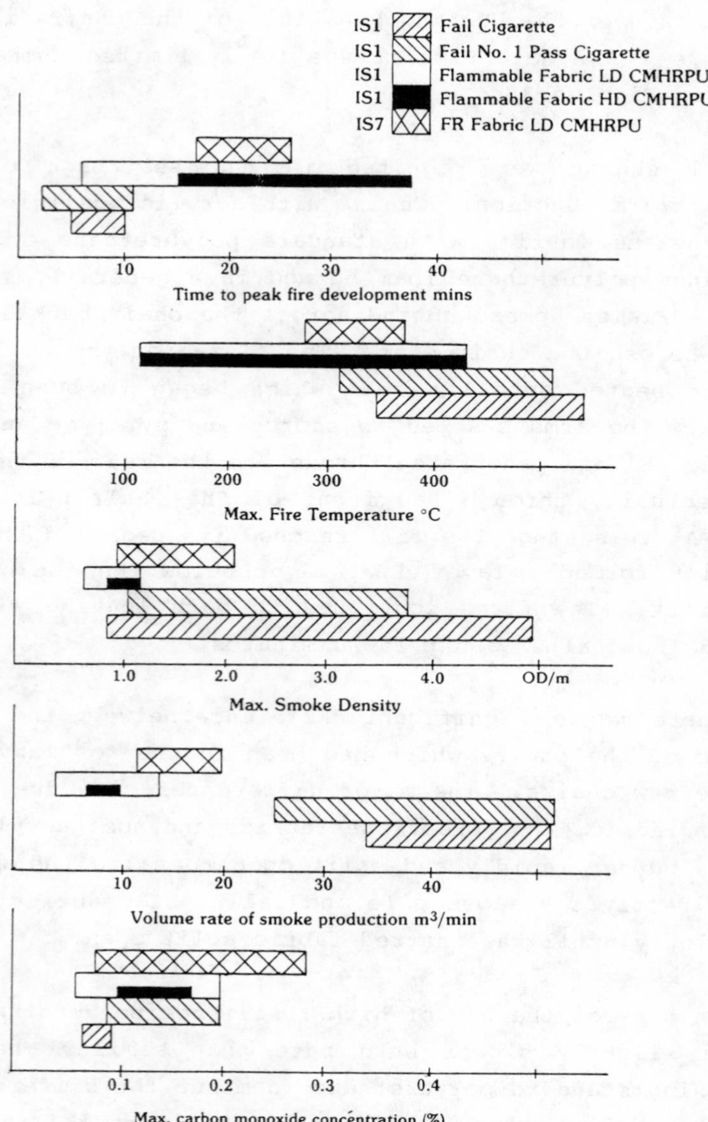

Fig. 2. Comparison of fire parameters of upholstered chairs containing polyurethane foams.

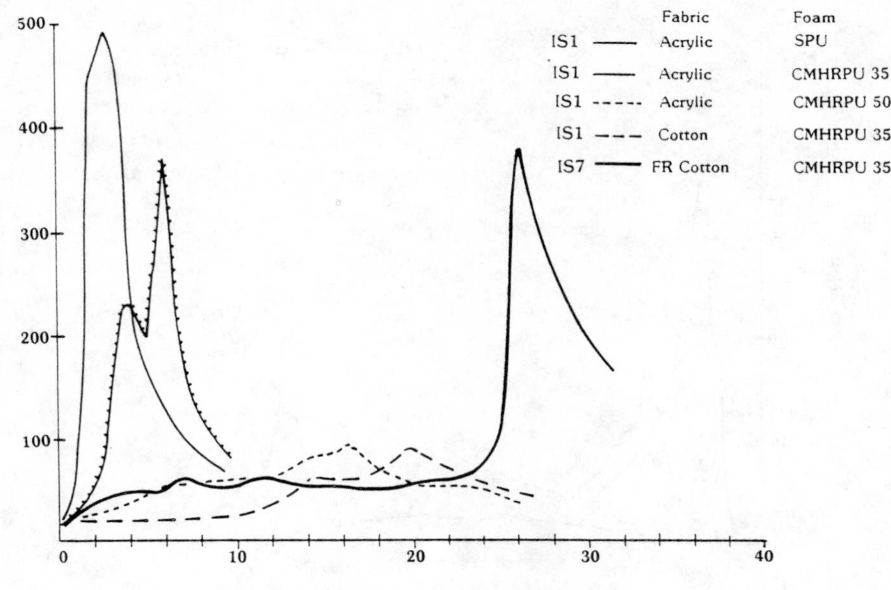

Fig. 3. Comparison of lintel temperatures from burning upholstered chairs containing polyurethane foams.

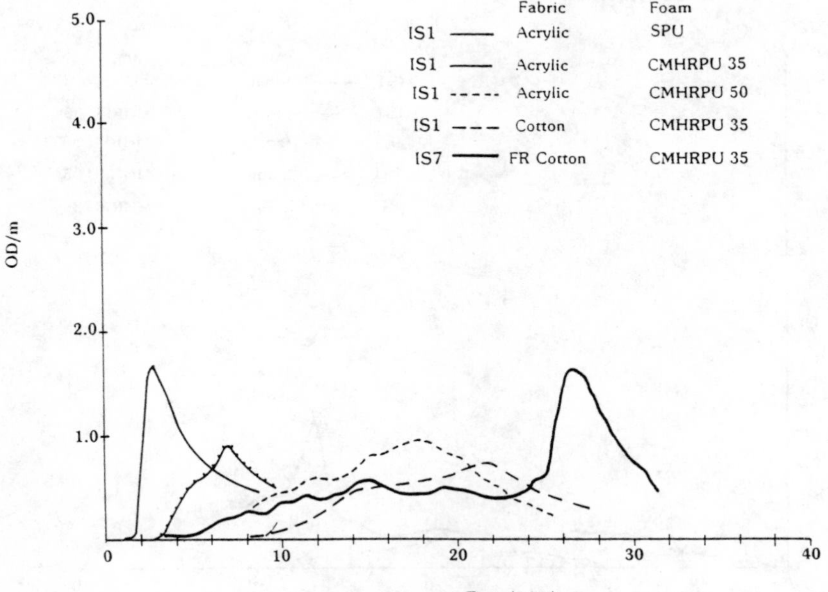

Fig. 4. Comparison of optical density of smoke from burning upholstered chairs containing polyurethane foams.

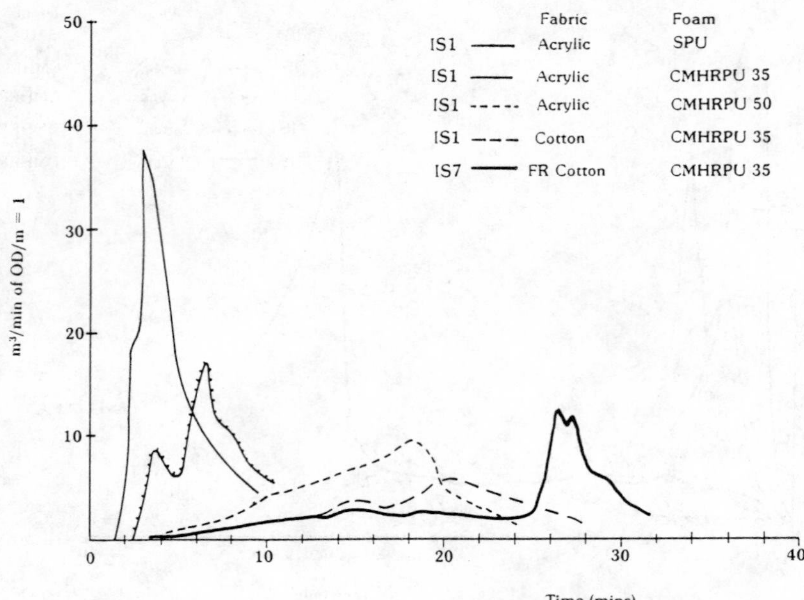

Fig. 5. Comparison of incremental smoke volume production rates from burning upholstered chairs containing polyurethane foams.

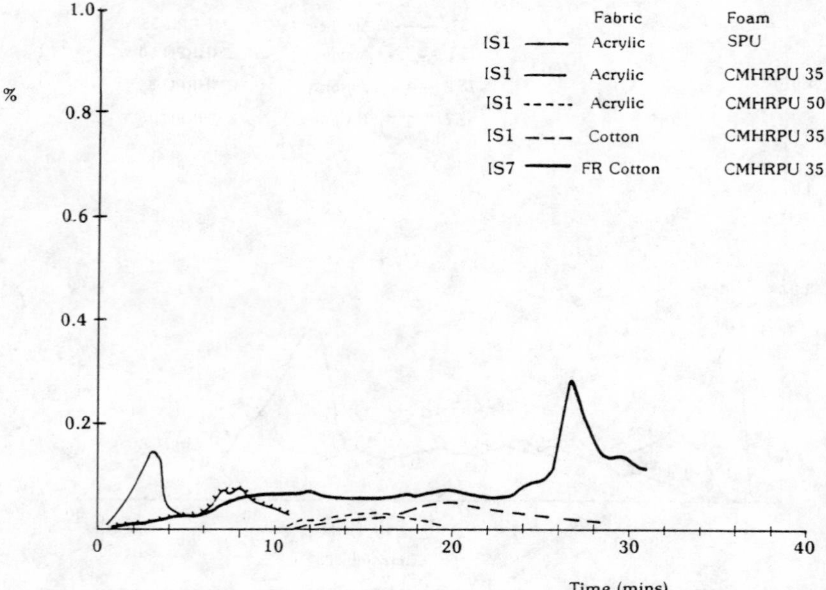

Fig. 6. Comparison of carbon monoxide concentrations from burning chairs containing polyurethane foams.

was considerably greater than that produced by standard polyurethane foam chairs. The peak carbon monoxide concentration was also higher. The relative values of peak temperatures differed with the different types of fabric.

Chairs covered with acrylic fabrics with the medium density combustion modified high resilience polyurethane foam burned in a similar manner to that described for the chairs containing standard and high resilience polyurethane foam except that the peak fire development was delayed by a further 1 to 2 minutes.

The use of the cotton fabric significantly decreased the initial burning rate and resulted in a slow burning fire in which the fabric and outer polyurethane foam layer burned leaving a charred surface to the underlying polyurethane foam. A similar pattern was observed with the acrylic covered chair with the high density combustion modified polyurethane foam.

Combining the cotton fabric with the high density combustion modified high resilience polyurethane foam increased the ignition resistance of the chair which did not sustain burning when ignited with the No.1 gas flame. The use of a larger ignition source gave a different burning pattern which was similar to that of the chairs with the ignition resistant fabrics described below.

Two chairs were burned in which medium density combustion modified high resilience polyurethane foam were covered with ignition resistant fabrics. The first chair was a Chesterfield design and was covered with a mixed wool/cotton fabric and the second chair was of the standard design with a flame retarded cotton fabric. The fabric was similar to the untreated cotton fabrics used for the second series of standard chairs. Both chairs were ignited and burned in a similar manner although the FR cotton covered chair took considerably longer to reach the peak fire development. Flames spread slowly over part of the back arm and seat and penetrated into the seat corner. The fire burned quite slowly with limited surface spread but developed below the corner in and below the platform. This fire burned steadily. Although it could not be observed, it is thought that the combustion modified polyurethane foam cushion tended to melt into the platform zone below the which contained the fire. As this fire built up, so it became hotter and the seat arms and back of the chair became involved. The resultant fire destroyed the chair upholstery leaving the wooden frame which was badly charred.

A summary of the main fire parameters is given in Figure 2.

Chairs containing standard or polyurethane foam in composites which failed or passed the cigarette test gave generally similar results although chairs with heavy viscose fabrics tended to burn more slowly than acrylic, polypropylene and lightweight cotton fabric fabrics. Used, dusty chairs burned in a similar manner to the new chairs.

The use of medium density combustion modified high resilience polyurethane foam even with match ignitable acrylic fabrics slightly increased the time to rapid fire development and reduced the fire smoke volume rate of production and density. The use of lightweight char-forming cotton fabric with medium density combustion modified polyurethane foam and the acrylic fabric with the high density combustion modified high resilience polyurethane foam changed the burning pattern. Relatively small flames burned across the chair and a considerable amount of upholstery foam remained after the test although this effect does not occur with higher intensity fires, e.g. acrylic fabric with medium density combustion modified high resilience polyurethane foam.

Rates of smoke and peak carbon monoxide concentrations were relatively low.

The use of ignition resistant, char-forming fabrics with combustion modified high resilience polyurethane foam gave the best results with the time to rapid fire growth increasing to 17-26 minutes even though a much larger ignition source (No.7) was used to cause sustained burning. It must be noted that this type of upholstery could not be ignited by the smaller sources which were used to ignite the earlier tests.

Peak carbon monoxide concentrations and peak temperatures were respectively similar and slightly lower than the chairs containing standard polyurethane foam but the smoke densities and the rates of smoke production were lower.

Although it was not possible to determine the rates of heat release in the chair tests, the maximum temperatures reflect this parameter. Babrauskas (12) has published values for the rates of heat release of polyurethane foams determined in the NBS cone calorimeter. The implications of these data are that chairs of similar design and with similar fabrics containing combustion modified high resilience polyurethane foam will generate heat at less than 70% of the rate of similar chairs containing standard polyurethane foam. The values in Table 9 were obtained at 25-35 kW/m^2 but the rates of heat release increase with increasing heat flux. Values for standard polyurethane foam increase from about 450 to 950 to 1800 kW/m^2 as the incident heat flux is increased from 25 to 50 to 75 kW/m^2. (12)

TABLE 9

Rates of Heat Release of Polyurethane Foam(12)

Polyurethane Foam	Rate of Heat Release kW/m^2
Standard	> 400
FR additive	> 400
Combustion Modified (melamine)	< 280

CONCLUSIONS

These conclusions are based on a relatively few (18) chair tests and relate to a series of single chairs burned in a brick room ($34m^3$ volume) ventilated by a single open doorway. The combustion modified high resilience polyurethane used in the chairs was Beaverco PLC Safeguard based on melamine/PIPA technology.

1. The ignitability and burning behaviour of upholstered chairs is affected by the covering fabric, the soft upholstery and the design. Used chairs appear to burn in a similar manner to new chairs.

2. With careful selection of covering fabrics, and soft upholstery it is possible to:-

(1) increase ignition resistance to give protection against cigarettes, matches and probably larger ignition sources

(2) significantly increase the time to rapid burning from 3-4 minutes to 17-26 minutes

(3) to improve the general burning behaviour of the chair by reducing smoke density and its rate of generation

(4) by implication to reduce the rate of heat generation by more than 30%.

3. The combination of ignition resistant fabrics and combustion modified high resilience polyurethane foam together represents a major improvement over upholstery with flammable fabrics with standard and high resilience polyurethane foams.

Comment

Although the use of ignition resistant fabrics and combustion modified high resilience polyurethane foams represents a very significant improvement over previous soft upholstery, the initially slow burning fire eventually increases and the resultant fire, although less serious than that of previous upholstered furniture may still cause a hazard to life. The use of smoke alarms will warn of the fire danger in the very early stages of a fire. It is suggested that the combination of ignition resistant fabrics, combustion modified polyurethane foam with a smoke alarm offers a major improvement in fire safety.

REFERENCES

(1) K.N.Palmer, W.Taylor, K.T.Paul, Fire Hazards of Plastics in Furniture and Furnishings BRE Garston. Current papers CP18/74, CP3/75 and CP21/76, 1974, 1975 and 1976.

(2) Flexible PU Foam, Its Uses and Misuses. British Rubber Manufacturers Association, London 1976, revised 1983.

(3) F.H.Prager, W.C. Darr, J.F. Wood, Cellular Polymers Vol.3, No.3 1984.

(4) Department of the Environment Crown Suppliers, London. Fire Technical FTS3, 5, 6 and 15.

(5) Home Office, London 1978.

(6) Consumer Protection, The Upholstered Furniture (Safety) Regulation 1980, HMSO, London.

(7) Draft Guide to Fire Precautions in Existing Residential Care Premises. Draft Guide to Fire Precaution in Hospitals. Home Office, Scottish Home and Health Departments, 1983.

(8) BS5852: Part 1. Methods of Test for Ignitability of Upholstered Composites for Seating by smokers materials. BSI London 1979.

(9) BS5852: Part 2. Methods of Test for Ignitability of Upholstered Composites for Seating by Flaming Sources. BSI London 1982.

(10) Consumer Protection. The Upholstered Furniture (Safety) (Amendment Regulations) 1983. HMSO, London.

(11) BS6807. Methods of Test for the Ignitability of Mattresses with Primary and Secondary Sources of Ignition.

(12) V.Babrouskas, First European Conference on Fire and Furniture, Brussels, 1988.

(13) Consumer Protection. The Furniture and Furnishings (Fire) (Safety) Regulations 1988.

(14) K.T.Paul, Urethanes Technology, June 1987.

(15) J.F.Szabat and J.A.Gaetano, 6th SPI Polyurethane Conf. San Diego, California. 2-4 November 1983.

(16) K.T.Paul and S.D.Christian. J.of Fire Science, Vol.5, No.3, May/June 1987.

Protozoan Parasites and Water

Protozoan Parasites and Water

Edited by

W.B. Betts

University of York, UK

D. Casemore

Public Health Laboratory, Rhyl, UK

C. Fricker

Thames Water Utilities, Reading, UK

H. Smith

Stobhill General Hospital, Glasgow, UK

J. Watkins

Yorkshire Water Enterprises Ltd, Bradford, UK

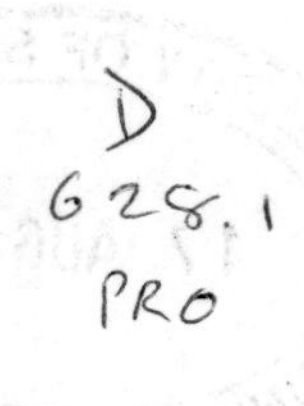

The proceedings of a meeting organised by the Royal Society of Chemistry Water Chemistry Forum, the Institution of Water and Environmental Management, the Society of Chemical Industry Environmental Biotechnology Group, the Institute of Chemical Engineers, and the Institute for Applied Biology. The meeting was held on 26–28 September, 1994 at the University of York.

Special Publication No. 168

ISBN 0-85404-755-7

A catalogue record of this book is available from the British Library.

Published by The Royal Society of Chemistry, Thomas Graham House, Science Park, Cambridge CB4 4WF

Typeset by IFAB Communications, York
Printed in Great Britain by Bookcraft (Bath) Ltd

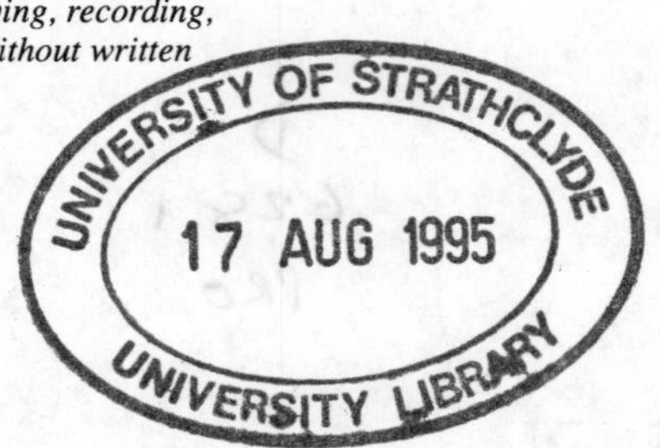

Preface

Protozoan parasites, particularly those of the gastrointestinal tract, are a major world-wide cause of human morbidity and a significant contributor to mortality. Over recent years knowledge of waterborne disease caused by parasites, particularly *Giardia lamblia* and *Cryptosporidium parvum*, has increased and there have been marked improvements in our understanding of parasite distribution and associated epidemiological and clinical aspects. Methods for the identification of these organisms are tedious and time consuming with the potential for inaccuracies, and there has been a great emphasis on improving detection and characterisation techniques, yielding a wide range of different systems to escape or confuse the microbial analyst. Although most parasites can be removed in treatment stages prior to disinfection it is known that free chlorine inactivation of residual cells of some organisms (especially *Cryptosporidium*) is not efficient and this disinfectant is used in the majority of water treatment systems. There has been much work to improve the removal and inactivation of parasites during water treatments, notably using filtration and ozonation methods, but a great deal more research is required.

The following proceedings represent the contributions of speakers at an international conference on Protozoan Parasites and Water held at the University of York, UK in September 1994. The objective of the conference was to promote an improved understanding of the occurrence, significance and detection of protozoan parasites in recreational, raw and potable water, with reference to water treatment and disinfection practices. This was achieved by inviting international experts to discuss the approaches adopted by various countries in handling the potentially difficult problem of protozoan parasites in water. The latest techniques of detection, confirmation and viability assessment for various parasites were described, and emerging pathogens that could represent a future health threat were highlighted. Certain case studies were also presented in order that lessons learned from these experiences could be disseminated to an international audience thus helping maintain or improve the quality of water world-wide.

We would like to express our thanks to the conference Organising Committee, and the Scientific Committee for refereeing all of the papers and posters submitted. We are indebted to Sir John Badenoch for the historical perspective provided in his opening address and to Sir Gordon Jones for his concluding remarks and recognition of the importance of the conference by Water Companies. Finally, my thanks go to Dr Julian White and his team at IFAB Communications at the University of York who had various significant roles in all aspects of the conference and proceedings.

W.B. Betts, D.P. Casemore, C.R. Fricker, H.V. Smith and J. Watkins
April 1995

Contents

Part 2: Distribution of Protozoan Parasites

Part 3: Detection Methods for Protozoan Parasites

Welcome Address

Sir John Badenoch DM, FRCP, FRCP Ed

It is a pleasure to welcome you all to this conference on Protozoan Parasites and Water, and especially to welcome our friends from overseas who have made such a great contribution to the subject. Their work is already well known to us, but it is good to have them here in person.

I think that you will also agree that the organisers of the conference are to be congratulated for putting together such an interesting and stimulating programme.

My interest in parasites began over fifty years ago when I was preparing my DM thesis. It was on the subject of malabsorption and I was determined to draw together all the known and probable causes of the disorder. In the course of my studies I came upon the case of a little boy who lived in an orphanage soon after the turn of the century - pretty grim places they were in those days - who appeared to be suffering from Coeliac Disease, the most common cause of malabsorption. His stools contained *Giardia lamblia* in large numbers and I could not help wondering if the parasites could have had anything to do with his condition.

Ten or fifteen years ago a conference on 'Protozoan Parasites and Water' would probably have aroused the reaction 'What on earth is all that about...? It is true, that with a few notable exceptions, scientists and for that matter the medical profession, were almost totally ignorant of the threat to the public health posed by these organisms if they entered the water supply in any numbers. We had some knowledge of giardiasis as it had affected returning travellers from the former Soviet Union and those that followed the 'hippy trail' across Eastern Europe to South East Asia, and of course the ravages of *Entamoeba histolytica* were well known, but there was little interest in these organisms as a cause of disease in this country. As is so often the case the veterinarians were ahead of us in recognising the hazard posed by parasites from domestic animals, but little of this reached the medical press.

For us in the United Kingdom at least, the outbreak of cryptosporidiosis in Oxford and Swindon at the end of 1988 and the beginning of 1989 changed all that. Possibly as many as 5000 persons, many of them children, were affected by a severe diarrhoeal illness and - awful thought - the disease was shown to have been spread through the public water supply.

As you can imagine, the media had an absolute 'field day' with tales of deadly viruses and 'horror bugs', but for once they were useful because the public outcry stimulated the government to set up a group of experts to look into the matter. Our remit was to examine the extent of the problem posed by the presence of *Cryptosporidium* in water, to assess its significance for the public health, and to formulate advice on what might be done to protect the water supplies in the future.

There were three aspects of the problem that had aroused particular public concern. It was generally accepted that the water supply was safe. You crossed the Channel at your peril, but anything that came out of the taps in this country could be drunk with safety. Now this was no longer the case. Secondly, some of those affected in Oxford and Swindon had been quite seriously ill and the doctors admitted that they had no specific treatment for the disease, and lastly and worst of all, chlorine that universal safety net of the water industry had been shown to be unable to kill the organism in any concentration that could be used for the treatment of drinking water.

The water industry faced with a new and unknown hazard urgently needed help. It appeared that the normal processes of water treatment were not enough to render the water supply safe and they were being pilloried by the Press and the media for not having dealt with a danger that they hardly knew existed.

For me personally, one of the best features of the expert group was that it contained representatives from many different disciplines, water scientists, practising engineers, clinical and environmental microbiologists, clinicians, community medical specialists, representatives of the Public Health Laboratory Service and Veterinary experts. I have always felt that scientific advances are most easily achieved when allied disciplines meet to tackle common problems and this soon proved to be the case. It became apparent that the answers to many of the questions about the organism itself, its occurrence in nature, pathogenicity for man and reaction to the processes of water treatment were unknown. As a result, largely due to the industry and foresight of Mike Healey, the then Director for the Drinking Water Inspectorate, a very large programme of research was put in hand in an attempt to find at least some of the answers.

Now, three years later, we are in a much stronger position. We know more about the biology of the organism, we are learning about its pathogenicity, although the infective dose for man is still proving elusive. We know that it occurs quite commonly in low numbers in virtually all surface waters, but that the massive contamination that was responsible for the outbreak in Swindon and Oxford was a most unusual event and we are slowly but surely beginning to improve on the traditional methods for the detection, separation, concentration and identification of the organism in environmental samples which, in the past, have been so inaccurate and time consuming and have demanded so much skill from the microscopists concerned.

This week we shall be discussing some of the results of this research and learning from our colleagues from overseas about the progress they are making in dealing not only with the problems posed by *Cryptosporidium* but also by *Giardia* and other protozoan parasites that are coming to the fore.

I am sure that we shall have a most interesting few days, but we live in a practical world, and we must remember as scientists that one of our main aims must be to help the water undertakings to provide a supply of water which is as safe as we can make it and in which the general public can have confidence.

Some Clinical Perspectives on Waterborne Parasitic Protozoa

R.W.A. Girdwood
Scottish Parasite Diagnostic Laboratory, Stobhill NHS Trust, Glasgow, G21 3UW, UK

Introduction

Human parasitic protozoans primarily affecting the gastrointestinal tract are a major cause of morbidity and contribute to significant mortality worldwide. The three most prevalent gastrointestinal protozoans; *Giardia duodenalis*, *Cryptosporidium parvum* and *Entamoeba histolytica* cause more than one thousand million infections and contribute to more than a million deaths annually (Walsh, 1986; Warhurst and Smith, 1992). All three parasites are transmitted by the faecal-oral route and inadequate sanitation, and potable water delivery systems play a major role in the epidemiology and transmission of these organisms. Symptoms vary according to the species and strain of the protozoan, and the age, immunological and nutritional status of the infected individual. Current methods of detecting cysts or oocysts in water are very inefficient. This, taken with the fact that only very small numbers of parasites are required to initiate human infection (cf. bacteria), means that the role of water in the transmission of the above parasites, *Balantidium coli, Toxoplasma gondii*, *Isospora belli* and *Cyclospora cayetanensis* remains to be elucidated.

Giardia duodenalis (Giardiasis)

The taxonomy of the species of *Giardia* is confusing. Based on morphological differences Filice (1952) described three species, *G. agilis*, *G. muris* and *G. duodenalis*. The human parasite has the morphology of *G.duodenalis* and has the synonyms *G. lamblia* and *G. intestinalis*. *G. duodenalis* is an intestinal flagellate parasite of the small intestine of man (and other mammals) which exists in two forms - the cyst which is the resistant transmissive stage and the trophozoite which is the feeding, multiplication and pathogenic stage. Cysts are voided in the faeces of infected individuals. Infection is by the faecal-oral route and waterborne outbreaks are well recognised (Craun, 1986). As apparently identical parasites are found in domestic, pet and wild animals the importance of these animals as zoonotic reservoirs for human infection is the subject of much investigation and debate (Faubert, 1988; Bemrick and Erlandsen, 1988).

G. duodenalis is currently the most common protozoan intestinal parasite of man with infection rates of up to 20% of children occurring in developing countries (Gilman *et al.* 1985). Ingested cysts release two trophozoites in the upper small intestine. The trophozoites multiply by binary fission and adhere to the mucosa by means of sucking discs. They do not invade the mucosal surface. Cysts are produced in the lower small intestine and are voided discontinuously in the faeces. In cases with profuse and frequent diarrhoea trophozoites are excreted. Infection can be asymptomatic (c.15%) but usually symptoms occur 1-2 weeks post infection. The acute phase of giardiasis is usually short-lived and is characterised by flatulence with sometimes sulphurous belching, abdominal distention and cramps. Diarrhoea is initially frequent and watery but later becomes bulky, sometimes frothy, greasy and offensive and the stools may float on water. Blood and mucus are usually absent and pus cells are not a feature on microscopy.

In the chronic stages of the disease malaise, weight loss and other features of malabsorption may become prominent. By this time, stools are usually pale or yellow and are frequent and of small volume. Occasionally episodes of constipation intervene with nausea and diarrhoea precipitated by the ingestion of food. Malabsorption of vitamins A and B12 and D-xylose can occur. In young children 'failure to thrive' is frequently due to giardiasis, and all infants being investigated for causes of malabsorption should have a diagnosis of giardiasis excluded.

Cyst excretion can approach 107 g-1 faeces (Danciger and Lopez, 1975). The prepatent period (time from infection to the initial detection of parasites in stools) is on average 9.1 days. The incubation period is usually 1-2 weeks. As the prepatent period can exceed the incubation period, initially a patient can have symptoms in the absence of cysts in the faeces (Jokipii and Jokipii, 1977).

Diagnosis of giardiasis is dependent upon the demonstration of intact parasites (cysts and/or trophozoites) by microscopy, parasite products by immunoassay and/or parasite DNA in faeces or duodenal/jejunal aspirates and serology. As cyst excretion can be intermittent, and some infected persons may be low cyst excretors, diagnosis, based on the detection of cysts in faecal concentrates can be inefficient. For example, the likelihood of detecting cysts, by bright-field microscopy, in a single stool sample from an infected human is between 35-50%, whereas between six and ten stool specimens from an infected human need to be examined to achieve a detection rate of 70-90% (Saveitz and Faust, 1942), reflecting the erratic nature of cyst excretion in symptomatic patients.

The erratic nature of cyst excretion, the requirement for experienced staff for microscopic identification and the low detection rate have precipitated the development of alternative methods for the diagnosis of giardiasis. Trophozoites can be demonstrated in duodenal/jejunal aspirates or biopsies when stool microscopy is negative, but it should be noted that on occasion positive stools have been found when aspirates are negative.

Fluorescence microscopy, using fluorescein isothiocynanate (FITC)-labelled monoclonal antibodies, reactive with surface-exposed genus-specific cyst wall epitopes has been reported to be more effective for detecting cysts than light microscopy (Perez *et al.* 1994). Similarly detection of *Giardia* antigen by ELISA in microscopically-negative stools is being increasingly utilised (e.g. Green *et al.* 1985).

Cryptosporidium parvum (Cryptosporidiosis)

C. parvum is a coccidian parasite with a world-wide distribution. The parasite is transmitted in the oocyst stage by the faecal-oral route. Water is important in disseminating the oocysts which are resistant to many potable water treatment processes and waterborne outbreaks are increasingly reported (D'Antonio *et al.* 1985). The zoonotic component of the epidemiology of cryptosporidiosis is well recognised and domestic cattle have been implicated in both direct (faecal-oral) and indirect (via water) human infection outbreaks (Tzipori, 1983).

The spherical oocysts measure c. 5 μm in diameter and release four sporozoites in the small intestine when ingested by a suitable host. The sporozoites invade the small intestinal epithelial cells and undergo successive asexual (merogonic) and sexual multiplication cycles. Mature meronts release merozoites which invade more epithelial cells to differentiate into micro- and macro-gamonts. The resultant gametocytes combine to produce immature oocysts. Unlike most coccidians the entire life cycle occurs in a single host. Human infection usually produces a self-limiting enteritis. Surveys of faecal excretion of oocysts indicate that asymptomatic infection is uncommon. An incubation period of 2-14 days is followed by watery diarrhoea which may be explosive at onset. Cramping abdominal pains and episodes of diarrhoea are frequently precipitated by the taking of food. Malaise, fever, anorexia, nausea, vomiting and flatulence are frequent symptoms while malabsorption is a less common feature. There is no peripheral leukocytosis. Symptoms usually last 10-14 days although faecal excretion can persist for a further two weeks. The incidence of infection is greatest in childhood and the decrease in infection with age is attributed to the acquisition of protective immunity (Current *et al.* 1983, Tzipori, 1988). In immunocompromised patients, especially AIDS patients, *C. parvum* infection causes severe intractable cholera-like diarrhoea with intense nausea. This is particularly distressing because, as yet, there is no specific effective treatment. The profuse diarrhoea results in dehydration and wasting and is frequently a terminal event in AIDS patients. In such severely compromised patients, infection of the entire length of the gastrointestinal tract from fauces to the anus can occur and biliary and respiratory epithelial involvement are sometimes found (Pitlaik *et al.* 1983).

Diagnosis is by the demonstration of oocysts in stained faecal smears or faecal concentrates. A modified Ziehl-Neelsen or the phenol auramine stain are most frequently used. The former stains the oocysts magenta while the latter makes oocysts fluoresce apple green when viewed with ultra-violet light (Garcia *et al.* 1983).

Entamobea histolytica (Amoebiasis)

The amoeba, *E. histolytica* is transmitted in the cystic stage by the faecal-oral route. Homosexual transmission is increasingly recognised but is globally a minor route of infection. While the organism has a worldwide distribution, amoebiasis is typically a disease which occurs most frequently where poor sanitation prevails. Direct waterborne transmission is thought to be relatively infrequent. Although *E. histolytica* has been described in monkeys, dogs, cats, pigs and rats there are no major reservoirs of animal infection. Some 10% of the world population is said to be infected, with c 50,000 deaths per annum (Walsh, 1986).

The trophozoites of *E. histolytica* emerge from the ingested cyst in the lower small intestine and typically live and multiply in the caecum and colon. The majority of infections are asymptomatic. Intestinal symptoms of colicky pains and abdominal tenderness result from acute proctocolitis with the passage of blood and mucus (dysentery).

Fever and leukocytosis are not usually a feature, although in fulminant amoebiasis, they are. Fulminant amoebiasis is a rare form of amoebiasis which occurs in the malnourished or otherwise compromised population and results in colonic necrosis and a high mortality.

In amoebic dysentery the symptoms maybe either self-limiting or run a more prolonged course. In the colon non-dysenteric colitis and amoeboma - a tumour like granulomatous response to the parasite, may occur. Acute complications include perforation of the colon with resulting amoebic peritonitis, intestinal haemorrhage and intussusception. Chronic intestinal sequelae are post-amoebic colitis and colonic stricture.

Extraintestinal manifestations of amoebic infection arise from haemotogenous spread via the portal system or by direct extension. In the former abscesses occur most frequently in the liver and less frequently in others sites such as lung and brain. Direct extension of infection results in mucocutaneous ulceration of the perianal region. The so-called abscesses consist of necrotic parenchymal tissue and stromal cells surrounded at the periphery by amoebic trophozoites and fibrin. Cysts are never found in extraintestinal amoebic lesions. Liver abscess occurs most frequently in areas of high amoebic endemicity such as India and Mexico. Abscesses occur predominantly in the right lobe (greater than 75%) and are usually single. Symptoms are very variable with fever the most constant feature. Pain and tenderness at the right costal margin increase as symptoms and signs as the abscess enlarges. Jaundice is unusual. Liver abscesses, as they enlarge, can 'point' and discharge through the skin, may extend through the diaphragm into the right lung or rupture in to the peritoneal cavity (Cook, 1992). The wide spectrum of amoebic infection from totally asymptomatic to aggressive invasive disease is still incompletely understood. The consensus view is that, based on enzyme electrophoresis, only nine of the currently recognised twenty two strains (zymodemes) have the intrinsic potential for pathogenically and pathogenic and non-pathogenic strains are immutable (Sargeaunt, 1988). Host factors such as intestinal flora, nutritional status and immunity have been invoked to attempt to explain the spectrum produced by pathogenic strains. Because of these varied manifestations the incubation period cannot be defined accurately. Earliest symptoms can occur 7-10 days after ingestion of cysts but the upper limit of incubation may extend to years. Diagnosis of intestinal amoebiasis is usually by the microscopic detection of trophozoites, which are only found in freshly voided faeces; or cysts, which being the transmissive stage, remain demonstrable in stools for some days. Trophozoites are readily recognisable by their characteristic movement and the presence of ingested erythrocytes within the cytoplasm. The cysts are c.12 μm in diameter and, when mature, contain four nuclei each with a central karyosome. A chromidial bar when present is diagnostic. Frequently special stains such as trichome or iron haematoxylin are required for the demonstration of the diagnostic nuclear details. Other diagnostic methods include characteristic sigmoidoscopic appearances and rectal biopsy. Invasive amoebiaisis - local or systemic - is usually diagnosed by the demonstration of serum antibodies by such methods as the fluorescent antibody test. The detection of trophozoites in 'aspirated' abscess material is less frequently used in current practice. In only about one third of proven amoebic abscesses are trophozoites found. Amoebic culture of aspirates demonstrated is similarly infrequently used (Cook, 1992).

Toxoplasma gondii (Toxoplasmosis)

T. gondii is a coccidian parasite with a complex life cycle and complex epidemiology. The only known definitive hosts are the Felidae. Cats become infected by either ingesting oocysts which can contaminate the environment after being voided in cat faeces or, more frequently, by the ingestion of tissue cysts contained in the carcasses of prey animals such as mice and birds. In either case released organisms invade the epithelial cells of the small intestine and undergo both asexual (schizogony) and sexual (sporogony) multiplication which culminate in the excretion of millions of oocysts in the faeces some 5 days after the ingestion of tissue cysts or 3 weeks after the ingestion of oocysts. Although faecal excretion is limited to some 3 weeks the oocysts can survive in a favourable environment for over 1 year. The oocysts which are subspherical, c. 10-12 µm in diameter, require some days in the environment to mature and become infective. The time for sporulation (and infectivity) to occur is dependent upon ambient temperature, moisture and oxygen. *T. gondii* is widely distributed in nature and because of the dual modes of transmission infection occurs in both herbivorous and carnivorous animals. The role of the cat in human infection cannot be ascertained definitively and must vary in different communities (Wallace, 1973). Seroepidemiological studies suggest that the eating of undercooked meat containing tissue cysts is the major route of human infection. The waterborne route for human infection has been documented (Benenson, *et al.* 1982) and *Toxoplasma*-like oocysts have been identified on potable water filtrates. The majority of human infections are asymptomatic and in many communities c. 90% of the healthy adult population have demonstrable circulating anti-*Toxoplasma* antibodies which indicate past infection or concurrent 'dormant' infection (Remington, 1974). Clinical manifestations cover a wide spectrum and will vary with the immunological status of the host. Only 20% of acute infections in adults are symptomatic and when present symptoms usually simulate an upper respiratory infection (i.e. fever, sore throat and enlarged cervical lymph glands) (McCabe *et al.* 1987). It seems likely that after recovery (with or without specific antiprotozoal treatment) tissue cysts remain dormant but viable in muscle, connective and nervous tissue. When such individuals become immunosuppressed either through therapy (e.g. steroids) or disease, (e.g. AIDS), reactivation of tissue cysts can result in dissemination of disease with the development of toxoplasmic encephalitis (Luft and Remington, 1988). Up to 25% of AIDS patients develop toxoplasmic encephalitis. Transplant patients are doubly vulnerable in that therapeutic immunosuppression can result in reactivation of latent infection in the recipient or the acquisition of new infection from the donated organ. Congenital infection is a major medical problem and occurs when the mother becomes infected (usually totally asymptomatically) during pregnancy. While congenital infection may have no sequelae congenital disease tends to be more severe the earlier the foetus is infected. Thus abortion, stillbirth, congenital heart defects, hydrocephalus and cataracts occur most frequently in foetuses infected during the first trimester. Choroidoretinitis is the most frequent complication of congenital toxoplasmosis and while such ocular disease may be apparent at birth it is now realised that congenitally acquired toxoplasmic choroidoretinitis can first become manifest at 10-20 yrs of age (Wilson *et al.* 1994).

Diagnosis of toxoplasmosis is usually by serological methods. Conventionally the presence of specific IgM indicates current or recent (in the first year) infection. More specific indicators of recently acquired infection of particular relevance in pregnancy depend on evaluation of specific IgE and IgA assays. Polymerase chain reaction (PCR) techniques for the detection of the parasite per se in immunosuppressed individuals have been developed and are being evaluated (Ashburton *et al.* 1994).

Balantidium coli (*Balantidiasis*)

B. coli is the only ciliate parasite of man. The epidemiology of human balantidiasis is not, as yet, understood. *B. coli* is a fairly common parasite of pigs in most parts of the world and it is widely believed that pigs act as a reservoir for human infection (Arean and Koppisch, 1956). However, attempts to produce experimental human infections using porcine isolates have, to date, consistently failed. It is postulated that man is usually innately resistant to *B. coli* and only changes in this resistance permit infection. Even when infection is established, disease symptoms are the exception (less than one fifth of infected individuals have symptoms). It has been suggested that diet, nutritional status and intestinal flora play roles in protecting against the establishment of infection. Transmission is usually by the faecal-oral route, the cysts being passed in human/animal faeces. A waterborne outbreak implicating pigs as the source has been described (Walzer *et al.* 1972). Morphologically-identical parasites have been found in monkeys, guinea pigs, cats, dogs and horses. The role of these animals and indeed the waterborne route in human infection is not known.

When human infection is established the trophozoites released from the ingested cysts live in the lower small intestine and extend into the colon where they invade the mucosa. Even when mucosal invasion occurs symptoms do not necessarily become manifest. When disease occurs it is frequently indistinguishable from other forms of dysentery (i.e. diarrhoea with the passage of blood and mucus). Nausea, epigastric pain, vomiting and intestinal colic can accompany these dysenteric symptoms. Chronic colitis as a result of balantidiasis has been described. The majority of patients recover even without treatment. Occasionally perforation of a colonic ulcer results in peritonitis.

Diagnosis is by the demonstration of the large unmistakable cysts c. 60 µm long. In dysenteric stools the motile trophozoites c. 50 - 300 µm long are similarly unmistakable.

Isospora belli (*Isosporiasis*)

I. belli is a coccidian parasite with a worldwide distribution. Man is thought to be the only host. Infection is most prevalent in Central and South America, the Caribbean Islands and Africa. Transmission is by the faecal-oral route and the role of water in transmission, whilst theoretically possible, is not known. The transmissive stage is the oocyst which is c. 30 x 15 µm and contains two sporocysts, each of which matures to produce four sporozoites. When ingested, the mature oocyst releases the sporocysts in the small intestine. The sporozoites invade the small intestinal mucosa when successive asexual (schizogony) and sexual (sporogony) cycles extend along the invaded epithelial surfaces. Following the sexual cycles oocysts are released into the intestinal lumen and voided in the faeces. Such oocysts are immature and require 2-3 days to become infective for a new host. The incubation period is about 7 days and infections are usually asymptomatic. Diarrhoea of varying severity is the main symptom and this may be accompanied by abdominal pain which again can vary from mild to severe. Malabsorption has been described (Brandborg, 1970). *I. belli* infections are usually self limiting and last about two weeks. Like many of the organisms of low pathogenicity, *I. belli* has assumed new importance as a cause of protracted diarrhoea in the immunocompromised host (De Hovitz *et al.* 1986).

Diagnosis is by the microscopic demonstration of the characteristic oocysts in faeces. Concentration techniques many be necessary as the oocysts are often scanty.

Cyclospora cayetanensis

This organism was first documented in 1979 by Ashford when it was thought to be a blue-green algae-like organism (cyanobacterium). Now recognised as a cyclosporan the life cycle in man has not been elucidated and the zooepidemiology is unknown. To date hundreds, rather than thousands, of human cases have been recognised. Cases have been described in inhabitants in, or visitors to Central and South America, Morocco, Nepal, India and Pakistan, South East Asia, the Solomon Islands and Papua New Guinea.

Indigenous cases have also been described in the USA and include a dormitory outbreak in Chicago where water was implicated. The incubation period is estimated at 2-11 days and symptoms resemble those of cryptosporidiosis with watery diarrhoea (c. six stools/day) nausea, anorexia, abdominal cramps and myalgia. Malabsorption with flatulence and bloating have also been described. Stools do not contain erythrocytes or leukcocytes and patients are usually afebrile. Symptoms, while frequently prolonged for up to six weeks, are usually self limiting in the immunologically-competent patient. Unsporulated spherical oocysts 8-10 μm in diameter and containing granular material are excreted in the stools in moderate numbers. Diagnosis is by the demonstration of these oocysts by conventional microscopy of stools. Scanty oocysts can be concentrated by the formol-ether technique (Wurtz, 1994).

Naegleria fowleri

N. fowleri is a free-living (non-parasitic) amoeba which is a rare cause of meningoencephalitis usually referred to as primary amoebic meningoencephalitis (PAM). The organisms have been found in soil, lakes, rivers and industrial cooling waters (John, 1982) throughout the world. The organism feeds and reproduces as a trophozoite but can transform to a flagellate stage when food is scarce or, under more adverse conditions such as low temperatures, encystment occurs. Cysts can survive for several months at 4°C. Infection is acquired by the trophozoites entering the olfactory region of the brain via the cribiform plate in the nose. Accordingly infection occurs in healthy children or young adults who have a recent history of having swum in or fallen into warm freshwater lakes or pools. The first three cases of infection were described from Australia (Fowler and Carter, 1965). Since then, more than one hundred cases have been described and only two are known to have survived the infection. Symptoms usually occur within a week of exposure and disturbances of smell or taste occur early to be followed by headache, fever, vomiting and neck stiffness. The disease is usually fulminant and fatal within a week of onset of symptoms (Martinez, 1985). At post mortem the olfactory bulbs are typically haemorrhagic and necrotic. Trophozoites are found in the perivascular spaces of small to medium sized arteries. A diffuse purulent meningitis with cerebral oedema is usually found. Because of the rarity of the condition the most important factor in making a diagnosis is to consider the possibility of a *N. fowleri* aetiology in the differential diagnosis of meningoencephalitis in previously healthy children and young adults. Examinations of wet films of cerebrospinal fluid reveals trophozoites in the majority of cases.

References

Arean,V.M., Koppisch, E. Balantidiasis - a review and report of cases. Am. J. Pathol. (1956) 32: 1089-108

Asburn, D., Chatterton J.M.W., Evans, R. *et al.* New techniques in *Toxoplasma* diagnosis. Comm. Dis. Hlth. Scot. Wkly. Rpt. (1994) 28 (50): 3-6

Bemrick, W.J., Erlandsen, S.L. Giardiasis - is it really a zoonosis. Parasitol. Today (1988) 4: 69-71

Brandborg, L.L., Goldberg S.B., Briedenbach W.C. Human coccidiosis - a possible cause of malabsorption N. Engl. J. Med. (1970) 283:1306-13

Cook, G.C. Invasive amoebiasis: dysentery and its major complications. Rev. in Med. Microbiol. (1992) 3: 137-44

Craun, G.F. Waterborne giardiasis in the United States 1965-1984 Lancet (1986) (ii): 513-4

Current, L., Reese, N.C., Ernst, J.V., *et al.* Human cryptosporidiosis in immunocompetent and immunodeficient persons: Studies of an outbreak and experimental transmission. N. Engl. J. Med. (1983) 308: 1252-7

Danciger, M., Lopez, M. Numbers of *Giardia* in the faeces of infected children. Am. J. Trop. Med. Hyg. (1975) 24: 237-242

D'Antonio, R.G., Winn, R.E., Taylor, J.P., *et al.* A waterborne outbreak of cryptosporidiosis in normal hosts. Ann. Intern. Med. (1985) 312: 647-8

De Hovitz, J.A., Pape, J.W., Boncy, M., *et al.* Clinical manifestations and therapy of *Isospora belli* infection in patients with acquired immunodeficiency syndrome. N. Engl. J. Med. (1986) 312: 647-8
Faubert, G.M. Evidence that giardiasis is a zoonosis. Parasitol. Today (1988) 4: 66-8
Filice, F.P. Studies on the cytology and life-history of a *Giardia* from the laboratory rat. University of California Publications in Zoology (1952) 57: 53-145
Fowler, M., Carter, R.F. Acute pyogenic meningitis probably due to Acanthamoeba sp. A preliminary report. Br. Med. J. (1965) ii : 7
Garcia, L.S., Bruckner, D.A., Brewer, T.C., *et al.* Techniques for the recovery and identification of *Cryptosporidium* oocysts from stool specimens. J. Clin. Microbiol. (1983) 18: 185-90
Gilman, R.H., Brown, K.H., Visvesvara, G.S., *et al.* Epidemiology and serology of *Giardia lamblia* in a developing country: Bangladesh. Trans. R. Soc.Trop. Med. Hyg. (1985) 79: 469-73
Green, E.L., Miles, M.A., Warhurst, D.C. Immunodiagnostic detection of *Giardia* antigen in faeces by a rapid visual enzyme linked immunosorbent assay. Lancet (1985). (ii): 691-693
John, D.T. Primary amoebic meningoencephalitis and the biology of *Naegleria fowleri.* Ann, Rev. Microbiol. (1982) 36: 101-3
Jokipii, A.M.M., Jokipii, L. Prepatency of giardiasis. Lancet. (1977) (i): 1095-7
Luft, B.J., Remington, J.S. Toxoplasmic encephalitis J. Infect. Dis. (1988) 157: 1-6
McCabe, R.E., Brooks, R.G., Dorfman, R.F., *et al.* Clinical spectrum in 107 cases of toxoplasmic lymphadenopathy Rev. Inf. Dis. (1987) 9: 74
Martinez, A.J. Free Living Amebas: Natural History, Prevention, Diagnosis, Pathology and Treatment of Disease. Boca Raton FL; CRC Press (1985)
Pitlik, S.D., Fainstein, V., Garza, D., *et al.* Human cryptosporidiosis: spectrum of disease. Report of six cases and review of the literature. Arch. Intern. Med. (1983) 143: 2269-76
Remington, J.S., Toxoplasmosis in the adult. Bull. N.Y. Acad. Med. 50:211
Sargeaunt, P.G. Zymodemes of Entamoeba histolytica. In: Ravdin, J.I., ed. Amoebiasis: human infection by *Entamoeba histolytica.* Edinburgh: Churchill Livingston. (1988) 370-387
Saveitz, W.G., Faust, E.C. The probability of detecting intestinal protozoa by successive stool examinations. Am. J. Trop. Med. (1942) 22: 130-2
Tzipori, S. Cryptosporidiosis in animals and humans. Microbiol. Rev. (1983) 47: 84- 96
Tzipori, S. Cryptosporidiosis in perspective. Adv. Parasitol. (1988) 27: 63-129
Wallace, G.D. The role of the cat in the natural history of *Toxoplasma gondii.* Am. J. Trop. Med. Hyg. (1973) 22: 313-9
Walsh, J.A. Problems in recognition and diagnosis of amoebiasis: estimation of the global magnitude of morbidity and mortality. Rev. Infect. Dis. (1986) 8: 228-38
Walzer, P.D., Judson, F.N., Murphy, K.B., *et al.* Balantidiasis outbreak in Truk. Am. J. Trop. Med. Hyg. (1973) 22:33-41
Wilson, C.D., Remington, J.S., Stagno, S. *et al.* Development of adverse sequelae in children born with subclinical congenital *Toxoplasma* infection. Paediatrics (1980) 66:67-71
Wurtz, R. Cyclospora: A newly identified intestinal pathogen of man. Clin. Inf. Dis. (1994) 18: 620-3

The Problem with Protozoan Parasites

D.P. Casemore
Public Health Laboratory Service, Rhyl, North Wales, UK

Introduction

Water has been recognised as a source of disease since early times and waterborne infection, particularly typhoid and cholera, was increasingly recognised with the emergence of the germ theory of causation of disease in the nineteenth century. Water treatment has, therefore, traditionally been based on the perceived need to control bacterial infections. The emergence of parasites as treatment resistant waterborne pathogens has opened a whole new chapter in the study of the epidemiology of transmission of disease by the water route.

The function of the PHLS is to diagnose and investigate infectious diseases and, by doing so, to attempt, with other agencies, to protect the health of the public. As a part of this work, the role of food and water in the transmission of infection, and more recently the role of enteric protozoa, have been given a high priority. The list of protozoal pathogens which may be transmitted by means of food and water is a long one (Casemore, 1990) and newly recognised species, such as *Cyclospora* and the microsporidia, are being described which are thought might be transmitted by the water route (Bendall and Chiodini, 1994; Sterling, 1994). In recent years outbreaks of water-associated and waterborne giardiasis and crypto-sporidiosis have been increasingly recognised as the most important species involved in both the United Kingdom and North America (Anon, 1990; Rose, 1990; Isaac-Renton *et al*, 1994; MacKenzie *et al* 1994; Anon 1994). In the United States, *Giardia* is the most commonly recognized cause of waterborne outbreaks although *Cryptosporidium* is the cause of the largest outbreaks. In England and Wales, *Giardia* is reported to the PHLS Communicable Disease Surveillance Centre rather more frequently year by year than is *Cryptosporidium*. *Giardia* seems, however, to be infrequently recognised as a cause of waterborne outbreaks here but *Cryptosporidium* increasingly is. Similar data are not generally available for other countries but this probably represents under-detection and reporting. While the several thousand, mainly apparently sporadic cases per year may be acceptable in terms of public perception, a few hundred cases in one locality at one time, or even contamination events, may result in public anxiety, media attention and questions in Parliament or Congress. Is this response, and indeed the wider response in terms of the United Kingdom and American Governments', and industry's investment in R&D, water treatment, etc, in proportion to the size and nature of the problem? What are the epidemiological aspects of these problems and how far have we come towards solving them?

The Badenoch report (Anon 1990) emphasised the importance of a multidisciplinary approach to investigating outbreaks, with input from medical public health specialists (CCDC's in the UK), environmental health departments, epidemiologists (for example, from the PHLS Communicable Disease Surveillance Centre), scientific experts on the parasite, MAFF, NRA, and water company specialists (scientists and operational staff). A mutual appreciation is required of the roles, responsibilities, and problems faced by these various groups. The epidemiological assessment of waterborne outbreaks of enteric protozoal infection requires an understanding not only of the principles and practice of epidemiology as applied to outbreaks of infectious diseases in general, but also of the peculiarities of the natural history of the parasites involved (Casemore 1990; Rose 1990; Hibler and Hancock 1990; Anon, 1992) and dynamics of transmission. Questions raised in various investigations have included: what is an outbreak, how do we define one and how do we tell that we have one? How many "sporadic" cases can be attributed to the water route? How are the data and their interpretation influenced by diagnostic laboratory practice or by public health investigations? What is the importance of the host response? How much is outcome influenced by their differing dynamics of transmission? The purpose of this paper was to address these questions, but not necessarily to provide answers to them all. Some of the answers would, hopefully, come from other presentations, or future research and developments.

The Numbers Game

Epidemiology is partly about measuring the numbers involved in disease frequency, and uses well-defined terms, as follows:

- Prevalence - Total number of infected individuals (carriers and cases, acute and recovering) over a defined period or at a point in time.
- Incidence - The number of new cases in a defined period. Both incidence and prevalence may be defined in terms of an absolute figure or as a rate, for example normalised to a rate per 100,000 population.
- Denominator - Total potentially exposed population.
- Laboratory "denominator" - Total number of samples submitted.
- Laboratory "incidence" (detection) rate -Percentage of laboratory samples found to be positive.
- In addition, a measure of the severity of an outbreak may be given as an attack rate which is a measure of transmission, both primary and secondary.

The epidemiologist studying an increase in case numbers follows well tried guidelines in investigating, and attempting to derive evidence of, an association between an event (exposure) and on outcome (illness). On being notified of a problem, the steps include (after Palmer and Swan, 1991):

- Set up field studies.
- Contact "players" to confirm existence of an outbreak (microbiological evidence and case numbers).
- Establish descriptive pattern (time, place, persons, etc).
- Formulate and test working hypotheses.
- Consider possible control measures.
- Follow-up studies and reporting.

Failure to understand this structured approach leads sometimes to accusations that water is unfairly being singled out for attention. Questions posed by the epidemiologist always include a wide variety of risk factors, including different foods and environmental exposures, as defined by previous case and outbreak studies (Casemore 1990, Palmer and Biffin, 1990). The most important of the epidemiological criteria for assessing an outbreak (after Palmer and Swan 1991) include:

- Strength of statistical association.
- Consistency with the known natural history of the infecting agent.
- Descriptive factors such as temporality and geographical distribution.
- Plausibility - often guided intuitively through experience.
- Analogy with other outbreaks investigated.

In addition, there may be a detectable response to control measures (the "John Snow pump handle" effect).

Water producers may suggest that insufficient attention has been paid to factors such as pets, for example. However, evidence of association in outbreaks, for example, with visits to educational farms, can normally be easily found. Intuitively, though, it would seem improbable that a cluster of cases over an area would all be exposed coincidentally to infected household pets (unless the pets were common victims for which, again, the most likely vehicle would seem to be water).

When enteric protozoal infection is introduced into a community, for example through the water supply, it can then be readily transmitted from person to person. Outbreaks are therefore not like the classical ones, such as cholera, where secondary transmission may be uncommon, especially in areas of generally good hygiene. They are more likely to be community propagated outbreaks initiated by water. What is meant by an outbreak? Some epidemiological definitions are:

- Two or more associated cases sharing a common source of infection (horizontal exposure).
- Two or more associated cases derived from a single source (vertical exposure - propagated outbreak).
- An increase in incidence above the expected (background) level.
- A cluster of cases in time and place without obvious common source.
- "Sporadic" cases over an extended period or area connected by a common outbreak strain. This can usually be detected only if an unusual or identifiable strain is involved - a key piece of epidemiological information not yet available for enteric parasites.

It is important to recognise that the rates determined by the laboratory are essentially artificial although trends can be deduced. Data are subject to many biases which need to be viewed critically and controlled for (Anon, 1990; Casemore and Roberts, 1993). Although some infectious agents may produce a characteristic clinical picture, individual cases can only be differentiated, from each other, and from the background of cases of diarrhoeal disease in the community, by laboratory tests. The recognition of an outbreak, unless unusually large, will thus be determined by ascertainment (based on clinical criteria for submission and laboratory criteria for the examination). "Outbreaks" can thus be artefacts created by changes in ascertainment practice. Pseudo-outbreaks can also be created by failure of good laboratory practice and the misidentification of artefacts (Casemore 1992). In this situation, one needs to be wary of circular arguments. For example, objects morphologically resembling cryptosporidial oocysts, viewed in the context of an apparent outbreak, are then falsely confirmed because "we know that *Cryptosporidium* causes waterborne outbreaks, therefore it must be oocysts we are looking at"! Reliability of laboratory data is thus crucial to the epidemiologist. Misidentification of oocyst-like bodies in water samples, by water company laboratories, has also occurred and led to unfounded concerns about "contamination" incidents.

Cases detected are likely to be a part of the "tip of the iceberg" of those occurring in the affected community. Estimates suggest that each case detected might represent from about 9-99 or more undetected cases. The identified cases represent part of a set of "nested squares", perhaps most easily understood by analogy, as the smallest of a set of (epidemiological) Russian dolls. The largest or outer one represents the denominator of the total population at risk (eg, within a water distribution area); inner ones representing, in turn, those with infective diarrhoea, those with *Cryptosporidium*, those with *Cryptosporidium* acquired from the source under investigation, and those which the laboratory succeeds in detecting. Of those cases, not all will be available, or agreeable to being investigated by an epidemiologist. This latter point raise various problems with the possible introduction of bias.

Dynamic Factors

The size of an outbreak will be determined, not only by the efficiency or otherwise of water treatment, following a challenge, but by both host and parasite factors described as the dynamics of transmission. By this is meant the fluctuations or flow of changes in parasite numbers and characteristics, and of host numbers, their susceptibility, and host exposure factors such as drinking habits.

Herd Immunity Factors

The term herd is used to describe any defined population of potential hosts, feral, livestock or human. Such factors are complex, and are indirect as well as specific. The term immunity to parasites refers to having experienced an immunological response to antigenic (eg parasite) challenge. The host's immune system will then recognise the parasite again (assuming it to be the same antigenic type) but the host is not necessarily refractory to re-infection. It is probable also, that a fully susceptible individual will require a smaller infective dose than a partially immune subject. What does seem to happen is that recurrent exposure is likely to lead to limited establishment of the parasite and asymptomatic infection. Such individuals will have a variable, but generally more limited, ability to transmit their infection. There is evidence that oocysts excreted late in the course of an infection are less viable than is the case earlier. There is thus a possibility that such immune infected subjects may limit the infectivity of the cysts excreted through poorly understood immune mechanisms. It might be said that, from the parasites' point of view, diarrhoea, with its uncontrolled out-flowing of bowel contents in an acute primary infection represents the ideal way to guarantee their passage to a new host.

Dynamically speaking, a person can therefore be placed in several categories (the so-called compartmental model):

- susceptible (variable, depending on their immune status);
- infected but whose infectiousness is limited (early incubation period);
- acutely ill and fully infectious;
- "immune" but infected (eg low-level asymptomatic carrier);
- immune and fully recovered (but increasingly re-infectable with time).

In reality, each one of these stages may merge into the next. One essential outcome is that the minimum inhibitory dose (MID) will vary according to the position of the exposed person in relation to this model.

Depending upon the status of the majority in a population, for a given infective challenge (ie number of oocysts in the water), several patterns of transmission are possible:

- Low herd immunity levels - highest probability that the oocysts will be ingested by a susceptible person; high secondary (person-to-person) transmission rates are possible (especially amongst children).
- Moderate herd immunity -Lower probability of ingestion by a susceptible person; some secondary cases likely but this is limited by immune individuals creating a secondary (indirect) barrier to transmission.
- High herd immunity - Low probability of ingestion by a susceptible person; situation commonly marked by a relatively high rate of asymptomatic infection. Waterborne transmission may occur but outbreaks are unlikely. Visitors may act as "sentinels", succumbing to symptomatic infection (travellers' diarrhoea).

If herd immunity is low to moderate, and the affected area is urban and in a developed country, then the routes of transmission to susceptible adults are limited. It would seem then, intuitively, that the water route would become relatively more important. The first indication that an outbreak has occurred may then be the observation of an increase in numbers of isolates from adults - a finding of a number of outbreak investigations (Aston *et al*, 1991; Joseph *et al*, 1991). For this to happen, it is essential that laboratories screen stool specimens for *Cryptosporidium* from adult patients as well as children (Casemore and Roberts, 1993).

Given an understanding of the complexity of the dynamics of transmission, it would be illogical to expect that transmission occurred only when a recognised outbreak followed. It is clearly likely from the above that the outcome of low-level intermittent contamination, especially in an area of moderate herd immunity, would be apparently sporadic cases with little secondary spread.

Parasite Dynamic Factors

It must be assumed that environmental isolates will differ in viability, in their potential infectivity for man, and possibly in their virulence (ability to cause severe disease), although little or nothing is yet known of this aspect. In addition, if strains of *C. parvum* are animal host-adapted, then the minimum infective dose (MID) may differ in respect to their potential for secondary transmission from person to person. In gnotobiotic (devoid of normal microbial flora and living in a sterile environment) lambs, which are a very susceptible host model the MID of a lamb adapted isolate, may be as low as one oocyst (Blewett *et al*, 1992). In normal, colostrum-fed lambs the same isolate still showed an MID in single figures but infection was somewhat slower to develop and was clinically less severe. Recent human feeding trials using a calf isolate showed an MID of <=30 and an ID_{50} (infecting 50% of those exposed) of 214 oocysts (Chappell *et al* 1994). Other isolates and younger subjects might well have shown a different MID. In addition, an ID50 is a standardised dose concept for use in scientific experiments. As water is almost universally consumed and a particular supply may be to millions of people, then an ID<=1% might well still expose significant numbers of consumers.

Parasite Environmental Dispersion and Host Consumption Factors

One may assume that parasites in water are not homogenously dispersed, and the dose ingested may thus vary considerably for any given count on a sample (which itself is subject to very wide statistical, sampling, and analytical variation). One might expect that a very low dose in the water would not be sufficient to infect consumers. Intuitively however, it would be expected that non-homogeneity of dispersal, resulting for example from a bolus of contaminated water, will lead to clusters of oocysts even when only small numbers of oocysts are present. This may then result in a susceptible consumer, especially one with AIDS, becoming infected. If one or two cases are thus caused, then waterborne transmission has occurred but is unlikely to be detected. If such a case is found by chance, the role of water is unlikely to be suspected, it could not be confirmed epidemiologically and would add to the background of apparently sporadic cases. Given the paucity and variability of ascertainment, only when large numbers of cases occur in an area, within a finite period of time, is an outbreak likely to be recognised. This does not mean that transmission is not occurring.

Because water is supplied to so many consumers within a distribution area, if oocysts are present the possibility of an MID being ingested by a susceptible individual are statistically higher than for other vehicles. The greater the number of oocysts, the greater the probability that a significant number of consumers will be exposed, including those with partial immunity. However, with the extreme variability and unpredictability of these events, one must assume for regulatory purposes, that the worst combination of factors will apply. That it does not do so in practice is a reason why outbreaks are not much more common.

Descriptive and Analytical Epidemiological Studies

An epidemiologist looks for clusters of cases in place and time (descriptive data) and then attempts to identify risk associations by statistical evaluation of questionnaires from groups of cases and appropriately defined controls (analytical study). The outcome will be an estimation of a probability of association, not proof of causation.

It is always important, as a first step, to ascertain whether an outbreak has really occurred, usually by comparison of laboratory data with current data for adjacent laboratories, and with data from previous months and the same period in previous years. This latter may reveal that there was in fact a problem in previous years at this time, cryptosporidiosis having seasonal peaks of incidence in many areas. However, although these may reflect, for example, farming events, transmission into the population affected still has to occur, directly or through a vehicle such as water. Active retrospective and prospective case-finding may be undertaken, for example by contacting local family practitioners to send in more specimens. Clearly subsequent findings need to be carefully assessed in the light of that action.

A number of difficulties arise in the investigation of community-wide outbreaks of cryptosporidiosis. When, for example, a salmonella outbreak involves a well defined group, for example a wedding feast, it is relatively easy to determine who has been exposed, to what, and when. Primary cases are therefore easily defined by a fixed time and place of exposure, and thus also secondary cases can be identified. If an outbreak of cryptosporidiosis results from contaminated potable water supplies, the time and place, and extent (except in general terms) of exposure is much less certain. One can define a household primary case but this individual may have become infected either from the primary vehicle (water), at home or elsewhere, or from an entirely different source (infected animal or human). The household primary case may thus not be an outbreak primary case (ie exposed to the suspected vehicle). This will tend to introduce a bias which, usually, will reduce the level of association found with the suspected vehicle of transmission.

If an analytical (case-control) study is set up, controls are sought from within that community who may be selected by several means including:

- case-nominated neighbourhood controls;
- Family Practitioner Committee (FPC) lists;
- by selection through systematic or "random" telephone number listings.

Each of these has particular merits or demerits. Close neighbours are likely to receive the same water supply and would seem, superficially, to be ideal as controls. However, if controls were found by chance to have had symptoms then they will be excluded. This is because they may have been undetected cases (ie, they were susceptible at the putative date of exposure). That being so, those who were asymptomatic and "acceptable" as controls must, intuitively, be more likely to have been immune and would not have become ill even though exposed to the same degree. This then introduces another bias reducing the significance of association. Family practitioner list selection (matched by age and sex) will generally draw from the same community but over a wider area. They are thus more likely to receive their water at home from a different supply. Such groups have, in practice, yielded more significant levels of association, as expected. Of course one also has to try to test for differences in levels of consumption of water, both at home and elsewhere, for example at work. Various socio-economic differences may influence outcome and this is seen with the third group of controls (and possibly also with other groups of controls) in that telephone ownership is determined by ability to afford to pay for the service. The epidemiologist has to be aware of, and will control for, these potential biases if necessary.

Portrait of Some Outbreaks

The possibility of an outbreak in an area depends on a combination of a number of factors:

- The parasite in sufficient numbers and of appropriate viability and infectivity;
- A sufficient number of susceptible persons for ingestion to lead to primary infection;
- A sufficient number of susceptible persons for ingestion to lead to secondary transmission, thus amplifying the incidence;
- Adequate laboratory surveillance and reporting.

To this must be added a number of specifically water-related factors which may include:

- abnormal weather conditions (eg, heavy rainfall) leading to agricultural wash off;
- high turbidity surface water, streaming in a reservoir, etc, leading to an increased challenge to treatment;
- break down in integrity of an aquifer (ground waters), possibly following heavy rain after a prolonged drought;
- sub-optimal working of water treatment;
- distribution pipework or service reservoir fault (ingress incident).

Outbreaks which illustrate some of these points are as follows.

1 In an arable farming area of eastern England the background laboratory detection rate was less than one case per week. A small cluster of some half dozen cases was noted and an investigation commenced (Brown *et al*, 1989). Retrospective case searching indicated that the first increase in cases occurred shortly after heavy rain in the locality had caused problems with the local water supply. In the succeeding few weeks small clusters and single cases were noted in the area. Partly because of the small number of cases involved a direct association with water consumption could not be demonstrated. However, this

small outbreak was the first in which the concept of a community-wide propagated outbreak initiated by water was thought to be the most probable explanation of events.

2 In a waterborne outbreak involving nearly 500 cases (Aston *et al*, 1991), the mean age for household primary cases was 23 years compared with the usual of <10 years. The modal age for the whole outbreak was somewhat lower, and the age of cases declined with time as secondary transmission occurred. The outbreak was found to be associated with a river water supply part of which, for operational reasons, had been allowed to by-bass slow sand filters at a time which coincided with increased turbidity following heavy rain. The two peaks of cases clearly mirrored the periods of filter bypassing. There was a marked dose-response effect (ie the more water a person was in the habit of drinking, the more likely they were, compared with controls, to have been ill). The level of significance for water exposure was greater for FPC than for neighbourhood controls. Interestingly, two-tailed statistical tests (which show both risk and protective effects) showed a protective effect from consumption of salad and raw vegetables. While this could not be identified then as anything more than a chance finding, it has been found in some other outbreaks and would be logical, since recurrent, possibly low-level, exposure from this route would be expected to lead to immunity.

3 In another area a gradual but marked increase was seen in incidence over several weeks compared with adjacent areas (Kealy, *et al*, unpublished report). The age-specific case data appeared, however, to be nearer to the UK average distribution. On closer inspection, several key facts emerged:

- a small cluster of adult cases had been identified in another part of the country, who had in common a history of recent travel to the affected area;
- a small increase was found in elderly cases (aged =>60 years) who were mainly people who had retired to the area, who generally lived in nursing homes and lacked other risk factors;
- a past history of an increased incidence each autumn for several years.

Thus, one could postulate that the visitors were like travellers to under developed countries acting as sentinels for the presence of a contaminated supply. Together with the elderly incomers, they acted as surrogates for the usual adult susceptible population, many of whom in this area would have become immune from previous uninvestigated episodes of transmission. On investigation, it was found that the area suffered a shortage of source water in the late summer each year, as a result of which water was abstracted from a river some distance away, in a dairying catchment area. Because it was abstracted from below river gravels it was treated as though it had been "filtered" and was then blended, prior to chlorination, with other supplies. Marked rises were noted to have occurred in that minor source in turbidity, to >4 NTU at times, although the blended supply met the required standard.

Other Epidemiological Considerations

Although epidemiology may provide proof of association but not proof of causation, that evidence alone may still be considered credible. However, the inference of causation is strengthened by complementary microbiological evidence. The epidemiological study of enteric protozoal outbreaks is currently constrained by the problems of sampling and detection (Fricker, 1994) and the absence of established "fingerprinting" techniques analogous to those used in tracking bacterial outbreaks. It has only recently begun to emerge, although first suggested many years ago, that *Entamoeba histolytica* is not one but two, morphologically indistinguishable, species, one a pathogen and one a commensal. The public health implications of this are huge (Anon, 1992). It is believed that so-called *Giardia intestinalis (lamblia)* is genetically at least as diverse. As a general point, "beaver fever" giardiasis cases could have resulted from the beaver transmitting infection which the beaver previously had acquired from water polluted by man. What, then, of *Cryptosporidium parvum*? Questions have been raised about the source of human cryptosporidiosis

(McDonald and Karriem, 1994). An important aspect of this variation in isolates is that they might well differ in their MID.

What can be done with cyst and oocyst monitoring results? What does routine sampling data mean in relation to what is known epidemiologically? Can "small numbers" of oocysts safely be ignored? What guidelines can be given and what preventative measures can be recommended (ie when should a "boil notice" be recommended)?

The primary purpose of epidemiology is to identify sources of infection, to control outbreaks, and to learn lessons which might prevent future outbreaks. What is the relationship between the prevalence of infection and incidence of disease, and oocysts numbers in water? Where prevalence is very high, oocysts may be commonly present but the risks to the community may be low. Conversely, if incidence is low, then oocysts are probably not often present, but may represent a greater risk when they are. One cannot safely define "permissible" oocysts numbers, or assess risk to communities from the numbers detected in water, at present, with any reliability. What can be done is to estimate risk based on "worse case scenarios" using certain assumptions (Rose, 1994). From this it follows that the regulators and the public need to understand the concept of an acceptable level of risk - a political and educational problem. When risk is defined in terms of both the probability of harm and the severity of harm produced, then it can be seen that a dual standard might be required. For the average otherwise healthy subject the occasional enteric infection is not especially serious, although unpleasant and disruptive. To an AIDS patient however, it may well be life threatening; the risk of ingesting a given number of oocysts may be no greater for an immunocompromised person but the MID, for them may actually be lower. The consequences of oocysts in the supply are thus more serious and the risk unacceptable. It may well be, therefore, that those who are immunocompromised should avoid exposure as much as possible, not drinking unboiled water and ensuring that, for example, salads and fruit, wherever possible, are washed in boiled water just as anyone might do in travel to underdeveloped countries.

The Legal Framework

Water producers are currently not able to guarantee freedom from risk of parasites in some supplies from time to time (Anon, 1990). However, it is clearly not in the interest of water producers to infect their customers. Admission that they might have done so might leave them open to civil action or even criminal prosecution. This implicit threat inhibits the free exchange of information and open discussion of possible contributory factors. What is the role of epidemiologists in the legal and regulatory framework, and in the public perception of these problems? Public health microbiologists and epidemiologists are not part of a forensic service. The criminalization of the water regulations in the UK, and the increasing threat of civil litigation, however, mean that they are increasingly expected to provide evidence and for which their studies were never intended to be applied. The primary function of disease detection, control and prevention are best conducted, not in the courts of law, but as pointed out in the Badenoch report, in an atmosphere of scientific collaboration, the aim of which is to protect the public health.

Few topics in water microbiology have led to so many problems, nor to such efforts, and money, to resolve them. Although much of the research has advanced our understanding, academic questions have sometimes been confused with public health needs. However, academic developments do benefit our understanding and evaluation of the problems which have been identified. Research, however, is increasingly constrained by reduced funding, potentially to the cost of the health of the public.

References

Anon. Addressing emerging infectious disease threats: a prevention strategy for the United States. Morbidity and Mortality Weekly Reports. 1994;43:1-18

Anon. *Cryptosporidium* in water supplies. Dept of Health/Dept of Environment. Report of the Group of Experts, Chairman, Sir John Badenoch. HMSO London 1990

Anon. World Health Organization. WHO/PAHO informal consultation on intestinal protozoal infections. 1992 WHO/CDS/IPI/92.2 pp1-42

Aston R, Mawer SL, Casemore DP, *et al.* Report of the Outbreak Control Team to co-ordinate the investigation of the outbreak of cryptosporidiosis in north Humberside, December 1989 - May 1990. Formal Report to the Local Authorities of Beverley and Kingston upon Hull, 1991

Bendall RP, Chiodini P. The epidemiology of human Cyclospora infection in the UK. 1994 (This volume)

Blewett DA, Wright SE, Casemore DP, Booth NE, Jones CE. Minimum infective dose size studies on *Cryptosporidium parvum* using gnotobiotic lambs. Proc IAWPRC International Symposium - Health related water microbiology. Water Science and Technology. 1993;27:61-4

Brown EAE, Casemore DP, Gerken A, Greatorex I. Cryptosporidiosis in Great Yarmouth - the investigation of an outbreak. Publ Hlth 1989;103:3-9

Casemore DP, Roberts C. Leader: Guidelines for screening for *Cryptosporidium* in stools: report of a joint working group. J Clin Pathol 1993;46: 2-4

Casemore DP. (1990) Foodborne protozoal infections. Lancet 336: 157-64

Casemore DP. A pseudo-outbreak of cryptosporidiosis. PHLS Communicable Disease Report. 1992; Review No 6;2: R84-5. Public Health Laboratory Service, London

Casemore DP. Broadsheet No 128: The laboratory diagnosis of human cryptosporidiosis. J Clin Pathol 1991;44:445-51

Casemore DP. Enteric protozoa and the water route of transmission - epidemiology and dynamics. In: Proceedings of Berzelius Conference, Water and Public Health, 1992. Royal Society of Medicine, London (In press)

Casemore DP. Epidemiological aspects of human cryptosporidiosis. Epidemiology and Infection 1990; 104: 1-28

Chappell C, Sterling CR, Rose JB, *et al. Cryptosporidium parvum*: the human model of infection. (abstract C63) 47th Annual Meeting Society of Protozoologists, Cleveland, USA, 1994

Dawson A, Lloyd A, eds. Proceedings of a workshop on *Cryptosporidium* in water supplies. The Drinking Water Inspectorate. HMSO, London, 1994

Fricker CR. Detection of *Cryptosporidium* and *Giardia* in Water 1994 (This volume)

Hibler CP, Hancock CM. Waterborne giardiasis. In: ed GA Mcfeters, Drinking water microbiology. Progress and recent developments. Springer-Verlag, New York, 1990, pp271-293

Isaac-Renton J, Moorhead W, Ross A. *Giardia* cyst concentrations and infectivity: longitudinal community drinking water studies. 1994 (This volume)

Joseph C, Hamilton G, O'Connor M, Nicholas S, Marshall R, Stanwell-Smith R, Sims R, Ndawula E, Casemore DP, Gallagher P, Harnett P. (1991) Cryptosporidiosis in the Isle of Thanet: an outbreak associated with local drinking water. Epidemiology and Infection 1991;107:509-19

MacKenzie WR, Hoxie NJ, Procter ME, *et al.* An outbreak of waterborne cryptosporidiosis associated with a filtered public water supply in Milwaukee, Wisconsin. 1994 (This volume)

McDonald V, Kariem FM. Strain variation in *Cryptosporidium parvum* and evidence for distinctive human and animal strains. 1994 (This volume)

Palmer SR, Biffin. Cryptosporidiosis in England and Wales: prevalence and clinical and epidemiological features. Public Health Laboratory Service Study Group report. Brit Med J 1990;300:774-7

Palmer SR, Swan AV. The epidemiological approach to infection control. Rev Med Microbiol. 1991; 2:187-93

Rose JB. Occurrence and control of *Cryptosporidium* in drinking water. In: ed GA Mcfeters, Drinking water microbiology. Progress and recent developments. Springer-Verlag, New York, 1990, pp294-321

Rose JB. Risk assessment for *Cryptosporidium*. 1994 (This volume)

Sterling CR. Emerging pathogens: Cyclospora, the microspora, and how many more? 1994 (This volume).

Epidemiologic Features and Implications of the Milwaukee Cryptosporidiosis Outbreak

D.G. Addiss[3], W.R. MacKenzie[1,3], N.J. Hoxie[1], M.S. Gradus[2], K.A. Blair[2], M.E. Proctor[1], J.J.Kazmierczak[1], W.L. Schell[1], P. Osewe[3], H. Frisby[1], H. Cicerello[3], R.L. Cordell[3], J.B. Rose[4] and J.P. Davis[1]
[1]The Wisconsin Division of Health, Madison, Wisconsin, USA
[2]The City of Milwaukee Department of Health, Milwaukee, Wisconsin, USA
[3]The U.S. Centers for Disease Control and Prevention, Atlanta, Georgia, USA
[4]The University of South Florida, Tampa, Florida, USA

Introduction

In March and April, 1993, the largest documented waterborne disease outbreak in U.S. history occurred in Milwaukee, Wisconsin. An estimated 403,000 people developed watery diarrhoea after drinking municipal water contaminated with *Cryptosporidium parvum* (MacKenzie *et al.* 1994). The magnitude of this outbreak and its association with a municipal water plant that was operating within existing state and federal regulatory standards heightened public concern about the quality of drinking water in the United States, highlighted the need for improved surveillance and coordination between public health agencies and water utilities, and revitalized efforts to develop regulatory standards for *Cryptosporidium* in drinking water. In this paper we review the major epidemiologic features of the Milwaukee outbreak and discuss its public health implications.

Milwaukee is the largest city in Wisconsin (population approximately 630,000), and is situated on the western shore of Lake Michigan. Drinking water is supplied by the Milwaukee Water Works (MWW), which has two water treatment plants, one in the north of the city and the other in the south. Both plants obtain their intake water from Lake Michigan, and either plant can supply water to the entire water district. When both plants are in operation, however, the South plant predominantly supplies water to the southern portion of the MWW service district.

On April 5, 1993, the Wisconsin Division of Health was notified about a substantial increase in the number of people who were absent from work because of gastrointestinal illness in Milwaukee. An epidemiologic investigation was begun, and on April 7, *Cryptosporidium* oocysts were detected in the stools of seven Milwaukee area residents. High levels of turbidity in the treated water from the South plant suggested the possibility of waterborne cryptosporidiosis, and a boil water advisory was issued on the evening of April 7. The South plant was temporarily closed on April 9 (MacKenzie *et al.* 1994).

Nursing Home Studies

To determine whether gastrointestinal illness was associated with drinking water supplied by the South plant, information was collected on rates of diarrhoeal illness in residents of 16 nursing homes throughout Milwaukee. Diarrhoea was defined as 3 or more loose stools in a 24 hour period. Among residents of 9 nursing homes in northern Milwaukee, the prevalence of diarrhoea remained less than 2% per week. In contrast, the prevalence of diarrhoea in 6 of the 7 nursing homes in southern Milwaukee increased to 16% during the first week of April and remained high until one week after the boil water advisory was issued on April 7. The remaining nursing home in southern Milwaukee, where the prevalence of diarrhoea remained less than 2% per week, obtained its drinking water from a private well. Of stools collected from 69 southern nursing home residents with diarrhoea, 51% were positive for *Cryptosporidium*, compared with none among 12 northern nursing home residents with diarrhoea (M. Proctor, unpublished data).

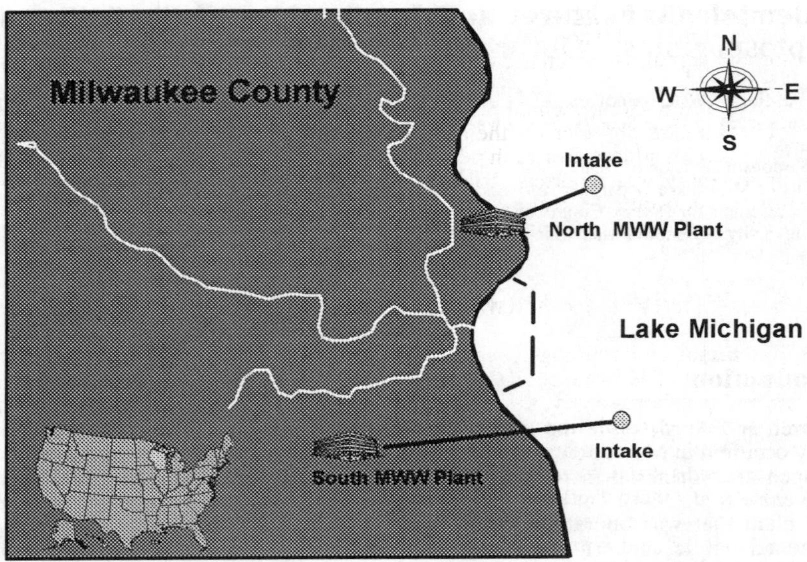

Figure 1. Location of the treatment plants and water intakes of the Milwaukee Water Works (MWW), Milwaukee, Wisconsin

Telephone Survey of the 5-County Metropolitan Area (MacKenzie *et al.* 1994)

To estimate the magnitude of the outbreak and collect information on the occurrence of diarrhoea illness in the community, a telephone survey using random digit dialling was conducted April 28 - May 2 in Milwaukee and the four surrounding counties. We asked to speak with the adult most knowledgeable about the health of all household members, and this person was asked about diarrhoea in all members of the household. Clinical cryptosporidiosis was defined as watery diarrhoea with onset between March 1 and April 28, 1993.

Interviews were completed with 613 respondents, a response rate of 73%, and information was collected on more than 1600 household members. The sample was demographically similar to the general population in the 1990 census for these counties. A total of 436 (26%) household members met the case definition for clinical cryptosporidiosis. The incidence of watery diarrhoea began to increase during the last week of March and reached a peak between April 1 and April 7.

For people living within the MWW service area, the attack rate of watery diarrhoea was highest among residents of southern Milwaukee, 52%, and lowest among residents of northern Milwaukee, 26%. The attack rate was 35% in the midzone, where water could be supplied by either the North or South treatment plant, depending on demand. People who lived outside the MWW service area had the lowest attack rate of watery diarrhoea, 15%.

The survey identified 644 household members who lived outside the MWW service area and who worked outside the home. Of the 28 who worked in southern Milwaukee and were possibly exposed to contaminated drinking water while at work, 11 (39%) had watery diarrhoea during the outbreak. In contrast, only 15% of those who worked outside the southern region had watery diarrhoea.

By applying the 26% overall attack rate of watery diarrhoea among survey participants to the total population of the 5-county area (1.61 million), we estimated that 419,000 persons in this area had watery diarrhoea during the survey period. From a subsequent survey in June,

1993, we estimated a background rate of watery diarrhoea among residents of 0.5% per month. Subtracting 16,000 non-outbreak-related cases that could have been expected during the two-month period, we estimated that 403,000 people had watery diarrhoea attributed to this outbreak.

Fifty (11%) of the 436 household members with watery diarrhoea in this survey reported visiting a health-care provider for their illness and five (1%) reported that they had been hospitalized for this illness. For each person with watery diarrhoea, an average of 1.8 days of lost productivity was reported. Applying these figures to the greater Milwaukee area population, we attribute an estimated 725,000 person-days of lost productivity to this outbreak (W. MacKenzie, personal communication).

Studies of Visitors to Milwaukee (MacKenzie *et al*, in press)

Several important epidemiologic questions were raised that could not be answered by studying residents of Milwaukee, including the duration of *Cryptosporidium* contamination of the Milwaukee water supply, the incubation period for illness, and the risk of secondary person-to-person transmission within households. Extensive national press coverage facilitated surveillance of outbreak-related cryptosporidiosis among short-term visitors from several states, and a standardized questionnaire was developed by the Wisconsin Division of Health to interview these visitors between April 12 and May 20, 1993.

Respondents were non-residents of Milwaukee County who visited Milwaukee once between March 15 and April 15, and who had developed either laboratory-confirmed cryptosporidiosis (considered a confirmed case) or watery diarrhoea (a clinical case) after their visit. Visitors were excluded from the study if any of their household members had travelled to Milwaukee during the month before their visit.

Ninety-four of the visitors with cryptosporidiosis had visited Milwaukee for less than 48 hours, and were considered short-term visitors. Of these, 54 had laboratory-confirmed cryptosporidiosis and 40 had clinical cryptosporidiosis (watery diarrhoea not confirmed as cryptosporidiosis), 32 (80%) of whom did not submit a stool specimen for examination. The clinical features of illness in these two groups were similar; the one exception was that the mean duration of diarrhoea was longer for confirmed cases (9 days) than for clinical cases (5 days).

All 94 short-term visitors reported drinking unboiled tap water or beverages containing unboiled tap water while in the southern MWW service area. The median volume was 16 ounces; 32% drank less than 8 ounces. March 24 was the earliest date of arrival in Milwaukee. For visitors with laboratory-confirmed cryptosporidiosis, exposure occurred every day for the next 12 days, suggesting that *Cryptosporidium* was present in the water for at least two consecutive weeks (MacKenzie *et al*, in press).

Onset of illness followed a similar pattern to that in Milwaukee residents, beginning the last week of March, reaching a maximum frequency during the first week of April, and, with one exception, ending within one week after the boil water advisory began. The median incubation period among short-term visitors was 7 days, with a range of 1-14 days.

Characteristics of Laboratory-Confirmed and Clinical Cryptosporidiosis(MacKenzie *et al.* 1994; MacKenzie *et al*, in press)

The large size of this outbreak presented an opportunity to collect information on the clinical spectrum of cryptosporidiosis, and to compare illnesses of people with laboratory confirmed and clinically defined infections. Information on laboratory-confirmed cases was collected by telephone interviews with 312 of 739 persons who were reported to the Milwaukee City Health Department as having laboratory-confirmed cryptosporidiosis. Of these, 285 had onset of diarrhoea between March 1 and May 15. Information on cryptosporidiosis in the community was obtained through a telephone survey of 482 adult Milwaukee County residents using random-digit dialling between April 9 and 12. Of these, 201 (42%) met the case definition of clinical cryptosporidiosis (watery diarrhoea with onset between March 1 and April 9).

Persons with laboratory-confirmed and clinical cases were similar with respect to mean age, sex, dates of onset of diarrhoea, and frequency of abdominal cramps, fatigue, and muscle aches. Not unexpectedly, however, laboratory-confirmed cases tended to be more severe than clinical cases of cryptosporidiosis. Duration of diarrhoea was greater for laboratory-confirmed cases (9 days vs. 3 days), as was the median maximum number of stools per day (12 vs. 5). Vomiting and fever were more commonly reported for laboratory-confirmed cases than clinical cases (48% vs. 18% for vomiting and 57% vs. 36% for fever, respectively). Among persons with laboratory confirmed cases, 17% were immunocompromised and 46% were hospitalized for their illness. By definition, all persons with laboratory-confirmed cases had seen a physician for their illness, compared with 6% of those with clinical cryptosporidiosis.

In a concomitant survey of HIV-infected persons in Milwaukee, the attack rate appeared to be no greater than that among the general population, regardless of CD4 count. However, increasing severity of illness was associated with decreasing CD4 counts (H. Frisby, unpublished data).

The rate of asymptomatic infection during the outbreak is unknown because persons without diarrhoea were not systematically tested for *Cryptosporidium* infection. In late April, however, 129 diapered children attending several day care centers in Milwaukee were screened. Of 35 children with *Cryptosporidium* identified in their stool, 29% had not had diarrhoea during or since the outbreak (R. Cordell, unpublished data). These limited data suggest that asymptomatic or mild infection may have been a common occurrence.

Recurrence of Watery Diarrhoea (MacKenzie *et al*, in press)

For several weeks after the boil water advisory was issued, a number of people telephoned the City of Milwaukee Health Department to report that they had had watery diarrhoea during the outbreak, and that their symptoms had resolved. However, after several days of normal stools, their diarrhoea recurred. Although intermittent diarrhoea or a "waxing and waning" pattern of cryptosporidiosis has been previously described, particularly in immunosuppressed patients, it seemed an unusually frequent occurrence during the Milwaukee outbreak. To determine the magnitude of this pattern, we asked persons with laboratory-confirmed cryptosporidiosis whether they had had a return of watery diarrhoea after at least two days of normal stools; 39% reported at least one recurrence of diarrhoea after a median interval of 2 days of normal stools (range, 2 to 14 days). Six percent had recurrence after at least 5 days of normal stools.

The similarity of this pattern to that among visitors suggested that recurrence could not be explained by reinfection through ongoing post-outbreak transmission in Milwaukee. Of 74 visitors contacted for a second interview, 24 (32%) reported recurrence of watery diarrhoea after at least 2 days of normal stools. They had a median of 3 days of normal stools before the diarrhoea recurred (range, 2-10 days). Six (8%) visitors reported recurrence of watery diarrhoea after at least 5 days of normal stools.

Secondary Household Transmission from Adults (MacKenzie *et al*, in press)

To assess the risk of secondary household transmission from adult (17 - 54 years old) visitors to Milwaukee, we contacted 74 visitors for a second telephone interview. They lived in 62 households with 74 other household members who had not visited Milwaukee during the outbreak. Four (5%) of these household members developed watery diarrhoea within 14 days after the visitor had returned from Milwaukee. Among 44 eligible household members who resided with a Milwaukee visitor who had laboratory-confirmed cryptosporidiosis, two (5%) developed watery diarrhoea.

Laboratory Test Results (MacKenzie *et al.* 1994)

In early April, intensive surveillance was established with 14 clinical laboratories in Milwaukee County. These laboratories retrospectively reported results from March 1 -April 6 and thereafter prospectively reported results of all stools submitted for bacterial or viral culture, examination for ova and parasites, or *Cryptosporidium* testing. Before the outbreak, only the City of Milwaukee Bureau of Laboratories routinely included acid fast staining for *Cryptosporidium* in ova and parasite examinations; after April 7, other laboratories expanded testing of stools to include *Cryptosporidium*. Thirteen laboratories used standard concentration techniques with modified acid fast staining and one laboratory used direct fluorescent antibody staining.

A reported 2300 stool specimens were cultured for bacterial enteric pathogens between March 1 and April 16, 1993. Less than 1% were positive for salmonella, shigella, or campylobacter. No more than 3% of stools tested were positive for yersinia, aeromonas, rotavirus, other enteric viruses, or giardia. Examination by electron microscopy of stools from 11 persons with watery diarrhoea did not detect viruses or other pathogens.

From March 1 through April 6, 12 (29%) of 42 stools specimens submitted for *Cryptosporidium* testing were positive; from April 8 to April 16, 331 (33%) of 1009 stool specimens were positive. These percentages may seem relatively low, and it has been suggested that other unidentified waterborne pathogens might have been involved in the outbreak. We consider this possibility unlikely for several reasons. First, intensive laboratory investigations identified no other organisms that could explain more than a small percentage of cases. Second, the sensitivity of acid fast testing for *Cryptosporidium* is known to be low. Third, in other waterborne outbreaks of cryptosporidiosis in the United States, comparable figures have been observed (e.g., 39% of diarrhoeal stool specimens submitted during the 1987 Carrollton, Georgia outbreak were positive for *Cryptosporidium*) (Hayes *et al* 1989).

Finally, in children evaluated at Wisconsin Children's Hospital during the outbreak, those who tested positive for *Cryptosporidium* submitted stool specimens more frequently and later during the course of their illness than did children who tested negative (H. Cicerello, unpublished data).

Examination of Ice for *Cryptosporidium* (MacKenzie *et al.* 1994)

A civic-minded ice manufacturer contacted the investigation team to volunteer a unique archival source of water for *Cryptosporidium* testing: 50-gallon blocks of ice that were intended for use in ice sculpture. Ice made on March 25 and April 9, 1993 was discolored and dirty. We melted and filtered these ice blocks using a 11.5-inch Millipore membrane filter with a porosity of 0.45-µm. The filter was eluted, the eluates centrifuged, the pellets resuspended, and suspensions were examined for *Cryptosporidium* oocysts using an immunofluorescent technique.

The concentration of oocysts in ice blocks made on March 25 and April 9 were 13.2 and 6.7 oocysts per 100 liters, respectively. The actual oocyst concentration in the Milwaukee water was probably much higher because freezing reduces the recovery of oocysts and the peak turbidity of treated water leaving the South plant on March 25 was relatively low, less than 0.5 nephelometric turbidity units (NTU). Oocyst concentration was likely to have been higher during the following week, when turbidity was higher.

Investigation of the South Water Treatment Plant (MacKenzie *et al.* 1994)

At the time of the outbreak, the South water treatment plant obtained its water from an intake pipe that extends 7600 feet offshore and rests on the bottom of Lake Michigan under 50 feet of water. The water in this pipe flows by gravity until it reaches a pumping station at the water's edge and is pumped 3.5 miles to the treatment plant.

Inside the plant, chlorine and a coagulant, polyaluminum chloride, were added to the water. This was followed by rapid mixing, mechanical flocculation, sedimentation, and rapid filtration in one of eight sand filters. After filtration, the effluent was stored in a 35 million gallon clearwell until it was supplied to customers. About six months before the outbreak, the plant had changed the coagulant from alum to polyaluminum chloride in an attempt to reduce levels of lead and copper leaching into the drinking water.

At the beginning of March, 1993, large fluctuations in the turbidity of the raw water for the South plant occurred with no major increases in turbidity of the treated water. On March 23, for the first time in more than 10 years, the turbidity of treated water from the South plant exceeded 0.4 NTU. The peak daily turbidity reached unprecedented levels of up to 1.7 NTU on March 28 and 30 despite adjustments in the dose of polyaluminum chloride. On April 2 the South plant switched to alum as the coagulant, but on April 5, the turbidity of treated water once again increased to 1.5 NTU. During March and April the daily maximum turbidity of the treated water leaving the North MWW plant did not exceed 0.45 NTU.

At all times during February, March, and April 1993, treated water samples from both Milwaukee water treatment plants were negative for coliforms and were in compliance with existing state and federal regulatory standards, as was the facility itself. However, several findings may have contributed to a delay in recognition of a problem or an inability to bring turbidity under control: coagulant dosing was determined without the aid of a continuous streaming current monitor; the finished water turbidity was continuously measured in the clearwell rather than as the water left each filter; and filter backwash water was recycled through the plant rather than being discarded.

Source of Oocysts in Lake Michigan

The source of oocysts in Lake Michigan remains speculative (J.P. Davis, unpublished data) (MacKenzie *et al.* 1994). The outbreak appears to have been an unfortunate confluence of several events. Heavy rainfall during early spring likely resulted in higher-than-usual levels of organic material, including cow manure that had been spread on fields within the watershed, being washed into streams that flow into Milwaukee's rivers. Even during years with more normal spring rainfall, lake water turbidity is high in the spring. A review of data from seven Wisconsin water treatment plants along the western shore of Lake Michigan revealed that finished water turbidity readings of > 0.5 NTU occur most frequently during March and April (W. MacKenzie, unpublished data). Other possible sources of oocysts include a slaughterhouse and meat packing plant in central Milwaukee, and the sewage treatment plant, which is located at the confluence of Milwaukee's three rivers as they flow into Lake Michigan. Combined sewage overflow is known to occur during heavy rains. Assuming that the oocysts entered Lake Michigan by these rivers, the natural currents of the lake and prevailing northeasterly winds during late March and early April would have favored their transport southward toward the water intake of the South MWW treatment plant rather than dispersal throughout the lake.

Post-Outbreak Transmission

The number of new cases of cryptosporidiosis dropped dramatically after the boil water advisory was announced. However, 60 confirmed cases were reported with onset during May and June, and there was concern of ongoing transmission in the Milwaukee area. We interviewed 33 of these patients and conducted a case-control study with neighborhood and household controls (P. Osewe, unpublished data).

Of the 33 confirmed cases in May and June, 79% had onset of diarrhoea during May. MWW water was not associated with illness. Case-patients were more likely than controls to live with a child less than 5 years old, a finding that suggests person-to-person transmission. Case-patients were also more likely to be immunosuppressed. Detection bias may explain this association, since people who are immunosuppressed may be more likely to have severe illness or may have physicians that are more likely to test for the organism.

Several swimming pool outbreaks were reported in Wisconsin during the spring and summer of 1993 (W. MacKenzie, unpublished data)(MMWR 1993) It was not determined whether this was a direct result of contamination by persons who had acquired their infections in Milwaukee, or whether increased awareness and testing allowed for identification of outbreaks that, in other years, would have gone undetected.

Impact of the Milwaukee Outbreak

The massive size of this outbreak and the fact that it occurred in an urban area with a large water treatment facility caught the attention of the U.S. public. The outbreak effectively served as a national "wake-up call" on the issue of water quality. More stringent federal water quality standards, which had been under development for several years, were implemented shortly after the outbreak. Since the outbreak, boil water advisories have been issued in several U.S. cities when finished water turbidity exceeded federal limits or *Cryptosporidium* was detected in finished water. The U.S. Environmental Protection Agency plans to implement an Information Collection Rule in early 1995, which will require utilities with surface water sources to test for *Cryptosporidium* routinely. The persons and agencies with authority to issue boil water advisories vary tremendously from state to state, and the need for communication and advance planning among public health agencies, water utilities, and other groups, such as physicians and representatives of immunosuppressed persons, has become obvious. These groups are beginning to come together at local, state, and national levels to develop effective prevention and research strategies, public education messages, and guidelines for prevention and early identification of waterborne cryptosporidiosis. For each answer provided by the investigation of the Milwaukee outbreak, many new questions were raised. Addressing these questions is the subject of intense research interest and public health activity.

Acknowledgement

We are indebted to all members of the outbreak investigation team for their tireless efforts and extraordinary contributions.

References

CDC. *Cryptosporidium* infections associated with swimming pools -- Dane County, Wisconsin, 1993. MMWR 1993; 43:561-563

Hayes EB, Matte TD, O'Brien TR, *et al.* Large community outbreak of cryptosporidiosis due to contamination of a filtered water supply. N Engl J Med 1989; 320:1372-1376

MacKenzie WR, Hoxie NJ, Proctor ME, *et al.* A massive waterborne outbreak of *Cryptosporidium* infection transmitted through the public water supply. N Engl J Med 1994; 331:161-167

MacKenzie WR, Schell WL, Blair KA, *et al.* Massive waterborne outbreak of cryptosporidiosis, Milwaukee, Wisconsin: Recurrence of illness and risk of secondary transmission. Clin Infect Dis (in press).

The Epidemiology of Human *Cyclospora* Infection in the UK

R.P. Bendall and P.L.Chiodini
Department of Clinical Parasitology, Hospital for Tropical Diseases, London, UK

Introduction

The Department of Clinical Parasitology, Hospital for Tropical Diseases, London, provides a national diagnostic service for parasitology. *Cyclospora* infection was first encountered at the Hospital in 1986 in a patient with diarrhoea who had returned from vacation in Pakistan. The oocysts were thought to be coccidian in nature and provisionally identified as *Sarcocystis*. Retrospective examination of the case has confirmed that they were in fact oocysts of *Cyclospora cayetanensis*. In 1986 Soave *et al.* reported the presence of a new coccidian, subsequently shown to be *Cyclospora* but it is now widely recognised that Ashford (1979) was the first to describe this organism, though it was not named until 1992 (Ortega *et al.* 1992).

Epidemiology

Table 1 shows the number of cases of *Cyclospora* infection diagnosed at the Hospital for Tropical Diseases (HTD) since 1986. Latterly, there is a trend towards laboratories outside HTD diagnosing the infection themselves or sending in samples for reference confirmation. Of the 43 cases microscopically diagnosed at HTD, age and sex were known for 41. Thirty nine patients were adults and two children; 22 male and 19 female.

Table 1. *Cyclospora cayetanensis* laboratory diagnosis at HTD 1986 - 15 September 1994

Year	HTD Total	HTD patients	Reference
1986	1	1	0
1991	5	5	0
1992	9	4	5
1993	11	8	3
1994	17	7	10
	43	25	18

Table 2. Hospital for Tropical Diseases, London. Travel history for patients with *Cyclospora* infection 1986 - September 1994

Pacific	Indonesia	5	
	Solomon Islands	1	6
Far East	Cambodia	1	
	Cambodia/Thailand/Vietnam	1	
	SE Asia	1	3
Indian Sub-Continent	Bangladesh	2	
	India	7	
	Nepal	5	
	Pakistan	4	
	India/Nepal	1	19
Africa	Morocco	1	
	Nigeria	1	
	Tanzania	1	3
Mediterranean	Turkey	1	
Europe	United Kingdom	3	
Central America	Mexico/Cuba	1	
More than one area	India/Nepal/Thailand	2	
	Indonesia/Hong Kong	1	
	Mexico/China	1	4
Total			40

A travel history was available for 40 of the 42 HTD diagnoses and is summarised in Table 2. The Indian sub-continent accounted for almost half the cases and this fits well with the knowledge that *Cyclospora* infection is endemic in Nepal, with cases confined largely to the period May through October (Hoge *et al.* 1993). Although three cases were reported from Africa, two of them from South of the Sahara, this continent as a whole is under represented in this series, since Sub-Saharan Africa is the commonest area visited by patients returning to the HTD either for clinical care or for Post Tropical Screening. Three of the HTD series had not travelled abroad recently.

Table 3. PHLS, Communicable Disease Surveillance Centre, Travel history for patients with *Cyclospora* infection 1994, weeks 1 to 37

Pacific	Indonesia	6	6
Far East	Cambodia	1	
	Thailand	1	
	Far East	1	
	SE Asia	1	4
Indian Sub-Continent	Bangladesh	2	
	India	2	
	Nepal	3	7
Mediterranean	Turkey	4	4
Europe	Bulgaria	1	1
More than one area	Indonesia/Hong Kong	1	
	SE Asia/S Africa	1	
	India/Nepal/Thailand	2	
	Nepal/Hong Kong	1	
	Mexico/China	1	6
Total			28

The Public Health Laboratory Service, Communicable Disease Surveillance Centre received 42 notifications of *Cyclospora* infection during weeks 1-37 of 1994. One incidence of double reporting was identified, leaving 41 cases. Of these, a travel history was available for 28 (Adak, personal communication 1994). Table 3 shows the travel history for the PHLS series and, though the preponderance of cases from the Indian Sub-continent is less pronounced, the overall pattern of travel is similar.

Three patients had no history of recent overseas travel:

1 In 1992, a case was reported from Worthing, West Sussex. The patient had visited Australia nine months prior to his illness, but there was no other travel history in the intervening period. He had his own swimming pool and an aliquot of the pool water was examined at HTD, but no *Cyclospora* were found.
2 In 1993, a case was diagnosed by microscopy on a sample from Yeovil in Somerset. The patient had visited a waterfall in North Devon and also drunk untreated well-water from the same county. There was no recent overseas travel.
3 In 1994, a case was recorded in Bury St Edmunds, Suffolk. The patient had a charcoal based water filter which was attached to her water system which she used for drinking. The filter was transported to the HTD, dismantled and examined, but no *Cyclospora* could be found in it.

Diagnosis

In order for epidemiological data to be accurate, a satisfactory level of diagnosis is required. There are a few clinical clues in the case of *Cyclospora* which point towards this particular organism. However, the prolonged nature of the illness, the infrequent fever, remission and relapse and malabsorption suggest a parasitic rather than bacterial or viral cause and point to *Cyclospora* or *Giardia* as possible causes.

The standard of diagnostic parasitology in the UK is monitored by the UK National External Quality Assessment Scheme (NEQAS). In September 1993, a faecal suspension for concentration was distributed which contained oocysts of *Cyclospora* species. As

Cyclospora had not been sent previously, it was not scored, though participants were not aware of this in advance of their reporting. Table 4 shows the results obtained. Twenty eight per cent of laboratories were able to diagnose this parasite, in many cases without ever having seen it before in the diagnostic laboratory. One hundred and forty two of 315 (45%) failed to see any cysts. In contrast, a distribution of fixed but unstained faecal smears was sent in June 1994 with instructions to participants that they should examine the specimen for *Cryptosporidium*, the specimen having come from a farmer with diarrhoea. Ninety seven per cent of the participants successfully detected the presence of *Cryptosporidium*. In August 1994 a fixed faecal smear containing *Cyclospora* stained with modified Ziehl-Neelsen stain was sent to participants with the request that they examine it for parasites, the specimen having come from a patient with diarrhoea following a visit to Nepal. Table 5 shows the results obtained. Eighty two per cent of laboratories were able to detect the presence of *Cyclospora*, but 36 laboratories reported an unexpected parasite only. Thirty three of these laboratories (11% of the total participants) reported the presence of *Cryptosporidium*. In a modified Ziehl-Neelsen stained faecal smear the size difference (4-6 µm for *Cryptosporidium*, 8-10 µm for *Cyclospora*) should alert microscopists to the presence of *Cyclospora* rather than *Cryptosporidium* (Chiodini, 1994).

Table 4. Participants' reports: UK NEQAS Parasitology, September 1993

Category of report	No. of reports
Oocysts of *Cyclospora* species (correct response)	89
Unspecified cysts seen	13
No parasites seen	142
One unexpected parasite only	66
Two unexpected parasites only	3
Three unexpected parasites only	2

Table 5. Participants' reports: UK NEQAS Parasitology, August 1994

Category of report	No. of reports
Oocysts of *Cyclospora* species (correct response)	236
Unspecified coccidian species	3
No parasites seen*	11
One unexpected parasite only	36

*Includes 4 reports of 'No oocysts of *Cryptosporidium* species'

Conclusions

Cyclospora infection in the UK is mostly imported. The infection is under-diagnosed in the laboratory and probably also by clinicians. *Cyclospora* is being confused in the laboratory with *Cryptosporidium*. *Cyclospora* infection in the UK merits more detailed surveillance with special attention to cases which do not have an overseas travel history. Although *Cyclospora* infection is thought to be water-borne (Hoge *et al.* 1993) more detailed attention to food and water histories in known cases, with targeted sampling should help to unravel the epidemiology.

Acknowledgements

We are grateful to Dr Bob Adak, Public Health Laboratory Service, Communicable Disease Surveillance Centre, for providing data on notifications of *Cyclospora* to the CDSC.

Results from the UK NEQAS Parasitology Sub-Scheme are reproduced with the permission of Mr J. J. S. Snell, Director of the QA Laboratory at the Central Public Health Laboratory, Colindale, London.

References

Ashford R W (1979). Occurrence of an undescribed coccidian in man in Papua New Guinea. Annals of Tropical Medicine and Parasitology, 73: 497-500

Chiodini P L (1994). A 'new' parasite: human infection with *Cyclospora cayetanensis*. Transactions of the Royal Society of Tropical Medicine and Hygiene, 88: 369-371

Hoge C W, Shlim D R , Rajah R, Triplett J, Shear M, Rabold J G and Echeverria P (1993) Epidemiology of diarrhoeal illness associated with coccidian-like organisms among travellers and foreign residents in Nepal. Lancet 341: 1175-1179

Ortega Y R, Sterling C R, Gutman R H, Cama V A and Diaz F (1992) *Cyclospora cayetanensis*: a new protozoan pathogen of humans. American Journal of Tropical Medicine and Hygiene 47, Supplement 210

Soave R, Dubey J P, Ramos L J, Tummings M (1986) A new intestinal pathogen? Clinical Research 34: 533A

UK National Study of *Legionella* Contamination of Hospital Transplant Unit Water Supplies: Relevance of Free-living Amoebae

I. Campbell[1], W. Tennant[1], D.V. Seal[2], J. Hay[2], I. McLuckie[3] and W. Patterson[4]
[1]CSA Building Division, Clifton House, Glasgow, UK
[2]Department of Ophthalmology, University of Glasgow, UK
[3]NHS Management Executive, The Scottish Office, UK
[4]North Yorkshire Health Authority, U.K

Introduction

L. pneumophila, the causative organism of Legionnaires' disease presents a considerable risk to hospitalised patients with compromised T-cell immunity. Potable water has been indicted as a source of this infection (Patterson *et al.* 1994). The legionellas proliferate within, for example, water heating or holding tanks. Despite implementation of containment procedures, nosocomial Legionnaires' disease continues to be a problem to the transplant patient (Hay and Seal, 1994a,b).

Infection control is complicated by the natural history of *Legionella* within the environment of hospital plumbing systems. One such problem is the known interaction of *Legionella* with certain free-living protozoa (Fields, 1993). It has even been suggested that *Legionella* does not proliferate in its ecosystem in the absence of protozoa, although this is unlikely in all situations.

This study permitted investigation of the prevalence of *Legionella* and such protozoa in the potable water supplies of certain UK transplant units.

Materials and Methods

Water from 72 hospital transplant units was examined. Two 5-litre water samples (1 hot, 1 cold) were collected immediately outside the unit and a similar two within the unit. This comprised the pre-point prevalence study (PPPS). Source of the cold and hot water (main, bore-hole, tank) was determined. Water chemistry including chlorine levels was obtained for each sample. Subsequently each unit had two 5-litre samples collected (1 hot, 1 cold) on one single day at an appointed time. This comprised the point prevalence study (PPS).
All water samples were processed for *Legionella* using culture (Harrison and Taylor, 1988) and for free-living amoebae (Page, 1988).

Results and Discussion

On the first visit to the 72 units (PPPS), 32 (44%) of cold water samples yielded *Legionella* (72% *L. pneumophila*, 28% *L. anisa*), as did 28 (39%) of hot water samples (89% *L. pneumophila*, 11% *L. anisa*). *L. pneumophila* serogroups 1 to 10 were present as determined by immunofluorescent staining. Other species of *Legionella* were not detected. On the PPS, 70 units returned samples. 22 (31%) of cold supplies yielded *Legionella* (36% L.pneumophila, 64% *L. anisa*) as did 22 (31%) of hot supplies (73% *L. pneumophila*, 27% *L. anisa*). On both occasions *L. pneumophila* and *L. anisa* were isolated together from cold supplies (7 on PPPS and 3 on PPS) or hot supplies (6 on PPPS and 4 on PPS).

Free-living amoebae including those of the genera *Acanthamoeba, Vahlkampfia, Hartmannella and Echinamoeba*, known to permit intracellular multiplication of *Legionella* (Fields 1993) were present in a number of samples as were various ciliates and flagellates.

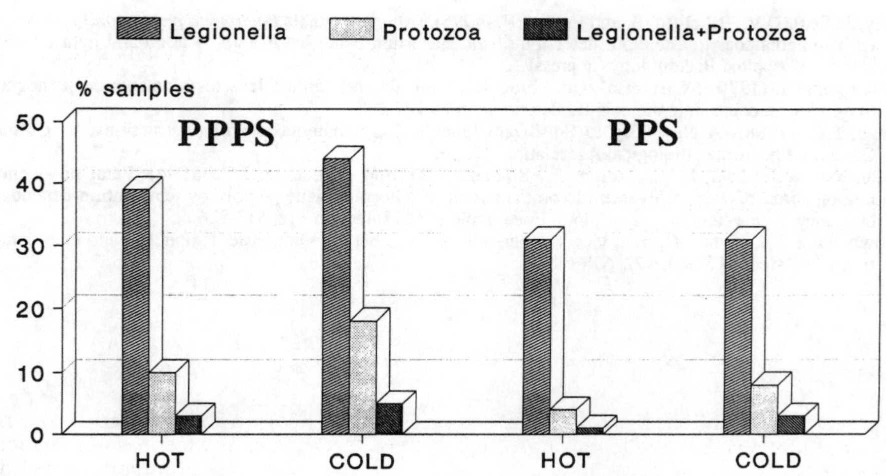

Figure 1. *Legionella* and Protozoa

The prevalence of protozoa was somewhat lower than that of *Legionella*, This may suggest that water sampling was collecting planktonic *Legionella* only, and not those associated with biofilm or protozoa.

It is generally recognised that elimination of *Legionella* from hosptal water supplies is exceedingly difficult. This may, at least in part, be the consequence of the protozoonotic relationship between *Legionella* and free-living amoebae (Rowbotham, 1986) in the water system. The presence of such protozoa within this habitat may have profound consequences from an infection control perspective. The cysts of, for example, *Acanthamoeba* are resistant to chlorine derived from hypochlorite at levels of 50 ppm (Kilvington, 1990). Furthermore, in the laboratory at least, the interaction of Acanthamoeba with *Legionella* may render the bacteria viable but not culturable on BCYE agar (Hay *et al.* 1995). The latter, should it occur with samples from hospital plumbing systems, may lead to erroneous conclusions regarding infection control procedures for *Legionella*.

The primary object of such infection control procedures in hospitals is to negate the risk of infection by *Legionella* in patients who may be at high risk of developing Legionnaires' disease. In order to accomplish this aim protozoa capable of harbouring *Legionella* and especially those permitting its proliferation must be eradicated from the plumbing system. This is especially so in the water supplies to transplant units.

The challenge at present is to identify a suitable biocide which will perform such a task but be innocuous at residual levels which may come into contact with patients.

References

Fields, B.S. (1993). *Legionella* and protozoa: interaction of a pathogen and its natural host. In: *Legionella* Current Status and Emerging Perspectives, Editors Barbaree, J.M., Brieman, R.F. and Dufour, A.P. American Society for Microbiology, Washington D.C., pp129-136

Harrison, T.G. and Taylor, A.G. Eds. (1988). A Laboratory Manual for *Legionella*. Wiley Interscience, New York., 181pp

Hay, J. and Seal D.V. (1994a). Surveying for legionnaires' disease bacterium. Current Opinion in Infectious Disease 7, 479-483

Hay, J. and Seal, D.V. (1994b). Monitoring of hospital water supplies for *Legionella*. Journal of Hospital Infection 26, 75-78

Hay, J., Seal, D.V., Billcliffe, B. and Freer, J.H. (1995). Non-cultivatable *Legionella pneumophila* associated with Acanthamoeba castellanii: detection of the bacterium using DNA amplification and hybridization. Journal of Applied Bacteriology (in press)

Kilvington, S. (1990). Activity of water biocide chemicals and contact lens disinfectants on pathogenic free-living amoebae. International Biodeterioration 26 127-138

Page, F.C. (1988). A New Key to Freshwater and Soil Gymnamoebae with Instructions for Culture. Cumbria, Freshwater Biological Association. 122pp

Patterson, W.J., Seal, D.V., Curran, E., Sinclair, T.M. and McLuckie, J.C. (1994). Fatal nosocomial Legionnaires' disease: relevance of contamination of a hospital water supply by temperature-dependany buoyancy-driven flow from spur pipes. Epidemiology and Infection 112, 513-526

Rowbotham, T.J. (1986). Current views on the relationships between amoebae, legionellae and man. Israeli Journal of Medical Science 22, 678-689

The Incidence of Cryptosporidiosis in Comparison with other Gastrointestinal Illnesses in Blackpool, Wyre and Fylde

L. Fewtrell[1] and A. Delahunty[2]
[1]Post Doctoral Research Fellow, CREH, 5 Quakers Coppice, Crewe, Cheshire, UK
[2]CREH Senior Research Fellow, Registrar in Public Health Medicine, East Dyfed and Pembrokeshire Health Authorities, UK

Introduction

At the request of the Blackpool, Wyre and Fylde Director of Public Health a study was conducted to look at the incidence of cryptosporidiosis in the area. Blackpool, Wyre and Fylde is a small health authority in the North West of England with a resident population of almost 320 000. Public water supplies are provided by North West Water, predominantly from the Barnacre, Franklaw, Hodder and Broughton water treatment works. These water treatment works receive their water from a variety of sources including upland impounding reservoirs, boreholes and the rivers Lune and Wyre.

The area has a higher than average rate of cryptosporidiosis reporting, and the study was conducted to see if it was possible to explain the pattern of illness in non-outbreak conditions.

Methodology

The study was conducted in two parts; the first part examined the incidence of the illness retrospectively over a six year period between 1987 and 1992; whilst the second part gathered prospective information, over the space of a year, on a number of gastrointestinal illnesses, including cryptosporidiosis and giardiasis.

Retrospective Study

In the retrospective study, information on the incidence of cryptosporidiosis was collected by examination of pathology laboratory records from Victoria Hospital in Blackpool. Age, sex, postcode, date of first isolation and lab number were reported for each identified case. Postcode data were converted to grid references, ward codes and also street names using 'Postcode Address Files' obtained from the Royal Mail. The grid references and street names allowed individual cases to be plotted on a map of water supply zone.

Prospective Study

In the prospective study data were gathered by the use of a specially designed questionnaire which was conducted on a one-to-one basis by local environmental health officers with people reporting laboratory-confirmed infections with *Campylobacter* spp., *Cryptosporidium* sp., *Giardia* sp., *Salmonella* spp. or *Shigella* spp. The questionnaire included questions on water sports participation, contact with animals and whether any trips away from home had been made in the two weeks prior to symptom onset. As with the retrospective study, postcode data were converted to grid references, ward codes and street names using 'Postcode Address Files'.

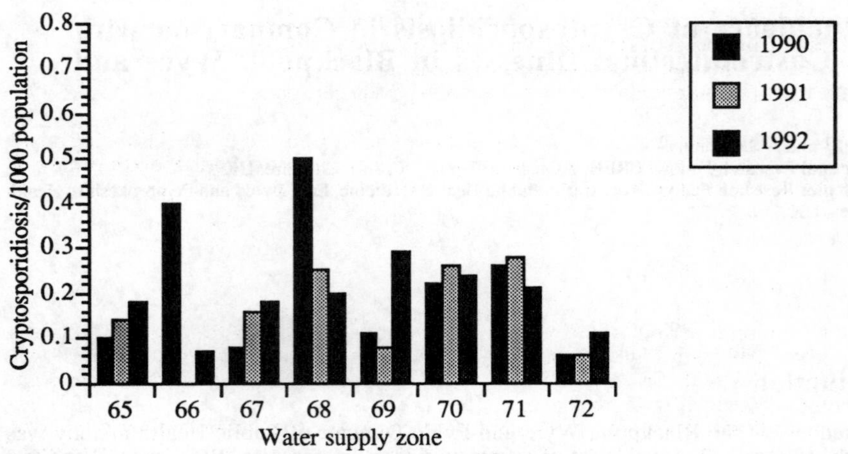

Figure 1. Cryptosporidiosis/1000 Population by Water Supply Zone (1990-1992)

Results

Retrospective Study

During the six year period of the retrospective study a total of 497 cases of laboratory-confirmed cryptosporidiosis were reported. The ages of the cases ranged from 4 months to 89 years old. Table 1 shows the annual incidence during the study period.

Table 1. Annual Incidence of Cryptosporidiosis between 1.1.87 and 31.12.92

Year	Index cases	Total cases
1987	62	86
1988	49	59
1989	131	162
1990	59	67
1991	51	54
1992	60	69

The number of cases is fairly stable, with the exception of 1989 where the number of cases was more than double that typically seen. Examination of the monthly incidence of cases showed that *Cryptosporidium* isolation was highest in late summer and autumn (it should be noted that the month identified is when the first isolation of the pathogen was made and NOT that of the onset of the symptoms). The greatest level of isolation was found in infants between the ages of 1 and 4, with a second smaller peak seen in 25 to 34 year olds.

Figure 1 shows the annual reporting of cryptosporidiosis for 1990, 1991 and 1992 per 1000 of the population by home water supply zone. It can be seen from this Figure that there is no consistent pattern of elevated reporting in any of the water supply zones. Statistical analysis showed very few differences between the zones.

Census wards were identified for each case of cryptosporidiosis reported over the study period. As there are over 70 wards in Blackpool, Wyre and Fylde the annual data were combined and the ward data compared with figures for the whole area for the six year period. Only one ward, Staining in the Fylde area, had a significantly higher level of cryptosporidiosis isolations than the other wards. Four so called 'deprivation' variables, based on Townsend *et al.* (1986), were calculated for each ward:

- the percentage of economically active residents who are unemployed;
- the percentage of households that do not possess a car;
- the percentage of households not owner occupied, and
- the percentage of households with more than one person per room.

For each calculated variable, wards were ranked and then examined to see if Staining could be considered to be a 'deprived' ward. Staining didn't appear in the bottom sixth of any of the ranking lists, suggesting that 'deprivation' is not a factor in the reporting of cryptosporidiosis.

Prospective Results

During the 12 month period, a total of 573 cases of the selected gastrointestinal illnesses were reported; 239 with *Campylobacter* spp., 71 with *Cryptosporidium* spp., 53 with *Giardia* spp., 186 with *Salmonella* spp. and 24 with *Shigella* spp. Ten people were concurrently infected with two pathogens.

Cryptosporidiosis reporting was once again greatest in the autumn. Campylobacter infections peaked in the summer whilst Salmonella infections were high during the summer and autumn, as were Shigella, Giardia showed no obvious peak. Overall there was very little difference in the incidence of the gastrointestinal illnesses in men and women with 50.2% recorded in women and 49.8% in men.

The figures obtained from the Blackpool, Wyre and Fylde area were compared with the national rate derived from the Communicable Disease Report produced by the Public Health Laboratory Service. Blackpool Wyre and Fylde had significantly lower levels of Campylobacter, Salmonella and Shigella infection when compared with national figures. There was no difference in the incidence of giardiasis, but cryptosporidiosis reporting was, for the seventh year in succession, significantly higher than the national level.

As with the retrospective study, postcode information was converted into grid references, street names and ward codes allowing the incidence of illness in individual water supply zones and census wards to be examined. Examining the incidence of gastrointestinal illness reporting (per 1000 population) by water supply zone showed that there were no marked differences between zones for *Cryptosporidium* sp. or *Shigella* spp. There were, however, marked differences for some of the pathogens, especially *Campylobacter* spp. and *Giardia* sp. Water supply zone 68 showed significantly elevated reporting of *Campylobacter* spp., *Giardia* sp. and *Salmonella* spp. Water supply zone 70 also showed elevated campylobacter isolations.

Whilst *Giardia* sp. may be transmitted by drinking water, neither campylobacter enteritis nor salmonellosis, which are also elevated in water supply zone 68, would be expected to be caused by the public water supply. This suggests that other factors may be contributing. To examine this it was hoped to compare the various rates of illness reporting between the census wards, but when the cases were split between 71 wards the numbers were to small to be meaningful.

Data on possible 'risk factors', obtained from the questionnaire, were examined for each index case. Individuals with shigellosis were significantly more likely to report recent travel abroad ($p<0.05$) and consumption of raw dairy produce ($p<0.01$). Over 30% of people suffering from cryptosporidiosis reported contact with farm animals in the period prior to their illness, whilst 40% reported participation in water sports. When compared with people suffering from other gastrointestinal illnesses, recreational water use and farm animal contact were both statistically significant at $p<0.01$ for cryptosporidiosis.

Discussion

Overall, the study showed an elevated incidence of cryptosporidiosis in the Blackpool, Wyre and Fylde area. Although the levels of reporting are fairly consistent, spatial analysis of the data did not demonstrate any trends when examined in relation to water supply zone or census ward. An examination of the water supply system in Blackpool, Wyre and Fylde, however, revealed that it is very complex with the supply zones being served by several different sources, making any pattern very difficult to identify. When data were combined from the six year period, Staining was the only ward which demonstrated an elevated incidence of cryptosporidiosis. Staining can not be considered to be a deprived area, and although it is a rural ward there does not seem to be an unusual concentration of livestock farming in the area which might explain the higher than expected level of cryptosporidiosis.

Although recreational water use was found to be a 'risk factor', local swimming pools are unlikely to be the source, since no single pool was consistently highlighted when individuals reported their swimming habits. Two people with cryptosporidiosis had been in contact with river water, one of whom attributed his illness to swallowing water from the river Ribble whilst boating.

Over 30% of people with cryptosporidiosis reported previous contact with farm animals, three-quarters of whom were under the age of ten. In this instance health education could have a role to play in reducing the incidence by making parents, teachers and farm staff more aware of the potential risk of cryptosporidiosis from farm visits.

Information on the national incidence of cryptosporidiosis and other gastrointestinal illnesses is collected by the Communicable Disease Surveillance Centre through a laboratory reporting system, with the 53 public health laboratories along with about 300 other laboratories reporting laboratory-confirmed infections. It is a PHLS recommendation that all acute diagnostic faecal samples are screened for *Cryptosporidium* sp.; this is also the policy in Blackpool Wyre and Fylde. This is not necessarily the case in all laboratories, with full screening often only done on faecal samples from children. It would seem likely that the consistently high rates of identified cryptosporidiosis cases in the area are due to a combination of the through screening procedures in Blackpool Wyre and Fylde, coupled with the semi-rural nature of the area.

References

Townsend, P., Phillimore, P. and Beattie, A. (1986) *Inequalities in health in the Northern Region: an interim report*. Northern Regional Health Authority.

Giardia Cyst Concentrations and Infectivity: Longitudinal Community Drinking Water Studies

J. Isaac-Renton[1], W. Moorehead[2] and A. Ross[3]
[1]Department of Pathology and Laboratory Medicine, University of British Columbia and British Columbia Centre for Disease Control, Vancouver, Canada
[2]South Okanagan and [3]North Okanagan Health Units, Ministry of Health, British Columbia, Canada.

Introduction

Waterborne outbreaks of giardiasis have occurred in several provinces in Canada and in British Columbia leading to over 1500 cases annually (Wallis 1994; Fisk 1987; Isaac-Renton 1987). Protozoal contamination of surface water supplies is a public health concern since most drinking water is obtained from unfiltered sources. A province-wide survey was carried out to determine the extent and distribution of *Giardia* contamination. Longitudinal community studies were then done with the aim of further studying the observation that cyst concentrations and viability decreased after settling in reservoirs and after chlorination. Study of seasonal trends in parasite concentrations and viability, sources of *Giardia* contamination, and health of the population using this drinking water were also studied.

Methods

Drinking Water Testing

Large volume water samples were collected and tested as described elsewhere (D-19 Proposal 1992). Because the basic method was developed for low-turbidity water (D-19 Proposal 1992; Riley *et al.* 1993) and high-turbidity water matrices are found throughout the province, some minor modifications were required. Sucrose flotation (Schaefer *et al.*1982) was used in the province-wide testing in the twelve months of the study based on then current recommendations. A Percoll-sucrose gradient (specific gravity 1.10) was used in the following two-year community projects (D-19 Proposal 1992). Cyst recovery efficiencies were determined. Cyst viability was assessed by infectivity in the Mongolian gerbil (*Meriones unguiculatus*) (Faubert and Belosevic 1990) and some samples were also assessed using a vital dye staining technique (Sauch *et al.* 1991).

Drinking Water Studies

Province-wide. Drinking water samples were collected from all regions of British Columbia over a 12-month period. No filtered drinking water supplies were tested.

Black Mountain Irrigation District (BMID). Drinking water samples were collected on the same day at three sites within the system (T values consistently exceeded the values recommended for 99.9% cyst removal. Samples collected were: raw water at the Mission Creek intake, water that had been settled in the 10.5 million gal reservoir, and water after chlorination (Fig. 1). Sampling was carried out twice a week for twelve months. Drinking water was also sampled "at tap" (a residence). Cyst-positive sediments were inoculated into pretreated gerbils.

Vernon Irrigation District (VID). This community is in a separate but adjacent watershed to BMID. Drinking water samples were collected weekly on the same day from two sites in the system: raw surface source water at the intake in the Duteau Creek and water that had been

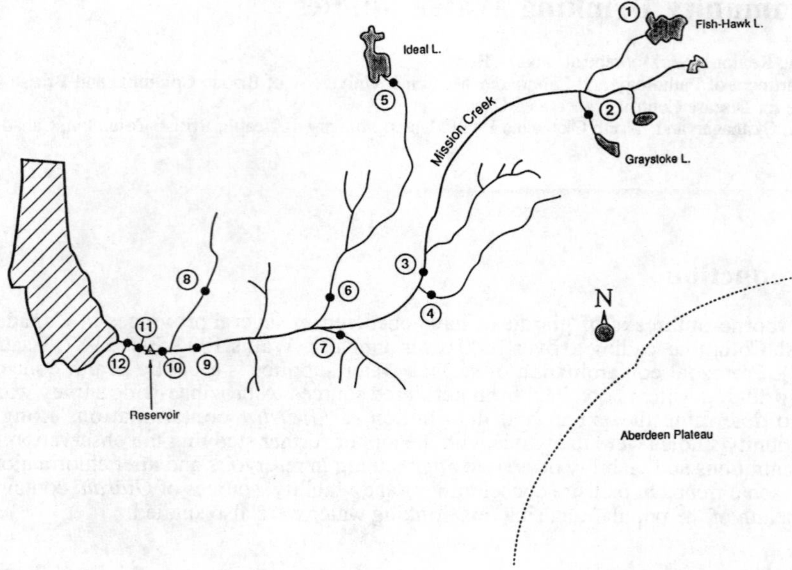

Figure 1. Black Mountain Irrigation District (BMID) watershed. Numbers indicate sites of watershed sampling (1-9) and community drinking water sampling (site 10 raw, site 11 settled in reservoir, and site 12 chlorinated). Cysts were detected at sites 3,4,5,6,7 and 9 as well as 10,11,12.

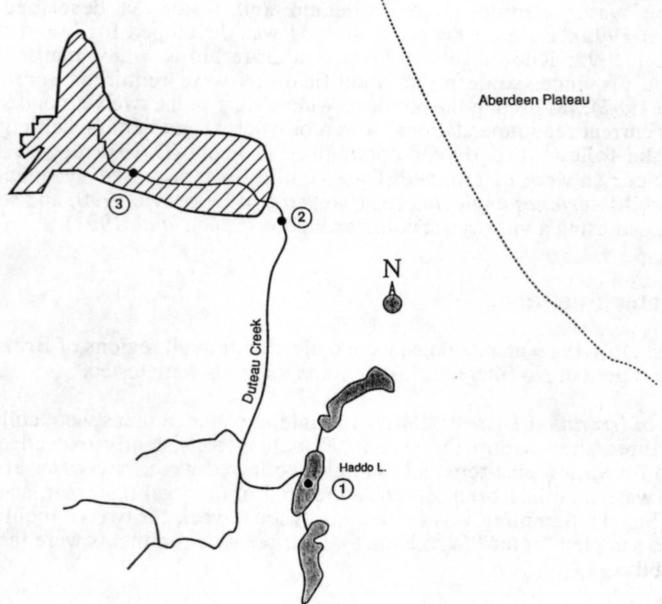

Figure 2. Vernon Irrigation District (VID) watershed. Numbers indicate sites of lake site sampling (1) and community drinking water sampling (site 2, raw and site 3, chlorinated).

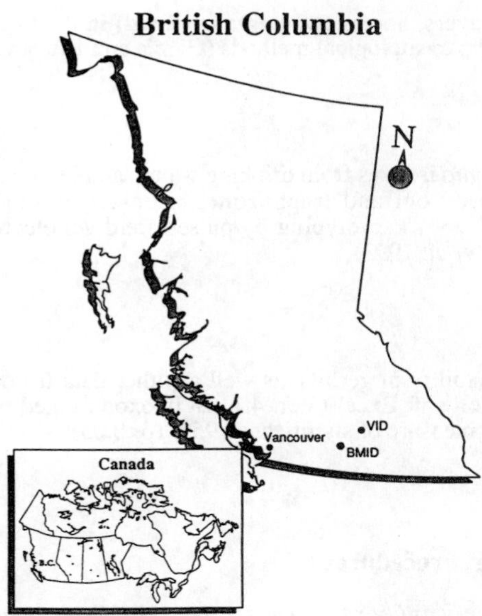

Figure 3. Map of British Columbia, Canada, indicating the location of the two communities studied.

chlorinated (Fig.2). Sampling was carried out for twelve months. Cyst-positive sediments were inoculated into gerbils. Ten pairs of raw and chlorinated samples were also stained with propidium iodide to assess viability.

Surveillance and Seroprevalence Studies

Province-wide. Giardiasis is a reportable disease in this western Canadian province (population 3,544,000, Fig.3). A province-wide serosurvey (1,122 persons) was carried out using an enzyme-linked immunosorbent assay (Isaac-Renton *et al.* 1994).

Black Mountain Irrigation District (BMID) Community. This community (population 17,000) is located in a ranching and orcharding region (Fig.3). Physicians in the community were reminded to report identified cases of giardiasis as well as to submit fecal samples on all patients with gastrointestinal symptoms. A seroprevalence study (IgM and IgG) of residents was carried out as in the province-wide study.

Vernon Irrigation District (VID) Community. Physicians in this ranching community (population 16,000, Fig.3) were also reminded to report all cases of giardiasis and encouraged to use diagnostic laboratory facilities in cases of gastrointestinal illness. A seroprevalence study (anti-*Giardia* IgG and IgM) of residents was also carried out as described above.

Watershed Investigations

Sampling sites were described in terms of resident animals (domestic and wild), human activity, and human sewage discharges. Water samples from 9 sites in the BMID watershed and 1 source site (VID) were tested for *Giardia* (Figs. 1, 2). Fecal specimens were collected from animals (cattle, beavers, horses and migratory fowl) in the two watersheds and were processed using standard parasitological methods (Garcia and Bruckner 1993).

Parasite Biotyping

Attempts to retrieve *Giardia* isolates from drinking water samples as well as from human and animal hosts were carried out and trophozoites axenized in culture characterized by isoenzyme analysis and DNA karyotyping by pulsed field gel electrophoresis as reported elsewhere (Isaac-Renton *et al.* 1993).

Data Analysis

Cyst quantitation and viability in gerbils, as well as other data from water samples tested, were analysed using Microsoft Excel (Ver. 4.1). Wilcoxon ranked pairs test and Student's t-test were used with the measure of significance 95% ($p<0.05$).

Results

Efficiency of Testing Procedures

The mean per cent recovery of *Giardia* cysts for the method using sucrose clarification (the first year's inventory) was 17.7% compared to 37.9% for Percoll-sucrose (the two year community studies).

Drinking Water Studies

Province-wide. Two hundred and forty-four drinking water samples (153 raw, 91 treated) from 86 sites were tested in the first stage of the study. Overall, 64% of samples (69% of sites) were *Giardia* cyst-positive. None of the sites were considered pristine (Rose *et al.* 1991) but all sites are in rural areas. No seasonal variation in raw water cyst concentrations was noted. Mean cyst concentrations from raw water samples (arithmetic mean 11.2 cysts/100L, geometric mean 2.9 cysts/100L) were greater than chlorinated samples (arithmetic mean 5.3 cysts/100L, geometric mean 2.1 cysts/100L). Sixty-eight per cent of raw water samples and 59% of treated (chlorinated) samples were cyst-positive. Forty-five (34%) of 133 cyst-positive samples inoculated into gerbils were infective (Fig.4). Infectivity of cysts was more frequently found when sediments from raw water were inoculated, compared with cysts from sediments from treated water samples.

Black Mountain Irrigation District. Two hundred and twenty-nine drinking water samples were tested. Seventy samples were of raw water, 75 samples were obtained after reservoir settling, and 77 were chlorinated. Seven other samples were collected as described (post-pressure reducing valve and "at tap"). Two hundred and eight samples (91%), including 70 (100%) raw, 74 (99%) settled, and 59 (77%) chlorinated, were cyst-positive. Cyst concentrations ranged from 7-2,215 cysts/100L (geometric mean 229 cysts/100L) for raw water, 12-626 cysts/100L (geometric mean 95 cysts/100L) for samples collected after reservoir settling, and 0.3-371/100L (geometric mean 31 cysts/100L) for chlorinated samples. Samples "at tap" were found to contain cysts.

Mean monthly cyst concentrations were calculated (Fig.5). Marked variation by month was observed with a seasonal trend to peak concentrations (maximum mean monthly concentration 1,500 cysts/100L, peak sample concentration 2,215/100 L) in late autumn and early winter. High raw water cyst concentrations were found more frequently during the peak months. Wide day-to-day variation in cyst concentrations was also observed (Fig.6). This "spiking" phenomenon (cyst concentrations higher than the overall trend) was observed

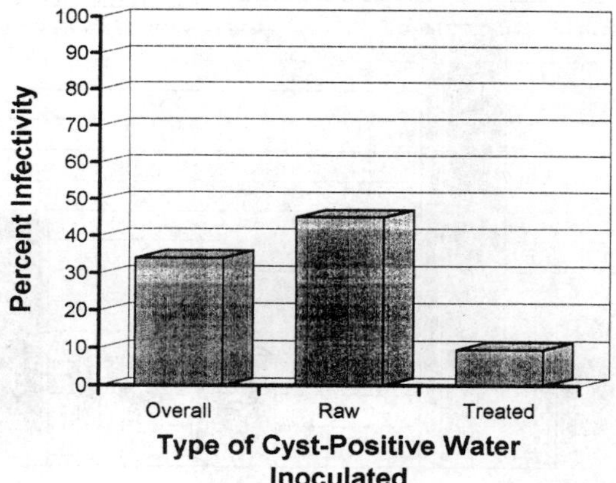

Figure 4. Per cent infectivity in gerbils of all-cyst-positive sediments in the province-wide study. Raw and treated samples were collected from the same site on the same day.

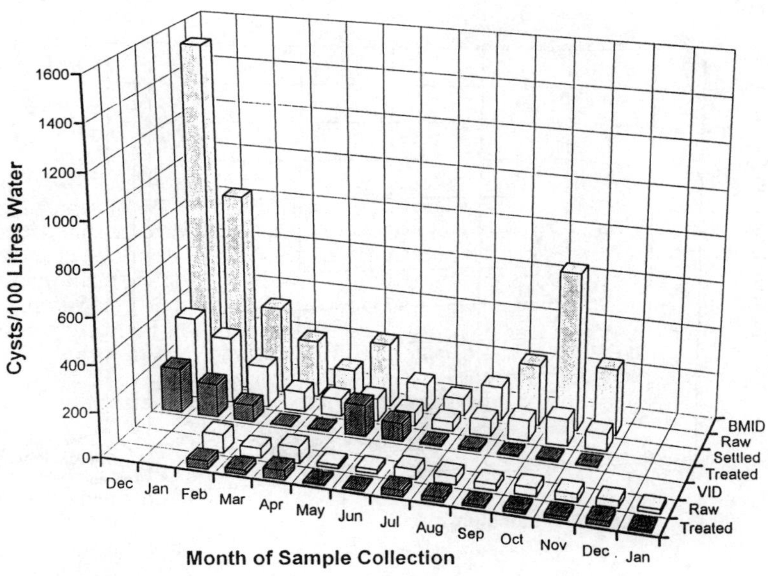

Figure 5. Mean monthly *Giardia* concentrations (cysts per 100 L) in Black Mountain Irrigation District (BMID raw, reservoir settled and chlorinated) and Vernon Irrigation District (VID raw and chlorinated) drinking water samples.

during months of both peak (December - January) and non-peak concentrations (May). In one 24 hr sampling period the number of cysts climbed from 493 to 1,424 cysts per 100 litres.

Comparison of raw, reservoir settled and treated water cyst concentrations showed significant differences (Student's t-test, $p < 0.05$) between each of the mean monthly cyst

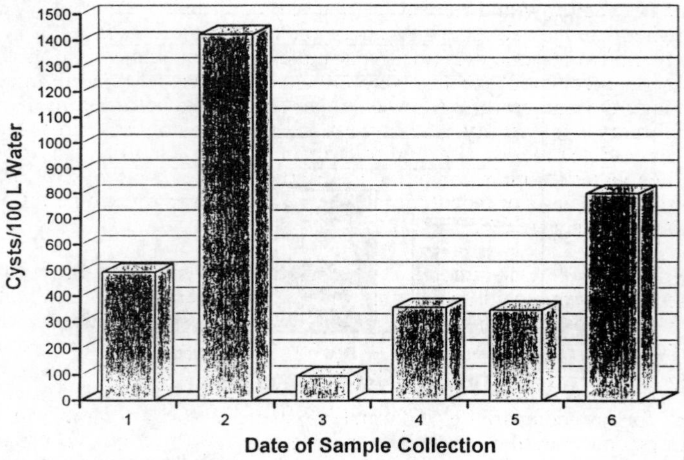

Figure 6. Day-to-day variation in raw water cyst concentrations in Black Mountain Irrigation District. Pair labelled 1-2 was collected in December, pair 3-4 was collected in January and pair 5-6 pair was collected in May.

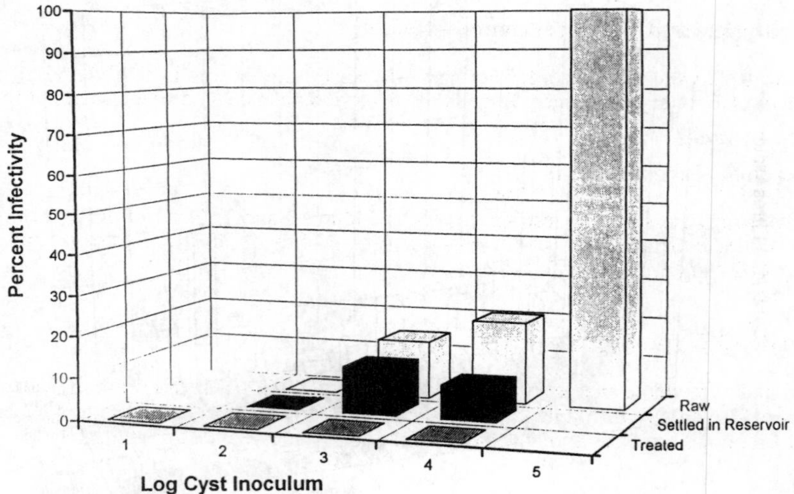

Figure 7. Per cent infectivity of BMID samples in Mongolian gerbils (*Meriones unguiculatus*) by type of water and number of cysts inoculated.

concentrations. Significance differences between these sample types occurred in both peak and non-peak months. When cyst removal between raw and chlorinated specimens was analysed, a two log or greater reduction in cyst numbers was achieved in 3 of 12 months. A one log reduction was achieved in 8 of 12 months. During peak cyst concentration months (December, January and October), a two log cyst removal concentration was seen only in October. Sets of peak cyst concentrations most frequently showed a one log reduction in cyst concentrations between raw and treated (settled and chlorinated water). CT values were consistently higher than the values recommended for 99.9% cyst removal.

One hundred and twenty-one cyst-positive samples were inoculated into gerbils. Eleven (11% of sediments inoculated) isolates were infective. A seasonal trend in infectivity was seen and although the number of cysts was higher in samples collected in winter months (December-February), infectivity was highest for samples collected in the autumn. A significant decrease (Student's t-test, $p < 0.1$) in percent viability was observed for chlorinated (0%) water samples compared to reservoir settled water (10%) or raw water (18%). Analysis on the basis of inoculum (number of cysts given to each gerbil) was carried out and the same results were seen (Fig.7).

Vernon Irrigation District. One hundred and seven samples were tested. Fifty-three samples were raw water and 54 were chlorinated. One hundred per cent (53/53) of raw water samples and 98%(53/54) of chlorinated samples were cyst-positive. Cyst concentrations ranged from 8-114/100L (geometric mean 30 cysts/100L) for raw water and 2-73/100L (geometric mean 14 cysts/100L) for chlorinated water. No clear seasonal trend was observed (Fig.5). Significant differences (Student's t-test, $p< 0.05$) were noted between mean monthly concentrations for raw compared to chlorinated water. There were no months, including times of peak cyst concentrations, in which a one log or greater cyst removal occurred.

None of the cyst-positive VID samples inoculated into gerbils was infective. Propidium iodide dye inclusion studies of ten raw-treated paired samples were carried out and 89% of cysts from raw water samples appeared viable by these microscopic standards compared to 68% from chlorinated samples ($p< 0.01$).

Surveillance and Seroprevalence Studies

No outbreaks were identified during the study period. Five cases in BMID and 20 cases in VID were laboratory confirmed. Results of the seroprevalence studies are seen in Fig.8.

Watershed Investigations

Results from watershed site testing are seen in Figures 1 and 2. Three of thirty fecal samples (10%) collected from BMID cattle (Fig 1, site 7), 3 of the 9 (33%) VID beaver and 5 of ten (50%) VID cattle were *Giardia*-positive.

Parasite Biotyping

PFGE and zymodeme analysis showed heterogeneity in the 9 *Giardia* drinking water isolates retrieved into culture from the one watershed. The raw water isolate and settled water isolate collected on the same day in the same distribution system were different (Fig. 9).

Discussion

The overall provincial results are similar to other studies (Rose *et al.* 1991; LeChevallier *et al.*). This data is consistent with widespread parasite contamination of raw water. All studies to date underestimate the level of environmental contamination since detection methods are insensitive, and intermittent contamination of source water probably occur in some watersheds. Comparison of data from study to study must also be done with caution and in the context of the laboratory methods used.

A striking seasonal variation was noted when mean monthly cyst concentrations (as well as when the frequency distribution of cysts) were calculated for BMID raw water samples. The consistently lower cyst concentrations in VID raw water showed no seasonal pattern although both VID and BMID systems obtained source water from small, fast-flowing

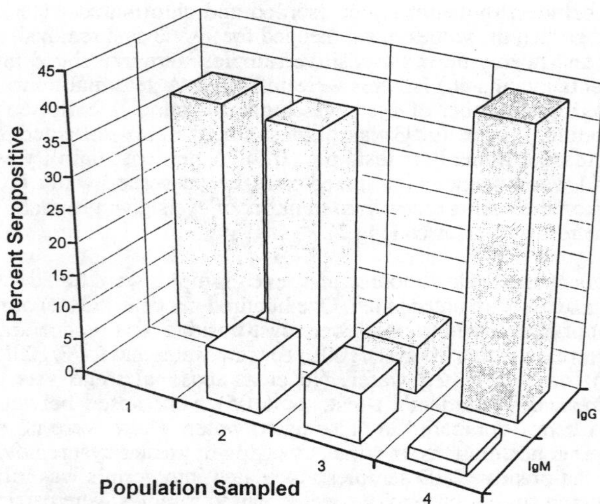

Figure 8. Seroprevalence study showing percent positive specimens (anti-*Giardia* immunoglobulin G and M) in different test populations. Lane 1 are results from the province-wide study, 2 are results from the BMID community, lane 3 the VID community and lane 4 the large urban center using chlorinated water obtained from a protected watershed.

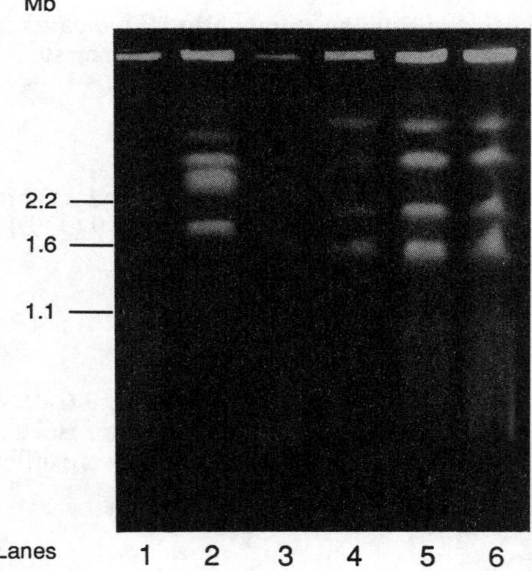

Figure 9. Heterogeneity of *Giardia* drinking water isolates from one community shown by pulsed field gel electrophoresis. Lane 1, *Saccharomyces cerevisiae* (arrows indicate molecular weight bands), lane 2, VANC/93/UBC/105, lane 3, VANC/92/UBC/100, lane 4, VANC/92/UBC/104, lane 5, VANC/92/UBC/101, lane 6, WB reference strain (ATCC #30957). Isolates in lanes 3 and 5 were collected on the same day but at different sites in the drinking water distribution system.

creeks, both of which had similar fluctuating flow rates and were in adjacent watersheds sharing most topographical features.

Both communities had *Giardia*-positive cattle identified in their watersheds although only VID's Duteau Creek had *Giardia*-infected water mammals (beavers). Range management practices differ considerably between the two watersheds. Mission Creek (BMID) is joined by creeks running through privately owned property used in some seasons for intensive ranching activities while cattle in the VID watershed are driven through Duteau Creek at specific points of the creek. It has been suggested that cattle may be a potential source of human infections (Buret *et al.* 1990). Unlike beavers, however, which can clearly act as reservoirs (Isaac-Renton *et al.* 1993), laboratory-based data is not yet available to confirm this. It is our opinion that many animals including cattle may act as reservoirs of human disease and that the zoonotic potential resides in the parasite not the host. Further attempts to retrieve and karyotype drinking water, cattle and human isolates are underway.

The present study also demonstrates heterogeneity of drinking water source isolates. The biological significance of this observation needs to be determined. At present there are no laboratory markers of virulence or host-specificity.

Besides the biological character of the parasite, other factors such as cyst concentrations and host population (herd immunity). Significant fluctuations or "spiking" levels of cyst concentrations were observed in the longitudinal studies. These fluctuations could not be accounted for by inter-test recovery differences. As well, paired raw and treated samples collected on the same day at the same site consistently showed this spiking phenomenon. The phenomenon may be an important risk factor and deserves further study.

Although a previous study reported that cysts were not removed by a large reservoir (Ongerth 1989), the present study showed that both cyst concentrations and parasite gerbil infectivity (corrected for cyst inoculum) decreased after settling. Further work, however, needs to be carried out.

Acquired protective immunity has been demonstrated in giardiasis (Isaac-Renton *et al.* 1994; Istre *et al.* 1984). Although the biological significance of anti-*Giardia* IgG as measured in the present study is not clear, it is possible that the VID community with the lower seroprevalence rate (7%) may be more susceptible to a bolus of viable, human-infective cysts than the BMID community (36%).

There is a need for more information on which to assess risk including the role of the host, the host-specificity and virulence of different strains of *Giardia* as well as the parasite's behaviour in the environment.

Acknowledgments

This work was supported by the Ministry of Health British Columbia and by British Columbia Health Research Foundation. The collaboration and support of provincial Health Unit staff, particularly Mrs. G. Volk, Mr. R. White (South Okanagan Health Unit) Mr. N. Clarkson (North Okanagan Health Unit) and Mr. P. Ruskowsky, Mr. B. Krause, Mr. M. Tomlinson, Mr. M. Nolan (BMID and VID) is gratefully acknowledged.

References

Buret A., N. den Hollander, P.M. Wallis, D. Befus and M.E. Olsen. 1990. Zoonotic potential of giardiasis in domestic ruminants. J. Infect. Dis. 162:231-237

D-19 Proposal P 229, Proposed test method for *Giardia* cysts and *Cryptosporidium* oocysts in low turbidity water by a fluorescent antibody procedure. 1992. Annual Book of ASTM Standards. Section 11, Water and Environmental Technology, Vol. 11.02, water (II), p.925-935, ASTM, Philadelphia, PA

Faubert G.M., and M. Belosevic. 1990. Animal models for *Giardia duodenalis* type organisms, p.77-90. *In* Meyer E.A.(ed.) Giardiasis;human parasitic diseases. Elsevier Science Publishing Co., Amsterdam

Fisk, R. 1987. Giardiasis in British Columbia. Can.Dis. Wkly.Rep. 13-47:211-213

Garcia L.S. and D.A Bruckner (ed.). 1993. Diagnostic procedures, p.487-535. *In* Diagnostic medical parasitology. American Society for Microbiology, Washington, D.C

Isaac-Renton J., L. Lewis, C.S.L. Ong, and M.F. Nulsen. 1994. A second community outbreak of waterborne giardiasis in Canada and serological investigation of patients. Trans. Roy. Soc. Trop. Med. Hyg. 88:33-35

Isaac-Renton J.L., C. Cordeiro, K. Sarafis and H.S. Shahriari. 1993. Characterization of *Giardia duodenalis* isolates from a waterborne outbreak. J. Infect. Dis. 167:431-40

Isaac-Renton, J.L. 1987. Giardiasis:a review. B.C. Med. J. 29:341-344

Istre, G.R., T.S. Dunlop, G.B. Gaspard and R.S. Hopkins. 1984. Waterborne giardiasis at a mountain resort: evidence for acquired immunity. Amer. J. Public Health. 74:602-604

LeChevallier, M.W., W.D. Norton and R.G. Lee. 1991 Occurrence of *Giardia* and *Cryptosporidium* species in surface water supplies. Appl. Environ. Microbiol. 57:2610-2616

Ongerth, J.E. 1989. *Giardia* cyst concentrations in river water. J Amer. Water Works. September:81-86

Riley, K., J. Oppenheimer, A. Cummings, and J. Jacangelo. 1993. Application of a modified method and quality control protocols for detection and enumeration of *Giardia* and *Cryptosporidium* seeded into variable water quality matrices. p. 1111-1130. *In* Proceedings of the 1993 Water Quality Conference

Rose, J.B., C.P. Gerba and W. Jakubowski. 1991. Survey of potable water supplies for *Cryptosporidium* and *Giardia*. Environ. Sci. Technol. 25:1393-1400

Sauch J.F., D. Flanigan, M.L. Galvin, D. Berman and W. Jakubowksi. 1991. Propidium iodide as an indicator of *Giardia* cyst viability. Appl. Environ. Microbiol. 57:3243-3247

Schaefer III, F.W. and E.W. Rice. 1982. *Giardia* methodology for water supply analysis, p. 143-147. *In* Proceedings of the American Water Works Association Water Technology Conference, American Water Works Association, Seattle

Wallis, P. M. 1994. Abiotic transmission - Is water really significant?, p. 99-122. *In* R.C.A. Thompson. J.A. Reynoldson, A.J. Lymbery (ed.), *Giardia*: From molecules to disease, CAB International, Oxon, UK

Occurrence of *Giardia* Cysts and *Cryptosporidium* Oocysts in Sewage Influent in Six Sewage Treatment Plants in Scotland and Prevalence of Cryptosporidiosis and Giardiasis Diagnosed in the Communities Served by those Plants

L.J. Robertson[1,2], H.V. Smith[1] and C.A. Paton[1,2]
[1]Scottish Parasite Diagnostic Laboratory, Stobhill NHS Trust, Springburn, Glasgow, G21 3UW, UK
[2]Division of Environmental Health, Department of Civil Engineering, University of Strathclyde, Glasgow, G1 1XQ, UK

Introduction

Giardia cysts and *Cryptosporidium* oocysts which occur in sewage may originate from a variety of sources (Table 1). If it is assumed that most human symptomatic infections of either species are diagnosed and that it is these infections which constitiute the major contribution of cysts and oocysts to sewage, then it should be possible to observe a correlation between the number of cases diagnosed in a community and the number of cysts or oocysts entering the sewage treatment plant serving that community.

Table 1. Potential sources of cysts and oocysts occurring in sewage

Human infections with*G. duodenalis/C. parvum*	- symptomatic	-diagnosed
		-not diagnosed
	- asymptomatic	
Animal infections with *G. duodenalis/C. parvum*	- symptomatic	- diagnosed
		- not diagnosed
	- asymptomatic	
Animal infections with other species of *Giardia* and *Cryptosporidium* (e.g. G. muris/C. muris)	- symptomatic	- diagnosed
		- not diagnosed
	- asymptomatic	

Previous research on the numbers of *Giardia* cysts entering sewage treatment plants and cases of giardiasis in the communities served (Jakubowski *et al.* 1991; Smith *et al.* 1994) have provided encouraging data. At one sewage treatment plant, Jakubowski *et al.* (1991) were able to demonstrate a significant and positive correlation between cases in a community and cyst concentration in sewage. However, intriguingly, a significant correlation at another plant was negative. The authors are unaware of similar studies having been conducted on *Cryptosporidium*.

Methods

In this study, 2L samples of sewage influent was collected from six treatment works in Strathclyde region at approximately monthly intervals, concentrated and clarified. A proportion of each sample was stained with FITC-labelled monoclonal antibodies for *Giardia* and *Cryptosporidium* and the cysts and oocysts enumerated by fluorescence microscopy. Neither monoclonal antibody used is species specific. The sewage works serving the home addresses of the individuals with diagnosed infections of cryptosporidiosis and giardiasis were traced from data from the public health offices and from the regional department of sewerage; no attempt was made to take into account the sewage works serving the work-place/school of individuals diagnosed with either of these infections, nor were general practitioners in the relevant communities alerted to this study.

Results

One immediately striking observation was that for most communities the total number of cases of cryptosporidiosis diagnosed over the year was higher than the total number of cases of giardiasis diagnosed over the year, but the mean concentration of oocysts detected in the sewage was considerably lower than the mean concentration of *Giardia* cysts detected. Correlation of cyst/oocyst concentration and numbers of cases of disease revealed low correlation coefficients for both infections, and an alternative method of analysing the data was attempted.

Table 2. Predicted and actual *Cryptosporidium* oocyst concentrations in sewage influent

	Bi-Monthly Sampling						
	M-J	J-A	S-O	N-D	J-F	M-A	M-J
Works A							
Predicted	735	90	60	15	-	60	150
Actual	30	52	n.d.	4	-	10	40
Works B							
Predicted	531	63	31	0	-	219	31
Actual	15	5	5	10	-	80	35
Works C							
Predicted	0	-	0	-	-	0	0
Actual	20	-	5	-	-	110	55
Works D							
Predicted	2567	-	0	-	-	0	0
Actual	20	-	8	-	-	150	30
Works E							
Predicted	0	0	0	-	0	0	0
Actual	10	n.d.	3	-	40	70	10
Works F							
Predicted	575	124	47	0	-	31	16
Actual	85	5	n.d.	7	-	30	39

Table 3. Predicted and actual *Giardia* cyst concentrations in sewage influent

	Bi-Monthly Sampling						
	M-J	J-A	S-O	N-D	J-F	M-A	M-J
Works A							
Predicted	0	45	45	0	-	0	15
Actual	620	450	170	800	-	1790	235
Works B							
Predicted	63	63	63	31	-	0	63
Actual	1085	135	570	1400	-	3040	1765
Works C							
Predicted	0	-	0	-	-	0	0
Actual	1670	-	1345	-	-	3500	43907
Works D							
Predicted	367	-	367	-	-	0	0
Actual	465	-	102	-	-	2450	3240
Works E							
Predicted	0	0	3158	-	0	0	0
Actual	535	2745	150	-	690	1160	135
Works F							
Predicted	108	16	47	0	-	62	62
Actual	730	520	690	2000	-	1000	2855

n.d.: none detected

Smith *et al.* (1994) have successfully used their data to predict the number of cases of giardiasis to be expected in the community given the concentration of cysts detected in the sewage, and here, a similar type of approach was used. The volume of sewage processed by each plant and the number of cases of giardiasis and cryptosporidiosis diagnosed in the community were used to predict the concentration of cysts and oocysts to be expected in the sewage, and these predictions were compared with actual figures (Tables 2 and 3). For *Cryptosporidium* (Table 2), the predicted oocyst concentration was almost always greater than the actual number of oocysts detected, whereas for *Giardia* (Table 3), the inverse occurred, with the predicted cyst concentration being almost always lower than the actual number of cysts detected.

Discussion

As the daily cyst and oocyst excretion in moderate infections of giardiasis and cryptosporidiosis are considered to be similar, and as the number of animal reservoirs considered to exist for both infections are also considered to be similar, these results might be considered surprising. However, there are several possible factors which might have contributed to these results. These include

1 reduced detection of *Cryptosporidium* oocysts in the sewage samples (possibly due to loss of oocysts during purification procedures),
2 high numbers of animal infections with *Giardia* (both duodenalis and other species, with both symptomatic and asymptomatic infection),
3 high numbers of asymptomatic *Giardia* infections in humans,
4 under-diagnosis of symptomatic *Giardia* infections in humans. It is probable that all these factors contributed to some extent to the results described.

Acknowledgements

We would like to acknowledge the ready assistance of the Department of Sewerage, Strathclyde Regional Council in the collection of sewage samples and also the Public Health laboratories in Strathclyde region for the provision of data.

References

Smith, H.V., Robertson, L.J., Reay, D. and Young, C.J. (1994). Occurrence of *Giardia* cysts in raw and treated sewage in relation to the prevalence of giardiasis in a Scottish community. In: *Giardia*: From Molecules to Disease. Part 3. Biotic and Abiotic Transmission. (Eds, Thompson, R.C.A., Reynoldson, J.A., and Lymbery, A.J.) CAB International, Wallingford. U.K. pp.128-129

Outbreak of Giardiasis Caused by a Contaminated Private Water Supply in the Worcester Area

C.L. Constantine,[1] D.Hales,[2] and D.J. Dawson [3]
[1]CCDC, Worcester and District Health Authority, Department of Public Health Medicine, Isaac Maddox House, Shrub Hill Rd., Worcester, WR4 9RW, UK
[2]Environmental Health Officer (retired), Wychavon District Council, UK
[3]Senior Microbiologist, Quality Assurance, Severn Trent Water, Mythe Treatment Works, Tewkesbury, Glos. GL20 6AA, UK

Introduction

A G.P. covering a rural area of South Worcestershire noticed six cases of severe unexplained diarrhoea in whom routine microbiological analysis was negative. Following discussion with the medical microbiologist, *Giardia lamblia* was identified and appropriate treatment with metronidazole began. No subsequent cases were identified in the following three weeks, however an earlier cluster of cases in November 1991 was recognised through checking practice records, suggesting a continuing source of infection.

Health Aspects

Cases (see fig. 1)

A total of 31 episodes (28 patients) of clinical giardiasis were identified, with clusters in November 1991 and April 1992.

The clinical case definition was as follows:- diarrhoea and steathorrea with one or more of; abdominal pain, bloating, fatigue, anorexia, flatulence, weight loss for more than 48 hours.

All cases who were treated with metronidazole (200 mg tds for 10-14 days) responded. Many cases were diagnosed retrospectively as the outbreak was not identified until March 1992. *Giardia lamblia* was seen in 5 cases and one symptomless excreter. The average age of those affected was 37 yrs 6 months (range 10 months - 73 yrs 1 month). 26% of cases were under the age of 14.

Epidemiology

A case finding exercise showed that all 28 cases lived in the same area supplied by a private water supply. No cases had been identified in the same period (November - April) in the previous year. There was no excess of cases in areas around the village. The local microbiology laboratory had not noticed any overall increase in the numbers of cases identified in their catchment area.

The village population is approximately 200, giving a clinical attack rate of 16%. No cases were seen amongst 60 children attending a day school in the village. No further cases occurred following the boil water notice and installation of a filtration system.

Aspects Relating to Water Supply

Source (see fig.2)

The source is a shallow spring. Springwater seeps directly from bedrock and also flows from a pipe in a brick-lined chamber. Anectdotal evidence described marked increases in

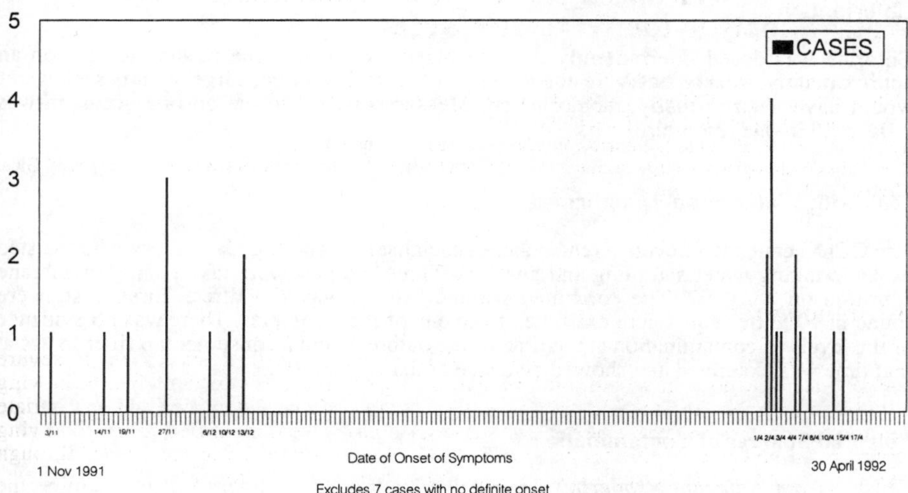

Figure 1. Worcestershire *Giardia* epidemic curve

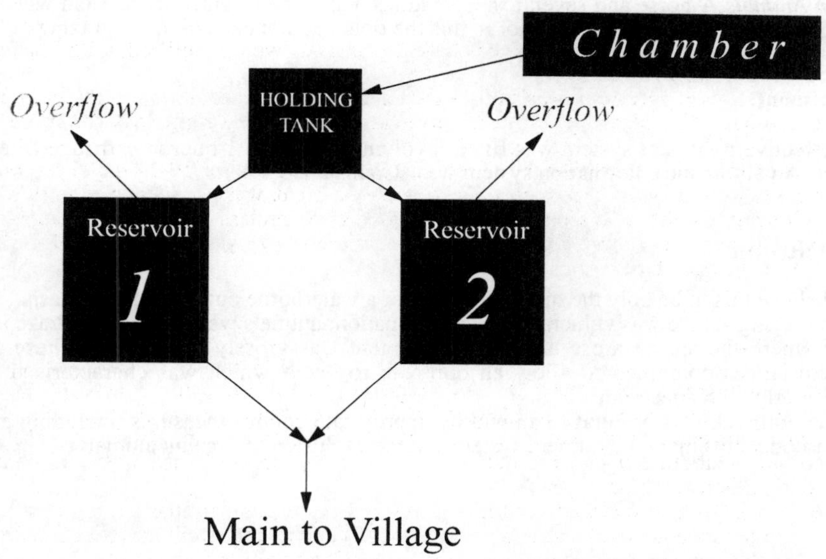

Figure 2. Layout at source

flow immediately after heavy rain, suggesting periodic surface water ingress. Water flows via an underground pipe to a holding tank and then to two covered reservoirs with 20,000 litres total capacity. The village is supplied by a gravity fed main. About 56,000 litres per day are supplied to the village.

Chlorination

Chlorine was dosed intermittently into the reservoirs at the time of the incident on an approximately weekly basis. In the absence of a dosing pump large volumes of water would have been virtually unchlorinated. Measured free chlorine on one occasion was < 0.1 mg/l in one reservoir.

Link with Water Supply Confirmed

The CCDC contacted Severn Trent Water's specialist microbiology laboratory who assisted by undertaking water sampling and analysis. Three samples were taken using membrane filtration on 28/04/92. The combined volume filtered was 773 litres. Three cysts were found in 100 litres equivalent examined from one of these samples. There was no evidence of the levels of contamination at the time of the outbreak, but a consumer tap filter in use at that time was examined and showed evidence of damaged cysts.

Potential Sources of Contamination

Sewage from Adjacent Properties Tracer dye studies were undertaken to examine the possibility of contamination from septic tank outflows above the spring; there was no evidence for this.

Farm Animals A horse and several sheep had been allowed to graze in the field where the spring rose from Autumn 1991. Prior to this the field had not been used for grazing.

Treatment

An effective treatment system was fitted involving 10, 5 and 1 micron cartridge filters in series. An automatic chlorination system was also installed.

Conclusion

We believe this to be only the third UK report of a waterborne outbreak of giardiasis.

The spring source was vulnerable to contamination; animals were allowed to graze in the field where the spring arose and water treatment was grossly inadequate. These three circumstances combined to allow an outbreak to occur which was characterised by a particularly high attack rate.

The outbreak was brought to an end by appropriate control measures, including a boil water notice, fitting of a treatment system and the exclusion of grazing animals.

Estimation of the *Cryptosporidium* Infection Risk via Drinking Water

G.J. Medema[1], P.F.M. Teunis[1], V. Gornik[2], A.H. Havelaar[1] and M. Exner[2]
[1]National Institute of Public Health and Environmental Protection, P.O. Box 1, 3720 BA, Bilthoven, The Netherlands
[2]Hygiene Institut der Universitüt, Sigmund Freudstrasse, 25, D-53127 Bonn, Germany

Introduction

The occurrence of epidemic and endemic transmission of waterborne disease via drinking water that meets the current standards for faecal indicator bacteria implies that a renewed concept is needed for the production of microbiologically safe drinking water. The concept that is emerging is to use risk analysis techniques to assess the risk of infection with pathogenic micro-organisms in drinking water. The presence of pathogenic micro-organisms, even at low concentrations, will pose a certain risk of infection to the consumers. The US Environmental Protection Agency has defined an infection risk of 10^{-4} per person per year as acceptable for drinking water. Using data from human (feeding) studies on the dose-response relationship (Haas andRose 1994), the maximum allowable dose of pathogenic micro-organisms can be calculated. The maximum allowable concentration for *Cryptosporidium* in drinking water (based on a daily consumption of 1 l unboiled drinking water) would be 5.5×10^{-5} oocysts per litre, which is in the same order of magnitude as *Giardia* and several enteric viruses. These very low concentrations make it impossible to assess the microbiological safety of drinking water by monitoring drinking water for these pathogens. Consequently, the concentration of pathogens in source water, combined with treatment efficiency, has to be used to estimate pathogen concentrations in drinking water. Together with data on water consumption and dose-response relationships for these pathogens the risk of infection can be calculated.

Aim

The aim of this study was to design a protocol to estimate the risk of infection with *Cryptosporidium* via drinking water produced by a (surface) water treatment plant and to analyse the contribution of the uncertainty present in every treatment step on the overall uncertainty of this risk estimate.

Methods

The risk analysis was performed on a conventional surface water treatment plant. The source water is reservoir water that is faecally contaminated by sewage effluents and agricultural run-off. The water is treated by alum-coagulation, followed by two subsequent rapid sand filtrations and chlorination.

To determine the concentration of *Cryptosporidium* oocysts in source water 300-1000 l samples were taken, processed and analysed according to the UK (SCA) standard method.

This data set gave information about only one step in the risk analysis. These data were therefore combined with the best available literature data to calculate the levels of uncertainty incorporated in the other steps: viability, recovery, treatment efficiency, drinking water consumption and dose-response. One or several distributions were fitted to the data and the best value(s) for the distribution parameter(s) were obtained by maximum likelihood estimation. For (unboiled) drinking water consumption the distribution parameters are published in the literature, and for the dose-response relationship the model (parameter) is published. These were used without modifications.

Raw Water Concentration

Data source: 14 samples were taken from October 1993 to April 1994 and analysed for the presence of *Cryptosporidium* oocysts.
Distribution: Likelihood ratio analysis of Poisson, negative binominal and Poisson with added zero's showed that the negative binominal distribution fits the experimental data best.
Parameters: Median: 31 oocysts per 100 l; 95% CI: 4-108 oocysts per 100 l
Causes of uncertainty:
- Small number of oocysts per sample.
- Variations in the emission of faecal pollution to the reservoirs.
- Variations in the survival rate of the oocysts at different temperatures.

Not incorporated sources of uncertainty: Detection of *Cryptosporidium* species that are not infective for mammals (man).

Recovery

Data source: LeChevallier *et al.* reported data on the variability of the recovery of the detection method using a single method in a single laboratory.
Distribution: Lognormal.
Parameters: Median: 41%; 95% CI: 28-59%
Causes of uncertainty: The recovery of the detection method depends largely on the presence of particulate matter in the sample (colloids, phyto- and zooplankton) which vary according to season, weather conditions, water flow etc.
Not incorporated sources of uncertainty: Variability of the recovery in our samples with our detection method.

Viability

Data source: LeChevallier *et al.*: the viability of *Cryptosporidium* oocysts isolated from surface water was expressed as the fraction of oocysts showing a 'viable type morphology'.
Distribution: Binomial distribution with Beta-distributed probability of success. LeChevallier *et al.* reported a high frequency at 0%, 50% and 100% viability, due to the low number of oocysts detected in the samples. In this study, the same viability data were weighed according to the total number of oocysts counted in each sample.
Parameters: Median: 38%; 95% CI: 5-84%
Causes of uncertainty:
- Viability upon excretion of the oocysts by infected man or animals.
- Loss of viability in the environment (sewage treatment, sunlight, energy or nutrient depletion, mechanical shear).

Not incorporated sources of uncertainty: Viability may be overestimated since the viability assay does not include metabolic activity or infectivity of the oocysts.

Treatment Efficiency

Data source: LeChevallier *et al.* have studied the removal of oocysts by coagulation/filtration plants in the USA. Data from a single plant (307) were used. The effect of chlorination was considered negligible, because of the very high resistance of oocysts to chlorine.

Distribution: Lognormal.
Parameters: Median: 96.4%; 95% CI: 0-99.91%
Causes of uncertainty: The efficiency of coagulation processes depends on many factors, such as pH, temperature, type and dose of coagulant, turbidity, mixing efficiency, coagulation additives etc.
Not included causes of uncertainty: The treatment efficiency at low water temperatures is not incorporated.

Drinking Water Consumption

Data source: The data on the consumption of untreated drinking water from Roseberry and Burmaster were used in this study.
Distribution: Lognormal.
Parameters: Median: 0.963 l per day; 95% CI: 0.341-2.721 l per day
Cause(s) of uncertainty: Person-to-person differences in drinking habits, health state, occupation etc.
Not incorporated sources of uncertainty: Differences in drinking habits, health state and age distribution in different countries.

Dose

From the data on raw water concentration of oocysts, the recovery, viability, removal efficiency and consumption the distribution of ingested doses can be calculated.

Dose-Response

Data source: Haas estimated the best value for the parameter for the exponential model for the dose-response relation found in the Dupont human feeding study.
Distribution: Exponential model.
Parameters: Median: r(=1/k) = 0.00494; 95% CI: 0.00261 - 0.0108
Causes of uncertainty: Variations in susceptibility between different hosts.
Not incorporated sources of uncertainty: The dose-response relationship may differ
- for sub-populations with a compromised immune system
- between different strains of *C. parvum* oocysts

Risk

Data source: To determine the daily risk of *Cryptosporidium* infection and its overall uncertainty, a Monte Carlo analysis was used: a combination of random samples was taken from each of the underlying distributions (raw water concentration, recovery, viability, removal, water consumption and dose-response parameter) and the resulting estimated daily risks were computed. This computation was repeated 10 000 times to estimate the uncertainty of the daily risk estimate.
Distribution: Lognormal.
Parameters: Median: 3.6 * 10-5 pppd; 95% CI: 3.5 * 10^{-7} - 1.8 8 10^{-3} pppd
Causes of uncertainty: The contribution of the uncertainty of the different steps in the risk analysis are presented in Table 1.

Conclusions

It is possible to estimate the risk of infection with *Cryptosporidium* (and other pathogens), and the uncertainty of this estimate, using the risk analysis concept.

Table 1. Best estimates with 95% confidence intervals (CI) for every parameter contributing to the risk of infection with *Cryptosporidium* via drinking water.

		Median	95% CI
Raw Water Concentration	(per 100 l)	31	4 - 108
Recovery	(%)	41	28 - 59
Viability	(%)	38	5 - 84
Treatment Efficiency	(DR)	1.42	0.17 - 2.59
Water Consumption	(l)	0.963	0.341 - 2.721
Dose Response		0.00494	0.00261 - 0.0182
Daily Risk	(pp)	$3.6*10^{-5}$	$3.5*10^{-7}$ - $1.8*10^{-3}$

In this study case, the estimated median daily risk of infection with *Cryptosporidium* was $3.6 * 10^{-5}$. The acceptable risk level defined by the USEPA is 10^{-4} per year. This indicates that the treatment under study could not reduce the *Cryptosporidium* oocysts in their source water to an acceptable level and more extensive treatment will be necessary.

Using our data on oocyst concentration in source water, in combination with the best available published data on recovery, viability, treatment efficiency, water consumption and dose-response relationship the uncertainty (95% confidence interval) of the risk estimate is a factor 50-100.

The factor that accounts for the largest part of the overall uncertainty in this risk analysis is treatment efficiency. In order to reduce the uncertainty of this risk estimate research should focus on obtaining more data on the removal of oocysts by water treatment processes, the value of surrogate parameters (particle counts, *Clostridium perfringens* spores) to determine treatment efficiency.

In general, to be able to perform an analysis of the risk of infection with *Cryptosporidium* (or any other pathogen) via a certain drinking water, data on raw water concentration, recovery, viability and treatment efficiency have to be collected simultaneously. The more data are collected on each of these parameters, the more the certainty of a risk estimate will be improved.

References

Haas CN, Rose JB. Reconciliation of microbial risk models and outbreak epidemiology: the case of the Milwaukee outbreak. Annual Conference AWWA, New York, USA, June 19-23, 1994

LeChevallier MW, Norton WD, Lee RG, Rose JB. *Giardia* and *Cryptosporidium* in water supplies. AWWA Research Foundation, Denver USA, 1991

Roseberry A, Burmaster D. Lognormal distribution for water intake by children and adults. Risk Analysis 1992; 242:29

The Occurrence of *Cryptosporidium* spp. Oocysts in Surface Waters and Factors Influencing their Levels, with Particular Reference to the United Kingdom

E.G. Carrington[1] and H.V. Smith[2]
[1]WRc plc, Medmenham, Marlow, Bucks, SL7 2HD,UK
[2]Scottish Parasite Diagnostic Laboratory, Stobhill NHS, Trust, Glasgow, G21 3UW, UK

Background

Cryptosporidiosis caused by *Cryptosporidium parvum* is widespread in man and farmed animals. Infected persons or animals excrete large numbers of oocysts in faeces. An infected calf, for example, may excrete up to 10^{10} oocysts per day for as long as 14 days. Many oocysts from animals and man enter surface waters via sewage effluent, farm drainage and runoff. Oocysts can survive long periods in the environment under adverse conditions, being resistant to the commonly used water disinfectants. The infective dose is very low, and may be less than 10 oocysts. The occurrence of waterborne outbreaks, notably those in Swindon and Oxfordshire in 1989 and in Milwaukee in 1993 indicate that oocysts may pass through water treatment systems and cause infection in a large number of consumers. Thus the presence of oocysts in source waters is of concern to the water supply authorities.

After the first waterborne outbreak in Carollton in the US in 1987 surveys of the occurrence and levels of oocysts have taken place initially in the US, but subsequently in the UK, other European countries and elsewhere including Australia.

The report of the Group of Experts on *Cryptosporidium* in Water (DoE/DH, 1990) which was established after the outbreak in Swindon and Oxfordshire included the recommendation that there should be a survey of occurrence of oocysts in waters used for abstraction. This led to comprehensive surveys being carried out in the UK.

There are a number of factors that can influence the levels of oocysts in surface waters such as the source and the age of the polluting material. Furthermore the current techniques for the recovery of oocysts, for example, the provisional method of the Standing Committee of Analysts (1990), are inconsistent in their reproducibility and sensitivity.

Levels of Oocysts in Surface Waters

United Kingdom

During a survey of lowland surface waters, 10 sites on 3 rivers in England were monitored 3 times each week during a 12-15 month period between January 1990 and March 1991. River A drained a mainly rural area, although sewage effluent from a large town entered the river some 60 km upstream of site A1. Site A2 was on a large tributary which entered the main river above site A1. River B drained a dairy farming area above site B3, but became progressively more urbanised downstream towards site B6. A major tributary including some drainage from a large conurbation entered the river between sites B3 and B4. A large town straddled a canal just above site C7 and sewage effluent from the town entered the canal between sites C7 and C8. Below this site the land use was mainly agricultural. The canal joined the main river, which bypassed the town, just above site C10. Site C9 was on the main river upstream of its confluence with the canal.

The results of this survey (National *Cryptosporidium* Survey Group 1992) are summarised in Table 1.

Table 1. Results of UK National *Cryptosporidium* Survey of Lowland Waters.

Site	Positive/Total	Mean(/l)	Range (/l)
A1	9/183	0.91	0.1-2.5
A2	8/192	0.99	0.1-4.0
B3	91/171	0.30	0.04-2.0
B4	90/160	0.41	0.06-1.59
B5	103/180	0.40	0.06-2.48
B6	79/180	0.40	0.06-3.0
C7	1/108	0.12	0.12
C8	7/106	0.38	0.08-0.73
C9	5/110	0.41	0.1-0.81
C10	5/106	1.09	0.1-2.75

Five sites on the River Severn have been monitored since 1991 by Dawson *et al.* (1994). The results for the period April 1993 to April 1994 (Table 2), show the upper reaches to contain fewer oocysts than the more urbanised lower reaches.

Table 2. Results of a 12-month Survey of a UK River.

Site	Levels of Oocysts (% of Samples)			
	<0.4/l	0.4-1/l	1-2/l	>2/l
Upstream				
Shelton	94.0	6.0		
Trimpley	100			
Barbourne	49.0	27.5	21.6	1.9
Mythe	46.3	35.2	6.7	1.9
Downstream				

Two tributaries, which partially drained a large conurbation, join the main river between Trimpley and Barbourne. These were monitored weekly over the same period. Some 80% of these samples were positive, mainly during late Spring and Summer, in the range of 0.4 - 82 oocysts/l.

As part of the UK survey a study was made of an upland water source (Parker *et al.* 1993). Water at the abstraction point of a Scottish loch was sampled over a 2-year period by continuously passing water through a Cuno filter, which was changed every 48-72 hours. Thirty two of the 279 samples were reported as positive, with a range of oocysts between 0.0019 and 0.12/l and a mean level of 0.018/l.

In an earlier study in Scotland by Smith *et al.* (1991), 34 of 84 raw water samples were found to contain oocysts at concentrations between 0.006 and 2.3 oocysts per litre.

United States

A number of researchers have reported surveys carried out in the US. These were not as intensive as the UK studies but they covered a wider range of geographic areas and water quality, from pristine mountain streams to heavily polluted rivers. The maximum levels of oocysts observed were generally higher than those reported in the UK. The results of a number of these studies have been drawn together in summary form in Table 3.

Table 3. Summary of Reports of US Surface Water Surveys.

Area	Sites	Positive Samples/Total samples	Mean(/l)	Range(/l)
Western USA (Ongerth and Stibbs 1987)	6	11/11	25	2-112
Western USA (Rose 1988)		56/74	8.1	
Western USA (Rose *et al.* 1988)	2	28/39	5.8	0.15-63.5
North East USA (LeChevallier *et al.* 1991)	64	71/82	2.7	0.07-484
California	1	2/2	1.72	0.38-3.05
Alberta (Canada)	1	1/1		0.34
North West USA (Rose *et al.* 1991)		5/12	0.05}	
North East USA		8/31	0.02}	
South West USA		29/77	12.9 }	0.03-290
South East USA		11/15	0.39}	
Hawaii	1	1/1	0.03}	

Other Countries

Until recently there has not been the same level of interest in other countries in the occurrence of oocysts in water as in the US and the UK. The studies generally followed the pattern of the UK studies of a small number of sites being sampled intensively over a long period, rather than a few samples being collected from a large number of sites. The results of some of these studies are summarised in Table 4.

Table 4. Levels of Oocysts in Surface Waters in other Countries.

Country	Sites	Positive/Total	Range(/l)
Canada (Northern) (Roach *et al.* 1993)	2	2/52	0.2-0.5
Netherlands (Ketelaars *et al.* 1994)	1	6/52	0.002-0.018
Australia (Hutton *et al.* 1994)	14	53/114	0.1-14.3
Israel (Armon *et al.* 1994)	2	11/16	0.006-0.52

Sources of *Cryptosporidium* spp. Oocysts

Sewage Effluents

Although infected persons excrete oocysts in large numbers, most of which will enter the sewer system and consequently may pollute a receiving water, there are few reported data on oocyst levels in sewage effluents. An early study in the US by Madore *et al.* (1987) found levels as high as 3960 per litre. During the survey of the upland catchment by Parker *et al.* (1993) the effluents from 7 small sewage works were examined periodically over the 2-year period. The concentrations of oocysts reported were considerably lower, in the range of 0.03 to 2.3 per litre. Oocysts were recovered from all the works, but none consistently produced positive samples.

At weekly intervals for a 12-month period Dawson *et al.* (1994), monitored the effluent from the sewage works of a moderately large town, which was not receiving any animal waste. Thirty seven of the 52 samples were positive with a range 1-321 oocysts per litre. Six plants in Scotland were sampled over one year by Robertson *et al.* (1994) who reported 65% of 117 samples as positive. These surveys of sewage effluents are summarised in Table 5.

Table 5. Levels of Oocysts in Sewage Effluents.

Region	Positive/Total	Range(/l)
US (Madore *et al.* 1987)	11/11	4-3960
England (Dawson *et al.* 1994)	37/50	1-321
Upland Catchment (Parker *et al.* 1994)	26/70	0.03-2.3
Scotland (Robertson *et al.* 1994)	76/117	5-60

Animal Excreta

Cryptosporidiosis has been reported in most species of domesticated animals. High infection rates occur in young animals and those infected excrete large numbers of oocysts over a short period of time. An infected calf, for example, may excrete upto 10^{10} oocysts per day. Animal waste may contaminate surface waters through storm run-off following manure application to the land or from drains originating in the farm buildings. A recent study has found oocysts in farm drains at concentrations ranging from 0.06 to 19.4 per litre (Kemp *et al.*, 1994).

Seasonal Variation

Cryptosporidiosis is more common in Spring, particularly in cattle. The manures, however, may not be spread on land until later in the year. This means that during dry periods sewage effluents contribute a high proportion of the oocysts found in surface waters, but at times of storm these numbers are diluted by the increased flow which itself is carrying oocysts arising from run-off.

Few of the surveys of surface waters have continued for more than one cycle of seasons. The study of the upland catchment by Parker *et al.* (1993) was carried out over two years. With the exception of the period from the end of November 1992 to the beginning of January 1993 and mid-May 1992 the occurrence of positive samples was sporadic, although there was a tendency for them to occur either late or early in the year. Data from the survey by Dawson *et al.*, (1994) indicates that in 1993 the levels of oocysts were greater between May and September than at other times.

The National *Cryptosporidium* Survey (1992) carried out some statistical analysis on the data from sites B3-B6, vide supra. A seasonal difference was found between the February-June 1990 samples and the July 1990-January 1991 samples, but this also coincided with a change in the protocol for the examination of the samples. No correlation between oocyst numbers or the occurrence of positive samples and rainfall or riverflow was observed.

Survival of Oocysts in the Environment

The survival of oocysts in the environment can influence their numbers in waters, particularly in the lower stretches of a river. Some authorities quote survival times as long as 1 year. Recent data on oocysts stored in semipermeable containers immersed in river water has shown that during a 31-week period of summer conditions, April to October 1993, there was a 99.997% reduction in oocyst numbers (Carrington and Ransome 1994). During that period the viability of the recovered oocysts declined from 94.1% to 47.2%. However during the preceding 22 weeks, November 1992 to April 1993, the numbers only declined by 96%, and the viability was reduced from 67% to 62%. The meteorological records, other parameters measured and other aspects of that study indicate that temperature is probably the major factor influencing oocyst survival. In an earlier study using oocysts from two sources and similar storage arrangements Robertson *et al.* (1992) reported declines in viability from 77.7% to 11% and from 83.8% to 1% over a 25-week period.

Limitations of Recovery Techniques

When drawing comparisons between surveys or similar studies the limitations of the techniques used for the recovery of the organism from the environment must be borne in mind. Parker *et al.* (1993) reported concentrations of oocysts as low as 0.03 per litre in the sewage effluents they examined, but Dawson *et al.* (1994) quote their lower limit of detection as being 1 per litre for similar samples.

Because of the apparent low infective dose of *Cryptosporidium* spp oocysts the presence of a few in source waters is a concern to water supply undertakings. Therefore it is necessary to examine large sample volumes. Typically, volumes of 10-100 litres are concentrated to small volume deposits, by the use of either depth filters followed by multiple centrifugations, membrane filtration and centrifugation or coagulation techniques. A portion of the final deposit is then examined by a skilled and experienced microscopist. The efficiency of recovery may be influenced by many factors, including the turbidity of the sampled water where extraneous debris can obscure oocysts during the microscopic examination. The size of the initial sample can influence the sensitivity of the results as can the portion of the final deposit that is examined.

A number of groups of workers have shown that the efficiency of recovery from spiked samples by the commonly used techniques to be imprecise. For example, Shepherd and Wynn-Jones (1994), showed a range of recovery from spiked tap water when using depth filters of between 9.6 and 16.5%, when using membrane filters of between 4.4 and 55.7% and between 70.8 and 75.2% when using a floculation technique.

Conclusions

Cryptosporidium spp. oocysts can be found in surface waters worldwide, including pristine waters in remote areas. Sewage effluents are major sources of oocysts in water, as are animal excreta which may pollute the water through farm drains or from storm runoff after manure has been applied to land.

The occurrence of oocysts in water is generally intermittent and not associated with any season.

Oocysts can survive long periods in water, but their survival time is less in periods of high temperature.

An improved method of recovery is desirable to give consistent, reproducible and reliable results.

References

Armon, R., Greenberg, Z. and Shelef, G., (1994). *Giardia lamblia* and *Cryptosporidium parvum* in surface waters of Israel; and their clinical prevalence for the period 1923-1991. This volume

Carrington, E.G. and Ransome, M.E.(1994). Factors influencing the survival of *Cryptosporidium* oocysts in the environment. Report No FR 0456, Foundation for Water Research, Marlow, Bucks

Dawson, D.J., Furness, M.L., Maddocks, M., Roberts, J. and Vidler,J .S., (1994). The impact of catchment events on levels of *Cryptosporidium* and *Giardia* in raw waters. AWWA Seminar, Watershed management and control of infectious organisms. New York, 20 June 1994

DoE/DH (Department of the Environment and the Department of Health) (1990) Report of the Group of Experts on *Cryptosporidium* in Water. HMSO, London

Hutton, P., Ashbolt, N., Vesey, G. and Walker, J., (1994). *Giardia* and *Cryptosporidium* in the aquatic environment of Sydney, Australia. This volume

Kemp, J,S., Wright, S.E. and Bukhari, Z., (1994). On farm detection of *Cryptosporidium parvum* in cattle, calves and environmental samples. This volume

Ketelaars, H.A.M., Medema, G., van Breman, L.W.C.A., van der Kooij, D., Nobel, P.J. and Nuhn, P., (1994). Occurrence of *Cryptosporidium* oocysts and *Giardia* cysts in the River Meuse and removal in the Biesbosch storage reservoirs (The Netherlands). Poster presented at IAWQ 17th Biennial International Conference, Budapest, 24-30 July 1994

LeChevallier, M.W., Norton, W.D. and Lee, R.G., (1991). occurrence of *Giardia* and *Cryptosporidium* spp. in surface water supplies. Applied and Environmental Microbiology, 57, 2610-2616

Madore, M.S., Rose,J .B., Gerba, C.P., Arrowood, M.J. and Sterling, C.R., (1987). Occurrence of *Cryptosporidium* in sewage effluents and selected surface waters. J. Parasitology, 73, 702-705

National *Cryptosporidium* Survey Group, (1992). A survey of *Cryptosporidium* oocysts in surface and groundwaters in the UK. J. IWEM, 6, 697-703

Ongerth, J.E. and Stibbs, H.H., (1987). Identification of *Cryptosporidium* oocysts in river water. Applied and Environmental Microbiology, 53, 672-676

Parker,J .F.W., Smith, H.V. and Girdwood, R.W.A., (1993). Survey of Loch Lomond to assess the occurrence and prevalence of *Cryptosporidium* spp. oocysts and their likely impact on human health. Report No. FR 0409. Foundation for Water Research, Marlow, Bucks

Roach, P.D., Olsen, M.E., Whitley, G. and Wallis, P.M., (1993). Waterborne *Giardia* cysts and *Cryptosporidium* oocysts in the Yukon, Canada. Applied and Environmental Microbiology, 59, 67- 73

Robertson, L.J., Campbell, A.T. and Smith, H.V., (1992). Survival of *Cryptosporidium parvum* oocysts under various environmental pressures. Applied and Environmental Microbiology, 58, 3494- 3500

Robertson, L.J., Smith, H.V. and Paton, C.A., (1994). Occurrence of *Giardia* cysts and *Cryptosporidium* oocysts in sewage influent in six sewage treatment plants in Scotland and the prevalence of cryptosporidiosis and giardiasis in the communities served by those plants. Paper presented at this conference

Rose, J.B., (1988). Occurrence and significance of *Cryptosporidium* in water. J. AWWA, 80, 53-58

Rose, J.B., Darbin, H. and Gerba, C.P., (1988). Correlations of the protozoa *Cryptosporidium* and *Giardia* with water quality variables in a watershed. Water Science and Technology, 20 11/12, 271-276

Rose, J.B., Gerba, C.P. and Jakubowski, W., (1991). Survey of potable water supplies for *Cryptosporidium* and *Giardia*. Environmental Science and Technology, 25, 1393-1400

Shepherd, K.M. and Wynn-Jones, A.P. (1994).A comparison of methods for the concentration of *Cryptosporidium* oocysts from water. Paper presented at IAWQ 17th Biennial International Conference, Budapest, 24-30 July 1994

Smith, H.V., Grimason, A.M., Benton, C. and Parker,J .F.W., (1991). The occurrence of *Cryptosporidium* spp. oocysts in Scottish waters, and the development of a fluorogenic viability assay for individual *Cryptosporidium* spp. oocysts. Water Science and Technology, 24, 169-172

Standing Committee of Analysts, (1990). Isolation and identification of *Giardia* cysts, *Cryptosporidium* oocysts and free living pathogenic amoebae in water etc., 1989. HMSO London

Rodent Reservoirs of *Cryptosporidium*

R.M. Chalmers[1], A.P. Sturdee[1], S.A. Bull[1] and A. Miller[2]
[1]Division of Biological Sciences, Coventry University, Priory Street, Coventry, CV1 5FB, UK.
[2]School of Biological and Molecular Sciences, Oxford Brookes University, Headington, Oxford, OX3 0BP, UK

Introduction

Cryptosporidiosis is a prolonged diarrhoeal disease of man and some other mammals caused by the parasitic protozoan *Cryptosporidium parvum*. Outbreaks are often associated with distributed water or recreational use of water. Although the original source of the environmentally resistant infective oocysts is generally unknown the parasite is frequently detected in livestock, especially calves and lambs. Smith and Rose, 1990, have drawn attention to the significance of current farming practices for contamination of water catchments either directly by fresh droppings or indirectly by spreading of farm effluents. However, wild animals can also be infected and some, such as several of the rodent species, often live uncomfortably close to man, livestock and water courses.

C. parvum is important for several reasons. Firstly, because cryptosporidiosis can be fatal to immunocompromised patients (Casemore, 1990). Secondly, when waterborne outbreaks of the disease occur hundreds of people may be affected at once (Smith and Rose, 1990). Finally, in the farming community significant economic losses are incurred when infected livestock suffer from diarrhoea, sometimes fatally (Fayer and Unger, 1986). A second species, *C. muris*, also infects mammals and although the consequences of infection with *C. muris* are not well documented affected livestock may fail to thrive (Anderson, 1991).

Unfortunately, very little is known about normal levels of occurrence of cryptosporidia in wildlife and healthy livestock, nor about the quantities of oocysts released into the environment. The first of these points has been addressed by a two year faecal sampling programme at the 250 hectare Warwickshire College Farm and Stud, Moreton Morrell, England. This paper focuses on the contribution small rodents might make as reservoirs of the parasite.

Materials and Methods

Faecal specimens were taken from randomly or semi-randomly selected but individually identified livestock (home-bred and market-bought calves, lambs, foals, dairy cows, beef bulls, sheep and horses) at approximately monthly intervals.

Wild house mice (*Mus musculus*) were caught in Longworth live mammal traps in the farm and stable buildings on a monthly basis, and wood mice (*Apodemus sylvaticus*) and bank voles (*Clethrionomys glareolus*) were caught in the hedgerows on seven occasions. Faecal pellets were collected from the traps and the animals weighed and marked prior to release at the point of capture. Wild rabbit (*Oryctolagus cuniculus*) faeces were collected from the latrines at six warrens in a pilot study.

The faecal samples were processed by a formol-ether sedimentation technique (Casemore, 1991) followed by a monoclonal antibody reacting with the oocyst wall (Shield Diagnostics, Dundee, UK) and fluorescence microscopy to detect *Cryptosporidium* species. Positive specimens were stained by a modified Ziehl-Neelsen method (Casemore, 1991) and the oocysts measured with a calibrated eyepiece graticule to differentiate between *C. parvum* and *C. muris* (Chalmers *et al*, 1994). Data on the faecal samples (for example, source, date, result) and on the animals (such as identification code, age, gender, cohort size, location, history) were logged on a relational database for later detailed analysis.

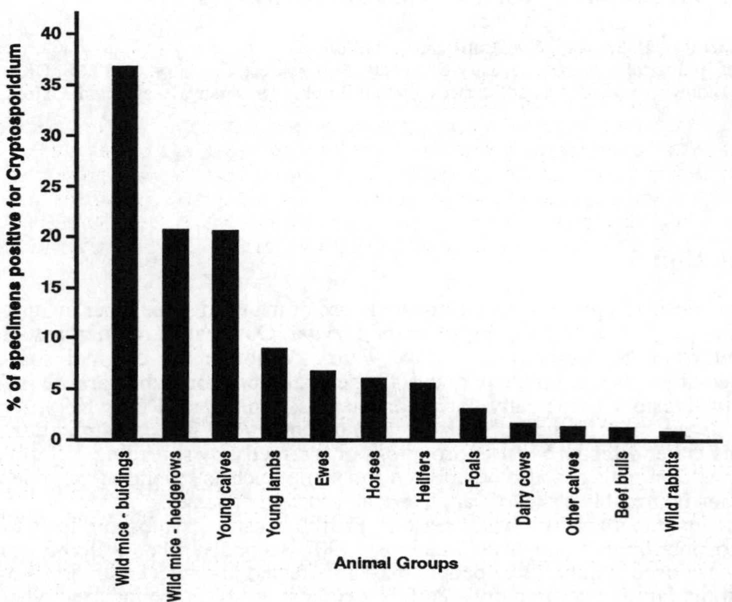

Figure 1. Percentage of faecal samples positive for cryptosporidia on the Warwickshire College Estate, 1992-4

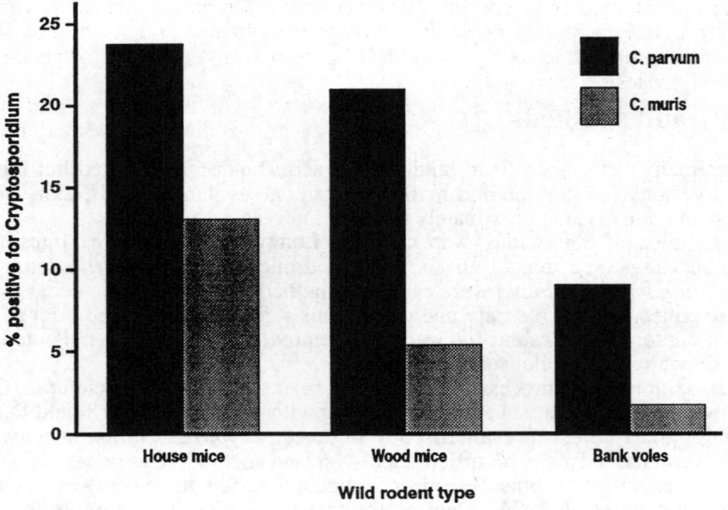

Figure 2. Mean infection rates of *C. parvum* and *C. muris* in wild rodents on the Warwickshire College Estate, 1992-4

Results

Of the 5060 specimens tested 480 (9.5%) were positive for *Cryptosporidium*. The parasite was detected at some stage in every animal group both livestock and wild but most frequently in mice and voles shown in the overall summary (Figure 1).

Cryptosporidium was detected on most mouse trapping occasions (22/29) in the buildings, and on six out of seven trapping sessions in the hedgerows. *C. muris* was present less often than *C. parvum* and only amongst the rodents. *C. parvum* oocysts were present in 71 of 300 (23.7%) house mouse specimens, 48 of 230 (20.9%) wood mouse specimens and 11 of 123 (8.9%) bank vole specimens. Corresponding figures for *C. muris* were 39/300 (13%) house mouse, 12/230 (5.2%) wood mouse and 2/123 (1.6%) for the bank vole (Figure 2).

Discussion

This survey at Warwickshire College has shown that cryptosporidia were detected in every animal population tested with rather high levels in wild rodents. To avoid possible mis-interpretation, percentages in Figure 1 represent the absolute number of positive specimens divided by the total accumulated for that animal category during the two year sampling period. Since some animals were sampled more than once the figures do not represent prevalence.

Nevertheless, the overall high levels in the rodents are particularly interesting; the values are similar to those of Sinski *et al* (1993) who provide the only other data for these species showing 20% animals infected with *C. parvum* among 330 trapped *Clethrionomys*, *Apodemus* and *Sorex* species. Mice and voles are ubiquitous, numerous and live in close proximity to man, livestock, food and water supplies, drainage and effluent routes leaving their droppings wherever they go. In America Klesius (1986) has demonstrated the infectivity of *C. parvum* from wild house mice for calves, which supports the view that mice could be a reservoir of infection for livestock.

Although studies in other countries have shown *C. muris* in cattle (Anderson, 1991; Pavlasek, 1994), at this site it was found only in the wild rodents, perhaps indicating a greater host specificity than *C. parvum*. However, it is worth noting that cattle with *C. muris* in Anderson's study suffered long term, chronic parasitism without obvious illness but probably causing gradual loss of performance. Livestock suffering "performance lethargy" might usefully be tested for *C. muris*.

It is too early to say whether the difference in overall levels of *Cryptosporidium* between the rodent groups in our study is significant. There could be differences due to the host, the parasite or a variety of unknown factors. However, the apparently higher proportion of infected house mice might be accounted for by their tendency to live a more colonial existence than wood mice or bank voles (Flowerdew, 1993).

The finding that all animal groups tested shed *C. parvum* at some time during the year suggests a potentially considerable and continuing source of environmental contamination. The UK has a large livestock population and probably a far greater one of rodents. The wild rodents were the only group persistently shedding oocysts in our study; thus they may provide a year round reservoir of infection for livestock and man in both rural and urban environments as well as a contributing oocysts to surface waters.

Acknowledgements

This work was funded by Coventry University, grant numbers 35009 and 35012. The authors particularly wish to thank the staff of Warwickshire College for their cooperation and Rachel Bishop for excellent technical assistance.

References

Anderson B.C. (1991): *Cryptosporidium muris* in cattle. Vet Rec., 129, 20

Casemore D.P. (1990): Epidemiological aspects of human cryptosporidiosis. Epidemiol. Infect. 104, 1-28

Casemore D.P. (1991): Laboratory methods for diagnosing cryptosporidiosis. J. Clin. Pathol. 44, 445-451

Chalmers R.M., Sturdee A.P., Casemore D.P., Curry A., Miller A., Parker N.D. and Richmond T.M. (1994): *Cryptosporidium muris* in wild house mice (*Mus musculus*): first report in the UK. Europ. J. Protistol. 30, 151-155

Fayer R. and Unger B.P.L. (1986): *Cryptosporidium* spp. and cryptosporidiosis. Microbiol. Rev. 50, 458-483

Flowerdew J. (1993): Mice and Voles. Whittet Books Ltd, London

Klesius P.H., Haynes T.B., and Malo K.L. (1986): Infectivity of *Cryptosporidium* species isolated from wild mice for calves and mice. J. Am. Vet. Med. Assoc. 189, 1992-3

Pavlasek I. (1994): The first cases of spontaneous infection of cattle by *C. muris* Tyzzer (1907), 1910 in the Czech Republic. Vet. Med. Czech. 39, 276-286

Sinski E., Hlebowicz E. and Bednarska M. (1993): Occurrence of *Cryptosporidium parvum* infection in wild small mammals in District of Mazury Lake (Poland). Acta Parasitologica 38(2), 59-61

Smith H.V. and Rose J.B. (1990): Waterborne cryptosporidiosis. Parasitol. Today. 6, 8-12

Occurrence of *Giardia* sp. Cysts in a Scottish Potable Water Supply and the Surface Water Source used for Abstraction

A.M.Grimason[1,2], J.F.W. Parker[1] and H.V.Smith[1]
[1]Scottish Parasite Diagnostic Laboratory, Stobhill NHS Trust, Glasgow G21 3UW, UK
[2]Division of Environmental Health, University of Strathclyde, Glasgow G4 0NG, UK

Introduction

In the United States of America more than 100 waterborne outbreaks of giardiasis have been reported over the last few decades (Craun 1991). Such outbreaks have shown that human infective cysts can pass through full conventional water treatment systems and yet still remain infective. In many of the outbreaks, disinfection was adequate in the control of coliform bacteria, however it was apparently insufficient for the inactivation of *Giardia*. In contrast, only three waterborne outbreaks of giardiasis have been recorded in the UK over a similar time period (Jephcott *et al.* 1986, Bell *et al.* 1991; Dawson *et al.* 1994). Nevertheless, concern has been expressed amongst water undertakers regarding the occurrence of pathogenic protozoan parasites in surface water sources used for the abstraction and production of potable water, especially as conventional water treatment processes cannot ensure their complete removal and inactivation. To this end, a one year study was conducted to determine the occurrence and concentration of *Giardia* sp. cysts in a Scottish treated potable water supply and the surface water supply used for abstraction.

Materials and Methods

Water Source Used for Abstraction: The loch is one of the largest freshwater sources in Europe with a surface area of 70.6 sq. Km, and a catchment area some 10 times greater at 769 sq. Km. The water from the loch is of good quality with low dissolved and suspended solids and little colour or turbidity (data not presented). It is classified, according to a European Community Directive (75/440) concerning the quality of surface water intended for consumption as A1.

Water Treatment: Water is drawn from the loch through an intake placed 229 m from the edge of the loch and 2.6 m below the lowest recorded loch level. Abstracted water is passed through coarse and mechanically operated fine screens to remove debris before being chlorinated and pumped to the Treatment Works (Figure 1). At both treatment works, water is passed through stainless steel microstrainers (nominal pore size 23 microns). The pH is raised to reduce plumbosolvency and a further dose of chlorine added to ensure the water remains of good bacterial quality while in distribution. All chemicals are dosed in proportion to the rate of flow through the works and the residual characteristics of the water.

Sample Collection: Over a period of 1 year (March 1989/1990), fortnightly samples of raw (n=26) and treated (n= 52) water from two different lines along the distribution network were taken and examined for the presence of *Giardia* cysts. Samples were procured and processed according to the large volume cartridge filtration method of Gilmour *et al* (1990). Up to 300 l of raw water and 1,000 l of treated water were filtered. Identification of *Giardia* sp. cysts was carried out by an immunofluorescent antibody technique according to Gilmour *et al.* (1990).

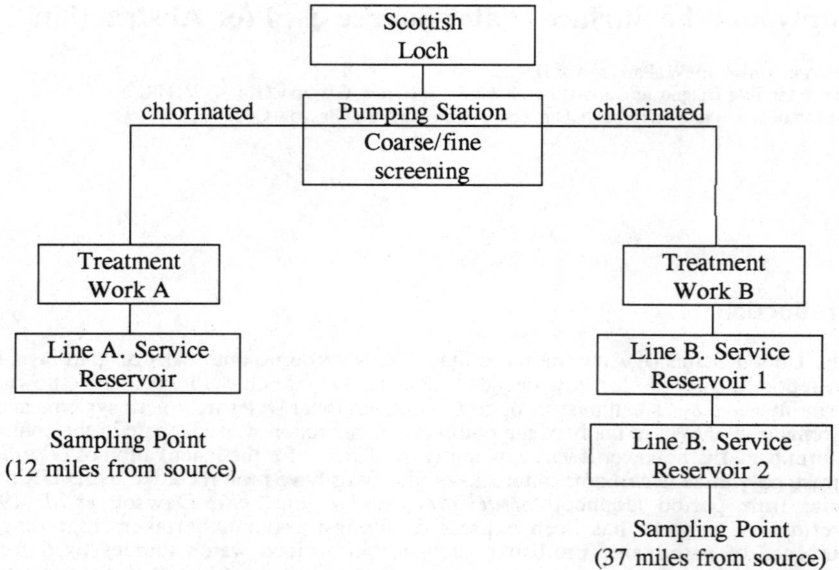

Figure 1. Schematic Flow Diagram of Loch, Water Treatment Works and Distribution Lines A and B.

Statistical Analysis

Data were analysed using a Minitab statistical package. The Mann-Whitney statistical test was used to evaluate the differences between concentrations of cysts detected. Significant associations were tested by chi-squared analysis. Differences were considered to be statistically significant when $p \leq 0.05$. Median and mean cyst concentrations were derived from positive samples only. Removal efficiencies were calculated by dividing the mean or median concentration of cysts detected in treated water by the mean or median concentration in surface water, and multiplied by 100.

Results

Recovery Efficiency of Method: The efficiency of the method for the recovery of cysts from spiked surface and potable water trials was 18.9 ± 4.5% and 27 ± 6%, respectively.

Occurrence and Concentration of Giardia cysts: Of 26 surface water samples examined, cysts (range 0.008 - 0.18 cyst/l) were detected in 22 (85%). Of 52 treated water samples examined from sites A (n=26) and B (n=26), cysts were found in 10 (19%); 5 at site A (cyst range 0.009 - 0.018 cyst/l) and B (cyst range 0.009 - 0.017 cyst/l), respectively. Both the occurrence and concentration of cysts detected in treated water were significantly lower than the levels detected in surface water (Table 1, Figure 2). Whereas the mean cyst concentration detected in surface water (0.065 cyst/l) was nearly 5 times the mean cyst concentration in treated water (site A 0.014 cyst/l; site B 0.013 cyst/l), the median cyst concentration (0.034 cyst/l) detected in surface water was less than twice the median cyst concentration in treated water (site A 0.015 cyst/l; site B 0.012 cyst/l).

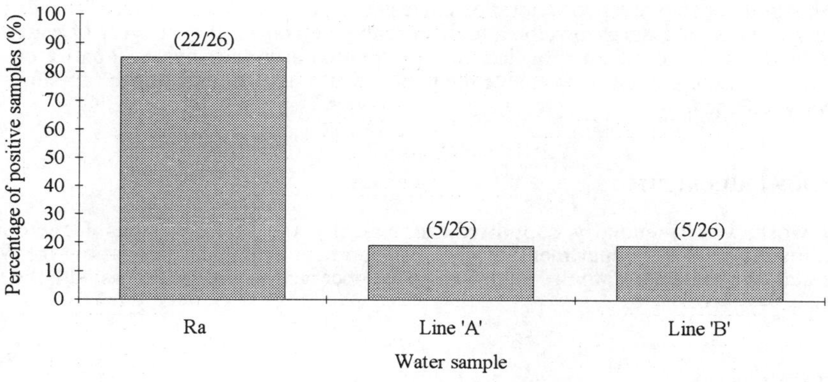

Figure 2. Occurrence of *Giardia* sp cysts in the Raw and Treated Water 1989 to 1990.

Table 1. Concentration of *Giardia* sp. cysts in Raw and Treated Water (1989/90).

Water sample	Number sampled	Range (cysts/l)	Mean (cysts/l)	Median (cysts/l)
Raw	26	0.009 - 0.18	0.065	0.034
Line A	26	0.009 - 0.018	0.014	0.015
Line B	26	0.009 - 0.017	0.013	0.012

Removal Efficiency of Water Treatment Process: Based upon the mean concentration of cysts detected in surface water used for abstraction for potable water and in the corresponding treated waters, microstraining and chlorination was estimated to reduce cyst numbers by between 78 and 80%. However, when based upon the median concentration of cysts detected in raw and treated waters, the removal efficiency was estimated to be lower, between 56 and 65%.

Discussion

Based upon the occurrence and concentration of cysts detected in raw and treated waters, such data would suggest partial removal of *Giardia* by the water treatment process (microstraining and chlorination). Endemic infections within the indigenous animal population, and wastewater discharges into rivers and tributaries from sewage treatment works were thought to be potential sources of contamination in the water catchment area, and subsequent studies have confirmed this hypothesis (data not presented).

Although cysts were sporadically detected in final waters, no epidemiological indications of clinical disease associated with waterborne transmission were reported. It is not yet clear what concentration of viable waterborne cysts constitute a risk to public health but outbreaks of waterborne disease indicate that such levels are exceeded from time to time. The presence of low concentrations of viable cysts in potable water, possibly inactivated by water treatment processes, may either contribute to an endemic level of disease or augment the level of herd immunity in the exposed population, or both. The rationale that the absence of faecal indicators denotes the absence of intestinal protozoan pathogens and thus the safety of the water, was not borne out by the results of this study in that cysts were detected in final water despite the absence of faecal indicators of pollution (data not presented). In the absence of an effective routine method for determining the viability of individual G. duodenalis-type cysts, the significance, to public health, of detecting these cysts cannot be assessed.

Current techniques of waterborne cyst enumeration and identification of organisms infectious to human beings are imprecise, which makes the interpretation of the public health significance of cyst concentrations detected in routine surveys such as this difficult. Further work is required to develop a more efficient method for the recovery of waterborne cysts; and a suitable method for determining the viability and species identity of small number of waterborne cysts, to enable the public health implications of such findings to be properly assessed.

Acknowledgements

This work was financially supported, in part, by the UK Overseas Development Administration, UK Department of the Environment and the Foundation for Water Research. We are grateful to the water authority concerned who provided us with the water samples.

References

Bell, T., Sibbald, C., and Booth, N. E. (1991). Giardiasis outbreak in Edinburgh. Environ. Hlth. Scotland, 3: 6-7

Craun, G. F. (1991). Causes of waterborne outbreaks in the United States. U.S.E.P.A., 26 M.L. King Dr., Cincinnati, Ohio, 45268. IAWPRC In: Wat. Sci. Tech., 22: Pt 2

Dawson, D, Hales, D. and Constantine, C. (1994). this volume

Gilmour, R. A., Smith, H. V., Smith, P. G., Morris, G. P. and Girdwood, R. W. A. (1989). A modified method for the detection of *Giardia* spp. cysts in water-related samples. Comm. Dis. (Scotland) Weekly Rep., 89/33: 5-10

Grimason, A.M. (1992). Occurrence and removal of Cryptosporidium sp. Oocysts and *Giardia* sp. Cysts in United Kingdom Surface, Potable and Wastewater. University of Strathclyde, Glasgow, PhD Thesis. 238pp

Jephcott, A. E., Begg, N. T., and Baker, I. A. (1986). Outbreak of giardiasis associated with mains water in the United Kingdom. Lancet ii, 730-732

Cryptosporidium and *Giardia* in the Aquatic Environment of Sydney, Australia

P. Hutton[1], N. Ashbolt[1], G. Vesey[2], J. Walker[3] and J. Ongerth[4]
[1]AWT EnSight West Ryde, NSW 2114, Australia
[2]School of Biological Sciences, Macquarie University, NSW 2109, Australia
[3]ICPMR, Westmead Hospital, Westmead, NSW 2145, Australia
[4]Dept of Environmental Health, University of Washington, WA 98115, USA

Introduction

The purpose of this paper is to summarise new information from the Sydney region of eastern Australia on the concentrations of the potentially waterborne disease agents, *Cryptosporidium* and *Giardia* and to compare on an equivalent basis, these data to those reported from elsewhere. Data on these organisms from the literature must be examined carefully to enable accurate interpretation because of significant differences in both the design of the studies producing the data and methods by which samples were analysed and the data reported.

Four sets of data from the literature were used here to provide a reasonably broad view of the concentrations of *Cryptosporidium* and *Giardia* found in Britain and the United States, the only areas for which substantial data have been published. The data include:

1 More than a year of monitoring by Thames Water prior to the current limited volume monitoring approach, (Poulton *et al.* 1991);
2 Results of a British national survey compiled by the Water Research Centre, (Miller and Carrington 1992);
3 Results of a large scale survey of water sources and filtered waters in the US, sponsored by the American Water Works Association Research Foundation, (LeChevallier *et al.* 1991a,b); and
4 Results of monitoring rivers from mountain sources in the Pacific northwest of the US, (Ongerth 1989; Hansen and Ongerth 1991).

Having no previous information on *Cryptosporidium* and *Giardia* in Australian waters, Sydney Water Board began to monitor sources of Sydney water supply to determine their presence in 1992. Information on their presence in the Sydney area population at annual incidence rates of approximately 2/100,000 for cryptosporidiosis and 15/100,000 for giardiasis was broadly similar to the incidence rates for these infections found in other developed countries, and suggested the likelihood of their presence at least in water sources affected by urban development and wastewater.

Sydney Water Board supplies water to approximately 3.6 million people over an area of about 13,000 square kilometres. Because of the erratic rainfall in the region, a large storage capacity is necessary. Sydney is supplied by 6 large reservoirs, the largest holding about 2 million ML, and 8 smaller reservoirs. In general the large reservoirs have well protected catchments with little human impact, while the smaller reservoirs have a variety of agricultural inputs and some have sewage discharges within their catchments. In addition some areas in the west of the city are supplied directly from the Hawkesbury Nepean River. It is the major river flowing through the city receiving urban drainage, with correspondingly poor quality water. This water is treated at North Richmond by a conventional rapid sand filtration plant and chlorinated before distribution. Water for most of the rest of the city, around 95% of the population, is not filtered, but is chloraminated before entering the distribution system.

The aim of the initial part of the project was to survey the variety of water sources supplying raw water to Sydney, and the distribution system in the city, to determine if *Cryptosporidium* and *Giardia* were present at measurable concentrations.

Methods

Raw water sample volumes were ten litres. The major storages were sampled approximately fortnightly between May and August 1992. The smaller storages were sampled fortnightly or monthly between February and August 1993. Ten litre samples of the raw water (Nepean R.) and 1000 litre samples of the filtered water were taken at the North Richmond water treatment plant, between February and October 1993. Distribution system samples (100L) were taken approximately monthly intervals at representative points through the system.

Water samples were concentrated using either the flocculation method developed at Thames Water for 10 litre samples (Vesey *et al.* 1993), or the flat membrane filter method developed by Dr. Jerry Ongerth at the University of Washington (Hansen and Ongerth 1991), for samples up to 1000L. The pellets obtained by these methods were analysed using a Coulter Elite flow cytometer (Vesey *et al.* 1994).

The referenced data were produced by two different types of studies and by two different methods of analysis. The first study type, used in the WRC and AWWA RF references, was a survey in which only one or at most a few samples were taken at a large number of locations. These studies also used the yarn-wound filter methods described as the UK Blue Book and the US Standard Methods. The method's principal feature is the yarn-wound cartridge and associated large water volume, ca. 100 L. The method is clearly documented to have a variable recovery efficiency for both *Cryptosporidium* and *Giardia* which is usually between 1 and 10% (Vesey and Slade 1991; Clancy *et al.* 1994; Fricker 1994), and recent data show the method precision is typically around 35% (Fricker 1994). Using a generous average recovery efficiency of 5%, the method would have a limit of detection of 1 organism in 5 L. The design of the surveys, analysing single or small numbers of samples, using an analysis method with a relatively high limit of detection has contributed to the misimpression that these organisms existed only in some locations or that their presence has been intermittent.

The second study type, used in the early Thames Water study (Poulton *et al.* 1991) and those of Ongerth (Ongerth 1989; Hansen and Ongerth 1991), was to take repeated samples at a single location over periods of months or years, and to apply methods recognizing the effect of the limit of detection. These studies show that for any surface water, even from pristine protected watersheds, these organisms are present continuously and that the concentrations can be measured, establishing a level and degree of variation that should reflect the nature of the watershed and organism sources in characteristic ways (Ongerth 1989; Hansen and Ongerth 1991).

The data presented here for the Sydney area are the actual concentrations of oocysts and cysts found corrected for recovery efficiency, typically 33% for *Cryptosporidium* and 50% for *Giardia*. Data from the literature are presented accounting for recovery efficiency. Data reported by Ongerth included recoveries (ca. 20%) which were reported (Ongerth 1989; Hansen and Ongerth 1991); data of Colbourne (Poulton *et al.* 1991) also included recovery efficiencies (ca. 0.3 to 1%) which were not reported but deduced from the reported mean limit of detection and sample volumes. Other data resulting from the cartridge method but not adjusted for recovery (Miller and Carrington 1992; LeChevallier *et al.*1991a,b), were adjusted using a value of 5% as suggested by other published work (Vesey and Slade 1991; Clancy *et al.* 1994; Fricker 1994).

Results

Sydney Storage Reservoirs In from 5 to 11 samples from the 14 reservoirs sampled, *Cryptosporidium* concentrations ranged from <0.3/L to 42.9/L. In the 6 large storages, the *Cryptosporidium* concentration averaged 2.4 oocysts/L (s=6.9, 60% above the limit of detection). In the 8 smaller reservoirs the mean concentration was 0.66 oocysts/L (s=1.44, 38% above the limit of detection). Almost all samples analysed for *Giardia* were below the limit of detection. The mean *Giardia* concentration in the larger storages was 0.006 cysts/L (s=0.04), while for the smaller reservoir samples the mean was 0.01 cysts/L (s=0.06). (Hutton *et al.* In prep).

Nepean R. and Warragamba Dam In 16 samples from the Nepean River, the average *Cryptosporidium* concentration was 0.87 oocysts/L (s=1.05, 69% above detection limit), only one *Giardia* cyst was isolated giving a concentration of 0.012 cysts/L. In a month long period of three per day sampling of Warragamba Dam water, the average *Cryptosporidium* concentration was 0.69 oocysts/L (s=0.90, 73% above detection limit).

Distribution System

From total of 13 100L samples from the distribution system mean *Cryptosporidium* concentration was 0.021 oocysts/L (s=0.03), with 30% of samples above the limit of detection. No *Giardia* cysts were isolated from any distribution system sites. In 14 samples of filtered water from the North Richmond water treatment plant the average was 0.021 oocysts/L (s=0.057, 29% above detection limit). No *Giardia* were isolated from the filtered water. The efficiency of *Cryptosporidium* removal for the North Richmond complete rapid sand treatment plant using water from the Nepean River was calculated to be 1.88 $\log_{10}$.

Cryptosporidium and *Giardia* in the UK and USA

Data from Great Britain (Miller and Carrington 1992) and raw and filtered drinking water from unprotected lowland catchments in the eastern USA (LeChevallier *et al* 1991a,b), show concentrations of oocysts that were considerably higher than those found in Sydney area waters, Table 1.

Table 1. Summary of *Cryptosporidium* oocyst levels found in raw source waters and filtered drinking waters.

Water Source	Water Type	No. of Samples	Crypto. Conc. Avg., No./litre	Crypto. Conc. Min., No./litre	Crypto. Conc. Max., No./litre	Reference
East USA	Raw	84	56	7	1940	3
East USA	Filtered Drinking	82	0.3	0.05	1.9	4
England	Raw	318	6.0	0.12	60	2

The data presented in Table 1 are from over 80 communities ranging in population from 50,000 to 1.5 million resulting from monitoring conducted over as much as 2 years. Monitoring of raw and filtered surface waters in Great Britain indicates that oocyst concentrations in surface waters there were similar to those reported in USA locations.

Data sets of the second type including numerous samples from the same location clearly demonstrate the continuous presence of these organisms. Data have been plotted in log-normal probability form to illustrate the range, median (50-percentile), and degree of variability (slope) (Figure 1). Data from rivers with agricultural drainage in the US (●) and UK (▲) had the highest *Cryptosporidium* concentrations. The concentrations on the UK River Tillingbourne (▲) were considerably more variable (steeper slope). The greater variability in the UK data could be due to higher variability of the analytical method (Fricker 1994). Both the median concentration and degree of variability observed for Warragamba water in Sydney (‡) were similar to those observed in rivers from protected watersheds in the Pacific Northwest of the USA shown here (Snoqualmie R.(◆), (Hansen and Ongerth 1991); and Green R.(⊕), (Ongerth unpublished)

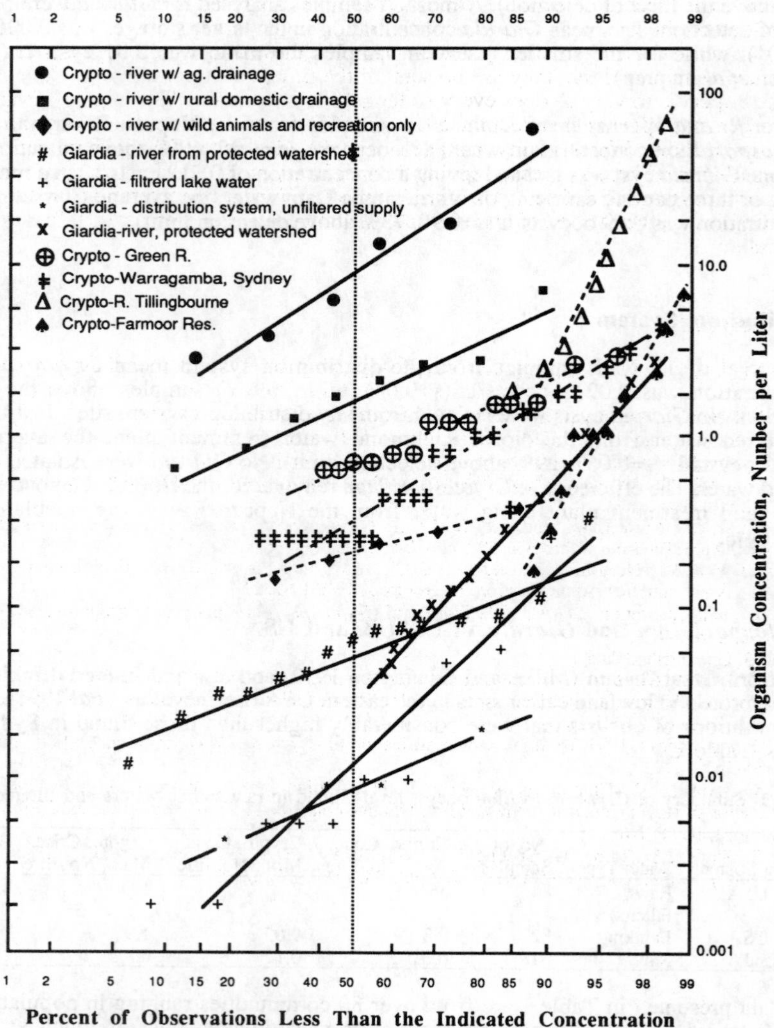

Figure 1. Log-transformed cumulative frequency distributions of *Cryptosporidium* and *Giardia* concentrations in rivers, reservoirs, filtered water, unfiltered distribution system water in the UK, USA, and Australia.

Discussion

The data presented show continuous *Cryptosporidium* presence in Sydney waters at concentrations similar to that found in waters in the USA and Britain. *Giardia* is also present in Sydney waters but at concentrations 50 to several hundred times lower than *Cryptosporidium*. The *Cryptosporidium* concentrations found in Australia, Britain, the USA cover a broad range. However, concentrations appear strikingly similar in waters from

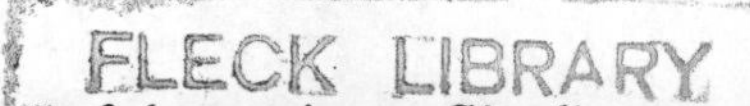

watersheds of similar character regardless of the continent. *Giardia* concentrations in Australia do not seem to follow this pattern, possibly due to their more rapid disintegration in warmer waters there.

The data summarised here clearly demonstrate that these organisms are present in virtually all surface waters, and that they are present all the time, not intermittently. Concentrations must be expected to vary as does every water quality constituent. The degree of variation in these organisms appears to reflect the characteristics of the watersheds above the individual sampling locations. Water quality managers can take advantage of the general concentration patterns illustrated here to guess at concentrations likely at an untested location, or to design a sampling program to define *Cryptosporidium* and *Giardia* concentrations at any selected location. Clearly, the method of analysis and the limit of detection are critical features to take into account.

References

Clancy J.L., Gollnitz, W.D., and Tabib, Z. 1994. Commercial labs: how accurate are they? J. AWWA, 86, 89-97

Fricker C. Detection, Protozoan Parasites and Water Conference,York, UK. October 1994

Hansen, J.S. and Ongerth, J.E. 1991. Effects of time and watershed characteristics on the concentration of *Cryptosporidium* oocysts in river water. Appl. Environ. Microbiol. 57, 2790-2795

Hutton, P., Ashbolt, N., Ongerth, J., Walker, J. *Cryptosporidium* and *Giardia* in waters in Sydney, Australia. In prep

LeChevallier, M., Norton, W., and Lee, R. 1991a. *Giardia* and *Cryptosporidium* spp. in surface water supplies. Appl. Environ. Microbiol. 57(9):2610-2616

LeChevallier, M.W., Norton, W.D. and Lee, R.G. 1991b. *Giardia* and *Cryptosporidium* spp. in filtered drinking water supplies. Appl. Environ. Microbiol., 57, 2617-2621

Miller D.J. and Carrington E.G.A., 1992 Survey of *Cryptosporidium* oocysts in groundwaters in the UK. JIWEM. 6, 697-703

Ongerth, J. Unpublished data

Ongerth, J.E. 1989. *Giardia* cyst concentrations in river water. J. AWWA, 81, (9) 81-86

Poulton, M., Colbourne, J. and Dennis, P.J. 1991. Thames Water's experiences with *Cryptosporidium*. Wat.Sci. Technol. 24, 21-26

Vesey, G. and Slade, J. 1991. Isolation and identification of *Cryptosporidium* from water. Wat. Sci. Technol. 24, 165-167

Vesey, G., Hutton, P., Champion, A., Ashbolt, N., Williams, K.L., Warton, A. and Veal, D. 1994. Application of flow cytometric methods for the routine detection of *Cryptosporidium* and *Giardia* in water. Cytometry, 16 (1) 1-6

Vesey, G., Slade, J.S., Byrne, M., Shepherd, K. and Fricker, C.R. 1993. A new method for the concentration of *Cryptosporidium* oocysts from water. J. Appl. Bacteriol., 75, 82-86

Giardia lamblia and *Cryptosporidium parvum* in Surface Waters of Israel, and their Clinical Prevalence for the Period 1923 - 1991

R. Armon[1] , Z. Greenberg[2] and G. Shelef[1]
[1]Environmental and Water Resources Engineering, Technion, Haifa 32000, Israel
[2]Public Health Laboratory, Ministry of Health, Jerusalem, Israel

Introduction

In Israel no major *Giardia* and *Cryptosporidium* outbreaks have been recorded during a period of 68 years due largely to an absence of appropriate detection methods. The bulk of the data on these two parasites is based on their prevalence in the population among diarrhoeic clinical cases. The present study was conducted to determine the presence and concentrations of *Giardia* cysts and *Cryptosporidium* oocysts in surface water, from northern Israel.

Materials and Methods

Concentration of Large Volumes of Surface Water

Concentration of 380 to 800 L of surface water was performed using the mobile laboratory vehicle equipment of the Viruses Central Laboratory, Tel-Hashomer. The concentration and elution of filtered samples was performed as described by Rose *et al.* (1991). Coliforms and fecal coliforms were detected using a standard membrane filtration method (Anon 1992).

Final Filtration and Fluorescent Staining

Small volumes of the final water concentrate (100 to 400 µl, depending on solution turbidity and filterability) were passed through 13 mm nylon filters (Schleicher and Schull, Germany). The porosity of the filters used were 5 µm for *Giardia* cysts and 1.2 µm for *Cryptosporidium* oocysts. The filter was stained with FITC-labelled monoclonal antibodies (Hydrofluor Combo, Meridian Diagnostics, Inc., U.S.A.) according to the manufacturer's instructions. The filter was placed on a clean microscope slide, covered and screened for cysts or oocysts using a Nikon Labophot 2 microscope (FITC filters, excitation 436 nm, with B2A barrier filter). In positive samples, both cysts and oocysts fluoresced apple-green, being brighter than the background and other interfering material. In parallel, controls supplied by the manufacturer, were also stained and observed for comparison. Presumptive fluorescent-positive cysts or oocysts were also observed under bright field illumination in order to attempt to confirm their morphology (for *Giardia*: 2-4 nuclei, axonemes, median bodies, and trophozoites). With highly polluted surface waters, cyst identification, using bright field microscopy was extremely difficult.

Calculation of Cysts/Oocysts Concentration

The calculation of cysts and oocysts numbers was done according to Rose *et al.*, (1991).

Results and Discussion

In surface water, *Giardia* cysts were found in 50% of the samples, while *Cryptosporidium* oocysts were detected in 68.7% of samples. The *Giardia* cyst numbers ranged from 1 to 14 and *Cryptosporidium* oocysts from 1 to 22 per volume tested (see Table 1).

Table 1. Enumeration of *Giardia* cysts and *Cryptosporidium* oocysts isolated from large surface water volumes.

Sampling site	Date	Sampled volume (L)	Total coliforms and Fecal coliforms Number/100 ml	*Giardia lamblia* cysts/volume (L)	*Cryptosporidium* oocysts/volume (L)
Tapwater (non-chlorinated) (Water supply from one of the Banias springs)	1.7.92	400	-	2/36.5	19/36.5
Aric Bridge (1)[a] (Jordan river)	1.7.92	380	-	0/160	0/160
Aric Bridge (2) (Jordan river)	1.7.92	450	-	0/160	0/160
Aric Bridge (3) (Jordan river)	1.7.92	400	-	0/160	0/160
Bnot Yaakov bridge (1) (Jordan river)	1.7.92	380	-	0/160	1/126.6
Bnot Yaakov bridge (2) (Jordan river)	1.7.92	450	-	0/160	2/112.5
Bnot Yaakov bridge (3) (Jordan river)	1.7.92	400	-	0/160	1/126.6
Jordan valley, Lake Kinneret pumping station	27.8.92	800	-	14/160	22/160
Dgania	27.8.92	800	-	1/160	18/160
Genosar	27.8.92	800	-	5/160	14/160
Jordan valley, Lake Kinneret pumping station	4.11.92	800	TC-10,FC-0	2/160	5/160
Dgania	4.11.92	800	TC-30,FC-1	1/160	9/160
Genosar	4.11.92	800	TC-420,FC-1	2/160	9/160
Jordan valley, Lake Kinneret pumping station	3.2.93	800	TC-8,FC-0	0/160	0/160
Dgania	3.2.93	800	TC-14,FC-0	0/160	1/160
Genosar	3.2.93	800	TC-375,FC-1	1/160	0/160

[a]Three samples from the same site; TC - Total coliforms; FC - Fecal coliforms

Table 2. Prevalence of *Giardia lamblia* positive cases in Mandatory Palestine for the period 1923-46 (Data from Health Department of Mandatory Government)

Year	No. of samples examined	*Giardia lamblia* positive samples (%)
1923	9602	16(0.16)
1924	20511	20(0.09)
1925	18245	95(0.52)
1926	22227	319(1.43)
1927	20762	383(1.8)
1928	15770	572(3.6)
1929	13629	525(3.85)
1930	12768	525(4.11)
1931	11073	409(3.69)
1932	13155	434(3.29)
1933	18333	428(2.33)
1934	17056	425(2.49)
1935	16292	308(1.89)
1936	20321	470(2.31)
1937	19705	307(1.55)
1938	19413	327(1.68)
1939	11109	413(3.71)
1946*	21207	419(1.97)

*During the years 1940-45 the reports did not contain parasites data

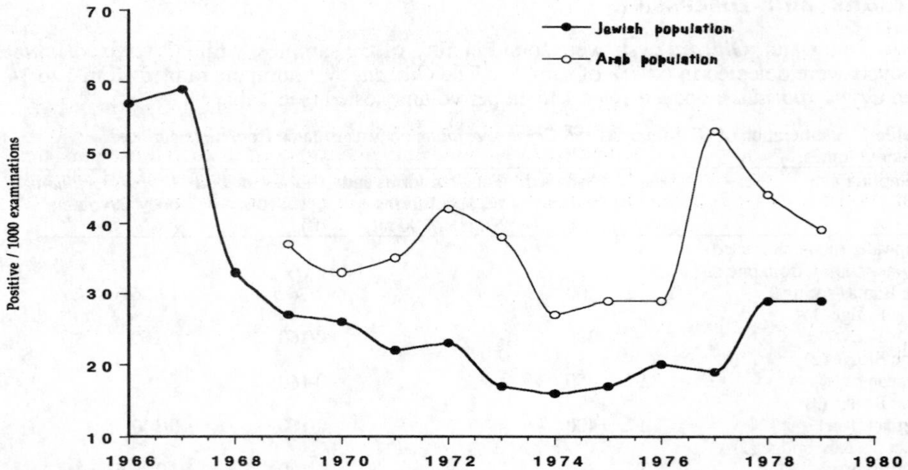

Figure 1. *Prevalence of *Giardia lamblia* in Jewish and Arab population in Jerusalem from 1966 to 1979 *From Public Health Laboratory, Ministry of Health, Jerusalem data for 67'-79'.

Table 3. Prevalance of *Giardia lamblia* in Jerusalem residents for the period 1946-1951

Year	1946	1947	1948	1949	1950	1951
Total stool examined	6005	4676	1562	4201	4796	3967
Intestinal parasites positive stools	3222	2683	613	1570	1857	1568
Giardia lamblia positive (%)	202(3.36)	150(3.2)	72(4.6)	376(8.9)	671(13.9)	466(11.7

Table 4. *Cryptosporidium* prevalence in Israel (1986-1991)

Year	Positive/Total tested (%)	Comments	Reference
1986		A Jewish Ethiopian origin baby (first report)	(Drucker *et al.*)
1986	30/221 (13.5%)	Malnourished children	(Sallon *et al.*)
1987	7/185 (3.7%)	Children with diarrhoea	(Dan and Gutman)
1987	2/35 (6%)	AIDS patients	(Siegman-Igra *et al.*)
1990	83/1073 (7.7%)	Children with acute gastroenteritis (<5 years higher prevalence)	(Miron and Kenes)
1991	13/382 (3.4%)	Bedouin and Jewish children (equal distribution)	(Dagan *et al.*)
1991	19%	Children admitted at Nasser's Children Hospital (*Cryptosporidium* excretion)	(Sallon *et al.*)

Prevalence of *Giardia* and *Cryptosporidium* in Human Beings

During the Mandatory Palestine period (1923-46), *Giardia* prevalence ranged from 0.09 to 4.11 % positive in samples tested (Table 2).

The prevalence of *Giardia* in the Jewish and Arab population in the Jerusalem district is presented in Fig. 1. The prevalence was higher in the Arab population (range 30-65 positive/1000 examinations).

After the second world war, the prevalence of *Giardia* infection increased, due to increased immigration, from 3 to 11.7 % positive in samples tested (Table 3).

Information on the prevalence of *Cryptosporidium* is listed in Table 4. The first published clinical data appeared only in 1986. The recognition that *Cryptosporidium* is a parasitic disease transmissible to human, causing clinical symptoms was slow, and no earlier data is available.

In summary, *Giardia* and *Cryptosporidium* are present in surface water in Northern Israel (the area including the main water reservoir of Israel, Lake Kinneret). Human farming activity (such as agricultural settlements) and wild animals may contribute to those parasites' presence in the environment. However, according to prevalence data, it seems that sporadic waterborne, as well as person to person transmission are the main infection routes.

Acknowledgement

We would like to thank to Mr.Y. Manor (Central Virus Laboratory, Tel-Hashomer) for helpful support in water sampling.

References

Anon. APHA,AWWA, and WPCF. 1992. *Standard Methods for the Examination of Water and Wastewater*. Washington, D.C., 18th ed

Rose JB, Gerba CP, Jakubowski W. Survey of potable water supplies for *Cryptosporidium* and *Giardia*. *Env Sci Tech* 1991; 25:1393-1400

Detection and Survival of Protozoan Parasites in Water in the Ottawa (Canada) Region

C. Chauret, V.S. Springthorpe and S.A. Sattar
Department of Microbiology and Immunology, University of Ottawa, Ottawa, Ontario, K1H 8M5, Canada

Introduction

Cryptosporidium oocysts and *Giardia lamblia* cysts are protozoa commonly detected in surface water samples. For instance, LeChevallier *et al.* (1991) detected *Cryptosporidium* oocysts in 97% of 66 raw water samples from 14 U.S. states and one Canadian province (Alberta). High densities of organisms were correlated with waters receiving sewage effluents. Nevertheless, sewage treatment by activated sludge generally reduces concentrations of oocysts by one or two orders of magnitude (Madore *et al.*, 1987). Rose (1988) noted that *Cryptosporidium* oocysts may be ubiquitous in aquatic environments. In a survey in the U.S., she detected *Cryptosporidium* oocysts in 91% of the sewage samples, and 77 and 75 % of the river and lake water samples, respectively. In addition, 83% of pristine water sources (without any human activities) contained oocysts. Rose (1990) concluded that "*Cryptosporidium* is commonly detected in surface waters; however it is unknown what factors are associated with peaks of contamination". In the latter study, *Giardia* cysts were routinely recovered from sewage and in water receiving sewage treatment plant effluents. Rose *et al.* (1991) found no relationship between the presence of either *Giardia* or *Cryptosporidium* and total coliforms.

Little is known about the occurrence of protozoan parasites in the aquatic systems of Eastern Ontario, Canada. The purpose of this study was to monitor the levels of *Cryptosporidium* oocysts and *Giardia lamblia* cysts in selected rivers in the Ottawa area and to determine if those levels correlate with the presence of other microbial pathogens and indicators. This study also examined the *in vitro* survival of *Cryptosporidium* oocysts in natural waters.

Materials and Methods

Samples were collected from three rivers, several wells, and the water treatment plants in the Ottawa (Canada) region during June 1994 and August 1994.

Sampling methods and procedures for protozoan parasites followed the proposed ICR method. One hundred and 400 L of water were sampled at the raw surface water sites and wells, respectively. Bacterial enumerations were performed by filtering 100 mL of the sampled water. Fecal coliforms were enumerated on mFC agar (Difco), total coliforms on m T7 (Difco), fecal streptococci on KF agar (Difco), *Pseudomonas aeruginosa* on Pseudomonas P agar (Difco), *Aeromonas* sp. on Ryan Agar (Oxoid), and *Clostridium perfringens* levels were determined by the method of Payment and Franco (1993). Levels of chlorophyll *a* and somatic coliphages (Escherichia coli C as the host) were determined as detailed in "Standard Methods for the Examination of Water and Wastewater (1992)".

Statistical analysis (Spearman correlation coefficient) was carried out using the SigmaStat™ Statistical Software.

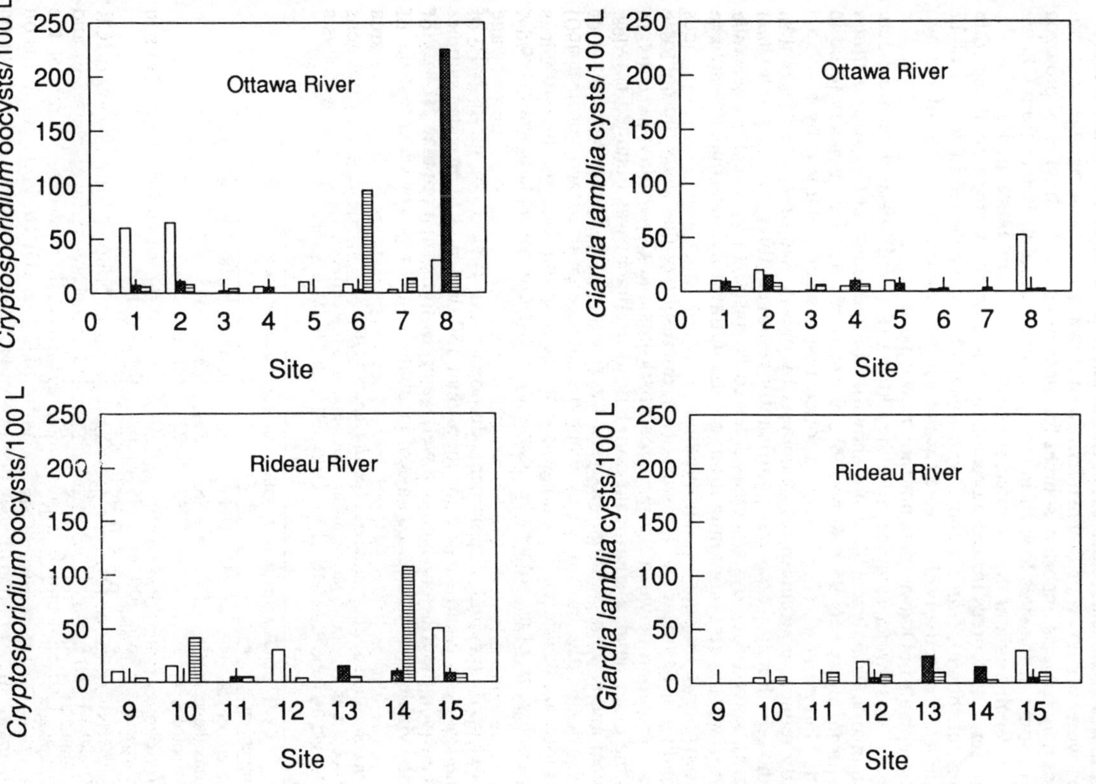

Figure 1. *Cryptosporidium* oocyst and *Giardia lamblia* cyst concentrations at various sites in the Ottawa and Rideau River watersheds. Sites 1 to 3 and 9 to 13 were located upstream from Ottawa. Sites 4 to 6 and 14-15 were located in Ottawa. Sites 7 and 8 were located downstream from Ottawa. Each site was sampled once a month in June (□), July (▩), or August (▥) 1994.

Results and Discussion

Both *Cryptosporidium* oocysts and *Giardia lamblia* cysts were routinely detected in raw surface water samples from the Ottawa and the Rideau River (Figure 1). This agrees with previous studies where these protozoan parasites were detected in high percentages of raw surface water samples in the U.S. (Rose 1990; LeChevallier *et al.* 1991). The highest levels of the protozoa were at sites in or downstream from downtown Ottawa, suggesting that human activities may serve as important sources for these protozoa. Both types of protozoa were detected in some of the sites located in the agricultural areas upstream from Ottawa on the Rideau River throughout the summer, suggesting that agricultural activities in the region may also serve as sources for these organisms. The protozoa were rarely detected in well water (data not shown); *Giardia* and *Cryptosporidium* were detected in 2 and 1 of 12 well water samples, respectively. No treated water sample (n=8) from either of the two water purification plants in Ottawa (data not shown) was positive.

Raw and treated wastewater samples from the Ottawa (Pickard) wastewater treatment plant were obtained and analyzed (data not shown). The reduction in *Cryptosporidium* oocysts and *Giardia* cysts was 96.8 % and 99.3 %, respectively. This appears to be in agreement with Madore *et al.* (1987) who reported that sewage treatment by activated sludge generally reduces concentrations of oocysts by one or two orders of magnitude. Therefore, although the protozoa are significantly removed through the wastewater treatment process, some of the cysts/oocysts detected downstream from Ottawa possibly originated from wastewater contamination of the Ottawa River. Further studies downstream from Ottawa may answer this question.

Unlike the finding of Payment and Franco (1993), the results of this study did not yield any significant correlation between the protozoan parasites and *Clostridium perfringens* (Table 1). On the other hand, a significant correlation coefficient was obtained between fecal streptococci and *Cryptosporidium* oocysts. Interestingly, the Spearman correlation coefficient varies drastically, in some cases, when the data are grouped by river instead of being analyzed together (Table 1). This suggests that a relationship between the protozoan levels and *C. perfringens*, or any other indicator, may vary from one aquatic system to the other.

Lastly, an *in vitro* survival experiment demonstrated that more than half of *Cryptosporidium* oocysts could survive for more than 150 days at 4°C in water samples from the Ottawa River, the Rideau River, and well water. In addition, more than 50% of the oocysts remained viable at 21°C after 60 days of incubation in all types of water tested.

Table 1. Spearman correlation coefficients among *Giardia lamblia* cysts, *Cryptosporidium* oocysts and various microorganisms enumerated in raw surface water samples collected from the Rideau River, the Ottawa River and the Mississippi River (Canada) [a].

		Giardia lamblia cysts			*Cryptosporidium* oocysts		
River	Microorganism	*n*	*r*	*P*	*n*	*r*	*P*
All	Fecal streptococci	49	0.240	NS	48	0.347	0.018
Rideau	Fecal streptococci	16	0.167	NS	16	0.395	NS
Ottawa	Fecal streptococci	22	-0.309	NS	22	0.132	NS
All	*C. perfringens*	20	0.254	NS	20	0.216	NS
Rideau	*C. perfringens*	6	0.116	NS	6	0.406	NS
Ottawa	*C.perfringens*	8	-0.105	NS	8	0.351	NS
All	Som. coliphages	37	0.344	0.037	39	0.254	NS
Rideau	Som. coliphages	14	0.429	NS	14	0.414	NS
Ottawa	Som. coliphages	16	0.412	NS	16	0.203	NS
All	Fecal coliforms	39	0.058	NS	39	0.261	NS
All	Total coliforms	41	0.131	NS	41	0.179	NS
All	*Aeromonas* sp.	37	0.014	NS	37	0.005	NS
All	*P. aeruginosa*	49	0.174	NS	49	0.089	NS
All	algae [b]	32	0.410	0.001	32	0.003	NS

[a]n, number of samples; *r*, Spearman correlation coefficient; *P*, *P* value associated with correlation coefficient; NS, not statistically significant (P > 0.05)
[b]chlorophyll *a*

Acknowledgements

This study was supported by funds from the Environmental Youth Corps of Ontario (Ministry of Environment and Energy), Health Canada, the Regional Municipality of Ottawa-Carleton, and CPRT, Inc. The authors wish to thank Neil Armstrong, Jason Fisher, and Ranu Sharma for their technical help.

References

LeChevallier, M.W., W.D. Norton, and R.G. Lee. 1991. Occurrence of *Giardia* and *Cryptosporidium* spp. in surface water supplies. Appl. Environ. Microbiol. 57: 2610-2616

Madore, M.S., J.B. Rose, C.P. Gerba, M.J. Arrowood, and C.R. Sterling. 1987. Occurrence of *Cryptosporidium* oocysts in sewage effluents and selected surface waters. J. Parasitol. 73: 702-705

Payment, P., and E. Franco. 1993. *Clostridium perfringens* and somatic coliphages as indicators of the efficiency of drinking water treatment for viruses and protozoan cysts. Appl. Environ. Mcrobiol. 59: 2418-2424

Rose, J.B. 1988. Occurrence and significance of *Cryptosporidium* in water. J. Amer. Water Works Assoc. 80: 53-58

Rose, J.B. 1990. Occurrence and control of *Cryptosporidium* in drinking water. In Drinking water Microbiology. Progress and Recent Developments. Edited by G.A. McFeters. Springer-Verlag, New York

Rose, J.B., C.P. Gerba, and W. Jakubowski. 1991. Survey of potable water supplies for *Cryptosporidium* and *Giardia*. Environ. Sci. Technol. 25: 1393-1400

Occurrence of *Cryptosporidium* and *Giardia* in Secondary and Tertiary Wastewater Effluents

V. Enriquez[1], J.B. Rose[3], C.E. Enriquez[2] and C.P. Gerba[1,2]
[1]Department of Soil and Water Science, and
[2]Department of Microbiology and Immunology, University of Arizona, Tucson, AZ, USA and
[3]Department of Marine Science, University of South Florida, Tampa, FL, USA

Introduction

Cryptosporidium and *Giardia* are pathogenic protozoa producing gastrointestinal illness which are transmitted via the fecal-oral route. These agents produce a stable infective stage, the cyst and oocyst, respectively, which enables them to survive in the environment while enhancing their potential for waterborne transmission (Rose, 1990; Hibler and Hancock, 1990). Waterborne outbreaks of cryptosporidiosis have, sometimes, originated from drinking water which had been treated by conventional coagulation, sedimentation, and filtration.

Large waterborne cryptosporidiosis outbreaks have been documented (Hayes *et al.*, 1989; Leland *et al.*, 1993; Edwards, 1993). Hayes *et al.* (1989) described a *Cryptosporidium* waterborne outbreak in a Georgia county, in which 13,000 people (20% of the total population) became ill. More recently, a very large *Cryptosporidium* waterborne outbreak occurred in the city of Milwaukee, where 403,000 residents experienced severe diarrhoea, nausea, and stomach cramps, resulting in at least 40 deaths (Edwards, 1993). Even though, cryptosporidiosis has become an important waterborne disease, giardiasis still leads as the most common (Hibler and Hancock, 1990). Most *Giardia* outbreaks have been associated to surface waters which have received disinfection as the only treatment (Craun, 1979), while *Cryptosporidium* waterborne outbreaks have resulted from filtered and disinfected drinking water supplies (Hayes *et al.*, 1989; Leland *et al.*, 1993). The ability to detect these protozoa in waste, ground, surface and drinking water, can aid in the control and reduction of waterborne outbreaks of disease. Little information exists on the occurrence of *Giardia* cysts and *Cryptosporidium* oocysts in secondarily treated sewage which is often discharged into recreational and surface waters that may serve as drinking water sources to downstream communities. This study monitored the occurrence of these agents in two activated sludge treatment plants and one waste water reclamation plant, on a monthly basis for a period of 3 years.

Materials and Methods

A total of 130 wastewater samples were collected, during a three year period, from two activated sludge treatment plants, with a capacity of 25 (Plant 1) and 35 MGD (Plant 2), respectively, and from a water reclamation plant, with a capacity of 8 MGD (Plant 3), which operated with secondary sewage from plant 1. In addition to activated sludge, plant 2 included biotower treatment. The tertiary treatment consisted of sand and coal filtration, and chlorination. Sample volumes of 378 liters of water were passed through yarn-wound polypropylene cartridge filters (Cuno Meridian, CT), with a flow rate adjusted to 15 to 19 liters/min. Filters were backflushed with a solution of 1% Tween 80, cut in half, and the fibers teased and washed into the original eluent (Musial *et al.*, 1986). Eluents were reconcentrated by centrifugation and the pellet divided into two, one part resuspended in 10% formalin for *Giardia* cyst, and the other in 2.5% potassium dichromate for *Cryptosporidium* oocysts analyses. A pellet size equivalent to 40 liters was washed, resuspended in a detergent solution, homogenized, and sonicated. Samples for *Cryptosporidium* oocysts were floated in a sucrose solution with a 1.24 specific gravity and for *Giardia* cysts in a potassium citrate solution with a 1.16 specific gravity (Rose *et al.*, 1988). Supernatants were passed through

13-mm diameter cellose-acetate membrane filters, with a pore size of 5 µm to recover *Giardia* cysts, and 1.2 µm to recover *Cryptosporidium* oocysts. Each filter was stained with a mixture of specific mouse-monoclonal antibodies to both *Cryptosporidium* oocysts and *Giardia* cysts walls (Meridian, Cincinnati, OH), and subsequently stained with goat anti-mouse antibodies conjugated to a fluorescent dye (Kirkegaard and Perry, Gaithersburg, MD). Filters were mounted on glass slides, and examined with the aid of an epifluorescence microscope. The recovery efficiency of the described procedure was evaluated by processing 113 l volumes of tap, or reclaimed waste water, seeded with known amounts of *Giardia* cysts and *Cryptosporidium* oocysts.

Results

Giardia cysts and *Cryptosporidium* oocysts were detected throughout the year in the effluents of the two secondary treatment plants studied. However, the concentration of *Giardia* cysts varied widely, while that of *Cryptosporidium* oocyst remained fairly constant. No seasonal distribution of either *Giardia* cysts or *Cryptosporidium* oocysts was observed in this study. The monthly average of *Giardia* cysts, in 40 liters of secondary sewage effluent from plant 1, ranged from 2 to 26, with a geometric average of 8.3 (Table 1), and from plant 2 fluctuated from 2 to 15, with a geometric average of 6.6 (Table 1). In contrast, *Cryptosporidium* oocysts were detected, in secondary effluents, in a much lower frequency and numbers than *Giardia* cysts, with a concentration of one or two oocysts most months of the year (data not shown). The combined geometric average of *Cryptosporidium* oocysts in secondary sewage effluents from the two studied treatment plants was one per 40 liters (Table 1). Tertiary treatment of sewage effluents resulted in approximately 50% reduction of *Giardia* cysts, from a geometric mean of 6.6 in the secondary effluent (Plant 2), to a geometric mean of 3 in the effluent from the water reclamation plant (Plant 3) (Table 1). However, the reduction of the concentration of *Cryptosporidium* oocysts, after tertiary treatment, was negligible, with a geometric mean of 1.7 *Cryptosporidium* oocysts in both secondary (Plant 2), and tertiary wastewater effluents (Plant 3) (Table 1). Our recovery efficiency experiments showed that *Cryptosporidium* oocysts and *Giardia* cysts can be recovered from tap water with an efficiency of 9.36 and 13.4%, respectively, or from reclaimed water with an efficiency of 8.7% for *Cryptosporidium* oocysts and 10.7% for *Giardia* cysts (Table 2).

Table 1. Average parasite concentrations in 40 liters of treated sewage effluent[1]

Plant	*Giardia* Cysts		*Cryptosporidium* Oocysts	
	Arithmetic	Geometric	Arithmetic	Geometric
1	17 ± 35	8.3 ± 3.3	1.0 ± 1.5	1.9 ± 1.6
2	12 ± 18.3	6.6 ± 3.8	1.2 ± 1.7	1.7 ± 2.1
3	2.7 ± 5.9	3.0 ± 2.9	0.7 ± 1.4	1.7 ± 2.1

[1]Geometric mean and geometric standard deviation are based on non-zero data.

Table 2. Average recovery efficiencies of *Giardia* cysts and *Cryptosporidium* oocysts from 113.5 l volumes of tap or reclaimed water

	Tap water[1]	Waste water[2]
Cryptosporidium oocysts	9.36±1.36	8.7±0.51
Giardia cysts	13.4±2.9	10.7±0.67

Three[1] and four trials[2]

Discussion

Although *Giardia* and *Cryptosporidium* have been associated with numerous waterborne gastroenteritis outbreaks (Smith, 1992; Richardson *et al*., 1991), information regarding the concentration of these organisms in secondary and tertiary treated sewage effluents is limited. This study showed that the concentration of *Giardia* cysts in secondary wastewater varied widely, with concentrations in 40 liters ranging from 0 to 160 cysts. In contrast, the concentration of *Cryptosporidium* oocysts remained relatively constant throughout this study, with values from 0 to 2 oocysts in 40 liters. Although Sykora *et al.*, (1991) reported a seasonal pattern of *Giardia* cysts in secondary sewage, with higher numbers during late summer to early winter, our results did not show a seasonal distribution of either pathogen. It was observed in this study that tertiary treatment of sewage reduced the concentration of *Giardia* cysts approximately 50%, from a geometric mean of 6.6 *Giardia* cysts in 40 liters of secondary sewage, to 3 cysts in 40 liters of tertiary wastewater. These results are in agreement with those reported by Casson *et al.* (1990), who found that *Giardia* cysts removal during secondary treatment can reach 50 %. In this study, the removal of *Cryptosporidium* oocyst during tertiary treatment, in contrast to *Giardia* cysts removal, was insignificant. This was not unexpected, as chlorine is an inefficient disinfectant against *Cryptosporidium* oocysts (Rose, 1990; Richardson *et al.*, 1991; Smith, 1992), and filtration may be inadequate under certain circumstances. This is further supported by Leland *et al.* (1993) who described a waterborne outbreak of cryptosporidiosis caused by a filtered water supply, in which the treatment plant rapid-mix unit was inoperative, and no alum was used during the coagulation/flocculation process. Moreover, Schuler *et al.* (1991), reported that a head loss of water greater than 1.5 m in a biologically immature filter, but not in a biologically mature one, resulted in failure to efficiently remove both *Giardia* cysts, and *Cryptosporidium* oocyst. LeChevalier *et al.* (1991), indicated that *Cryptosporidium* oocysts and *Giardia* cysts can be recovered from effluents of well operated and maintained drinking water treatment plants, in particular, if the influent is of poor quality. The observed lack of removal of *Cryptosporidium* oocysts after tertiary treatment may be related, in addition to the remarkable resistance of *Cryptosporidium* oocyst, to its small size (4-6μm), making the filtration process less effective. Furthermore, it has been reported (Rose, 1990), that *Cryptosporidium* oocysts are flexible, and capable of passing through membranes with a pore size of 3 μm. It was concluded in this investigation, that tertiary treatment in the studied treatment plant, based on filtration and chlorination, significantly reduced the concentration of *Giardia* cysts, but the number of *Cryptosporidium* oocysts remains unaffected.

References

Casson, L. W., Sorber, C. A., Sykora, J. L., Gavahan, P. D., Shapiro, M. A., and Jakubowski, W. (1991). Giardia in wastewater-effect of treatment. Res. J. WPCF. 62: 670-675

Craun, G. F. (1979). Waterborne giardiasis in the United States: a review. Am. J. Pub. Health. 69: 817-819

Edwards, D. D. (1993). Troubled waters in Milwaukee. ASM News. 59: 342-345

Grimason, A. M., Smith, H. V., Thitai, W. N., Smith, P. G., Jackson, M. H., and Girwood, R. W. A. (1993). Occurrence and removal of Cryptosporidium spp. oocysts and Giardia spp. cysts in Kenyan waste stabilization ponds. Wat. Sci. Tech. 27: 97-104

Hayes, E. B., Matte, T. D., O'Brien, T. R., McKinley, T. W., Logsdon, G. S., Rose, J. B., Ungar, B. L. P., Word, D. M., Pinsky, P. F., Cummings, M. L., Wilson, M. A., Long, E. G., Hurwitz, E. S., and Juranek, D. D. (1989). Large community outbreak of cryptosporidiosis due to contamination of a filtered public water supply. New England J. Med. 320: 1372-1376

Hibler, C. P., and Hancock, C. M. (1990). Waterborne gaiardiasis. In: Drinking water microbiology. Edited by McFeters, G. A. Springer-Verlag, New York

Leland, D., McAnulty, J., Keene, W., and Stevens, G. (1993). A cryptosporidiosis outbreak in a filtered-water supply. J. AWWA. 85: 34-42

Musial, C.E., Arrowood, M.J., Sterling, C.R., and Gerba C.P. (1987). Detection of *Cryptosporidium* in water using Polypropylene cartridge filters. Appl. Environ. Microbiol. 53: 687-692

Richardson, A.J., Frankenberg, R.A. Buck, A.C., Selkon, J.B., Colbourne, J.S. (1991). Outbreak of waterborne *Cryptosporidiosis* in Swindon and Oxfordshire. Epidem. Infec. 107: 485-495

Rose, J. B. (1990). Occurrence and control of Cryptosporidium in drinking water. In: Drinking water microbiology. Edited by McFeters, G. A. Springer-Verlag, New York

Rose, J.B., Kayed, D., Madore, M.S., Gerba, C.P., Arrowood, M.J., and Sterling, C.R. (1988). Methods for recovery of *Giardia* and *Cryptosporidium* from Environmental Waters and their Comparative Occurrence. Advances in Giardia research., P. Wallis and B. Hammond. Univ. Calgary Press, 1988. pp 205-209

Schuler, P. F., Ghosh, M. M., and Gopalan. (1991). Slow sand and diatomaceous earth filtration of cysts and other particulates. Wat. Res. 25: 995-1005

Smith, H. V. (1992). *Cryptosporidium* and water: a review. J. IWEM. 6:443-451

Sykora, J.L., Sorber, C.A., Jakubowski, W., Casson, L.W., and Gavaghan, P.D. (1991). Distribution of *Giardia* cysts in wastewater. Wat. Sci. Tech. 24: 187-192

The Occurrence and Viability of *Cryptosporidium* Sp. Oocysts in an Upland Raw Water Source in Central Scotland

S.W. Humphreys[1], S. McCreadie[2] and H.V. Smith[1]
[1]Scottish Parasite Diagnostic Laboratory, Stobhill NHS Trust, Glasgow G21 3UW, UK
[2]Central Scotland Water Development Board, Balmore Village, Torrance, Glasgow G64 4AJ, UK

Introduction

Over the past 15 years, the protozoan parasite *Cryptosporidium parvum* has been recognised as a significant pathogen of medical and veterinary importance. The environmentally robust and transmissive stage of the parasite (oocyst) favours waterborne transmission. This has resulted in at least eight waterborne outbreaks of cryptosporidiosis as a result of consuming oocyst-contaminated potable water and has affected over 418,000 individuals in both the U.K. and U.S.A. In the Milwaukee outbreak, over 400,000 individuals were affected, and the cost was estimated to be over $153 million.

In the first two outbreaks in the U.K. in which oocysts were detected in treated water, agricultural wastes were implicated. In 1989 an increase in cases of cryptosporidiosis in Central Scotland was detected and a possible association was made between those suffering from cryptosporidiosis and the water supplied to them (Anon., 1990a). However, the evidence was not conclusive as to the waterborne source of the infection, and other factors such as post-treatment contamination could not be ruled out (Parker *et al.*, 1993). In order to determine the impact of waterborne oocysts in this water source, which had been monitored on a monthly basis since 1989, a programme of continuous monitoring was instigated in January 1991. The aim of this study was to assess the seasonal occurrence of *Cryptosporidium* sp. oocysts in the raw water. Between June 1990 and February 1994 a survey of the occurrence and viability of *Cryptosporidium* sp. oocysts in the raw and potable water was conducted in conjunction with a Water Authority in Central Scotland.

Materials and Methods

Sampling, filter processing and detection: A filter housing containing a polypropylene microwynd depth filter (CUNO, DPPPY) of 1m nominal pore size was fitted on-line at the abstraction point. The flow rate was kept at approximately 1L min^{-1}. From January 1991, it has been sampled continuously, with three samples being collected weekly (each over a period of 2-3 days) until April 1993, when two samples were collected weekly (each over a period of 3-4 days). Sample volumes ranging from 100 to 6296 litres of either raw or potable water were collected and analysed. Filter processing and detection was performed according to the U.K. Standing Committee of Analysts Standard Method (Anon. 1990b). The overall recovery efficiencies of oocysts from CUNO filters by the SCA method was 7.5%-26.0%, with oocyst recoveries ranging between 30.3% and 91.5% for the centrifugation stages. At least 10% of the water concentrate was analysed. Diamidino-2-phenylindole (DAPI), which binds to DNA, thus highlighting sporozoite nuclei was used as an adjunct to morphometrics for identifying oocysts of *Cryptosporidium* spp. (Campbell *et al.*, 1992, Grimason *et al.*, 1994).

Microscopy: An Olympus BH-2 fluorescence microscope, equipped with Nomarski/DIC optics was used. Additional filter blocks were used for viability assessment, a blue filter block was used for FITC (excitation 490 nm; emission 510 nm), ultra-violet filter block for DAPI (excitation 350 nm; emission 450 nm), and a green filter block for PI (excitation 500 nm; emission 610 nm).

Oocyst viability: Viability was determined by the inclusion or exclusion of two fluorogenic vital dyes (DAPI and propidium iodide (PI)) according to the method of Campbell *et al.* (1992). A 100 l aliquot of the sample was placed in a 1.5 ml Eppendorf tube, containing 1ml of acidified Hanks Balanced Salt Solution (HBSS) (pH 2.75) and incubated for 1 h at 37°C. The samples were washed x3 with HBSS, (pH 7.2), concentrated to 100 l, then 10 l of DAPI (2mg/ml) and 10 l PI (1mg/ml) were added and the samples incubated for 2h at 37°C. Optimally diluted FITC anti-*Cryptosporidium* sp. Mab was added for the final 30 min of incubation. Samples were washed x3 with HBSS (pH 7.2), and 10 l aliquots were placed onto glass microscope slides, a coverslip added, and examined by fluorescence and DIC microscopy.

Results

Between June 1990 and February 1994, 403 raw water and 15 final (potable) waters were analysed for the presence of *Cryptosporidium* sp. oocysts. In raw water samples, 15% (61 of 403) samples contained oocysts, with a mean concentration of 0.02 oocysts/L (range 0.0012/L - 0.12/L). Only one of fifteen final water samples examined contained oocysts at a concentration of 0.006/L.

Viability was assessed for 22 raw water samples (between April 1991 and February 1994), which contained oocysts (range 0.006/L-0.12/L). Viable and non-viable oocysts were detected in 6 of 22 (27.3%) raw water samples, whereas in 10 of 22 (45.4%) samples all oocysts detected were non-viable. Oocysts were not recovered from the remaining 6 raw water samples.

Discussion

This is the first report of the continuous monitoring of an upland raw water entering water treatment for a period of 45 months (June 1990-February 1994). Individual samples were collected over periods of between two and three days and analysed within three days of receipt at the SPDL. Of a total of 403 raw water samples examined for the presence of oocysts, 61 (15%) were positive, containing oocysts at very low concentrations. The viability of the oocysts in 22 of these (later) samples was assessed. Most of the oocysts detected in raw water concentrates (10/22) were non-viable; however, six samples contained low numbers of viable oocysts. An epidemiological study set up to monitor human cryptosporidiosis in communities served by treated water from this source failed to identify any correlation between the occurrence of oocysts in raw water and the occurrence of cryptosporidiosis in those communities. Two potential sources of raw water contamination were identified between April 1991 and February 1993. Firstly, oocysts from sewage treatment works discharging into the source water via a river could be detected sporadically and, secondly, oocysts were detected in stools from two diarrhoeic animals pastured in the South of the catchment (Parker *et al.*, 1993). Thus both human and animal-derived oocysts could have contributed to the raw water contamination. Robertson *et al.*, (1992) demonstrated that viable oocysts survived well both in faeces and river water, whilst Parker *et al.*, (1995) estimated their rate constants (min^{-1}) for loss of viability to be 4.05×10^{-6} and 7.88×10^{-6} respectively. Both non-viable and viable oocysts were detected at the abstraction point, the majority being non-viable. Whilst it is possible that the non-viable oocysts were contributed by animals (or possibly humans) excreting non-viable oocysts (Bukhari *et al.*, 1994) it is as likely that viable oocysts, killed in the environment, were subsequently washed into the water course, reaching the abstraction point much later. At present, the most likely explanation is the latter, with oocysts being excreted onto pasture and subsequently being washed into the water course. Further analyses, using techniques such as those identified by McDonald and Kariem (1994), may help elucidate the source of such waterborne oocysts.

With the exception of an increase in oocyst numbers in raw water in the Winter of 1992/3, no statistically significant seasonal peaks were observed. In 1992 and 1993,

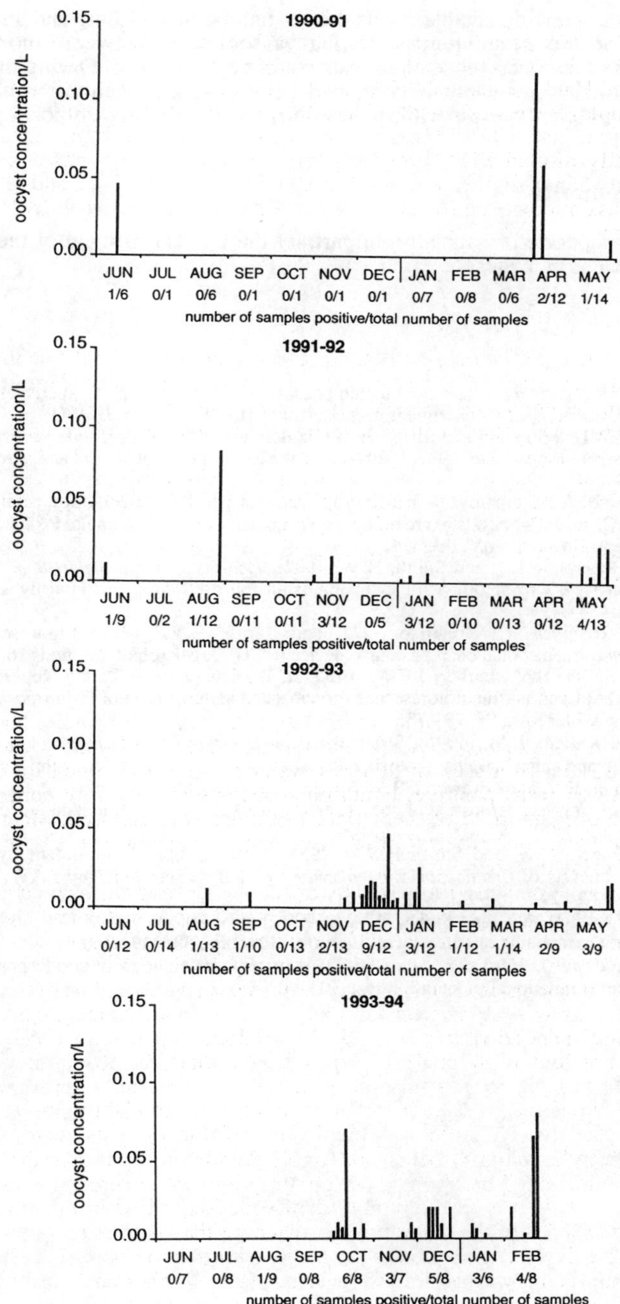

Figure 1. Concentration of oocysts in positive samples

oocysts declined below detectable levels during the months of June and July. During the sampling period no consistent statistical association between monthly rainfall measurements and the occurrence of oocysts could be established. During this survey only one of fifteen final water samples contained oocysts at a concentration of 0.006/L. No outbreak of waterborne cryptosporidiosis was attributed to this oocyst-positive final water.

Acknowledgements

This work was supported financially, in part, by the UK Department of the Environment and the Foundation for Water Research.

References

Anonymous (1990a). *Cryptosporidium* in water supplies. Report of the group of experts; chairman, Sir John Badenoch. Department of the Environment, Department of Health. London: HMSO

Anonymous (1990b) Isolation and identification of Giardia cysts, *Cryptosporidium* oocysts and free living pathogenic amoebae in water etc. 1989. Methods for the examination of waters and associated materials. London: HMSO

Bukhari, Z., Smith, H.V., Humphreys, S.W., Kemp, J. and Wright, S.E. (1994). Comparative evaluation of the viability of C. parvum oocysts excreted by experimentally infected animals. Protozoan Parasites and Water, 26-28 Sept. University of York, U.K

Campbell, A.T., Robertson, L.J. and Smith, H.V. (1992) Viability of *Cryptosporidium parvum* oocysts: correlation of i*n vitro* excystation with inclusion/exclusion of fluorogenic vital dyes. Appl. Environ. Microbiol., 58, 3488-3493

Campbell, A.T., Haggart, R., Robertson, L.J. and Smith, H.V. (1992) Fluorescent imaging of *Cryptosporidium* using a cooled charged couple device (CCD). J. Microbiol. Methods 16, 169-174

Grimason, A.M., Smith, H.V., Parker, J.F.W., Bukhari, Z., Campbell, A.T. and Robertson, L.J (1994). Application of DAPI and Immunofluorescence for enhanced identification of *Cyptosporidium* spp oocysts in water samples. Water Res., 28, 733-736

McDonald, V. and Kariem, F.M. (1994). Strain variation in *Cryptosporidium parvum* and evidence for distinctive human and animal strains. Protozoan Parasites and Water, 26-28 Sept. University of York, U.K

Parker, J.F.W., Smith, H.V. and Girdwood, R.W.A. (1993). Survey of Loch Lomond to assess the occurrence and prevalence of *Cryptosporidium* spp. oocysts and their likely impact on human health. Foundation for Water Research, FR 0409

Parker, J.F.W., Ongerth J.E. and Smith H.V. (1995). Authors' reply to comment by Haas, C.N. on "Destruction of oocysts of *Cryptosporidium parvum* by sand and chlorine" by J.F.W. Parker and H.V. Smith. Wat. Res. 27: 729-31 (1993). Wat. Res. In press

Robertson, L.J., Campbell, A.T. and Smith, H.V. (1992). Survival of oocysts of *Cryptosporidium parvum* under various environmental pressures. Appl. Environ. Microbiol. 58. 3494-3500

Smith, H.V., Patterson, W.J., Hardie, R., *et al.*, (1989). A waterborne outbreak of cryptosporidiosis caused by post treatment contamination. Epidemiol. Infect. 103, 703-715

Detection of *Cryptosporidium* and *Giardia* in Water

C.R. Fricker
Thames Water Utilities, Spencer House, Manor Farm Road, Reading, RG2 0JN, UK

Introduction

The increasing awareness that both *Cryptosporidium* spp. and *Giardia* spp. can cause waterborne outbreaks of disease has led to an intensive effort to develop methods for the detection of these organisms in water samples and substantial progress has been made in the few years that have elapsed since the first waterborne outbreak was reported. However, the development of these methods has not been simple and one of the major problems with evaluating the significance of the waterborne route of transmission of these organisms has been the difficulties associated with the available methods.

As methods are not available for the routine culture of either cryptosporidia or giardia from environmental samples, detection relies upon direct examination of water samples. Since the infective dose of the organism is thought to be low, large volumes of water need to be concentrated and subsequently examined. This type of procedure was not commonly used in the water industry where most microbiology consisted of culture of small volumes of water for heterotrophic plate count (1 ml) or coliforms and *E.coli* (100 ml). A relatively small number of utility facilities had experienced the need to concentrate and examine large volumes of water for detection of viruses, although these concentrates were subsequently examined by culture.

The procedure for detecting protozoan parasites in water can be divided into three basic sections, namely concentration, purification and detection. This paper will describe some of the available methods, discuss their advantages and shortcomings and address the issue of performance characteristics of various methods.

Concentration

Three methods of concentration are in widespread use, cartridge filtration (Rose *et al.*, 1988), membrane filtration (Ongerth and Stibbs (1987) and calcium carbonate flocculation (Vesey *et al.*, 1993a). The cartridge filtration method is the most commonly used procedure, both in Europe and in the United States, and the procedure allows the concentration of large volumes of water prior to examination. Water is passed through either a yarn wound filter or a pleated membrane filter at a flow rate of approximately 1.5 l per minute. When the desired volume of water has been filtered, the cartridge is returned to the laboratory for examination. The volume of water filtered can vary from site to site depending largely on water quality. Typical sample volumes are around 100 l for a raw water and up to 1000 l for treated water. Once in the laboratory, the concentrated material is eluted from the filter either by backflushing or more commonly by cutting up the filter and washing. For yarn wound filters, the strands of filter matrix are teased apart, washed in a detergent solution and often treated in a stomacher. For pleated membrane filters, the individual layers of each filter are separated, washed by hand and then treated in a stomacher. With both types of cartridge, several washes may be necessary to remove the particulate matter. After washing the filter it is not uncommon to have a total volume of 4 l of washings which are then concentrated by centrifugation.

The membrane filtration technique described by Ongerth and Stibbs (1987) is suitable for smaller volumes of water (10-20 l). The water sample is collected, returned to the laboratory and filtered through a 2 μ polycarbonate filter. The retained material is collected into a plastic tray by carefully scraping the surface of the membrane with a suitably shaped piece of rubber, somewhat like a car windscreen wiper blade and washing with detergent solution. The collected material is then further concentrated by centrifugation.

The calcium carbonate flocculation method is a simple procedure suitable for concentrating small (10-20 l) volumes of water. Sodium bicarbonate (100 ml of 1M) and calcium chloride (100 ml of 1 M) are added to 10 l of water and thoroughly mixed. The pH of the water is then increased to approximately pH 10 by the addition of sodium hydroxide (100 ml of 1 M). This causes the formation of insoluble calcium carbonate crystals which slowly settle, taking with them particulates in suspension. The sample is left for a minimum of four hours before the supernatant fluid is removed by vacuum. The precipitated calcium carbonate is then dissolved in sulphamic acid (10%) and the fluid decanted into a 1 l centrifuge pot. The original container is then rinsed with Tween solution (to ensure that all particulate material is recovered) and the washings added to the centrifuge pot. Centrifugation is then use to concentrate the material still further.

Each of the three methods have been used extensively and there is no "best" method for every situation. In the United States in particular, monitoring programs are largely based upon examination of small numbers of high volume samples and thus the cartridge filtration system is employed. In other areas such as Australia, larger numbers of smaller volume samples are preferred (N. Ashbolt, personal communication) and indeed others use a combination of small and large volume samples. In some situations it is not practical to take samples by the cartridge filtration method, for example when taking samples from customer taps. In these situations it is much more convenient to take 10 or 20 l samples. Also when large numbers of samples are required from a number of points within a distribution system it is unlikely that a utility would have sufficient sampling equipment (flow restrictors, filter holders etc) to take sufficient cartridge samples simultaneously and therefore smaller samples which are much more easily collected are more appropriate. A further benefit of collecting smaller samples is that they can be processed much more easily in the laboratory using the flocculation or membrane filtration methods.

The decision as to which sample collection procedure to use is therefore a matter for the local utility, based on experience, limit of detection required and practicalities. What though of the relative sensitivities of the three methods? Little work has been performed to compare the methods and a wide range of recovery rates have been quoted for the cartridge filtration method. In the original description of the calcium carbonate flocculation method, recoveries in the order of 70% were demonstrated and the ability to obtain such recoveries was confirmed by Campbell *et al* . (1994). More recent studies (Ongerth *et al*., unpublished) have confirmed these recovery rates with the flocculation method and have demonstrated similar recoveries for some samples with the membrane filtration method. The cartridge filtration method however, tended to give lower recoveries of both *Giardia* cysts and *Cryptosporidium* oocysts, in the order of 0-30%. Similar data have been generated by other workers in the U.K (K.Shepherd, personal communication). Furthermore when studying the reproducibility of results obtained by cartridge filtration, membrane filtration and flocculation (Fricker and Ongerth, unpublished) considerably more variability was demonstrated in the recovery of *Cryptosporidium* oocysts and *Giardia* cysts when using the cartridge method, than with the other two methods. One of the major reasons for this is that large numbers of cysts and oocysts either pass through the cartridge filters or adhere so tightly to the filter matrix that they cannot be recovered by washing (Vesey and Slade 1990).

Purification

Having concentrated a water sample in the laboratory, the volume of material obtained varies tremendously depending on the quality of the water and the volume concentrated. It is however not unusual to obtain 2-3 ml of concentrate from a raw surface water. Clearly it is not possible to examine all of this material by fluorescent microscopy and thus either only a small proportion can be examined or the cysts and oocysts must in some way be purified or "enriched". The most common way in which this is achieved is by density flotation using Percoll, Percoll-sucrose or sucrose (1.18 g/ml), the latter being the method employed in the U.K. Samples are underlayed with sucrose and subjected to a short low speed centrifugation step. The principle behind this technique is that dense particulates will sink whilst the less dense cysts and oocysts will be retained by the sucrose cushion. The supernatant and

Table 1. Results of experiments investigating oocyst recovery from water samples after various time periods and treatments

Water type	No. of trials	Oocyst seed	Examined immediately after seeding			Examined 6 hours after seeding			Examined 48 hours after seeding		
			With flotation	Without flotation	Sediment	With flotation	Without flotation	Sediment	With flotation	Without flotation	Sediment
Raw	4	162	91 (56)	137 (85)	33 (20)	27 (17)	118 (73)	79 (49)	18 (11)	107 (66)	78 (48)
Raw	5	368	202 (55)	284 (77)	122 (33)	166 (45)	273 (74)	169 (46)	88 (24)	264 (72)	162 (44)
Reservoir	4	157	106 (68)	132 (84)	23 (15)	84 (54)	108 (69)	49 (31)	39 (25)	118 (75)	62 (39)
Reservoir	5	329	216 (66)	265 (81)	67 (20)	153 (47)	244 (74)	104 (32)	106 (32)	237 (72)	129 (39)
Treated	4	144	112 (78)	111 (77)	15 (10)	102 (71)	128 (89)	27 (19)	89 (62)	121 (84)	24 (17)
Treated	5	342	278 (81)	294 (86)	18 (5)	243 (71)	288 (84)	37 (11)	186 (54)	242 (71)	47 (14)

interface can then be collected, resulting, in theory, in a more pure suspension of the material of interest. However, recoveries of cysts and oocysts after sucrose density flotation can be extremely variable. In our laboratory, recoveries with sucrose flotation have ranged from <5-81% depending on a number of factors. The turbidity of the water had a significant effect on recovery, samples with higher turbidities generally giving lower recoveries and this has been demonstrated elsewhere (H.V. Smith, personal communication). Furthermore experimental design can have a significant effect on recovery. Unpublished data from our laboratory has demonstrated that the period between adding cysts and oocysts to a water sample and subsequent processing by sucrose flotation can have a marked effect on recovery. In one experiment, oocysts were added to a raw water concentrate and mixed thoroughly. A portion was removed immediately, treated by sucrose flotation and examined by epifluorescent microscopy. A further portion was removed after six hours and another after 48 hours. The percentage recoveries obtained were 72, 49 and 9 respectively. These results were obtained presumably because the longer the cysts or oocysts are present in a suspension together with other material, the more likely they are to bind to other particulates. Thus if they bind to larger particles of dense material they may well be lost during "purification". Clearly in naturally contaminated waters there is considerable potential for cysts and oocysts to adhere to other particulates and thus we must suppose that the use of the sucrose flotation technique will cause significant under reporting of the presence of *Cryptosporidium* and *Giardia*.

Clearly in the experiment described above, binding of oocysts to particulates was not the only plausible explanation for the losses incurred and thus further experiments were performed using the same experimental design. In these experiments, not only was the supernatant and interface material examined by microscopy, but also the material which sedimented and a portion of the suspension which had not been subjected to sucrose flotation. The results of these experiments are shown in Table 1.

In this particular set of experiments, the recovery of oocysts after sucrose flotation ranged from 11-81%. In general, lower recoveries were obtained with high turbidity water and recovery decreased after oocysts had been in contact with the pellet for extended periods of time. Almost 50% of oocysts could be recovered from the pellet obtained during sucrose flotation with some samples, presumably because they had bound to more dense particulates and had thus passed through the sucrose. However, the maximum recovery of oocysts from both floated material together with that found in the pellet was 91% and in some cases was as low as 59%. Presumably the remaining oocysts were either masked by other particulates, were missed by the microscopist or floated off of the slide during staining. All of these factors can, and do, contribute to the losses seen during routine parasite recovery procedures. The comparisons made during these experiments were somewhat unrealistic since much more time was necessarily spent on microscopy for those samples which were not treated by sucrose flotation, due to the larger volume of pellet obtained, some samples requiring up to three hours microscopy. In a busy routine monitoring laboratory it is not realistic for such periods of time to be taken for routine analyses of a single sample and thus either sucrose flotation or some other "purification" method is required. Initial trials undertaken at Thames Water Utilities (Vesey *et al.*, 1991) showed that flow cytometry may be a suitable procedure for detecting or "purifying" *Cryptosporidium* oocysts and *Giardia* cysts. However, in the early experiments using an instrument which could detect but not sort fluorescent particles, the sensitivity which was achievable was too low and there was considerable difficulty in separating "background noise" from genuine signals. Further studies identified that with a suitable protocol, flow cytometry together with fluorescent activated cell sorting was indeed a suitable method for "sorting" oocysts and cysts from background debris (Vesey *et al.*, 1993b; 1994). Concentrated material is stained in suspension with a fluorescent-labelled monoclonal antibody, run through the flow cytometer and fluorescent material of the correct size is collected onto a microscope slide for later microscopic examination. The benefits of this procedure are that the amount of time for microscopical examination is greatly reduced, sensitivity is increased, larger samples can be examined and some oocysts stain better than when stained fixed to a microscope slide. The procedure is now widely used in several U.K. water utilities together with others in Australia and the U.S. The major drawback of the procedure is the expense of the instrument which is in the order of £150,000. However, when costed over a period of five years, the instrument easily pays for itself by the reduction in labour costs.

Detection

Detection of *Cryptosporidium* oocysts and *Giardia* cysts relies largely on direct microscopical examination. Here, as with all stages of the procedure, experience is required and inexperienced staff can lead to false positive or false negative results being reported. The basis of correct identification is the size and shape of the cyst or oocyst and other features such as the "suture line" on *Cryptosporidium* oocysts should be regarded as potentially useful but not diagnostic. Extreme care is required when examining potential oocysts of *Cryptosporidium parvum* as there are many organisms (particularly algae and yeasts) which can mimic the appearance of these oocysts. Careful measurement of the organism is required together with examination by phase contrast or Normarski microscopy. Furthermore, oocysts of other species of *Cryptosporidium* may appear very similar to oocysts of *C.parvum* notably *C. bailiae*. In fact there is considerable overlap in the size of oocysts from these two species (Smith, H.V., personal communication). It is a useful practice to keep records of the size of all oocysts reported and whenever possible to take photomicrographs.

The antibodies available for fluorescent labelling of the cysts and oocysts are remarkably similar regardless of source. The anti-*Cryptosporidium* antibodies which are commercially available all appear to recognise a similar epitope which is immunodominant. These antibodies will often bind to other organisms or to other particulate matter in the sample. These "cross reactions" may be genuinely due to other organisms possessing the same or similar epitopes or may be due to the expression of antibody binding proteins (e.g. protein A) on the surface of some cells, particularly yeasts. Non-specific antibody binding also occurs and as with other immunological methods this can be reduced to a certain extent by incorporation of blocking agents such as bovine serum albumen, into the staining protocol, and the use of mild detergents.

Conclusion

Considerable advances have been made in the methodologies available for detecting protozoan parasites in water in recent years. However, despite these advances our ability to detect these organisms is, at best, variable and could probably be more accurately described as "inconsistent and poor". In addition, the process is time consuming, expensive and requires a high degree of training, resulting in relatively low numbers of samples being examined. This considerably reduces our understanding of the role of water in the epidemiology of human protozoan disease.

On a more positive note, there is continuing research aimed at improving sensitivity, reproducibility and repeatability. The application of modern technologies such as flow cytometry has helped considerably and further research into the potential of modern molecular methods such as the polymerase chain reaction and fluorescent in situ hybridisation is warranted. However, if one were to identify the areas of greatest need they would have to be the concentration and purification steps. All of the detection technologies currently available suffer from the same problem, the large amount of contaminating material which makes identification of cysts and oocysts difficult. We can, therefore, look forward to much progress over the coming years but the time when parasite analysis becomes as frequent and simple as that for the indicator bacteria is many years away.

References

Campbell, A.T., Robertson, L.J., Smith,H.V. and Girdwood, R.W.A. 1994 Viability of *Cryptosporidium parvum* oocysts concentrated by calcium carbonate flocculation. Journal of Applied Bacteriology, 76, 638-639

Ongerth, J.E. and Stibbs, H.H. 1987 Identification *Cryptosporidium* oocysts in river water. Applied and Environmental Microbiology, 53, 672-676

Rose, J.B., Darbin, H. and Gerba, C.P. 1988 Correlations of the protozoa *Cryptosporidium* and *Giardia*, with water quality variables in a watershed. Water Science and Technology, 20, 271-276

Vesey, G. and Slade, J.S. 1990 Isolation and identification of *Cryptosporidium* from water. Water Science and Technology, 24, 165-167

Vesey, G., Slade, J.S. and Fricker, C.R. 1991 Taking the eye strain out of environmental *Cryptosporidium* analysis. Letters in Applied Microbiology

Vesey, G., Slade, J.S., Byrne, M., Shepherd, K., Dennis, P.J. and Fricker, C.R. 1993a A new method for the concentration of *Cryptosporidium* oocysts from water. Journal of Applied Bacteriology, 75, 87-90

Vesey, G., Slade, J.S., Byrne, M., Shepherd, K., Dennis, P.J. and Fricker, C.R. 1993b Routine monitoring of *Cryptosporidium* oocysts in water using flow cytometry. Journal of Applied Bacteriology, 75, 82-86

Vesey, G., Slade, J.S., Byrne, M., Shepherd, K., and Fricker, C.R. 1994 New techniques for the detection of protozoan parasites in water. In: Rapid Methods in Microbiology eds Kroll, R. *et al.*

Viability of *Giardia* Cysts and *Cryptosporidium* Oocysts

L.J. Robertson
Scottish Parasite Diagnostic Laboratory, Stobhill NHS Trust, Springburn, Glasgow, G21 3UW, UK

Introduction

The microbiological safety of a potable water supply to the consumer is normally inferred by surrogate parameters such as turbidity, particle counts, chlorine residuals, coliform counts etc. However, cysts and oocysts of the parasitic protozoa *Giardia duodenalis* and *Cryptosporidium parvum* are resistant to chlorine disinfection, and furthermore, the coliform standard is unreliable as an indicator of either the presence or viability of cysts and oocysts. The public health hazard from cysts or oocysts revolves around their infectivity to man, which, as it cannot be addressed directly requires the need for the development of a surrogate method of assessment. It should be realised that whatever approach is used in developing such an assay, it must always be acknowledged that it is a surrogate. Whilst there are a number of such surrogate techniques for assessing viability, not all are applicable to small numbers or individual parasites which are normally isolated from raw and potable water.

The objective of this paper is to describe both the approach used at the Scottish Parasite Diagnostic Laboratory in attempting to develop and use viability assays for *Giardia* cysts and *Cryptosporidium* oocysts and also to outline why this approach has been used. The approach that we have used in developing a surrogate assay is based upon microscopy using fluorogenic vital dyes, a technique whose value lies not only in assisting in identification by enhancing the visualisation of the morphology, but, by leaving the organism intact allows further testing of the parasite by other methods. To date, we have had some success in developing and using such a viability assay for individual *C. parvum* oocysts (Campbell *et al.* 1992a) and we have attempted to use the experiences gained in developing this assay to develop a similarly user-friendly assay for *Giardia* cysts.

Why Assess Viability?

The transmission stages of the protozoan parasites *Giardia* and *Cryptosporidium*, the cyst and oocyst respectively, are known to be robust and capable of surviving a range of environmental pressures. The robust nature of the cyst and oocyst is an important factor in the success of these parasitic infections and means that they are capable of surviving for relatively long periods of time in water bodies (which may be a vehicle for transmission) and can withstand the application of some disinfectants (DeRegnier *et al.* 1989; Korich *et al.* 1990; Hoff, 1986; Robertson *et al.* 1992). Thus it is frequently important to be able to assess whether cysts and oocysts isolated from environmental samples are viable and, furthermore, assessment of viability is an important tool in experimental situations and in devising protocols for inactivating cysts and oocysts.

What is Meant by Viability?

When an organism is referred to as viable, this generally refers to a state of being alive, recognised by one of a number of criteria usually indicating either respiration or metabolic activity, possibly basal. However, for the transmission stages of protozoan parasites, viability is frequently understood to mean being capable of progressing to the next stage of the life cycle i.e. capable of excystation. However, in terms of the life-cycle of *Giardia* and *Cryptosporidium*, excystation is insufficient if the sporozoites (in the case of *Cryptosporidium*) or the trophozoites (in the case of *Giardia*) do not proceed to establish infection. Furthermore, as those species of *Giardia* cysts and *Cryptosporidium* oocysts which may infect man (*G. duodenalis* and *C. parvum*) occurring in the environment are only of public health significance if they are infective, infectivity status, rather than viability, is frequently of interest.

What Techniques are Available for Assessing Viability of *Cryptosporidium* Oocysts and *Giardia* Cysts: Infection, Excystation or a Surrogate?

The success or failure of attempting to initiate infection in a susceptible host species is the only definitive test for infectivity, but there are problems in attempting to assess infectivity (Table 1). As *in vitro* excystation has been shown to correlate with infectivity (Blewett, 1989; Labatuik *et al.* 1991), this is considered to be a suitable surrogate. However, *in vitro* excystation as an index of viability also has a range of associated problems. These problems include:

1 selection of *in vitro* excystation protocol to use;
2 technique for enumeration of excystation;
3 the expense in time;
4 the lack of suitability of such an approach to small numbers of cysts/oocysts which may be isolated from environmental samples.

Table 1. Problems using infectivity to measure *Giardia* cyst or *Cryptosporidium* oocyst viability

Selection of infective dose to use
Route of infection to use (the importance, if any, of salivary contact in establishing infection)
Interpretation of kinetics of infections with different doses
Selection of host animal to use and relevance of selected host to establishment of human infection
Interpretation of lack of establishment of infection
Expense (both in time and consumables)
Ethical considerations
Not applicable to individual/small numbers of organisms isolated from environmental samples

Furthermore, whilst *in vitro* excystation of *C. parvum* oocysts seems to be relatively straighforward and consistent (Robertson *et al.* 1993), the *in vitro* excystation of *Giardia duodenalis* cysts seems to be more complex and less consistent, with different research groups apparently having different degrees of success with different excystation protocols (e.g. Bingham & Meyer, 1979; Rice & Schaefer, 1982; Sauch, 1988). This could be because the optimum *in vitro* excystation assay(s) for this species of *Giardia* has yet to be described, but it also probably reflects differences between isolates of *G.duodenalis* which may require different triggers for excystation. In contrast, *G. muris* seems relatively simple to excyst *in vitro*, and the marked differences between isolates of *G. duodenalis* have not been noted for this species.

Despite these difficulties, infectivity must remain the "gold standard" and *in vitro* excystation the "silver standard" for assessment of cyst and oocyst viability. However, because of these difficulties, and in particular because of the need to have means of assessing the viability of small numbers or individual organisms isolated from environmental samples, in recent years there has been considerable effort directed at developing a surrogate method for viability assessment.

Developing a Surrogate Method for Viability Assessment of *Giardia* Cysts and *Cryptosporidium* Oocysts Suitable for Small Numbers or Individual Parasites Isolated from the Environment

In order to overcome the difficulties associated with infectivity and *in vitro* excystation, the development of sensitive and user-friendly techniques for the viability of individual or small numbers of cysts and oocysts is required. Such a test would, ideally, leave the cyst or oocyst intact for verification of the viability by another technique and also it would be beneficial if it could, simultaneously, be useful for assisting in identification of the organism. The approaches so far investigated by different research groups have included molecular techniques (e.g. *in situ* hybridisation and polymerase chain reaction (PCR)), biophysical techniques (e.g. dielectrophoresis and electro-rotation) and microscopic techniques (morphology and fluorescent probes). Whilst the first two of these approaches indubitably have utility and exciting progress has been made with them, there are associated problems. For example, many molecular techniques tend not to be holistic and thus the potential for verification of results, obtained from individual organisms, by another technique may be lost; PCR-based techniques are frequently qualitative rather than quantitative. As yet, both bio-physical and molecular approaches require considerable further evaluation before they can be of use for a routine laboratory and there is an urgent need for devising an assay which can be used as soon as possible. Therefore, the approach that has been used at SPDL has focused upon visualisation techniques using microscopy.

Table 2. Rationale behind developing a microscope-based technique for assessing the viability of cysts and oocysts

Holistic approach - cyst/oocyst remains intact for further testing e.g. excystation, electrorotation
Uses same technology as presently used for identification
May be used to enhance morphology and thus aid in identification; a link between identification and assessment of viability
May be used in conjunction with other technologies e.g. dielectrophoresis, flow cytometry
Possibility of multiple parameter probes
Relatively simple technology: readily adopted by laboratories of varying technological status

There are a number of reasons why a microscopy-based approach has been used (Table 2), and this approach has the potential to encompass not only assessment of morphology using light microscopy, but by using fluorogenic dyes has enabled the enhanced visualisation of some morphological features. Thus, as well as indicating markers which may provide indices of viability, fluorogenic dyes may be useful in assisting in the identification of cysts and oocysts in environmental samples.

Morphology as an Indicator of Viability

The most simple approach to using microscopy to assess the viability of cysts and oocysts, is to examine them by light microscopy, preferably with improved optics (DIC/Nomarski or phase contrast) and compare their morphology with strictly defined morphological criteria indicative of viability or lack of viability (Table 3).

Table 3. Morphological criteria for viability or lack of viability in cysts and oocysts.
(derived from data accumulated at the SPDL and from Deng and Cliver, 1992; Schupp *et al.* 1988)

Viable cysts/oocysts	Non-viable cysts/oocysts
Correct morphometry	Misshapen or collapsed
Intact cyst/oocyst wall	Broken cyst/oocyst wall
Cytoplasm distinct	Cytoplasm either contracted from wall or closely applied to wall
Refractile	Empty shell or cytoplasm contracted and/or granular
Smooth surface morphology	Rough surface morphology

Although it is relatively simple to recognise a non-viable cyst or oocyst if it is clearly collapsed or misshapen, it may be more difficult if the degree of disintegration is slight, and this difficulty is probably greater with oocysts than cysts because of their smaller size. Furthermore, this difficulty may often be exacerbated in environmental samples by occluding debris. The effects of ageing and sub-lethal doses of disinfectants on the morphology of cysts and oocysts, which, whilst still remaining viable, may be considered to be dying may also present further problems, and the effect of the isolation technique on the organism must also be addressed.

Why use Fluorogenic Dyes as Surrogate Indicators of Viability?

The use of fluorogenic vital dyes is suggested firstly, because of the difficulties in using morphology alone, secondly, because of the potential for highlighting some marker for viability, and thirdly, in order to improve visualisation of the morphology and thereby assist in identification. Fluorogenic dyes may be used to indicate viability by a number of possible approaches, some of which have the potential to be used in tandem, or, preferably, simultaneously, and may be used at the nucleic acid level, the cytoplasmic level, or the whole organism level, depending on the probe(s) (Table 4). Some dyes may be used to indicate intactness as a measure of viability by dye exclusion (negative indicators of viability) or other dyes may be used to indicate various cellular functions (positive indicators of viability).

Table 4. Potential indicators of viability which may be assessed by use of fluorogenic dyes

	Dye excluded	Dye included
Intactness of cell	√	
Active enzyme systems		√
Oxidative potential		√
Ion pump activity		√
Cellular permeability		√
Maintenance of homeostasis		√

What Problems are Associated with using Fluorogenic Dyes as Surrogate Indicators of Viability?

There are, however, a range of potential problems to be addressed when attempting to use fluorogenic vital dyes as indicators of viability for cysts and oocysts. One of the major problems is posed by the robust wall which cysts and oocysts possess and which is largely responsible for the ability of these organisms to exist for relatively long periods of time under a range of environmental conditions. For those dyes which must be incorporated into the cell before being used as a viability indicator, the cell wall may prevent ingress of the dye, and for those dyes which indicate viability by their exclusion, again the cell wall may prevent the dye ingress despite cell membranes being ruptured.

Other problems which may be encountered in using dyes are that the dye or dye solvent may affect the viability of the cyst/oocyst; environmental factors may prevent the uptake of the dye or the binding of the dye to its substrate (e.g. aldehydes such as formalin can cross-link the proteins of cell membranes and may therefore inhibit the inclusion and intercalation of certain dyes; Campbell *et al.* 1993); dyes may leach from cells; the background demand for the dyes used must be taken into account, particularly in dirty samples; spectral isolation of the dye both from the fluorochrome (commonly FITC) on the distinguishing monoclonal antibody and, if more than one dye is used, between dyes, is required.

Dye Exclusion as an Indicator of Viability

Dye exclusion (e.g. propidium iodide (PI) or dansyl lysine) is considered to underestimate consistently the viability of *G. duodenalis* cysts (Smith and Smith, 1989) and has provided variable results in some experiments for *G. muris* cysts (Sauch *et al.* 1991; Schupp and Erlandsen, 1987). Whilst we can be convinced that a cyst or oocyst which includes such a dye is non-viable and has ruptured membranes, uncertainty arises over those cysts or oocysts which exclude the dye; either the cyst or oocyst is indeed viable, or it is non-viable but, for some reason, has not included/bound the dye. Also, when dye exclusion is used to indicate viability the dye would be of greater use if it could also assist in identification by highlighting an organelle (e.g. PI will high-light the nuclei of cysts and oocysts) in those cysts or oocysts which include the dye and are, therefore, dead. Dye exclusion would, therefore, be a useful negative measure of viability provided that it was used in conjunction with another positive indicator of viability, which may also be of use in assisting in identification.

Positive Indicators of Viability

One such positive indicator that has frequently been suggested is enzymatic activity. The basis of such an assay is the supposition that viable cells will have active enzyme systems and non-viable cells will not. Fluorescein diacetate (FDA) is one of the more frequently cited dyes which could be used to indicate enzymatic activity, and has been considered for assessment of *Giardia* cyst viability (Schupp and Erlandsen, 1987; Schupp *et al.* 1988; Smith and Smith, 1989); taken into the cell in a non-fluorescent form, non-specific esterases will cleave the dye and the fluorescein fluorescence indicates enzymatic activity. A major problem with this is that cysts/oocysts which are considered to be non-viable by morphology or dye exclusion may still show enzymatic activity. This could be due to non-specific esterases from the environment penetrating the ruptured cells, or, more probably, the enzyme system remains active even after cell death. Thus, even in conjunction with dye exclusion, this assay is not wholly satisfactory, although the dual-assay has been used with some success with non-human isolates of *Giardia* cysts (Deng and Cliver, 1992). Similar problems to those described for FDA also arise with probes to measure oxidative potential and ion pump activity.

For *Cryptosporidium*, the viability assay developed at the SPDL also relies on two parameters which are assessed simultaneously, as well as upon morphology. The first parameter is the exclusion of PI by intact cells, and the second parameter is the incorporation of 4',6-diamidino-2-phenylindole (DAPI) into the nuclei of the sporozoites. Viable cells will not only exclude the PI but also include the DAPI into the sporozoite nuclei with a characteristically defined sky blue fluorescence. When the DAPI staining of the sporozoites is cytoplasmic, without the nuclei being specifically high-lighted, the oocysts are still considered non-viable even if the PI has not apparently been included. With this two-pronged approach, with both negative and positive indicators of viability, the likelihood of the viability of an oocyst being assessed incorrectly is diminished. This assay has been correlated with viability as assessed by *in vitro* excystation and correlation coefficients in excess of 0.99 been described (Campbell *et al.* 1992a; Robertson *et al.* 1992). Difficulties with permeation of the DAPI through the oocyst wall have been overcome by treatments which have also been found to be essential for *in vitro* excystation (Robertson *et al.* 1993). Furthermore, in the viability assay for *C. parvum,* the positive indicator for viability (DAPI) provides a useful adjunct for identification by highlighting the four sporozoite nuclei (Campbell *et al.* 1992b).

The Difficulties with *Giardia* and the Potential for Success

To date, we have not had a similar success in the development of a viability assay for *Giardia* cysts. This is perhaps in part due to the difficulties with *in vitro* excystation of human isolates of *Giardia* cysts which mean that correlation of potential assays with *in vitro* excystation is difficult and also due to the difficulty in obtaining sufficient numbers of viable *Giardia* cysts of the *duodenalis* species for exhaustive testing. However, we have been able to identify a range of probes which enhance the morphology of the cyst and may have potential for indicating cyst viability (Table 5). As there are more organelles present in *Giardia* cysts(2-4 nuclei, flagella axonemes, median body) than *Cryptosporidium* oocysts (4 sporozoite nuclei), the potential for using fluorogenic probes which assist in identification by enhancing visualisation of morphology is increased. Dyes with potential utility have been identified and it is anticipated that a combination of these, probably using a negative indicator of viability such as dansyl lysine or dimeric nuclei acid stains, in conjunction with a positive indicator viability, will be able to provide a simple, reliable and user-friendly technique for assessment of *Giardia* cyst viability. Furthermore, it is anticipated that at least one of the selected dyes will highlight organelles within the cyst, thus providing a tool for enhancing visualisation of the cyst morphology for improvement of identification.

Table 5. Fluorogenic probes with potential for indicating viability in *Giardia* cysts and assisting identification by high-lighting organelles

Probe	Organelles high-lighted	Indicator
BCECF-diacetate	Flagellar axonemes	Enzymatic activity
Dihydroethidium	Nuclei	Oxidative potential
SNAFL-diacetate	Flagella axonemes, median body, nuclei	Enzymatic activity Cellular homeostasis
Thiolites	Nuclei and cytoplasmic staining	Free sulphydryl
AMCA-peptides	Cytoplasmic staining	Proteases
DAPI	Nuclei	Permeability

Acknowledgements

I would like to acknowledge that the work described above is the result of the combined efforts of all the members of the Scottish Parasite Diagnostic Laboratory, with particular in-put from A.T. Campbell and H.V. Smith.

References

Bingham, A.K. and Meyer, E.A. (1979). *Giardia* excystation can be induced *in vitro* in acidic solutions. *Nature (London)* 277 301-302

Blewett, D.A. (1989). Disinfection and oocysts. In: *Cryptosporidiosis. Proceedings of the First International workshop*. (Angus, K.W. and Blewett, D.A., editors). The Animal Disease Research Association, Edinburgh. pp. 107-116

Campbell, A.T., Haggart, R., Robertson, L.J. and Smith, H.V. (1992b). Fluorescent imaging of *Cryptosporidium* using a cooled charge couple device (CCD). *J. Micro. Methods* 16 169-174

Campbell, A.T., Robertson, L.J., Smith, H.V. (1992a). Viability of *Cryptosporidium parvum* oocysts: correlation of *in vitro* excystation with inclusion/exclusion of fluorogenic vital dyes. *Appl. Env. Microbiol.*58 3488-3493

Campbell, A.T., Robertson, L.J. and Smith, H.V. (1993). Effects of preservatives on viability of *Cryptosporidium parvum* oocysts. *Appl. Env. Microbiol.* 59 4361-4362

Deng, M.Y. and Cliver, D.O. (1992). Degradation of *Giardia lamblia* cysts in mixed human and swine wastes. *App. Env. Microbiol.* 58 2368-2374

DeRegnier, D.P., Cole, L., Schupp, D.G. and Erlandsen, S.L. (1989). Viability of Giardia cysts suspended in lake, river and tap water. *Appl. Env. Microbiol.* 55 1223-1229

Hoff, J.C. (1986). Inactivation of microbial agents by chemical disinfectants. EPA-600/2-86-067, US Environmental Protection Agency, Cincinnati, Ohio

Korich, D.G., Mead, J.R., Madore, M.S., Sinclair, N.A., and Sterling, C.R. (1990). Effects of ozone, chlorine dioxide, chlorine and monochloramine on *Cryptosporidium* oocyst viability. *Appl. Env. Microbiol.* 56 1423-1428

Labatuik, C.W., Schaefer III, F.W., Finch, G. R., Belosevic, M. (1991). Comparison of animal infectivity, excystation and fluorogenic dye as measures of *Giardia muris* cyst inactivation by ozone. *Appl. Env. Microbiol.* 57 3187-3192

Rice, E.W. and Schaefer, F.W. (1982). An improved *in vitro* excystation procedure of *Giardia lamblia* cysts. *J. Clin. Microbiol.* 14 709-710

Robertson, L.J., Campbell, A.T. and Smith, H.V. (1992). Survival of oocysts of *Cryptosporidium parvum* under various environmental pressures. *Appl. Env. Microbiol.* 58 3494-3500

Robertson, L.J., Campbell, A.T. and Smith, H.V. (1993). *In vitro* excystation of *Cryptosporidium parvum*. *Parasitology* 106 13-19

Sauch, J.F. (1988). A new method of excystation of *Giardia*. In: *Advances in Giardia Research* (ed.s Wallis, P.M. and Hamond, B.R.) The University of Calgary Press, Calgary, Canada. pp. 261-264

Sauch, J.L., Flanigan, D., Galvin, M.L., Berman, D. and Jakubowski, W. (1991). Propidium iodide as an indicator of *Giardia* cyst viability. *Appl. Env. Microbiol.* 57 3243-3247

Schupp, D.G. and Erlandsen, S.L. (1987). A new method to determine Giardia cyst viability: correlation of fluorescein diacetate and propidium iodide staining with animal infectivity. *Appl. Env. Microbiol.* 53 704-707

Schupp, D.G., Januschka, M.M. and Erlandsen, S.L. (1988). Assessing *Giardia* cyst viability with fluorogenic dyes: comparisons to animal infectivity and cyst morphology by light and electron microscopy. In: *Advances in Giardia Research* (ed.s Wallis, P.M. and Hamond, B.R.) The University of Calgary Press, Calgary, Canada. pp. 265-269

Smith, A.L. and Smith, H.V. (1989). A comparison of fluorescein diacetate and propidium iodide staining and *in vitro* excystation for determining *Giardia intestinalis* cyst viability. *Parasitology* 99 329-331

Strain Variation in *Cryptosporidium parvum* and Evidence for Distinctive Human and Animal Strains

V. McDonald and F.M. Awad-El-Kariem
London School of Hygiene and Tropical Medicine, Department of Clinical Sciences, Keppel St., London WC1E 7HT, UK

Cryptosporidium is a parasitic protozoan of the Subclass Coccidia which develops in epithelial cells, normally in the gastrointestinal tract or respiratory tract, of vertebrates. Parasite development in the host may result in serious pathophysiological effects, depending on the site of development. *Cryptosporidium parvum*, an important species which infects man and many other species of mammals, inhabits mainly the small intestine and causes an unpleasant watery diarrhoea. The infection is transmitted in a faecal-oral manner through the oocyst (Tzipori, 1988).

The epidemiology of the disease has been closely examined in recent years, but there are many gaps in our knowledge, particularly concerning details of the mechanisms of transmission. It has been suggested, with good evidence, that the transmission of *C. parvum* to man is primarily zoonotic, either through direct contact with animals or consumption of contaminated water (PHLS Study Group, 1990). Person to person contact is also known to be a common route of transmission. Advances in epidemiology will be facilitated through the development of simple and sensitive methods for differentiating between species and strains of Cryptosporidium.

Since the genus *Cryptosporidium* was first described in the early 1900's until relatively recently, new species of the parasite were named for every host species found to be infected, based on the assumption that, like some other coccidia, *Cryptosporidium* was highly host-specific. In the 1980's, however, it became clear that the same species of *Cryptosporidium* could infect more than one host species (Tzipori, 1988). For example, it was shown experimentally that *C. parvum* infected a variety of mammalian species while *C. baileyi* produced infections in a number of species of birds. A small number of species were eventually characterised; this was based mainly on parasite morphology, host range and site of infection in the host. The species which are still generally recognised are: *C. parvum*, which infects the gastrointestinal tract of mammals; *C. muris*, a gastric parasite of rodents, cattle and some other mammals; *C. baileyi*, commonly infecting the bursa, intestine or respiratory tract of chickens and turkeys; and *C. meleagridis*, an avian parasite which is found in the intestine. These descriptive approaches have been valuable up to a point but further elucidation is required. It has not been satisfactorily established, for example, whether *C. parvum* is indeed single species or a number of species or subspecies. Even if it is one species, we know very little concerning intraspecies variation. Increased knowledge in these areas could be informative about detection of virulence or preferred host range and may provide molecular markers which would be valuable in epidemiology.

In recent years molecular studies of *Cryptosporidium* have become common and new approaches have been adopted in attempts to differentiate between species and strains of Cryptosporidium. From oocyst studies, *C. parvum*, *C. muris* and *C. baileyi* have now been readily differentiated according to polypeptide composition (Nina *et al.*, 1992a), electrophoretic mobility of chromosomes (Mead *et al.*, 1988), polymerase chain reaction (Webster *et al.*, 1993; Awad-El-Kariem *et al.*, 1994) and enzyme electrophoresis (Ogunkolade *et al.*, 1993).

Recently, our laboratory has been studying strain variation in *C. parvum* and, using oocysts purified from infected hosts and employing different molecular techniques, we have been able to demonstrate strain variation within this species. This variation was particularly clear when comparing parasite isolates from man and other host species, suggesting that there may be distinctive human strains of *C. parvum*.

Western blotting

The first technique that we used to examine strain variation was Western blotting. Homogenised oocysts of each isolate were first subjected to electrophoresis in a sodium dodecyl sulphate polyacrylamide gel to separate their polypeptides according to molecular mass. Direct comparison between isolates was obtained by running samples in lanes side by side. Western blotting was then performed to transfer electrophoretically an imprint of the polypeptide profiles of the oocyst samples to a sheet of nitrocellolose paper. Antibodies are able to bind quite efficiently to the polypeptides in the nitrocellulose paper. The antigen bands in the blot with which specific antibodies react were observed via a colorimetric reaction involving a second antibody, specific for the first antibody, which was covalently linked to an enzyme that produces a colour after addition of its substrate.

In our Western blot studies, we examined the interaction between *C. parvum* parasite antigens and a number of monoclonal antibodies developed against the oocyst stage of this species isolated from a human infection (McDonald *et al.*, 1991). The pattern of antigen bands of different oocyst isolates in adjacent lanes could then be compared. The antigenic profiles varied between isolates with a number of antibodies tested. One antibody, 2A6, which reacted specifically with the sporozoite (but not the wall surrounding the sporozoites in the oocyst), was tested against 8 oocyst isolates from animals (four bovine and four ovine) and 11 isolates from humans (Nina *et al.* 1992b). In the blots only one major antigen band was observed for each isolate, located at a position corresponding to a molecular mass of just over 45 kD. There was some variation in the actual size of this band between isolates, however. Consistently, the band in animal isolates was always the same size, 48 kD. The equivalent band from human isolates was always of a slightly different size, the majority (ten out of eleven) being smaller (about 47 kD - ie the band had migrated a little further down the gel), but one antigen band of a human isolate was larger (51 kD) than the bands from animal isolates. The antigen recognized by 2A6 is located on the sporozoite surface and is an immunodominant glycoprotein (unpublished data). Another antibody which recognised the sporozoite, 182C1, reacted with a number of bands in oocyst samples, but two in particular were strongly detected - at 150 and 140 kD. The 140 kD band was observed in human isolates but not in any of the animal isolates tested.

These results demonstrated, therefore, that Western blotting with monoclonal antibodies could differentiate between human and animal isolates of *C. parvum*.

Enzyme Electrophoresis

In this technique oocyst homogenates were placed in wells in a thin slab of starch gel and subjected to electrophoresis to separate out the proteins according to their electrical charge. Sporozoites were excysted from oocysts by incubation at 37°C with bile salts, washed in medium to remove the bile salts and homogenised by freeze-thawing using liquid nitrogen. Such material from a number of isolates was applied to wells along one end of a starch gel and a electric current was applied to allow migration of proteins through the gel. Following this, the particular enzyme of interest was detected by addition to the gel of the enzyme substrate which on reaction with the enzyme produced a colour, the enzyme appearing as a discrete coloured band. Variation in the migration distance between isoenzymes from related organisms normally indicates differences in amino acid composition and this technique has been used successfully to identify and distinguish strains or species of organisms (Godfrey and Kilgour, 1976).

Several enzymes of *C. parvum* have been examined by us in starch gel electrophoresis. Examination of the enzyme glucose phosphate isomerase had previously allowed us to differentiate between the three species, *C. parvum*, *C. muris* and *C. baileyi* (Ogunkolade *et al.*, 1993). More than twenty isolates of both human and animal (predominantly bovine) isolates of *C. parvum* have now been tested, but a single enzyme type has been observed in all isolates. A similar result was obtained with lactate dehydrogenase. In contrast, two isoenzyme forms in *C. parvum* were clearly observed with phosphoglucomutase and hexokinase. With PGM all twelve animal isolates examined had the same enzyme; out of twelve human isolates, however, only two had the "animal" strain enzyme, while the other ten had a different, "human", strain enzyme type (e.g. Awad-El-Kariem *et al.*, 1993). Similarly, with hexokinase the four human isolates tested had a single enzyme type quite different from the one observed from six animal isolates (Awad-El-Kariem *et al.*, 1995).

This technique provided further evidence of strain variation in *C. parvum* and, as with Western blotting, appears to distinguish between some strains from humans and others from animals.

Conclusions

The oocyst isolates examined in our studies came from a wide geographic area, mostly from within the United Kingdom, but samples were also obtained from other parts of Europe and two were from Africa. A distinctive pattern was obtained with each experimental approach, indicating that there were two major parasite types, one associated with man, the other with animals (particularly cattle). These differences were based on phenotypic observations but similar results were obtained following genotypic analysis by Ortega *et al.* (1991) using DNA restriction fragment length polymorphism and, in our laboratory, using arbitrary primed polymerase chain reaction (Awad-El-Kariem *et al.*, unpublished data).

Two important and related questions arise from these investigations of strain variation. The first concerns the phylogenetic relationship of the human and animal isolates of *C. parvum*. If strains of *C. parvum* are not to be differentiated according to the host of origin then the parasite phenotype must alter in different host types as a result of selection pressure created by the host environment. This may explain minor alterations to the sporozoite surface, but it is unlikely to explain changes in the "housekeeping" glycolytic enzymes studied. Alternatively, if "human" strains do exist it might be expected that they vary in virulence within a separate host species. Indeed, there is some indirect evidence for this: Pozio *et al.* (1992) reported that parasites from AIDS patients with severe cryptosporidial infections produced relatively mild infections in calves whereas parasites from other AIDS patients with mild infections produced severe infections in calves.

The second question concerns the epidemiological significance of the existence of putative human strains. As mentioned earlier, both zoonotic and anthroponotic transmission are important in human cryptosporidiois (PHLS Study Group, 1990). The comparative frequencies of human infections produced by animal versus human strains probably depend on factors such as the geographic area of parsite isolation (e.g. rural or urban) or on the immediate source of infection (e.g. animal, person or water). So far the detection rate in our survey of animal strains in human cases of disease was low, but the relative importance of each form of infection will only be established after examination of many oocyst isolates. In future, it will be important to determine to what extent these human isolates are infective to animals. Failure to infect animals would indicate an exclusive cycle of infection in man with no animal reservoir. Preliminary studies by us (unpublished data) suggested some human isolates were not infective to immunosuppressed mice or they induced very mild infections whereas all animal isolates produced a heavy infection (cf the results of Pozio *et al.*, 1992).

Further investigations are required to build on our observations on strain variation in *C. parvum*, and to assess the epidemiological or taxonomic implications of variation.

References

Awad-El-Kariem F.M., Robinson H.A., McDonald V., Evans D. and Dyson D.A. (1993) Lancet 341: 1535

Awad-El-Kariem F.M., Warhurst D.C. and McDonald V. (1994) Parasitol. 109: 19-22

Awad-El-Kariem F.M., Robinson H.A., Dyson D.A., Evans D., Wright S., Fox M.T. and McDonald V. (1995) Parasitol., in press

Godfrey D.G. and Kilgour V.K. (1976) Trans. Roy. Soc. Trop. Med. Hyg. 70: 219-224

McDonald V, Deer R.M.A., Nina J.M.S., Wright S., Chiodini P.L. and McAdam K.P.W.J. (1991) Parasite Immunol. 13:251-259

Mead J.R., Arrowood M.J., Current W.L. and Sterling C.R. (1988) J. Parasitol. 74: 366-399
Nina J.M.S., McDonald V., Dyson D.A., Catchpole J., Uni S., Iseki M., Chiodini P.L. and McAdam K.P.W.J. (1992a) Infect. Immun. 60: 1509-13
Nina J.M.S., McDonald V., Deer R.M.A., Wright S.E., Dyson D.A. Chiodini P.L. and McAdam K.P.W.J. (1992b) Parasite Immunol. 14: 227-232
Ortega Y.R., Sheehy R.R., Cama V.A., Oishi K.K. and Sterling C.R. (1991) J. Protozool. 38:540-541
Ogunkolade B.W., Robinson H.A., McDonald V., Webster K. and Evans D.A. (1993) Parasitol. Res. 79: 385-388
PHLS Study Group (1990) Brit. Med. J. 300:774-777
Pozio. E., Gomez Moralez M.A. Barbiera F.M. and La Rosa G. (1992) Trans. Roy. Soc. Trop. Med. Hyg. 86: 636-638
Tzipori S. (1988) Adv. Parasitol. 27: 63-129
Webster K.A., Pow J.D.E., Giles M., Catchpole J. and Woodward M.J. (1993) Vet. Parasitol. 50: 35-44

Emerging Technologies for the Detection of Protozoan Parasites in Water

H.V. Smith
Scottish Parasite Diagnostic Laboratory, Stobhill Hospital NHS Trust, Glasgow G21 3UW, UK

Introduction

Specific methods for the isolation and enumeration of the cysts and oocysts of the intestinal protozoan parasites *Giardia duodenalis* and *Cryptosporidium parvum* from water are required for the following reasons: first, their chlorine insensitivity; second, the inability to augment their numbers prior to identification and third, the low minimum infectious dose for human beings. Generally, with the exception of wastewaters and filter backwash waters, cysts and oocysts occur in low numbers in the aquatic environment (reviewed in Smith *et al.*, 1993; Wallis, 1994; Smith, 1995) and diverse techniques employing large volume sampling followed by sample concentration have been employed in an attempt to concentrate them. Interestingly, Jakubowski and Ericksen (1979) describe a variety of isolation and concentration methods developed between the 1950's and the 1970's for *Giardia* and *Entamoeba* cysts, including flocculation, pre-filtration followed by membrane filtration and cartridge filtration. Nearly twenty years later, similar methods are being evaluated for *Cryptosporidium* (Fricker, 1995). Although methods based upon flocculation, membrane and cartridge filtration have various advantages and disadvantages, each has been used successfully to determine the occurrence of cysts and oocysts. There is no universally accepted procedure however, most methods are based on that described by Jakubowski and Eriksen (1979) which can be sub-divided into:

a sampling
b elution, clarification and concentration
c identification.

Methods for Concentrating Cysts and Oocysts

Concentration by size alone results in the accumulation of a variety of other similar and larger-sized extraneous particulates which can interfere with organism detection and identification. Partial separation of cysts and oocysts from other particulates can be achieved by density flotation however, many researchers identify this clarification step to be inefficient, with organisms being sedimented, rather than being retained at the water/flotation fluid interface, and prefer to omit it if the water concentrate is not too turbid. Work at the Scottish Parasite Diagnostic Laboratory (SPDL) has identified that non-viable cysts and oocysts are more likely to penetrate the sucrose flotation interface than viable cysts and oocysts, and that viable organisms are concentrated on the sucrose density interface (Bukhari and Smith, 1995; Robertson *et al.*, unpublished observations). Thus the 'inefficiency' of the sucrose flotation method may be a reflection of the numbers of non-viable cysts and oocysts in a water concentrate and clarification by sucrose flotation should be regarded as a method for the enrichment of viable organisms rather than as a method for concentrating and/or purifying all cysts and oocysts present in a water concentrate. Using a recently developed $CaCO_3$ flocculation method, better recoveries of seeded oocysts can be obtained than when using cartridge or membrane filtration techniques, although oocyst viability is reduced (Fricker, 1995).

Concentration methods based upon physical properties of oocysts have been reviewed by Smith *et al.*, (1993) and, in that review, the authors stated that methods based on specific biological properties of cysts and oocysts were finding favour. Although a critical knowledge of the biochemistry and biophysics of the cyst and oocyst wall is fundamental to the success of such an approach, little information is available (Smith *et al.*, 1993; Smith, 1995). The use of fluorescence-labelled monoclonal antibodies (mAbs), reactive with genus-specific surface-exposed epitopes on cysts of *Giardia* and oocysts of *Cryptosporidium* have found application in the purification of organisms. For example, flow cytometers with cell sorting (FCCS) capabilities which can concentrate particles of defined size and fluorescence intensity have been used to concentrate cysts and oocysts. Currently, fluorescent "sorted" objects are automatically deposited on a microscope slide, but require verification as being cysts or oocysts by microscopy (Campbell *et al.*, 1993a; Vesey *et al.*, 1993). By providing a sample with maximum separation of fluorescent oocysts from contaminating material, Vesey *et al.*, (1993) demonstrated that FCCS made subsequent microscopical analysis and identification easier and less time consuming.

Another approach to concentration has utilised the technology of immuno-magnetisable separation (IMS), in which cysts and oocysts are bound immunologically to beads coated with commercially available mAbs and which can be concentrated by magnet (Bifulco and Schaeffer, 1993; Smith *et al.*, 1993; Parker and Smith, 1994; Smith, 1995). Using antibody-coated paramagnetic colloidal (40 nm) magnetite particles, Bifulco and Schaeffer demonstrated that an average of 82% of mAb-coated *Giardia* cysts (seeded at 500 cysts ml^{-1} into water concentrates with turbidities from 6 - 6,000 NTU), could be recovered. Using iron-cored latex beads (Dynabeads®) coated with anti-FITC mAb to separate oocysts coated with FITC-anti-*Cryptosporidium* mAb from samples seeded with between 2 and 100 oocysts ml^{-1}, recoveries, averaging 83% in raw water, were achieved (Parker and Smith, 1994). Further work using a *Cryptosporidium* mAb directly conjugated onto Dynabeads indicated recovery efficiencies of up to 80% in samples seeded with either 50 or 100 oocysts ml^{-1}.

Dielectrophoresis has also been suggested for concentrating oocysts. In dielectrophoresis, organisms are polarised by the application of a non-uniform alternating current (a.c.) electric field. Polarisation is dependent upon the interaction of the individual make-up of the cyst or oocyst and the conductivity of the suspending medium. The electrical field is applied across two electrodes so that polarised organisms will migrate toward one or other electrode and collect there. Altering the frequency of the applied voltage alters the extent of the migration and the subsequent collection of cysts/oocysts. The use of novel electrodes has shown promise in the development of a concentrator for oocysts (Archer *et al.*, 1995).

Detection Based on Antibody Selection

A major drawback of standard methods for detecting cysts and oocysts is that all samples have to be read microscopically. Whilst developments such as FCCS may be capable of automating identification in the future, the single channel format of these machines dictates that samples have to be analysed consecutively, with sufficient quality assurance to prevent cross-contamination of samples. Microplate systems which would be capable of analysing up to 96 samples simultaneously, by using amplification systems such as colorimetric and luminescence-based enzyme immunoassays, have also been proposed (Siddons *et al.*, 1992; Campbell *et al.*, 1993b; Smith *et al.*, 1993; Smith, 1995). A sensitive enhanced chemiluminescence (ECL) detection system, which could detect between two and six oocysts, using either X-ray film or a luminometer for imaging light emissions from mAb-coated *C. parvum* oocysts was developed by Campbell *et al.*, (1993b).

Electronic imaging using cooled charge couple devices (CCDs) can provide a basis for the development of a sensitive, reliable and rapid technique for detecting fluorescence and/or luminescence-labelled cysts and oocysts (Campbell *et al.*, 1992b; Smith *et al.*, 1993). CCD's can detect fluorescent emissions from fluorogens which can enhance morphological detail, at low total magnification (x20-x30), and can reconstruct accurately the spatial organisation of the intact fluorescent organism, thus providing the means for electronic measurement (Campbell *et al.*, 1992b; Smith *et al.*, 1993; Smith, 1995).

One definite advantage of the emerging technologies identified is that they have the potential to be fused together. The ability of CCDs to detect luminescent as well as fluorescent emissions makes them suitable candidates for consideration for a variety of the antibody-based novel technologies identified. Coupling of a CCD to a FCCS would provide a sensible solution by combining the advantages of both to produce a system which could not only sort fluorescent organisms, but which could also, with the inclusion of DNA-intercalating fluorogenic vital dyes, biotype and spatially reconstruct individual cysts and oocysts.

Although immunofluorescence techniques have enhanced our ability to detect cysts and oocysts in water concentrates, the specific fluorescence of similar-sized objects and non-specific antibody binding will decrease accurate identification. Furthermore, the lack of species-specificity, apparent with the majority of mAbs, will limit our abilities to detect organisms of significance to human health. The potential for reducing cross-reactions due to Fc binding has been investigated by producing FITC-labelled Fab fragments, containing the antibody paratope, from a commercially available mAb. The reagent, on a weight to weight basis, has a higher working dilution than the whole molecule (Smith, 1995). Currently, our ability to determine criteria such as the species, infectivity and virulence of cysts and oocysts, necessary for the interpretation of results, is lacking. We must assume that each intact cyst and oocyst detected in potable water is potentially infectious to man. In order to overcome such difficulties and to present regulators with more definite information regarding the biological status of cysts and oocysts, the use of more discriminating techniques has been advocated.

Nucleic Acid-based Detection Methods

Nucleic acid-based methods offer the potential for (a) increased sensitivity and specificity and (b) addressing issues such as species identity, infectivity and virulence. Abbaszadegan *et al.*, (1991) used a 265 bp genus-specific fragment to detect the presence of *Giardia* nucleic acid, liberated from disrupted cysts; this was as sensitive as a standard immunofluorescence method. Mahbubani *et al.*, (1991), (1992) and Webster *et al.*, (1993) detected small numbers of *Giardia* cysts and *Cryptosporidium* oocysts, respectively, by amplifying [polymerase chain reaction (PCR)] specific regions of DNA. Mahbubani *et al.* (1992), were able to distinguish *G. duodenalis* from *G. muris* and *G. ardeae* under ideal laboratory conditions by amplifying a 218 bp region of the *Giardia* giardin coding gene, and detecting the amplified product with a 28 mer oligonucleotide probe. Whilst this method could detect 250 cysts per litre of water, it failed to detect species differences when 105 cysts were present in a concentrated 400 litre sample (Erlandsen, 1994). The method of Webster *et al.*, (1993) amplifies a genus-specific 330 bp fragment which, following hybridisation to a 30 mer oligonucleotide probe and autoradiography, detects small numbers (~20) of *C. parvum* oocysts. Probing the PCR product with either a 280 bp insert probe or the oligonucleotide probe enables amplified *C. parvum* DNA to be differentiated from amplified *C. baileyi* DNA however, the method does not detect smaller numbers of oocysts consistently. The sensitivity of amplification by PCR is compromised when used to detect organisms in environmental samples. Using the method of Webster *et al.*, (1993) we have demonstrated that the transfer of *C. parvum* oocysts from the 'inhibitory' water concentrate by IMS (Parker and Smith, 1994), into a non-inhibitory buffer prior to nucleic acid extraction and PCR amplification can overcome such problems, and that a *C. parvum*-specific band can be detected reproducibly, following Southern blotting, from oocysts isolated from environmental water concentrates seeded with between two and five *C. parvum* oocysts (Smith, H.V. and Webster, K., unpublished).

Recently, Erlandsen and co-workers have addressed the requirement to determine the species of individual *Giardia* cysts. A series of species-specific oligonucleotide rDNA probes to the small subunit rDNA of *G. duodenalis*, *G. muris* and *G. ardeae* (cited in Erlandsen *et al.*, 1994) was developed, and using the techniques of fluorescence *in situ* hybridisation (FISH) and laser confocal scanning microscopy, they demonstrated that individual cysts of the above species could be discriminated using these species-specific probes. The benefits of both FITC-mAbs and FISH to determine both morphometry and species of the organism were used in their approach. Thus, using 17 - 22 mer probes to the

16S-like rRNA of *G. duodenalis*, *G. muris* and *G. ardeae* linked to either FITC or high quantum yield carboxymethylindocyanine dyes, together with an FITC-labelled mAb to the cyst wall of *Giardia*, they were able to identify individual *G. duodenalis* cysts present in a sewage lagoon concentrate by laser confocal scanning microscopy (Erlandsen, *et al.*, 1994).

Isaac-Renton and colleagues used molecular techniques to investigate waterborne outbreaks of giardiasis, and to attempt to determine whether transmission of *Giardia* was zoonotic (e.g. Isaac-Renton, 1994). Cysts were collected from contaminated water, infected individuals and beavers epidemiologically-linked to an outbreak, and the trophozoites were excysted and expanded. Analysis of trophozoite extracts by isoenzyme electrophoresis indicated that all samples were in the same zymodeme and pulsed-field gel electrophoresis (PFGE) revealed that they were of the same karyotype, although PFGE discriminated between isolates within zymodemes, thus providing evidence of the potential for zoonotic transmission.

Biophysical/Biochemical-based Detection Methods

The make up of organisms is thought to be unique, based on the diversity, orientation, density, composition, fluidity of molecules and the interactions between them. When exposed to electrical fields, interactions between molecules produce identifiable electrical patterns which can be characterised. The usefulness of dielectrophoresis and electrorotation, both based on movement within a.c. electrical fields, has been assessed for identifying, concentrating and/or assessing the viability status of cysts and/or oocysts. Both dielectrophoresis and electrorotation are dependent upon the relative conductive properties of the particle and the suspending medium and produce a 'fingerprint' of the organism in question which is thought to be unique. Knowledge of this fingerprint can be used either to attract (collect) organisms to an electrode (dielectrophoresis) where their images can be captured on videotape (Archer *et al.*, 1993), or to repel them from electrodes.

Whereas dielectrophoresis can be described as the motion imparted on electrically neutral, but polarised particles, which are subjected to non-uniform electrical fields, electrorotation occurs as a result of rotational torque exerted on polarised particles subjected to rotating electrical fields. Based on the work of Pethig and co-workers (e.g. Pethig *et al.*, 1991), the possibility of characterising cysts and oocysts by measuring relative rotational forces induced by a.c. electrical fields has been suggested (Coghlan, 1993). In this approach, oocysts, when bound to antibody-coated beads and subjected to defined rotating a.c. electrical fields, can be differentiated from the background of unbound beads and other contaminants because they rotate at a speed different from the speed of the other contaminating particles. This is due to the interaction of the rotating field with the induced dipole of the bead-bound particle which induces a physical torque on that particle, causing it to spin at a speed different from that of the background beads.

Viability

Little can be inferred of the likely impact of cysts and oocysts on human health without knowing their viability status. As the minimum infectious dose for both *Giardia* and *Cryptosporidium* is low, it is important to be able to determine the viability of individual (or small numbers of) organisms, which precludes the use of either animal infectivity or excystation *in vitro*. The microscopical observation of the inclusion or exclusion of specific fluorogens has been used as an objective estimate of organism viability. A fluorogenic vital dye assay, based upon the inclusion/exclusion of two fluorogenic dyes, 4',6-diamidino-2-phenylindole (DAPI) and PI which correlated well with optimised *in vitro* excystation (Robertson *et al.*, 1993a) was developed by Campbell *et al.*, (1992a). Discrimination between viable and non-viable oocysts revolves around the former including DAPI into the nuclei of the four sporozoites, but excluding PI, whilst the latter include PI either into the nuclei or cytoplasm as well as DAPI. Its usefulness has also been documented both in the water industry and for assessing the survival of *C. parvum* oocysts under various environmental pressures (Robertson *et al.*, 1992, Campbell *et al.*, 1994b). Vesey *et al.*, (1995) used a fluorescence-labelled oligonucleotide probe (conserved eukaryotic, Euk) and FISH to determine the viability of *C. parvum* oocysts by FCCS. FISH staining of oocysts correlated well with excystation *in vitro* and overcame problems with DAPI demand in turbid samples, but is unsuitable for monitoring purposes because the Euk probe is complementary to an 18sRNA sequence in all eukaryotes (Vesey *et al.*, 1995).

Less consistent findings have been reported for *Giardia* (reviewed by Smith, 1995). Whilst the fluorogens fluorescein diacetate (FDA) and PI were used successfully to determine the viability of *G. muris* cysts, Smith and Smith (1989) could not demonstrate a correlation between the inclusion of FDA and the viability of *G. intestinalis* cysts as determined by *in vitro* excystation. They found that PI inclusion consistently underestimated dead *G. intestinalis* cysts, and suggested that a combination of PI inclusion/exclusion and assessment of morphology by DIC, according to the criteria of Schupp and Erlandsen (1987b) would be a more suitable method. Thompson and Boreham (1994) also concluded that this was the most satisfactory way to proceed. The lack of consistent findings with fluorogenic vital dyes for *Giardia* viability has led to other molecular approaches being investigated. Mahbubani *et al.*, (1991) measured the amount of giardin mRNA using a cDNA-PCR before and after acid induction and suggested that viable cysts, having a greater signal than non-viable cysts, could be distinguished from the latter.

Despite such developments, infectivity must remain the 'gold standard' and other surrogates such as *in vitro* excystation, inclusion/exclusion of vital dyes, assessment of mRNA or rRNA, etc. are lesser standards for assessment of the potential of individual cysts and oocysts to infect susceptible hosts. The holistic approach adopted at the SPDL (Smith and Smith, 1989; Campbell *et al.*, 1992; Robertson, 1995) identifies the need to maintain the integrity of the parasite as far as possible, and that destructive techniques should be used only when non-destructive techniques are not available. For example, for *Cryptosporidium*, we have demonstrated a good correlation between the non-destructive technique of the fluorogenic vital dye assay and *in vitro* excystation which retains the intactness of the organism. Further analyses for infectivity such as the amplification of genes coding for adherence, penetration and virulence factors may well require the need for more destructive techniques. One possibility might be to develop a combined viability and infectivity assay based on the inclusion of fluorogenic vital dyes and *in vitro* culture. Oocysts exposed to excystation stimuli would be transferred by magnetisable particle technology to a culture of human-derived cells which support the invasion and asexual development of *Cryptosporidium in vitro*. The vital dye chosen for assessing the infectivity of the sporozoite would highlight its cytoplasm, producing a fluorescent banana-shaped image. Infection of the host cell would result in the development of a (fluorescent) spherical trophozoite. Identification of either banana-shaped, or spherical fluorescent objects in the cell monolayer, would determine infectivity. Further biotyping might revolve around *in situ* PCR in infected host cells. Whilst we have had partial success developing this concept with *Eimeria* sp. sporozoites, to date, we have been less successful with *C. parvum* sporozoites.

The awareness that both the biochemistry and the biophysics of an organism contribute to its viability status has stimulated renewed interest in other holistic approaches to viability. The recent work by Pethig and co-workers and Betts and co-workers has identified that the approaches of dielectrophoresis and electrorotation may have application for the assessment of *Giardia* and *Cryptosporidium* viability. Whilst the physico-chemical principles underlying dielectrophoresis and electrorotation may not be understood completely, the documented evidence indicates that viable and non-viable organisms can be made to behave differently using these techniques. Archer *et al.*, (1993) suggested that discrimination would be dependent upon the dielectrophoretic "finger-print" spectra of viable and non-viable organisms being sufficiently different to allow for differentiation between them, and recent work has suggested that ozone-treated, chlorine-treated and untreated oocysts produce different spectra (Quinn *et al.*, 1995).

The usefulness of electrorotation for assessing the viability of *G. intestinalis* and *C. parvum* oocysts is generating interest. Our preliminary data indicate that those *C. parvum* oocysts which were viable (i.e. included DAPI, excluded PI and were capable of excysting *in vitro*) could be differentiated from those oocysts which were non-viable (i.e. included DAPI and PI and which did not excyst *in vitro*) (Smith *et al.*, 1994b). Furthermore, we were able to rotate viable oocysts clockwise and non-viable oocysts counterclockwise at a pre-determined frequency. Thus, whilst little evidence is available regarding the usefulness of non-uniform a.c. electrical fields for the determination of the viability of *Giardia* and *Cryptosporidium*, it will be interesting to await the outcome of further research.

Conclusions

There is little doubt that methods for the isolation, enumeration and biotyping of the parasitic protozoa *Giardia* and *Cryptosporidium* have attracted the attention of regulators, epidemiologists, water industry personnel and researchers alike. Indeed, the advent of a multidisciplinary approach to these problems has brought about a plethora of novel technologies which have the capability of being included into future standard methods. Some of the present limitations have been overcome however, others remain to be addressed. Specificity and sensitivity remain our objectives. Technologies as diverse as *in situ* PCR and non-uniform a.c. electrical fields, which can address specific biological issues, may well interdigitate to provide more effective methods in the future. Further flurries of research may well achieve the ultimate goal of on-line monitoring.

References

Abbaszadegan, M., Gerba, C.P. and Rose, J.B. (1991). Detection of *Giardia* cysts with a cDNA probe and applications to water samples. Applied and Environmental Microbiology 57: 927-931

Archer, G.P., Betts, W.B. and Haig, T. (1993). Rapid differentiation of untreated, autoclaved and ozone-treated *Cryptosporidium parvum* oocysts using dielectrophoresis. Microbios 73: 165-172

Archer, G.P., Quinn, C.M., Betts, W.B., Sancho, M., Martinez G., Llamas M, Neill, J.G. (1995) An electrical filter for the selective concentration of *Cryptosporidium parvum* oocysts from water, this volume

Bukhari, Z. and Smith, H.V. (1995). The effect of water-ether concentration and sucrose density flotation on the viability of *Cryptosporidium parvum* oocysts recovered from bovine faeces. (submitted)

Bifulco, J.M. and Schaefer, F.W., III. (1993). Antibody-magnetite method for selective concentration of *Giardia lamblia* cysts from water samples. Applied and Environmental Microbiology 59: 772-776

Campbell, A.T., Robertson, L.J. and Smith, H.V. (1992a). Viability of *Cryptosporidium parvum* oocysts: correlation of *in vitro* excystation with inclusion/exclusion of fluorogenic vital dyes. Journal of Applied and Environmental Microbiology 58: 3488-3493

Campbell, A.T., Haggart, R., Robertson, L.J. and Smith, H.V. (1992b). Fluorescent imaging of *Cryptosporidium* using a cooled charge couple device (CCD). Journal of Microbiological Methods 16 169-174

Campbell, A.T., Robertson, L.J. and Smith, H.V. (1993a). Novel methodology in the detection of *Cryptosporidium parvum*: a comparison of cooled charge couple devices (CCD) and flow cytometry. Water Science and Technology 27: 89-92

Campbell, A.T., Robertson, L.J. and Smith, H.V. (1993b). Detection of oocysts of *Cryptosporidium* by enhanced chemiluminescence. Journal of Microbiological Methods 17: 297-303

Campbell, A.T., Robertson, L.J. and Smith, H.V. (1993c). Effects of preservatives on viability of *Cryptosporidium parvum* oocysts. Journal of Applied and Environmental Microbiology 59: 4361-4362

Campbell, A.T., Robertson, L.J., Smith, H.V. and Girdwood, R.W.A. (1994b). Viability of *Cryptosporidium parvum* oocysts concentrated by calcium carbonate flocculation. Journal of Applied Bacteriology 76: In press

Coghlan, A. (1993). Sticky beads put bacteria in a spin. New Scientist 15th May: 21

Erlandsen, S.L., van Keulen, H., Brelje,T., Gurien, A., Jakubowski,W., Schaefer, F.W., Wallis, P., Feely, D. and Jarroll, E. (1994). Molecular approach to the speciation and detection of *Giardia*: fluorochrome-rDNA probes for identification of *Giardia lamblia* , *Giardia muris*, and *Giardia ardeae* in laboratory and environmental samples by *in situ* hybridisation. In: *Giardia*: From Molecules to Disease (eds. Thompson, R.C.A., Reynoldson, J.A. and Lymbery, A.J.), CAB International, Oxon, UK. pp. 64-66

Fricker, C.R. (1995) Detection of *Cryptosporidium* and *Giardia* in Water, this volume

Grimason, A.M., Smith, H.V., Parker, J.F.W., Bukhari, Z., Campbell, A.T. and Robertson, L.J. (1994). Application of DAPI and immunofluorescence for enhanced identification of *Cryptosporidium* spp. oocysts in water samples. Water Research 28: 733-736

Isaac-Renton, J.L. (1994). Giardiasis in British Columbia: studies in an area of endemnicity in Canada. In: *Giardia*: From Molecules to Disease. (eds. Thompson, R.C.A., Reynoldson, J.A. and Lymbery, A.J.) CAB International, Oxon, U.K. pp. 123-124

Jakubowski, W. and Eriksen, T.H. (1979). Methods for the detection of *Giardia* cysts in water supplies. 193-210. In: Waterborne Transmission of Giardiasis. (eds. Jakubowski, W. and Hoff, J.C.), US Environmental Protection Agency, Office of Research and Development, Environmental Research Centre, Cincinnati, OH. EPA 600/9-79-001

Mahbubani, M.H., Bej, A.K., Perlin, M., Schaeffer, F.W., III, Jakubowski, W. and Atlas, R.M. (1991). Detection of *Giardia* cysts by using the polymerase chain reaction and distinguishing live from dead cysts. Applied and Environmental Microbiology 57: 3456-3461

Mahbubani, M.H., Bej, A.K., Perlin, M., Schaefer, F.W., III, Jakubowski, W. and Atlas, R.M. (1992). Differentiation of *Giardia duodenalis* from other *Giardia* spp. cysts by using polymerase chain reaction and gene probes. Journal of Clinical Microbiology 30: 74-78

Parker, J.F.W. and Smith, H.V. (1994). The recovery of *Cryptosporidium* sp. oocysts from water samples by immunomagnetic separation. Transactions of the Royal Society of Tropical Medicine and Hygiene. 88: 25

Pethig, R. (1991). Application of A.C. electrical fields to the manipulation and characterisation of cells. In: Automation in Biotechnology (ed. I. Karube), Elsevier, Amsterdam. pp. 159-185

Robertson, L.J., Campbell, A.T. and Smith, H.V. (1992). Survival of oocysts of *Cryptosporidium parvum* under various environmental pressures. Applied and Environmental Microbiology 58: 3494-3500

Quinn, C.M., Archer, G.P., Betts, W.B.,1 and O'Neill, J.G. (1995)

Robertson, L.J., Campbell, A.T. and Smith, H.V. (1993a). In vitro excystation of *Cryptosporidium parvum*. Parasitology 106: 13-29

Schupp, D.E. and Erlandsen, S.L. (1987a). A new method to determine *Giardia* cyst viability: correlation between fluorescein diacetate/propidium iodide staining and animal infectivity. Applied and Environmental Microbiology 55: 704-707

Schupp, D.E. and Erlandsen, S.L. (1987b). Determination of *Giardia muris* cyst viability by differential interference contrast, phase or bright field microscopy. Journal of Parasitology 73: 723-729

Schupp, D.E., Januschka, M.M. and Erlandsen, S.L. (1988). Assessing *Giardia* cyst viability with fluorogenic dyes: comparisons to animal infectivity and cyst morphology by light and electron microscopy. pp. 265-269. In: Advances in *Giardia* Research. (eds. Wallis, P.M. and Hammond, B.R.), University of Calgary Press, Calgary, Canada

Siddons, C.A., Chapman, P.A. and Rush, B.A. (1992). Evaluation of an enzyme immunoassay kit for detecting cryptosporidium in faeces and environmental samples. Journal of Clinical Pathology 45: 479-482

Smith, A.L. and Smith, H.V. (1989). A comparison of fluorescein diacetate and propidium iodide staining and *in vitro* excystation for determining *Giardia intestinalis* cyst viability. Parasitology 99: 329-331

Smith, H.V. and Rose, J.B. (1990). Waterborne cryptosporidiosis. Parasitology Today 6: 8-12

Smith, H.V., Robertson, L.J. and Campbell, A.T. (1993b). *Cryptosporidium* and cryptosporidiosis. Part 2: Future technologies and state of the art research. European Microbiology 2: 22-29

Smith H.V., Burt, J.P.H., Bukhari, Z. Pethig, R. and Parton, A. (1994b). Non-uniform alternating current electrical fields and *Cryptosporidium parvum* oocyst viability. Transactions of the Royal Society of Tropical Medicine and Hygiene. 88: 619

Thompson, R.C.A. and Boreham, P.F.L. (1994). Discussants Report: Biotic and abiotic transmission. In: *Giardia*: From Molecules to Disease (eds. Thompson, R.C.A., Reynoldson, J.A. and Lymbery, A.J.), CAB International, Oxon, UK. p. 135

Vesey, G. Byrne, M., Shepherd, K., Slade, J.S. and Fricker, C. R. (1993). Routine monitoring of *Cryptosporidium* oocysts in water using flow cytometry. Journal of Applied Bacteriology 75: 87-90

Wallis, P.M. (1994). Abiotic transmission - is water really significant? In: *Giardia*: From Molecules to Disease (eds. Thompson, R.C.A., Reynoldson, J.A. and Lymbery, A.J.), CAB International, Oxon, UK. pp. 99-122

Vesey, G., Ashbolt, N., Wallner, G., Dorsch, M., Williams, K. and Veal, D. (1995) Assessing *Cryptosporidium parvum* oocyst viability with fluorescent *in-situ* hybridisation using ribosomal RNA probes and flow cytometry, this volume

Webster, K.A., Pow, J.D.E., Giles, M., Catchpole, J. and Woodward, M.J. (1993) Detection of *Cryptosporidium parvum* using a specific polymerase chain reaction. Veterinary Parasitology 50: 35-44

Analysis of Water Samples for *Cryptosporidium* Including the Use of Flow Cytometry

J. Watkins, P. Kemp and K. Shepherd
Yorkshire Environmental, Bradford and University of Sunderland, UK

Introduction

Cryptosporidium is a recognised cause of outbreaks of waterborne disease. Following an outbreak in Oxford and Swindon (Richardson *et. al.*, 1991) a panel of scientists was asked by the Standing Committee of Analysts to provide a reference method for the detection of *Cryptosporidium* and *Giardia* in water (Anon, 1989). This document, whilst providing the only method that the water industry had, contained a number of shortcomings. There was no guide to the recovery efficiency of the various techniques described although an overall recovery of 30-50% is advised. In addition no advice was given on detection limits and individual Water Companies were left to set their own acceptable limits for raw and treated waters. This has led to a wide range of standards being set, from none in 1 litre to none in 200 litres. Furthermore the methods have been shown to be time consuming and inefficient. More recently, much time and effort has been spent on improving the efficiency of methods and the speed of analysis and detection. Flow cytometry has played a useful role in improving detection and in defining detection limits and sample volumes. We are becoming much better at understanding how good we are and how good we need to be.

Methods of Analysis

The different methods of analysis and recovery efficiency are given in Table 1 and are discussed briefly below.

Table 1. Recovery efficiencies for various sample treatment processes

Process	Treatment	Percentage recovery
Sampling	Cuno Filter	70 - 95%
Elution	Cuno Filter	0.2 - 40%
Elution	Vokes Filter	0.3 - 10.5%
Settlement	4°C 1 - 3 days	8 - 40%
Filtration	Cellulose Nitrate 3.0 µm	5.4 - 31.6%
	Cellulose Nitrate 1.2 µm	5 - 40%
Filtration	Cellulose Acetate 1.2 µm	5 - 60%
Centrifugation	1500g for 10 min	16 - 75%
Flocculation	Calcium Carbonate	60 - 80%
Cross Flow Filtration		10 - 50%
Sucrose Cleaning	Sucrose Solution	25%
Staining	Slide Preparation	58 - 100%
Staining	Suspension	83 - 100%
Staining and Counting	AQC Exercise	0 - 150%
IMS	Magnetic Particles	20 - 60% from concentrate

Sampling

Seeding trials have shown that large sample volumes taken through Cuno Micro-wynd filters can allow up to 50% of oocysts to pass through the filters. In addition the filtration efficiency can vary from filter to filter even using a flow restrictor. This agrees with results obtained by Vesey and Slade (1991) who showed a 5-30% loss through Cuno cartridge filters. Musial *et. al.* (1987) demonstrated 80 - 90% retention with seeded 20 l volumes although larger volumes had reduced retention possibly because of water forcing oocysts through the filter material. Restricting the flow to 1.5 litres per minute means that it can take up to 24 hours to obtain a large volume sample. Reducing the sample volume to 10 l makes processing easier, offers a wider range of analytical techniques and defines a minimum detection level below which, detection is not considered to be a problem. This type of sample demands good, consistent recovery efficiency if results are to be meaningful.

Sample Concentration

Elution

The elution process with Cuno filters recovers between 0.2% and 40% of seeded oocysts. The efficiency can be improved by washing in larger volumes of eluent and increasing the number of washings used in the recovery process.

Sedimentation

Calculations from the Badenoch Report (1990) show that oocysts settle only slowly in water (463 days to settle 20 metres). Sedimentation at 4°C offers an easy way of concentrating samples. Marshall (pers. comm.) has shown that 8% of seeded oocysts in 10 l samples can be recovered with overnight sedimentation improving to 38% if samples are left for up to 3 days.

Filtration

Membranes or tangential flow filtration provide simple alternatives for concentrating 10 litre samples. Filtration of 5 - 10 litre samples through 1.2 µm, or 3.0 µm 142 mm cellulose acetate or cellulose nitrate membranes takes between 5 - 10 min. Recovery efficiency varies from 10-60%, the critical factor being elution of oocysts from the filter surface. Scraping, brushing and manual massage give better recovery efficiencies than stomaching and minimise break-up of the filter. A number of different membranes have been tested; cellulose nitrate and cellulose acetate give the best recovery (Shepherd and Wyn-Jones, 1994). Vortex flow filtration (Whitmore, 1993) gives consistent recovery efficiencies of 30 - 40%.

Flocculation

Vesey *et. al.* (1993) describe a calcium carbonate flocculation process which recovers 70 - 80% of seeded oocysts. Solution of the calcium carbonate with sulphamic acid may however affect oocyst viability (Smith, *et. al.*, 1994). This method has been shown to be consistent across a number of laboratories (see Fricker, C. R. 1995).

Centrifugation

Smith *et. al.* (1994) have shown that centrifugation recovers up to 75% of oocysts. Seeding trials suggest that at 1500 g for 10 min, approximately 30% of oocysts are pelleted. Shepherd and Wyn-Jones (1994) demonstrated up to 84% loss of oocysts at this stage of the SCA method. The remainder are still in suspension and may be removed with the supernatant. Increasing the speed to 5,000 g for 15 min increases recovery up to about 55% but may cause the break up of old environmental oocysts.

Sample Cleaning

Sucrose density gradient centrifugation may be used to clean samples and remove organic and inorganic particulate material. The cleaning process loses up to 75% of oocysts and should only be used where the degree of contamination makes detection by microscopy or flow cytometry impractical.

Staining

Concentrates which are applied to slides for staining are not fixed. Staining and washing procedures can readily remove oocysts and vigorous washing may remove up to 90% of oocysts. Coating slides with egg yolk, egg albumen or bovine serum albumen helps unfixed material to stick to the slide during staining and washing. Samples may be filtered onto polycarbonate membranes and stained *in situ.* Staining in suspension and then applying to microscope slides can give up to 18% increase in recovery efficiency. Oocysts stain well in suspension due to the monoclonal antibody being able to gain access to specific epitope sites whereas staining on the slide permits binding in one plane only (Shepherd and Wyn-Jones, 1994).

Detection

Direct microscopy Microcopy is time consuming, tiring and prone to reader error. An individual examining replicates of a single suspension can derive a reproducible mean value. Distribution of a single suspension to a number of laboratories results in a wide range of counts about a mean value varying from 0 - 150% of the mean (see Thompson *et al.* 1995). Microscopists need a considerable amount of training and expertise in scanning slides and identifying bodies as oocysts. Contaminating material greatly reduces the efficiency of microscopy and Rose *et. al.* (1989) report that at turbidities of greater than 150 NTU, detection of oocysts is reduced by up to 95% using membrane filtration staining.

Flow Cytometry

Vesey *et. al.* (1993) reported flow cytometry as a means of detecting protozoan parasites in water. The technique developed by Yorkshire Environmental uses a Becton Dickinson FACS-Vantage fitted with a water-cooled Coherent Enterprise laser producing 200 mW of light at 488 nm.

Basic Principles of Flow Cytometry

The sample is run through the laser in a continuous stream of a phosphate buffered saline solution (sheath fluid). The stream is extruded from a ceramic nozzle at a velocity of 10 m/s. Information about light scatter and light emission is collected by a series of detectors. The information is converted into signal pulses which can be plotted either as a dot plot or dot histogram (Fig. 1). Electronic gates can be set on dot plots and dot histograms defining specific regions where events may occur. Material can then be sorted from the gated region and unwanted material discarded. The nozzle can be vibrated using a piezoelectric crystal to produce droplets. Any droplet containing material that produces a pulse within the electronic gate is charged and pulled out of the main stream by two electrically charged plates. In practice, 3 droplets are sorted to minimise the risk of the machine sorting the wrong droplet.

Pulse data is normally related to the height of the pulse of light produced. The pulse data may be processed and pulse width used instead of pulse height. Pulse processing of the

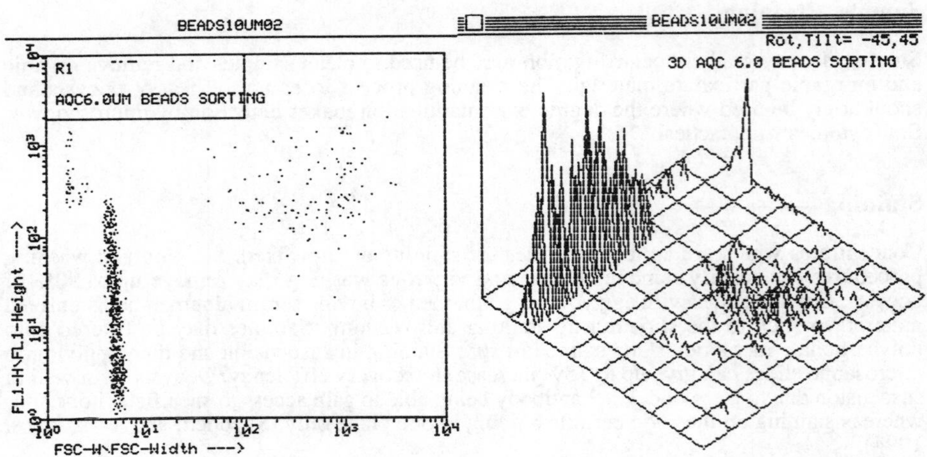

Figure 1. Dot plot and dot histogram showing the sort region used for the detection of *Cryptosporidium* oocysts.

forward scattered light was found to give a more tightly clustered sort region for *Cryptosporidium* whilst minimising the amount of unwanted material sorted. The parameters used for analysis are therefore forward scatter width and pulse height on the FLI (green light) detector. Using these parameters both strongly and weakly stained oocysts as well as clumps are sorted. The sorted sample is collected on a 4 well teflon coated microscope slide which is mounted once analysis is complete and examined microscopically. The amount of material sorted usually covers less than one well although material other than oocysts may be sorted.

Calibration

The machine is calibrated with 10 µm DNA check beads (Coulter Electronics, UK) to give a coefficient of variance of dot histograms of less than 3.0 with a minimum instrument setting for each parameter used. Optimisation of the fluidics and sorting is assessed by replicate test sorts of a suspension of 6 µm Fluoresbrite calibration beads (Polyscience Inc, USA) containing approximately 25 beads. The machine is cleaned between samples by running 10% v/v sodium hypochlorite for one min. This will remove the epitopes of remaining oocysts and prevent their visualisation in subsequent samples. The hypochlorite is removed by rinsing with detergent for 1 min.

Analysis

Once calibration and test sorting is complete samples can be run. Samples are stained in suspension with Crypto-Cel (Bradsure Biologicals, Shepshed, UK) at 37°C for 30 minutes followed by dilution to approximately 1 ml with sheath fluid and analysis on the machine. Analysis time varies with the amount of material in the sample. Clean samples take approximately 5 min whilst very turbid samples can take up to 45 min. A small filter with a nominal pore size of 30 µm is incorporated into the sample line to remove large particulate material. To prevent blocking the filter can be back flushed after each sample and cleaned as described above. Oocysts do not appear to be trapped by the filter nor do they carry over to subsequent samples if the system is properly cleaned. The filter can be back-flushed at regular intervals. Any remaining material after sorting can be removed from the sample tube with a pipette and spotted onto a slide.

In using the machine as part of an analytical proficiency scheme counts obtained by flow cytometry match those of manual microscopy (Table 2). Where samples are very dirty the machine is better at detecting oocysts by having the ability to examine the sample particle by particle. Duplicate analysis of over 200 environmental samples gave 19 positive by both methods, 3 positive by manual microscopy and 2 positive by flow cytometry. All 5 samples contained very low levels of oocysts.

Table 2. Comparison of manual microscopy and flow cytometry for the detection of *Cryptosporidium* oocysts.

Exercise Number	Manual Counting	Flow Cytometer Counting
	(Numbers of oocysts/10 µl aliquot)	
6	54, 37, 90, 31, 31, 64, 53, 88	53, 38, 91, 33, 86, 57, 61, 38
7	17, 18, 17, 19, 18, 21, 16, 18	17, 18, 16, 18, 17, 17, 18, 18
8	26, 18, 25, 23, 20, 21, 26, 21	22, 25, 22, 23
9	26, 25, 13, 17, 22, 18, 17, 14	24, 17, 14, 11

The flow cytometer is expensive to purchase and maintain. Advantages are outweighed by time and cost without a high sample turnover. When a relatively large number of samples need to be examined however eg. during a catchment contamination or an outbreak situation, the machine enables samples to be scanned quickly and efficiently without the need for continuous repetitive microscopy. In addition, with very turbid samples requiring extensive microscopy, there can be a considerable amount of time saved.

Environmental Investigation

The machine was used to study the contamination of an upland catchment area with *Cryptosporidium* oocysts. (Table 3). Following heavy rainfall in the catchment attention focused on 2 water treatment works, No 1 being placed higher up the catchment than No 2. Contamination can be seen to move from works No 1 to works No 2 on 9 and 10 September following heavy rain and again between 13 and 14 September following further heavy rain. By 15 September the contamination was no longer evident and a routine monitoring programme could have missed it. Intensive monitoring in the catchment (Table 4) revealed widespread contamination of feeder streams and several ingress points. In particular heavy surface contamination was demonstrated at a cattle feeding station.

Discussion

Many of the processes used in the examination of water samples for *Cryptosporidium* and *Giardia* are time consuming and inefficient. They do not lend themselves to providing rapid results and with low recovery efficiencies, results are often meaningless. Flow cytometry particularly when coupled with flocculation or membrane filtration allows 10 litre grab samples to be examined quickly and providing that recovery efficiencies are reasonable i.e. 30% or better, results can be provided quickly allowing operational decisions to be made about water quality and the need for advice to the public to boil water. In addition, large scale catchment investigations can be undertaken to determine possible sources of ingress into surface waters and the incidence of cryptosporidiosis in farm stock. Such information collected during or just after heavy rainfall can provide valuable information about potential catchment contamination and help to prevent outbreaks occurring.

Flow cytometers are, however, expensive to purchase and maintain and the learning curve to successful operation is often a long and painful road. The flow cytometer must be backed up by efficient, rapid laboratory techniques. However, once the machine has been mastered and routine analysis implemented we can sit back and ask 'What shall we develop next?'. The water industry currently has ample scope for other applications.

Table 3. Water quality results during a catchment contamination.

Date of sample	Location	Manual Microscopy	Flow Cytometer
		Oocyst Count/Litre	
09.09.93	Raw Water No: 1	0.6	0.6
	Treated Water No: 1	< 0.1	
10.09.93	Raw Water No: 1	< 0.2	0.2
	Treated Water No:1	< 0.1	
	Raw Water No: 2	2.8	22.8
	Treated Water No: 2	< 0.1	
11.09.93	Raw Water No: 2	< 0.2	
	Treated Water No: 2	< 0.1	
13.09.93	Raw Water No: 1	14	
	Treated Water No: 1	< 0.1	
	Raw Water No: 2	< 0.2	
	Treated Water No: 2	< 0.1	
	Distribution	< 0.1	
14.09.93	Raw Water No: 1	0.6	
	Treated Water No: 1	< 0.1	
	Raw Water No: 2	18	
	Treated Water No: 2	< 0.1	
	Raw Water No: 2	2.4	
	Treated Water No: 2	< 0.1	
15.09.93	Raw Water No: 1	0.8	
	Treated Water No: 1	< 0.1	
	Raw Water No: 2	3	
	Treated Water No: 2	< 0.1	
	Raw Water No: 2	0.2	
	Treated Water No: 2	< 0.1	
	Distribution	< 0.1	
16.09.93	Raw Water No: 1	0.2	
	Treated Water No: 1	< 0.1	
	Raw Water No: 2	< 0.2	
	Treated Water No: 2	< 0.1	
18.09.93	Raw Water No: 1	< 0.2	
	Treated Water No: 1	< 0.1	
	Raw Water No: 2	< 0.2	
	Treated Water No: 2	< 0.1	

Table 4. Environmental samples analysed for *Cryptosporidium* during a catchment contamination.

Date of sample	Location	Manual Microscopy	Flow Cytometer
		Oocyst Count/Litre	
14.09.93	Feeder Stream	11	
14.09.93	Catchment Ingress	4,400	
14.09.93	Farmyard Run-off	< 100	
14.09.93	Aqueduct Sample	9.4	6
16.09.93	Feeder Stream		110
16.09.93	Catchment Ingress	500	450
16.09.93	Catchment Ingress	475	390
16.09.93	Aqueduct Sample	150	250
16.09.93	Aqueduct Sample	4	
18.09.93	Aqueduct Sample		3.2
18.09.93	Aqueduct Sample		< 1.0
18.09.93	Aqueduct Sample		< 1.0
18.09.93	Aqueduct Sample		< 1.0
18.09.93	Aqueduct Sample		< 1.0
18.09.93	Aqueduct Sample		< 1.0
18.09.93	Aqueduct Sample		1.0
17.09.94	Cattle Feeding Station		350,000

Acknowledgements

The opinions expressed in this paper are those of the authors and not necessarily the organisations that they represent. The authors would like to thank Yorkshire Water and the University of Sunderland for permission to publish this paper and to Alison Bird, Liz Woods, Jian Xiangrong and Jim Marshall for all their help with the preparation of data.

References

Anon (1989). Isolation and Identification of *Giardia* Cysts, *Cryptosporidium* Oocysts and Free-living Pathogenic Amoebae in Water etc. HMSO, London. ISBN 0-11-752282-1

Badenoch, J. (1990). *Cryptosporidium* in Water Supplies. HMSO, London. ISBN 0-11-752322-4

Campbell, A. T., Robertson, L. J., Smith, H. V. and Girdwood, R. W. A. (1994). Viability of *Cryptosporidium parvum* Oocysts Concentrated by Calcium Carbonate Flocculation. Journal of Applied Bacteriology, 76, 638-639

Fricker, C. R., (1995) Detection of *Cryptosporidium* and *Giardia* in water, this volume

Musial, C. E., Arrowood, M. J., Sterling, C. R. and Gerba, C. P. (1987) Detection of *Cryptosporidium* in Water using Polypropylene Cartridge Filters. Applied and Environmental Microbiology, 53, 687-692

Richardson, A. J., Frankenberg. R. A., Buck, A. C., Selkon, J. B., Colbourne, J. S., Parsons, J. W. and Mayon-white, R. T. (1991). An Outbreak of Waterborne Cryptosporidiosis in Swindon and Oxfordshire. Epidemiology and Infection, 107, 485-495

Rose, J. B., Landers, L. K., Riley, K. R. and Gerba, C. P. (1989). Evaluation of Immunofluorescence Techniques for Detection of *Cryptosporidium* Oocysts and *Giardia* Cysts from Environmental Samples. Applied and Environmental Microbiology, 55, 3189-3196

Shepherd, K. and Wyn-Jones, P. (1994). Evaluation of Different Filtration Techniques for the Concentration of *Cryptosporidium* Oocysts from Water. Proceedings of the 17th Biennial Conference of the International Association on Water Quality, Budapest

Thompson, C., May, B., and Corscadden, D. (1995) Development of a *Cryptosporidium* proficiency scheme, this volume

Vesey, G., Slade, J. S., Byrne, M., Shepherd, K. and Fricker, C. R. (1993). New Techniques for the Detection of Protozoan Parasites in Water, In New Techniques in Food and Beverage Microbiology. Eds. Kroll, R. G., *et al.* Society for Applied Microbiology, Technical Series 31, Blackwell Scientific Publications, London. ISBN 0-632-03755-5

Vesey, G. and Slade, J. (1990). Isolation and Identification of *Cryptosporidium* from Water. Water Science and Technology, 24, 2, 165-167

Whitmore, T. N. and Carrington, E. G. (1993). Comparison of Methods for the Recovery of *Cryptosporidium* from Water. Water Science and Technology, 27, 3-4, 69-76

Non-cultivatable *Legionella pneumophila* Associated with *Acanthamoeba castellanii*: Detection of the Bacterium using DNA Amplification and Hybridization

J. Hay, D.V. Seal, B. Billcliffe[1] and J.H. Freer[1]
Department of Ophthalmology and [1]Division of Molecular and Cellular Biology, University of Glasgow, UK

Introduction

Certain strains of five genera of amoebae (*Acanthamoeba, Naegleria, Hartmannella, Vahlkampfia, Echinamoeba*) and one genus of ciliated protozoa (*Tetrahymena*) have been shown to support the growth of legionellae (Fields 1993).

This inter-relationship can make *Legionella* viable but non-cultivatable on BCYE agar-based systems (Connor *et al.* 1993). DNA amplification and hybridization was used to detect *L. pneumophila* rendered non-cultivatable by association with the free-living protozoan *Acanthamoeba castellanii*.

Materials and Methods

Interaction between *A. castellanii* and *L. pneumophila*

Cysts of *Acanthamoeba castellanii* were seeded with *Legionella pneumophila* 1. After incubation *A. castellanii* trophozoites contained intracellular *L. pneumophila*. Cysts were induced and washed with acid to remove any extracystic bacteria. The cysts were permitted to differentiate into trophozoites and the cycle repeated on one further occasion.

After incubation no bacteria were detected on blood or BYCE agar.

DNA Amplification and Hybridization

Trophozoites were lysed and *Legionella* DNA liberated using three cycles of boiling and freezing in liquid nitrogen. The bacterial DNA was amplified by PCR utilising two 19-mer primers (LEG1 and LEG2) specific for a *L. pneumophila* chromosomal DNA sequence of unknown function and 35 cycles of amplification (Starnbach *et al.* 1989).

Amplification mixtures were spotted onto nitrocellulose membranes and detected using a radiolabelled 5' end labelled 25-mer probe (LEG 3, Starnbach *et al* 1989).

The specificity of the reaction was determined using a range of bacterial species and the sensitivity identified as approximately 35 cfu.

Determination of *L. pneumophila* Viability

Three methods were used to determine viability of *L. pneumophila* in all samples which yielded an amplified product.

1 separate incubation of the freeze thawed trophozoite lysate with *Legionella* naive *A. polyphaga* or *Hartmannella vermiformis* (Sanden *et al.* 1992);
2 incubation of the lysate for 5 days at 37°C in an defined liquid medium (Pine *et al.* 1979); and
3 addition of excess of catalase to the lysate (Connor *et al.* 1993).

Each treatment was followed by plating the treated lysate onto supplemented BCYE agar and incubation in 5% CO2 at 37°C for 21 days.

Results and Discussion

Amplification products (0.8kb) characteristic of those expected from *L. pneumophila* serogroup 1 were obtained in 29 out of the 36 (approximately 81%) of samples which were originally recorded as culture negative for *L. pneumophila.* In each case the product was confirmed as *L. pneumophila* by hybridization using dot blots.

Cocultivation, enrichment, or a combination of these, or catalase treatment, revealed that nine (approximately 31%) of the 29 samples with a specific amplification product, contained culturable *L. pneumophila.*

The findings clearly indicate that *L. pneumophila* localized within *A. castellanii* are not always detectable by plating onto appropriate laboratory agar.

Failure to detect *Legionella* by conventional culture methods in these two latter studies may have been the consequence of either:

1 amoebal respiratory burst oxidants acting upon the *Legionella*; or,
2 other unknown factors which may render *Legionella* viable, but non-cultivatable on agar-based media (Hussong *et al.* 1987; McKay, 1992).

Identification of specific DNA sequences is an alternative strategy for detection of *Legionella* in biological or environmental samples in cases where conventional culture methods may fail.

PCR and hybridization yielded positive results for *L. pneumophila* in approximately 81% (29/36) samples where the bacteria had not been detected using culture. The remaining 19% may not have been identifiable using the molecular procedure possibly as a consequence of the sensitivity limit of the method.

A combination of co-cultivation of these samples with *Legionella*-naive *A. polyphaga* or *H. vermiformis* , incubation in a defined medium which permits enrichment for enhanced growth of *Legionella* and use of catalase (Connor *et al.* 1993), indicated that approximately 31% (9/29) of the samples which were PCR positive for *L. pneumophila* contained the bacteria, which after initial incubation with amoebae were viable but not cultivatable on BCYE agar.

Use of PCR and hybridization for detection of *L. pneumophila* is preferable to culture in environments where free-living amoebae are present. This is especially so with samples from water supplies to transplant units (Hay and Seal 1994a,b; Patterson *et al.* 1994) where 'at risk' patients are located. Surveillance systems for hospital water supplies based on agar-culture detection (Liu *et al.* 1992) will be inaccurate and under-estimate the problem of *Legionella* contamination, since the natural history of *Legionella*, and specifically its protozoonotic relationship with free-living protozoa, is not generally considered in such audits.

Thus if free-living amoebae are present in a water sample to be tested for the presence of *L. pneumophila,* agar cultivation alone may be inaccurate and the method may underestimate the problem of *L. pneumophila* contamination. PCR and hybridisation as well as enrichment and amoebal co-cultivation of the sample can be used in some instances to determine the viability of samples producing PCR products.

References

Connor, R., Hay, J., Mead, A.J.C. and Seal, D.V. (1993) Reversal of inhibitory effects of *Acanthamoeba castellanii* lysate for *Legionella pneumophila* using catalase. Journal of Microbiological Methods 18, 311-316

Fields, B.S. (1993) *Legionella* and protozoa: interaction of a pathogen and its natural host. In: *Legionella* Current Status and Emerging Perspectives, Editors Barbaree, J.M., Breiman, R.F. and Dufour, A.P. American Society for Microbiology, Washington D.C., pp129-136

Hay, J. and Seal, D.V. (1994a) Surveying for legionnaires' disease bacterium. Current Opinion in Infectious Diseases 7, 479-483

Hay, J. and Seal, D.V. (1994b) Monitoring of hospital water supplies for *Legionella*. Journal of Hospital Infection 26, 75-78

Hussong, D., Colwell, R.R., O'Brien, M., Weiss, E., Pearson, A.D., Weiner, R.M. and Burge, W.D. (1987) Viable *Legionella pneumophila* not detectable by culture on agar media. Biotechnology 5, 947-950

McKay, A.M. (1992) Viable but non-cultivatable forms of potentially pathogenic bacteria in water. Letters in Applied Bacteriology 14, 129-135

Patterson, W.J., Seal, D.V., Curran, E., Sinclair, T.M. and McLuckie, J.C. (1994) Fatal nosocomial Legionnaires' disease: relevance of contamination of a hospital water supply by temperature-dependent buoyancy-driven flow from spur pipes. Epidemiology and Infection 112, 513-526

Pine, L., George, J.R., Reeves, M.W. and Harrell, W.K. (1979) Development of a chemically defined liquid medium for growth of *Legionella pneumophila*. Journal of Clinical Microbiology 9, 615-626

Sanden, G.N., Morrill, W.E., Fields, B.S., Breiman, R.F. and Barbaree, J.M. (1992) Incubation of water samples containing amoebae improves detection of legionellae by the culture method. Applied and Environmental Microbiology 58, 2001-2004

Starnbach, M.N., Falkow, S. and Tomkins, L.S. (1989) Species-specific detection of *Legionella pneumophila* in water by DNA amplification and hybridisation. Journal of Clinical Microbiology 27, 1257-1261

An Image Analysis Enhanced Rapid Dielectrophoretic Assessment of *Cryptosporidium parvum* Oocyst Treatment

C.M. Quinn[1], G.P. Archer[1], W.B. Betts[1] and J. G. O'Neill[2]
[1]Department of Biology, University of York, Heslington, York, YO1 5DD, UK
[2]Yorkshire Water, Water Quality, 32/34 Monkgate, York YO3 7RH, UK

Introduction

Cryptosporidium oocysts cannot be completely removed during the sedimentation and filtration stages of water treatment and are not efficiently killed by chlorination (Anon, 1990). As the infective dose of oocysts in human is small (Miller *et al.*, 1990) it is vital that they are rendered non-viable in potable water. Ozonation has been suggested as a practical method to achieve this (Anon, 1990).

The analysis of viable and non-viable oocysts at low concentrations is important to assess the efficiency of any treatment process. Methods are under development for this purpose (Smith *et al.*, 1993) but many do not provide a rapid and reproducible analysis of viable oocysts in voluminous samples. Analysis of *Cryptosporidium* using dielectrophoresis has shown promise (Hawkes *et al.*, 1993).

Dielectrophoresis is a term used to describe the motion of neutral particles within a non-uniform electric field (Pohl, 1951). Using a.c. electric fields the different levels of particle collection at electrodes over a frequency range provide characteristic spectra. Absorbance measurements of collection (Betts & Hawkes, 1991; Hawkes *et al.* 1993; Price *et al.* 1988) using suspensions containing $< 10^7$ particles per ml is problematic but a recent video method to capture microscope images of collected *Cryptosporidium* oocysts enabled the analysis of low concentrations (Archer *et al.* 1993). This apparatus could distinguish between oocysts treated in various ways, but the procedure was rather laborious. It has now been improved dramatically by incorporating an image analysis system with automated particle counting.

Materials and methods

Micro-organism

Cryptosporidium parvum oocysts, purified using a standard procedure (Hill *et al*, 1990) were supplied by the Moredun Research Institute, Edinburgh, U.K. and received from Yorkshire Water Service plc, York, U.K. as a suspension (typically 10^9 oocysts ml^{-1}) in phosphate buffered saline.

Preparation of Oocysts

Untreated. A stock suspension of oocysts was vortexed and a 50 ml sample containing approximately 10^7 oocysts obtained. This was centrifuged for 10 min at 1000 x g and resuspended in 3-4 ml of deionized water. A routine count of untreated oocyst samples was performed in order to assess the number of empty oocyst shells present in the stock suspension.

Chlorine-treated. Chlorine demand-free water and glassware were used throughout (Korich *et al.*, 1990). 50 µl of untreated oocyst suspension was re-suspended in 10 ml of buffered sodium hypochlorite solution at pH 7.0. The oocyst suspension was vortexed and left for

40 min to provide a *Ct* value of 20. The required chlorine concentration of 0.5 mgl^{-1} had previously been quantified using a comparator (Lovibond 2000 Mk. II, Tintometer Ltd., Salisbury, U.K.). The reaction was quenched by adding 2 ml of 10% (w/v) sodium thiosulphate solution. It had been previously established that a residual level of chlorine remained after the contact time had expired. The procedure was repeated using an oocyst sample been treated with 5.0 mg l^{-1} chlorine providing a *Ct* value of 200. A control experiment using untreated oocysts exposed to 2 ml 10% (w/v) sodium thiosulphate solution alone was performed to demonstrate that this treatment did not change the dielectrophoretic response of disinfectant-treated oocysts. The oocyst suspensions were washed twice in deionized water and resuspended in 3-4 ml of deionized water.

Ozonated. Ozonation was performed with a laboratory ozonator (Model DA 023, Wallace and Tiernan, U.K.), using an air flow rate into the ozonator of 150 l h^{-1} for 10 min. The dosage employed (approximately 1.5 mg l^{-1} ozone) was determined by the indigo method (Bader and Hoigné, 1982). A 30 ml volume of ozone-demand-free water in a 50 ml ozone demand-free flask (Korich *et al.*, 1990) was spiked with a 2 ml suspension containing *Cryptosporidium* oocysts to provide a residual concentration of approximately 10^7 oocysts after accounting for losses in the ozonation procedure. Ozone was bubbled through the oocyst suspension which was maintained at 25°C with constant stirring. Immediately upon completion of the ozone treatment the oocyst suspension was transferred to a centrifuge tube containing 2 ml 10% (w/v) sodium thiosulphate in order to quench the reaction. The ozonated oocyst suspension was washed twice and re-suspended in 3-4 ml deionized water.

Correlation with Viability

Previous work, using both *in vitro* excystation assays and mouse infectivity experiments to assess oocyst viability, examined the disinfection effect of 1 mg l^{-1} ozone (Korich *et al.*, 1990). This indicated that a *Ct* value of 5-10 rendered 99.0-99.9% of *Cryptosporidium parvum* oocysts inactive. The effects of ozone treatments performed in the current study were assessed using the *in vitro* excystation method of Robertson *et al.* (1993). An excystation mixture was incubated at 37°C with shaking for a minimum of 4 h and the extent of excystation subsequently examined using Hoffman Modulation Contrast microscopy (Hoffman, 1977) . The percentage excystation was calculated from (Number of excysted oocysts/Number of excysted + intact oocysts) x 100. Sporozoite ratios were not calculated as many of these were lysed by the end of the 4h incubation period.

Dielectrophoresis Apparatus

Aluminium electrodes (50 µm wide separated by a 50 µm or 5 µm space) were constructed using a photolithographic technique and laid down on a glass microscope slide. A chamber was constructed over them to allow suspensions of oocysts to pass through the arrangement (Betts & Hawkes, 1991; Hawkes *et al.*, 1993). The walls of the chamber were produced from a layer of photoresist, built up using double-sided sticky-tape and a perspex lid (with two holes for the inward and outward flow of the sample) was placed on top and the edges glued to prevent leakage. Two further blocks of perspex with pre-drilled holes were glued on top of the inlet and outlet holes to secure the tubes. Connector wires were attached to tabs on either side of electrodes in order to link them to a signal generator (Hewlett Packard 8116A, Germany).

The experimental equipment was arranged as shown in Fig. 1. The oocyst suspension was recirculated through the electrode chamber and back to the reservoir by the peristaltic pump (Gilson Minipuls 3, France). The electrodes were mounted on a microscope (Nikon Labophot 2, Japan) to which a high resolution charge coupled device (CCD) camera (Ikegami ICD-42E, Japan) was attached. The electrode bars were observed in bright field using a 10 x objective providing an image on the monitor with a total magnification of 1360 x. This magnification was sufficient to allow oocyst detection although morphological

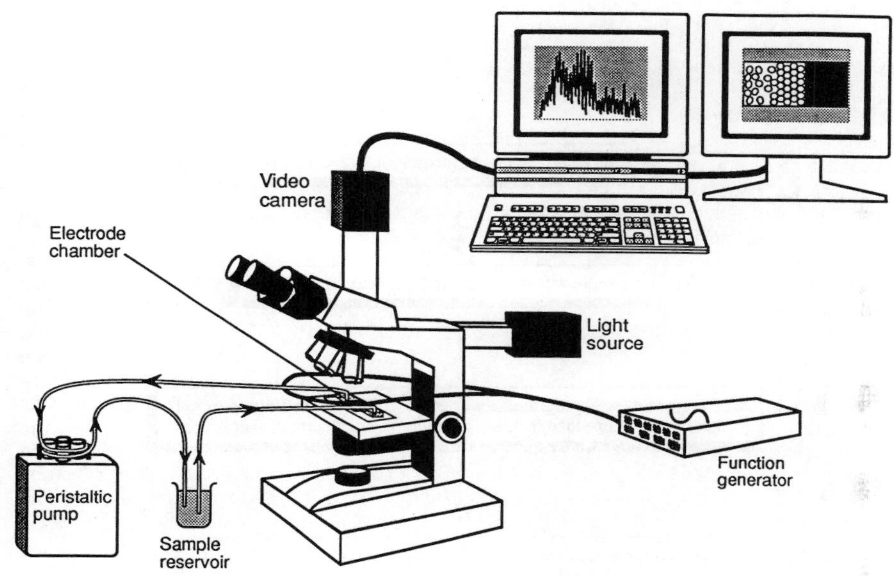

Figure 1. The dielectrophoretic system incorporating image analysed measurements of collection.

detail including excystation status could not be distinguished (this was determined subsequent to dielectrophoretic experimentation). A signal generator was connected by leads attached to tabs on the electrodes. The whole system was managed by a personal computer (AST 486 Bravo) which housed software controlling all parameters including frequency, pulse voltage and period, and timing and speed of the pump. A second monitor was used to set and control the experimental parameters. The software used in this part of the system was developed "in-house".

The Image Analysis System

The image analysis package selected was "Domino" (Perceptive Instruments, U.K.) originally designed as an automatic colony counting system (Pover, 1990). This was specifically modified for use with the dielectrophoretic system and an image analysis board was installed in the computer in order to provide accessibility to software suitable for data analysis and storage.

Video signals from the CCD camera were fed to the image analysis board which contained circuitry to condition the signal before digitising it into a binary image memory. This was then accessed by special digital processing logic allowing measurements to be obtained in real-time from each successive frame of the video picture. The video signal was displayed on the monitor used to view the electrodes, with colour coded overlays showing the objects detected by the system and allowing the operator to define regions within which they were to be measured. A dedicated control and data processing software programme communicated with the board via the computer expansion bus and converted measurements into calibrated data which could then be displayed, printed or transferred to proprietary spreadsheet or statistical analysis packages.

The programme was operated through the use of a menu screen, called up on the control monitor, which invited the user to select the various parameters desired. The size of the frame on the monitor within which cell counts were made could be varied, as could the level

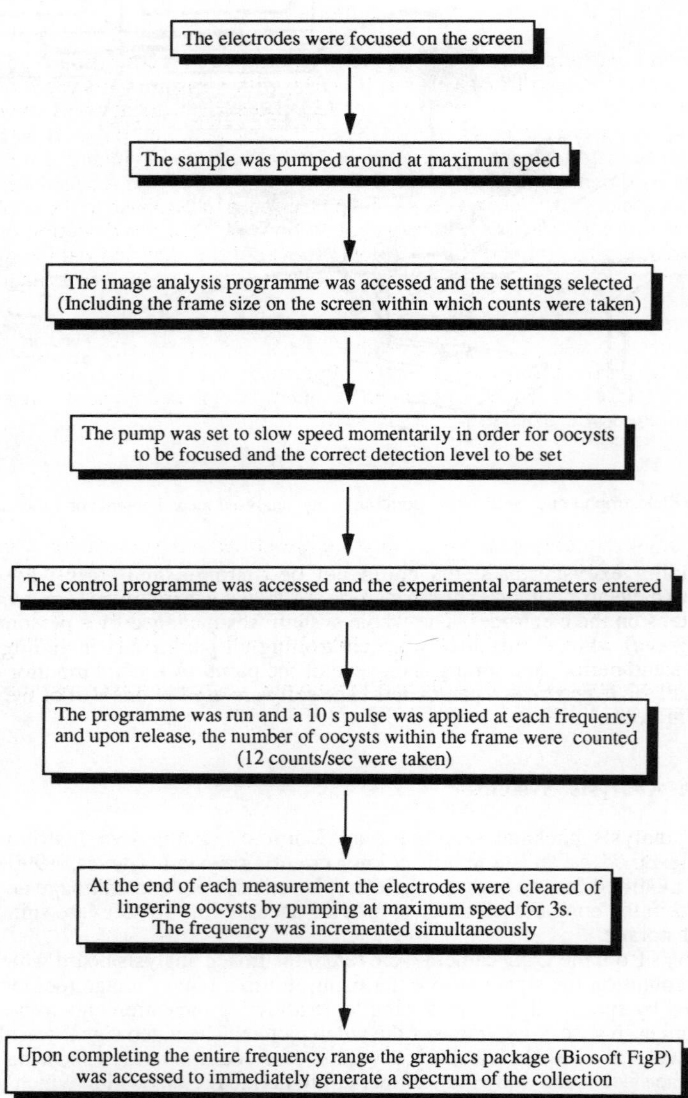

Figure 2. Experimental sequence to create a dielectrophoretic spectrum of *Cryptosporidium* oocysts.

of detection required. Oocysts were detected by virtue of contrast differences with the suspending medium. The "Domino" software operated in conjunction with the in-house software designed to control the timing of an experimental sequence.

Dielectrophoretic Collection Measurements

The parameters used were chosen so as to yield optimum oocyst collection. The frequencies of the applied pulse ranged from 1 kHz to 10 MHz, with measurements taken ten times per decade of log frequency. A count of oocysts collected at each frequency was taken upon their subsequent release from the electrodes at the end of each applied pulse. It was found that counting oocysts after release rather than counting collection yielded a more accurate measurement by the image analysis system. One reason for this was the formation of 'pearl-chain' patterns of oocyst collection between the electrodes in response to the applied electric field. These occurred particularly at frequencies above 10 kHz and detection of oocysts as single entities was made more difficult. Upon removal of the electric field the oocysts were released from the electrodes and passed by the counting frame of the image analysis system as individual objects.

A typical experimental sequence is presented in Fig. 2. Each replicate experiment was completed in approximately 13 min. To establish the statistical significance of differences in the spectra obtained from untreated and ozone-treated oocyst samples, a series of 58 pairs of measurements were made. Each pair detailed the levels of collection that resulted when using applied field frequencies of 100 kHz and 10 MHz.

Results

Untreated oocyst samples generated reproducible collection spectra for a given set of electrodes under similar conditions of pH, conductivity and oocyst concentration. The extent of collection was observed to rise within a frequency range below 100 kHz.

Treatment of oocysts with increasing concentrations of chlorine (C*t* values of 20 [0.5 mg^{-1}, 40 min] and 200 [5.0 mg l^{-1}, 40 min]) reduced the level of dielectrophoretic collection (Fig. 3).

Ozone-treated oocysts (Fig. 4) collected to a greater degree at lower frequencies (below 200 kHz) than their untreated counterparts. At the higher frequency range (3-10 MHz) a decrease in the collection levels of the ozone treated oocysts was observed. This latter difference was examined further by performing multiple measurements at two frequencies (100 kHz and 10 MHz). The collection level at 100 kHz was divided by the amount of collection at 10 MHz to form a ratio (Fig. 5). The ratios obtained from the ozonated and untreated samples were compared and found to be significantly different (t-test, $p \ll 0.05$).

The number of empty oocysts in the untreated and chlorine-treated samples subjected to the excystation procedure was high whereas the number of empty oocysts in the ozone-treated sample was low implying low and high levels of inactivation, respectively. The proportion of empty shells already present in the untreated samples (6.6%; s.d. = 2.1, n = 3) was not observed to vary over the time that the oocysts were used for experimental and control purposes.

Discussion

The dielectrophoretic response of oocysts is dependent on the extent to which they can be polarised by a non-uniform electric field. The surface charge composition of oocysts is unique and composed of charged species associated with specific structural features together with a loosely bound counterion layer. When oocysts are exposed to treatments, the electronic features of the surface are altered, for example by a change in the composition of the surrounding medium and the presence of disinfectants which may disrupt surface structural features.

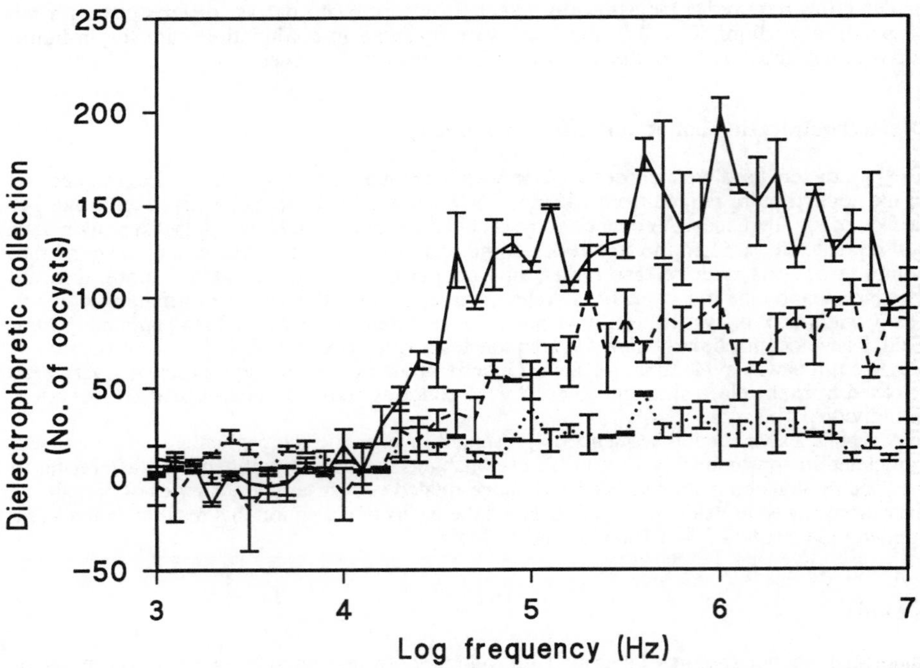

Figure 3. Dielectrophoretic spectra of *Cryptosporidium* oocysts treated with chlorine. Untreated oocysts (conductivity 3.8-3.9 mS cm^{-1}); 0.5 mg l^{-1} Cl treated oocysts (conductivity 3.9 mS cm^{-1}); 5.0 mg l^{-1} Cl treated oocysts (conductivity 3.7-3.8 mS cm^{-1}). Electrode separation = 5 mm, pulselength 10 s and 10 V. Error bars represent standard error of the mean.

The treatment of oocysts with chlorine influenced their collection. It has been suggested that chlorine may act by stripping away portions of the outer surface of the oocyst wall altering its permeability (Reduker and Speer, 1985) although the concentrations used to achieve this were much higher than those employed in the present study. The C*t* values of 20 and 200 used were not sufficient to remove the outer layer but a more subtle effect upon the surface could have influenced the dielectrophoretic response. It is thought that there is a high proportion of carbohydrate present on the oocyst surface which extends down beyond the immediate outer layer (Smith, Personal communication). It may be possible that such molecules are involved in the polarisability of oocysts and their modification by the action of chlorine could reduce dielectrophoretic collection.

A detailed explanation for the mode of action of ozone as a disinfectant is yet to be determined, although free radicals are likely to be involved which could change the outer chemistry of oocysts markedly. Dielectrophoretic experiments showing a decrease at the highest frequencies cannot as yet be explained but higher frequency fields may penetrate the oocysts and internal structures could influence the response, in which case the physiological state of the sporozoites may be important. The statistical significance found upon repeated investigation of ozone treatment indicates the potential of dielectrophoresis for viability assessment of *Cryptosporidium* after ozonation.

Different electrodes of the same design were used to generate the results in Fig. 3 (chlorination) and Fig. 4 (ozonation) due to failure of the electrodes in the period between the two experiments. These electrodes are short-lived elements designed to be inexpensive and disposable. Electrodes are currently manufactured individually and small differences are inevitable during manufacture. Consequently no detailed comparison can be made between

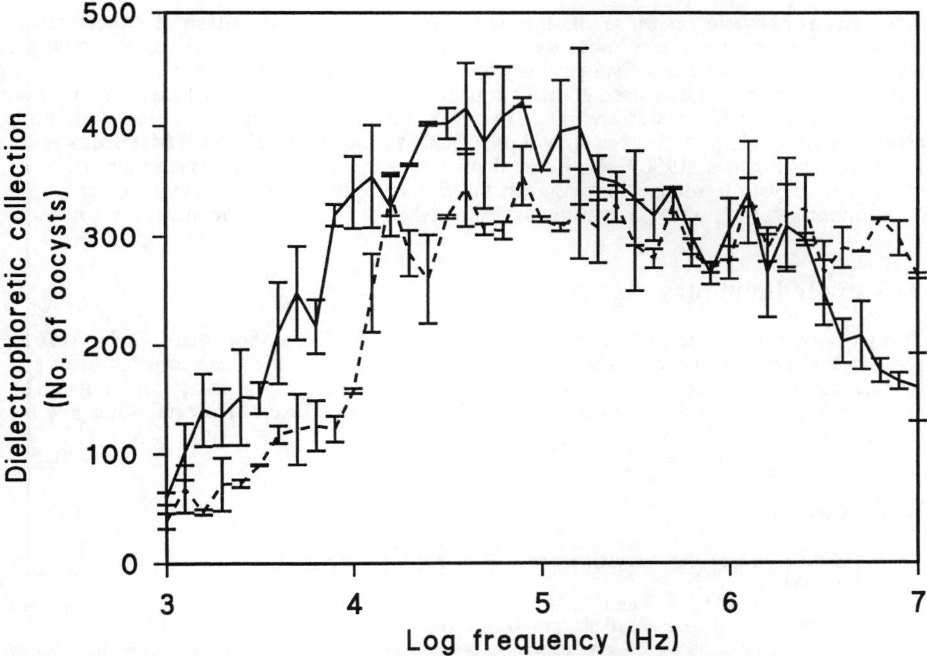

Figure 4. Dielectrophoretic spectra of *Cryptosporidium* oocysts treated with ozone. Untreated oocysts (conductivity 3.0-3.9 mS cm^{-1}); ozone treated oocysts (conductivity 2.9-3.1 mS cm^{-1}). Electrode separation = 5 mm, pulselength 10 s and 10 V. Error bars represent standard error of the mean.

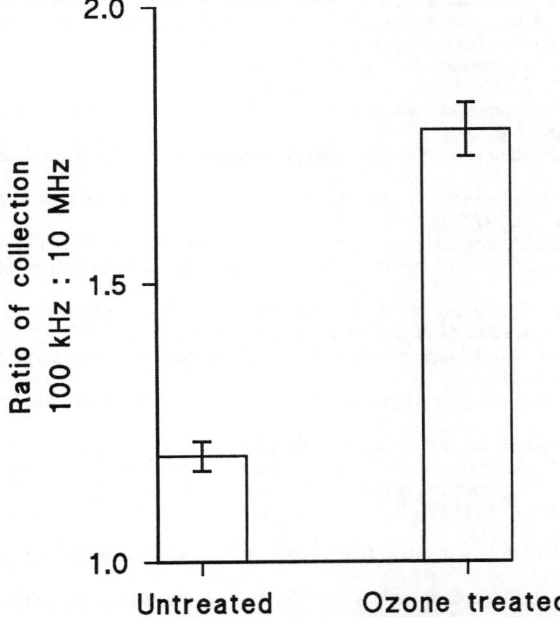

Figure 5. Comparison between collection levels of ozone-treated and untreated *C. parvum* oocysts at two key frequencies.

the dielectrophoretic response of untreated oocyst samples in different experiments. However, the same set of electrodes were used for each independent experiment, allowing a comparison of untreated and disinfectant-treated oocyst samples in each case.

The oocyst concentrations used in dielectrophoretic experiments were far greater than those found in any potable water sample. However, the measurement of dielectrophoretic properties of single particles has shown previously (Dimitrov *et al.* 1984; Marszalek *et al.* 1989; Kaler & Jones, 1990) which could prove useful in the rapid assessment of even individual oocysts. Evidence now suggests that dielectrophoresis could provide a very rapid assessment of the viability status of oocysts in very low concentration samples.

Acknowledgements

This work was supported by Yorkshire Water Services plc. The authors thank Dr D. Allsopp and Mr J. Cremer (Dept. of Electronics, University of York) for clean room facilities and manufacture of electrodes and Dr J. Graves (Dept. of Biology) for statistical advice. The authors are also grateful to Professor Huw Smith, Stobhill General Hospital, Glasgow for helpful comments and criticisms.

References

Anon (1990) Cryptosporidium in water supplies. *Report of the group of experts*. Her Majesty's Stationery Office, London

Archer, G.P., Betts, W.B. & Haigh, T. [1] (1993) Rapid Differentiation of untreated, autoclaved and ozone-treated *Cryptosporidium parvum* oocysts using dielectrophoresis. *Microbios* 73, 165-172

Bader, H and Hoigné, J (1982) Determination of ozone in water by the indigo method. *Ozone Science and Engineering*. 4, 169-176

Betts, W.B. and Hawkes, J.J. (1991) An Electronic Method for the Identification and Characterisation of Micro-organisms and other particles. *U.K. Patent Application* Number 9025785.8

Dimitrov, D.S., Tsoneva, I., Stoicheva, N. & Zhelev, D. (1984) An assay for dielectrophoresis: applications to electromagnetically induced membrane adhesion and fusion *Journal of Biological Physics* 12, 26-30.

Hawkes, J.J., Archer, G.P. and Betts, W.B. (1993) A dielectrophoretic spectrometer for characterising micro-organisms and other particles. *Microbios* 73, 81-86

Hill, B.D.; Blewett, D.A.; Dawson, A.M. & Wright, S. (1990) Analysis of the kinetics, isotype and specificity of serum and coproantibody in lambs infected with *Cryptosporidium parvum*. *Research in Veterinary Science*, 48, 76-81

Hoffman, R. (1977) The modulation contrast microscope: principles and performance. *Journal of Microscopy*, 110 (3), 205-222

Kaler, K.V. & Jones, T.B. (1990) Dielectrophoretic spectra of single cells determined by feedback-controlled levitation. *Biophysical Journal* 57, 173-182

Korich, D.G., Mead, J.R., Madore, M.S., Sinclair, N.A. and Sterling, C.R. (1990) Effects of ozone, chlorine dioxide and monochloramine on *Cryptosporidium parvum* oocyst viability. *Appl. Environ. Microbiol.* 56, 1423-1428

Marszalek, P., Zielinski, J.J. & Fikus, M. (1989) Experimental verification of a theoretical treatment of the mechanism of dielectrophoresis. *Bioelectrochemistry & Bioenergtics* 22, 289-298

Miller, R.A., Bronson, M.A. and Morton, W.R. (1990) Experimental cryptosporidiosis in a primate model. *J. Infect. Dis.* 161, 312-315

Pohl, H.A. (1951) The motion and precipitation of suspensions in divergent electric fields. *J. Appl. Phys.* 22, 869-871

Pover P.S. (1990) Colony counting and other petri dish applications of image analysis. *Binary* 2, 77-79

Price, J.A.R., Burt, J.P.H. and Pethig, R. (1988) Applications of a novel optical technique for measuring the dielectrophoretic behaviour of micro-organisms. *Biochimica et Biophysica Acta* 964, 221-230

Reduker, D.W. and Speer, C.A. (1985) Factors influencing excystation in Cryptosporidium oocysts from cattle. *J. Parasitol.* 71, 112-115

Robertson, L.J., Campbell, A.T. and Smith, H.V. (1993). *In vitro* excystation of *Cryptosporidium parvum*. *Parasitology* 106, 13-19

Smith, H.V., Robertson, L.J. and Campbell, A.T. (1993). *Cryptosporidium* and Cryptosporidiosis. Part II: Future technologies and state-of-the-art research in laboratory detection. *European Microbiology*. 2, 22-29

Assessing *Cryptosporidium parvum* Oocyst Viability with Fluorescent *in situ* Hybridisation using Ribosomal RNA Probes and Flow Cytometry

G. Vesey, [1]N. Ashbolt, [2]G. Wallner, [1]M. Dorsch, K.Williams and D. Veal
MUCAB, School of Biological Sciences, Macquarie University, Sydney 2109, Australia
[1]University of New South Wales, Sydney 2052, Australia
[2]GSF - Institut für Biophysikalische Strahlenforschung, 85764 Oberschleißheim, Germany

Introduction

The detection of *Cryptosporidium* oocysts in water relies on the concentration of particulate matter from large volumes of water prior to staining with fluorescently labelled monoclonal antibodies. Until recently, detection and identification of fluorescently labelled oocysts required examination of the sample using epifluorescence microscopy. The tedious and labour intensive nature of this detection method, in particular the amount of fluorescent microscopy required, limited the monitoring work which could be performed. The development of flow cytometric assisted detection methods has alleviated some of these problems and enabled the routine monitoring of water for the presence of *Cryptosporidium* oocysts (Vesey *et al.*, 1994A). However, a major limitation of all these methodologies is the lack of oocyst viability measurements.

The presence of dead *Cryptosporidium* oocysts in drinking water is of little significance to public health, however if oocysts are viable the risk to public health is enormous. There is, therefore, an urgent requirement to develop an effective method for determining the viability of *Cryptosporidium* oocysts in water. A method for assessing oocyst viability that is applicable to flow cytometry would enable the technique to be applied to the routine monitoring of water.

Fluorescent *in situ* hybridisation (FISH) is a relatively new method by which microorganisms can be specifically labelled. The technique is reliant upon the identification of a specific sequence of RNA within the target organism. Probes targeting a specific rRNA sequence are then synthesised and labelled with a fluorochrome. The cell is then permeabilised and the complementary sequence allowed to hybridise with the target sequence resulting in specific fluorescent labelling of the target cell.

The use of ribosomal RNA (rRNA) targeted oligonucleotide probes with FISH and flow cytometry has been reported by Amann *et al.* (1990B). Molecules of rRNA are ideal targets for fluorescently labelled nucleic acid probes for several reasons:

1 high sensitivity can be achieved since the target molecules are present in very high numbers;
2 a denaturation step is not required during the procedure as the target region is single stranded; and
3 rRNA has a short half life and will only be present in a high copy number in viable cells.

Here we describe the use of FISH with a oligodeoxynucleotide probe complementary to an 18S rRNA region, conserved for eukarya, to determine the viability of small numbers of *Cryptosporidium* oocysts and compare the technique to viability measured by *in vitro* excystation. We also discuss the application of these methodologies to flow cytometry for the routine monitoring of water.

Materials and Methods

Cryptosporidium oocysts. Cryptosporidium parvum oocysts cultured in lambs and purified by density gradient centrifugation were purchased from the Moredun Animal Research Institute, Edinburgh, UK.

Oligodeoxynucleotide probes. A probe (Euk) complementary to an 18S rRNA region conserved for eukarya (5'-ACCAGACTTGCCCTCC-3') (Amann *et al.* 1990A) was used to stain *Cryptosporidium* oocysts. A second probe (Bac) complementary to an 16S rRNA region conserved for all bacteria (5'-GCTGCCTCCCGTAGGAGT-3') (Amann *et al.*, 1990A) was used as a negative control for non-specific binding in all experiments. The probes were synthesised and labelled with fluorescein isothiocyanate as described previously (Amann *et al.*, 1990B).

Fixation of oocysts. Fixation of oocysts was performed using a modified method of that described previously by Wallner *et al.* (1993) for the fixation of yeasts and bacteria. One volume of oocyst suspension was mixed with 3 volumes of fresh cold 4% paraformaldehyde in phosphate buffered saline (PBS), pH 7.2, and kept at 4°C for 1 h. The oocysts were washed three times by centrifugation (13,000 g, 30 s) and then resuspending in PBS. The sample was then mixed with an equal volume of cold (-20°C) absolute ethanol and stored at 4°C. All samples, unless stated otherwise were hybridised within 1 h.

Hybridisation. Fixed oocysts were hybridised with the probe by mixing 10 µl of oocyst suspension with 100 µl of hybridisation buffer (0.9 M NaCl, 20 mM Tris/HCL, 0.5% sodium dodecylsulfate) prewarmed to 48°C and 10 µl of probe (25 ng/µl in distilled water). The sample was mixed and incubated at 48°C for 1 hour. The sample was then washed by centrifugation (13,000 g, 30 s) and resuspending in hybridisation buffer, without sodium dodecylsulfate, prewarmed to 48°C. Samples were then analysed immediately using flow cytometry or epifluorescence microscopy.

Sample analysis. Flow cytometry was performed using a Coulter Elite flow cytometer or a Coulter XL flow cytometer as described previously (Vesey *et al.*, 1993; Vesey *et al.*, 1994A; Vesey *et al.*, 1994B).Epifluorescence microscopy was performed using a Nikon Optiphot-2 microscope fitted with differential interference contrast (DIC) optics and excitation and emission filters suitable for the examination of FITC. Oocysts were detected using DIC and then examined for fluorescence. A minimum of 100 oocysts were examined in all samples.

Excystation. In vitro excystation was performed as described by Campbell *et al.* (1992). To a 100 µl volume of oocyst suspension (approximately 10^4 oocysts) 10 µl of 1% (w/v) sodium deoxycholate in Hanks minimal essential medium and 10 µl of 2.2% sodium hydrogen carbonate in Hanks balanced salt solution was added. After incubation, 37°C for 4 h, samples were examined microscopically using DIC optics. The proportion of empty oocysts, partially excysted oocysts and non-excysted oocysts was determined. At least 100 oocysts were counted in all samples. The percent excystation was calculated as follows:

[(number of empty oocysts + number of partially excysted oocysts)/total number of oocysts counted] X 100,

where the number of empty oocysts equalled the number preexcystation subtracted from the number post excystation.

Stored samples. To determine if samples could be fixed and then stored before analysis, storage experiments were performed. Aliquots (100 µl) of fixed oocysts suspensions were stored at 4°C for 1 month. Samples were removed at time intervals, stained with FISH and analysed using flow cytometry. All experiments were performed in triplicate.

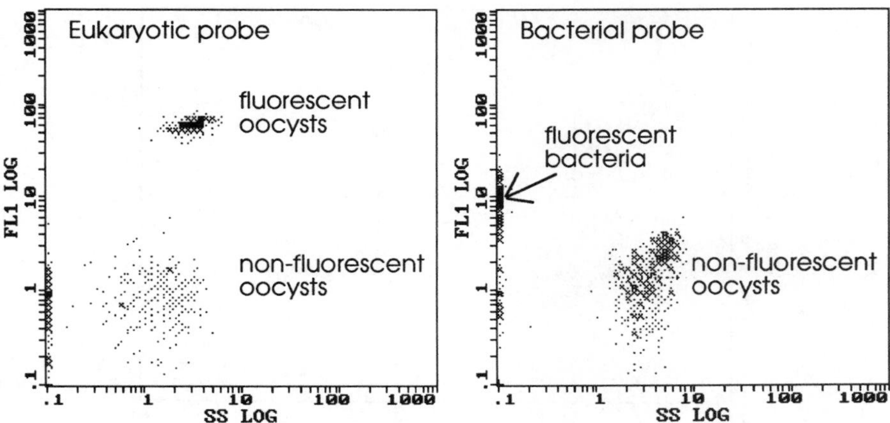

Figure 1. Flow cytometric analysis of FISH stained oocysts using the Euk probe and the Bac probe.

Aging of oocysts. Aliquots (10 µl) of oocyst suspension containing 10^8 oocysts were diluted in 10 ml of PBS and stored at 22°C in the dark. Samples (0.5 ml) were taken at time intervals and the viability of oocysts assessed using both FISH and excystation. All experiments were performed in triplicate.

Results

Staining of oocysts with FISH. Microscopic examination of oocysts, which had been stained using fluorescent *in situ* hybridisation with the Euk rRNA probe revealed brightly fluorescent oocysts together with oocysts which showed no fluorescence. Fluorescence staining was located within the sporozoites. Examination of the fluorescent oocysts using DIC optics revealed intact oocysts with a small gap between the oocyst wall and the internal structures. In comparison, non-fluorescent oocysts frequently appeared to have a ruptured oocyst wall and a large gap between the oocyst wall and the internal structures. Empty oocysts did not fluoresce.Flow cytometric analysis of oocysts stained by FISH with the Euk rRNA probe resulted in two distinct populations, a brightly fluorescence population and a non-fluorescent population. This is illustrated in the scatter plot (Figure 1) on which the Y axis represents fluorescence and the X-axis side scatter. Analysis by epifluorescence microscopy and flow cytometry of samples which had been stained with the Bac probe resulted in no fluorescence in any oocysts above that of the autofluorescence of unstained oocysts (Figure 1).

Stored samples. Samples of fixed oocysts which had been stored at 4°C for up to 4 weeks and then stained with FISH showed no reduction in the number of oocysts which fluoresced and no reduction in the brightness of the fluorescence (Table 1).

Table 1. A comparison of the fluorescence intensity of freshly fixed oocysts and oocysts fixed and stored at 4°C for up to 3 weeks, before staining with FISH and analysing using flow cytometry.

Day	Mean Fluorescence
0	17.1
7	17.3
14	16.6
21	17.8

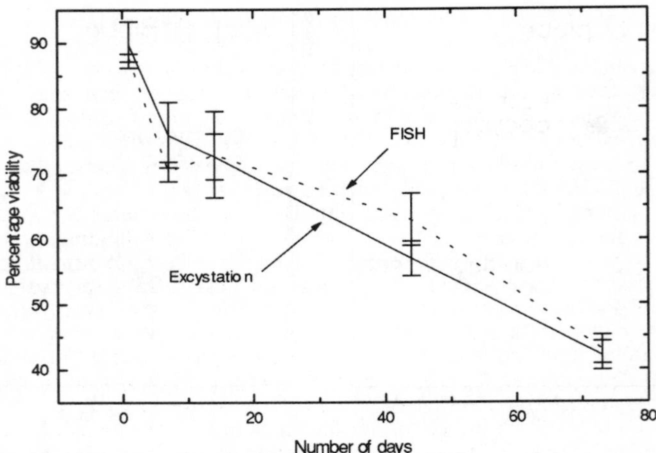

Figure 2. Comparison of oocyst viability as measured by excystation and viability determined by FISH on oocysts following storage at 22°C in the dark and sampled over a 74 day period.

Comparison of viability determined by FISH and in vitro excystation. A comparison of oocyst viability, measured by excystation and by staining by FISH with an rRNA targetted probe, on three batches of oocysts obtained from Moredun Animal Research Institute are presented in Table 2. Results are very similar for both methods of assessing oocyst viability indicating that the rRNA probes only stain viable oocysts.

Table 2. Comparison of oocyst percentage viability determined by excystation and viability determined by FISH on three different batches of oocysts.[1]

	Batch 1	Batch 2	Batch 3
FISH	56%	76%	95%
Excystation	54%	79%	92%

[1]100 oocysts were examined for each determination

Comparison of FISH and excystation for determining oocysts viability on suspensions of oocysts stored at 22°C in the dark are presented in Figure 2. Results are very similar for both methods. A gradual decline in the viability of the oocysts from 90% to 40% over the 74 day period was observed with both methods. Correlation of the two sets of results was highly significant, with a calculated correlation coefficient (r) of 0.998.

Discussion

A major limitation of the methods used to detect *Cryptosporidium* oocysts in water is the inability to distinguish between live and dead organisms. Methods to determine viability such as animal infectivity and excystation, are impractical because of the low number of oocysts normally present in water samples.

The results of this study clearly demonstrate that FISH using a rRNA directed probe can be used for assessing the viability of *Cryptosporidium* oocysts. Oocysts containing fluorescing sporozoites after hybridisation with the probes are viable and oocysts which do not fluoresce are dead. The reason that dead oocysts do not stain is because the rRNA which the probes bind to deteriorates rapidly and in dead oocysts is not present in sufficient copy numbers to be detected.

In vitro excystation is currently considered the gold standard to which methods for determining oocyst viability are compared. Results from comparing measurement of oocysts viability using FISH and measuring viability using *in vitro* excystation produced very similar results with both methods for all samples of oocysts analysed. Correlation of the FISH assay with excystation was highly statistically significant, with a calculated correlation coefficient of 0.998. Furthermore, the FISH method was found to be easy to perform and the results easily interpreted. Oocysts were either fluorescent, indicating a viable oocyst, or did not fluoresce at all, indicating a dead oocyst.

Alternative methods for determining the viability of small numbers of *Cryptosporidium* oocysts based on the uptake or exclusion of the fluorescent DNA binding dyes propridium iodide (PI) and 4',6-diamidino-2-phenylindole (DAPI) have been reported (Campbell *et al.* 1992). The authors report that dead oocysts take up PI and fluoresce red, whereas live oocysts exclude PI but are permeable to DAPI resulting in the sporozoites within the oocysts fluorescing blue. The method requires an acidification pretreatment to permeate the oocyst wall enabling uptake of the dyes. The method has proven useful for viability studies on pure oocysts (Campbell *et al.*, 1993A; Robertson *et al.*, 1992). However, the application of the method to the routine monitoring of *Cryptosporidium* oocysts in water has been limited due to problems with incorporating the technique into flow cytometric detection methods (Campbell *et al.*, 1993B). We have experienced problems with the method when analysing turbid environmental samples. In particular, the demand for DAPI by some of the particulate matter present in these samples is higher than the demand for DAPI by the oocysts. This results in the particulate matter staining bright blue and the oocysts not staining. Increasing the concentration of DAPI to tens times that recommended by Campbell *et al.* (1992) results in fluorescent oocysts but the fluorescence of the background becomes unacceptably high. FISH techniques have the potential to alleviate these problems and are ideal staining methods for analysis by flow cytometry.

Another significant advantage of the FISH method described is that samples can be fixed and then stored at 4°C prior to analysis. By contrast, samples which are to be analysed using the DAPI/PI method must be analysed immediately as storage or fixation of the samples will result in a reduction in the viability of the oocysts as measured by this technique.

The rRNA targeted probe used in this study to stain *Cryptosporidium* oocysts is complementary to a sequence of 18S rRNA present in all eukaryots. Due to the large amount of algal and other eukaryot cells present in water samples the application of this probe to the detection of oocysts in water is limited. However, the development of a rRNA probe specific to *Cryptosporidium* would enable the detection of viable oocysts in water samples.

Acknowledgments

This work would not have been performed without the financial support from the Water Board, Sydney, Illawarra and Blue Mountains, Australia.

References

Amann, R.I.. Binder, B.J., Olson, R.J., Chisholm, S.W., Devereux, R., and Stahl, D. (1990A): Combination of 16S rRNA-targeted oligonucleotide probes with flow cytometry for analysing mixed microbial populations. Appl. Environ. Microbiol. 56, 1919-1925

Amann, R.I., Krumholz, L., and Stahl, D.A. (1990B). Fluorescent-oligonucleotide probing of whole cells for determinative, phlogentic, and environmental studies in microbiology. J. Bacteriol. 172:762-770

Campbell, A.T., Robertson, L.J., and Smith, H.V. 1992. Viability of *Cryptosporidium parvum* oocysts: correlation of *in vitro* excystation with inclusion of fluorogenic vital dyes. Appl. Environ. Microbiol., 58:3488-3493

Campbell, A.T.; Robertson, L.J., Smith, H.V. 1993A. Effects of preservatives on viability of *Cryptosporidium parvum* oocysts. Appl. Environ. Microbiol. 59: 4361-4362

Campbell, A.T., Robertson, L.J., and Smith, H.V. 1993B. Novel methodology for the detection of *Cryptosporidium parvum*: A comparison of cooled charge coupled devices (CCD) and flow cytometry. Wat. Sci. Tech. 27:89-92

Robertson, L.J.; Campbell, A.T.; Smith, H.V. 1992. Survival of *Cryptosporidium parvum* oocysts under various environmental pressures. Appl. Environ. Microbiol. 58: 3494-3500.

Vesey, G., Slade, J.S, Byrne, M., Shepherd, K., Dennis, P.J. and Fricker, C.R. 1993. Routine monitoring of *Cryptosporidium* oocysts in water using flow cytometry. J. Appl. Bacteriol. 75: 87-90

Vesey, G., Hutton, P.E., Champion, A.C., Ashbolt, N.J., Williams, K.L., Warton, A. and Veal, D.A. 1994A. Application of flow cytometric methods for the routine detection of *Cryptosporidium* and Giardia in water. Cytometry, 16: 1-6

Vesey, G., Narai, J., Ashbolt, N., Williams, K.L. and Veal, D. 1994B. Detection of specific microorganisms in environmental samples using flow cytometry, p.489-522. In Methods in Cell Biology -Flow Cytometry Second Edition. Academic Press Inc., New York

Wallner, G., Amann, R. and Beisker, W. 1993. Optimizing fluorescent *in-situ* hybridization with rRNA-targeted oligonucleotide probes for flow cytometric identification of microorganisms. Cytometry, 14: 136-43

Rapid Techniques for the Recovery of *Cryptosporidium*

T.N. Whitmore
WRc plc, Marlow, Buckinghamshire, SL7 2HD, UK

Introduction

The deficiencies of current techniques for the concentration of micro-organisms from water are particularly evident when applied to *Cryptosporidium* recovery, because, since there are no *in vitro* culture techniques available for oocyst amplification, it is necessary to concentrate large volumes of water.

The recovery technique in widespread use, which has been provisionally recommended by the Department of the Environment, involves the filtration of large (100-500 l) volumes of water through a 25 cm spun polypropylene cartridge filter of nominal pore size 1 µm at a flow rate of 1-1.5 l min^{-1} (Anon 1990). The subsequent elution, recovery and purification of the entrapped oocysts from the filter fibres is a time-consuming and tedious process of low and variable efficiency.

An investigation into potential alternative techniques for the recovery of *Cryptosporidium* oocysts from water was initiated to address these shortcomings. Large volume recovery techniques tested were continuous flow centrifugation, vortex flow filtration, and cross flow filtration. Immunomagnetic separation was evaluated for the specific recovery of oocysts from small volume samples.

Continuous Flow Centrifugation

The capacity of conventional centrifuges is a few litres which limits their use to processing small sample volumes. A benchtop continuous centrifuge was evaluated (Alfa-Laval Sharples Gyrotester) for the recovery of oocysts from seeded tap and river water samples. The rotational speed of the centrifuge is fixed (equivalent to 9600 g) and hence the efficiency of retention of particles is dependent upon the rate of fluid flow into the centrifuge bowl.

The results indicated that the recovery of oocysts from seeded tap and river water samples seeded oocysts was optimal at an input flow of approximately 0.3 l min^{-1}, when a recovery of approximately 30% was obtained from tap water and 11% from river water. However the retention efficiency appeared to be very sensitive to the rate of input to the centrifuge.

Vortex Flow Filtration

A vortex flow filtration apparatus consists of a cylindrical filter which rotates at high speed and is contained within a second cylinder. The sample is circulated under pressure around the cavity between the cylinders forcing the liquid phase to permeate through the filter. Vortices created over the filter surface tend to suppress fouling of the filter surface. The unit used in this study was a Membrex Benchmark rotary biofiltration unit equipped with a polysulphone membrane cartridge of 0.45 µm nominal pore size. A mean recovery of 37% was obtained from treated water and 30% from river water. The permeate flow, which is dependent upon the inflow rate and operating pressure and determines the rate of sample throughput was within the range 50-100 ml min^{-1}.

Cross Flow Filtration

Cross flow (tangential flow) filtration is potentially a more efficient technique than conventional filtration because the bulk of the liquid flow is parallel to the filter surface rather than perpendicular to it. A tangential flow thus continuously sweeps the membrane and matter is prevented from accumulating on the surface which would otherwise lead to a reduction in liquid flow. An Anotec Ansep cross-flow filtration module, equipped with either inorganic (alumina) or polymeric (polycarbonate) membranes was used to concentrate *Cryptosporidium* oocysts from 100 l aliquots of spiked treated and river water.

Trials using the cross-flow module with treated water samples demonstrated that the technique yielded oocyst recoveries within the range 40-50% at a net flow rate of around 1 l min^{-1}, with marginally higher recoveries obtained when the polymeric membranes were used. However since the oocysts adhered to the polymeric membrane it was necessary to incorporate an additional elution step for their recovery by washing the membranes in a solution of Tween 80. The recovery of oocysts from river water using either membrane was, however, markedly reduced to around 10% or less.

Immunomagnetic Separation

Dynabeads

Density gradient centrifugation is currently used to recover and purify *Cryptosporidium* oocysts from the filter washings. This technique can, however, lead to substantial losses of oocysts due to contamination of the sample with material of similar density and adherence of oocysts to other particles.

Immunomagnetic separation (IMS) utilised 4.5 μm Dynabeads M450 (Dynal UK Ltd.) which are supplied complexed to rat anti-mouse IgM. The Dynabeads were conjugated to an anti-*Cryptosporidium* antibody (Crypto-Cel, Bradsure Biologicals Ltd.). Cells thus labelled immunologically with the Dynabeads can, potentially, be easily separated from unlabelled particles by a simple permanent magnet.

High recoveries (80-100%) were obtained when the Dynabead-antibody complex was incubated with a suspension of *Cryptosporidium* oocysts using a Dynabead/oocyst ratio of 40:1. Simulated environmental water samples were prepared by filtering 100 l of river water through a Cuno filter and concentrating the filter washings to 10 ml. However IMS of oocysts from spiked 1 ml aliquots resulted in substantially lower recoveries in the range 8-15%. Magnetically active debris was found to interfere with the recovery and the suspension containing the separated oocysts was contaminated with particulates.

Ferrofluid

Ferrofluids are superparamagnetic microparticles (diameter approxmately 50 nm) which are claimed to possess a number of potentially superior characteristics compared with the larger immunomagnetic particles. Binding to the target cell is more rapid, the cells can be labelled quantitatively and the optical parameters of the labelled cell remain essentially unchanged.

Two magnetic separation devices were used in this study. The Miltenyi MiniMACS (Eurogenetics UK Ltd.) which is a flow-through device in a column format and the static Immunicon system (Scotlab Ltd.)

Streptavidin coated ferrofluids were obtained from Immunicon or Miltenyi Biotec. A three stage protocol was required for labelling the oocysts with ferrofluid for IMS. *Cryptosporidium* oocysts were conjugated to a fluorescein isothiocyanate (FITC) anti-*Cryptosporidium* antibody (Crypto-Cel) and the resulting complex was in turn conjugated to a biotinylated anti-fluorescein antibody (Molecular Probes Inc.). Magnetic labelling was accomplished through conjugation of the antibody/oocyst complex to the streptavidin ferrofuid, which occurs via the biotin moieties of the secondary antibody.

The recovery of oocysts from suspensions using the MiniMACS and Immunicon IMS systems resulted in recoveries of 98% and 83% respectively. Lower recoveries of oocysts from spiked Cuno filter washings were obtained using both formats. The MiniMACS column quickly became blocked with particulate and magnetically active matter in the sample. However using smaller (100 µl) aliquots recoveries of 63% and 82% were obtained. Oocyst recoveries of around 10% were obtained using the Immunicon system.

Discussion

These studies have demonstrated that certain techniques warrant further investigation for the recovery of *Cryptosporidium* oocysts from water samples.

Continuous centrifugation and vortex flow filtration required careful optimisation before reasonable oocyst recovery efficiencies (30-40%) were obtained. The operational complexity of the latter machine may, however, negate any advantages for routine use.

The most promising method for the concentration of large volumes of treated water was cross flow filtration. The filtration rates are comparable and the recovery efficiencies compare well with current cartridge filtration techniques. However, further experimentation is required to assess its utility to recover low numbers of oocysts. In addition units from other manufacturers should be evaluated since the design of the Ansep module renders it particularly susceptible to blockage. Cross flow filtration could also be applied to recover oocysts from the several litres of cartridge filter washings obtained during the standard technique, thus obviating a number of centrifugation steps.

The only published work on the recovery of protozoa using cross flow filtration relates to *Giardia*. Isaac-Renton *et al.* (1986) used a Millipore Pellicon cassette system to recover *Giardia* cysts from seeded distilled water and obtained recoveries of around 30%. In a comparative study Hastie *et al.* (1992) concluded, however, that centrifugation rather than cross flow filtration was more efficient for *Giardia* cyst recovery.

IMS technology has been extensively applied in clinical research for the recovery of mammalian cells and in microbiology to the recovery of bacteria of public-health significance. Recently presented work from the Scottish Parasite Diagnostic Laboratory (Parker 1994) has demonstrated the potential of the technique for the recovery of oocysts from spiked samples of buffer, pond water and sewage effluent. Ferrofluids have been been applied to the recovery of *Giardia* cysts from 1 ml aliquots of water samples with various turbidities (Bifulco and Schaefer 1993). The average recovery obtained was 82% with significantly higher recoveries from less turbid water samples.

Both IMS techiques evaluated during this study (Dynabeads and ferrofluid) yielded high and reproducible oocyst recoveries from seeded samples. IMS using ferrofluid would appear to offer advantages if flow cytometry is employed for subsequent detection of the oocysts, since their optical parameters would remain unchanged.

The recovery efficiency of both systems was markedly reduced from cartridge filter washings seeded with oocysts. Particulate matter and magnetically active debris were believed to be responsible. However, the results of this preliminary study indicate that IMS shows promise and warrants further investigation, particularly for the recovery of low numbers of oocysts from a variety of water types. The application of IMS to recover oocysts directly from large volume water samples also requires examination.

This study has shown that it is feasible to apply alternative technologies to recover *Cryptosporidium* oocysts from water. Further fundamental research is required into, for example, the physico-chemical properties of the oocyst wall and the development of antibodies of high affinity and specificity, in order that new recovery techniques can be tailored to this demanding application.

Acknowledgements

The author gratefully acknowledges the Foundation for Water Research for funding part of this study. Additional thanks are due to Anotec Separations Ltd. for the loan of the cross flow filtration unit.

References

Anon (1990) Methods for the examination of water and associated materials.Isolation and identification of *Giardia* cysts, *Cryptosporidium* oocysts and free living pathogenic amoeba in water etc. Standing Committee of Analysts, London, HMSO

Bifulco, J.M. and Schaefer, F.W. III (1993) Antibody-magnetite method for selective concentration of *Giardia lamblia* cysts from water samples. Applied and Environmental Microbiology 59, 772-776

Hastie, J.C., Kelly, P.J. and Brown, T.J. (1992) Concentrating *Giardia* cysts in water by tangential flow filtration compared with centrifugation. New Zealand Journal of Marine and Freshwater Research 26, 275-278

Isaac-Renton, J.L., Fung, C.P.J. and Lochan, A (1986) Evaluation of a tangential flow multiple-filter technique for detection of *Giardia lamblia* in water. Applied and Environmental Microbiology 52, 400-402

Parker, J. (1994) *Cryptosporidium*. Presented at Isolation of Pathogenic Organisms by Immunomagnetic Separation, Dynal (UK) seminar. Liverpool, March 1994

Physical Separation of Untreated and Ozone-treated *Cryptosporidium parvum* Oocysts using Non-uniform Electric Fields

G.P. Archer,[1] C. M. Quinn, [1] W.B. Betts,[1] D.W.E. Allsopp[2] and J.G. O' Neill[3]
[1]Institute for Applied Biology, Dept. of Biology, University of York, York YO1 5DD, UK
[2]Department of Electronics, University of York, York YO1 5DD, UK
[3]Yorkshire Water, Water Quality, 32-34 Monkgate, York YO3 7RH, UK

Introduction

Dielectrophoresis occurs when neutral particles are placed in non-uniform electric fields. The particles move towards electrodes, as determined by the dielectric properties of the particles (conductivity and permittivity). The accepted description of the dielectric force F is given as F = pv (E.del)E, where p = the effective polarisability of the suspended particle, v = the volume of the particle, E = the local root mean square electric field and del = the del vector operator. If the effective polarisability of a particle exceeds that of its surrounding medium it will experience a dielectrophoretic force when subjected to a non-uniform electric field, causing the particle to move towards the regions of greatest field intensity (e.g. an electrode). The polarisability of the cell, and therefore the polarity and magnitude of the dielectrophoretic force, varies as a function of the frequency of the applied field.

The dielectric properties of all materials have characteristic frequency-dependent components. For this reason, when the level of particle (e.g. microbial cell) collection at the electrodes is observed across a frequency range, the collection spectrum is characteristic for that particle type (Archer *et al.*, 1993; Hawkes *et al.*, 1993). At the molecular level the dielectric properties of cells are determined by the polarisability of their mobile charges. Research results suggest that it is polarisation of charges at the surface of cells that is the major contributor to the dielectrophoresis force. The dielectrophoretic collection spectrum is therefore a reflection of the characteristic polarisability of the surface charge of the cells.

Dielectrophoresis has been shown to be capable of directing microscopic particles into pre-defined positions within an electrode chamber. If the effective conductivity of a particle exceeds that of the suspending medium the dielectrophoretic force is positive and the particle will move towards the area of highest non-uniformity in the applied electric field. If the converse is true, then the particle will be extruded into the region with least divergence in the electric field.

Numerical modelling methods have shown that with microelectrodes of the form shown in Figure 1, regions of high field divergence are located on the each edge of the electrode bars. Two regions of low field divergence are situated close to the electrodes, above each electrode bar and midway between the electrode bars. This in principle provides a method by which a mixture of particles which differ in their dielectrophoretic response may be spatially separated.

The spatial separation capability of dielectrophoresis is demonstrated in this paper using a mixture of *Escherichia coli* cells and *Cryptosporidium parvum* oocysts. Preliminary work carried out using a mixture of untreated and ozone-treated oocysts is also presented. The results are interpreted with the assistance of numerical modelling of the field configuration generated by microelectrodes of the form used in these experiments.

Materials and Methods

Micro-organisms

Escherichia coli was grown overnight in nutrient broth at 37°C. The bacteria were harvested and washed twice in deionised water before being suspended in deionised water.

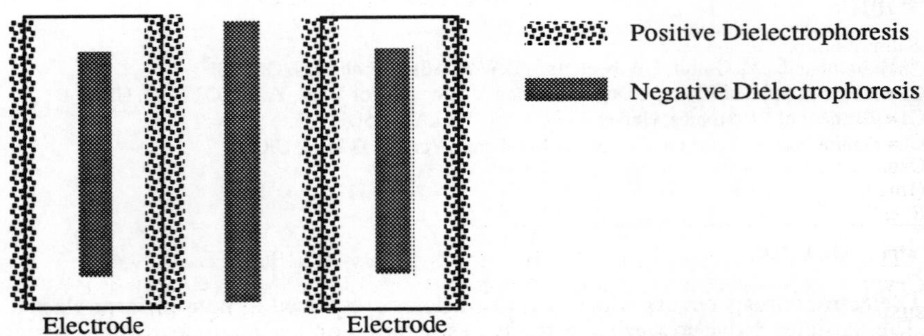

Figure 1. Diagram showing the regions of the microelectrodes where particles are directed to when undergoing dielectrophoresis.

Cryptosporidium parvum oocysts were obtained from the Moredun Research Institute, Edinburgh, U.K. through Yorkshire Water Service plc, York, U.K. The preparation of untreated and ozone-treated oocysts for use in dielectrophoresis experiments was performed as previously described (Quinn *et al.*, 1994). The excystation rates of the oocysts used in these experiments were 65% and 7% (as measured by the proportion of empty oocyst shells) for the untreated and ozonated samples, respectively. No change in these rates was caused by the effect of the electrical fields used in the experiments.

Dielectrophoresis

The effect of electric fields of various frequencies between 1 kHz and 10 MHz on a sample of untreated oocysts suspended in deionised water was observed. The conductivity of the cell and oocyst suspending medium was adjusted to 10 μS cm^{-1} by addition of 0.01M KCl.

A pin and plate microelectrode design, laid down onto a glass microscope slide using a photolithographic technique, was used for dielectrophoresis experiments. The slide was fitted to the stage of a microscope and sample suspensions were pipetted onto the electrodes and covered with a glass coverslip. Dielectrophoretic responses were recorded using a video camera attached to the microscope.

Results

At lower frequencies (below 5 kHz) the oocysts were seen to demonstrate negative dielectrophoresis. Above this frequency, positive dielectrophoresis was observed.

At a frequency of 100 kHz the dielectrophoretic response of biological particles is thought to be controlled by ionic relaxation and conduction at the cell wall and dipolar and dielectric losses occurring at the cell wall (Burt *et al.*, 1990; Huang *et al.*, 1992). Above 1 MHz the electric field can penetrate the cell and internal structures and properties begin to control dielectrophoretic collection.

Using a frequency of 100 kHz the dielectrophoretic responses will reflect properties of the oocyst shell. Observations of oocysts undergoing dielectrophoresis were made microscopically. The conductivity of the suspending medium was gradually increased by additions of 0.01M KCl. The conductivity at which positive dielectrophoresis ceased to occur was noted. At this conductivity the suspending medium and particle had the same effective conductivity. The results for untreated, chlorine- and ozone-treated oocysts as well as *E. coli* are shown in Table 1.

Table 1. The conductivity at which positive dielectrophoresis ceased to occur for untreated, chlorine- and ozone-treated oocysts, and *E. coli* .

Sample	Effective Conductivity at 100 kHz (μS cm-1)
Untreated *C. parvum* oocysts	39
Chlorine-treated *C. parvum* oocysts:	
Ct = 20	39
Ct = 200	34
Ct = 2000	33
Ozone-treated *C. parvum* oocysts (1mg.ml-1 for 10 min)	40
E. coli	400

The large difference in effective conductivity at 100 kHz between *E. coli* and *Cryptosporidium* oocysts suggested that these should be easily separated. By selecting a suspending medium with a conductivity between 40 and 400 μS cm^{-1} (60 μScm^{-1}) we observed and video-recorded oocysts undergoing negative dielectrophoresis whilst bacteria simultaneously collected at the electrodes by positive dielectrophoresis. Choosing a higher frequency (1 MHz) caused both micro-organisms to undergo positive dielectrophoresis.

The finding that untreated and ozone-treated oocysts possessed very similar effective conductivities at 100 kHz precludes the use of this frequency for separation purposes. It also suggests that any damage inflicted upon the oocysts by ozone treatment at the levels used in this study does not affect the shell conduction processes significantly enough to be detected by dielectrophoresis. Another study (Quinn *et al.*, 1994) showed that ozone-treated oocysts respond differently to untreated oocysts when electric fields of frequency greater than 1 MHz were applied.

The effect of fields at frequencies of 1 MHz and 10 MHz upon a 50:50 mix of untreated and ozone-treated oocysts was video-recorded. The experiment conducted using a medium conductivity of 10 μScm^{-1} showed that a 1 MHz field caused all the oocysts in the vicinity of the electrodes to undergo positive dielectrophoresis. When the frequency of the field was switched to 100 kHz, approximately 50% of the oocysts were forced away from the electrode by negative dielectrophoresis.

As the experiments of Quinn *et al.* (1994) showed reduced collection of ozone-treated oocysts in fields of 10 MHz compared to untreated oocysts, it can be speculated that this field frequency caused the ozone-treated oocysts to be displaced whilst the untreated oocysts remained collected at the electrodes. These findings are currently under intense investigation.

Acknowledgements

The authors wish to acknowledge Yorkshire Water Services plc for financial support, the British Council and Spanish Department of Education for funding scientific exchanges through the Accion Integrada program, Jonathan Cremer (Dept. of Electronics, University of York) for clean room facilities and development of electrodes, Drs Miguel Sancho, Geneveva Martinez and Margarita Llamas (Departmento de Fisica Aplicada III, Universidad Complutense, Madrid) for electric field configuration modelling.

References

Archer, G.P., Betts, W.B. & Haigh, T. (1993) *Microbios* 73, 165-172

Burt, J. P. H., Pethig, R., Gasgoyne, P. R. C. and Becker, F. F. (1990), *Biochim. Biophys. Acta* 1034, 93-101

Hawkes, J.J., Archer, G.P. and Betts, W.B. (1993) *Microbios* 73, 81-86

Huang, Y., Holzel, R., Pethig, R. and Wang, X. B. (1992) *Phys. Med. Biol.* 37, 1499-1517

Quinn, C. M., Archer, G. P., Betts, W. B. and O' Neill, J. G. (1994) Oral Paper presented at Royal Society of Chemistry Conference *"Protozoan Parasites in Water"*, University of York

An Electrical Filter for the Selective Concentration of *Cryptosporidium parvum* Oocysts from Water

G.P. Archer[1], C.M. Quinn[1], W.B. Betts[1] , M. Sancho[2] , G. Martinez[2], M.Llamas[2] and J.G. O'Neill[3]
[1]Institute for Applied Biology, Dept. of Biology, The University of York, York, Y01 5DD U.K
[2]Departmento de Fisica Aplicada III, Universidad Complutense, 28040 Madrid, Spain
[3]Yorkshire Water, Water Quality, 32-34 Monkgate, York YO3 7RH UK

Introduction

The phenomenon dielectrophoresis is the motion of neutral particles in non-uniform electric fields (Pohl, 1951). When a.c. electric fields are employed it is found that the level of particle collection at electrodes is frequency dependent (Hawkes *et al.*, 1993). It has been shown previously that dielectrophoresis can be used to distinguish between ozone-treated and untreated *Cryptosporidium parvum* oocysts (Archer *et al.*, 1993a, Quinn *et al.*, 1994). These studies were carried out using micro-electrodes fabricated upon glass microscope slides and several types of system incorporating these have been described in the literature (Price *et al.*, 1988; Betts and Hawkes, 1994).

This paper describes work carried out using electrodes which have been designed to concentrate micro-organisms from larger sample volumes (Archer *et al.*, 1993b; Betts and Hawkes, 1992). The collection (filtration) efficiency of these electrodes has been measured using suspensions of *Cryptosporidium parvum* oocysts and this has been compared to those obtained using micro-electrodes.

Materials and Methods

Micro-organisms

Cryptosporidium parvum oocysts were originally supplied by the Moredun Research Institute, Edinburgh, U.K. through Yorkshire Water Service plc, York, U.K. The preparation of untreated and ozone-treated oocysts for use in dielectrophoresis experiments was performed as previously described (Quinn *et al.*, 1994)

Table 1. Characteristics of the grid electrodes

Characteristic	Dimension
Diameter	25 mm
Thickness	200 µm
Pore density	5 per mm^2
Pore Diameter	150 µm

Electrodes and Electrode Chamber

The electrodes consisted of two identical stainless steel membrane support screens (Costar Ltd, UK), the charactersitics of which are shown in Table 1. These were held in a purpose-built electrode chamber (Figure 1).

Dielectrophoretic Procedure

The apparatus and experimental procedure have been described previously (Archer *et al.*, 1993b). An electric field was applied at 16 V and at a frequencies of between 1 MHz and 4 Mhz as detailed in the results section.

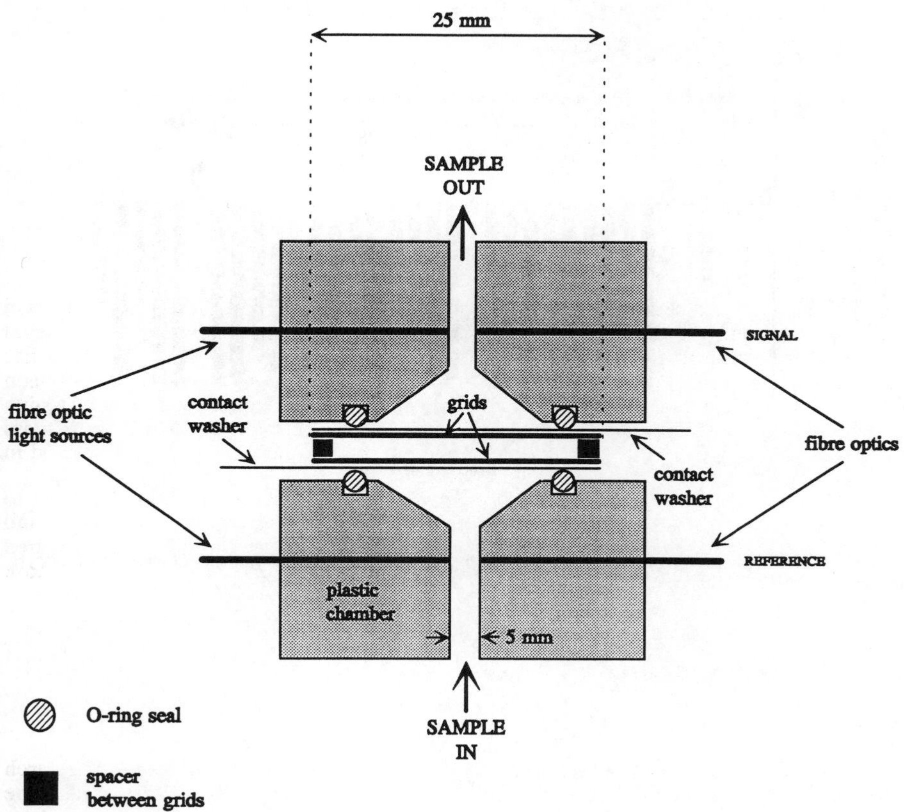

Figure 1. Diagram showing the arrangement of grid electrodes (25 mm diameter) within the support chamber.

Oocyst Enumeration

Samples of the oocyst suspension (2 x 10^6 untreated oocyst ml^{-1}) were collected into micro-centrifuge tubes from an outlet tube downstream of the grid electrodes. Aliquots (20 µl) of these samples were added to 10 ml volumes of Isoton (Coulter, UK) and their concentration determined using a Coulter counter.

Results

Efficiency of Dielectrophoretic Collection

Coulter Counter analyses of particles with diameters of 4-6 µm were made using samples taken prior to and during the application of a 1 MHz electric field to a suspension of oocysts flowing through the electrodes. The counts were subsequently manipulated according to the following formula:

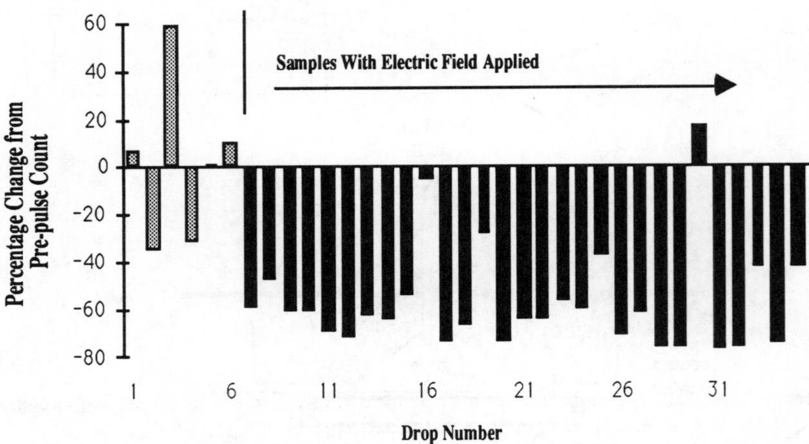

Figure 2. Dielectrophoretic response (% change from pre-pulse counts) of *Cryptosporidium parvum* oocysts. Frequency = 1MHz, Voltage = 16V.

$$\Delta\% = \frac{N_P - N_b}{N_b} \times 100$$

where:

N_P = Count per ml when pulse applied,
N_b = Count during pre-pulse period and
$\Delta\%$ = % change in oocyst concentration.

The results of the experiment are shown in Figure 2. The effect of the electric field was to reduce the oocyst concentration downstream of the electrodes. This was calculated on average to be 58%. In control experiments, when the electric field was turned off, no change in oocyst concentration was observed.

Dielectrophoretic Response of Untreated and Ozone-treated Oocysts

Various frequencies between 1 and 4 MHz were applied to two suspensions of oocysts both at a concentration of 2 x 10^6 oocysts ml^{-1}. One suspension contained untreated oocysts, the other ozone-treated oocysts (Ct = 15). Again, Coulter Counter values were obtained for samples of oocysts which passed through the electrode chamber. These were used to calculate the percentage change in oocyst concentration due to the applied electric fields. The results in Figure 3 show that above 3 MHz the ozone-treated oocysts have a greatly reduced dielectrophoretic response compared to the untreated oocysts.

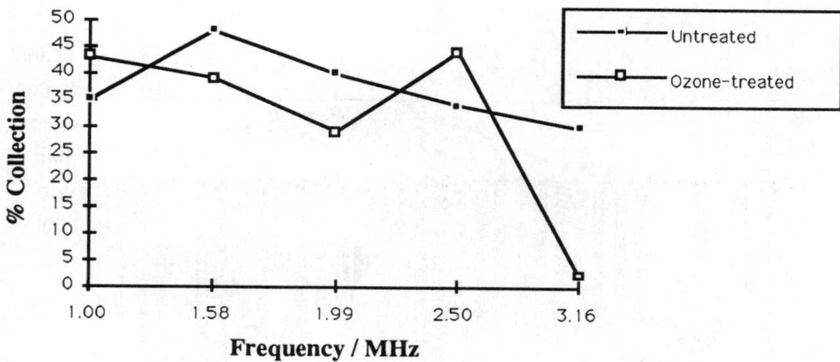

Figure 3. Effect of ozonation upon dielectrophoretic abstraction of *Cryptosporidium parvum* oocysts at different frequencies.

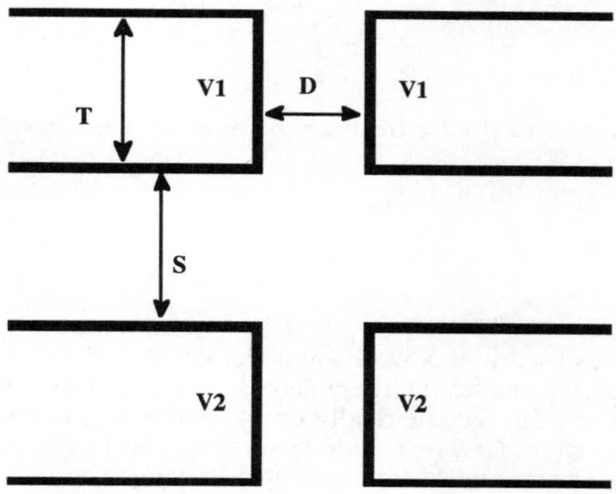

Figure 4. Basic geometry representing a cross section of a unit cell of the electrodes, set to potentials V_1 and V_2.

Computation of Field Configuration

The field configuration around grid type electrodes has been computed using a numerical approach based on an integral equation for the electrostatic potential (Martinez and Sancho, 1990, 1991). The geometry of the electrodes for which the calculations have been performed is shown in Figure 4 and the resulting three dimensional plot of E^2 verses radial and axial coordinates (r,z) is depicted in Figure 5. Since dielectrophoretic force is proportional to the gradient of E^2, the results suggest that particles will tend to be concentrated between the electrodes close to the pore edge.

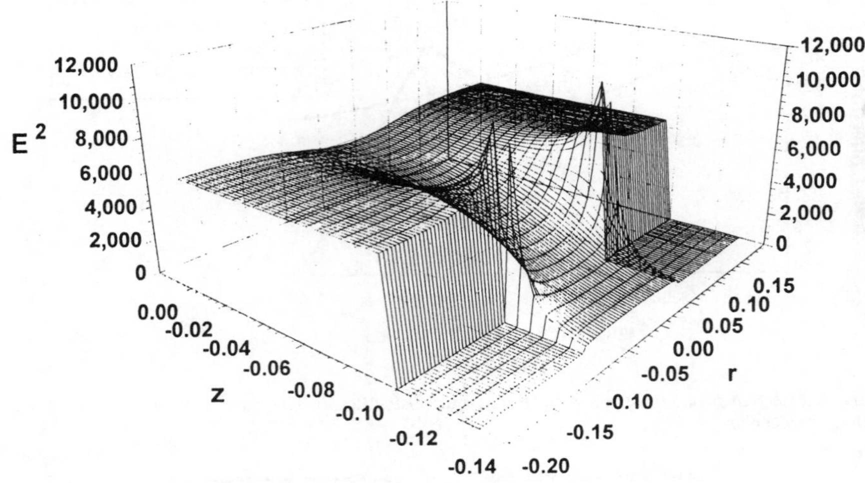

Figure 5. Three dimensional plot of E2 = constant surfaces in the pore region (V2 = 16V, V1 = 0V, S=T=4/3D).

Discussion

The grid-type electrodes used in this work are under developed as a means of selectively concentrating micro-organisms from large volumes of water. Although the electrodes are not presently optimised either geometrically or by choice of construction material they have been shown to abstract *Cryptosporidium* oocysts. Over 50% of untreated oocysts (2×10^6 oocysts ml^{-1}) were removed from a sample flowing at a rate of 0.5 ml min^{-1}. This figure compares with a figure of less than 3% for micro-electrodes using similar voltages and sample flow rates.

The ability of these electrodes to distinguish between oocysts which have undergone treatment using ozone from those which have not, suggests that selective concentration of untreated or treated oocysts from a sample containing a mixture of the two may also be possible. With further refinements this might be extended to viable and non-viable oocyst mixtures, which would be valuable in providing an assessment of the effectiveness of potable water treatment processes and the potential of contaminated water to cause cryptosporidiosis.

Acknowledgements

The authors acknowledge the financial support of Yorkshire Water Services plc for this program of work, the British Technology Group Ltd for initial funding of several dielectrophoretic studies and subsequent patent applications, and the British Council and Spanish Department of Education for funding scientific exchanges through the Accion Integrada program. We are also grateful to Dr Mark Render for his work developing the electrode chamber, and Andrew Brown, Adrian Harrison and Geoff Stimson for their technical support.

References

Archer, G. P., Betts, W. B. and Haigh, T. (1993a) *Microbios* 75, 165-172

Archer, G. P., Render, M. C., Betts, W. B. and Sancho, M. (1993b) *Microbios* 76, 237-244

Betts, W.B. and Hawkes, J.J. (1992) U.K. Patent Application Number 9208357.8

Betts, W.B. and Hawkes, J.J. (1994)*U.K. Patent* GB 2238619B

Hawkes, J.J., Archer, G.P. and Betts, W.B. (1993) Microbios 73, 81-86

Martinez, G. and Sancho, M. (1990) *Nuclear Instrumentation and Methods* A298, 70-77

Martinez, G. and Sancho, M. (1991) *Advances in Electronics and Electronic Physics* 81, 1-41

Price, J.A.R., Burt, J.P.H. and Pethig, R. (1988) *Biochim. Biophys. Acta* 964, 221-230

Quinn, C. M., Archer, G. P., Betts, W. B. and O' Neill, J. G. (1994) Oral Paper presented at Royal Society of Chemistry Conference *"Protozoan Parasites in Water"*, University of York

The Detection of *Cryptosporidium* Oocysts in Milk and Beverages

P. Bankes
Campden Food and Drink Research Association,Chipping Campden, Gloucestershire, Gl55 6lD, UK

Introduction

Pathogenic protozoa such as *Cryptosporidium* have been responsible for gastroenteritis in humans. Tentative links have been made between cryptosporidiosis and the consumption of raw milk and meat but have not been proven. Outbreaks have, however, been attributed to contaminated drinking water. This could lead to contamination of food and drink as large volumes of water are often used in their production. A large outbreak of cryptosporidiosis in the USA in 1993 was associated with the water supply and resulted in the voluntary recall of processed meat products. Local restaurants and supermarkets were urged to discard all foods made with contaminated water. It was believed that local food and drink manufacturers were able to keep the organism out of the production facilities by filtering the water. There are no *in vitro* enrichment methods to cultivate oocysts and detectable numbers of oocysts are therefore obtained by separation and concentration, usually by filtration and centrifugation. Detection is often done using fluorescently-labelled antibodies.

Method

In this research, whole milk, orange juice and white wine were inoculated with oocysts and analysed using a commercially-available immunofluorescence test combined with membrane filtration.

Pretreatment was needed to render samples filterable, to remove food particles and to facilitate the analysis of large sample volumes. This included the use of centrifugation (1200 *g* for 10 min.), prefiltration (0.1 mm nylon mesh), enzyme (trypsin), heat (60°C for 10 min.) and surfactant (sodium dodecyl sulphate (SDS) 1% aq.) (see Table1). Pretreated samples were filtered using a 1.2 μm pore size, 25 mm diameter polycarbonate membrane. Oocysts present in the sample were trapped on the surface of the membrane. The membrane was stained using the Crypto-Cel fluorescent antibody technique (Cellabs Diagnostics) and examined using epifluorescence microscopy.

Table 1. The detection of *Cryptosporidium* oocysts in pretreated samples.

Sample product	Pre-treatment	Oocysts/ml Inoculated	Oocysts/ml Detected
milk	heat, enzyme, surfactant and centrifugation	10	0.4
wine	centrifugation	10	4
orange juice	filtration and centrifugation	100	9

Results

Oocysts on the filter membrane appeared fluorescent green, spherical and 4-6 μm in diameter. Pretreatment did not affect the staining characteristics of oocysts but affected the numbers of oocysts recovered from inoculated samples. Oocysts were detected in milk samples inoculated with as few as 10 oocysts/ml but recovery was only 4% (see Table 2).

Pretreatment, using SDS, trypsin and heat allowed the analysis of 70 ml of milk. Only 0.1 ml milk samples could be examined without pretreatment. Oocysts were detected in orange juice inoculated with 100 oocysts/ml but recovery was <10%. The use of centrifugation and filtration allowed the analysis of 200 ml samples of orange juice. Only 1ml samples of untreated juice could be examined. Wine needed little pretreatment and 200 ml samples could be filtered onto the membrane following centrifugation. Oocysts were detected in samples inoculated with 10 oocysts/ml and recovery was >40%. Storage of inoculated wine or orange juice samples at 8°C for 3 weeks did not affect the detection of oocysts.

Table 2. The detection of *Cryptosporidium* oocysts in 200 ml milk

Pre-treatment	Oocysts/ml Inoculated	Oocysts/ml Detected	% oocysts detected
2xCentrifuge[1]	100	0	0
Surfactant[2] and 2xCentrifuge	1000	2	0.2
Surfactant and	100	0	0
Heat[3] and	1000	7	0.7
2xCentrifuge	1000	17	1.7
	1000	3	0.3
Surfactant and	10	0.4	4
Heat and Enzyme[4]	100	5.0	5
and 2xCentrifuge	1000	82	8.2
	1000	95	9.5

Key; 1=1200 g/ 10 min
2=SDS (1%aq.)
3=60°C/10 min
4=trypsin (10 ml)

Conclusion

Results indicate that a commercial test kit can be used effectively for the detection of *Cryptosporidium* oocysts in food and drink. Pretreatment, which is needed to separate and concentrate oocysts from food and drink, does not appear to affect antibody binding. Methods need to be optimised to improve levels of recovery and detection and to give an indication of oocyst viability.

On Farm Detection of *Cryptosporidium parvum* in Cattle, Calves and Environmental Samples

J.S. Kemp[1], S.E. Wright[1] and Z. Bukhari[2]
[1]Moredun Research Institute, Edinburgh, UK
[2]Scottish Parasite Diagnostic Laboratory, Glasgow, UK

Introduction

Cryptosporidium parvum is a coccidian parasite of worldwide distribution capable of infecting many mammalian species including man. Cryptosporidial infection may produce clinical symptoms of acute diarrhoea, nausea, vomiting and fever which in immunocompetent individuals is normally self limiting, but is potentially life threatening in immunocompromised individuals. To date no effective chemotherapeutic agents have been found. Infection is by ingestion of oocysts (4-6 µm diameter) shed in the faeces of infected individuals. Oocysts are highly resistant to disinfection. Human outbreaks of cryptosporidiosis have been attributed to direct contact with infected animals/humans, and increasingly from waterborne outbreaks via contaminated drinking water. One source suspected of contributing to contamination of potable water supplies is agriculture. To minimise the risks of environmental contamination from farms with cryptosporidial infections requires better understanding of the epidemiology and spread of infection within livestock, and the routes by which such pathogens may reach water courses. The aim of this ongoing study is to examine a dairy farm with a history of clinical cryptosporidial infection to determine the epidemiology of infection within neonatal calves and adult dairy cattle, and to assess the dissemination of oocysts from the farm to the surrounding aqueous environment.

Materials and Methods

Faecal samples were taken weekly throughout the calving season from neonatal calves. Samples were examined for the presence of *Cryptosporidium* oocysts using direct faecal smears stained with phenol auramine and viewed under incident (x40 objective) fluorescence light microscopy. Samples were quantified by dilution counts using an improved Neubauer haemocytometer. Enumeration of smaller numbers of oocysts (< 10^4/gram faeces) required the use of ether sedimentation techniques and counting of fixed volume smears stained with phenol auramine. Faecal samples from adult cattle were examined for the presence of oocysts by concentration techniques using ether sedimentation and saturated salt floatation and enumerated by counts from fixed volume smears stained with a FITC labelled anti-*Cryptosporidium* monoclonal antibody. Drainage water samples ranging from 58 to 948 liters were collected weekly by filtration using Cuno Microwynd filters (1 µm nominal porosity) from 4 catchment sites around the study farm. Samples were processed to elute *Cryptosporidium* oocysts according to the SCA method (Anon, 1990) and identified by staining 10 to 20 % of resulting pellet with FITC labelled monoclonal antibody.

Results

1 Epidemiology of cryptosporidial infection in neonatal calves.

Of 88 calves examined, 85 (96%) developed clinical cryptosporidiosis. Oocysts were detected in faeces of calves from 6 to 23 days old, with numbers shed ranging from 24 to 9.88x108/gram faeces (wet weight). Figure 1 illustrates the spread of infection throughout the calves and number of oocysts shed.

Individual calf No.	9/3	17/3	24/3	31/3	7/4	16/4
46						+++
45						
44						++++
43						++++
42						++++
41						++++
40					I	+++
39					I	I
38					+++	I
37					+++	I
37					++++	I
35					++++	I
34					+++	I
33					+++	I
32					++++	I
31					++	I
30					++	I
29			I	++++	+++	I
28			I	+++	I	I
27			I	++++	I	I
26			I	++++	I	I
25			I	++	I	I
24			I	+++	I	I
23			I	++++	I	I
22			I	++++	I	I
21			I	+++	I	I
20			+++	+	I	I
19		I	+++++	+	I	I
18		I	+++	I	I	I
17		I	+++	I	I	I
16		I	++	I	I	I
15		+++	I	I	I	I
14	I	++++	I	I	I	I
13	I	++++	I	I	I	I
12	I	+++++	I	I	I	I
11	I	++++	I	I	I	I
10	+++	++	I	I	I	I
9	+++++	I	I	I	I	I
8	+++	I	I	I	I	I
7	+++	I	I	I	I	I
6	++++	I	I	I	I	I
5	+++++	I	I	I	I	I
4	I	I	I	I	I	I
3	I	I	I	I	I	I

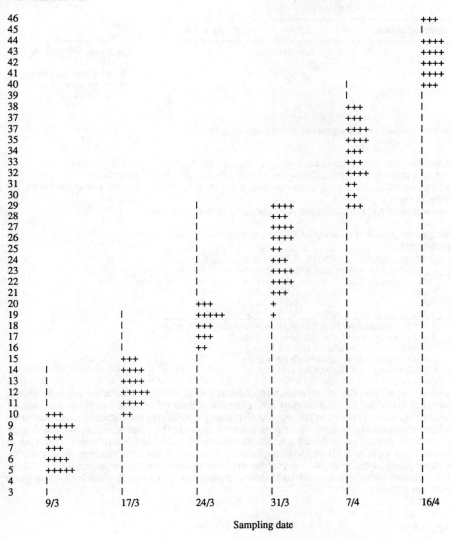

Sampling date

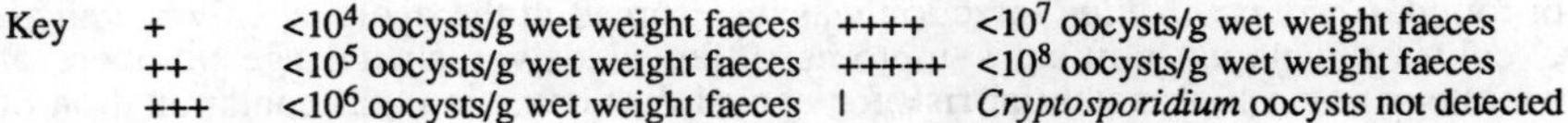

Key
+ $<10^4$ oocysts/g wet weight faeces
++ $<10^5$ oocysts/g wet weight faeces
+++ $<10^6$ oocysts/g wet weight faeces
++++ $<10^7$ oocysts/g wet weight faeces
+++++ $<10^8$ oocysts/g wet weight faeces
I *Cryptosporidium* oocysts not detected

Figure 1. Spread of *Cryptosporidium* infection in neonatal calves on study farm with time

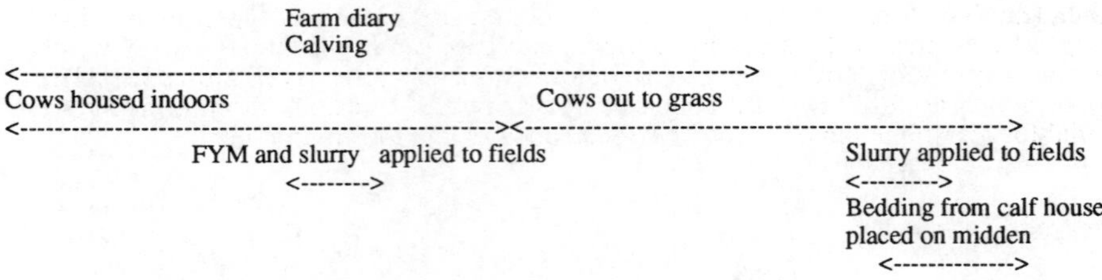

Figure 2. Movement of drainage water through various farm areas

2 Detection of *Cryptosporidium* oocysts in adult cow faeces.
From a total 89 cow faecal samples examined, 52 were found to contain *Cryptosporidium* oocysts, with numbers shed ranging from 0.5 to 19 per gram faeces (wet weight).
3 Detection of *Cryptosporidium parvum* in farm drainage water.

Table 1. Concentration of oocysts found in farm drainage water over a 6 month period.

Site	February	March	April	May	June	July
	Average weekly oocyst concentration/litre					
1	0.51	13.31	2.31	1.85	1.54	0.49
2	0.08	0.45	1.75	0.88	0.93	0.08
3	NS	5.39	2.10	0.81	2.65	0.68
4	NS	0.23	0.02	ND	NS	ND

Key Site 1 - Drainage from farm buildings (including dairy wash run-off)
Site 2 - Drainge from fields receiving cattle slurry
Site 3 - Collective drainage from sites 1 and 2
Site 4 - Drainage from fields receiving manure
NS - Not sampled; ND - Not detected

Average weekly oocyst concentrations were greatest from March to June at site 1, coinciding with the calving season and peak incidence of clinical cryptosporidiosis. A similar trend was observed at site 3, (see also slurry spreading) the increased concentration resulting predominantly from increased oocyst output at the farm steading. At collection site 2 oocyst concentration was greatest in the months of March and June. This rise in concentration may be attributable to application of slurry to the fields during these months. Oocyst concentration at site 4 was consistently low throughout the sampling period. These fields received farm yard manure in March and were not grazed by livestock to allow grass growth for silage.

Discussion

Cryptosporidium parvum was found to be the major enteropathogen and cause of diarrhoea on the study farm. Other causes of neonatal diarrhoea, such as rotavirus and salmonella were not found. *Cryptosporidium* infection was widespread in the neonatal calves, and all infected calves developed clinical symptoms. Infected calves shed large numbers of oocysts representing a high potential risk for oocyst dissemination and contamination of the environment. More than 50 percent of cows examined were shedding oocysts in their faeces. Numbers shed per gram faeces were very low, but represent a significant oocyst burden to the environment since cows excrete between 30 to 40 kilograms of faeces per day, and may also act as an initial source of infection for neonatal calves. Oocysts were detected in farm drainage water from all 4 sites examined. Oocyst concentrations varied depending on sampling site and month, with highest concentrations detected from the farm steading and lowest from the silage fields. Peak oocyst concentrations appeared to coincide with specific events, such as calving periods, and application of animal wastes to land. Since the majority of farm drainage and runoff ultimately joins river and lake systems, many of which are used for abstraction of potable water, livestock farming has a great potential for dissemination of *Cryptosporidium* oocysts into the environment.

Acknowledgements

This study forms part of CSA 2064, a project jointly funded by the Scottish Office Agriculture Fisheries Department and the Ministry of Agriculture Fisheries and Food.

References

Anon, (1990). Methods for the examination of waters and associated materials. Isolation and identification of Giardia cysts, *Cryptosporidium* oocysts and Free Living Pathogenic Amoebae in water etc 1989. Department of the Environment, Standing Committee of Analysts. H.M.S.O. publication ISBN 0 11 752282 1, London

Ultrasonic Isolation of *Cryptosporidium* Oocysts

J.C. Laughton, R.W. Owen, D.J. Clarke and A.F. Zamani
Detection Group, Microbial Technology Department, Centre for Applied Microbiology & Research (CAMR), Porton Down, Salisbury, Wiltshire, SP4 OJG, UK

Introduction

Cryptosporidium is a protozoan parasite that causes diarrhoeal disease. Transmission is via environmentally robust oocysts that are excreted in large numbers in the faeces (Robertson and Smith, 1992). The water industry is required to screen water supplies and source waters for the presence of oocysts. However, the standard recovery techniques are unreliable, with erratic recovery rates sometimes as low as 10% (Whitmore and Carrington, 1993).

Aim

To develop an efficient system to recover oocysts from water and deliver them to a small volume for identification. This was done in two phases. Firstly by ultrasound enhanced filtration, followed by further concentration using ultrasonic banding to deliver the oocysts to a small detection point.

Method [A] - Ultrasound Enhanced Filtration

Cryptosporidium parvum oocysts (heat inactivated, supplied by Moredun Animal Health Institute) were added to 1 L Demin water (6.0 x 10^5 oocysts).The oocyst containing water was filtered through an asymmetric ceramic filter (0.2 µl membrane pore size and 1 µm support pore size, 25 cm by 10 cm diameter, supplied by Fairey Industrial Ceramics.) using a peristaltic pump. The filter was placed inside the water filled ultrasound bath (Figure 1). The oocysts were then recovered from the filter by backwashing with sub-lethal pulsed ultrasound. 50 ml samples were collected sequentially. (The samples were further concentrated to 100 µl by two centrifugation steps of 4500 rpm for 15 minutes and 15000 rpm for 10 minutes.) The resuspended oocysts were stained with fluorescently labelled monoclonal antibodies (Bradsure FITC *C. parvum* 20 µl 50:50 ratio) and incubated for 30 minutes at 37°C. The oocysts were then counted under UV light using KOVA 10 Grid slides (Bertholf and Kao, 1991).

Results [A]

The ceramic filter retained more than 99.9 % of oocysts (no oocysts could be detected in the filtrate). Few oocysts were recovered by backwashing alone without ultrasound (Figure 2). Recoveries of 81 - 93 % of oocysts were achieved in 100 ml backwash using ultrasound power setting 11 with Tween 80 (0.01 % v/v), during backwashing (Figure 3). High recoveries (approx. 100 %) have also been achieved using viable counts from yeast suspensions (*Rhodotorula glutinis*).

The oocysts stained well with the FITC reagent despite exposure to ultrasound (Figure 4). Examination of samples by electron microscopy showed some damage to the surface of some oocysts but it did not show any shearing damage of the oocysts (Figure 5).

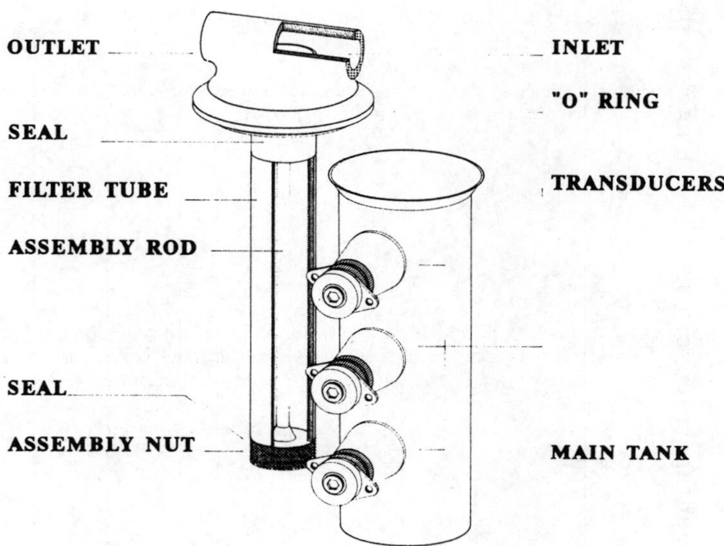

Figure 1. Ultrasound bath with the filter. (2 L bath, with three 35 Khz pillar transducers driven by a 50 W electronic output.)

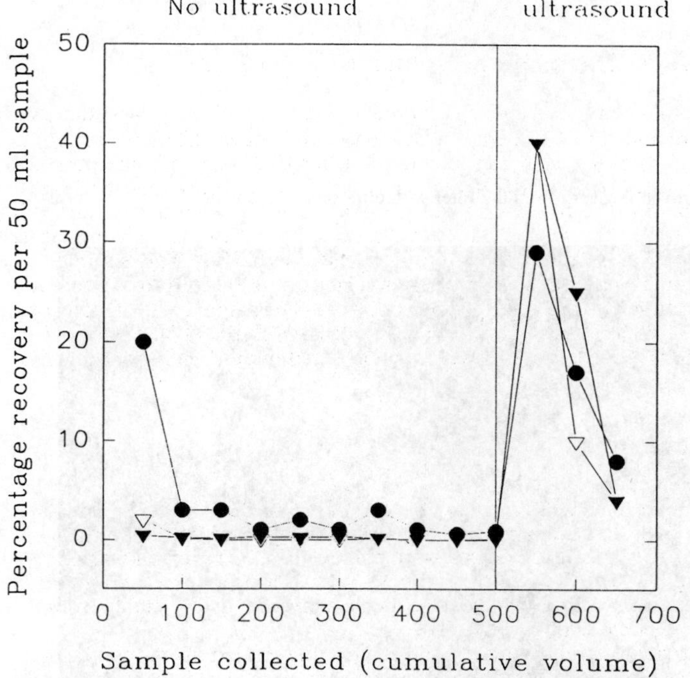

Figure 2. Comparison of the recovery rates from the filter with and without ultrasound treatment.

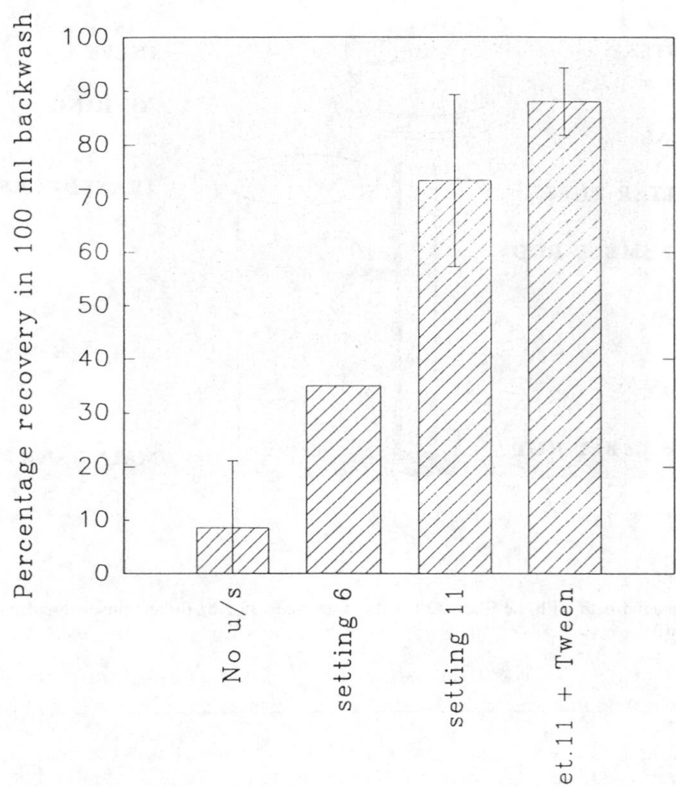

Figure 3. Improved recovery from the filter with ultrasound treatment.

Figure 4. Fluorescently stained oocysts after ultrasonication.

Figure 5. Electron micrograph of oocysts recovered from the filter using ultrasound.

Method [B] - Concentration Using Ultrasonic Banding

Rhodotorula glutinis was used as a model organism for the banding experiments. High concentrations were used in order to visualise the banding. The yeast suspension was gently flowed into the glass resonance vessel of the ultrasonic banding apparatus (Figure 6a). The yeasts were entrained in an ultrasound standing wave, with the yeasts forming bands at the low pressure nodes (Figure 6b). The bands were then moved to the collection point by modulation of the frequency of the ultrasonic field. The yeast suspension was then sampled using a hypodermic syringe. The samples were enumerated by total viable counts.

Results [B]

The yeasts were concentrated at the collection point. The remaining yeast suspension was clarified by 63 - 95 %. The ultrasound banding appeared to be more effective at entraining the yeasts at lower concentration levels (Table 1).

Table 1. Clarification of yeast suspension by ultrasonic banding.

Pre-banding (Yeasts per ml.)	Post-banding (Yeasts per ml.)	Clarification
6.4×10^7	2.1×10^7	67 %
4.4×10^4	3.9×10^3	91 %

Discussion and Conclusions

By combining the above techniques of ultrasonic filtration and banding it will be possible to recover oocysts (and other pathogens) from water samples and concentrate them into a small detection volume. The process shows potential for a high recovery rate and high reproducibility. It would remove the need for time-consuming manual filter extraction and oocyst concentration steps (eg. centrifugation) and the losses resulting from these steps.

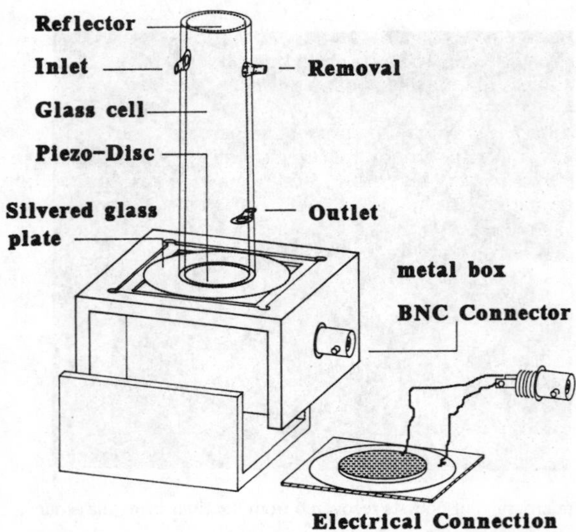

Figure 6a. Ultrasound banding apparatus Glass resonance vessel (35 ml) on an ultrasound transducer.

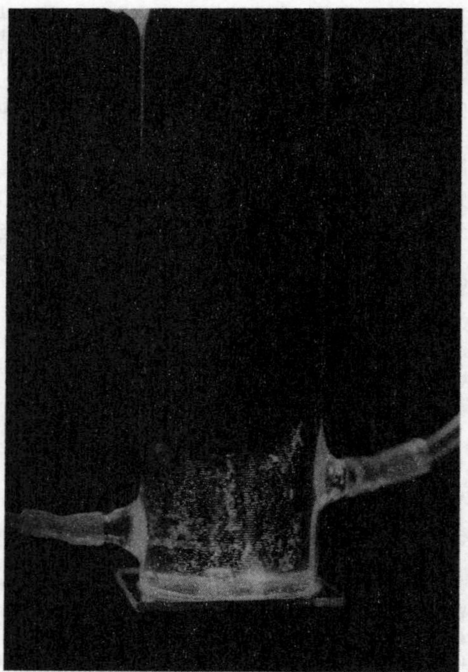

Figure 6b. Formation of bands of yeasts in ultrasound standing wave.

We are developing a small portable model of the filtration system which has a larger pore size (0.2 μm membrane pores and 12 μm support pores). This will increase the flow rate and enable large volumes of water (10 - 100 l) to be analysed. It will also reduce the background material in the sample and reduce any damage caused the oocysts by compaction against the filter.

The ultrasound banding apparatus appears to be particularly effective at concentrating lower levels of yeasts. This is important for monitoring water supplies since the infectious dose for *Cryptosporidium* may be as low as one oocyst in susceptible individuals (Blewett *et al.* 1993). We have started banding trials with FITC stained oocysts (heat inactivated).

It should be possible remove the background debris found in environmental samples by flowing Tween 80 through the vessel while the oocysts are entrained in the ultrasound standing wave. This would facilitate identification and enumeration of oocysts by microscopy or flow cytometry.

Acknowledgements

The electron microscopy was performed by Barry Dowsett at CAMR.

We are grateful to PHLS and MAFF for their support of this work.

References

Bertholf M.F. and Kao K.J. (1991), Laboratory Medicine, 22 (12), 864-868. "Disposable plastic and reusable glass haemacytometers for cell counts"

Blewett D.A. et al. (1993), Wat. Sci. Tech., 27 (3-4), 61-64. "Infective dose size studies on *Cryptosporidium parvum* using gnotobiotic lambs."

Robertson L.J. and Smith H.V. (1992), European microbiology, Nov./Dec. "*Cryptosporidium* and Cryptosporidiosis. Part I: Current perspective and present technologies."

Whitmore T.N. and Carrington E.G. (1993), Wat. Sci. Tech., 27 (3-4), 69-76."Comparison of methods for recovery of *Cryptosporidium* from water."

The PHLS External Quality Assessment Scheme for *Cryptosporidium* in Water

N.F. Lightfoot [1], B. Place [1], I.R. Richardson [1], D.P. Casemore [2] and P.J. Tynan [2]
[1]Regional Public Health Laboratory, Newcastle General Hospital, Newcastle Upon Tyne, NE4 6BE, UK
[2]Cryptosporidium Reference Unit, Rhyl Public Health Laboratory, Glan Clwyd District General Hospital, Rhyl, Clwyd, LL18 5UJ, UK

Introduction

The need for a national *Cryptosporidium* External Quality Assessment Scheme was first suggested by the Badenoch Expert Group in 1990. This was shortly after the outbreak in 1989 in the Swindon/Oxford area when there were over 500 confirmed cases of cryptosporidiosis. Oocysts had been found in raw water from a reservoir and also in potable water.

The examination of water samples is difficult and subjective and there are several sources of error. False positives are alarming for the general public and have very expensive consequences; low numbers of oocysts present in large volumes of water may pose a significant health risk . Percentage recovery of oocysts is low by current methods and false negatives are clearly a public health hazard. There is a definite need for external quality assessment.

The development of a PHLS EQA scheme had two main objectives: to enable laboratories to compare their performance with one another, and to improve general performance.

Following the successful completion of a pilot study initiated by Newcastle Upon Tyne PHL and the PHLS Cryptosporidium Reference Unit at Rhyl, a larger trial involving 46 Public Health Laboratories and 32 Water Authority laboratories was performed in January 1992. Since that succesful trial there have been eight distributions, three per year in January, May and September. The number of participants currently stands at 59 which includes 34 Public Health Laboratories and two from Europe.

Scheme Methodology

Each distribution consists of three simulated samples prepared with a background of either river or tap water and samples have been prepared over a wide range of levels including some negatives to give participants confidence in reporting zeros (Table 1).

Table 1. *Cryptosporidium* External Quality Assessment Scheme Samples 1991 - 1994

Water Source	Number of samples	Oocysts per litre
River	4	0
River	3	5-8
River	7	17-80
River	4	140-220
Tap	1	0
Tap	8	0.7-2.1

Background concentrates are screened for oocysts using a monoclonal immunofluorescent stain before diluting to the desired volume and density of solids. The required number of oocysts are added from a suspension in 2% potassium dichromate held at 4°C which was supplied by the Moredun Research Institute, Edinburgh. At this stage, multiple aliquots of each sample are examined for oocysts to obtain a good average count before being dispensed

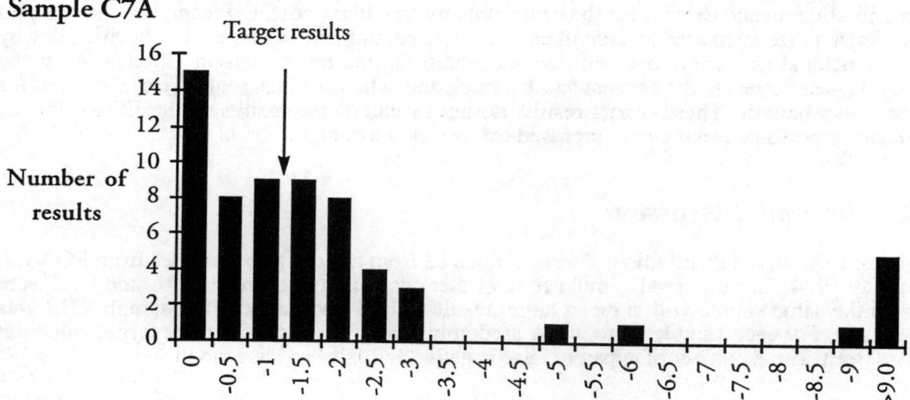

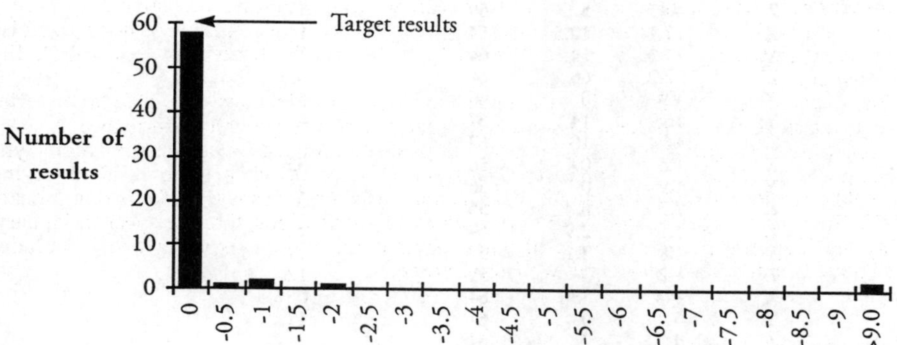

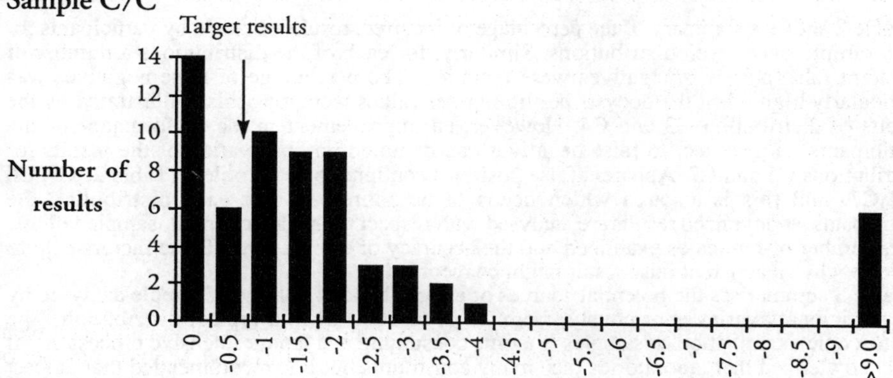

Figure 1. Distribution C7 May 1994

in 1ml aliquots and distributed to participants by first class post. On receipt of the samples participants are instructed to store them in the refrigerator and examine on a specified day by a monoclonal immunofluorescent method, returning the results within 12 days. After the closing date target results are sent to the participants who may then request extra samples for their own benefit. These repeat results do not influence the results in the EQA scheme. Finally, a personalised report is prepared for each participant.

Results and Discussion

Figure 1 shows the distribution of results obtained from a set of three samples from EQA C7, in May 1994. These were all simulated tap water concentrates. Samples C7A and C7C were from the same source with a mean target result of 1.08 oocysts per litre, sample C7B was negative. For each sample there was a predominance of results around the target value but there were also a number of apparent false negative and false positive results.

Table 2. Summary of wrong results

Distribution	Sample	Target	Median	Number of results	False Pos/N %
		Oocysts per litre			
C1	X	5.92	6	69	12
	Y	0	0	68	15
	Z	5.42	5	69	17
C2	X	17.1	10.5	64	16
	Y	17.3	14.5	64	17
	Z	72.2	66	64	6
C3	X	1.9	0	66	57
	Y	16.9	14	67	4
	Z	14.4	10	67	5
C4	X	1.6	0	56	55
	Y	1.9	0	56	55
	Z	7.5	6.2	56	9
C5	X	2.1	2.9	59	17
	Y	1.8	2.1	59	17
	Z	1.2	3	59	12
C6	X	144	130	64	0
	Y	0	0	64	17
	Z	0	0	64	9
C7	X	1.08	1.1	64	23
	Y	0	0	64	9
	Z	0.71	1.2	63	23

Table 2 shows a summary of the percentage of incorrect results obtained by participants for each sample over seven distributions. Similarly, for each of the distributions a number of apparent false positives/negatives were recorded. The percentage of false negatives was particularly high when the oocysts per litre target values were low; this is illustrated by the results of distribution C3 and C4. However, an improvement in the performance of the participants with respect to false negatives can be noted on observation of the results for distributions C5 and C7. Apparent false positives continue to be recorded (Table 2, C1, C6 and C7) and this is an area which needs to be addressed. For each distribution the participants' anonymized results are analysed with respect to the detection kit, sample volume size, number of replicates examined and the accuracy of calculations. These factors help to indicate why an apparent false result might be recorded.

Table 3 summarises the potential sources of error. The total volume of sample analysed by the participants varies enormously, from 25 µl to 1000 µl in a typical distribution. The microscopic examination of samples is a time consuming and labour intensive process and it is acknowledged that laboratories face many constraints but it is recommended that at least 200 µl should be examined. Despite the recommendations of some detection kit manufacturers the HMSO guidelines (Department of Environment 1990) do not recommend

Table 3. Sources of Error

Sample Preparation	Counting	Optical System	Reagents
mixing	technique	ultra violet source	monoclonal antibody
volume	recording	objective lenses	mountant
drying	features		
washing technique	background		
	counting twice		

fixing of the slides as this may distort the characteristic morphology of the oocysts, i.e. a size of 4-6 µm, bright green fluorescence of the wall and the presence of the diagnostic fold or suture line in the wall, although this latter feature is variably present. Slides should be carefully rinsed after staining and not washed in baths. Examination of the whole of all wells and accurate identification and counting are essential as are care of the optical system and reagents in order to achieve good results.

It is intended to carry out an assessment of the performance of participants over a number of distributions since in any distribution the number of oocysts will vary between samples. Therefore, from time to time any participant could expect to record a high or low value. By means of an assessment of this type, it can be determined whether a given participant is recording more outlying results than would be expected by chance indicating a need to look at materials and methodologies. There is much ongoing research in the field of *Cryptosporidium* detection. Some requirements for the future are outlined in Table 4. Undoubtedly, good training and support services are required but the way forward is for more rapid and less subjective methods for the detection of *Cryptosporidium* in environmental samples.

Table 4. Future Developments

1	Carry out further statistical analyses e.g. duplicates and repeatability.
2	Use fresh oocysts.
3	Provide more training.
4	Provide internal controls/reference material.
5	Improve immunofluorescent reagents.
6	Develop ELISA screening.
7	Develop molecular methods.
8	Extend interlaboratory trials to Europe and U.S.
9	Develop NETWORK of expert laboratories internationally.

References

Anon, Department of Environment. Isolation and Identification of Giardia Cysts, Cryptosporidium Oocysts and Free Living Pathogenic Amoeboe in Water etc, 1989. Methods for the Examination of Waters and Associated Materials, HMSO (1990)

Detection of *Cryptosporidium* Antigens on SDS-PAGE Western Blots using Enhanced Chemiluminescence

S. Moran, D.P. Casemore[1], J. McLauchlin and G.L. Nichols[2]
PHLS Food Hygiene Laboratory, Central Public Health Laboratory, Colindale Avenue, London NW9 5HT, UK
[1]Cryptosporidium Reference Laboratory, Public Health Laboratory, Rhyl, UK
[2]Environmental Services, PHLS Headquarters, UK

Introduction

The study of the epidemiology of cryptosporidiosis has been hampered by the lack of subtyping methods for the parasite (Casemore, 1990).

Systems based on SDS-PAGE western blotting (Nichols *et al.*, 1991) and isoenzyme analysis (Awad-El-Kariem *et al.*, 1993) have been described but these techniques present problems in obtaining sufficient parasite material for analysis.

The ECL system (Amersham) is a sensitive and non-radioactive method for the detection of horseradish peroxidase on membranes by the generation of light. The advantage of this system over conventional colorimetric detection methods is that a single sample may be retested on multiple occasions.

In this study, results from conventional colorimetrically stained gel and dot blots were compared with those achieved by using an enhanced chemiluminescence system.

Methods

Forty-one human faecal samples were supplied by the *Cryptosporidium* Reference Unit, Rhyl Public Health Laboratory, including 22 stools positive for *Cryptosporidium*, and other stools positive for *Giardia* (5), Salmonella (3), *Campylobacter* (4), *Cyclospora* (3), *Clostridium difficile* (1) and *Shigella sonnei* (3).

Samples of faeces (0.1 ml or 0.1 g) were homogenised in a microcentrifuge tube with 1 ml of extraction buffer (10% w/v SDS, 10 µl 2-mercaptoethanol, 0.5 M Tris-HCl pH 6.8), vortexed and heated to 100°C for 5 min. The mixture was cooled to room temperature, spun for 10 min and the pellet discarded. 1 µl and 4 µl volumes of faecal extract were 'dotted' onto nitrocellulose, allowed to dry and incubated in blocking buffer (phosphate buffered saline (PBS) with 1% w/v bovine serum albumin (BSA), 1% v/v Tween-20 and 5% w/v skimmed milk powder) at 4°C overnight. The probe used was a monoclonal antibody (MAb-C1) against an oocyst wall antigen (McLauchlin *et al.*, 1987).

The blots were incubated for 1 h at room temperature in MAb-C1 in whole ascitic fluid diluted 1/500 in blocking buffer followed by HRP-labelled anti-mouse antibody (Sigma). The blot was washed between antibodies in PBS buffer with 1% v/v Tween-20 (PBS-T).

Colorimetric staining was carried out with 3,3'-Diaminobenzidine (DAB) using a standard method (Sigma ImmuNotes sheet No. 5). Bound HRP was detected with the ECL system using the manufacturers' instructions. The light emission was detected using Hyperfilm-ECL (Amersham).

Following ECL detection, both primary and secondary antibodies were removed by placing the blot in stripping buffer (100 mM 2- mercaptoethanol, 2% SDS, 62.5 mM Tris-HCl pH 6.7) for 1 h at room temperature with occasional shaking. The membrane was washed for 2 X 10 min in large volumes of PBS-T prior to reblocking and testing as described above.

Oocyst isolates from lamb faeces (3), calf faeces (3), human faeces (2) and from an egg culture of *C. baileyi* were prepared using a modification of the formol-ether technique (Ridley *et al.*, 1956), using water instead of 10% formalin. The isolates were analysed by SDS-PAGE Western blotting as described previously (Nichols *et al.*, 1991).

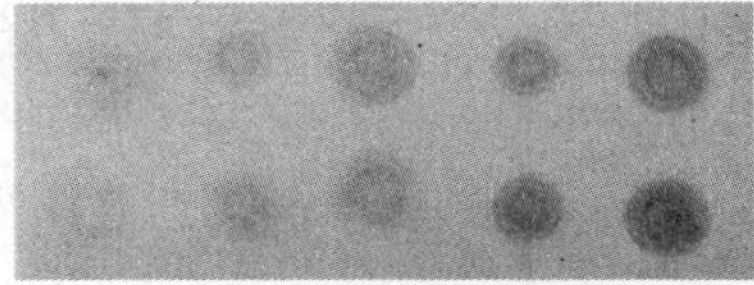

Figure 1. Dot blot of faecal extracts stained with MAb-C1 and HRP-labelled anti-mouse antibody. Bound HRP was detected using DAB.

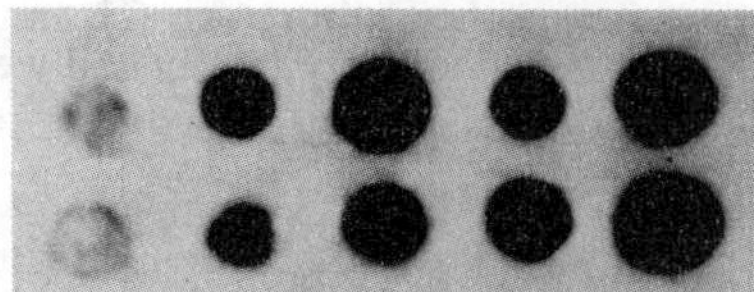

Figure 2. Dot blot of faecal extracts stained with MAb-C1 and HRP-labelled anti-mouse antibody after stripping and reprobing five times. Bound HRP was detected using ECL.

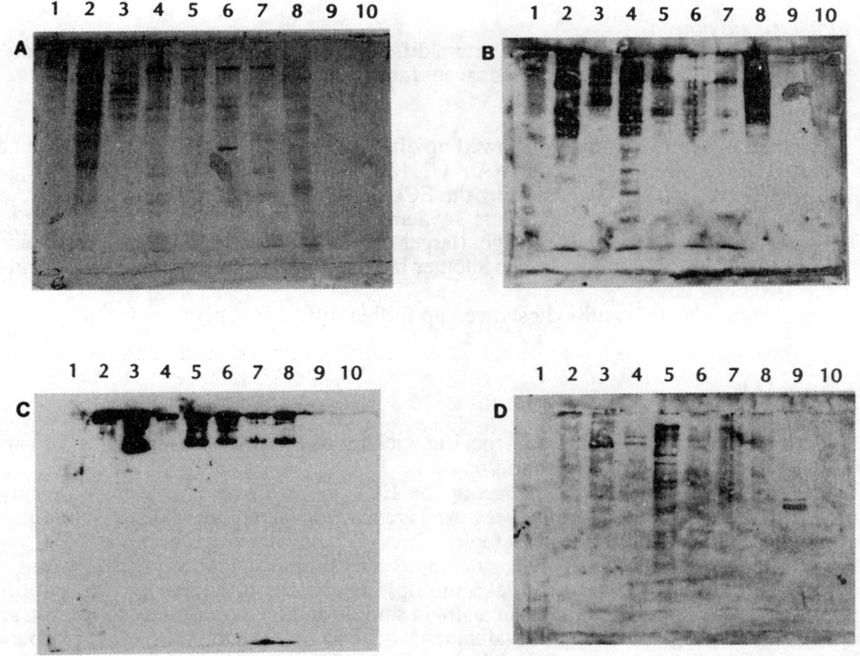

Figure 3. SDS-PAGE Western Blots of antigens stained with; **A**: anti-*Cryptosporidium* rabbit serum and AP-labelled anti-rabbit antibody. The AP was detected using NBT/BCIP. **B**: The same antigens stained with anti-*Cryptosporidium* rabbit serum and HRP-labelled anti-rabbit antibody. The HRP was detected using ECL. **C**: The same blot stained with MAbC1 and HRP-labelled anti-mouse antibody. Bound HRP was detected using ECL. **D**: The same blot stained with anti-*Cryptosporidium* human serum and HRP-labelled anti-human antibody. Bound HRP was detected using ECL.
The antigens were **1)** Lamb 405, **2)** Human 3455, **3)** *C. baileyi* culture, **4)** Calf 447, **5)** Lamb 450, **6)** Calf 394, **7)** Lamb 451, **8)** SDS 7B standards, **9)** Calf 433, **10)** Human 5111.

Western blots were treated as described above, or were probed using either MAb-C1, polyvalent rabbit antiserum raised against a purified oocyst suspension, or a convalescent phase serum from a human patient with cryptosporidiosis. Bound antibody was detected using the appropriate antibody conjugate (Sigma).

The Western blot was stripped as described above.

Results

The Dot Blot

Colorimetric staining The blot was probed with MAb-C1 and anti-mouse-HRP before staining with DAB. Some of the dots stained very faintly and were difficult to distinguish from the background.

ECL staining The blot was stained with MAb-C1 and stripped and reprobed seven times with other antibodies before restaining with MAb-C1. Although some mechanical damage is apparent, the pattern of staining remained similar. Positive results were far easier to distinguish from a lower background using the ECL than that produced using the DAB stain.

The Gel Blots

Colorimetric staining

a Using anti-*Cryptosporidium* rabbit serum, differences between the calf and lamb isolates were observed but many of the bands were faint.

ECL staining

a Rabbit antibody. This antibody showed up differences between calf isolates and bands of lower molecular weights than the MAb- C1. Most of the bands stained using the NBT/BCIP method also stained using the ECL detection method with this antibody.

b MAb-C1. Except in the human isolate 3455 and the calf isolate 447, the majority of bands stained were of high molecular weight (larger than 180 kDa). Bands stained in the lamb and calf isolates were similar to one another but the lower molecular weight bands in both isolates stained faintly.

c Human antibody. This antibody showed up further differences between isolates.

Discussion

In the dot blots, there was some non-specific sticking of MAb-C1 to material from patients with infections other than cryptosporidiosis.

There are several advantages of using the ECL system over the more conventional colorimetric methods. Many chromogens used are hazardous, require multiple solutions to be prepared and irreversibly stain each sample.

The advantages of using the ECL system are the simple preparation of substrates and recording of results, the ability to take multiple exposures to adjust for overstaining or different concentrations of antigens in a single sample and the opportunity to retest a single blot. Work is in progress to further evaluate this method for the subtyping of cryptosporidia.

This work is supported by the PHLS Central R & D Fund and by PHLS Core Funding.

References

Awad-El-Kariem FM, Robinson HA, McDonald V, Evans D, Dyson DA. Is human cryptosporidiosis a zoonotic disease? Lancet 1993; 341: 1535

Casemore DP. Epidemiological aspects of human cryptosporidiosis. Epidemiol Infect 1990; 104: 1-28

McLauchlin J, Casemore DP, Harrison TG, Gerson PJ, Samuel D, Taylor AG. Identification of *Cryptosporidium* oocysts by monoclonal antibody. Lancet 1987; i: 51

Nichols GL, McLauchlin J, Samuel D. A technique for typing cryptosporidium isolates. J Protozool 1991; 38: 237S-40S

Ridley DS, Hawgood BC. The value of formol-ether concentration of faecal cysts and ova. J Clin Pathol 1956; 9: 14-16

Giardia Cysts in Sewage : Distinguishing Between Species

C.A. Paton,[1,2] A.T. Campbell,[1] L.J. Robertson,[1,2] H.H. Stibbs[3] and H.V. Smith[1]
[1]Scottish Parasite Diagnostic Laboratory Stobhill Hospital NHS Trust, Springburn, Glasgow, G21 3UW, UK
[2]Division of Environmental Health, Department of Civil Engineering University of Strathclyde, Glasgow, G1 1XQ, UK
[3]Waterborne Inc. Hurst Street, New Orleans, La 70118, USA

Introduction

Differences in both trophozoite morphological form and median body type allow discrimination between at least three species of *Giardia* namely, *G. agilis*, *G. muris* and *G. duodenalis* (Filice, 1952; Thompson *et al.*, 1993).

Up to 165,000 *Giardia* spp. cysts per litre were found in sewage influent, but, at present, we are unable to determine what proportion of these cysts are of human origin. Infected sewer-dwelling rodents may contribute *G. muris* cysts to sewage which could account for a proportion of cysts detected. In order to assess the risk to public health of viable cysts in sewage effluent discharges, it is important to be able to identify the species of the parasite since cysts from various *Giardia* species are similar in morphology .

Stibbs (1994) proposed a method whereby either an FITC-conjugated anti-G. *muris*-specific monoclonal antibody (MAb) or an FITC-conjugated anti-*Giardia* spp. MAb could be used to assess the respective occurrence of *G. muris* and *G. lamblia* cysts in environmental samples.

We have developed a simultaneous dual antibody/fluorochrome labelling regime to assess the relative occurrence of *G. muris* and *G. duodenalis*-type cysts in sewage samples from six sewage works in the West of Scotland. This involved the use of an anti-*G. muris*-specific MAb and an anti-*Giardia* spp. MAb conjugated to two different fluorochromes with discrete spectral emission patterns.

Materials and Methods

Purification of Sewage Samples

Both crude and final effluent sewage were obtained from six treatment works. These works ranged from small to large scale and were located within both urban and rural communities. Two litre volumes were taken as either grab samples or 24 hour composite samples. Purification was by ether sedimentation and/or sucrose flotation.

Source of Antibodies

A commercially available FITC-conjugated anti-*Giardia* spp. MAb [without Evans Blue (EB)] was obtained from Bradsure Biologicals and used according to the manufacturer's instructions. An anti-*G. muris* specific MAb, obtained from Waterborne Inc., was conjugated to Texas Red (TR).

Source of *Giardia* Cysts

An isolate of the Roberts-Thompson strain of *G. muris* was obtained from H. H. Stibbs, Waterborne Inc. *G. duodenalis* cysts from symptomatic human excretors were purified from stools submitted to the SPDL.

Conjugation of anti-*G. muris* MAb to Texas Red

The anti-G. *muris* MAb was conjugated to TR using a modified version of the method described by Titus *et al.*, (1981).

Antibody Labelling of Sewage Samples

Sewage concentrates were dual-labelled using the FITC-conjugated anti-*Giardia* spp. MAb and the TR-conjugated anti-*G. muris* MAb at optimal assay concentrations (Paton *et al.*, 1994).

Microscopy

Dual-labelled samples were examined using an Olympus BH-2 epifluorescence microscope equipped with a blue filter block for visualisation of FITC (480 nm excitation; 520 nm emission) and a green filter block for visualisation of TR (545 nm excitation; >590 nm emission) to determine the number of *G. muris* and *G. duodenalis*-type cysts present in each sample. Each sample presumed to be positive for *G. muris* (i.e. with red rim fluorescence) when examined under the green filter block was then examined under an interference yellow filter block for visualisation of TR (565 nm excitation; >610 nm emission). Cyst fluorescence was scored positive (+), dubious (+/-), or negative (-) for each fluorochrome.

Confirmation of *G. muris* Positive Samples

An aliquot of the sample which contained 2 *G. muris* cysts was labelled with the same anti-*G. muris* specific MAb conjugated to FITC and examined under the blue filter block of an Olympus BH-2 epifluorescence microscope.

Results

Controls

The FITC-conjugated anti-*Giardia* spp. MAb reacted with *G. duodenalis* and *G. muris* cysts. The TR-conjugated anti-*G. muris* MAb reacted with *G. muris* cysts but not with *G. duodenalis* cysts at the concentrations used.

Sewage samples

Forty eight influent and effluent sewage samples collected from 6 treatment works were labelled using the FITC-conjugated anti-*Giardia* spp. MAb and the TR-conjugated anti-*G. muris* MAb.

Thirty five out of 48 samples (73%) were positive for cysts. Twelve of the 35 samples (34%) contained *G. duodenalis*-type cysts (FITC only) but no *G. muris* cysts. The remaining 23 samples (66%) contained *G. duodenalis*-type cysts together with cysts which had either a strong TR rim fluorescence (n = 2 (9%); possibly *G. muris* cysts) or a weak TR rim fluorescence (n = 21 (91%); too weak to be considered dual-labelled *G. muris* cysts).

These 23 samples which contained either strong or weak dual-labelled cysts were re-labelled and examined under the interference yellow filter block.

Under the interference yellow filter block 20 out of 23 samples (87%) were positive for cysts. Thirteen of the 20 samples (65%) contained *G. duodenalis*-type cysts but no *G. muris* cysts, 6 samples (30%) contained *G. duodenalis*-type cysts (FITC only) together with cysts which had a weak TR rim fluorescence (too weak to be considered dual-labelled *G. muris* cysts). One sample, No. 3, [5% (table)] contained one cyst which had a strong TR rim fluorescence (possible *G. muris* cyst) and another which had a weak TR rim fluorescence (too weak to be considered a dual-labelled *G. muris* cyst).

Table. Samples labelled with the FITC-conjugated anti-*Giardia* app. MAb and the TR-conjugated anti-*G. muris* MAb, and examined under the interference yellow filter block.

Sample No.& Date	Sample Type	Total No cysts detected (FITC)	Dual Label TR-	TR+/-	TR+
(3) 15/6/94	Raw (E)	16	14	1	1
(8) 15/6/94	Raw (S)	49	48	1	-
(11) 15/6/94	Raw (E)	24	24	-	-
(17) 2/6/94	Raw (E)	5	5	-	-
(26) 4/6/94	Raw (S)	8	7	1	-
(30) 5/6/94	Raw (S)	6	5	1	-
(38) 7/6/94	Raw (S)	4	4	-	-
(51) 18/5/94	Raw (E)	19	18	1	-
(57) 2/5/94	Raw (S)	5	2	3	-
(60) 3/5/94	Raw (E)	3	3	-	-
(66) 4/5/94	Effluent (E)	4	4	-	-
(68) 9/5/94	Raw (E)	8	8	-	-
(70) 10/5/94	Raw (E)	3	3	-	-
(72) 10/5/94	Effluent (E)	10	10	-	-
(77) 11/5/94	Effluent (S)	32	32	-	-
(79) 12/5/94	Raw (S)	8	8	-	-
(81) 12/5/94	Effluent (S)	17	17	-	-
(83) 14/4/94	Raw (S)	14	14	-	-
(85) 14/4/94	Raw (S)	8	7	1	-
(88) 14/4/94	Raw (E)	2	2	-	-

KEY: (S) = Sucrose flotation; (E) = Ether sedimentation; (TR+) = Strong TR fluorescence of cysts; (TR+/-) = Weak TR fluorescence of cysts; (TR-) = No TR fluorescence of cysts

A further aliquot of sample No. 3 was analysed and, again, one cyst (possible *G. muris*) with a strong TR rim fluorescence (7.5 x 9m) was observed (760/L *G. duodenalis*-type cysts and 20/L *G. muris* cysts). This sample of raw sewage was collected from a sewage works within an urban community. The works serves a population of 331,333 and the effluent is discharged into a major river in the West of Scotland.

Analysis of a further aliquot of sample No. 3 labelled with the anti-*G. muris* MAb conjugated to FITC failed to reveal further fluorescent cysts. Ten randomly selected samples (all containing "dubious" TR-positive (+/-) cysts) were labelled with the FITC-conjugated anti-*G. muris* MAb, but no fluorescent cysts were observed.

Discussion

G. muris cysts do not occur frequently in the sewage works sampled for this study. One sample of raw sewage contained two cysts which dual-labelling experiments indicated as being *G. muris*. The presence of further *G. muris* cysts could not be confirmed on subsequent re-analysis using the same anti-*G. muris* specific MAb labelled with FITC. This could be because of the paucity of *G. muris* cysts.

In dual labelling experiments, both Evans Blue and FITC conjugates can interfere with the signal emissions of Texas Red conjugates (Paton *et al.*, 1994). Evans Blue should therefore not be used in this dual-labelling study. The FITC interference could account for the high numbers of "dubious" *G. muris* cysts observed using the green filter block. An interference yellow filter block is recommended for separating TR and FITC emissions.

This reduced the signal crossover of FITC emissions when assessing TR binding to cysts, and decreased the number of encounters with "dubious" (+/-) TR conjugated anti-*G. muris* MAb-labelled cysts. Bandpass filters would increase TR emission specificity further.

It is possible to dual label *G. muris* cysts with a genus specific FITC-conjugated anti-*Giardia* MAb and a species specific TR MAb. This results in a decrease in FITC visualisation in 90% of the cysts detected Paton *et al.*, 1994), although these dual-labelled cysts are still readably detectable by FITC fluorescence. However, it does provide a method for distinguishing between and enumerating the occurrence of *G. duodenalis*-type cysts and *G. muris* cysts simultaneously in environmental samples.

Acknowledgements

We would like to thank Strathclyde Regional Council Department of Sewerage for their co-operation, and John Bradsure of Bradsure Biologicals for supplying the FITC-conjugated anti-*Giardia* spp. MAb without Evans Blue.

References

Filice, F.P. (1952). Studies on the cytology and life history of a *Giardia* from the laboratory rat. University of California Publication in Zoology 57, 53-146

Paton, C.A., Campbell, A.T., Robertson, L.J., Stibbs, H.H. and Smith, H.V. (1994). Development of a dual label for identification of *Giardia* cysts at a species level (abstract). Transactions of the Royal society for Tropical Medicine and Hygiene. In press

Stibbs, H. H. (1993). Detection and differentiation of G. lamblia and *G. muris* cysts in surface water by immunofluorescence flow cytometry. Proceedings of the Joint Annual Meeting of the American Society of Tropical Medicine and Hygiene and the American Society of Parasitologists. October/November 1993, Abstract 663

Thompson, R.C.A., Reynoldson, J.A., and Mendis A.H.W. (1993). *Giardia* and Giardiasis. Advances in Parasitology 32, 71-160

Titus, J.A., Haugland, R., Sharrow, S.O., and Segal, D.M. (1982). Texas Red, a hydrophilic, red-emitting fluorophore for use with fluorescein in dual parameter flow microfluorometric and fluorescence microscopic studies. Journal of Immunological Methods 50, 193-204

Development of a *Cryptosporidium* Proficiency Scheme

C. Thompson, B. May and D. Corscadden
LEAP Scheme Yorkshire Environmental, Eccup Moor Road, Leeds LS17 7RJ, UK

Introduction

Yorkshire Environmental (prior to 1989, Yorkshire Water Authority) has run a monthly chemical proficiency scheme since 1974 which in 1992 became the LEAP (Laboratory Environmental Analysis Proficiency) Scheme. In 1987 the first microbiological proficiency scheme (coliform) was introduced. This was followed by Faecal streptococcus, colony counts at 37°C and colony counts at 22°C and finally *Cryptosporidium* in 1993.

The Standing Committee of Analysts (Anon 1990) have produced a 'Blue Book' method for the isolation and identification of *Cryptosporidium* oocysts using a Cuno Microwynd polypropylene (1 µm) filter. Section 8.3 on quality control states: 'The sample concentration and processing procedures should be validated by running experiments with 100 litre samples of water seeded with oocysts. The recovery of the seed should be close to 50% of the total inoculum, and not less than 30%.' A number of workers (Vesey and Slade 1991; Anon 1991; Le Chevallier *et al.* 1991) have reported significantly poorer recoveries of *Cryptosporidium* oocysts from waters using methods incorporating similar filters. (Typically 5 - 12%.)

The initial purpose of this proficiency scheme is to establish the typical results obtained by laboratories carrying out routine *Cryptosporidium* analysis using standard accepted methods over a significant time period. It was also hoped that examination of the results, at meetings of the participants, would indicate methods of improving the overall accuracy of the analysis.

Development of a *Cryptosporidium* Proficiency Scheme

In 1993 a bi-monthly *Cryptosporidium* proficiency scheme was instituted. It consisted of two samples seeded with oocysts from the Moredun Institute:

Sample A which was a 0.5 ml phosphate buffered saline (PBS) seeded sample inoculated with a *Cryptosporidium* suspension. Four 10 µl individual counts were requested from each laboratory.

Sample B which was a Cuno Microwynd polypropylene (1µm) cartridge filter. Ten litres of tap water were inoculated with a known number of oocysts. The resulting oocyst suspension was then passed through the filter. The procedure was then repeated for each filter.

Alternative Sample B which was a PBS oocyst suspension. The participant added this to 10 litres of their tap water and mixed it thoroughly. This was then filtered through a membrane filter. The oocysts subsequently being eluted from the filter.

Initially the alternative Sample B was a 10 litre tap water sample inoculated with oocysts.

This was changed in February 1994 (from Exercise C1) to a concentrated PBS suspension because of transport difficulties with 10 litre samples. Participants were requested to count all oocysts observed with or without sutures. All prepared samples were prepared on a Friday stored for two days over the weekend at less than 8°C and then distributed to all participants on the same day (Monday).

It is felt that because of the inherent variability of microbiological techniques for both the preparation of and determination of parasite samples, the results for a laboratory should be judged over a number of exercises rather than individual exercises. Isolated failures may not be of any real significance.

Potential Errors

Table 1 lists a number of potential errors that can occur in the determination of *Cryptosporidium* in raw and potable waters. Most potential errors will result in a negative bias. However there have been a number of real life instances of positive bias from mis-identification of *Cryptosporidium*-like bodies (CLB's). To date no attempt has been made to circulate a sample containing known CLB's, although an exercise is planned.

The relatively large number of potential errors in the determination of *Cryptosporidium* in typical waters (and especially raw waters) would indicate that routine analysis of *Cryptosporidium* is likely to be fraught with errors (Vesey and Slade 1991; Anon 1991; Le Chevallier *et al.* 1991). The initial results from the LEAP Scheme exercises would appear to substantiate this conclusion.

Table 1 Potential Errors in the Determination of *Cryptosporidium* in Waters

1	Filtration efficiency
2	Filter manufacture reproducibility
3	Pressure/rate of filtration
4	Elution step from filter
5	Clean up step
6	Concentration step
7	Staining step (including shedding and/or destruction of epitopes during storage or sample processing)
8	Identification step
9	Counting step

Results and Discussion

Stability and Reproducibility of the P B S Suspension (Sample A)

A suspension of Cryptosporidium oocysts was prepared in PBS. The oocyst concentration in the suspension was counted. The initial count of 4 x 10 µl aliquots was 11, 11, 8 and 14 with a mean of 11.0 oocysts in 10 µl. The suspension was mixed thoroughly and dispensed in 1 ml volumes into 10 sterile Universal containers. Containers were stored at < 8°C and at regular intervals 10 µl was removed from each container, stained and counted. The results clearly demonstrated that the daily means of 10 µl aliquots taken from the 10 replicates do not demonstrate any significant decrease in the number of oocysts detected over 27 days. (Range 9.9 - 12.5/10 µl). The mean counts for each replicate over the 27 days also appear to be consistent. (Range 9.6 - 12.7/10 µl).

Table 2 Summary of Results for Sample A

Exercise Number	Number of Labs	Expected Number of Oocysts per 10 µl	Pooled Mean Oocysts per 10 µl	Pooled Standard Deviation Oocysts per 10 µl	Range of Laboratory Means Oocysts per 10 µl
3	4	8.8	9.3	5.1	8.0 - 13.0
4	4	352	285	15.2	93 - 334
5	3	5	3.9	0.33	2.5 - 5.2
6	6	40	38.8*	12.8*	27.3 - 56.6*
7	7	20	11.2	6.2	2.0 - 17.7
8**	6	25	13.4	9.2	0.25 - 22.8
C1	9	18.5	8.6	7.4	0 - 19.9
C2	9	21	11.1	9.6	0 - 27.0
C3	8	54	28.8	16.2	9.0 - 54.4
C4	8	5.5	6.0	3.1	2.2 - 11.5

Notes: * = After exclusion of outlier ** = Raw water concentrate matrix

Table 2 summarises the raw data for the circulated Sample A for both 1993 and 1994 to date. It can be seen that there was a significant variation between laboratories. The very low and zero results give cause for concern. Laboratories that obtain a significant number of low results should examine their procedures.

In general reasonable agreement was observed between results from different analysts in the same laboratory or replicate determinations by the same analyst. However a number of these duplicate in-house results did show significant (GT 50%) variations. Further within-laboratory testing is recommended.

Reproducibility of Seeding and Subsequent Analysis of Cuno Microwynd Filters

Ten Cuno Microwynd filters were seeded with 9600 oocysts contained in 10 litres of tap water using a pressure of 10 psig with a flow restrictor valve. The filters were then analysed following the standard analysis procedure. Two of the filters were processed after 2 days storage. A further 6 were processed after 9 days storage. The processing of the remaining 2 filters took place over 4 days, starting on day 6. The filtrates of all the filters were analysed on the day of filtration.

The percentage of oocysts retained by the filter ranged from 68 - 99%. It is generally accepted that the efficiency of filtration (but not elution) will increase with the filtrate volume of sample (i.e. as the pores block up). In practice sample volumes of 100-500 litres would normally be used. Vesey and Slade, 1991 reported that 5 - 30% of oocysts passed through a Microwynd filter cartridge. Another report (Anon 1991) quoted a figure of 15 ± 4%. These two figures are similar to that found in this study. (15 ±11%).

The overall percentage recoveries for each filter ranged from LT 0.3 to 10.9% with a mean recovery of 4.2 %. The variability of overall recovery for *Cryptosporidium* was a cause of concern. Possibly a delay in commencing the analysis may cause a decrease in recovery, but further work is required to confirm if storage of the filters adversely affects the recovery. Other workers have reported recoveries of *Cryptosporidium* oocysts from Microwynd filters of 13% (Anon 1991) and 5.8% (Le Chevallier 1991). It has been suggested (Clark, personal communication) that the epitopes recognised by most commercially available monoclonal antibodies are readily shed from the oocysts and this will obviously result in low recoveries. Vesey and Slade (1991) have suggested that the relevant epitopes are damaged by shear forces generated during centrifugation.

Recovery from the Circulated Cuno Microwynd Filters

The percentage recoveries obtained by each participant in 1994 are given in Table 3. All results relate to the actual number of oocysts in the 10 litre sample prior to filtration through the Microwynd filter. No correction factor for filtration efficiency has been used. Thus the results relate to overall efficiency of the *Cryptosporidium* determination. This is considered to be the key parameter to be determined. The mean recovery was 4.3 % with a standard deviation of 4.7%.

Table 3 Percentage Recovery for Seeded Cuno Filters (Jan - Aug 1994)

		Percentage	Recovery	(%)	
Exercise Number		C1	C2	C3	C4
No. of Oocysts/filter		9937	4300	5400	5000
Laboratory	Method of Analysis				
10	(FC)	37	14.5	9.3	58
27	(M)	1.8	3.2	9.4	9.0
29	(M)	7	LT 0.1	0.2	4.3
35	(M)	LT 0.1	4.6	0.2	0
37	(M)	24	LT 0.1	0.9	27
40	(M)	5.4	2.1	4.2	1.9
40	(FC)	---	2.1	3.7	---
42	(M)	1.1	0.3	2.3	2.8
43	(M)	2.2	LT 0.1	0.7	3
Leap Result	(M)	16.8	11.9	8.8	14

(M) = Microscopy (FC) = Flow Cytometry

A recent blind trial in the USA (Clancey *et al.* 1994) gave a mean recovery for *Cryptosporidium* oocysts from a supplied filter of 2.8% for the 4 out of the 16 laboratories that managed to detect *Cryptosporidium* oocysts. In general the overall recoveries from the Cuno Microwynd filters were very variable. It is recommended that laboratories that consistently obtained low recoveries should closely examine their procedures.

Recovery from Membrane Filters

Some preliminary tests have been carried out on the overall recovery from 142 mm 1.2 μm cellulose nitrate filters. The LEAP scheme organisers obtained a mean percentage recovery of 24.0% (Range 7.2 - 46.2%) with a standard deviation of 14.5%. During 1994 the scheme participants obtained a mean value of 22.4% (Range 0.6 - 77.0%) with a standard deviation of 24.4%. The recoveries were highly variable. Discussions of the participants highlighted the fact that there was a significant variation in the method of eluting the oocysts from the filters. Also there were some differences of results between analysts in a given laboratory following the documented method in use.

Conclusions

1 After the first year of the proficiency scheme it would appear that further validation work is required. Lower seeding levels are to be tried.
2 The overall recoveries using Microwynd filters are considered poor. This technique does not appear to be very robust. The overall recoveries quoted in reference 1 (the SCA Blue Book) for cartridge filters would appear to be somewhat optimistic.
3 Membrane filters gave better recoveries than the Microwynd cartridge filters. However the overall recoveries for both filters were very variable. It is recommended that a standard agreed elution procedure is agreed between participating laboratories.
4 Laboratories that consistently obtain poor results should examine their procedures.
5 Efforts should be made to test the reproducibility between analysts in a given laboratory as well as between different laboratories.
6 The LEAP Scheme would welcome any suggestions or comments on how the Scheme could be improved.

References

Anon. Isolation and identification of Giardia cysts, *Cryptosporidium* oocysts and free living pathogenic amoebae in water etc. 1989, HMSO, 1990

Anon. Recovery of *Cryptosporidium* from water, Report, FR0189, Foundation for Water Research, March 1991

Clancy. J.L., Gollnitz, W. D., and Tabib, Z., JAWWA, 1994, 86, 89

Clark, S., Personal communication (CAMR Porton Down)

Le Chevallier, M. W., Norton, W.D., and Lee, R.G., Evaluation of a method to detect Giardia and *Cryptosporidium* in Water, 'Monitoring Water in the 1990s' : Meeting New Challenges, ASTM STP 1102, Hall, J.R., and Glysson, G.D., Eds ASTM, 1991

Vesey, G. and Slade, J., Wat. Sci. Tech., 1991, 24, 165

Plant Optimization using Particle Counting for Treatment of *Giardia* and *Cryptosporidium*

M.W. LeChevallier and W.D. Norton
American Water Works Service Company, Inc. 1025 Laurel Oak Rd, Voorhees, NJ 08045 USA

Introduction

The use of particle counting and sizing provides water operators with a powerful tool to fine tune treatment plant performance and ensure maximal protection from waterborne protozoan disease. The level of treatment provided by a water supplier should be commensurate with the level of contamination of the raw water supply. To determine the source water levels of *Giardia* and *Cryptosporidium*, a monitoring program must be conducted to evaluate the occurrence and variation in cyst and oocyst densities. Once these values are obtained, the appropriate level of treatment can be computed to achieve a predetermined level of microbial safety. Particle counting can be a convenient, rapid, on-line method to monitor treatment processes and optimize plant operations for maximum cyst and oocyst removal.

This report describes the results of a five-year survey of *Giardia* and *Cryptosporidium* levels in 63 surface water sites located in the Midwestern United States. Concurrent with the protozoan analyses, particle count data were collected from raw and settled water, the effluent of each individual filter, and the combined plant effluent. Analysis of the data shows that particle counting can be used to predict the removal of cysts and oocysts within the treatment process. Optimization of treatment processes for particle count removal can reduce the reliance on chemical inactivation and the potential formation of disinfection by-products.

Materials and Methods

Sample Collection

Samples were collected from 67 surface water treatment plants that withdraw water from 63 surface water locations in 14 states. Raw water samples were typically collected from pressurized taps at the intake to the treatment process. Samples for *Giardia* and *Cryptosporidium* were filtered through 10-in. (inch) (25.4 cm[centimeter]) wound polypropylene cartridge filters having a nominal porosity of 1µm (Memtek Corp., Timonium, MD, Cat. #U1A10U). Flow rates averaged 4.5 L/min and ranged from 0.18 - 18.5 L/min. The total volume collected averaged 499 L and ranged from 86.6 - 3,394 L. Samples were processed by the immunofluorescence method as previously described (ASTM, 1991; LeChevallier *et al.*, 1992b). Plant effluent samples used a separate sampling system and chlorine residuals were neutralized prior to filtration through injection of a sodium thiosulfate solution using a Dema in-line injector (Dema Engineering Co., St. Louis). Flow rates averaged 4.5 L/min and ranged from 0.59 - 11.82 L/min. The total volume collected averaged 3,863 L and ranged from 378 - 7,862 L.

The recovery efficiency of the procedure was evaluated by spiking 151 L samples with known concentrations of cysts and oocysts. For tap water samples (turbidity <1 NTU), the geometric mean for recovery of *Giardia* cysts was 42.4 percent (range, 18.2 - 118.3%; n=58) and the geometric mean for recovery of *Cryptosporidium* oocysts was 23.6 percent (range, 8.7 - 74.7%; n=57). To simulate raw water samples, filter concentrates were added to tap water to achieve a 150 NTU solution. The geometric mean for recovery of *Giardia* cysts from the high turbidity solution was 50.1 percent (range, 36.7 - 75.3%; n=5) and the geometric mean for recovery of *Cryptosporidium* oocysts was 40.9 percent (range, 34.5 - 59.3%; n=6).

Densities of cysts and oocysts were reported as the number per liter for surface water and number per 100 L for plant effluent water. When parasites were not detected, the parasite level was reported as less than the detection limit. The geometric mean of the detection limit was 0.99 organisms/L (range 0.004 - 42 cysts/L) for raw water, and 1.79 organisms/100 L (range 0.02 - 52 organisms/100 L) for plant effluent water. Unless stated differently, total cyst and oocyst counts are presented, and values are not adjusted to reflect recovery efficiencies.

Particle Counts

Concurrent with the testing for *Giardia* and *Cryptosporidium*, particle count data were collected from the raw water, settled water (from each basin, if more than one), each individual filter effluent, and the plant effluent. Particle counting and sizing was performed using a Hiac/Royco model 8000A particle counter equipped with a HRLD-150 sensor and the Automatic Bottle Sampler (Pacific Scientific, Silver Springs, MD). Particle counts were determined by calculating the average count/mL from triplicate 25-mL volumes.

Samples were collected in pre-rinsed plastic bottles and shipped by overnight courier to the Belleville Lab for analysis. The plastic bottle produced an insignificant number of particles in the size range of interest (particle counts >3 μm were 1.68/mL for plastic bottles compared to 1.03/mL for glass bottles). Quality assurance data indicated that there was no significant change in particle count data for raw, settled or filter effluent samples, even when stored for 5 days. Particle counts were performed in the following size (in μm) ranges: 1-3, 3-5, 5-7, 7- 10, 10-15, 15-20, 20-40, >40. The particle counter was recalibrated by the manufacturer every 6 months and checked with each use using 3.0 and 9.8 μm latex beads. Samples were processed cleanest (plant effluent) to dirtiest (raw) and with a rinse of particle-free water in between each sample. Dilutions were typically made on raw and settled water with filtered, reagent-grade water. Particle counts were collected as grab-samples but could be related to filter performance by noting the length of the filter run (in hours) when the sample was collected.

Data Analysis

The data from the two-year biannual monitoring (from March, 1991 to January, 1993) was combined with a previous dataset (October, 1988 to June, 1990) collected from the same systems (LeChevallier *et al.*, 1991a, 1991b). Therefore, most systems (94%) had five or more analyses performed on both raw and plant effluent samples.

Results and Discussion

Giardia and *Cryptosporidium* Levels

Giardia were detected in 118 of the 262 (45.0 percent) of the raw water samples collected between March, 1991 and January, 1993. The geometric mean of (detectable) *Giardia* was 2.0 cysts/L with levels ranging from 0.02 to 43.8 cysts/L. *Cryptosporidium* were detected in 135 of the 262 (51.5 percent) of the raw water samples collected between March, 1991 and January, 1993. The geometric mean of (detectable) *Cryptosporidium* was 2.4 oocysts/L with levels ranging from 0.065 to 65.1 oocysts/L. A total of 183 samples (69.8 percent) were positive for either *Giardia* (47), *Cryptosporidium* (65), or both (71).

When the data from this study (n=262) are combined with the previous investigation (LeChevallier *et al.*, 1991a, 1991b)(n=85), the occurrence of *Giardia* and *Cryptosporidium* in 347 samples was 53.9 percent and 60.2 percent, respectively. These values are consistent with the findings of other investigators (Ongerth and Stibbs, 1987; Poulton *et al.*, 1992;

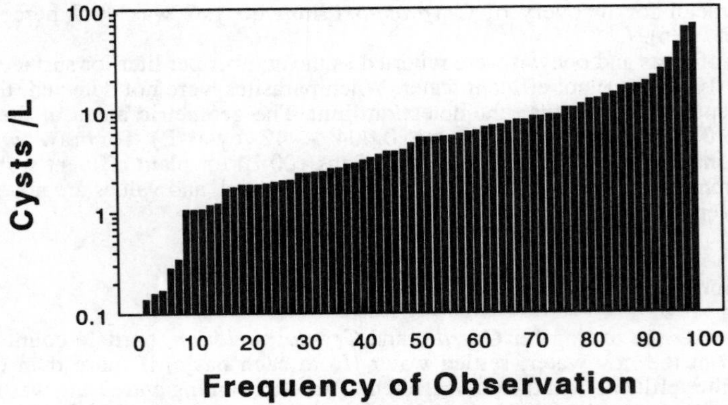

Figure 1. Distribution of Maximum *Giardia* Levels Observed at the 63 Sites Tested.

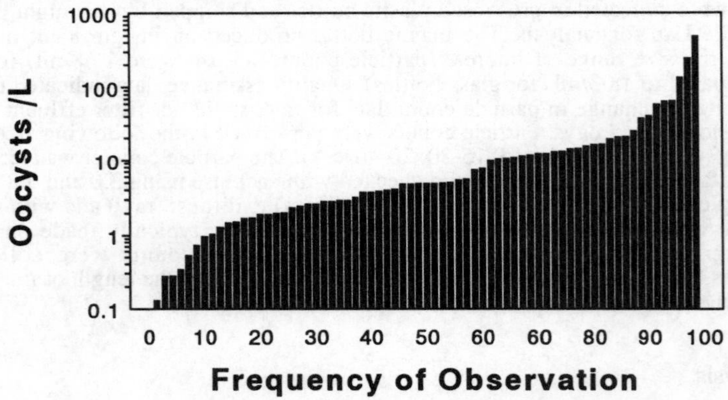

Figure 2. Distribution of Maximum *Cryptosporidium* Levels Observed at the 63 Sites Tested.

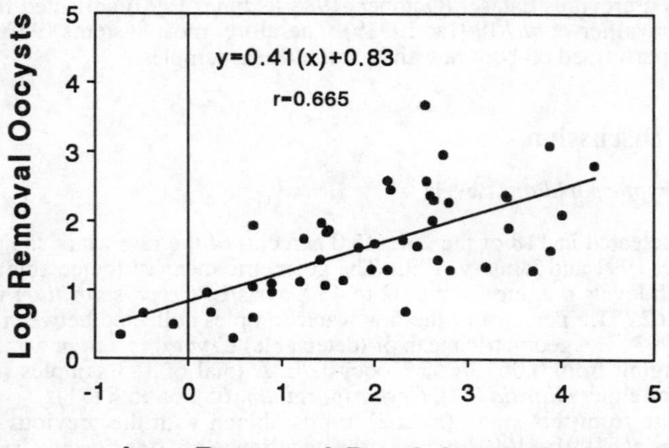

Figure 3. Relationship Between Removal of *Cryptosporidium* and Particles >3 μm.

Boutros, 1989; Hansen *et al.*, 1991; Rose, 1988). Ongerth (1989) reported detecting *Giardia* cysts in 43 percent of 222 samples collected from 17 sampling stations on three Pacific Northwest rivers. Rose *et al.* (1991) recovered *Cryptosporidium* oocysts in 51.4 percent of 111 surface water samples collected in 13 states.

Figures 1 and 2 show that maximum level of cysts and oocysts in raw water for each site tested. Because water utilities must provide a sufficient level of treatment to ensure the safety of potable supplies, the maximum count helps define the level of treatment needed to provide microbially-safe water. The median level of cysts and oocysts was 5/L (Figures 1 and 2). Using risk analysis models for *Giardia* and *Cryptosporidium* (Rose *et al.*, 1991, Haas 1994), it can be calculated that the average utility would need to provide 5.85 and 4.95 $\log_{10}$ treatment for *Giardia* and *Cryptosporidium*, respectively.

Particle Counting

The fundamental purpose of water treatment processes with regard to particle removal is the reduction of pathogenic microorganisms or particles that could shield microorganisms from disinfection. As a surrogate for microorganisms and particulates, turbidity levels were assigned a health-based standard through the promulgation of a maximum contaminant level (MCL). With the development of reliable particle counting technology, it is widely recognized that particle counts are a more sensitive measure of filter performance (Beard *et al.*, 1977; Tate *et al.*, 1978; Teefy, 1991; Hargesheimer *et al.*, 1992).

The relationship between reduction in particle counts and *Giardia* and *Cryptosporidium* in natural waters has not been widely studied. Studies using spiked cysts and oocysts in pilot plant trials have yielded mixed results. Some investigators have reported good relationships between particle count reductions and parasite reductions (Teefy, 1991; Nieminski, 1992), while other researchers have observed poor correlations between the two parameters (Hendricks *et al.*, 1984; Schuler *et al.*, 1991). Spiked studies, however, are replete with potential pitfalls and methodological differences can probably explain much of the variation.

In the only published studies to date comparing the removal of naturally-occurring cysts and oocysts with particle count reductions for four full-scale treatment plants, LeChevallier *et al.* (1991c) and LeChevallier and Norton (1992a) found significant correlations between reduction of particle counts (>5 µm) and *Giardia* and *Cryptosporidium*. By collecting particle count data along with the *Giardia* and *Cryptosporidium* testing in this study, the relationship between particle counts and parasite removals could be extended to a larger number of water systems.

Figure 3 shows a statistically significant relationship ($p<0.01$; $n=46$) between removal of *Cryptosporidium* oocysts and particle counts >3 µm for data collected from 22 plants. For this analysis the dataset was limited to only those occasions when *Cryptosporidium* was observed in the raw water and either settled water or plant effluent samples, and when particle count examinations were performed. The >3 µm size range was chosen because it would encompass both *Giardia* and *Cryptosporidium* sized particles (on-going research is examining other size categories). The relationship between particle count reductions (>3 µm) and *Giardia* cyst removal is presented in Figure 4. The data, collected from raw, settled and finished water at 14 plants, shows a statistically significant ($p<0.01$; $n=40$) relationship between removal of particle counts >3 µm, and *Giardia* cysts.

Although the data in Figures 3 and 4 show a significant correlation between the parasites and particle counts, the slope of the best-fit regression line does not suggest a 1:1 relationship. To further investigate the relationship between particle count reductions and treatment of *Cryptosporidium*, a ratio of $\log_{10}$ reduction in particle counts to $\log_{10}$ reduction in oocysts was developed (Figure 5). Ideally, if the reduction in particle counts corresponded exactly with reductions in *Cryptosporidium* levels, the ratio would be 1.0. Figure 5 shows that nearly 70 percent of the samples ranged between a ratio of 0.8 and 1.6, with a mean of 1.2. The ratio of particle count and *Giardia* removals in showed a similar 1.2 ratio (data not shown).

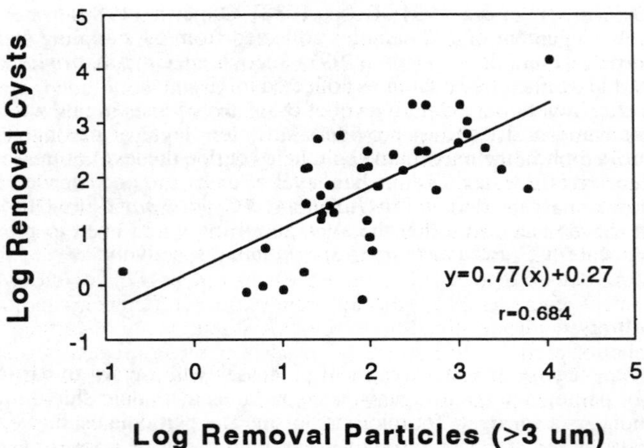

Figure 4. Relationship Between Removal of *Giardia* and Particles >3 μm.

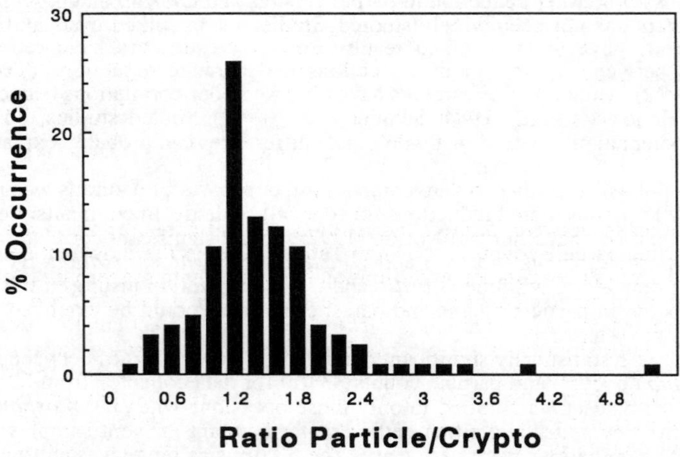

Figure 5. Ratio of the Log_{10} Removal of Particles (>3 μm) and *Cryptosporidium*. The limit of detection was used to calculate the oocyst effluent water value.

The reasons for the variation in results are numerous, and most obvious is the accuracy of the parasite assay, where recovery efficiencies averaged between 24 and 42 percent. In addition, between 64 and 81 percent of the raw and plant effluent counts were based on observing 1 or 2 organisms in the sample. Therefore, the statistical confidence intervals for these values are large (between 5 and 10 fold).

Although the measurement of particle counts is very accurate, the assumption that the difference in counts between the raw water and plant effluent is indicative of treatment performance may not always be valid. It must be recognized that measurement of particles in raw and treated effluents does not determine the "removal" of the particles, but is the net result of both the removal of raw water particulates and the generation of particles within the treatment process. For example, coagulation and flocculation may aggregate small particles into larger, *Giardia*-sized, particles. Therefore, the difference between raw and filtered particle counts in the size range of a *Giardia* cyst, may be impacted by aggregates of smaller particles. Ginn *et al.* (1992) presented a theoretical model describing detachment of aggregated particles from filter media. The authors concluded that particle size distribution data was controlled by filter detachment mechanisms. Not considered, however, was the possibility that penetration of cysts and oocysts through filter media may also be controlled by detachment mechanisms. Additionally, particulates associated with treatment chemicals (lime, soda ash, powdered activated carbon, hydrofluosilicic acid, etc.) may also alter apparent "removal" efficiencies. Plants that employ biologically active filtration may have increased effluent particle counts in the 1-3 µm range due to bacterial growth within the filter beds (Goldgrabe *et al.*, 1992). Recycle of washwater can result in higher cyst and oocyst levels within the treatment process (Cornwell *et al.*, 1993). The point is, treatment processes may affect apparent removal efficiencies and that these factors need to be addressed when evaluating the regulatory application of particle counting.

If the number of particles originating within the treatment process is small, or unrelated to the *Giardia* or *Cryptosporidium* size range (as in biologically active filters), compared to the number of particles in the raw water, then the overall impact on the apparent removal efficiency may be unimportant. However, if the number of particles in the raw water is low, or if the generation of particles within the treatment process is significant (as in lime, or powdered activated carbon addition), then the relationship between removal of *Giardia* and *Cryptosporidium* and apparent particle count removals may be skewed.

Table 1. Relationship Between Removal of Particle Counts and Parasites in Various Waters

Log_{10} Raw Water Particle Range	Avg Raw Water Turbidity	N	Log_{10} Particle Reduction by Sedimentation	Log_{10} Particle Reduction by Filtration	Log_{10} Reduction Cysts	Log_{10} Reduction Oocysts
1.5 - 3.5	1.6	29	-0.13	1.91	1.40	1.38
3.5 - 4.0	6.9	50	0.01	2.23	1.87	1.84
4.0 - 4.5	6.6	61	0.38	2.61	1.98	1.97
4.5 - 5.0	18	50	0.80	3.05	1.99	1.99
>5.0	55	49	1.35	3.55	2.20	2.30

The relationship between particle count removals and parasites for raw water having different starting particle counts is shown in Table 1. The results show that better removals are achieved through coagulation and filtration for waters with higher initial particle count levels. These high particle count waters also tended to have higher cyst and oocyst counts, and therefore better parasite removals. The ratio of particle count to parasite removal tended to increase slightly in waters with higher raw water particle counts, indicating a probable loss of sensitivity for cysts and oocysts due to interference by debris in the sample. Although there is little reason to suggest that the relationship between removal of particles and parasites change at higher densities, the impact of particles generated within the treatment process is more severe at lower particle count levels. Specifically, systems with low turbidity (i.e. <7 NTU), low particle count raw water may not be given the same treatment credit as high turbidity, high particle count systems because generation of particles within the treatment process prevents the low particle count systems from demonstrating a 2, 3, or 4 log reduction in particle counts. While further research is necessary to elucidate the relationship between low levels of parasites and particle counts, this uncertainty over the interpretation of the results should not stop water utilities from attempting to optimize treatment processes for maximum particle count removal.

Given the errors associated with parasite measurements and the interpretation of particle count data, the general assumption of a 1:1 (or conservatively, a 1.2:1) relationship between particle count and parasite removal appears to be justified. On-going research will attempt to further clarify this relationship further.

Average particle count removals for each surface water treatment plant studied was based on four replicate analyses. Overall, the 67 plants averaged 2.7 log_{10} removal of particles >3.0 µm (Figure 6). Importantly, data from Figure 6 indicate that 61.3 percent of the plants exceeded the 2.5 log_{10} removal credit assigned by the SWTR (USEPA, 1989) and 36.8 percent exceeded 3.0 log_{10} removal of particles >3 µm. Documentation of plant

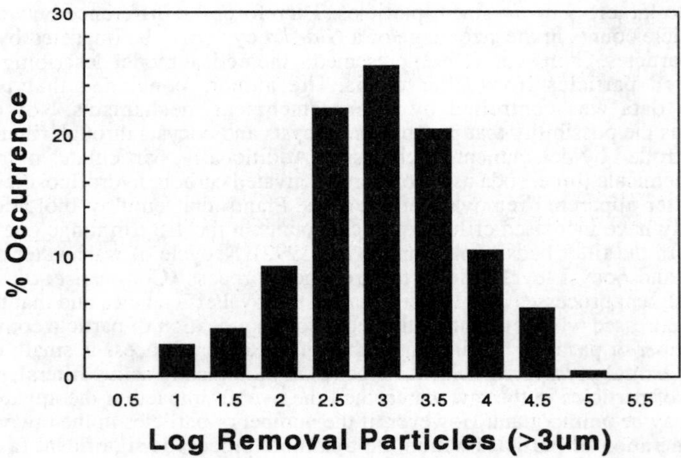

Figure 6. Histogram of Treatment Plant Performance for Particle Count Removal.

performance using particle count analysis will be helpful for demonstrating increased treatment credit.

The impact of water temperature on particle removal is shown in Table 2. Plant performance for particle count removal increased more than 2-fold (0.32 $\log_{10}$) when water temperature increased from 5°C to >20°C. Interestingly, the variation in plant performance (the difference between the average filter performance and the filter producing the lowest level of particle count removal) increased 56 percent with increasing water temperature. Efforts to improve overall plant performance for particle removal will also need to focus on reducing the variation between individual filters.

Table 2. Effect of Temperature on Treatment Plant Performance for Particle Removal

Temperature °C	N	$\log_{10}$ Removal of Particles >3 µm	Variation
1 - 5	32	2.58	0.64
5 - 10	43	2.63	0.66
10 - 15	43	2.78	0.78
15 - 20	42	2.65	0.73
20 - 25	48	2.90	0.80
25 - 30	23	2.86	1.00

The variation was calculated as the difference between the average $\log_{10}$ removal of particles >3µm, and the maximum value for each temperature range.

Conclusions

The concentrations of *Giardia* and *Cryptosporidium* in many surface water supplies are sufficient to require careful monitoring of treatment plant operations to ensure the safety of potable supplies. Particle counting is a rapid and sensitive surrogate for predicting cyst and oocyst removal. The results of this study show that the average system achieved a 2.7 $\log_{10}$ removal of particles >3 µm. Future optimization of treatment process for particle removal should be able to produce removals >3.0 $\log_{10}$ particle removal.

Acknowledgements

This study was funded by the American Water System, Voorhees, New Jersey, USA.

References

ASTM. 1991. Proposed test method for *Giardia* cysts and *Cryptosporidium* oocysts in low-turbidity water by a fluorescent antibody procedure. Ann. Book of ASTM Standards 11.01:925-935

Beard, J. D. and T. S. Tanaka. 1977. A comparison of particle counting and nephelometry. J. Amer. Water Works Assoc. 69:533-538

Boutros, S. N. 1989. Sampling and Analysis for *Cryptosporidium* in PA Public Surface Water Supply Sources, Report to Pennsylvania division of water supply, Harrisburg, PA

Cornwell, D. A. and R. G. Lee. 1993. Recycle Stream Effects on Water Treatment, AWWA Research Foundation, Denver, CO

Ginn, T. M., A. Amirtharajah, and P. R. Karr. 1992. Effects of particle detachment in granular-media filtration. J. Amer. Water Works Assoc. 84(2):66-76

Goldgrabe, J. C., R. S. Summers, R. J. Miltner, and K. R. Fox. 1992. Particle counting as a method of evaluating conventional and biological filter performance, p.1527-1557. In Proc. AWWA Water Quality Tech. Conf, Toronto, Ont

Haas, C. N. 1994. Personal Communication

Hansen, J. S. and J. E. Ongerth. 1991. Effects of time and watershed characteristics on the concentration of *Cryptosporidium* oocysts in river water. Appl. Environ. Microbiol. 57(10):2790-2795

Hargesheimer, E. E., C. M. Lewis, and C. M. Yentsch. 1992. Evaluation of Particle Counting as a Measure of Treatment Plant Performance, AWWA Research Foundation, Denver, CO

Hendricks, D. W., M. Y. Al-Ani, W. D. Bellamy, C. P. Hibler, and J. M. McElroy. 1984. Surrogate indicators of assessing removal of *Giardia* cysts, Proc. AWWA Water Quality Tech. Conf, Denver, CO

LeChevallier, M. W., W. D. Norton, and R. G. Lee. 1991a. Occurrence of *Giardia* and *Cryptosporidium* spp. in surface water supplies. Appl. Environ. Microbiol. 57(9):2610-2616

LeChevallier, M. W., W. D. Norton, and R. G. Lee. 1991b. *Giardia* and *Cryptosporidium* spp. in filtered drinking water supplies. Appl. Environ. Microbiol. 57(9):2617-2621

LeChevallier, M. W., W. D. Norton, R. G. Lee, and J. B. Rose. 1991c. *Giardia* and *Cryptosporidium* in Water, AWWA Research Foundation, Denver, CO

LeChevallier, M. W. and W. D. Norton. 1992a. Examining Relationships Between Particle Counts and *Giardia*, *Cryptosporidium*, and Turbidity. J. Amer. Water Works Assoc. 84(12):54-60

LeChevallier, M. W., W. D. Norton, and R. G. Lee. 1992b. Evaluation of a Method to Detect *Giardia* and *Cryptosporidium* in Water, p.483-498. In J. R. Hall and G. D. Glysson (eds.), Monitoring Water in the 199's: Meeting New Challenges, ASTM STP 1102, American Society for Testing and Materials, Philadelphia, PA

Nieminski, E. C. 1992. *Giardia & Cryptosporidium* - where do the cysts go? p.205-217. In Proc. AWWA Water Quality Tech. Conf, Toronto, Ont.

Ongerth, J. E. and H. H. Stibbs. 1987. Identification of *Cryptosporidium* oocysts in river water. Appl. Environ. Microbiol. 53:672-676

Ongerth, J. E. 1989. *Giardia* cyst concentrations in river water. J. Amer. Water Works Assoc. 81(9):81-86

Poulton, M. J., J. S. Colbourne, and J. B. Rose. 1992. *Cryptosporidium* monitoring in the UK and risk assessment, p.589-598. In Proc. AWWA Water Quality Tech. Conf, AWWA, Toronto, Ont

Rose, J. B. 1988. Occurrence and significance of *Cryptosporidium* in water. J. Amer. Water Works Assoc. 80(2):53-58

Rose, J. B., C. P. Gerba, and W. Jakubowski. 1991. Survey of potable water supplies for *Cryptosporidium* and *Giardia*. Env. Sci. Tech. 25(8):1393-1400

Schuler, P. F. and M. M. Ghosh. 1991. Slow filtration of cysts and other particulates, p.235-252. Proc. AWWA Annual. Conf, Philadelphia, PA

Tate, C. H. and R. R. Trussell. 1978. The use of particle counting in developing plant design criteria. J. Amer. Water Works Assoc. 70:691-698

Teefy, S. M. 1991. Full scale particle counting study to determine *Giardia* cyst removal efficiency, p.253-275. AWWA Annual. Conf. Proc, Philadelphia, PA

USEPA. 1989. National primary drinking water regulations: filtration and disinfection; turbidity, *Giardia* lamblia, viruses, Legionella and heterotrophic bacteria; proposed rule. Federal Register 54(124):27486-27541

Comparison of Excretion and Viability Patterns in Experimentally Infected Animals: Potential for Release of Viable *C.Parvum* Oocysts into the Environment

Z. Bukhari[1], H.V. Smith[1], S.W. Humphreys[1], J. Kemp[2] and S.E. Wright[2]
[1]Scottish Parasite Diagnostic Laboratory, Stobhill NHS Trust, Glasgow. G31 3UW, UK
[2]Moredun Research Institute, Gilmerton Road, Edinburgh. EH17 7JH, UK

Introduction

Cryptosporidiosis can cause severe diarrhoea in calves and lambs, and can be fatal. Consequently, *Cryptosporidium parvum* infections can have a considerable economic impact, which, for calves, has been estimated to approach US $6.2 million per annum in the USA (Fayer and Ungar, 1986). Infection in calves can result in the excretion of large numbers of oocysts (up to 10^{10}), over a period of 4 to 14 days (Blewett, 1989), which have the potential to cause infection from the time of excretion. Although isolated incidents of human cryptosporidiosis have been reported following contact with infected animals, over the past six years the waterborne route of oocyst transmission has received particular attention.

In the UK, in two reported waterborne outbreaks of human cryptosporidiosis (Smith *et al*, 1988; Richardson *et al*, 1989), contamination from agricultural discharges was implicated. In three separate surveys of surface waters, where samples from agricultural sources could be distinguished from human sewage discharges, the concentrations of oocysts were 1.5-1.9 fold greater in waters polluted by agricultural run-off (Ongerth and Stibbs, 1987; Madore *et al*, 1987).

A fundamental question which has not been addressed is that of the viability status of oocysts excreted during the course of infection. This information is of paramount importance when attempting to assess the significance of environmental pollution by oocysts with respect to public health.

The fluorogenic vital dye assay of Campbell *et al*. (1992) can assess the viability of individual oocysts. It demonstrates a good correlation with in vitro excystation ($r = 0.997$), and, unlike in vitro excystation, does not require highly purified oocyst suspensions for analysis.

Faecal material from calves, lambs and mice which had been experimentally infected with *C. parvum* oocysts was examined to:

a determine the percentage viability of excreted oocysts over time,
b compare the viability patterns of excreted oocysts from calves, lambs and mice, and
c assess the effect of the pen straw bedding environment on oocyst viability.

Material and Methods

Animals and infectious doses. Calves (n=5), lambs (n=11) and mice (n=8) were infected at 4-5 days of age with 10^7, 10^6 and 10^5 viable (>85%) *C. parvum (cervine/ ovine)* oocysts, respectively. These doses were similar to the infectious doses utilised in previously published infectivity trials (Whitmire and Harp, 1991; Snodgrass *et al*, 1984).

Faecal collection. Total faecal output from male calves and lambs was collected in faecal collection bags, attached by means of harnesses. Individual faecal samples were recovered from the mice daily. A pre-weighed sub-sample of daily voided faeces from each animal was purified and screened for the presence of oocysts.

Faecal purification procedure. Diethyl-ether (2 ml) was added to diluted faecal samples (10% in Grade 1 water) and the samples vortexed and centrifuged (1050g, 5 min). Both fat layer and fluid were discarded and the pellet washed in Grade 1 water (x 3). The volume of the concentrated pellet was adjusted to between 1.0 ml and 5.0 ml, dependent upon the amount of contaminating faecal debris.

Microscopic examination. An Olympus BH2 fluorescence microscope (x 40 objective and x 12.5 eyepieces), equipped with Nomarski DIC optics was used. A blue filter (490 nm-excitation, 510 nm-emission) was utilised for the detection of oocysts labelled with fluorescein-isothiocyanate conjugated monoclonal anti-*Cryptosporidium* sp antibody and viability was assessed with a UV filter block for DAPI (350 nm-excitation, 450 nm-emission) and a green filter block for propidium iodide (PI) (488 nm-excitation, 610 nm-emission).

Enumeration of purified oocysts. Oocysts in the purified samples were identified by DIC microscopy. Enumeration was performed with an improved Neubaur haemocytometer. The minimum detection limit of this method is 10^4 oocysts per 1.0 ml.

C. parvum oocyst viability. The viability of partially-purified oocysts was assessed by the assay of Campbell *et al.* (1992). In addition, for approximately 50% of the samples containing oocysts, viability was also assessed by maximised *in vitro* excystation (Robertson *et al*, 1993).

Results and Discussion

Although the mean number of oocysts excreted by the three animal species was of the same order of magnitude, total daily oocyst output exceeded 10^8 from day 1 of oocyst excretion for calves and lambs, whereas in mice, oocyst excretion was considerably lower until day 4. Furthermore, in mice faeces low numbers of oocysts ($<10^3$) continued to be detected (by monoclonal antibody labelling) for a considerably longer period (broken line in Figure 1). Despite these differences in the oocyst excretion profiles of calves or lambs when compared to mice, similarities in the viability patterns of excreted oocysts were observed in these three animal species (Figure 2). The mean percentage viability of excreted oocyst populations was highest during the first week of oocyst excretion and subsequently (10-12 days post infection) declined gradually. It is possible that the decline in oocyst viability is associated with the development of immunity in the host. The results from experimentally infected calves, lambs and mice indicate the percentages of viable oocysts excreted were 69.4%, 50.9% and 71.4% respectively, and suggest that environmental contamination with potentially infective oocysts may not be as high as previously conceived.

One potential route by which farm animals with cryptosporidiosis can release oocysts in to the environment is by leaching from faecally contaminated pen straw bedding. We applied faeces containing oocysts of known viability (from our experimentally-infected calves) onto the pen straw bedding on which these animals were housed, and noted a considerable decline in the viability of oocysts which leached from the bottom of these pens within a few days. Composting of straw bedding often commences whilst the straw is on the pen floor and can lead to an elevation in temperature and ammonia production. Both these factors can reduce the viability and infectivity of oocysts (Anderson,1985; Blewett,1989). Viable oocysts that leach out of the straw bedding probably experience further adverse environmental pressures such as temperature fluctuations, desiccation and physical abrasion, which would further reduce their viability.

It is important to recognise that there are numerous potential routes by which oocysts from agricultural waste may contaminate water courses. Identification and investigation of the significance of such routes should provide a better understanding of the likelihood of environmental contamination with viable oocysts from agricultural discharges.

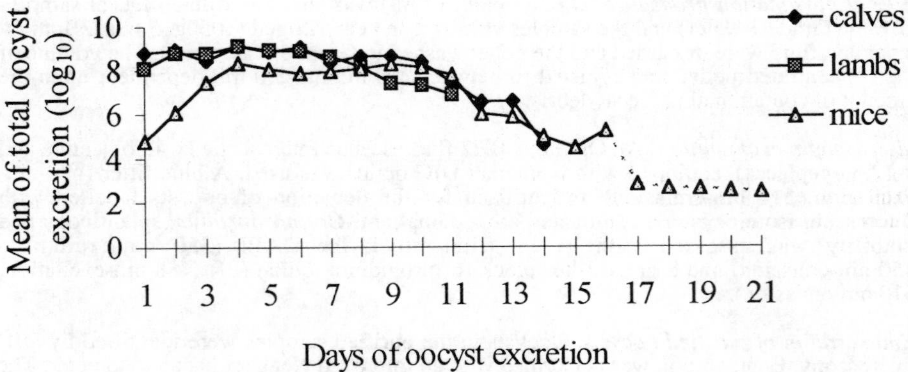

Figure 1. Comparison of mean total oocyst output by infected calves, lambs and mice.

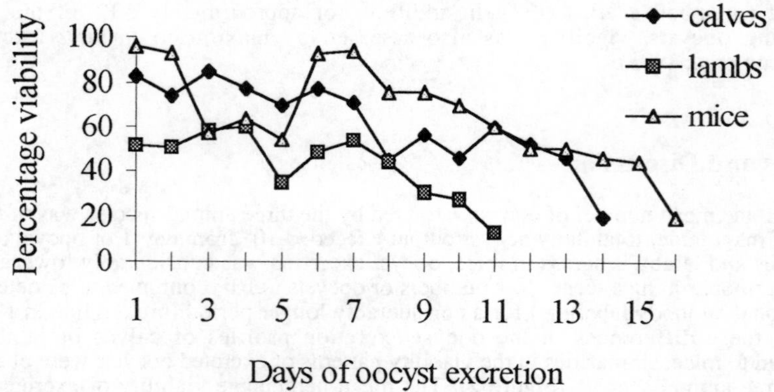

Figure 2. Comparison of excreted oocyst viability for calves, lambs and mice.

Acknowledgments

This project was supported in part by a joint grant from the Ministry of Agriculture Fisheries & Food and the Scottish Office Agriculture & Fisheries Department.

References

Anderson B.C. (1985) Moist heat inactivation of *Cryptosporidium* sp. Am. J. Public Health, 75: 1433

Blewett D.A. (1989) Disinfection and oocysts, in Proc. 1st Int. Workshop on Cryptosporidiosis, Angus K.W. and Blewett D.A. Eds. Sept 7-8, 1988, Edinburgh

Campbell A.T., Robertson L.J., and Smith H.V. (1992) Viability of *Cryptosporidium parvum* oocysts: Correlation of *In Vitro* Excystation with Inclusion or Exclusion of Fluorogenic Vital Dyes. Appl. Environ. Microbiol. 58: 3488

Fayer R., and Ungar B.L.P. (1986) *Cryptosporidium* sp and cryptosporidiosis. Microbiol Rev., 50: 458

Mador M.S., Rose J.B., Gerba C.P., Arrowood M.J., and Sterling C.R. (1987). Occurrence of *Cryptosporidium* oocysts in sewage effluents and selected surface waters. J.Parasitol. 73: 702

Ongerth J.E., and Stibbs. H.H. (1987). Identification of *Cryptosporidium* oocysts in river water. Appl. Environ. Microbiol. 53: 672

Richardson A.J., Frankenberg R.A., Buck A.C., Selkon J.B., Colbourne J.S., Parsons J.W., and Mayon-White R.T. (1991). An outbreak of waterborne cryptosporidiosis in Swindon and Oxfordshire. Epidemiol. infect. 107: 485

Robertson L.J., Campbell A.T., and Smith H.V. (1993) In vitro excystation of *Cryptosporidium parvum*. Parasitology. 106: 13

Smith H. V., Girdwood R. W. A., Patterson W. J., Hardie R., Greene L. A., Benton C., Tulloch W., Sharp J. C. M., and Forbes G. I. (1988). Waterborne outbreak of cryptosporidiosis. Lancet 2: 1484

Snodgrass D.R., Angus K.W., and Gray E.W. (1984) Experimental cryptosporidiosis in germ free lambs. J. Comp. Pathol. 94: 141

Whitmire W.M., and Harp J.A. (1991) Characterisation of bovine cellular and serum antibody responses during infection of *Cryptosporidium parvum*. Infect. and Immun. 59: 990

Removal of *Cryptosporidium* During Water Treatment

T. Hall, J. Pressdee and E. Carrington
WRc plc, Frankland Road, Blagrove, Swindon, Wiltshire, UK

Introduction

The most commonly used disinfectant in water treatment, chlorine, is known to be ineffective against *Cryptosporidium* oocysts. Because of the absence of this disinfection barrier, control of *Cryptosporidium* in water supplies relies on removal during treatment. There is some evidence that conventional water treatment processes should be effective for removing oocysts, typically giving a degree of removal of over 99% (UK Drinking Water Inspectorate, 1992). Some of this information is based on results of monitoring full scale plants in the USA (LeChevallier, 1991). However, there is generally insufficient information available to quantify with any confidence the degree of removal that would be expected. Furthermore, the operating regime of the process is also likely to influence the removal.

WRc is carrying out large scale pilot plant trials to investigate the performance of conventional water treatment for oocyst removal. The work was funded by the Water Industry through the Foundation for Water Research (FWR) between 1991 and 1994, and is continuing in 1994/5 with funding from UK Water Industry Research Ltd (UKWIRL). The pilot plant operation commenced in 1992, and this paper discusses results obtained until the end of the FWR contract in March 1994.

Pilot Plant Description

The pilot plant treats water abstracted directly from the River Thames, and consists of three treatment streams operating in parallel:

- slow sand filtration (SSF) preceded by primary rapid gravity filtration (RGF) using single media sand,
- chemical coagulation, clarification by dissolved air flotation (DAF), and RGF using single media sand, dual media, or granular activated carbon (GAC),
- chemical coagulation, clarification by floc blanket clarification (FBC), and RGF using single media sand.

A schematic of the plant is shown in Figure 1. The design flow to the plant is $120m^3/d$, with approximately $80m^3/d$ treated on the DAF stream, $30m^3/d$ on the FBC stream, and the remainder on the SSF stream. Typical hydraulic loadings to the DAF, FBC and RGFs are 8 m/h, 1.2 m/h and 6 m/h respectively. A proprietary design of textile cartridge filter (Kalsep Fibrotex) is used as a polishing filter to remove any remaining oocysts prior to discharge of the final treated water to soakaways alongside the River Thames. Sludge from the plant is pasteurised to destroy oocysts before disposal.

Experimental Conditions and Summary of Results

The performance of each of the treatment streams was assessed by dosing oocysts into the feed water to the plant, and taking samples along the treatment streams for measurement of oocyst concentrations using a standard method (Standing Committee of Analysts, 1990). The oocysts were obtained from a commercial supplier in a purified form isolated from bovine faeces. The objectives of the work were to compare the treatment streams and provide general data on the performance of conventional water treatment for oocyst

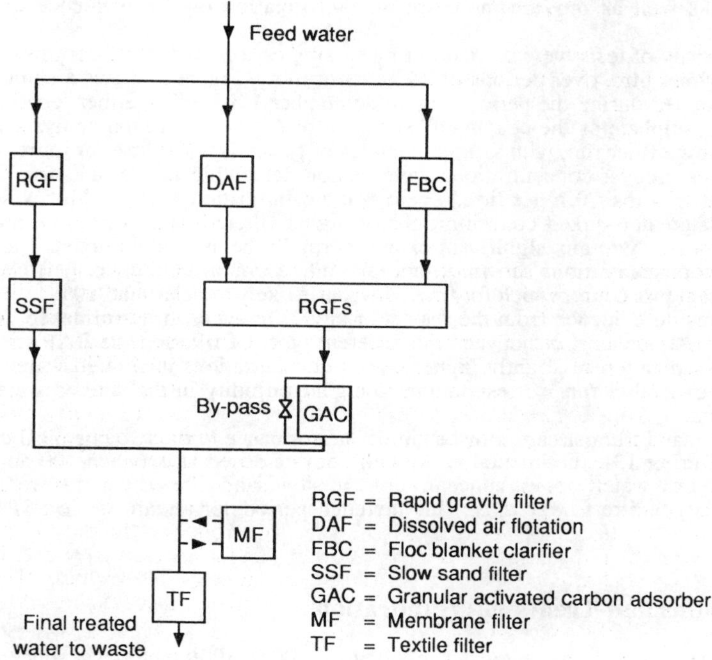

Figure 1. Pilot plant schematic

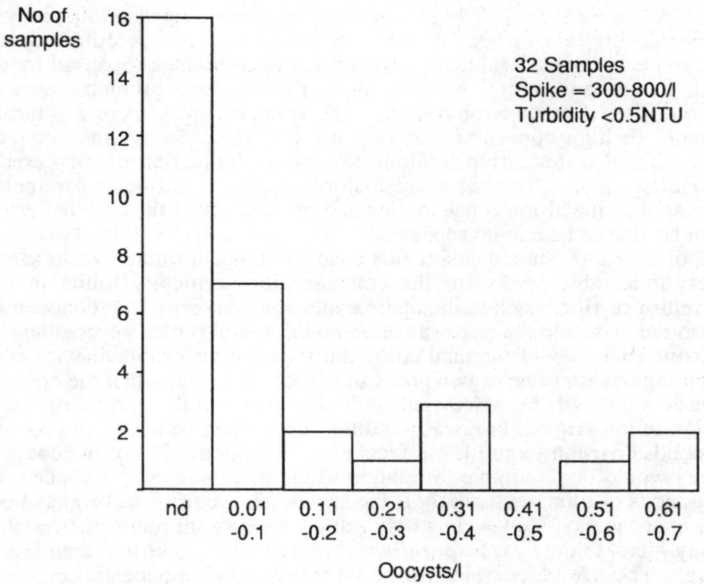

Figure 2. Summary of filtered water results from 32 experimental runs on DAF and FBC streams.

removal, as well as provide more specific information on the influence of operating conditions.

The majority of tests were carried out by spiking concentrations of oocysts in the range 300 to 800 per litre, over periods of 24 hours or more. Figure 2 shows a summary of the results obtained during the period May to September 1993, using either ferric sulphate or aluminium sulphate as the coagulant. Samples for *Cryptosporidium* analysis were taken throughout the filter run, with sample volumes of typically 1000 litres or more. For half of the samples, oocyst concentrations were at non-detectable levels, and for 70% of the samples at less than 0.1 per litre. There was no indication that the higher levels were because of greater spiked concentrations or higher filtered water turbidity, although the latter did not vary to any significant extent, normally being in the range 0.2 to 0.4 NTU. The oocyst concentrations shown do not take into account the recovery efficiency of the measurement procedure, which for filtered water is likely to be around 10%.

There was no evidence from the results of any differences in performance between the FBC and DAF streams, or between the different types of filter on the DAF stream. There was some indication of slightly higher oocyst concentrations in filtered water during the first hour of a filter run, corresponding to higher turbidity in the filtered water over the same period.

The slow sand filter stream showed similar performance to the two chemical coagulation streams. During 13 experimental runs, with oocysts dosed at between 400 and 1400 per litre to the raw water, oocyst concentrations in slow sand filtered water were at less than 0.1 oocysts per litre for 11 runs. This included periods of restart of the SSF after sand scraping.

Conclusions and Treatment Implications

With oocyst dosing to the raw water in the range 300 to 800/l the oocyst concentrations in the filtered water samples were measured at less than 0.1 oocysts/l for the majority of the dosing experiments. Assuming a 10% recovery for the *Cryptosporidium* measurement procedure, there would be less than one oocysts/l for most of the time. This represents greater than 99.8% removal (2.7 log reduction) for a dosed level of 500 oocysts/l, in the middle of the dosing range used. Greater concentrations were sometimes detected in the filtered waters, but this was usually at times of treatment problems, caused for example by high turbidity in the raw water. At these times, the treatment problems were not always apparent from filtered water turbidity, but were associated with increased turbidity in the clarified water or high concentrations of coagulant metal-ion in the filtered water. A reliance on filtered water turbidity alone to give an indication of increased risk from *Cryptosporidium* is therefore not a satisfactory approach, and other parameters such as dissolved coagulant metal-ion concentration and the stability of the clarified water turbidity level should be also be taken into account.

Removal of over 99% should ensure that concentrations in filtered water samples would be at barely detectable levels for the concentrations typically found in raw waters. However, return of filter backwash supernatants could increase the concentration in the feed water to the plant and the risk of breakthrough. A well settled supernatant will contain typically about 1% or 2% of the total coagulant solids in the original backwash water, the majority settling out after one or two hours settlement. It is likely that the cryptosporidia in the backwash water will be associated with coagulant solids, and therefore the oocyst concentration in the original backwash and the supernatant would be in proportion to the coagulant solids concentrations. The effects of recycling only 2% of the oocysts removed by the filters would be negligible in relation to the incoming oocyst concentration, even over long periods of time, particularly if the supernatant return was balanced out as much as possible over the day. However, poorly settled supernatant returned over short periods could greatly increase the *Cryptosporidium* loading to the works and therefore the risk of breakthrough. The use of polyelectrolyte to reduce solids concentrations in backwash supernatants, and avoidance of high flowrates for supernatant return, should reduce this risk.

There may be an increased risk of oocyst breakthrough at the beginning of a filter run, when turbidity can be at higher level than normal for the filter. Slow start-up procedures might be used to minimise the turbidity in the filtered water and therefore the degree of risk from cryptosporidia.

Work is continuing on the pilot plant to investigate aspects of plant operation in more detail. These investigations include slow start-up of rapid gravity filters to reduce risks of breakthrough at the beginning of the run, potential problems associated with stop/start operation of rapid gravity filters, and measurement of oocyst concentrations in backwash supernatants to assess the risks related to recycling of backwash waters.

References

LeChevallier, M.W., Norton, W.D. and Lee, R.G. (1991). Occurrence of *Giardia* and *Cryptosporidium* in surface water supplies. App. Environ. Microbiology, 57, 2610-2616

Standing Committee of Analysts. (1990). Isolation and identification of *Giardia* cysts, *Cryptosporidium* oocysts and free living pathogenic amoebae in waters. HMSO. London

UK Drinking Water Inspectorate. (1992). *Cryptosporidium* in water supplies - progress with the National Research Programme

An Evaluation of the Effectiveness of the Fibrotex Filter in Removing Cryptosporidial Oocysts from a Surface Water Supply

K.J. Ives[1], N. Smetham[2], G. Pearce[3] and J. Allam[3]
[1]Department of Civil and Environmental Engineering, University College London, Gower Street, London WC1E 6BT, UK
[2]Southern Water Services Ltd, Southern House, Yeoman Road, Worthing, West Sussex BN13 3NX, UK
[3]Kalsep Ltd, Doman Road, Yorktown Industrial Estate, Camberley, Surrey GU15 3DF, UK

Introduction

The raw water source supplying the Plucks Gutter water treatment works was shown to be vulnerable to the occasional presence of *Cryptosporidium* oocysts. Consequently trials were initiated to treat the filtrate from the conventional plant, which comprised flocculation - dissolved air flotation - filtration ('Purac' process), to removal any oocysts, and to provide a safe washwater discharge from the downstream unit.

Equipment

A Fibrotex filter unit was connected to the filtrate of the conventional water treatment works. Fibrotex filters comprise a thick bundle of fibres, with a hollow core within the bundle. In the filtration mode, the Fibrotex is rotated and compressed by a twisting action to hold the individual strands of fibrous yarn together. Feed water is then passed radially inwards through the fibre bundle, producing a clarified filtrate in the central core. With the interfibre openings of about 15 micron, the filter is not a strainer relative to oocysts (5 micron) and other fine particles. It is effectively a depth filter, as the flow encounters about 100 fibrous collectors sequentially in passing through. When the filter becomes clogged, as indicated by an increased pressure drop, the bundle is relaxed by untwisting, and then alternately stretched and squeezed to displace the trapped particles. Reverse flow of washwater under pressure carries away the retained deposits. If required a process of vacuum steam pasteurisation can be applied before backwashing, to ensure an even temperature of 60°C, thus killing oocysts and most other micro-organisms.

The trial has a flow capacity of 0.84 Ml/d (35 m^3/h), and was identical to those in a set of 12 units to provide a capacity of 10 ml/d to be capable of treating the entire filtrate of the conventional water treatment works (a 'Purac' installation).

Preliminary Test

Although the test unit was identical to the units installed in the main plant, it was felt prudent to check its performance relative to the main plant units. This was accomplished by monitoring the particle counts at the 5 micron size in the water (Purac filtrate) entering the Fibrotex units, and in the filtrate from the Fibrotex units over a run of 5 hours with a Hiac Royco particle analyser. With inlet counts of a few thousand per litre, the test unit averaged 84% removal providing an average filtrate turbidity of 0,08 NTU, and the plant unit averaged 89% removal, with 0.06 NTU. Thus the plant units were established as being able to achieve at least as good a particle removal as the test unit.

Oocyst Counting

A test protocol was established using triple validation with three cartridges (Vokes Polyfill) in parallel, pumping given concentration of oocysts at a controlled flowrate of 4 l/min for each cartridge for 20 min (80 l/cartridge). Deactivated oocysts (from Moredun Institute, Edinburgh) (deactivated for reasons of health and safety on a production waterworks) were dosed at levels of 20 and 20,000 oocysts/l, and the cartridges were sent for oocyst counting to the Rhyl PHLS laboratory, using the Standing Committee of Analysts (SCA) Blue Book method (Badenoch Report, 1990).

Table 1. Cartridge Validation Tests

A. Input concentration 20 oocysts/l

No. of oocysts recovered from each cartridge			
	Test 1	Test 2	Combined 1 and 2
	1.17	1.17	
	0.76	0.825	
	1.96	1.24	
mean	1.30	1.08	1.19 (S.D. 32.87%)
% recovery	6.5	5.4	5.96

B. Input concentration 20,000 oocysts/l

No. of oocysts recovered from each cartridge			
	Test 3	Test 4	Combined 3 and 4
	10710	9208	
	10354	9738	
	5866	5343	
mean	8977	8096	8537 (S.D. 34.97%)
% recovery	44.88	40.48	42.68

These triple validation data show consistency among the parallel three cartridges, and between two replicated for each input concentration level. But the percentage recovery is dependent on the concentration in the water.

Conditioning of Fibrotex Element

Experience with other Fibrotex applications has shown that new filters require conditioning with the water to be filtered, to bring them to maximum filtration efficiency. This is analogous to the ripening of other depth filters, such as sand filters. Accordingly, the test unit was conditioned with Purac filtrate for 6 days at 8 h/day. It is not necessary to condition again after each backwashing as is the case with the ripening of sand filters).

Test Runs

In the test procedure, oocysts at 1.67×10^4 per litre together with flocculating aluminium hydroxide (from aluminium sulphate) at 0.021 mg/l at Al, were added to the feed water (Purac filtrate) flowing at 35 m^3/h, with a dilution factor of 92.4. The alum was added to simulate the effect in a real situation that the oocysts passing through the Purac filter would have encountered a flocculation process and would be associated with very small levels of residual floc. A sample of 40 l/cartridge was pumped directly into 3 cartridges in parallel, and 30 min later a similar sample a Fibrotex filtrate was fed into 3 cartridges. After the test the Fibrotex unit was backwashed, and another test run was made the next day, with fresh cartridges.

Table 2. Test Runs Results

Test 1	No of oocysts/l			Test 2	No of oocysts/l	
	Inlet	Outlet	%removal	Inlet	Outlet	%removal
	194300	1.7		301000	10.6	
	83000	13.5		265000	10.4	
	*	5.6		*	7.95	
mean	138000	6.93		283000	9.65	
mean conc	1494.19+	6.93	99.54	3064.08+	9.65	99.69

* faulty cartridge housing, no data
+ allowing for dilution of 92.4

The two percentage removals, as log values were 99.54%, 2.34 log and 99.69%, 2.50 log.

Conclusions

1 A Fibrotex test unit performed identically to a plant installation unit.
2 A new (test) unit must be conditioned be several cycles of filtration. This conditioning (ripening) remains in repeated runs, even after backwashing.
3 Triple validation of cartridges (counted by SCA method) assumes consistency.
4 Oocysts must be added with residual Al to stimulate works behaviour, ie. in operation oocysts would have been exposed to Al flocculation in passing through a Purac system.
5 In two test runs at full scale flowrate (35 m^3/h per unit) oocyst removal efficiencies were 99.54% (2.34 log) and 99.69% (2.50 log).

Reference

Anon. *Cryptosporidium* in water supplies. Dept of Health/Dept of Environment. Report of the Group of Experts, Chairman, Sir John Badenoch. HMSO London 1990

An Evaluation of Fibrous Depth Filters for Removal of *Cryptosporidium* Oocysts from Water

J.G. O'Neill
Yorkshire Water Services Ltd, Leeds, UK

Experimental

Two Kalsep systems were assessed as pilot plants - the AX12 and AX50, designed to treat 12 and 50 m^3/hr respectively. Two units were used in each plant with both series and parallel use assessed. The smaller units were used to assess the removal of:

a live *Cryptosporidium*;
b 5 μm particles found in tapwater, predominantly iron and manganese; and
c 5 μm polystyrene beads.

The larger units were used to assess the removal of algae, particularly chlorophycean flagellates, as possible surrogates for *Cryptosporidium* oocysts.

The AX12 plant incorporated a $12m^3$ supply tank, a tank for clean backwashing water and two tanks which collected backwash water separately from the two units. For sampling, cartridge filter housings were installed upstream and downstream of the Fibrotex units.

The AX50 plant was installed at a water treatment works and operated on-line over a 9 month period.

Removal of Particles and Polystyrene Beads from Tapwater

This work was carried out on the AX12 plant. The feed tank was filled with tap water (turbidity 0.8 NTU) and continuously recirculated for 10 hours through the 2 units in parallel. Particle counts in the raw and cleaned water were measured using a Hiac-Royco 8000 and the results for particles in the 5 μm range are set out in Table 1.

Polystyrene beads, 5 μm diameter, were then added to the cleaned water which was pumped through the two units in series, and the beads enumerated in the 5 μm range of the Particle Size Analyser. These results are also given in Table 1.

Removal of *Cryptosporidium* Oocysts

This work was carried out with AX12 units. The feed tank was filled with a suspension of *Cryptosporidium* oocysts at a concentration of 10,000/l. The two units, in series, were fed at a rate of 7.5 m^3/hr, until the supply tank was empty (ca 1.6 hours). The cartridge filters, fitted for sample collection, were switched on-line after 30 minutes and switched off 5 minutes before the end of each run. The two units were backwashed with clean water and the filtrates collected. The results, from 8 runs, of:

a the numbers of oocysts detected in the feed and Fibrotex filtrates;
b the calculations of the recovery of oocysts from the feed tank, and;
c removal of oocysts by the Fibrotex units,

are set out in Table 2. The standard analytical method (Pearce 1993) was used throughout.

The oocysts present in the two backwash waters were counted directly and these results are set out in Table 3.

The initial concentration of 10,000/l and all recovery calculations are based on the figure of 10^9/ml for oocysts as supplied by the Moredun Institute.

Table 1

Removal of 5 μm particles from water by fibrotex units				
Particles per 20ml			Percentage Removal	
Feed	Unit 1	Unit 2	Unit 1	Unit 2
27,626	13	17	99.95	99.94
Removal of 5 μm polystyrene beads				
3809	389	111	89.8	71.3

Table 2

Removal of oocysts by fibrotex filters			
Trial	Oocysts per Litre		
Number	Feed	Unit 1	Unit 2
1	350 (3.5)	12	5
2	339 (3.4)	155	43
3	153 (1.5)	79	30
4	569 (5.7)	30	1.5
5	328 (3.3)	<0.1	0.1
6	78 (0.8)	<0.1	<0.1
7	34 (0.3)	9	5
8	389 (3.9)	8.2	1.2
( ) = percent recovery (see text)			
Mean Percentage Removal		Unit 1 = 86% Unit 2 = 70% Overall = 96%	

Table 3

Oocysts in backwash water from fibrotex filters		
Trial Number	Oocysts per litre in Backwash	
	Unit 1	Unit 2
1	6750	130
2	4582	8060
3	22050	6038
4	57500	9600
5	8680	3238
6	6650	4860
7	4166	2210
Mean Values	15768	4877

Table 4

Comparison Of Fibrotex With Slow Sand Filters				
		Percentage Removal		
		Unit 1 (28 m^3/h)	Unit 2 (10 m^3/h)	Slow Sand
Chlorophycean Flagellates	2.5 μm	12	29	70
	5.0 μm	28	49	86
	7.5 μm	39	53	94
Anabaena		90	98	99.9
Melosira		15	86	99
Centric Diatoms		23	78	91
Turbidity		8	41	86
Escherichia coli		7	29	99

Removal of Algae, and Comparison with Slow Sand Filters

Using the AX50 system with the two units running in parallel at 10 and 28 m^3/h, 65 sets of data were accumulated and the results are set out in Table 4. All values are arithmetic means.

The mean turbidity of the feed water over the trial was 1.3 NTU, with a maximum of 2.5 NTU. There were no significant operating problems with the system. Backwash was typically triggered every 8 hours but reducing to 1.7 hours during a bloom of the filamentous blue-green algae, *Anabaena*.

Discussion

Particle and Bead Removal

The Fibrotex unit removed greater than 99.9% of the 5 μm iron and manganese particles present in the feed water. This level of removal reflects the claims of the manufacturer (Anon 1990). However, the removal of polystyrene beads was significantly poorer: 90% removal from the first unit and 70% for the second in series. This indicates that there could be a significant interaction between the nature of the particle and the effectiveness of the Fibrotex process in removing it. The measurement of particle counts was by a well-proven and reliable method.

Removal of *Cryptosporidium* Oocysts

The data presented is highly variable with removal through Unit 1 between 49% and 99.7% and then through Unit 2 between 37 and 95%. It is very likely that these variations relate to the sampling/analytical method and not to variation in the operation of, or performance of, the Fibrotex units. However, assuming that the sampling and analytical errors are random, it can nonetheless be seen that the mean oocyst removals from Units 1 and 2 are very close to the mean removals of polystyrene beads as measured by a reliable method.

This observation is supported by the direct oocyst counts in the second unit backwash, which suggest that the removal from Unit 1 is no more than 78%. In addition, the highest apparent level of removal of 99.7% is contradicted by the high level of oocysts measured in the backwash from that particular run.

Even with the doubts about the analytical method for direct measurement of oocysts, the supplementary evidence indicates that a single Fibrotex unit operated as described can be expected to remove somewhere between 70% and 90% of *Cryptosporidium* oocysts. However, this is not to suggest that the process operated differently (Ives *et al.*) could not be more effective.

Removal of Algae

In the trial with the AX50 units where algae were used as surrogates for *Cryptosporidium*, the unit run at 10 m^3/hr was always significantly more effective than that run at 28 m^3/hr; but neither approached the performance of slow sand filters. This applies not only to the flagellates of similar size to *Cryptosporidium* but also to any of the other algal species monitored. This reduction in removal efficiency of live organisms with increased loading raises the question of how process control would be carried out if the Fibrotex system were to be used for *Cryptosporidium* oocysts, which are unlikely to be present for much of the time.

Conclusions

Although accepting limitations of the analytical methodology, it was concluded that the Fibrotex process could remove *Cryptosporidium* oocysts by around an order of magnitude. In addition, as removal of algae by the Fibrotex process was significantly lower than by slow sand filters, it was concluded that removal of *Cryptosporidium* would be similarly less effective.

Acknowledgements

I would like to acknowledge the contributions, assistance and co-operation of Kalsep staff in this work. The opinions expressed are those of the Author and not necessarily those of Yorkshire Water Services Limited.

References

Anon - Isolation and Identification of *Giardia* Cysts, *Cryptosporidium* Oocysts and Free Living Pathogenic Amoeba in Water etc: Methods for the Examination of Water and Related Substances, London HMSO, 1990

Ives K J, Smetham N, Pearce G K, Allam J. (ibid)

Pearce G K - Water Services, p23 - March 1993

An Integrated Water Utility Approach to Minimising the Risks Associated with Waterborne Cryptosporidiosis

M. J. Porter, R. A. Breach, M. L. Furness, D. Dawson, V. W. Howells and D. W. Black
Severn Trent Water Ltd. 2297 Coventry Road. Birmingham, B27 3PU, UK

Introduction

Cryptosporidium as an organism has been known for many years; however it is only relatively recently that it has become recognised as a common human pathogen. Probably the most usual route of infection is animal to person, or person to person, but water can also be a vehicle as witnessed by the major and serious waterborne incidents that have been reported both in the UK and US. In principle, many of the measures adopted to prevent *Cryptosporidium* contamination are no different to those for other waterborne pathogens. The main differences are the higher environmental stability, and resistance to chlorine of *Cryptosporidium* and the relatively low infective dose.

Severn Trent Water has embarked on a fundamental strategic review of the potential risks within its area from waterborne cryptosporidiosis and ways that these risks could be kept to an absolute minimum. The supply area of the company is large (around 8000 square miles) and has around 8 million customers. The water resources are varied with 26 upland and lowland surface water treatment plants providing around 65% of our total output, with the remainder derived from 161 groundwater abstractions. Because of this our approach has had to be flexible to accommodate the potentially different degrees of risk in different areas.

The Nature of Cryptosporidium Risks

Cryptosporidium is relatively common in many surface water environments and also potentially in some shallow or fissured groundwaters. The predominant sources are animal wastes, particularly from intensive livestock farming, and in some areas municipal waste water plants. In general the existing systems of watershed control and water treatment appear to cope with the day to day challenges of *Cryptosporidium*. Problems seem most likely to occur when one or more adverse factors are present, including for example a change in organism virulence, increased raw water oocyst challenge to the water treatment plant, treatment inefficiency or post treatment contamination.

In developing our own risk management strategy we have therefore used a model which assumes two different scenarios of *Cryptosporidium* risk.

i The "background" situation
ii The "abnormal challenge" situation

An Integrated Strategy

Management of *Cryptosporidium* risks is a complex task which must be dealt with on an integrated basis, from raw water to the customer's tap. It is also critically important to have effective two-way liaison arrangements with health officials. Much of the strategy is not just about technology, it is about management procedures, training and awareness. Indeed while it is vitally important to have effective treatment technology in place it could be argued that it is these other factors which are the most important and the most difficult to deal with in minimising the risk of waterborne *Cryptosporidium*.

Analytical Method Development

The ability to rapidly, easily and reliably detect and quantify *Cryptosporidium* oocysts in water is fundamental to any system of risk management. Many laboratories have been involved in improving current methodologies although difficulties still occur.

In our own laboratory we have made significant improvements to the recovery of oocysts using membrane based systems. Studies have shown that this results in typical recoveries of between 25-60%, and samples can be processed more quickly, generally in 4-5 hours. Detection and quantification of oocysts is currently carried out by fluorescence microscopy. However we are currently working in a joint research venture with a commercial manufacturer to develop a more effective methodology, based on an electro rotation assay (ERA).

It is important to be able to assess the viability of oocysts, particularly if contamination of final water is suspected. Using a procedure based on vital dye staining (3), a sample of oocysts can now be assessed for viability in our laboratory. In the future we are hopeful that novel methodology based on ERA will provide an integrated recovery, detection and viability assay within 1-2 hours.

Watershed Risk Assessment

A key element of our strategy is a systematic assessment of the risk and pattern of oocyst occurrence at the point of abstraction, based on both a knowledge of the watershed and a routine raw water monitoring programme.

At all of our raw water abstraction points we have introduced a monitoring programme to assess the overall pattern of occurrence. It is important to know the relative variation in raw water oocyst level because generally the treatment provision should be geared to the highest values normally expected. Currently we are sampling around 3000 times per year. However, the need for sampling at this relatively high frequency will be reviewed as our background knowledge of the catchments increases.

Whilst raw water monitoring will give a good picture of general background levels of oocysts, it will not necessarily provide a good idea of the likelihood of sudden oocyst challenge being present in the raw water. For this reason it is also necessary to have a knowledge of *Cryptosporidium* risks within the catchment. Typically this would include the patterns of farming and particularly livestock density; centres of livestock concentration eg cattle housing, abattoirs; animal waste storage/treatment facilities; and presence of municipal wastewater plants.

In assessing the relative risks from major sources of oocysts, the potential for oocyst attenuation must be considered. Although oocysts are relatively environmentally stable they can and do degrade and can also be diluted, for example in passage down rivers. The distance from the oocyst source to the intake must therefore be taken into account. For example a relatively small cattle slurry store close to a reservoir abstraction point probably poses a much greater risk than a major cattle facility many miles upstream on a large river system.

In trying to assess the relative risk of raw water *Cryptosporidium* to each abstraction point we have developed an empirical risk matrix which scores various catchment risk factors against treatment plant capability.

Watershed Risk Management

In seeking to manage the risk of *Cryptosporidium* within the watershed it is important to set realistic and achievable goals. In many catchments it would be difficult if not impossible to maintain raw water *Cryptosporidium* at very low levels and treatment plants will have to be designed and operated accordingly. However depending on the proximity of the oocyst risk to the abstraction a number of pragmatic approaches to risk minimisation are possible.

Crucial to this process is identifying the target groups, eg farmers, wastewater plant operators or abattoirs. Dialogue and awareness raising with these groups is essential, since often the nature of the potential risk from *Cryptosporidium* to water supply abstractions is simply not understood.

Provision of Optimised Treatment Barriers

A fundamental element of any *Cryptosporidium* strategy is provision of adequate and optimised treatment processes, according to the relative degree of risk within the raw water. However, a full discussion of the design and operation of surface water plants is outside the scope of this paper

Operator Training

Training of operators is a vital component of any *Cryptosporidium* risk management strategy, since maloperation of an otherwise adequate plant could potentially pose one of the greatest risks of contamination of treated water.

Within our Company we have therefore developed two structured training programmes, one for plant operators and one for distribution operators and maintenance teams. This has involved the preparation of simple training manuals as well as a cascaded presentation programme to all relevant staff.

Incident Management

Despite the most rigorous procedures it is possible that waterborne outbreaks of cryptosporidiosis could occur, or that oocysts could be detected in final water which could under some circumstances give rise to health risk.

This reinforces the importance of having well defined joint procedures with health authorities, not only to deal with *Cryptosporidium* but indeed any incident involving actual or potential contamination of treated water supplies.

For that reason, working in close co-operation with health and municipal authorities, Severn Trent has developed a model Outbreak Control Plan which has been refined into specific local Outbreak Control Plans for each of our area Health Districts.

Conclusions

Under normal circumstances the risk of significant *Cryptosporidium* contamination of treated water seems to be generally rare. Nevertheless because of the potential significance of even one waterborne outbreak, utilities must do all that is possible to keep the risk as low as is practicable.

As with many water quality issues, the risk can only be properly managed by an integrated strategy which looks at each stage of the water supply process from watershed to tap. The approach described in this paper has evolved from practical and research experience, and has involved many staff with a wide range of skill. The strategy is still being refined as our knowledge increases.

Practicalities of Disinfection for Control of *Cryptosporidium* and *Giardia*

J.R. Pressdee, T. Hall and E. Carrington
WRc, Frankland Road, Blagrove, Swindon, Wiltshire SN5 8YF, UK

Introduction

Whilst control of *Cryptosporidium* and *Giardia* in water supplies will rely heavily on achieving good removal during treatment, disinfectants may still have an important role to play as part of an overall strategy for control, in conjunction with water treatment solids-liquid separation processes. This paper reviews some of the published results for disinfection in relation to *Cryptosporidium* and *Giardia*, and summarises the considerations and costs associated with using these disinfectants for this purpose on water treatment works.

Review of Results for *Cryptosporidium*

Most of the recently reported work on *Cryptosporidium* disinfection has investigated ozone, which has shown some promise as an effective disinfectant. Table 1 compares the results of some of these studies.

Table 1. Comparison of ozone results for the inactivation of *Cryptosporidium* oocysts

Workers	Ozone Residual (C, mg/l)	Contact Time (t, mins)	Ct Value (mg.min/l)	Temperature (°C)	Inactivation (%)	Analytical Method
Korich *et al* (1990)	1	5	5	25	90 - 99	Mouse
	1	10	10	25	> 99	infectivity
HMSO (1990)	0.77	6	4.6	'Room'	> 99	Mouse
	1.49	8	11.9		> 99	infectivity
Finch and Black (1993)	0.5	18	9	7	> 99	Mouse
	0.5	7.8	3.9	22	> 99	infectivity
Parker *et al* (1993)	1	10	10	5	27.4	Stain
	3	10	30	5	18.2	
	5	10	50	5	38.8	
	1	10	10	20	70	
	3	10	30	20	>99	
Hall *et al* (1994)	0.7	14	9.8	8 to 10	42	Stain
	0.7	18	12.6		52	
	1.1	14	15.4		44	
	1.0	25	25.0		67	
	1.5	18	27.0		84	

The Ct values shown in Table 1 are the product of residual concentration, C, after the contact time period, t, which is a standard approach for comparing the efficiency of disinfection. The influence of temperature on the disinfection efficiency is demonstrated by the results of Parker *et al.* (1993). However, of more significance are the apparent differences between the results from investigations using mouse infectivity compared with those using the staining technique (Campbell *et al.* 1992) to estimate oocyst viability. It is not known which of these methods most closely models human infectivity and is therefore the more appropriate for assessing the effectiveness of disinfectants. Because the two methods give different conclusions regarding the effectiveness of disinfection, some caution should be applied when developing strategies for *Cryptosporidium* control involving ozone.

Table 2 gives example of the performance of disinfectants other than ozone. The concentrations of chlorine dioxide given in the table are greater than the doses currently allowed under UK Regulations, which stipulate that the combined concentration of chlorine dioxide, chlorate and chlorite compounds must not exceed 0.5 mg/l. The concentrations of the others are unsuitable for water treatment, both in terms of cost and the effect they would have on water quality.

Table 2. Summary of disinfection conditions required to give a reduction in viability of more than 90 %

Disinfectant	Concentration at the end of contact period (mg/l)	Contact time (mins)
Chlorine	c 3000	1440
Chlorine Dioxide	1.8	10
	0.8	15
Hydrogen peroxide	327	10
Iodine	120	60

Review of Results for *Giardia*

Results given in Table 3 suggest that a high degree of inactivation of *Giardia* can be achieved by the chemical disinfectants in common use, although the conditions required for chlorine and UV are more stringent than those normally used in water treatment, shown on Table 4.

Table 3. Summary of Ct (mg/min/l) or UV (mJ/cm^2) dose values required to achieve 90% and 99% inactivation of *Giardia lamblia*

Disinfectant	90%	99%
Chlorine	-	30-630
Ozone	0.63	1.3 - 2.0
Chlorine Dioxide	-	7.2 - 18.5
UV	80	-

Practicalities and Costs of Achieving Disinfection for *Cryptosporidium* and *Giardia*

Costs associated with achieving disinfection for *Cryptosporidium* and *Giardia* are outlined on Table 4, based on the Ct or UV dose values shown on the table, which should be sufficient to provide more than 90% inactivation. This level of inactivation would be adequate provided that a high degree of removal of *Cryptosporidium* oocysts and *Giardia* cysts is achieved during water treatment. The costs shown on the table also assume that the water exerts a low oxidants demand, which should be the case for most treated waters. The costs for ozone are based on the results from work in which viability was assessed using animal infectivity models. The costs for chlorine dioxide assume that the current maximum dose would not apply, which would require a change in the Regulations. Costs for UV irradiation assume that the costs are a direct function of the dose required. To put the costs shown in Table 4 into perspective, direct operating costs for treatment of a surface water source would be in the order of £50 per Ml. Table 4 does not include capital costs. Typical costs for ozonation plant are of the order of £ 600,000 for a 20 Ml/day works, and costs for UV equipment for a similar sized works vary from £ 50,000 to £ 150,000 depending on the type of UV lamps used and the configuration of the system.

Table 4. Estimated operating costs for disinfectants

Disinfectant	Typical cost for water treatment (£/Ml)	Cost for *Giardia* disinfection (£/Ml)	Cost for *Cryptosporidium* disinfection (£/Ml)
Chlorine	1.25 Ct = 15	6 Ct = 300	-
Chlorine Dioxide	1.0 (0.5 mg/l dose) Ct = 10	4 Ct = 15	5 Ct = 20
Ozone	10 Ct = 1.6	12 Ct = 2	15 Ct = 5
UV irradiation	3.3 (25 mJ/cm^2 dose)	13.2 (100 mJ/cm^2)	-

Consideration must also be given to the potential for by-product formation from the chemical oxidants. Limitations on the use of chlorine dioxide with regard to chlorate and chlorite production have already been mentioned. Chlorine reacts with natural organic material in the water to produce a range of regulated by-products, the most well known of which are the trihalomethanes. Production of chlorination by-products can be minimised by avoiding excessive use of chlorine on untreated waters with high chlorine demand. Generally, raw water is unsuitable for application of disinfectants because of the high demand for chlorine and other oxidants, and because of the influence of turbidity and colour on the effectiveness of UV. Ozone reacts with natural organics in the water to produce biodegradable material, Assimilable Organic Carbon (AOC), which, if present in the distribution system, can encourage undesirable bacterial growth. This AOC should be removed by appropriate water treatment before the water enters supply, and the use of ozone should therefore be avoided on final waters immediately before distribution. There is also concern over the production of bromate by ozonation, and WHO have set a provisional Guideline value of 25 µg/l.

Conclusions

A review of published results has suggested that some of the disinfectants currently used in water treatment could be used as part of an overall disinfection strategy to control *Cryptosporidium* and *Giardia* without incurring excessive operating costs. The potential for increased by-product formation needs to be taken into account, and, with regard to the use of chlorine dioxide, a change in the current UK Regulations would be needed to allow higher dose levels to be used. The assumption has been made that animal infectivity is the more applicable method for measuring oocyst viability. However, until information is available to assess which method most closely models human infectivity, some caution would be advisable in establishing strategies reliant on ozone.

References

Campbell A T, Robertson L J and Smith H V. Viability of *Cryptosporidium* parvum oocysts: correlation with in vitro excystation with inclusion or exclusion of fluorogenic vital dyes. Applied and Environmental Microbiology, 58, 3488-3943, 1992

Finch G R and Black E K. Inactivation of *Giardia* and *Cryptosporidium* using ozone. Proceedings of the Eleventh Ozone World Congress, Vol. 2, S-19-1 toS-19-17, San Francisco, 1993

Hall T, Pressdee J R and Carrington E. Removal of *Cryptosporidium* oocysts by water treatment processes. FWR final report FR 0457, 1994

HMSO. *Cryptosporidium* in water supplies. Department of the Environment and Department of Health, London 1990

Korich, DG, Mead, JR, Madore, MS, Sinclair, NA And Sterling CR. Effects of ozone, chlorine dioxide, chlorine and monochloramine on *Cryptosporidium* parvum oocyst viability, Applied and Environmental Microbiology 56(5): 1423 - 1428 , 1990

Parker J F W, Greaves G F and Smith H V. The effect of ozone on the viability of *Cryptosporidium* parvum oocysts and a comparison of experimental methods. Water Science and Technology, 27, 93-96, 1993

Survival of *Cryptosporidium parvum* Oocysts in Biofilm and Planktonic Samples in a Model System

J. Rogers and C.W. Keevil
CAMR, Porton Down, Salisbury, Wiltshire, SP4 OJG, UK

Introduction

The presence of oocysts of *Cryptosporidium parvum* within drinking water has led to outbreaks of human infection (Hayes *et al.*, 1989). In immunocompetent patients cryptosporidiosis occurs as a self-limiting diarrhoea, but in immunocompromised patients infection may lead to death (Navin and Juranek, 1984). In natural waters, oocysts occur in low numbers, even in waters where outbreaks have occurred. In the Milwaukee outbreak, where 403, 000 people had diarrhoea directly attributable to the contamination of the public water supply, only 6.7 to 13.2 to oocysts were detected per 100 L of water (MacKenzie *et al.*, 1994).

Ecological investigations involving the presence of oocysts in water are difficult to perform since their appearance in water is often sporadic and even when oocysts are present their numbers are low. If studies are undertaken, results are often difficult to interpret because large numbers of samples are negative and, due to the poor sampling efficiencies, even those which contain oocysts are often underestimated (Smith and Rose, 1990). Comparison of environmental conditions in a natural ecosystem is also difficult because of the large number of parameters which are variable. In the past ecological investigations into the viability of oocysts could only be determined by excystation (Blewett, 1989), and this was problematic in actual water samples which contained high backgrounds of microorganisms. These problems have often led to a simplified approach being undertaken by investigators, with most studies examining survival in purified oocyst suspensions (Blewett, 1989). The correlation of excystation to vital staining in pure cultures of oocysts, has led to the development of a viability method that can be used in actual water samples (Campbell *et al.*, 1992) and the examination of oocysts under various environmental conditions (Robertson *et al.*, 1992), but as yet this work has been carried out under sterile conditions.

Natural and potable waters are not sterile: they contain diverse populations of microoganisms. Therefore, the aim of this work was to develop a suitable laboratory model system so that the ecology and survival of *C. parvum* oocysts could be studied within a microbial consortium. The model system needed to reproduce the environmental conditions found within surface waters, so that the organisms could be studied under conditions that realistically simulated the aquatic habitat in which they occur. An essential requirement of the model system was that microbial growth was achieved using sterile water as the sole source of nutrient; it was thought that any addition would have resulted in the artificial selection of a microbial population. Batch culture was considered unsuitable, since there are inevitable accumulations of toxic metabolites, shifts in pH or changes in microbial growth rate, making those environmental parameters important to survival difficult to distinguish. These problems can be overcome by the use of continuous culture techniques which have the additional advantage that the model intends to simulate a flowing system. Another major advantage of chemostat culture is that environmental conditions are closely defined, controlled and reproducible. This ensures that results can be directly comparable between experiments and those environmental parameters which are important for survival can be elucidated. Pulsing the chemostat with a suspension of oocysts was considered to be the equivalent to oocysts being washed into a water course or reservoir. Aquatic ecosystems are composed of two distinct but interactive phases, unattached microorganisms within the planktonic culture, and microorganisms which are attached to surfaces in biofilms (in reservoirs this may be plant material and other suspended solids). In order to establish a representative model of the ecosystem, it was therefore thought necessary to include surfaces to allow a biofilm component to be investigated. Although glass is rarely present in reservoirs it was selected as the material of choice because it is biologically inert and suitable for viewing under all types of microscope; stained biofilm could be visualised easily and unstained biofilm could be easily removed from the surfaces for microbiological analysis. The use of glass coupons also enabled standardised samples of biofilm to be examined.

The use of sterile water as the sole source of nutrient, for the attached and unattached growth, of a mixed community of microorganisms was therefore combined with the chemostat approach for the study of the survival of *C. parvum* oocysts within the aquatic ecosystem.

Method

The model system was a modification of that used previously for the culture of *Legionella pneumophila* (Rogers *et al*., 1994). The inoculum consisted of a naturally occurring mixed population of microorganisms; this had been concentrated by filtration from a reservoir source and contained a diverse range of bacteria, protozoa and algae. The growth medium for the model system was filter-sterilised reservoir water from the same source. The model consisted of two 500 ml glass vessels linked in series. The first vessel was used to supply a constant inoculum of microorganisms to the second vessel and had a dilution rate (D) 0.05 h^{-1}. The second vessel was used to test the survival of the *Cryptosporidium* and was supplied with additional filter-sterilised water to give a total dilution rate of 0.2 h^{-1}. Effluent from this vessel was pumped via a weir into the collection vessel.

Environmental conditions within the vessels were controlled and monitored using Anglicon microprocessor control units (Brighton Systems, Newhaven). The temperature in the vessels was maintained at 20.0 ± 0.1°C using proportional integral and derivative controllers and was externally heated by an electrical pad. The stirrer speed in both vessels was maintained at 250 ± 5 rpm to maintain a fluid velocity of 1-2 m s^{-1} flow across the surface of the biofilms. Biofilms were generated on the surface of glass tiles, which had a 1 cm^2 surface area and a 1 mm hole drilled. These tiles were suspended in groups of three from silicone bungs using titanium wire. The tile assemblies were cleaned in acetone to remove any surface dirt or grease, placed in bottles of deionised water and autoclaved.

Sets of these tiles were suspended into the culture in the first and second vessels at day 0 of the experiment. Biofilms were allowed to develop on the surface of the glass tiles for 16 days prior to the inclusion of the oocysts into the vessel. After 16 days, vessel two was pulsed with a single dose of 10^8 oocysts obtained from calves (Moredun Institute, Edinburgh) and suspended in 10 ml of sterile water. Inlet and exit pumps were turned off for a 24 h period to allow oocysts attachment to occur. Oocysts were not added to the contents of the first vessel and tiles from that vessel were used to provide negative control samples. Planktonic and biofilm samples were periodically removed from both vessels.

Biofilms was aseptically removed from the surface of the glass tiles using a sterile dental probe. The biofilm was resuspended in 1.0 ml of sterile water and vortexed for 30 s to disperse the microorganisms. The numbers of oocysts in planktonic and resuspended biofilm samples was determined by direct immunolabelling. A 100 µl aliquot of the sample was incubated at 37°C for 40 min with a 50 µl aliquot of FITC conjugated monoclonal antibody against *C. parvum* (Bradsure Biologicals, Derby, UK). Vital staining was carried out as described by Campbell *et al*. (1992).

Unstained, intact biofilms were examined directly using Hoffman Modulation Contrast optics fitted to a Nikon Labophot microscope. Biofilms were immunolabelled by incubating in a solution containing 100 µl of sterile water and 50 µl of the FITC conjugated monoclonal antibody. Immunolabelled and vitally stained samples were viewed under a Nikon fluorescence microscope fitted with appropriate fluorescence filters.

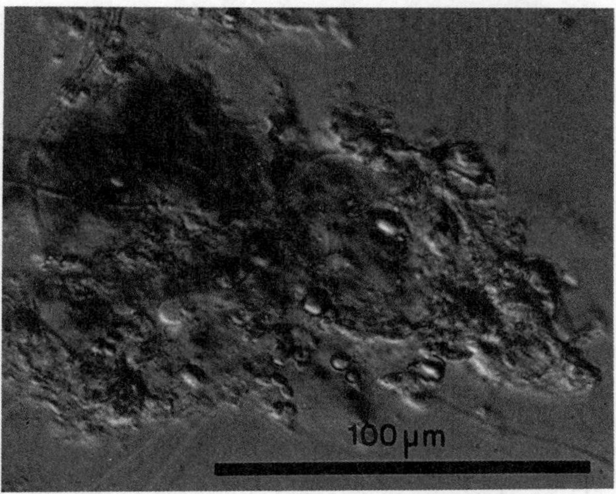

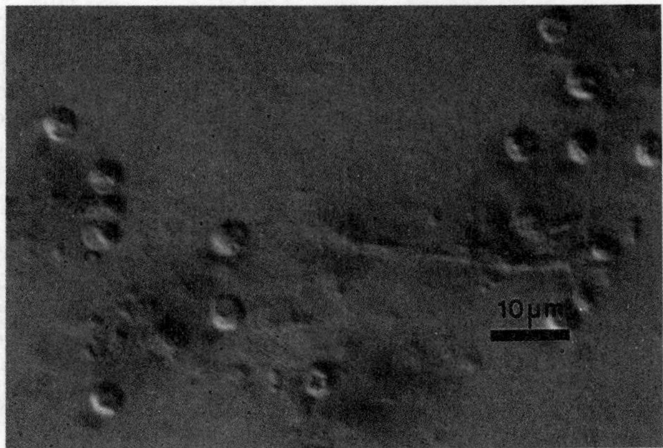

Figure 1. Dense regions of biofilm occurred on the surface of the glass tile (a) with a maximum depth of 100 µm. Even in unstained biofilms, there were sufficient oocysts to allow their discrimination within the basal layer of the biofilm (b).

Results

Biofilms were rapidly developed on the surface of the glass tiles and these supported a diverse range of microorganisms. When oocysts were added to the second vessel these were found to have adhered after the 24 h period at a concentration of 1400 oocysts cm^{-2}. The oocysts were shown to remain adherent within the biofilm for the duration of the trial period of one month at a concentration at least equal to that at the onset. A significant proportion of the oocysts were shown to remain viable even after one month within the chemostat culture.

Unstained biofilms were found to be similar to those previously examined (Rogers *et al.*, 1991). The biofilm consisted of a basal layer of microorganisms which had a depth of approximately 5 µm. Raising out of this basal layer were tall, finger-like stacks of biofilm which had a maximum height of 100 μm. Microscopic examination suggested the presence of microcolonies of bacteria within these stacks; this was indicated by the presence of bacteria of similar morphology and colour occurring in clusters. In some areas of the substratum denser regions of biofilm occurred (Fig 1a). Although staining was necessary to ensure the accurate determination of oocyst numbers cm^{-2}, oocysts could be identified in unstained biofilms (Fig 1b). The oocysts were found to adhere to the denser regions of the biofilm in groups but on the relatively uncolonised areas they occurred as single organisms spaced over the surface.

Discussion

Using this model system it has been demonstrated that a significant numbers of *C. parvum* oocysts exist attached to surfaces within the aquatic environment. It has been established that the oocysts are able to persist and survive for several weeks within that biofilm community at 20°C. This has important implications for the occurrence of waterborne *C. parvum* infection because it implies that the retention time of oocysts through a distribution system is considerably longer than the actual flow of water. Oocysts which enter water distribution systems may reside for several weeks within biofilms. Their subsequent sloughing in biofilm could possibly lead to infection, even long after source waters are considered safe. It was notable that biofilm-associated oocysts occurred in clusters, this would suggest that biofilm sloughing may well release a small but effective dose of oocysts into the water system. This may be one explanation of the occasional, sporadic cases of *C. parvum* infection which occur within the community and whose source cannot be identified.

In order for the results of any ecological investigation to be valid, the model system has to be representative of the ecosystem it intended to study. This was achieved in this study by the use of a continuous culture biofilm model, which utilised reservoir water for the growth of a naturally occurring microbial consortia to which *C. parvum* oocysts were added. The attachment and persistence of high numbers of oocysts on surfaces enables the investigation of the important factors which effect their survival to be examined under realistic conditions whilst maintaining sufficiently high numbers to ensure that results are statistically valid. This model system could be used to determine the important environmental factors for the survival of *C. parvum* oocysts in water systems and to determine suitable control measures. The use of a two-stage model is particularly useful since it provided a constant inoculum of microorganisms for the vessel which contained the oocysts and therefore would sustain a microbial population despite water treatment regimes. In addition, the first stage of the model system enables oocyst-free, control biofilms to be produced in the first vessel. This would be particularly necessary when investigating infectivity. Future work should consider the use of *in situ* excystation and infection into SCID mice to confirm results obtained by vital staining techniques.

References

Blewett D. A. 1989. Disinfection and oocysts, p. 107-116. In K. W. Angus and D. A. Blewett (ed.), Cryptosporidiosis. Proceedings of the First International Workshop. The Animal Disease Research Association, Edinburgh

Campbell, A. T., L. J. Robertson and H. V. Smith. 1992. Viability of *Cryptosporidium parvum* oocysts: correlation of *in vitro* excystation with inclusion or exclusion of fluorogenic vital dyes. Appl. Environ. Microbiol. 58:3488-3493

Hayes, E. B., T. D. Matte, T. R. O'Brien *et al.* 1989. A large community outbreak of cryptosporidiosis due to contamination of a filtered public water supply. N. Engl. J. Med. 320:1372-6

Mac Kenzie W. R., N. J. Hoxie, M. E. Proctor, M. S. Gradus, K. A. Blair, D. E. Peterson, J. J. Kazmierczak,. D. G. Addiss, K. R. Fox, J. B. Rose and J. P. Davis. 1994. A massive outbreak in Milwaukee of *Cryptosporidium* infection transmitted through the public water supply. N. Engl. J. Med. 331:161-7

Navin, T. R. and D. D. Juranek. 1984. Cryptosporidiosis: clinical, epidemiological and parasitological review. Rev. Infec. Dis. 6:313-27

Robertson, L. J., A. T. Campbell and H. V. Smith. Survival of *Cryptosporidium parvum* oocysts under various environmental pressures. Appl. Environ. Microbiol. 58:3494-3500

Rogers, J., A. B. Dowsett, P. J. Dennis, J. V. Lee and C. W. Keevil. 1994. Influence of materials on biofilm formation and growth of *Legionella pneumophila* in potable water systems. Appl. Environ. Microbiol. 60:1842-1851

Rogers, J., J. V. Lee, P. J. Dennis and C. W. Keevil. 1991. Continuous culture biofilm model for the survival and growth of *Legionella pneumophila* and associated protozoa in potable water systems, p.192-200. In R. Morris, L. M. Alexander, P. Wyn-Jones and J. Sellwood (ed.), Proceedings of the UK Symposium on Health-Related Water Microbiology, IAWPRC, Glasgow

Smith, H. V. and J. B. Rose. 1990. Waterborne cryptosporidiosis. Parasitol. Today. 6:8-12

Using Redox Potential to Assess *Cryptosporidium* Inactivation by Chlorine

V. Rasmussen[1], B. Nissen[1], E. Lund[1] and R.L. Strand[2]
[1]Laboratory of Virology and Immunology, Department of Veterinary Microbiology, The Royal Veterinary and Agricultural University, Copenhagen, Denmark
[2]Stranco Inc., Bradley, Ill., USA

Introduction

Chlorine is the most commonly used oxidizer for the disinfection of water supplies because it is relatively cheap and easy to apply. The mechanism through which chlorine inactivates pathogenic microorganisms is generally accepted to be oxidation. The management of a chlorine disinfection program is currently and typically accomplished by maintaining a measurable residual (concentration) of chlorine over a period of time known to be effective in achieving the disinfection goal. This practice has given rise to the concept of Ct or concentration multiplied by the contact time.

A titration or other residual analysis technique is the principal tool in disinfection management, with or without the rigorous application of Ct guidelines for plant design and operation. Unfortunately, the correlation between residual concentration and actual degree of disinfection is weak, particularly in soiled water. This is particularly vexing in light of current concerns with *Cryptosporidium*.

This paper details recent research into *Cryptosporidium*, virus and bacteria inactivation, th former having greater resistance to chlorine disinfection. It compares inactivation rates to both chlorine residuals and redox potentials. These studies show that redox potentials offer a more consistent method for predicting the results of an oxidant treatment program than do chlorine residuals.

Redox

In 1960 Hallum and Younger published a paper that dealt with the oxidation of influenza virus, Newcastle disease virus and poliovirus. They found a pronounced inactivation of these viruses by controlled potential electrolysis; however, they were only concerned with surface changes of the virus particles. In a series of publications (Lund and Lycke 1961) starting in 1961, the results of chemical oxidation studies of viruses were presented and expressed in terms of both redox (oxidation reduction) potentials and residual concentrations. These works clearly showed a close correlation between virus inactivation and redox potential. They were also the first papers to show the relatively poor correlation between inactivation and residual concentration. In 1965 Hasselbarth and Carlson studied chlorination on *E. coli* and found the same effect, again expressed in terms of redox potential. After this early period, little work was presented due to the difficulty in determining redox potentials in the laboratory. Using a potentiometer to measure between a calomel reference electrode and a platinum wire, the redox potential could be measured, but only intermittently, and the procedure required severe cleaning of the platinum between the measurements.

One of the most significant findings of this early research is that the rate of inactivation is dependent not only on the oxidant species (e.g. free or combined chlorine or permanganate) but as much on the reducing compounds present and other conditions.

A redox reaction equilibrium can in general be expressed with an equation like

$$Red + qH_2O \approx Ox + mH^+ + ne \qquad (a)$$

where Red is the concentration of reducing ions, Ox is the corresponding oxidant, e is one electron and q, m and n are the numbers of water molecules, hydrogen ions and electrons participating in the redox reaction, respectively. The law of mass action applied to the reaction leads to

$$E = E_o + \frac{RT}{nF} \ln \frac{Ox}{Red} - \frac{mRT}{nF} pH \quad \text{(b)}$$

Here E is the resultant oxidation potential and E_0 the normal oxidation potential (i.e. a constant of integration). Considering the findings stated earlier, that the rate of inactivation of virus is dependent on the oxidation reduction potential (ORP), it may now be seen why not only the concentration of an oxidant, but also the concentration of the reduced form, the temperature and pH influence the rate of reaction employing various oxidants.

In spite of these early studies, the idea of employing ORP rather than residual analysis to disinfection management has been implemented in industrial wastewater and public pool applications, but is not yet widespread in drinking water management.

Oxidation of *Cryptosporidium*

There is an established belief that *Cryptosporidium* is unaffected by chlorination. Alternatives to chlorine such as ozonation, flocculation and filtration are presently considered viable treatment plans to prevent this parasite from infecting public water supplies.

Because of the previous success in relating disinfection kinetics to redox potentials, new experiments were conducted in 1993/94 with the intent of discovering whether controlled-potential chlorination could effectively inactivate *Cryptosporidium*. New experiments were also conducted on several bacteria and viruses to form a common point of reference.

Materials and Methods

The testing of *Cryptosporidium* was carried out by counting the number of excysted oocysts (i.e. counting the number of empty shells).

A sample of the material containing 2.0×10^5 oocysts was centrifuged in an Eppendorf tube at 500 g for 10 minutes. The supernatant was drawn off and 1 ml 1% 37°C warmed trypsin in HBSS adjusted to pH 4 was added. After 1 hour at 37°C the sample was centrifuged for 10 minutes at 500 g at room temperature and the supernatant was drawn completely off. To a 37°C warm HBSS solution (in an amount of 950 µl) was added 50 µl of 2.2% $NaHCO_3$ and 100 µl of 1% nataurocholate in HBSS (employ a water heater box) and the solution was mixed. After 1 hour at 37°C, 100 oocysts were counted and the procentual amount of empty shells were determined. The sporazoites did not need to be counted.

To prepare trypsin and nataurocholate solutions, 200 mg of trypsin and of taurocholic acid (nb T-0750) were dissolved in 2 x 20 ml Hanks' Balanced Salt Solution (CHBSS). The trypsin solution was adjusted into pH 4.0 samples and kept in the freezer.

Determinations of chlorine were carried out employing a Hach battery driven colorimeter, which was calibrated to measure free or total chlorine content. The colorimeter permitted a direct reading in milligrams per liter of chlorine.

ORP measurements were obtained employing a Strantrol 751 (Stranco Inc.). A basic ORP system may consist of a highly sensitive potentiometer with a silver/silver chloride reference electrode and platinum electrode. The platinum employed was 99.9995% pure (over 200 times more pure than conventional ORP sensors). With the electrodes immersed in water, a liquid junction (salt bridge) and the medium being analyzed complete the electrical connection between the electrodes. The potential measured is then converted and displayed on a meter.

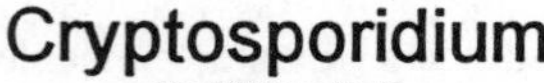

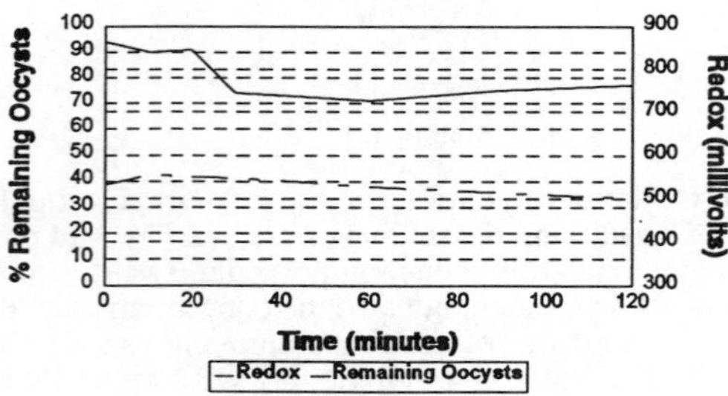

Figure 1.

Cryptosporidium

0.01% Sodium Hypochlorite

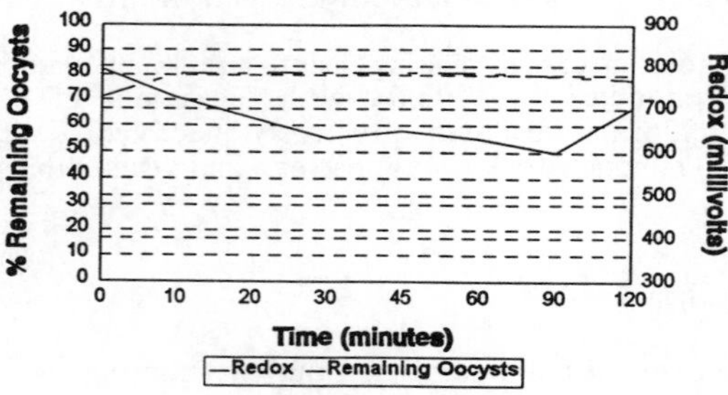

Figure 2.

Cryptosporidium

0.1% Sodium Hypochlorite

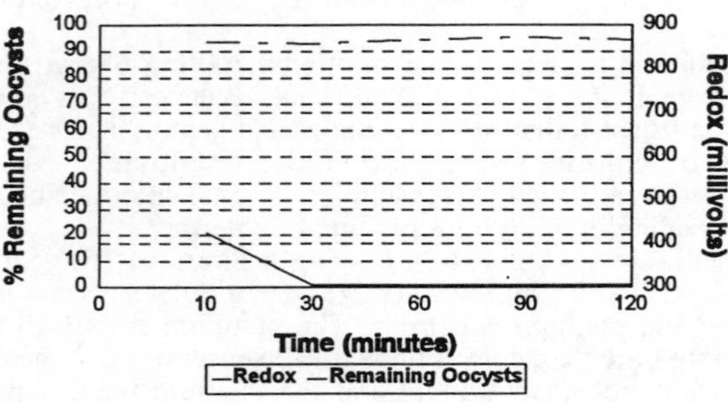

Figure 3.

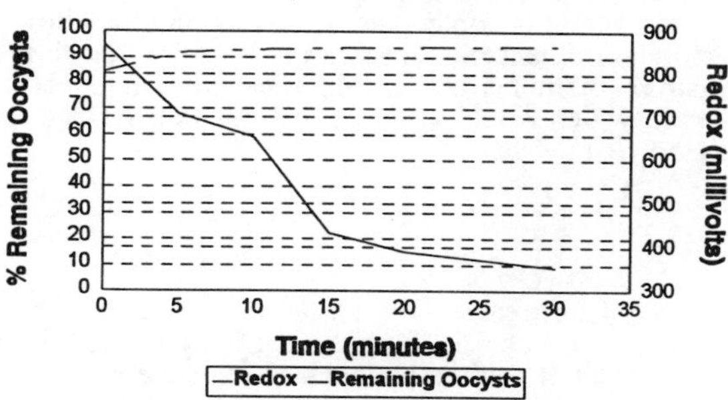

Figure 4.

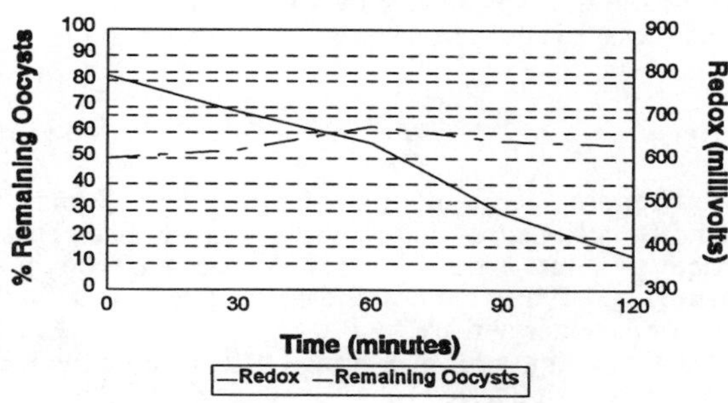

Figure 5.

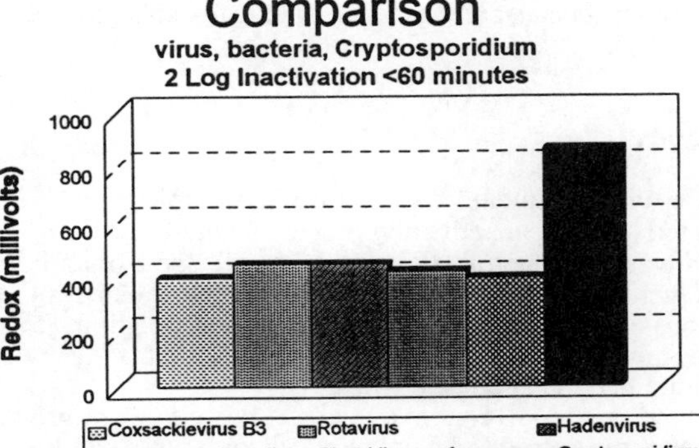

Figure 6.

The ORP measurement equipment made the whole process of potential determination reliable and convenient. In the earlier research it was necessary to constantly rework a detachable platinum electrode in order to get proper results. It had to be cleaned in acid, rinsed, glowed to high temperature, cooled and reset. This did not allow fast measurement and never continuous measurement. Some researchers omitted such procedures and got completely false positive results after having measured in a solution with a high concentration of chlorine, which would attach to the platinum surface. This fouling of the platinum was a very serious drawback.

Results

Cryptosporidium oocysts were treated with chloramine T. 1.0 g/l. (Fig 1) and sodium hypochlorite, 0.01% (Fig 2). Free chlorine was about 1.0 mg/l. The ORP of the chloramine T. treatment was 550 mV, and of sodium hypochlorite treatment was 770 mV. Very little excystment took place within 2 hours, in fact very little above the control. A new experiment employing 0.1% sodium hypochlorite (Fig 3) was conducted. An ORP of 800-850 mV was obtained at a free chlorine of 15-17 mg/l. Starting with 10^6 to 10^7 oocysts per ml., less than 1% remained after 30 minutes of treatment. This 2-log inactivation in 30 minutes was very surprising based on other reported research findings. In another experiment (Fig 4), 10^6 oocysts were reduced to less than 10% in 30 minutes at 800 mV and a free chlorine of 8-9 mg/l. Employing chloramine T (5 g/l) (Fig 5) an ORP of 600-650 mV was obtained resulting in an excystation of 13% in 2 hours. With 10 g/l of chloramine T an ORP of 730 mV was obtained giving about 15 mg/l of free chlorine. The resultant excystation was less than 10% in 2 hours.

Oxidation of Viruses

In the aforementioned reports, the oxidation of *poliovirus* (Lund 1964) as well as *coxsackieviruses* A and B, *echoviruses* and reovirus were studied. These viruses follow similar patterns of inactivation rate and trend when compared to redox potential. This was also true for *adenovirus* (Lund 1966), but in this case the rate of inactivation was found to be 10 times faster than for the enteroviruses.

In the present work, new techniques for measuring ORP and chlorine were employed and three different types of viruses were tested. The *coxsackievirus* B3 was selected because it may be useful as an indicator virus for faecally polluted water. The *rotavirus* was chosen, because it has been difficult to cultivate (Butchaiah *et al.* 1984) and there is a suspicion that the rotaviruses are not easily removed during wastewater treatment. They also remain active in the environment longer than enteroviruses. In addition, the bovine parvovirus (*Hadenvirus*) was chosen because it has been found resistant to chemical inactivation (Ravindra and Lund 1980).

Materials and Methods

Virus Filtrations The viruses studied were all titrated employing 10-fold dilution steps, with dilutions estimated to fit the inactivation process studies.

Coxsackievirus B3 was cultivated in HeLa cells, a cell line from a human carcinoma of the cervix. The cells were grown in Nunclon microtiter plates with 1 ml of medium in each well. The medium consisted of Eagle minimum essential medium, to which 2 per cent newborn calf serum, bicarbonate and antibodies were added. Final readings were made when the control culture had the stipulated titres.

Rotavirus was titrated in MA-104 monkey cells. The cells were grown with 2 per cent newborn calf serum and transferred to Nunclon plates with 2 per cent serum. The virus was activated with trypsin by mixing one part of virus suspension with one part of trypsin (Sigma No. T-6763) diluted 1:100. At the transfer to microplates, trypsin was added in a concentration of 1:10,000. The medium in the microplates had a confluent layer of cells, but was devoid of serum when virus suspensions were added.

Bovine parvovirus *(Hadenvirus)* was grown in secondary calf kidney cells. The medium contained 8 per cent of fetal calf serum. The virus titrations were carried out in tube cultures containing 2 ml medium without serum and 50,000-100,000 cells.

Results

Coxsackievirus B3 was grown to a high titre, 10^9 $TCID_{10}$ per ml. The virus was diluted 1:10,000 in buffer. Then chloramine T was added to a level of 0.1 g per liter. The ORP was stable from 343 mV to 380 mV. As in all cases of the present report, the inactivation of the virus was followed for 2 hours, taking in all 8 samples and controls without any oxidant at the beginning and the end of each test. The total chlorine level was 3 mg/l and the free chlorine 0.8 mg/l. The pH was 7.1 increasing to 7.8. The rate of inactivation started at 1 log unit per 10 minutes, but then remained unchanged after a 3 log unit reduction. Employing 1.0 g chloramine per liter, the virus was inactivated in 60 minutes (5 log units in 60 minutes). This fits rather well with previous experiments.

Employing 0.001 per cent sodium hypochlorite, a millivolt value of around 400 mV was obtained at a pH of 7.5-8.0. Although the free chlorine level was 0.1 mg/l, no inactivation was observed. 0.006 per cent hypochlorite resulted in 400- 500 mV at 0.1 mg free chlorine. The virus dilution was only 1:10 and it therefore took 10 minutes to reduce the virus titre 3 log units even in the most efficient case.

The results of the tests were thus rather unsatisfactory. The virus suspensions should have been more purified or diluted. The rates found were, however, in agreement with previous results.

Rotavirus experiment schedules were like those for *Coxsackievirus*. The virus dilution of 1:1000 permitted only 400 mV in spite of the presence of 1.2-1.8 mg/l of free chlorine when 0.1g/l of chloramine T. was employed. The pH was kept at 7.5 and the rate of inactivation of the rotavirus was 1 log unit reduction in 30 minutes. In fact, this was a value quite similar to what has been found for enteroviruses.

Another experiment permitted a higher potential and a 4 log unit reduction within 30 minutes. Employing 0.001 per cent sodium hypochlorite, one experiment gave 4 log units reduction of virus in 50 minutes, whereas another gave only 1 log unit reduction in 10 minutes and then stopped. Consequently, it seems that the rotavirus behaved more or less like the enteroviruses.

Hadenvirus was studied with the same schedule as for the other viruses: Inactivation was followed for 2 hours taking 8 samples. At an ORP of 300-400 mV and 0.7-0.9 free chlorine with 0.1 g of chloramine T added, a titer reduction of 2 log units was obtained in 60 minutes, but then no further reduction was obtained.

Employing 0.005 per cent of sodium hypochlorite, an ORP of above 450 mV was obtained with free chlorine of 0.05-0.07 mg/l. 1-2 log units of virus reduction were obtained in 45 minutes, but no further reduction was observed. It seems necessary to carry out more experiments with *Hadenvirus* before any conclusion may be drawn, but the general impression is that the virus is quite resistant to chlorine inactivation.

Oxidation Of Bacteria

Materials and Methods

E. coli suspensions were prepared in the following way: 4 ml of meat extract broth was inoculated with an agar slant culture of *E. coli* and incubated at 37°C for 4 hours. The broth was then transferred to a bottle containing 100 ml of fresh broth, which was incubated at 37°C for 18 hours. The culture was spun down, and the cells were washed twice in phosphate buffer (pH 7) and resuspended in the same buffer. The final suspension contained about 109 bacteria per ml.

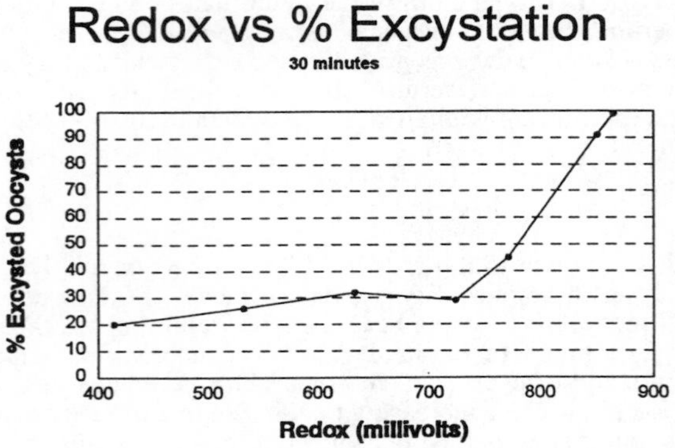
Redox vs % Excystation
30 minutes
% Excysted Oocysts
100
90
80
70
60
50
40
30
20
10
0
400
500
600
700
800
900
Redox (millivolts)

Figure 7

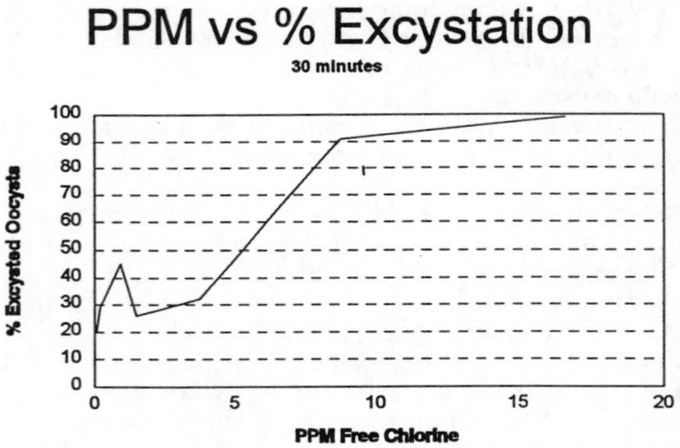
PPM vs % Excystation
30 minutes
% Excysted Oocysts
100
90
80
70
60
50
40
30
20
10
0
0
5
10
15
20
PPM Free Chlorine

Figure 8.

In the chlorination experiments, a diluted suspension of bacteria was mixed with a dilution of chlorine. Serial, tenfold dilutions were prepared from this mixture and from each dilution step, four aliquots of 1 ml were mixed with RVG agar and poured into petri dishes. The dishes were incubated at 37°C and 44°C and colony counts were made after 24 and 48 hours. The numbers of viable bacteria were calculated from the counts obtained on the plates showing 30-300 colonies.

Results

Employing 0.005 per cent hypochlorite against *E. coli*, no disinfection was obtained in 2 hours in spite of a total chlorine of 0.8 mg/l and a free chlorine of 0.1 mg/l. The ORP was 150-200 mV. These results repeated at both 37°C and 44°C. With 0.1 g/l of chloramine T the infectivity went down from 10^6 bacteria per ml in 45-60 minutes. The free chlorine was 0.5 mg/l and the total chlorine 3.0 mg/l. The ORP was around 200-300 mV.

For *Enterococcus faecalis* no disinfection was obtained with 0.05 per cent sodium hypochlorite, although the potential was 300-400 mV, the free chlorine 0.1 mg/l and the total around 1.0 mg/l. Employing chloramine T (0.1 g/l) the potential was around 400 mV, the free chlorine 0.8 mg/l, the total 3 mg/l. Here the bacteria titer went from 6.7 per ml to <10 after 45 minutes.

For *Clostridium perfrungens* the bacterial titer went from 1.6 x 10^7 to 1.4 x 10^1 in 60 minutes when chloramine T was employed in 0.1 g/l. The ORP was 400 mV, free chlorine 0.5-0.8 mg/l and total chlorine 2.5-3.0 mg/l.

Discussion

When free chlorine is present, the combined chlorine does not influence the results because the ORP is so much lower for combined chlorine than for free chlorine. Therefore, in spite of the measurement of total chlorine carried out, these measurements are not included in the descriptions of the results as they are considered unimportant.

The importance of the theory of ORP can be seen from equation b. The factors that are so conveniently a part of the potential show that redox depends not only on the oxidant and the corresponding reducing compound(s), but also the temperature, the pH and the character of equation a.

It is apparent from the data (Fig 6) that *Cryptosporidium* is much more resistant to chlorine than are the bacteria and viruses studied here. This would also hold true for viruses studied in previous research. It does, however, seem possible to inactivate at reasonable dosages and within practical contact times. Figures 7 and 8 show excystation rates after 30 minutes of contact time, plotted against redox and chlorine concentration. The shape of the redox curve is typical for microorganism disinfection. Very little kill takes place up to a lower threshold, after which inactivation rate increases in linear proportion to redox increase. Chlorine concentration does not seem to show this same proportionality.

Why does this research suggest that 2 logs of *Cryptosporidium* inactivation can be accomplished in 30 minutes at 17 PPM free chlorine when other studies seem to indicate much higher concentrations and longer contact times are required? The key appears to be the maintenance of a constant redox potential for the duration of the contact time, as has been true with numerous experiments with viruses. The reported 17 PPM free chlorine is merely incidental to this particular experiment. Another experiment at different pH, temperature, chlorine species or reductant load could easily require a different average residual to achieve the same redox potential. As long as the same redox potential is maintained, the same results should be achieved. Since earlier research on *Cryptosporidium* did not include redox potential data, it can only be assumed that potentials were not measured during the experiments. We cannot know what the potentials were or if they were constant over the contact time. Based on the high chlorine concentration required, we can only surmise that the potentials were lower than reported here. Redox potentials should be considered critical data in future research on *Cryptosporidium* inactivation.

Conclusions

Cryptosporidium is much more resistant to chlorination than bacteria or viruses. However, it is the opinion of the authors that it may not be so resistant that chlorination cannot be used to combat this parasite.

Assuming 2 logs of inactivation are sufficient to protect potable water supplies against *Cryptosporidium*, the authors suggest that safe water can be provided without major modification to the treatment plant. Further we propose that 30 minutes of contact time is not unreasonable. If the chlorine level is brought down to normal levels immediately after the contact time, the development of undue levels of disinfection byproducts (DBP) may also be avoided.

Redox has proven to be a direct indicator of virus inactivation rate in experiments conducted over the last 35 years. This research indicates that it is also an indicator of *Cryptosporidium* inactivation rate. This rate-predicting ability, along with its proven field reliability record, makes redox potential measurement and control a valuable tool in disinfection management applications. It also should allow engineers to design and implement disinfection management systems that will meet safe-water needs now and in the future.

References

Butchaiah G, Bøtner A. G. and Lund E. Studies on the growth of bovine rotavirus in cell cultures. Zbl. Vet. Med B. 31, 760-769 (1984)
Hallum J.V and Younger J.S. The effect of oxidative controlled potential electrolysis on viruses. Virology 12, 283-308 (1960)
Hasselbarth U and Carlson S. Die Beschaffenheit des Badewassers in einem vertikal durchströmten Becken in Abhängigkeit von Belastung Aufbereitung. Arch. Badewesen. 18, 6 (1965)
Lund E and Lycke E. The effect of oxidation and reduction on the infectivity of polyomyelitis virus. Arch. ges. Virusforsch. XI, 100-110 (1961)
Lund E. Oxidative inactivation of adenovirus. Arch ges. Virusforsch. XIX, 32-37 (1966)
Lund E. Oxidative inactivation of different types of enteroviruses. Am. J. Hyg. 80, 1-10 (1964)
Ravindra N. S. and Lund E. The stability of bovine parvovirus and its possible use as an indicator for the persistence of enteric viruses. Water Res. 14, 1017-1021 (1980)

Acanthamoeba keratitis: a Water-borne Disease

D.V. Seal, J. Hay and C.M. Kirkness
Department of Ophthalmology, University of Glasgow, UK

Introduction

If not diagnosed early (Bacon *et al.* 1993), ocular disease associated with the free-living protozoan *Acanthamoeba* can be devastating. The amoebae are introduced onto the cornea in contaminated water or from dirt or by association with contact lenses which have transferred to the ocular surface from a storage case containing the amoebae (Seal, 1994).

The Organism

There are about 17 known species of *Acanthamoeba* and of these 7 have so far been indicted as causing disease in humans. Four species have so far been found in association with keratitis (John, 1993) but this is likely to be an underestimate.

Of further importance when considering the dynamics of an *Acanthamoeba* infection is that a predator-prey relationship can exist between the protozoan and certain bacterial species and other microbes in the environment (Rodriguez-Zaragoza, 1994). This can also occur within the storage case (Devonshire *et al.* 1993). *Acanthamoeba* also have a protozoonotic interaction with other human pathogens such as members of the genus *Legionella*. Transfer of such bacteria to the ocular surface within the amoebae may have a profound effect on the pathogenic processes which are generally attributed to the amoebae only.

The Infection

Patients with *Acanthamoeba* infection of the cornea typically present with an inflammed eye and are in considerable pain which is exacerbated by exposure of the eye to light. Initially there is an epithelial infection with punctate lesions and often a dendritiform type of infiltrate that may later ulcerate.

An alternative clinical appearance is the occurrence of micro-abscesses that can be observed in a circular pattern or as a 'snow-storm' effect on slit lamp microscopy. If *Acanthamoeba* has not been identified as the cause of these ocular changes, the infection will progress remorselessly. There is infiltration by the protozoan into the corneal stroma, thus resulting in a deep stromal ring abscess, which can involve the whole of the cornea. Perforation may ensue with consequent loss of vision.

Early intervention even with a regimen comprising chlorhexidine and propamidine isethionate (Hay *et al.* 1994) is essential. Treatment commenced at later stages in the disease process will usually require corneal grafting on one or more occasion. This may be due to cyst forms of *Acanthamoeba* being retained within the remaining host corneal tissue undergoing excystation with migration into the graft, thus inducing recrudescence of ocular disease.

The Ecology of the Infection

Acanthamoeba can be found in a wide range of very diverse environments including soil and water. Infection of the eye has occurred in some instances without contact lens wear. In such circumstances previous corneal disease such as that associated with trachoma or *Herpes simplex* infection cannot be discounted in the aetiology of the subsequent infection with *Acanthamoeba*. There is no doubt, however, that in the majority of individuals who acquire this fairly rare corneal infection, contact lens wear plays a major role.

The primary source of *Acanthamoeba* infection of the cornea in contact lens wearers is domestic tap water (Hay and Seal, 1994) and potable water derived from the workplace, used to clean or rinse the storage case or to dilute inappropriate disinfecting agents. This is not to discount completely the fact that *Acanthamoeba* can also be found in dust and dirt around wash-basins and in hot-tubs and swimming pools, the latter even in the presence of chlorine.

There are two major problems that appear to be of considerable importance in the acquisition of contact lens associated *Acanthamoeba keratitis*. First, use of inappropriate disinfection practice. A number of disinfection solutions are completely ineffective against *Acanthamoeba*, especially in its cyst form (Hay *et al.* 1995). Cysts are resistant to commercially-available chlorine-generating systems used in contact lens disinfection practice (Seal *et al.* 1993). Under no circumstances whatever, should tap water or any other non-sterile aqueous material containing tap water come into contact with the lenses. Some products are efficacious against the amoebae under optimum laboratory conditions for the particular chemical agent but may be considerably less so when there are fluctuations in pH or organic loading. Further, some products may be acanthamoebacidal only at higher concentrations than are present in a commercial preparation of the contact lens disinfection system.

Secondly, many users of contact lenses admit to washing their lenses and/or storage cases in non-sterile water from the domestic tap. This usually, but not invariably, occurs with the cold-water supply in the bathroom.

Once in the storage case, the *Acanthamoeba* trophozoite may find a very favourable environment for its survival and replication. The solution in which it is located is generally stored at temperatures which greatly suit its growth. Gram negative bacteria, yeasts, algae and other organisms will provide it with a ready source of nutrition. Mechanical transfer to the eye of the *Acanthamoeba* can then occur since they can adhere to the polymers used for contact lens manufacture (Kilvington and Larkin, 1990). If local conditions permit, the amoebae are capable of invading the cornea to produce ocular pathology associated with their infection of this structure.

Thus an almost closed cycle of events appears to be associated with development of *Acanthamoeba keratitis*. This commences with the amoebae within the domestic water supply being decanted into the contact lens storage case. There will be multiplication of these amoebae within the biologically favourable conditions that they often find within the case. With inappropriate cleaning and disinfection the population and their resources may be reduced but not removed completely, so that the organisms may soon proliferate. It is then from the contact lens stored within this environment that transfer of the offending amoebae to the ocular surface occurs with potentially disastrous effects should the cornea be susceptible to invasion by the *Acanthamoeba*.

The Solution

Potable or other water taken from especially the cold water tap supply should never be part of contact lens hygiene practice. Storage cases can be cleaned using boiled-cool water (used at about 70°C) from the domestic kettle (Hay and Seal, 1994). The only truly effective cold chemical acanthamoebacidal agent available commercially is 3% hydrogen peroxide. Chlorhexidine at a concentration as low as 0.002% in a solution of around neutral pH and with no organic load is also a highly efficacious agent for killing *Acanthamoeba*.

Acanthamoeba is undoubtedly a water-borne pathogen. Its effect on the human eye would be best eliminated by prevention of direct or indirect interaction of contaminated water with the cornea.

References

Bacon AS, Dart JKG, Ficker LA, Matheson MM, Wright P. (1993). *Acanthamoeba keratitis* the value of early diagnosis. Ophthalmology, 100: 1238-1243

Devonshire P, Munro FA, Abernethy C, Clark BJ (1993). Microbial contamination of contact lens cases in the West of Scotland. British Journal of Ophthalmology, 77: 41-45

Hay J and Seal DV (1994). Contact lens wear by hospital health care staff: is there cause for concern? British Journal of Optometry and Dispensing, 2, 145-148

Hay J, Kirkness CM, Seal DV, Wright P (1994). Drug resistance and *Acanthamoeba keratitis*: the quest for alternative antiprotozoal chemotherapy. Eye (in press)

Hay J, Seal DV, Connor R, Simmons PA, Tomlinson A (1995). Disinfection and sonication: effect on *Acanthamoeba* cyst adherence to ionic, high water content hydrogel contact lens. Journal of the British Contact Lens Association, (in press)

John DT (1993). Opportunistically pathogenic free-living amoebae. In Parasitic Protozoa, 2nd Edition, Volume 3. Eds Kreier JP and Baker JR, Academic Press, Inc., San Diego pp143-246

Kilvington S and Larkin DFP (1990). *Acanthamoeba* adherence to contact lenses and removal by cleaning agents. Eye, 4: 589-593

Rodriguez-Zaragoza S (1994). Ecology of free-living amoebae. Critical Reviews in Microbiology, 20: 225-241

Seal DV (1994). *Acanthamoeba keratitis* A problem for contact lens wearers that is here to stay. British Medical Journal (Editorial), 308: 1116-1117

Seal DV, Hay J, Devonshire P, Kirkness CM (1993). *Acanthamoeba* and contact lens disinfection: should chlorine be discontinued? British Journal of Ophthalmology, 77, 128

Disinfection of *Cryptosporidium parvum* with Ozone at High Concentrations

D.C. Armstrong[1], D.P. Casemore[2], A.M. Couper[1], A.D. Martin[1] and P.J. Naylor[3]
[1]ICI Chemicals & Polymers Ltd, PO Box 8, The Heath, Runcorn, Cheshire WA7 4QG, UK
[2]Public Health Laboratory, Ysbyty Glan Clwyd, Bodelwyddan, Rhyl, Clwyd, UK
[3]Acer Environmental, Acer House, Howard Court, Manor Park, Nr Daresbury, Warrington, Cheshire WA7 1SJ, UK

Introduction

Work on strategies for dealing with *Cryptosporidium parvum* in potable water treatment systems have shown that ozone is an effective disinfectant (Peeters *et al.* 1989; Ransome *et al.* 1993). However, laboratory studies to determine the required concentration - time product (CT value) have shown that this will need to be higher than that for other organisms (Finch *et al.* 1993). This situation is likely to be worse in practice because of factors such as temperature, natural range of the organism's robustness and competing reactions. ICI has been working on the development and scale-up of an ozone generator that is capable of generating gaseous ozone at concentrations up to 40% wt which is much higher than conventional methods (Couper and Bullen 1992; Couper 1993). Contacting this with water can readily produce high concentrations of dissolved ozone.

The availability of this technology and the acknowledged difficulties with the disinfection of *Cryptosporidium* showed that an investigation into its use for this application would be of interest.

Ozone as a Disinfectant

The use of ozone at high concentration would generate conditions very different from those normally used and so consideration had to be given to the interpretation of the data and how it would be used for equipment design. The observed disinfection process with ozone is a combination of several individual processes. It is commonly simplified to a CT value, but this assumes that the process is zero order for the organism. In practice for an organism like *Cryptosporidium* this has been found to be incorrect, probably due to the oxidation reactions required to break down the oocyst's shell (Finch *et al.* 1993).

Also in this work the aim was to use gaseous ozone in a practical contactor/reactor which would more closely represent a working system. Hence a more rigorous approach was used where the process was divided into four steps: injuring, killing, lysing and fragmenting. Each step has a rate (r) which can be expressed by an equation of the form:

$$r = k\, c^{n}_{\text{oocyst}}\, c^{m}_{\text{dissolved ozone}}$$

where k is a rate constant and c the concentration of subscripted species with reaction orders of n and m. The changes taking place in each step are illustrated in Figure 1. In the excystation process an injured oocyst is capable of producing between 1 and 4 active sporozoites, a killed oocyst gives none, and a lysed oocyst gives none but has the appearance of being excysted to give active sporozoites. With extensive ozonation fragmentation of the oocyst's shell can occur but this need not be considered in detail for the disinfection process. Finally, the rate equations for the steps can be summed as a set of series of parallel processes to describe the overall process. In this study data was obtained to test this model for a batch system so that it could be extended to a continuous flow situation.

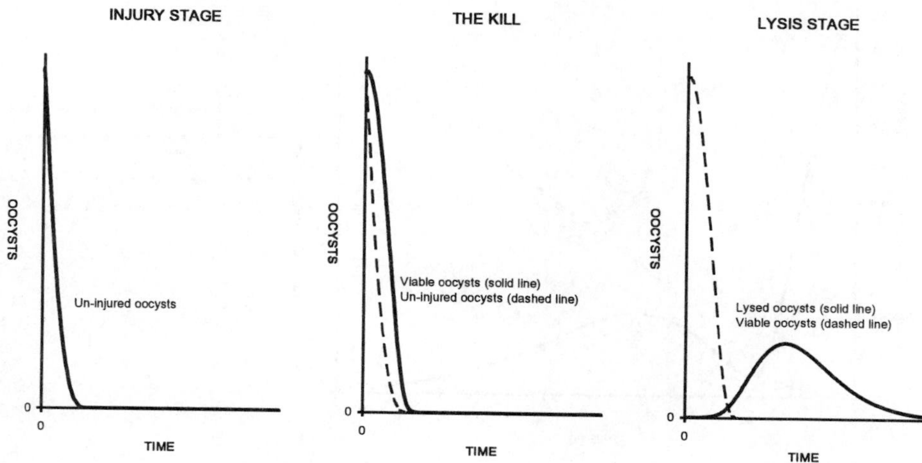

Figure 1. Four stage model of cryptosporidium parvum disinfection

Experimental

The tests were carried out in a glass 1.5 litre stirred batch reactor/contactor. Separate measurements were used to determine the mass transfer characteristics of the system. Ozone gas was supplied at 0.5 g/h with concentrations of 2, 10 and 20% wt. Fresh tap water was inoculated with oocysts to give a concentration of about 10^4 oocysts/ml. To provide additional data on the effectiveness of the ozone and some ozone demand 10^6 poliovirus/ml was also added. Initial samples were taken and the ozone started, further samples were withdrawn for analysis of dissolved ozone and microbiological measurements.

The dissolved ozone was determined using the standard DPD colorimetric method with dilution at higher concentrations (Anon). The oocysts were separated by centrifugation, excysted in phosphate buffered saline solution and fixed in glutaraldehyde for counting. Counts were performed by phase - contrast microscopy, to determine the numbers of whole oocysts (non-viable), empty oocysts and sporozoites. Note was also taken of incomplete excystation.

Results

The results for the experiment using 20% wt ozone are presented in Figure 2 as the change with time for the number of oocysts that excysted to leave empty shells and the dissolved ozone concentration. As expected in this batch experiment, the dissolved ozone concentration increased but did not reach a stable value. The disinfection process for the oocysts took place surprisingly quickly. The poliovirus was extinguished at the first sample point i.e. within 20s. Similar data was obtained at the other ozone concentrations. A control run with only poliovirus showed that air only in the contactor/reactor system had no detectable effect.

Discussion

In all the tests, a rapid disinfection was observed with kills in the range 120 to 420 secs. The paradoxical result of apparently increasing excystation following a fall in the number of viable oocysts is spurious. Exposure which is just sufficient to kill the sporozoites usually

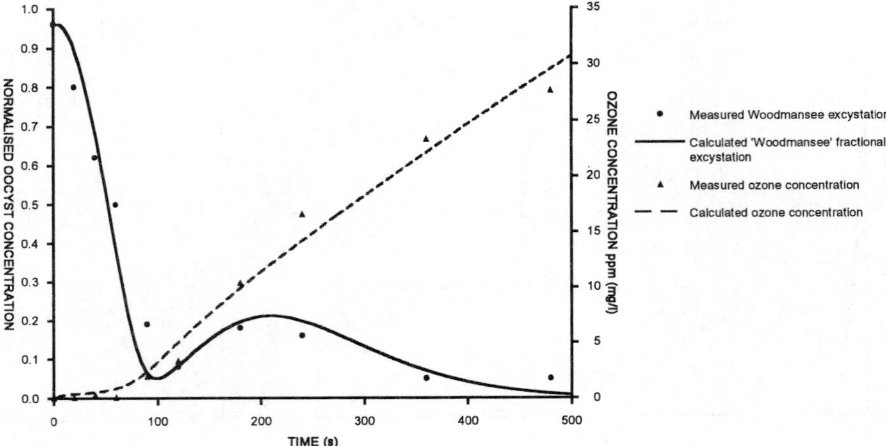

Figure 2. Four stage model fitted to 20% w/w ozone disinfection data

results in whole, intact but dead oocysts. Increased length of exposure may cause the sporozoite to lyse within the oocyst and for the suture to open when exposed to excystation fluid. It is then difficult to distinguish dead but empty or partially empty oocysts from the empty shells which have released viable sporozoites. The sporozoite numbers found following the excystation process declined rapidly to <2/shell and very few sporozoites could be detected after 60 to 90 seconds.

Using these results and the characterisation of the reactor/contactor, curves could be calculated for the various stages of the process and combined to give the overall observed curve as shown in Figure 2 for the test with 20% wt ozone. It can be seen that a good fit to the observed data was obtained; consistent results were also obtained for 10% wt but were less good for 2% wt; Table 1 summarises the disinfection times and utilisations.

Table 1

Disinfection of *Cryptosporidium*			
Reduction in viable oocysts (Log)	Ozone in gas phase (% wt)	Disinfection Time (s)	Utilisation (%)
3	2	238	65
	20	130	96
6	2	300	52
	20	167	94

These disinfection times are very short and are due to the efficient mass transfer that can be achieved by the combination of ozone at high concentration and the design of the contactor/reactor. It is difficult to compare these results with other available data because other work has generally used an ozonated solution that is inoculated, and in this case the concentration will decline during the experiment. Parker (Parker *et al.* 1993) describes a high degree of disinfection by 120s with 5 mg ozone/l and refers to the continuous addition of ozone being a preferable method.

Conclusions

The ability to analyse experimental data in this way means that investigations can be carried out in the laboratory and on pilot plants in conditions that are more realistic and comparable to those encountered in practice, and can yield valuable design data. The use of ozone at 20% wt is probably not economically viable for use in the main treatment line. However, recent considerations of possible methods has suggested that using a multiple barrier approach will be best (Robertson *et al.* 1994). In this the oocysts are filtered out and then purged from the system by backwashing. These backwash waters can contain 10^4 oocysts/litre and a high degree of disinfection will be required before the water can be re-used or returned to the environment.

Based on these results it is proposed that the combination of 20% wt ozone with an intensive contacting/reacting system would provide a way of treating these backwash waters. Such a system would have a small reaction volume with a low residence time and less by-product formation, a high degree of disinfection from the high residual ozone concentration at the point of injection and a higher utilisation of the ozone.

The next stage is to carry out larger scale field trials. To this end, ICI has proposed a mobile trailer mounted unit specifically designed for the treatment of backwash waters. This would use ICI's electrochemical ozone generator to produce high concentration ozone with a venturi contactor followed by a helical pipe reactor which provides an intense contacting/reacting system.

References

Anon, Chemical disinfecting agents in water and effluents. HMSO, ISBN 011 7514934, 1980

Couper A M, Bullen S; I.CHEM.E. Symposium Series No. 127, 1992

Couper A M; 11th Ozone World Congress, San Francisco, 1993

Finch G R, Black E K, Gyurek L, Belosevic M; Applied Environ. Microbiol., vol 59, p4203, 1993

Parker J F W, Greaves G F, Smith H V; Wat Sci Tech, vol 27, p93, 1993

Peeters, J E, Elvira A M, Masschelein, W J, Martinez de Maturana I V, Debacker E; Applied Environ. Microbiol., vol 55, p1519, 1989

Ransome M E, Whitmore T N, Carrington E G; Water Supply, vol 11, p103, 1993

Robertson L J, Smith H V, Ongerth J E; Microbiology Europe, Jan/Feb 1994, p18

Wessex Water's Approach to the Treatment of Sand Filter Backwashings

D. Craft
Wessex Water Science and Technology, Kingston Seymour, Clevedon, Avon BS21 6UY, UK

Introduction

Wessex Water has a policy of re-using backwash water, where applicable, from rapid gravity and pressure sand filters on its surface water treatment works. Recycling backwash water conserves a valuable resource in areas where abstraction licence quantities are limited and customer demand is increasing.

During the last few years, the issue of cryptosporidium contamination of surface water sources has caused Wessex Water to reconsider the conventional approach to recycling of backwash water. Experience elsewhere has shown that recycling the washwater from sand filters can create a significant problem on concentrating *Cryptosporidium* oocysts within the water treatment works (WTW) to such an extent that ultimately a breakthrough of oocysts can occur.

Wessex Water's approach has been to adopt a policy of filtering the backwash water to ensure that the *Cryptosporidium* oocysts are removed from the cycle. The filtration system also provides the benefit of reducing turbidity and hence increasing the quality of the recycled stream.

Outlined below are details of the evaluation of the Kalsep Fibrotex filter for the treatment of sand filter backwashings carried out and a description of the Fibrotex system installed at Ashford WTW in 1992.

Ashford Water Treatment Works

The new Ashford WTW was completed and commissioned in 1992. Source water is primarily run-off from the Quantock hills and is collected in Ashford and Hawkridge reservoirs. The new works incorporates dissolved air flotation followed by pressure sand filtration, rapid gravity granular activated carbon filters (GAC) and final chlorination to achieve the required treated water quality standards. Ferric chloride is currently used as coagulant.

The pressure sand filters are backwashed regularly, typically every twenty four hours, and the GAC filters backwashed every two weeks. The backwash water from the filters is then allowed to settle for a minimum period of two hours. The settled sludge is removed and dewatered by centrifuge. The supernatant water is fed directly to the multi-vessel Fibrotex unit from which the filtrate is returned to Ashford raw water reservoir.

The Fibrotex Filter

Background

Fibrotex is a finely rated fibrous filter capable of achieving 98% removal of particles down to 2 μm in a standard test dust challenge. This compares to a standard dual media filter (sand + anthracite) which typically achieves 83% for the same challenge. Of particular importance for *Cryptosporidium* removal is the 5 μm removal efficiency which is approximately 99.9% for the Fibrotex filter compared to 94% for a dual media filter.

During the filtration cycle, the nylon yarn filter element is twisted and compressed, with the feed passing from the outside of the element to the central core. When fully loaded with solids, the element is automatically backwashed by untwisting and extending the yarn, and reversing the flow.

Initial Wessex Water trials

Wessex Water carried out initial trials on Fibrotex for the treatment of sand filter backwashings at Durleigh WTW. The objectives of the trial were expressed as a set of agreed performance criteria for the Fibrotex unit:

1 Filtrate quality
   - 70-75% reduction of suspended solids
   - reduction of turbidity of the settled backwash water feed from 10 NTU to 4 NTU
   - high removal efficiency of dosed *Cryptosporidium* oocysts
2 Throughput
   - 1 m^3/hr from AX5 trial unit
3 Backwash water requirement
   - less than 10% of the throughput of the filtration cycle

The results of the trial were encouraging with a filtrate quality of better than 4 NTU at a flowrate of 1.1 m^3/hr. Run times of 50-55 minutes were achieved, equating to a 9% backwash water requirement. *Cryptosporidium* oocysts dosed at 10^3/litre were removed by Fibrotex, with none detected in the filtrate. Thus all of the performance criteria set were met.

The Fibrotex system at Ashford WTW

The installed AX200 Fibrotex system has the capacity to treat up to 1 Ml/d of settled filter backwash water. Since installation in the summer of 1992, good filtrate quality has been achieved, meeting the performance targets set. Run times have resulted in a backwash water requirement of approximately 10% of the throughput of the filtration cycle. Typical plant performance is illustrated in the table below.

Table 1. Typical performance of Fibrotex filter at Ashford WTW

Run time	Feed quality			Filtrate quality		
(minutes)	Suspended Solids (mg/l)	Turbidity (NTU)	Total Iron (mgFe/l)	Suspended Solids (mg/l)	Turbidity (NTU)	Total Iron (mgFe/l)
0	-	-	-	<2	0.9	0.02
15	11	2.8	0.17	<2	0.9	0.02
40	10	3.7	0.39	2	1.2	0.06
60	13	4.6	0.51	7	2.1	0.19
62	13	5.2	0.59	5	1.9	0.15
64	....backwash initiated..					
Mean	11.8	4.1	0.42	3.2	1.4	0.09
Mean removal during cycle (%)				73%	66%	79%

On line time has also been high despite having to cope with variable conditions generated during the commissioning of the new works. A major benefit of the Fibrotex is the ability to deal automatically with variable feed conditions. Backwash frequency may increase temporarily with high feed turbidity however the system soon returns to steady state operation without operator intervention.

Since commissioning the plant, no *Cryptosporidium* has been detected in the treated water supply from the works, even though it is known that the catchment can be contaminated occasionally.

The Effect of Aerobic Treatment on the Survival of *Cryptosporidium parvum* Oocysts in Cattle Slurry

I.A. Read and I.F. Svoboda
Dept. Biochem. Sci. 1, Scottish Agricultural College, Auchincruive, Ayr, UK

Scott, Smith and Gibbs (1994) found that 14 apparently healthy beef suckler cows excreted an average of 900 oocysts per gram of faeces (range 25-1.8x10^4). This represents a vast reservoir of oocysts, especially at times such as slurry spreading with the subsequent run-off to water courses.

Calves may excrete up to 10^{10} oocysts during the course of their infection (Blewett, 1988a) and pen run-off and subsequent midden run-off, when the bedding is composted, may also be contaminated with oocysts. Ideally this run-off would be diverted to the slurry tank reception pit.

In cases of heavy infection within herds there is a case for treating the slurry and run-off.

As part of a SOAFD/MAFF open contract, entitled 'Protozoan, bacterial and viral pathogens, farm animal wastes and water quality', an investigation is being carried out into the efficacy of aerobic treatment systems for the inactivation of *Cryptosporidium parvum* oocysts in cattle slurry.

Slurry used for these experiments was collected, from one cow, as the total output of faeces and urine over a 24 hour period. The bulk solids were removed using a slurry separator, and the separated liquid phase diluted to a chemical oxygen demand (COD) of 38g/l.

Continuous culture aerobic treatment was performed in two 3 litre aerobic reactors (Plate 1). The steady state conditions for this treatment were:

i A residence time of 4.7 days
ii A treatment temperature of 15°C
iii Minimal aeration, with a dissolved oxygen level (DO) of 0%. (Redox potential = -100mV E_{cal}).

These conditions maintained the ammonia content at approximately 0.9 g/l and the pH at 8.8.

Oocysts (cervine:ovine, obtained from the Moredun Research Institute) were introduced into the reactors in containers bound with Vokes Nylon 6 membrane. Sub-samples were excysted using the method of Blewett (1988b) and observed under phase contrast microscopy at a magnification of x400. Unexcysted and excysted oocysts were counted, as were sporozoites. Control samples, stored in Hanks' Balanced Salt Solution (HBSS) at 15°C, were assessed by the same technique.

The results showed that there was no statistically significant difference between the counts in samples from the two reactors (Figures 1 and 2). However, there was a statistically significant difference between the two reactors and the control (Figure 3). Die off rates for *Cryptosporidium* were deduced from regression analysis of the data on the basis of sporozoite ratios. These indicated that continuous culture aerobic treatment of cattle slurry, with the above parameters, could render *Cryptosporidium* oocysts non-viable during 4.1 days of treatment.

Further data will be generated from the ongoing research with aerobic treatment at higher temperatures, various residence times and various DO concentrations.

References

Blewett, D.A. Disinfection and oocysts. Cryptosporidiosis: Proceedings of the first international workshop. 1988b

Blewett, D.A. Quantitative techniques in *Cryptosporidium* research. Cryptosporidiosis: Proceedings of the first international workshop. 1988a

Scott, C.A., Smith, H.V., Gibbs, H.A. Excretion of *Cryptosporidium parvum* oocysts by a herd of beef suckler cows. Veterinary Record (1994),134, 172

Plate 1. The Aerobic Reactor System.

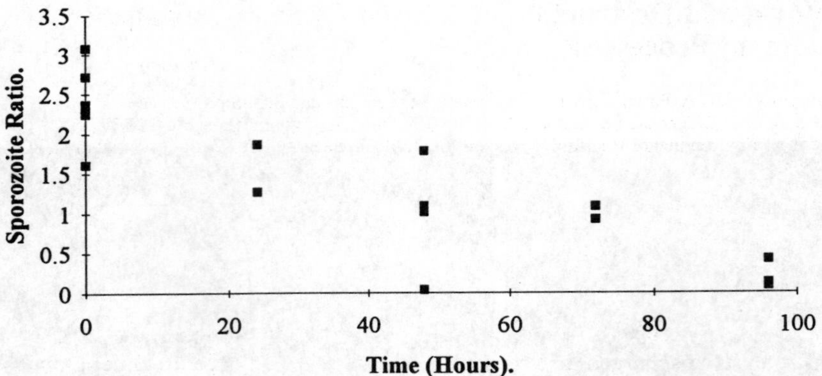

Figure 1. Fermenter 4. (15°C, 0% D.O., Redox = -100mV).

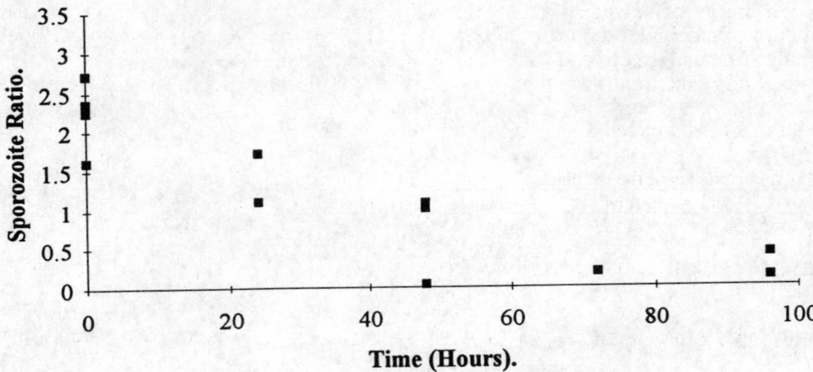

Figure 2. Fermenter 5. (15°C, 0% D.O., Redox = -100mV).

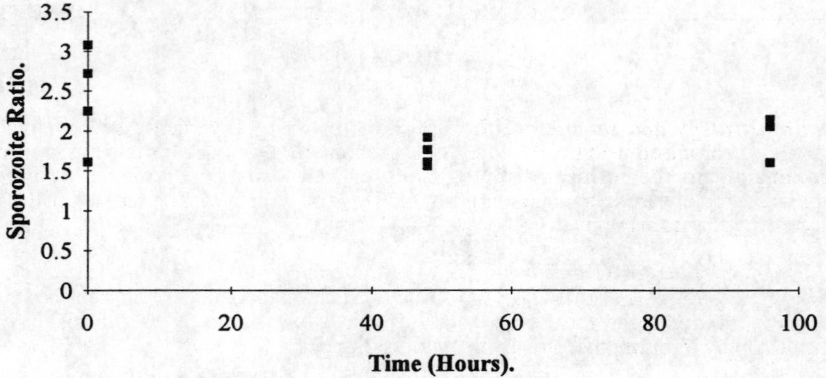

Figure 3. Control. (15°C).

Removal and Destruction of *Giardia* Cysts by Sewage Treatment Processes

L.J. Robertson[1,2], C.A. Paton[1,2], A.T. Campbell[1,2], H.V. Smith[1] and P.G. Smith[2]
[1]Scottish Parasite Diagnostic Laboratory, Stobhill NHS Trust, Springburn, Glasgow G21 3UW, UK
[2]Division of Environmental Health, Department of Civil Engineering, University of Strathclyde, Glasgow. G1 1XQ, UK

Introduction

Giardia cysts discharged in the final effluent from sewage treatment plants can contaminate water which may be used for abstraction for potable water supplies or for recreational purposes; sewage effluents containing cysts have been implicated in waterborne outbreaks of disease and pilot studies in Glasgow area have indicated that *Giardia* cysts can be detected throughout the year in treated sewage effluent (Smith *et al*, 1994). Discharge of sewage effluent must therefore be considered of importance in the formulation of catchment control directives and it is of importance to know which sewage treatments are most effective at removing and/or inactivating *Giardia* cysts.

In this study, six treatment plants in the Glasgow area incorporating different sewage treatment regimes (see table 1) have been studied for their efficiency in removing and inactivating *Giardia* cysts.

Table 1. Characteristics of the six plants

	Plant A	Plant B	Plant C	Plant D	Plant E	Plant F
Holding time (hrs)	7	11	18	25	36	26
Population equivalent served	452,966	41,303	644,000	331,333	5,763	2,100
Dry weather flow (L/day)	1.9×10^8	8.2×10^6	2.0×10^8	9.6×10^7	9.5×10^5	4.5×10^5
Treatments in place	Primary settlement only	Primary settlement then trickling filters	Primary settlement then activated sludge	Primary settlement then activated sludge	Activated sludge only	Primary settlement then trickling filters Tertiary treatment

Methods

Sampling strategy and sample purification Samples were taken using twenty four hour samplers synchronised using the holding times so that effluent samples taken corresponded approximately to the influent samples taken earlier. Two litre volumes of the 24 h composite sample were taken and concentrated by centrifugation and clarified using ether. Final pellet volumes were usually between 0.5-4.0 ml.

Analysis of samples for Giardia cysts 50µl aliquots were analysed for *Giardia* cysts by labelling fixed aliquots with FITC-labelled anti-*Giardia* spp.-monoclonal antibody and a DNA-stain to highlight the nuclei and screening by fluorescence microscopy with confirmation by light microscopy using Nomarski optics.

Assessment of viability of Giardia cysts In our experience, contact with ether has proved lethal to *Giardia* cysts. Therefore, samples in which cyst viability was assessed were clarified using sucrose flotation. Viability of cysts was assessed by morphology and inclusion/exclusion of the vital stain propidium iodide in a method adapted from Smith *et al* (1993) and recently recommended as the most satisfactory method presently available for asssessing the viability of *Giardia* cysts isolated from environmental samples (Thomas and Boreham, 1994).

Results

Removal of Giardia cysts during sewage treatment Giardia cyst concentrations detected in influent and effluent samples and the removal efficiencies for matched pairs of influent and effluent are described in table 2. Cyst removal efficiency varied between plants, with the highest removal efficiency and least variation in removal efficiency recorded at treatment plant C and the lowest removal efficiency and greatest variation recorded at plants A, B and F. Statistical analysis revealed that whereas plants A, B and F had significantly lower cyst removal efficiencies than plants D and E ($P \leq 0.05$) and plant C ($P \leq 0.001$), the cyst removal efficiency from plant E was also significantly lower than from plant C. No significant difference in cyst removal efficiency was detected between plants A, B and F, plants C and D, and plants D and E.

Table 2. *Giardia* cyst concentration in influent and effluent of treatment plants and removal efficiency

Treatment plant	n	Mean concentration of cysts in influent (range)	Mean concentration of cysts in effluent (range)	Mean cyst removal efficiency (range)
A	7	1403/L (520-2840/L)	445/L (35-820/L)	67% (22-93%)
B	13	1063/L (80-2880/L)	333/L (20-960)	57% (<0*-98%)
C	10	991/L (540-1580/L)	24/L (<5-70/L)	97% (87-99%)
D	8	1124/L (320-2960/L)	69/L (<10-430/L)	89% (30-99%)
E	9	1281/L (70-6000/L)	43/L (10-110/L)	86% (35-98%)
F	9	1238/L (290-2150/L)	248/L (110-540/L)	69% (34-94%)

*<0: On 3 occasions the concentration of cysts detected in the effluent was higher than the concentration of cysts detected in the influent.

Destruction of Giardia cysts during sewage treatment Frequently insufficient *Giardia* cysts were detected in liquid mounts of sucrose-purified effluent concentrate to allow realistic estimation of the viability of the cyst population. However, viability of the cysts detected in matched pairs of influent and effluent could be estimated on 8 occasions at 4 treatment plants and the results are presented in table 3.

Table 3. Percentage viability of *Giardia* cysts detected in influent and effluent

Sewage Works	Percentage of cysts considered viable	
	At influent	At effluent
Plant A	39 (n=56)	27 (n=55)
	18 (n=103)	41 (n=39)
	49 (n=80)	21 (n=19)
Plant B	29 (n=79)	88 (n=80)
	52 (n=96)	33 (n=24)
	7 (n=56)	71 (n=42)
Plant E	16 (n=32)	55 (n=11)
Plant F	52 (n=23)	41 (n=34)

Combination of these results indicates that frequently the percentage of viable cysts detected at effluent was higher than that detected at influent. However, it should be noted that these results may be an over-estimate of percentage viability at both influent and effluent as it is probable that the sucrose-flotation technique used for sample purification selects for viable cysts.

Discussion

Of the six sewage treatment plants examined during this study, those which had the highest cyst removal efficiencies incorporated primary settlement treatment followed by activated sludge, whereas those which were either primary settlement only or primary settlement followed by trickling filters, with or without tertiary treatment, had the lowest removal efficiencies. If it is assumed that 1000 *Giardia* cysts challenge each of the treatment plants per litre of sewage influent, then the number of *Giardia* cysts discharged daily by each of the sewage treatment plants can be estimated to range from 1.3×10^8 cysts/day (plant E) to 6.3×10^{10} cysts/day (plant A)

Although sucrose flotation probably selects for viable *Giardia* cysts, a considerable proportion of cysts in both influent and, more importantly, effluent were considered to be viable. As the proportion of viable cysts in the effluent was frequently found to be higher than in the influent, it should be considered that some sewage treatment processes may selectively remove non-viable cysts.

Even if as few as 20% of the *Giardia* cysts discharged in sewage effluent are considered to be viable, then from plant E (which of these six treatment plants discharges the least cysts on a daily basis) up to twenty million viable *Giardia* cysts will be released from it every day into a water course. However, whether these cysts, which are considered viable, are also infective and, if so, whether man or animals are their potential hosts is not addressed by this research.

Acknowledgements

We would like to acknowledge the ready assistance of the Department of Sewerage, Strathclyde Regional Council in the collection of this data and the Science and Engineering Research Council for financial support of this research under grant no. GR/J17456.

References

Smith, H.V., Robertson, L.J., Gilmour, R.A., Morris, G.P., Girdwood, R.W.A. & Smith, P.G. (1993). The occurrence and viability of *Giardia* cysts in Scottish raw and final waters. Journal of the Institute of Water and Environmental Mangagement 7 (6) 632-635

Smith, H.V., Robertson, L.J., Reay, D. & Young, C.J. (1994). Occurrence of *Giardia* cysts in raw and treated sewage in relation to the prevalence of giardiasis in a Scottish community. In: *Giardia*: From Molecules to Disease. Part 3. Biotic and Abiotic Transmission. (Ed.s, Thompson, R.C.A., Reynoldson, J.A., & Lymbery, A.J.) CAB International, Wallingford. U.K. pp.128-129

Thompson, R.C.A. & Boreham, P.F.L. (1994). Discussants report: biotic and abiotic transmission. In: *Giardia*: From Molecules to Disease. Part 3. Biotic and Abiotic Transmission. (Ed.s, Thompson, R.C.A., Reynoldson, J.A., & Lymbery, A.J.) CAB International, Wallingford. U.K. pp.131-136

Risk Assessment Methods for *Cryptosporidium* and *Giardia* in Contaminated Water

J. B. Rose[1], J. T. Lisle[1] and C. N. Haas[2]
[1]University of South Florida, Department of Marine Sciences, St. Petersburg, FL, 33701, USA
[2]Environmental Studies Institute, Bldg. 29-W, Drexel University, Philadelphia, PA 19104, USA

Introduction

As technological advancements in microbial detection and knowledge of microbial interactions in drinking water increases, directors of municipalities and health officials will be called upon to ensure that the public is adequately protected from epidemic and endemic waterborne disease. Risk assessment is a tool by which environmental microbiologists, engineers, water quality managers and health officials can communicate. Risk assessment approaches can be used to interpret water quality surveys and assist in defining the adequacy of drinking water treatment and acceptable public health risks.

Previous dose-response data have been used to develop risk estimates for microbiological infections after exposure to contaminated water. This has included viruses and *Giardia* (Rose *et al*., 1991a, Regli *et al*., 1991 and Haas *et al*., 1993). These models have been used to set treatment goals in the United States under the Environmental Protection Agency's "Surface Water Treatment Rule" for *Giardia*. This rule established a goal of 10^{-4} annual risk for determining the microbiological quality of drinking water in the United States. To meet this goal various treatment configurations, which could include new treatment processes, may be required depending on source water quality.

Cryptosporidium and *Giardia* are the most significant cause of waterborne disease in the United States. This is due to the wide spread occurrence in animals, humans and environmental waters (Rose, 1993). The oocyst and cyst (the structures which are found in water and cause the infections) are resistant to disinfectants. While, with the proper contact time the cysts of *Giardia* can be inactivated through water disinfection, the oocysts of *Cryptosporidium* are not inactivated by current chlorination procedures used in water treatment (Korick *et al*., 1991; Peeters *et al*., 1991). Ozone has been shown to have potential use for inactivating oocysts.

The waterborne outbreak of cryptosporidiosis last year in Milwaukee was associated with 400,000 illnesses (MacKenzie *et al*. 1994). Many of those who were immunocompromised died. This has spurred an interest in assessing the occurrence of protozoan cysts and oocysts in source and treated waters. Surveys have found that up to 80% of the surface waters and 45% of the treated waters will contain cysts and oocysts at various concentrations (LeChevallier *et al*., 1991 & 1991a). The risk to the public is difficult to evaluate in these cases through the current public health surveillance system. Therefore risk assessment models can be used to contrast varying levels of contamination, evaluating relative-risk.

Risk Assessment Models

The *Cryptosporidium* risk assessment model has recently been developed based upon research at the University of Texas, lead by Dr. Herbert Dupont (Dupont *et al*., 1995; Haas and Rose, 1994). The human dose-response came from studies on infectivity and morbidity resulting from oral ingestion of *Cryptosporidium* oocysts in sets of human volunteers. This study demonstrated that a dose of 30 oocysts would initiate infection in 20% of those exposed. The risk equation may be described as follows, in terms of the probability of infection (P_i):

$$P_i = 1 - e^{(-rN)}$$

where r is the fraction of microorganisms that are ingested which survive to initiate infection (which is organism specific) and N is the daily exposure, assumed to be 2 liters of drinking water per day. For *Cryptosporidium*, r = 0.00467 (0.00195-0.0097, 95% conf. limits). The *Giardia* risk assessment model was previously published (Rose *et al.*, 1991) and the parameter for *Giardia* was r=0.0198 (0.009798-0.03582, 95% conf. limits). Table 1 shows the risk estimates for these two models in comparison to other models which have been developed in a variety of species and hosts. These data show that some animals such as the muskrat for *G. lamblia* would not be appropriate to examine human isolates and in each case the animal models predicted a lower risk than the human dose-response data sets. The models were also used to show that during a *Giardia* outbreak there was a dose-response relationship between the numbers of glasses of water consumed per day and the potential for infection suggesting that each glass of water may have contained 2 cysts.

Table 1. Dose-response assessment for a variety of enteric protozoa data sets and animal hosts.

Infectious Agent	Host	Probability of Infection*
Giardia lamblia	Humans	$2.0x10^{-2}$
Giardia lamblia	Gerbils	$2.0x10^{-3}$
Giardia lamblia	Muskrats	$2.7x10^{-6}$
Giardia lamblia	Humans (in glasses of water)	$9.3x10^{-2}$**
Cryptosporidium parvum	Mice	$1.8x10^{-3}$
Cryptosporidium parvum	Humans	$4.7x10^{-3}$

*Probability of infection with exposure to 1 organism.
**Probability of infection with exposure to 1 glass of water.

Application of the Risk Assessment Models

Table 2 shows the daily risk estimates for varying levels of *Giardia* cysts in drinking water. In order to meet the current safety goal of 10^{-4} annual risk as suggested in the "Surface Water Treatment Rule", less than 1 cyst per 150,000 litre is desirable. Because detection of cysts at this level is difficult with the current methodology, source water levels may be monitored along with treatment reductions for calculation of the levels which may be found in drinking water.

Table 2. *Giardia* cyst levels in drinking water associated with risk

Levels/100 l	Vol. Required for Detection of 1 cyst	Daily Risk (95% conf.limits)
$6.75x10^{-4}$	150,000 l (1.3-4.8)	$2.67x10^{-7}$
	Meets annual risk safety levels of 10^{-4} (range 0.5-1.8 x 10^{-4})	
0.67	150 l	$2.6x10^{-4}$ (1.3-4.8)
10	10 l	$3.95x10^{-3}$ (2-7.1)
100	1 l	$3.95x10^{-2}$ (2-7.1)

Annual Risk is $P_i = 1- [e^{(-rN)}]^{365}$, where N is the average exposure.

Table 3 shows the daily risk estimates for *Cryptosporidium*. The data suggest that oocysts may be slightly less infectious than cysts. The minimum concentration of oocysts that could be present in drinking water and still meet the annual risk safety level of 10^{-4} was found to be $\leq$1 oocyst per 34,000 litre. In terms of monitoring criteria, if a utility monitored the finished water daily, the occurrence of 1 oocyst per 340 liters for not more than 8-10 days (2-2.8% of the time) would still be within the annual safety goal of 10^{-4}.

Table 3. *Cryptosporidium* oocyst levels in drinking water associated with risk

Levels/100 l	Vol. Required for Detection of 1 oocyst	Daily Risk (95% conf.limits)
$2.93x10^{-3}$	34,000 l	$2.67x10^{-7}$ (1.1-5.7)
Meets annual risk safety levels of 10^{-4} (range 0.4-2.1 x 10^{-4})		
0.3	340 l	$2.8x10^{-5}$ (1.1-5.7)
8 to 10 days exposure at this level would exceed annual safety level of 10^{-4}		
1	100 l	$9.3x10^{-5}$ (3.9-19)
10	10 l	$9.3x10^{-4}$ (3.9-19)

The data from the survey of finished drinking water by LeChevallier, *et al.*(1991a) was evaluated using the risk assessment models. In this study 27% of the finished drinking water samples were positive for the presence of oocysts in the range of 0.1 to 40 oocysts/100l, while 17% were positive for *Giardia* cysts in the range of 0.2 to 64 cysts/100l. The risk estimates associated with the averages and ranges are shown in Table 4. For *Cryptosporidium*, the calculated daily risk estimate was $1.4x10^{-4}$ with a range of $0.12x10^{-4}$ to $44x10^{-4}$. *Giardia* risks averaged approximately $20x10^{-4}$ and were as high as $250x10^{-4}$. These risks levels would be difficult to ascertain in this population due to passive surveillance. In addition, in most States, cryptosporidiosis is a non-reportable disease throughout the United States. These risk estimates are well above the annual risk of 10^{-4} (shown in Tables 2 and 3).

Table 4. Risk levels associated with *Giardia* cyst and *Cryptosporidium* oocyst detection in drinking water

Averages: (Ranges)	*Giardia* Cysts/100 l	*Cryptosporidium* Oocysts/100 l
	4.45 (0.29-64)	1.52 (0.13-48)
Daily Risk (Ranges)	$1.8x10^{-3}$ (0.1-25)	$1.4x10^{-4}$ (0.12-44)

Data on Occurrence from LeChevallier *et al.*,(1991) 17% and 27% of the samples were positive for cysts and oocysts, respectively.

The models have potential use during epidemiological investigations to further evaluate environmental monitoring information. A large contamination event is necessary, compounded by poor treatment removals to end up with levels in drinking water which would lead to an outbreak. Often the contamination event, peak exposure values are missed during outbreak investigations. The *Cryptosporidium* model was used to determine the most likely level of contamination present during the Milwaukee outbreak (Haas and Rose, 1994). The following assumptions were used to complete the risk assessment analysis:

1 the morbidity ratio (illness:infection) was 100%,
2 daily water ingestion rate was 1948 ml,
3 the contamination event lasted 21 days,
4 each day during the outbreak represents an independent identical exposure event.

Oocyst levels/litre were calculated for 1, 10 and 30 days exposure, using the risk model with an attack rate of 0.14 to 0.52 (as the P_i in the model) (Table 4). Based on duplicate ice samples corrected for loss of oocysts due to freezing, thawing and method recovery deficiencies, the geometric mean oocyst concentration was 0.79/litre. In this case the 30 day exposure value matched closely the predictions from the risk model (0.54 compared to 0.79 oocysts/litre), and the estimates fell within the 95% confidence limits of the model.

Table 5. Potential levels of *Cryptosporidium* oocysts in treated drinking water during the Milwaukee outbreak

	Exposure Duration (Days of Exposure)		
	1	10	30
Attack Rates	Oocyst Levels Per 100 l		
0.14	1615	161	54
0.52	7858	786	262

Note: Ice melted and sampled in Milwaukee contained 6 to 13 oocysts/100 l, and research has shown that during the freeze/thaw process 90% of the oocysts can be lost. Given the recoveries anywhere from 60 to 130 oocysts/100 l may have been in the tap water according to the environmental monitoring data.

Conclusions

The risk assessment process is divided into 4 steps:

1 Hazard identification has been defined for the enteric protozoa; the type of illness and the risk to the immunocompromised population particularly for cryptosporidiosis infections have been reported on. Prevalence of infections and risk of varying transmission routes (i.e. the role of pets) needs to be further elucidated.
2 Dose-response data are scarce in humans as well as animals. Most studies have focused on an infectious dose at one particular point (i.e. level at which 50% of the population becomes infected). The idea of the minimum infectious dose is no longer valid and experiments in appropriate animal models in the future need to be designed and conducted to evaluate the response curve, particularly at low dose levels.
3 Exposure is the area where there is the greatest need for adequate data. The level of infectious cysts and oocysts at the tap where the consumer is exposed is unknown. Contamination events, transport patterns, survival and removal during treatment processes needs to be studied.
4 Risk characterization, the last step in the process can only be accomplished when the previous three steps have been defined.

The better the scientific information on hazard identification, dose-response, and exposure, the better and more definitive the risk assessment.

The risk assessment and control of endemic waterborne disease needs further study. However, recommendations do need to be developed for detection of varying low levels in finished water, particularly for the immunocompromised. Epidemic disease and outbreaks should be controlled. In order to control both endemic and epidemic disease, three lines of defense need to be developed. First assessment of faecal sources impacting source waters and the control of these to the extent possible are needed. Some watersheds may need to treat wastewaters to a greater extent in the future. Second, filtration needs to be optimized. Removal of 85% is no longer appropriate and 99.9% should be achieved with enhanced reliability. Finally, new disinfectants, combination of disinfectants and alternative treatment processes will be needed by utilities with polluted source waters, or with the potential for large contamination events effecting their intake waters.

Risk assessment has become a valuable tool for evaluating a variety of health hazards associated with food and water. Risk estimation can provide a useful means for decision makers in the development of standards, treatment requirements, for risk management and risk/benefit analysis. However, the risk assessment approach has only been used on a limited scale for judging the risks associated with waterborne pathogenic microorganisms (Haas *et al.*, 1993; Rose *et al.*, 1991a and Regli *et al.*, 1991). Such strategy is needed and could be used by the water utilities to meet regulatory requirements under the Safe Drinking Water Act, Water Pollution Control Act, and other acts of regulatory needs which deal with the treatment of microbial contaminants in water. Now that models are available for the enteric protozoa, this will aid in further elucidating the importance of water in their transmission.

References

Anon., National primary drinking water regulations: monitoring requirements for public drinking water supplies: *Cryptosporidium*, *Giardia*, viruses, disinfection byproducts, water treatment plant data and other information requirements. In: *Federal Register* 59(#28), 1994

Dupont H, Chappell C, Sterling C, Okhuysen P, Rose J, Jakubowski W. Infectivity of *Cryptosporidium parvum* for adult humans. *New Engl J Med* 1995; (submitted)

Haas C, Rose J. Reconciliation of microbial risk models and outbreak epidemiology: the case of the Milwaukee outbreak. In: *Proceedings of the Annual Conference for the American Water Works Association*, New York (June 5-9). American Water Works Association, Denver, 1994; 517

Haas C, Rose J, Gerba C, Regli S. Risk assessment of viruses in drinking water. *Risk Analysis* 1993; 13: 545

Korich D, Mead J, Madore M, Sinclair N, Sterling C. Effects of ozone, chlorine dioxide, chlorine, and monochloramine on *Cryptosporidium parvum* oocyst viability. *Appl Env Microbiol* 1990; 56: 1423

LeChevallier MW, Norton WD, Lee RG. Occurrence of *Giardia* and *Cryptosporidium spp.* in surface water supplies. *Appl Env Microbiol* 1991; 57: 2610

LeChevallier MW, Norton WD, Lee RG. *Giardia* and *Cryptosporidium spp.* in filtered drinking water supplies. *Appl Env Microbiol* 1991a; 57: 2617

MacKenzie W, Neil M, Hoxie N, Proctor M, Gradus M, Blair K, Peterson D, Kazmierczak J, Addiss D, Fox K, Rose J, Davis J. A massive outbreak in Milwaukee of *Cryptosporidium* infection transmitted through the public water supply. *New Engl J Med* 1994; 331: 161

Peeters J, Mazas E, Masschelein W, Martinez I, Debacker E. Effect of disinfection of drinking water with ozone or chlorine dioxide on survival of *Cryptosporidium parvum* oocysts. *Appl Env Microbiol* 1989; 55: 1519

Regli S, Rose J, Haas C, Gerba C. Modeling the risk from *Giardia* and viruses in drinking water. *J Am Water Works Assoc* 1991; 83: 76

Rose JB, Gerba CP, Jakubowski W. Survey of potable water supplies for *Cryptosporidium* and *Giardia*. *Env Sci Technol* 1991; 25: 1393

Rose J, Haas C, Regli S. Risk assessment and control of waterborne giardiasis. *Am J Public Health* 1991a; 81: 709

Rose, J. Enteric Waterborne Protozoa: Hazard and Exposure Assessment. Safety of Water Disinfection: Balancing Chemical & Microbial Risks. Craun, G. F.(ed.). ISLI Press. Washington, D.C. 1993, p. 115

Surface water treatment rule, guidance manual for compliance with the filtration and disinfection requirements for public water systems using surface water sources. *Federal Register* 1989; 54

Emerging Pathogens: *Cyclospora*, the Microspora, and How Many More?

C.R. Sterling
Dept. of Veterinary Science, University of Arizona, Tucson, AZ 85721, USA

Waterborne disease outbreaks caused by protozoan parasites appear to be on the rise. This can be attributed, in part, to an enhanced ability to isolate and detect the parasites responsible for such outbreaks. While outbreaks caused by *Giardia* and *Cryptosporidium* head the list, ongoing studies in immunocompromised individuals, such as AIDS patients and the malnourished of developing countries, indicate the presence of new opportunistic agents of disease that require attention. Two, *Cyclospora cayetanensis* and several genera of the Phylum Microspora, are now being detected in patients with diarrheal illness and have great potential for waterborne transmission.

The protozoan identity of organisms previously referred to as "*Cyanobacterium*-like bodies or CLBs" and now recognized as *C. cayetanensis* and causing protracted diarrhea in humans globally was make in 1993 (Ortega *et al.* 1993). Organisms of the genus *Cyclospora*, however, were likely first recognized in 1870 in the intestine of moles (Eimer 1870). The genus was created in 1881 for a parasite, *Cyclospora glomerica*, which was described from a myriapod (Schneider 1881). The first life cycle study of parasites in this genus was made from moles in which *C. caryolytica* was described developing in the intestinal epithelium and producing a severe enteritis (Schaudinn 1902). Subsequent descriptions of cyclosporan species have been made from snakes (Pellérdy 1965), insectivores (Pellérdy and Tanyi 1968; Duszynski and Wattam 1988; Ford and Duszynski 1988,1989; Mohamed andMolyneux 1990), rodents (Ford *et al.* 1990), and most recently, humans (Ortega *et al.* 1993).

Very strong evidence implicating organisms of the genus *Cyclospora* with infection and disease in humans comes from a recent study characterizing the complete sporulation, excystation, and detailed fine structure of the organism obtained from the feces of diarrheic Peruvians (Ortega *et al.* 1993). This evidence, along with microscopic size and appearance following application of modified acid-fast stains or following visualization under UV epifluorescence, division in culture, patient symptoms, and refractoriness to conventional antimicrobial therapy links previous reports of "cyanobacterium-like body" or "coccidian-like body (CLB) infections in humans from different parts of the world to this newly described *Cyclospora* of humans in Peru (Soave *et al.* 1986; Naranjo *et al.* 1988; Taylor *et al.* 1988; Hart *et al.* 1990; Long *et al.*1990; MMWR 1991; Long *et al.* 1991; Shlim *et al.* 1991; Weekly Epidemiological Record 1991; Butcher 1992; Pollock *et al.* 1992; Albert *et al.* 1993; Ashford *et al.* 1993; Catchpole *et al.* 1993; Connor *et al.*1993; Gascón *et al* 1993; Hoge *et al.* 1993; McDougall and Tandy 1993; Wurtz *et al.* 1993). Verification of this assumption has been made through collaborative efforts with researchers in Los Angeles, Chicago, Nepal and elsewhere.

Initial observations of CLB infections from humans was probably made in 1977. Organisms isolated from patients of Papua New Guinea were morphologically identical to CLBs and at that time were though to possibly represent a new species of *Isospora* (Ashford 1979). Subsequent reports of CLB infections were made during the course of studies to define the role of *Cryptosporidium parvum* and other enteropathogens as responsible for diarrheal disease outbreaks (Soave *et al.* 1986; Naranjo *et al.* 1988). A striking similarity between this new organism and *C. muris* in stained fecal smears was also noted (Naranjo *et al.* 1988). Initial attempts to sporulate these CLB's were unsuccessful, however, and identities other than coccidian were reported in the literature.

Most reports detailing CLB infections have come from patients who were tourists or expatriates visiting countries which normally have high diarrheal disease rates. A few have come from immunocompromised (AIDS) patients. Sporadic as these reports have been, however, there has been a high degree of suspicion that perhaps many cases involving this organism have been overlooked because many laboratories in developing countries do not place a great emphasis on making microscopic size measurements of organisms encountered. *Cyclospora*, therefore, could have been mistakenly reported as *Cryptosporidium*. Oocysts of *C. cayetanensis* measure 8-10 µm in diameter while those of *C. parvum* measure only 4-6 µm. Symptoms of infection produced by *Cyclospora* infection also mimic those of *Cryptosporidium* with the exception of being frequently intermittent and more protracted. Our experience with *Cyclospora* in Peru confirms this assumption.

Fecal samples from patients containing CLBs and sent to us from around the world have confirmed that the organism in question was *C. cayetanensis*. A noteworthy feature of this organism's life cycle, which in part contributed to the delay in identifying it, is the prolonged sporulation time. *Cyclospora*, like *Cryptosporidium*, has an environmentally resistant oocyst with 4 sporozoites. *Cryptosporidium*, however, is fully sporulated when passed from an infected host. The sporulation time for *Cyclospora*, from two weeks at 25°C and up to 4-6 months at 4°C, implies that oocysts must be in a moist environment to ensure their survival. Hence, the implication for waterborne transmission.

An unusual disease outbreak with *Cyclospora* occurred in a Chicago hospital in which evidence pointed to water as a likely source of infection (MMWR 1991). It must be kept in mind that in almost 50% of waterborne disease outbreaks the responsible organism is never identified. In the Chicago hospital based outbreak contaminated water from a rooftop reservoir was implicated in relation to illness observed among hospital residents. Direct and acid-fast stained microscopic examination of stool specimens from nine of the house staff physicians and one other employee showed the presence of CLB's. The symptoms among the staff included explosive watery diarrhea, anorexia, severe abdominal cramping, nausea, and occasional vomiting. Chronic diarrhea continued for at least 4 weeks. Because clinical presentation of *Cyclospora* mimics *Cryptosporidium* infections so strongly, it is highly recommended that all laboratories screening for *Cryptosporidium*, especially when acid-fast staining is used for the diagnostic identification, provide precise oocyst measurements. In one other incident that appeared to be related to waterborne transmission, an eight year old Chicago youth acquired illness and presented with CLB's one week after swimming in Lake Michigan. Water samples taken from near the inlet of the Chicago municipal water supply system showed the presence of CLB-like bodies. In this case the organism's identity from water was not confirmed. In addition, most reports dealing with infection with this organism have come from cities or regions of countries which are predominantly coastal, both near fresh and salt water. Very other little information is available on this new parasite infecting humans at this time. It is still not know precisely where the organism resides within the body and if there are reservoir hosts which serve to aid in the transmission of this agent or not.

Cyclospora should be of keen interest to the water industry as a possible new waterborne pathogen. Because of its size, morphology, and autofluorescent characteristics, this organism may well have seen by technicians screening for *Giardia* and *Cryptosporidium*. One recommendation that might be added to the current method for detecting parasites in water samples is that a portion of the final sample be viewed by fluorescent microscopy before application of any specific fluorescent detection probes. Not only might this serve to possibly identify an organism such as *Cyclospora*, but it would also serve to indicate what the background level on non-specific fluorescence was in a given sample. At present, sporulation and excystation procedures are the only methods of positively identifying *Cyclospora*. Specific detection tests based on the use of monoclonal antibodies and other technologies are being developed. Use of these techniques should enable us to better define the epidemiology of this new organism and determine to what extent water plays a role in its transmission.

The Microspora are newcomers to the infectious disease scene. They too produce resistant forms, called spores, which can survive for extended periods in the environment. Organisms in this phylum are obligate intracellular parasites which are principally known through their association with disease of aquatic invertebrates and vertebrates (Canning 1977). Because of AIDS, they are gaining attention as opportunistic pathogens in humans (Shadduck 1989; Orenstein 1991; Bryan *et al.* 1991). At least five genera are known to infect and produce disease in man: *Encephalitozoon*, *Enterocytozoon*, *Nosema*, *Pleistophora* (Bryan *et al.* 1991), and *Septata* (Cali *et al.* 1993). Two of these, *Enterocytozoon* and *Septata*, produce severe diarrheal disease in AIDS patients and indeed are the most frequently encountered microsporidia of immunocompromised patients. It is not known if the microsporidia can also cause disease in the immunocompetent population. One can't help but recall the early history of the association of *Cryptosporidium* with disease in humans. This parasite rose to importance because of its association with AIDS patients and secondarily was shown to cause disease in the general population. Will the same hold true for the microsporidia? At present it is not known if the microsporidia which produce disease in humans have reservoir hosts, although many aquatic animals serve as hosts for microsporidian species (Canning 1977). The spores are smaller than oocysts of *Cryptosporidium* and, therefore, are more likely to breach filtration barriers. At present, we also know very little about their disinfection resistance. One can't help but wonder how many more organisms, with the potential for waterborne transmission, await discovery.

References

Albert MJ, I Dabir, T Azim, A Hossain, M Ansaruzzaman, L Unicomb. Diag. Microbiol. Inf. Dis. submitted, 1993

Ashford RW, DC Warhurst, GDF Reid. The Lancet 341: 1034, 1993

Ashford RW. Ann. Trop. Med. Parasitol. 73: 497-500, 1979

Bryan RT, A Cali, RT Owen, HC Spencer. Microsporidia: opportunistic pathogens in patients with AIDS, in Progress in Clinical Parasitology, Sun T, ed., Field & Wood Medical Pub, Inc., New York, NY, pp. 1-26, 1991

Butcher, A. personal communication, 1992

Cali A, DP Kotler, JM Orenstein. J. Eukar. Micro. 40: 101-112, 1993

Canning EU. Microsporidia, in *Parasitic Protozoa*, Kreier JP, ed., Academic Press, Orlando, FL, pp. 155-191, 1977

Catchpole R, C Toomey, R Thomson. [Abs.] 93rd ASM meeting #C-436, 1993

Connor BA, DR Shlim, JV Scholes, JL Rayburn, J Reidy, R Rajah. Ann. Intern. Med. 119: 377-382, 1993

Duszynski DW, AR Wattam. J. Protozool. 35: 58-62, 1988

Eimer, T. A. Stuber's Verlangshandlung, Würzburg. pp. 1-58, 1870

Ford PL, DW Duszynski, CT McAllister. J. Parasitol. 76: 325-331, 1990

Ford PL, DW Duszynski. J. Protozool. 35: 223-226, 1988

Ford PL, DW Duszynski. J. Protozool. 75: 508-513, 1989

Gascón J, M Corachan, ME Valls, A Gene, JA Bombi. Scan. J. Inf. Dis. 25: 253-257, 1993

Hart AS, MT Redinger, R Soundarajan, CS Peters, AL Swiatlo, FE Kocka. The Lancet 335: 169-170, 1990

Hoge CW, DR Shlim, R Rajah, J Triplett, M Shear, JG Rabold, P Echeverria. The Lancet 341: 1175-1179, 1993

Long EG, A Ebrahimzadeh, EH White, B Swisher, CS Callaway. J. Clin. Microbiol. 28: 1101-1104, 1990

Long EG, E White, WW Carmichael, PM Quinlisk, R Raja, BL Swisher, H Daugharty, M.T. Cohen. J. Infect. Dis. 164: 199-202, 1991

McDougall RJ, MW Tandy. personal communication. 1993

MMWR. Morb. Mortal. Wkly. Rep. 40: 325-327, 1991

Mohamed HA, DH Molyneux. Parasitology. 101: 345-350, 1990

Naranjo J, CR Sterling, R Gilman, E Miranda, F Diaz, M Cho, A Benel. [Abs. 324] In: Abstracts of the 38th annual meeting of the American Society of Tropical Medicine and Hygiene, Honolulu, 1988

Orenstein JM. J. Parasitol. 77: 843-864, 1991

Ortega YR, CR Sterling, RH Gilman, VA Cama, F Diaz. New. Eng. J. Med. 328: 1308- 1312, 1993

Pellérdy, L, J Tanyi. Folia Parasitologica (Praha). 15: 275-277, 1968

Pellérdy, LP. *Coccidia and coccidiosis* . 2nd ed., Verlag Paul Parey, Berlin, 959pp., 1965

Pollock RCG, RP Bendall, A Moody, PL Chiodini, DR Churchill. The Lancet 340: 556- 557, 1992

Schaudinn, F. Arb. Kais. Gesundh. 18: 378-416, 1902

Schneider, A. Arch. Zool. Exp. generale 9: 387-404, 1881

Shadduck J. Rev. Inf. Dis. 11: 203-207, 1989

Shlim DR, MT Cohen, M Eaton, R Rajah, E Long, B Ungar. Am. J. Trop. Med. Hyg. 45:383-389, 1991

Soave R, JP Dubey, LJ Ramos, M Tummings. [Abs.] Clin. Res. 34: 533A, 1986

Taylor DN, R Houston, DR Shlim, M Bhaibulaya, BL Ungar, P Echevarria. JAMA 260: 1245-1248, 1988

Weekly Epidemiological Record. 33: 241-243, 1991

Wurtz RM, FE Kocka, CS Peters, CM Weldon-Linne, A Kuritza, P Yungbluth. Clin. Inf. Dis. 16: 136-138, 1993

Protozoan Parasites and Water: Veterinary Aspects

M.A. Taylor
Central Veterinary Laboratory, Weybridge, UK

Introduction

Parasites are an important cause of morbidity and mortality in domestic animals and of considerable economic importance to the farming industry. Helminths and ectoparasites are generally the most significant in terms of pathogenicity, but there are a number of protozoa which are of both veterinary and public health importance.

Grazing animals are host to many commensal protozoa within the gastrointestinal tract which aid in the breakdown of cellulose. Of the parasitic protozoa, Apicomplexan or coccidian parasites, can be a significant cause of disease and death in young cattle, sheep and poultry raised under intensive conditions. These animals may be infected with many different species of coccidia of varying pathogenicity. The majority belong to the genus *Eimeria*, which are characteristically highly host-specific, undergoing development within a single host species. Sheep and goats for example, are infected with 11 morphologically distinct species of *Eimeria* respectively, but studies have demonstrated that sheep species do not infect goats and vice versa. Cats and dogs are the final host for a wide range of coccidian parasites including *Isospora*, which are generally host-specific, and Sarcocystis, in which asexual and sexual development occur in different hosts.

Protozoan parasites also exist which show little host specificity and which may be capable of producing widespread environmental contamination because of the potentially large host population. Contamination may possibly be increased through the spread of sewage, slurry or manure on land. In this context, animals have been incriminated in outbreaks of waterborne protozoan infections of *Cryptosporidium* and *Giardia*.

This paper will discuss the taxonomy and incidence of these protozoa in domestic animals and review the clinical and pathological aspects of infections.

Cryptosporidiosis

Parasites of the coccidial genus *Cryptosporidium* are small intracellular parasites which occur throughout the animal kingdom and have been reported in more than 40 species of mammals, birds, reptiles and fish. Since their discovery in mice in 1907, the importance of these parasites was for a long time overlooked, until the recognition of infection in young livestock in the 1970s in various species of domestic animals especially cattle and sheep. The taxonomic status of *Cryptosporidium* is still not fully resolved but it is generally accepted that the species that occur in mammals are *C. parvum*, *C. muris* and *C. wrairi*. Infection in man and domestic livestock, particularly calves, is usually associated with *C. parvum*. Cryptosporidiosis is very prevalent in young calves and appears to be age related. Seasonal peaks of disease coincide with birth peaks in spring and autumn. It is predominantly found in young calves less than 3 weeks old. The first calves to be born often become infected without showing clinical signs. In these calves the parasite multiplies producing large numbers of oocysts in the faeces which contaminate the environment for calves that follow. Infection spreads rapidly, and later-born calves can become so heavily infected that clinical disease results. Symptoms of profuse watery diarrhoea, abdominal pain and dehydration may be followed by recovery and immunity to further clinical episodes. Disease is often associated with the presence of other organisms, notably enterotoxogenic *Escherichia coli*, *Salmonella* spp., *Clostridium perfringens*, rotavirus and coronavirus, all of which may contribute to the neonatal diarrhoea complex (calf scours) although evidence suggests that *C. parvum* is a primary pathogen in its own right. Disease associated with *C. parvum* has also been reported in neonates of sheep, goats and deer and in non-domestic ruminants including antelope and oryx (Gregory 1990). Symptoms in all species included diarrhoea, dehydration and death in a number cases. In young calves infected with *Cryptosporidium parvum*, pathological signs include inflammation and distension of the intestines with enlargement of the mediastinal lymph nodes. Histopathological changes occur mainly in the jejunum and ileum with parasitic stages seen on the surface of epithelial cells lining the jejunum, ileum and caecum and occasionally in severe infections, the colon and rectum.

Pigs, goats and horses can also be infected. Most porcine cryptosporidial infections are asymptomatic with the majority of infections occurring in 6 to 12 week old pigs (Lindsay and Blagburn 1991). Clinical signs where they do occur include diarrhoea and unthriftiness although these are usually associated with the presence of other pathogens such as *Salmonella* spp., *E. coli*, adenovirus or *Isospora suis*. Cryptosporidiosis has been reported in immunodeficient foals (Gibson *et al.* 1983) as a cause of diarrhoea. Other findings indicate that apparently immunocompetent horses can develop patent infections and that *Cryptosporidium* can contribute to mortality in the young foal (Coleman *et al.* 1989). There are few reports of *Cryptosporidium* infections in companion animals. Dogs, cats and other pets are occasionally infected but they do not seem to be an important source of infection to other hosts. Given their ubiquitous occurrence, there is a large potential reservoir of infection to man and domestic animals. A survey in cats in Scotland suggested that infection is common among young and new-born kittens but that the disease was usually asymptomatic (Mtambo *et al.* 1991). As such, cats may be potential carriers of infection for human or other animal hosts. Clinical cryptosporidiosis has been reported in cats occurring in immunosuppressed individuals infected with feline leukaemia virus (FeLV) or feline immunodeficiency virus (FIV) (Angus 1988).

C. muris, which was first described in the stomach of mice (Tyzzer 1907), has also been reported from cattle although its significance is unknown (Anderson 1991). As in mice, the predilection site is the glandular abomasum (or ruminant 4th stomach). Parasite stages are found attached predominantly to cells of the gastric gland mucosa.

In birds, two species *C. baileyi* and *C. meleagridis* have been reported although other species may exist. *C. baileyi* is usually associated with infections of the cloacal bursa, cloaca and respiratory tract in a number of species of birds (Lindsay *et al.* 1986). In infected birds, parasites are on epithelial cells of the cloaca and Bursa of Fabricius (the site of B cell maturation in the bird), and occasionally the caecae and trachea. Heavy infections produce epithelial hyperplasia and hypertrophy, particularly of the bursa, and the ensuing inflammatory exudate occasionally produces bursal casts. *C. meleagridis* is thought to be the species associated with gut related infections in turkeys (Goodwin *et al.* 1988). The avian cryptosporidia appear to have a high host specificity for birds. However, a report of infection with *C. baileyi* in an immunosuppressed human patient (Ditrich *et al.* 1991) suggests that under certain circumstances cross-transmission to mammalian hosts may occur.

A number of chemotherapeutic agents have been tested in animals and man but to date no effective specific treatment for cryptosporidiosis has been found. In immunocompetent individuals, the infection is self-limiting and requires supportive treatment only to prevent dehydration. Prevention in animals is primarily aimed at limiting exposure and also reducing stress in young neonates which are the most susceptible.

In many instances where *Cryptosporidium* is diagnosed, it appears that infections usually originate from the same host species. In animals, the primary route of infection is likely to be the direct animal-to-animal faecal-oral route. Thus in calves for example, overcrowding, stress of early weaning, transport and marketing, together with low levels of hygiene will increase the risk of clinical infections. In lambs, chilling due to adverse weather conditions in the neonatal period, intercurrent infections or nutritional or mineral deficiencies could exacerbate or increase the likelihood of disease. Infection in these cases is likely to occur through grooming, nuzzling, coprophagy, faecal soiling by direct contact with infected animals, or indirectly through consumption of contaminated foods or environmental sources including pasture and water. Heavy infections can lead to high levels of environmental contamination which influences the rate of infection in susceptible hosts. The role of rodents in transmission of cryptosporidiosis has been little investigated.

In man person-to-person transmission is now recognised to be common, thus indicating that cryptosporidiosis is not necessarily a zoonosis (Casemore 1990). Zoonotic transmission has been reported from calves and lambs particularly following educational visits to farms. Companion animals such as cats and dogs have also been implicated in human disease. In Australia, RAPD-PCR has demonstrated geographical differences in strain isolates from different hosts which suggests local endemnicity and zoonotic transmission. Isoenzyme analysis in the UK, has shown differences in human isolates and animal isolates. It is not clear at this stage whether this represents strain variation in cross-species transmission between Australian or UK isolates, or just differences in the strain typing methods.

Giardiosis

Giardia infections are frequently overlooked in domestic animals despite being isolated from a variety of mammalian, avian, reptilian, amphibian and fish hosts. The host specificity of *Giardia* is still undecided and as such the zoonotic potential of animal infection is the subject of much research. For a long time it was considered that *Giardia* spp. were host specific and this resulted in the description of over 40 species based on the host species in which they were found. It is now generally accepted that there are just three structural types or species. The species affecting man and the majority of domestic animals, is *Giardia duodenalis* (*intestinalis*). The other morphologically different species are *G. muris* identified in rodents, birds and reptiles and *G. agilis* from amphibians.

Biochemical and immunological differences in *Giardia* isolated from humans suggest that there is a great deal of heterogeneity within these strains, whilst at the same time relatively close relationships exist between certain human and animal strains.

Giardia are flagellate protozoans normally found adherent to epithelial surfaces of the small intestine especially the middle to lower areas of the villi. The life cycle is simple and direct, the trophozoite stage dividing by binary fission to produce further trophozoites. Species variation exists in the size of the trophozoite, and the shape and size of the median bodies. Intermittently, trophozoites encyst forming resistant cyst stages that pass out in the faeces of the host.

Giardia infections in many species of animals are often asymptomatic. When disease does occur, the signs often include chronic, pasty diarrhoea, weight loss, lethargy and failure to thrive. The diarrhoea may be continuous or intermittent. The existence of *Giardia* in domestic animals has been known for many years but during that time little information has become available on prevalence, pathogenicity and the disease caused by these parasites in their hosts. *Giardia* has been reported in cattle, sheep, goats, horses, dogs, cats, rodents, and psittacines. Based on limited investigations, the incidence of these parasites varies but can be assumed to be higher in some species than has been reported. Studies in Canada (Buret *et al* 1990) indicate infections in sheep and cattle of 18% and 10% respectively. A more recent study in the UK (Taylor *et al* 1993) indicated that nearly 70% of a flock of lambs to be infected with *Giardia* although the presence of the organism was not necessarily associated with clinical signs of disease. A survey of dogs attending a charity animal hospital in London (Sykes and Fox 1989) showed an overall prevalence of infection of 15% with the highest prevalence in dogs less than 12 months of age (30%). In aviary birds, *Giardia* is frequently encountered in psittacines such as cockatiels, budgerigars and lovebirds causing enteropathy, weight loss and death (Fudge and McEntee, 1986). Treatment of *Giardia* in animals is usually with one of the nitroimidazole compounds metronidazole, dimetridazole, ronidazole, carnidazole, or tinidazole.

Limited epidemiological studies suggest that direct animal-to-animal transmission is the most likely method of transmission although water contamination can also be considered as a possible route. Human infection in the USA has been reported from drinking water contaminated with *Giardia* thought to have originated from beavers (Dykes *et al.* 1980). Other wild animals may act as reservoirs of infection. The role of farm animals in the overall epidemiology of human giardiosis has yet to be investigated.

References

Anderson C. (1991). *Cryptosporidium muris* in cattle. Veterinary Record 129, 20

Angus K.W. (1988) Mammalian Cryptosporidiosis: a veterinary perspective. In: Cryptosporidiosis. Proceedings of the First International Workshop (Ed. K W Angus and D A Blewett) Animal Diseases Research Association, Edinburgh, Scotland, pp 43-53

Buret A., derHollander N., Wallis P.M., Befus D. and Olsen M.E. (1990). Zoonotic Potential of Giardiasis in Domestic Ruminants. Journal of Infectious Diseases 162, 232-237

Casemore D.P. (1990) Epidemiological aspects of human cryptosporidiosis. Epidemiol Infect 104, 1-28

Coleman S.U., Klei T.R., French D.D., Chapman M.R. and Corstret R.E. (1989). Prevalence of *Cryptosporidium* spp. in equids in Louisiana. American Journal of Veterinary Research 505, 575-577

Ditrich O., Palkovic L., Sterba J., Prokopic J., Loudova J. and Giboda M. (1991). The first finding of *Cryptosporidium baileyi* in man. Parasitology Research 77, 44-47

Dykes A.C., Juranek D.D., Lorenz R.A., Sinclair S., Jakubowski W. and Davies R. (1980). Municipal waterborne giardiosis. Epidemiologic investigation - beavers implicated as a possible reservoir. Annals of Internal. Medicine. 92, 165-170

Fudge A.M. and MCEntree L (1986). Avian Giardiasis: Syndromes, diagnosis and therapy. 1986 Proceedings of the Association of Avian Veterinarians, Miami

Gibson J.A., Hill M.W.M. and Huber M.J. (1983). Cryptosporidiosis in Arabian foals with severe combined immunodeficiency. Australian Veterinary Journal 60, 378-379

Goodwin M.A., Steffens W.L., Russell I.D. and Brown J, (1988). Diarrhoea associated with intestinal cryptosporidiosis in turkeys. Avian Diseases 32, 63-67

Gregory M.W. (1990). Epidemiology of cryptosporidiosis in animals. Cryptosporidiosis in water supplies. Report of the group of experts (chairman Sir John Badenoch). HM Stationery Office, London.

Lindsay D.S. and Blagburn B.L. (1991). *Cryptosporidium parvum* infections in swine. Compendium of continuing education of the practising veterinarian 13 (5), 891-894

Lindsay D.S. and Blagburn B.L., Sundermann C.A., Hoerr F.J. and Ernst J.A. (1986). Experimental *Cryptosporidium* infections in chickens: oocysts structure and site specificity. American Journal of Veterinary Research 47, 876-879

Mtambo M.M.A., Nash A. S., Blewett D.A., Smith H.V. and Wright S. (1991). *Cryptosporidium* infection in cats: prevalence of infection in domestic and feral cats in the Glasgow area. Veterinary Record 129, 502-504

Sykes T.J. and Fox M.T. (1989). Patterns of infection with *Giardia* in dogs in London Trans. Royal Soc. Trop. Med. and Hyg. 83, 239-240

Taylor M A , Catchpole J, Marshall R.N. and Green J. (1993). Giardiasis in lambs at pasture. Vet. Rec. 133, 131-133

Tyzzer E.E. (1907) A sporozoan found in peptic glands of the common mouse. Proceedings of the Society for Experimental Biology and Medicine 5, 12

Prevention of Environmental Contamination by *Cryptosporidium parvum* Oocysts after Treatment of Neonatal Meat Calves with Halofuginone Lactate

J.E. Peeters and D. Vandergheynst
National Institute of Veterinary Research, Section of Parasitology, Groeselenberg 99, B-1180 Brussels, Belgium

Introduction

Cryptosporidium parvum causes neonatal diarrhoea in mammals. In calves *C. parvum* has been identified as the second most common infectious agent in outbreaks of diarrhoea (Angus 1988). Infected animals excrete large numbers of oocysts. As the parasite is non-host specific, it can be transmitted from one species to another. The overall distribution in ruminants causes contamination of surface and ground water. Contaminated drinking water is an important source of human cryptosporidiosis (Hayes *et al.* 1989). This stresses the importance to clear drinking water of the parasite, but also to take preventive measures in intensive animal production units.

Prevention of cryptosporidiosis is difficult. Whereas most other species of enteric coccidia are incapable of recycling within the host, *C. parvum* has two stages that initiate auto-infectivity. These stages are believed to be responsible for the development of severe infections in hosts exposed to a small number of oocysts (Current and Garcia 1991). No commercially available drugs are approved for treatment of cryptosporidiosis. Naciri *et al.* reported promising results with halofuginone lactate in lambs. Villacorta *et al.* showed the drug to strongly reduce oocyst output and clinical signs in naturally infected calves. Medication with low doses may result in small numbers of oocysts passed in the faeces after withdrawing. Lower doses do not completely arrest the cycle of the parasite and allow immunity (Peeters *et al.* 1993). Therefore, the optimal dose has been set between 60 and 120 µg/kg of live weight in mixed milk and meat calves. Yet, pure meat breeds such as the Belgian Blue-White, Charolais and Limousin breeds are more susceptible to *Cryptosporidium* infection. This paper will deal with the efficacy of a curative and a preventive program on oocyst output and local immunity in a pure meat breed after natural infection.

Materials and Methods

Animals

In two calves breeding and fattening farms 118 neonatal Belgian Blue-White meat calves were monitored from birth until four weeks of age. Both farms were selected based on reports of the treating veterinarian and on the demonstration of the parasite in faecal samples.

Drug

Halofuginone lactate was supplied as a 3.1 % (w/v) concentrate by Hoechst (lot nr 350 A 013). To perform a blind study, the different drug concentrations were masked by adding methylene blue and by marking the bottles with only the ear number of the calf for which the dose was intended to. As a consequence the farmers were not aware if they were giving the animals a placebo or the drug. Three working solutions containing 0, 60 and 120 µg/kg were prepared twice a week. Each calf received 70 ml of working solution during seven days according to the details of the experimental design. Drug dosage was calculated on an estimated mean body weight of 50 kg. In farm Durand the drug was administered directly in the mouth by a 50 ml syringe, whereas the drug was administered through the milk in farm Lummen.

Experimental Design

The calves were allocated randomly to one of three treatment groups. First a preventive treatment was installed in farm Durand: from the 4th day after birth, calves received one of the three drug dosages during 7 consecutive days. Three groups of 17 animals were tested. Mean body weight at start was 49.7 ± 8.9 kg. A curative treatment was assayed in both farms: the drug was administered for 7 consecutive days from the first signs of diarrhoea. Medication was started resp. 8 ± 1 and 8 ± 3 days after birth in farms Durand and Lummen. In the first farm 3 groups of 11 or 12 animals were tested and one control group of 17 and two medicated groups of 8 calves in the second farm. Mean body weight at birth was 54.6 ± 9.5 kg and 41.7 ± 5.8 kg resp. Animals were observed daily. Diarrhoea was assessed as follows: 0 = pastose; 1 = semi-liquid and 2 = liquid stools. During 4 weeks, fresh faecal material was collected twice a week by rectal sampling. The infection rate was evaluated semi-quantitatively by carbol fuchsin stain as previous experiments showed a close relationship between numbers of oocysts present and semi-quantitative scores (Villacorta *et al.* 1991). After this step, 2 g of faecal material was homogenised by shaking in 8 ml of PBS-pH 7.2 and spun down at 650 x g for 15 min. The supernatant was stored at - 30 °C until tested on IgA, IgG and IgM by ELISA as described before (Peeters et al. 1993).

Results

Preventive Treatment

Non medicated calves showed diarrhoea between 4 and 21 days after birth. Clinical signs were most severe on day +7 and coincided with maximal output of cryptosporidial oocysts. Medication with halofuginone significantly reduced clinical signs, although only 120 µg/kg prevented them almost completely (Fig. 1): only four out of 17 animals showed discrete signs of diarrhoea against 11 in 60 µg/kg medicated calves. In 120 µg/kg medicated animals an episode of diarrhoea was established only between 11 and 21 days after birth, with a peak on day 14. This peak was not associated with rising *C. parvum* (Fig. 2). All 17 unmedicated calves passed cryptosporidial oocysts in the faeces. Maximal levels were established 7 days after birth, suggesting that most animals became infected at birth or shortly afterwards (Fig. 2). Medications with 60 or 120 µg of halofuginone lactate per kg live weight reduced mean oocyst excretion significantly. Yet, all 60 µg/kg medicated calves excreted detectable quantities of oocysts during the first 4 weeks after birth, against only 9 out of 17 calves medicated with 120 µg/kg. None of the medicated calves showed an increase of oocyst output after withdrawing the drug and oocyst output followed the same excretion pattern as in unmedicated calves.

The first few days after birth high levels of specific faecal IgG and IgM and moderate levels of IgA were detected. Then levels of IgG declined progressively in all three groups and became almost negative four weeks after birth (Fig 3). IgM showed a similar evolution in the 120 µg/kg group, whereas an increase was detected in non medicated calves between seven and 11 days after birth and between 11 and 14 days in the 60 µg/kg group. Afterwards titers declined. IgA titers showed a decline during the first four days in the unmedicated group, the first seven days in the 60 µg/kg group and the first 11 days in the 120 µg/kg group. Then IgA titers rose again with peak values on resp. 11 and 14 days after birth. Once the oocyst output dropped, IgA titers declined. This confirms that preventive treatment with halofuginone lactate allows development of a specific local antibody response.

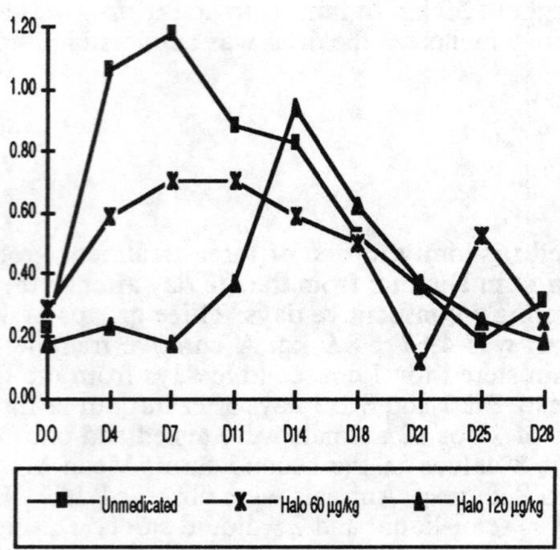

Figure 1. Farm Durand : influence of preventive treatment on diarrhoea score

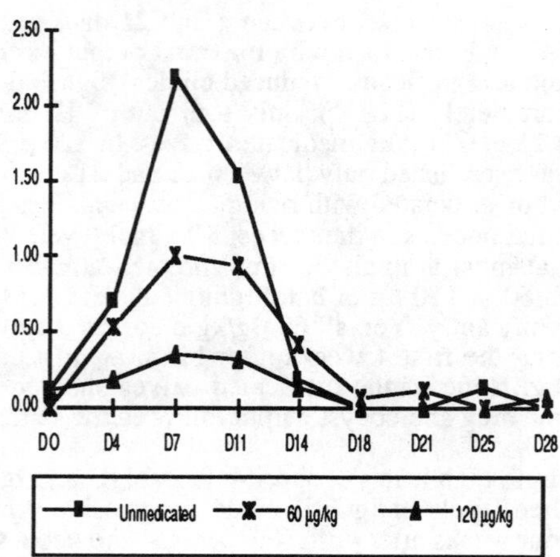

Figure 2. Farm Durand : influence of preventive treatment on oocyst output

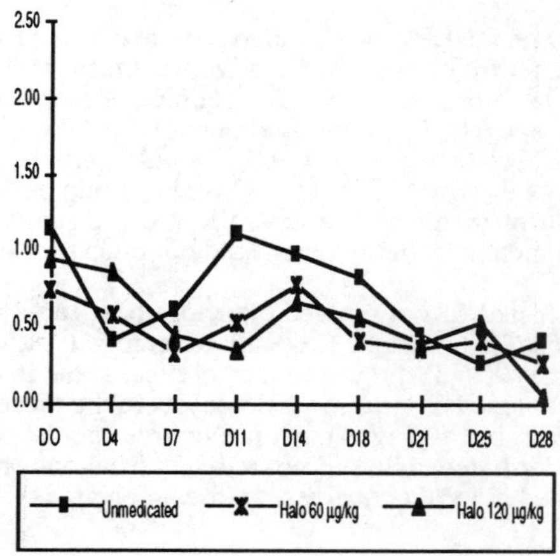

Figure 3. Farm Durand : influence of preventive treatment on kinetics of specific faecal anti-*C. parvum* IgA

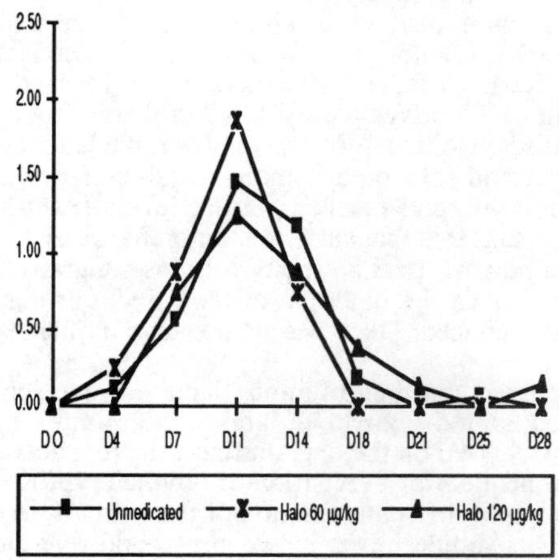

Figure 4. Farm Lummen : influence of preventive treatment on oocyst output

Curative Treatment

Farm Durand Non medicated calves showed diarrhoea between 11 and 21 days after birth. Clinical signs were most severe on day 14. Curative treatment with halofuginone from the first signs of diarrhoea (day 8 ± 1) did not reduce clinical signs. Almost all calves (32/34) excreted cryptosporidial oocysts. Curative treatments with 60 or 120 μg weight reduced faecal passage of oocysts between days + 11 and +14 only partially. After withdrawing the drug, a slight increase was established in the 120 μg/kg group between day +14 and +18. Afterwards oocyst output of medicated calves followed the same excretion pattern as in unmedicated calves. Treatment with halofuginone did not impair local antibody response.

Farm Lummen Non medicated calves showed diarrhoea between 4 and 21 days after birth. Clinical signs were most severe on day 11. Curative treatment with halofuginone from the first signs of diarrhoea (day 8 ± 3) did not reduce clinical signs in either treatment group. Almost all calves (31/33) passed cryptosporidial oocysts in the faeces. Maximal output was established 11 days after birth (Fig 4). Curative treatments with 60 or 120 μg of halofuginone lactate per kg live weight did not reduce faecal oocyst scores. No significant differences were established in local antibody response among the three groups.

Discussion

The data confirm the activity of 60-120 μg halofuginone lactate per kg l.w. against *C. parvum* in neonatal Belgian Blue-White meat calves. When the drug was administered preventively from the 4th day after birth, it strongly reduced oocyst output during the clinical phase of the disease and prevented clinical signs. Moreover, the drug allowed development of a local antibody response after natural infection. During a former trial in a mixed milk and meat cattle breed it was not possible to establish clear differences between both doses, nor concerning antiparasitic activity against the parasite, nor concerning the kinetics of local antibodies. This trial on the contrary clearly indicates an insufficient action of 60 μg/kg against the parasite in a pure meat breed: although diarrhoea scores are reduced to a certain extent, all animals excreted cryptosporidial oocysts during and after medication and 11 out of 17 animals showed diarrhoea (severe diarrhoea in 6/17). In the 120 μg/kg group on the contrary only nine out of 17 calves passed low numbers of oocysts in the faeces and only four of them showed discrete clinical signs. Moreover, the latter dose allowed a local immune response: although IgA and IgM titers remained stable or declined during treatment, they increased after withdrawing and reached similar levels seven days later as those of non medicated calves. This suggests that sufficient antigenic activity remains after withdrawing the drug that allows a normal local antibody response. Curative treatment on the contrary showed no distinct effect on the outcome of the infection: nor clinical signs, nor oocyst output was significantly reduced. There was no negative influence on local antibody response either.

So, it may be concluded that halofuginone lactate is particularly useful in preventing cryptosporidiosis associated diarrhoea and contamination of the environment by cryptosporidial oocysts. Based on the data outlined above a dose of 120 μg/kg during seven days should be recommended for prevention of bovine cryptosporidiosis. It is advisable to estimate first the mean onset of contamination of the animals, to determine the optimal start time of medication. This should be set between two and five days post-infection. Yet, the results do not support the use of halofuginone lactate as a curative drug. Probably the drug comes too late to avoid the consequences of intestinal damage caused by the parasite.

References

Angus, K.W. 1988. Mammalian cryptosporidiosis : a veterinary perspective. In: Cryptosporidiosis. Proceedings of the First International Workshop. Ed. K.W. Angus & D.A. Blewett, Moredun Research Institute, Edinburgh 1989, pp. 43-53

Current, W.L., and Garcia, L.S. 1991. Cryptosporidiosis. Clin. Microbiol. Rev. 4:325-358

Hayes, E.B., Matte, T.D., O'Brien, T.R., McKinley, T.W., Logsdon, G.S., Fose, J.B. ,Ungar, B.L.P., Word, D.M.,P Pinsky, .F., Cummings, M.S., Wilson, M.A., Long, E.G., Hurwitz, E.S., and Juranek, D.D. 1989. Large community outbreak of cryptosporidiosis due to contamination of a filtered public water supply, N. Engl. J. Med. 320:1372-1376

Naciri M,.Yvoré P. 1989. Efficacité du lactate d'halofuginone dans le traitement de la cryptosporidiose chez l'agneau. Rec. Méd. Vét. 165, 823-826

Peeters J.E., Villacorta I., Naciri M., Vanopdenbosch E. (1993). Specific serum and local antibody responses against *Cryptosporidium parvum* during medication of calves with halofuginone lactate. Infect. Immun., 61, 4440-4445

Villacorta, I., Peeters J.E., Vanopdenbosch E., Ares-Mazás E., and H. Theys. 1991. Efficacy of halofuginone lactate against *Cryptosporidium parvum* in calves. J. Antimicrob. Agents Chemotherapy., 35:283-287

Closing Address

Sir Gordon Jones
Chairman, Yorkshire Water plc

I am delighted to have the opportunity of giving the closing address to this prestigious conference and I would like to thank the Royal Society of Chemistry Water Chemistry Forum for inviting me to do so. I was especially gratified that the conference was held in Yorkshire, and hope you find your visit to this historic City of interest.

The sponsors' names have an illustrious ring, and I am very pleased that some of my colleagues in Yorkshire Water have been able to offer help and support. If only because many of the issues being considered are of the greatest possible relevance and importance to water companies in many - probably most - countries around the world.

I have noted from some of the papers that there have been outbreaks of cryptosporidiosis in various parts of the world, most notably, perhaps, in the United States, but also here in this region, and Yorkshire Water has learned the hard way about the issues involved in minimising the possible spread and distribution of waterborne outbreaks, and dealing with the concerns and fears of communities affected.

The scientific community has devoted considerable effort to supporting research into detection techniques. However, I fear that we are still some way off seeing a reliable on-line operational device for detecting *Cryptosporidium* and other micro-organisms in water in time to do something about them, and prevent them from entering into the supply. Whilst this situation continues, the policy of preventing contamination by adherence to the strictest water quality operational standards and the vigorous implementation of preventative measures during water treatment is commended, and employed by Yorkshire Water.

It is, of course, a reflection of today's society that, as the health of the population continues to improve because of such things as better food, personal care and hygiene and more sophisticated medication, we see very much highlighted such things as *Cryptosporidium* outbreaks that would hardly have been noticed in previous years. This is a situation thrown into even greater relief by the fact that drinking water these days is of such extraordinarily high quality, and laboratory techniques for the detection and identification of minute traces of chemicals are so much more reliable.

Quite apart, however, from the actual presence of organisms in water, I feel that analytical techniques are, today, becoming so sophisticated as to be able to detect almost infinitesimal concentrations of such things as pesticides in drinking water to the point where quality standards for some chemicals and other impurities are set so as to be near, or sometimes at, the limit of detection. Indeed, today there is a widespread feeling among many people that if something can be detected in drinking water, no matter how great the dilutions, then it should not be there.

This is only one manifestation of wider public concern about socio-environmental issues, and we see something similar, perhaps, in the current feelings of many people about the danger of dioxins. Many people - perhaps fed by the media - fail to appreciate the complexity of dioxin chemistry, and that there are, in fact, hundreds of dioxins, only a few of which are alleged to have any harmful effects on health. It is also assumed by some people that dioxins result only from incineration, whereas, in fact, they have been around probably since time immemorial, and there is an ever-present background dioxin level in the atmosphere, in soil, and even in river water.

Similarly, it is interesting that the *Cryptosporidium* organism was only identified for the first time in - I think - 1974, yet although it has been around possibly forever, there is widespread public concern about outbreaks of cryptosporidiosis, although thankfully they are quite rare.

So we are seeking to strike a balance between the providers of drinking water, who are obliged to spend more and more on producing ever purer water (95% of which is thrown away) which, in any case, people are unwilling to pay more for, and consumers who are becoming more concerned about the minute levels of impurities that have sometimes existed for many years and, perhaps, only today can be detected by the more extensive use of sophisticated laboratory techniques.

It is a measure, I think, of the importance of the subjects discussed at this conference that over 160 delegates and contributors have attended from such countries as the USA, Canada, Israel, Belgium, The Netherlands, Australia, France and elsewhere. I am especially delighted that South Africa is represented.

My Company - Yorkshire Water - is vitally interested in the matters discussed at this conference, and works closely with health authorities and environmental health departments to investigate and manage outbreaks whenever they occur.

It is a measure of the importance that Yorkshire Water attaches to the whole subject that we have done our best to support the conference, and to present papers. My colleague, Clive Thompson and Dr Julian White of the University of York were largely responsible for the organisation of the conference, and I am sure that you would wish to join me in thanking them for making it so successful.

Subject Index